Laurie G. Kirszner
University of the Sciences in Philadelphia

Stephen R. Mandell
Drexel University

Portable
Literature

READING ◆ REACTING ◆ WRITING

Sixth Edition

WADSWORTH
CENGAGE Learning™

Australia • Brazil • Japan • Korea • Mexico • Singapore • Spain• United Kingdom • United States

WADSWORTH
CENGAGE Learning™

**Portable Literature:
Reading, Reacting, Writing
Sixth Edition
Kirszner & Mandell**

Publisher: Michael Rosenberg

Acquisitions Editor: Aron Keesbury

Development Editor: Karen R. Smith

Managing Developmental Editor:
Karen Judd

Editorial Assistant: Cheryl Forman

Managing Marketing Manager:
Mandee Eckersley

Marketing Manager: Kate Edwards

Marketing Assistant:
Dawn Giovanneillo

Advertising Project Manager:
Patrick Rooney

Editorial Production Manager:
Michael Burggren

Manufacturing Manager:
Marcia Locke

Senior Permissions Editor:
Isabel Alves

Permissions Freelancer:
Stephen Jordan

Senior Art Director: Bruce Bond

Photo Manager: Sheri Blaney

Photo Researcher: Jill Engebretson

Technology Project Manager:
Tim Smith

Production Service/Compositor:
Nesbitt Graphics

Text Designer: Jerilyn Bockorick

Cover Designer: Suzanne Heiser

Cover Quilt Creator: Greta Vaught

For product information and technology assistance, contact us at **Cengage Learning Customer & Sales Support, 1-800-354-9706**

For permission to use material from this text or product, submit all requests online at **cengage.com/permissions**
Further permissions questions can be emailed to **permissionrequest@cengage.com**

Library of Congress Control Number: 2005937961
ISBN-13: 978-1-4130-2281-0
ISBN-10: 1-4130-2281-2

Wadsworth
25 Thomson Place
Boston, MA 02210-1202
USA

Cengage Learning is a leading provider of customized learning solutions with office locations around the globe, including Singapore, the United Kingdom, Australia, Mexico, Brazil, and Japan. Locate your local office at: **international.cengage.com/region**

Cengage Learning products are represented in Canada by Nelson Education, Ltd.

For your course and learning solutions, visit **academic.cengage.com**

Purchase any of our products at your local college store or at our preferred online store **www.ichapters.com**

Printed in the United States of America
4 5 6 7 8 9 10 09 08

BRIEF CONTENTS

CONTENTS

16 | VOICE   459

PREFACE

Portable Literature: Reading, Reacting, Writing is a response to the many instructors who told us they wanted a book with the core selections and pedagogical features of the full and compact versions of *Literature: Reading, Reacting, Writing* in a size better suited for their one-semester or one-quarter courses. *Portable Literature* is that book. It is designed to be extensive enough to provide the stories, poems, and plays essential to the study of literature, accompanied by the introductions and study questions that have helped students begin to read literature more closely over five editions of the larger volumes—all in a book compact enough for students to bring to class.

To keep *Portable Literature* short, we do not include the extensive instructional guidance that characterizes the other two versions of our text. For example, we do not include a discussion of the process of writing a research paper (although we do provide full coverage of MLA documentation in Chapter 3). Similarly, we have removed the literary selections that in the larger editions simply provide a depth of choice, retaining the selections essential to a survey of literature—stories by Hawthorne, Poe, and O'Connor, for example—as well as a sampling of contemporary works that help give students a taste of how literature has developed. Thus, students are still exposed to a rich variety of literature, but are not asked to pay for selections they may not read or for pedagogical features they may not use.

Despite the relatively small size of *Portable Literature*, its purpose is the same as that of the more comprehensive anthologies: to expand students' appreciation of literature and to suggest the many possibilities for self-discovery that literature offers. Other features enhance and strengthen the text's emphasis on reading and writing about literature. For example, each section of the book begins with a chapter that orients readers to fiction, poetry, and drama. Some of the other elements that instructors and students will find useful in *Portable Literature: Reading, Reacting, Writing* are listed below.

Balanced Selections

The stories, poems, and plays collected here represent a balance of old and new, with works by classic authors placed alongside works by more contemporary writers. In addition, a wide variety of nations and cultures and a wide range of styles are represented in *Portable Literature: Reading, Reacting, Writing*.

- **39 essential stories.** Including classic stories by Ernest Hemingway, Joyce Carol Oates, William Faulkner, and Flannery O'Connor, as well as contemporary works by literary lights such as Jonathan Safran Foer, Margaret

Atwood, and T. Coraghessan Boyle, the fiction section of *Portable Literature* provides a solid selection of works and helps students approach a rich variety of literature. New to this edition are stories by Toni Cade Bambara, Hisaye Yamamoto, and Gabriel García Márquez. In addition, a new Fiction Sampler (Chapter 5) introduces students to six contemporary short-short stories.

- **Over 200 essential poems.** This edition includes poems by celebrated contemporary poets such as Billy Collins, Robert Pinsky, and Louise Glück alongside classic favorites by Shakespeare, Keats, Whitman, Dickinson, and Hughes. New to this edition, poems by such poets as Wanda Coleman, Adam Zagajewski, and José Juan Tablada add a contemporary touch to the poetry section, and a new Poetry Sampler (Chapter 15) highlights visual poetry.

- **13 essential plays.** Shakespeare's *Hamlet*, Miller's *Death of a Salesman*, Ibsen's *A Doll House*, Sophocles's *Oedipus*, and Williams's *The Glass Menagerie* make up the backbone of the drama section, which also includes a new Drama Sampler (Chapter 26) showcasing four contemporary ten-minute plays that will engage instructors and students alike.

Thorough Coverage of Writing

Central to our approach is the idea that writing is a vital part of understanding literature. For this reason, we include writing instruction not as an afterthought, tucked away in an appendix, but in the book's opening chapters and integrated throughout.

- **Chapter 1, "Reading and Writing about Literature."** This introductory chapter discusses reading, interpreting, and evaluating literature, illustrating the process of gathering and arranging ideas, drafting, and revising and explaining how these concepts apply specifically to writing about literature. We believe this chapter will prepare students to approach the literary works in this anthology with confidence and to write about them intelligently and creatively.

- **New chapter on literary argument.** Chapter 2, "Writing Literary Arguments," helps students to think critically about their writing and build logical arguments about literary works. This chapter takes students through the process of writing a literary argument and concludes with a new annotated student paper, "The Politics of 'Everyday Use.'"

- **New chapter on MLA documentation.** Chapter 3, "Documenting Sources and Avoiding Plagiarism," includes practical strategies for avoiding plagiarism as well as the most up-to-date documentation and format guidelines from the Modern Language Association (including many examples of MLA-style citations for electronic sources).

- **Three model student papers.** At the end of Chapter 1, we include three model student papers, one on a short story, Alberto Alvaro Ríos's "The Secret Lion" (p. 23); one comparing two poems, Robert Hayden's "Those Winter Sundays" (p. 27) and Seamus Heaney's "Digging" (p. 27); and one analyzing a play, Susan Glaspell's *Trifles* (p. 31).
- **Checklists for Writing.** Most chapter introductions end with a checklist designed to help students measure their understanding of concepts introduced in the chapter. These checklists can also guide students as they generate, explore, focus, and organize ideas for writing about works of literature.
- **Reading and Reacting questions.** Useful and engaging Reading and Reacting questions (including journal prompts) follow many selections throughout the text. These questions ask students to interpret and evaluate what they have read, sometimes encouraging them to make connections between the literary work being studied and other works in the text.
- **Related Works.** A Related Works list following each set of Reading and Reacting questions includes works linked (by theme, author, or genre) to the particular work under study. This feature encourages students to see connections between works by different authors, between works in different genres, or between two themes—connections they can explore in class discussions and in writing.
- **Writing Suggestions with Web activities.** Imaginative suggestions for paper topics are included at the end of each chapter. Corresponding Web activities are provided on the book's companion Web site <http://kirsznermandell.wadsworth.com> to spark students' interest and generate engaged writing.

A Full Package of Supplementary Materials

To support students and instructors who use the sixth edition of *Portable Literature: Reading, Reacting, Writing*, the following ancillary materials are available from Wadsworth:

- **Instructor's Resource Manual** A comprehensive instructor's manual provides all the materials necessary to support a variety of teaching styles. This resource includes discussion and activities for every short story, poem, and play in the anthology; a thematic table of contents; semester and quarter sample syllabi; and articles on the evolution of the literary canon and reader-response theory. In addition, this edition includes a section called "Do Your Students Know?"— brief, entertaining notes that provide interesting, sometimes offbeat contextual information.

- **Lit21: Literature in the Twenty-First Century** *Lit21* is a CD-ROM designed to provide students with a unique interactive environment that can supplement the many aspects of the study of literature. In addition to sixty-eight stories, poems, and scenes from plays read aloud on the disc, *Lit21* offers thirty video clips of poetry readings, interviews, and selected scenes. Quizzes for every story, play, and element of literature help students review for class and complement the "brush-up" instruction on the elements of literature. Finally, a unique program, the Explicator, actually guides students step by step through the process of close literary analysis while helping them prepare notes for an explication paper.

Film Series

DVD

- **The Wadsworth Original Film Series in Literature** Original adaptations of Tillie Olsen's "I Stand Here Ironing," Alice Walker's "Everyday Use," Raymond Carver's "Cathedral," Eudora Welty's "A Worn Path," and John Updike's "A&P," accompanied by interviews with the authors, are available on DVD or VHS.

- **The Wadsworth Casebook Series for Reading, Research, and Writing** (previously titled *The Harcourt Brace Casebook Series in Literature*) Fourteen complete casebooks, each providing all the materials students need to jumpstart a literary research project, are available:

Fiction
Raymond Carver's "Cathedral"
William Faulkner's "A Rose for Emily"
Charlotte Perkin's Gilman's "The Yellow Wallpaper"
Flannery O'Connor's "A Good Man Is Hard to Find"
Edgar Allan Poe's "The Cask of Amontillado"
John Updike's "A&P"
Eudora Welty's "A Worn Path"

Poetry
Emily Dickinson, A Collection of Poems
Robert Frost, A Collection of Poems
Langston Hughes, A Collection of Poems
Walt Whitman, A Collection of Poems

Drama
Athol Fugard's *Master Harold and the Boys*
Susan Glaspell's *Trifles*
William Shakespeare's *Hamlet*

- **Arden Shakespeare** Nine plays from the Arden Shakespeare Series can be packaged with *Portable Literature: Reading, Reacting, Writing*, Sixth Edition, including *Hamlet, King Lear, A Midsummer Night's Dream, The Tempest, Othello*, and *Twelfth Night*.

ACKNOWLEDGMENTS

From start to finish, this book has been a true collaboration, not only with each other, but also with our students and colleagues. We have worked hard on this book, and many people at Wadsworth have worked hard along with us.

We would like to begin by thanking our incredibly creative and talented Development Editor, Karen Smith, who has always been there for us (and who we hope always will be there). She is one of a kind, and we are simply in awe of her abilities.

We continue to be grateful to Acquisitions Editor Aron Keesbury for his enthusiasm and persistence as well as for his belief in the book. And we remain very grateful as well to our publisher, Michael Rosenberg, for coming back just in time.

Also at Wadsworth, we thank Mike Burggren for guiding the manuscript through production, with skilled help from the team at Nesbitt Graphics, especially Sherry Berg, Barbara Lipson, and Susan McIntyre. We owe a special debt to Susan, our first-rate project manager, for her expertise as well as for her thoroughness and her patience.

We also very much appreciate the help we got on this project from William Coyle on the Instructor's Resource Manual; from Stacey Brown on updating the headnotes, footnotes, Cultural Contexts, and Critical Perspective questions; from Tony Perriello on the research and review process; and from Jessie Swigger on the new student papers.

We would like to thank the following reviewers of the sixth edition: Joy L. Blom, Montclair State University; Terri Bourus, Indiana University–Kokomo; Jennifer Brown, University of Hartford; Sheryl Chisamore, State University of New York–Ulster; Wayne Christensen, Florida Memorial College; Kirk Colvin, American River College; Susan Cornett, St. Petersburg College; Joseph A. Correro Jr., Delta State University; Carl C. Curtis III, Liberty University; Patricia A. Daskivich, Los Angeles Harbor College; Tammy DiBenedetto, Riverside Community College; Josh Dickinson, Jefferson Community College (SUNY); Michael M. Dinielli, Chaffey College; Ellen Gross, Central Virginia Community College; Susan Isaac, Georgia Military College; Deborah Israel, University of Central Oklahoma; Susan A. Johnson, Sierra College; Jane Anderson Jones, Manatee Community College–Venice; Jason B. Jones, Central Connecticut State University; Kerrie Kawasaki-Hull, Ohlone College; Kevin Kelly, Andover College; James Kirkpatrick, Central Piedmont Community College; Judith Kleck, Central Washington University; Mark Kosinski, Manchester Community College; Mary Kramer, University of Massachusetts–Lowell; David Kucher, Westchester Community College; Carol Kushner, Dutchess Community College; Noreen Lace, California State University–Northridge; Paul Long, Baltimore City Community College; Martha B. Macdonald, York Technical College; Deanna Mascle, Morehead State University; Robert Mitchell, Ohlone College; Deborah Montuori, Shippensburg University; Robbi Muckenfuss, Durham Technical Community College; Michail W. Mulvey, Central Connecticut State University; L. J. Nutter, Liberty University; Nancy K. Pennell, McPherson College; Renee Pigeon, California State University–San Bernardino; David Schwankle, Riverside Community College–Norco; Shant Shahoian, Oxnard College; Andy Solomon, University of Tampa; Donald R. Stinson, Northern Oklahoma College; Carolyn Stonewell, Middlesex Community College; Gary Thomas, University of North Carolina–Charlotte; Regina Williams, Arkansas State University–Heber Springs; and David Winsper, Springfield Technical Community College.

We would also like to thank the following reviewers of the fifth edition: Jane Anderson Jones, Manatee Community College–Venice; Lee Barnes, Community College of Southern Nevada; Robin Calitri, Merced College; Janet Eber, County College of Morris; Charles Fisher, Aims Community College; Maryanne Garbowsky, County College of Morris; Clinton Gardner, Salt Lake City Community College; Diana Gatz, St. Petersburg College; Dawn Marie Hershberger, University of Indianapolis; Isara Kelley Tyson, Manatee Community College; Andrew Kozma, University of Florida; Bernard Morris, Modesto College; David Neff, University of Alabama–Huntsville; Diana Nystedt, Palo Alto College; Roger Platizky, Austin College; Angela M. Rhoe, Prince George's Community College; Mark Rollins, University of Ohio; Christine Roth, University of Wisconsin; David A. Salomon, Black Hills State University; Ann Spurlock, Mississippi State University; and Pam Sutton, Union University.

We continue to be grateful to the reviewers of the fourth edition: Crystal V. Bacon, Glouchester County College; Gwen Barklay-Toy, North Carolina State University; Eric Birdsall, University of Akron; John Doyle, Quinnipiac College; David Fear, Valencia Community College; Elizabeth Keats Flores, College of Lake Country; Linda Gruber, Kishwaukee College; Lynn Hildenbrand, Chesapeake College; Teresa Kennedy, Mary Washington College; Michael Kraus, Marian College of Fond du Lac; Teri Maddox, Jackson State Community College; Judith P. Moray, Moraine Valley Community College; Mary Beth Namm, North Carolina State University; Rodney D. Newton, Central Texas College; Monte Prater, Tulsa Community College–Northeast; Gail Rung, Black Hawk College; Robert M. Temple, Manatee Community College; Maria W. Warren, University of West Florida; Donnie Yeilding, Central Texas College; and Laura Mandell Zaidman, University of South Carolina–Sumter.

We would also like to thank all the reviewers who made valuable contributions to the third edition: Ben Accardi, University of Kansas; Thomas Bailey, Western Michigan University; John Bails, University of Sioux Falls; Leigh Boyd, Temple Junior College; Cathy Cowan, Cabrillo College; Pat Cowart, Frostburg State University; Kitty Dean, Nassau Community College; Jo Devine, University of Alaska–Southeast; Jack Doyle, University of South Carolina–Sumter; Lynn Fauth, Oxnard College; David Fear, Valencia Community College; Mary Fleming, Jackson State Community College; Ann Fogg, University of Maine; Wayne Gilbert, Community College of Aurora; Shain Graham, Orange Coast College; Linda Gruber, Kishwaukee College; Chris Hacskaylo, University of Alaska–Ketchikan; Richard Hascal, Contra Costa College; Gwen Hauk, Temple Junior

College; Michael Herzog, Gonzaga University; Andrew Kelly, Jackson State Community College; Benna Kime, Jackson State Community College; Army Sparks Kolker, University of Kansas; Michael Kraus, Marian College of Fond du Lac; Heidi Ledett, Ulster County Community College; Teri Maddox, Jackson State Community College; Jeanne Mauzy, Valencia Community College; Fred Milley, Anderson University; Robert Milliken, University of Southern Maine; Andrew Moody, University of Kansas; Paul Perry, Palo Alto Community College; Angela Rapkin, Manatee Community College; Jean Reynolds, Polk Community College; Ellen Robbins, Ulster County Community College; Paul Rogauls, Plymouth State College; Neil Sebacher, Valencia Community College; Larry Severeid, College of Eastern Utah; Sharon Small, Des Moines Area Community College; Virginia Streamer, Dundalk Community College; Robert Temple, Manatee Community College; Margie Whelan, Mt. San Antonio College; Mike White, Odessa College; Rebecca Yancey, Jackson State Community College; Donnie Yielding, Central Texas College; and Martha Zamorano, Miami Dade–Kendall.

Reviewers of the second edition included Deborah Barberousse, Horry-Georgetown Technical College; Bob Mayberry, University of Nevada–Las Vegas; Shireen Carroll, University of Miami; Stephen Wright, Seminole Community College; Robert Dees, Orange Coast College; Larry Gray, Southeastern Louisiana University; Nancy Rayl, Cypress College; James Clemmer, Austin Peay State University; Roberta Kramer, Nassau Community College.

Reviewers of the first edition included Anne Agee, Anne Arundel Community College; Lucien Agosta, California State University–Sacramento; Diana Austin, University of New Brunswick; Judith Bechtel; Northern Kentucky University; Laureen Belmont, North Idaho College; Vivian Brown, Laredo Junior College; Rebecca Butler, Dalton Junior College; Susan Coffey, Central Virginia Community College; Douglas Crowell, Texas Tech University; Shirley Ann Curtis, Polk Community College; Kitty Dean, Nassau Community College; Robert Dees, Orange Coast College; Joyce Dempsey, Arkansas Tech University; Mindy Doyle, Orange County Community College; James Egan, University of Akron; Susan Fenyves, University of North Carolina–Charlotte; Marvin Garrett, University of Cincinnati; Ann Gebhard, State University of New York–Cortland; Emma Givaltney, Arkansas Tech University; Corrinne Hales, California State University–Fresno; Gary Hall, North Harris County College; Iris Hart, Santa Fe Community College; James Helvey, Davidson County Community College; Chris Henson, California State University–Fresno; Gloria Hochstein, University of Wisconsin–Eau Claire; Angela Ingram, Southwest Texas State University; John Iorio, University of South Florida; George Ives, North Idaho College; Lavinia Jennings, University of North Carolina–Chapel Hill; Judy Kidd, North Carolina State University; Leonard Leff, Oklahoma State University; Michael Matthews, Tarrant County Junior College–Northeast; Craig McLuckie, Okanagan College; Candy Meier, Des Moines Area Community College; Judith Michna, DeKalb College–North; Christopher O'Hearn, Los Angeles Harbor

College; James O'Neil, Edison Community College; Melissa Pennell, University of Lowell; Sam Phillips, Gaston College; Robbie Pinter, Belmont College; Joseph Sternberg, Harper College; Kathleen Tickner, Brevard Community College; Betty Wells, Central Virginia Community College; Susan Yaeger, Monroe Business Institute.

We would also like to thank our families—Mark, Adam, and Rebecca Kirszner and Demi, David, and Sarah Mandell—for being there when we needed them. And finally, we each thank the person on the other side of the ampersand for making our collaboration work one more time.

1 | A GUIDE TO WRITING ABOUT LITERATURE

CHAPTER 1

READING AND WRITING
ABOUT LITERATURE

Reading Literature

Most of the time, readers are passive; they expect the text to give them everything they need, and they do not expect to contribute much to the reading process. In contrast, **active reading** means participating in the reading process: thinking about what you read, asking questions, and challenging ideas. Active reading is excellent preparation for the discussion and writing you will do in college literature classes. And, because it helps you understand and appreciate the works you read, active reading will continue to be of value to you long after your formal classroom study of literature has ended.

Three strategies in particular —*previewing, highlighting,* and *annotating*— will help you to become a more effective reader. Keep in mind, though, that reading and responding to what you read is not an orderly process — or even a sequential one. You will most likely find yourself doing more than one thing at a time — annotating at the same time you highlight, for example.

Previewing

You begin active reading by **previewing** a work to get a general idea of what to look for later, when you read it more carefully.

Start your prewriting with the work's most obvious physical characteristics. How long is a short story? How many acts and scenes does a play have? Is a poem divided into stanzas? The answers to these and similar questions will help you begin to notice more subtle aspects of the work's form. For example, previewing may reveal that a contemporary short story is presented entirely in a question-and-answer format, that it is organized as diary entries, or that it is divided into sections by headings. Previewing may identify poems that seem to lack formal structure, such as E. E. Cummings's unconventional "l(a" (p. 449); poems written in traditional forms (such as **sonnets**) or in experimental forms, such as the numbered list of questions and answers in Denise Levertov's "What Were They Like?" (p. 641); or **visual poetry,** such as George Herbert's "Easter Wings" (p. 454). Your awareness of these and other distinctive features at this point may help you gain insight into a work later on.

3

Perhaps the most physically distinctive element of a work is its title. Not only can the title give you a general idea of what the work is about, as straightforward titles like "Miss Brill" and "The Cask of Amontillado" do, but it can also isolate (and thus call attention to) a word or phrase that emphasizes an important idea. For example, the title of Amy Tan's short story "Two Kinds" (p. 416) refers to two kinds of daughters — Chinese and American — suggesting the two perspectives that create the story's conflict. A title can also be an allusion to another work. Thus, *The Sound and the Fury*, the title of a novel by William Faulkner, alludes to a speech from Shakespeare's *Macbeth* that reinforces the major theme of the novel. Finally, a title can introduce a symbol that will gain meaning in the course of a work — as the quilt does in Alice Walker's "Everyday Use" (p. 282).

Other physical elements — such as paragraphing, capitalization, italics, and punctuation — can also provide clues about how to read a work. In William Faulkner's short story "Barn Burning" (p. 209), for instance, previewing would help you to notice passages in italic type, indicating the protagonist's thoughts, which occasionally interrupt the narrator's story.

Finally, previewing can enable you to see some of the more obvious stylistic and structural features of a work — the point of view used in a story, how many characters a play has and where it is set, or the repetition of certain words or lines in a poem, for example. Such features may or may not be important; at this stage, your goal is to observe, not to analyze or evaluate.

Previewing is a useful strategy not because it provides answers but because it suggests questions to ask later, as you read more closely. For instance, *why* does Faulkner use italics in "Barn Burning," and *why* does Herbert shape his poem like a pair of wings? Elements such as those described above will gain significance as you read more carefully and review your notes.

Highlighting

When you read a work closely, you will notice additional, more subtle, elements that you may want to examine further. At this point, you should begin **highlighting** — physically marking the text to identify key details and to note relationships among ideas.

What should you highlight? As you read, ask yourself whether repeated words or phrases form a pattern, as they do in Tim O'Brien's short story "The Things They Carried" (p. 251), in which the word *carried* appears again and again. Because this word appears so frequently, and because it appears at key points in the story, it helps to reinforce a key theme of the story: the burdens and responsibilities soldiers carry in wartime. Repeated words and phrases are particularly important in poetry. In Dylan Thomas's "Do not go gentle into that good night" (p. 627), for example, the repetition of two of the poem's nineteen lines four times each enhances the poem's rhythmic, almost monotonous, cadence. As you read, highlight your text to identify such repeated words and phrases. Later, you can consider *why* these elements are repeated.

During the highlighting stage, also pay particular attention to **images** that occur repeatedly, keeping in mind that such repeated images may form patterns that can help you to interpret the work. When you reread, you can begin to determine what pattern the images form and perhaps decide how this pattern enhances the work's ideas. When highlighting Robert Frost's "Stopping by Woods on a Snowy Evening" (p. 672), for instance, you might identify the related images of silence, cold, and darkness. Later, you can consider their significance.

✔ **CHECKLIST**   **Using Highlighting Symbols**

- Underline important ideas.
- Box or circle words, phrases, or images that you want to think more about.
- Put question marks beside confusing passages, unfamiliar references, or words that need to be defined.
- Circle related words, ideas, or images and draw lines or arrows to connect them.
- Number incidents that occur in sequence.
- Set off a key portion of the text with a vertical line in the margin.
- Place stars beside particularly important ideas.

The following poem by Maya Angelou has been highlighted by a student preparing to write about it. Notice how the student uses highlighting symbols to help him identify stylistic features, key ideas, and patterns of repetition that he may want to examine later.

MAYA ANGELOU (1928 –   )

My Arkansas (1978)

There is a deep brooding
in Arkansas.
Old crimes like moss pend ?
from poplar trees.
The sullen earth   5
is much too
red for comfort.

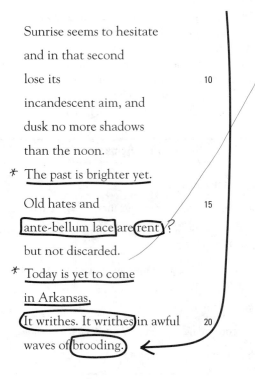

Sunrise seems to hesitate
and in that second
lose its   10
incandescent aim, and
dusk no more shadows
than the noon.
* The past is brighter yet.
Old hates and   15
ante-bellum lace are rent ?
but not discarded.
* Today is yet to come
in Arkansas,
It writhes. It writhes in awful   20
waves of brooding.

This student identifies repeated words and phases ("brooding"; "It writhes") and places question marks beside the two words ("pend" and "rent") that he plans to look up in a dictionary. He also boxes two phrases —"Old crimes" and "ante-bellum lace"— that he needs to think more about. Finally, he stars what he tentatively identifies as the poem's key ideas. When he rereads the poem, his highlighting will make it easier for him to react to and interpret the writer's ideas.

Annotating

At the same time you highlight a text, you also **annotate** it, recording your reactions as marginal notes. In these notes, you may define new words, identify allusions and patterns of language or imagery, summarize plot relationships, list a work's possible themes, suggest a character's motivation, examine the possible significance of particular images or symbols, or record questions that occur to you as you read. Ideally, your annotations will help you find ideas to write about.

The following paragraph from John Updike's 1961 short story "A&P" (p. 128) was highlighted and annotated by a student in an Introduction to Literature course who was writing in response to the question "Why does Sammy really quit his job?" Because the instructor had discussed the story in class and given the class a specific assignment, the student's annotations are quite focused.

In addition to highlighting important information, she notes her reactions to the story and tries to interpret Sammy's actions.

Action isn't the result of thought.

Lengel sighs and begins to look very patient and old and gray. He's been a friend of my parents for years. "Sammy, you don't want to do this to your Mom and Dad," he tells me. It's true, I don't. But it seems to me that once you begin a gesture it's fatal not to go through with it. I fold the apron, "Sammy" stitched in red on the pocket, and put it on the counter, and drop the bow tie on top of

Sammy reacts to the girl's embar-rassment.

it. The bow tie is theirs, if you've ever wondered. "You'll feel this for the rest of your life," Lengel* says, and I know that's true, too, but remembering how he made the pretty girl blush makes me so scrunchy inside I punch the No Sale tab and the machine whirs "pee-pul" and the drawer splats out. One advantage to this scene taking place in summer, I can follow this up with a clean exit, there's no fumbling around getting your coat and galoshes, I just saunter into the electric eye in my white shirt that my mother ironed the night before, and the door heaves itself open, and outside the sunshine is skating around on the asphalt.

Need for a clean exit— romantic idea.

Romantic cowboy, but his mother irons his shirt (irony).

Sometimes you annotate a work before you have decided on a topic. In fact, the process of reading and responding to the text can help you to find a topic to write about. In the absence of a topic, your annotations are likely to be somewhat unfocused, so you will probably need to repeat the process when your paper's direction is clearer.

Writing about Literature

Writing about literature — or about anything else — is an idiosyncratic process during which many activities occur at once: as you write, you think of ideas; as you think of ideas, you clarify the focus of your essay; and as you clarify your focus, you reshape your paragraphs and sentences and refine your word choice. Even though this process sounds chaotic, it has three stages: *planning, drafting,* and *revising and editing.*

Planning an Essay

Considering Your Audience

Sometimes you write primarily for yourself —for example, when you write a journal entry. At other times, you write for others. As you write an essay, consider the special requirements of your **audience.** Is your audience your classmates or your instructor? Can you assume your readers are familiar with your paper's topic and with any technical terms you will use, or will they need brief plot summaries or definitions of key terms? If your audience is your instructor, remember that he or she is a representative of a larger academic audience and therefore expects accurate information; standard English; correct grammar, mechanics, and spelling; logical arguments; and a certain degree of stylistic fluency. In addition, your instructor expects you to support your statements with specific information, to express yourself clearly and explicitly, and to document your sources. In short, your instructor wants to see how clearly you think and whether you are able to arrange your ideas into a well-organized, coherent essay.

In addition to being a member of a general academic audience, your instructor is also a member of a particular community of scholars — in this case, those who study literature. By writing about literature, you engage in a dialogue with this community. For this reason, you need to follow certain specific **conventions**—procedures that by habitual use have become accepted practice. Many of the conventions that apply specifically to writing about literature — matters of style, format, and the like — are discussed in this book. (The checklist on pages 21–22 addresses some of these conventions.)

Understanding Your Purpose

Sometimes you write with a single **purpose** in mind. At other times, you may have more than one purpose. In general terms, you may write for any of the following three reasons:

1. *Writing to respond:*   When you write to **respond,** your goal is to discover and express your reactions to a work. To record your responses, you engage in relatively informal activities, such as brainstorming, listing, and journal writing (see pp. 10–13). As you write, you explore your own ideas, forming and re-forming your impressions of the work.

2. *Writing to interpret:*   When you write to **interpret,** your aim is to explain a work's possible meanings. To do so, you may summarize, give examples, or compare and contrast the work to other works or to your own experiences. Then, you may go on to analyze the work: studying each of its elements in turn, putting complex statements into your own words, defining difficult concepts, and placing ideas in context.

3. *Writing to evaluate:*   When you write to **evaluate,** your purpose is to assess a work's literary merits. You may consider not only its aesthetic appeal, but

also its ability to retain that appeal over time and across national or cultural boundaries. As you write, you use your own critical sense and the opinions of experts to help you make judgments about the work.

> **NOTE:** When you write a **literary argument**, your purpose is to **persuade**. See Chapter 2.

Choosing a Topic

When you write an essay about literature, you develop and support an idea about one or more literary works. Before you begin writing, you should make certain that you understand your assignment. Do you know how much time you have to complete your essay? Are you expected to rely on your own ideas, or are you able to consult outside sources? Is your essay to focus on a specific work or on a particular element of literature? Do you have to write on an assigned topic, or are you free to choose a topic? About how long should your essay be? Do you understand exactly what the assignment is asking you to do?

Sometimes your assignment limits your options by telling you what you should discuss:

- Write an essay analyzing Thomas Hardy's use of irony in his poem "The Man He Killed."
- Discuss Hawthorne's use of allegory in his short story "Young Goodman Brown."
- Write a short essay explaining Nora's actions at the end of Ibsen's *A Doll House*.

At other times, your instructor may give you few guidelines other than a paper's required length and format. In such situations, when you must choose a topic on your own, you can often find a topic by brainstorming or by writing journal entries. As you engage in these activities, keep in mind that you have many options for writing papers about literature. Among them are the following:

- You can explicate a poem or a passage of a play or short story, doing a close reading and analyzing the text.
- You can compare two works of literature. (The Related Works list at the end of each "Reading and Reacting" section in this book suggests possible connections.)
- You can compare two characters or discuss some trait those characters share.
- You can trace a common theme — jealousy, revenge, power, coming of age — in several works.
- You can consider how a common subject — war, love, nature — is treated in several works.
- You can examine a single literary element in one or more works — for instance, plot, point of view, or character development.

- You can focus on a single aspect of a literary element, such as the use of flashbacks, the effect of a shifting narrative perspective, or the role of a minor character.
- You can apply a critical theory to a work of literature —for instance, a feminist perspective to Tillie Olsen's "I Stand Here Ironing" (p. 174).
- You can examine connections between an issue treated in a work of literature —for instance, racism in Richard Wright's "Big Black Good Man" (p. 192) or postpartum psychosis in Charlotte Perkins Gilman's "The Yellow Wallpaper" (p. 372)— and that same issue as it is treated in sociological or psychological journals or in the popular press.
- You can examine some aspect of history or biography and consider its relationship to a literary work —for instance, the influence of World War I on Wilfred Owen's poems.
- You can explore a problem within a work and propose a possible solution —for example, Montresor's actual reason for killing Fortunato in Edgar Allan Poe's "The Cask of Amontillado" (p. 203).
- You can explore similarities and differences between a literary work and a film version of the work —for example, the different endings in Joyce Carol Oates's short story "Where Are You Going, Where Have You Been?" (p. 384) and the film *Smooth Talk*.

Any of those options may lead you to an interesting topic. Remember, however, that you may have to narrow the scope of your topic so that it fits within the limits of your assignment.

Finding Something to Say

Once you have a topic, you have to find something to say about it. The information you collected when you highlighted and annotated will help you formulate the statement that will be the central idea of your essay and will help you find ideas that can support that statement.

You can use a variety of strategies to find supporting material:

- You can discuss ideas with others —friends, classmates, instructors, or parents, for example.
- You can ask questions.
- You can do research, either in the library or on the Internet.
- You can **freewrite**— that is, write on a topic for a given period of time without pausing to consider style, structure, or content.

Two additional strategies —*brainstorming* and *keeping a journal*— are especially helpful at this stage of the writing process.

Brainstorming   When you **brainstorm,** you record ideas — single words, phrases, or sentences (in the form of statements or questions)— as they occur to you, moving as quickly as possible. Your starting point may be a general assignment, a particular work (or works) of literature, or a specific topic. You can brainstorm at any stage of the writing process (alone or in a group), and you can repeat this activity as often as you like.

The brainstorming notes that follow were made by a student preparing to write a paper on the relationships between children and parents in four poems. She began by brainstorming separately about each poem and went on to consider thematic relationships among the poems. These notes are her preliminary reactions to one of the four poems she planned to study, Adrienne Rich's 1984 poem "A Woman Mourned by Daughters."

```
Memory: then and now
    Then: leaf, straw, dead insect (= light);
        ignored
    Now: swollen, puffed up, weight (= heavy);
        focus of attention controls their
        movements.
*
 Kitchen = a "universe"
    Teaspoons, goblets, etc. = concrete
        representations of mother; also =
        obligations, responsibilities (like
        plants and father)
(weigh on them, keep them under her spell)
Milestones of past: weddings, being fed as
children "You breathe upon us now"
    PARADOX? (Dead, she breathes, has weight,
    fills house and sky. Alive, she was a dead
    insect, no one paid attention to her.)
```

Keeping a journal You can record ideas in a journal (a notebook, a small notepad, or a computer file) — and, later, you can use these ideas in your paper. In a **journal,** you expand your marginal annotations, recording your responses to works you have read, noting questions, exploring emerging ideas, experimenting with possible paper topics, trying to paraphrase or summarize difficult concepts, or speculating about a work's ambiguities. A journal is the place to take chances, to try out ideas that may initially seem frivolous or irrelevant; here you can think on paper (or on your computer) until connections become clear or ideas crystallize. You can also use your journal as a convenient place to collect your brainstorming notes and, later, your lists of related ideas.

As he prepared to write a paper analyzing the role of Jim, the "gentleman caller" in Tennessee Williams's play *The Glass Menagerie* (p. 1153), a student explored ideas in the following journal entry.

> When he tells Laura that being disappointed is not the same as being discouraged, and that he's disappointed but not discouraged, Jim reveals his role as a symbol of the power of newness and change—a "bulldozer" that will clear out whatever is in its path, even delicate people like Laura. But the fact that he is disappointed shows Jim's human side. He has run into problems since high school, and these problems have blocked his progress toward a successful future. Working at the warehouse, Jim needs Tom's friendship to remind him of what he used to be (and what he still can be?), and this shows his insecurity. He isn't as sure of himself as he seems to be.

Seeing Connections: Listing

Listing is the process of reviewing your notes, deciding which ideas are most interesting, and arranging related ideas into lists. Listing enables you to discover patterns: to see repeated images, similar characters, recurring words and phrases, and interrelated themes or ideas. Identifying these patterns can help you to decide which points to make in your paper and what information you will use to support these points.

A student preparing a paper about D. H. Lawrence's short story "The Rocking-Horse Winner" (p. 340) made the following list of related details.

<u>Secrets</u>
    Mother can't feel love
    Paul gambles
    Paul gives mother money
    Family lives beyond means
    Paul gets information from horse
<u>Religion</u>
    Gambling becomes like a religion
    They all worship money
    Specific references: "serious as a church"; "It's as if he had it from heaven"; "secret, religious voice"
<u>Luck</u>
    Father is unlucky
    Mother is desperate for luck
    Paul is lucky (ironic)

This kind of listing can be a helpful preliminary organizing strategy, but remember that the lists you make now will not necessarily determine the order or emphasis of ideas in your paper. As your thoughts become more focused, you will add, delete, and rearrange material.

Deciding on a Thesis

Whenever you are ready, you should try to express the main idea of your emerging essay in a **thesis statement** — an idea, usually expressed in a single sentence, that the rest of your essay will support. This idea should emerge logically out of your highlighting, annotating, brainstorming notes, journal entries, and lists. Eventually, you will write a **thesis-and-support paper:** stating your thesis in your introduction, supporting the thesis in the body paragraphs of your essay, and reinforcing the thesis or summarizing your paper's key points in your conclusion.

An effective thesis statement tells readers what your essay will discuss and how you will approach your material. Consequently, it should be precisely worded, making its point clear to your readers, and it should contain no vague words or imprecise phrases that will make it difficult for readers to follow your discussion. For example, consider the following statement: `The use of sound in Tennyson's poem "The Eagle" is interesting.` Although this statement is accurate, it does not convey a precise idea to your readers because the words *sound* and *interesting* are not specific. A more effective thesis statement would be, `Unity in "The Eagle" is achieved through Tennyson's use of alliteration, assonance, and rhyme throughout the poem.`

In addition to being specific, your thesis statement should give your readers an accurate sense of the scope and direction of your essay. It should not make promises that you do not intend to fulfill or include extraneous details that might confuse your readers. If, for example, you are going to write a paper about the dominant image in a poem, your thesis should not imply that you will focus on the poem's setting or tone.

Remember that as you organize your ideas and as you write, you will probably modify and sharpen your thesis. Sometimes you will even begin planning your essay with one thesis in mind and end it with an entirely different one. If this happens, be sure to revise your support paragraphs so that they are consistent with your changes and so that the examples you include support your new thesis. If you find that your thoughts about your topic are changing, don't be concerned; this is how the writing process works.

Preparing an Outline

Once you have decided on a thesis and have some idea how you will support it, you can begin to plan your essay's structure. At this stage of the writing process, an **outline** can help you to clarify your ideas and the relationship of these ideas to one another.

A **scratch outline** is perhaps the most useful kind of outline for a short paper. An informal list of the main points you will discuss in your essay, a scratch outline is more focused than a simple list of related points because it presents ideas in the order in which they will be introduced. As its name implies, however, a scratch outline lacks the detail and the degree of organization of a more formal outline. The main purpose of a scratch outline is to give you a sense of the shape and order of your paper and thus enable you to begin writing.

A student writing a short essay on Edwin Arlington Robinson's use of irony in his 1910 poem "Miniver Cheevy" used this scratch outline as a guide.

```
Speaker's Attitude
    Ironic
    Cynical
    Critical
Use of Diction
    Formal
    Detached
Use of Allusions
    Thebes
    Camelot
    Priam
    Medici
Use of Repetition
    "Miniver"
    "thought"
    regular rhyme scheme
```

Once this outline was complete, the student was ready to write a first draft.

Drafting an Essay

A first draft is a preliminary version of your paper, something to react to and revise. Even before you actually begin drafting your paper, however, you should review the material you have collected. To make sure you are ready to begin drafting, take the following three steps:

1. *Make sure you have collected enough information to support your thesis.* The points you make are only as convincing as the evidence you present to support them. As you read and take notes, you collect supporting examples—in the form of summary, paraphrase, or quotation—from the work or works about which you are writing. How many of these examples you need to use in your draft depends on the breadth of your thesis and how skeptical you believe your audience to be. In general, the broader your thesis, the more material you need to support it. For example, if you were supporting the rather narrow thesis that the speech of a certain character in the second scene of a play reveals important information about his motivation, only a

few examples would be needed. However, if you wanted to support the broader thesis that Nora and Torvald Helmer in Henrik Ibsen's *A Doll House* (p. 784) are trapped in their roles, you would need to present a wide range of examples.

2. *See if the work includes any details that contradict your thesis.* Before you begin writing, test the validity of your thesis by looking for details that contradict it. For example, if you plan to support the thesis that in *A Doll House*, Ibsen makes a strong case for the rights of women, you should look for counterexamples. Can you find subtle hints in the play that suggest women should remain locked in their traditional roles and continue to defer to their fathers and husbands? If so, you will want to modify your thesis accordingly.

3. *Consider whether you need to use outside sources to help you support your thesis.* You could, for example, strengthen the thesis that *A Doll House* challenged contemporary attitudes about marriage by including the information that when the play first opened, Ibsen was convinced by an apprehensive theater manager to write an alternative ending. In this new ending, Ibsen had Nora decide, after she stopped briefly to look in at her sleeping children, that she could not leave her family. Sometimes information from another source can even lead you to change your thesis. For example, after reading *A Doll House*, you might have decided that Ibsen's purpose was to make a strong case for the rights of women. In class, however, you might learn that Ibsen repeatedly said that his play was about the rights of all human beings, not just of women. This information could lead you to a thesis that suggests Torvald is just as trapped in his role as Nora is in hers. Naturally, Ibsen's interpretation of his own work does not invalidate your first judgment, but it does suggest another conclusion that is worth investigating.

After carefully evaluating the completeness, relevance, and validity of your supporting material, you can begin drafting your essay, using your scratch outline as a guide. In this first draft, your focus should be on the body of your essay; this is not the time to worry about constructing the "perfect" introduction and conclusion. (Many writers, knowing that their ideas will change as they write, postpone writing these paragraphs until a later draft, preferring instead to begin simply by stating their tentative thesis.) As you write, remember that your first draft is going to be rough and will probably not be as clear as you would like it to be; still, it will enable you to see the ideas you have outlined begin to take shape.

Revising and Editing an Essay

Revision

When you **revise,** you literally "re-see" your draft and, in many cases, you go on to reorder and rewrite substantial portions of your essay. Before you are satisfied with your essay, you will probably write several drafts, each more closely focused and more coherent than the previous one.

As you move through successive drafts, the task of revising your essay will be easier if you follow a systematic process. As you read and react to your essay, begin by assessing the effectiveness of the larger elements — for example, your thesis statement and your key supporting ideas — and then move on to examine increasingly smaller elements.

Thesis Statement First, reconsider your **thesis statement.** Is it carefully and precisely worded? Does it provide a realistic idea of what your essay will cover? Does it make a point that is worth supporting?

Strategies for Revision

Two strategies can help you to revise your drafts: *peer review* and *a dialogue with your instructor:*

1. **Peer review** is a process in which students assess each other's work-in-progress. This activity may be carried out in informal sessions during which one student comments on another's draft, or it may be a formal process in which students respond to specific questions on a form supplied by the instructor or participate in an electronic exchange. In either case, one student's reactions can help another student revise.
2. **A dialogue with your instructor** — in conference or by email — can give you a sense of how to proceed with your revision. Establishing such an oral or written dialogue can help you learn how to respond critically to your own writing, and your reactions to your instructor's comments on any draft can help you to clarify your essay's goals and write drafts that are increasingly consistent with these goals. (If your instructor is not available, try to schedule a conference with a writing center tutor.)

The following thesis statements are imprecise and unfocused.

Vague: Many important reasons exist to explain why Margot Macomber's shooting of her husband was probably intentional.

Vague: Dickens's characters are a lot like those of Addison and Steele.

To give focus and direction to your essay, a thesis statement must be more pointed and specific.

Revised: Although Hemingway's text states that Margot Macomber "shot at the buffalo," a careful analysis of her relationship with her husband suggests that in fact she intended to kill him.

Revised: With their extremely familiar physical and moral traits, many of Charles Dickens's minor characters reveal that Dickens owes a debt to the "characters" created by the eighteenth-century essayists Joseph Addison and Richard Steele for the newspaper The Spectator.

Supporting ideas   Next, assess the appropriateness of your **supporting ideas,** considering whether you present enough support for your thesis and whether all the details you include are relevant to that thesis. Make sure you have supported all points with specific, concrete examples from the work or works you are discussing, briefly summarizing key events, quoting dialogue or description, describing characters or settings, or paraphrasing important ideas. Make certain, however, that your own ideas are central to the essay and that you have not substituted plot summary for analysis and interpretation. Your goal is to draw a conclusion about one or more works and to support that conclusion with pertinent details. If an event in a story you are analyzing supports a point you wish to make, include a *brief* summary and then explain its relevance to the point you are making.

In the following excerpt from a paper on a short story by James Joyce, the first sentence briefly summarizes a key event, and the second sentence explains its significance.

At the end of James Joyce's "Counterparts," when Farrington returns home after a day of frustration and abuse at work, his reaction is to strike out at his son Tom. This act shows that although he and his son are similarly victimized, Farrington is also the counterpart of his tyrannical boss.

Topic sentences   Now, turn your attention to the **topic sentences** that present the main ideas of your body paragraphs. Make sure that each topic sentence is clearly worded and that it signals the direction of your discussion and indicates the precise relationships of ideas to one another.

Be especially careful to avoid abstractions and vague generalities in topic sentences.

Vague: One similarity revolves around the dominance of the men by women. (What is the similarity?)

Revised: In both stories, a man is dominated by a woman.

Vague: There is one reason for the fact that Jay Gatsby remains a mystery. (What is the reason?)

Revised: Because The Great Gatsby is narrated by the outsider Nick Carraway, Jay Gatsby himself remains a mystery.

When revising topic sentences that are intended to move readers from one point (or one section of your paper) to another, be sure the relationship between the ideas they link is clear.

Unclear: Now the poem's imagery will be discussed.

Revised: Another reason for the poem's effectiveness is its unusual imagery.

Unclear: The sheriff's wife is another interesting character.

Revised: Like her friend Mrs. Hale, the sheriff's wife also has mixed feelings about what Mrs. Wright has done.

Introduction and conclusion When you are satisfied with the body of your essay, you can turn your attention to your paper's *introduction* and *conclusion*.

The **introduction** of an essay about literature should identify the works to be discussed and their authors and indicate the emphasis of the discussion to follow. Depending on your purpose and on your paper's topic, you may want to provide some historical background or biographical information or to briefly discuss the work in relation to similar works. Like all introductions, the one you write for an essay about literature should create interest in your topic and include a clear thesis statement.

The following introduction, though acceptable for a first draft, is in need of revision.

Draft: Revenge, which is defined as "the chance to retaliate, get satisfaction, take vengeance, or inflict damage or injury in return for an injury, insult, etc.," is a major component in many of the stories we have read. The stories that will be discussed here deal with a variety of ways to seek revenge. In my essay, I will show some of these differences.

Although the student clearly identifies her paper's topic, she does not identify the works she will discuss or the particular point she will make about revenge. Her tired opening strategy, a dictionary definition, is not likely to create interest in her topic, and her announcement of her intention in the last sentence is awkward and unnecessary. The following revision is much more effective.

Revised: In Edgar Allan Poe's "The Cask of Amontillado," Montresor vows revenge on Fortunato for an unspecified "insult"; in Ring Lardner's "Haircut," Paul, a young retarded man, gets even with a cruel practical joker who has taunted him for years. Both

of these stories present characters who seek
revenge, and both stories end in murder. However,
the murderers' motivations are presented very
differently. In "Haircut," the narrator is unaware
of the significance of many events, and his ignorance
helps to create sympathy for the murderer; in "The
Cask of Amontillado," where the narrator is the
murderer himself, Montresor's inability to offer a
convincing motive turns the reader against him.

In your **conclusion,** you restate your thesis or sum up your essay's main points; then, you make a graceful exit.

The concluding paragraph that follows is acceptable for a first draft, but it needs further development.

Draft: Although the characters of Montresor and Paul were
created by different authors at different times, they
do have similar motives and goals. However, they are
portrayed very differently.

The following revision reinforces the essay's main point, effectively incorporating a brief quotation from "The Cask of Amontillado" (p. 203):

Revised: In fact, what is significant is not whether each
murderer's act is justified, but rather how each
murderer, and each victim, is portrayed by the
narrator. Montresor—driven by a thirst to avenge
"a thousand injuries" (p.203) as well as a final
insult—is shown to be sadistic and unrepentant; in
"Haircut," it is Jim, the victim, whose sadism and
lack of remorse are revealed to the reader.

Sentences and words Now, focus on the individual sentences and words of your essay. Begin by evaluating your **transitions,** the words and phrases that link sentences and paragraphs. Be sure that every necessary transitional element has been supplied and that each word or phrase you have selected accurately conveys the exact relationship (sequence, contradiction, and so on) between ideas.

When you are satisfied with the clarity and appropriateness of your paper's transitions, consider sentence variety and word choice:

- Be sure you have varied your sentence structure. You will bore your readers if all your sentences begin with the subject ("He. . . . He. . . ."; "The story. . . . The story. . . .").
- Make sure that all the words you have selected communicate your ideas accurately and that you have not used vague, inexact diction. For example,

saying that a character is *bad* is a lot less helpful than describing him or her as *ruthless*, *conniving*, or *malicious*.

- Eliminate subjective expressions, such as *I think, in my opinion, I believe, it seems to me,* and *I feel.* These phrases weaken your essay by suggesting that its ideas are "only" your opinions and have no objective validity.

Using and documenting sources   Make certain that all references to sources are integrated smoothly into your sentences and that all information that is not your own is documented appropriately.

✔ CHECKLIST   Using Sources

☐ Acknowledge all material from sources, including the work or works under discussion, using the documentation style of the Modern Language Association (MLA).

☐ Combine paraphrases, summaries, and quotations with your own interpretations, weaving quotations smoothly into your paper. Introduce the words or ideas of others with a phrase that identifies their source (`According to Richard Wright's biographer, . . .`) and end with appropriate parenthetical documentation.

☐ Use quotations *only* when something vital would be lost if you did not reproduce the author's exact words.

☐ Integrate short quotations (four lines or fewer of prose or three lines or fewer of poetry) smoothly into your paper. Use a slash (/) with one space on either side to separate lines of poetry. Be sure to enclose quotations in quotation marks.

☐ Set off quotations of more than four lines of prose or three lines of poetry by indenting one inch (ten spaces) from the left-hand margin. Double-space, and do not use quotation marks. If you are quoting just one paragraph, do not indent the first line.

☐ Use ellipses — three spaced periods — to indicate that you have omitted material within a quotation (but never use ellipses at the beginning of a quoted passage).

☐ Use brackets to indicate that you have added words to a quotation: `As Earl notes, "[Willie] is a modern-day Everyman"` (201). Use brackets to alter a quotation so that it fits grammatically into your sentence: `Wilson says that Miller "offer[s] audiences a dark view of the present"` (74).

☐ Place commas and periods *inside* quotation marks: `According to Robert Coles, the child could "make others smile."`

☐ Place punctuation marks other than commas and periods *outside* quotation marks: `What does Frost mean when he says, "a poem must ride` on its own melting"? If the punctuation mark is part of the quoted material, place it *inside* the quotation marks: In "Mending Wall," Frost asks, "Why do they make good neighbors?"

- When citing part of a short story or novel, supply the page number (143). For a poem, supply line numbers (3-5), including the word *line* or *lines* just in the first reference. For a play, supply act, scene, and line numbers (2.2.17-22).

- Include a works-cited list (unless your instructor tells you not to).

Editing and Proofreading

Once you have finished revising, you **edit**— that is, you make certain that your paper's grammar, punctuation, spelling, and mechanics are correct. Always run a spell check —but remember that you still have to **proofread**—look carefully for errors that the spell checker will not identify. These include homophones (*brake* incorrectly used instead of *break*), typos that create correctly spelled words (*work* instead of *word*), and words (such as a technical or foreign term or a writer's name) that may not be in your computer's dictionary. If you use a grammar checker, remember that although grammar programs may identify potential problems — long sentences, for example — they may not be able to determine whether a particular long sentence is grammatically correct (let alone stylistically pleasing). Always keep a style handbook as well as a dictionary nearby so that you can double-check any problems a spell checker or grammar checker highlights in your writing.

As you edit, pay particular attention to the mechanical conventions of literary essays, some of which are addressed in the checklist below. When your editing is complete, give your essay a descriptive title. Before you print your final copy, be sure that its format conforms to your instructor's requirements.

✔ CHECKLIST   Conventions of Writing about Literature

- Use present-tense verbs when discussing works of literature:
  The character of Mrs. Mallard's husband *is* not developed. . . .

- Use past-tense verbs only when discussing historical events (Owen's poem conveys the destructiveness of World War I, which at the time the poem *was* written *was* considered to be . . .); when presenting historical or biographical data (Her first novel, which *was* published in 1811 when Austen *was* thirty-six, . . .); or when identifying events that occurred prior to

---

continued on next page

the time of the story's main action (`"Miss Emily is a recluse; since her father's death she has lived alone except for a servant"`).

- Support all points with specific, concrete examples from the work you are discussing, briefly summarizing key events, quoting dialogue or description, describing characters or setting, or paraphrasing ideas.

- Avoid unnecessary plot summary. Your goal is to draw a conclusion about one or more works and to support that conclusion with pertinent details. If a plot detail supports a point you wish to make, a *brief* summary is acceptable. But remember, plot summary is no substitute for analysis.

- Use literary terms accurately. For example, be careful not to confuse *narrator* or *speaker* with *author;* feelings or opinions expressed by a narrator or character do not necessarily represent those of the author. You should not say, `"In the poem's last stanza, Frost expresses his indecision"` when you mean that the poem's *speaker* is indecisive.

- Underline titles of novels and plays; place titles of short stories and poems within quotation marks.

- Refer to authors of literary works by their full names (`Edgar Allan Poe`) in your first reference to them and by their last names (`Poe`) in subsequent references. Never refer to authors by their first names, and never use titles that indicate marital status (`Flannery O'Connor` or `O'Connor`, never `Flannery` or `Miss O'Connor`).

Three Model Student Papers

The three papers in this section were written by students in an Introduction to Literature course. The first, by John Frei, analyzes the short story "The Secret Lion" (p. 412); the second, by Catherine Whittaker, compares the poems "Those Winter Sundays" (p. 623) and "Digging" (p. 624); the third, by Kimberly Allison, discusses the play *Trifles* (p. 770). As they planned, drafted, and revised these papers, the students followed the writing process described in this chapter.

John Frei

Professor Nyysola

English 102

1 May 2006

"The Secret Lion": Everything Changes

The first paragraph of Alberto Alvaro Ríos's "The Secret Lion" presents a twelve-year-old's view of growing up: everything changes. When the magician pulls a tablecloth out from under a pile of dishes, the child is amazed at the "staying-the-same part" (412); adults focus on the tablecloth. As adults, we have the benefit of experience; we know the trick will work as long as the technique is correct. We gain confidence, but we lose our innocence, and we lose our sense of wonder. The price we pay for knowledge is a permanent sense of loss, and this tradeoff is central to "The Secret Lion," a story whose key symbols reinforce its central theme: that change is inevitable and that change is always accompanied by loss.

The golf course is one symbol that helps to convey this theme. When the boys first see the golf course, it is "heaven" (415). Lush and green and carefully tended, it is the antithesis of the dry, brown Arizona landscape and the polluted arroyo. In fact, to the boys it is another world, as exotic as Oz and ultimately as unreal. Before long, the Emerald City becomes black and white again. They learn that there is no such thing as a "Coke-holder," that their "acting 'rich'" is just an act, and that their heaven is only a golf course (416). As the narrator acknowledges,

Opening paragraph identifies work and author. Parenthetical documentation identifies source of quotation.

Thesis statement

Topic sentence identifies one key symbol.

Frei 2

"Something got taken away from us that moment. Heaven" (416).

Topic sentence identifies another key symbol.

The arroyo, a dry gulch that can fill up with water, is another symbol that reflects the idea of the inevitability of change and of the loss that accompanies change. It is a special, Edenlike place for the boys—a place where they can rebel by shouting forbidden words and by swimming in forbidden waters. Although it is a retreat from the disillusionment of the golf course, it is still their "personal Mississippi" (413), full of possibilities. Eventually, though, the arroyo too disappoints the boys, and they stop going there. As the narrator says, "Nature seemed to keep pushing us around one way or another, teaching us the same thing every place we ended up" (414). The lesson they keep learning is that nothing is permanent.

Topic sentence identifies another key symbol.

The grinding ball, round and perfect, suggests permanence and stability. But when the boys find it, they realize at once that they cannot keep it forever, just as they cannot remain balanced forever between childhood and adulthood. Like a child's life, the ball is perfect—but temporary. Burying it is their desperate attempt to stop time, to preserve perfection in an imperfect world, innocence in an adult world. But the boys are already twelve years old, and they have learned nature's lesson well enough to know that this action will not work. Even if they had been able to find the ball, the perfection and the

Frei 3

innocence it suggests to them would still be unattainable. Perhaps that is why they do not try very hard to find it.

Like the story's other symbols, the secret lion itself suggests the most profound kind of change: the movement from innocence to experience, from childhood to adulthood, from expectation to disappointment to resignation. The narrator explains that when he was twelve, "something happened that we didn't have a name for, but it was there nonetheless like a lion, and roaring, roaring that way the biggest things do. Everything changed" (412). School was different, girls were different, language was different. Despite its loud roar, the lion remained paradoxically "secret," unnoticed until it passed. Like adolescence, the secret lion is a roaring disturbance that unsettles everything for a brief time and then passes, leaving everything changed.

Topic sentence identifies final (and most important) symbol.

In an attempt to make things stay the same, to make time stand still, the boys bury the grinding ball "because it was perfect. . . . It was the lion" (416). The grinding ball is "like that place, that whole arroyo" (414): secret and perfect. The ball and the arroyo and the lion are all perfect, but all, ironically, are temporary. The first paragraph of "The Secret Lion" tells us "Everything changed" (412); by the last paragraph we learn what this change means: "Things get taken away" (416). In other words, change implies loss. Heaven turns out to be just a golf course; the round, perfect object only "a cannonball thing used

Conclusion

Frei 4

in mining" (413); the arroyo just a polluted
stream; and childhood just a phase. "Things get
taken away," and this knowledge that things do not
last is the lion, secret yet roaring.

Catherine Whittaker

Professor Jackson

English 102

6 May 2006

Digging for Memories

Robert Hayden's "Those Winter Sundays" and Seamus Heaney's "Digging" are two literary pieces that are tributes to the speakers' fathers. Although the depiction of the families and the tones of the two poems are different, the common thread of love between fathers and children extends through the two poems, and each speaker is inspired by his father's example.

Many other poets have written about children and their fathers. In "Do not go gentle into that good night," Dylan Thomas writes a touching tribute to a father who struggles to resist his approaching death. In other poems, such as Theodore Roethke's "My Papa's Waltz," fathers are depicted as imperfect, vulnerable people who try to cope with life as well as possible.

As all these poems reveal, reflections on childhood can bring complex memories to light, as they do for Hayden's and Heaney's speakers. Now adults, they reminisce about their childhoods with a mature sense of enlightenment not found in childhood. Both speakers describe their fathers' hard work and dedication to their families. Hayden's speaker remembers that even after working hard all week, his father would get up early on Sunday to warm the house in preparation for his

Thesis statement

References to poems in this text include complete authors' names and titles.

First point of similarity: Both poems focus on memory.

Whittaker 2

Parenthetical reference cites line numbers. (First reference to lines of poetry includes word lines. *Subsequent references include just line numbers.)*

Second point of similarity: Both fathers are hard workers.

sleeping children. The speaker vividly portrays his father's hands, describing "cracked hands that ached / from labor in the weekday weather" (lines 3-4). And yet, these same hands not only built the fires that drove out the cold but also polished his children's good shoes. In a similar way, Heaney's speaker reminisces about his father's and grandfather's digging of soil and sod, pointing out their skill and their dedication to their tasks.

The fathers in these poems appear to be hard workers, laborers who struggled to support their families. Not only were they dedicated to their work, but they also loved their children. Looking back, Hayden's speaker realizes that, although his childhood may not have been perfect and his family life was not entirely without problems, his father loved him. Heaney's description of the potato picking makes us imagine a loving family led by a father and grandfather who worked together and included the children in both work and celebration. Heaney's speaker grows into a man who has nothing but respect for his father and grandfather, wishing to be like them and to somehow fill their shoes.

Although some similarities exist between the sons and fathers in the poems, the family life the two poems depict is very different. Perhaps it is the tone of the poems that best reveals the family atmosphere. The tone of "Digging" is wholesome, earthy, natural, and happy, emphasizing the healthy and caring nature of the speaker's childhood. Heaney's speaker seems to have no bad

memories of his father or family. In contrast,
the tone of Hayden's poem is very much like the
coldness of the Sunday mornings. Even though the
father warmed the house, the "chronic angers of
that house" (9) did not leave with the cold. The
speaker, as a child, seems to have resented his
father, no doubt blaming him for the family's
problems. The reader senses that the warm
relationship between the father and the son in
Heaney's poem is absent in Hayden's.

In spite of these differences, the reader
cannot go away from either poem without the
impression that both speakers learned important
lessons from their fathers. Both fathers had a
great amount of inner strength and dedication to
their families. As the years pass, Hayden's
speaker has come to realize the depth of his
father's devotion to his family. He uses the image
of the "blueblack cold" (2) that was splintered
and broken by the fires lovingly prepared by his
father to suggest the father's efforts to keep his
family free from harm. The cold suggests the
tensions of the family that the father is
determined to force out of the house through his
"austere and lonely offices" (14).

In Heaney's poem, the father and grandfather
have also had a profound impact on the young
speaker. As the memories come pouring back, the
speaker's admiration for the men who came before
him forces him to reflect on his own life and
work. He realizes that he will never have the

Focus returns
to parallels
between the
two poems.
Third point
of similarity:
Both speakers
learn from
grandfathers
(discussed
in two para-
graphs).

Whittaker 4

ability (or the desire) to do the physical labor of his relatives: "I've no spade to follow men like them" (28). However, just as the spade was the tool of his father and grandfather, the pen will be the tool with which the speaker will work. The shovel suggests the hard work, effort, and determination of the men who came before him, and the pen is the literary equivalent of the shovel. Heaney's speaker has been inspired by his father and grandfather and hopes to accomplish with a pen in the world of literature what they accomplished with a shovel on the land.

Conclusion reinforces thesis.

"Digging" and "Those Winter Sundays" are poems written from the perspective of sons who are admiring and appreciating their fathers. Childhood memories not only act as images of the past but also evoke the speakers' self-realization and enlightenment. Even after childhood, the fathers' influence over their sons is evident; only now, however, do the speakers appreciate its true importance.

Kimberly Allison

English 1013

Professor Johnson

3 Mar. 2006

Desperate Measures: Acts of Defiance in Trifles

Susan Glaspell wrote her best-known play,
Trifles, in 1916, at a time when married women
were beginning to challenge their socially defined
roles, realizing that their identities as wives kept
them in a subordinate position in society. Because
women were demanding more autonomy, traditional
institutions such as marriage, which confined women
to the home and made them mere extensions of their
husbands, were beginning to be reexamined.

Evidently touched by these concerns, Glaspell
chose as her play's protagonist a married woman,
Minnie Foster (Mrs. Wright), who challenged
society's expectations in a very extreme way: by
murdering her husband. Minnie's defiant act has
occurred before the action begins, and during the
play, two women, Mrs. Peters and Mrs. Hale, who
accompany their husbands on an investigation of
the murder scene, piece together the details of
the situation surrounding the murder. As the
events unfold, however, it becomes clear that the
focus of Trifles is not on who killed John Wright
but on the themes of the subordinate role of
women, the confinement of the wife in the home,
and the experiences all women share. With these
themes, Glaspell shows her audience the desperate
measures women had to take to achieve autonomy.

Opening sentence identifies author and work.

Introduction places play in historical context.

Thesis statement

Allison 2

Topic sentence identifies first point paper will discuss: women's subordinate role.

The subordinate role of women, particularly Minnie's role in her marriage, becomes evident in the first few minutes of the play, when Mr. Hale observes that the victim, John Wright, had little concern for his wife's opinions: "I didn't know as what his wife wanted made much difference to John—" (771). Here Mr. Hale suggests that Minnie was powerless against the wishes of her husband. Indeed, as these characters imply, Minnie's every act and thought were controlled by her husband, who tried to break her spirit by forcing her to perform repetitive domestic chores alone in the home. Minnie's only source of power in the household was her kitchen work, a situation that Mrs. Peters and Mrs. Hale understand because each of these women's behavior is also determined by her husband. Therefore, when Sheriff Peters makes fun of Minnie's concern about her preserves, saying, "Well, can you beat the women! Held for murder and worryin' about her preserves" (774), he is, in a sense, criticizing all three of the women for worrying about domestic matters rather than about the murder that has been committed. Indeed, the sheriff's comment suggests that he assumes women's lives are trivial, an assumption that influences the thoughts and speech of all three men.

Topic sentence introduces second point paper will discuss: women's confinement.

Mrs. Peters and Mrs. Hale are similar to Minnie in another way as well: throughout the play, they are confined to the kitchen of the Wrights' house. As a result, the kitchen becomes

Allison 3

the focal point of the play—and, ironically, the women find that the kitchen holds the clues to Mrs. Wright's loneliness and to the details of the murder. Mrs. Peters and Mrs. Hale remain confined to the kitchen while their husbands enter and exit the house at will. This scenario mirrors Minnie's daily life, as she remained in the home while her husband went to work and into town. The two women discuss Minnie's isolation: "Not having children makes less work—but it makes a quiet house, and Wright out to work all day, and no company when he did come in" (778). Beginning to identify with Minnie's loneliness, Mrs. Peters and Mrs. Hale recognize that, busy in their own homes, they have, in fact, participated in isolating and confining Minnie. Mrs. Hale declares, "Oh, I <u>wish</u> I'd come over here once in a while! That was a crime! That was a crime! Who's going to punish that? . . . I might have known she needed help!" (781).

Soon the two women discover that Minnie's only connection to the outside world was her bird, the symbol of her confinement; Minnie herself was a caged bird who was kept from singing and communicating with others because of her husband. And piecing together the evidence—the disorderly kitchen, the misstitched quilt pieces, and the dead canary—the women come to believe that John Wright broke the bird's neck just as he had broken Minnie's spirit. At this point, Mrs. Peters and Mrs. Hale figure out the connection between the dead canary and Minnie's situation. The stage

Transitional paragraph discusses women's observations and conclusions.

Allison 4

directions describe the moment when the women
become aware of the truth behind the murder: "<u>Their
eyes meet</u>," and the women share "<u>A look of growing
comprehension, of horror</u>" (779).

Topic
sentence
introduces
third point
paper will
discuss:
commonality
of women's
experiences.

Through their observations and discussions in
Mrs. Wright's kitchen, Mrs. Hale and Mrs. Peters
come to understand the commonality of women's
experiences. Mrs. Hale speaks for both of them when
she says, "I know how things can be—for women.
. . . We all go through the same things—it's all
just a different kind of the same thing" (781).
And once the two women realize the experiences
they share, they begin to recognize that they must
join together in order to challenge a male-oriented
society; although their experiences may seem
trivial to the men, the "trifles" of their lives
are significant to them. They realize that Minnie's
independence and identity were crushed by her
husband and that their own husbands have asserted
that women's lives are trivial and unimportant as
well. This realization leads them to commit an act
as defiant as the one that got Minnie into trouble:
they conceal their discovery from their husbands
and from the law.

Significantly, Mrs. Peters does acknowledge
that "the law is the law" (776), yet she still
understands that because Mr. Wright treated his
wife badly, Minnie is justified in killing him. They
also realize, however, that for men the law is
black and white and that an all-male jury will not
take into account the extenuating circumstances

Allison 5

that prompted Minnie to kill her husband. And even if Minnie were allowed to communicate to the all-male court the psychological abuse she has suffered, the law would undoubtedly view her experience as trivial because a woman who complained about how her husband treated her would be seen as ungrateful.

Nevertheless, because Mrs. Hale and Mrs. Peters empathize with Minnie's condition, they suppress the evidence they find, enduring their husbands' condescension rather than standing up to them. And through this desperate action, the women break through the boundaries of their social role, just as Minnie has done. Although Minnie is imprisoned for her crime, she has freed herself; and although Mrs. Peters and Mrs. Hale conceal their knowledge, fearing the men will laugh at them, these women are really challenging society and freeing themselves as well.

In <u>Trifles</u>, Susan Glaspell addresses many of the problems shared by early-twentieth-century women, including their subordinate status and their confinement in the home. In order to emphasize the pervasiveness of these problems and the desperate measures women had to take to break out of restrictive social roles, Glaspell does more than focus on the plight of a woman who has ended her isolation and loneliness by committing a heinous crime against society. By presenting male and female characters who demonstrate the vast differences between male

Conclusion places play in historical context.

Allison 6

and female experience, she illustrates how men define the roles of women and how women must challenge these roles in search of their own significance in society and their eventual independence.

CHAPTER 2

WRITING LITERARY ARGUMENTS

Most of the essays you write about literature are **expository**— that is, you write to give information to readers. For example, you might discuss the rhyme or meter of a poem or examine the interaction of two characters in a play. (Most of the student essays in this book are expository.) Other essays you write, however, may be **literary arguments**— that is, you take a position on a debatable topic and attempt to change readers' minds about it. The more persuasive your argumentative essay, the more likely readers will be to concede your points and grant your conclusion.

When you write a literary argument, you follow the same process you do when you write any essay about a literary topic. However, because the purpose of an argument is to convince readers, you need to use some additional strategies to present your ideas.

Planning a Literary Argument

Choosing a Debatable Topic

Your first step in writing a literary argument will be to decide on a specific topic to write about. Because an argumentative essay attempts to change the way readers think, it must focus on a **debatable topic,** one about which reasonable people may disagree. **Factual statements**— statements about which reasonable people do *not* disagree — are therefore inappropriate as topics for argument.

> **Factual Statement:** Linda Loman is Willy Loman's long-suffering wife in Arthur Miller's play <u>Death of a Salesman</u>.

> **Debatable Topic:** More than a stereotype of the long-suffering wife, Linda Loman in Arthur Miller's play <u>Death of a Salesman</u> is a multidimensional character.

In addition to being debatable, your topic should be narrow enough for you to develop within your page limit. After all, in an argumentative essay, you will have to present your own ideas and supply convincing support while possibly also pointing out the strengths and weaknesses of opposing arguments. If your topic is too broad, you will not be able to discuss it in enough detail.

Finally, your topic should be interesting. Keep in mind that some topics — such as the significance of the wall in Robert Frost's poem "Mending Wall"—have been written about so often that you will probably not be able to say anything very new or interesting about them. Instead of relying on an overused topic, choose one that enables you to write something original.

Developing an Argumentative Thesis

After you have chosen your topic, your next step is to state your position in an **argumentative thesis**— one that takes a strong stand. Properly worded, this thesis statement will lay the foundation for the rest of your argument.

One way to make sure that your thesis actually does take a stand is to formulate an **antithesis**— a statement that takes an arguable position opposite from yours. If you can construct an antithesis, you can be certain that your thesis statement takes a stand. If you cannot, your thesis statement needs further revision to make it an argumentative thesis.

Thesis Statement: The last line of Richard Wright's short story "Big Black Good Man" indicates that Jim was fully aware all along of Olaf's deep-seated racial prejudice.

Antithesis: The last line of Richard Wright's short story "Big Black Good Man" indicates that Jim remained unaware of Olaf's feelings toward him.

> **NOTE:** Your thesis statement is an assertion that your entire essay supports. Keep in mind, however, that you can never prove your thesis conclusively—if you could, there would be no argument. The best you can do is provide enough evidence to establish a high probability that your thesis is reasonable.

Defining Your Terms

You should always define the key terms you use in your argument. For example, if you are using the term *narrator* in an essay, make sure that readers know whether you are referring to a first-person or a third-person narrator. In addition, you may need to clarify the distinction between an **unreliable narrator**— someone who misrepresents or misinterprets events — and a **reliable narrator** — someone who accurately describes events. Without a clear definition of the terms you are using, readers may have a very difficult time understanding the point you are making.

Defining Your Terms

Be especially careful to use precise terms in your thesis statement. Avoid vague and judgmental words, such as *wrong, bad, good, right,* and *immoral.*

Vague: The poem "Birmingham Sunday (September 15, 1963)" by Langston Hughes shows how bad racism can be.

Clearer: The poem "Birmingham Sunday (September 15, 1963)" by Langston Hughes makes a moving statement about how destructive racism can be.

Considering Your Audience

As you plan your essay, keep your audience in mind. For example, if you are writing about a work that has been discussed in class, you can assume that your readers are familiar with it; include a plot summary only when it is needed to explain or support a point you are making. Keep in mind that you will be addressing an academic audience—your instructor and possibly some students. For this reason, you should be sure to follow the conventions of writing about literature as well as the conventions of standard written English (for information on the conventions of writing about literature, see the checklist in Chapter 1, pp. 21–22).

When you write an argumentative essay, always assume that you are addressing a skeptical audience. Remember, your thesis is debatable, so not everyone will agree with you — and even if your readers are sympathetic to your position, you cannot assume that they will accept your ideas without question.

The strategies you use to convince your readers will vary according to your relationship with them. Somewhat skeptical readers may need to see only that your argument is logical and that your evidence is solid. More skeptical readers, however, may need to see that you understand their reservations and that you concede some of their points. Of course, you may never be able to convince hostile readers that your conclusions are legitimate. The best you can hope for is that these readers will acknowledge the strengths of your argument even if they do not accept your conclusion.

Refuting Opposing Arguments

As you develop your literary argument, you may need to **refute**— that is, to disprove — opposing arguments by demonstrating that they are false, misguided, or illogical. By summarizing and refuting opposing views, you make opposing arguments seem less credible to readers; thus, you strengthen your case. When an opposing argument is so strong that it cannot be easily dismissed, however, you should concede the strength of the argument and then point out its limitations.

Notice in the following paragraph how a student refutes the argument that Homer Barron, a character in William Faulkner's short story "A Rose for Emily," is gay.

Opposing argument — A number of critics have suggested that Homer Barron, Miss Emily's suitor, is gay. Certainly, there is some evidence in the story to support this *Concession* interpretation. For example, the narrator points out that Homer "liked men" (Faulkner 118) and that he was not "a marrying man" (Faulkner 118). In addition, the narrator describes Homer as wearing yellow gloves when he took Emily for drives. According to the critic William Greenslade, in the 1890s yellow was associated *Refutation* with homosexuality (24). This evidence, however, does not establish that Homer is gay. During the nineteenth century, many men preferred the company of other men (as many do today). This, in itself, did not mean they were gay. Neither does the fact that Homer wore yellow gloves. According to the narrator, Homer was a man who liked to dress well. It is certainly possible that he wore these gloves to impress Miss Emily, a woman he was trying to attract.

Using Evidence Effectively

Supporting Your Literary Argument

Many literary arguments are built on **assertions**—statements made about a debatable topic—backed by **evidence**—supporting examples in the form of references to the text, quotations, and the opinions of literary critics. For example, if you stated that Torvald Helmer, Nora's husband in Henrik Ibsen's play *A Doll House*, is as much a victim of society as his wife is, you could support this assertion with relevant quotations and examples from the play. You could also paraphrase, summarize, or quote the ideas of literary critics who also hold this opinion. Remember, only assertions that are **self-evident** (All plays include characters and dialogue) or **factual** (A Doll House was published in 1879) need no supporting evidence. All other kinds of assertions require support.

Establishing Credibility

Some people bring **credibility** with them whenever they write. When a well-known literary critic evaluates the contributions of a particular writer, you can assume that he or she speaks with authority. (Although you might question the critic's opinions, you do not question his or her expertise.) But most people do not have this kind of credibility. When you write a literary argument, you must constantly work to establish credibility.

Clear reasoning, compelling evidence, and strong refutations go a long way toward making an argument solid. But these elements in themselves are not enough to create a convincing literary argument. In order to persuade readers, you have to satisfy them that you have credibility — which you can do by *demonstrating knowledge*, *maintaining a reasonable tone*, and *presenting yourself as someone worth listening to*.

Demonstrating Knowledge One way to establish credibility is by presenting your own carefully considered ideas about a subject. A clear argument and compelling support can demonstrate to readers that you know what you are talking about.

You can also show readers that you have thoroughly researched your subject. By referring to important sources and by providing accurate documentation for your information, you present evidence that you have done the necessary background reading. Including a range of sources — not just one or two — suggests that you are well acquainted with your subject. Remember, however, that questionable sources, inaccurate (or missing) documentation, and factual errors can undermine your credibility. For many readers, an undocumented quotation or even an incorrect date can call an entire argument into question.

Maintaining a Reasonable Tone Your **tone** — your attitude toward your readers or subject — is almost as important as the information you convey. Talk *to* your readers not *at* them. If you lecture your readers or appear to talk down to them, you will alienate them. Generally speaking, readers are more likely to respond to a writer who seems balanced and respectful than one who seems strident or condescending.

As you write your essay, use moderate language, and qualify your statements so that they seem reasonable. Try to avoid words and phrases such as *all*, *never*, *always*, and *in every case*, which can make your points seem simplistic, exaggerated, or unrealistic. Also, avoid absolute statements. For example, the statement, `In "Doe Season," the ocean symbolizes Andy's attachment to her mother,` leaves no room for other possible interpretations. A more measured and accurate statement might be, `In "Doe Season," the symbol of the ocean seems to suggest Andy's identification with her mother and her realization that she is becoming a woman.`

Presenting Yourself as Someone Worth Listening To When you write a literary argument, you should try to present yourself as someone your readers will want to listen to. Make your argument confidently, and don't apologize for your views. For example, do not use phrases such as "In my opinion" and "It seems to me," which undercut your credibility. Be consistent, and be careful not to contradict yourself. Finally, avoid the use of *I* (unless you are asked to give your opinion or to write a reaction statement), and avoid slang and colloquialisms.

Being Fair

Argument promotes one point of view over all others, so it is seldom objective. However, college writing requires that you stay within the bounds of fairness and that you avoid **bias**— conclusions based on preconceived ideas rather than on evidence. To make sure that the support for your argument is not misleading or distorted, you should follow the guidelines below:

- *Avoid distorting evidence.* Distortion is misrepresentation. Writers sometimes misrepresent the extent to which critical opinion supports their thesis. For example, by saying that "many critics" think that something is so when only one or two do, they try to make a weak case stronger than it actually is.

- *Avoid quoting out of context.* When you take words from their original setting and use them in another, you are quoting out of context. When you quote a source's words out of their original context, you can change the meaning of what someone has said or suggested. For example, you are quoting out of context if you say, "Emily Dickinson's poems are so idiosyncratic that they do not appeal to readers" when your source says, "Emily Dickinson's poems are so idiosyncratic that they do not appeal to readers *who are accustomed to safe, conventional subjects.*" By eliminating a key portion of the sentence, you alter the meaning of the original.

- *Avoid slanting.* When you select only information that supports your case and ignore information that does not, you are guilty of slanting. You can eliminate this problem by including a full range of examples, not just examples that support your thesis. Be sure to consult books and articles that represent a cross-section of critical opinion about your subject. If you find that such a cross-section does not exist, you may need to modify your thesis. Only by doing this can you be sure that you are not misleading readers.

- *Avoid using unfair appeals.* Traditionally, writers of arguments use three types of appeals to influence readers: **logical appeals,** which address a reader's sense of reason, **emotional appeals,** which play on a reader's emotions, and **ethical appeals,** which emphasize the credibility of the writer. Problems arise, however, when these appeals are used unfairly. For example, writers can use **logical fallacies**— flawed arguments — to fool readers into thinking a conclusion is logical when it is not. Writers can also use inappropriate emotional appeals — appeals to prejudice, for example — to influence readers. And finally, writers can undercut their credibility if they use questionable support — books and articles written by people who have little or no expertise on the topic. This is especially true when information is obtained from the Internet, where the credentials of the writer may be difficult or impossible to assess.

Using Visuals as Evidence

Visuals— pictures, drawings, diagrams, and the like — can add a persuasive dimension to your essay. Because visual images have an immediate impact, they can sometimes make a good literary argument even better. In a sense, visuals are another type of evidence that can support your thesis. For example, suppose you are writing an essay about the play *Trifles* in which you argue that Mrs. Wright's quilt is an important symbol in the play. In fact, your research leads you to conclude that the process of creating the quilt by piecing together its log cabin pattern parallels the process by which the two female characters in the play determine why Mrs. Wright murdered her husband. The addition of a photograph of a quilt with a log cabin pattern could not only eliminate several paragraphs of description but also help support your conclusion.

Of course, not all visuals will be appropriate or effective for a literary argument. Before using a visual, make certain it actually supports the point you make. If it does not, it will distract readers and thereby undercut your argument. To ensure that readers understand the purpose the visual is supposed to serve, introduce it with a sentence that establishes its context; then, discuss its significance, paying particular attention to how it helps you make your point. Finally, be sure to include full documentation for any visual that is not your original creation.

Organizing a Literary Argument

In its simplest form, a literary argument —like any argumentative essay — consists of a thesis statement and supporting evidence. Like other argumentative essays, however, literary arguments frequently use additional strategies to win audience approval and to overcome potential opposition.

Elements of Literary Arguments

- **Introduction:** The introduction should orient readers to the subject of your essay, presenting the issue you will discuss and explaining its significance.
- **Thesis statement:** In most literary arguments, you will present your thesis statement in your introduction. However, if you think your readers may not be familiar with the issue you are discussing (or if it is very controversial), you may want to postpone stating your thesis until later in the essay — perhaps until after the background section.
- **Background:** In this section, you can survey critical opinion about your topic, perhaps pointing out the shortcomings of these opinions. You can also define key terms, review basic facts, or briefly summarize the plot of the work or works you will discuss.
- **Arguments in support of your thesis:** Here you present your assertions and the evidence to support them. It makes sense to move from least controversial

continued on next page

to most controversial point or from most familiar to least familiar idea. In other words, you should begin with arguments that your readers are most likely to accept and then deal with those that require more discussion and more evidence.

- **Refutation of opposing arguments:** In a literary argument, you may want to summarize and refute the most obvious arguments against your thesis. If you do not address these opposing arguments, doubts about your position will remain in your readers' minds. If the opposing arguments are relatively weak, refute them after you have presented your own arguments. However, if the opposing arguments are strong, concede their strengths and discuss their limitations *before* you present your own arguments.

- **Conclusion:** Your conclusion will often restate your thesis as well as the major arguments you have made in support of it. Your conclusion can also summarize key points, remind readers of the weaknesses of opposing arguments, or underscore the logic of your position. Many writers like to end their essays with a strong last line—for example, a quotation or a memorable statement that they hope will stay with readers after they finish the essay.

Sample Student Paper: Writing a Literary Argument

The following student paper presents a literary argument about Dee, a character in Alice Walker's short story "Everyday Use." The student author supports her thesis with ideas she developed as she read the story as well as with information she found when she did research. She also includes two visuals from a DVD of the story.

Margaret Chase

Professor Sierra

English 1001

6 May 2006

The Politics of "Everyday Use"

Alice Walker's "Everyday Use" focuses on a
mother, Mrs. Johnson, and her two daughters,
Maggie and Dee, and how they view their heritage.
The story's climax comes when Mrs. Johnson rejects
Dee's request to take a hand-stitched quilt with
her so that she can hang it on her wall. Knowing
that Maggie will put the quilt to "everyday use,"
Dee is horrified, and she tells her mother and
Maggie that they do not understand their heritage.
Although many literary critics see Dee's desire
for the quilt as materialistic and shallow, a
closer examination of the social and historical
circumstances in which Walker wrote this 1973
story suggests a more generous interpretation of
Dee's behavior.

On the surface, "Everyday Use" is a story
about two sisters, Dee and Maggie, and Mrs.
Johnson, their mother. Mrs. Johnson tells the
reader that "Dee, . . . would always look anyone
in the eye. Hesitation was no part of her nature"
(283). Unlike her sister, Maggie is shy and
introverted. She is described as looking like a
lame animal that has been run over by a car.
According to the narrator, "She has been like
this, chin on chest, eyes on ground, feet in
shuffle" (283) ever since she was burned in a fire.

[margin annotations: Introduction; Thesis statement; Background]

Unlike Dee, Mrs. Johnson never received an
education. After second grade, she explains, the
school closed down. She says, "Don't ask me why: in
1927 colored asked fewer questions than they do
now" (283). Mrs. Johnson admits that she accepts
the status quo even though she knows that it is
unjust. This admission further establishes the
difference between Mrs. Johnson and Dee: Mrs.
Johnson has accepted her circumstances, while Dee
has worked to change hers. Their differences are
illustrated in a film version of the story by their
contrasting dress. As shown in fig. 1, Dee and her
boyfriend Hakim-a-barber dress in the Afro-American

Fig. 1. Dee and Hakim-a-barber arrive at the
family home. "Everyday Use," The Wadsworth
Original Film Series in Literature: "Everyday
Use," dir. Bruce R. Schwartz, DVD, Wadsworth,
2005.

Chase 3

style of the late 1960s, embracing their African heritage; Mrs. Johnson and Maggie dress in plain, conservative clothing.

When Dee arrives home with her new boyfriend, it soon becomes obvious that her character is, for the most part, unchanged. As she eyes her mother's belongings and asks Mrs. Johnson if she can take the top of the butter churn home with her, it is clear that she is still very materialistic. However, her years away from home have also politicized her. Dee now wants to be called "Wangero" because she believes (although mistakenly) that her given name comes from whites who owned her ancestors. She wears African clothing and talks about how a new day is dawning for African-Americans.

The meaning and political importance of Dee's decision to adopt an African name and wear African clothing cannot be fully understood without a knowledge of the social and political context in which Walker wrote this story. Walker's own comments about this time period explain Dee's behavior and add meaning to it. In her interview with White, Walker explains that the late 1960s was a time of cultural and intellectual awakening for African-Americans. Many turned ideologically and culturally to Africa, adopting the dress, hairstyles, and even the names of their African ancestors. Walker admits that as a young woman she too became interested in discovering her African heritage. (In fact, she herself was given the name

[margin note:] Background continued

[margin note:] Social and historical context used as evidence to support thesis

Chase 4

<u>Wangero</u> during a visit to Kenya in the late 1960s.)
Walker tells White that she considered keeping
this new name, but eventually realized that to do
so would be to "dismiss" her family and her
American heritage. When she researched her
American family, she found that her great-great-
grandmother had walked from Virginia to Georgia
carrying two children. "If that's not a Walker,"
she says, "I don't know what is." Thus, Walker
realized that, over time, African-Americans had
actually transformed the names they had originally
taken from their enslavers. To respect the
ancestors she knew, Walker says, she decided it
was important to retain her name.

Along with adopting symbols of their African
heritage, many African-Americans also worked to
elevate these symbols, such as the quilt shown in
fig. 2, to the status of high art. According to
Salaam, one way of doing this was to put these
objects in museums; another was to hang them on
the walls of their homes. Such acts were aimed at
convincing whites that African-Americans had an
old and rich culture and that consequently they
deserved not only basic civil rights, but also
respect. These gestures were also meant to
improve self-esteem and pride within black
communities (Salaam 42-43).

Concession
and
presentation
of opposing
argument

Admittedly, as some critics have pointed out,
Dee is more materialistic than political. For
example, although Mrs. Johnson makes several
statements throughout the story that suggest her

Fig. 2. Traditional hand-stitched quilt.
Alice Walker, "Alice Walker: Stitches in
Time," interview with Evelyn C. White,
<u>The Wadsworth Original Film Series in
Literature: "Everyday Use,"</u> dir. Bruce
R. Schwartz, DVD, Wadsworth, 2005.

admiration of Dee's defiant character, she also
identifies incidents that highlight Dee's
materialism and selfishness. When their first house
burned down, Dee watched it burn while she stood
under a tree with "a look of concentration" (283)
rather than remorse. Mrs. Johnson knows that Dee
hated their small, dingy house, and she knows too
that Dee was glad to see it destroyed. Furthermore,
Walker acknowledges in an interview with her
biographer, Evelyn C. White, that as she was
writing the story, she imagined that Dee might even
have set the fire that destroyed the house and
scarred her sister. Even now, Dee is ashamed of the
tin-roofed house her family lives in, and she has

Chase 6

said that she would never bring her friends there.
Mrs. Johnson has always known that Dee wanted

Refutation
of opposing
argument

"nice things" (283); even at sixteen, "she had a
style of her own: and knew what style was" (283).
However, although these examples indicate that Dee
is materialistic and self-serving, they also show
positive traits: pride and a strong will. Knowing
that she will encounter strong opposition wherever
she goes, she works to use her appearance to
establish power. Thus, her desire for the quilt
can be seen as an attempt to establish herself and
her African-American culture in a society
dominated by whites.

Analysis of
Mrs. Johnson's
final act

Mrs. Johnson knows Dee wants the quilt, but
she decides instead to give it to Maggie.
According to literary critics Houston Baker and
Charlotte Pierce-Baker, when Mrs. Johnson decides
to give the quilt to Maggie, she is challenging
Dee's understanding of her heritage. Unlike Dee,
Mrs. Johnson recognizes that quilts signify
"sacred generations of women who have made their
own special kind of beauty separate from the
traditional artistic world" (qtd. in Piedmont-
Marton 45). According to Baker and Pierce-Baker,
Mrs. Johnson realizes that her daughter Maggie,
whom she has long dismissed because of her quiet
nature and shyness, understands the true meaning
of the quilt in a way that Dee never will
(Piedmont-Marton 45). Unlike Dee, Maggie has paid
close attention to the traditions and skills of
her mother and grandmother: she has actually

learned to quilt. More important, by staying with her mother instead of going to school, she has gotten to know her family. She poignantly underscores this fact when she tells her mother that Dee can have the quilt because she does not need it to remember her grandmother. Even though Maggie's and Mrs. Johnson's understanding of heritage may be more emotionally profound than Dee's, it is important not to dismiss Dee's interest in elevating the quilt to the level of high art. The political stakes of defining an object as art in the late 1960s and early 1970s were high, and the fight for equality went beyond basic civil rights.

Although there is much in the story that indicates Dee's materialism, her desire to hang the quilt should not be dismissed as simply a selfish act. Like Mrs. Johnson and Maggie, Dee is a complicated character. At the time the story was written, displaying the quilt would have been not only a personal act, but also a political act—an act with important, positive results. The final message of "Everyday Use" may just be that in order to create an accurate view of the quilt (and, by extension, of African-American culture) you need both views—Maggie's and Mrs. Johnson's everyday use and Dee's elevation of the quilt to art.

Conclusion restating thesis

Chase 8

Works Cited

Piedmont-Marton, Elisabeth. "An Overview of
    'Everyday Use.'" <u>Short Stories for Students</u> 2
    (1997): 42-45. <u>Literature Resource Center</u>.
    Gale Group Databases. U of Texas Lib. System,
    TX. 20 Apr. 2006 <http://www.galegroup.com>.

Salaam, Kalamu Ya. "A Primer of the Black Arts
    Movement: Excerpts from <u>The Magic of Juju: An
    Appreciation of the Black Arts Movement</u>."
    <u>Black Renaissance/Renaissance Noire</u> (2002):
    40-59. <u>Expanded Academic ASAP</u>. Gale Group
    Databases. U of Texas Lib. System, TX. 21
    Apr. 2006 <http://www.galegroup.com>.

Walker, Alice. "Alice Walker: Stitches in Time."
    Interview with Evelyn C. White. <u>The Wadsworth
    Original Film Series in Literature: "Everyday
    Use."</u> Dir. Bruce R. Schwartz. DVD. Boston:
    Wadsworth, 2005.

---. "Everyday Use." <u>Portable Literature: Reading,
    Reacting, Writing</u>. Ed. Laurie G. Kirszner and
    Stephen R. Mandell. 6th ed. Boston: Wadsworth,
    2007. 282-88.

CHAPTER 3

DOCUMENTING SOURCES AND AVOIDING PLAGIARISM

Documentation is the formal acknowledgment of the sources in a research paper. This chapter explains and illustrates the documentation style recommended by the Modern Language Association (MLA), the style used by students of literature.

What to Document

In general, you must document the following types of information:

- *All word-for-word quotations from a source.* Whenever you use a writer's exact words, you must document them. Even if you quote only a word or two within a paraphrase or summary, you must document the quoted words separately, after the final quotation marks.
- *All ideas from a source (print or electronic) that you put into your own words.* Be sure to document all paraphrases or summaries of a source's ideas, including the author's judgments, conclusions, and debatable assertions.
- *All visuals—tables, charts, and photographs—from a source.* Because visuals are almost always someone's original creation, they must be documented.

NOTE: Certain items do not require documentation: **common knowledge** (information most readers probably know), facts available from a variety of reference sources, familiar sayings and well-known quotations, and your own ideas and conclusions.

Avoiding Plagiarism

Plagiarism is the presentation of another person's words or ideas as if they were your own. Most plagiarism is **unintentional plagiarism**—for example, inserting a passage from a downloaded document directly into your paper and forgetting to include quotation marks and documentation. However, there is a difference between

53

an honest mistake and **intentional plagiarism**—for example, copying sentences from a journal article or submitting as your own an essay that someone else has written. The penalties for unintentional plagiarism may sometimes be severe, but intentional plagiarism is almost always dealt with harshly.

The best way to avoid unintentional plagiarism is to start your research early, keep careful notes, and make sure you distinguish between your words and ideas and those of your sources. The guidelines that follow can help you avoid mistakes that lead to unintentional plagiarism.

Document All Material That Requires Documentation

Original: In Oates's stories there are no safe relationships, but the most perilous of all possibilities is sex. Sex is always destructive. (Tierce, Mike, and John Michael Crafton. "Connie's Tambourine Man: A New Reading of Arnold Friend." *Studies in Short Fiction* 22 (1985): 219–24.)

Plagiarism: In many of Oates's stories, relationships— especially sexual relationships—are dangerous.

In the example above, the writer uses ideas from a source but does not include documentation. As a result, she gives readers the mistaken impression that the source's ideas are actually her own.

Correct: Tierce and Crafton point out that in many of Oates's stories, relationships—especially sexual relationships—are dangerous (220).

Enclose Borrowed Words in Quotation Marks

Original: "The Yellow Wallpaper," which Gilman herself called "a description of a case of nervous breakdown," recalls in the first person the experiences of a woman who is evidently suffering from postpartum psychosis. (Gilbert, Sandra M., and Susan Gubar. *The Madwoman in the Attic: The Woman Writer and the Nineteenth-Century Literary Imagination.* New Haven: Yale UP, 1984.)

Plagiarism: As Gilbert and Gubar point out, the narrator in "The Yellow Wallpaper" is evidently suffering from postpartum psychosis (212).

Even though the writer documents the passage, he uses the source's exact words without putting them in quotation marks.

Correct: As Gilbert and Gubar point out, the narrator in "The Yellow Wallpaper" is "evidently suffering from postpartum psychosis" (212).

Do Not Imitate a Source's Syntax and Phrasing

Original: Tennessee Williams's *The Glass Menagerie*, though it has achieved a firmly established position in the canon of American plays, is often distorted, if not misunderstood, by readers, directors, and audiences. (King, Thomas. "Irony and Distance in *The Glass Menagerie*." *Educational Theatre Journal* 31 (1992): 123–34.)

Plagiarism: Although The Glass Menagerie has a well-established place in the American theater, it is often misinterpreted by those who read it, see it, and direct it (King 125).

Although the student does not use the exact words of the source, he closely follows the sentence structure of the original and simply substitutes synonyms for the writer's key words. Remember, acceptable paraphrases and summaries do more than change words; they use original phrasing and syntax to convey the source's meaning.

Correct: According to Thomas King, although The Glass Menagerie has become an American classic, it is still not fully appreciated (125).

Differentiate Your Words from Those of Your Source

Original: At some colleges and universities, traditional survey courses of world and English literature . . . have been scrapped or diluted. . . . What replaces them is sometimes a mere option of electives, sometimes "multicultural" courses introducing material from Third World cultures and thinning out an already thin sampling of Western writings, and sometimes courses geared especially to issues of class, race, and gender. (Howe, Irving. "The Value of the Canon." *The New Republic* 2 Feb. 1991: 40–47.)

Plagiarism: At many universities, the Western literature survey courses have been edged out by courses that emphasize minority concerns. These courses are "thinning an already thin sampling of Western writings" in favor of courses geared especially to issues of "class, race, and gender" (Howe 40).

Because the student writer does not differentiate his ideas from those of his source, it appears that only the two quotations in the last sentence are borrowed when, in fact, the first sentence also owes a debt to the original. The student should have identified the boundaries of the borrowed material by introducing it with an identifying phrase and ending with documentation. (Note that a quotation always requires its own documentation.)

Correct: According to Irving Howe, at many universities the Western literature survey courses have been edged out by courses that emphasize minority concerns (41). These courses, says Howe, are "thinning an already thin sampling of Western writings" in favor of courses geared especially to issues of "class, race, and gender" (40).

✔ **CHECKLIST   Plagiarism and Internet Sources**

When you download any text from the Internet, you risk plagiarism. To avoid this problem, follow these guidelines:

☐ Download material into individual files so you can easily keep track of your sources.

☐ Do not cut and paste blocks of downloaded text directly into your paper. Summarize or paraphrase this material first.

☐ If you download the exact words of your source, enclose them in boldface quotation marks. If you do this, you will know when you are working with a direct quotation.

☐ Record full documentation information for emails, Web sites, and online postings.

Documenting Sources

Many instructors of English and other languages, as well as instructors in other humanities disciplines, require MLA-style documentation. MLA documentation has three parts: *parenthetical references in the body of the paper* (also known as *in-text citations*), a *works-cited list*, and *content notes.**

Parenthetical References in the Text

MLA documentation style uses parenthetical references within the text to refer to an alphabetical works-cited list at the end of the paper. A parenthetical reference should contain just enough information to guide readers to the appropriate entry on your works-cited list. A typical parenthetical reference consists of the author's last name and a page number.

Gwendolyn Brooks uses the sonnet form to create poems that have a wide social and aesthetic range (Williams 972).

---

*For more information, see the *MLA Handbook for Writers of Research Papers*, 6th ed. (New York: MLA, 2003). You can also consult the MLA Web site at <http://www.mla.org>.

✔ **CHECKLIST**   Guidelines for Punctuating Parenthetical References

---

Paraphrases and Summaries
Place the parenthetical reference after the last word of the sentence and before the final punctuation.

In her poems, Brooks combines the pessimism of modernist poetry with the optimism of the Harlem Renaissance (Smith 978).

Direct Quotations Run in with the Text
Place the parenthetical reference after the quotation marks and before the final punctuation.

According to Gary Smith, Brooks's A Street in Bronzeville "conveys the primacy of suffering in the lives of poor Black women" (980).

According to Gary Smith, the poems in A Street in Bronzeville "served notice that Brooks had learned her craft..." (978).

Along with Thompson, we must ask, "Why did it take so long for critics to acknowledge that Gwendolyn Brooks is an important voice in twentieth-century American poetry" (123)?

Quotations Set off from the Text
Omit the quotation marks, and place the parenthetical reference one space after the final punctuation. (For guidelines for setting off long quotations, see p. 20.)

For Gary Smith, the identity of Brooks's African-American women is inextricably linked with their sense of race and poverty:

> For Brooks, unlike the Renaissance poets, the victimization of poor Black women becomes not simply a minor chord but a predominant theme of A Street in Bronzeville. Few, if any, of her female characters are able to free themselves from a web of poverty that threatens to strangle their lives. (980)

If you mention the author's name or the title of the work in your paper, only a page reference is needed.

> According to Gladys Margaret Williams in "Gwendolyn
> Brooks's Way with the Sonnet," Brooks combines a
> sensitivity to poetic forms with a depth of emotion
> appropriate for her subject matter (972-73).

If you use more than one source by the same author, include a shortened title in the parenthetical reference.

> Brooks knows not only Shakespeare, Spenser, and Milton,
> but also the full range of African-American poetry
> (Williams, "Brooks's Way" 972).

SAMPLE PARENTHETICAL REFERENCES

An entire work

When citing an entire work, state the name of the author in your paper instead of in a parenthetical reference.

> August Wilson's play Fences treats many themes frequently
> expressed in modern drama.

A work by two or three authors

> Myths cut across boundaries and cultural spheres and
> reappear in strikingly similar forms from country to country
> (Feldman and Richardson 124).

> The effect of a work of literature depends on the audience's
> predispositions that derive from membership in various
> social groups (Hovland, Janis, and Kelley 87).

A work by more than three authors

State the last name of the first author, and use the abbreviation *et al.* (Latin for "and others") for the rest.

> Hawthorne's short stories frequently use a combination of
> allegorical and symbolic methods (Guerin et al. 91).

A work in an anthology

> In his essay "Flat and Round Characters," E. M. Forster
> distinguishes between one-dimensional characters and those
> that are well developed (Stevick 223-31).

Note that the parenthetical reference cites the anthology (edited by Stevick) that contains Forster's essay; full information about the anthology appears in the works-cited list.

A work with volume and page numbers

Critics consider <u>The Zoo Story</u> to be one of Albee's best plays (Eagleton 2: 17).

An indirect source

Use the abbreviation *qtd. in* ("quoted in") to indicate that the quoted material was not taken directly from the original source.

Wagner observed that myth and history stood before him "with opposing claims" (qtd. in Winkler 10).

A play with numbered lines

The parenthetical reference should contain the act, scene, and line numbers (in arabic numerals), separated by periods. When included in parenthetical references, titles of the books of the Bible and well-known literary works are often abbreviated — *Gen.* for *Genesis* and *Ham.* for *Hamlet* for example.

"Give thy thoughts no tongue," says Polonius, "Nor any unproportioned thought his act" (<u>Ham</u>. 1.3.64-65).

A poem

Use a slash (/) to separate lines of poetry run in with the text. (The slash is preceded and followed by one space.) The parenthetical reference should cite the lines quoted. Include the word *line* or *lines* in the first reference but just the numbers in subsequent references.

"I muse my life-long hate, and without flinch / I bear it nobly as I live my part," says the speaker in Claude McKay's bitterly ironic poem "The White City" (lines 3-4).

An electronic source

If you are citing a source from the Internet or from an online subscription service, remember that these sources frequently do not contain page numbers. If the source uses paragraph, section, or screen numbers, use the abbreviation "par." or "sec." or the full word "screen."

The earliest type of movie censoring came in the form of licensing fees, and in Deer River, Minnesota, "a licensing fee of $200 was deemed not excessive for a town of 1000" (Ernst, par. 20).

If the source has no page numbers or markers of any kind, cite the entire work. (When readers consult your works-cited list, they will be able to determine the nature of the source.)

In her article "Limited Horizons," Lynne Cheney says that schools do best when students read literature not for what it tells them about the workplace, but for its insights into the human condition.

Because of its parody of communism, the film <u>Antz</u> is actually an adult film masquerading as a child's tale (Clemin).

The Works-Cited List

Parenthetical references refer to a **works-cited list** that includes all the sources you refer to in your paper. Begin the works-cited list on a new page, continuing the page numbers of the paper. For example, if the text of the paper ends on page 6, the works-cited list will begin on page 7.

Center the title Works Cited one inch from the top of the page. Arrange entries alphabetically, according to the last name of each author. Use the first word of the title if the author is unknown (articles —*a, an,* and *the*— at the beginning of a title are not considered first words). Double-space the entire works-cited list between and within entries. Begin typing each entry at the left margin, and indent subsequent lines five spaces (or one-half inch). Each works-cited entry has three divisions —*author, title,* and *publishing information*— separated by periods. The *MLA Handbook for Writers of Research Papers* shows a single space after all end punctuation.

Informal Documentation

Sometimes—for example, when you are writing a paper that includes quotations from a single source that the entire class has read, or when all your sources are from your textbook— your instructor may give you permission to use *informal documentation.* Because both the instructor and the class are familiar with the sources, you supply the authors' last names and page numbers in parenthetical references but do not include a works-cited list.

Below is a directory of the sample MLA works-cited list entries that begin on page 62.

DIRECTORY OF MLA WORKS-CITED LIST ENTRIES

Print Sources: Entries for Books

1. A book by a single author
2. A book by two or three authors
3. A book by more than three authors
4. Two or more works by the same author
5. An edited book
6. A book with a volume number
7. A short story, poem, or play in a collection of the author's work
8. A short story in an anthology
9. A poem in an anthology

10. A play in an anthology
11. An article in an anthology
12. More than one selection from the same anthology
13. A translation

Print Sources: Entries for Articles

14. An article in a journal with continuous pagination throughout an annual volume
15. An article with separate pagination in each issue
16. An article in a magazine
17. An article in a daily newspaper
18. An article in a reference book

Entries for Other Sources

19. A film, videocassette, DVD, or CD-ROM
20. An interview
21. A lecture or an address

Electronic Sources: Entries from Internet Sites

22. A scholarly project or information database on the Internet
23. A document within a scholarly project or information database on the Internet
24. A personal site on the Internet
25. A book on the Internet
26. An article in a scholarly journal on the Internet
27. An article in an encyclopedia on the Internet
28. An article in a newspaper on the Internet
29. An article in a magazine on the Internet
30. A painting or photograph on the Internet
31. An email
32. An online posting

Electronic Sources: Entries from Subscription Services

33. A scholarly journal article with separate pagination in each issue from an online service
34. A scholarly journal article with continuous pagination throughout an annual volume from an online service
35. A monthly magazine article from an online service
36. A newspaper article from an online service
37. A reference book article from an online service
38. A dictionary definition from an online service

Entries for Other Electronic Sources

39. A nonperiodical publication on DVD or CD-ROM
40. A periodical publication on DVD or CD-ROM

MLA • Print Sources: Entries for Books

Book citations include the author's name; book title (underlined); and publication information (place, publisher, date). Capitalize all major words in the title except articles, prepositions, and the *to* of an infinitive (unless it is the first or last word of the title or subtitle). MLA requires that you abbreviate publishers' names — for example, *Basic* for Basic Books and *Oxford UP* for Oxford University Press.

1. A book by a single author
```
Kingston, Maxine Hong. The Woman Warrior: Memoirs of a
     Girlhood among Ghosts. New York: Knopf, 1976.
```

2. A book by two or three authors
```
Feldman, Burton, and Robert D. Richardson. The Rise of
     Modern Mythology. Bloomington: Indiana UP, 1972.
```

Note that only the *first* author's name is in reverse order.

3. A book by more than three authors
```
Guerin, Wilfred, et al., eds. A Handbook of Critical
     Approaches to Literature. 3rd ed. New York: Harper,
     1992.
```

Note that instead of using *et al.*, you may list all the authors' names in the order in which they appear on the title page.

4. Two or more works by the same author
List two or more works by the same author in alphabetical order by *title*. Include the author's full name in the first entry; use three unspaced hyphens followed by a period to take the place of the author's name in second and subsequent entries.

```
Novoa, Juan-Bruce. Chicano Authors: Inquiry by Interview.
     Austin: U of Texas P, 1980.
---. "Themes in Rudolfo Anaya's Work." Address given at
     New Mexico State University, Las Cruces. 11 Apr.
     1987.
```

5. An edited book
```
Oosthuizen, Ann, ed. Sometimes When It Rains: Writings by
     South African Women. New York: Pandora, 1987.
```

Note that here the abbreviation *ed.* stands for *editor*.

6. A book with a volume number
When all the volumes of a multivolume work have the same title, list the number of the volume you used.

```
Eagleton, T. Allston. A History of the New York Stage.
     Vol. 2. Englewood Cliffs: Prentice, 1987.
```

When each volume of a multivolume work has a separate title, list the title of the volume you used.

```
Durant, Will, and Ariel Durant. The Age of Napoleon: A
     History of European Civilization from 1789 to 1815.
     New York: Simon, 1975.
```

(*The Age of Napoleon* is volume 2 of *The Story of Civilization*. You need not provide documentation for the entire multivolume work.)

7. A short story, poem, or play in a collection of the author's work

```
Gordimer, Nadine. "Once upon a Time." "Jump" and Other
     Stories. New York: Farrar, 1991. 23-30.
```

8. A short story in an anthology

```
Salinas, Marta. "The Scholarship Jacket." Nosotros:
     Latina Literature Today. Ed. Maria del Carmen Boza,
     Beverly Silva, and Carmen Valle. Binghamton:
     Bilingual, 1986. 68-70.
```

Note that here the abbreviation *Ed.* stands for *Edited by*. The inclusive page numbers follow the year of publication.

9. A poem in an anthology

```
Simmerman, Jim. "Child's Grave, Hale County, Alabama."
     The Pushcart Prize, X: Best of the Small Presses.
     Ed. Bill Henderson. New York: Penguin, 1986. 198-99.
```

10. A play in an anthology

```
Hughes, Langston. Mother and Child. Black Drama
     Anthology. Ed. Woodie King and Ron Miller. New
     York: NAL, 1986. 399-406.
```

11. An article in an anthology

```
Forster, E. M. "Flat and Round Characters." The Theory of
     the Novel. Ed. Philip Stevick. New York: Free, 1980.
     223-31.
```

12. More than one selection from the same anthology

If you are using more than one selection from an anthology, cite the anthology in a separate entry. Then, list each individual selection separately, including the author and title of the selection, the anthology editor's last name, and the inclusive page numbers.

Baxter, Charles. "Gryphon." Kirszner and Mandell 139-52.

Kirszner, Laurie G., and Stephen R. Mandell, eds. <u>Portable Literature: Reading, Reacting, Writing</u>. 6th ed. Boston: Wadsworth, 2007.

Rich, Adrienne. "Diving into the Wreck." Kirszner and Mandell 606-08.

13. A translation

Carpentier, Alejo. <u>Reasons of State</u>. Trans. Francis Partridge. New York: Norton, 1976.

MLA • Print Sources: Entries for Articles

Article citations include the author's name; the title of the article (in quotation marks); the name of the periodical (underlined); the month (abbreviated, except for May, June, and July) and the year; and the pages on which the full article appears (without the abbreviations *p.* or *pp.*).

14. An article in a journal with continuous pagination throughout an annual volume

LeGuin, Ursula K. "American Science Fiction and the Other." <u>Science Fiction Studies</u> 2 (1975): 208-10.

15. An article with separate pagination in each issue

Grossman, Robert. "The Grotesque in Faulkner's 'A Rose for Emily.'" <u>Mosaic</u> 20.3 (1987): 40-55.

Note that *20.3* signifies volume 20, issue 3.

16. An article in a magazine

Milosz, Czeslaw. "A Lecture." <u>New Yorker</u> 22 June 1992: 32.

An article with no listed author is entered by title on the works-cited list.

"Solzhenitsyn: An Artist Becomes an Exile." <u>Time</u> 25 Feb. 1974: 34+.

Note that *34+* indicates that the article appears on pages that are not consecutive; in this case, the article begins on page 34 and continues on page 37.

17. An article in a daily newspaper

Omit the article *the* from the title of a newspaper even if the newspaper's actual title includes the article.

```
Oates, Joyce Carol. "When Characters from the Page Are
     Made Flesh on the Screen." New York Times 23 Mar.
     1986, late ed.: C1+.
```

Note that *C1+* indicates that the article begins on page 1 of Section C and continues on a subsequent page.

18. An article in a reference book

Do not include publication information for well-known reference books.

```
"Dance Theatre of Harlem." The New Encyclopaedia
Britannica: Micropaedia. 15th ed. 1987.
```

Include publication information when citing reference books that are not well known.

```
Grimstead, David. "Fuller, Margaret Sarah." Encyclopedia
     of American Biography. Ed. John A. Garraty. New York:
     Harper, 1974.
```

Entries for Other Sources

19. A film, videocassette, DVD, or CD-ROM

```
The Heinle Original Film Series in Literature: Eudora Welty's
"A Worn Path." Dir. Bruce R. Schwartz. DVD. Heinle, 2003.
```

20. An interview

```
Brooks, Gwendolyn. "An Interview with Gwendolyn Brooks."
     Triquarterly 60 (1984): 405-10.
```

21. A lecture or an address

```
Novoa, Juan-Bruce. "Themes in Rudolfo Anaya's Work."
     Literature Colloquium. New Mexico State University.
     Las Cruces. 11 Apr. 2002.
```

MLA • Electronic Sources: Entries from Internet Sites

MLA style recognizes that publication information is not always available for electronic sources. Include in your citation whatever information you can reasonably obtain: the title of the Internet site (underlined); the editor of the site (if available); the version number of the source (if applicable); the date of electronic publication (or update); the number of pages, paragraphs, or sections (if available); the name of any sponsoring institution; the date of access; and the URL (within angle brackets). If you have to carry the URL over to the next line, divide it after a slash. If the URL is excessively long, use just the URL of the site's search page, or use the URL of the site's home page, followed by the word *path* and a colon and then the sequence of links to follow.

22. A scholarly project or information database on the Internet

> Philadelphia Writers Project. Ed. Miriam Kotzen Green.
>   May 1998. Drexel U. 12 June 1999 <http://
>   www.Drexel.edu/letrs/wwp/>.

23. A document within a scholarly project or information database on the Internet

> "D-Day: June 7th, 1944." The History Channel Online.
>   1999. History Channel. 7 June 1999 <http://
>   historychannel.com/thisday/today/997690.html>.

24. A personal site on the Internet

> Yerkes, James. Chiron's Forum: John Updike Home Page. 23
>   June 2000. 30 June 2000 <http://www.users.fast.net/
>   ~joyerkers/item9.html>.

25. A book on the Internet

> Douglass, Frederick. My Bondage and My Freedom. Boston:
>   Houghton, 1855. 8 June 2005 <gopher://
>   gopher.vt.edu:10024/22/178/3>.

26. An article in a scholarly journal on the Internet

> Dekoven, Marianne. "Utopias Limited: Post-Sixties and
>   Postmodern American Fiction." Modern Fiction Studies
>   41.1 (1995): 13 pp. 17 Mar. 2002 <http://muse.jhu.edu/
>   journals/mfs.v041/41.1dwkovwn.html>.

When you cite information from the print version of an electronic source, include the publication information for the printed source, the number of pages or paragraphs (if available), and the date of access.

27. An article in an encyclopedia on the Internet

> "Hawthorne, Nathaniel." Britannica Online. Vers. 98.2.
>   Apr. 1998. Encyclopedia Britannica. 16 May 1998
>   <http://www.eb/com/:220>.

28. An article in a newspaper on the Internet

> Lohr, Steve. "Microsoft Goes to Court." New York Times on
>   the Web 19 Oct. 1998. 29 Apr. 2000 <http://
>   www.nytimes.com/web/docroot/library.cyber/week/
>   1019business.html>.

29. An article in a magazine on the Internet

> Weiser, Jay. "The Tyranny of Informality." Time 26 Feb.
>   1996. 1 Mar. 1999 <http://www.enews.com/
>   magazines.tnr/current/022696.3.html>.

30. A painting or photograph on the Internet

> Lange, Dorothea, <u>Looking at Pictures</u>. 1936. Museum of
>   Modern Art, New York. 17 July 2005 <http://moma.org/
>   exhibitions/lookingatphotographs/lang-fr.html>.

31. An email

> Adkins, Camille. Email to the author. 28 June 2005.

32. An online posting

> Gilford, Mary. "Dog Heroes in Children's Literature."
>   Online posting. 17 Mar. 2004. 12 Apr. 2004
>   <news:alt.animals.dogs>.

MLA • Electronic Sources:
Entries from Subscription Services

Online subscription services can be divided into those you subscribe to, such as
America Online, and those your college library subscribes to, such as Expanded
Academic ASAP, LexisNexis, and ProQuest.

To cite information from an online service (such as AOL) to which you subscribe, you have two options. If the service provides a URL, follow the examples in
entries 22 through 30. If the service enables you to use a keyword to access material, provide the keyword (following the date of access) at the end of the entry.

> "Kafka, Franz." <u>Compton's Encyclopedia Online</u>. Vers.
>   3.0. 2000. America Online. 8 June 2001. Keyword:
>   Compton's.

If, instead of a keyword, you follow a series of topic labels, list them (separated by
semicolons) after the word *Path*.

> "Elizabeth Adams." <u>History Resources</u>. 11 Nov. 2001.
>   America Online. 28 Apr. 2001. Path: Research; Biology;
>   Women in Science; Biographies.

To cite information from an online service to which your library subscribes,
supply the publication information (including page numbers, if available) followed by the underlined name of the database (if known), the name of the service, the library at which you accessed the database, the date of access, and the
URL of the online service's home page.

> Luckenbill, Trent. "Environmental Litigation: Down the
>   Endless Corridor." <u>Environment</u> 17 July 2001: 34-42.
>   <u>ABI/INFORM GLOBAL</u>. ProQuest Direct. Drexel U Lib.,
>   Philadelphia. 12 Oct. 2001 <http://www.proquest.com>.

**33. A scholarly journal article with separate pagination in each issue from
an online service**

Schaefer, Richard J. "Editing Strategies in Television
News Documentaries." Journal of Communication 47.4
(1997): 69-89. InfoTrac OneFile Plus. Gale Group
Databases. Augusta R. Kolwyck Lib., Chattanooga, TN.
2 Oct. 2002 <http://www.galegroup.com>.

34. A scholarly journal article with continuous pagination throughout an annual volume from an online service

Hudson, Nicholas. "Samuel Johnson, Urban Culture, and the
Geography of Postfire London." Studies in English
Literature 42 (2002): 557-80. MasterFILE Premier.
EBSCOhost. Augusta R. Kolwyck Lib., Chattanooga, TN.
2 Oct. 2002 <http://www.ebscohost.com>.

35. A monthly magazine article from an online service

Livermore, Beth. "Meteorites on Ice." Astronomy July 1993:
54-58. Expanded Academic ASAP Plus. Gale Group
Databases. Augusta R. Kolwyck Lib., Chattanooga,
TN. 2 Oct. 2003 <http://www.galegroup.com>.

36. A newspaper article from an online service

Meyer, Greg. "Answering Questions about the West Nile
Virus." Dayton Daily News 11 July 2002: Z3-Z7.
LexisNexis Academic. Augusta R. Kolwyck Lib.,
Chattanooga, TN. 2 Oct. 2003 <http://
www.web.lexis-nexis.com>.

37. A reference book article from an online service

Laird, Judith. "Geoffrey Chaucer." Cyclopedia of World
Authors. 1997. MagillOnLiterature. EBSCOhost.
Augusta R. Kolwyck Lib., Chattanooga, TN. 2 Oct.
2003 <http://www.ebscohost.com>.

38. A dictionary definition from an online service

"Migraine." Mosby's Medical, Nursing, and Allied Health
Dictionary. 1998 ed. Health Reference Center. Gale
Group Databases. Augusta R. Kolwyck Lib., Chattanooga,
TN. 2 Oct. 2003 <http://www.galegroup.com>.

**MLA • Electronic Sources:
Entries for Other Electronic Sources**

39. A nonperiodical publication on DVD or CD-ROM

"Windhover." The Oxford English Dictionary. 2nd ed.
DVD. Oxford: Oxford UP, 2001.

40. A periodical publication on DVD or CD-ROM

Zurbach, Kate. "The Linguistic Roots of Three Terms."
    Linguistic Quarterly 37 (1994): 12-47. InfoTrac:
    Magazine Index Plus. CD-ROM. Information Access.
    Jan. 2001.

> **WARNING:** Using information from an Internet source can be risky. Contributors are not necessarily experts, and they frequently are inaccurate or misinformed. Unless you can be certain that the information you are obtaining from these sources is reliable, do not use it. You can check the reliability of an Internet source by asking your instructor or librarian for guidance.

Content Notes

Use **content notes,** indicated by a superscript (a raised number) in the text, to cite several sources at once or to provide commentary or explanations that do not fit smoothly into your paper. The full text of these notes appears on the first numbered page following the last page of the paper. (If your paper has no content notes, the works-cited page follows the last page of the paper.) Like works-cited entries, content notes are double-spaced within and between entries. However, the first line of each explanatory note is indented five spaces (or one-half inch), and subsequent lines are flush with the left-hand margin.

To Cite Several Sources

In the paper

Surprising as it may seem, there have been many attempts
to define literature.[1]

In the note

    [1]For an overview of critical opinion, see Arnold 72;
Eagleton 1-2; Howe 43-44; and Abrams 232-34.

To Provide Explanations

In the paper

In recent years, gothic novels have achieved great
popularity.[3]

In the note

    [3]Gothic novels, works written in imitation of
medieval romances, originally relied on supernatural
occurrences. They flourished in the late eighteenth and
early nineteenth centuries.

2| FICTION

CHAPTER 4

UNDERSTANDING FICTION

A **narrative** tells a story by presenting events in some logical or orderly way. A work of **fiction** is a narrative that originates in the imagination of the author rather than in history or fact. Certainly some fiction — historical or autobiographical fiction, for example — focuses on real people and is grounded in actual events, but the way the characters interact, what they say, and how the plot unfolds are largely the author's invention.

Even before they know how to read, most people have learned how narratives are structured. As children learn how to tell a story, they start to experiment with its form, learning the value of exaggerating, adding or deleting details, rearranging events, and bending facts. In other words, they learn how to *fictionalize* a narrative to achieve a desired effect. This kind of informal, personal narrative is similar to more structured literary narratives.

Origins of Modern Fiction

The earliest examples of narrative fiction are linked with our understanding of stories in general. Human beings have always had stories to tell, and as our species evolved, so did our means of self-expression. Our early ancestors depicted the stories of their daily lives and beliefs in primitive drawings that used pictures as symbols. As language evolved, so too did our means of communicating — and our need to preserve what we understood to be our past.

Stories and songs emerged as an oral means of communicating and preserving the past: tales of heroic battles or struggles, myths, or religious beliefs. In a society that was not literate, and in a time before mass communication, the oral tradition enabled people to pass down these stories, usually in the form of rhyming poems. These poems used various literary devices — including **rhyme** and **alliteration** as well as **anaphora** (the repetition of key words or phrases) — to make the poems easier to remember. Thus, the earliest forms of fiction were in fact poetry.

Eventually written down, these extended narratives developed into **epics**— long narrative poems about heroic figures whose actions determine the fate of a nation or of an entire race. Homer's *Iliad* and *Odyssey*, the ancient Babylonian *Epic of Gilgamesh*, the Hindu *Bhagavad Gita*, and the Anglo-Saxon *Beowulf* are examples. Many of the tales of the Old Testament also came out of this tradition.

Engraving of Ulysses Slaying Penelope's Suitors, from Homer's
Odyssey.

Engraving of the Trojan horse from Homer's *Iliad.*

The setting of an epic is vast — sometimes worldwide or cosmic, including heaven and hell — and the action commonly involves a battle or a perilous journey. Quite often, divine beings participate in the action and influence the outcome of events, as they do in the Trojan War in the *Iliad* and in the founding of Rome in Virgil's *Aeneid*.

During the Middle Ages, these early epics were supplanted by the **romance.** Written initially in verse and later in prose, the romance replaced the gods, goddesses, and central heroic characters of the epic with knights, kings, and damsels in distress. Events were controlled by enchantments rather than by the will of divine beings. The anonymously written *Sir Gawain and the Green Knight* and Thomas Malory's *Le Morte d'Arthur* are examples of romances based upon the legend of King Arthur and the Knights of the Round Table.

Other significant texts of the Middle Ages were Geoffrey Chaucer's *The Canterbury Tales* and Giovanni Boccaccio's *The Decameron*, both written in the fourteenth century. These works contained extended poems and stories, respectively, that were integrated into a larger narrative framework; in this respect, they had much in common with today's collections of short stories.

The History of the Novel

The evolution of the **novel** has been a gradual but steady process. Early forms of literature share many of the characteristics of the novel (although not necessarily

he Lady Guinevere

Portrait of Queen Guinevere, King Arthur's wife and Sir Lancelot's mistress.

sharing its recognizable form, style, or focus). Epics and romances, for instance, often had broad plots, heroic characters, and moral themes, and in this way, they were precursors of what we call the novel today.

Perhaps the most notable event in the development of the novel, and of literature as a whole, was the invention of the printing press by Johannes Gutenberg in 1440. Before this milestone, printing was a costly and impractical process that was largely reserved for medical books and sacred texts. In fact, invention made the production and distribution of longer works a practical possibility and forever changed, broadened, and expanded the scope of what we consider literature to be—and how we access it. In fact, the printing press was one of the factors that made the Renaissance possible. During this period, philosophy, science, literature, and the arts, flowered. The **pastoral romance,** a prose tale set in an idealized rural world, and the **character,** a brief satirical sketch illustrating a type of personality, both became popular in Renaissance England. The **picaresque novel,** an episodic, often satirical work about a rogue or rascal (such as Miguel de Cervantes' *Don Quixote*) emerged in seventeenth-century Spain. Other notable Renaissance-era

An 1863 engraving by Gustave Doré depicting a scene from Miguel de Cervantes's *Don Quixote*.

texts included Sir Philip Sidney's *Arcadia*, Edmund Spenser's *The Faerie Queen*, and John Bunyan's *The Pilgrim's Progress*. Each of these texts had elements of the novel—longer narrative, extended plot, the development of characters over time, and a hero/protagonist—and the form continued to evolve.

The English writer Daniel Defoe is commonly given credit for writing the first novel. His *Robinson Crusoe* (1719) is an episodic narrative similar to a picaresque but unified by a single setting as well as by a central character. Jonathan Swift's *Gulliver's Travels*, which followed Defoe, is a satirical commentary on the undesirable outcomes of science. During this time, the **epistolary novel** also flourished. This kind of novel told a story in the format of letters, or included letters as a means of disseminating information. Henry Fielding's *Tom Jones* is an example from the eighteenth century; a contemporary example is Alice Walker's *The Color Purple*.

By the nineteenth century, the novel had reached a high point in its development, and its influence and importance were widespread. During the Victorian era in England (1837–1901), many novels reflected the era's preoccupation with propriety and manners. The most notable examples of these **novels of manners** were Jane Austen's *Sense and Sensibility* and *Pride and Prejudice*. Beyond the world of the aristocracy, members of the middle class clamored for novels that mirrored their own experiences, and writers such as George Eliot, Charles Dickens, William Thackeray, and Charlotte and Emily Brontë appealed to this desire by creating large fictional worlds populated by many different characters who reflected the complexity—and at times the melodrama—of Victorian society. Other writers addressed the dire consequences of science and ambition, as Mary Wollstonecraft Shelley did in her Gothic tale *Frankenstein*.

Nineteenth-century woodcut by J. Mahoney depicting a scene from Charles Dickens's *Oliver Twist*.

In the United States, the early nineteenth century was marked by novels that reflected the concerns of a growing country with burgeoning interests. **Realism,** which strove to portray everyday events and people in a realistic fashion, began in France with Honoré de Balzac and Gustav Flaubert and spread to the United States, influencing writers such as Henry James, Stephen Crane, and Mark Twain. James Fenimore Cooper (*Last of the Mohicans*) and Nathaniel Hawthorne wrote historical fiction, while Herman Melville (*Moby-Dick*) and Edgar Allan Poe confronted issues of good and evil, madness and sanity.

Other writers of the nineteenth century had a slightly different set of concerns. Many addressed social, historical, or even feminist themes in their work. In the United States, writers who addressed such concerns included Harriet Beecher Stowe (*Uncle Tom's Cabin*), Louisa May Alcott (*Little Women*), and Kate Chopin (*The Awakening*). Meanwhile, in Russia, novelists such as Fyodor Dostoyevsky (*Crime and Punishment*) and Leo Tolstoy (*War and Peace*) examined the everyday lives, as well as the larger struggles and triumphs, of their people.

The early twentieth century marked the beginning of a literary movement known as **modernism,** in which writers reacted to the increasing complexity of a changing world and mourned the passing of old ways under the pressures of modernity. World War I, urbanization, and the rise of industrialism all contributed to a sense that new things needed to be told in new ways, and writers such as James Joyce (*Ulysses*), Virginia Woolf (*To the Lighthouse*), and D. H. Lawrence (*Sons and Lovers*) experimented with both form and content.

In the United States, the Roaring Twenties and the Great Depression inspired numerous novelists who set out to write The Great American Novel and capture the culture and concerns of the times, often in very gritty and realistic ways. These authors included F. Scott Fitzgerald (*The Great Gatsby*), Ernest Hemingway (*The Sun Also Rises*), William Faulkner (*The Sound and the Fury*), and John Steinbeck (*The Grapes of Wrath*). A little later, novelists such as Richard Wright (*Native Son*) and Ralph Ellison (*Invisible Man*) made important literary contributions by addressing the sociopolitical climate for African-Americans in a segregated society.

In the aftermath of modernism, a movement called **postmodernism** emerged. Postmodern artists reacted to the confines and limitations placed upon form and meaning by opening ideas of interpretation. Often, the search for meaning in a text became the meaning itself, and in this way, the work's meaning became relative and subjective. Postmodern novelists, such as George Orwell (*1984*), Aldous Huxley (*Brave New World*), and William Golding (*Lord of the Flies*), confronted the changing society, the future, and the impact of technology.

Contemporary fiction has been marked and influenced by the developments of the latter part of the twentieth century, including globalization, the rise of technology, and the advent of the Internet and the Age of Communication. As our ability to interact and communicate with other societies has increased exponentially, so too has our access to the literature of other cultures. Contemporary fiction is a world that mirrors the diversity of its participants in terms of form, content, themes, styles, and language. There are many writers worthy of mention, as each culture makes its own invaluable contributions. Some particularly note-worthy postmodern writers include Gabriel Garcia Marquez, Salman Rushdie, Milan Kundera, Chinua Achebe, Saul Bellow, Toni Morrison, and V. S. Naipul. As we continue into the twenty-first century, the only thing that remains certain about the future of the novel, and of fiction in general, is its past.

The History of the Short Story

Early precursors for the short story include **anecdotes, parables, fables, folk tales, and fairy tales.** What all of these forms have in common is brevity and a moral. The ones that have survived, such as "Cinderella" and Aesop's *Fables,* are con-temporary versions of old, even ancient, tales that can be traced back centuries through many different cultures.

Undated woodcut of Cinderella

Folktales and fairy tales share many different characteristics. First, they feature simple charac-ters who illustrate a quality or trait that can be summed up in a few words. Much of the appeal of "Cinderella," for example, depends on the con-trast between the selfish, sadistic stepsisters and the poor, gentle, victimized Cinderella. In addi-tion, the folktale or fairy tale has an obvious theme or moral—good triumphing over evil, for instance. The stories move directly to their conclusions, never interrupted by ingenious or unexpected twists of plot. (Love is temporarily thwarted, but the prince eventually finds Cin-derella and marries her.) Finally, these tales are anchored not in specific times or places but in "Once upon a time" settings, green worlds of prehistory filled with royalty, talk-ing animals, and magic.

Giovanni Boccaccio's *The Decameron* and Geoffrey Chaucer's *The Canterbury Tales,* both written in the fourteenth century, were precursors of the modern short story in that they included individual stories worked together thematically within a larger narrative framework. *Grimm's Fairy Tales* (1824–1826), an early collec-tion of short narratives and folk stories, also helped to pave the way for the development of the genre, but it was not until the nineteenth century that the contemporary version of the short story emerged.

During the last quarter of the nineteenth century, a proliferation of literary and popular magazines and journals created a demand for short fiction (between 3,000 and 15,000 words) that could be encapsulated and published as a whole rather than in serial installments, as most novels at the time were. Nathaniel Hawthorne's *Twice Told Tales* (1842) and Edgar Allan Poe's *Tales of the Grotesque and Arabesque* (1836) were early collections of short stories. Americans in partic-ular hungrily consumed the written word, and short stories soared in popularity.

In fact, because the short story was embraced so readily and developed so quickly in the United States, it is commonly (although not quite accurately) thought of as an American literary form.

Defining the Short Story

Like the novel, the short story evolved from various forms of narrative and has its roots in an oral tradition. However, whereas the novel is an extended piece of narrative fiction, the **short story** is distinguished by its relative brevity, which creates a specific set of expectations and possibilities. Unlike the novelist, the short story writer cannot devote a great deal of space to developing a highly complex plot or a large number of characters. As a result, the short story often begins close to or at the height of action and is more limited in the number of characters it can develop. Usually focusing on a single incident, the writer develops one or more characters by showing their reactions to events. This attention to character development, as well as its detailed description of setting, is what distinguishes the short story from earlier short narrative forms.

In many contemporary short stories, a character experiences an **epiphany,** a moment of illumination in which something hidden or not understood becomes immediately clear. In other short stories, the thematic significance, or meaning, is communicated through the way in which the characters develop, or react, over time. Regardless of the specifics of its format or its theme, a short story offers readers an open window to a world that they can enter—if only briefly.

The short story that follows, Ernest Hemingway's "Hills Like White Elephants" (1927), illustrates many of the characteristics of the modern **short story.** Although it is so brief that it might be more accurately called a **short-short story,** it uses its limited space to establish a setting and develop two characters. From the story's first paragraph, readers know where the story takes place and whom it is about: "The American and the girl with him sat at a table in the shade, outside the building. It was very hot and the express from Barcelona would come in forty minutes." As time elapses and the man and woman wait for the train to Madrid, their strained dialogue reveals the tension between them and hints at the serious conflict they must resolve.

ERNEST HEMINGWAY (1898–1961) grew up in Oak Park, Illinois, and after high school graduation began his writing career as a cub reporter on the *Kansas City Star.* While working as a volunteer ambulance driver in World War I, eighteen-year-old Hemingway was wounded. As Hemingway himself told the story, he was hit by machine-gun fire while carrying an Italian soldier to safety. (Hemingway biographer Michael Reynolds, however, reports that Hemingway was wounded when a mortar shell fell and killed the man next to him.)

Success for Hemingway came early, with publication of the short story collection *In Our Time* (1925) and his first and most acclaimed novel, *The Sun Also Rises* (1926), a portrait of a postwar "lost generation" of Americans adrift in Europe. This group was based on his own circle of friends and their experiences, and thus the novel established Hemingway's ability to create fiction and art out of the reality of his own life. *A Farewell to Arms* (1929) harks back to his war experiences; *For Whom the Bell Tolls* (1940) emerged out of his experiences as a journalist in Spain during the Spanish Civil War. Later in life, he made his home in Key West, Florida, and then in Cuba, where he wrote *The Old Man and the Sea* (1952). In 1954, Hemingway won the Nobel Prize in Literature. In 1961, plagued by poor health and mental illness—and perhaps also by the difficulty of living up to his own image—Hemingway took his own life.

Hills Like White Elephants   (1927)

The hills across the valley of the Ebro° were long and white. On this side there was no shade and no trees and the station was between two lines of rails in the sun. Close against the side of the station there was the warm shadow of the building and a curtain, made of strings of bamboo beads, hung across the open door into the bar, to keep out flies. The American and the girl with him sat at a table in the shade, outside the building. It was very hot and the express from Barcelona would come in forty minutes. It stopped at this junction for two minutes and went on to Madrid.

"What should we drink?" the girl asked. She had taken off her hat and put it on the table.

"It's pretty hot," the man said.

"Let's drink beer."

5   "Dos cervezas," the man said into the curtain.

"Big ones?" a woman asked from the doorway.

"Yes. Two big ones."

The woman brought two glasses of beer and two felt pads. She put the felt pads and the beer glasses on the table and looked at the man and the girl. The girl was looking off at the line of hills. They were white in the sun and the country was brown and dry.

"They look like white elephants," she said.

10   "I've never seen one," the man drank his beer.

"No, you wouldn't have."

"I might have," the man said. "Just because you say I wouldn't have doesn't prove anything."

The girl looked at the bead curtain. "They've painted something on it," she said. "What does it say?"

"Anis del Toro.° It's a drink."

15   "Could we try it?"

Ebro: A river in northern Spain.

Anis del Toro: A dark alcoholic drink made from anise, an herb that tastes like licorice.

The man called "Listen" through the curtain. The woman came out from the bar.

"Four reales."°

"We want two Anis del Toro."

"With water?"

"Do you want it with water?"

"I don't know," the girl said. "Is it good with water?"   20

"It's all right."

"You want them with water?" asked the woman.

"Yes, with water."

"It tastes like licorice," the girl said and put the glass down.   25

"That's the way with everything."

"Yes," said the girl. "Everything tastes of licorice. Especially all the things you've waited so long for, like absinthe."

"Oh, cut it out."

"You started it," the girl said. "I was being amused. I was having a fine time."

"Well, let's try and have a fine time."   30

"All right I was trying. I said the mountains looked like white elephants. Wasn't that bright?"

"That was bright."

"I wanted to try this new drink. That's all we do, isn't it—look at things and try new drinks?"

"I guess so."

The girl looked across at the hills.   35

"They're lovely hills," she said. "They don't really look like white elephants. I just meant the coloring of their skin through the trees."

"Should we have another drink?"

"All right."

The warm wind blew the bead curtain against the table.

"The beer's nice and cool," the man said.   40

"It's lovely," the girl said.

"It's really an awfully simple operation, Jig," the man said. "It's not really an operation at all."

The girl looked at the ground the table legs rested on.

"I know you wouldn't mind it, Jig. It's really not anything. It's just to let the air in."

The girl did not say anything.   45

"I'll go with you and I'll stay with you all the time. They just let the air in and then it's all perfectly natural."

"Then what will we do afterward?"

"We'll be fine afterward. Just like we were before."

---

reales: Spanish coins.

"What makes you think so?"

50   "That's the only thing that bothers us. It's the only thing that's made us unhappy."

The girl looked at the bead curtain, put her hand out and took hold of two of the strings of beads.

"And you think then we'll be all right and be happy."

"I know we will. You don't have to be afraid. I've known lots of people that have done it."

"So have I," said the girl. "And afterward they were all so happy."

55   "Well," the man said, "if you don't want to you don't have to. I wouldn't have you do it if you didn't want to. But I know it's perfectly simple."

"And you really want to?"

"I think it's the best thing to do. But I don't want you to do it if you don't really want to."

"And if I do it you'll be happy and things will be like they were and you'll love me?"

"I love you now. You know I love you."

60   "I know. But if I do it, then it will be nice again if I say things are like white elephants, and you'll like it?"

"I'll love it. I love it now but I just can't think about it. You know how I get when I worry."

"If I do it you won't ever worry?"

"I won't worry about that because it's perfectly simple."

"Then I'll do it. Because I don't care about me."

65   "What do you mean?"

"I don't care about me."

"Well, I care about you."

"Oh, yes. But I don't care about me. And I'll do it and then everything will be fine."

"I don't want you to do it if you feel that way."

70   The girl stood up and walked to the end of the station. Across, on the other side, were fields of grain and trees along the banks of the Ebro. Far away beyond the river, were mountains. The shadow of a cloud moved across the field of grain and she saw the river through the trees.

"And we could have all this," she said. "And we could have everything and everyday we make it more impossible."

"What did you say?"

"I said we could have everything."

"We can have everything."

75   "No, we can't."

"We can have the whole world."

"No, we can't."

"We can go everywhere."

80   "No, we can't. It isn't ours any more."

"It's ours."

"No, it isn't. And once they take it away, you never get it back."

"But they haven't taken it away."

"We'll wait and see."

"Come on back in the shade," he said. "You mustn't feel that way."

"I don't feel any way," the girl said. "I just know things."   85

"I don't want you to do anything that you don't want to do —."

"Nor that isn't good for me," she said. "I know. Could we have another beer?"

"All right. But you've got to realize —"

"I realize," the girl said. "Can't we maybe stop talking?"

They sat down at the table and the girl looked across at the hills on the dry side 90
of the valley and the man looked at her and at the table.

"You've got to realize," he said, "that I don't want you to do it if you don't want
to. I'm perfectly willing to go through with it if it means anything to you."

"Doesn't it mean anything to you? We could get along."

"Of course it does. But I don't want anybody but you. I don't want any one else.
And I know it's perfectly simple."

"Yes, you know it's perfectly simple."

"It's all right for you to say that, but I do know it."   95

"Would you do something for me now?"

"I'd do anything for you."

"Would you please please please please please please please stop talking?"

He did not say anything but looked at the bags against the wall of the station.
There were labels on them from all the hotels where they had spent nights.

"But I don't want you to," he said, "I don't care anything about it."   100

"I'll scream," the girl said.

The woman came out through the curtains with two glasses of beer and put
them down on the damp felt pads. "The train comes in five minutes," she said.

"What did she say?" asked the girl.

"That the train is coming in five minutes."

The girl smiled brightly at the woman, to thank her.   105

"I'd better take the bags over to the other side of the station," the man said.
She smiled at him.

"All right. Then come back and we'll finish the beer."

He picked up the two heavy bags and carried them around the station to the
other tracks. He looked up the tracks but could not see the train. Coming back, he
walked through the barroom, where people waiting for the train were drinking. He
drank an Anis at the bar and looked at the people. They were all waiting reasonably for the train. He went out through the bead curtain. She was sitting at the
table and smiled at him.

"Do you feel better?" he asked.

"I feel fine," she said. "There's nothing wrong with me. I feel fine."   110

❖ ❖ ❖

Recognizing Kinds of Fiction

As noted earlier, a **short story** is a work of fiction that is marked by its brevity, its relatively limited scope of temporal and character development, and its ability to achieve thematic significance in a relatively short space. A **novella,** such as Herman Melville's "Bartleby, the Scrivener" (1853), is an extended short story that shares some characteristics (for example, concentrated action) with a short story while retaining some qualities of a novel, including greater character development. At the other end of the spectrum are **short-short stories,** such as those collected in Chapter 5, which are under 1,500 words (about five pages) in length, and **flash fiction,** or **micro-fiction,** which can vary in length from 200 to 500 words. **Prose poems,** such as Carolyn Forché's, "The Colonel" (p. 593), are hybrid versions of literature that have characteristics of both prose (being written in paragraphs) and poetry (being written in verse form, often using imagery, meter, and rhyme to convey lyrical beauty). Today, the Internet has given rise to new possibilities for arranging, presenting, and disseminating text.

There are, it seems, as many different ways to tell a story as there are stories to be told. A short story may be comic or tragic; its subject may be growing up, marriage, crime and punishment, war, sexual awakening, death, or any number of other human concerns. The setting can be an imaginary world, the old West, rural America, the jungles of Uruguay, nineteenth-century Russia, precommunist China, or modern Egypt. The story may have a conventional form, with a definite beginning, middle, and end, or it may be structured as a letter, as a diary entry, or even as a collection of random notes. The narrator of a story may be trustworthy or unreliable, involved in the action or a disinterested observer, sympathetic or deserving of scorn, extremely ignorant or highly insightful, limited in vision or able to see inside the minds of all the characters. As the selections in this anthology show, the possibilities of the short story are infinite.

CHAPTER 5

FICTION SAMPLER: THE SHORT-SHORT

This chapter will focus on the **short-short story,** a short story that is fewer than 1,500 words in length. Some short-shorts are quite conventional (that is, they include recognizable characters and have an identifiable beginning, middle, and end); others are experimental, perhaps lacking a definite setting or a clear plot. As defined by James Thomas (who, along with Robert Shepard, edited the short-short story collection *Sudden Fiction*), short-shorts are "Highly compressed, highly charged, insidious, protean, sudden, alarming, tantalizing"; they can "confer form on small corners of chaos, and, at their best, can do in a page what a novel does in two hundred."

Perhaps the most traditional of the six short-shorts that follow is Gary Gildner's "Sleepy Time Gal," which specifies a setting, develops several distinct characters, and traces a plot in a logical order. Jonathan Safran Foer's "A Primer for the Punctuation of Heart Disease" seems at first to be extremely unconventional: it uses punctuation marks and other symbols as shorthand for language and therefore has a very unusual appearance on the page. Still, despite its unconventional appearance, it has a universal theme and all-too-human characters. Essentially, it is a realistic story about a family's struggle to communicate.

The other four stories in this chapter are more experimental. Margaret Atwood's "Happy Endings" is **metafiction,** a story about the process of writing fiction, with a narrator who offers readers a choice of possible plots. In fact, Atwood herself did not quite know what to make of it. "When I wrote 'Happy Endings'" she remembers, "I did not know what sort of creature it was. It was not a poem, a short story, or a prose poem. It was not quite a condensation, a commentary, a questionnaire, and it missed being a parable, a proverb, a paradox. It was a mutation." Jamaica Kincaid's "Girl," **a stream-of-consciousness** monologue, is also unusual (the entire story is a single extended sentence), as is Amanda Holzer's "Love and Other Catastrophes: A Mix Tape," consisting entirely of a list of song titles, with no information about character or setting. Finally, Monica Ware's "Mislaid Plans" is only six sentences long; in a sense, the story's real action, which readers must infer, precedes these sentences.

Despite their brevity, the stories in this chapter have much in common with the stories that appear elsewhere in this book. Each, after all, "tells a story": characters act and events unfold.

GARY GILDNER (1938 –   ) is an award-winning writer whose work includes *Blue Like the Heavens: New and Selected Poems* (1984), *Clackamas* (1991), and *The Swing* (1996), as well as a novel, *The Second Bridge* (1987), and two collections of stories, *The Crush* (1983) and *A Week in South Dakota* (1987). His popular memoir *The Warsaw Sparks* (1990) recounts his experiences as a baseball coach in Warsaw, Poland. Another memoir, *My Grandfather's Book*, was published in 2002 and was named a Top Ten University Press Book of the Year by *ForeWord Magazine*, and his most recent collection of stories, *Somewhere Geese Are Flying*, was published in 2004.

Sleepy Time Gal (1979)

In the small town in northern Michigan where my father lived as a young man, he had an Italian friend who worked in a restaurant. I will call his friend Phil. Phil's job in the restaurant was as ordinary as you can imagine — from making coffee in the morning to sweeping up at night. But what was not ordinary about Phil was his piano playing. On Saturday nights my father and Phil and their girlfriends would drive ten or fifteen miles to a roadhouse by a lake where they would drink beer from schooners and dance and Phil would play an old beat-up piano. He could play any song you named, my father said, but the song everyone waited for was the one he wrote, which he would always play at the end before they left to go back to the town. And everyone knew of course that he had written the song for his girl, who was as pretty as she was rich. Her father was the banker in their town, and he was a tough old German, and he didn't like Phil going around with his daughter.

My father, when he told the story, which was not often, would tell it in an off-hand way and emphasize the Depression and not having much, instead of the important parts. I will try to tell it the way he did, if I can.

So they would go to the roadhouse by the lake, and finally Phil would play his song, and everyone would say, Phil, that's a great song, you could make a lot of money from it. But Phil would only shake his head and smile and look at his girl. I have to break in here and say that my father, a gentle but practical man, was not inclined to emphasize the part about Phil looking at his girl. It was my mother who said the girl would rest her head on Phil's shoulder while he played, and that he got the idea for the song from the pretty way she looked when she got sleepy. My mother was not part of the story, but she had heard it when she and my father were younger and therefore had that information. I would like to intrude further and add something about Phil writing the song, maybe show him whistling the tune and going over the words slowly and carefully to get the best ones, while peeling onions or potatoes in the restaurant; but my father is already driving them home from the roadhouse, and saying how patched up his tires were, and how his car's engine was a gingerbread of parts from different makes, and some parts were his own invention as well. And my mother is saying that the old German had made his daughter promise not to get involved with any man until after college, and they couldn't be late. Also my mother likes the sad parts and is eager to get to their last night before the girl goes away to college.

So they all went out to the roadhouse, and it was sad. The women got tears in their eyes when Phil played her song, my mother said. My father said that Phil spent his week's pay on a new shirt and tie, the first tie he ever owned, and people kidded him. Somebody piped up and said, Phil, you ought to take that song down to Bay City — which was like saying New York City to them, only more realistic — and sell it and take the money and go to college too. Which was not meant to be cruel, but that was the result because Phil had never even got to high school. But you can see people were trying to cheer him up, my mother said.

Well, she'd come home for Thanksgiving and Christmas and Easter and they'd 5 all sneak out to the roadhouse and drink beer from schooners and dance and everything would be like always. And of course there were the summers. And everyone knew Phil and the girl would get married after she made good her promise to her father because you could see it in their eyes when he sat at the old beat-up piano and played her song.

That last part about their eyes was not, of course, in my father's telling, but I couldn't help putting it in there even though I know it is making some of you impatient. Remember that this happened many years ago in the woods by a lake in northern Michigan, before television. I wish I could put more in, especially about the song and how it felt to Phil to sing it and how the girl felt when hearing it and knowing it was hers, but I've already intruded too much in a simple story that isn't even mine.

Well, here's the kicker part. Probably by now many of you have guessed that one vacation near the end she doesn't come home to see Phil, because she meets some guy at college who is good-looking and as rich as she is and, because her father knew about Phil all along and was pressuring her into forgetting about him, she gives in to this new guy and goes to his hometown during the vacation and falls in love with him. That's how the people in town figured it, because after she graduates they turn up, already married, and right away he takes over the old German's bank — and buys a new Pontiac at the place where my father is the mechanic and pays cash for it. The paying cash always made my father pause and shake his head and mention again that times were tough, but here comes this guy in a spiffy white shirt (with French cuffs, my mother said) and pays the full price in cash.

And this made my father shake his head too: Phil took the song down to Bay City and sold it for twenty-five dollars, the only money he ever got for it. It was the same song we'd just heard on the radio and which reminded my father of the story I just told you. What happened to Phil? Well, he stayed in Bay City and got a job managing a movie theater. My father saw him there after the Depression when he was on his way to Detroit to work for Ford. He stopped and Phil gave him a box of popcorn. The song he wrote for the girl has sold many millions of records, and if I told you the name of it you could probably sing it, or at least whistle the tune. I wonder what the girl thinks when she hears it. Oh yes, my father met Phil's wife too. She worked in the movie theater with him, selling tickets and cleaning the carpet after the show with one of those sweepers you push. She was also big and loud and nothing like the other one, my mother said.

❖   ❖   ❖

JONATHAN SAFRAN FOER (1977–   ) is an author, editor, and illustrator born in Washington, D.C. Winner of a Zoetrope Award for short fiction, Foer has had stories published in the *Paris Review, Conjunctions,* and *The New Yorker.* He edited the best-selling anthology *A Convergence of Birds: Original Fiction and Poetry Inspired by the Work of Joseph Cornell* (2001). For his first novel, *Everything Is Illuminated* (2002), Foer embarked on a journey to the Ukraine to research his grandfather's life. Among other things, the book concerns Foer's attempt to find out about the woman who may or may not have saved his grandfather from the Nazis. *Everything Is Illuminated* won The Guardian First Book Award and the National Jewish Book Award and was named Book of the Year by the *Los Angeles Times.* His second novel, *Extremely Loud and Incredibly Close,* released in 2005, relates the reactions of a nine-year-old boy to the events of 9/11.

A Primer for the Punctuation of Heart Disease   (2002)

The "silence mark" signifies an absence of language, and there is at least one on every page of the story of my family life. Most often used in the conversations I have with my grandmother about her life in Europe during the war, and in conversations with my father about our family's history of heart disease—we have forty-one heart attacks between us, and counting—the silence mark is a staple of familial punctuation. Note the use of silence in the following brief exchange, when my father called me at college, the morning of his most recent angioplasty:

"Listen," he said, and then surrendered to a long pause, as if the pause were what I was supposed to listen to. "I'm sure everything's gonna be fine, but I just wanted to let you know —"

"I already know," I said.

"□"

"□"

5   "□"

"□"

"O.K.," he said.

"I'll talk to you tonight," I said, and I could hear, in the receiver, my own heartbeat.

10   He said, "Yup."

The "willed silence mark" signifies an intentional silence, the conversational equivalent of building a wall over which you can't climb, through which you can't see, against which you break the bones of your hands and wrists. I often inflict willed silences upon my mother when she asks about my relationships with girls. Perhaps this is because I never have *relationships* with girls—only *relations.* It depresses me to think that I've never had sex with anyone who really loved me. Sometimes I wonder if having sex with a girl who doesn't love me is like felling a tree, alone, in a forest: no one hears about it; it didn't happen.

?? The "insistent question mark" denotes one family member's refusal to yield to
a willed silence, as in this conversation with my mother:

"Are you dating at all?"

"☐"

"But you're seeing people, I'm sure. Right?"   15

"☐"

"I don't get it. Are you ashamed of the girl? Are you ashamed of me?"

"■"

"??"

As it visually suggests, the "unxclamation point" is the opposite of an exclama-   20
tion point; it indicates a whisper.

The best example of this usage occurred when I was a boy. My grandmother
was driving me to a piano lesson, and the Volvo's wipers only moved the rain
around. She turned down the volume of the second side of the seventh tape of an
audio version of "Shoah,"° put her hand on my cheek, and said, "I hope that you
never love anyone as much as I love you¡"

Why was she whispering? We were the only ones who could hear.

Theoretically, the "extraunxclamation points" would be used to denote twice
an unxclamation point, but in practice any whisper that quiet would not be
heard. I take comfort in believing that at least some of the silences in my life were
really extraunxclamations.

The "extraexclamation points" are simply twice an exclamation point. I've
never had a heated argument with any member of my family. We've never
yelled at each other, or disagreed with any passion. In fact, I can't even remember
a difference of opinion. There are those who would say that this is unhealthy. But,
since it is the case, there exists only one instance of extraexclamation points in
our family history, and they were uttered by a stranger who was vying with my father for a parking space in front of the National Zoo.

"Give it up, fucker!!" he hollered at my father, in front of my mother, my   25
brothers, and me.

"Well, I'm sorry," my father said, pushing the bridge of his glasses up his nose,
"but I think it's rather obvious that we arrived at this space first. You see, we were
approaching from —"

"Give . . . it . . . up . . . fucker!!"

"Well, it's just that I think I'm in the right on this particu —"

"GIVE IT UP, FUCKER!!"   30

"Give it up, Dad¡" I said, suffering a minor coronary event as my fingers
clenched his seat's headrest.

"Je-sus!" the man yelled, pounding his fist against the outside of his car door.
"Giveitupfucker!!"

Shoah: A 1985 documentary about the Holocaust.

Ultimately, my father gave it up, and we found a spot several blocks away. Before we got out, he pushed in the cigarette lighter, and we waited, in silence, as it got hot. When it popped out, he pushed it back in. "It's never, ever worth it," he said, turning back to us, his hand against his heart.

~ Placed at the end of a sentence, the "pedal point" signifies a thought that dissolves into a suggestive silence. The pedal point is distinguished from the ellipsis and the dash in that the thought it follows is neither incomplete nor interrupted but an outstretched hand. My younger brother uses these a lot with me, probably because he, of all the members of my family, is the one most capable of telling me what he needs to tell me without having to say it. Or, rather, he's the one whose words I'm most convinced I don't need to hear. Very often he will say, "Jonathan~" and I will say, "I know."

A few weeks ago, he was having problems with his heart. A visit to his university's health center to check out some chest pains became a trip to the emergency room became a week in the intensive-care unit. As it turns out, he's been having one long heart attack for the last six years. "It's nowhere near as bad as it sounds," the doctor told my parents, "but it's definitely something we want to take care of."

35   I called my brother that night and told him that he shouldn't worry. He said, "I know. But that doesn't mean there's nothing to worry about~"

"I know~" I said.

"I know~" he said.

"I~"

"I~"

40   "□"

Does my little brother have relationships with girls? I don't know.

↓ Another commonly employed familial punctuation mark, the "low point," is used either in place — or for accentuation at the end — of such phrases as "This is terrible," "This is irremediable," "It couldn't possibly be worse."

"It's good to have somebody, Jonathan. It's necessary."

"□"

45   "It pains me to think of you alone."

"■↓"

"??↓"

Interestingly, low points always come in pairs in my family. That is, the acknowledgment of whatever is terrible and irremediable becomes itself something terrible and irremediable — and often worse than the original referent. For example, my sadness makes my mother sadder than the cause of my sadness does. Of course, her sadness then makes me sad. Thus is created a "low-point chain": ↓↓↓↓ . . . ∞.

❄ The "snowflake" is used at the end of a unique familial phrase — that is, any sequence of words that has never, in the history of our family life, been assembled as such. For example, "I didn't die in the Holocaust, but all of my siblings did, so where does that leave me? ✳" Or, "My heart is no good, and I'm afraid of dying, and I'm also afraid of saying I love you.✳"

☺ The "corroboration mark" is more or less what it looks like. But it would be   50
a mistake to think that it simply stands in place of "I agree," or even "Yes."
Witness the subtle usage in this dialogue between my mother and my father:

"Could you add orange juice to the grocery list, but remember to get the kind with reduced acid. Also some cottage cheese. And that bacon-substitute stuff. And a few Yahrzeit candles."

"☺"

"The car needs gas. I need tampons."

"☺"

"Is Jonathan dating anyone? I'm not prying, but I'm very interested."   55

"☺"

My father has suffered twenty-two heart attacks — more than the rest of us combined. Once, in a moment of frankness after his nineteenth, he told me that his marriage to my mother had been successful because he had become a yes-man early on.

"We've only had one fight," he said. "It was in our first week of marriage. I realized that it's never, ever worth it."

My father and I were pulling weeds one afternoon a few weeks ago. He was disobeying his cardiologist's order not to pull weeds. The problem, the doctor says, is not the physical exertion but the emotional stress that weeding inflicts on my father. He has dreams of weeds sprouting from his body, of having to pull them, at the roots, from his chest. He has also been told not to watch Orioles games and not to think about the current Administration.

As we weeded, my father made a joke about how my older brother, who, bar-   60
ring a fatal heart attack, was to get married in a few weeks, had already become a yes-man. Hearing this felt like having an elephant sit on my chest — my brother, whom I loved more than I loved myself, was surrendering.

"Your grandfather was a yes-man," my father added, on his knees, his fingers pushing into the earth, "and your children will be yes-men."

I've been thinking about that conversation ever since, and I've come to understand — with a straining heart — that I, too, am becoming a yes-man, and that, like my father's and my brother's, my surrender has little to do with the people I say yes to, or with the existence of questions at all. It has to do with a fear of dying, with rehearsal and preparation.

✂🕸 The "severed web" is a Barely Tolerable Substitute, whose meaning approximates "I love you," and which can be used in place of "I love you." Other Barely Tolerable Substitutes include, but are not limited to:

→|←, which approximates "I love you."

🍐☐, which approximates "I love you."   65

🔒, which approximates "I love you."

✕✈, which approximates "I love you."

I don't know how many Barely Tolerable Substitutes there are, but often it feels as if they were everywhere, as if everything that is spoken and done — every "Yup," "O.K.," and "I already know," every weed pulled from the lawn, every sexual act — were just Barely Tolerable.

∶ Unlike the colon, which is used to mark a major division in a sentence, and to indicate that what follows is an elaboration, summation, implication, etc., of what precedes, the "reversible colon" is used when what appears on either side elaborates, summates, implicates, etc., what's on the other side. In other words, the two halves of the sentence explain each other, as in the cases of "Mother::Me," and "Father::Death." Here are some examples of reversible sentences:

70 My eyes water when I speak about my family::I don't like to speak about my family.

I've never felt loved by anyone outside of my family::my persistent depression. 1938 to 1945::□.

Sex::yes.

My grandmother's sadness::my mother's sadness::my sadness::the sadness that will come after me.

To be Jewish::to be Jewish.

75 Heart disease::yes.

←Familial communication always has to do with failures to communicate. It is common that in the course of a conversation one of the participants will not hear something that the other has said. It is also quite common that one of the participants will not understand what the other has said. Somewhat less common is one participant's saying something whose words the other understands completely but whose meaning is not understood at all. This can happen with very simple sentences, like "I hope that you never love anyone as much as I love you¡"

But, in our best, least depressing moments, we *try* to understand what we have failed to understand. A "backup" is used: we start again at the beginning, we replay what was missed and make an effort to hear what was meant instead of what was said:

"It pains me to think of you alone."

"← It pains me to think of me without any grandchildren to love."

80 { A related set of marks, the "should-have brackets," signify words that were not spoken but should have been, as in this dialogue with my father:

"Are you hearing static?"

"{I'm crying into the phone.}"

"Jonathan?"

85 "□"

"Jonathan~"

"■"

"??"

"I::not myself~"

"{A child's sadness is a parent's sadness.}"   90
"{A parent's sadness is a child's sadness.}"
"←"
"I'm probably just tired¡"
"{I never told you this, because I thought it might hurt you, but in my dreams it was *you*. Not me. *You* were pulling the weeds from my chest.}"
"{I want to love and be loved.}"
"☺"   95
"☺"
"↓"
"↓"
"♨"
"☺"   100
"□↔□↔□"
"↓"
"↓"
"▶▶○◀◀"
"■+■→■"   105
"☺"
"👂□"
"⊠⊠"
"◉□❖●◆○□◆☉●"
"■"   110
"{I love you.}"
"{I love you, too. So much.}"

Of course, my sense of the should-have is unlikely to be the same as my brothers', or my mother's, or my father's. Sometimes — when I'm in the car, or having sex, or talking to one of them on the phone — I imagine their should-have versions. I sew them together into a new life, leaving out everything that actually happened and was said.

❖ ❖ ❖

MARGARET ATWOOD (1939–) is one of the most widely read Canadian writers of her generation. Born in Ottawa, Ontario, she was educated at Victoria College in the University of Toronto, at Radcliffe College, and at Harvard University. Her first collection of poems, *The Circle Game*, appeared in 1964. Since then she has produced works in many genres, including poetry, short stories, novels, children's books, nonfiction, and scripts for television. Her most recent novel is *Oryx and Crake* (2003); other novels include *The Blind Assassin* (2000), *Cat's Eye* (1989) and *The Handmaid's Tale* (1985), adapted for the screen and released as a film in 1990. Her poetry collections include *Selected Poems* (1976), *Selected Poems II* (1986), and *Eating Fire: Selected Poems 1965–1995*.

Happy Endings   (1983)

John and Mary meet.
What happens next?
If you want a happy ending, try A.

A. John and Mary fall in love and get married. They both have worthwhile and remunerative jobs which they find stimulating and challenging. They buy a charming house. Real estate values go up. Eventually, when they can afford live-in help, they have two children, to whom they are devoted. The children turn out well. John and Mary have a stimulating and challenging sex life and worthwhile friends. They go on fun vacations together. They retire. They both have hobbies which they find stimulating and challenging. Eventually they die. This is the end of the story.

5 B. Mary falls in love with John but John doesn't fall in love with Mary. He merely uses her body for selfish pleasure and ego gratification of a tepid kind. He comes to her apartment twice a week and she cooks him dinner, you'll notice that he doesn't even consider her worth the price of a dinner out, and after he's eaten the dinner he fucks her and after that he falls asleep, while she does the dishes so he won't think she's untidy, having all those dirty dishes lying around, and puts on fresh lipstick so she'll look good when he wakes up, but when he wakes up he doesn't even notice, he puts on his socks and his shorts and his pants and his shirt and his tie and his shoes, the reverse order from the one in which he took them off. He doesn't take off Mary's clothes, she takes them off herself, she acts as if she's dying for it every time, not because she likes sex exactly, she doesn't, but she wants John to think she does because if they do it often enough surely he'll get used to her, he'll come to depend on her and they will get married, but John goes out the door with hardly so much as a good-night and three days later he turns up at six o'clock and they do the whole thing over again.

Mary gets run-down. Crying is bad for your face, everyone knows that and so does Mary but she can't stop. People at work notice. Her friends tell her John is a rat, a pig, a dog, he isn't good enough for her, but she can't believe it. Inside John, she thinks, is another John, who is much nicer. This other John will emerge like a butterfly from a cocoon, a Jack from a box, a pit from a prune, if the first John is only squeezed enough.

One evening John complains about the food. He has never complained about the food before. Mary is hurt.

Her friends tell her they've seen him in a restaurant with another woman, whose name is Madge. It's not even Madge that finally gets to Mary: it's the restaurant. John has never taken Mary to a restaurant. Mary collects all the sleeping pills and aspirins she can find, and takes them and a half a bottle of sherry. You can see what kind of a woman she is by the fact that it's not even whiskey. She leaves a note for John. She hopes he'll discover her and get her to the hospital in time and repent and then they can get married, but this fails to happen and she dies.

John marries Madge and everything continues as in A.

C. John, who is an older man, falls in love with Mary, and Mary, who is only 10 twenty-two, feels sorry for him because he's worried about his hair falling out. She sleeps with him even though she's not in love with him. She met him at work. She's in love with someone called James, who is twenty-two also and not yet ready to settle down.

John on the contrary settled down long ago: this is what is bothering him. John has a steady, respectable job and is getting ahead in his field, but Mary isn't impressed by him, she's impressed by James, who has a motorcycle and a fabulous record collection. But James is often away on his motorcycle, being free. Freedom isn't the same for girls, so in the meantime Mary spends Thursday evenings with John. Thursdays are the only days John can get away.

John is married to a woman called Madge and they have two children, a charming house which they bought just before the real estate values went up, and hobbies which they find stimulating and challenging, when they have the time. John tells Mary how important she is to him, but of course he can't leave his wife because a commitment is a commitment. He goes on about this more than is necessary and Mary finds it boring, but older men can keep it up longer so on the whole she has a fairly good time.

One day James breezes in on his motorcycle with some top-grade California hybrid and James and Mary get higher than you'd believe possible and they climb into bed. Everything becomes very underwater, but along comes John, who has a key to Mary's apartment. He finds them stoned and entwined. He's hardly in any position to be jealous, considering Madge, but nevertheless he's overcome with despair. Finally he's middle-aged, in two years he'll be bald as an egg and he can't stand it. He purchases a handgun, saying he needs it for target practice — this is the thin part of the plot, but it can be dealt with later — and shoots the two of them and himself.

Madge, after a suitable period of mourning, marries an understanding man called Fred and everything continues as in A, but under different names.

D. Fred and Madge have no problems. They get along exceptionally well and are 15 good at working out any little difficulties that may arise. But their charming house is by the seashore and one day a giant tidal wave approaches. Real estate values go down. The rest of the story is about what caused the tidal wave and how they escape from it. They do, though thousands drown, but Fred and Madge are virtuous and lucky. Finally on high ground they clasp each other, wet and dripping and grateful, and continue as in A.

E. Yes, but Fred has a bad heart. The rest of the story is about how kind and understanding they both are until Fred dies. Then Madge devotes herself to charity work until the end of A. If you like, it can be "Madge," "cancer," "guilty and confused," and "bird watching."

F. If you think this is all too bourgeois, make John a revolutionary and Mary a counterespionage agent and see how far that gets you. Remember, this is Canada. You'll still end up with A, though in between you may get a lustful brawling saga of passionate involvement, a chronicle of our times, sort of.

You'll have to face it, the endings are the same however you slice it. Don't be deluded by any other endings, they're all fake, either deliberately fake, with malicious intent to deceive, or just motivated by excessive optimism if not by downright sentimentality.

The only authentic ending is the one provided here:
John and Mary die. John and Mary die. John and Mary die.

20 So much for endings. Beginnings are always more fun. True connoisseurs, however, are known to favor the stretch in between, since it's the hardest to do anything with.

That's about all that can be said for plots, which anyway are just one thing after another, a what and a what and a what.

Now try How and Why.

❖   ❖   ❖

JAMAICA KINCAID (1949–   ) was born Elaine Potter Richardson on the island of Antigua, where she received a British education and was often at the top of her class. In early childhood, she was very close to her mother, but when she was nine, her mother gave birth to three sons in quick succession, which altered their relationship forever. According to Kincaid, she was treated badly and neglected, and she left Antigua in 1965 to work as an au pair in Westchester, New York. She went on to study photography at the New York School for Social Research and attended Franconia College in New Hampshire for a year. In 1973, after having begun her writing career, she changed her name to Jamaica Kincaid because her family disapproved of her writing. She soon began writing a regular column for the *New Yorker*. Her best-known works include the novel *Annie John* (1986) and the non-fiction book *A Small Place* (1988), which criticizes British Colonialism in Antigua. Her most recent books are *Talk Stories* (2001) and *My Favorite Tool* (2005).

Girl (1984)

Wash the white clothes on Monday and put them on the stone heap; wash the color clothes on Tuesday and put them on the clothesline to dry; don't walk bare-head in the hot sun; cook pumpkin fritters in very hot sweet oil; soak your little clothes right after you take them off; when buying cotton to make yourself a nice blouse, be sure that it doesn't have gum on it, because that way it won't hold up well after a wash; soak salt fish overnight before you cook it; is it true that you sing benna° in Sunday School?; always eat your food in such a way that it won't turn

---

benna: Calypso music.

someone else's stomach; on Sundays try to walk like a lady and not like the slut you are so bent on becoming; don't sing benna in Sunday School; you mustn't speak to wharf-rat boys, not even to give directions; don't eat fruits on the street — flies will follow you; *but I don't sing benna on Sundays at all and never in Sunday school;* this is how to sew on a button; this is how to make a buttonhole for the button you have just sewed on; this is how to hem a dress when you see the hem coming down and so to prevent yourself from looking like the slut I know you are so bent on becoming; this is how you iron your father's khaki shirt so that it doesn't have a crease; this is how you iron your father's khaki pants so that they don't have a crease; this is how you grow okra — far from the house, because okra tree harbors red ants; when you are growing dasheen, make sure it gets plenty of water or else it makes your throat itch when you are eating it; this is how you sweep a corner; this is how you sweep a whole house; this is how you sweep a yard; this is how you smile to someone you don't like too much; this is how you smile to someone you don't like at all; this is how you smile to someone you like com- pletely; this is how you set a table for tea; this is how you set a table for dinner; this is how you set a table for dinner with an important guest; this is how you set a table for lunch; this is how you set a table for breakfast; this is how to behave in the presence of men who don't know you very well, and this way they won't rec- ognize immediately the slut I have warned you against becoming; be sure to wash every day, even if it is with your own spit; don't squat down to play marbles — you are not a boy, you know; don't pick people's flowers — you might catch something; don't throw stones at blackbirds, because it might not be a blackbird at all; this is how to make a bread pudding; this is how to make doukona;° this is how to make pepper pot; this is how to make a good medicine for a cold; this is how to make a good medicine to throw away a child before it even becomes a child; this is how to catch a fish; this is how to throw back a fish you don't like, and that way some- thing bad won't fall on you; this is how to bully a man; this is how a man bullies you; this is how to love a man, and if this doesn't work there are other ways, and if they don't work don't feel too bad about giving up; this is how to spit up in the air if you feel like it, and this is how to move quick so that it doesn't fall on you; this is how to make ends meet; always squeeze bread to make sure it's fresh; *but what if the baker won't let me feel the bread?;* you mean to say that after all you are really going to be the kind of woman who the baker won't let near the bread?

◇ ◇ ◇

AMANDA HOLZER (1981–) is a graduate of Emerson College. "Love and Other Catastro- phes" was first published in 2002 in *Story Quarterly* and was reprinted in *Best American Non- Required Reading 2003.*

---

doukona: Spicy plantain pudding.

Love and Other Catastrophes: A Mix Tape   (2002)

"All By Myself" (Eric Carmen). "Looking for Love" (Lou Reed). "I Wanna Dance With Somebody" (Whitney Houston). "Let's Dance" (David Bowie). "Let's Kiss" (Beat Happening). "Let's Talk About Sex" (Salt N' Pepa). "Like A Virgin" (Madonna). "We've Only Just Begun" (The Carpenters). "I Wanna Be Your Boyfriend" (The Ramones). "I'll Tumble 4 Ya" (Culture Club). "Head Over Heels" (The Go-Go's). "Nothing Compares To You" (Sinéad O'Connor). "My Girl" (The Temptations). "Could This Be Love?" (Bob Marley). "Love and Marriage" (Frank Sinatra). "White Wedding" (Billy Idol). "Stuck in the Middle with You" (Steelers Wheel). "Tempted" (The Squeeze). "There Goes My Baby" (The Drifters). "What's Going On?" (Marvin Gaye). "Where Did You Sleep Last Night?" (Leadbelly) "Whose Bed Have Your Boots Been Under?" (Shania Twain). "Jealous Guy" (John Lennon). "Your Cheatin' Heart" (Tammy Wynette). "Shot Through the Heart" (Bon Jovi). "Don't Go Breaking My Heart" (Elton John and Kiki Dee). "My Achy Breaky Heart" (Billy Ray Cyrus). "Heartbreak Hotel" (Elvis Presley), "Stop, In the Name of Love" (The Supremes). "Try a Little Tenderness" (Otis Redding). "Try (Just a Little Bit Harder)" (Janis Joplin). "All Apologies" (Nirvana). "Hanging on the Telephone" (Blondie). "I Just Called to Say I Love You" (Stevie Wonder). "Love Will Keep Us Together" (Captain and Tennille). "Let's Stay Together" (Al Green). "It Ain't Over 'Till It's Over" (Lenny Kravitz). "What's Love Got To Do With It? (Tina Turner). "You Don't Bring Me Flowers Anymore" (Barbara Streisand and Neil Diamond). "I Wish You Wouldn't Say That" (Talking Heads). "You're So Vain" (Carly Simon). "Love is a Battlefield" (Pat Benatar). "Heaven Knows I'm Miserable Now" (The Smiths). "(Can't Get No) Satisfaction" (Rolling Stones). "Must Have Been Love (But It's Over Now)" (Roxette). "Breaking Up is Hard to Do" (Neil Sedaka). "I Will Survive" (Gloria Gaynor). "Hit the Road, Jack" (Mary McCaslin and Jim Ringer). "These Boots Were Made for Walking" (Nancy Sinatra). "All Out of Love" (Air Supply). "All By Myself" (Eric Carmen).

◇ ◇ ◇

MONICA WARE

Mislaid Plans

A rash of new bills came that morning. The letter from their insurance company announced the cancellation of their policies.

She sighed and rose wearily to tell her husband. The kitchen smelled of gas. On his desk she found the note.

"... the money from my life insurance will be enough for you and the children..."

◇ ◇ ◇

Reading and Reacting

1. Aside from "Sleepy Time Gal," which of the six short-short stories in this chapter seems most conventional? Which seems least conventional? Explain.

2. Does each story seem complete? What, if anything, seems to be missing from each story that might be present in a longer story?

3. If you were going to add material to "Mislaid Plans," what would you add? Why?

4. How would "A Primer for the Punctuation of Heart Disease" be different without the highlighted punctuation marks and other symbols? Are they necessary to the story, or are they just embellishment?

5. How would "Girl" be different if the story were told by the person whom the narrator is addressing? If the story included dialogue?

6. Consider the writing "advice" presented in "Happy Endings." Does the advice seem to apply to the other stories in this chapter? Explain.

WRITING SUGGESTIONS

1. Write an explication of another short-short story in this book—for example, Kate Chopin's "Story of an Hour."

2. Compare "A Primer for the Punctuation of Heart Disease" with another story about family relationships— or, compare "Love and Other Catastrophes: A Mix Tape" with one of the love poems in Chapter 23.

3. Write a "mix tape" story about an experience in your own life.

CHAPTER 6

PLOT

> It's a truism that there are only two basic plots in fiction: one, somebody takes a trip; two, a stranger comes to town.
>
> —attributed to American novelist John Gardner

Alfred Hitchcock's 1951 film *Strangers on a Train,* based on a suspense novel by Patricia Highsmith, offers an intriguing premise: two men, strangers, each can murder someone the other wishes dead; because they have no apparent connection to their victims, both can escape suspicion. Many people would describe this ingenious scheme as the film's "plot," but in fact it is simply the gimmick around which the complex plot revolves. Certainly a clever twist can be an important ingredient of a story's plot, but plot is more than "what happens"; it is how what happens is revealed, the way in which a story's events are arranged. Plot is shaped by causal connections — historical, social, and personal — by the interaction between characters, and by the juxtaposition of events. In *Strangers on a Train,* the plot that unfolds is complex: one character directs the events and determines their order while the other character is drawn into the action against his will. The same elements that enrich the plot of the film — unexpected events, conflict, suspense, flashbacks, foreshadowing — can also enrich the plot of a work of short fiction.

Conflict

Readers' interest and involvement are heightened by a story's **conflict,** the struggle between opposing forces that emerges as the action develops. This conflict is a clash between the **protagonist,** a story's principal character, and an **antagonist,** someone or something presented in opposition to the protagonist. Sometimes the antagonist is a villain; more often, it is a character who represents a conflicting point of view or advocates a course of action different from the one the protagonist follows. Sometimes the antagonist is not a character at all but a situation (for instance, war or poverty) or an event (a natural disaster, such as a flood or a storm, for example) that challenges the protagonist. In other stories, the protagonist may struggle against a supernatural force, or the conflict may occur within a character's mind. It may, for example, be a struggle between two

100

moral choices, such as whether to stay at home and care for an aging parent or to leave and make a new life.

Stages of Plot

A work's plot explores one or more conflicts, moving from *exposition* through a series of *complications* to a *climax* and, finally, to a *resolution*.

During a story's **exposition,** the writer presents the basic information readers need to understand the events that follow. Typically, the exposition sets the story in motion: it establishes the scene, introduces the major characters, and perhaps suggests the major events or conflicts to come.

Sometimes a single sentence can present a story's exposition clearly and economically, giving readers information vital to their understanding of the plot that will unfold. For example, the opening sentence of Amy Tan's "Two Kinds" (p. 416) — "My mother believed you could be anything you wanted to be in America"— reveals an important trait of a central character. Similarly, the opening sentence of Shirley Jackson's "The Lottery" (p. 274) — "The morning of June 27th was clear and sunny, with the fresh warmth of a full-summer day; the flowers were blossoming profusely and the grass was richly green"— introduces the picture-perfect setting that is essential to the story's irony. At other times, as in John Updike's "A&P" (p. 128), a more fully developed exposition section establishes the story's setting, introduces the main characters, and suggests possible conflicts. In some experimental stories, a distinct exposition component may be absent, as it is in Amanda Holzer's "Love and Other Catastrophes: A Mix Tape" (p. 98).

As the plot progresses, the story's conflict unfolds through a series of complications that eventually lead readers to the story's climax. As it develops, the story may include several crises. A **crisis** is a peak in the story's action, a moment of considerable tension or importance. The **climax** is the point of greatest tension or importance, the scene that presents a story's decisive action or event.

The final stage of plot, the **resolution,** or **denouement** (French for "untying of the knot"), draws the action to a close and accounts for all remaining loose ends. Sometimes this resolution is achieved with the help of a **deus ex machina** (Latin for "a god from a machine"), an intervention of some force or agent previously extraneous to the story — for example, the sudden arrival of a long-lost relative or a fortuitous inheritance, the discovery of a character's true identity, or a last-minute rescue by a character not previously introduced. Usually, however, the resolution is more plausible: all the events lead logically and convincingly (though not necessarily predictably) to the resolution. Sometimes the ending of a story is indefinite — that is, readers are not quite sure what the protagonist will do or what will happen next. This kind of resolution, although it may leave some readers feeling cheated, has its advantages: it mirrors the complexity of life, where closure rarely occurs, and it can keep readers involved in the action as they try to understand the significance of the story's ending or to decide how conflicts should have been resolved.

Order and Sequence

A writer may present a story's events in strict chronological order, presenting each event in the sequence in which it actually takes place. More often, however, especially in relatively modern fiction, writers do not present events chronologically. Instead, they present incidents out of expected order, or in no apparent order. For example, a writer may choose to begin **in medias res** (Latin for "in the midst of things"), starting with a key event and later going back in time to explain events that preceded it, as Tillie Olsen does in "I Stand Here Ironing" (p. 174). Or, a writer can decide to begin a work of fiction at the end and then move back to reconstruct events that led up to the final outcome, as William Faulkner does in "A Rose for Emily" (p. 113). Many sequences are possible as the writer manipulates events to create interest, suspense, confusion, wonder, or some other effect.

Writers who wish to depart from strict chronological order use *flashbacks* and *foreshadowing*. A **flashback** moves out of sequence to examine an event or situation that occurred before the time in which the story's action takes place. A character can remember an earlier event, or a story's narrator can re-create an earlier situation. For example, in Alberto Alvaro Ríos's "The Secret Lion" (p. 412), the adult narrator looks back at events that occurred when he was twelve years old and then moves farther back in time to consider related events that occurred when he was five. In Edgar Allan Poe's "The Cask of Amontillado" (p. 203), the entire story is told as a flashback. Flashbacks are valuable because they can substitute for or supplement formal exposition by presenting background readers need to understand a story's events. One disadvantage of flashbacks is that, because they interrupt the natural flow of events, they may be intrusive or distracting. Such distractions, however, can be an advantage if the writer wishes to reveal events gradually and subtly or to obscure causal links.

Foreshadowing is the introduction early in a story of situations, events, characters, or objects that hint at things to come. Typically, a seemingly simple element — a chance remark, a natural occurrence, a trivial event — is eventually revealed to have great significance. For example, a dark cloud passing across the sky during a wedding can foreshadow future problems for the marriage. Foreshadowing allows a writer to hint provocatively at what is to come, so that readers only gradually become aware of a particular detail's role in a story. Thus, foreshadowing helps readers sense what will occur and grow increasingly involved as they see the likelihood (or even the inevitability) of a particular outcome.

In addition to using conventional techniques like flashbacks and foreshadowing, writers may experiment with sequence by substantially tampering with — or even dispensing with — chronological order. (An example is the scrambled chronology of "A Rose for Emily.") In such instances, the experimental form enhances interest and encourages readers to become involved with the story as they work to untangle or reorder the events and determine their logical and causal connections.

Today, the computer has given a new fluidity to the nature of plot, with hypertext stories appearing on the Internet and stories constructed to permit readers to actually participate in the creation of plot.

✔ CHECKLIST   Writing about Plot

- What happens in the story?

- Where does the story's formal exposition section end? What do readers learn about characters in this section? What do readers learn about setting? What possible conflicts are suggested here?

- What is the story's central conflict? What other conflicts are presented? Who is the protagonist? Who (or what) serves as the antagonist?

- Identify the story's crisis or crises.

- Identify the story's climax.

- How is the story's central conflict resolved? Is this resolution plausible? Satisfying?

- Which part of the story constitutes the resolution? Do any problems remain unresolved? Does any uncertainty remain? If so, does this uncertainty strengthen or weaken the story? Would another ending be more effective?

- How are the story's events arranged? Are they presented in chronological order? What events are presented out of logical sequence? Does the story use foreshadowing? Flashbacks? Are the causal connections between events clear? Logical? If not, can you explain why?

KATE CHOPIN (1851–1904) was born Katherine O'Flaherty, the daughter of a wealthy Irish-born merchant and his aristocratic Creole wife. She was married at nineteen to Oscar Chopin, a Louisiana cotton broker, who took her to live first in New Orleans and later on a plantation in central Louisiana. Chopin's representations of the Cane River region and its people in two volumes of short stories — *Bayou Folk* (1894) and *A Night in Arcadie* (1897) — are the foundation of her reputation as a local colorist, a writer dedicated to creating an accurate picture of a particular region and its people.

Her honest, sexually frank stories (many of them out of print for more than half a century) were rediscovered in the 1960s and 1970s, influencing a new generation of writers. Though she was a popular contributor of stories and sketches to the magazines of her day, Chopin scandalized many critics with her outspoken novel *The Awakening* (1899), in which a woman seeks sexual and emotional fulfillment with a man who is not her husband. The book was removed from the shelves of the public library in St. Louis, where Chopin was born.

"The Story of an Hour" depicts a brief event in a woman's life, but in this single hour, Chopin reveals both a lifetime's emotional torment and the momentary joy of freedom.

The Story of an Hour (1894)

Knowing that Mrs. Mallard was afflicted with a heart trouble, great care was taken to break to her as gently as possible the news of her husband's death.

It was her sister Josephine who told her, in broken sentences, veiled hints that revealed in half concealing. Her husband's friend Richards was there, too, near her. It was he who had been in the newspaper office when intelligence of the railroad disaster was received, with Brently Mallard's name leading the list of "killed." He had only taken the time to assure himself of its truth by a second telegram, and had hastened to forestall any less careful, less tender friend in bearing the sad message.

She did not hear the story as many women have heard the same, with a paralyzed inability to accept its significance. She wept at once, with sudden, wild abandonment, in her sister's arms. When the storm of grief had spent itself she went away to her room alone. She would have no one follow her.

There stood, facing the open window, a comfortable, roomy armchair. Into this she sank, pressed down by a physical exhaustion that haunted her body and seemed to reach into her soul.

5   She could see in the open square before her house the tops of trees that were all aquiver with the new spring life. The delicious breath of rain was in the air. In the street below a peddler was crying his wares. The notes of a distant song which some one was singing reached her faintly, and countless sparrows were twittering in the eaves.

There were patches of blue sky showing here and there through the clouds that had met and piled one above the other in the west facing her window.

She sat with her head thrown back upon the cushion of the chair, quite motionless, except when a sob came up into her throat and shook her, as a child who has cried itself to sleep continues to sob in its dreams.

She was young, with a fair, calm face, whose lines bespoke repression and even a certain strength. But now there was a dull stare in her eyes, whose gaze was fixed away off yonder on one of those patches of blue sky. It was not a glance of reflection, but rather indicated a suspension of intelligent thought.

There was something coming to her and she was waiting for it, fearfully. What was it? She did not know; it was too subtle and elusive to name. But she felt it, creeping out of the sky, reaching toward her through the sounds, the scents, the color that filled the air.

10   Now her bosom rose and fell tumultuously. She was beginning to recognize this thing that was approaching to possess her, and she was striving to beat it

back with her will — as powerless as her two white slender hands would have been.

When she abandoned herself a little whispered word escaped her slightly parted lips. She said it over and over under her breath: "Free, free, free!" The vacant stare and the look of terror that had followed it went from her eyes. They stayed keen and bright. Her pulses beat fast, and the coursing blood warmed and relaxed every inch of her body.

She did not stop to ask if it were not a monstrous joy that held her. A clear and exalted perception enabled her to dismiss the suggestion as trivial.

She knew that she would weep again when she saw the kind, tender hands folded in death; the face that had never looked save with love upon her, fixed and gray and dead. But she saw beyond that bitter moment a long procession of years to come that would belong to her absolutely. And she opened and spread her arms out to them in welcome.

There would be no one to live for during those coming years; she would live for herself. There would be no powerful will bending her in that blind persistence with which men and women believe they have a right to impose a private will upon a fellow creature. A kind intention or a cruel intention made the act seem no less a crime as she looked upon it in that brief moment of illumination.

And yet she had loved him — sometimes. Often she had not. What did it   15 matter! What could love, the unsolved mystery, count for in face of this possession of self-assertion which she suddenly recognized as the strongest impulse of her being.

"Free! Body and soul free!" she kept whispering.

Josephine was kneeling before the closed door with her lips to the key-hole, imploring for admission. "Louise, open the door! I beg; open the door — you will make yourself ill. What are you doing, Louise? For heaven's sake open the door."

"Go away. I am not making myself ill." No; she was drinking in a very elixir of life through that open window.

Her fancy was running riot along those days ahead of her. Spring days, and summer days, and all sorts of days that would be her own. She breathed a quick prayer that life might be long. It was only yesterday she had thought with a shudder that life might be long.

She arose at length and opened the door to her sister's importunities. There   20 was a feverish triumph in her eyes, and she carried herself unwittingly like a goddess of Victory. She clasped her sister's waist, and together they descended the stairs. Richards stood waiting for them at the bottom.

Some one was opening the front door with a latchkey. It was Brently Mallard who entered, a little travel-stained, composedly carrying his grip-sack and umbrella. He had been far from the scene of the accident, and did not even know there had been one. He stood amazed at Josephine's piercing cry; at Richards' quick motion to screen him from the view of his wife.

But Richards was too late.

When the doctors came they said she had died of heart disease — of joy that kills.

Reading and Reacting

1. The story's basic exposition is presented in its first two paragraphs. What additional information about character or setting would you like to know? Why do you suppose Chopin does not supply this information?

2. "The Story of an Hour" is a very economical story, with little action or dialogue. Do you see this economy as a strength or a weakness? Explain.

3. When "The Story of an Hour" was first published in *Vogue* magazine in 1894, the magazine's editors titled it "The Dream of an Hour." A film version, echoing the last words of the story, is called *The Joy That Kills*. Which of the three titles do you believe most accurately represents what happens in the story? Why?

4. Do you think Brently Mallard abused his wife? Did he love her? Did she love him? Exactly why was she so relieved to be rid of him? Can you answer any of these questions with certainty?

5. What is the nature of the conflict in this story? Who, or what, do you see as Mrs. Mallard's antagonist?

6. What emotions does Mrs. Mallard experience during the hour she spends alone in her room? What events do you imagine take place during this same period outside her room? Outside her house?

7. Do you find the story's ending satisfying? Believable? Contrived?

8. Was the story's ending unexpected, or were you prepared for it? What elements in the story foreshadow this ending?

9. **JOURNAL ENTRY** Rewrite the story's ending, substituting a few paragraphs of your own for the last three paragraphs.

10. **CRITICAL PERSPECTIVE** Kate Chopin is widely viewed today as an early feminist writer whose work often addressed the social injustices and inequalities that women faced during her time, the second half of the nineteenth century. According to literary critic Elaine Showalter, this story was written during a period in which women writers were able to "reject the accommodating postures of femininity and to use literature to dramatize the ordeals of wronged womanhood." Do you think this story rejects the "postures of femininity"? What "ordeals of wronged womanhood" are being dramatized here?

Related Works: "The Storm" (p. 158), "The Yellow Wallpaper" (p. 372), "Women" (p. 455), *A Doll House* (p. 784)

STEPHEN DOBYNS (1941–   ) is a prolific writer in a variety of genres — poetry, novels, short stories, essays — whose work has been translated into ten languages. Dobyns was educated at Wayne State University, and he went on to obtain his MFA from the University of Iowa. Of his ten books of poetry and twenty novels, the most recent are *Pallbearers Envying the One Who Rides* and *Boy in the Water* (both 1999). His collection of short stories, *Eating Naked,* was published in 2000; his essays appear in *Best Words, Best Order* (1996). His most recent book is *Mystery, So Long* (2005), a collection of poems. The recipient of numerous literary awards, Dobyns has taught at a variety of schools, including the University of Iowa, Boston University, Sarah Lawrence College, and Emerson College.

Kansas   (1999)

The boy hitchhiking on the back-country Kansas road was nineteen years old. He had been dropped there by a farmer in a Model T Ford who had turned off to the north. Then he waited for three hours. It was July and there were no clouds. The wheat fields were flat and went straight to the horizon. The boy had two plums and he ate them. A blue Plymouth coupe° went by with a man and a woman. They were laughing. The woman had blond hair and it was all loose and blew from the window. They didn't even see the boy. The strands of straw-colored hair seemed to be waving to him. Half an hour later a farmer stopped in a Ford pickup covered with a layer of dust. The boy clambered into the front seat. The farmer took off again without glancing at him. A forty-five revolver lay next to the farmer's buttocks on the seat. Seeing it, the boy felt something electric go off inside of him. The revolver was old and there were rust spots on the barrel. Black electrician's tape was wrapped around the handle.

"You seen a woman and a man go by here in a Plymouth coupe?" asked the farmer. He pronounced it "koo-pay."

The boy said he had.

"How long ago?"

"About thirty minutes."   5

The farmer had light blue eyes and there was stubble on his chin. Perhaps he was forty, but to the boy he looked old. His skin was leather-colored from the sun. The farmer pressed his foot to the floor and the pickup roared. It was a dirt road and the boy had to hold his hands against the dashboard to keep from being bounced around. It was hot and both windows were open. There was grit in the boy's eyes and on his tongue. He kept glancing sideways at the revolver.

---

coupe: A two-door car, often one that seats only two people.

"They friends of yours?" asked the boy.

The farmer didn't look at him. "That's my wife," he said. "I'm going to put a bullet in her head." He put a hand to the revolver to make sure it was still there. "The man too," he added.

The boy didn't say anything. He was hitchhiking back to summer school from Oklahoma. He was the middle of three boys and the only one who had left home. He had already spent a year at the University of Oklahoma and was spending the summer at Lawrence. And there were other places, farther places. The boy played the piano. He intended to go to those farther places.

10   "What did they do?" the boy asked at last.

"You just guess," said the farmer.

The pickup was going about fifty miles per hour. The boy was afraid of seeing the dust cloud from the Plymouth up ahead, but there was only straight road. Then he was afraid that the Plymouth might have pulled off someplace. He touched his tongue to his upper lip but it was just one dry thing against another. Getting into the pickup, the boy had had a clear idea of the direction of his life. He meant to go to New York City at the end of summer. He meant to play the piano in Carnegie Hall.° The farmer and his forty-five seemed to stand between him and that future. They formed a wall that the boy was afraid to climb over.

"Do you have to kill them?" the boy asked. He didn't want to talk but he felt unable to remain silent.

The farmer had a red boil on the side of his neck and he kept touching it with two fingers. "When you have something wicked, what do you do?" asked the farmer.

15   The boy wanted to say he didn't know or he wanted to say he would call the police, but the farmer would have no patience with those answers. And the boy also wanted to say he would forgive the wickedness, but he was afraid of that answer as well. He was afraid of making the farmer angry and so he only shrugged.

"You stomp it out," said the farmer. "That's what you do — you stomp it out."

The boy stared straight ahead, searching for the dust cloud and hoping not to see it. The hot air seemed to bend in front of them. The boy was so frightened of seeing the dust cloud that he was sure he saw it. A little puff of gray getting closer. The pickup went straight down the middle of the road. There was no other traffic. Even if there had been other cars, the boy felt certain that the farmer wouldn't have moved out of the way. The wheat on either side of the road was coated with layers of dust, making it a reddish color, the color of dried blood.

"What about the police?" asked the boy.

"It's my wife," said the farmer. "It's my problem."

20   The boy never did see the dust cloud. They reached Lawrence and the boy got out as soon as he could. His shirt was stuck to his back and he kept rubbing his palms on his dungarees. He thanked the farmer but the man didn't look at him, he just kept staring straight ahead.

Carnegie Hall: A famous concert hall in New York City.

"Don't tell the police," said the farmer. His hand rested lightly on the forty-five beside him on the seat.

"No," said the boy. "I promise." He slammed shut the dusty door of the pickup.

The boy didn't tell the police. For several days he didn't tell anyone at all. He looked at the newspapers twice a day for news of a killing, but he didn't find anything. More than the farmer's gun, he had been frightened by the strength of the farmer's resolve. It had been like a chunk of stone and compared to it the boy had felt as soft as a piece of white bread. The boy never knew what happened. Perhaps nothing had happened.

The summer wound to its conclusion. The boy went to New York. He never did play in Carnegie Hall. His piano playing never got good enough. The war came and went. He wasn't a boy any longer. He was a married man with two sons. The family moved to Michigan. The man was a teacher, then a minister. His own parents died. He told his sons the story about the farmer in the pickup. "What do you think happened?" they asked. Nobody knew. Perhaps the farmer caught up with them; perhaps he didn't. The man's sons went off to college and began their own lives. The man and his wife moved to New Hampshire. They grew old. Sixty years went by between that summer in Kansas and the present. The man entered his last illness. He stayed at home but he couldn't get out of bed. His wife gave him shots of morphine. He began to have dreams even when he was awake. The visiting nurse was always chipper. "Feeling better today?" she would ask. He tried to be polite, but he had no illusions. He went from one shot a day to two, and then three. The doctor said, "Give him as many as he needs." His wife started to ask about the danger of addiction, then she said nothing.

The man hardly knew when he was asleep or awake. He hardly knew if one 25 day had passed or many. He had oxygen. He didn't eat. The space between his eyes and the bedroom wall was always occupied with people of his invention, people of his past. He would lift his hand to wave them away, only to find his hand still lying motionless on the counterpane. Even music distracted him now. Always he was listening for something in the distance.

The boy was standing by the side of a dirt road. A Ford pickup stopped beside him and he got in. The farmer lifted a forty-five revolver. "I'm going to shoot my wife in the head."

"No," said the boy, "don't do it!"

The farmer drove fast. He had a red boil on the side of his neck and he kept touching it with two fingers. They found the Plymouth coupe pulled off into a hollow. There were shade trees and a brook. The farmer jammed down the brakes and the pickup slid sideways across the dirt. The man and woman were in the front seat of the Plymouth. Their clothes were half off. They jumped out of the car. The woman had big red breasts. The farmer jumped out with his forty-five. "No!" shouted the boy. The farmer shot the man in the head. His whole head exploded and he fell down in the dust. His head was just a broken thing on the ground. The woman covered her face and tried to cover her breasts as well. The farmer shot her as well. Bits of dust floated on the surface of her blood. "One last for me," said the farmer. He put the barrel of the gun in his mouth. "No, no!" cried the boy.

The boy was standing by the side of a dirt road. A Ford pickup stopped beside him and he got in. "I'm going to shoot my wife," said the farmer. He had a big revolver on the seat beside him.

30   "You can't," said the boy.

They talked all the way to Lawrence. The farmer was crying. "I've always been good to her," he said. He had a red boil on the side of his neck and he kept touching it.

"Give the gun to the police," said the boy.

"I'm afraid," said the farmer.

"You needn't be," said the boy. "The police won't hurt you."

35   They drove to the police station. The boy told the desk sergeant what had happened. The sergeant shook his head. He took the revolver away from the farmer. "We'll get her back, sir," he said. "Wife stealing's not permitted around here."

"I could have got in real trouble," said the farmer.

The boy was standing by the side of a dirt road. A pickup stopped beside him and he got in. The farmer said, "I'm going to kill my wife."

The boy was too frightened to say anything. He kept looking at the forty-five revolver. He was sure that he would be shot himself. He regretted not staying in Oklahoma, where he had friends and family. He couldn't imagine why he had moved away. The farmer drove straight to Lawrence. The boy was bounced all over the cab of the pickup but he didn't say anything. He was afraid that something would happen to his hands and he wouldn't be able to play the piano. It seemed to him that playing the piano was the only important thing in the entire world. The farmer had a red boil on the side of his neck and he kept touching it.

When they got to Lawrence, the boy jumped out of the pickup and ran. He saw a policeman and told him what had happened. An hour later he was getting a hamburger at a White Tower restaurant. He heard shooting. He ran out and saw the farmer's dusty pickup. There were police cars with their lights flashing. The boy pushed through the crowd. The farmer was hanging half out of the door of his pickup truck. There was blood all over the front of his workshirt. The forty-five revolver lay on the pavement. The policemen were clapping each other on the back. They had big grins. The boy began cracking his knuckles. They made snapping noises.

40   The boy was standing by the side of a dirt road. A pickup stopped beside him and he got in. The farmer pointed a forty-five revolver at his head. "Get in here," he said. They drove toward Lawrence.

"I'm going to shoot my wife for wickedness," said the farmer.

"No," said the boy, "you must forgive her."

"I'm going to kill her," said the farmer, "and her fancy man besides."

The boy said, "You can't take the law into your own hands."

The farmer raised his forty-five revolver. "They're as good as dead." He had a 45
red boil on the side of his neck.

The boy was a college student. It was the Depression. He wanted to go to
New York and become a classical pianist. He had already been accepted by Juilliard.° "Justice does not belong to you," said the boy.

"Wickedness must be punished," said the farmer.

They argued all the way to Lawrence. The boy stayed with the farmer. He
could have jumped out of the pickup, but he didn't. The boy kept trying to convince him that he was wrong. The farmer drove to the train station.

The farmer's wife was in the waiting room with the man who had been driving the Plymouth coupe. She was very pretty, with blond hair and milky pink
skin. She screamed when she saw the farmer. Her companion put his arms
around her to protect her.

The boy hurried to stand between the woman and her husband. "Think of 50
what you are doing," he said. "Think how you are throwing your life away." The
first bullet struck him in the shoulder and whipped him around. He could see the
woman open her mouth in a startled *Oh* of surprise. The second bullet caught
him in the small of his back.

The man's family was with him in New Hampshire when he died: his wife and
his two sons, neither of them young anymore. It was early evening in October at
the very height of color. Even after sundown the maple trees seemed bright. The
older son watched his father breathing. He kept twisting and trying to kick his
feet. His face was very thin, his whole body was just a ridge under the middle of
the sheet. He didn't talk anymore. He didn't want anyone to touch him. He
seemed to be focusing his attention. He took a breath and they waited. He exhaled slowly. They continued to wait. He didn't breathe again. They waited several minutes. Then his wife removed the oxygen tubes from his nose, doing it
quickly, as if afraid of doing something wrong.

The older son went back into the bedroom with the two men from the funeral home. They had a collapsible stretcher which they put next to the bed.
They unrolled a dark blue body bag. They shifted the dead man onto the
stretcher and wrestled him into the body bag, one at his feet, one at his head.
The son stood in the doorway. The men from the funeral home muttered directions to each other. They were breathing heavily and their hair was mussed. At
last they got him into the body bag. The son watched closely as the zipper was
drawn up and across his father's face. It was a large silver zipper and the son
watched it being pulled across his father's forehead. All the days after that he
kept seeing its glittering progress, a picture repeating itself in his mind.

Juilliard: A highly respected school for the performing arts in New York City.

Reading and Reacting

1. Paragraph 1 presents the story's exposition. List the specific pieces of information this paragraph presents. How will each detail be important later in the story? Are any details unnecessary? Are any important details *not* introduced in paragraph 1?

2. Summarize the story's plot in three sentences.

3. In paragraph 12, the narrator says, "Getting into the pickup, the boy had had a clear idea of the direction of his life. . . . The farmer and his forty-five seemed to stand between him and that future." What direction do you think the boy imagined his life would take? What direction did it actually take? Were "the farmer and his forty-five" in any way responsible for this change of direction? Explain.

4. How would the story be different without the presence of the revolver lying on the seat?

5. What specific information are readers told in the story's first twenty-five paragraphs about the boy? The farmer? The couple in the blue Plymouth? Is all this information essential to the story's plot? What additional information might you want to know? Why?

6. The first twenty-five paragraphs present the story's basic plot; then, this section of the story is followed by three alternate versions of the boy's experience, each beginning with the sentence "The boy was standing by the side of a dirt road." What is the point of these alternate versions? What is the writer trying to accomplish?

7. How are the three alternate versions of events similar to and different from the boy's story as it is first presented? Which version is most satisfying? Most logical? Most believable? Explain.

8. At the end of paragraph 25, as the boy (now a man) is dying, he is "listening for something in the distance." What do you suppose he might be listening for?

9. The red boil on the side of the farmer's neck is mentioned several times. What other physical details are repeated in the story's descriptions of characters and setting? What is the effect of these repetitions? Are any important physical details omitted?

10. What does the last sentence add to the story?

11. JOURNAL ENTRY In paragraph 23, the narrator says, "The boy never knew what happened. Perhaps nothing had happened." What does he mean by this? What do you think really happened to the boy that day?

12. CRITICAL PERSPECTIVE In reviewing *Eating Naked*, the collection in which "Kansas" appeared, Roger Boylan says that Dobyns "almost gleefully imposes life's unpredictability on his characters." Boylan then goes on to give examples of the ways in which Dobyns "imposes life's unpredictability":

> Cancer ends a life in one story; a car crash does so in another. A kidnapping goes ludicrously wrong. People betray each other. Lust overrides good sense. Absur-

dity rules. Marriages fall apart with depressing regularity—and if yours doesn't seem to be on the rocks, well, can you be sure you know what your better half's up to when you're away?

Do you think "Kansas" fits the pattern Boylan has identified? Is it a story in which "absurdity rules"?

Related Works: "Sleepy Time Gal" (p. 86), "A Good Man Is Hard to Find" (p. 238), "Do not go gentle into that good night" (p. 627), "The Road Not Taken" (p. 671), *Beauty* (p. 736), *Tape* (p. 741)

WILLIAM FAULKNER (1897–1962), winner of the 1949 Nobel Prize in Literature and the 1955 and 1963 Pulitzer Prizes for fiction, was a Southern writer whose work continues to transcend the regional label. His nineteen novels, notably *The Sound and the Fury* (1929), *As I Lay Dying* (1930), *Light in August* (1932), *Absalom, Absalom!* (1936), and *The Reivers* (1962), explore a wide range of human experience — from high comedy to tragedy — as seen in the life of one community, the fictional Yoknapatawpha County (modeled on the area around Faulkner's own hometown of Oxford, Mississippi). Faulkner's Yoknapatawpha stories — a fascinating blend of complex Latinate prose and  primitive Southern dialect — paint an extraordinary portrait of a community bound together by ties of blood, by a shared belief in moral "verities," and by an old grief (the Civil War). Faulkner's grandfather raised "Billy" on Civil War tales and local legends, including many about the "Old Colonel," the writer's great-grandfather, who was a colorful Confederate officer. Although Faulkner's stories elegize the agrarian virtues of the Old South, they look unflinchingly at that world's tragic flaw: the "peculiar institution" of slavery.

Local legends and gossip frequently served as the spark for Faulkner's stories. As John B. Cullen, writing in *Old Times in Faulkner Country*, notes, "A Rose for Emily," Faulkner's first nationally published short story, was based on the tale of Oxford's aristocratic "Miss Mary" Neilson, who married Captain Jack Hume, the charming Yankee foreman of a street-paving crew, over her family's shocked protests. According to Cullen, one of Faulkner's neighbors said he created his story "out of fears and rumors" — the dire predictions of what *might* happen if Mary Neilson married her Yankee.

A Rose for Emily (1930)

I

When Miss Emily Grierson died, our whole town went to her funeral: the men through a sort of respectful affection for a fallen monument, the women mostly out of curiosity to see the inside of her house, which no one save an old manservant — a combined gardener and cook — had seen in at least ten years.

It was a big, squarish frame house that had once been white, decorated with cupolas and spires and scrolled balconies in the heavily lightsome style of the seventies, set on what had once been our most select street. But garages and cotton gins had encroached and obliterated even the august names of that neighborhood; only Miss Emily's house was left, lifting its stubborn and coquettish decay above the cotton wagons and the gasoline pumps — an eyesore among eyesores. And now Miss Emily had gone to join the representatives of those august names where they lay in the cedar-bemused cemetery among the ranked and anonymous graves of Union and Confederate soldiers who fell at the battle of Jefferson.

Alive, Miss Emily had been a tradition, a duty, and a care; a sort of hereditary obligation upon the town, dating from that day in 1894 when Colonel Sartoris, the mayor — he who fathered the edict that no Negro woman should appear on the streets without an apron — remitted her taxes, the dispensation dating from the death of her father on into perpetuity. Not that Miss Emily would have accepted charity. Colonel Sartoris invented an involved tale to the effect that Miss Emily's father had loaned money to the town, which the town, as a matter of business, preferred this way of repaying. Only a man of Colonel Sartoris' generation and thought could have invented it, and only a woman could have believed it.

When the next generation, with its more modern ideas, became mayors and aldermen, this arrangement created some little dissatisfaction. On the first of the year they mailed her a tax notice. February came, and there was no reply. They wrote her a formal letter, asking her to call at the sheriff's office at her convenience. A week later the mayor wrote her himself, offering to call or to send his car for her, and received in reply a note on paper of an archaic shape, in a thin, flowing calligraphy in faded ink, to the effect that she no longer went out at all. The tax notice was also enclosed, without comment.

5 They called a special meeting of the Board of Aldermen. A deputation waited upon her, knocked at the door through which no visitor had passed since she ceased giving china-painting lessons eight or ten years earlier. They were admitted by the old Negro into a dim hall from which a stairway mounted into still more shadow. It smelled of dust and disuse — a close, dank smell. The Negro led them into the parlor. It was furnished in heavy, leather-covered furniture. When the Negro opened the blinds of one window, they could see that the leather was cracked; and when they sat down, a faint dust rose sluggishly about their thighs, spinning with slow motes in the single sun-ray. On a tarnished gilt easel before the fireplace stood a crayon portrait of Miss Emily's father.

They rose when she entered — a small, fat woman in black, with a thin gold chain descending to her waist and vanishing into her belt, leaning on an ebony cane with a tarnished gold head. Her skeleton was small and spare; perhaps that was why what would have been merely plumpness in another was obesity in her. She looked bloated, like a body long submerged in motionless water, and of that pallid hue. Her eyes, lost in the fatty ridges of her face, looked like two small pieces of coal pressed into a lump of dough as they moved from one face to another while the visitors stated their errand.

She did not ask them to sit. She just stood in the door and listened quietly until the spokesman came to a stumbling halt. Then they could hear the invisible watch ticking at the end of the gold chain.

Her voice was dry and cold. "I have no taxes in Jefferson. Colonel Sartoris explained it to me. Perhaps one of you can gain access to the city records and satisfy yourselves."

"But we have. We are the city authorities, Miss Emily. Didn't you get a notice from the sheriff, signed by him?"

"I received a paper, yes," Miss Emily said. "Perhaps he considers himself the sheriff . . . I have no taxes in Jefferson." 10

"But there is nothing on the books to show that, you see. We must go by the —"

"See Colonel Sartoris. I have no taxes in Jefferson."

"But, Miss Emily —"

"See Colonel Sartoris." (Colonel Sartoris had been dead almost ten years.) "I have no taxes in Jefferson. Tobe!" The Negro appeared. "Show these gentlemen out."

II

So she vanquished them, horse and foot, just as she had vanquished their fa- thers thirty years before about the smell. That was two years after her father's 15 death and a short time after her sweetheart — the one we believed would marry her — had deserted her. After her father's death she went out very little; after her sweetheart went away, people hardly saw her at all. A few of the ladies had the temerity to call, but were not received, and the only sign of life about the place was the Negro man — a young man then — going in and out with a market basket.

"Just as if a man — any man — could keep a kitchen properly," the ladies said; so they were not surprised when the smell developed. It was another link between the gross, teeming world and the high and mighty Griersons.

A neighbor, a woman, complained to the mayor, Judge Stevens, eighty years old.

"But what will you have me do about it, madam?" he said.

"Why, send her word to stop it," the woman said. "Isn't there a law?"

"I'm sure that won't be necessary," Judge Stevens said. "It's probably just a snake or a rat that nigger of hers killed in the yard. I'll speak to him about it." 20

The next day he received two more complaints, one from a man who came in diffident deprecation. "We really must do something about it, Judge. I'd be the last one in the world to bother Miss Emily, but we've got to do something." That night the Board of Aldermen met — three graybeards and one younger man, a member of the rising generation.

"It's simple enough," he said. "Send her word to have her place cleaned up. Give her a certain time to do it in, and if she don't . . ."

"Dammit, sir," Judge Stevens said, "will you accuse a lady to her face of smelling bad?"

So the next night, after midnight, four men crossed Miss Emily's lawn and slunk about the house like burglars, sniffing along the base of the brickwork and at the cellar openings while one of them performed a regular sowing motion with his hand out of a sack slung from his shoulder. They broke open the cellar door and sprinkled lime there, and in all the outbuildings. As they recrossed the lawn, a window that had been dark was lighted and Miss Emily sat in it, the light behind her, and her upright torso motionless as that of an idol. They crept quietly across the lawn and into the shadow of the locusts that lined the street. After a week or two the smell went away.

25   That was when people had begun to feel really sorry for her. People in our town, remembering how old lady Wyatt, her great-aunt, had gone completely crazy at last, believed that the Griersons held themselves a little too high for what they really were. None of the young men were quite good enough for Miss Emily and such. We had long thought of them as a tableau, Miss Emily a slender figure in white in the background, her father a spraddled silhouette in the foreground, his back to her and clutching a horsewhip, the two of them framed by the back-flung front door. So when she got to be thirty and was still single, we were not pleased exactly, but vindicated; even with insanity in the family she wouldn't have turned down all of her chances if they had really materialized.

When her father died, it got about that the house was all that was left to her; and in a way, people were glad. At last they could pity Miss Emily. Being left alone, and a pauper, she had become humanized. Now she too would know the old thrill and the old despair of a penny more or less.

The day after his death all the ladies prepared to call at the house and offer condolence and aid, as is our custom. Miss Emily met them at the door, dressed as usual and with no trace of grief on her face. She told them that her father was not dead. She did that for three days, with the ministers calling on her, and the doctors, trying to persuade her to let them dispose of the body. Just as they were about to resort to law and force, she broke down, and they buried her father quickly.

We did not say she was crazy then. We believed she had to do that. We remembered all the young men her father had driven away, and we knew that with nothing left, she would have to cling to that which had robbed her, as people will.

III

She was sick for a long time. When we saw her again, her hair was cut short, making her look like a girl, with a vague resemblance to those angels in colored church windows — sort of tragic and serene.

The town had just let the contracts for paving the sidewalks, and in the sum- 30 mer after her father's death they began the work. The construction company came with niggers and mules and machinery, and a foreman named Homer Barron, a Yankee — a big, dark, ready man, with a big voice and eyes lighter than his face. The little boys would follow in groups to hear him cuss the niggers, and the niggers singing in time to the rise and fall of picks. Pretty soon he knew everybody in town. Whenever you heard a lot of laughing anywhere about the square, Homer Barron would be in the center of the group. Presently we began to see him and Miss Emily on Sunday afternoons driving in the yellow-wheeled buggy and the matched team of bays from the livery stable.

At first we were glad that Miss Emily would have an interest, because the ladies all said, "Of course a Grierson would not think seriously of a Northerner, a day laborer." But there were still others, older people, who said that even grief could not cause a real lady to forget *noblesse oblige*° — without calling it *noblesse oblige*. They just said, "Poor Emily. Her kinsfolk should come to her." She had some kin in Alabama; but years ago her father had fallen out with them over the estate of old lady Wyatt, the crazy woman, and there was no communication between the two families. They had not even been represented at the funeral.

And as soon as the old people said, "Poor Emily," the whispering began. "Do you suppose it's really so?" they said to one another. "Of course it is. What else could . . ." This behind their hands; rustling of craned silk and satin behind jalousies closed upon the sun of Sunday afternoon as the thin, swift clop-clop-clop of the matched team passed: "Poor Emily."

She carried her head high enough — even when we believed that she was fallen. It was as if she demanded more than ever the recognition of her dignity as the last Grierson; as if it had wanted that touch of earthiness to reaffirm her imperviousness. Like when she bought the rat poison, the arsenic. That was over a year after they had begun to say "Poor Emily," and while the two female cousins were visiting her.

"I want some poison," she said to the druggist. She was over thirty then, still a slight woman, though thinner than usual, with cold, haughty black eyes in a face the flesh of which was strained across the temples and about the eye-sockets as you imagine a lighthouse-keeper's face ought to look. "I want some poison," she said.

"Yes, Miss Emily. What kind? For rats and such? I'd recom —" 35

"I want the best you have. I don't care what kind."

The druggist named several. "They'll kill anything up to an elephant. But what you want is —"

"Arsenic," Miss Emily said. "Is that a good one?"

"Is . . . arsenic? Yes, ma'am. But what you want —"

---

noblesse oblige: The obligation of those of high birth or rank to behave honorably.

40   "I want arsenic."

The druggist looked down at her. She looked back at him, erect, her face like a strained flag. "Why, of course," the druggist said. "If that's what you want. But the law requires you to tell what you are going to use it for."

Miss Emily just stared at him, her head tilted back in order to look him eye for eye, until he looked away and went and got the arsenic and wrapped it up. The Negro delivery boy brought her the package; the druggist didn't come back. When she opened the package at home there was written on the box, under the skull and bones: "For rats."

IV

So the next day we all said, "She will kill herself"; and we said it would be the best thing. When she had first begun to be seen with Homer Barron, we had said, "She will marry him." Then we said, "She will persuade him yet," because Homer himself had remarked — he liked men, and it was known that he drank with the younger men in the Elks' Club — that he was not a marrying man. Later we said, "Poor Emily" behind the jalousies as they passed on Sunday afternoon in the glittering buggy, Miss Emily with her head high and Homer Barron with his hat cocked and a cigar in his teeth, reins and whip in a yellow glove.

Then some of the ladies began to say that it was a disgrace to the town and a bad example to the young people. The men did not want to interfere, but at last the ladies forced the Baptist minister — Miss Emily's people were Episcopal — to call upon her. He would never divulge what happened during that interview, but he refused to go back again. The next Sunday they again drove about the streets, and the following day the minister's wife wrote to Miss Emily's relations in Alabama.

45   So she had blood-kin under her roof again and we sat back to watch developments. At first nothing happened. Then we were sure that they were to be married. We learned that Miss Emily had been to the jeweler's and ordered a man's toilet set in silver, with the letters H. B. on each piece. Two days later we learned that she had bought a complete outfit of men's clothing, including a nightshirt, and we said, "They are married." We were really glad. We were glad because the two female cousins were even more Grierson than Miss Emily had ever been.

So we were not surprised when Homer Barron — the streets had been finished some time since — was gone. We were a little disappointed that there was not a public blowing-off, but we believed that he had gone on to prepare for Miss Emily's coming, or to give her a chance to get rid of the cousins. (By that time it was a cabal, and we were all Miss Emily's allies to help circumvent the cousins.) Sure enough, after another week they departed. And, as we had expected all along, within three days Homer Barron was back in town. A neighbor saw the Negro man admit him at the kitchen door at dusk one evening.

And that was the last we saw of Homer Barron. And of Miss Emily for some time. The Negro man went in and out with the market basket, but the front door remained closed. Now and then we would see her at a window for a moment, as the men did that night when they sprinkled the lime, but for almost six months she did not appear on the streets. Then we knew that this was to be expected too; as if that quality of her father which had thwarted her woman's life so many times had been too virulent and too furious to die.

When we next saw Miss Emily, she had grown fat and her hair was turning gray. During the next few years it grew grayer and grayer until it attained an even pepper-and-salt iron-gray, when it ceased turning. Up to the day of her death at seventy-four it was still that vigorous iron-gray, like the hair of an active man.

From that time on her front door remained closed, save for a period of six or seven years, when she was about forty, during which she gave lessons in china-painting. She fitted up a studio in one of the downstairs rooms, where the daughters and granddaughters of Colonel Sartoris' contemporaries were sent to her with the same regularity and in the same spirit that they were sent to church on Sundays with a twenty-five-cent piece for the collection plate. Meanwhile her taxes had been remitted.

Then the newer generation became the backbone and the spirit of the town, 50 and the painting pupils grew up and fell away and did not send their children to her with boxes of color and tedious brushes and pictures cut from the ladies' magazines. The front door closed upon the last one and remained closed for good. When the town got free postal delivery, Miss Emily alone refused to let them fasten the metal numbers above her door and attach a mailbox to it. She would not listen to them.

Daily, monthly, yearly we watched the Negro grow grayer and more stooped, going in and out with the market basket. Each December we sent her a tax notice, which would be returned by the post office a week later, unclaimed. Now and then we would see her in one of the downstairs windows — she had evidently shut up the top floor of the house — like the carven torso of an idol in a niche, looking or not looking at us, we could never tell which. Thus she passed from generation to generation — dear, inescapable, impervious, tranquil, and perverse.

And so she died. Fell ill in the house filled with dust and shadows, with only a doddering Negro man to wait on her. We did not even know she was sick; we had long since given up trying to get any information from the Negro. He talked to no one, probably not even to her, for his voice had grown harsh and rusty, as if from disuse.

She died in one of the downstairs rooms, in a heavy walnut bed with a curtain, her gray head propped on a pillow yellow and moldy with age and lack of sunlight.

V

The Negro met the first of the ladies at the front door and let them in, with their hushed, sibilant voices and their quick, curious glances, and then he disappeared. He walked right through the house and out the back and was not seen again.

55   The two female cousins came at once. They held the funeral on the second day, with the town coming to look at Miss Emily beneath a mass of bought flowers, with the crayon face of her father musing profoundly above the bier and the ladies sibilant and macabre; and the very old men — some in their brushed Confederate uniforms — on the porch and the lawn, talking of Miss Emily as if she had been a contemporary of theirs, believing that they had danced with her and courted her perhaps, confusing time with its mathematical progression, as the old do, to whom all the past is not a diminishing road but, instead, a huge meadow which no winter ever quite touches, divided from them now by the narrow bottleneck of the most recent decade of years.

   Already we knew that there was one room in that region above stairs which no one had seen in forty years, and which would have to be forced. They waited until Miss Emily was decently in the ground before they opened it.

   The violence of breaking down the door seemed to fill this room with pervading dust. A thin, acrid pall as of the tomb seemed to lie everywhere upon this room decked and furnished as for a bridal: upon the valance curtains of faded rose color, upon the rose-shaded lights, upon the dressing table, upon the delicate array of crystal and the man's toilet things backed with tarnished silver, silver so tarnished that the monogram was obscured. Among them lay collar and tie, as if they had just been removed, which, lifted, left upon the surface a pale crescent in the dust. Upon a chair hung the suit, carefully folded; beneath it the two mute shoes and the discarded socks.

   The man himself lay in the bed.

   For a long while we just stood there, looking down at the profound and fleshless grin. The body had apparently once lain in the attitude of an embrace, but now the long sleep that outlasts love, that conquers even the grimace of love, had cuckolded him. What was left of him, rotted beneath what was left of the nightshirt, had become inextricable from the bed in which he lay; and upon him and upon the pillow beside him lay that even coating of the patient and biding dust.

60   Then we noticed that in the second pillow was the indentation of a head. One of us lifted something from it, and leaning forward, that faint and invisible dust dry and acrid in the nostrils, we saw a long strand of iron-gray hair.

Reading and Reacting

1. Arrange these events in the sequence in which they actually occur: Homer's arrival in town, the aldermen's visit, Emily's purchase of poison, Colonel Sartoris's decision to remit Emily's taxes, the development of the odor around Emily's house, Emily's father's death, the arrival of Emily's relatives, Homer's disappearance. Then, list the events in the sequence in which they are introduced in the story. Why do you suppose Faulkner presents these events out of their actual chronological order?

2. Despite the story's confusing sequence, many events are foreshadowed. Give some examples of this technique. How does foreshadowing enrich the story?

3. Where does the exposition end and the movement toward the story's climax begin? Where does the resolution stage begin?

4. Emily is clearly the story's protagonist. In the sense that he opposes her wishes, Homer is the antagonist. What other characters — or what larger forces — are in conflict with Emily?

5. Explain how each of these phrases moves the story's plot along: "So she vanquished them, horse and foot . . ." (par. 15); "After a week or two the smell went away" (par. 24); "And that was the last we saw of Homer Barron" (par. 47); "And so she died" (par. 52); "The man himself lay in the bed" (par. 58).

6. The narrator of the story is an observer, not a participant. Who might this narrator be? How do you suppose the narrator might know so much about Emily? Why do you think the narrator uses *we* instead of *I*?

7. The original version of "A Rose for Emily" included a two-page deathbed scene revealing that Tobe, Emily's servant, has shared her terrible secret all these years, and that Emily has left her house to him. Why do you think Faulkner deleted this scene? Do you think he made the right decision?

8. Some critics have suggested that Miss Emily Grierson is a kind of symbol of the Old South, with its outdated ideas of chivalry, formal manners, and tradition. Do you see her also as a victim of those values? Explain.

9. JOURNAL ENTRY When asked at a seminar at the University of Virginia about the meaning of the title "A Rose for Emily," Faulkner replied, "Oh, it's simply the poor woman had no life at all. Her father had kept her more or less locked up and then she had a lover who was about to quit her, she had to murder him. It was just 'A Rose for Emily'— that's all." In another interview, asked the same question, he replied, "I pitied her and this was a salute, just as if you were to make a gesture, a salute, to anyone; to a woman you would hand a rose, as you would lift a cup of *sake* to a man." What do you make of Faulkner's responses? What else might the title suggest?

10. CRITICAL PERSPECTIVE In his essay "William Faulkner: An American Dickens," literary critic Leslie A. Fiedler characterizes Faulkner as "primarily . . . a sentimental writer; not a writer with the occasional vice of sentimentality, but one whose basic mode of experience is sentimental." He continues, "In a writer whose very method is self-indulgence, that sentimentality becomes sometimes downright embarrassing." Fiedler also notes Faulkner's "excesses of maudlin feelings and absurd indulgences in overripe rhetoric."

Do you think these criticisms apply to "A Rose for Emily"? If so, does the "vice of sentimentality" diminish the story, or do you agree with Fiedler — who calls Faulkner a "supereminently good 'bad' writer"— that the author is able to transcend these excesses?

Related Works: "Miss Brill" (p. 134), "Porphyria's Lover" (p. 480), "Richard Cory" (p. 695), *Trifles* (p. 770)

WRITING SUGGESTIONS: Plot

1. Write a sequel to "The Story of an Hour," telling the story in the voice of Brently Mallard. Use flashbacks to provide information about his view of the Mallards' marriage.

2. "The Story of an Hour" includes a **deus ex machina,** an outside force or agent that suddenly appears to change the course of events. Consider the possible effects of a deus ex machina on the other two stories in this chapter. What might this outside force be in each story? How might it change the story's action? How plausible would such a dramatic turn of events be in each case?

3. In "Kansas," a character's actual life unfolds alongside his memories and fantasies. Write an essay in which you compare "Kansas" with another story in which a character's imaginative life is a significant part of the story—for example, "The Rocking-Horse Winner" (p. 340) or "The Yellow Wallpaper" (p. 372).

4. Read the following article from the January 30, 1987, *Philadelphia Inquirer*. After listing some similarities and differences between the events in the article's story and those in "A Rose for Emily," write an essay in which you discuss how the presentation of events differs. Can you draw any conclusions about the differences between journalistic and fictional treatments of similar incidents?

DICK POTHIER AND THOMAS J. GIBBONS JR.

A Woman's Wintry Death Leads to a Long-Dead Friend

For more than two years, Frances Dawson Hamilton lived with the body of her long-time companion, draping his skeletonized remains with palm fronds and rosary beads.

Yesterday, the 70-year-old woman was found frozen to death in the home in the 4500 block of Higbee Street where she had lived all her life — the last year without heat or hot water. Her body was found by police accompanying a city social worker who came bearing an order to have her taken to a hospital.

Police investigators said the body of Bernard J. Kelly, 84, was found in an upstairs bedroom of the two-story brick home in the Wissinoming section, on the twin bed where he apparently died at least two years ago.

Two beds had been pushed together, and Hamilton apparently had been sleeping beside Kelly's remains since he died of unknown causes, police said.

Kelly's remains were clothed in long johns and socks, investigators said. The body was draped with rosary beads and palm fronds, and on the bed near his body were two boxes of Valentine's Day candy.

"It was basically a funeral — we've seen it before in such cases," said one investigator who was at the scene but declined to be identified.

Neighbors and investigators said Hamilton and Kelly had lived together in the house for at least 15 years. Several neighbors said Hamilton came from an affluent family, was educated in Europe, and lived on a trust fund until a year or so ago.

Last winter, said John Wasniewski, Hamilton's next-door neighbor, the basement of the home was flooded and the heater destroyed. "There was no heat in that house last winter or this winter," he said.

An autopsy will be performed on Hamilton today, but she apparently froze to death sometime since Monday, when a friend spoke to her on the telephone, investigators said.

Over the last two years, neighbors said, Hamilton had become increasingly reclusive and irrational. Just last week, a city social worker summoned by a friend arranged for a Philadelphia Gas Works team to visit the home and try to repair the furnace — but she refused to let them in.

The friend was James Phillips, 44, of Horsham, a salesman for Apex Electric in Souderton.

In October 1985, he said, Hamilton visited the Frankford Avenue electrical shop where he was then working, told him that she had an electrical problem in her house and had no lights, and asked whether he could help.

Phillips said he visited the house, fixed the problem and gave her some light bulbs.

"She was really paranoid," Phillips said. "She believed that all her problems were from people doing things to her. For some reason or other, she took to me."

Phillips said that he began visiting her, taking her shopping and doing some shopping for her. But, he said, he never saw the body on the second floor.

Hamilton told him there was a man up there. "I thought it was a story she was telling to protect herself," Phillips said.

He provided her with electric heaters and also contacted a caseworker with the city's Department of Human Services whom Phillips identified as Albert Zbik.

Between the two of them, he said, "we got her through last winter." Phillips said Zbik helped her obtain food stamps and Social Security assistance.

When the snowstorm hit last week, Phillips became concerned because he knew Hamilton would have trouble getting food. On Saturday, he took her a plate of hot food and bought more food from a local store.

On Monday, she telephoned him. "I didn't like the way she sounded," he said. He called Zbik and told him he felt it was time that they forced her to go to a hospital.

Phillips said Zbik went to her home yesterday, carrying a form authorizing an involuntary admission to a hospital for observation or required medical treatment.

Phillips told police that he was never allowed above the first floor and was often told by Hamilton that "Bernie is not feeling well today."

Neighbors and police investigators said Kelly was last seen alive about two years ago, and appeared to be quite ill at the time.

"As recently as last month, I asked Frances how Bernard was and whether she should get a doctor, and she said it wasn't necessary. She said 'He's sick, but I'm taking care of him — I'm feeding him with an eyedropper,'" Wasniewski said.

"I told her in December that if he was that sick, she should call a doctor, but she'd say she was taking care of him very well," Wasniewski said.

CHAPTER 7

CHARACTER

> Every real writer . . . starts with people and their emotions and actions and lets them make their own stories.
>
> — Martha Foley, *Best American Short Stories*

A **character** is a fictional representation of a person — usually (but not necessarily) a psychologically realistic depiction. Writers may develop characters through their actions, through their reactions to situations or to other characters, through their physical appearance, through their speech and gestures and expressions, and even through their names.

Generally speaking, characters' physical traits, as well as their feelings and beliefs, are communicated to readers in two ways. First, readers can be *told* about characters. Third-person narrators can provide information about what characters are doing, saying, and thinking; what experiences they have had; what they look like; how they are dressed; and so on. Sometimes they also offer analysis of and judgments about a character's behavior or motivation. Similarly, first-person narrators can tell us about themselves or about other characters. Thus, Sammy in John Updike's "A&P" (p. 128) tells readers what he thinks about his job and about the girls who come into the supermarket where he works. He also tells us what various characters look like and describes their actions, attitudes, speech, and gestures. (For more information about first-person narrators, see Chapter 9, "Point of View.")

Alternatively, a character's personality traits and motivation may be revealed through actions, dialogue, or thoughts. For instance, Sammy's vivid fantasies and his disapproval of his customers' lives suggest to readers that he is something of a nonconformist; however, Sammy himself does not actually tell us this.

Round and Flat Characters

In his influential 1927 work *Aspects of the Novel*, English novelist E. M. Forster classifies characters as either **round** (well developed, closely involved in and responsive to the action) or **flat** (barely developed or stereotypical). To a large extent, these categories are still useful. In an effective story, the major characters are usually complex and fully developed; if they are not, readers do not care what happens to them. Sometimes, readers are encouraged to become involved with the characters, even to identify with them, and this empathy is possible only when we know something about the characters — their strengths and weaknesses, their likes and dislikes. In some cases, of course, a story can be effective even when its central characters are not well developed. Sometimes, in fact, a story's effectiveness is enhanced by an *absence* of character development, as in Shirley Jackson's "The Lottery" (p. 274).

Readers often expect characters to behave as "real people" in their situation might behave. Real people are not perfect, and realistic characters cannot be perfect either. The flaws that are revealed as round characters are developed — greed, gullibility, naïveté, shyness, a quick temper, or a lack of insight or judgment or tolerance or even intelligence — make them believable. In modern fiction, the protagonist is seldom if ever the noble "hero"; more often, he or she is at least partly a victim, someone to whom some unpleasant things happen, and someone who is sometimes ill equipped to cope with events.

Unlike major characters, minor characters are frequently not well developed. Often they are flat, perhaps acting as *foils* for the protagonist. A **foil** is a supporting character whose role in the story is to highlight a major character by presenting a contrast with him or her. For instance, in "A&P," Stokesie, another young checkout clerk, is a foil for Sammy. Because he is a little older than Sammy and seems to have none of Sammy's imagination, restlessness, or nonconformity, Stokesie suggests what Sammy might become if he were to continue to work at the A&P. Some flat characters are **stock characters,** easily identifiable types who behave so predictably that readers can readily recognize them. The kindly old priest, the tough young bully, the ruthless business executive, and the reckless adventurer are all stock characters. Some flat characters can even be **caricatures,** characterized by a single dominant trait, such as miserliness, or even by one physical trait, such as nearsightedness.

Dynamic and Static Characters

Characters may also be classified as either *dynamic* or *static*. A **dynamic character** grows and changes in the course of a story, developing as he or she reacts to events and to other characters. In "A&P," for instance, Sammy's decision to speak out in defense of the girls — as well as the events that lead him to do so — changes him. His view of the world has changed at the end of the story, and as a result his position in the world will change too. A **static character** may face the same challenges a dynamic character might face but will remain essentially unchanged: a static character who was selfish and arrogant will remain selfish and arrogant, regardless of the nature of the story's conflict. In the fairy tale "Cinderella," for example, the title character is as sweet and good-natured at the end of the story — despite her mistreatment by her family — as she is at the beginning. Her situation may have changed, but her character has not.

Whereas round characters tend to be dynamic, flat characters tend to be static. But even a very complex, well-developed major character may be static; sometimes, in fact, the point of a story may hinge on a character's inability to change. A familiar example is the title character in William Faulkner's "A Rose for Emily" (p. 113), who lives a wasted, empty life, at least in part because she is unwilling or unable to accept that the world around her and the people in it have changed.

A story's minor characters are often static; their growth is not usually relevant to the story's development. Moreover, we usually do not learn enough about a minor character's traits, thoughts, actions, or motivation to determine whether the character changes significantly.

Motivation

Because round characters are complex, they are not always easy to understand. They may act unpredictably, just as real people do. They wrestle with decisions, resist or succumb to temptation, make mistakes, ask questions, search for answers, hope and dream, rejoice and despair. What is important is not whether we approve of a character's actions but whether those actions are *plausible* — whether the actions make sense in light of what we know about the character. We need to see a character's **motivation** — the reasons behind his or her behavior — or we will not believe or accept that behavior. For instance, given Sammy's age, his dissatisfaction with his job, and his desire to impress the young woman he calls Queenie, the decision he makes at the end of the story is perfectly plausible. Without having established his motivation, Updike could not have expected readers to accept Sammy's actions.

Of course, even when readers get to know a character, they still are not able to predict how a complex, round character will behave in a given situation; only a flat character is predictable. The tension that develops as readers wait to see how a character will act or react, and thus how a story's conflict will be resolved, is what holds readers' interest and keeps them involved as a story's action unfolds.

✔ CHECKLIST   Writing about Character

☐ Who is the story's protagonist? Who (or what) is the antagonist? Who are the other major characters?

☐ Who are the minor characters? What roles do they play in the story? How would the story be different without them?

☐ What do the major characters look like? Is their physical appearance important?

☐ What are the major characters' most noticeable personality traits?

---

continued on next page

- What are the major characters' likes and dislikes? Their strengths and weaknesses?

- What are we told about the major characters' backgrounds and prior experiences? What can we infer?

- Are the characters round or flat?

- Are the characters dynamic or static?

- Does the story include any stock characters? Any caricatures? Does any character serve as a foil?

- Do the characters act in a way that is consistent with how readers expect them to act?

- With which characters are readers likely to be most sympathetic? Least sympathetic?

JOHN UPDIKE (1932–   ) is a prolific writer of novels, short stories, essays, poems, plays, and children's tales. Updike's earliest ambition was to be a cartoonist for the *New Yorker*. He attended Harvard hoping to draw cartoons for the *Harvard Lampoon,* studied drawing and fine art at Oxford, and in 1955 went to work for the *New Yorker*— not as a cartoonist but as a "Talk of the Town" reporter. Updike left the *New Yorker* after three years to write full-time but (over forty years later) is still contributing stories, reviews, and essays to the magazine. Among his novels are *Rabbit, Run* (1960), *The Centaur* (1963), *Rabbit Redux* (1971), *Rabbit Is Rich* (1981), *The Witches of Eastwick* (1985), and *Rabbit at Rest* (1990). His most recent novels are *Seek My Face* (2002) and *Villages* (2004). Updike has also published *Collected Poems 1953–1993* (1993) and a collection of essays titled *The Afterlife and Other Stories* (1994). In 1998, Updike received the National Book Foundation Medal for Distinguished Contribution to American Letters.

In early stories such as "A&P" (1961), Updike draws on memories of his childhood and teenage years for the sort of "small" scenes and stories for which he quickly became famous. "There is a great deal to be said about almost anything," Updike comments in an interview in *Contemporary Authors.* "All people can be equally interesting. . . . Now either nobody is a hero or everybody is. I vote for everybody. My subject is the American Protestant small-town middle class. I like middles. It is in middles that extremes clash."

A&P   (1961)

In walks these three girls in nothing but bathing suits. I'm in the third check-out slot, with my back to the door, so I don't see them until they're over by the bread. The one that caught my eye first was the one in the plaid green two-piece. She was a chunky kid, with a good tan and a sweet broad soft-looking can with those two crescents of white just under it, where the sun never seems to hit, at the top of the backs of her legs. I stood there with my hand on a box of HiHo crackers trying to remember if I rang it up or not. I ring it up again and the customer starts giving me hell. She's one of these cash-register-watchers, a witch about fifty with rouge on her cheekbones and no eyebrows, and I know it made her day to trip me up. She'd been watching cash registers for fifty years and probably never seen a mistake before.

By the time I got her feathers smoothed and her goodies into a bag — she gives me a little snort in passing, if she'd been born at the right time they would have burned her over in Salem — by the time I get her on her way the girls had circled around the bread and were coming back, without a push-cart, back my way along the counters, in the aisle between the check-outs and the Special bins. They didn't even have shoes on. There was this chunky one, with the two-piece — it was bright green and the seams on the bra were still sharp and her belly was still pretty pale so I guessed she just got it (the suit) — there was this one, with one of those chubby berry-faces, the lips all bunched together under her nose, this one, and a tall one, with black hair that hadn't quite frizzed right, and one of these sunburns right across under the eyes, and a chin that was too long — you know, the kind of girl other girls think is very "striking" and "attractive" but never quite makes it, as they very well know, which is why they like her so much — and then the third one, that wasn't quite so tall. She was the queen. She kind of led them, the other two peeking around and making their shoulders round. She didn't look around, not this queen, she just walked straight on slowly, on these long white prima-donna legs. She came down a little hard on her heels, as if she didn't walk in her bare feet that much, putting down her heels and then letting the weight move along to her toes as if she was testing the floor with every step, putting a little deliberate extra action into it. You never know for sure how girls' minds work (do you really think it's a mind in there or just a little buzz like a bee in a glass jar?) but you got the idea she had talked the other two into coming in here with her, and now she was showing them how to do it, walk slow and hold yourself straight.

She had on a kind of dirty-pink — beige maybe, I don't know — bathing suit with a little nubble all over it and, what got me, the straps were down. They were off her shoulders looped loose around the cool tops of her arms, and I guess as a result the suit had slipped a little on her, so all around the top of the cloth there was this shining rim. If it hadn't been there you wouldn't have known there could have been anything whiter than those shoulders. With the straps pushed off, there was nothing between the top of the suit and the top of her head except just *her*, this clean bare plane of the top of her chest down from the shoulder bones like a dented sheet of metal tilted in the light. I mean, it was more than pretty.

She had sort of oaky hair that the sun and salt had bleached, done up in a bun that was unravelling, and a kind of prim face. Walking into the A&P with your straps down, I suppose it's the only kind of face you *can* have. She held her head so high her neck, coming out of those white shoulders, looked kind of stretched, but I didn't mind. The longer her neck was, the more of her there was.

5   She must have felt in the corner of her eye me and over my shoulder Stokesie in the second slot watching, but she didn't tip. Not this queen. She kept her eyes moving across the racks, and stopped, and turned so slow it made my stomach rub the inside of my apron, and buzzed to the other two, who kind of huddled against her for relief, and they all three of them went up the cat-and-dog-food-breakfast-cereal-macaroni-rice-raisins-seasonings-spreads-spaghetti-soft-drinks-crackers-and-cookies aisle. From the third slot I look straight up this aisle to the meat counter, and I watched them all the way. The fat one with the tan sort of fumbled with the cookies, but on second thought she put the packages back. The sheep pushing their carts down the aisle — the girls were walking against the usual traffic (not that we have one-way signs or anything)— were pretty hilarious. You could see them, when Queenie's white shoulders dawned on them, kind of jerk, or hop, or hiccup, but their eyes snapped back to their own baskets and on they pushed. I bet you could set off dynamite in an A&P and the people would by and large keep reaching and checking oatmeal off their lists and muttering "Let me see, there was a third thing, began with A, asparagus, no, ah, yes, applesauce!" or whatever it is they do mutter. But there was no doubt, this jiggled them. A few houseslaves in pin curlers even looked around after pushing their carts past to make sure what they had seen was correct.

You know, it's one thing to have a girl in a bathing suit down on the beach, where what with the glare nobody can look at each other much anyway, and another thing in the cool of the A&P, under the fluorescent lights, against all those stacked packages, with her feet paddling along naked over our checkerboard green-and-cream rubber-tile floor.

"Oh Daddy," Stokesie said beside me. "I feel so faint."

"Darling," I said. "Hold me tight." Stokesie's married, with two babies chalked up on his fuselage already, but as far as I can tell that's the only difference. He's twenty-two, and I was nineteen this April.

"Is it done?" he asks, the responsible married man finding his voice. I forgot to say he thinks he's going to be manager some sunny day, maybe in 1990 when it's called the Great Alexandrov and Petrooshki Tea Company or something.

10   What he meant was, our town is five miles from a beach, with a big summer colony out on the Point, but we're right in the middle of town, and the women generally put on a shirt or shorts or something before they get out of the car into the street. And anyway these are usually women with six children and varicose veins mapping their legs and nobody, including them, could care less. As I say, we're right in the middle of town, and if you stand at our front doors you can see two banks and the Congregational church and the newspaper store and three real-estate offices and about twenty-seven old freeloaders tearing up Central Street because the sewer broke again. It's not as if we're on the Cape; we're

north of Boston and there's people in this town haven't seen the ocean for twenty years.

The girls had reached the meat counter and were asking McMahon something. He pointed, they pointed, and they shuffled out of sight behind a pyramid of Diet Delight peaches. All that was left for us to see was old McMahon patting his mouth and looking after them sizing up their joints. Poor kids, I began to feel sorry for them, they couldn't help it.

Now here comes the sad part of the story, at least my family says it's sad but I don't think it's sad myself. The store's pretty empty, it being Thursday afternoon, so there was nothing much to do except lean on the register and wait for the girls to show up again. The whole store was like a pinball machine and I didn't know which tunnel they'd come out of. After a while they come around out of the far aisle, around the light bulbs, records at discount of the Caribbean Six or Tony Martin Sings or some such gunk you wonder they waste the wax on, sixpacks of candy bars, and plastic toys done up in cellophane that fall apart when a kid looks at them anyway. Around they come, Queenie still leading the way, and holding a little gray jar in her hand. Slots Three through Seven are unmanned and I could see her wondering between Stokes and me, but Stokesie with his usual luck draws an old party in baggy gray pants who stumbles up with four giant cans of pineapple juice (what do these bums *do* with all that pineapple juice? I've often asked myself) so the girls come to me. Queenie puts down the jar and I take it into my fingers icy cold. Kingfish Fancy Herring Snacks in Pure Sour Cream: 49. Now her hands are empty, not a ring or a bracelet, bare as God made them, and I wonder where the money's coming from. Still with that prim look she lifts a folded dollar bill out of the hollow at the center of her nubbled pink top. The jar went heavy in my hand. Really, I thought that was so cute.

Then everybody's luck begins to run out. Lengel comes in from haggling with a truck full of cabbages on the lot and is about to scuttle into that door marked MANAGER behind which he hides all day when the girls touch his eye. Lengel's pretty dreary, teaches Sunday school and the rest, but he doesn't miss that much. He comes over and says, "Girls, this isn't the beach."

Queenie blushes, though maybe it's just a brush of sunburn I was noticing for the first time, now that she was so close. "My mother asked me to pick up a jar of herring snacks." Her voice kind of startled me, the way voices do when you see the people first, coming out so flat and dumb yet kind of tony, too, the way it ticked over "pick up" and "snacks." All of a sudden I slid right down her voice into her living room. Her father and the other men were standing around in ice-cream coats and bow ties and the women were in sandals picking up herring snacks on toothpicks off a big plate and they were all holding drinks the color of water with olives and sprigs of mint in them. When my parents have somebody over they get lemonade and if it's a real racy affair Schlitz in tall glasses with "They'll Do It Every Time" cartoons stencilled on.

15   "That's all right," Lengel said. "But this isn't the beach." His repeating this struck me as funny, as if it had just occurred to him, and he had been thinking all these years the A&P was a great big dune and he was the head lifeguard. He didn't like my smiling — as I say he doesn't miss much — but he concentrates on giving the girls that sad Sunday-school-superintendent stare.

Queenie's blush is no sunburn now, and the plump one in plaid, that I liked better from the back — a really sweet can — pipes up, "We weren't doing any shopping. We just came in for the one thing."

"That makes no difference," Lengel tells her, and I could see from the way his eyes went that he hadn't noticed she was wearing a two-piece before. "We want you decently dressed when you come in here."

"We *are* decent," Queenie says suddenly, her lower lip pushing, getting sore now that she remembers her place, a place from which the crowd that runs the A&P must look pretty crummy. Fancy Herring Snacks flashed in her very blue eyes.

"Girls, I don't want to argue with you. After this come in here with your shoulders covered. It's our policy." He turns his back. That's policy for you. Policy is what the kingpins want. What the others want is juvenile delinquency.

20   All this while, the customers had been showing up with their carts but, you know, sheep, seeing a scene, they had all bunched up on Stokesie, who shook open a paper bag as gently as peeling a peach, not wanting to miss a word. I could feel in the silence everybody getting nervous, most of all Lengel, who asks me, "Sammy, have you rung up this purchase?"

I thought and said "No" but it wasn't about that I was thinking. I go through the punches, 4, 9, GROC, TOT — it's more complicated than you think, and after you do it often enough, it begins to make a little song, that you hear words to, in my case "Hello (*bing*) there, you (*gung*) hap-py *pee*-pul (*splat*)!" — the *splat* being the drawer flying out. I uncrease the bill, tenderly as you may imagine, it just having come from between the two smoothest scoops of vanilla I had ever known were there, and pass a half and a penny into her narrow pink palm, and nestle the herrings in a bag and twist its neck and hand it over, all the time thinking.

The girls, and who'd blame them, are in a hurry to get out, so I say "I quit" to Lengel quick enough for them to hear, hoping they'll stop and watch me, their unsuspected hero. They keep right on going, into the electric eye; the door flies open and they flicker across the lot to their car, Queenie and Plaid and Big Tall Goony-Goony (not that as raw material she was so bad), leaving me with Lengel and a kink in his eyebrow.

"Did you say something, Sammy?"

"I said I quit."

25   "I thought you did."

"You didn't have to embarrass them."

"It was they who were embarrassing us."

I started to say something that came out "Fiddle-de-doo." It's a saying of my grandmother's, and I know she would have been pleased.

"I don't think you know what you're saying," Lengel said.

"I know you don't," I said. "But I do." I pull the bow at the back of my apron 30 and start shrugging it off my shoulders. A couple customers that had been heading for my slot begin to knock against each other, like scared pigs in a chute.

Lengel sighs and begins to look very patient and old and gray. He's been a friend of my parents for years. "Sammy, you don't want to do this to your Mom and Dad," he tells me. It's true, I don't. But it seems to me that once you begin a gesture it's fatal not to go through with it. I fold the apron, "Sammy" stitched in red on the pocket, and put it on the counter, and drop the bow tie on top of it. The bow tie is theirs, if you've ever wondered. "You'll feel this for the rest of your life," Lengel says, and I know that's true, too, but remembering how he made that pretty girl blush makes me so scrunchy inside I punch the No Sale tab and the machine whirs "pee-pul" and the drawer splats out. One advantage to this scene taking place in summer, I can follow this up with a clean exit, there's no fumbling around getting your coat and galoshes, I just saunter into the electric eye in my white shirt that my mother ironed the night before, and the door heaves itself open, and outside the sunshine is skating around the asphalt.

I look around for my girls, but they're gone, of course. There wasn't anybody but some young married screaming with her children about some candy they didn't get by the door of a powder-blue Falcon station wagon. Looking back in the big windows, over the bags of peat moss and aluminum lawn furniture stacked on the pavement, I could see Lengel in my place in the slot, checking the sheep through. His face was dark gray and his back stiff, as if he'd just had an injection of iron, and my stomach kind of fell as I felt how hard the world was going to be to me hereafter.

Reading and Reacting

1. Summarize the information Sammy gives readers about his tastes and background. Why is this exposition vital to the story's development?
2. List some of the most obvious physical characteristics of the A&P's customers. How do these characteristics make them foils for Queenie and her friends?
3. What is it about Queenie and her friends that appeals to Sammy?
4. Is Queenie a stock character? Explain.
5. What rules and conventions are customers expected to follow in a supermarket? How does the behavior of Queenie and her friends violate these conventions?
6. Is the supermarket setting vital to the story? Could the story have been set in a car wash? In a fast-food restaurant? In a business office?
7. How accurate are Sammy's judgments about the other characters? How might the characters be portrayed if the story were told by Lengel?

8. Given what you learn about Sammy during the course of the story, what do you see as his *primary* motivation for quitting his job? What other factors motivate him?

9. Journal Entry Where do you think Sammy will find himself in ten years? Why?

10. Critical Perspective In her 1976 book *The Necessary Blackness*, critic Mary Allen observes, "Updike's most tender reverence is reserved for women's bodies. The elegant style with which he describes female anatomy often becomes overwrought, as his descriptions do generally. But it always conveys wonder."

In what passages in "A&P" does Updike (through Sammy) convey this sense of wonder? Do you think today's audience, reading the story forty-five years after Updike wrote it, and thirty years after Allen's essay was published, would still see such passages as conveying "tender reverence"? Or do you think readers might now see Sammy (and, indeed, Updike) as sexist? How do you see these passages?

Related Works: "Araby" (p. 232), "A Supermarket in California" (p. 543), "The Road Not Taken" (p. 671), *The Glass Menagerie* (p. 1153).

KATHERINE MANSFIELD (1888–1923), one of the pioneers of the modern short story, was born in New Zealand and educated in England. Very much a "modern young woman," she began living on her own in London at the age of nineteen, soon publishing stories and book reviews in many of the most influential literary magazines of the day.

A short story writer of great versatility, Mansfield produced sparkling social comedies as well as more intellectually and technically complex works intended for "perceptive readers." According to one critic, her best works "[w]ith delicate plainness . . . present elusive moments of decision, defeat, and small triumph." Her last two story collections — *Bliss and Other Stories* (1920) and *The Garden Party and Other Stories* (1922) — were met with immediate critical acclaim, but Mansfield's career was cut short in 1923 when she died of complications from tuberculosis at the age of thirty-five.

One notable theme in Mansfield's work is the *dame seule,* the "woman alone," which provides the basis for the poignant "Miss Brill."

Miss Brill   (1922)

Although it was so brilliantly fine — the blue sky powdered with gold and great spots of light like white wine splashed over the Jardins Publiques° — Miss Brill was glad that she had decided on her fur. The air was motionless, but when you opened

---

Jardins Publiques: "Public Gardens" (French).

your mouth there was just a faint chill, like a chill from a glass of iced water before you sip, and now and again a leaf came drifting — from nowhere, from the sky. Miss Brill put up her hand and touched her fur. Dear little thing! It was nice to feel it again. She had taken it out of its box that afternoon, shaken out the moth-powder, given it a good brush, and rubbed the life back into the dim little eyes. "What has been happening to me?" said the sad little eyes. Oh, how sweet it was to see them snap at her again from the red eiderdown! . . . But the nose, which was of some black composition, wasn't at all firm. It must have had a knock, somehow. Never mind — a little dab of black sealing-wax when the time came — when it was absolutely necessary. . . . Little rogue! Yes, she really felt like that about it. Little rogue biting its tail just by her left ear. She could have taken it off and laid it on her lap and stroked it. She felt a tingling in her hands and arms, but that came from walking, she supposed. And when she breathed, something light and sad — no, not sad, exactly — something gentle seemed to move in her bosom.

There were a number of people out this afternoon, far more than last Sunday. And the band sounded louder and gayer. That was because the Season had begun. For although the band played all year round on Sundays, out of season it was never the same. It was like some one playing with only the family to listen; it didn't care how it played if there weren't any strangers present. Wasn't the conductor wearing a new coat, too? She was sure it was new. He scraped with his foot and flapped his arms like a rooster about to crow, and the bandsmen sitting in the green rotunda blew out their cheeks and glared at the music. Now there came a little "flutey" bit — very pretty! — a little chain of bright drops. She was sure it would be repeated. It was; she lifted her head and smiled.

Only two people shared her "special" seat: a fine old man in a velvet coat, his hands clasped over a huge carved walking-stick, and a big old woman, sitting upright, with a roll of knitting on her embroidered apron. They did not speak. This was disappointing, for Miss Brill always looked forward to the conversation. She had become really quite expert, she thought, at listening as though she didn't listen, at sitting in other people's lives just for a minute while they talked round her.

She glanced, sideways, at the old couple. Perhaps they would go soon. Last Sunday, too, hadn't been as interesting as usual. An Englishman and his wife, he wearing a dreadful Panama hat and she button boots. And she'd gone on the whole time about how she ought to wear spectacles; she knew she needed them; but that it was no good getting any; they'd be sure to break and they'd never keep on. And he'd been so patient. He'd suggested everything — gold rims, the kind that curved round your ears, little pads inside the bridge. No, nothing would please her. "They'll always be sliding down my nose!" Miss Brill wanted to shake her.

The old people sat on the bench, still as statues. Never mind, there was always 5 the crowd to watch. To and fro, in front of the flower-beds and the band rotunda, the couples and groups paraded, stopped to talk, to greet, to buy a handful of flowers from the old beggar who had his tray fixed to the railings. Little children ran among them, swooping and laughing; little boys with big white silk bows under their chins, little girls, little French dolls, dressed up in velvet and lace. And sometimes a tiny staggerer came suddenly rocking into the open from under the trees, stopped, stared, as suddenly sat down "flop," until its small high-stepping mother, like a young hen, rushed scolding to its rescue. Other people sat on the benches and green chairs, but they were nearly always the same, Sunday after Sunday, and — Miss Brill had often noticed — there was something funny about nearly all of them. They were odd, silent, nearly all old, and from the way they stared they looked as though they'd just come from dark little rooms or even — even cupboards!

Behind the rotunda the slender trees with yellow leaves down drooping, and through them just a line of sea, and beyond the blue sky with gold-veined clouds.

Tum-tum-tum tiddle-um! tiddle-um! tum tiddley-um tum ta! blew the band.

Two young girls in red came by and two young soldiers in blue met them, and they laughed and paired and went off arm-in-arm. Two peasant women with funny straw hats passed, gravely, leading beautiful smoke-colored donkeys. A cold, pale nun hurried by. A beautiful woman came along and dropped her bunch of violets, and a little boy ran after to hand them to her, and she took them and threw them away as if they'd been poisoned. Dear me! Miss Brill didn't know whether to admire that or not! And now an ermine toque° and a gentleman in grey met just in front of her. He was tall, stiff, dignified, and she was wearing the ermine toque she'd bought when her hair was yellow. Now everything, her hair, her face, even her eyes, was the same color as the shabby ermine, and her hand, in its cleaned glove, lifted to dab her lips, was a tiny yellowish paw. Oh, she was so pleased to see him — delighted! She rather thought they were going to meet that afternoon. She described where she'd been — everywhere, here, there, along by the sea. The day was so charming — didn't he agree? And wouldn't he, perhaps? . . . But he shook his head, lighted a cigarette, slowly breathed a great deep puff into her face, and, even while she was still talking and laughing, flicked the match away and walked on. The ermine toque was alone; she smiled more brightly than ever. But even the band seemed to know what she was feeling and played more softly, played tenderly, and the drum beat, "The Brute! The Brute!" over and over. What would she do? What was going to happen now? But as Miss Brill wondered, the ermine toque turned, raised her hand as though she'd seen some one else, much nicer, just over there, and pattered away. And the band changed again and played more quickly, more gaily than ever, and the old couple on Miss Brill's seat got up and marched away, and such a funny old man with long whiskers hobbled along in time to the music and was nearly knocked over by four girls walking abreast.

Oh, how fascinating it was! How she enjoyed it! How she loved sitting here, watching it all! It was like a play. It was exactly like a play. Who could believe the sky at the back wasn't painted? But it wasn't till a little brown dog trotted on solemn and then slowly trotted off, like a little "theatre" dog, a little dog that had been drugged, that Miss Brill discovered what it was that made it so exciting. They were

---

toque: Small, close-fitting woman's hat.

all on the stage. They weren't only the audience, not only looking on; they were acting. Even she had a part and came every Sunday. No doubt somebody would have noticed if she hadn't been there; she was part of the performance after all. How strange she'd never thought of it like that before! And yet it explained why she made such a point of starting from home at just the same time each week — so as not to be late for the performance — and it also explained why she had quite a queer, shy feeling at telling her English pupils how she spent her Sunday afternoons. No wonder! Miss Brill nearly laughed out loud. She was on the stage. She thought of the old invalid gentleman to whom she read the newspaper four afternoons a week while he slept in the garden. She had got quite used to the frail head on the cotton pillow, the hollowed eyes, the open mouth and the high pinched nose. If he'd been dead she mightn't have noticed for weeks; she wouldn't have minded. But suddenly he knew he was having the paper read to him by an actress! "An actress!" The old head lifted; two points of light quivered in the old eyes. "An actress — are ye?" And Miss Brill smoothed the newspaper as though it were the manuscript of her part and said gently: "Yes, I have been an actress for a long time."

The band had been having a rest. Now they started again. And what they   10
played was warm, sunny, yet there was just a faint chill — a something, what was it?— not sadness — no, not sadness — a something that made you want to sing. The tune lifted, lifted, the light shone; and it seemed to Miss Brill that in another moment all of them, all the whole company, would begin singing. The young ones, the laughing ones who were moving together, they would begin, and the men's voices, very resolute and brave, would join them. And then she too, she too, and the others on the benches — they would come in with a kind of accompaniment — something low, that scarcely rose or fell, something so beautiful —moving. . . . And Miss Brill's eyes filled with tears and she looked smiling at all the other members of the company. Yes, we understand, we understand, she thought — though what they understood she didn't know.

Just at that moment a boy and a girl came and sat down where the old couple had been. They were beautifully dressed; they were in love. The hero and heroine, of course, just arrived from his father's yacht. And still soundlessly singing, still with that trembling smile, Miss Brill prepared to listen.

"No, not now," said the girl. "Not here, I can't."

"But why? Because of that stupid old thing at the end there?" asked the boy. "Why does she come here at all — who wants her? Why doesn't she keep her silly old mug at home?"

"It's her fu-fur which is so funny," giggled the girl. "It's exactly like a fried whiting."°

"Ah, be off with you!" said the boy in an angry whisper. Then: "Tell me, my   15
petite chérie —"°

"No, not here," said the girl. "Not yet."

----

whiting: Food fish related to the cod.

petite chérie: "Little darling" (French).

On her way home she usually bought a slice of honeycake at the baker's. It was her Sunday treat. Sometimes there was an almond in her slice, sometimes not. It made a great difference. If there was an almond it was like carrying home a tiny present — a surprise — something that might very well not have been there. She hurried on the almond Sundays and struck the match for the kettle in quite a dashing way.

But to-day she passed the baker's boy, climbed the stairs, went into the little dark room — her room like a cupboard — and sat down on the red eiderdown. She sat there for a long time. The box that the fur came out of was on the bed. She unclasped the necklet quickly; quickly, without looking, laid it inside. But when she put the lid on she thought she heard something crying.

Reading and Reacting

1. What specific details can you infer about Miss Brill's character (and, perhaps, about her life) from this statement: "She had become really quite expert, she thought, at listening as though she didn't listen, at sitting in other people's lives just for a minute while they talked round her" (par. 3)?

2. How do Miss Brill's observations of the people around her give us insight into her own character? Why do you suppose she doesn't interact with any of the people she observes?

3. In paragraph 9, Miss Brill realizes that the scene she observes is "exactly like a play" and that "Even she had a part and came every Sunday." What part does Miss Brill play? Is she a stock character in this play, or is she a three-dimensional character? Does she play a lead role or a supporting role?

4. What do you think Miss Brill means when she says, "I have been an actress for a long time" (par. 9)? What does this comment reveal about how she sees herself? Is her view of herself similar to or different from the view the other characters have of her?

5. What role does Miss Brill's fur piece play in the story? In what sense, if any, does it function as a character?

6. What happens in paragraphs 11–16 to break Miss Brill's mood? Why is the scene she observes so upsetting to her?

7. At the end of the story, has Miss Brill changed as a result of what she has overheard, or is she the same person she was at the beginning? Do you think she will return to the park the following Sunday?

8. The story's last paragraph describes Miss Brill's room as being "like a cupboard." Where else has this image appeared in the story? What does its repetition in the conclusion tell us?

9. JOURNAL ENTRY   Write a character sketch of Miss Brill, inventing a plausible family and personal history that might help to explain the character you see in the story.

10. CRITICAL PERSPECTIVE Critic Gillian Boddy, in *Katherine Mansfield: The Woman, The Writer*, offers the following analysis of Mansfield's fiction:

> The story evolves through the characters' minds. The external narrator is almost eliminated. As so often in her work, the reader is dropped into the story and simply confronted by a particular situation. There is no preliminary establishing and identification of time and place. The reader is immediately involved; it is assumed that he or she has any necessary prerequisite knowledge and is, in a sense, part of the story too.

Do you see this absence of conventional exposition as a problem in "Miss Brill"? Do you think the story would be more effective if Mansfield had supplied more preliminary information about setting and character? Or do you believe that what Boddy calls Mansfield's "concentration on a moment or episode" is a satisfactory substitute for the missing exposition, effectively shifting interest from "*what* happens" to "*why* it happens"?

Related Works: "Rooming houses are old women" (p. 524), "Aunt Jennifer's Tigers" (p. 555), *The Stronger* (p. 853)

CHARLES BAXTER (1947–) was born in Minneapolis and educated at Macalester College and at the State University of New York, Buffalo. Currently a professor of English at The University of Michigan, Baxter is the author of four critically praised collections of short stories: *Harmony of the World* (1984), *Through the Safety Net* (1985), *A Relative Stranger: Stories* (1990), and *Believers: A Novella and Stories* (1997). He is also the author of four novels, *First Light* (1987), *Shadow Play* (1993), *The Feast of Love* (2002), and *Saul and Patsy* (2003), and one book of poetry, *Imaginary Paintings and Other Poems* (1989). Baxter has also written *Burning Down the House* (1997), a collection of essays on fiction.

Baxter's critics often mention the compassion he shows in writing about his fictional characters: a couple who lose their child, a hospital worker who wants to be famous, a tired businessman who really wants to paint. In many of his short stories in *Through the Safety Net* (in which "Gryphon" appeared), unexpected events jar Baxter's characters out of their routines, forcing them to consider different choices, to call on inner strength, or to swim against the tide of "middle America's" conventions.

Gryphon (1985)

On Wednesday afternoon, between the geography lesson on ancient Egypt's hand-operated irrigation system and an art project that involved drawing a model city next to a mountain, our fourth-grade teacher, Mr. Hibler, developed a cough. This cough began with a series of muffled throat clearings and progressed to propulsive noises contained within Mr. Hibler's closed mouth. "Listen to him," Carol Peterson whispered to me. "He's gonna blow up." Mr. Hibler's laughter — dazed and infrequent — sounded a bit like his cough, but as we worked on our model cities we would look up, thinking he was enjoying a joke, and see Mr. Hibler's face turning red, his cheeks puffed out. This was not laughter. Twice he bent over, and his loose tie, like a plumb line, hung down straight from his neck as he exploded himself into a Kleenex. He would excuse himself, then go on coughing. "I'll bet you a dime," Carol Peterson whispered, "we get a substitute tomorrow."

Carol sat at the desk in front of mine and was a bad person — when she thought no one was looking she would blow her nose on notebook paper, then crumble it up and throw it into the wastebasket — but at times of crisis she spoke the truth. I knew I'd lose the dime.

"No deal," I said.

When Mr. Hibler stood us up in formation at the door just prior to the final bell, he was almost incapable of speech. "I'm sorry, boys and girls," he said. "I seem to be coming down with something."

5   "I hope you feel better tomorrow, Mr. Hibler," Bobby Kryzanowicz, the faultless brown-noser said, and I heard Carol Peterson's evil giggle. Then Mr. Hibler opened the door and we walked out to the buses, a clique of us starting noisily to hawk and cough as soon as we thought we were a few feet beyond Mr. Hibler's earshot.

Five Oaks being a rural community, and in Michigan, the supply of substitute teachers was limited to the town's unemployed community college graduates, a pool of about four mothers. These ladies fluttered, provided easeful class days, and nervously covered material we had mastered weeks earlier. Therefore it was a surprise when a woman we had never seen came into the class the next day, carrying a purple purse, a checkerboard lunchbox, and a few books. She put the books on one side of Mr. Hibler's desk and the lunchbox on the other, next to the Voice of Music phonograph. Three of us in the back of the room were playing with Heever, the chameleon that lived in the terrarium and on one of the plastic drapes, when she walked in.

She clapped her hands at us. "Little boys," she said, "why are you bent over together like that?" She didn't wait for us to answer. "Are you tormenting an animal? Put it back. Please sit down at your desks. I want no cabals this time of the day." We just stared at her. "Boys," she repeated, "I asked you to sit down."

I put the chameleon in his terrarium and felt my way to my desk, never taking my eyes off the woman. With white and green chalk, she had started to draw a tree on the left side of the blackboard. She didn't look usual. Furthermore, her tree was outsized, disproportionate, for some reason.

"This room needs a tree," she said, with one line drawing the suggestion of a leaf. "A large, leafy, shady, deciduous . . . oak."

10   Her fine, light hair had been done up in what I would learn years later was called a chignon, and she wore gold-rimmed glasses whose lenses seemed to have the faintest blue tint. Harold Knardahl, who sat across from me, whispered "Mars," and I nodded slowly, savoring the imminent weirdness of the day. The substitute drew another branch with an extravagant arm gesture, then turned around and said, "Good morning. I don't believe I said good morning to all you yet."

Facing us, she was no special age — an adult is an adult — but her face had two prominent lines, descending vertically from the sides of her mouth to her chin. I knew where I had seen those lines before: *Pinocchio*. They were marionette lines. "You may stare at me," she said to us, as a few more kids from the last bus came into the room, their eyes fixed on her, "for a few more seconds, until the bell rings. Then I will permit no more staring. Looking I will permit. Staring, no. It is impolite to stare, and a sign of bad breeding. You cannot make a social effort while staring."

Harold Knardahl did not glance at me, or nudge, but I heard him whisper "Mars" again, trying to get more mileage out of his single joke with the kids who had just come in.

When everyone was seated, the substitute teacher finished her tree, put down her chalk fastidiously on the phonograph, brushed her hands, and faced us. "Good morning," she said. "I am Miss Ferenczi, your teacher for the day. I am fairly new to your community, and I don't believe any of you know me. I will therefore start by telling you a story about myself."

While we settled back, she launched into her tale. She said her grandfather had been a Hungarian prince; her mother had been born in some place called Flanders, had been a pianist, and had played concerts for people Miss Ferenczi referred to as "crowned heads." She gave us a knowing look. "Grieg," she said, "the Norwegian master, wrote a concerto for piano that was," she paused, "my mother's triumph at her debut concert in London." Her eyes searched the ceiling. Our eyes followed. Nothing up there but ceiling tile. "For reasons that I shall not go into, my family's fortunes took us to Detroit, then north to dreadful Saginaw, and now here I am in Five Oaks, as your substitute teacher, for today, Thursday, October the eleventh. I believe it will be a good day: All the forecasts coincide. We shall start with your reading lesson. Take out your reading book. I believe it is called *Broad Horizons*, or something along those lines."

Jeannie Vermeesch raised her hand. Miss Ferenczi nodded at her. "Mr. Hibler 15 always starts the day with the Pledge of Allegiance," Jeannie whined.

"Oh, does he? In that case," Miss Ferenczi said, "you must know it *very* well by now, and we certainly need not spend our time on it. No, no allegiance pledging on the premises today, by my reckoning. Not with so much sunlight coming into the room. A pledge does not suit my mood." She glanced at her watch. "Time *is* flying. Take out *Broad Horizons*."

She disappointed us by giving us an ordinary lesson, complete with vocabulary word drills, comprehension questions, and recitation. She didn't seem to care for the material, however. She sighed every few minutes and rubbed her glasses with a frilly perfumed handkerchief that she withdrew, magician style, from her left sleeve.

After reading we moved on to arithmetic. It was my favorite time of the morning, when the lazy autumn sunlight dazzled its way through ribbons of clouds past the windows on the east side of the classroom, and crept across the linoleum floor.

On the playground the first group of children, the kindergartners, were running on the quack grass just beyond the monkey bars. We were doing multiplication tables. Miss Ferenczi had made John Wazny stand up at his desk in the front row. He was supposed to go through the tables of six. From where I was sitting, I could smell the Vitalis soaked into John's plastered hair. He was doing fine until he came to six times eleven and six times twelve. "Six times eleven," he said, "is sixty-eight. Six times twelve is . . ." He put his fingers to his head, quickly and secretly sniffed his fingertips, and said, "seventy-two." Then he sat down.

"Fine," Miss Ferenczi said. "Well now. That was very good."

20   "Miss Ferenczi!" One of the Eddy twins was waving her hand desperately in the air. "Miss Ferenczi! Miss Ferenczi!"

"Yes?"

"John said that six times eleven is sixty-eight and you said he was right!"

"*Did* I?" She gazed at the class with a jolly look breaking across her marionette's face. "Did I say that? Well, what *is* six times eleven?"

"It's sixty-six!"

25   She nodded. "Yes. So it is. But, and I know some people will not entirely agree with me, at some times it is sixty-eight."

"When? When is it sixty-eight?"

We were all waiting.

"In higher mathematics, which you children do not yet understand, six times eleven can be considered to be sixty-eight." She laughed through her nose. "In higher mathematics numbers are . . . more fluid. The only thing a number does is contain a certain amount of something. Think of water. A cup is not the only way to measure a certain amount of water, is it?" We were staring, shaking our heads. "You could use saucepans or thimbles. In either case, the water *would be the same*. Perhaps," she started again, "it would be better for you to think that six times eleven is sixty-eight only when I am in the room."

"Why is it sixty-eight," Mark Poole asked, "when you're in the room?"

30   "Because it's more interesting that way," she said, smiling very rapidly behind her blue-tinted glasses. "Besides, I'm your substitute teacher, am I not?" We all nodded. "Well, then, think of six times eleven equals sixty-eight as a substitute fact."

"A substitute fact?"

"Yes." Then she looked at us carefully. "Do you think," she asked, "that anyone is going to be hurt by a substitute fact?"

We looked back at her.

"Will the plants on the windowsill be hurt?" We glanced at them. There were sensitive plants thriving in a green plastic tray, and several wilted ferns in small clay pots. "Your dogs and cats, or your moms and dads?" She waited. "So," she concluded, "what's the problem?"

35   "But it's wrong," Janice Weber said, "isn't it?"

"What's your name, young lady?"

"Janice Weber."

"And you think it's wrong, Janice?"

"I was just asking."

"Well, all right. You were just asking. I think we've spent enough time on this 40 matter by now, don't you, class? You are free to think what you like. When your teacher, Mr. Hibler, returns, six times eleven will be sixty-six again, you can rest assured. And it will be that for the rest of your lives in Five Oaks. Too bad, eh?" She raised her eyebrows and glinted herself at us. "But for now, it wasn't. So much for that. Let us go to your assigned problems for today, as painstakingly outlined, I see, in Mr. Hibler's lesson plan. Take out a sheet of paper and write your names in the upper left-hand corner."

For the next half hour we did the rest of our arithmetic problems. We handed them in and went on to spelling, my worst subject. Spelling always came before lunch. We were taking spelling dictation and looking at the clock. "Thorough," Miss Ferenczi said. "Boundary." She walked in the aisles between the desks, holding the spelling book open and looking down at our papers. "Balcony." I clutched my pencil. Somehow, the way she said those words, they seemed foreign, Hungarian, mis-voweled and mis-consonanted. I stared down at what I had spelled. *Balconie.* I turned my pencil upside down and erased my mistake. *Balconey.* That looked better, but still incorrect. I cursed the world of spelling and tried erasing it again and saw the paper beginning to wear away. *Balkony.* Suddenly I felt a hand on my shoulder.

"I don't like that word either," Miss Ferenczi whispered, bent over, her mouth near my ear. "It's ugly. My feeling is, if you don't like a word, you don't have to use it." She straightened up, leaving behind a slight odor of Clorets.

At lunchtime we went out to get our trays of sloppy joes, peaches in heavy syrup, coconut cookies, and milk, and brought them back to the classroom, where Miss Ferenczi was sitting at the desk, eating a brown sticky thing she had unwrapped from tightly rubber-banded wax paper. "Miss Ferenczi," I said, raising my hand. "You don't have to eat with us. You can eat with the other teachers. There's a teachers' lounge," I ended up, "next to the principal's office."

"No, thank you," she said. "I prefer it here."

"We've got a room monitor," I said. "Mrs. Eddy." I pointed to where Mrs. 45 Eddy, Joyce and Judy's mother, sat silently at the back of the room, doing her knitting.

"That's fine," Miss Ferenczi said. "But I shall continue to eat here, with you children. I prefer it," she repeated.

"How come?" Wayne Razmer asked without raising his hand.

"I talked with the other teachers before class this morning," Miss Ferenczi said, biting into her brown food. "There was a great rattling of the words for the fewness of ideas. I didn't care for their brand of hilarity. I don't like ditto machine jokes."

"Oh," Wayne said.

"What's that you're eating?" Maxine Sylvester asked, twitching her nose. "Is 50 it food?"

"It most certainly *is* food. It's a stuffed fig. I had to drive almost down to Detroit to get it. I also bought some smoked sturgeon. And this," she said, lifting some green leaves out of her lunchbox, "is raw spinach, cleaned this morning before I came out here to the Garfield-Murry school."

"Why're you eating raw spinach?" Maxine asked.

"It's good for you," Miss Ferenczi said. "More stimulating than soda pop or smelling salts." I bit into my sloppy joe and stared blankly out the window. An almost invisible moon was faintly silvered in the daytime autumn sky. "As far as food is concerned," Miss Ferenczi was saying, "you have to shuffle the pack. Mix it up. Too many people eat . . . well, never mind."

"Miss Ferenczi," Carol Peterson said, "what are we going to do this afternoon?"

55   "Well," she said, looking down at Mr. Hibler's lesson plan, "I see that your teacher, Mr. Hibler, has you scheduled for a unit on the Egyptians." Carol groaned. "Yessss," Miss Ferenczi continued, "that is what we will do: the Egyptians. A remarkable people. Almost as remarkable as the Americans. But not quite." She lowered her head, did her quick smile, and went back to eating her spinach.

After noon recess we came back into the classroom and saw that Miss Ferenczi had drawn a pyramid on the blackboard, close to her oak tree. Some of us who had been playing baseball were messing around in the back of the room, dropping the bats and the gloves into the playground box, and I think that Ray Schontzeler had just slugged me when I heard Miss Ferenczi's high-pitched voice quavering with emotion. "Boys," she said, "come to order right this minute and take your seats. I do not wish to waste a minute of class time. Take out your geography books." We trudged to our desks and, still sweating, pulled out *Distant Lands and Their People*. "Turn to page forty-two." She waited for thirty seconds, then looked over at Kelly Munger. "Young man," she said, "why are you still fossicking in your desk?"

Kelly looked as if his foot had been stepped on. "Why am I what?"

"Why are you . . . burrowing in your desk like that?"

"I'm lookin' for the book, Miss Ferenczi."

60   Bobby Kryzanowicz, the faultless brown-noser who sat in the first row by choice, softly said, "His name is Kelly Munger. He can't ever find his stuff. He always does that."

"I don't care what his name is, especially after lunch," Miss Ferenczi said. *"Where is your book?"*

"I just found it." Kelly was peering into his desk and with both hands pulled at the book, shoveling along in front of it several pencils and crayons, which fell into his lap and then to the floor.

"I hate a mess," Miss Ferenczi said. "I hate a mess in a desk or a mind. It's . . . unsanitary. You wouldn't want your house at home to look like your desk at school, now, would you?" She didn't wait for an answer. "I should think not. A house at home should be as neat as human hands can make it. What were we talking about? Egypt. Page forty-two. I note from Mr. Hibler's lesson plan that you have been discussing the modes of Egyptian irrigation. Interesting, in my view, but not so interesting as what we are about to cover. The pyramids and Egyptian slave labor. A plus on one side, a minus on the other." We had our books open to page forty-two, where there was a picture of a pyramid, but Miss Ferenczi wasn't looking at the book. Instead, she was staring at some object just outside the window.

"Pyramids," Miss Ferenczi said, still looking past the window. "I want you to think about the pyramids. And what was inside. The bodies of the pharaohs, of course, and their attendant treasures. Scrolls. Perhaps," Miss Ferenczi said, with something gleeful but unsmiling in her face, "these scrolls were novels for the pharaohs, helping them to pass the time in their long voyage through the centuries. But then, I am joking." I was looking at the lines on Miss Ferenczi's face. "Pyramids," Miss Ferenczi went on, "were the repositories of special cosmic powers. The nature of a pyramid is to guide cosmic energy forces into a concentrated point. The Egyptians knew that; we have generally forgotten it. Did you know," she asked, walking to the side of the room so that she was standing by the coat closet, "that George Washington had Egyptian blood, from his grandmother? Certain features of the Constitution of the United States are notable for their Egyptian ideas."

Without glancing down at the book, she began to talk about the movement 65 of souls in Egyptian religion. She said that when people die, their souls return to Earth in the form of carpenter ants or walnut trees, depending on how they behaved — "well or ill" — in life. She said that the Egyptians believed that people act the way they do because of magnetism produced by tidal forces in the solar system, forces produced by the sun and by its "planetary ally," Jupiter. Jupiter, she said, was a planet, as we had been told, but had "certain properties of stars." She was speaking very fast. She said that the Egyptians were great explorers and conquerors. She said that the greatest of all the conquerors, Genghis Khan, had had forty horses and forty young women killed on the site of his grave. We listened. No one tried to stop her. "I myself have been in Egypt," she said, "and have witnessed much dust and many brutalities." She said that an old man in Egypt who worked for a circus had personally shown her an animal in a cage, a monster, half bird and half lion. She said that this monster was called a gryphon and that she had heard about them but never seen them until she traveled to the outskirts of Cairo. She said that Egyptian astronomers had discovered the planet Saturn, but had not seen its rings. She said that the Egyptians were the first to discover that dogs, when they are ill, will not drink from rivers, but wait for rain, and hold their jaws open to catch it.

*   *   *

"She lies."

We were on the school bus home. I was sitting next to Carl Whiteside, who had bad breath and a huge collection of marbles. We were arguing. Carl thought she was lying. I said she wasn't, probably.

"I didn't believe that stuff about the bird," Carl said, "and what she told us about the pyramids? I didn't believe that either. She didn't know what she was talking about."

"Oh yeah?" I had liked her. She was strange. I thought I could nail him. "If she was lying," I said, "what'd she say that was a lie?"

70   "Six times eleven isn't sixty-eight. It isn't ever. It's sixty-six, I know for a fact."

"She said so. She admitted it. What else did she lie about?"

"I don't know," he said. "Stuff."

"What stuff?"

"Well." He swung his legs back and forth. "You ever see an animal that was half lion and half bird?" He crossed his arms. "It sounded real fakey to me."

75   "It could happen," I said. I had to improvise, to outrage him. "I read in this newspaper my mom bought in the IGA about this scientist, this mad scientist in the Swiss Alps, and he's been putting genes and chromosomes and stuff together in test tubes, and he combined a human being and a hamster." I waited, for effect. "It's called a humster."

"You never." Carl was staring at me, his mouth open, his terrible bad breath making its way toward me. "What newspaper was it?"

"The *National Enquirer*," I said, "that they sell next to the cash registers." When I saw his look of recognition, I knew I had bested him. "And this mad scientist," I said, "his name was, um, Dr. Frankenbush." I realized belatedly that this name was a mistake and waited for Carl to notice its resemblance to the name of the other famous mad master of permutations, but he only sat there.

"A man and a hamster?" He was staring at me, squinting, his mouth opening in distaste. "Jeez. What'd it look like?"

When the bus reached my stop, I took off down our dirt road and ran up through the back yard, kicking the tire swing for good luck. I dropped my books on the back steps so I could hug and kiss our dog, Mr. Selby. Then I hurried inside. I could smell Brussels sprouts cooking, my unfavorite vegetable. My mother was washing other vegetables in the kitchen sink, and my baby brother was hollering in his yellow playpen on the kitchen floor.

80   "Hi, Mom," I said, hopping around the playpen to kiss her, "Guess what?"

"I have no idea."

"We had this substitute today, Miss Ferenczi, and I'd never seen her before, and she had all these stories and ideas and stuff."

"Well. That's good." My mother looked out the window behind the sink, her eyes on the pine woods west of our house. Her face and hairstyle always reminded other people of Betty Crocker, whose picture was framed inside a gigantic spoon on the side of the Bisquick box; to me, though, my mother's face just looked white. "Listen, Tommy," she said, "go upstairs and pick your clothes off the bathroom floor, then go outside to the shed and put the shovel and ax away that your father left outside this morning."

"She said that six times eleven was sometimes sixty-eight!" I said. "And she said she once saw a monster that was half lion and half bird." I waited. "In Egypt, she said."

"Did you hear me?" my mother asked, raising her arm to wipe her forehead with   85
the back of her hand. "You have chores to do."

"I know," I said. "I was just telling you about the substitute."

"It's very interesting," my mother said, quickly glancing down at me, "and we can talk about it later when your father gets home. But right now you have some work to do."

"Okay, Mom." I took a cookie out of the jar on the counter and was about to go outside when I had a thought. I ran into the living room, pulled out a dictionary next to the TV stand, and opened it to the G's. *Gryphon:* "variant of griffin." *Griffin:* "a fabulous beast with the head and wings of an eagle and the body of a lion." Fabulous was right. I shouted with triumph and ran outside to put my father's tools back in their place.

Miss Ferenczi was back the next day, slightly altered. She had pulled her hair down and twisted it into pigtails, with red rubber bands holding them tight one inch from the ends. She was wearing a green blouse and pink scarf, making her difficult to look at for a full class day. This time there was no pretense of doing a reading lesson or moving on to arithmetic. As soon as the bell rang, she simply began to talk.

She talked for forty minutes straight. There seemed to be less connection be-   90
tween her ideas, but the ideas themselves were, as the dictionary would say, fabulous. She said she had heard of a huge jewel, in what she called the Antipodes, that was so brilliant that when the light shone into it at a certain angle it would blind whoever was looking at its center. She said that the biggest diamond in the world was cursed and had killed everyone who owned it, and that by a trick of fate it was called the Hope diamond. Diamonds are magic, she said, and this is why women wear them on their fingers, as a sign of the magic of womanhood. Men have strength, Miss Ferenczi said, but no true magic. That is why men fall in love with women but women do not fall in love with men; they just love being loved. George Washington had died because of a mistake he made about a diamond. Washington was not the first *true* President, but she did not say who was. In some places in the world, she said, men and women still live in the trees and eat monkeys for breakfast. Their doctors are magicians. At the bottom of the sea are creatures thin as pancakes which have never been studied by scientists because when you take them up to the air, the fish explode.

There was not a sound in the classroom, except for Miss Ferenczi's voice, and Donna DeShano's coughing. No one even went to the bathroom.

Beethoven, she said, had not been deaf; it was a trick to make himself famous, and it worked. As she talked, Miss Ferenczi's pigtails swung back and forth. There are trees in the world, she said, that eat meat: their leaves are sticky and close up on bugs like hands. She lifted her hands and brought them together, palm to palm. Venus, which most people think is the next closest planet to the sun, is not always closer, and, besides, it is the planet of greatest mystery because of its thick cloud cover. "I know what lies underneath those clouds," Miss Ferenczi said, and waited. After the silence, she said, "Angels. Angels live under those clouds." She said that angels were not invisible to everyone and were in fact smarter than most people. They did not dress in robes as was often claimed but instead wore formal evening clothes, as if they were about to attend a concert. Often angels *do* attend concerts and sit in the aisles where, she said, most people pay no attention to them. She said the most terrible angel had the shape of the Sphinx. "There is no running away from that one," she said. She said that unquenchable fires burn just under the surface of the earth in Ohio, and that the baby Mozart fainted dead away in his cradle when he first heard the sound of a trumpet. She said that someone named Narzim al Harrardim was the greatest writer who ever lived. She said that planets control behavior, and anyone conceived during a solar eclipse would be born with webbed feet.

"I know you children like to hear these things," she said, "these secrets, and that is why I am telling you all this." We nodded. It was better than doing comprehension questions for the readings in *Broad Horizons*.

"I will tell you one more story," she said, "and then we will have to do arithmetic." She leaned over, and her voice grew soft. "There is no death," she said. "You must never be afraid. Never. That which is, cannot die. It will change into different earthly and unearthly elements, but I know this as sure as I stand here in front of you, and I swear it: you must not be afraid. I have seen this truth with these eyes. I know it because in a dream God kissed me. Here." And she pointed with her right index finger to the side of her head, below the mouth, where the vertical lines were carved into her skin.

95   Absent-mindedly we all did our arithmetic problems. At recess the class was out on the playground, but no one was playing. We were all standing in small groups, talking about Miss Ferenczi. We didn't know if she was crazy, or what. I looked out beyond the playground, at the rusted cars piled in a small heap behind a clump of sumac, and I wanted to see shapes there, approaching me.

On the way home, Carl sat next to me again. He didn't say much, and I didn't either. At last he turned to me. "You know what she said about the leaves that close up on bugs?"

"Huh?"

"The leaves," Carl insisted. "The meat-eating plants. I know it's true. I saw it on television. The leaves have this icky glue that the plants have got smeared all

over them and the insects can't get off 'cause they're stuck. I saw it." He seemed
demoralized. "She's tellin' the truth."

"Yeah."

"You think she's seen all those angels?" 100

I shrugged.

"I don't think she has," Carl informed me. "I think she made that part up."

"There's a tree," I suddenly said. I was looking out the window at the farms
along County Road H. I knew every barn, every broken windmill, every fence,
every anhydrous ammonia tank, by heart. "There's a tree that's . . . that I've seen
. . ."

"Don't you try to do it," Carl said. "You'll just sound like a jerk."

I kissed my mother. She was standing in front of the stove. "How was your 105
day?" she asked.

"Fine."

"Did you have Miss Ferenczi again?"

"Yeah."

"Well?"

"She was fine. Mom," I asked, "can I go to my room?" 110

"No," she said, "not until you've gone out to the vegetable garden and picked
me a few tomatoes." She glanced at the sky. "I think it's going to rain. Skedaddle
and do it now. Then you come back inside and watch your brother for a few minutes while I go upstairs. I need to clean up before dinner." She looked down at
me. "You're looking a little pale, Tommy." She touched the back of her hand to
my forehead and I felt her diamond ring against my skin. "Do you feel all right?"

"I'm fine," I said, and went out to pick the tomatoes.

Coughing mutedly, Mr. Hibler was back the next day, slipping lozenges into
his mouth when his back was turned at forty-five minute intervals and asking us
how much of the prepared lesson plan Miss Ferenczi had followed. Edith Atwater took the responsibility for the class of explaining to Mr. Hibler that the substitute hadn't always done exactly what he would have done, but we had worked
hard even though she talked a lot. About what? he asked. All kinds of things,
Edith said. I sort of forgot. To our relief, Mr. Hibler seemed not at all interested
in what Miss Ferenczi had said to fill the day. He probably thought it was woman's
talk; unserious and not suited for school. It was enough that he had a pile of
arithmetic problems from us to correct.

For the next month, the sumac turned a distracting red in the field, and the
sun traveled toward the southern sky, so that its rays reached Mr. Hibler's Halloween display on the bulletin board in the back of the room, fading the scarecrow with a pumpkin head from orange to tan. Every three days I measured how
much farther the sun had moved toward the southern horizon by making small
marks with my black Crayola on the north wall, ant-sized marks only I knew
were there, inching west.

115   And then in early December, four days after the first permanent snowfall, she appeared again in our classroom. The minute she came in the door, I felt my heart begin to pound. Once again, she was different: this time, her hair hung straight down and seemed hardly to have been combed. She hadn't brought her lunchbox with her, but she was carrying what seemed to be a small box. She greeted all of us and talked about the weather. Donna DeShano had to remind her to take her overcoat off.

    When the bell to start the day finally rang, Miss Ferenczi looked out at all of us and said, "Children, I have enjoyed your company in the past, and today I am going to reward you." She held up the small box. "Do you know what this is?" She waited. "Of course you don't. It is a tarot pack."

    Edith Atwater raised her hand. "What's a tarot pack, Miss Ferenczi?"

    "It is used to tell fortunes," she said. "And that is what I shall do this morning. I shall tell your fortunes, as I have been taught to do."

    "What's fortune?" Bobby Kryzanowicz asked.

120   "The future, young man. I shall tell you what your future will be. I can't do your whole future, of course. I shall have to limit myself to the five-card system, the wands, cups, swords, pentacles, and the higher arcanes. Now who wants to be first?"

    There was a long silence. Then Carol Peterson raised her hand.

    "All right," Miss Ferenczi said. She divided the pack into five smaller packs and walked back to Carol's desk, in front of mine. "Pick one card from each of these packs," she said. I saw that Carol had a four of cups, a six of swords, but I couldn't see the other cards. Miss Ferenczi studied the cards on Carol's desk for a minute. "Not bad," she said. "I do not see much higher education. Probably an early marriage. Many children. There's something bleak and dreary here, but I can't tell what. Perhaps just the tasks of a housewife life. I think you'll do very well, for the most part." She smiled at Carol, a smile with a certain lack of interest. "Who wants to be next?"

    Carl Whiteside raised his hand slowly.

    "Yes," Miss Ferenczi said, "let's do a boy." She walked over to where Carl sat. After he picked his five cards, she gazed at them for a long time. "Travel," she said. "Much distant travel. You might go into the Army. Not too much romantic interest here. A late marriage, if at all. Squabbles. But the Sun is in your major arcana, here, yes, that's a very good card." She giggled. "Maybe a good life."

125   Next I raised my hand, and she told me my future. She did the same with Bobby Kryzanowicz, Kelly Munger, Edith Atwater, and Kim Foor. Then she came to Wayne Razmer. He picked his five cards, and I could see that the Death card was one of them.

    "What's your name?" Miss Ferenczi asked.

    "Wayne."

    "Well, Wayne," she said, you will undergo a *great* metamorphosis, the greatest, before you become an adult. Your earthly element will leap away, into thin air, you sweet boy. This card, this nine of swords here, tells of suffering and desolation. And this ten of wands, well, that's certainly a heavy load."

"What about this one?" Wayne pointed to the Death card.

"That one? That one means you will die soon, my dear." She gathered up the cards. We were all looking at Wayne. "But do not fear," she said. "It's not really death, so much as change." She put the cards on Mr. Hibler's desk. "And now, let's do some arithmetic." 130

At lunchtime Wayne went to Mr. Faegre, the principal, and told him what Miss Ferenczi had done. During the noon recess, we saw Miss Ferenczi drive out of the parking lot in her green Rambler. I stood under the slide, listening to the other kids coasting down and landing in the little depressive bowl at the bottom. I was kicking stones and tugging at my hair right up to the moment when I saw Wayne come out to the playground. He smiled, the dead fool, and with the fingers of his right hand he was showing everyone how he had told on Miss Ferenczi.

I made my way toward Wayne, pushing myself past two girls from another class. He was watching me with his little pinhead eyes.

"You told," I shouted at him. "She was just kidding."

"She shouldn't have," he shouted back. "We were supposed to be doing arithmetic."

"She just scared you," I said. "You're a chicken. You're a chicken, Wayne. You are. Scared of a little card," I singsonged. 135

Wayne fell at me, his two fists hammering down on my nose. I gave him a good one in the stomach and then I tried for his head. Aiming my fist, I saw that he was crying. I slugged him.

"She was right," I yelled. "She was always right! She told the truth!" Other kids were whooping. "You were just scared, that's all!"

And then large hands pulled at us, and it was my turn to speak to Mr. Faegre.

In the afternoon Miss Ferenczi was gone, and my nose was stuffed with cotton clotted with blood, and my lip had swelled, and our class had been combined with Mrs. Mantei's sixth-grade class for a crowded afternoon science unit on insect life in ditches and swamps. I knew where Mrs. Mantei lived: she had a new house trailer just down the road from us, at the Clearwater Park. She was no mystery. Somehow she and Mr. Bodine, the other fourth-grade teacher, had managed to fit forty-five desks into the room. Kelly Munger asked if Miss Ferenczi had been arrested, and Mrs. Mantei said no, of course not. All that afternoon, until the buses came to pick us up, we learned about field crickets and two-striped grasshoppers, water bugs, cicadas, mosquitoes, flies, and moths. We learned about insects' hard outer shell, the exoskeleton, and the usual parts of the mouth, including the labrum, mandible, maxilla, and glossa. We learned about compound eyes and the four-stage metamorphosis from egg to larva to pupa to adult. We learned something, but not much, about mating. Mrs. Mantei drew, very skillfully, the internal anatomy of the grasshopper on the blackboard. We learned about the dance of the honeybee, directing other bees in the hive to pollen. We found out about which insects were pests to man, and which were not. On lined white pieces of paper we made lists of insects we might actually see, then a list of insects too small to be clearly visible, such as fleas; Mrs. Mantei said that our assignment would be to memorize these lists for the next day, when Mr. Hibler would certainly return and test us on our knowledge.

Reading and Reacting

1. In classical mythology, a gryphon (also spelled *griffin*) is a monster that has the head and wings of an eagle and the body of a lion. Why is this story called "Gryphon"?

2. Describe Miss Ferenczi's physical appearance. Why is her appearance important to the story? How does it change as the story progresses?

3. How is Miss Ferenczi different from other teachers? From other substitute teachers? From other people in general? How is her differentness communicated to her pupils? To the story's readers?

4. What is the significance of the narrator's comment, in paragraph 11, that the lines on Miss Ferenczi's face remind him of Pinocchio?

5. Is Miss Ferenczi a round or a flat character? Explain.

6. In what sense is the narrator's mother a foil for Miss Ferenczi?

7. Why does the narrator defend Miss Ferenczi, first in his argument with Carl Whiteside and later on the playground? What does his attitude toward Miss Ferenczi reveal about his character?

8. Are all of Miss Ferenczi's "substitute facts" lies, or is there some truth in what she says? Is she correct when she says that substitute facts cannot hurt anyone? Could it be argued that much of what is taught in schools today could be viewed as "substitute facts"? Explain.

9. JOURNAL ENTRY Is Miss Ferenczi a good teacher? Why or why not?

10. CRITICAL PERSPECTIVE Writing in the *New York Times Book Review*, critic William Ferguson characterizes *A Relative Stranger*, a more recent collection of Baxter's short stories than the one in which "Gryphon" appeared, as follows:

> The thirteen stories in *A Relative Stranger*, all quietly accomplished, suggest a mysterious yet fundamental marriage of despair and joy. Though in one way or another each story ends in disillusionment, the road that leads to that dismal state is so richly peopled, so finely drawn, that the effect is oddly reassuring.

Do you think this characterization of Baxter's work in *A Relative Stranger* applies to "Gryphon" as well? For example, how are despair and joy joined? Do you find the story reassuring in any way, or does it convey only a sense of disillusionment?

Related Works: "The Secret Lion" (p. 412), "A&P" (p. 128), "A Worn Path" (p. 319), "When I Heard the Learn'd Astronomer" (p. 491), "On First Looking into Chapman's Homer" (p. 575), *I Dream Before I Take the Stand* (p. 745)

WRITING SUGGESTIONS: Character

1. In both "A&P" and "Gryphon" the main characters (Sammy and Tommy, respectively) struggle against rules, authority figures, and inflexible social systems. Compare and contrast the struggles in which these two characters are engaged.

2. Write an essay in which you contrast the character of Miss Brill (p. 134) with the character of Emily Grierson in "A Rose for Emily" (p. 113) or with Phoenix Jackson in "A Worn Path" (p. 319). Consider how each character interacts with those around her as well as how each seems to see her role or mission in the world.

3. Sammy, Miss Brill, and Miss Ferenczi all use their active imaginations to create scenarios that help get them through the day. None of them is able to sustain the illusion, however. As a result, all three find out how harsh reality can be. How are these scenarios alike, and how are they different? What steps could these three characters take to fit more comfortably into the worlds they inhabit? *Should* they take such steps? Are they able to do so?

CHAPTER 8

SETTING

> The earth was here before I was. When I came, I simply identified place by living in it or looking at it. One does create place in the same way that the storyteller creates himself, creates his listener. The writer creates a place.
>
> —N. Scott Momaday, *Ancestral Voices*

The **setting** of a work of fiction establishes its historical, geographical, and physical context. *Where* a work is set — on a tropical island, in a dungeon, at a crowded party, in the woods — influences our reactions to the story's events and characters. *When* a work takes place — during the French Revolution, during the Vietnam War, today, or in the future — is equally important. Setting, however, is more than just the approximate time and place in which a work is set; setting also encompasses a wide variety of physical and cultural elements.

Clearly, setting is more important in some works than in others. In some stories, no particular time or place is specified or even suggested, perhaps because the writer does not consider a specific setting to be important or because the writer wishes the story's events to seem timeless and universal. This is the case in Nathaniel Hawthorne's "Young Goodman Brown" (p. 302), which is set in a forest in an unidentified location. In other stories, a writer may provide only minimal information about setting, telling readers little more than where and when the action takes place. Sometimes, however, a particular setting may be vital to the story, perhaps influencing characters' behavior, as it does in the stories in this chapter.

Sometimes a story's central conflict is between the protagonist and the setting — for example, Alice in Wonderland, a northerner in the South, an unsophisticated American tourist in an old European city, a sane person in a mental hospital, a moral person in a corrupt environment, an immigrant in a new world, or a city dweller in the country. Such a conflict may drive the story's plot and also help to define the characters. (A conflict between events and setting — for example, the arrival of a mysterious stranger in a typical suburban neighborhood, the intrusion of modern social ideas into an old-fashioned world, or the intrusion of a brutal murder into a peaceful village — can also enrich a story.)

Historical Setting

A particular historical period, and the events and customs associated with it, can be vital to a story; therefore, some knowledge of the period is useful (or even essential) to readers who wish to understand the story fully. The historical context establishes a story's social, cultural, economic, and political environment. Knowing, for instance, that Charlotte Perkins Gilman's "The Yellow Wallpaper" (p. 372) was written in the late nineteenth century, when doctors treated women as delicate and dependent creatures, helps to explain the narrator's emotional state. Likewise, it may be important to know that a story is set during a particularly volatile (or static) political era, during a time of permissive (or repressive) attitudes toward sex, during a war, or during a period of economic prosperity or recession. Any one of these factors may help to explain characters' actions and motivation. Historical events or cultural norms may, for instance, limit or expand a character's options, and our knowledge of history may reveal to us a character's incompatibility with his or her milieu. For example, in F. Scott Fitzgerald's "Bernice Bobs Her Hair," set in the 1920s in a midwestern town, a young girl is goaded into cutting her long hair. To understand the significance of Bernice's act — and to understand the reactions of others to that act — readers must know that during that era only racy "society vampires," not nice girls from good families, bobbed their hair.

The approximate year or historical period during which a story takes place can explain forces that act on characters and account for their behavior, clarify circumstances that influence the story's action, and justify a writer's use of plot devices that might otherwise seem improbable. For instance, stories set before the development of modern transportation and communication systems may hinge on plot devices readers would not accept in a modern story. Thus, in "Paul's Case," a 1904 story by Willa Cather, a young man who steals a large sum of money in Pittsburgh is able to spend several days enjoying it before the news of the theft reaches New York, where he has fled. In other stories, we see characters threatened by diseases that have now been eradicated (or subjected to outdated medical or psychiatric treatment) or constrained by social conventions very different from those that operate in our own society.

Geographical Setting

In addition to knowing *when* a work takes place, readers need to know *where* it takes place. Knowing whether a story is set in the United States, in Europe, or in a developing nation can help to explain anything from why language and customs are unfamiliar to us to why characters act in ways we find improbable. Even in stories set in our own country, regional differences may account for differences in plot development and characters' motivation. For example, knowing that William Faulkner's "A Rose for Emily" (p. 113) is set in the post–Civil War American South helps to explain why the townspeople are so chivalrously protective of Miss Emily. Similarly, the fact that Bret Harte's "The Outcasts of Poker Flat" (1869) is set in a California mining camp accounts for its varied cast of characters — including a gambler, a prostitute, and a traveling salesman.

The size of the town or city in which a story takes place may also be important. In a small town, for example, a character's problems are more likely to be subject to intense scrutiny by other characters, as they are in stories of small-town life such as those in Sherwood Anderson's *Winesburg, Ohio*. In a large city, characters may be more likely to be isolated and anonymous, like Mrs. Miller in Truman Capote's "Miriam" (1945), who is so lonely that she creates an imaginary companion. Characters may also be alienated by their big-city surroundings, as Gregor Samsa is in Franz Kafka's classic novella "The Metamorphosis" (1915).

Of course, a story may not have a recognizable geographical setting: its location may not be specified, or it may be set in a fantasy world. Choosing unusual settings may free writers from the constraints placed on them by familiar environments, allowing them to experiment with situations and characters, unaffected by readers' expectations or associations with familiar settings.

Physical Setting

Physical setting can clearly influence a story's mood as well as its development. For example, *time of day* can be important. The gruesome murder described in Edgar Allan Poe's "The Cask of Amontillado" (p. 203) takes place in an appropriate setting: not just underground but in the darkness of night. Conversely, the horrifying events of Shirley Jackson's "The Lottery" (p. 274) take place in broad daylight, contrasting dramatically with the darkness of the society that permits — and even participates in — such events. Many stories, of course, move through several time periods as the action unfolds, and changes in time may also be important. For instance, the approach of evening, or of dawn, can signal the end of a crisis in the plot.

Whether a story is set primarily *inside* or *out-of-doors* may also be significant. The characters may be physically constrained by a closed-in setting or liberated by an expansive landscape. Some interior settings may be psychologically limiting. For instance, the narrator in "The Yellow Wallpaper" feels suffocated by her room, whose ugly wallpaper comes to haunt her. In many of Poe's stories, the central character is trapped, physically or psychologically, in a confined, suffocating space. In other stories, an interior setting may have a symbolic function. For instance, in "A Rose for Emily," the house is for Miss Emily a symbol of the South's past glory as well as a refuge, a fortress, and a hiding place. Similarly, a building or house may represent society, with its rules, norms, and limitations. In John Updike's "A&P" (p. 128), for instance, the supermarket establishes social as well as physical limits.

Conversely, an outdoor setting can free a character from social norms of behavior, as it does for Ernest Hemingway's Nick Adams, a war veteran who, in "Big Two-Hearted River" (1925), finds order, comfort, and peace only when he is away from civilization. An outdoor setting can also expose characters to physical dangers, such as untamed wilderness, uncharted seas, and frighteningly empty open spaces, as is the case in Stephen Crane's 1897 story, "The Open Boat."

Weather can be another important aspect of setting. A storm can threaten a character's life or just make the character — and readers — *think* danger is present, distracting us from other, more subtle threats. Extreme weather conditions can make characters act irrationally or uncharacteristically, as in Kate Chopin's "The Storm" (p. 158), where a storm provides the story's complication and determines the characters' actions. In numerous stories set in hostile landscapes, where extremes of heat and cold influence the action, weather may serve as a test for characters, as it does in Jack London's "To Build a Fire" (1908), in which the main character struggles unsuccessfully against the brutally cold, hostile environment of the Yukon.

The various physical attributes of setting combine to create a story's **atmosphere** or **mood.** In "The Cask of Amontillado," for example, several factors work together to create the story's eerie, intense atmosphere: it is nighttime; it is the hectic carnival season; and the catacombs are dark, damp, and filled with the bones of the narrator's ancestors. Sometimes the mood or atmosphere that is created helps to convey a story's central theme — as the ironic contrast between the pleasant atmosphere and the shocking events that unfold communicates the theme of "The Lottery." A story's atmosphere may also be linked to a character's mental state, perhaps reflecting his or her mood. For example, darkness and isolation can reflect a character's depression, whereas an idyllic, peaceful atmosphere can express a character's joy. And, of course, a story's atmosphere may also *influence* the characters' state of mind, causing them to react one way in a crowded, busy, urban atmosphere but to react very differently in a peaceful rural atmosphere.

CHECKLIST   Writing about Setting

- Is the setting specified or unidentified? Is it fully described or only suggested?

- Is the setting just background, or is it a key force in the story?

- Are any characters in conflict with their environment?

- How does the setting influence the story's plot? Does it cause characters to act?

continued on next page

- In what time period does the story take place? How can you tell? What social, political, or economic characteristics of the historical period might influence the story?

- In what geographical location is the story set? Is this location important to the story?

- At what time of day is the story set? Is time important to the development of the story?

- Is the story set primarily inside or outside? What role does this aspect of the setting play in the story?

- What role do weather conditions play in the story?

- What kind of atmosphere or mood does the setting create?

- How does the setting influence the characters? Does it affect (or reflect) their emotional state? Does it help to explain their motivation?

- Does the atmosphere change as the story progresses? Is this change significant?

KATE CHOPIN (1851–1904) (picture and biography on p. 103) wrote in a style that was realistic yet infused with a dense, sensual texture that was perhaps, in part, her artistic response to her memories of the exotic Louisiana bayou country. Like her contemporary Gustave Flaubert (Chopin's short novel *The Awakening* has often been called a "Creole *Bovary*"), Chopin used the physical world — as in the charged atmosphere of "The Storm" — to symbolize the inner truths of her characters' minds and hearts. Unlike Flaubert, however, she depicted sex not as a frantic and destructive force but as a joyous, elemental part of life. Apparently Kate Chopin knew how daring "The Storm" was: she never submitted it for publication.

The Storm   (c. 1899)

I

The leaves were so still that even Bibi thought it was going to rain. Bobinôt, who was accustomed to converse on terms of perfect equality with his little son, called the child's attention to certain sombre clouds that were rolling with sinister intention from the west, accompanied by a sullen, threatening roar. They were at Friedheimer's store and decided to remain there till the storm had passed. They sat within the door on two empty kegs. Bibi was four years old and looked very wise.

"Mama'll be 'fraid, yes," he suggested with blinking eyes.

"She'll shut the house. Maybe she got Sylvie helpin' her this evenin'," Bobinôt responded reassuringly.

"No; she ent got Sylvie. Sylvie was helpin' her yistiday," piped Bibi.

Bobinôt arose and going across to the counter purchased a can of shrimps, of 5 which Calixta was very fond. Then he returned to his perch on the keg and sat stolidly holding the can of shrimps while the storm burst. It shook the wooden store and seemed to be ripping great furrows in the distant field. Bibi laid his little hand on his father's knee and was not afraid.

II

Calixta, at home, felt no uneasiness for their safety. She sat at a side window sewing furiously on a sewing machine. She was greatly occupied and did not notice the approaching storm. But she felt very warm and often stopped to mop her face on which the perspiration gathered in beads. She unfastened her white sacque at the throat. It began to grow dark, and suddenly realizing the situation she got up hurriedly and went about closing windows and doors.

Out on the small front gallery she had hung Bobinôt's Sunday clothes to air and she hastened out to gather them before the rain fell. As she stepped outside, Alcée Laballière rode in at the gate. She had not seen him very often since her marriage, and never alone. She stood there with Bobinôt's coat in her hands, and the big rain drops began to fall. Alcée rode his horse under the shelter of a side projection where the chickens had huddled and there were plows and a harrow piled up in the corner.

"May I come and wait on your gallery till the storm is over, Calixta?" he asked.

"Come 'long in, M'sieur Alcée."

His voice and her own startled her as if from a trance, and she seized Bobinôt's 10 vest. Alcée, mounting to the porch, grabbed the trousers and snatched Bibi's braided jacket that was about to be carried away by a sudden gust of wind. He expressed an intention to remain outside, but it was soon apparent that he might as well have been out in the open: the water beat in upon the boards in driving sheets, and he went inside, closing the door after him. It was even necessary to put something beneath the door to keep the water out.

"My! what a rain! It's good two years sence it rain' like that," exclaimed Calixta as she rolled up a piece of bagging and Alcée helped her to thrust it beneath the crack.

She was a little fuller of figure than five years before when she married; but she had lost nothing of her vivacity. Her blue eyes still retained their melting quality; and her yellow hair, dishevelled by the wind and rain, kinked more stubbornly than ever about her ears and temples.

The rain beat upon the low, shingled roof with a force and clatter that threatened to break an entrance and deluge them there. They were in the dining room — the sitting room — the general utility room. Adjoining was her bed room, with Bibi's couch along side her own. The door stood open, and the room with its white, monumental bed, its closed shutters, looked dim and mysterious.

Alcée flung himself into a rocker and Calixta nervously began to gather up from the floor the lengths of a cotton sheet which she had been sewing.

15   "If this keeps up, *Dieu sait*° if the levees° goin' to stan' it!" she exclaimed.

"What have you got to do with the levees?"

"I got enough to do! An' there's Bobinôt with Bibi out in that storm — if he only didn't left Friedheimer's!"

"Let us hope, Calixta, that Bobinôt's got sense enough to come in out of a cyclone."

She went and stood at the window with a greatly disturbed look on her face. She wiped the frame that was clouded with moisture. It was stiflingly hot. Alcée got up and joined her at the window, looking over her shoulder. The rain was coming down in sheets obscuring the view of far-off cabins and enveloping the distant wood in a gray mist. The playing of the lightning was incessant. A bolt struck a tall chinaberry tree at the edge of the field. It filled all visible space with a blinding glare and the crash seemed to invade the very boards they stood upon.

20   Calixta put her hands to her eyes, and with a cry, staggered backward. Alcée's arm encircled her, and for an instant he drew her close and spasmodically to him.

"*Bonté!*"° she cried, releasing herself from his encircling arm and retreating from the window, "the house'll go next! If I only knew w'ere Bibi was!" She would not compose herself; she would not be seated. Alcée clasped her shoulders and looked into her face. The contact of her warm, palpitating body when he had unthinkingly drawn her into his arms, had aroused all the old-time infatuation and desire for her flesh.

"Calixta," he said, "don't be frightened. Nothing can happen. The house is too low to be struck, with so many tall trees standing about. There! aren't you going to be quiet? say, aren't you?" He pushed her hair back from her face that was warm and steaming. Her lips were as red and moist as pomegranate seed. Her white neck and a glimpse of her full, firm bosom disturbed him powerfully. As she glanced up at him the fear in her liquid blue eyes had given place to a drowsy gleam that unconsciously betrayed a sensuous desire. He looked down into her eyes and there was nothing for him to do but to gather her lips in a kiss. It reminded him of Assumption.

"Do you remember — in Assumption, Calixta?" he asked in a low voice broken by passion. Oh! she remembered; for in Assumption he had kissed her and kissed and kissed her; until his senses would well nigh fail, and to save her he would resort to a desperate flight. If she was not an immaculate dove in those days, she was still inviolate; a passionate creature whose very defenselessness had made her defense, against which his honor forbade him to prevail. Now — well, now — her lips seemed in a manner free to be tasted, as well as her round, white throat and her whiter breasts.

Dieu sait: "God knows" (French).

levees: Raised embankments designed to keep a river from overflowing.

Bonté: "Goodness!" (French).

They did not heed the crashing torrents, and the roar of the elements made her laugh as she lay in his arms. She was a revelation in that dim, mysterious chamber; as white as the couch she lay upon. Her firm, elastic flesh that was knowing for the first time its birthright, was like a creamy lily that the sun invites to contribute its breath and perfume to the undying life of the world.

The generous abundance of her passion, without guile or trickery, was like a 25
white flame which penetrated and found response in depths of his own sensuous nature that had never yet been reached.

When he touched her breasts they gave themselves up in quivering ecstasy, inviting his lips. Her mouth was a fountain of delight. And when he possessed her, they seemed to swoon together at the very borderland of life's mystery.

He stayed cushioned upon her, breathless, dazed, enervated, with his heart beating like a hammer upon her. With one hand she clasped his head, her lips lightly touching his forehead. The other hand stroked with a soothing rhythm his muscular shoulders.

The growl of the thunder was distant and passing away. The rain beat softly 30
upon the shingles, inviting them to drowsiness and sleep. But they dared not yield.

The rain was over; and the sun was turning the glistening green world into a palace of gems. Calixta, on the gallery, watched Alcée ride away. He turned and smiled at her with a beaming face; and she lifted her pretty chin in the air and laughed aloud.

III

Bobinôt and Bibi, trudging home, stopped without at the cistern to make themselves presentable.

"My! Bibi, w'at will yo' mama say! You ought to be ashame'. You oughtn' put on those good pants. Look at 'em! An' that mud on yo' collar! How you got that mud on yo' collar, Bibi? I never saw such a boy!" Bibi was the picture of pathetic resignation. Bobinôt was the embodiment of serious solicitude as he strove to remove from his own person and his son's the signs of their tramp over heavy roads and through wet fields. He scraped the mud off Bibi's bare legs and feet with a stick and carefully removed all traces from his heavy brogans. Then, prepared for the worst — the meeting with an over-scrupulous housewife, they entered cautiously at the back door.

Calixta was preparing supper. She had set the table and was dripping coffee at the hearth. She sprang up as they came in.

"Oh, Bobinôt! You back! My! but I was uneasy. W'ere you been during the rain? An' Bibi? he ain't wet? he ain't hurt?" She had clasped Bibi and was kissing him effusively. Bobinôt's explanations and apologies which he had been composing all along the way, died on his lips as Calixta felt him to see if he were dry, and seemed to express nothing but satisfaction at their safe return.

"I brought you some shrimps, Calixta," offered Bobinôt, hauling the can from his ample side pocket and laying it on the table.

35   "Shrimps! Oh, Bobinôt! you too good fo' anything!" and she gave him a smacking kiss on the cheek that resounded. *"J'vous réponds,*° we'll have a feas' tonight! umph-umph!"

Bobinôt and Bibi began to relax and enjoy themselves, and when the three seated themselves at table they laughed much and so loud that anyone might have heard them as far away as Laballière's.

IV

Alcée Laballière wrote to his wife, Clarisse, that night. It was a loving letter, full of tender solicitude. He told her not to hurry back, but if she and the babies liked it at Biloxi, to stay a month longer. He was getting on nicely; and though he missed them, he was willing to bear the separation a while longer — realizing that their health and pleasure were the first things to be considered.

V

As for Clarisse, she was charmed upon receiving her husband's letter. She and the babies were doing well. The society was agreeable; many of her old friends and acquaintances were at the bay. And the first free breath since her marriage seemed to restore the pleasant liberty of her maiden days. Devoted as she was to her husband, their intimate conjugal life was something which she was more than willing to forego for a while.

So the storm passed and everyone was happy.

Reading and Reacting

1. Trace the progress of the storm through the five parts of the story. Then, trace the stages of the story's plot. How does the progress of the storm parallel the developing plot?

2. How does the weather help to create the story's atmosphere? How would you characterize this atmosphere?

3. In Part I, the "sombre clouds . . . rolling with sinister intention" introduce the storm. In what sense does this description introduce the story's action as well?

4. In what ways does the storm *cause* the events of the story? List specific events that occur because of the storm. Is the presence of the storm essential to the story? Explain.

5. In what sense does the storm act as a character in the story?

6. The weather is the most obvious element of the story's setting. What other aspects of setting are important to the story?

7. After Part II, the storm is not mentioned again until the last line of the story. What signs of the storm remain in Parts III, IV, and V?

8. Besides denoting the weather, what else might the title suggest?

J'vous réponds: "I tell you" (French).

9. **JOURNAL ENTRY** The storm sets in motion the chain of events that leads to the characters' adultery. Do you think the storm excuses the characters in any way from responsibility for their actions?

10. **CRITICAL PERSPECTIVE** Kate Chopin is widely considered to be a regional, or "local color" writer. This term refers to writing in which descriptions of a particular geographic region are prominent. Local color writers strive to incorporate accurate speech patterns and dialects, as well as descriptions of local scenery, dress, and social customs, in their writing. In their introduction to her work, Prentice Hall educators note the following:

> Through her vivid descriptions and use of dialect, Chopin captured the local color of the region. In her stories, published in *Bayou Folk* (1894) and *Acadie* (1897), she exhibited her deep understanding of the different attitudes and concerns of the Louisiana natives. Yet her charming portraits of Louisiana life often obscured the fact that she explored the themes considered radical at the time: the nature of marriage, racial prejudice, and women's desire for social, economic, and political equality.

In what ways is "The Storm" an example of local color writing? In what ways is it more than just a "charming portrait of Louisiana life"?

Related Works: "Hills Like White Elephants" (p. 80), "What Lips My Lips Have Kissed" (p. 636), "General Review of the Sex Situation" (p. 636), *The Stronger* (p. 853).

SHERMAN J. ALEXIE (1966–   ), a Spokane/Coeur d'Alene Indian, grew up on the Spokane Indian Reservation in Wellpinit, Washington, about fifty miles northwest of Spokane, where approximately 1,100 Spokane Tribal members live. Alexie has published short stories, novels, and poetry. He was named one of Granta's Best of Young American Novelists, and his first novel, *Reservation Blues* (1995), won the Before Columbus Foundation's American Book Award and the Murray Morgan Prize. His second novel, *Indian Killer* (1996), was named one of *People's* Best of Pages and was a *New York Times* Notable Book. In 1997, he and Native American director Chris Eyre collaborated on a film project based on parts of Alexie's 1993 short story  collection *The Lone Ranger and Tonto Fistfight in Heaven;* the film, *Smoke Signals,* was released in 1998. To date, Alexie has written sixteen books, including poetry collections, novels, and short story collections. His most recent book is *Ten Little Indians* (2003), a collection of short stories.

Commenting on Native American culture, Alexie has said, "One of the biggest misconceptions about Indians is that we're stoic, but humor is an essential part of our culture." "This Is What It Means to Say Phoenix, Arizona" (from *The Lone Ranger and Tonto Fistfight in Heaven*) demonstrates this unique use of humor to transcend the harsh realities of life on the reservation and of the struggle to adapt to contemporary American life.

This Is What It Means to Say Phoenix, Arizona (1993)

Just after Victor lost his job at the Bureau of Indian Affairs,° he also found out that his father had died of a heart attack in Phoenix, Arizona. Victor hadn't seen his father in a few years, had only talked to him on the telephone once or twice, but there still was a genetic pain, which was as real and immediate as a broken bone. Victor didn't have any money. Who does have money on a reservation, except the cigarette and fireworks salespeople? His father had a savings account waiting to be claimed, but Victor needed to find a way to get from Spokane to Phoenix. Victor's mother was just as poor as he was, and the rest of his family didn't have any use at all for him. So Victor called the tribal council.

"Listen," Victor said. "My father just died. I need some money to get to Phoenix to make arrangements."

5   "Now Victor," the council said, "you know we're having a difficult time financially."

"But I thought the council had special funds set aside for stuff like this."

"Now, Victor, we do have some money available for the proper return of tribal members' bodies. But I don't think we have enough to bring your father all the way back from Phoenix."

"Well," Victor said. "It ain't going to cost all that much. He had to be cremated. Things were kind of ugly. He died of a heart attack in his trailer and nobody found him for a week. It was really hot, too. You get the picture."

"Now, Victor, we're sorry for your loss and the circumstances. But we can really only afford to give you one hundred dollars."

"That's not even enough for a plane ticket."

"Well, you might consider driving down to Phoenix."

10   "I don't have a car. Besides, I was going to drive my father's pickup back up here."

"Now, Victor," the council said, "we're sure there is somebody who could drive you to Phoenix. Or could anybody lend you the rest of the money?"

"You know there ain't nobody around with that kind of money."

"Well, we're sorry, Victor, but that's the best we can do."

Victor accepted the tribal council's offer. What else could he do? So he signed the proper papers, picked up his check, and walked over to the Trading Post to cash it.

15   While Victor stood in line, he watched Thomas Builds-the-Fire standing near the magazine rack talking to himself. Like he always did. Thomas was a storyteller whom nobody wanted to listen to. That's like being a dentist in a town where everybody has false teeth.

Bureau of Indian Affairs: The division of the U.S. Department of the Interior that manages Native American matters; the bureau is operated by government officials, not tribal leaders.

Victor and Thomas Builds-the-Fire were the same age, had grown up and played in the dirt together. Ever since Victor could remember, it was Thomas who had always had something to say.

Once, when they were seven years old, when Victor's father still lived with the family, Thomas closed his eyes and told Victor this story: "Your father's heart is weak. He is afraid of his own family. He is afraid of you. Late at night, he sits in the dark. Watches the television until there's nothing but that white noise. Sometimes he feels like he wants to buy a motorcycle and ride away. He wants to run and hide. He doesn't want to be found."

Thomas Builds-the-Fire had known that Victor's father was going to leave, known it before anyone. Now Victor stood in the Trading Post with a one-hundred-dollar check in his hand, wondering if Thomas knew that Victor's father was dead, if he knew what was going to happen next.

Just then, Thomas looked at Victor, smiled, and walked over to him.

"Victor, I'm sorry about your father," Thomas said.   20

"How did you know about it?" Victor asked.

"I heard it on the wind. I heard it from the birds. I felt it in the sunlight. Also, your mother was just in here crying."

"Oh," Victor said and looked around the Trading Post. All the other Indians stared, surprised that Victor was even talking to Thomas. Nobody talked to Thomas anymore because he told the same damn stories over and over again. Victor was embarrassed, but he thought that Thomas might be able to help him. Victor felt a sudden need for tradition.

"I can lend you the money you need," Thomas said suddenly. "But you have to take me with you."

"I can't take your money," Victor said. "I mean, I haven't hardly talked to you   25
in years. We're not really friends anymore."

"I didn't say we were friends. I said you had to take me with you."

"Let me think about it."

Victor went home with his one hundred dollars and sat at the kitchen table. He held his head in his hands and thought about Thomas Builds-the-Fire, remembered little details, tears and scars, the bicycle they shared for a summer, so many stories.

                              *   *   *

Thomas Builds-the-Fire sat on the bicycle, waiting in Victor's yard. He was ten years old and skinny. His hair was dirty because it was the Fourth of July.

"Victor," Thomas yelled. "Hurry up. We're going to miss the fireworks."   30

After a few minutes, Victor ran out of his family's house, vaulted over the porch railing, and landed gracefully on the sidewalk.

Thomas gave him the bike and they headed for the fireworks. It was nearly dark and the fireworks were about to start.

"You know," Thomas said, "it's strange how us Indians celebrate the Fourth of July. It ain't like it was our independence everybody was fighting for."

"You think about things too much," Victor said. "It's just supposed to be fun. Maybe Junior will be there."

35   "Which Junior? Everybody on this reservation is named Junior."

The fireworks were small, hardly more than a few bottle rockets and a fountain. But it was enough for two Indian boys. Years later, they would need much more.

Afterward, sitting in the dark, fighting off mosquitoes, Victor turned to Thomas Builds-the-Fire.

"Hey," Victor said. "Tell me a story."

Thomas closed his eyes and told this story: "There were these two Indian boys who wanted to be warriors. But it was too late to be warriors in the old way. All the horses were gone. So the two Indian boys stole a car and drove to the city. They parked the stolen car in the front of the police station and then hitchhiked back home to the reservation. When they got back, all their friends cheered and their parents' eyes shone with pride. 'You were very brave,' everybody said to the two Indian boys. 'Very brave.'"

40   "Ya-hey," Victor said. "That's a good one. I wish I could be a warrior."

"Me too," Thomas said.

Victor sat at his kitchen table. He counted his one hundred dollars again and again. He knew he needed more to make it to Phoenix and back. He knew he needed Thomas Builds-the-Fire. So he put his money in his wallet and opened the front door to find Thomas on the porch.

"Ya-hey, Victor," Thomas said. "I knew you'd call me."

Thomas walked into the living room and sat down in Victor's favorite chair.

45   "I've got some money saved up," Thomas said. "It's enough to get us down there, but you have to get us back."

"I've got this hundred dollars," Victor said. "And my dad had a savings account I'm going to claim."

"How much in your dad's account?"

"Enough. A few hundred."

"Sounds good. When we leaving?"

50   When they were fifteen and had long since stopped being friends, Victor and Thomas got into a fistfight. That is, Victor was really drunk and beat Thomas up for no reason at all. All the other Indian boys stood around and watched it happen. Junior was there and so were Lester, Seymour, and a lot of others.

The beating might have gone on until Thomas was dead if Norma Many Horses hadn't come along and stopped it.

"Hey, you boys," Norma yelled and jumped out of her car. "Leave him alone."

If it had been someone else, even another man, the Indian boys would've just ignored the warnings. But Norma was a warrior. She was powerful. She could have picked up any two of the boys and smashed their skulls together. But worse than that, she would have dragged them all over to some tepee and made them listen to some elder tell a dusty old story.

The Indian boys scattered, and Norma walked over to Thomas and picked him up.

"Hey, little man, are you O.K.?" she asked.   55

Thomas gave her a thumbs-up.

"Why they always picking on you?"

Thomas shook his head, closed his eyes, but no stories came to him, no words or music. He just wanted to go home, to lie in his bed and let his dreams tell the stories for him.

Thomas Builds-the-Fire and Victor sat next to each other in the airplane, coach section. A tiny white woman had the window seat. She was busy twisting her body into pretzels. She was flexible.

"I have to ask," Thomas said, and Victor closed his eyes in embarrassment.   60

"Don't," Victor said.

"Excuse me, miss," Thomas asked. "Are you a gymnast or something?"

"There's no something about it," she said. "I was first alternate on the 1980 Olympic team."

"Really?" Thomas asked.

"Really."   65

"I mean, you used to be a world-class athlete?" Thomas asked.

"My husband thinks I still am."

Thomas Builds-the-Fire smiled. She was a mental gymnast too. She pulled her leg straight up against her body so that she could've kissed her kneecap.

"I wish I could do that," Thomas said.

Victor was ready to jump out of the plane. Thomas, that crazy Indian story- 70
teller with ratty old braids and broken teeth, was flirting with a beautiful Olympic gymnast. Nobody back home on the reservation would ever believe it.

"Well," the gymnast said. "It's easy. Try it."

Thomas grabbed at his leg and tried to pull it up into the same position as the gymnast's. He couldn't even come close, which made Victor and the gymnast laugh.

"Hey," she asked. "You two are Indian, right?"

"Full-blood," Victor said.

"Not me," Thomas said. "I'm half magician on my mother's side and half 75
clown on my father's."

They all laughed.

"What are your names?" she asked.

"Victor and Thomas."

"Mine is Cathy. Pleased to meet you all."

The three of them talked for the duration of the flight. Cathy the gymnast 80
complained about the government, how they screwed the 1980 Olympic team by boycotting the games.

"Sounds like you all got a lot in common with Indians," Thomas said.

Nobody laughed.

After the plane landed in Phoenix and they had all found their way to the terminal, Cathy the gymnast smiled and waved goodbye.

"She was really nice," Thomas said.

85   "Yeah, but everybody talks to everybody on airplanes," Victor said.

"You always used to tell me I think too much," Thomas said. "Now it sounds like you do."

"Maybe I caught it from you."

"Yeah."

Thomas and Victor rode in a taxi to the trailer where Victor's father had died.

90   "Listen," Victor said as they stopped in front of the trailer. "I never told you I was sorry for beating you up that time."

"Oh, it was nothing. We were just kids and you were drunk."

"Yeah, but I'm still sorry."

"That's all right."

Victor paid for the taxi, and the two of them stood in the hot Phoenix summer. They could smell the trailer.

95   "This ain't going to be nice," Victor said. "You don't have to go in."

"You're going to need help."

Victor walked to the front door and opened it. The stink rolled out and made them both gag. Victor's father had lain in that trailer for a week in hundred-degree temperatures before anyone had found him. And the only reason anyone found him was the smell. They needed dental records to identify him. That's exactly what the coroner said. They needed dental records.

"Oh, man," Victor said. "I don't know if I can do this."

"Well, then don't."

100   "But there might be something valuable in there."

"I thought his money was in the bank."

"It is: I was talking about pictures and letters and stuff like that."

"Oh," Thomas said as he held his breath and followed Victor into the trailer.

When Victor was twelve, he stepped into an underground wasps' nest. His foot was caught in the hole and no matter how hard he struggled, Victor couldn't pull free. He might have died there, stung a thousand times, if Thomas Builds-the-Fire had not come by.

105   "Run," Thomas yelled and pulled Victor's foot from the hole. They ran then, hard as they ever had, faster than Billy Mills, faster than Jim Thorpe, faster than the wasps could fly.

Victor and Thomas ran until they couldn't breathe, ran until it was cold and dark outside, ran until they were lost and it took hours to find their way home. All the way back, Victor counted his stings.

"Seven," Victor said. "My lucky number."

*   *   *

Victor didn't find much to keep in the trailer. Only a photo album and a stereo. Everything else had that smell stuck in it or was useless anyway. "I guess this is all," Victor said. "It ain't much."

"Better than nothing," Thomas said.

"Yeah, and I do have the pickup." 110

"Yeah," Thomas said. "It's in good shape."

"Dad was good about that stuff."

"Yeah, I remember your dad."

"Really?" Victor asked. "What do you remember?"

Thomas Builds-the-Fire closed his eyes and told this story: "I remember when 115
I had this dream that told me to go to Spokane, to stand by the falls in the middle of the city and wait for a sign. I knew I had to go there but I didn't have a car. Didn't have a license. I was only thirteen. So I walked all the way, took me all day, and I finally made it to the falls. I stood there for an hour waiting. Then your dad came walking up. 'What the hell are you doing here?' he asked me. I said, 'Waiting for a vision.' Then your father said, 'All you're going to get here is mugged.' So he drove me over to Denny's, bought me dinner, and then drove me home to the reservation. For a long time, I was mad because I thought my dreams had lied to me. But they hadn't. Your dad was my vision. *Take care of each other* is what my dreams were saying. *Take care of each other*."

Victor was quiet for a long time. He searched his mind for memories of his father, found the good ones, found a few bad ones, added it all up, and smiled.

"My father never told me about finding you in Spokane," Victor said.

"He said he wouldn't tell anybody. Didn't want me to get in trouble. But he said I had to watch out for you as part of the deal."

"Really?"

"Really. Your father said you would need the help. He was right." 120

"That's why you came down here with me, isn't it?" Victor asked.

"I came because of your father."

Victor and Thomas climbed into the pickup, drove over to the bank, and claimed the three hundred dollars in the savings account.

Thomas Builds-the-Fire could fly.

Once, he jumped off the roof of the tribal school and flapped his arms like a 125
crazy eagle. And he flew. For a second he hovered, suspended above all the other Indian boys, who were too smart or too scared to jump too.

"He's flying," Junior yelled, and Seymour was busy looking for the trick wires or mirrors. But it was real. As real as the dirt when Thomas lost altitude and crashed to the ground.

He broke his arm in two places.

"He broke his wing, he broke his wing, he broke his wing," all the Indian boys chanted as they ran off, flapping their wings, wishing they could fly too. They hated Thomas for his courage, his brief moment as a bird. Everybody has dreams about flying. Thomas flew.

One of his dreams came true for just a second, just enough to make it real.

*   *   *

Victor's father, his ashes, fit in one wooden box with enough left over to fill a cardboard box.

"He always was a big man," Thomas said.

Victor carried part of his father out to the pickup, and Thomas carried the rest. They set him down carefully behind the seats, put a cowboy hat on the wooden box and a Dodgers cap on the cardboard box. That was the way it was supposed to be.

"Ready to head back home?" Victor asked.

"It's going to be a long drive."

"Yeah, take a couple days, maybe."

135   "We can take turns," Thomas said.

"O.K.," Victor said, but they didn't take turns. Victor drove for sixteen hours straight north, made it halfway up Nevada toward home before he finally pulled over.

"Hey, Thomas," Victor said. "You got to drive for a while."

"O.K."

140   Thomas Builds-the-Fire slid behind the wheel and started off down the road. All through Nevada, Thomas and Victor had been amazed at the lack of animal life, at the absence of water, of movement.

"Where is everything?" Victor had asked more than once.

Now, when Thomas was finally driving, they saw the first animal, maybe the only animal in Nevada. It was a long-eared jackrabbit.

"Look," Victor yelled. "It's alive."

Thomas and Victor were busy congratulating themselves on their discovery when the jackrabbit darted out into the road and under the wheels of the pickup.

145   "Stop the goddamn car," Victor yelled, and Thomas did stop and backed the pickup to the dead jackrabbit.

"Oh, man, he's dead," Victor said as he looked at the squashed animal.

"Really dead."

"The only thing alive in this whole state and we just killed it."

"I don't know," Thomas said. "I think it was suicide."

150   Victor looked around the desert, sniffed the air, felt the emptiness and loneliness, and nodded his head.

"Yeah," Victor said. "It had to be suicide."

"I can't believe this," Thomas said. "You drive for a thousand miles and there ain't even any bugs smashed on the windshield. I drive for ten seconds and kill the only living thing in Nevada."

"Yeah," Victor said. "Maybe I should drive."

"Maybe you should."

155   Thomas Builds-the-Fire walked through the corridors of the tribal school by himself. Nobody wanted to be anywhere near him because of all those stories. Story after story.

Thomas closed his eyes and this story came to him: "We are all given one thing by which our lives are measured, one determination. Mine are the stories that can change or not change the world. It doesn't matter which, as long as I continue to tell the stories. My father, he died on Okinawa° in World War II, died fighting for this country, which had tried to kill him for years. My mother, she died giving birth to me, died while I was still inside her. She pushed me out into the world with her last breath. I have no brothers or sisters. I have only my stories, which came to me before I even had the words to speak. I learned a thousand stories before I took my first thousand steps. They are all I have. It's all I can do."

Thomas Builds-the-Fire told his stories to all those who would stop and listen. He kept telling them long after people had stopped listening.

Victor and Thomas made it back to the reservation just as the sun was rising. It was the beginning of a new day on earth, but the same old shit on the reservation.

"Good morning," Thomas said.

"Good morning."   160

The tribe was waking up, ready for work, eating breakfast, reading the newspaper, just like everybody else does. Willene LeBret was out in her garden, wearing a bathrobe. She waved when Thomas and Victor drove by.

"Crazy Indians made it," she said to herself and went back to her roses.

Victor stopped the pickup in front of Thomas Builds-the-Fire's HUD° house. They both yawned, stretched a little, shook dust from their bodies.

"I'm tired," Victor said.

"Of everything," Thomas added.   165

They both searched for words to end the journey. Victor needed to thank Thomas for his help and for the money, and to make the promise to pay it all back.

"Don't worry about the money," Thomas said. "It don't make any difference anyhow."

"Probably not, enit?"

"Nope."

Victor knew that Thomas would remain the crazy storyteller who talked to   170 dogs and cars, who listened to the wind and pine trees. Victor knew that he couldn't really be friends with Thomas, even after all that had happened. It was cruel but it was real. As real as the ash, as Victor's father, sitting behind the seats.

"I know how it is," Thomas said. "I know you ain't going to treat me any better than you did before. I know your friends would give you too much shit about it."

Victor was ashamed of himself. Whatever happened to the tribal ties, the sense of community? The only real thing he shared with anybody was a bottle and broken dreams. He owed Thomas something, anything.

Okinawa: Largest island of the Ryukyus, a chain of Japanese islands in the western Pacific Ocean.

HUD: The U.S. Department of Housing and Urban Development.

"Listen," Victor said and handed Thomas the cardboard box that contained half of his father. "I want you to have this."

Thomas took the ashes and smiled, closed his eyes, and told this story: "I'm going to travel to Spokane Falls one last time and toss these ashes into the water. And your father will rise like a salmon, leap over the bridge, over me, and find his way home. It will be beautiful. His teeth will shine like silver, like a rainbow. He will rise, Victor, he will rise."

175   Victor smiled.

"I was planning on doing the same thing with my half," Victor said. "But I didn't imagine my father looking anything like a salmon. I thought it'd be like cleaning the attic or something. Like letting things go after they've stopped having any use."

"Nothing stops, cousin," Thomas said. "Nothing stops."

Thomas Builds-the-Fire got out of the pickup and walked up his driveway. Victor started the pickup and began the drive home.

"Wait," Thomas yelled suddenly from his porch. "I just got to ask one favor."

180   Victor stopped the pickup, leaned out the window, and shouted back.

"What do you want?" he asked.

"Just one time when I'm telling a story somewhere, why don't you stop and listen?" Thomas asked.

"Just once?"

"Just once."

185   Victor waved his arms to let Thomas know that the deal was good. It was a fair trade. That's all Thomas had ever wanted from his whole life. So Victor drove his father's pickup toward home while Thomas went into his house, closed the door behind him, and heard a new story come to him in the silence afterward.

Reading and Reacting

1. In paragraph 1, readers are told that Victor lives on an Indian reservation. What details elsewhere in the story establish this setting? What associations does this setting have for you? Do you think the story could take place anywhere else?

2. In addition to various locations on the reservation, the story's settings include an airplane, a trailer in Phoenix, and a road through Nevada. What does each of these settings contribute to the story's plot?

3. Is the scene on the plane necessary? Intrusive? Distracting? Farfetched?

4. How would you characterize the story's mood or atmosphere? How do Thomas's stories help to create this mood? How do they help to establish his character? Do you think Alexie should have included more of these stories?

5. Why do you suppose Victor and Thomas cannot be friends when they get back to the reservation? Why are they able to be friends when they are traveling to Phoenix?

6. Do the flashbacks to the two men's childhood add something vital to the story? What purpose do these flashbacks serve?

7. In Native American culture, the storyteller holds an important position, telling tales that transmit and preserve the tribe's basic beliefs. Do you think Thomas's stories serve such a function? Or, do you think that he is, as Victor characterizes him, simply "the crazy storyteller who talked to dogs and cars, who listened to the wind and pine trees" (par. 170)?

8. What do you think the story's title means?

9. JOURNAL ENTRY At the end of the story, when Thomas returns home, he hears "a new story come to him in the silence" after he closes the door. What kind of story do you think comes to him at this point?

10. CRITICAL PERSPECTIVE In the introduction to a collection of Native American literature, Clifford E. Trafzer, the collection's editor, discusses the unique characteristics of Native American writers:

> Due to their grounding in the oral tradition of their people, Native American writers do not follow the literary canon of the dominant society in their approach to short stories. Rather than focusing on one theme or character in a brief time frame, or using one geographical area, they often use multiple themes and characters with few boundaries of time or place. Their stories do not always follow a linear and clear path, and frequently the past and present, real and mythic, and conscious and unconscious are not distinguishable. Multidimensional characters are common, and involved stories usually lack absolute conclusions. Native American writers may also play tricks with language, deliberately misusing grammar, syntax, and spelling — sometimes in defiance of the dominant culture — in order to make English reflect the language of their peoples.

Do you think "This Is What It Means to Say Phoenix, Arizona" has the characteristics Trafzer associates with Native American writers?

Related Works: "Sleepy Time Gal" (p. 86), "Defending Walt Whitman" (p. 645), "Indian Boarding School: The Runaways" (p. 669), *The Glass Menagerie* (p. 1153)

TILLIE OLSEN (1912 or 1913–   ) is known for her works of fiction about working-class Americans. Her short stories and one novel are inhabited by those she called the "despised people" — coal miners, farm laborers, packinghouse butchers, and housewives. Olsen was born in Nebraska into a working-class family. Though she has been described as a Depression-era dropout, Olsen has observed that she educated herself, with libraries as her college. According to an account in her nonfiction work *Silences* (1978), Olsen at age fifteen was inspired to write about working-class people when she read Rebecca Harding Davis's *Life in the Iron Mills,* a tale of the effects of industrialization on workers, in an 1861 issue of *Atlantic Monthly* bought for ten cents in a junk shop.

Shortly after she left high school, she was jailed for helping to organize packinghouse workers. Motivated by her experiences, she began to write a novel, *Yonnondio*. Under her maiden name, Tillie Lerner, she published two poems, a short story, and part of her novel during the 1930s. After her marriage, she did not publish again for twenty-two years, spending her time raising four children and working at a variety of jobs. The collection of short stories *Tell Me a Riddle* (1961), which includes "I Stand Here Ironing" (originally titled "Help Her to Believe"), was published when she was fifty. Her only other work of fiction is *Yonnondio* (1974), which she pieced together from drafts she wrote in the 1930s and edited for publication in 1974.

In 1984, she edited *Mother to Daughter, Daughter to Mother: Mothers on Mothering*, a collection of poems, letters, short fiction, and diary excerpts written by famous and not-so-famous women, and in 1995, she collaborated with Estelle Jussim on *Mothers & Daughters: That Special Quality: An Exploration in Photographs*.

I Stand Here Ironing (1961)

I stand here ironing, and what you asked me moves tormented back and forth with the iron.

"I wish you would manage the time to come and talk with me about your daughter. I'm sure you can help me understand her. She's a youngster who needs help and whom I'm deeply interested in helping."

"Who needs help." . . . Even if I came, what good would it do? You think because I am her mother I have a key, or that in some way you could use me as a key? She has lived for nineteen years. There is all that life that has happened outside of me, beyond me.

And when is there time to remember, to sift, to weigh, to estimate, to total? I will start and there will be an interruption and I will have to gather it all together again. Or I will become engulfed with all I did or did not do, with what should have been and what cannot be helped.

5   She was a beautiful baby. The first and only one of our five that was beautiful at birth. You do not guess how new and uneasy her tenancy in her now-loveliness. You did not know her all those years she was thought homely, or see her poring over her baby pictures, making me tell her over and over how beautiful she had been — and would be, I would tell her — and was now, to the seeing eye. But the seeing eyes were few or nonexistent. Including mine.

I nursed her. They feel that's important nowadays. I nursed all the children, but with her, with all the fierce rigidity of first motherhood, I did like the books then said. Though her cries battered me to trembling and my breasts ached with swollenness, I waited till the clock decreed.

Why do I put that first? I do not even know if it matters, or if it explains anything.

She was a beautiful baby. She blew shining bubbles of sound. She loved motion, loved light, loved color and music and textures. She would lie on the floor in her blue overalls patting the surface so hard in ecstasy her hands and feet would blur. She was a miracle to me, but when she was eight months old I had to leave her daytimes with the woman downstairs to whom she was no miracle at all, for I worked or looked for work and for Emily's father, who "could no longer endure" (he wrote in his good-bye note) "sharing want with us."

I was nineteen. It was the pre-relief, pre-WPA° world of the depression. I would start running as soon as I got off the streetcar, running up the stairs, the place smelling sour, and awake or asleep to startle awake, when she saw me she would break into a clogged weeping that could not be comforted, a weeping I can hear yet.

After a while I found a job hashing at night so I could be with her days, and 10 it was better. But it came to where I had to bring her to his family and leave her.

It took a long time to raise the money for her fare back. Then she got chicken pox and I had to wait longer. When she finally came, I hardly knew her, walking quick and nervous like her father, looking like her father, thin, and dressed in a shoddy red that yellowed her skin and glared at the pockmarks. All the baby loveliness gone.

She was two. Old enough for nursery school they said, and I did not know then what I know now — the fatigue of the long day, and the lacerations of group life in the kinds of nurseries that are only parking places for children.

Except that it would have made no difference if I had known. It was the only place there was. It was the only way we could be together, the only way I could hold a job.

And even without knowing, I knew. I knew the teacher that was evil because all these years it has curdled into my memory, the little boy hunched in the corner, her rasp, "why aren't you outside, because Alvin hits you? that's no reason, go out, scaredy." I knew Emily hated it even if she did not clutch and implore "don't go Mommy" like the other children, mornings.

She always had a reason why we should stay home. Momma, you look sick. 15 Momma, I feel sick. Momma, the teachers aren't there today, they're sick. Momma, we can't go, there was a fire there last night. Momma, it's a holiday today, no school, they told me.

But never a direct protest, never rebellion. I think of our others in their three-, four-year-oldness — the explosions, the tempers, the denunciations, the demands — and I feel suddenly ill. I put the iron down. What in me demanded that goodness in her? And what was the cost, the cost to her of such goodness?

The old man living in the back once said in his gentle way: "You should smile at Emily more when you look at her." What *was* in my face when I looked at her? I loved her. There were all the acts of love.

WPA: The Works Progress Administration, created in 1935 as part of President Franklin D. Roosevelt's New Deal program. The purpose of the WPA (renamed the Works Projects Administration in 1939) was to provide jobs for the unemployed during the Great Depression.

It was only with the others I remembered what he said, and it was the face of joy, and not of care or tightness or worry I turned to them — too late for Emily. She does not smile easily, let alone almost always as her brothers and sisters do. Her face is closed and sombre, but when she wants, how fluid. You must have seen it in her pantomimes, you spoke of her rare gift for comedy on the stage that rouses laughter out of the audience so dear they applaud and applaud and do not want to let her go.

Where does it come from, that comedy? There was none of it in her when she came back to me that second time, after I had had to send her away again. She had a new daddy now to learn to love, and I think perhaps it was a better time.

20   Except when we left her alone nights, telling ourselves she was old enough.

"Can't you go some other time, Mommy, like tomorrow?" she would ask. "Will it be just a little while you'll be gone? Do you promise?"

The time we came back, the front door open, the clock on the floor in the hall. She rigid awake. "It wasn't just a little while. I didn't cry. Three times I called you, just three times, and then I ran downstairs to open the door so you could come faster. The clock talked loud. I threw it away, it scared me what it talked."

She said the clock talked loud again that night I went to the hospital to have Susan. She was delirious with the fever that comes before red measles, but she was fully conscious all the week I was gone and the week after we were home when she could not come near the new baby or me.

She did not get well. She stayed skeleton thin, not wanting to eat, and night after night she had nightmares. She would call for me, and I would rouse from exhaustion to sleepily call back: "You're all right, darling, go to sleep, it's just a dream," and if she still called, in a sterner voice, "now go to sleep, Emily, there's nothing to hurt you." Twice, only twice, when I had to get up for Susan anyhow, I went in to sit with her.

25   Now when it is too late (as if she would let me hold and comfort her like I do the others) I get up and go to her at once at her moan or restless stirring. "Are you awake, Emily? Can I get you something?" And the answer is always the same: "No, I'm all right, go back to sleep, Mother."

They persuaded me at the clinic to send her away to a convalescent home in the country where "she can have the kind of food and care you can't manage for her, and you'll be free to concentrate on the new baby." They still send children to that place. I see pictures on the society page of sleek young women planning affairs to raise money for it, or dancing at the affairs, or decorating Easter eggs or filling Christmas stockings for the children.

They never have a picture of the children so I do not know if the girls still wear those gigantic red bows and the ravaged looks on the every other Sunday when parents can come to visit "unless otherwise notified" — as we were notified the first six weeks.

Oh it is a handsome place, green lawns and tall trees and fluted flower beds. High up on the balconies of each cottage the children stand, the girls in their red bows and white dresses, the boys in white suits and giant red ties. The parents stand below shrieking up to be heard and the children shriek down to be heard, and between them the invisible wall: "Not to Be Contaminated by Parental Germs or Physical Affection."

There was a tiny girl who always stood hand in hand with Emily. Her parents never came. One visit she was gone. "They moved her to Rose Cottage," Emily shouted in explanation. "They don't like you to love anybody here."

She wrote once a week, the labored writing of a seven-year-old. "I am fine. 30 How is the baby. If I write my leter nicly I will have a star. Love." There never was a star. We wrote every other day, letters she could never hold or keep but only hear read — once. "We simply do not have room for children to keep any personal possessions," they patiently explained when we pieced one Sunday's shrieking together to plead how much it would mean to Emily, who loved so to keep things, to be allowed to keep her letters and cards.

Each visit she looked frailer. "She isn't eating," they told us.

(They had runny eggs for breakfast or mush with lumps, Emily said later, I'd hold it in my mouth and not swallow. Nothing ever tasted good, just when they had chicken.)

It took us eight months to get her released home, and only the fact that she gained back so little of her seven lost pounds convinced the social worker.

I used to try to hold and love her after she came back, but her body would stay stiff, and after a while she'd push away. She ate little. Food sickened her, and I think much of life too. Oh she had physical lightness and brightness, twinkling by on skates, bouncing like a ball up and down up and down over the jump rope, skimming over the hill; but these were momentary.

She fretted about her appearance, thin and dark and foreign-looking at a 35 time when every little girl was supposed to look or thought she should look a chubby blonde replica of Shirley Temple. The doorbell sometimes rang for her, but no one seemed to come and play in the house or be a best friend. Maybe because we moved so much.

There was a boy she loved painfully through two school semesters. Months later she told me how she had taken pennies from my purse to buy him candy. "Licorice was his favorite and I brought him some every day, but he still liked Jennifer better'n me. Why, Mommy?" The kind of question for which there is no answer.

School was a worry to her. She was not glib or quick in a world where glibness and quickness were easily confused with ability to learn. To her overworked and exasperated teachers she was an overconscientious "slow learner" who kept trying to catch up and was absent entirely too often.

I let her be absent, though sometimes the illness was imaginary. How different from my now-strictness about attendance with the others. I wasn't working. We had a new baby, I was home anyhow. Sometimes, after Susan grew old enough, I would keep her home from school, too, to have them all together.

Mostly Emily had asthma, and her breathing, harsh and labored, would fill the house with a curiously tranquil sound. I would bring the two old dresser mirrors and her boxes of collections to her bed. She would select beads and single earrings, bottle tops and shells, dried flowers and pebbles, old postcards and scraps, all sorts of oddments; then she and Susan would play Kingdom, setting up landscapes and furniture, peopling them with action.

40   Those were the only times of peaceful companionship between her and Susan. I have edged away from it, that poisonous feeling between them, that terrible balancing of hurts and needs I had to do between the two, and did so badly, those earlier years.

Oh there are conflicts between the others too, each one human, needing, demanding, hurting, taking — but only between Emily and Susan, no, Emily toward Susan that corroding resentment. It seems so obvious on the surface, yet it is not obvious. Susan, the second child, Susan, golden- and curly-haired and chubby, quick and articulate and assured, everything in appearance and manner Emily was not; Susan, not able to resist Emily's precious things, losing or sometimes clumsily breaking them; Susan telling jokes and riddles to company for applause while Emily sat silent (to say to me later: that was *my* riddle, Mother, I told it to Susan); Susan, who for all the five years' difference in age was just a year behind Emily in developing physically.

I am glad for that slow physical development that widened the difference between her and her contemporaries, though she suffered over it. She was too vulnerable for that terrible world of youthful competition, of preening and parading, of constant measuring of yourself against every other, of envy, "If I had that copper hair," "If I had that skin. . . ." She tormented herself enough about not looking like the others, there was enough of the unsureness, the having to be conscious of words before you speak, the constant caring — what are they thinking of me? without having it all magnified by the merciless physical drives.

Ronnie is calling. He is wet and I change him. It is rare there is such a cry now. That time of motherhood is almost behind me when the ear is not one's own but must always be racked and listening for the child cry, the child call. We sit for a while and I hold him, looking out over the city spread in charcoal with its soft aisles of light. "*Shoogily*," he breathes and curls closer. I carry him back to bed, asleep. *Shoogily.* A funny word, a family word, inherited from Emily, invented by her to say: *comfort.*

In this and other ways she leaves her seal, I say aloud. And startle at my saying it. What do I mean? What did I start to gather together, to try and make coherent? I was at the terrible, growing years. War years. I do not remember them well. I was working, there were four smaller ones now, there was not time for her. She had to help be a mother, and housekeeper, and shopper. She had to set her seal. Mornings of crisis and near hysteria trying to get lunches packed, hair combed, coats and shoes found, everyone to school or Child Care on time, the baby ready for transportation. And always the paper scribbled on by a smaller one, the book looked at by Susan then mislaid, the homework not done. Running out to that huge school where she was one, she was lost, she was a drop; suffering over the unpreparedness, stammering and unsure in her classes.

There was so little time left at night after the kids were bedded down. She 45 would struggle over books, always eating (it was in those years she developed her enormous appetite that is legendary in our family) and I would be ironing, or preparing food for the next day, or writing V-mail° to Bill, or tending the baby. Sometimes, to make me laugh, or out of her despair, she would imitate happenings or types at school.

I think I said once: "Why don't you do something like this in the school amateur show?" One morning she phoned me at work, hardly understandable through the weeping: "Mother, I did it. I won, I won; they gave me first prize; they clapped and clapped and wouldn't let me go."

Now suddenly she was Somebody, and as imprisoned in her difference as she had been in anonymity.

She began to be asked to perform at other high schools, even in colleges, then at city and statewide affairs. The first one we went to, I only recognized her that first moment when thin, shy, she almost drowned herself into the curtains. Then: Was this Emily? The control, the command, the convulsing and deadly clowning, the spell, then the roaring, stamping audience, unwilling to let this rare and precious laughter out of their lives.

Afterwards: You ought to do something about her with a gift like that — but without money or knowing how, what does one do? We have left it all to her, and the gift has as often eddied inside, clogged and clotted, as been used and growing.

She is coming. She runs up the stairs two at a time with her light graceful 50 step, and I know she is happy tonight. Whatever it was that occasioned your call did not happen today.

"Aren't you ever going to finish the ironing, Mother? Whistler painted his mother in a rocker. I'd have to paint mine standing over an ironing board." This is one of her communicative nights and she tells me everything and nothing as she fixes herself a plate of food out of the icebox.

She is so lovely. Why did you want me to come in at all? Why were you concerned? She will find her way.

She starts up the stairs to bed. "Don't get me up with the rest in the morning." "But I thought you were having midterms." "Oh, those," she comes back in, kisses me, and says quite lightly, "in a couple of years when we'll all be atom-dead they won't matter a bit."

She has said it before. She *believes* it. But because I have been dredging the past, and all that compounds a human being is so heavy and meaningful in me, I cannot endure it tonight.

I will never total it all. I will never come in to say: She was a child seldom 55 smiled at. Her father left me before she was a year old. I had to work her first six years when there was work, or I sent her home and to his relatives. There were

---

V-mail: Mail sent to or from members of the armed forces during World War II. Letters were reduced onto microfilm and enlarged and printed out at their destination.

years she had care she hated. She was dark and thin and foreign-looking in a world where the prestige went to blondeness and curly hair and dimples, she was slow where glibness was prized. She was a child of anxious, not proud, love. We were poor and could not afford for her the soil of easy growth. I was a young mother, I was a distracted mother. There were other children pushing up, demanding. Her younger sister seemed all that she was not. There were years she did not want me to touch her. She kept too much in herself, her life was such she had to keep too much in herself. My wisdom came too late. She has much to her and probably little will come of it. She is a child of her age, of depression, of war, of fear.

Let her be. So all that is in her will not bloom — but in how many does it? There is still enough left to live by. Only help her to know — help make it so there is cause for her to know — that she is more than this dress on the ironing board, helpless before the iron.

Reading and Reacting

1. "I Stand Here Ironing" focuses on incidents that took place in the "pre-relief, pre-WPA world" of the Depression (par. 9). In light of social, political, and economic changes that have occurred since the 1930s, do you think the events the story presents could occur today? Explain.

2. In what sense is the image of a mother at an ironing board appropriate for this story?

3. The narrator is overwhelmed by guilt. What does she believe she has done wrong? What, if anything, do *you* think she has done wrong? Do you think she has been a good mother? Why or why not?

4. Who, or what, do you blame for the narrator's problems? For example, do you blame Emily's father? The Depression? The social institutions and "experts" to which the narrator turns?

5. Do you see the narrator as a victim limited by the times in which she lives? Do you agree with the narrator that Emily is "a child of her age, of depression, of war, of fear" (par. 55)? Or do you believe both women have some control over their own destinies, regardless of the story's historical setting?

6. What do you think the narrator wants for her daughter? Do you think her goals for Emily are realistic? Why or why not?

7. Paragraph 28 describes the physical setting of the convalescent home to which Emily was sent. What does this description add to the story? Why do you suppose there is no physical description of the apartment in which Emily lived as a child? How do you picture this apartment?

8. To whom do you think the mother is speaking in this story?

9. **JOURNAL ENTRY** Put yourself in Emily's position. What do you think she would like to tell her mother?

10. CRITICAL PERSPECTIVE Writing in *The Red Wheelbarrow*, psychologist Robert Coles discusses the complex family relationships depicted in "I Stand Here Ironing" and reaches an optimistic conclusion:

> But the child did not grow to be a mere victim of the kind so many of us these days are rather eager to recognize — a hopeless tangle of psychopathology. The growing child, even in her troubled moments, revealed herself to be persistent, demanding, and observant. In the complaints we make, in the "symptoms" we develop, we reveal our strengths as well as our weaknesses. The hurt child could summon her intelligence, exercise her will, smile and make others smile.

Do you agree with Coles's psychological evaluation of Emily? Do you find the story's ending as essentially uplifting as he seems to? Why or why not?

Related Works: "A Primer for the Punctuation of Heart Disease" (p. 88), "Kansas" (p. 107), "Everyday Use" (p. 282), "Seventeen Syllables" (p. 425), "Those Winter Sundays" (p. 623), *The Glass Menagerie* (p. 1153)

WRITING SUGGESTIONS: Setting

1. In both "The Storm" and "I Stand Here Ironing," social constraints determined by the story's historical setting limit a woman's options. Explore the options each woman might reasonably exercise in order to break free of the limits that social institutions impose on her.

2. Write an essay in which you consider how "This Is What It Means to Say Phoenix, Arizona" would be different if its geographical and physical setting were changed to a setting of your choice. In your essay, examine the changes (in plot development as well as in the characters' conflicts, reactions, and motivation) that might occur as a result of the change in setting.

3. Select a story from another chapter, and write an essay in which you consider how setting affects its plot — for example, how it creates conflict or crisis, how it forces characters to act, or how it determines how the plot is resolved.

4. "The Storm" uses rich descriptive language to create a mood that dominates the story. Analyze this use of language, explicating two or three short passages. How does language help to create and enrich the story's setting?

POINT OF VIEW

> Even if [a writer] has decided on a narrator who will fit one of the critic's classifications—"omniscient," "first-person," "limited omniscient," "objective," . . . and so on—his troubles have just begun.
>
> —Wayne C. Booth, *"Distance and Point of View"*

All stories are told by a **narrator,** and one of the first choices writers make is who tells the story. This choice determines the story's **point of view**—the vantage point from which events are presented. The implications of this choice are far-reaching. Consider, for example, the following scenario. Five people witness a crime and are questioned by the police. Their stories agree on certain points: a crime was committed, a body was found, and the crime occurred at noon. But in other ways their stories are different. The man who fled the scene was either tall or of average height; his hair was either dark or light; he either was carrying an object or was empty-handed. The events that led up to the crime and even the description of the crime itself are markedly different, depending on who tells the story. Thus, the perspective from which a story is told determines what details are included in the story and how they are arranged—in short, the plot. In addition, the perspective of the narrator affects the story's style, language, and themes.

The narrator of a work of fiction is not the same as the writer—even when a writer uses the first-person *I*. Writers create narrators to tell their stories. Often the personalities and opinions of narrators are far different from those of the author. The term **persona**—which literally means "mask"—is used for such narrators. By assuming this mask, a writer expands the creative possibilities of a work.

When deciding on a point of view for a work of fiction, a writer can choose to tell the story either in the *first person* or in the *third person*.

First-Person Narrators

Sometimes the narrator is a character who uses the **first person** (*I* or sometimes *we*) to tell the story. Often this narrator is a **major character**— Sammy in John Updike's "A&P" (p. 128) and the boy in James Joyce's "Araby" (p. 232), for

182

example — who tells his or her own story and is the focus of that story. Sometimes, however, a first-person narrator tells a story that is primarily about someone else. Such a narrator may be a **minor character** who plays a relatively small part in the story or simply an **observer** who reports events experienced or related by others. The narrator of William Faulkner's "A Rose for Emily" (p. 113), for example, is an unidentified witness to the story's events. By using *we* instead of *I*, this narrator speaks on behalf of all the town's residents, expressing their shared views of their neighbor, Emily Grierson:

> We did not say she was crazy then. We believed she had to do that. We remembered all the young men her father had driven away, and we knew that with nothing left, she would have to cling to that which had robbed her, as people will.

Writers gain a number of advantages when they use first-person narrators. First, they are able to present incidents convincingly. Readers are more willing to accept a statement like "My sister changed a lot after that day" than they are to accept the impersonal observations of a third-person narrator. The first-person narrator also simplifies a writer's task of selecting details. Only the events and details that the narrator could actually have seen or experienced can be introduced into the story.

Another major advantage of first-person narrators is that their restricted view can create **irony** — a discrepancy between what is said and what readers believe to be true. Irony may be *dramatic, situational,* or *verbal.* **Dramatic irony** occurs when a narrator (or character) perceives less than readers do; **situational irony** occurs when what happens is at odds with what readers are led to expect; **verbal irony** occurs when the narrator says one thing but actually means another.

"Gryphon," by Charles Baxter (p. 139), illustrates all three kinds of irony. Baxter creates **dramatic irony** when he has his main character see less than readers do. For example, at the end of the story, the young boy does not yet realize what readers already know — that he has learned more from Miss Ferenczi's way of teaching than from Mr. Hibler's. The setting of the story — a conventional school — creates **situational irony** because it contrasts with the unexpected events that unfold there. In addition, many of the narrator's comments create **verbal irony** because they mean something different from what they seem to mean. At the end of the story, for example, after the substitute, Miss Ferenczi, has been fired, the narrator relates another teacher's comment that life will now return to "normal" and that their regular teacher will soon return to test them on their "knowledge." This comment is ironic in light of all Miss Ferenczi has done to redefine the narrator's ideas about "normal" education and about "knowledge."

Unreliable Narrators

Sometimes first-person narrators are self-serving, mistaken, confused, unstable, or even insane. These **unreliable narrators,** whether intentionally or unintentionally, misrepresent events and misdirect readers. In Edgar Allan Poe's "The Cask of Amontillado" (p. 203), for example, the narrator, Montresor, tells his story to justify a crime he committed fifty years before. Montresor's version of what happened is not accurate, and perceptive readers know it: his obvious self-deception, his sadistic manipulation of Fortunato, his detached description of the cold-blooded murder, and his lack of remorse lead readers to question his sanity and, therefore, to distrust his version of events. This distrust creates an ironic distance between readers and narrator.

The narrator of Charlotte Perkins Gilman's "The Yellow Wallpaper" (p. 372) is also an unreliable narrator. Suffering from "nervous depression," she unintentionally distorts the facts when she says that the shapes in the wallpaper of her bedroom are changing and moving. Moreover, she does not realize what is wrong with her or why, or how her husband's "good intentions" are hurting her. Readers, however, see the disparity between the narrator's interpretation of events and their own, and this irony enriches their understanding of the story.

Some narrators are unreliable because they are naive. Because they are immature, sheltered, or innocent of evil, these narrators are not aware of the significance of the events they are relating. Having the benefit of experience, readers interpret events differently from the way these narrators do. When we read a passage by a child narrator — such as the following one from J. D. Salinger's novel *The Catcher in the Rye* — we are aware of the narrator's innocence, and we know his interpretation of events is flawed:

> Anyway, I keep picturing all these little kids playing some game in this big field of rye and all. Thousands of little kids, and nobody's around — nobody big, I mean — except me. And I'm standing on the edge of some crazy cliff. What I have to do, I have to catch everybody if they start to go over the cliff — I mean if they're running and they don't look where they're going I have to come out from somewhere and catch them. I'd just be the catcher in the rye. . . .

The irony in the preceding passage comes from our knowledge that the naive narrator, Holden Caulfield, cannot stop children from growing up. Ultimately, they all fall off the "crazy cliff" and mature into adults. Although Holden is not aware of the futility of trying to protect children from the dangers of adulthood, readers know that his efforts are doomed from the start.

A naive narrator's background can also limit his or her ability to understand a situation. The narrator in Sherwood Anderson's short story "I'm a Fool," for example, lies to impress a rich girl he meets at a racetrack. At the end of the story, the boy regrets the fact that he lied, believing that if he had told the truth, he could have seen the girl again. The reader knows, however, that the narrator (a laborer at the racetrack) is deceiving himself because the social gap that separates him and the girl could never be bridged.

Keep in mind that all first-person narrators are, in a sense, unreliable because they present a situation as only one person sees it. "In a Grove," a story by the Japanese author Ryūnosuke Akutagawa, illustrates this idea. In this story, seven characters act as narrators and give different accounts of a murder. Some of the characters seem to be lying or bending the facts to suit their own needs, but others simply have an incomplete or mistaken understanding of events. No character, of course, has all the information the story's author has.

When you read, you should look for discrepancies between a narrator's view of events and your own. Discovering that a story has an unreliable narrator enables you not only to question the accuracy of the narrative but also to recognize the irony in the narrator's version of events. By doing so, you gain insight into the story and learn something about the writer's purpose.

Third-Person Narrators

Sometimes a writer uses the **third person** (*he, she, they*) to tell the story from the point of view of a narrator who is not also a character. Third-person narrators fall into three categories: **omniscient, limited omniscient,** and **objective.**

Omniscient Narrators

Some third-person narrators are **omniscient** (all-knowing) narrators, moving at will from one character's mind to another. One advantage of omniscient narrators is that they have none of the naïveté, dishonesty, gullibility, or mental instability that can characterize first-person narrators. In addition, because omniscient narrators are not characters in the story, their perception is not limited to what any one character can observe or comprehend. As a result, they can present a more inclusive view of events and characters than first-person narrators can. Omniscient narrators can also convey their attitude toward their subject matter. For example, the omniscient narrator in "Once upon a Time," Nadine Gordimer's chilling 1991 story about South Africa under apartheid, uses sentence structure, word choice, and repetition to express her distaste for the scene she describes:

> In a house, in a suburb, in a city, there were a man and his wife who loved each other very much and were living happily ever after. They had a little boy, and they loved him very much. They had a cat and a dog that the little boy loved very much. They had a car and a caravan trailer for holidays, and a swimming-pool which was fenced so that the little boy and his playmates would not fall in and drown. They had a housemaid who was absolutely trustworthy and an itinerant gardener who was highly recommended by the neighbours. For when they began to live happily ever after they were warned, by that wise old witch, the husband's mother, not to take on anyone off the street.

Occasionally, omniscient narrators move not only in and out of the minds of the characters but also in and out of a **persona** (representing the voice of the author) that speaks directly to readers. This narrative technique was popular with writers during the eighteenth century, when the novel was a new literary form. It permitted writers to present themselves as masters of artifice, able to know and control all aspects of experience. Few contemporary writers would give

themselves the license that Henry Fielding does in the following passage from
Tom Jones (1749):

> And true it was that [Mr. Alworthy] did many of these things; but had he done
> nothing more I should have left him to have recorded his own merit on some
> fair freestone over the door of that hospital. Matters of a much more extraordi-
> nary kind are to be the subject of this history, or I should grossly misspend my
> time in writing so voluminous a work; and you my sagacious friend, might with
> equal profit and pleasure travel through some pages which certain droll authors
> have been facetiously pleased to call *The History of England*.

A contemporary example of this type of omniscient point of view occurs in
Ursula K. LeGuin's "The Ones Who Walk Away from Omelas" (1975). This story
presents a description of a city that in the narrator's words is "like a city in a fairy
tale." As the story proceeds, however, the description of Omelas changes, and the
narrator's tone changes as well: "Do you believe? Do you accept the festival, the
city, the joy? No? Then let me describe one more thing." By undercutting her own
narrative, the narrator underscores the ironic theme of the story, which suggests
that it is impossible for human beings to ever achieve an ideal society.

Limited Omniscient Narrators

Third-person narrators can have **limited omniscience,** focusing on only what a
single character experiences. In other words, events are limited to one character's
perspective, and nothing is revealed that the character does not see, hear, feel, or
think. Andy in David Michael Kaplan's "Doe Season" (p. 327) is just such a
limited-focus character. Limited omniscient narrators, like all third-person narrators, have certain advantages over first-person narrators. When a writer uses a
first-person narrator, the narrator's personality and speech color the story, creating a personal or even an idiosyncratic narrative. Also, the first-person narrator's
character flaws or lack of knowledge may limit his or her awareness of the
significance of events. Limited omniscient narrators are more flexible: they take
readers into a particular character's mind just as a first-person narrator does, but
without the first-person narrator's subjectivity, self-deception, or naïveté.

In the following example from Anne Tyler's 1984 story "Teenage Wasteland,"
the limited omniscient narrator presents the story from the point of view of a single character, Daisy:

> Daisy and Matt sat silent, shocked. Matt rubbed his forehead with his finger-
> tips. Imagine, Daisy thought, how they must look to Mr. Lanham: an over-
> weight housewife in a cotton dress and a too-tall, too-thin insurance agent in a
> baggy, frayed suit. Failures, both of them — the kind of people who are always
> hurrying to catch up, missing the point of things that everyone else grasps at
> once. She wished she'd worn nylons instead of knee socks.

Here the point of view gives readers the impression that they are standing off to
the side watching Daisy and her husband Matt. However, at the same time we

have the advantage of this objective view, we are also able to see into the mind of one character.

Objective Narrators

Third-person narrators who tell a story from an *objective* (or *dramatic*) point of view remain entirely outside the characters' minds. With **objective narrators,** events unfold the way they would in a play or a movie: narrators tell the story only by presenting dialogue and recounting events; they do not reveal the characters' (or their own) thoughts or attitudes. Thus, they allow readers to interpret the actions of the characters without any interference. Ernest Hemingway uses the objective point of view in his short story "A Clean, Well-Lighted Place" (1933):

> The waiter took the brandy bottle and another saucer from the counter inside the café and marched out to the old man's table. He put down the saucer and poured the glass full of brandy.
> "You should have killed yourself last week," he said to the deaf man. The old man motioned with his finger. "A little more," he said. The waiter poured on into the glass so that the brandy slopped over and ran down the stem into the top saucer of the pile. "Thank you," the old man said. The waiter took the bottle back inside the café. He sat down at the table with his colleague again.

The story's narrator is distant, seemingly emotionless, and this perspective is consistent with the author's purpose: for Hemingway, the attitude of the narrator reflects the stunned, almost anesthetized condition of people in the post–World War I world.

Selecting an Appropriate Point of View

Writers of short stories often maintain a consistent point of view. The main criterion writers use when they decide on a point of view is how the distance they maintain from their material will affect their narrative. The passages that follow illustrate the options writers have.

Limited Omniscient Point of View

In the following passage from the short story "Doe Season," David Michael Kaplan uses a third-person limited omniscient narrator to tell the story of Andy, a nine-year-old girl who is going hunting with her father for the first time.

> They were always the same woods, she thought sleepily as they drove through the early morning darkness — deep and immense, covered with yesterday's snowfall, which had frozen overnight. They were the same woods that lay behind her house, *and they stretch all the way to here,* she thought, *for miles and miles, longer than I could walk in a day, or a week even, but they are still the same woods.* The thought made her feel good: it was like thinking of God; it was like thinking of the space between here and the moon; it was like thinking of all the foreign countries from her geography book where even now, Andy knew,

people were going to bed, while they — she and her father and Charlie Spoon and Mac, Charlie's eleven-year-old son — were driving deeper into the Pennsylvania countryside, to go hunting.

They had risen long before dawn. Her mother, yawning and not trying to hide her sleepiness, cooked them eggs and French toast. Her father smoked a cigarette and flicked ashes into his saucer while Andy listened, wondering *Why doesn't he come?* and *Won't he ever come?* until at last a car pulled into the graveled drive and honked. "That will be Charlie Spoon," her father said; he always said "Charlie Spoon," even though his real name was Spreun, because Charlie was, in a sense, shaped like a spoon, with a large head and a narrow waist and chest.

Here the limited omniscient point of view has the advantage of allowing the narrator to focus on the thoughts, fears, and reactions of the child while at the same time giving readers information about Andy that she herself is too immature or unsophisticated to know. Rather than simply presenting the thoughts of the child (represented in the story by italics), the third-person narrator makes connections between ideas and displays a level of language and a degree of insight that readers would not accept from Andy as a first-person narrator. In addition, the limited omniscient perspective enables the narrator to maintain some distance.

First-Person Point of View (Child)

Consider how different the passage would be if it were narrated by nine-year-old Andy.

"I like the woods," I thought. "They're big and scary. I wonder if they're the same woods that are behind my house. They go on for miles. They're bigger than I could walk in a day, or a week even." It was neat to think that while we were driving into the woods people were going to bed in other countries.

When I woke up this morning, I couldn't wait to go hunting. My mother was cooking breakfast, but all I could think of was, "When will he come?" and "Won't he ever come?" Finally, I heard a car honk. "That will be Charlie Spoon," my father said. I think he called him "Charlie Spoon" because he thought Charlie was shaped like a big spoon.

As a first-person narrator, nine-year-old Andy must have the voice of a child; moreover, she is restricted to only those observations that a nine-year-old could reasonably make. Because of these limitations, the passage lacks the level of vocabulary, syntax, and insight necessary to develop the central character and the themes of the story. This point of view could succeed only if Andy's words established an ironic contrast between her naive sensibility and the reality of the situation.

First-Person Point of View (Adult)

Kaplan could have avoided these problems and still gained the advantages of using a first-person narrator by having Andy tell her story as an adult looking back on a childhood experience. (This technique is used by James Joyce in "Araby," p. 232; Charles Baxter in "Gryphon," p. 139; and Alberto Alvaro Ríos in "The Secret Lion," p. 412.)

> "They are always the same woods," I thought sleepily as we drove through the
> early morning darkness — deep and immense, covered with yesterday's snowfall,
> which had frozen overnight. "They're the same woods that lie behind my house,
> and they stretch all the way to here," I thought. I knew that they stretched for
> miles and miles, longer than I could walk in a day, or even in a week but that they
> were still the same woods. Knowing this made me feel good: I thought it was like
> thinking of God; it was like thinking of the space between that place and the
> moon; it was like thinking of all the foreign countries from my geography book
> where even then, I knew, people were going to bed, while we — my father and I
> and Charlie Spoon and Mac, Charlie's eleven-year-old son — were driving deeper
> into the Pennsylvania countryside, to go hunting.
>
> We had risen before dawn. My mother, who was yawning and not trying to
> hide her sleepiness, cooked us eggs and French toast. My father smoked a cigarette
> and flicked ashes into his saucer while I listened, wondering, "Why doesn't he
> come?" and "Won't he ever come?" until at last a car pulled into our driveway and
> honked. "That will be Charlie Spoon," my father said. He always said "Charlie
> Spoon," even though his real name was Spreun, because Charlie was, in a sense,
> shaped like a spoon, with a large head and a narrow waist and chest.

Although this passage presents the child's point of view, it does not use a child's
voice; the language and scope of the passage are too sophisticated for a child. By
using a mature style, the adult narrator considers ideas that a child could not possibly understand, such as the symbolic significance of the woods. In so doing, however, he sacrifices the degree of objectivity that characterizes the third-person
limited omniscient narrator of the original story.

Omniscient Point of View

Kaplan could also have used an omniscient narrator to tell his story. In this case,
the narrator would be free to reveal and comment not only on Andy's thoughts
but also on those of her father, and possibly even on the thoughts of her mother
and Charlie Spoon.

In the following passage, the omniscient narrator interprets the behavior of
the characters and tells what each one is thinking.

> They were always the same woods, she thought sleepily as they drove through
> the early morning darkness — deep and immense, covered with yesterday's
> snowfall, which had frozen overnight. They were the same woods that lay
> behind her house, and they stretch all the way to here, she thought, for miles
> and miles, longer than I could walk in a day, or a week even, but they are still
> the same woods.
>
> They had risen before dawn. The mother, yawning and not trying to hide
> her sleepiness, cooked them eggs and French toast. She looked at her husband
> and her daughter and wondered if she was doing the right thing by allowing
> them to go hunting together. "After all," she thought, "he's not the most
> careful person. Will he watch her? Make sure that no harm comes to her?"
>
> The father smoked a cigarette and flicked ashes into his saucer. He was
> listening to the sounds of the early morning. "I know everything will be all
> right," he thought. "It's about time Andy went hunting. When I was her

age. . . ." Andy listened, wondering Why doesn't he come? and Won't he ever come? until at last a car pulled into the graveled drive and honked. Suddenly the father cocked his head and said, "That will be Charlie Spoon."

Andy thought it was funny that her father called Charlie "Spoon" even though his real name was Spreun, because Charlie was, in a sense, shaped like a spoon, with a large head and a narrow waist and chest.

Certainly this point of view has its advantages; for example, the wide scope of this perspective provides a great deal of information about the characters. However, the use of an omniscient point of view deprives the story of its focus on Andy.

Objective Point of View

Finally, Kaplan could have used an objective narrator. This point of view would eliminate all interpretation by the narrator and force readers to make judgments solely on the basis of what the characters say and do.

Andy sat sleepily staring into her cereal. She played with the dry flakes of bran as they floated in the surface of the milk.

Andy's mother, yawning, cooked them eggs and French toast. She looked at her husband and her daughter, paused for a second, and then went about what she was doing.

Andy's father smoked a cigarette and flicked ashes into his saucer. He looked out the window and said, "I wonder where Charlie Spoon is?"

Andy squirmed restlessly and repeatedly looked up at the clock that hung above the stove.

The disadvantage of this point of view is that it creates a great deal of distance between the characters and the readers. Instead of gaining the intimate knowledge of Andy that the limited omniscient point of view provides — knowledge even greater than she herself has — readers must infer what she thinks and feels without any help from the narrator.

✔ **CHECKLIST   Selecting an Appropriate Point of View: Review**

First-Person Narrators (use *I* or *WE*)

▶ *Major character telling his or her own story*   "Every morning I lay on the floor in the front parlour watching her door." (James Joyce, "Araby")

▶ *Minor character as witness*   "And so she died. . . . We did not even know she was sick; we had long since given up trying to get information. . . ." (William Faulkner, "A Rose for Emily")

Third-Person Narrators (use *HE*, *SHE*, and *THEY*)

▶ *Omniscient — able to move at will from character to character and comment about them*   "Although they lived in style, they felt always an anxiety in the house. There was never enough money." (D. H. Lawrence, "The Rocking-Horse Winner")

▶ *Limited Omniscient — restricts focus to a single character* "The wagon went on. He did not know where they were going." (William Faulkner, "Barn Burning")

▶ *Objective (Dramatic)— simply reports the dialogue and the actions of characters* "'You'll be drunk,' the waiter said. The old man looked at him. The waiter went away." (Ernest Hemingway, "A Clean, Well-Lighted Place")

✔ CHECKLIST   Writing about Point of View

What is the dominant point of view from which the story is told?

Is the narrator a character in the story? If so, is he or she a participant in the story's events or just a witness?

Does the story's point of view create irony?

If the story has a first-person narrator, is the narrator reliable or unreliable? Are there any inconsistencies in the narrator's presentation of the story?

If the story has a third-person narrator, is he or she omniscient? Does he or she have limited omniscience? Is the narrator objective?

What are the advantages of the story's point of view? How does the point of view accomplish the author's purpose?

Does the point of view remain consistent throughout the story, or does it shift?

How might a different point of view change the story?

RICHARD WRIGHT (1908–1960) was born near Natchez, Mississippi, the son of sharecroppers. He had little formal schooling but as a young man was a voracious reader, especially of naturalistic fiction. Relocating to Chicago in the late 1920s, Wright worked as a postal clerk until 1935, when he joined the Federal Writers' Project, an association that took him to New York City. Deeply troubled by the economic and social oppression of African-Americans, Wright joined the Communist Party in 1932, and his early poems and stories reflect a distinctly Marxist perspective. In 1944, he broke with the party because of its stifling effect on his creativity.

Wright began to reach a mainstream audience when a group of four long stories on the theme of racial oppression and violence was judged best manuscript in a contest sponsored by *Story* magazine; these stories were published as *Uncle Tom's Children* in 1938.

Two years later, Wright published his most famous work, *Native Son,* an angry and brutal novel exploring the moral devastation wrought by a racist society. The autobiographical *Black Boy* was published in 1945. In later years, Wright abandoned the United States for Paris in protest against the treatment of African-Americans in his native country and focused his work on reports about national independence movements in Africa and elsewhere in the third world.

The following story, published in the posthumous collection *Eight Men* (1961), is uncharacteristic of Wright's work in a number of ways — not least of which is that it is told through the eyes of a white protagonist.

Big Black Good Man   (1957)

Through the open window Olaf Jenson could smell the sea and hear the occasional foghorn of a freighter; outside, rain pelted down through an August night, drumming softly upon the pavements of Copenhagen,° inducing drowsiness, bringing dreamy memory, relaxing the tired muscles of his work-wracked body. He sat slumped in a swivel chair with his legs outstretched and his feet propped atop an edge of his desk. An inch of white ash tipped the end of his brown cigar and now and then he inserted the end of the stogie° into his mouth and drew gently upon it, letting wisps of blue smoke eddy from the corners of his wide, thin lips. The watery gray irises behind the thick lenses of his eyeglasses gave him a look of abstraction, of absentmindedness, of an almost genial idiocy. He sighed, reached for his half-empty bottle of beer, and drained it into his glass and downed it with a long slow gulp, then licked his lips. Replacing the cigar, he slapped his right palm against his thigh and said half aloud:

"Well, I'll be sixty tomorrow. I'm not rich, but I'm not poor either . . . Really, I can't complain. Got good health. Traveled all over the world and had my share of girls when I was young . . . And my Karen's a good wife. I own my home. Got no debts. And I love digging in my garden in the spring . . . Grew the biggest carrots of anybody last year. Ain't saved much money, but what the hell . . . Money ain't everything. Got a good job. Night portering ain't too bad." He shook his head and yawned. "Karen and I could of had some children, though. Would of been good company . . . 'Specially for Karen. And I could of taught 'em languages . . . English, French, German, Danish, Dutch, Swedish, Norwegian, and Spanish . . ." He took the cigar out of his mouth and eyed the white ash critically. "Hell of a lot of good language learning did me . . . Never got anything out of it. But those ten years in New York were fun . . . Maybe I could of got rich if I'd stayed in America . . . Maybe. But I'm satisfied. You can't have everything."

Behind him the office door opened and a young man, a medical student occupying room number nine, entered.

Copenhagen: The capital of Denmark.
stogie: A cheap cigar.

"Good evening," the student said.

"Good evening," Olaf said, turning.   5

The student went to the keyboard and took hold of the round, brown knob that anchored his key.

"Rain, rain, rain," the student said.

"That's Denmark for you," Olaf smiled at him.

"This dampness keeps me clogged up like a drainpipe," the student complained.

"That's Denmark for you," Olaf repeated with a smile.   10

"Good night," the student said.

"Good night, son," Olaf sighed, watching the door close.

Well, my tenants are my children, Olaf told himself. Almost all of his children were in their rooms now . . . Only seventy-two and forty-four were missing . . . Seventy-two might've gone to Sweden . . . And forty-four was maybe staying at his girl's place tonight, like he sometimes did . . . He studied the pear-shaped blobs of hard rubber, reddish brown like ripe fruit, that hung from the keyboard, then glanced at his watch. Only room thirty, eighty-one, and one hundred and one were empty . . . And it was almost midnight. In a few moments he could take a nap. Nobody hardly ever came looking for accommodations after midnight, unless a stray freighter came in, bringing thirsty, women-hungry sailors. Olaf chuckled softly. Why in hell was I ever a sailor? The whole time I was at sea I was thinking and dreaming about women. Then why didn't I stay on land where women could be had? Hunh? Sailors are crazy . . .

But he liked sailors. They reminded him of his youth, and there was something so direct, simple, and childlike about them. They always said straight out what they wanted, and what they wanted was almost always women and whisky . . . "Well, there's no harm in that . . . Nothing could be more natural," Olaf sighed, looking thirstily at his empty beer bottle. No; he'd not drink any more tonight; he'd had enough; he'd go to sleep . . .

He was bending forward and loosening his shoelaces when he heard the office   15
door crack open. He lifted his eyes, then sucked in his breath. He did not straighten; he just stared up and around at the huge black thing that filled the doorway. His reflexes refused to function; it was not fear; it was just simple astonishment. He was staring at the biggest, strangest, and blackest man he'd ever seen in all his life.

"Good evening," the black giant said in a voice that filled the small office. "Say, you got a room?"

Olaf sat up slowly, not to answer but to look at this brooding black vision; it towered darkly some six and a half feet into the air, almost touching the ceiling, and its skin was so black that it had a bluish tint. And the sheer bulk of the man! . . . His chest bulged like a barrel; his rocklike and humped shoulders hinted of mountain ridges; the stomach ballooned like a threatening stone; and the legs were like telephone poles . . . The big black cloud of a man now lumbered into the office, bending to get its buffalolike head under the door frame, then advanced slowly upon Olaf, like a stormy sky descending.

"You got a room?" the big black man asked again in a resounding voice.

Olaf now noticed that the ebony giant was well dressed, carried a wonderful new suitcase, and wore black shoes that gleamed despite the raindrops that peppered their toes.

20 "You're American?" Olaf asked him.

"Yeah, man; sure," the black giant answered.

"Sailor?"

"Yeah. American Continental Lines."

Olaf had not answered the black man's question. It was not that the hotel did not admit men of color; Olaf took in all comers — blacks, yellows, whites, and browns . . . To Olaf, men were men, and, in his day, he'd worked and eaten and slept and fought with all kinds of men. But this particular black man . . . Well, he didn't seem human. Too big, too black, too loud, too direct, and probably too violent to boot . . . Olaf's five feet seven inches scarcely reached the black giant's shoulder and his frail body weighed less, perhaps, than one of the man's gigantic legs . . . There was something about the man's intense blackness and ungainly bigness that frightened and insulted Olaf; he felt as though this man had come here expressly to remind him how puny, how tiny, and how weak and how white he was. Olaf knew, while registering his reactions, that he was being irrational and foolish; yet, for the first time in his life, he was emotionally determined to refuse a man a room solely on the basis of the man's size and color . . . Olaf's lips parted as he groped for the right words in which to couch his refusal, but the black giant bent forward and boomed:

25 "I asked you if you got a room. I got to put up somewhere tonight, man."

"Yes, we got a room," Olaf murmured.

And at once he was ashamed and confused. Sheer fear had made him yield. And he seethed against himself for his involuntary weakness. Well, he'd look over his book and pretend that he'd made a mistake; he'd tell this hunk of blackness that there was really no free room in the hotel, and that he was so sorry . . . Then, just as he took out the hotel register to make believe that he was poring over it, a thick roll of American bank notes, crisp and green, was thrust under his nose.

"Keep this for me, will you?" the black giant commanded. "Cause I'm gonna get drunk tonight and I don't wanna lose it."

Olaf stared at the roll; it was huge, in denominations of fifties and hundreds. Olaf's eyes widened.

"How much is there?" he asked.

30 "Two thousand six hundred," the giant said. "Just put it into an envelope and write 'Jim' on it and lock it in your safe, hunh?"

The black mass of man had spoken in a manner that indicated that it was taking it for granted that Olaf would obey. Olaf was licked. Resentment clogged the pores of his wrinkled white skin. His hands trembled as he picked up the money. No; he couldn't refuse this man . . . The impulse to deny him was strong, but each time he was about to act upon it something thwarted him, made him shy off. He clutched about desperately for an idea. Oh yes, he could say that if he planned to stay for only one night, then he could not have the room, for it was against the policy of the hotel to rent rooms for only one night . . .

"How long are you staying? Just tonight?" Olaf asked.

"Naw. I'll be here for five or six days, I reckon," the giant answered off handedly.

"You take room number thirty," Olaf heard himself saying. "It's forty kroner 35 a day."

"That's all right with me," the giant said.

With slow, stiff movements, Olaf put the money in the safe and then turned and stared helplessly up into the living, breathing blackness looming above him. Suddenly he became conscious of the outstretched palm of the black giant; he was silently demanding the key to the room. His eyes downcast, Olaf surrendered the key, marveling at the black man's tremendous hands . . . He could kill me with one blow, Olaf told himself in fear.

Feeling himself beaten, Olaf reached for the suitcase, but the black hand of the giant whisked it out of his grasp.

"That's too heavy for you, big boy; I'll take it," the giant said.

Olaf let him. He thinks I'm nothing . . . He led the way down the corridor, 40 sensing the giant's lumbering presence behind him. Olaf opened the door of number thirty and stood politely to one side, allowing the black giant to enter. At once the room seemed like a doll's house, so dwarfed and filled and tiny it was with a great living blackness . . . Flinging his suitcase upon a chair, the giant turned. The two men looked directly at each other now. Olaf saw that the giant's eyes were tiny and red, buried, it seemed, in muscle and fat. Black cheeks spread, flat and broad, topping the wide and flaring nostrils. The mouth was the biggest that Olaf had ever seen on a human face; the lips were thick, pursed, parted, showing snow-white teeth. The black neck was like a bull's . . . The giant advanced upon Olaf and stood over him.

"I want a bottle of whiskey and a woman," he said. "Can you fix me up?"

"Yes," Olaf whispered, wild with anger and insult.

But what was he angry about? He'd had requests like this every night from all sorts of men and he was used to fulfilling them; he was a night porter in a cheap, water-front Copenhagen hotel that catered to sailors and students. Yes, men needed women, but this man, Olaf felt, ought to have a special sort of woman. He felt a deep and strange reluctance to phone any of the women whom he habitually sent to men. Yet he had promised. Could he lie and say that none was available? No. That sounded too fishy. The black giant sat upon the bed, staring straight before him. Olaf moved about quickly, pulling down the window shades, taking the pink coverlet off the bed, nudging the giant with his elbow to make him move as he did so . . . That's the way to treat 'im . . . Show 'im I ain't scared of 'im . . . But he was still seeking for an excuse to refuse. And he could think of nothing. He felt hypnotized, mentally immobilized. He stood hesitantly at the door.

"You send the whiskey and the woman quick, pal?" the black giant asked, rousing himself from a brooding stare.

"Yes," Olaf grunted, shutting the door.

45   Goddamn, Olaf sighed. He sat in his office at his desk before the phone. Why did *he* have to come here? . . . I'm not prejudiced . . . No, not at all . . . But . . . He couldn't think any more. God oughtn't make men as big and black as that . . . But what the hell was he worrying about? He'd sent women of all races to men of all colors . . . So why not a woman to the black giant? Oh, only if the man were small, brown, and intelligent-looking . . . Olaf felt trapped.

With a reflex movement of his hand, he picked up the phone and dialed Lena. She was big and strong and always cut him in for fifteen per cent instead of the usual ten per cent. Lena had four small children to feed and clothe. Lena was willing; she was, she said, coming over right now. She didn't give a good goddamn about how big and black the man was . . .

"Why you ask me that?" Lena wanted to know over the phone. "You never asked that before . . ."

"But this one is *big*," Olaf found himself saying.

"He's just a man," Lena told him, her voice singing stridently, laughingly over the wire. "You just leave that to me. You don't have to do anything. *I'll* handle 'im."

50   Lena had a key to the hotel door downstairs, but tonight Olaf stayed awake. He wanted to see her. Why? He didn't know. He stretched out on the sofa in his office, but sleep was far from him. When Lena arrived, he told her again how big and black the man was.

"You told me that over the phone," Lena reminded him.

Olaf said nothing. Lena flounced off on her errand of mercy. Olaf shut the office door, then opened it and left it ajar. But why? He didn't know. He lay upon the sofa and stared at the ceiling. He glanced at his watch; it was almost two o'clock . . . She's staying in there a long time . . . Ah, God, but he could do with a drink . . . Why was he so damned worked up and nervous about a nigger and a white whore? . . . He'd never been so upset in all his life. Before he knew it, he had drifted off to sleep. Then he heard the office door swinging creakingly open on its rusty hinges. Lena stood in it, grim and businesslike, her face scrubbed free of powder and rouge. Olaf scrambled to his feet, adjusting his eyeglasses, blinking.

"How was it?" he asked her in a confidential whisper.

Lena's eyes blazed.

55   "What the hell's that to you?" she snapped. "There's your cut," she said, flinging him his money, tossing it upon the covers of the sofa. "You're sure nosy tonight. You wanna take over my work?"

Olaf's pasty cheeks burned red.

"You go to hell," he said, slamming the door.

"I'll meet you there!" Lena's shouting voice reached him dimly.

He was being a fool; there was no doubt about it. But, try as he might, he could not shake off a primitive hate for that black mountain of energy, of muscle, of bone;

he envied the easy manner in which it moved with such a creeping and powerful motion; he winced at the booming and commanding voice that came to him when the tiny little eyes were not even looking at him; he shivered at the sight of those vast and clawlike hands that seemed always to hint of death . . .

Olaf kept his counsel. He never spoke to Karen about the sordid doings at the 60 hotel. Such things were not for women like Karen. He knew instinctively that Karen would have been amazed had he told her that he was worried sick about a nigger and a blonde whore . . . No; he couldn't talk to anybody about it, not even the hard-bitten° old bitch who owned the hotel. She was concerned only about money; she didn't give a damn about how big and how black a client was as long as he paid his room rent.

Next evening, when Olaf arrived for duty, there was no sight or sound of the black giant. A little later after one o'clock in the morning he appeared, left his key, and went out wordlessly. A few moments past two the giant returned, took his key from the board, and paused.

"I want that Lena again tonight. And another bottle of whiskey," he said boomingly.

"I'll call her and see if she's in," Olaf said.

"Do that," the black giant said and was gone.

He thinks he's God, Olaf fumed. He picked up the phone and ordered Lena 65 and a bottle of whiskey, and there was a taste of ashes in his mouth. On the third night came the same request: Lena and whiskey. When the black giant appeared on the fifth night, Olaf was about to make a sarcastic remark to the effect that maybe he ought to marry Lena, but he checked it in time . . . After all, he could kill me with one hand, he told himself.

Olaf was nervous and angry with himself for being nervous. Other black sailors came and asked for girls and Olaf sent them, but with none of the fear and loathing that he sent Lena and a bottle of whiskey to the giant . . . All right, the black giant's stay was almost up. He'd said that he was staying for five or six nights; tomorrow night was the sixth night and that ought to be the end of this nameless terror.

On the sixth night Olaf sat in his swivel chair with his bottle of beer and waited, his teeth on edge, his fingers drumming the desk. But what the hell am I fretting for? . . . The hell with 'im . . . Olaf sat and dozed. Occasionally he'd awaken and listen to the foghorns of freighters sounding as ships came and went in the misty Copenhagen harbor. He was half asleep when he felt a rough hand on his shoulder. He blinked his eyes open. The giant, black and vast and powerful, all but blotted out his vision.

"What I owe you, man?" the giant demanded. "And I want my money."

"Sure," Olaf said, relieved, but filled as always with fear of this living wall of black flesh.

With fumbling hands, he made out the bill and received payment, then gave 70 the giant his roll of money, laying it on the desk so as not to let his hands touch

---

hard-bitten: Stubborn, tough.

the flesh of the black mountain. Well, his ordeal was over. It was past two o'clock in the morning. Olaf even managed a wry smile and muttered a guttural "Thanks" for the generous tip that the giant tossed him.

Then a strange tension entered the office. The office door was shut and Olaf was alone with the black mass of power, yearning for it to leave. But the black mass of power stood still, immobile, looking down at Olaf. And Olaf could not, for the life of him, guess at what was transpiring in that mysterious black mind. The two of them simply stared at each other for a full two minutes, the giant's tiny little beady eyes blinking slowly as they seemed to measure and search Olaf's face. Olaf's vision dimmed for a second as terror seized him and he could feel a flush of heat overspread his body. Then Olaf sucked in his breath as the devil of blackness commanded:

"Stand up!"

Olaf was paralyzed. Sweat broke on his face. His worst premonitions about this black beast were coming true. This evil blackness was about to attack him, maybe kill him . . . Slowly Olaf shook his head, his terror permitting him to breathe:

"What're you talking about?"

75   "Stand up, I say!" the black giant bellowed.

As though hypnotized, Olaf tried to rise; then he felt the black paw of the beast helping him roughly to his feet.

They stood an inch apart. Olaf's pasty-white features were glued to the giant's swollen black face. The ebony ensemble of eyes and nose and mouth and cheeks looked down at Olaf, silently; then, with a slow and deliberate movement of his gorillalike arms, he lifted his mammoth hands to Olaf's throat. Olaf had long known and felt that this dreadful moment was coming; he felt trapped in a nightmare. He could not move. He wanted to scream, but could find no words. His lips refused to open; his tongue felt icy and inert. Then he knew that his end had come when the giant's black fingers slowly, softly encircled his throat while a horrible grin of delight broke out on the sooty face . . . Olaf lost control of the reflexes of his body and he felt a hot stickiness flooding his underwear . . . He stared without breathing, gazing into the grinning blackness of the face that was bent over him, feeling the black fingers caressing his throat and waiting to feel the sharp, stinging ache and pain of the bones in his neck being snapped, crushed . . . He knew all along that I hated 'im . . . Yes, and now he's going to kill me for it, Olaf told himself with despair.

The black fingers still circled Olaf's neck, not closing, but gently massaging it, as it were, moving to and fro, while the obscene face grinned into his. Olaf could feel the giant's warm breath blowing on his eyelashes and he felt like a chicken about to have its neck wrung and its body tossed to flip and flap dyingly in the dust of the barnyard . . . Then suddenly the black giant withdrew his fingers from Olaf's neck and stepped back a pace, still grinning. Olaf sighed, trembling, his body seeming to shrink; he waited. Shame sheeted him for the hot wetness that was in his trousers. Oh, God, he's teasing me . . . He's showing me how easily he can kill me . . . He swallowed, waiting, his eyes stones of gray.

The giant's barrel-like chest gave forth a low, rumbling chuckle of delight.
"You laugh?" Olaf asked whimperingly.   80
"Sure I laugh," the giant shouted.
"Please don't hurt me," Olaf managed to say.
"I wouldn't hurt you, boy," the giant said in a tone of mockery. "So long."
And he was gone. Olaf fell limply into the swivel chair and fought off losing
consciousness. Then he wept. He was showing me how easily he could kill me . . .
He made me shake with terror and then laughed and left . . . Slowly, Olaf recov-
ered, stood, then gave vent to a string of curses:
"Goddamn 'im! My gun's right there in the desk drawer; I should of shot 'im.   85
Jesus, I hope the ship he's on sinks . . . I hope he drowns and the sharks eat 'im . . ."
Later, he thought of going to the police, but sheer shame kept him back; and,
anyway, the giant was probably on board his ship by now. And he had to get home
and clean himself. Oh, Lord, what could he tell Karen? Yes, he would say that his
stomach had been upset . . . He'd change clothes and return to work. He phoned
the hotel owner that he was ill and wanted an hour off; the old bitch said that she
was coming right over and that poor Olaf could have the evening off.
Olaf went home and lied to Karen. Then he lay awake the rest of the night
dreaming of revenge. He saw that freighter on which the giant was sailing; he saw
it springing a dangerous leak and saw a torrent of sea water flooding, gushing into
all the compartments of the ship until it found the bunk in which the black giant
slept. Ah, yes, the foamy, surging waters would surprise that sleeping black bastard
of a giant and he would drown, gasping and choking like a trapped rat, his tiny
eyes bulging until they glittered red, the bitter water of the sea pounding his lungs
until they ached and finally burst . . . The ship would sink slowly to the bottom of
the cold, black, silent depths of the sea and a shark, a *white* one, would glide aimlessly about the shut portholes until it found an open one and it would slither inside and nose about until it found that swollen, rotting, stinking carcass of the
black beast and it would then begin to nibble at the decomposing mass of tarlike
flesh, eating the bones clean . . . Olaf always pictured the giant's bones as being
jet black and shining.
Once or twice, during these fantasies of cannibalistic revenge, Olaf felt a little guilty about all the many innocent people, women and children, all white
and blonde, who would have to go down into watery graves in order that that
white shark could devour the evil giant's black flesh . . . But, despite feelings of
remorse, the fantasy lived persistently on, and when Olaf found himself alone, it
would crowd and cloud his mind to the exclusion of all else, affording him the
only revenge he knew. To make me suffer just for the pleasure of it, he fumed.
Just to show me how strong he was . . . Olaf learned how to hate, and got pleasure out of it.
Summer fled on wings of rain. Autumn flooded Denmark with color. Winter
made rain and snow fall on Copenhagen. Finally spring came, bringing violets
and roses. Olaf kept to his job. For many months he feared the return of the black

giant. But when a year had passed and the giant had not put in an appearance, Olaf allowed his revenge fantasy to peter out, indulging in it only when recalling the shame that the black monster had made him feel.

90   Then one rainy August night, a year later, Olaf sat drowsing at his desk, his bottle of beer before him, tilting back in his swivel chair, his feet resting atop a corner of his desk, his mind mulling over the more pleasant aspects of his life. The office door cracked open. Olaf glanced boredly up and around. His heart jumped and skipped a beat. The black nightmare of terror and shame that he had hoped that he had lost forever was again upon him . . . Resplendently dressed, suitcase in hand, the black looming mountain filled the doorway. Olaf's thin lips parted and a silent moan, half a curse, escaped them.

"Hi," the black giant boomed from the doorway.

Olaf could not reply. But a sudden resolve swept him: this time he would even the score. If this black beast came within so much as three feet of him, he would snatch his gun out of the drawer and shoot him dead, so help him God . . .

"No rooms tonight," Olaf heard himself announcing in a determined voice.

The black giant grinned; it was the same infernal grimace of delight and triumph that he had had when his damnable black fingers had been around his throat . . .

95   "Don't want no room tonight," the giant announced.

"Then what are you doing here?" Olaf asked in a loud but tremulous voice.

The giant swept toward Olaf and stood over him; and Olaf could not move, despite his oath to kill him . . .

"What do you want then?" Olaf demanded once more, ashamed that he could not lift his voice above a whisper.

The giant still grinned, then tossed what seemed the same suitcase upon Olaf's sofa and bent over it; he zippered it open with a sweep of his clawlike hand and rummaged in it, drawing forth a flat, gleaming white object done up in glowing cellophane. Olaf watched with lowered lids, wondering what trick was now being played on him. Then, before he could defend himself, the giant had whirled and again long, black, snakelike fingers were encircling Olaf's throat . . . Olaf stiffened, his right hand clawing blindly for the drawer where the gun was kept. But the giant was quick.

100   "Wait," he bellowed, pushing Olaf back from the desk.

The giant turned quickly to the sofa and, still holding his fingers in a wide circle that seemed a noose for Olaf's neck, he inserted the rounded fingers into the top of the flat, gleaming object. Olaf had the drawer open and his sweaty fingers were now touching the gun, but something made him freeze. The flat, gleaming object was a shirt and the black giant's circled fingers were fitting themselves into its neck . . .

"A perfect fit!" the giant shouted.

Olaf stared, trying to understand. His fingers loosened about the gun. A mixture of a laugh and a curse struggled in him. He watched the giant plunge his hands into the suitcase and pull out other flat, gleaming shirts.

"One, two, three, four, five, six," the black giant intoned, his voice crisp and businesslike. "Six nylon shirts. And they're all yours. One shirt for each time Lena came . . . See, Daddy-O?"

The black, cupped hands, filled with billowing nylon whiteness, were ex- 105
tended under Olaf's nose. Olaf eased his damp fingers from his gun and pushed
the drawer closed, staring at the shirts and then at the black giant's grinning face.

"Don't you like 'em?" the giant asked.

Olaf began to laugh hysterically, then suddenly he was crying, his eyes so
flooded with tears that the pile of dazzling nylon looked like snow in the dead of
winter. Was this true? Could he believe it? Maybe this too was a trick? But, no.
There were six shirts, all nylon, and the black giant had had Lena six nights.

"What's the matter with you, Daddy-O?" the giant asked. "You blowing your
top? Laughing and crying . . ."

Olaf swallowed, dabbed his withered fists at his dimmed eyes; then he realized
that he had his glasses on. He took them off and dried his eyes and sat up. He
sighed, the tension and shame and fear and haunting dread of his fantasy went
from him, and he leaned limply back in his chair . . .

"Try one on," the giant ordered.   110

Olaf fumbled with the buttons of his shirt, let down his suspenders, and pulled
the shirt off. He donned a gleaming nylon one and the giant began buttoning it
for him.

"Perfect, Daddy-O," the giant said.

His spectacled face framed in sparkling nylon, Olaf sat with trembling lips. So
he'd not been trying to kill me after all.

"You want Lena, don't you?" he asked the giant in a soft whisper. "But I don't
know where she is. She never came back here after you left —"

"I know where Lena is," the giant told him. "We been writing to each other. 115
I'm going to her house. And, Daddy-O, I'm late." The giant zipped the suitcase
shut and stood a moment gazing down at Olaf, his tiny little red eyes blinking
slowly. Then Olaf realized that there was a compassion in that stare that he had
never seen before.

"And I thought you wanted to kill me," Olaf told him. "I was scared of you
. . ."

"Me? Kill you?" the giant blinked. "When?"

"That night when you put your fingers around my throat —"

"What?" the giant asked, then roared with laughter. "Daddy-O, you're a
funny little man. I wouldn't hurt you. I like you. You a *good* man. You helped
me."

Olaf smiled, clutching the pile of nylon shirts in his arms.   120

"You're a good man too," Olaf murmured. Then loudly, "You're a big black
good man."

"Daddy-O, you're crazy," the giant said.

He swept his suitcase from the sofa, spun on his heel, and was at the door in
one stride.

"Thanks!" Olaf cried after him.

The black giant paused, turned his vast black head, and flashed a grin.   125

"Daddy-O, drop dead," he said and was gone.

Reading and Reacting

1. Why do you suppose Wright presents events through Olaf's eyes? How would the story be different if the sailor told it?

2. This story was published in 1957. What attitudes about race does Wright expect his American readers to have? Do these attitudes predispose readers to identify with the sailor or with Olaf? Explain.

3. Why does Olaf dislike the sailor? What does the narrator mean in paragraph 24 when he says that the sailor's "intense blackness and ungainly bigness . . . frightened and insulted Olaf"?

4. In what ways do the sailor's words and actions contribute to Olaf's fears? Do you think Olaf's reactions are reasonable, or do you believe he is overreacting?

5. The sailor's name is Jim, but this name is almost never used in the story. Why not? List some words used to describe Jim. Why are these words used? How do they affect your reaction to Jim?

6. Do you think the story's title is ironic? In what other respects is the story ironic?

7. How would "Big Black Good Man" be different if Jim were white? Would there even *be* a story?

8. Why do you think Wright set the story in Copenhagen? Could it have been set in the United States in 1957?

9. What do you think Jim thinks of Olaf? Do you suppose he realizes the effect he has on him? How do you explain Jim's last comment?

10. JOURNAL ENTRY What point do you think the story makes about racial prejudice? Do you think Wright seems optimistic or pessimistic about race relations in the United States?

11. CRITICAL PERSPECTIVE In his 1982 article "The Short Stories: *Uncle Tom's Children, Eight Men*," Edward Margolies notes that "Big Black Good Man" was somewhat of a departure for Wright:

> "Big Black Good Man," which first appeared in *Esquire* in 1957, is the last short story Wright published in his lifetime. Possibly it is the last he ever wrote. In any event it represents a more traditional approach to storytelling in that Wright here avoids confining himself exclusively to dialogue. On the other hand, "Big Black Good Man" deviates from the usual Wright short story. For one thing, the narrative, by Wright's standards at least, is practically pointless. Scarcely anything "happens." There is no violence, practically no external narrative action, and no change of milieu.

Do you agree that the story is "practically pointless"? If not, what point do you think the story makes?

Related Works: "The Lesson" (p. 353), "We Wear the Mask" (p. 665), *The Brute* (p. 723)

EDGAR ALLAN POE (1809–1849) profoundly influenced many writers all over the world. His tales of psychological terror and the macabre, his hauntingly musical lyric poems, and his writings on the craft of poetry and short story writing affected the development of symbolic fiction, the modern detective story, and the gothic horror tale. In most of Poe's horror tales (as in "The Cask of Amontillado"), readers vicariously "live" the story through the first-person narrator who tells the tale.

Poe was born in 1809, the son of a talented English-born actress who, deserted by her actor husband, died of tuberculosis before her son's third birthday. Although Poe was raised in material comfort by foster parents in Richmond, Virginia, his life was increasingly uncertain: his foster mother loved him, but her husband became antagonistic. He kept the young Poe so short of money at the University of Virginia (and later at West Point) that Poe resorted to gambling to raise money for food and clothing. Finally, disgraced and debt-ridden, he left school altogether.

Poe found work as a magazine editor, gaining recognition as a literary critic. In 1836, he married his frail thirteen-year-old cousin, Virginia Clemm. Poe produced many of his most famous stories and poems in the next few years, working feverishly to support his tubercular wife, but although his stories were widely admired, financial success never came. His wife died in 1847. Less than two years after her death, Poe was found barely conscious in a Baltimore street after a mysterious disappearance; three days later, he was dead at age forty.

The Cask of Amontillado (1846)

The thousand injuries of Fortunato I had borne as I best could, but when he ventured upon insult I vowed revenge. You, who so well know the nature of my soul, will not suppose, however, that I gave utterance to a threat. *At length* I would be avenged; this was a point definitely settled — but the very definitiveness with which it was resolved precluded the idea of risk. I must not only punish but punish with impunity. A wrong is unredressed when retribution overtakes its redresser. It is equally unredressed when the avenger fails to make himself felt as such to him who has done the wrong.

It must be understood that neither by word nor deed had I given Fortunato cause to doubt my good will. I continued, as was my wont, to smile in his face, and he did not perceive that my smile *now* was at the thought of his immolation.

He had a weak point — this Fortunato — although in other regards he was a man to be respected and even feared. He prided himself on his connoisseurship in wine. Few Italians have the true virtuoso spirit. For the most part their enthusiasm is adopted to suit the time and opportunity, to practise imposture upon the British and Austrian *millionaires*. In painting and gemmary, Fortunato, like his countrymen, was a quack, but in the matter of old wines he was sincere. In this respect I did not differ from him materially; — I was skillful in the Italian vintages myself, and bought largely whenever I could.

It was about dusk, one evening during the supreme madness of the carnival sea-son, that I encountered my friend. He accosted me with excessive warmth, for he had been drinking much. The man wore motley.° He had on a tight-fitting parti-striped dress, and his head was surmounted by the conical cap and bells. I was so pleased to see him that I thought I should never have done wringing his hand.

5   I said to him — "My dear Fortunato, you are luckily met. How remarkably well you are looking to-day. But I have received a pipe° of what passes for Amontillado,° and I have my doubts."

"How?" said he. "Amontillado? A pipe? Impossible! And in the middle of the carnival!"

"I have my doubts," I replied; "and I was silly enough to pay the full Amontillado price without consulting you in the matter. You were not to be found, and I was fearful of losing a bargain."

"Amontillado!"

"I have my doubts."

10   "Amontillado!"

"And I must satisfy them."

"Amontillado!"

"As you are engaged, I am on my way to Luchresi. If any one has a critical turn it is he. He will tell me —"

"Luchresi cannot tell Amontillado from Sherry."

15   "And yet some fools will have it that his taste is a match for your own."

"Come, let us go."

"Whither?"

"To your vaults."

"My friend, no; I will not impose upon your good nature. I perceive you have an engagement. Luchresi —"

20   "I have no engagement; — come."

"My friend, no. It is not the engagement, but the severe cold with which I perceive you are afflicted. The vaults are insufferably damp. They are encrusted with nitre."°

"Let us go, nevertheless. The cold is merely nothing. Amontillado! You have been imposed upon. And as for Luchresi, he cannot distinguish Sherry from Amontillado."

Thus speaking, Fortunato possessed himself of my arm; and putting on a mask of black silk and drawing a *roquelaire*° closely about my person, I suffered him to hurry me to my palazzo.

---

motley: The many-colored attire of a court jester.

pipe: In the United States and England, a cask containing a volume equal to 126 gallons.

Amontillado: A pale, dry sherry; literally, a wine "from Montilla" (Spain).

nitre: Mineral deposits.

roquelaire: A short cloak.

There were no attendants at home; they had absconded to make merry in honor of the time. I had told them that I should not return until the morning, and had given them explicit orders not to stir from the house. These orders were sufficient, I well knew, to insure their immediate disappearance, one and all, as soon as my back was turned.

I took from their sconces two flambeaux, and giving one to Fortunato, bowed 25 him through several suites of rooms to the archway that led into the vaults. I passed down a long and winding staircase, requesting him to be cautious as he followed. We came at length to the foot of the descent, and stood together upon the damp ground of the catacombs of the Montresors.

The gait of my friend was unsteady, and the bells upon his cap jingled as he strode.

"The pipe," he said.

"It is farther on," said I; "but observe the white web-work which gleams from these cavern walls."

He turned towards me, and looked into my eyes with two filmy orbs that distilled the rheum of intoxication.

"Nitre?" he asked at length. 30

"Nitre," I replied. "How long have you had that cough?"

"Ugh! ugh! ugh! — ugh! ugh! ugh! — ugh! ugh! ugh! — ugh! ugh! ugh! — ugh! ugh! ugh!"

My poor friend found it impossible to reply for many minutes.

"It is nothing," he said at last.

"Come," I said, with decision, "we will go back; your health is precious. You 35 are rich, respected, admired, beloved; you are happy, as once I was. You are a man to be missed. For me it is no matter. We will go back; you will be ill, and I cannot be responsible. Besides, there is Luchresi —"

"Enough," he said; "the cough is a mere nothing; it will not kill me. I shall not die of a cough."

"True — true," I replied; "and, indeed, I had no intention of alarming you unnecessarily — but you should use all proper caution. A draught of this Médoc° will defend us from the damps."

Here I knocked off the neck of a bottle which I drew from a long row of its fellows that lay upon the mould.

"Drink," I said, presenting him the wine.

He raised it to his lips with a leer. He paused and nodded to me familiarly, 40 while his bells jingled.

"I drink," he said, "to the buried that repose around us."

"And I to your long life."

He again took my arm, and we proceeded.

Médoc: A red wine from the Médoc district, near Bordeaux, France.

"These vaults," he said, "are extensive."

45   "The Montresors," I replied, "were a great and numerous family."

"I forget your arms."

"A huge human foot d'or, in a field azure; the foot crushes a serpent rampant whose fangs are imbedded in the heel."

"And the motto?"

"*Nemo me impune lacessit.*"°

50   "Good!" he said.

The wine sparkled in his eyes and the bells jingled. My own fancy grew warm with the Médoc. We had passed through long walls of piled skeletons, with casks and puncheons° intermingling, into the inmost recesses of the catacombs. I paused again, and this time I made bold to seize Fortunato by an arm above the elbow.

"The nitre!" I said; "see, it increases. It hangs like moss upon the vaults. We are below the river's bed. The drops of moisture trickle among the bones. Come, we will go back ere it is too late. Your cough —"

"It is nothing," he said; "let us go on. But first, another draught of the Médoc."

I broke and reached him a flagon of De Grâve.° He emptied it at a breath. His eyes flashed with a fierce light. He laughed and threw the bottle upwards with a gesticulation I did not understand.

55   I looked at him in surprise. He repeated the movement — a grotesque one.

"You do not comprehend?" he said.

"Not I," I replied.

"Then you are not of the brotherhood."

"How?"

60   "You are not of the masons."°

"Yes, yes," I said; "yes, yes."

"You? Impossible! A mason?"

"A mason," I replied.

"A sign," he said, "a sign."

65   "It is this," I answered, producing from beneath the folds of my *roquelaire* a trowel.

"You jest," he exclaimed, recoiling a few paces. "But let us proceed to the Amontillado."

"Be it so," I said, replacing the tool beneath the cloak and again offering him my arm. He leaned upon it heavily. We continued our route in search of the

---

Nemo me impune lacessit: "No one insults me with impunity" (Latin); this is the legend on the royal coat of arms of Scotland.

puncheons: Barrels.

De Grâve: Correctly, "Graves," a light wine from the Bordeaux area.

masons: Freemasons (members of a secret fraternity). The trowel is a symbol of their alleged origin as a guild of stonemasons.

Amontillado. We passed through a range of low arches, descended, passed on, and descending again, arrived at a deep crypt, in which the foulness of the air caused our flambeaux rather to glow than flame.

At the most remote end of the crypt there appeared another less spacious. Its walls had been lined with human remains, piled to the vault overhead, in the fashion of the great catacombs of Paris. Three sides of this interior crypt were still ornamented in this manner. From the fourth side the bones had been thrown down, and lay promiscuously upon the earth, forming at one point a mound of some size. Within the wall thus exposed by the displacing of the bones, we perceived a still interior crypt or recess, in depth about four feet, in width three, in height six or seven. It seemed to have been constructed for no especial use within itself, but formed merely the interval between two of the colossal supports of the roof of the catacombs, and was backed by one of their circumscribing walls of solid granite.

It was in vain that Fortunato, uplifting his dull torch, endeavored to pry into the depth of the recess. Its termination the feeble light did not enable us to see.

"Proceed," I said; "herein is the Amontillado. As for Luchresi — " 70

"He is an ignoramus," interrupted my friend, as he stepped unsteadily forward, while I followed immediately at his heels. In an instant he had reached the extremity of the niche, and finding his progress arrested by the rock, stood stupidly bewildered. A moment more and I had fettered him to the granite. In its surface were two iron staples, distant from each other about two feet, horizontally. From one of these depended a short chain, from the other a padlock. Throwing the links about his waist, it was but the work of a few seconds to secure it. He was too much astounded to resist. Withdrawing the key I stepped back from the recess.

"Pass your hand," I said, "over the wall; you cannot help feeling the nitre. Indeed, it is *very* damp. Once more let me *implore* you to return. No? Then I must positively leave you. But I must first render you all the little attentions in my power."

"The Amontillado!" ejaculated my friend, not yet recovered from his astonishment.

"True," I replied; "the Amontillado."

As I said these words I busied myself among the pile of bones of which I have 75 before spoken. Throwing them aside, I soon uncovered a quantity of building stone and mortar. With these materials and with the aid of my trowel, I began vigorously to wall up the entrance of the niche.

I had scarcely laid the first tier of the masonry when I discovered that the intoxication of Fortunato had in a great measure worn off. The earliest indication I had of this was a low moaning cry from the depth of the recess. It was *not* the cry of a drunken man. There was a long and obstinate silence. I laid the second tier, and the third, and the fourth; and then I heard the furious vibrations of the chain. The noise lasted for several minutes, during which, that I might hearken to it with the more satisfaction, I ceased my labors and sat down upon the bones. When at last the clanking subsided, I resumed the trowel, and finished without interruption the fifth, the sixth, and the seventh tier. The wall was now nearly upon a level with my breast. I again paused, and holding the flambeaux over the mason-work, threw a few feeble rays upon the figure within.

A succession of loud and shrill screams, bursting suddenly from the throat of the chained form, seemed to thrust me violently back. For a brief moment I hesitated, I trembled. Unsheathing my rapier, I began to grope with it about the recess; but the thought of an instant reassured me. I placed my hand upon the solid fabric of the catacombs, and felt satisfied. I reapproached the wall; I replied to the yells of him who clamoured. I re-echoed, I aided, I surpassed them in volume and in strength. I did this, and the clamourer grew still.

It was now midnight, and my task was drawing to a close. I had completed the eighth, the ninth and the tenth tier. I had finished a portion of the last and the eleventh; there remained but a single stone to be fitted and plastered in. I struggled with its weight; I placed it partially in its destined position. But now there came from out the niche a low laugh that erected the hairs upon my head. It was succeeded by a sad voice, which I had difficulty in recognizing as that of the noble Fortunato. The voice said —

"Ha! ha! ha! — he! he! he! — a very good joke, indeed — an excellent jest. We will have many a rich laugh about it at the palazzo — he! he! he! — over our wine — he! he! he!"

80   "The Amontillado!" I said.

"He! he! he! — he! he! he! — yes, the Amontillado. But is it not getting late? Will not they be awaiting us at the palazzo, the Lady Fortunato and the rest? Let us be gone."

"Yes," I said, "let us be gone."

"For the love of God, Montresor!"

"Yes," I said, "for the love of God."

85   But to these words I hearkened in vain for a reply. I grew impatient. I called aloud —

"Fortunato!"

No answer. I called again —

"Fortunato!"

No answer still. I thrust a torch through the remaining aperture and let it fall within. There came forth in return only a jingling of the bells. My heart grew sick; it was the dampness of the catacombs that made it so. I hastened to make an end of my labour. I forced the last stone into its position; I plastered it up. Against the new masonry I re-erected the old rampart of bones. For the half of a century no mortal has disturbed them. *In pace requiescat!*°

Reading and Reacting

1. Montresor cites a "thousand injuries" and an "insult" as his motivation for murdering Fortunato. Given what you learn about the two men during the course of the story, what do you suppose the "injuries" and "insult" might be?

pace requiescat: "May he rest in peace" (Latin).

2. Do you find Montresor to be a reliable narrator? If not, what makes you question his version of events?

3. What is Montresor's concept of personal honor? Is it consistent or inconsistent with the values of contemporary American society? How relevant are the story's ideas about revenge and guilt to present-day society? Explain.

4. Does Fortunato ever understand why Montresor hates him? What is Fortunato's attitude toward Montresor?

5. What is the significance of Montresor's family coat of arms and motto? What is the significance of Fortunato's costume?

6. In what ways does Montresor manipulate Fortunato? What weaknesses does Montresor exploit?

7. Why does Montresor wait fifty years to tell his story? How might the story be different if he had told it the morning after the murder?

8. Why does Montresor wait for a reply before he puts the last stone in position? What do you think he wants Fortunato to say?

9. JOURNAL ENTRY Do you think the use of a first-person point of view makes you more sympathetic toward Montresor than you would be if his story were told by a third-person narrator? Why or why not?

10. CRITICAL PERSPECTIVE In his discussion of this story in *Edgar Allan Poe: A Study of the Short Fiction*, Charles E. May says, "We can legitimately hypothesize that the listener is a priest and that Montresor is an old man who is dying and making final confession. . . ."

Do you agree or disagree with May's hypothesis? Do you think that Montresor has atoned for his sin? Who else could be listening to Montresor's story?

Related Works: "A Rose for Emily" (p. 113), "Porphyria's Lover" (p. 480), *Tape* (p. 741), *Trifles* (p. 770)

WILLIAM FAULKNER (1897–1962) (picture and biography on p. 113) "Barn Burning" (1939) marks the first appearance of the Snopes clan in Faulkner's fiction. These crafty and unappealing tenant farmers and traders run roughshod over the aristocratic families of Yoknapatawpha County in three Faulkner novels: *The Hamlet* (1940), *The Town* (1957), and *The Mansion* (1959). According to Ben Wasson in *Count No Count*, Faulkner once told a friend that "somebody said I was a genius writer. The only thing I'd claim genius for is thinking up that name *Snopes*." In Southern literary circles, at least, the name "Snopes" still serves as a shorthand term for the graceless and greedy (but frequently successful) opportunists of the "New South."

Barn Burning   (1939)

The store in which the Justice of the Peace's court was sitting smelled of cheese. The boy, crouched on his nail keg at the back of the crowded room, knew he smelled cheese, and more: from where he sat he could see the ranked shelves close-packed with the solid, squat, dynamic shapes of tin cans whose labels his stomach read, not from the lettering which meant nothing to his mind but from the scarlet devils and the silver curve of fish — this, the cheese which he knew he smelled and the hermetic° meat which his intestines believed he smelled coming in intermittent gusts momentary and brief between the other constant one, the smell and sense just a little of fear because mostly of despair and grief, the old fierce pull of blood. He could not see the table where the Justice sat and before which his father and his father's enemy (*our enemy* he thought in that despair; *ourn! mine and hisn both! He's my father!*) stood, but he could hear them, the two of them that is, because his father had said no word yet:

"But what proof have you, Mr. Harris?"

"I told you. The hog got into my corn. I caught it up and sent it back to him. He had no fence that would hold it. I told him so, warned him. The next time I put the hog in my pen. When he came to get it I gave him enough wire to patch up his pen. The next time I put the hog up and kept it. I rode down to his house and saw the wire I gave him still rolled on to the spool in his yard. I told him he could have the hog when he paid me a dollar pound fee. That evening a nigger came with the dollar and got the hog. He was a strange nigger. He said, 'He say to tell you wood and hay kin burn. I said, 'What?' 'That whut he say to tell you,' the nigger said. 'Wood and hay kin burn.' That night my barn burned. I got the stock out but I lost the barn."

"Where is the nigger? Have you got him?"

5   "He was a strange nigger, I tell you. I don't know what became of him."

"But that's not proof. Don't you see that's not proof?"

"Get that boy up here. He knows." For a moment the boy thought too that the man meant his older brother until Harris said, "Not him. The little one. The boy," and, crouching, small for his age, small and wiry like his father, in patched and faded jeans even too small for him, with straight, uncombed, brown hair and eyes gray and wild as storm scud, he saw the men between himself and the table part and become a lane of grim faces, at the end of which he saw the Justice, a shabby, collarless, graying man in spectacles, beckoning him. He felt no floor under his bare feet; he seemed to walk beneath the palpable weight of the grim turning faces. His father, stiff in his black Sunday coat donned not for the trial but for the moving, did not even look at him. *He aims for me to lie*, he thought, again with that frantic grief and despair. *And I will have to do hit.*

"What's your name, boy?" the Justice said.

"Colonel Sartoris Snopes," the boy whispered.

10   "Hey?" the Justice said. "Talk louder. Colonel Sartoris? I reckon anybody named for Colonel Sartoris in this country can't help but tell the truth, can they?" The boy said nothing. *Enemy! Enemy!* he thought; for a moment he could not even see, could not see that the Justice's face was kindly nor discern that his voice was troubled when he spoke to the man named Harris: "Do you want me to ques-

---

hermetic: Canned.

tion this boy?" But he could hear, and during those subsequent long seconds while there was absolutely no sound in the crowded little room save that of quiet and intent breathing it was as if he had swung outward at the end of a grape vine, over a ravine, and at the top of the swing had been caught in a prolonged instant of mesmerized gravity, weightless in time.

"No!" Harris said violently, explosively. "Damnation! Send him out of here!" Now time, the fluid world, rushed beneath him again, the voices coming to him again through the smell of cheese and sealed meat, the fear and despair and the old grief of blood:

"This case is closed. I can't find against you, Snopes, but I can give you advice. Leave this country and don't come back to it."

His father spoke for the first time, his voice cold and harsh, level, without emphasis: "I aim to. I don't figure to stay in a country among people who . . ." he said something unprintable and vile, addressed to no one.

"That'll do," the Justice said. "Take your wagon and get out of this country before dark. Case dismissed."

His father turned, and he followed the stiff black coat, the wiry figure walking 15 a little stiffly from where a Confederate provost's man's° musket ball had taken him in the heel on a stolen horse thirty years ago, followed the two backs now, since his older brother had appeared from somewhere in the crowd, no taller than the father but thicker, chewing tobacco steadily, between the two lines of grim-faced men and out of the store and across the worn gallery and down the sagging steps and among the dogs and half-grown boys in the mild May dust, where as he passed a voice hissed:

"Barn burner!"

Again he could not see, whirling; there was a face in a red haze, moonlike, bigger than the full moon, the owner of it half again his size, he leaping in the red haze toward the face, feeling no blow, feeling no shock when his head struck the earth, scrabbling up and leaping again, feeling no blow this time either and tasting no blood, scrabbling up to see the other boy in full flight and himself already leaping into pursuit as his father's hand jerked him back, the harsh, cold voice speaking above him: "Go get in the wagon."

It stood in a grove of locusts and mulberries across the road. His two hulking sisters in their Sunday dresses and his mother and her sister in calico and sunbonnets were already in it, sitting on and among the sorry residue of the dozen and more movings which even the boy could remember — the battered stove, the broken beds and chairs, the clock inlaid with mother-of-pearl, which would not run, stopped at some fourteen minutes past two o'clock of a dead and forgotten day and time, which had been his mother's dowry. She was crying, though when she saw him she drew her sleeve across her face and began to descend from the wagon. "Get back," the father said.

"He's hurt. I got to get some water and wash his . . ."

---

provost's man's: Military policeman's.

20   "Get back in the wagon," his father said. He got in too, over the tail-gate. His father mounted to the seat where the older brother already sat and struck the gaunt mules two savage blows with the peeled willow, but without heat. It was not even sadistic; it was exactly that same quality which in later years would cause his descendants to overrun the engine before putting a motor car into motion, striking and reining back in the same movement. The wagon went on, the store with its quiet crowd of grimly watching men dropped behind; a curve in the road hid it. *Forever* he thought. *Maybe he's done satisfied now, now that he has* . . . stopping himself, not to say it aloud even to himself. His mother's hand touched his shoulder.

"Does hit hurt?" she said.

"Naw," he said. "Hit don't hurt. Lemme be."

"Can't you wipe some of the blood off before hit dries?"

"I'll wash to-night," he said. "Lemme be, I tell you."

25   The wagon went on. He did not know where they were going. None of them ever did or ever asked, because it was always somewhere, always a house of sorts waiting for them a day or two days or even three days away. Likely his father had already arranged to make a crop on another farm before he . . . Again he had to stop himself. He (the father) always did. There was something about his wolf-like independence and even courage when the advantage was at least neutral which impressed strangers, as if they got from his latent ravening ferocity not so much a sense of dependability as a feeling that his ferocious conviction in the rightness of his own actions would be of advantage to all whose interest lay with his.

That night they camped, in a grove of oaks and beeches where a spring ran. The nights were still cool and they had a fire against it, of a rail lifted from a nearby fence and cut into lengths — a small fire, neat, niggard almost, a shrewd fire; such fires were his father's habit and custom always, even in freezing weather. Older, the boy might have remarked this and wondered why not a big one; why should not a man who had not only seen the waste and extravagance of war, but who had in his blood an inherent voracious prodigality with material not his own, have burned everything in sight? Then he might have gone a step farther and thought that that was the reason: that niggard blaze was the living fruit of nights passed during those four years in the woods hiding from all men, blue or gray, with his strings of horses (captured horses, he called them). And older still, he might have divined the true reason: that the element of fire spoke to some deep mainspring of his father's being, as the element of steel or of powder spoke to other men, as the one weapon for the preservation of integrity, else breath were not worth the breathing, and hence to be regarded with respect and used with discretion.

But he did not think this now and he had seen those same niggard blazes all his life. He merely ate his supper beside it and was already half asleep over his iron plate when his father called him, and once more he followed the stiff back, the stiff and ruthless limp, up the slope and on to the starlit road where, turning, he could see his father against the stars but without face or depth — a shape black, flat, and bloodless as though cut from tin in the iron folds of the frockcoat which had not been made for him, the voice harsh like tin and without heat like tin:

"You were fixing to tell them. You would have told him." He didn't answer. His father struck him with the flat of his hand on the side of the head, hard but without heat, exactly as he had struck the two mules at the store, exactly as he would strike either of them with any stick in order to kill a horse fly, his voice still without fear or anger: "You're getting to be a man. You got to learn. You got to learn to stick to your own blood or you ain't going to have any blood to stick to you. Do you think either of them, any man there this morning, would? Don't you know all they wanted was a chance to get at me because they knew I had them beat? Eh?" Later, twenty years later, he was to tell himself, "If I had said they wanted only truth, justice, he would have hit me again." But now he said nothing. He was not crying. He just stood there. "Answer me," his father said.

"Yes," he whispered. His father turned.

"Get on to bed. We'll be there tomorrow." 30

Tomorrow they were there. In the early afternoon the wagon stopped before a paintless two-room house identical almost with the dozen others it had stopped before even in the boy's ten years, and again, as on the other dozen occasions, his mother and aunt got down and began to unload the wagon, although his two sisters and his father and brother had not moved.

"Likely hit ain't fitten for hawgs," one of the sisters said.

"Nevertheless, fit it will and you'll hog it and like it," his father said. "Get out of them chairs and help your Ma unload."

The two sisters got down, big, bovine, in a flutter of cheap ribbons; one of them drew from the jumbled wagon bed a battered lantern, the other a worn broom. His father handed the reins to the older son and began to climb stiffly over the wheel. "When they get unloaded, take the team to the barn and feed them." Then he said, and at first the boy thought he was still speaking to his brother: "Come with me."

"Me?" he said.

"Yes," his father said. "You." 35

"Abner," his mother said. His father paused and looked back — the harsh level stare beneath the shaggy, graying, irascible brows.

"I reckon I'll have a word with the man that aims to begin tomorrow owning me body and soul for the next eight months."

They went back up the road. A week ago — or before last night, that is — he would have asked where they were going, but not now. His father had struck him before last night but never before had he paused afterward to explain why; it was as if the blow and the following calm, outrageous voice still rang, repercussed, divulging nothing to him save the terrible handicap of being young, the light weight of his few years, just heavy enough to prevent his soaring free of the world as it seemed to be ordered but not heavy enough to keep him footed solid in it, to resist it and try to change the course of its events.

Presently he could see the grove of oaks and cedars and the other flowering 40 trees and shrubs, where the house would be, though not the house yet. They walked beside a fence massed with honeysuckle and Cherokee roses and came to a gate swinging open between two brick pillars, and now, beyond a sweep of drive, he saw the house for the first time and at that instant he forgot his father and the terror and despair both, and even when he remembered his father again (who had not stopped) the terror and despair did not return. Because, for all the twelve movings, they had sojourned until now in a poor country, a land of small farms and fields and houses, and he had never seen a house like this before. *Hit's big as a courthouse* he thought quietly, with a surge of peace and joy whose reason he could not have thought into words, being too young for that: *They are safe from him. People whose lives are a part of this peace and dignity are beyond his touch, he no more to them than a buzzing wasp: capable of stinging for a little moment but that's all; the spell of this peace and dignity rendering even the barns and stable and cribs which belong to it impervious to the puny flames he might contrive* . . . this, the peace and joy, ebbing for an instant as he looked again at the stiff black back, the stiff and implacable limp of the figure which was not dwarfed by the house, for the reason that it had never looked big anywhere and which now, against the serene columned backdrop, had more than ever that impervious quality of something cut ruthlessly from tin, depthless, as though, sidewise to the sun, it would cast no shadow. Watching him, the boy remarked the absolutely undeviating course which his father held and saw the stiff foot come squarely down in a pile of fresh droppings where a horse had stood in the drive and which his father could have avoided by a simple change of stride. But it ebbed only for a moment, though he could not have thought this into words either, walking on in the spell of the house, which he could even want but without envy, without sorrow, certainly never with that ravening and jealous rage which unknown to him walked in the ironlike black coat before him: *Maybe he will feel it too. Maybe it will even change him now from what maybe he couldn't help but be.*

They crossed the portico. Now he could hear his father's stiff foot as it came down on the boards with clocklike finality, a sound out of all proportion to the displacement of the body it bore and which was not dwarfed either by the white door before it, as though it had attained to a sort of vicious and ravening minimum not to be dwarfed by anything — the flat, wide, black hat, the formal coat of broadcloth which had once been black but which had now that friction-glazed greenish cast of the bodies of old house flies, the lifted sleeve which was too large, the lifted hand like a curled claw. The door opened so promptly that the boy knew the Negro must have been watching them all the time, an old man with neat grizzled hair, in a linen jacket, who stood barring the door with his body, saying, "Wipe yo foots, white man, fo you come in here. Major ain't home nohow."

"Get out of my way, nigger," his father said, without heat too, flinging the door back and the Negro also and entering, his hat still on his head. And now the boy saw the prints of the stiff foot on the doorjamb and saw them appear on the pale rug behind the machinelike deliberation of the foot which seemed to bear (or transmit) twice the weight which the body compassed. The Negro was shouting "Miss Lula! Miss Lula!" somewhere behind them, then the boy, deluged as though

by a warm wave by a suave turn of carpeted stair and a pendant glitter of chande-
liers and a mute gleam of gold frames, heard the swift feet and saw her too, a
lady — perhaps he had never seen her like before either — in a gray, smooth gown
with lace at the throat and an apron tied at the waist and the sleeves turned back,
wiping cake or biscuit dough from her hands with a towel as she came up the hall,
looking not at his father at all but at the tracks on the blond rug with an expression of incredulous amazement.

"I tried," the Negro cried, "I tole him to . . ."

"Will you please go away?" she said in a shaking voice. "Major de Spain is not
at home. Will you please go away?"

His father had not spoken again. He did not speak again. He did not even look 45
at her. He just stood stiff in the center of the rug, in his hat, the shaggy iron-gray
brows twitching slightly above the pebble-colored eyes as he appeared to examine the house with brief deliberation. Then with the same deliberation he turned;
the boy watched him pivot on the good leg and saw the stiff foot drag round the
arc of the turning, leaving a final long and fading smear. His father never looked
at it, he never once looked down at the rug. The Negro held the door. It closed
behind them, upon the hysteric and indistinguishable woman-wail. His father
stopped at the top of the steps and scraped his boot clean on the edge of it. At the
gate he stopped again. He stood for a moment, planted stiffly on the stiff foot,
looking back at the house. "Pretty and white, ain't it?" he said. "That's sweat. Nigger sweat. Maybe it ain't white enough yet to suit him. Maybe he wants to mix
some white sweat with it."

Two hours later the boy was chopping wood behind the house within which
his mother and aunt and the two sisters (the mother and aunt, not the two girls,
he knew that; even at this distance and muffled by walls the flat loud voices of the
two girls emanated an incorrigible idle inertia) were setting up the stove to prepare a meal, when he heard the hooves and saw the linen-clad man on a fine sorrel mare, whom he recognized even before he saw the rolled rug in front of the
Negro youth following on a fat bay carriage horse — a suffused, angry face vanishing, still at full gallop, beyond the corner of the house where his father and
brother were sitting in the two tilted chairs; and a moment later, almost before he
could have put the axe down, he heard the hooves again and watched the sorrel
mare go back out of the yard, already galloping again. Then his father began to
shout one of the sisters' names, who presently emerged backward from the
kitchen door dragging the rolled rug along the ground by one end while the other
sister walked behind it.

"If you ain't going to tote, go on and set up the wash pot," the first said.

"You, Sarty!" the second shouted. "Set up the wash pot!" His father appeared
at the door, framed against that shabbiness, as he had been against that other
bland perfection, impervious to either, the mother's anxious face at his shoulder.

"Go on," the father said. "Pick it up." The two sisters stooped, broad, lethargic; stooping, they presented an incredible expanse of pale cloth and a flutter of
tawdry ribbons.

50   "If I thought enough of a rug to have to git hit all the way from France I wouldn't keep hit where folks coming in would have to tromp on hit," the first said. They raised the rug.

"Abner," the mother said. "Let me do it."

"You go back and git dinner," his father said. "I'll tend to this."

From the woodpile through the rest of the afternoon the boy watched them, the rug spread flat in the dust beside the bubbling wash-pot, the two sisters stooping over it with that profound and lethargic reluctance, while the father stood over them in turn, implacable and grim, driving them though never raising his voice again. He could smell the harsh homemade lye° they were using; he saw his mother come to the door once and look toward them with an expression not anxious now but very like despair; he saw his father turn, and he fell to with the axe and saw from the corner of his eye his father raise from the ground a flattish fragment of field stone and examine it and return to the pot, and this time his mother actually spoke: "Abner. Abner. Please don't. Please, Abner."

Then he was done too. It was dusk; the whippoorwills had already begun. He could smell coffee from the room where they would presently eat the cold food remaining from the mid-afternoon meal, though when he entered the house he realized they were having coffee again probably because there was a fire on the hearth, before which the rug now lay spread over the backs of the two chairs. The tracks of his father's foot were gone. Where they had been were now long, water-cloudy scoriations resembling the sporadic course of a Lilliputian mowing machine.

55   It still hung there while they ate the cold food and then went to bed, scattered without order or claim up and down the two rooms, his mother in one bed, where his father would later lie, the older brother in the other, himself, the aunt, and the two sisters on pallets on the floor. But his father was not in bed yet. The last thing the boy remembered was the depthless, harsh silhouette of the hat and coat bending over the rug and it seemed to him that he had not even closed his eyes when the silhouette was standing over him, the fire almost dead behind it, the stiff foot prodding him awake. "Catch up the mule," his father said.

When he returned with the mule his father was standing in the black door, the rolled rug over his shoulder. "Ain't you going to ride?" he said.

"No. Give me your foot."

He bent his knee into his father's hand, the wiry, surprising power flowed smoothly, rising, he rising with it, on to the mule's bare back (they had owned a saddle once; the boy could remember it though not when or where) and with the same effortlessness his father swung the rug up in front of him. Now in the starlight they retraced the afternoon's path, up the dusty road rife with honeysuckle, through the gate and up the black tunnel to the drive to the lightless

---

lye: A soap made from wood ashes and water, unsuitable for washing fine fabrics.

house, where he sat on the mule and felt the rough warp of the rug drag across his thighs and vanish.

"Don't you want me to help?" he whispered. His father did not answer and now he heard again that stiff foot striking the hollow portico with that wooden and clocklike deliberation, that outrageous overstatement of the weight it carried. The rug, hunched, not flung (the boy could tell that even in the darkness) from his father's shoulder struck the angle of wall and floor with a sound unbelievably loud, thunderous, then the foot again, unhurried and enormous; a light came on in the house and the boy sat, tense, breathing steadily and quietly and just a little fast, though the foot itself did not increase its beat at all, descending the steps now; now the boy could see him.

"Don't you want to ride now?" he whispered. "We kin both ride now," the **60** light within the house altering now, flaring up and sinking. *He's coming down the stairs now,* he thought. He had already ridden the mule up beside the horse block; presently his father was up behind him and he doubled the reins over and slashed the mule across the neck, but before the animal could begin to trot the hard, thin arm came round him, the hard, knotted hand jerking the mule back to a walk.

In the first red rays of the sun they were in the lot, putting plow gear on the mules. This time the sorrel mare was in the lot before he heard it at all, the rider collarless and even bareheaded, trembling, speaking in a shaking voice as the woman in the house had done, his father merely looking up once before stooping again to the hame° he was buckling, so that the man on the mare spoke to his stooping back:

"You must realize you have ruined that rug. Wasn't there anybody here, any of your women . . ." he ceased, shaking, the boy watching him, the older brother leaning now in the stable door, chewing, blinking slowly and steadily at nothing apparently. "It cost a hundred dollars. But you never had a hundred dollars. You never will. So I'm going to charge you twenty bushels of corn against your crop. I'll add it in your contract and when you come to the commissary you can sign it. That won't keep Mrs. de Spain quiet but maybe it will teach you to wipe your feet off before you enter her house again."

Then he was gone. The boy looked at his father, who still had not spoken or even looked up again, who was now adjusting the loggerhead in the hame.

"Pap," he said. His father looked at him — the inscrutable face, the shaggy brows beneath which the gray eyes glinted coldly. Suddenly the boy went toward him, fast, stopping as suddenly. "You done the best you could!" he cried. "If he wanted hit done different why didn't he wait and tell you how? He won't git no twenty bushels! He won't git none! We'll gether hit and hide hit! I kin watch . . ."

"Did you put the cutter back in that straight stock like I told you?" **65**

"No, sir," he said.

---

hame: Harness.

"Then go do it."

That was Wednesday. During the rest of that week he worked steadily, at what was within his scope and some which was beyond it, with an industry that did not need to be driven nor even commanded twice; he had this from his mother, with the difference that some at least of what he did he liked to do, such as splitting wood with the half-size axe which his mother and aunt had earned, or saved money somehow, to present him with at Christmas. In company with the two older women (and on one afternoon, even one of the sisters), he built pens for the shoat and the cow which were a part of his father's contract with the landlord, and one afternoon, his father being absent, gone somewhere on one of the mules, he went to the field.

They were running a middle buster now, his brother holding the plow straight while he handled the reins, and walking beside the straining mule, the rich black soil shearing cool and damp against his bare ankles, he thought *Maybe this is the end of it. Maybe even that twenty bushels that seems hard to have to pay for just a rug will be a cheap price for him to stop forever and always from being what he used to be*; thinking, dreaming now, so that his brother had to speak sharply to him to mind the mule: *Maybe he even won't collect the twenty bushels. Maybe it will all add up and balance and vanish — corn, rug, fire; the terror and grief, the being pulled two ways like between two teams of horses — gone, done with for ever and ever.*

70   Then it was Saturday; he looked up from beneath the mule he was harnessing and saw his father in the black coat and hat. "Not that," his father said. "The wagon gear." And then, two hours later, sitting in the wagon bed behind his father and brother on the seat, the wagon accomplished a final curve, and he saw the weathered paintless store with its tattered tobacco- and patent-medicine posters and the tethered wagons and saddle animals below the gallery. He mounted the gnawed steps behind his father and brother, and there again was the lane of quiet, watching faces for the three of them to walk through. He saw the man in spectacles sitting at the plank table and he did not need to be told this was a Justice of the Peace; he sent one glare of fierce, exultant, partisan defiance at the man in collar and cravat now, whom he had seen but twice before in his life, and that on a galloping horse, who now wore on his face an expression not of rage but of amazed unbelief which the boy could not have known was at the incredible circumstance of being sued by one of his own tenants, and came and stood against his father and cried at the Justice: "He ain't done it! He ain't burnt . . ."

"Go back to the wagon," his father said.

"Burnt?" the Justice said. "Do I understand this rug was burned too?"

"Does anybody here claim it was?" his father said. "Go back to the wagon." But he did not, he merely retreated to the rear of the room, crowded as that other had been, but not to sit down this time, instead, to stand pressing among the motionless bodies, listening to the voices:

"And you claim twenty bushels of corn is too high for the damage you did to the rug?"

"He brought the rug to me and said he wanted the tracks washed out of it. I 75 washed the tracks out and took the rug back to him."

"But you didn't carry the rug back to him in the same condition it was in before you made the tracks on it."

His father did not answer, and now for perhaps half a minute there was no sound at all save that of breathing, the faint, steady suspiration of complete and intent listening.

"You decline to answer that, Mr. Snopes?" Again his father did not answer. "I'm going to find against you, Mr. Snopes. I'm going to find that you were responsible for the injury to Major de Spain's rug and hold you liable for it. But twenty bushels of corn seems a little high for a man in your circumstances to have to pay. Major de Spain claims it cost a hundred dollars. October corn will be worth about fifty cents. I figure that if Major de Spain can stand a ninety-five dollar loss on something he paid cash for, you can stand a five-dollar loss you haven't earned yet. I hold you in damages to Major de Spain to the amount of ten bushels of corn over and above your contract with him, to be paid to him out of your crop at gathering time. Court adjourned."

It had taken no time hardly, the morning was but half begun. He thought they would return home and perhaps back to the field, since they were late, far behind all other farmers. But instead his father passed on behind the wagon, merely indicating with his hand for the older brother to follow with it, and crossed the road toward the blacksmith shop opposite, pressing on after his father, overtaking him, speaking, whispering up at the harsh, calm face beneath the weathered hat: "He won't git no ten bushels neither. He won't git one. We'll . . ." until his father glanced for an instant down at him, the face absolutely calm, the grizzled eyebrows tangled above the cold eyes, the voice almost pleasant, almost gentle:

"You think so? Well, we'll wait till October anyway." 80

The matter of the wagon — the setting of a spoke or two and the tightening of the tires — did not take long either, the business of the tires accomplished by driving the wagon into the spring branch behind the shop and letting it stand there, the mules nuzzling into the water from time to time, and the boy on the seat with the idle reins, looking up the slope and through the sooty tunnel of the shed where the slow hammer rang and where his father sat on an upended cypress bolt, easily, either talking or listening, still sitting there when the boy brought the dripping wagon up out of the branch and halted it before the door.

"Take them on to the shade and hitch," his father said. He did so and returned. His father and the smith and a third man squatting on his heels inside the door were talking, about crops and animals; the boy, squatting too in the ammoniac dust and hoof-parings and scales of rust, heard his father tell a long and unhurried story out of the time before the birth of the older brother even when he had been a professional horsetrader. And then his father came up beside him where he stood before a tattered last year's circus poster on the other side of the store, gazing rapt and quiet at the scarlet horses, the incredible poisings and convolutions of tulle and tights and the painted leers of comedians, and said, "It's time to eat."

But not at home. Squatting beside his brother against the front wall, he watched his father emerge from the store and produce from a paper sack a segment of cheese and divide it carefully and deliberately into three with his pocket knife and produce crackers from the same sack. They all three squatted on the gallery and ate, slowly, without talking; then in the store again, they drank from a tin dipper tepid water smelling of the cedar bucket and of living beech trees. And still they did not go home. It was a horse lot this time, a tall rail fence upon and along which men stood and sat and out of which one by one horses were led, to be walked and trotted and then cantered back and forth along the road while the slow swapping and buying went on and the sun began to slant westward, they — the three of them — watching and listening, the older brother with his muddy eyes and his steady, inevitable tobacco, the father commenting now and then on certain of the animals, to no one in particular.

It was after sundown when they reached home. They ate supper by lamplight, then, sitting on the doorstep, the boy watched the night fully accomplish, listening to the whippoorwills and the frogs, when he heard his mother's voice: "Abner! No! No! Oh, God. Oh, God. Abner!" and he rose, whirled, and saw the altered light through the door where a candle stub now burned in a bottle neck on the table and his father, still in the hat and coat, at once formal and burlesque as though dressed carefully for some shabby and ceremonial violence, emptying the reservoir of the lamp back into the five-gallon kerosene can from which it had been filled, while the mother tugged at his arm until he shifted the lamp to the other hand and flung her back, not savagely or viciously, just hard, into the wall, her hands flung out against the wall for balance, her mouth open and in her face the same quality of hopeless despair as had been in her voice. Then his father saw him standing in the door.

85   "Go to the barn and get that can of oil we were oiling the wagon with," he said. The boy did not move. Then he could speak.

"What . . ." he cried. "What are you . . ."

"Go get that oil," his father said. "Go."

Then he was moving, running, outside the house, toward the stable: this the old habit, the old blood which he had not been permitted to choose for himself, which had been bequeathed him willy nilly and which had run for so long (and who knew where, battening on what of outrage and savagery and lust) before it came to him. *I could keep on,* he thought. *I could run on and on and never look back, never need to see his face again. Only I can't. I can't,* the rusted can in his hand now, the liquid sploshing in it as he ran back to the house and into it, into the sound of his mother's weeping in the next room, and handed the can to his father.

"Ain't you going to even send a nigger?" he cried. "At least you sent a nigger before!"

90   This time his father didn't strike him. The hand came even faster than the blow had, the same hand which had set the can on the table with almost excruciating care flashing from the can toward him too quick for him to follow it, gripping him by the back of his shirt and on to tiptoe before he had seen it quit the

can, the face stooping at him in breathless and frozen ferocity, the cold, dead voice speaking over him to the older brother who leaned against the table, chewing with that steady, curious, sidewise motion of cows:

"Empty the can into the big one and go on. I'll catch up with you."

"Better tie him to the bedpost," the brother said.

"Do like I told you," the father said. Then the boy was moving, his bunched shirt and the hard, bony hand between his shoulderblades, his toes just touching the floor, across the room and into the other one, past the sisters sitting with spread heavy thighs in the two chairs over the cold hearth, and to where his mother and aunt sat side by side on the bed, the aunt's arms about his mother's shoulders.

"Hold him," the father said. The aunt made a startled movement. "Not you," the father said. "Lennie. Take hold of him. I want to see you do it." His mother took him by the wrist. "You'll hold him better than that. If he gets loose don't you know what he is going to do? He will go up yonder." He jerked his head toward the road. "Maybe I'd better tie him."

"I'll hold him," his mother whispered.   95

"See you do then." Then his father was gone, the stiff foot heavy and measured upon the boards, ceasing at last.

Then he began to struggle. His mother caught him in both arms, he jerking and wrenching at them. He would be stronger in the end, he knew that. But he had no time to wait for it. "Lemme go!" he cried. "I don't want to have to hit you!"

"Let him go!" the aunt said. "If he don't go, before God, I am going up there myself!"

"Don't you see I can't?" his mother cried. "Sarty! Sarty! No! No! Help me, Lizzie!"

Then he was free. His aunt grasped at him but it was too late. He whirled,   100 running, his mother stumbled forward on to her knees behind him, crying to the nearest sister: "Catch him, Net! Catch him!" But that was too late too, the sister (the sisters were twins, born at the same time, yet either of them now gave the impression of being, encompassing as much living meat and volume and weight as any other two of the family) not yet having begun to rise from the chair, her head, face, alone merely turned, presenting to him in the flying instant an astonishing expanse of young female features untroubled by any surprise even, wearing only an expression of bovine interest. Then he was out of the room, out of the house, in the mild dust of the starlit road and the heavy rifeness of honeysuckle, the pale ribbon unspooling with terrific slowness under his running feet, reaching the gate at last and turning in, running, his heart and lungs drumming, on up the drive toward the lighted house, the lighted door. He did not knock, he burst in, sobbing for breath, incapable for the moment of speech; he saw the astonished face of the Negro in the linen jacket without knowing when the Negro had appeared.

"De Spain!" he cried, panted. "Where's . . ." then he saw the white man too emerging from a white door down the hall. "Barn!" he cried. "Barn!"

"What?" the white man said. "Barn?"

"Yes!" the boy cried. "Barn!"

"Catch him!" the white man shouted.

105   But it was too late this time too. The Negro grasped his shirt, but the entire sleeve, rotten with washing, carried away, and he was out that door too and in the drive again, and had actually never ceased to run even while he was screaming into the white man's face.

Behind him the white man was shouting, "My horse! Fetch my horse!" and he thought for an instant of cutting across the park and climbing the fence into the road, but he did not know the park nor how high the vine-massed fence might be and he dared not risk it. So he ran on down the drive, blood and breath roaring; presently he was in the road again though he could not see it. He could not hear either: the galloping mare was almost upon him before he heard her, and even then he held his course, as if the very urgency of his wild grief and need must in a moment more find him wings, waiting until the ultimate instant to hurl himself aside and into the weed-choked roadside ditch as the horse thundered past and on, for an instant in furious silhouette against the stars, the tranquil early summer night sky which, even before the shape of the horse and rider vanished, stained abruptly and violently upward: a long, swirling roar incredible and soundless, blotting the stars, and he springing up and into the road again, running again, knowing it was too late yet still running even after he heard the shot and, an instant later, two shots, pausing now without knowing he had ceased to run, crying "Pap! Pap!", running again before he knew he had begun to run, stumbling, tripping over something and scrabbling up again without ceasing to run, looking backward over his shoulder at the glare as he got up, running on among the invisible trees, panting, sobbing, "Father! Father!"

At midnight he was sitting on the crest of a hill. He did not know it was midnight and he did not know how far he had come. But there was no glare behind him now and he sat now, his back toward what he had called home for four days anyhow, his face toward the dark woods which he would enter when breath was strong again, small, shaking steadily in the chill darkness, hugging himself into the remainder of his thin, rotten shirt, the grief and despair now no longer terror and fear but just grief and despair. *Father. My father,* he thought. "He was brave!" he cried suddenly, aloud but not loud, no more than a whisper: "He was! He was in the war! He was in Colonel Sartoris' cav'ry!" not knowing that his father had gone to that war a private in the fine old European sense, wearing no uniform, admitting the authority of and giving fidelity to no man or army or flag, going to war as Malbrouck° himself did: for booty — it meant nothing and less than nothing to him if it were enemy booty or his own.

The slow constellations wheeled on. It would be dawn and then sunup after a while and he would be hungry. But that would be tomorrow and now he was only cold, and walking would cure that. His breathing was easier now and he decided

---

Malbrouck: A character in a popular eighteenth-century nursery rhyme about a famous warrior.

to get up and go on, and then he found that he had been asleep because he knew it was almost dawn, the night almost over. He could tell that from the whippoorwills. They were everywhere now among the dark trees below him, constant and inflectioned and ceaseless, so that, as the instant for giving over to the day birds drew nearer and nearer, there was no interval at all between them. He got up. He was a little stiff, but walking would cure that too as it would the cold, and soon there would be the sun. He went on down the hill, toward the dark woods within which the liquid silver voices of the birds called unceasing — the rapid and urgent beating of the urgent and quiring heart of the late spring night. He did not look back.

Reading and Reacting

1. Is the third-person narrator of "Barn Burning" omniscient, or is his omniscience limited? Explain.

2. What is the point of view of the italicized passages? What do you learn from them? Do they create irony? How would the story have been different without these passages?

3. "Barn Burning" includes a great deal of dialogue. How would you characterize the level of diction of this dialogue? What information about various characters does it provide?

4. What conflicts are presented in "Barn Burning"? Which, if any, are resolved in the story? Are the conflicts avoidable? Explain.

5. Why does Ab Snopes burn barns? Do you think his actions are justified? Explain your reasoning.

6. What role does the Civil War play in "Barn Burning"? What does Abner Snopes's behavior during the war tell readers about his character?

7. In the First and Second books of Samuel in the Old Testament, Abner was a relative of King Saul and commander in chief of his armies. Abner supported King Saul against David and was killed as a result of his own jealousy and rage. What, if any, significance is there in the fact that Faulkner names Ab Snopes — loyal to no man, fighter "for booty, and father of the Snopes clan" — after this mighty biblical leader?

8. Why does Sarty Snopes insist that his father was brave? How does your knowledge of events unknown to the boy affect your reactions to his defense of his father?

9. JOURNAL ENTRY How would the story be different if it were told from Ab's point of view? From Sarty's? From the point of view of Ab's wife? From the point of view of a member of a community in which the Snopeses have lived?

10. CRITICAL PERSPECTIVE Critic Edmond L. Volpe argues in his article "'Barn Burning': A Definition of Evil" that "Barn Burning" is not really about the class conflict between the sharecropping Snopeses and landowners like the de Spains but rather about Sarty:

The story is centered upon Sarty's emotional dilemma. His conflict would not have been altered in any way if the person whose barn Ab burns had been a simple poor farmer, rather than an aristocratic plantation owner. . . . Sarty's struggle is against the repressive and divisive force his father represents. The boy's anxiety is created by his awakening sense of his own individuality. Torn between strong emotional attachment to the parent and his growing need to assert his own identity, Sarty's crisis is psychological and his battle is being waged far below the level of his intellectual and moral awareness.

Do you believe "Barn Burning" is, as Volpe suggests, essentially a coming-of-age story, or do you believe it is about something else — class conflict, for example?

Related Works: "A Worn Path" (p. 319), "Baca Grande" (p. 500), "Child's Grave, Hale County, Alabama" (p. 599), *Fences* (p. 1096)

WRITING SUGGESTIONS: Point of View

1. How would Poe's "The Cask of Amontillado" be different if it were told by a minor character who observed the events? Rewrite the story from this point of view — or tell the story that precedes the story, explaining the "thousand injuries" and the "insult."

2. Assume that you are the sailor in "Big Black Good Man" and that you are keeping a journal of your travels. Write the journal entries for the time you spent in Copenhagen. Include your impressions of Olaf, Lena, the hotel, and anything else that caught your attention. Make sure you present your version of the key events described in the story — especially Olaf's reaction to you.

3. Both "The Cask of Amontillado" and "Barn Burning" deal with crimes that essentially go unpunished and with the emotions that accompany these crimes. In what sense does each story's use of point of view shape its treatment of the crime in question? For instance, how does point of view determine how much readers know about the motives for the crime, the crime's basic circumstances, and the extent to which the crime is justified?

CHAPTER 10

STYLE, TONE, AND LANGUAGE

The difference between the right word and the nearly right word is the same as that between lightning and the lightning bug.

— Mark Twain

Style and Tone

One of the qualities that gives a work of literature its individuality is its **style,** the way in which a writer uses language, selecting and arranging words to say what he or she wants to say. Style encompasses elements such as word choice; syntax; sentence length and structure; and the presence, frequency, and prominence of imagery and figures of speech.

Closely related to style is **tone,** the attitude of the narrator or author of a work toward the subject matter, characters, or audience. Word choice and sentence structure help to create a work's tone, which may be intimate or distant, bitter or affectionate, straightforward or cautious, supportive or critical, respectful or condescending. (Tone may also be **ironic;** see Chapter 9, "Point of View," for a discussion of irony.)

The Uses of Language

Language offers almost limitless possibilities to a writer. Creative use of language (such as unusual word choice, word order, or sentence structure) can enrich a story and add to its overall effect. Sometimes, in fact, a writer's use of language can expand a story's possibilities through its very inventiveness. For example, James Joyce's innovative **stream-of-consciousness** style mimics thought, allowing ideas to run into one another as random associations are made so that readers may follow and participate in the thought processes of the narrator. Here is a stream-of-consciousness passage from Joyce's experimental 1922 novel *Ulysses*.

frseeeeeeeeefronnnng train somewhere whistling the strength those engines
have in them like big giants and the water rolling all over and out of them all
sides like the end of Loves old sweet sonnnng the poor men that have to be out
all the night from their wives and families in those roasting engines stifling it
was today. . . .

Most often, language is used to enhance a story's other elements. It may, for example, help to create an atmosphere that is important to the story's plot or theme,
as Kate Chopin's lush, rhythmic sentences help to create the sexually charged atmosphere of "The Storm" (p. 158)—an atmosphere that overpowers the characters and thus drives the plot. Language may also help to delineate character,
perhaps by conveying a character's mental state to readers. For instance, the
breathless, disjointed style of Edgar Allan Poe's "The Tell-Tale Heart" (p. 409) suggests the narrator's increasing emotional instability: "Was it possible they heard not?
Almighty God!—no, no! They heard!—they suspected!—they *knew!*—they
were making a mockery of my horror!" In his 1925 short story "Big Two-Hearted
River," Ernest Hemingway uses sentences without transitions to create a flat, emotionless prose style that reveals his character's alienation and fragility as he struggles
to maintain control: "Now things were done. There had been this to do. Now it was
done. It had been a hard trip. He was very tired. That was done. He had made his
camp. He was settled. Nothing could touch him."

Language that places emphasis on the sounds and rhythm of words and sentences can also enrich a work of fiction. Consider the use of such language in the
following sentence from James Joyce's "Araby" (p. 232).

> The light from the lamp opposite our door caught the white curve of her neck,
> lit up her hair that rested there and, falling, lit up the hand upon the railing.

Here the narrator is describing his first conversation with a girl who fascinates
him, and the lush, lyrical, almost musical language reflects his enchantment.
Note in particular the **alliteration** (light/lamp; caught/curve; hair/hand), the
repetition (lit up/lit up), and the rhyme (lit up her *hair*/that rested *there*) and **near
rhyme** (falling/railing); these poetic devices connect the words of the sentence
into a smooth, rhythmic whole.

Another example of this emphasis on sound may be found in the measured **parallelism** of this sentence from Nathaniel Hawthorne's 1843 story "The Birthmark."

> He had left his laboratory to the care of an assistant, cleared his fine counte-
> nance from the furnace smoke, washed the stain of acids from his fingers, and
> persuaded a beautiful woman to become his wife.

The style of this sentence, conveying methodical precision and order, reflects the
compulsive personality of the character being described.

The following passage from Alberto Alvaro Ríos's story "The Secret Lion"
(p. 412) illustrates the power of language to enrich a story.

> We had read the books, after all; we knew about bridges and castles and
> wildtreacherousraging alligatormouth rivers. We wanted them. So we were
> going to go out and get them. We went back that morning into that kitchen

and we said, "We're going out there, we're going into the hills, we're going away for three days, don't worry." She said, "All right."

"You know," I said to Sergio, "if we're going to go away for three days, well, we ought to at least pack a lunch."

But we were two young boys with no patience for what we thought at the time was mom-stuff: making sa-and-wiches. My mother didn't offer. So we got out little kid knapsacks that my mother had sewn for us, and into them we put the jar of mustard. A loaf of bread. Knivesforksplates, bottles of Coke, a can opener. This was lunch for the two of us. And we were weighed down, humped over to be strong enough to carry this stuff. But we started walking anyway, into the hills. We were going to eat berries and stuff otherwise. "Goodbye." My mom said that.

Through language, the adult narrator of the preceding paragraphs recaptures the bravado of the boys in search of "wildtreacherousraging alligatormouth rivers" even as he suggests to readers that the boys are not going far. The story's use of language is original and inventive: words are blended together ("getridofit," "knivesforksplates"), linked to form new words ("mom-stuff"), and drawn out ("sa-and-wiches") to mimic speech. These experiments with language show the narrator's willingness to move back into a child's frame of reference while maintaining the advantage of distance. The adult narrator uses sentence fragments ("A loaf of bread."), colloquialisms ("kid," "mom," "stuff"), and contractions. He also includes conversational elements such as *you know* and *well* in the story's dialogue, accurately re-creating the childhood scene at the same time he sees its folly and remains aware of the disillusionment that awaits him. Thus, the unique style permits the narrator to bring readers with him into the child's world even as he maintains his adult stance: "But we were two young boys with no patience for what we thought at the time was mom-stuff. . . ."

Although many stylistic options are available to writers, a story's language must be consistent with the writer's purpose and with the effect he or she hopes to create. Just as writers may experiment with point of view or manipulate events to create a complex plot, so they can adjust language to suit a particular narrator or character or to convey a particular theme. In addition to the creative uses of language described above, writers also frequently experiment with *formal and informal diction*, *imagery*, and *figures of speech*.

Formal and Informal Diction

The level of diction — how formal or informal a story's language is — can reveal a good deal about those who use the language.

Formal diction is characterized by elaborate, complex sentences; a learned vocabulary; and a serious, objective, detached tone. The speaker avoids contractions, shortened word forms (like *phone*), regional expressions, and slang, and he or she may use *one* or *we* in place of *I*. At its most extreme, formal language is stiff and stilted, far removed from everyday speech.

Formal diction, whether used by a narrator or by a character, may indicate erudition, a high educational level, a superior social or professional position, or emotional detachment. When one character's language is significantly more formal than others', he or she may seem old-fashioned or stuffy; when language is inappropriately elevated or complex, it may reveal the character to be pompous or ridiculous; when a narrator's language is noticeably more formal than that of the characters, the narrator may seem superior or even condescending. Thus, the choice of a particular level (or levels) of diction in a story conveys information about characters and about the narrator's attitude toward them.

The following passage from Hawthorne's "The Birthmark" illustrates formal style.

> In the latter part of the last century there lived a man of science, an eminent proficient in every branch of natural philosophy, who not long before our story opens had made experience of a spiritual affinity more attractive than any chemical one. He had left his laboratory to the care of an assistant, cleared his fine countenance from the furnace smoke, washed the stain of acids from his fingers, and persuaded a beautiful woman to become his wife. In those days when the comparatively recent discovery of electricity and other kindred mysteries of Nature seemed to open paths into the region of miracle, it was not unusual for the love of science to rival the love of woman in its depth and absorbing energy. The higher intellect, the imagination, the spirit, and even the heart might all find their congenial ailment in pursuits which, as some of their ardent votaries believed, would ascend from one step of powerful intelligence to another, until the philosopher should lay his hand on the secret of creative force and perhaps make new worlds for himself.

The long and complex sentences, learned vocabulary ("countenance," "ailment," "votaries"), and absence of colloquialisms suit Hawthorne's purpose well, recreating the formal language of the earlier era in which his story is set. The omniscient narrator is aloof and controlled, and his diction makes this clear to readers.

Informal diction, consistent with everyday speech, is characterized by slang, contractions, colloquial expressions like *you know* and *I mean,* shortened word forms, incomplete sentences, and a casual, conversational tone. A first-person narrator may use an informal style, or characters may speak informally; in either case, informal style tends to narrow the distance between readers and text.

Informal language can range from the distinctive contemporary style of the narrator's voice in T. Coraghessan Boyle's "Greasy Lake" (p. 359) to the regionalisms and dialect used in Flannery O'Connor's "A Good Man Is Hard to Find" ("aloose"; "you all"; "britches"). In "Greasy Lake," the narrator's self-consciously slangy, conversational style reveals the naivete and false bravado that characterized his adolescence; in "A Good Man Is Hard to Find" (p. 238), speech patterns and diction help to identify the region in which the characters live and their social class. Informal language may also include language readers find offensive. In this case, a character's use of obscenities may suggest his or her crudeness or adolescent bravado, and the use of racial or ethnic slurs indicates that a character is insensitive and bigoted.

The following passage from John Updike's "A&P" (p. 128) illustrates informal style.

> She had sort of oaky hair that the sun and salt had bleached, done up in a bun that was unravelling, and a kind of prim face. Walking into the A&P with your straps down, I suppose it's the only kind of face you *can* have. She held her head so high her neck, coming out of those white shoulders, looked kind of stretched, but I didn't mind. The longer her neck was, the more of her there was.

Here, the first-person narrator, a nineteen-year-old supermarket checkout clerk, uses a conversational style, including colloquialisms ("sort of," "I suppose," "kind of"), contractions ("it's," "didn't"), and the imprecise, informal *you* ("Walking into the A&P with *your* straps down. . . ."). The narrator uses neither elaborate syntax nor a learned vocabulary.

Imagery

Imagery — words and phrases that describe what is seen, heard, smelled, tasted, or touched — can have a significant impact in a story. A writer may use a pattern of repeated imagery to convey a particular impression about a character or situation or to communicate or reinforce a story's theme. For example, the theme of newly discovered sexuality can be conveyed through repeated use of words and phrases suggesting blooming or ripening.

In "Greasy Lake," the narrator's vivid description of Greasy Lake uses rich visual imagery to evoke a scene.

> Through the center of town, up the strip, past the housing developments and shopping malls, street lights giving way to the thin streaming illumination of the headlights, trees crowding the asphalt in a black unbroken wall: that was the way out to Greasy Lake. The Indians had called it Wakan, a reference to the clarity of its waters. Now it was fetid and murky, the mud banks glittering with broken glass and strewn with beer cans and the charred remains of bonfires. There was a single ravaged island a hundred yards from shore, so stripped of vegetation it looked as if the air force had strafed it. We went up to the lake because everyone went there, because we wanted to snuff the rich scent of possibility on the breeze, watch a girl take off her clothes and plunge into the festering murk, drink beer, smoke pot, howl at the stars, savor the incongruous full-throated roar of rock and roll against the primeval susurrus of frogs and crickets. This was nature.

By characterizing a natural setting with surprising words like "fetid," "murky," and "greasy" and unpleasant images such as the "glittering of broken glass," the "ravaged island," and the "charred remains of bonfires," Boyle creates a picture that is completely at odds with the traditional view of nature. The incongruous images are nevertheless perfectly consistent with the sordid events that take place at Greasy Lake.

Figures of Speech

Figures of speech— such as *similes, metaphors,* and *personification*— can enrich a story, subtly revealing information about characters and themes.

By using **metaphors** and **similes**—figures of speech that compare two dissimilar items — writers can indicate a particular attitude toward characters and events. Thus, Flannery O'Connor's many grotesque similes in "A Good Man Is Hard to Find" help to dehumanize her characters; the children's mother, for instance, has a face "as broad and innocent as a cabbage." In Tillie Olsen's "I Stand Here Ironing" (p. 174), an extended metaphor in which a mother compares her daughter to a dress waiting to be ironed expresses the mother's attitude toward her child, effectively suggesting to readers the daughter's vulnerability. Similes and metaphors are used throughout in Kate Chopin's "The Storm" (p. 158). In a scene of sexual awakening, Calixta's skin is "like a creamy lily," her passion is "like a white flame," and her mouth is "a fountain of delight"; these figures of speech add a lushness and sensuality to the story.

Personification— a figure of speech, closely related to metaphor, that endows inanimate objects or abstract ideas with life or with human characteristics — is used in "Araby" (p. 232), where houses, "conscious of decent lives within them, gazed at one another with brown imperturbable faces." This use of figurative language expands readers' vision of the story's setting and gives a dreamlike quality to the passage. (Other figures of speech, such as **hyperbole** and **understatement,** can also enrich works of fiction. See Chapter 19, "Figures of Speech," for further information.)

Allusions— references to familiar historical, cultural, literary, or biblical texts, figures, or events — may also expand readers' understanding and appreciation of a work. An allusion widens a work's context by bringing it into the context of a related subject or idea. For instance, in Charles Baxter's short story "Gryphon" (p. 139), the narrator's allusions to Pinocchio and Betty Crocker enable readers who recognize the references to gain a deeper understanding of what a central character is really like.

> **NOTE:** In analyzing the use of language in a work of fiction, you may occasionally encounter obscure allusions (or foreign words and phrases or unfamiliar regional expressions), particularly in works treating cultures and historical periods other than your own. Frequently, such language will be clarified by the context, or by explanatory notes in your text. When it is not, you should consult a dictionary, encyclopedia, or other reference work.

> ✔ **CHECKLIST**   **Writing about Style, Tone, and Language**
>
> ☐ Does the writer make any unusual creative use of word choice, word order, or sentence structure?
>
> ☐ Is the story's tone intimate? Distant? Ironic? How does the tone advance the writer's purpose?
>
> ☐ Does the style emphasize the sound and rhythm of language? For example, does the writer use alliteration and assonance? Repetition and parallelism? What do such techniques add to the story?
>
> ☐ Is the level of diction generally formal, informal, or somewhere in between?
>
> ☐ Is there a difference between the style of the narrator and the style of the characters' speech? If so, what is the effect of this difference?
>
> ☐ Do any of the story's characters use regionalisms, colloquial language, or nonstandard speech? If so, what effect does this language have?
>
> ☐ What do different characters' levels of diction reveal about them?
>
> ☐ What kind of imagery predominates? Where, and why, is imagery used?
>
> ☐ Does the story develop a pattern of imagery? How does this pattern of imagery relate to the story's themes?
>
> ☐ Does the story use simile and metaphor? Personification? What is the effect of these figures of speech?
>
> ☐ Do figures of speech reinforce the story's themes? Reveal information about characters?
>
> ☐ Does the story make any historical, literary, or biblical allusions? What do these allusions contribute to the story?
>
> ☐ Are any unfamiliar, obscure, or foreign words, phrases, or images used in the story? What do these words or expressions contribute to the story?

JAMES JOYCE (1884–1941) was born in Dublin but lived his entire adult life in self-imposed exile from his native Ireland. Though his parents sent him to schools that trained young men for the priesthood, Joyce saw himself as a religious and artistic rebel and fled to Paris soon after graduation in 1902. Recalled briefly to Dublin by his mother's fatal illness, Joyce returned to the Continent in 1904, taking with him an uneducated Irish country girl named Nora Barnacle, who became his wife in 1931. In dreary quarters in Trieste, Zurich, and Paris, Joyce struggled to support a growing family, sometimes teaching classes in Berlitz language schools.

Though Joyce never again lived in Ireland, he continued to write about Dublin. Publication of *Dubliners* (1914), a collection of short stories that included "Araby," was delayed for seven years because the Irish publisher feared libel suits from local citizens who were thinly disguised as characters in the stories. Joyce's autobiographical *Portrait of the Artist as a Young Man* (1916) tells of a young writer's rejection of family, church, and country. *Ulysses* (1922), the comic tale of eighteen hours in the life of a wandering Dublin advertising salesman, was banned when the United States Post Office brought charges of obscenity against the book, and it remained banned in the United States and England for more than a decade. With *Ulysses,* Joyce began a revolutionary journey away from traditional techniques of plot and characterization to the interior monologues and stream-of-consciousness style that mark his last great novel, *Finnegans Wake* (1939).

Araby (1914)

North Richmond Street, being blind,° was a quiet street except at the hour when the Christian Brothers' School set the boys free. An uninhabited house of two storeys stood at the blind end, detached from its neighbours in a square ground. The other houses of the street, conscious of decent lives within them, gazed at one another with brown imperturbable faces.

The former tenant of our house, a priest, had died in the back drawing-room. Air, musty from having been long enclosed, hung in all the rooms, and the waste room behind the kitchen was littered with old useless papers. Among these I found a few paper-covered books, the pages of which were curled and damp: *The Abbot,* by Walter Scott, *The Devout Communicant* and *The Memoirs of Vidocq.*° I liked the last best because its leaves were yellow. The wild garden behind the house contained a central apple-tree and a few straggling bushes under one of which I found the late tenant's rusty bicycle-pump. He had been a very charitable priest; in his will he had left all his money to institutions and the furniture of his house to his sister.

When the short days of winter came dusk fell before we had well eaten our dinners. When we met in the street the houses had grown sombre. The space of sky above us was the colour of ever-changing violet and towards it the lamps of the street lifted their feeble lanterns. The cold air stung us and we played till our bodies glowed. Our shouts echoed in the silent street. The career of our play brought us through the dark muddy lanes behind the houses where we ran the gauntlet of the rough tribes from the cottages, to the back doors of the dark drip-

---

blind: Dead-end.

The Abbot . . . Vidocq: Sir Walter Scott (1771–1832) — an English Romantic novelist; *The Devout Communicant* — a variant title for *Pious Meditations,* written by an eighteenth-century English Franciscan friar, Pacificus Baker; *The Memoirs of Vidocq* — an autobiography of François-Jules Vidocq (1775–1857), a French criminal turned police agent.

ping gardens where odours arose from the ashpits, to the dark odorous stables where a coach-man smoothed and combed the horse or shook music from the buckled harness. When we returned to the street light from the kitchen windows had filled the areas. If my uncle was seen turning the corner we hid in the shadow until we had seen him safely housed. Or if Mangan's sister came out on the doorstep to call her brother in to his tea we watched her from our shadow peer up and down the street. We waited to see whether she would remain or go in and, if she remained, we left our shadow and walked up to Mangan's steps resignedly. She was waiting for us, her figure defined by the light from the half-opened door. Her brother always teased her before he obeyed and I stood by the railings looking at her. Her dress swung as she moved her body and the soft rope of her hair tossed from side to side.

Every morning I lay on the floor in the front parlour watching her door. The blind was pulled down to within an inch of the sash so that I could not be seen. When she came out on the doorstep my heart leaped. I ran to the hall, seized my books and followed her. I kept her brown figure always in my eye and, when we came near the point at which our ways diverged, I quickened my pace and passed her. This happened morning after morning. I had never spoken to her, except for a few casual words, and yet her name was like a summons to all my foolish blood.

Her image accompanied me even in places the most hostile to romance. On 5 Saturday evenings when my aunt went marketing I had to go to carry some of the parcels. We walked through the flaring streets, jostled by drunken men and bargaining women, amid the curses of labourers, the shrill litanies of shop-boys who stood on guard by the barrels of pigs' cheeks, the nasal chanting of street-singers, who sang a *come-all-you* about O'Donovan Rossa,° or a ballad about the troubles in our native land. These noises converged in a single sensation of life for me: I imagined that I bore my chalice safely through a throng of foes. Her name sprang to my lips at moments in strange prayers and praises which I myself did not understand. My eyes were often full of tears (I could not tell why) and at times a flood from my heart seemed to pour itself out into my bosom. I thought little of the future. I did not know whether I would ever speak to her or not or, if I spoke to her, how I could tell her of my confused adoration. But my body was like a harp and her words and gestures were like fingers running upon the wires.

One evening I went into the back drawing-room in which the priest had died. It was a dark rainy evening and there was no sound in the house. Through one of the broken panes I heard the rain impinge upon the earth, the fine incessant needles of water playing in the sodden beds. Some distant lamp or lighted window gleamed below me. I was thankful that I could see so little. All my senses

---

O'Donovan Rossa: Any popular song beginning "Come all you gallant Irishmen . . ."; O'Donovan Rossa was an Irish nationalist who was banished in 1870 for advocating violent rebellion against the British.

seemed to desire to veil themselves and, feeling that I was about to slip from them, I pressed the palms of my hands together until they trembled, murmuring: "*O love! O love!*" many times.

At last she spoke to me. When she addressed the first words to me I was so confused that I did not know what to answer. She asked me was I going to *Araby*. I forgot whether I answered yes or no. It would be a splendid bazaar, she said she would love to go.

"And why can't you?" I asked.

While she spoke she turned a silver bracelet round and round her wrist. She could not go, she said, because there would be a retreat that week in her convent.° Her brother and two other boys were fighting for their caps and I was alone at the railings. She held one of the spikes, bowing her head towards me. The light from the lamp opposite our door caught the white curve of her neck, lit up her hair that rested there and, falling, lit up the hand upon the railing. It fell over one side of her dress and caught the white border of a petticoat, just visible as she stood at ease.

"It's well for you," she said.

10   "If I go," I said, "I will bring you something."

What innumerable follies laid waste my waking and sleeping thoughts after that evening! I wished to annihilate the tedious intervening days. I chafed against the work of school. At night in my bedroom and by day in the classroom her image came between me and the page I strove to read. The syllables of the word *Araby* were called to me through the silence in which my soul luxuriated and cast an Eastern enchantment over me. I asked for leave to go to the bazaar on Saturday night. My aunt was surprised and hoped it was not some Freemason° affair. I answered few questions in class. I watched my master's face pass from amiability to sternness; he hoped I was not beginning to idle. I could not call my wandering thoughts together. I had hardly any patience with the serious work of life which, now that it stood between me and my desire, seemed to me child's play, ugly monotonous child's play.

On Saturday morning I reminded my uncle that I wished to go to the bazaar in the evening. He was fussing at the hallstand, looking for the hatbrush, and answered me curtly:

"Yes, boy, I know."

15   As he was in the hall I could not go into the front parlour and lie at the window. I left the house in bad humour and walked slowly towards the school. The air was pitilessly raw and already my heart misgave me.

When I came home to dinner my uncle had not yet been home. Still it was early. I sat staring at the clock for some time and, when its ticking began to irri-

---

convent: Her convent school.

Freemason: At the time the story takes place, many Catholics in Ireland thought the Masonic Order was a threat to the church.

tate me, I left the room. I mounted the staircase and gained the upper part of the house. The high cold empty gloomy rooms liberated me and I went from room to room singing. From the front window I saw my companions playing below in the street. Their cries reached me weakened and indistinct and, leaning my forehead against the cool glass, I looked over at the dark house where she lived. I may have stood there for an hour, seeing nothing but the brown-clad figure cast by my imagination, touched discreetly by the lamplight at the curved neck, at the hand upon the railings and at the border below the dress.

When I came downstairs again I found Mrs. Mercer sitting at the fire. She was an old garrulous woman, a pawnbroker's widow, who collected used stamps for some pious purpose. I had to endure the gossip of the tea-table. The meal was prolonged beyond an hour and still my uncle did not come. Mrs. Mercer stood up to go: she was sorry she couldn't wait any longer, but it was after eight o'clock and she did not like to be out late, as the night air was bad for her. When she had gone I began to walk up and down the room, clenching my fists. My aunt said:

"I'm afraid you may put off your bazaar for this night of Our Lord."

At nine o'clock I heard my uncle's latchkey in the halldoor. I heard him talking to himself and heard the hallstand rocking when it had received the weight of his overcoat. I could interpret these signs. When he was midway through his dinner I asked him to give me the money to go to the bazaar. He had forgotten.

"The people are in bed and after their first sleep now," he said. 20

I did not smile. My aunt said to him energetically:

"Can't you give him the money and let him go? You've kept him late enough as it is."

My uncle said he was very sorry he had forgotten. He said he believed in the old saying: "All work and no play makes Jack a dull boy." He asked me where I was going and, when I had told him a second time he asked me did I know *The Arab's Farewell to his Steed.*° When I left the kitchen he was about to recite the opening lines of the piece to my aunt.

I held a florin tightly in my hand as I strode down Buckingham Street towards the station. The sight of the streets thronged with buyers and glaring with gas recalled to me the purpose of my journey. I took my seat in a third-class carriage of a deserted train. After an intolerable delay the train moved out of the station slowly. It crept onward among ruinous houses and over the twinkling river. At Westland Row Station a crowd of people pressed to the carriage doors; but the porters moved them back, saying that it was a special train for the bazaar. I remained alone in the bare carriage. In a few minutes the train drew up beside an improvised wooden platform. I passed out on to the road and saw by the lighted dial of a clock that it was ten minutes to ten. In front of me was a large building which displayed the magical name.

The Arab's Farewell to his Steed: A sentimental poem by Caroline Norton (1808–1877) that tells the story of a nomad's heartbreak after selling his much-loved horse.

25   I could not find any sixpenny entrance and, fearing that the bazaar would be closed, I passed in quickly through a turnstile, handing a shilling to a weary-looking man. I found myself in a big hall girdled at half its height by a gallery. Nearly all the stalls were closed and the greater part of the hall was in darkness. I recognised a silence like that which pervades a church after a service. I walked into the centre of the bazaar timidly. A few people were gathered about the stalls which were still open. Before a curtain, over which the words *Café Chantant*° were written in coloured lamps, two men were counting money on a salver. I listened to the fall of the coins.

Remembering with difficulty why I had come I went over to one of the stalls and examined porcelain vases and flowered tea-sets. At the door of the stall a young lady was talking and laughing with two young gentlemen. I remarked their English accents and listened vaguely to their conversation.

"O, I never said such a thing!"

"O, but you did!"

"O, but I didn't!"

30   "Didn't she say that?"

"Yes. I heard her."

"O, there's a . . . fib!"

Observing me the young lady came over and asked me did I wish to buy anything. The tone of her voice was not encouraging; she seemed to have spoken to me out of a sense of duty. I looked humbly at the great jars that stood like eastern guards at either side of the dark entrance to the stall and murmured:

"No, thank you."

35   The young lady changed the position of one of the vases and went back to the two young men. They began to talk of the same subject. Once or twice the young lady glanced at me over her shoulder.

I lingered before her stall, though I knew my stay was useless, to make my interest in her wares seem the more real. Then I turned away slowly and walked down the middle of the bazaar. I allowed the two pennies to fall against the sixpence in my pocket. I heard a voice call from one end of the gallery that the light was out. The upper part of the hall was now completely dark.

Gazing up into the darkness I saw myself as a creature driven and derided by vanity; and my eyes burned with anguish and anger.

Reading and Reacting

1. How would you characterize the story's level of diction? Is this level appropriate for a story about a young boy's experiences? Explain.

2. Identify several figures of speech in the story. Where is Joyce most likely to use this kind of language? Why?

Café Chantant: A Paris café featuring musical entertainment.

3. What words and phrases express the boy's extreme idealism and romantic view of the world? How does such language help to communicate the story's major theme?

4. In paragraph 4, the narrator says, "her name was like a summons to all my foolish blood." In the story's last sentence, he sees himself as "a creature driven and derided by vanity." What other expressions does he use to describe his feelings? How would you characterize these feelings?

5. How does the narrator's choice of words illustrate the contrast between his day-to-day life and the exotic promise of the bazaar?

6. What does each of the italicized words suggest: "We walked through the *flaring* streets" (par. 5); "I heard the rain *impinge* upon the earth" (par. 6); "I *chafed* against the work of school" (par. 12); "I found myself in a big hall *girdled* at half its height by a gallery" (par. 25)? What other examples of unexpected word choice can you identify in the story?

7. What is it about the events in this story that causes the narrator to remember them years later?

8. Identify words and phrases in the story that are associated with religion. What purpose do these references to religion serve? Do you think they are intentional?

9. JOURNAL ENTRY Rewrite a brief passage from this story in the voice of the young boy. Use informal style, simple figures of speech, and vocabulary appropriate for a child.

10. CRITICAL PERSPECTIVE In *Notes on the American Short Story Today*, Richard Kostelanetz discusses the **epiphany,** one of Joyce's most significant contributions to literature:

> In Joyce's pervasively influential theory of the short story we remember, the fiction turned upon an epiphany, a moment of revelation in which, in [critic] Harry Levin's words, "amid the most encumbered circumstances it suddenly happens that the veil is lifted, the . . . mystery laid bare, and the ultimate secret of things made manifest." The epiphany, then, became a technique for jelling the narrative and locking the story's import into place. . . . What made this method revolutionary was the shifting of the focal point of the story from its end . . . to a spot within the body of the text, usually near (but not at) the end.

Where in "Araby" does the story's epiphany occur? Does it do all that Kostelanetz believes an epiphany should do? Or do you think that, at least in the case of "Araby," the epiphany may not be as significant a force as Kostelanetz suggests?

Related Works: "The Secret Lion" (p. 412), "A&P" (p. 128), "Gryphon" (p. 139), "Cathedral" (p. 289), "Doe Season" (p. 327), "Shall I compare thee to a summer's day?" (p. 521), *Beauty* (p. 736)

(MARY) FLANNERY O'CONNOR (1925–1964) was born to a prosperous Catholic family in Savannah, Georgia, and spent most of her adult life on a farm near the town of Milledgeville. She left the South to study writing at the University of Iowa, moving to New York to work on her first novel, *Wise Blood* (1952). On a train going south for Christmas, O'Connor became seriously ill; she was diagnosed as having lupus, the immune system disease that had killed her father and would cause O'Connor's death when she was only thirty-nine years old.

While her mother ran the farm, O'Connor spent mornings writing and afternoons wandering the fields with cane or crutches. Her short story collection *A Good Man Is Hard to Find* (1955) and an excellent French translation of *Wise Blood* established her international reputation, which was solidified with the publication of a second novel, *The Violent Bear It Away* (1960), and a posthumously published book of short stories, *Everything That Rises Must Converge* (1965).

O'Connor, said a friend, believed that an artist "should face all the truth down to the worst of it." Yet however dark, her stories are infused with grim humor and a fierce belief in the possibility of spiritual redemption, even for her most tortured characters. A line from her short story "A Good Man Is Hard to Find" says much about what O'Connor perceived about both natural things and her characters: "The trees were full of silver-white sunlight and the meanest of them sparkled." In O'Connor's work, the "meanest" things and people can sparkle, touched by a kind of holy madness and beauty.

A Good Man Is Hard to Find (1955)

The grandmother didn't want to go to Florida. She wanted to visit some of her connections in east Tennessee and she was seizing at every chance to change Bailey's mind. Bailey was the son she lived with, her only boy. He was sitting on the edge of his chair at the table, bent over the orange sports section of the *Journal*. "Now look here, Bailey," she said, "see here, read this," and she stood with one hand on her thin hip and the other rattling the newspaper at his bald head. "Here this fellow that calls himself The Misfit is aloose from the Federal Pen and headed toward Florida and you read here what it says he did to these people. Just you read it. I wouldn't take my children in any direction with a criminal like that aloose in it. I couldn't answer to my conscience if I did."

Bailey didn't look up from his reading so she wheeled around then and faced the children's mother, a young woman in slacks, whose face was as broad and innocent as a cabbage and was tied around with a green headkerchief that had two points on the top like a rabbit's ears. She was sitting on the sofa, feeding the baby his apricots out of a jar. "The children have been to Florida before," the old lady said. "You all ought to take them somewhere else for a change so they would see different parts of the world and be broad. They never have been to east Tennessee."

The children's mother didn't seem to hear her but the eight-year-old boy, John Wesley, a stocky child with glasses, said, "If you don't want to go to Florida, why dontcha stay at home?" He and the little girl, June Star, were reading the funny papers on the floor.

"She wouldn't stay at home to be queen for a day," June Star said without raising her yellow head.

"Yes and what would you do if this fellow, the Misfit, caught you?" the grand- 5
mother asked.

"I'd smack his face," John Wesley said.

"She wouldn't stay at home for a million bucks," June Star said. "Afraid she'd miss something. She has to go everywhere we go."

"All right, Miss," the grandmother said. "Just remember that the next time you want me to curl your hair."

June Star said her hair was naturally curly.

The next morning the grandmother was the first one in the car, ready to go. 10
She had her big black valise that looked like the head of a hippopotamus in one corner, and underneath it she was hiding a basket with Pitty Sing, the cat, in it. She didn't intend for the cat to be left alone in the house for three days because he would miss her too much and she was afraid he might brush against one of the gas burners and accidentally asphyxiate himself. Her son, Bailey, didn't like to arrive at a motel with a cat.

She sat in the middle of the back seat with John Wesley and June Star on either side of her. Bailey and the children's mother and the baby sat in front and they left Atlanta at eight forty-five with the mileage on the car at 55890. The grandmother wrote this down because she thought it would be interesting to say how many miles they had been when they got back. It took them twenty minutes to reach the outskirts of the city.

The old lady settled herself comfortably, removing her white cotton gloves and putting them up with her purse on the shelf in front of the back window. The children's mother still had on slacks and still had her head tied up in a green kerchief, but the grandmother had on a navy blue straw sailor hat with a bunch of white violets on the brim and a navy blue dress with a small white dot in the print. Her collars and cuffs were white organdy trimmed with lace and at her neckline she had pinned a purple spray of cloth violets containing a sachet. In case of an accident, anyone seeing her dead on the highway would know at once that she was a lady.

She said she thought it was going to be a good day for driving, neither too hot nor too cold, and she cautioned Bailey that the speed limit was fifty-five miles an hour and that the patrolmen hid themselves behind billboards and small clumps of trees and sped out after you before you had a chance to slow down. She pointed out interesting details of the scenery: Stone Mountain; the blue granite that in some places came up to both sides of the highway; the brilliant red clay banks slightly streaked with purple; and the various crops that made rows of green lacework on the ground. The trees were full of silver-white sunlight and the meanest of them sparkled. The children were reading comic magazines and their mother had gone back to sleep.

"Let's go through Georgia fast so we won't have to look at it much," John Wesley said.

15   "If I were a little boy," said the grandmother, "I wouldn't talk about my native state that way. Tennessee has the mountains and Georgia has the hills."

"Tennessee is just a hillbilly dumping ground," John Wesley said, "and Georgia is a lousy state too."

"You said it," June Star said.

"In my time," said the grandmother, folding her thin veined fingers, "children were more respectful of their native states and their parents and everything else. People did right then. Oh look at the cute little pickaninny!" she said and pointed to a Negro child standing in the door of a shack. "Wouldn't that make a picture, now?" she asked and they all turned and looked at the little Negro out of the back window. He waved.

"He didn't have any britches on," June Star said.

20   "He probably didn't have any," the grandmother explained. "Little niggers in the country don't have things like we do. If I could paint, I'd paint that picture," she said.

The children exchanged comic books.

The grandmother offered to hold the baby and the children's mother passed him over the front seat to her. She set him on her knee and bounced him and told him about the things they were passing. She rolled her eyes and screwed up her mouth and stuck her leathery thin face into his smooth bland one. Occasionally he gave her a faraway smile. They passed a large cotton field with five or six graves fenced in the middle of it, like a small island. "Look at the graveyard!" the grandmother said, pointing it out. "That was the old family burying ground. That belonged to the plantation."

"Where's the plantation?" John Wesley asked.

"Gone With the Wind,"° said the grandmother. "Ha. Ha."

25   When the children finished all the comic books they had brought, they opened the lunch and ate it. The grandmother ate a peanut butter sandwich and an olive and would not let the children throw the box and the paper napkins out the window. When there was nothing else to do they played a game by choosing a cloud and making the other two guess what shape it suggested. John Wesley took one the shape of a cow and June Star guessed a cow and John Wesley said, no, an automobile, and June Star said he didn't play fair, and they began to slap each other over the grandmother.

The grandmother said she would tell them a story if they would keep quiet. When she told a story, she rolled her eyes and waved her head and was very dramatic. She said once when she was a maiden lady she had been courted by a Mr. Edgar Atkins Teagarden from Jasper, Georgia. She said he was a very good-look-

---

Gone with the Wind: A 1936 novel by Margaret Mitchell about the Civil War.

ing man and a gentleman and that he brought her a watermelon every Saturday afternoon with his initials cut in it, E. A. T. Well, one Saturday, she said, Mr. Teagarden brought the watermelon and there was nobody at home and he left it on the front porch and returned in his buggy to Jasper, but she never got the watermelon, she said, because a nigger boy ate it when he saw the initials, E. A. T.! This story tickled John Wesley's funny bone and he giggled and giggled but June Star didn't think it was any good. She said she wouldn't marry a man that just brought her a watermelon on Saturday. The grandmother said she would have done well to marry Mr. Teagarden because he was a gentleman and had bought Coca-Cola stock when it first came out and that he died only a few years ago, a very wealthy man.

They stopped at The Tower for barbecued sandwiches. The Tower was a part stucco and part wood filling station and dance hall set in a clearing outside of Timothy. A fat man named Red Sammy Butts ran it and there were signs stuck here and there on the building and for miles up and down the highway saying, TRY RED SAMMY'S FAMOUS BARBECUE. NONE LIKE FAMOUS RED SAMMY'S! RED SAM! THE FAT BOY WITH THE HAPPY LAUGH. A VETERAN! RED SAMMY'S YOUR MAN!

Red Sammy was lying on the bare ground outside The Tower with his head under a truck while a gray monkey about a foot high, chained to a small chinaberry tree, chattered nearby. The monkey sprang back into the tree and got on the highest limb as soon as he saw the children jump out of the car and run toward him.

Inside, The Tower was a long dark room with a counter at one end and tables at the other and dancing space in the middle. They all sat down at a board table next to the nickelodeon and Red Sam's wife, a tall burnt-brown woman with hair and eyes lighter than her skin, came and took their order. The children's mother put a dime in the machine and played "The Tennessee Waltz," and the grandmother said that tune always made her want to dance. She asked Bailey if he would like to dance but he only glared at her. He didn't have a naturally sweet disposition like she did and trips made him nervous. The grandmother's brown eyes were very bright. She swayed her head from side to side and pretended she was dancing in her chair. June Star said play something she could tap to so the children's mother put in another dime and played a fast number and June Star stepped out onto the dance floor and did her tap routine.

"Ain't she cute?" Red Sam's wife said, leaning over the counter. "Would you like to come be my little girl?"

"No I certainly wouldn't," June Star said. "I wouldn't live in a broken-down place like this for a million bucks!" and she ran back to the table.

"Ain't she cute?" the woman repeated, stretching her mouth politely.

"Aren't you ashamed?" hissed the grandmother.

Red Sam came in and told his wife to quit lounging on the counter and hurry up with these people's order. His khaki trousers reached just to his hip bones and his stomach hung over them like a sack of meal swaying under his shirt. He came over and sat down at a table nearby and let out a combination sigh and yodel. "You can't win," he said. "You can't win," and he wiped his sweating red face off with a gray handkerchief. "These days you don't know who to trust," he said. "Ain't that the truth?"

35   "People are certainly not nice like they used to be," said the grandmother.

"Two fellers come in here last week," Red Sammy said, "driving a Chrysler. It was a old beat-up car but it was a good one and these boys looked all right to me. Said they worked at the mill and you know I let them fellers charge the gas they bought? Now why did I do that?"

"Because you're a good man!" the grandmother said at once.

"Yes'm, I suppose so," Red Sam said as if he were struck with this answer.

His wife brought the orders, carrying the five plates all at once without a tray, two in each hand and one balanced on her arm. "It isn't a soul in this green world of God's that you can trust," she said. "And I don't count nobody out of that, not nobody," she repeated, looking at Red Sammy.

40   "Did you read about that criminal, The Misfit, that's escaped?" asked the grandmother.

"I wouldn't be a bit surprised if he didn't attact this place right here," said the woman. "If he hears about it being here, I wouldn't be none surprised to see him. If he hears it's two cent in the cash register, I wouldn't be at all surprised if he . . ."

"That'll do," Red Sam said. "Go bring these people their Co'-Colas," and the woman went off to get the rest of the order.

"A good man is hard to find," Red Sammy said. "Everything is getting terrible. I remember the day you could go off and leave your screen door unlatched. Not no more."

He and the grandmother discussed better times. The old lady said that in her opinion Europe was entirely to blame for the way things were now. She said the way Europe acted you would think we were made of money and Red Sam said it was no use talking about it, she was exactly right. The children ran outside into the white sunlight and looked at the monkey in the lacy chinaberry tree. He was busy catching fleas on himself and biting each one carefully between his teeth as if it were a delicacy.

45   They drove off again into the hot afternoon. The grandmother took cat naps and woke up every few minutes with her own snoring. Outside of Toombsboro she woke up and recalled an old plantation that she had visited in this neighborhood once when she was a young lady. She said the house had six white columns across the front and that there was an avenue of oaks leading up to it and two little wooden trellis arbors on either side in front where you sat down with your suitor after a stroll in the garden. She recalled exactly which road to turn off to get to it. She knew that Bailey would not be willing to lose any time looking at an old house, but the more she talked about it, the more she wanted to see it once again and find out if the little twin arbors were still standing. "There was a secret panel in this house," she said craftily, not telling the truth but wishing that she were,

"and the story went that all the family silver was hidden in it when Sherman came through but it was never found . . ."

"Hey!" John Wesley said. "Let's go see it! We'll find it! We'll poke all the woodwork and find it! Who lives there? Where do you turn off at? Hey Pop, can't we turn off there?"

"We never have seen a house with a secret panel!" June Star shrieked. "Let's go to the house with the secret panel! Hey Pop, can't we go see the house with the secret panel!"

"It's not far from here, I know," the grandmother said. "It wouldn't take over twenty minutes."

Bailey was looking straight ahead. His jaw was as rigid as a horseshoe. "No," he said.

The children began to yell and scream that they wanted to see the house with the secret panel. John Wesley kicked the back of the front seat and June Star hung over her mother's shoulder and whined desperately into her ear that they never had any fun even on their vacation, that they could never do what THEY wanted to do. The baby began to scream and John Wesley kicked the back of the seat so hard that his father could feel the blows in his kidney. 50

"All right!" he shouted and drew the car to a stop at the side of the road. "Will you all shut up? Will you all just shut up for one second? If you don't shut up, we won't go anywhere."

"It would be very educational for them," the grandmother murmured.

"All right," Bailey said, "but get this: this is the only time we're going to stop for anything like this. This is the one and only time."

"The dirt road that you have to turn down is about a mile back," the grandmother directed. "I marked it when we passed."

"A dirt road," Bailey groaned. 55

After they had turned around and were headed toward the dirt road, the grandmother recalled other points about the house, the beautiful glass over the front doorway and the candle-lamp in the hall. John Wesley said that the secret panel was probably in the fireplace.

"You can't go inside this house," Bailey said. "You don't know who lives there."

"While you all talk to the people in front, I'll run around behind and get in a window," John Wesley suggested.

"We'll all stay in the car," his mother said.

They turned onto the dirt road and the car raced roughly along in a swirl of pink dust. The grandmother recalled the times when there were no paved roads and thirty miles was a day's journey. The dirt road was hilly and there were sudden washes in it and sharp curves on dangerous embankments. All at once they would be on a hill, looking down over the blue tops of trees for miles around, then the next minute, they would be in a red depression with the dust-coated trees looking down on them. 60

"This place had better turn up in a minute," Bailey said, "or I'm going to turn around."

The road looked as if no one had traveled on it in months.

"It's not much farther," the grandmother said and just as she said it, a horrible thought came to her. The thought was so embarrassing that she turned red in the face and her eyes dilated and her feet jumped up, upsetting her valise in the corner. The instant the valise moved, the newspaper top she had over the basket under it rose with a snarl and Pitty Sing, the cat, sprang onto Bailey's shoulder.

The children were thrown to the floor and their mother, clutching the baby, was thrown out the door onto the ground; the old lady was thrown into the front seat. The car turned over once and landed right-side-up in a gulch off the side of the road. Bailey remained in the driver's seat with the cat — gray-striped with a broad white face and an orange nose — clinging to his neck like a caterpillar.

65   As soon as the children saw they could move their arms and legs, they scrambled out of the car, shouting, "We've had an ACCIDENT!" The grandmother was curled up under the dashboard, hoping she was injured so that Bailey's wrath would not come down on her all at once. The horrible thought she had had before the accident was that the house she had remembered so vividly was not in Georgia but in Tennessee.

Bailey removed the cat from his neck with both hands and flung it out the window against the side of a pine tree. Then he got out of the car and started looking for the children's mother. She was sitting against the side of the red gutted ditch, holding the screaming baby, but she only had a cut down her face and a broken shoulder. "We've had an ACCIDENT!" the children screamed in a frenzy of delight.

"But nobody's killed," June Star said with disappointment as the grandmother limped out of the car, her hat still pinned to her head but the broken front brim standing up at a jaunty angle and the violet spray hanging off the side. They all sat down in the ditch, except the children, to recover from the shock. They were all shaking.

"Maybe a car will come along," said the children's mother hoarsely.

"I believe I have injured an organ," said the grandmother, pressing her side, but no one answered her. Bailey's teeth were clattering. He had on a yellow sport shirt with bright blue parrots designed in it and his face was as yellow as the shirt. The grandmother decided that she would not mention that the house was in Tennessee.

70   The road was about ten feet above and they could see only the tops of the trees on the other side of it. Behind the ditch they were sitting in there were more woods, tall and dark and deep. In a few minutes they saw a car some distance away on top of a hill, coming slowly as if the occupants were watching them. The grandmother stood up and waved both arms dramatically to attract their attention. The car continued to come on slowly, disappeared around a bend and appeared again, moving even slower, on top of the hill they had gone over. It was a big black battered hearse-like automobile. There were three men in it.

It came to a stop just over them and for some minutes, the driver looked down with a steady expressionless gaze to where they were sitting, and didn't speak.

Then he turned his head and muttered something to the other two and they got out. One was a fat boy in black trousers and a red sweat shirt with a silver stallion embossed on the front of it. He moved around on the right side of them and stood staring, his mouth partly open in a kind of loose grin. The other had on khaki pants and a blue striped coat and a gray hat pulled down very low, hiding most of his face. He came around slowly on the left side. Neither spoke.

The driver got out of the car and stood by the side of it, looking down at them. He was an older man than the other two. His hair was just beginning to gray and he wore silver-rimmed spectacles that gave him a scholarly look. He had a long creased face and didn't have on any shirt or undershirt. He had on blue jeans that were too tight for him and was holding a black hat and a gun. The two boys also had guns.

"We've had an ACCIDENT!" the children screamed.

The grandmother had the peculiar feeling that the bespectacled man was someone she knew. His face was as familiar to her as if she had known him all her life but she could not recall who he was. He moved away from the car and began to come down the embankment, placing his feet carefully so that he wouldn't slip. He had on tan and white shoes and no socks, and his ankles were red and thin. "Good afternoon," he said. "I see you all had you a little spill."

"We turned over twice!" said the grandmother.   75

"Oncet," he corrected. "We seen it happen. Try their car and see will it run, Hiram," he said quietly to the boy with the gray hat.

"What you got that gun for?" John Wesley asked. "Watcha gonna do with that gun?"

"Lady," the man said to the children's mother, "would you mind calling them children to sit down by you? Children make me nervous. I want all you all to sit down right together there where you're at."

"What are you telling US what to do for?" June Star asked.

Behind them the line of woods gaped like a dark open mouth. "Come here,"   80 said their mother.

"Look here now," Bailey began suddenly, "we're in a predicament! We're in . . ."

The grandmother shrieked. She scrambled to her feet and stood staring. "You're The Misfit!" she said. "I recognized you at once!"

"Yes'm," the man said, smiling slightly as if he were pleased in spite of himself to be known, "but it would have been better for all of you, lady, if you hadn't of reckernized me."

Bailey turned his head sharply and said something to his mother that shocked even the children. The old lady began to cry and The Misfit reddened.

"Lady," he said, "don't you get upset. Sometimes a man says things he don't   85 mean. I don't reckon he meant to talk to you thataway."

"You wouldn't shoot a lady, would you?" the grandmother said and removed a clean handkerchief from her cuff and began to slap at her eyes with it.

The Misfit pointed the toe of his shoe into the ground and made a little hole and then covered it up again. "I would hate to have to," he said.

"Listen," the grandmother almost screamed, "I know you're a good man. You don't look a bit like you have common blood. I know you must come from nice people!"

"Yes mam," he said, "finest people in the world." When he smiled he showed a row of strong white teeth. "God never made a finer woman than my mother and my daddy's heart was pure gold," he said. The boy with the red sweat shirt had come around behind them and was standing with his gun at his hip. The Misfit squatted down on the ground. "Watch them children, Bobby Lee," he said. "You know they make me nervous." He looked at the six of them huddled together in front of him and he seemed to be embarrassed as if he couldn't think of anything to say. "Ain't a cloud in the sky," he remarked, looking up at it. "Don't see no sun but don't see no cloud neither."

90   "Yes, it's a beautiful day," said the grandmother. "Listen," she said, "you shouldn't call yourself The Misfit because I know you're a good man at heart. I can just look at you and tell."

"Hush!" Bailey yelled. "Hush! Everybody shut up and let me handle this!" He was squatting in the position of a runner about to sprint forward but he didn't move.

"I pre-chate that, lady," The Misfit said and drew a little circle in the ground with the butt of his gun.

"It'll take a half a hour to fix this here car," Hiram called, looking over the raised hood of it.

"Well, first you and Bobby Lee get him and that little boy to step over yonder with you," The Misfit said, pointing to Bailey and John Wesley. "The boys want to ast you something," he said to Bailey. "Would you mind stepping back in them woods there with them?"

95   "Listen," Bailey began, "we're in a terrible predicament! Nobody realizes what this is," and his voice cracked. His eyes were as blue and intense as the parrots in his shirt and he remained perfectly still.

The grandmother reached up to adjust her hat brim as if she were going to the woods with him but it came off in her hand. She stood staring at it and after a second she let it fall on the ground. Hiram pulled Bailey up by the arm as if he were assisting an old man. John Wesley caught hold of his father's hand and Bobby Lee followed. They went off toward the woods and just as they reached the dark edge, Bailey turned and supporting himself against a gray naked pine trunk, he shouted, "I'll be back in a minute, Mamma, wait on me!"

"Come back this instant!" his mother shrilled but they all disappeared into the woods.

"Bailey Boy!" the grandmother called in a tragic voice but she found she was looking at The Misfit squatting on the ground in front of her. "I just know you're a good man," she said desperately. "You're not a bit common!"

"Nome, I ain't a good man," The Misfit said after a second as if he had considered her statement carefully, "but I ain't the worst in the world neither. My daddy said I was a different breed of dog from my brothers and sisters. 'You know,' Daddy said, 'it's some that can live their whole life out without asking about it and it's others has to know why it is, and this boy is one of the latters. He's going to be into everything!'" He put on his black hat and looked up suddenly and then away deep into the woods as if he were embarrassed again. "I'm sorry I don't have on a shirt before you ladies," he said, hunching his shoulders slightly. "We buried our clothes that we had on when we escaped and we're just making do until we can get better. We borrowed these from some folks we met," he explained.

"That's perfectly all right," the grandmother said. "Maybe Bailey has an ex- 100
tra shirt in his suitcase."

"I'll look and see terrectly," The Misfit said.

"Where are they taking him?" the children's mother screamed.

"Daddy was a card himself," The Misfit said. "You couldn't put anything over on him. He never got in trouble with the Authorities though. Just had the knack of handling them."

"You could be honest too if you'd only try," said the grandmother. "Think how wonderful it would be to settle down and live a comfortable life and not have to think about somebody chasing you all the time."

The Misfit kept scratching in the ground with the butt of his gun as if he 105
were thinking about it. "Yes'm, somebody is always after you," he murmured.

The grandmother noticed how thin his shoulder blades were just behind his hat because she was standing up looking down on him. "Do you ever pray?" she asked.

He shook his head. All she saw was the black hat wiggle between his shoulder blades. "Nome," he said.

There was a pistol shot from the woods, followed closely by another. Then silence. The old lady's head jerked around. She could hear the wind move through the tree tops like a long satisfied insuck of breath. "Bailey Boy!" she called.

"I was a gospel singer for a while," The Misfit said. "I been most everything. Been in the arm service, both land and sea, at home and abroad, been twict married, been an undertaker, been with the railroads, plowed Mother Earth, been in a tornado, seen a man burnt alive oncet," and he looked up at the children's mother and the little girl who were sitting close together, their faces white and their eyes glassy; "I even seen a woman flogged," he said.

"Pray, pray," the grandmother began, "pray, pray . . ." 110

"I never was a bad boy that I remember of," The Misfit said in an almost dreamy voice, "but somewheres along the line I done something wrong and got sent to the penitentiary. I was buried alive," and he looked up and held her attention to him by a steady stare.

"That's when you should have started to pray," she said. "What did you do to get sent to the penitentiary that first time?"

"Turn to the right, it was a wall," The Misfit said, looking up again at the cloudless sky. "Turn to the left, it was a wall. Look up it was a ceiling, look down it was a floor. I forget what I done, lady. I set there and set there, trying to re-member what it was I done and I ain't recalled it to this day. Oncet in a while, I would think it was coming to me, but it never come."

"Maybe they put you in by mistake," the old lady said vaguely.

115   "Nome," he said. "It wasn't no mistake. They had the papers on me."

"You must have stolen something," she said.

The Misfit sneered slightly. "Nobody had nothing I wanted," he said. "It was a head-doctor at the penitentiary said what I had done was kill my daddy but I known that for a lie. My daddy died in nineteen ought nineteen of the epidemic flu and I never had a thing to do with it. He was buried in the Mount Hopewell Baptist churchyard and you can go there and see for yourself."

"If you would pray," the old lady said, "Jesus would help you."

"That's right," The Misfit said.

120   "Well then, why don't you pray?" she asked trembling with delight suddenly.

"I don't want no hep," he said. "I'm doing all right by myself."

Bobby Lee and Hiram came ambling back from the woods. Bobby Lee was dragging a yellow shirt with bright blue parrots in it.

"Thow me that shirt, Bobby Lee," The Misfit said. The shirt came flying at him and landed on his shoulder and he put it on. The grandmother couldn't name what the shirt reminded her of. "No, lady," The Misfit said while he was buttoning it up, "I found out the crime don't matter. You can do one thing or you can do another, kill a man or take a tire off his car, because sooner or later you're going to forget what it was you done and just be punished for it."

The children's mother had begun to make heaving noises as if she couldn't get her breath. "Lady," he asked, "would you and that little girl like to step off yon-der with Bobby Lee and Hiram and join your husband?"

125   "Yes, thank you," the mother said faintly. Her left arm dangled helplessly and she was holding the baby, who had gone to sleep, in the other. "Hep that lady up, Hiram," The Misfit said as she struggled to climb out of the ditch, "and Bobby Lee, you hold onto that little girl's hand."

"I don't want to hold hands with him," June Star said. "He reminds me of a pig."

The fat boy blushed and laughed and caught her by the arm and pulled her off into the woods after Hiram and her mother.

Alone with The Misfit, the grandmother found that she had lost her voice. There was not a cloud in the sky nor any sun. There was nothing around her but woods. She wanted to tell him that he must pray. She opened and closed her mouth several times before anything came out. Finally she found herself saying, "Jesus, Jesus," meaning, Jesus will help you, but the way she was saying it, it sounded as if she might be cursing.

"Yes'm," The Misfit said as if he agreed. "Jesus thown everything off balance. It was the same case with Him as with me except He hadn't committed any crime and they could prove I had committed one because they had the papers on me. Of course," he said, "they never shown me my papers. That's why I sign myself now. I said long ago, you get you a signature and sign everything you do and keep a copy of it. Then you'll know what you done and you can hold up the crime to the punishment and see do they match and in the end you'll have something to prove you ain't been treated right. I call myself The Misfit," he said, "because I can't make what all I done wrong fit what all I gone through in punishment."

There was a piercing scream from the woods, followed closely by a pistol re-   130
port. "Does it seem right to you, lady, that one is punished a heap and another ain't punished at all?"

"Jesus!" the old lady cried. "You've got good blood! I know you wouldn't shoot a lady! I know you come from nice people! Pray! Jesus, you ought not to shoot a lady. I'll give you all the money I've got!"

"Lady," The Misfit said, looking beyond her far into the woods, "there never was a body that give the undertaker a tip."

There were two more pistol reports and the grandmother raised her head like a parched old turkey hen crying for water and called, "Bailey Boy, Bailey Boy!" as if her heart would break.

"Jesus was the only One that ever raised the dead," The Misfit continued, "and He shouldn't have done it. He thown everything off balance. If He did what He said, then it's nothing for you to do but thow away everything and follow Him, and if He didn't, then it's nothing for you to do but enjoy the few minutes you got left the best way you can — by killing somebody or burning down his house or doing some other meanness to him. No pleasure but meanness," he said and his voice became almost a snarl.

"Maybe He didn't raise the dead," the old lady mumbled, not knowing what   135
she was saying and feeling so dizzy that she sank down in the ditch with her legs twisted under her.

"I wasn't there so I can't say He didn't," The Misfit said. "I wisht I had of been there," he said, hitting the ground with his fist. "It ain't right I wasn't there because if I had of been there I would of known. Listen, lady," he said in a high voice, "if I had of been there I would of known and I wouldn't be like I am now." His voice seemed about to crack and the grandmother's head cleared for an instant. She saw the man's face twisted close to her own as if he were going to cry and she murmured, "Why you're one of my babies. You're one of my own children!" She reached out and touched him on the shoulder. The Misfit sprang back as if a snake had bitten him and shot her three times through the chest. Then he put his gun down on the ground and took off his glasses and began to clean them.

Hiram and Bobby Lee returned from the woods and stood over the ditch, looking down at the grandmother who half sat and half lay in a puddle of blood with her legs crossed under her like a child's and her face smiling up at the cloudless sky.

Without his glasses, The Misfit's eyes were red-rimmed and pale and defenseless-looking. "Take her off and thow her where you thown the others," he said, picking up the cat that was rubbing itself against his leg.

"She was a talker, wasn't she?" Bobby Lee said, sliding down the ditch with a yodel.

140   "She would of been a good woman," The Misfit said, "if it had been somebody there to shoot her every minute of her life."

"Some fun!" Bobby Lee said.

"Shut up, Bobby Lee," The Misfit said. "It's no real pleasure in life."

Reading and Reacting

1. How are the style and tone of the narrator's voice different from those of the characters? What, if anything, is the significance of this difference?

2. The figures of speech used in this story sometimes create unflattering, even grotesque, pictures of the characters. Find several examples of such negative figures of speech. Why do you think the author uses them?

3. What does the grandmother's use of the words *pickaninny* and *nigger* reveal about her? How are readers expected to reconcile this language with her very proper appearance and her preoccupation with manners? How does her use of these words affect your reaction to her?

4. Explain the **irony** in this statement: "In case of an accident, anyone seeing her dead on the highway would know at once that she was a lady" (par. 12).

5. How does The Misfit's dialect characterize him?

6. What does the allusion to *Gone with the Wind* (par. 24) contribute to the story?

7. How do the style and tone of the two-paragraph description of the three men in the car (pars. 71–72) help to prepare readers for the events that follow?

8. When The Misfit tells the grandmother about his life, his language takes on a measured, rhythmic quality: "Been in the arm service, both land and sea, at home and abroad, been twict married, been an undertaker, been with the railroads, plowed Mother Earth, been in a tornado, seen a man burnt alive oncet . . ." (par. 109). Find other examples of parallelism and rhythmic repetition in this character's speech. How does this style help to develop The Misfit's character?

9. **Journal Entry** Why do you think the grandmother tells The Misfit she recognizes him? Why does she fail to realize the danger of her remark?

10. **Critical Perspective** In his 2002 essay "Light and Shadow: Religious Grace in Two Stories by Flannery O'Connor," David Allen Cook writes:

> The literary works of Flannery O'Connor often contend that religious belief can only be consummated by direct confrontation with evil, and for those uncommitted and unprepared, tragedy seems inevitable. For O'Connor's religious "pretenders," a moment of religious grace — a revelation of Truth — often does

come, but at a devastating price. In . . . "A Good Man Is Hard to Find," we are presented with main characters that experience a deep epiphany after being spiritually challenged by the darker side of human nature.

In this story, who are the religious "pretenders," and who has true faith? What is the price of achieving a moment of religious grace? What role does violence play in this equation?

Related Works: "The Lottery" (p. 274), "Where Are You Going, Where Have You Been?" (p. 384), "Everything That Rises Must Converge" (p. 397), "The Tell-Tale Heart" (p. 409), *Tape* (p. 741)

TIM O'BRIEN (1946–   ) is sometimes described as a writer whose books are on the short list of essential fiction about the Vietnam War. After graduating summa cum laude from Macalester College in 1968, O'Brien was immediately drafted into the United States Army and sent to Vietnam, where he served with the 198th Infantry Brigade. He was promoted to sergeant and awarded a Purple Heart after receiving a shrapnel wound in a battle near My Lai. In 1970, after his discharge from the army, he attended Harvard graduate school to study government. He worked as a reporter for the *Washington Post* before pursuing a full-time career as a writer.

O'Brien's plots focus on danger, violence, courage, endurance, despair, and other topics often associated with war fiction, but he treats these topics with an emphasis on the contemporary dilemmas faced by those who may be unwilling participants in an unpopular war. O'Brien calls *If I Die in a Combat Zone, Box Me Up and Ship Me Home* (1979) a memoir because it relates his war experiences as a naive young college graduate who suddenly finds himself facing bullets and land mines rather than sitting behind a desk. *Northern Lights* (1975) concentrates on the wilderness survival experiences of two brothers, one of whom has just returned from the Vietnam War. A fantastic daydream of an American soldier, *Going after Cacciato* (1978), won a National Book Award. *The Things They Carried* (1990) is a quasi-fictional collection of interrelated stories that deal with a single platoon. *The Vietnam in Me* (1994) emphasizes the destructive effects of war on a soldier, even after he has returned home, and *In the Lake of the Woods* (1994) tells a dramatic story of a couple missing in Minnesota. O'Brien's most recent books are *Tomcat in Love* (1998) and *July, July* (2002).

The Things They Carried (1986)

First Lieutenant Jimmy Cross carried letters from a girl named Martha, a junior at Mount Sebastian College in New Jersey. They were not love letters, but Lieutenant Cross was hoping, so he kept them folded in plastic at the bottom of his rucksack. In the late afternoon, after a day's march, he would dig his foxhole, wash his hands under a canteen, unwrap the letters, hold them with the tips of his fingers, and spend the last hour of light pretending. He would imagine romantic camping trips into the White Mountains in New Hampshire. He would sometimes taste the envelope flaps, knowing her tongue had been there. More than anything, he wanted Martha to love him as he loved her, but the letters were mostly chatty, elusive on the matter of love. She was a virgin, he was almost sure. She was an English major at Mount Sebastian, and she wrote beautifully about her professors and roommates and midterm exams, about her respect for Chaucer and her great affection for Virginia Woolf. She often quoted lines of poetry; she never mentioned the war, except to say, Jimmy, take care of yourself. The letters weighed ten ounces. They were signed "Love, Martha," but Lieutenant Cross understood that "Love" was only a way of signing and did not mean what he sometimes pretended it meant. At dusk, he would carefully return the letters to his rucksack. Slowly, a bit distracted, he would get up and move among his men, checking the perimeter, then at full dark he would return to his hole and watch the night and wonder if Martha was a virgin.

The things they carried were largely determined by necessity. Among the necessities or near necessities were P-38 can openers, pocket knives, heat tabs, wrist watches, dog tags, mosquito repellent, chewing gum, candy, cigarettes, salt tablets, packets of Kool-Aid, lighters, matches, sewing kits, Military Payment Certificates, C rations, and two or three canteens of water. Together, these items weighed between fifteen and twenty pounds, depending upon a man's habits or rate of metabolism. Henry Dobbins, who was a big man, carried extra rations; he was especially fond of canned peaches in heavy syrup over pound cake. Dave Jensen, who practiced field hygiene, carried a toothbrush, dental floss, and several hotel-size bars of soap he'd stolen on R&R in Sydney, Australia. Ted Lavender, who was scared, carried tranquilizers until he was shot in the head outside the village of Than Khe in mid-April. By necessity, and because it was SOP,° they all carried steel helmets that weighed five pounds including the liner and camouflage cover. They carried the standard fatigue jackets and trousers. Very few carried underwear. On their feet they carried jungle boots — 2.1 pounds — and Dave Jensen carried three pairs of socks and a can of Dr. Scholl's foot powder as a precaution against trench foot. Until he was shot, Ted Lavender carried six or seven ounces of premium dope, which for him was a necessity. Mitchell Sanders, the RTO,° carried condoms. Norman Bowker carried a diary. Rat Kiley carried comic books. Kiowa, a devout Baptist, carried an illustrated New Testament that had been presented to him by his father, who taught Sunday school in Oklahoma City, Oklahoma. As a hedge against bad times, however, Kiowa also carried his grandmother's distrust of the white man, his grandfather's old hunt-

SOP: Standard operating procedure.
RTO: Radio telephone operator.

ing hatchet. Necessity dictated. Because the land was mined and booby-trapped, it was SOP for each man to carry a steel-centered, nylon-covered flak jacket, which weighed 6.7 pounds, but which on hot days seemed much heavier. Because you could die so quickly, each man carried at least one large compress bandage, usually in the helmet band for easy access. Because the nights were cold, and because the monsoons were wet, each carried a green plastic poncho that could be used as a raincoat or ground sheet or makeshift tent. With its quilted liner, the poncho weighed almost two pounds, but it was worth every ounce. In April, for instance, when Ted Lavender was shot, they used his poncho to wrap him up, then to carry him across the paddy, then to lift him into the chopper that took him away.

They were called legs or grunts.

To carry something was to "hump" it, as when Lieutenant Jimmy Cross humped his love for Martha up the hills and through the swamps. In its intransitive form, "to hump" meant "to walk," or "to march," but it implied burdens far beyond the intransitive.

Almost everyone humped photographs. In his wallet, Lieutenant Cross carried two photographs of Martha. The first was a Kodachrome snapshot signed "Love," though he knew better. She stood against a brick wall. Her eyes were gray and neutral, her lips slightly open as she stared straight-on at the camera. At night, sometimes, Lieutenant Cross wondered who had taken the picture, because he knew she had boyfriends, because he loved her so much, and because he could see the shadow of the picture taker spreading out against the brick wall. The second photograph had been clipped from the 1968 Mount Sebastian yearbook. It was an action shot — women's volleyball — and Martha was bent horizontal to the floor, reaching, the palms of her hands in sharp focus, the tongue taut, the expression frank and competitive. There was no visible sweat. She wore white gym shorts. Her legs, he thought, were almost certainly the legs of a virgin, dry and without hair, the left knee cocked and carrying her entire weight, which was just over one hundred pounds. Lieutenant Cross remembered touching that left knee. A dark theater, he remembered, and the movie was *Bonnie and Clyde,* and Martha wore a tweed skirt, and during the final scene, when he touched her knee, she turned and looked at him in a sad, sober way that made him pull his hand back, but he would always remember the feel of the tweed skirt and the knee beneath it and the sound of the gunfire that killed Bonnie and Clyde, how embarrassing it was, how slow and oppressive. He remembered kissing her good night at the dorm door. Right then, he thought, he should've done something brave. He should've carried her up the stairs to her room and tied her to the bed and touched that left knee all night long. He should've risked it. Whenever he looked at the photographs, he thought of new things he should've done.

What they carried was partly a function of rank, partly of field specialty.

As a first lieutenant and platoon leader, Jimmy Cross carried a compass, maps, code books, binoculars, and a .45-caliber pistol that weighed 2.9 pounds fully loaded. He carried a strobe light and the responsibility for the lives of his men.

As an RTO, Mitchell Sanders carried the PRC-25 radio, a killer, twenty-six pounds with its battery.

As a medic, Rat Kiley carried a canvas satchel filled with morphine and plasma and malaria tablets and surgical tape and comic books and all the things a medic must carry, including M&M's for especially bad wounds, for a total weight of nearly twenty pounds.

10   As a big man, therefore a machine gunner, Henry Dobbins carried the M-60, which weighed twenty-three pounds unloaded, but which was almost always loaded. In addition, Dobbins carried between ten and fifteen pounds of ammunition draped in belts across his chest and shoulders.

As PFCs or Spec 4s, most of them were common grunts and carried the standard M-16 gas-operated assault rifle. The weapon weighed 7.5 pounds unloaded, 8.2 pounds with its full twenty-round magazine. Depending on numerous factors, such as topography and psychology, the riflemen carried anywhere from twelve to twenty magazines, usually in cloth bandoliers, adding on another 8.4 pounds at minimum, fourteen pounds at maximum. When it was available, they also carried M-16 maintenance gear — rods and steel brushes and swabs and tubes of LSA oil — all of which weighed about a pound. Among the grunts, some carried the M-79 grenade launcher, 5.9 pounds unloaded, a reasonably light weapon except for the ammunition, which was heavy. A single round weighed ten ounces. The typical load was twenty-five rounds. But Ted Lavender, who was scared, carried thirty-four rounds when he was shot and killed outside Than Khe, and he went down under an exceptional burden, more than twenty pounds of ammunition, plus the flak jacket and helmet and rations and water and toilet paper and tranquilizers and all the rest, plus the unweighed fear. He was dead weight. There was no twitching or flopping. Kiowa, who saw it happen, said it was like watching a rock fall, or a big sandbag or something — just boom, then down — not like the movies where the dead guy rolls around and does fancy spins and goes ass over teakettle — not like that, Kiowa said, the poor bastard just flat-fuck fell. Boom. Down. Nothing else. It was a bright morning in mid-April. Lieutenant Cross felt the pain. He blamed himself. They stripped off Lavender's canteens and ammo, all the heavy things, and Rat Kiley said the obvious, the guy's dead, and Mitchell Sanders used his radio to report one U.S. KIA and to request a chopper. Then they wrapped Lavender in his poncho. They carried him out to a dry paddy, established security, and sat smoking the dead man's dope until the chopper came. Lieutenant Cross kept to himself. He pictured Martha's smooth young face, thinking he loved her more than anything, more than his men, and now Ted Lavender was dead because he loved her so much and could not stop thinking about her. When the dust-off arrived, they carried Lavender aboard.

Afterward they burned Than Khe. They marched until dusk, then dug their holes, and that night Kiowa kept explaining how you had to be there, how fast it was, how the poor guy just dropped like so much concrete. Boom-down, he said. Like cement.

*   *   *

In addition to the three standard weapons — the M-60, M-16, and M-79 — they carried whatever presented itself, or whatever seemed appropriate as a means of killing or staying alive. They carried catch-as-catch-can. At various times, in various situations, they carried M-14s and CAR-15s and Swedish Ks and grease guns and captured AK-47s and Chi-Coms and RPGs and Simonov carbines and black-market Uzis and .38-caliber Smith & Wesson handguns and 66 mm LAWs and shotguns and silencers and blackjacks and bayonets and C-4 plastic explosives. Lee Strunk carried a slingshot; a weapon of last resort, he called it. Mitchell Sanders carried brass knuckles. Kiowa carried his grandfather's feathered hatchet. Every third or fourth man carried a Claymore antipersonnel mine — 3.5 pounds with its firing device. They all carried fragmentation grenades — fourteen ounces each. They all carried at least one M-18 colored smoke grenade — twenty-four ounces. Some carried CS or tear-gas grenades. Some carried white-phosphorus grenades. They carried all they could bear, and then some, including a silent awe for the terrible power of the things they carried.

In the first week of April, before Lavender died, Lieutenant Jimmy Cross received a good-luck charm from Martha. It was a simple pebble, an ounce at most. Smooth to the touch, it was a milky-white color with flecks of orange and violet, oval-shaped, like a miniature egg. In the accompanying letter, Martha wrote that she had found the pebble on the Jersey shoreline, precisely where the land touched water at high tide, where things came together but also separated. It was this separate-but-together quality, she wrote, that had inspired her to pick up the pebble and to carry it in her breast pocket for several days, where it seemed weightless, and then to send it through the mail, by air, as a token of her truest feelings for him. Lieutenant Cross found this romantic. But he wondered what her truest feelings were, exactly, and what she meant by separate-but-together. He wondered how the tides and waves had come into play on that afternoon along the Jersey shoreline when Martha saw the pebble and bent down to rescue it from geology. He imagined bare feet. Martha was a poet, with the poet's sensibilities, and her feet would be brown and bare, the toenails unpainted, the eyes chilly and somber like the ocean in March, and though it was painful, he wondered who had been with her that afternoon. He imagined a pair of shadows moving along the strip of sand where things came together but also separated. It was phantom jealousy, he knew, but he couldn't help himself. He loved her so much. On the march, through the hot days of early April, he carried the pebble in his mouth, turning it with his tongue, tasting sea salts and moisture. His mind wandered. He had difficulty keeping his attention on the war. On occasion he would yell at his men to spread out the column, to keep their eyes open, but then he would slip away into daydreams, just pretending, walking barefoot along the Jersey shore, with Martha, carrying nothing. He would feel himself rising. Sun and waves and gentle winds, all love and lightness.

What they carried varied by mission.

15   When a mission took them to the mountains, they carried mosquito netting, machetes, canvas tarps, and extra bug juice.

If a mission seemed especially hazardous, or if it involved a place they knew to be bad, they carried everything they could. In certain heavily mined AOs,° where the land was dense with Toe Poppers and Bouncing Betties, they took turns humping a twenty-eight-pound mine detector. With its headphones and big sensing plate, the equipment was a stress on the lower back and shoulders, awkward to handle, often useless because of the shrapnel in the earth, but they carried it anyway, partly for safety, partly for the illusion of safety.

On ambush, or other night missions, they carried peculiar little odds and ends. Kiowa always took along his New Testament and a pair of moccasins for silence. Dave Jensen carried night-sight vitamins high in carotin. Lee Strunk carried his slingshot; ammo, he claimed, would never be a problem. Rat Kiley carried brandy and M&M's. Until he was shot, Ted Lavender carried the starlight scope, which weighed 6.3 pounds with its aluminum carrying case. Henry Dobbins carried his girlfriend's panty-hose wrapped around his neck as a comforter. They all carried ghosts. When dark came, they would move out single file across the meadows and paddies to their ambush coordinates, where they would quietly set up the Claymores and lie down and spend the night waiting.

Other missions were more complicated and required special equipment. In mid-April, it was their mission to search out and destroy the elaborate tunnel complexes in the Than Khe area south of Chu Lai. To blow the tunnels, they carried one-pound blocks of pentrite high explosives, four blocks to a man, sixty-eight pounds in all. They carried wiring, detonators, and battery-powered clackers. Dave Jensen carried earplugs. Most often, before blowing the tunnels, they were ordered by higher command to search them, which was considered bad news, but by and large they just shrugged and carried out orders. Because he was a big man, Henry Dobbins was excused from tunnel duty. The others would draw numbers. Before Lavender died there were seventeen men in the platoon, and whoever drew the number seventeen would strip off his gear and crawl in head first with a flashlight and Lieutenant Cross's .45-caliber pistol. The rest of them would fan out as security. They would sit down or kneel, not facing the hole, listening to the ground beneath them, imagining cobwebs and ghosts, whatever was down there — the tunnel walls squeezing in — how the flashlight seemed

°AOs: Areas of operation.

impossibly heavy in the hand and how it was tunnel vision in the very strictest sense, compression in all ways, even time, and how you had to wiggle in — ass and elbows — a swallowed-up feeling — and how you found yourself worrying about odd things — will your flashlight go dead? Do rats carry rabies? If you screamed, how far would the sound carry? Would your buddies hear it? Would they have the courage to drag you out? In some respects, though not many, the waiting was worse than the tunnel itself. Imagination was a killer.

On April 16, when Lee Strunk drew the number seventeen, he laughed and muttered something and went down quickly. The morning was hot and very still. Not good, Kiowa said. He looked at the tunnel opening, then out across a dry paddy toward the village of Than Khe. Nothing moved. No clouds or birds or people. As they waited, the men smoked and drank Kool-Aid, not talking much, feeling sympathy for Lee Strunk but also feeling the luck of the draw. You win some, you lose some, said Mitchell Sanders, and sometimes you settle for a rain check. It was a tired line and no one laughed.

Henry Dobbins ate a tropical chocolate bar. Ted Lavender popped a tranquil- 20 izer and went off to pee.

After five minutes, Lieutenant Jimmy Cross moved to the tunnel, leaned down, and examined the darkness. Trouble, he thought — a cave-in maybe. And then suddenly, without willing it, he was thinking about Martha. The stresses and fractures, the quick collapse, the two of them buried alive under all that weight. Dense, crushing love. Kneeling, watching the hole, he tried to concentrate on Lee Strunk and the war, all the dangers, but his love was too much for him, he felt paralyzed, he wanted to sleep inside her lungs and breathe her blood and be smothered. He wanted her to be a virgin and not a virgin, all at once. He wanted to know her. Intimate secrets — why poetry? Why so sad? Why that grayness in her eyes? Why so alone? Not lonely, just alone — riding her bike across campus or sitting off by herself in the cafeteria. Even dancing, she danced alone — and it was the aloneness that filled him with love. He remembered telling her that one evening. How she nodded and looked away. And how, later, when he kissed her, she received the kiss without returning it, her eyes wide open, not afraid, not a virgin's eyes, just flat and uninvolved.

Lieutenant Cross gazed at the tunnel. But he was not there. He was buried with Martha under the white sand at the Jersey shore. They were pressed together, and the pebble in his mouth was her tongue. He was smiling. Vaguely, he was aware of how quiet the day was, the sullen paddies, yet he could not bring himself to worry about matters of security. He was beyond that. He was just a kid at war, in love. He was twenty-two years old. He couldn't help it.

A few moments later Lee Strunk crawled out of the tunnel. He came up grinning, filthy but alive. Lieutenant Cross nodded and closed his eyes while the others clapped Strunk on the back and made jokes about rising from the dead.

Worms, Rat Kiley said. Right out of the grave. Fuckin' zombie.

The men laughed. They all felt great relief.

Spook City, said Mitchell Sanders.

25

Lee Strunk made a funny ghost sound, a kind of moaning, yet very happy, and right then, when Strunk made that high happy moaning sound, when he went *Ahhooooo,* right then Ted Lavender was shot in the head on his way back from peeing. He lay with his mouth open. The teeth were broken. There was a swollen black bruise under his left eye. The cheekbone was gone. Oh shit, Rat Kiley said, the guy's dead. The guy's dead, he kept saying, which seemed profound — the guy's dead. I mean really.

The things they carried were determined to some extent by superstition. Lieutenant Cross carried his good-luck pebble. Dave Jensen carried a rabbit's foot. Norman Bowker, otherwise a very gentle person, carried a thumb that had been presented to him as a gift by Mitchell Sanders. The thumb was dark brown, rubbery to the touch, and weighed four ounces at most. It had been cut from a VC corpse, a boy of fifteen or sixteen. They'd found him at the bottom of an irrigation ditch, badly burned, flies in his mouth and eyes. The boy wore black shorts and sandals. At the time of his death he had been carrying a pouch of rice, a rifle, and three magazines of ammunition.

You want my opinion, Mitchell Sanders said, there's a definite moral here.
30   He put his hand on the dead boy's wrist. He was quiet for a time, as if counting a pulse, then he patted the stomach, almost affectionately, and used Kiowa's hunting hatchet to remove the thumb.

Henry Dobbins asked what the moral was.

Moral?

You know. *Moral.*

Sanders wrapped the thumb in toilet paper and handed it across to Norman Bowker. There was no blood. Smiling, he kicked the boy's head, watched the flies scatter, and said, It's like with that old TV show — Paladin. Have gun, will travel.

35   Henry Dobbins thought about it.

Yeah, well, he finally said. I don't see no moral.

There it *is,* man.

Fuck off.

They carried USO stationery and pencils and pens. They carried Sterno, safety pins, trip flares, signal flares, spools of wire, razor blades, chewing tobacco, liberated joss sticks and statuettes of the smiling Buddha, candles, grease pencils, *The Stars and Stripes,* fingernail clippers, Psy Ops leaflets, bush hats, bolos, and much more. Twice a week, when the resupply choppers came in, they carried hot chow in green Mermite cans and large canvas bags filled with iced beer and soda pop. They carried plastic water containers, each with a two-gallon capacity. Mitchell Sanders carried a set of starched tiger fatigues for special occasions. Henry Dobbins carried Black Flag insecticide. Dave Jensen carried empty sandbags that could be filled at night for added protection. Lee Strunk carried tanning lotion.

Some things they carried in common. Taking turns, they carried the big PRC-77 scrambler radio, which weighed thirty pounds with its battery. They shared the weight of memory. They took up what others could no longer bear. Often, they carried each other, the wounded or weak. They carried infections. They carried chess sets, basketballs, Vietnamese-English dictionaries, insignia of rank, Bronze Stars and Purple Hearts, plastic cards imprinted with the Code of Conduct. They carried diseases, among them malaria and dysentery. They carried lice and ring-worm and leeches and paddy algae and various rots and molds. They carried the land itself — Vietnam, the place, the soil — a powdery orange-red dust that covered their boots and fatigues and faces. They carried the sky. The whole atmosphere, they carried it, the humidity, the monsoons, the stink of fungus and decay, all of it, they carried gravity. They moved like mules. By daylight they took sniper fire, at night they were mortared, but it was not battle, it was just the endless march, village to village, without purpose, nothing won or lost. They marched for the sake of the march. They plodded along slowly, dumbly, leaning forward against the heat, unthinking, all blood and bone, simple grunts, soldiering with their legs, toiling up the hills and down into the paddies and across the rivers and up again and down, just humping, one step and then the next and then another, but no volition, no will, because it was automatic, it was anatomy, and the war was entirely a matter of posture and carriage, the hump was everything, a kind of inertia, a kind of emptiness, a dullness of desire and intellect and conscience and hope and human sensibility. Their principles were in their feet. Their calculations were biological. They had no sense of strategy or mission. They searched the villages without knowing what to look for, not caring, kicking over jars of rice, frisking children and old men, blowing tunnels, sometimes setting fires and sometimes not, then forming up and moving on to the next village, then other villages, where it would always be the same. They carried their own lives. The pressures were enormous. In the heat of early afternoon, they would remove their helmets and flak jackets, walking bare, which was dangerous but which helped ease the strain. They would often discard things along the route of march. Purely for comfort, they would throw away rations, blow their Claymores and grenades, no matter, because by nightfall the resupply choppers would arrive with more of the same, then a day or two later still more, fresh watermelons and crates of ammunition and sunglasses and woolen sweaters — the resources were stunning — sparklers for the Fourth of July, colored eggs for Easter. It was the great American war chest — the fruits of science, the smokestacks, the canneries, the arsenals at Hartford, the Minnesota forests, the machine shops, the vast fields of corn and wheat — they carried like freight trains; they carried it on their backs and shoulders — and for all the ambiguities of Vietnam, all the mysteries and unknowns, there was at least the single abiding certainty that they would never be at a loss for things to carry.

*   *   *

40   After the chopper took Lavender away, Lieutenant Jimmy Cross led his men into the village of Than Khe. They burned everything. They shot chickens and dogs, they trashed the village well, they called in artillery and watched the wreckage, then they marched for several hours through the hot afternoon, and then at dusk, while Kiowa explained how Lavender died, Lieutenant Cross found himself trembling.

He tried not to cry. With his entrenching tool, which weighed five pounds, he began digging a hole in the earth.

He felt shame. He hated himself. He had loved Martha more than his men, and as a consequence Lavender was now dead, and this was something he would have to carry like a stone in his stomach for the rest of the war.

All he could do was dig. He used his entrenching tool like an ax, slashing, feeling both love and hate, and then later, when it was full dark, he sat at the bottom of his foxhole and wept. It went on for a long while. In part, he was grieving for Ted Lavender, but mostly it was for Martha, and for himself, because she belonged to another world, which was not quite real, and because she was a junior at Mount Sebastian College in New Jersey, a poet and a virgin and uninvolved, and because he realized she did not love him and never would.

Like cement, Kiowa whispered in the dark. I swear to God — boom-down. Not a word.

I've heard this, said Norman Bowker.

A pisser, you know? Still zipping himself up. Zapped while zipping.

All right, fine. That's enough.

Yeah, but you had to see it, the guy just —

I *heard*, man. Cement. So why not shut the fuck *up?*

45   Kiowa shook his head sadly and glanced over at the hole where Lieutenant Jimmy Cross sat watching the night. The air was thick and wet. A warm, dense fog had settled over the paddies and there was the stillness that precedes rain.

After a time Kiowa sighed.

One thing for sure, he said. The Lieutenant's in some deep hurt. I mean that crying jag — the way he was carrying on — it wasn't fake or anything, it was real heavy-duty hurt. The man cares.

Sure, Norman Bowker said.

Say what you want, the man does care.

We all got problems.

Not Lavender.

No, I guess not, Bowker said. Do me a favor, though.

Shut up?

That's a smart Indian. Shut up.

50   Shrugging, Kiowa pulled off his boots. He wanted to say more, just to lighten up his sleep, but instead he opened his New Testament and arranged it beneath his head as a pillow. The fog made things seem hollow and unattached. He tried not to think about Ted Lavender, but then he was thinking how fast it was, no

drama, down and dead, and how it was hard to feel anything except surprise. It seemed un-Christian. He wished he could find some great sadness, or even anger, but the emotion wasn't there and he couldn't make it happen. Mostly he felt pleased to be alive. He liked the smell of the New Testament under his cheek, the leather and ink and paper and glue, whatever the chemicals were. He liked hearing the sounds of night. Even his fatigue, it felt fine, the stiff muscles and the prickly awareness of his own body, a floating feeling. He enjoyed not being dead. Lying there, Kiowa admired Lieutenant Jimmy Cross's capacity for grief. He wanted to share the man's pain, he wanted to care as Jimmy Cross cared. And yet when he closed his eyes, all he could think was Boom-down, and all he could feel was the pleasure of having his boots off and the fog curling in around him and the damp soil and the Bible smells and the plush comfort of night.

After a moment Norman Bowker sat up in the dark.

What the hell, he said. You want to talk, *talk*. Tell it to me.

Forget it.

No, man, go on. One thing I hate, it's a silent Indian.

For the most part they carried themselves with poise, a kind of dignity. Now 55 and then, however, there were times of panic, when they squealed or wanted to squeal but couldn't, when they twitched and made moaning sounds and covered their heads and said Dear Jesus and flopped around on the earth and fired their weapons blindly and cringed and sobbed and begged for the noise to stop and went wild and made stupid promises to themselves and to God and to their mothers and fathers, hoping not to die. In different ways, it happened to all of them. Afterward, when the firing ended, they would blink and peek up. They would touch their bodies, feeling shame, then quickly hiding it. They would force themselves to stand. As if in slow motion, frame by frame, the world would take on the old logic — absolute silence, then the wind, then sunlight, then voices. It was the burden of being alive. Awkwardly, the men would reassemble themselves, first in private, then in groups, becoming soldiers again. They would repair the leaks in their eyes. They would check for casualties, call in dust-offs, light cigarettes, try to smile, clear their throats and spit and begin cleaning their weapons. After a time someone would shake his head and say, No lie, I almost shit my pants, and someone else would laugh, which meant it was bad, yes, but the guy had obviously not shit his pants, it wasn't that bad, and in any case nobody would ever do such a thing and then go ahead and talk about it. They would squint into the dense, oppressive sunlight. For a few moments, perhaps, they would fall silent, lighting a joint and tracking its passage from man to man, inhaling, holding in the humiliation. Scary stuff, one of them might say. But then someone else would grin or flick his eyebrows and say, Roger-dodger, almost cut me a new asshole, *almost*.

There were numerous such poses. Some carried themselves with a sort of wistful resignation, others with pride or stiff soldierly discipline or good humor or macho zeal. They were afraid of dying but they were even more afraid to show it.

They found jokes to tell.

They used a hard vocabulary to contain the terrible softness. *Greased*, they'd say. *Offed, lit up,*° *zapped while zipping.*° It wasn't cruelty, just stage presence. They were actors and the war came at them in 3-D. When someone died, it wasn't quite dying, because in a curious way it seemed scripted, and because they had their lines mostly memorized, irony mixed with tragedy, and because they called it by other names, as if to encyst and destroy the reality of death itself. They kicked corpses. They cut off thumbs. They talked grunt lingo. They told stories about Ted Lavender's supply of tranquilizers, how the poor guy didn't feel a thing, how incredibly tranquil he was.

There's a moral here, said Mitchell Sanders.

They were waiting for Lavender's chopper, smoking the dead man's dope.

60   The moral's pretty obvious, Sanders said, and winked. Stay away from drugs. No joke, they'll ruin your day every time.

Cute, said Henry Dobbins.

Mind-blower, get it? Talk about wiggy — nothing left, just blood and brains.

They made themselves laugh.

65   There it is, they'd say, over and over, as if the repetition itself were an act of poise, a balance between crazy and almost crazy, knowing without going. There it is, which meant be cool, let it ride, because oh yeah, man, you can't change what can't be changed, there it is, there it absolutely and positively and fucking well *is*.

They were tough.

They carried all the emotional baggage of men who might die. Grief, terror, love, longing — these were intangibles, but the intangibles had their own mass and specific gravity, they had tangible weight. They carried shameful memories. They carried the common secret of cowardice barely restrained, the instinct to run or freeze or hide, and in many respects this was the heaviest burden of all, for it could never be put down, it required perfect balance and perfect posture. They carried their reputations. They carried the soldier's greatest fear, which was the fear of blushing. Men killed, and died, because they were embarrassed not to. It was what had brought them to the war in the first place, nothing positive, no dreams of glory or honor, just to avoid the blush of dishonor. They died so as not to die of embarrassment. They crawled into tunnels and walked point and advanced under fire. Each morning, despite the unknowns, they made their legs move. They endured. They kept humping. They did not submit to the obvious alternative, which was simply to close the eyes and fall. So easy, really. Go limp and tumble to the ground and let the muscles unwind and not speak and not budge until your buddies picked you up and lifted you into the chopper that would roar and dip its nose and carry you off to the world. A mere matter of falling, yet no one ever fell. It was not courage, exactly; the object was not valor. Rather, they were too frightened to be cowards.

Offed, lit up: Killed.

zapped while zipping: Killed while urinating.

By and large they carried these things inside, maintaining the masks of composure. They sneered at sick call. They spoke bitterly about guys who had found release by shooting off their own toes or fingers. Pussies, they'd say. Candyasses. It was fierce, mocking talk, with only a trace of envy or awe, but even so, the image played itself out behind their eyes.

They imagined the muzzle against flesh. They imagined the quick, sweet pain, then the evacuation to Japan, then a hospital with warm beds and cute geisha nurses.

They dreamed of freedom birds.

70

At night, on guard, staring into the dark, they were carried away by jumbo jets. They felt the rush of takeoff. *Gone!* they yelled. And then velocity, wings and engines, a smiling stewardess — but it was more than a plane, it was a real bird, a big sleek silver bird with feathers and talons and high screeching. They were flying. The weights fell off, there was nothing to bear. They laughed and held on tight, feeling the cold slap of wind and altitude, soaring, thinking *It's over, I'm gone!* — they were naked, they were light and free — it was all lightness, bright and fast and buoyant, light as light, a helium buzz in the brain, a giddy bubbling in the lungs as they were taken up over the clouds and the war, beyond duty, beyond gravity and mortification and global entanglements — *Sin loi!* they yelled, *I'm sorry, motherfuckers, but I'm out of it, I'm goofed, I'm on a space cruise, I'm gone!* — and it was a restful, disencumbered sensation, just riding the light waves, sailing that big silver freedom bird over the mountains and oceans, over America, over the farms and great sleeping cities and cemeteries and highways and the golden arches of McDonald's. It was flight, a kind of fleeing, a kind of falling, falling higher and higher, spinning off the edge of the earth and beyond the sun and through the vast, silent vacuum where there were no burdens and where everything weighed exactly nothing. *Gone!* they screamed, *I'm sorry but I'm gone!* And so at night, not quite dreaming, they gave themselves over to lightness, they were carried, they were purely borne.

On the morning after Ted Lavender died, First Lieutenant Jimmy Cross crouched at the bottom of his foxhole and burned Martha's letters. Then he burned the two photographs. There was a steady rain falling, which made it difficult, but he used heat tabs and Sterno to build a small fire, screening it with his body, holding the photographs over the tight blue flame with the tips of his fingers.

He realized it was only a gesture. Stupid, he thought. Sentimental, too, but mostly just stupid.

Lavender was dead. You couldn't burn the blame.

Besides, the letters were in his head. And even now, without photographs, Lieutenant Cross could see Martha playing volleyball in her white gym shorts and yellow T-shirt. He could see her moving in the rain.

75

When the fire died out, Lieutenant Cross pulled his poncho over his shoulders and ate breakfast from a can.

There was no great mystery, he decided.

In those burned letters Martha had never mentioned the war, except to say, Jimmy, take care of yourself. She wasn't involved. She signed the letters "Love," but it wasn't love, and all the fine lines and technicalities did not matter.

The morning came up wet and blurry. Everything seemed part of everything else, the fog and Martha and the deepening rain.

80   It was a war, after all.

Half smiling, Lieutenant Jimmy Cross took out his maps. He shook his head hard, as if to clear it, then bent forward and began planning the day's march. In ten minutes, or maybe twenty, he would rouse the men and they would pack up and head west, where the maps showed the country to be green and inviting. They would do what they had always done. The rain might add some weight, but otherwise it would be one more day layered upon all the other days.

He was realistic about it. There was that new hardness in his stomach.

No more fantasies, he told himself.

Henceforth, when he thought about Martha, it would be only to think that she belonged elsewhere. He would shut down the daydreams. This was not Mount Sebastian, it was another world, where there were no pretty poems or midterm exams, a place where men died because of carelessness and gross stupidity. Kiowa was right. Boom-down, and you were dead, never partly dead.

85   Briefly, in the rain, Lieutenant Cross saw Martha's gray eyes gazing back at him. He understood.

It was very sad, he thought. The things men carried inside. The things men did or felt they had to do.

He almost nodded at her, but didn't.

Instead he went back to his maps. He was now determined to perform his duties firmly and without negligence. It wouldn't help Lavender, he knew that, but from this point on he would comport himself as a soldier. He would dispose of his good-luck pebble. Swallow it, maybe, or use Lee Strunk's slingshot, or just drop it along the trail. On the march he would impose strict field discipline. He would be careful to send out flank security, to prevent straggling or bunching up, to keep his troops moving at the proper pace and at the proper interval. He would insist on clean weapons. He would confiscate the remainder of Lavender's dope. Later in the day, perhaps, he would call the men together and speak to them plainly. He would accept the blame for what had happened to Ted Lavender. He would be a man about it. He would look them in the eyes, keeping his chin level, and he would issue the new SOPs in a calm, impersonal tone of voice, an officer's voice, leaving no room for argument or discussion. Commencing immediately, he'd tell them, they would no longer abandon equipment along the route of march. They would police up their acts. They would get their shit together, and keep it together, and maintain it neatly and in good working order.

90   He would not tolerate laxity. He would show strength, distancing himself.

Among the men there would be grumbling, of course, and maybe worse, because their days would seem longer and their loads heavier, but Lieutenant Cross reminded himself that his obligation was not to be loved but to lead. He would dispense with love; it was not now a factor. And if anyone quarreled or complained, he would simply tighten his lips and arrange his shoulders in the correct command posture. He might give a curt little nod. Or he might not. He might just shrug and say Carry on, then they would saddle up and form into a column and move out toward the villages west of Than Khe.

Reading and Reacting

1. Although the setting and the events described in "The Things They Carried" are dramatic and moving, its tone is often flat and emotionless. How is this tone created? Why do you think the narrator adopts this kind of tone?

2. Consider the different meanings of the word *carry*, which can refer to burdens abstract or concrete as well as to things carried physically or emotionally, actively or passively. Give one or two examples of each of the different senses in which O'Brien uses the word. How does his repeated use of the word enhance the story?

3. A striking characteristic of the story's style is its thorough catalogs of the concrete, tangible "things" the soldiers carry. Why do you suppose such detailed lists are included? What does what each man carries tell you about him? In a less literal, more abstract sense, what else do these men "carry"?

4. One stylistic technique O'Brien uses is intentional repetition — of phrases ("they carried"); people's names and identifying details (Martha's virginity, for example); and pieces of equipment. What effect do you think O'Brien hopes to achieve through such repetition? Is he successful?

5. Interspersed among long paragraphs crammed with detail are short one- or two-sentence paragraphs. What function do these brief paragraphs serve?

6. What role does Martha play in the story? Why does Lieutenant Cross burn her letters?

7. In paragraph 68, the narrator says of the soldiers, "They used a hard vocabulary to contain the terrible softness." What do you think he means by this? Do you think this "hard vocabulary" is necessary? How does it affect your reaction to the characters?

8. Describing Lieutenant Cross's new sense of purpose in the story's final paragraph, the narrator uses the phrase "Carry on." Do you think this phrase is linked in any way to the story's other uses of the word *carry*, or do you believe it is unrelated? Explain.

9. **Journal Entry** "The Things They Carried" is a story about war. Do you think it is an antiwar story? Why or why not?

10. **Critical Perspective** In an essay about war memoirs, Clayton W. Lewis questions O'Brien's decision to present "the nightmare [he] faced in a Vietnam rice paddy" as fiction. Lewis believes that some of O'Brien's stories "dissolve into clever artifice" and, therefore, are not as effective as actual memoirs of the Vietnam experience would be. He concludes that "for all its

brilliance and emotional grounding, [the stories do not] satisfy one's appetite to hear what happened rendered as it was experienced and remembered."

Do you think Lewis has a point? Or do you think O'Brien's "artifice" communicates his emotions and experiences more effectively than a straightforward memoir could? Explain your position.

Related Works: "The Soldier" (p. 638), "For the Union Dead" (p. 639), "Facing It" (p. 642), "Dulce et Decorum Est" (p. 638)

WRITING SUGGESTIONS: Style, Tone, and Language

1. In "The Things They Carried," Tim O'Brien considers his characters' emotional and psychological burdens as well as the physical "things they carry." Applying O'Brien's criteria to Charlotte Perkins Gilman's "The Yellow Wallpaper" (p. 372), write an essay in which you consider what the narrator "carries" (and what her husband "carries") and why.

2. Both "A Good Man Is Hard to Find" and "The Things They Carried" depict high-stakes struggles for survival. Other works in this anthology depict similar struggles — some intellectual and some physical, even violent. Choose two or three works in which a physical or intellectual contest between two individuals is central, and write an essay in which you compare the nature of the struggles and their outcomes.

3. Imagine The Misfit in a prison cell, relating the violent incident at the end of "A Good Man Is Hard to Find" to another prisoner — or to a member of the clergy. Would his tone be boastful? Regretful? Apologetic? Defiant? Would he use the elaborate poetic style he sometimes uses in the story or more straightforward language? Tell his version of the incident in his own words.

4. Both "Araby" and "The Things They Carried" deal, at least in part, with infatuation. Compare and contrast the infatuations described in the two stories. How does the language used by the narrators in the two stories communicate the two characters' fascination and subsequent disillusionment?

CHAPTER 11

SYMBOL, ALLEGORY, AND MYTH

> Symbols have to spring from the work direct, and stay alive. Symbols for the sake of symbols are counterfeit, and were they all stamped on the page in red they couldn't any more quickly give themselves away.
>
> —Eudora Welty, "*Words into Fiction*"

Symbol

A **symbol** is a person, object, action, place, or event that, in addition to its literal meaning, suggests a more complex meaning or range of meanings. **Universal** or **archetypal symbols,** such as the Old Man, the Mother, or the Grim Reaper, are so much a part of human experience that they suggest the same thing to most people. **Conventional symbols** are also likely to suggest the same thing to most people (a rose suggests love, a skull and crossbones denotes poison), provided the people have common cultural and social assumptions. Such symbols are often used as a kind of shorthand in films, popular literature, and advertising, where they encourage predictable responses.

A conventional symbol such as the stars and stripes of the American flag can evoke powerful feelings of pride and patriotism in a group of people who share a culture, just as the maple leaf and the Union Jack can. Symbols used in works of literature can function in much the same way, enabling writers to convey particular emotions or messages with a high degree of predictability. Thus, spring can be expected to suggest rebirth and promise; autumn, declining years and powers; summer, youth and beauty. Because a writer expects a dark forest to evoke fear, or a rainbow to communicate hope, he or she can be quite confident in using such images to convey a particular idea or mood (provided the audience shares the writer's frame of reference).

Many symbols, however, suggest different things to different people, and different cultures may react differently to the same symbols. (In the United States, for example, an owl suggests wisdom; in India it suggests the opposite.) Thus, symbols enrich meaning, expanding the possibilities for interpretation and for

267

readers' interaction with the text. Because they are so potentially rich, symbols have the power to open up a work of literature.

Literary Symbols

Both universal and conventional symbols can function as **literary symbols** that take on additional meanings in particular works. For instance, a watch or clock denotes time; as a conventional symbol, it suggests the passing of time; as a literary symbol in a particular work, it might also convey anything from a character's inability to recapture the past to the idea of time running out — or it might suggest something else.

Considering an object's possible symbolic significance can suggest a variety of ways to interpret a text. For instance, William Faulkner focuses attention on an unseen watch in a pivotal scene in "A Rose for Emily" (p. 113). The narrator first describes Emily Grierson as "a small, fat woman in black, with a thin gold chain descending to her waist and vanishing into her belt." Several sentences later, the narrator returns to the watch, noting that Emily's visitors "could hear the invisible watch ticking at the end of the gold chain." Like these visitors, readers are drawn to the unseen watch as it ticks away. Because Emily is portrayed as a woman living in the past, readers can assume that the watch is intended to reinforce the impression that she cannot see that time (the watch) has moved on. The vivid picture of the pale, plump woman in the musty room with the watch invisibly ticking does indeed suggest both that she has been left back in time and that she remains unaware of the progress around her. Thus, the symbol enriches both the depiction of character and the story's theme.

In "Barn Burning" (p. 209), another Faulkner story, the clock is a more complex symbol. The itinerant Snopes family is without financial security and apparently without a future. The clock the mother carries from shack to shack — "The clock inlaid with mother-of-pearl, which would not run, stopped at some fourteen minutes past two o'clock of a dead and forgotten day and time, which had been [Sarty's] mother's dowry" — is their only possession of value. The fact that the clock no longer works seems at first to suggest that time has run out for the family. On another level, the clock stands in stark contrast to Major de Spain's grand home, with its gold and glitter and Oriental rugs. Knowing that the clock was part of the mother's dowry, and that a dowry suggests a promise, readers may decide that the broken clock symbolizes lost hope. The fact that the mother still clings to the clock, however, could suggest just the opposite: her refusal to give up.

As you read, you should not try to find one exact equivalent for each symbol; that kind of search is limiting and unproductive. Instead, consider the different meanings a symbol might suggest. Then, consider how these various interpretations enrich other elements of the story and the work as a whole.

Recognizing Symbols

When is a clock just a clock, and when is it also a symbol with a meaning (or meanings) beyond its literal significance? If a character waiting for a friend glances once at a watch to verify the time, there is probably nothing symbolic about the watch or about the act of looking at it. If, however, the watch keeps appearing again and again in the story, at key moments; if the narrator devotes a good deal of time to describing it; if it is placed in a conspicuous physical location; if characters keep noticing it and commenting on its presence; if it is lost (or found) at a critical moment; if its function in some way parallels the development of plot or character (for instance, if it stops as a relationship ends or when a character dies); if the story's opening or closing paragraph focuses on the timepiece; or if the story is called "The Watch"— the watch most likely has symbolic significance. In other words, considering how an image is used, how often it is used, and when it appears will help you to determine whether or not it functions as a symbol.

Symbols expand the possible meanings of a story, thereby heightening interest and actively involving readers in the text. In "The Lottery" (p. 274), for example, the mysterious black box has symbolic significance. It is mentioned prominently and repeatedly, and it plays a pivotal role in the story's action. Of course, the black box is important on a purely literal level: it functions as a key component of the lottery. But the box has other associations as well, and it is these associations that suggest what its symbolic significance might be.

The black wooden box is very old, a relic of many past lotteries; the narrator observes that it represents tradition. It is also closed and closely guarded, suggesting mystery and uncertainty. It is shabby, "splintered badly along one side . . . and in places faded or stained," and this state of disrepair could suggest that the ritual it is part of has also deteriorated or that tradition itself has deteriorated. The box is also simple in construction and design, suggesting the primitive (and therefore perhaps outdated) nature of the ritual. Thus, this symbol encourages readers to probe the story for values and ideas, to consider and weigh the suitability of a variety of interpretations. It serves as a "hot spot" that invites questions, and the answers to these questions reinforce and enrich the story's theme.

Allegory

An **allegory** communicates a doctrine, message, or moral principle by making it into a narrative in which the characters personify ideas, concepts, qualities, or other abstractions. Thus, an allegory is a story with two parallel and consistent levels of meaning — one literal and one figurative. The figurative level, which offers some moral or political lesson, is the story's main concern. The allegorical figures are significant only because they represent something beyond their literal meaning in a fixed system.

Whereas a symbol has multiple symbolic associations as well as a literal meaning, an **allegorical figure**— a character, object, place, or event in the allegory — has just one meaning within an **allegorical framework,** the set of ideas that conveys the allegory's message. (At the simplest level, for instance, one character can stand for good and another can stand for evil.) For this reason, allegorical figures do not open up a text to various interpretations the way symbols do. Because the purpose of allegory is to communicate a particular lesson, readers are not encouraged to speculate about the allegory's possible meanings; each element has only one equivalent, which readers must discover if they are to make sense of the story.

Naturally, the better a reader understands the political, religious, and literary assumptions of a writer, the easier it will be to recognize the allegorical significance of his or her work. John Bunyan's *The Pilgrim's Progress,* for example, is a famous seventeenth-century allegory based on the Christian doctrine of salvation. In order to appreciate the complexity of Bunyan's work, you would have to familiarize yourself with this doctrine—possibly by consulting an encyclopedia or a reference work such as *The Oxford Companion to English Literature*.

One type of allegory, called a **beast fable,** is a short tale, usually including a moral, in which animals assume human characteristics. Aesop's fables are the best-known examples of beast fables. More recently, contemporary writers have used beast fables to satirize the political and social conditions of our time. In one such tale, "The Gentlemen of the Jungle" by the Kenyan writer Jomo Kenyatta, an elephant is allowed to put his trunk inside a man's hut during a rainstorm. Not content with keeping his trunk dry, the elephant pushes his entire body inside the hut, displacing the man. When the man protests, the elephant takes the matter to the lion, who appoints a Commission of Enquiry to settle the matter. Eventually, the man is forced not only to abandon his hut to the elephant, but also to build new huts for all the animals on the Commission. Even so, the jealous animals occupy the man's new hut and begin fighting for space; while they are arguing, the man burns down the hut, animals and all. Like the tales told by Aesop, "The Gentlemen of the Jungle" has a moral: "Peace is costly," says the man as he walks away happily, "but it's worth the expense." The following passage from Kenyatta's tale reveals how the allegorical figures work within the framework of the allegory:

> The elephant, obeying the command of his master (the lion), got busy with the other ministers to appoint a Commission of Enquiry. The following elders of the jungle were appointed to sit in the Commission: (1) Mr. Rhinoceros; (2) Mr. Buffalo; (3) Mr. Alligator; (4) The Rt. Hon. Mr. Fox to act as chairman; and (5) Mr. Leopard to act as Secretary of the Commission. On seeing the personnel, the man protested and asked if it was not necessary to include in this Commission a member from his side. But he was told that it was impossible, since no one from his side was well enough educated to understand the intricacy of jungle law.

From this excerpt we can see that each character represents a particular idea. For example, the members of the Commission stand for bureaucratic smugness and inequity, and the man stands for the citizens who are victimized by the government. In order to fully understand the allegorical significance of each figure in this story, of course, readers would have to know something about government bureaucracies, colonialism in Africa, and possibly a specific historical event in Kenya.

Some works contain both symbolic elements *and* allegorical elements, as Nathaniel Hawthorne's "Young Goodman Brown" (p. 302) does. The names of the story's two main characters, "Goodman" and "Faith," suggest that they fit within an allegorical system of some sort: Young Goodman Brown represents a good person who, despite his best efforts, strays from the path of righteousness; his wife, Faith, represents the quality he must hold on to in order to avoid temptation. As characters, they have no significance outside of their allegorical functions. Other elements of the story, however, are not so clear-cut. The older man whom Young Goodman Brown meets in the woods carries a staff that has carved on it "the likeness of a great black snake, so curiously wrought, that it might almost be seen to twist and wriggle itself like a living serpent." This staff, carried by a Satanic figure who represents evil and temptation, suggests the snake in the Garden of Eden, an association that neatly fits into the allegorical framework of the story. Alternately, however, the staff could suggest the "slippery," ever-changing nature of sin, the difficulty people have in perceiving sin, or even sexuality (which may explain Young Goodman Brown's susceptibility to temptation). This range of possible meanings suggests that the staff functions as a symbol (not an allegorical figure) that enriches Hawthorne's allegory.

Other stories work entirely on a symbolic level and contain no allegorical figures. "The Lottery," despite its moral overtones, is not an allegory because its characters, events, and objects are not arranged to serve one rigid, didactic purpose. In fact, many different interpretations have been suggested for this story. When it was first published in June 1948 in the *New Yorker*, some readers believed it to be a story about an actual custom or ritual. As Shirley Jackson reports in her essay "Biography of a Story," even those who recognized it as fiction speculated about its meaning, seeing it as (among other things) an attack on prejudice, a criticism of society's need for a scapegoat, or a treatise on witchcraft, Christian martyrdom, or village gossip. The fact is that no single allegorical interpretation will account for every major character, object, and event in the story.

MYTH

Throughout history, human beings have been makers of myths. For the purpose of this discussion, a **myth** is a story that is central to a culture; it embodies the values on which a culture or society is built. Thus, myths are not synonymous with falsehoods or fairy tales. They are stories that contain ideas that inform a culture and that give that culture meaning. In this sense, then, both an ancient epic and a contemporary religious text can convey a "myth."

Although many myths have to do with religion, myths are not limited to the theological. Myths explain everything from natural phenomena — such as the creation of the world — to the existence of human beings and the beginnings of agriculture. The importance of myths rests on their ability to embody a set of beliefs that unifies both individuals and the society in which they live. By examining myths, we can learn much about our own origins and our most deeply held beliefs.

One of the most prevalent types of myth is the **creation myth**. Almost every culture has an explanation for how the earth, sun, and stars — not to mention people — came into being. According to the ancient Greeks, for example, the world began as an empty void from which Nyx, a bird with black wings, emerged. She laid a golden egg, and out of it Eros, the god of love, arose. The two halves of the eggshell became the earth and the sky, who fell in love with each other and had many children and grandchildren. These offspring became the gods of the Greek pantheon, who eventually created humans beings in their own likeness. Each of these gods had a role to play in the creation and maintenance of the world, and their actions — in particular, their constant meddling in the lives of people — comprise the myths of ancient Greece.

In various cultures all over the world, creation myths take different forms. To the ancient Japanese, for example, the world emerged from a single seed, which grew to form a god who, in turn, created other gods and eventually the islands of Japan and their inhabitants. Several Native American tribes share common beliefs about "sky ancestors," who they believe created the people on the planet.

In Western culture, the most recognizable creation myth appears in Genesis, the first book of the Old Testament. According to Genesis, God created the heavens and the earth as well as all living creatures — including Adam and Eve. Other stories, also part of the oral tradition of Judaism, do not appear in Genesis. An example of such a story is the tale of Lilith, which emerged sometime between the eighth and eleventh centuries. According to this Hebrew myth, Lilith, who was created before Eve, was Adam's first wife. However, she refused to be subservient to Adam, and so she left Eden, eventually to be replaced by Eve. Talmudic tradition holds that she later mated with demons and gave birth to a legion of demonic offspring who inhabit the dark places of the earth.

The influence of mythology on literature is profound, and our contemporary understanding of narrative fiction owes a great deal to mythology. In fact, many of the short stories in this anthology contain allusions to myth. Consider, for example, the role of myth in "The Lottery" by Shirley Jackson, "Cathedral" by Raymond Carver, and "Young Goodman Brown" by Nathaniel Hawthorne. In each of these short stories, myth is central to the characters' behavior, sensibility, and understanding of the world in which they live.

✔ CHECKLIST   Writing about Symbol, Allegory, and Myth

▪ Are any universal symbols used in the work? Any conventional symbols? What is their function?

▪ Is any character, place, action, event, or object given unusual prominence or emphasis in the story? If so, does this element seem to have symbolic as well as literal significance?

▪ What possible meanings does each symbol suggest?

▪ How do symbols help to depict the story's characters?

▪ How do symbols help to characterize the story's setting?

▪ How do symbols help to advance the story's plot?

▪ Does the story have a moral or didactic purpose? What is the message, idea, or moral principle the story seeks to convey? Is the story an allegory?

▪ What equivalent may be assigned to each allegorical figure in the story?

▪ What is the allegorical framework of the story?

▪ Does the story combine allegorical figures and symbols? How do they work together in the story?

▪ Does the story have any references to myth? If so, what do they add?

SHIRLEY JACKSON (1916–1965) is best known for her restrained tales of horror and the supernatural, most notably her novel *The Haunting of Hill House* (1959) and the short story "The Lottery" (1948). Among her other works are two novels dealing with divided personalities — *The Bird's Nest* (1954) and *We Have Always Lived in the Castle* (1962) — and two collections of comic tales about her children and family life, *Life among the Savages* (1953) and *Raising Demons* (1957). A posthumous collection of stories, *Just an Ordinary Day* (1997), was published after the discovery of a box of some of Jackson's unpublished papers in a Vermont barn and her heirs' subsequent search for her other uncollected works.

With her husband, literary critic Stanley Edgar Hyman, she settled in the small town of Bennington, Vermont, but was never accepted by the townspeople. "The Lottery" is set in much the same kind of small, hidebound town. Despite the story's matter-of-fact tone and familiar setting, its publication in the *New Yorker* provoked a torrent of letters from enraged and shocked readers. In her quiet way, Jackson presented the underside of village life and revealed to readers the dark side of human nature. Future writers of gothic tales recognized their great debt to Jackson. Horror master Stephen King dedicated his book *Firestarter* "to Shirley Jackson, who never had to raise her voice."

The Lottery   (1948)

The morning of June 27th was clear and sunny, with the fresh warmth of a full-summer day; the flowers were blossoming profusely and the grass was richly green. The people of the village began to gather in the square, between the post office and the bank, around ten o'clock; in some towns there were so many people that the lottery took two days and had to be started on June 26th, but in this village, where there were only about three hundred people, the whole lottery took less than two hours, so it could begin at ten o'clock in the morning and still be through in time to allow the villagers to get home for noon dinner.

The children assembled first, of course. School was recently over for the summer, and the feeling of liberty sat uneasily on most of them; they tended to gather together quietly for a while before they broke into boisterous play, and their talk was still of the classroom and the teacher, of books and reprimands. Bobby Martin had already stuffed his pockets full of stones, and the other boys soon followed his example, selecting the smoothest and roundest stones; Bobby and Harry Jones and Dickie Delacroix — the villagers pronounced this name "Dellacroy" — eventually made a great pile of stones in one corner of the square and guarded it against the raids of the other boys. The girls stood aside, talking among themselves, looking over their shoulders at the boys, and the very small children rolled in the dust or clung to the hands of their older brothers or sisters.

Soon the men began to gather, surveying their own children, speaking of planting and rain, tractors and taxes. They stood together, away from the pile of stones in the corner, and their jokes were quiet and they smiled rather than laughed. The women, wearing faded house dresses and sweaters, came shortly after their menfolk. They greeted one another and exchanged bits of gossip as they went to join their husbands. Soon the women, standing by their husbands, began to call to their children, and the children came reluctantly, having to be called four or five times. Bobby Martin ducked under his mother's grasping hand and ran, laughing, back to the pile of stones. His father spoke up sharply, and Bobby came quickly and took his place between his father and his oldest brother.

The lottery was conducted — as were the square dances, the teen-age club, the Halloween program — by Mr. Summers, who had time and energy to devote to civic activities. He was a round-faced, jovial man and he ran the coal business, and people were sorry for him, because he had no children and his wife was a scold. When he arrived in the square, carrying the black wooden box, there was a murmur of conversation among the villagers, and he waved and called, "Little late today, folks." The postmaster, Mr. Graves, followed him, carrying a three-legged stool, and the stool was put in the center of the square and Mr. Summers set the black box down on it. The villagers kept their distance, leaving a space between themselves and the stool, and when Mr. Summers said, "Some of you fellows want to give me a hand?" there was a hesitation before two men, Mr. Martin and his oldest son, Baxter, came forward to hold the box steady on the stool while Mr. Summers stirred up the papers inside it.

The original paraphernalia for the lottery had been lost long ago, and the 5
black box now resting on the stool had been put into use even before Old Man
Warner, the oldest man in town, was born. Mr. Summers spoke frequently to the
villagers about making a new box, but no one liked to upset even as much tradition as was represented by the black box. There was a story that the present box
had been made with some pieces of the box that had preceded it, the one that
had been constructed when the first people settled down to make a village here.
Every year, after the lottery, Mr. Summers began talking again about a new box,
but every year the subject was allowed to fade off without anything's being done.
The black box grew shabbier each year; by now it was no longer completely black
but splintered badly along one side to show the original wood color, and in some
places faded or stained.

Mr. Martin and his oldest son, Baxter, held the black box securely on the
stool until Mr. Summers had stirred the papers thoroughly with his hand. Because so much of the ritual had been forgotten or discarded, Mr. Summers had
been successful in having slips of paper substituted for the chips of wood that had
been used for generations. Chips of wood, Mr. Summers had argued, had been all
very well when the village was tiny, but now that the population was more than
three hundred and likely to keep on growing, it was necessary to use something
that would fit more easily into the black box. The night before the lottery, Mr.
Summers and Mr. Graves made up the slips of paper and put them in the box,
and it was then taken to the safe of Mr. Summers's coal company and locked up
until Mr. Summers was ready to take it to the square next morning. The rest of
the year, the box was put away, sometimes one place, sometimes another; it had
spent one year in Mr. Graves's barn and another year underfoot in the post office,
and sometimes it was set on a shelf in the Martin grocery and left there.

There was a great deal of fussing to be done before Mr. Summers declared the
lottery open. There were the lists to make up—of heads of families, heads of
households in each family, members of each household in each family. There was
the proper swearing-in of Mr. Summers by the postmaster, as the official of the
lottery; at one time, some people remembered, there had been a recital of some
sort, performed by the official of the lottery, a perfunctory, tuneless chant that
had been rattled off duly each year; some people believed that the official of the
lottery used to stand just so when he said or sang it, others believed that he was
supposed to walk among the people, but years and years ago this part of the ritual had been allowed to lapse. There had been, also, a ritual salute, which the
official of the lottery had had to use in addressing each person who came up to
draw from the box, but this also had changed with time, until now it was felt necessary only for the official to speak to each person approaching. Mr. Summers was
very good at all this; in his clean white shirt and blue jeans, with one hand resting carelessly on the black box, he seemed very proper and important as he
talked interminably to Mr. Graves and the Martins.

Just as Mr. Summers finally left off talking and turned to the assembled villagers, Mrs. Hutchinson came hurriedly along the path to the square, her sweater

thrown over her shoulders, and slid into place in the back of the crowd. "Clean forgot what day it was," she said to Mrs. Delacroix, who stood next to her, and they both laughed softly. "Thought my old man was out back stacking wood," Mrs. Hutchinson went on, "and then I looked out the window and the kids was gone, and then I remembered it was the twenty-seventh and came a-running." She dried her hands on her apron, and Mrs. Delacroix said, "You're in time, though. They're still talking away up there."

Mrs. Hutchinson craned her neck to see through the crowd and found her husband and children standing near the front. She tapped Mrs. Delacroix on the arm as a farewell and began to make her way through the crowd. The people separated good-humoredly to let her through; two or three people said, in voices just loud enough to be heard across the crowd, "Here comes your Missus, Hutchinson," and "Bill, she made it after all." Mrs. Hutchinson reached her husband, and Mr. Summers, who had been waiting, said cheerfully, "Thought we were going to have to get on without you, Tessie." Mrs. Hutchinson said, grinning, "Wouldn't have me leave m'dishes in the sink, now, would you, Joe?," and soft laughter ran through the crowd as the people stirred back into position after Mrs. Hutchinson's arrival.

10   "Well, now," Mr. Summers said soberly, "guess we better get started, get this over with, so's we can go back to work. Anybody ain't here?"

"Dunbar," several people said. "Dunbar, Dunbar."

Mr. Summers consulted his list. "Clyde Dunbar," he said. "That's right. He's broke his leg, hasn't he? Who's drawing for him?"

"Me, I guess," a woman said, and Mr. Summers turned to look at her. "Wife draws for her husband," Mr. Summers said. "Don't you have a grown boy to do it for you, Janey?" Although Mr. Summers and everyone else in the village knew the answer perfectly well, it was the business of the official of the lottery to ask such questions formally. Mr. Summers waited with an expression of polite interest while Mrs. Dunbar answered.

"Horace's not but sixteen yet," Mrs. Dunbar said regretfully. "Guess I gotta fill in for the old man this year."

15   "Right," Mr. Summers said. He made a note on the list he was holding. Then he asked, "Watson boy drawing this year?"

A tall boy in the crowd raised his hand. "Here," he said. "I'm drawing for m'mother and me." He blinked his eyes nervously and ducked his head as several voices in the crowd said things like "Good fellow, Jack," and "Glad to see your mother's got a man to do it."

"Well," Mr. Summers said, "guess that's everyone. Old Man Warner make it?"

"Here," a voice said, and Mr. Summers nodded.

A sudden hush fell on the crowd as Mr. Summers cleared his throat and looked at the list. "All ready?" he called. "Now, I'll read the names — heads of families first — and the men come up and take a paper out of the box. Keep the paper folded in your hand without looking at it until everyone has had a turn. Everything clear?"

The people had done it so many times that they only half listened to the di- 20
rections; most of them were quiet, wetting their lips, not looking around. Then
Mr. Summers raised one hand high and said, "Adams." A man disengaged himself from the crowd and came forward. "Hi, Steve," Mr. Summers said, and Mr.
Adams said, "Hi, Joe." They grinned at one another humorlessly and nervously.
Then Mr. Adams reached into the black box and took out a folded paper. He
held it firmly by one corner as he turned and went hastily back to his place in the
crowd, where he stood a little apart from his family, not looking down at his
hand.

"Allen," Mr. Summers said. "Anderson. . . . Bentham."

"Seems like there's no time at all between lotteries any more," Mrs. Delacroix
said to Mrs. Graves in the back row. "Seems like we got through with the last one
only last week."

"Time sure goes fast," Mrs. Graves said.

"Clark. . . . Delacroix."

"There goes my old man," Mrs. Delacroix said. She held her breath while her 25
husband went forward.

"Dunbar," Mr. Summers said, and Mrs. Dunbar went steadily to the box while
one of the women said, "Go on, Janey," and another said, "There she goes."

"We're next," Mrs. Graves said. She watched while Mr. Graves came around
from the side of the box, greeted Mr. Summers gravely, and selected a slip of paper from the box. By now, all through the crowd there were men holding the
small folded papers in their large hands, turning them over and over nervously.
Mrs. Dunbar and her two sons stood together, Mrs. Dunbar holding the slip of
paper.

"Harburt. . . . Hutchinson."

"Get up there, Bill," Mrs. Hutchinson said, and the people near her laughed.

"Jones." 30

"They do say," Mr. Adams said to Old Man Warner, who stood next to him,
"that over in the north village they're talking of giving up the lottery."

Old Man Warner snorted. "Pack of crazy fools," he said. "Listening to the
young folks, nothing's good enough for *them*. Next thing you know, they'll be
wanting to go back to living in caves, nobody work any more, live *that* way for a
while. Used to be a saying about 'Lottery in June, corn be heavy soon.' First thing
you know, we'd all be eating stewed chickweed and acorns. There's *always* been
a lottery," he added petulantly. "Bad enough to see young Joe Summers up there
joking with everybody."

"Some places have already quit lotteries," Mrs. Adams said.

"Nothing but trouble in *that*," Old Man Warner said stoutly. "Pack of young
fools."

"Martin." And Bobby Martin watched his father go forward. "Overdyke. . . . 35
Percy."

"I wish they'd hurry," Mrs. Dunbar said to her older son. "I wish they'd hurry."

"They're almost through," her son said.

"You get ready to run tell Dad," Mrs. Dunbar said.

Mr. Summers called his own name and then stepped forward precisely and selected a slip from the box. Then he called, "Warner."

40 "Seventy-seventh year I been in the lottery," Old Man Warner said as he went through the crowd. "Seventy-seventh time."

"Watson." The tall boy came awkwardly through the crowd. Someone said, "Don't be nervous, Jack," and Mr. Summers said, "Take your time, son."

"Zanini."

After that, there was a long pause, a breathless pause, until Mr. Summers, holding his slip of paper in the air, said, "All right, fellows." For a minute, no one moved, and then all the slips of paper were opened. Suddenly, all the women began to speak at once, saying, "Who is it?," "Who's got it?," "Is it the Dunbars?," "Is it the Watsons?" Then the voices began to say, "It's Hutchinson. It's Bill," "Bill Hutchinson's got it."

"Go tell your father," Mrs. Dunbar said to her older son.

45 People began to look around to see the Hutchinsons. Bill Hutchinson was standing quiet, staring down at the paper in his hand. Suddenly, Tessie Hutchinson shouted to Mr. Summers, "You didn't give him time enough to take any paper he wanted. I saw you. It wasn't fair!"

"Be a good sport, Tessie," Mrs. Delacroix called, and Mrs. Graves said, "All of us took the same chance."

"Shut up, Tessie," Bill Hutchinson said.

"Well, everyone," Mr. Summers said, "that was done pretty fast, and now we've got to be hurrying a little more to get done in time." He consulted his next list. "Bill," he said, "you draw for the Hutchinson family. You got any other households in the Hutchinsons?"

"There's Don and Eva," Mrs. Hutchinson yelled, "Make *them* take their chance!"

50 "Daughters draw with their husbands' families, Tessie," Mr. Summers said gently. "You know that as well as anyone else."

"It wasn't *fair*," Tessie said.

"I guess not, Joe," Bill Hutchinson said regretfully. "My daughter draws with her husband's family, that's only fair. And I've got no other family except the kids."

"Then, as far as drawing for families is concerned, it's you," Mr. Summers said in explanation, "and as far as drawing for households is concerned, that's you, too. Right?"

"Right," Bill Hutchinson said.

55 "How many kids, Bill?" Mr. Summers asked formally.

"Three," Bill Hutchinson said. "There's Bill, Jr., and Nancy, and little Dave. And Tessie and me."

"All right, then," Mr. Summers said. "Harry, you got their tickets back?"

Mr. Graves nodded and held up the slips of paper. "Put them in the box, then," Mr. Summers directed. "Take Bill's and put it in."

"I think we ought to start over," Mrs. Hutchinson said, as quietly as she could. "I tell you it wasn't *fair*. You didn't give him time enough to choose. *Every*body saw that."

Mr. Graves had selected the five slips and put them in the box, and he dropped 60 all the papers but those onto the ground, where the breeze caught them and lifted them off.

"Listen, everybody," Mrs. Hutchinson was saying to the people around her.

"Ready, Bill?" Mr. Summers asked, and Bill Hutchinson, with one quick glance around at his wife and children, nodded.

"Remember," Mr. Summers said, "take the slips and keep them folded until each person has taken one. Harry, you help little Dave." Mr. Graves took the hand of the little boy, who came willingly with him up to the box. "Take a paper out of the box, Davy," Mr. Summers said. Davy put his hand into the box and laughed. "Take just *one* paper," Mr. Summers said. "Harry, you hold it for him." Mr. Graves took the child's hand and removed the folded paper from the tight fist and held it while little Dave stood next to him and looked at him wonderingly.

"Nancy next," Mr. Summers said. Nancy was twelve, and her school friends breathed heavily as she went forward, switching her skirt, and took a slip daintily from the box. "Bill, Jr.," Mr. Summers said, and Billy, his face red and his feet overlarge, nearly knocked the box over as he got a paper out. "Tessie," Mr. Summers said. She hesitated for a minute, looking around defiantly, and then set her lips and went up to the box. She snatched a paper out and held it behind her.

"Bill," Mr. Summers said, and Bill Hutchinson reached into the box and felt 65 around, bringing his hand out at last with the slip of paper in it.

The crowd was quiet. A girl whispered, "I hope it's not Nancy," and the sound of the whisper reached the edges of the crowd.

"It's not the way it used to be," Old Man Warner said clearly. "People ain't the way they used to be."

"All right," Mr. Summers said. "Open the papers. Harry, you open little Dave's."

Mr. Graves opened the slip of paper and there was a general sigh through the crowd as he held it up and everyone could see that it was blank. Nancy and Bill, Jr., opened theirs at the same time, and both beamed and laughed, turning around to the crowd and holding their slips of paper above their heads.

"Tessie," Mr. Summers said. There was a pause, and then Mr. Summers 70 looked at Bill Hutchinson, and Bill unfolded his paper and showed it. It was blank.

"It's Tessie," Mr. Summers said, and his voice was hushed. "Show us her paper, Bill."

Bill Hutchinson went over to his wife and forced the slip of paper out of her hand. It had a black spot on it, the black spot Mr. Summers had made the night before with the heavy pencil in the coal-company office. Bill Hutchinson held it up, and there was a stir in the crowd.

"All right, folks," Mr. Summers said. "Let's finish quickly."

Although the villagers had forgotten the ritual and lost the original black box, they still remembered to use stones. The pile of stones the boys had made earlier was ready; there were stones on the ground with the blowing scraps of paper that had come out of the box. Mrs. Delacroix selected a stone so large she had to pick it up with both hands and turned to Mrs. Dunbar. "Come on," she said. "Hurry up."

75   Mrs. Dunbar had small stones in both hands, and she said, gasping for breath, "I can't run at all. You'll have to go ahead and I'll catch up with you."

The children had stones already, and someone gave little Davy Hutchinson a few pebbles.

Tessie Hutchinson was in the center of a cleared space by now, and she held her hands out desperately as the villagers moved in on her. "It isn't fair," she said. A stone hit her on the side of the head.

Old Man Warner was saying, "Come on, come on, everyone." Steve Adams was in the front of the crowd of villagers, with Mrs. Graves beside him.

"It isn't fair, it isn't right," Mrs. Hutchinson screamed, and then they were upon her.

Reading and Reacting

1. What possible significance, beyond their literal meaning, might each of the following have:

- The village square
- Mrs. Hutchinson's apron
- Old Man Warner
- The slips of paper
- The black spot

2. "The Lottery" takes place in summer, a conventional symbol that has a positive connotation. What does this setting contribute to the story's plot? To its atmosphere?

3. What, if anything, might the names *Graves*, *Adams*, *Summers*, and *Delacroix* signify in the context of this story? Do you think these names are intended to have any special significance? Why or why not?

4. What role do the children play in the ritual? How can you explain their presence in the story? Do they have any symbolic role?

5. What symbolic significance might be found in the way the characters are dressed? In their conversation?

6. In what sense is the story's title ironic?

7. Throughout the story, there is a general atmosphere of excitement. What indication is there of nervousness or apprehension?

8. Early in the story, the boys stuff their pockets with stones, foreshadowing the attack in the story's conclusion. What other examples of foreshadowing can you identify?

9. JOURNAL ENTRY How can a ritual like the lottery continue to be held year after year? Why does no one move to end it? Can you think of a modern-day counterpart to this lottery — a situation in which people continue to act in ways they know to be wrong rather than challenge the status quo? How can you account for such behavior?

10. CRITICAL PERSPECTIVE When "The Lottery" was published in the June 26, 1948, issue of the *New Yorker,* its effect was immediate. The story, as the critic Judy Oppenheimer notes in her book *Private Demons: The Life of Shirley Jackson,* "provoked an unprecedented outpouring of fury, horror, rage, disgust, and intense fascination." As a result, Jackson received hundreds of letters, which included (among others) the following interpretations of the story:

- The story is an attack on small-town America.
- The story is a parable about the perversion of democracy.
- The story is a criticism of prejudice, particularly anti-Semitism.
- The story has no point at all.

How plausible do you think each of these interpretations is? Which comes closest to your interpretation of the story? Why?

Related Works: "Young Goodman Brown" (p. 302), "Where Are You Going, Where Have You Been?" (p. 384), "Patterns" (p. 473), *Nine Ten* (p. 760)

ALICE WALKER (1944–   ) was the youngest of eight children born to Willie Lee and Minnie Tallulah Grant Walker, sharecroppers who raised cotton. She left the rural South to attend Spelman College in Atlanta (1961–1963) and Sarah Lawrence College in Bronxville, New York (1963–1965).

In 1967, Walker moved to Mississippi, where she was supported in the writing of her first novel, *The Third Life of Grange Copeland* (1970), by a National Endowment for the Arts grant. Her short story "Everyday Use" was included in *Best American Short Stories 1973* and has been widely anthologized and studied. Other novels and collections of short stories followed, including *In Love & Trouble: Stories of Black Women* (1973), *Meridian* (1976), *You Can't Keep a Good Woman Down* (1981), *The Temple of My Familiar* (1989), *Possessing the Secret of Joy* (1993), *The Complete Stories* (1994), *By the Light of My Father's Smile* (1998), *The Way Forward Is with a Broken Heart* (2000), and *Now Is the Time to Open Your Heart* (2004). Her third novel, *The Color Purple* (1982), won the American Book Award and a Pulitzer Prize and was made into an award-winning movie.

In the third year of her marriage, Walker took back her maiden name because she wanted to honor her great-great-great-grandmother who had walked, carrying her two children, from Virginia to Georgia. Walker's renaming is consistent with one of her goals in writing, which is to further the process of reconnecting people to their ancestors. She has said that "it is fatal to see yourself as separate" and that if people can reaffirm the past, they can "make a different future."

Everyday Use   (1973)

For Your Grandmama

I will wait for her in the yard that Maggie and I made so clean and wavy yesterday afternoon. A yard like this is more comfortable than most people know. It is not just a yard. It is like an extended living room. When the hard clay is swept clean as a floor and the fine sand around the edges lined with tiny, irregular grooves, anyone can come and sit and look up into the elm tree and wait for the breezes that never come inside the house.

Maggie will be nervous until after her sister goes: she will stand hopelessly in corners, homely and ashamed of the burn scars down her arms and legs, eying her sister with a mixture of envy and awe. She thinks her sister has held life always in the palm of one hand, that "no" is a word the world never learned to say to her.

You've no doubt seen those TV shows where the child who has "made it" is confronted, as a surprise, by her own mother and father, tottering in weakly from backstage. (A pleasant surprise, of course: What would they do if parent and child came on the show only to curse out and insult each other?) On TV mother and child embrace and smile into each other's faces. Sometimes the mother and father weep, the child wraps them in her arms and leans across the table to tell how she would not have made it without their help. I have seen these programs.

Sometimes I dream a dream in which Dee and I are suddenly brought together on a TV program of this sort. Out of a dark and soft-seated limousine I am ushered into a bright room filled with many people. There I meet a smiling, gray, sporty man like Johnny Carson who shakes my hand and tells me what a fine girl I have. Then we are on the stage and Dee is embracing me with tears in her eyes. She pins on my dress a large orchid, even though she has told me once that she thinks orchids are tacky flowers.

5   In real life I am a large, big-boned woman with rough, man-working hands. In the winter I wear flannel nightgowns to bed and overalls during the day. I can kill and clean a hog as mercilessly as a man. My fat keeps me hot in zero weather. I can work outside all day, breaking ice to get water for washing; I can eat pork liver cooked over the open fire minutes after it comes steaming from the hog. One winter I knocked a bull calf straight in the brain between the eyes with a sledge hammer and had the meat hung up to chill before nightfall. But of course all this does not show on television. I am the way my daughter would want me to be: a hundred pounds lighter, my skin like an uncooked barley pancake. My

hair glistens in the hot bright lights. Johnny Carson has much to do to keep up with my quick and witty tongue.

But that is a mistake. I know even before I wake up. Who ever knew a Johnson with a quick tongue? Who can even imagine me looking a strange white man in the eye? It seems to me I have talked to them always with one foot raised in flight, with my head turned in whichever way is farthest from them. Dee, though. She would always look anyone in the eye. Hesitation was no part of her nature.

"How do I look, Mama?" Maggie says, showing just enough of her thin body enveloped in pink skirt and red blouse for me to know she's there, almost hidden by the door.

"Come out into the yard," I say.

Have you ever seen a lame animal, perhaps a dog run over by some careless person rich enough to own a car, sidle up to someone who is ignorant enough to be kind to him? That is the way my Maggie walks. She has been like this, chin on chest, eyes on ground, feet in shuffle, ever since the fire that burned the other house to the ground.

Dee is lighter than Maggie, with nicer hair and a fuller figure. She's a woman 10 now, though sometimes I forget. How long ago was it that the other house burned? Ten, twelve years? Sometimes I can still hear the flames and feel Maggie's arms sticking to me, her hair smoking and her dress falling off her in little black papery flakes. Her eyes seemed stretched open, blazed open by the flames reflected in them. And Dee. I see her standing off under the sweet gum tree she used to dig gum out of; a look of concentration on her face as she watched the last dingy gray board of the house fall in toward the red-hot brick chimney. Why don't you do a dance around the ashes? I'd wanted to ask her. She had hated the house that much.

I used to think she hated Maggie, too. But that was before we raised the money, the church and me, to send her to Augusta to school. She used to read to us without pity; forcing words, lies, other folks' habits, whole lives upon us two, sitting trapped and ignorant underneath her voice. She washed us in a river of make-believe, burned us with a lot of knowledge we didn't necessarily need to know. Pressed us to her with the serious way she read, to shove us away at just the moment, like dimwits, we seemed about to understand.

Dee wanted nice things. A yellow organdy dress to wear to her graduation from high school; black pumps to match a green suit she'd made from an old suit somebody gave me. She was determined to stare down any disaster in her efforts. Her eyelids would not flicker for minutes at a time. Often I fought off the temptation to shake her. At sixteen she had a style of her own, and knew what style was.

I never had an education myself. After second grade the school was closed down. Don't ask me why: in 1927 colored asked fewer questions than they do now. Sometimes Maggie reads to me. She stumbles along good-naturedly but can't see well. She knows she is not bright. Like good looks and money, quickness passed her by. She will marry John Thomas (who has mossy teeth in an earnest face) and then I'll be free to sit here and I guess just sing church songs to myself. Although I never was a good singer. Never could carry a tune. I was always better at a man's job. I used to love to milk till I was hooked in the side in '49. Cows are soothing and slow and don't bother you, unless you try to milk them the wrong way.

I have deliberately turned my back on the house. It is three rooms, just like the one that burned, except the roof is tin; they don't make shingle roofs any more. There are no real windows, just some holes cut in the sides, like the portholes in a ship, but not round and not square, with rawhide holding the shutters up on the outside. This house is in a pasture, too, like the other one. No doubt when Dee sees it she will want to tear it down. She wrote me once that no matter where we "choose" to live, she will manage to come see us. But she will never bring her friends. Maggie and I thought about this and Maggie asked me, "Mama, when did Dee ever *have* any friends?"

15   She had a few. Furtive boys in pink shirts hanging about on washday after school. Nervous girls who never laughed. Impressed with her they worshiped the well-turned phrase, the cute shape, the scalding humor that erupted like bubbles in lye. She read to them.

When she was courting Jimmy T she didn't have much time to pay to us, but turned all her faultfinding power on him. He *flew* to marry a cheap city girl from a family of ignorant flashy people. She hardly had time to recompose herself.

When she comes I will meet — but there they are!

Maggie attempts to make a dash for the house, in her shuffling way, but I stay her with my hand. "Come back here," I say. And she stops and tries to dig a well in the sand with her toe.

It is hard to see them clearly through the strong sun. But even the first glimpse of leg out of the car tells me it is Dee. Her feet were always neat-looking, as if God himself had shaped them with a certain style. From the other side of the car comes a short, stocky man. Hair is all over his head a foot long and hanging from his chin like a kinky mule tail. I hear Maggie suck in her breath. "Uhnnnh," is what it sounds like. Like when you see the wriggling end of a snake just in front of your foot on the road. "Uhnnnh."

20   Dee next. A dress down to the ground, in this hot weather. A dress so loud it hurts my eyes. There are yellows and oranges enough to throw back the light of the sun. I feel my whole face warming from the heat waves it throws out. Earrings gold, too, and hanging down to her shoulders. Bracelets dangling and making noises when she moves her arm up to shake the folds of the dress out of her armpits. The dress is loose and flows, and as she walks closer, I like it. I hear Maggie go "Uhnnnh" again. It is her sister's hair. It stands straight up like the wool on a sheep. It is black as night and around the edges are two long pigtails that rope about like small lizards disappearing behind her ears.

"Wa-su-zo-Tean-o!"° she says, coming on in that gliding way the dress makes her move. The short stocky fellow with the hair to his navel is all grinning and he follows up with "Asalamalakim,° my mother and sister!" He moves to hug Maggie but she falls back, right up against the back of my chair. I feel her trembling there and when I look up I see the perspiration falling off her chin.

"Don't get up," says Dee. Since I am stout it takes something of a push. You can see me trying to move a second or two before I make it. She turns, showing white heels through her sandals, and goes back to the car. Out she peeks next with a Polaroid. She stoops down quickly and lines up picture after picture of me sitting there in front of the house with Maggie cowering behind me. She never takes a shot without making sure the house is included. When a cow comes nibbling around the edge of the yard she snaps it and me and Maggie *and* the house. Then she puts the Polaroid in the back seat of the car, and comes up and kisses me on the forehead.

Meanwhile Asalamalakim is going through motions with Maggie's hand. Maggie's hand is as limp as a fish, and probably as cold, despite the sweat, and she keeps trying to pull it back. It looks like Asalamalakim wants to shake hands but wants to do it fancy. Or maybe he don't know how people shake hands. Anyhow, he soon gives up on Maggie.

"Well," I say. "Dee."

"No, Mama," she says. "Not 'Dee,' Wangero Leewanika Kemanjo!"   25

"What happened to 'Dee'?" I wanted to know.

"She's dead," Wangero said. "I couldn't bear it any longer, being named after the people who oppress me."

"You know as well as me you was named after your aunt Dicie," I said. Dicie is my sister. She named Dee. We called her "Big Dee" after Dee was born.

"But who was *she* named after?" asked Wangero.

"I guess after Grandma Dee," I said.   30

"And who was she named after?" asked Wangero.

"Her mother," I said, and saw Wangero was getting tired. "That's about as far back as I can trace it," I said. Though, in fact, I probably could have carried it back beyond the Civil War through the branches.

"Well," said Asalamalakim, "there you are."

"Uhnnnh," I heard Maggie say.

"There I was not," I said, "before 'Dicie' cropped up in our family, so why   35 should I try to trace it that far back?"

He just stood there grinning, looking down on me like somebody inspecting a Model A car. Every once in a while he and Wangero sent eye signals over my head.

Wa-su-zo-Tean-o: A greeting in Swahili; Dee sounds it out one syllable at a time.

Asalamalakim: A greeting in Arabic: "Peace be upon you."

"How do you pronounce this name?" I asked.

40 "You don't have to call me by it if you don't want to," said Wangero.

"Why shouldn't I?" I asked. "If that's what you want us to call you, we'll call you."

"I know it might sound awkward at first," said Wangero.

"I'll get used to it," I said. "Ream it out again."

Well, soon we got the name out of the way. Asalamalakim had a name twice as long and three times as hard. After I tripped over it two or three times he told me to just call him Hakim-a-barber. I wanted to ask him was he a barber, but I didn't really think he was, so I didn't ask.

"You must belong to those beef-cattle peoples down the road," I said. They said "Asalamalakim" when they met you, too, but they didn't shake hands. Always too busy: feeding the cattle, fixing the fences, putting up salt-lick shelters, throwing down hay. When the white folks poisoned some of the herd the men stayed up all night with rifles in their hands. I walked a mile and a half just to see the sight.

Hakim-a-barber said, "I accept some of their doctrines, but farming and raising cattle is not my style." (They didn't tell me, and I didn't ask, whether Wangero [Dee] had really gone and married him.)

45 We sat down to eat and right away he said he didn't eat collards and pork was unclean. Wangero, though, went on through the chitlins and corn bread, the greens and everything else. She talked a blue streak over the sweet potatoes. Everything delighted her. Even the fact that we still used the benches her daddy made for the table when we couldn't afford to buy chairs.

"Oh, Mama!" she cried. Then turned to Hakim-a-barber. "I never knew how lovely these benches are. You can feel the rump prints," she said, running her hands underneath her and along the bench. Then she gave a sigh and her hand closed over Grandma Dee's butter dish. "That's it!" she said. "I knew there was something I wanted to ask you if I could have." She jumped up from the table and went over in the corner where the churn stood, the milk in it clabber by now. She looked at the churn and looked at it.

"This churn top is what I need," she said. "Didn't Uncle Buddy whittle it out of a tree you all used to have?"

"Yes," I said.

"Uh huh," she said happily. "And I want the dasher, too."

50 "Uncle Buddy whittle that, too?" asked the barber.

Dee (Wangero) looked up at me.

"Aunt Dee's first husband whittled the dash," said Maggie so low you almost couldn't hear her. "His name was Henry, but they called him Stash."

"Maggie's brain is like an elephant's," Wangero said, laughing. "I can use the churn top as a centerpiece for the alcove table," she said, sliding a plate over the churn, "and I'll think of something artistic to do with the dasher."

When she finished wrapping the dasher the handle stuck out. I took it for a moment in my hands. You didn't even have to look close to see where hands pushing the dasher up and down to make butter had left a kind of sink in the wood. In fact, there were a lot of small sinks; you could see where thumb and fingers had sunk into the wood. It was beautiful light yellow wood, from a tree that grew in the yard where Big Dee and Stash had lived.

After dinner Dee (Wangero) went to the trunk at the foot of my bed and 55 started rifling through it. Maggie hung back in the kitchen over the dishpan. Out came Wangero with two quilts. They had been pieced by Grandma Dee and then Big Dee and me had hung them on the quilt frames on the front porch and quilted them. One was in the Lone Star pattern. The other was Walk Around the Mountain. In both of them were scraps of dresses Grandma Dee had worn fifty and more years ago. Bits and pieces of Grandpa Jarrell's Paisley shirts. And one teeny faded blue piece, about the size of a penny matchbox, that was from Great Grandpa Ezra's uniform that he wore in the Civil War.

"Mama," Wangero said sweet as a bird. "Can I have these old quilts?"

I heard something fall in the kitchen, and a minute later the kitchen door slammed.

"Why don't you take one or two of the others?" I asked. "These old things was just done by me and Big Dee from some tops your grandma pieced before she died."

"No," said Wangero. "I don't want those. They are stitched around the borders by machine."

"That'll make them last better," I said. 60

"That's not the point," said Wangero. "These are all pieces of dresses Grandma used to wear. She did all this stitching by hand. Imagine!" She held the quilts securely in her arms, stroking them.

"Some of the pieces, like those lavender ones, come from old clothes her mother handed down to her," I said, moving up to touch the quilts. Dee (Wangero) moved back just enough so that I couldn't reach the quilts. They already belonged to her.

"Imagine!" she breathed again, clutching them closely to her bosom.

"The truth is," I said, "I promised to give them quilts to Maggie, for when she 65 marries John Thomas."

She gasped like a bee had stung her. "Maggie can't appreciate these quilts!" she said. "She'd probably be backward enough to put them to everyday use."

"I reckon she would," I said. "God knows I been saving 'em for long enough with nobody using 'em. I hope she will!" I didn't want to bring up how I had offered Dee (Wangero) a quilt when she went away to college. Then she had told me they were old-fashioned, out of style.

"But, they're *priceless!*" she was saying now, furiously; for she has a temper. "Maggie would put them on the bed and in five years they'd be in rags. Less than that!"

"She can always make some more," I said. "Maggie knows how to quilt."

Dee (Wangero) looked at me with hatred. "You just will not understand. The point is these quilts, *these* quilts!"

70   "Well," I said, stumped. "What would *you* do with them?"

"Hang them," she said. As if that was the only thing you *could* do with quilts. Maggie by now was standing in the door. I could almost hear the sound her feet made as they scraped over each other.

"She can have them, Mama," she said, like somebody used to never winning anything, or having anything reserved for her. "I can 'member Grandma Dee without the quilts."

I looked at her hard. She had filled her bottom lip with checkerberry snuff and it gave her face a kind of dopey, hangdog look. It was Grandma Dee and Big Dee who taught her how to quilt herself. She stood there with her scarred hands hidden in the folds of her skirt. She looked at her sister with something like fear but she wasn't mad at her. This was Maggie's portion. This was the way she knew God to work.

75   When I looked at her like that something hit me in the top of my head and ran down to the soles of my feet. Just like when I'm in church and the spirit of God touches me and I get happy and shout. I did something I never had done before: hugged Maggie to me, then dragged her on into the room, snatched the quilts out of Miss Wangero's hands and dumped them into Maggie's lap. Maggie just sat there on my bed with her mouth open.

"Take one or two of the others," I said to Dee.

But she turned without a word and went out to Hakim-a-barber.

"You just don't understand," she said, as Maggie and I came out to the car.

"What don't I understand?" I wanted to know.

80   "Your heritage," she said. And then she turned to Maggie, kissed her, and said, "You ought to try to make something of yourself, too, Maggie. It's really a new day for us. But from the way you and Mama still live you'd never know it."

She put on some sunglasses that hid everything above the tip of her nose and her chin.

Maggie smiled; maybe at the sunglasses. But a real smile, not scared. After we watched the car dust settle I asked Maggie to bring me a dip of snuff. And then the two of us sat there just enjoying, until it was time to go in the house and go to bed.

Reading and Reacting

1. In American culture, what does a patchwork quilt symbolize?

2. What is the literal meaning of the two quilts to Maggie and her mother? To Dee? Beyond this literal meaning, what symbolic meaning, if any, do they have to Maggie and her mother? Do the quilts have any symbolic meaning to Dee?

3. How does the contrast between the two sisters' appearances, personalities, lifestyles, and feelings about the quilts help to convey the story's theme?

4. What does the name *Wangero* signify to Dee? To her mother and sister? Could the name be considered a symbol? Why or why not?

5. Why do you think Maggie relinquishes the quilts to her sister?

6. What is Dee's opinion of her mother and sister? Do you agree with her assessment?

7. What does the story's title suggest to you? Is it ironic? What other titles would be effective?

8. Discuss the possible meanings, aside from their literal meanings, that each of the following suggest: the family's yard, Maggie's burn scars, the trunk in which the quilts are kept, Dee's Polaroid camera. What symbolic functions, if any, do these items serve in the story?

9. JOURNAL ENTRY What objects have the kind of symbolic value to you that the quilts have to Maggie? What gives these objects this value?

10. CRITICAL PERSPECTIVE In her article "The Black Woman Artist as Wayward," critic Barbara Christian characterizes "Everyday Use" as a story in which Alice Walker examines the "creative legacy" of ordinary African-American women. According to Christian, the story "is about the use and misuse of the concept of heritage. The mother of two daughters, one selfish and stylish, the other scarred and caring, passes on to us its true definition."

What definition of *heritage* does the mother attempt to pass on to her children? How is this definition like or unlike Dee's definition?

Related Works: "Two Kinds" (p. 416), "Digging" (p. 624), "My Grandmother Would Rock Quietly and Hum" (p. 462), "Aunt Jennifer's Tigers" (p. 555), *Trifles* (p. 770), *Fences* (p. 1096)

RAYMOND CARVER (1938–1988), one of the most influential and widely read writers of our time, fashioned his stories from the stuff of common life uncommonly perceived. He married at nineteen and fathered two children by the time he was twenty; during this period, he also began to write. He received a degree from Humboldt State University and later from the University of Iowa. His first collection of stories, *Will You Please Be Quiet, Please* (1976), was nominated for a National Book Award. Five more collections of stories followed, including *Cathedral* (1983)— nominated for both a Pulitzer Prize and a National Book Critics Circle Award — and *Where I'm Calling From: New and Selected Stories* (1988). Carver was also the author of five books of poetry. In his  last years, Carver was praised as the best American short story writer since Ernest Hemingway; novelist Robert Stone called him "a hero of perception." He was made an Honorary Doctor of Letters at the University of Hartford and was inducted into the American Academy and Institute of Arts and Letters.

Cathedral (1983)

This blind man, an old friend of my wife's, he was on his way to spend the night. His wife had died. So he was visiting the dead wife's relatives in Connecticut. He called my wife from his in-laws'. Arrangements were made. He would come by train, a five-hour trip, and my wife would meet him at the station. She hadn't seen him since she worked for him one summer in Seattle ten years ago. But she and the blind man had kept in touch. They made tapes and mailed them back and forth. I wasn't enthusiastic about his visit. He was no one I knew. And his being blind bothered me. My idea of blindness came from the movies. In the movies, the blind moved slowly and never laughed. Sometimes they were led by seeing-eye dogs. A blind man in my house was not something I looked forward to.

That summer in Seattle she had needed a job. She didn't have any money. The man she was going to marry at the end of the summer was in officers' training school. He didn't have any money, either. But she was in love with the guy, and he was in love with her, etc. She'd seen something in the paper: HELP WANTED — *Reading to Blind Man*, and a telephone number. She phoned and went over, was hired on the spot. She'd worked with this blind man all summer. She read stuff to him, case studies, reports, that sort of thing. She helped him organize his little office in the county social-service department. They'd become good friends, my wife and the blind man. How do I know these things? She told me. And she told me something else. On her last day in the office, the blind man asked if he could touch her face. She agreed to this. She told me he touched his fingers to every part of her face, her nose — even her neck! She never forgot it. She even tried to write a poem about it. She was always trying to write a poem. She wrote a poem or two every year, usually after something really important had happened to her.

When we first started going out together, she showed me the poem. In the poem, she recalled his fingers and the way they had moved around over her face. In the poem, she talked about what she had felt at the time, about what went through her mind when the blind man touched her nose and lips. I can remember I didn't think much of the poem. Of course, I didn't tell her that. Maybe I just don't understand poetry. I admit it's not the first thing I reach for when I pick up something to read.

Anyway, this man who'd first enjoyed her favors, the officer-to-be, he'd been her childhood sweetheart. So okay. I'm saying that at the end of the summer she let the blind man run his hands over her face, said goodbye to him, married her childhood etc., who was now a commissioned officer, and she moved away from Seattle. But they'd kept in touch, she and the blind man. She made the first contact after a year or so. She called him up one night from an Air Force base in Alabama. She wanted to talk. They talked. He asked her to send a tape and tell him about her life. She did this. She sent the tape. On the tape, she told the blind man about her husband and about their life together in the military. She told the blind man she loved her husband but she didn't like it where they lived and she didn't like it that he was part of the military-industrial thing. She told the blind man she'd written a poem and he was in it. She told him that she was writing a poem about what it was like to be an Air Force officer's wife. The poem wasn't finished yet. She was still writing it. The blind man made a tape. He sent her the tape. She made a tape. This went on for years. My wife's officer was posted to one base and then another. She sent tapes from Moody AFB, McGuire, McConnell, and finally Travis,° near Sacramento, where one night she got to feeling lonely and cut off from people she kept losing in that moving-around life. She got to feeling she couldn't go it another step. She went in and swallowed all the pills and capsules in the medicine chest and washed them down with a bottle of gin. Then she got into a hot bath and passed out.

But instead of dying, she got sick. She threw up. Her officer — why should he 5 have a name? he was the childhood sweetheart, and what more does he want? — came home from somewhere, found her, and called the ambulance. In time, she put it all on a tape and sent the tape to the blind man. Over the years, she put all kinds of stuff on tapes and sent the tapes off lickety-split. Next to writing a poem every year, I think it was her chief means of recreation. On one tape, she told the blind man she'd decided to live away from her officer for a time. On another tape, she told him about her divorce. She and I began going out, and of course she told her blind man about it. She told him everything, or so it seemed to me. Once she asked me if I'd like to hear the latest tape from the blind man. This was a year ago. I was on the tape, she said. So I said okay, I'd listen to it. I got us drinks and we settled down in the living room. We made ready to listen. First she inserted the tape into the player and adjusted a couple of dials. Then she pushed a lever. The tape squeaked and someone began to talk in this loud voice. She lowered the volume. After a few minutes of harmless chitchat, I heard my own name in the mouth of this stranger, this blind man I didn't even know! And then this: "From all you've said about him, I can only conclude — " But we were interrupted, a knock at the door, something, and we didn't ever get back to the tape. Maybe it was just as well. I'd heard all I wanted to.

Now this same blind man was coming to sleep in my house.

"Maybe I could take him bowling," I said to my wife. She was at the draining board doing scalloped potatoes. She put down the knife she was using and turned around.

"If you love me," she said, "you can do this for me. If you don't love me, okay. But if you had a friend, any friend, and the friend came to visit, I'd make him feel comfortable." She wiped her hands with the dish towel.

"I don't have any blind friends," I said.

"You don't have *any* friends," she said. "Period. Besides," she said, "goddamn 10 it, his wife's just died! Don't you understand that? The man's lost his wife!"

I didn't answer. She'd told me a little about the blind man's wife. Her name was Beulah. Beulah! That's a name for a colored woman.

"Was his wife a Negro?" I asked.

"Are you crazy?" my wife said. "Have you just flipped or something?" She picked up a potato. I saw it hit the floor, then roll under the stove. "What's wrong with you?" she said. "Are you drunk?"

Moody . . . Travis: United States Air Force bases.

"I'm just asking," I said.

15   Right then my wife filled me in with more detail than I cared to know. I made a drink and sat at the kitchen table to listen. Pieces of the story began to fall into place.

Beulah had gone to work for the blind man the summer after my wife had stopped working for him. Pretty soon Beulah and the blind man had themselves a church wedding. It was a little wedding — who'd want to go to such a wedding in the first place?—just the two of them, plus the minister and the minister's wife. But it was a church wedding just the same. It was what Beulah had wanted, he'd said. But even then Beulah must have been carrying the cancer in her glands. After they had been inseparable for eight years — my wife's word, *inseparable*— Beulah's health went into a rapid decline. She died in a Seattle hospital room, the blind man sitting beside the bed and holding on to her hand. They'd married, lived and worked together, slept together — had sex, sure — and then the blind man had to bury her. All this without his having ever seen what the goddamned woman looked like. It was beyond my understanding. Hearing this, I felt sorry for the blind man for a little bit. And then I found myself thinking what a pitiful life this woman must have led. Imagine a woman who could never see herself as she was seen in the eyes of her loved one. A woman who could go on day after day and never receive the smallest compliment from her beloved. A woman whose husband could never read the expression on her face, be it misery or something better. Someone who could wear makeup or not — what difference to him? She could, if she wanted, wear green eye-shadow around one eye, a straight pin in her nostril, yellow slacks, and purple shoes, no matter. And then to slip off into death, the blind man's hand on her hand, his blind eyes streaming tears — I'm imagining now — her last thought maybe this: that he never even knew what she looked like, and she on an express to the grave. Robert was left with a small insurance policy and a half of a twenty-peso Mexican coin. The other half of the coin went into the box with her. Pathetic.

So when the time rolled around, my wife went to the depot to pick him up. With nothing to do but wait — sure, I blamed him for that — I was having a drink and watching the TV when I heard the car pull into the drive. I got up from the sofa with my drink and went to the window to have a look.

I saw my wife laughing as she parked the car. I saw her get out of the car and shut the door. She was still wearing a smile. Just amazing. She went around to the other side of the car to where the blind man was already starting to get out. This blind man, feature this, he was wearing a full beard! A beard on a blind man! Too much, I say. The blind man reached into the backseat and dragged out a suitcase. My wife took his arm, shut the car door, and, talking all the way, moved him down the drive and then up the steps to the front porch. I turned off the TV. I finished my drink, rinsed the glass, dried my hands. Then I went to the door.

My wife said, "I want you to meet Robert. Robert, this is my husband. I've told you all about him." She was beaming. She had this blind man by his coat sleeve.

20   The blind man let go of his suitcase and up came his hand.

I took it. He squeezed hard, held my hand, and then he let it go.

"I feel like we've already met," he boomed.

"Likewise," I said. I didn't know what else to say. Then I said, "Welcome. I've heard a lot about you." We began to move then, a little group, from the porch into the living room, my wife guiding him by the arm. The blind man was carrying his suitcase in his other hand. My wife said things like, "To your left here, Robert. That's right. Now watch it, there's a chair. That's it. Sit down right here. This is the sofa. We just bought this sofa two weeks ago."

I started to say something about the old sofa. I'd liked that old sofa. But I didn't say anything. Then I wanted to say something else, small-talk, about the scenic ride along the Hudson.° How going *to* New York, you should sit on the right-hand side of the train, and coming *from* New York, the left-hand side.

"Did you have a good train ride?" I said. "Which side of the train did you sit 25 on, by the way?"

"What a question, which side!" my wife said. "What's it matter which side?" she said.

"I just asked," I said.

"Right side," the blind man said. "I hadn't been on a train in nearly forty years. Not since I was a kid. With my folks. That's been a long time. I'd nearly forgotten the sensation. I have winter in my beard now," he said. "So I've been told, anyway. Do I look distinguished, my dear?" the blind man said to my wife.

"You look distinguished, Robert," she said. "Robert," she said. "Robert, it's just so good to see you."

My wife finally took her eyes off the blind man and looked at me. I had the 30 feeling she didn't like what she saw. I shrugged.

I've never met, or personally known, anyone who was blind. This blind man was late forties, a heavy-set, balding man with stooped shoulders, as if he carried a great weight there. He wore brown slacks, brown shoes, a light-brown shirt, a tie, a sports coat. Spiffy. He also had this full beard. But he didn't use a cane and he didn't wear dark glasses. I'd always thought dark glasses were a must for the blind. Fact was, I wished he had a pair. At first glance, his eyes looked like anyone else's eyes. But if you looked close, there was something different about them. Too much white in the iris, for one thing, and the pupils seemed to move around in the sockets without his knowing it or being able to stop it. Creepy. As I stared at his face, I saw the left pupil turn in toward his nose while the other made an effort to keep in one place. But it was only an effort, for that eye was on the roam without his knowing it or wanting it to be.

I said, "Let me get you a drink. What's your pleasure? We have a little of everything. It's one of our pastimes."

"Bub, I'm a Scotch man myself," he said fast enough in this big voice.

"Right," I said. Bub! "Sure you are. I knew it."

Hudson: A river in New York State.

35 He let his fingers touch his suitcase, which was sitting alongside the sofa. He was taking his bearings. I didn't blame him for that.

"I'll move that up to your room," my wife said.

"No, that's fine," the blind man said loudly. "It can go up when I go up."

"A little water with the Scotch?" I said.

"Very little," he said.

40 "I knew it," I said.

He said, "Just a tad. The Irish actor, Barry Fitzgerald? I'm like that fellow. When I drink water, Fitzgerald said, I drink water. When I drink whiskey, I drink whiskey." My wife laughed. The blind man brought his hand up under his beard. He lifted his beard slowly and let it drop.

I did the drinks, three big glasses of Scotch with a splash of water in each. Then we made ourselves comfortable and talked about Robert's travels. First the long flight from the West Coast to Connecticut, we covered that. Then from Connecticut up here by train. We had another drink concerning that leg of the trip.

I remembered having read somewhere that the blind didn't smoke because, as speculation had it, they couldn't see the smoke they exhaled. I thought I knew that much and that much only about blind people. But this blind man smoked his cigarette down to the nubbin and then lit another one. This blind man filled his ashtray and my wife emptied it.

When we sat down at the table for dinner, we had another drink. My wife heaped Robert's plate with cube steak, scalloped potatoes, green beans. I buttered him up two slices of bread. I said, "Here's bread and butter for you." I swallowed some of my drink. "Now let us pray," I said, and the blind man lowered his head. My wife looked at me, her mouth agape. "Pray the phone won't ring and the food doesn't get cold," I said.

45 We dug in. We ate everything there was to eat on the table. We ate like there was no tomorrow. We didn't talk. We ate. We scarfed. We grazed that table. We were into serious eating. The blind man had right away located his foods, he knew just where everything was on his plate. I watched with admiration as he used his knife and fork on the meat. He'd cut two pieces of meat, fork the meat into his mouth, and then go all out for the scalloped potatoes, the beans next, and then he'd tear off a hunk of buttered bread and eat that. He'd follow this up with a big drink of milk. It didn't seem to bother him to use his fingers once in a while, either.

We finished everything, including half a strawberry pie. For a few moments, we sat as if stunned. Sweat beaded on our faces. Finally, we got up from the table and left the dirty plates. We didn't look back. We took ourselves into the living room and sank into our places again. Robert and my wife sat on the sofa. I took the big chair. We had us two or three more drinks while they talked about the major things that had come to pass for them in the past ten years. For the most part, I just listened. Now and then I joined in. I didn't want him to think I'd left the room, and I didn't want her to think I was feeling left out. They talked of things that had happened to them — to them! — these past ten years. I waited in vain to hear my name on my wife's sweet lips: "And then my dear husband came into my life"— something like that. But I heard nothing of the sort. More talk of Robert. Robert had done a little of everything, it seemed, a regular blind jack-of-all-trades. But most recently he and his wife had had an Amway distributorship, from which, I gathered, they'd earned their living, such as it was. The blind man was also a ham radio operator.° He talked in his loud voice about conversations he'd had with fellow operators in Guam, in the Philippines, in Alaska, and even in Tahiti. He said he'd have a lot of friends there if he ever wanted to go visit those places. From time to time, he'd turn his blind face toward me, put his hand under his beard, ask me something. How long had I been in my present position? (Three years.) Did I like my work? (I didn't.) Was I going to stay with it? (What were the options?) Finally, when I thought he was beginning to run down, I got up and turned on the TV.

My wife looked at me with irritation. She was heading toward a boil. Then she looked at the blind man and said, "Robert, do you have a TV?"

The blind man said, "My dear, I have two TVs. I have a color set and a black-and-white thing, an old relic. It's funny, but if I turn the TV on, and I'm always turning it on, I turn on the color set. It's funny, don't you think?"

I didn't know what to say to that. I had absolutely nothing to say to that. No opinion. So I watched the news program and tried to listen to what the announcer was saying.

"This is a color TV," the blind man said. "Don't ask me how, but I can tell." 50

"We traded up a while ago," I said.

The blind man had another taste of his drink. He lifted his beard, sniffed it, and let it fall. He leaned forward on the sofa. He positioned his ashtray on the coffee table, then put the lighter to his cigarette. He leaned back on the sofa and crossed his legs at the ankles.

My wife covered her mouth, and then she yawned. She stretched. She said, "I think I'll go upstairs and put on my robe. I think I'll change into something else. Robert, you make yourself comfortable," she said.

"I'm comfortable," the blind man said.

"I want you to feel comfortable in this house," she said.   55

"I am comfortable," the blind man said.

After she'd left the room, he and I listened to the weather report and then to the sports roundup. By that time, she'd been gone so long I didn't know if she was going to come back. I thought she might have gone to bed. I wished she'd come back downstairs. I didn't want to be left alone with a blind man. I asked him if he wanted another drink, and he said sure. Then I asked if he wanted to smoke some dope with me. I said I'd just rolled a number. I hadn't, but I planned to do so in about two shakes.

---

ham radio operator: A licensed amateur radio operator.

"I'll try some with you," he said.

"Damn right," I said. "That's the stuff."

60 I got our drinks and sat down on the sofa with him. Then I rolled us two fat numbers. I lit one and passed it. I brought it to his fingers. He took it and inhaled.

"Hold it as long as you can," I said. I could tell he didn't know the first thing.

My wife came back downstairs wearing her pink robe and her pink slippers.

"What do I smell?" she said.

"We thought we'd have us some cannabis," I said.

65 My wife gave me a savage look. Then she looked at the blind man and said, "Robert, I didn't know you smoked."

He said, "I do now, my dear. There's a first time for everything. But I don't feel anything yet."

"This stuff is pretty mellow," I said. "This stuff is mild. It's dope you can reason with," I said. "It doesn't mess you up."

"Not much it doesn't, bub," he said, and laughed.

My wife sat on the sofa between the blind man and me. I passed her the number. She took it and toked° and then passed it back to me. "Which way is this going?" she said. Then she said, "I shouldn't be smoking this. I can hardly keep my eyes open as it is. That dinner did me in. I shouldn't have eaten so much."

70 "It was the strawberry pie," the blind man said. "That's what did it," he said, and he laughed his big laugh. Then he shook his head.

"There's more strawberry pie," I said.

"Do you want some more, Robert?" my wife said.

"Maybe in a little while," he said.

We gave our attention to the TV. My wife yawned again. She said, "Your bed is made up when you feel like going to bed, Robert. I know you must have had a long day. When you're ready to go to bed, say so." She pulled his arm. "Robert?"

75 He came to and said, "I've had a real nice time. This beats tapes, doesn't it?"

I said, "Coming at you," and I put the number between his fingers. He inhaled, held the smoke, and then let it go. It was like he'd been doing it since he was nine years old.

"Thanks, bub," he said. "But I think this is all for me. I think I'm beginning to feel it," he said. He held the burning roach out for my wife.

"Same here," she said. "Ditto. Me, too." She took the roach and passed it to me. "I may just sit here for a while between you two guys with my eyes closed. But don't let me bother you, okay? Either one of you. If it bothers you, say so. Otherwise, I may just sit here with my eyes closed until you're ready to go to bed," she said. "Your bed's made up, Robert, when you're ready. It's right next to our room at the top of the stairs. We'll show you up when you're ready. You wake me up now, you guys, if I fall asleep." She said that and then she closed her eyes and went to sleep.

---

toked: Inhaled.

The news program ended. I got up and changed the channel. I sat back down on the sofa. I wished my wife hadn't pooped out. Her head lay across the back of the sofa, her mouth open. She'd turned so that her robe slipped away from her legs, exposing a juicy thigh. I reached to draw her robe back over her, and it was then that I glanced at the blind man. What the hell! I flipped the robe open again.

"You say when you want some strawberry pie," I said.   80

"I will," he said.

I said, "Are you tired? Do you want me to take you up to your bed? Are you ready to hit the hay?"

"Not yet," he said. "No, I'll stay up with you, bub. If that's all right. I'll stay up until you're ready to turn in. We haven't had a chance to talk. Know what I mean? I feel like me and her monopolized the evening." He lifted his beard and he let it fall. He picked up his cigarettes and his lighter.

"That's all right," I said. Then I said, "I'm glad for the company."

And I guess I was. Every night I smoked dope and stayed up as long as I could   85
before I fell asleep. My wife and I hardly ever went to bed at the same time. When I did go to sleep, I had these dreams. Sometimes I'd wake up from one of them, my heart going crazy.

Something about the church and the Middle Ages was on the TV. Not your run-of-the-mill TV fare. I wanted to watch something else. I turned to the other channels. But there was nothing on them, either. So I turned back to the first channel and apologized.

"Bub, it's all right," the blind man said. "It's fine with me. Whatever you want to watch is okay. I'm always learning something. Learning never ends. It won't hurt me to learn something tonight. I got ears," he said.

We didn't say anything for a time. He was leaning forward with his head turned at me, his right ear aimed in the direction of the set. Very disconcerting. Now and then his eyelids drooped and then they snapped open again. Now and then he put his fingers into his beard and tugged, like he was thinking about something he was hearing on the television.

On the screen, a group of men wearing cowls was being set upon and tormented by men dressed in skeleton costumes and men dressed as devils. The men dressed as devils wore devil masks, horns, and long tails. This pageant was part of a procession. The Englishman who was narrating the thing said it took place in Spain once a year. I tried to explain to the blind man what was happening.

"Skeletons," he said. "I know about skeletons," he said, and nodded.   90

The TV showed this one cathedral. Then there was a long, slow look at another one. Finally, the picture switched to the famous one in Paris, with its flying buttresses and its spires reaching up to the clouds. The camera pulled away to show the whole of the cathedral rising above the skyline.

There were times when the Englishman who was telling the thing would shut up, would simply let the camera move around the cathedrals. Or else the camera would tour the countryside, men in fields walking behind oxen. I waited as long as I could. Then I felt I had to say something. I said, "They're showing the outside of this cathedral now. Gargoyles. Little statues carved to look like monsters. Now I guess they're in Italy. Yeah, they're in Italy. There's paintings on the walls of this one church."

"Are those fresco° paintings, bub?" he asked, and he sipped from his drink.

I reached for my glass. But it was empty. I tried to remember what I could remember. "You're asking me are those frescoes?" I said. "That's a good question. I don't know."

95   The camera moved to a cathedral outside Lisbon.° The differences in the Portuguese cathedral compared with the French and Italian were not that great. But they were there. Mostly the interior stuff. Then something occurred to me, and I said, "Something has occurred to me. Do you have any idea what a cathedral is? What they look like, that is? Do you follow me? If somebody says cathedral to you, do you have any notion what they're talking about? Do you know the difference between that and a Baptist church, say?"

He let the smoke dribble from his mouth. "I know they took hundreds of workers fifty or a hundred years to build," he said. "I just heard the man say that, of course. I know generations of the same families worked on a cathedral. I heard him say that, too. The men who began their life's work on them, they never lived to see the completion of their work. In that wise, bub, they're no different from the rest of us, right?" He laughed. Then his eyelids drooped again. His head nodded. He seemed to be snoozing. Maybe he was imagining himself in Portugal. The TV was showing another cathedral now. This one was in Germany. The Englishman's voice droned on. "Cathedrals," the blind man said. He sat up and rolled his head back and forth. "If you want the truth, bub, that's about all I know. What I just said. What I heard him say. But maybe you could describe one to me? I wish you'd do it. I'd like that. If you want to know, I really don't have a good idea."

I stared hard at the shot of the cathedral on the TV. How could I even begin to describe it? But say my life depended on it. Say my life was being threatened by an insane guy who said I had to do it or else.

I stared some more at the cathedral before the picture flipped off into the countryside. There was no use. I turned to the blind man and said, "To begin with, they're very tall." I was looking around the room for clues. "They reach way up. Up and up. Toward the sky. They're so big, some of them, they have to have these supports. To help hold them up, so to speak. These supports are called buttresses. They remind me of viaducts,° for some reason. But maybe you don't know viaducts, either? Sometimes the cathedrals have devils and such carved into the front. Sometimes lords and ladies. Don't ask me why this is," I said.

---

fresco: Painted plaster.

Lisbon: The capital of Portugal.

viaducts: Long, elevated roadways.

He was nodding. The whole upper part of his body seemed to be moving back and forth.

"I'm not doing so good, am I?" I said.   100

He stopped nodding and leaned forward on the edge of the sofa. As he listened to me, he was running his fingers through his beard. I wasn't getting through to him, I could see that. But he waited for me to go on just the same. He nodded, like he was trying to encourage me. I tried to think what else to say. "They're really big," I said. "They're massive. They're built of stone. Marble, too, sometimes. In those olden days, when they built cathedrals, men wanted to be close to God. In those olden days, God was an important part of everyone's life. You could tell this from their cathedral-building. I'm sorry," I said, "but it looks like that's the best I can do for you. I'm just no good at it."

"That's all right, bub," the blind man said. "Hey, listen. I hope you don't mind my asking you. Can I ask you something? Let me ask you a simple question, yes or no. I'm just curious and there's no offense. You're my host. But let me ask if you are in any way religious? You don't mind my asking?"

I shook my head. He couldn't see that, though. A wink is the same as a nod to a blind man. "I guess I don't believe in it. In anything. Sometimes it's hard. You know what I'm saying?"

"Sure, I do," he said.

"Right," I said.

The Englishman was still holding forth. My wife sighed in her sleep. She   105
drew a long breath and went on with her sleeping.

"You'll have to forgive me," I said. "But I can't tell you what a cathedral looks like. It just isn't in me to do it. I can't do any more than I've done."

The blind man sat very still, his head down, as he listened to me.

I said, "The truth is, cathedrals don't mean anything special to me. Nothing. Cathedrals. They're something to look at on late-night TV. That's all they are."

It was then that the blind man cleared his throat. He brought something   110
up. He took a handkerchief from his back pocket. Then he said, "I get it, bub. It's okay. It happens. Don't worry about it," he said. "Hey, listen to me. Will you do me a favor? I got an idea. Why don't you find us some heavy paper? And a pen. We'll do something. We'll draw one together. Get us a pen and some heavy paper. Go on, bub, get the stuff," he said.

So I went upstairs. My legs felt like they didn't have any strength in them. They felt like they did after I'd done some running. In my wife's room, I looked around. I found some ballpoints in a little basket on her table. And then I tried to think where to look for the kind of paper he was talking about.

Downstairs, in the kitchen, I found a shopping bag with onion skins in the bottom of the bag. I emptied the bag and shook it. I brought it into the living room and sat down with it near his legs. I moved some things, smoothed the wrinkles from the bag, spread it out on the coffee table.

The blind man got down from the sofa and sat next to me on the carpet.

He ran his fingers over the paper. He went up and down the sides of the paper.
The edges, even the edges. He fingered the corners.

115   "All right," he said. "All right, let's do her."

He found my hand, the hand with the pen. He closed his hand over my hand.
"Go ahead, bub, draw," he said. "Draw. You'll see. I'll follow along with you. It'll
be okay. Just begin now like I'm telling you. You'll see. Draw," the blind man said.

So I began. First I drew a box that looked like a house. It could have been the
house I lived in. Then I put a roof on it. At either end of the roof, I drew spires.
Crazy.

"Swell," he said. "Terrific. You're doing fine," he said. "Never thought anything like this could happen in your lifetime, did you, bub? Well, it's a strange life,
we all know that. Go on now. Keep it up."

I put in windows with arches. I drew flying buttresses. I hung great doors.
I couldn't stop. The TV station went off the air. I put down the pen and closed and
opened my fingers. The blind man felt around over the paper. He moved the tips
of his fingers over the paper, all over what I had drawn, and he nodded.

120   "Doing fine," the blind man said.

I took up the pen again, and he found my hand. I kept at it. I'm no artist. But
I kept drawing just the same.

My wife opened up her eyes and gazed at us. She sat up on the sofa, her robe
hanging open. She said, "What are you doing? Tell me, I want to know."

I didn't answer her.

The blind man said, "We're drawing a cathedral. Me and him are working on
it. Press hard," he said to me. "That's right. That's good," he said. "Sure. You got
it, bub, I can tell. You didn't think you could. But you can, can't you? You're cooking with gas now. You know what I'm saying? We're going to really have us something here in a minute. How's the old arm?" he said. "Put some people in there
now. What's a cathedral without people?"

125   My wife said, "What's going on? Robert, what are you doing? What's going on?"

"It's all right," he said to her. "Close your eyes now," the blind man said to me.

I did it. I closed them just like he said.

"Are they closed?" he said. "Don't fudge."

"They're closed," I said.

130   "Keep them that way," he said. He said, "Don't stop now. Draw."

So we kept on with it. His fingers rode my fingers as my hand went over the
paper. It was like nothing else in my life up to now.

Then he said, "I think that's it. I think you got it," he said. "Take a look. What
do you think?"

But I had my eyes closed. I thought I'd keep them that way for a little longer.
I thought it was something I ought to do.

"Well?" he said. "Are you looking?"

135   My eyes were still closed. I was in my house. I knew that. But I didn't feel like
I was inside anything.

"It's really something," I said.

Reading and Reacting

1. Who is the narrator? What do we know about him? Why does the impend-ing visit by the blind man disturb him?

2. At several points in the story, the narrator's wife loses patience with him. What causes her displeasure? What do her reactions reveal about the wife? About the narrator?

3. Why did the narrator's wife leave her first husband? What qualities in the narrator might have led his wife to marry him?

4. Why is the narrator's wife so devoted to the blind man? What does she gain from her relationship with him?

5. According to the narrator, his wife never forgot the blind man's running his fingers over her face. Why is this experience so important to her?

6. Toward the end of the story, the blind man asks the narrator to describe a cathedral. Why is the narrator unable to do so? What does his inability to do so reveal about him?

7. Why does the blind man tell the narrator to close his eyes while he is draw-ing? What does he hope to teach him? What is the narrator able to "see" with his eyes shut that he cannot see with them open?

8. In paragraph 96, the blind man observes that the men who began work on a cathedral never lived to see it completed. In this way, he says, "they're no different from the rest of us." What does the cathedral symbolize to the blind man? What does it come to symbolize to the narrator?

9. What other symbols are present in the story? How do these symbols help to develop the central theme of the story?

10. JOURNAL ENTRY The blind man is an old friend of the narrator's wife. Why then does he focus on the narrator? In what way is the narrator's spiritual de-velopment the blind man's gift to the narrator's wife?

11. CRITICAL PERSPECTIVE Critic Kirk Nesset, in his discussion of "Cathedral," notes that the narrator becomes more open as the story progresses, and that this coming out is mirrored by rhetoric of the story. Early on in the story, the narrator feels momentarily "sorry for the blind man," his insulated hardness beginning to soften. As the walls of his resentment noticeably crack, he watches with "admiration" as Robert eats, recognizing Robert's handicap to be "no impairment to his performance at the dinner table. . . . Like Robert, who is on a journey by train, dropping in on friends and relatives, trying to get over the loss of his wife, the narrator is also on a journey, one signaled by signposts in his language and played out by the events of the story he tells."

Do you agree that the narrator becomes more open? If so, can you cite any other instances where the words he chooses reflect this increasing openness?

Related Works: "Gryphon" (p. 139), "Doe Season" (p. 327), "When I Heard the Learn'd Astronomer" (p. 491), "On First Looking into Chapman's Homer" (p. 575), "Batter My Heart, Three-Personed God" (p. 662), "God's Grandeur" (p. 676)

NATHANIEL HAWTHORNE (1804–1864) was born in Salem, Massachusetts, the great-great-grandson of a judge who presided over the infamous Salem witch trials. After his sea captain father was killed on a voyage when Hawthorne was four years old, his childhood was one of genteel poverty. An uncle paid for his education at Bowdoin College in Maine, where Hawthorne's friends included a future president of the United States, Franklin Pierce, who in 1853 appointed him U.S. consul in Liverpool, England. Hawthorne published four novels — *The Scarlet Letter* (1850), *The House of the Seven Gables* (1851), *The Blithedale Romance* (1852), and *The Marble Faun* (1860) — and more than one hundred short stories and sketches.

Hawthorne referred to his own work as *romance*. He used this term to mean not an escape from reality but rather a method of confronting "the depths of our common nature" and "the truth of the heart." His stories probe the dark side of human nature and frequently paint a world that is virtuous on the surface but (as Young Goodman Brown comes to believe) "one stain of guilt, one mighty blood spot" beneath. Hawthorne's stories often emphasize the ambiguity of human experience. For example, the reader is left to wonder whether Goodman Brown actually saw a witch's coven or dreamed about the event. For Hawthorne, what is important is Brown's recognition that evil may be found everywhere. "Young Goodman Brown," as Hawthorne's neighbor and friend Herman Melville once said, is a tale "as deep as Dante."

Young Goodman° Brown   (1835)

Young Goodman Brown came forth at sunset, into the street of Salem village, but put his head back, after crossing the threshold, to exchange a parting kiss with his young wife. And Faith, as the wife was aptly named, thrust her own pretty head into the street, letting the wind play with the pink ribbons of her cap, while she called to Goodman Brown.

"Dearest heart," whispered she, softly and rather sadly, when her lips were close to his ear, "prithee, put off your journey until sunrise, and sleep in your own bed to-night. A lone woman is troubled with such dreams and such thoughts, that she's afeard of herself, sometimes. Pray, tarry with me this night, dear husband, of all nights in the year!"

"My love and my Faith," replied young Goodman Brown, "of all nights in the year, this one night must I tarry away from thee. My journey, as thou callest it, forth and back again, must needs be done 'twixt now and sunrise. What, my sweet, pretty wife, dost thou doubt me already, and we but three months married!"

"Then God bless you!" said Faith with the pink ribbons, "and may you find all well, when you come back."

Goodman: A form of address, similar to *Mr.*, meaning "husband."

"Amen!" cried Goodman Brown. "Say thy prayers, dear Faith, and go to bed 5
at dusk, and no harm will come to thee."

So they parted; and the young man pursued his way, until, being about to turn
the corner by the meeting-house, he looked back and saw the head of Faith still
peeping after him, with a melancholy air, in spite of her pink ribbons.

"Poor little Faith!" thought he, for his heart smote him. "What a wretch am I,
to leave her on such an errand! She talks of dreams, too. Methought, as she spoke,
there was trouble in her face, as if a dream had warned her what work is to be done
to-night. But no, no! 't would kill her to think it. Well; she's a blessed angel on
earth; and after this one night, I'll cling to her skirts and follow her to Heaven."

With this excellent resolve for the future, Goodman Brown felt himself
justified in making more haste on his present evil purpose. He had taken a dreary
road, darkened by all the gloomiest trees of the forest, which barely stood aside to
let the narrow path creep through, and closed immediately behind. It was as
lonely as could be; and there is this peculiarity in such a solitude, that the traveller knows not who may be concealed by the innumerable trunks and the thick
boughs overhead; so that, with lonely footsteps, he may yet be passing through an
unseen multitude.

"There may be a devilish Indian behind every tree," said Goodman Brown to
himself; and he glanced fearfully behind him, as he added, "What if the devil
himself should be at my very elbow!"

His head being turned back, he passed a crook of the road, and looking for- 10
ward again, beheld the figure of a man, in grave and decent attire, seated at the
foot of an old tree. He arose at Goodman Brown's approach, and walked onward,
side by side with him.

"You are late, Goodman Brown," said he. "The clock of the Old South° was
striking, as I came through Boston; and that is full fifteen minutes agone."

"Faith kept me back awhile," replied the young man, with a tremor in his
voice, caused by the sudden appearance of his companion, though not wholly
unexpected.

It was now deep dusk in the forest, and deepest in that part of it where these
two were journeying. As nearly as could be discerned, the second traveller was
about fifty years old, apparently in the same rank of life as Goodman Brown, and
bearing a considerable resemblance to him, though perhaps more in expression
than features. Still, they might have been taken for father and son. And yet,
though the elder person was as simply clad as the younger, and as simple in manner too, he had an indescribable air of one who knew the world, and would not
have felt abashed at the governor's dinner-table, or in King William's court,°
were it possible that his affairs should call him thither. But the only thing about

---

Old South: Old South Church in Boston, renowned meeting place for American patriots during the Revolution.
King William: William III, king of England from 1689 to 1702.

him that could be fixed upon as remarkable, was his staff, which bore the likeness of a great black snake, so curiously wrought, that it might almost be seen to twist and wriggle itself like a living serpent. This, of course, must have been an ocular deception, assisted by the uncertain light.

"Come, Goodman Brown!" cried his fellow-traveller, "this is a dull pace for the beginning of a journey. Take my staff, if you are so soon weary."

15   "Friend," said the other, exchanging his slow pace for a full stop, "having kept covenant by meeting thee here, it is my purpose now to return whence I came. I have scruples, touching the matter thou wot'st of."

"Sayest thou so?" replied he of the serpent, smiling apart. "Let us walk on, nevertheless, reasoning as we go, and if I convince thee not, thou shalt turn back. We are but a little way in the forest, yet."

"Too far, too far!" exclaimed the goodman, unconsciously resuming his walk. "My father never went into the woods on such an errand, nor his father before him. We have been a race of honest men and good Christians, since the days of the martyrs. And shall I be the first of the name of Brown that ever took this path and kept —"

"Such company, thou wouldst say," observed the elder person, interrupting his pause. "Well said, Goodman Brown! I have been as well acquainted with your family as with ever a one among the Puritans; and that's no trifle to say. I helped your grandfather, the constable, when he lashed the Quaker woman so smartly through the streets of Salem. And it was I that brought your father a pitch-pine knot, kindled at my own hearth, to set fire to an Indian village, in King Philip's war.° They were my good friends, both; and many a pleasant walk have we had along this path, and returned merrily after midnight. I would fain be friends with you, for their sake."

"If it be as thou sayest," replied Goodman Brown, "I marvel they never spoke of these matters. Or, verily, I marvel not, seeing that the least rumor of the sort would have driven them from New England. We are a people of prayer, and good works to boot, and abide no such wickedness."

20   "Wickedness or not," said the traveller with the twisted staff, "I have a very general acquaintance here in New England. The deacons of many a church have drunk the communion wine with me; the selectmen, of divers towns, make me their chairman; and a majority of the Great and General Court are firm supporters of my interest. The governor and I, too — but these are state secrets."

"Can this be so!" cried Goodman Brown, with a stare of amazement at his undisturbed companion. "Howbeit, I have nothing to do with the governor and council; they have their own ways, and are no rule for a simple husbandman like me. But, were I to go on with thee, how should I meet the eye of that good old

---

King Philip's war: A war of Indian resistance led by Metacomet of the Wampanoags, known to the English as "King Philip." The war, intended to halt expansion of English settlers in Massachusetts, collapsed after Metacomet's death in August 1676.

man, our minister, at Salem village? Oh, his voice would make me tremble, both
Sabbath-day and lecture-day!"°

Thus far, the elder traveller had listened with due gravity, but now burst into
a fit of irrepressible mirth, shaking himself so violently, that his snakelike staff
actually seemed to wriggle in sympathy.

"Ha, ha, ha!" shouted he, again and again; then composing himself, "Well, go
on, Goodman Brown, go on; but, prithee, don't kill me with laughing!"

"Well, then, to end the matter at once," said Goodman Brown, considerably
nettled, "there is my wife, Faith. It would break her dear little heart; and I'd rather
break my own!"

"Nay, if that be the case," answered the other, "e'en go thy ways, Goodman   25
Brown. I would not, for twenty old women like the one hobbling before us, that
Faith should come to any harm."

As he spoke, he pointed his staff at a female figure on the path, in whom
Goodman Brown recognized a very pious and exemplary dame, who had taught
him his catechism in youth, and was still his moral and spiritual adviser, jointly
with the minister and Deacon Gookin.

"A marvel, truly, that Goody° Cloyse should be so far in the wilderness, at
nightfall!" said he. "But, with your leave, friend, I shall take a cut through the
woods, until we have left this Christian woman behind. Being a stranger to you,
she might ask whom I was consorting with, and whither I was going."

"Be it so," said his fellow-traveller. "Betake you to the woods, and let me keep
the path."

Accordingly, the young man turned aside, but took care to watch his companion, who advanced softly along the road, until he had come within a staff's
length of the old dame. She, meanwhile, was making the best of her way, with sin-
gular speed for so aged a woman, and mumbling some indistinct words, a prayer,
doubtless, as she went. The traveller put forth his staff, and touched her withered
neck with what seemed the serpent's tail.

"The devil!" screamed the pious old lady.   30

"Then Goody Cloyse knows her old friend?" observed the traveller, confronting her, and leaning on his writhing stick.

"Ah, forsooth, and is it your worship, indeed?" cried the good dame. "Yea, truly
is it, and in the very image of my old gossip, Goodman Brown, the grandfather of
the silly fellow that now is. But, would your worship believe it? my broomstick
hath strangely disappeared, stolen, as I suspect, by that unhanged witch, Goody
Cory, and that, too, when I was all anointed with the juice of smallage and
cinque-foil and wolf's bane —"°

---

lecture-day. The day of the midweek sermon, usually Thursday.   *Goody:* A contraction of "Goodwife," a term of
politeness used in addressing a woman of humble station. Goody Cloyse, like Goody Cory and Martha Carrier, who
appear later in the story, was one of the Salem "witches" sentenced in 1692.

smallage . . . wolf's bane: Plants believed to have magical powers. Smallage is wild celery.

"Mingled with fine wheat and the fat of a new-born babe," said the shape of old Goodman Brown.

"Ah, your worship knows the recipe," cried the old lady, cackling aloud. "So, as I was saying, being all ready for the meeting, and no horse to ride on, I made up my mind to foot it; for they tell me there is a nice young man to be taken into communion to-night. But now your good worship will lend me your arm, and we shall be there in a twinkling."

35   "That can hardly be," answered her friend. "I may not spare you my arm, Goody Cloyse, but here is my staff, if you will."

So saying, he threw it down at her feet, where, perhaps, it assumed life, being one of the rods which its owner had formerly lent to the Egyptian Magi. Of this fact, however, Goodman Brown could not take cognizance. He had cast his eyes in astonishment, and looking down again, beheld neither Goody Cloyse nor the serpentine staff, but his fellow-traveller alone, who waited for him as calmly as if nothing had happened.

"That old woman taught me my catechism!" said the young man; and there was a world of meaning in this simple comment.

They continued to walk onward, while the elder traveller exhorted his companion to make good speed and persevere in the path, discoursing so aptly, that his arguments seemed rather to spring up in the bosom of his auditor, than to be suggested by himself. As they went he plucked a branch of maple, to serve for a walking-stick, and began to strip it of the twigs and little boughs, which were wet with evening dew. The moment his fingers touched them, they became strangely withered and dried up, as with a week's sunshine. Thus the pair proceeded, at a good free pace, until suddenly, in a gloomy hollow of the road, Goodman Brown sat himself down on the stump of a tree, and refused to go any farther.

"Friend," said he, stubbornly, "my mind is made up. Not another step will I budge on this errand. What if a wretched old woman do choose to go to the devil, when I thought she was going to Heaven! Is that any reason why I should quit my dear Faith, and go after her?"

40   "You will think better of this by and by," said his acquaintance, composedly. "Sit here and rest yourself awhile; and when you feel like moving again, there is my staff to help you along."

Without more words, he threw his companion the maple stick, and was as speedily out of sight as if he had vanished into the deepening gloom. The young man sat a few moments by the roadside, applauding himself greatly, and thinking with how clear a conscience he should meet the minister, in his morning walk, nor shrink from the eye of good old Deacon Gookin. And what calm sleep would be his, that very night, which was to have been spent so wickedly, but purely and sweetly now, in the arms of Faith! Amidst these pleasant and praiseworthy meditations, Goodman Brown heard the tramp of horses along the road, and deemed it advisable to conceal himself within the verge of the forest, conscious of the guilty purpose that had brought him thither, though now so happily turned from it.

On came the hoof-tramps and the voices of the riders, two grave old voices, conversing soberly as they drew near. These mingled sounds appeared to pass along the road, within a few yards of the young man's hiding-place; but owing, doubtless, to the depth of the gloom, at that particular spot, neither the travellers nor their steeds were visible. Though their figures brushed the small boughs by the wayside, it could not be seen that they intercepted, even for a moment, the faint gleam from the strip of bright sky, athwart which they must have passed. Goodman Brown alternately crouched and stood on tiptoe, pulling aside the branches, and thrusting forth his head as far as he durst, without discerning so much as a shadow. It vexed him the more, because he could have sworn, were such a thing possible, that he recognized the voices of the minister and Deacon Gookin, jogging along quietly, as they were wont to do, when bound to some ordination or ecclesiastical council. While yet within hearing, one of the riders stopped to pluck a switch.

"Of the two, reverend Sir," said the voice like the deacon's, "I had rather miss an ordination dinner than to-night's meeting. They tell me that some of our community are to be here from Falmouth and beyond, and others from Connecticut and Rhode Island; besides several of the Indian powwows, who, after their fashion, know almost as much deviltry as the best of us. Moreover, there is a goodly young woman to be taken into communion."

"Mighty well, Deacon Gookin!" replied the solemn old tones of the minister. "Spur up, or we shall be late. Nothing can be done, you know, until I get on the ground."

The hoofs clattered again, and the voices, talking so strangely in the empty 45 air, passed on through the forest, where no church had ever been gathered, nor solitary Christian prayed. Whither, then, could these holy men be journeying, so deep into the heathen wilderness? Young Goodman Brown caught hold of a tree, for support, being ready to sink down on the ground, faint and over-burthened with the heavy sickness of his heart. He looked up to the sky, doubting whether there really was a Heaven above him. Yet, there was the blue arch, and the stars brightening in it.

"With Heaven above, and Faith below, I will yet stand firm against the devil!" cried Goodman Brown.

While he still gazed upward, into the deep arch of the firmament, and had lifted his hands to pray, a cloud, though no wind was stirring, hurried across the zenith, and hid the brightening stars. The blue sky was still visible, except directly overhead, where this black mass of cloud was sweeping swiftly northward. Aloft in the air, as if from the depths of the cloud, came a confused and doubtful sound of voices. Once, the listener fancied that he could distinguish the accents of townspeople of his own, men and women, both pious and ungodly, many of whom he had met at the communion-table, and had seen others rioting at the tavern. The next moment, so indistinct were the sounds, he doubted whether he had heard aught but the murmur of the old forest, whispering without a wind. Then came a stronger swell of those familiar tones, heard daily in the sunshine, at Salem village, but never, until now, from a cloud at night. There was one voice, of a young woman, uttering lamentations, yet with an uncertain sorrow, and en-treating for some favor, which, perhaps, it would grieve her to obtain. And all the unseen multitude, both saints and sinners, seemed to encourage her onward.

"Faith!" shouted Goodman Brown, in a voice of agony and desperation; and the echoes of the forest mocked him, crying —"Faith! Faith!" as if bewildered wretches were seeking her, all through the wilderness.

The cry of grief, rage, and terror was yet piercing the night, when the un-happy husband held his breath for a response. There was a scream, drowned im-mediately in a louder murmur of voices fading into far-off laughter, as the dark cloud swept away, leaving the clear and silent sky above Goodman Brown. But something fluttered lightly down through the air, and caught on the branch of a tree. The young man seized it and beheld a pink ribbon.

50 "My Faith is gone!" cried he, after one stupefied moment. "There is no good on earth, and sin is but a name. Come, devil! for to thee is this world given."

And maddened with despair, so that he laughed loud and long, did Goodman Brown grasp his staff and set forth again, at such a rate, that he seemed to fly along the forest path, rather than to walk or run. The road grew wilder and drearier, and more faintly traced, and vanished at length, leaving him in the heart of the dark wilderness, still rushing onward, with the instinct that guides mortal man to evil. The whole forest was peopled with frightful sounds: the creaking of the trees, the howling of wild beasts, and the yell of Indians; while, sometimes, the wind tolled like a distant church bell, and sometimes gave a broad roar around the traveller, as if all Nature was laughing him to scorn. But he was himself the chief horror of the scene, and shrank not from its other horrors.

"Ha! ha! ha!" roared Goodman Brown, when the wind laughed at him. "Let us hear which will laugh loudest! Think not to frighten me with your deviltry! Come witch, come wizard, come Indian powwow, come devil himself! and here comes Goodman Brown. You may as well fear him as he fear you!"

In truth, all through the haunted forest, there could be nothing more fright-ful than the figure of Goodman Brown. On he flew, among the black pines, brandishing his staff with frenzied gestures, now giving vent to an inspiration of horrid blasphemy, and now shouting forth such laughter, as set all the echoes of the forest laughing like demons around him. The fiend in his own shape is less hideous, than when he rages in the breast of man. Thus sped the demoniac on his course, until, quivering among the trees, he saw a red light before him, as when the felled trunks and branches of a clearing have been set on fire, and throw up their lurid blaze against the sky, at the hour of midnight. He paused, in a lull of the tempest that had driven him onward, and heard the swell of what seemed a hymn, rolling solemnly from a distance, with the weight of many voices. He knew the tune. It was a familiar one in the choir of the village meet-ing-house. The verse died heavily away, and was lengthened by a chorus, not of human voices, but of all the sounds of the benighted wilderness, pealing in aw-ful harmony together. Goodman Brown cried out; and his cry was lost to his own ear, by its unison with the cry of the desert.

In the interval of silence, he stole forward, until the light glared full upon his eyes. At one extremity of an open space, hemmed in by the dark wall of the forest, arose a rock, bearing some rude, natural resemblance either to an altar or a pulpit, and surrounded by four blazing pines, their tops aflame, their stems untouched, like candles at an evening meeting. The mass of foliage, that had overgrown the summit of the rock, was all on fire, blazing high into the night, and fitfully illuminating the whole field. Each pendent twig and leafy festoon was in a blaze. As the red light arose and fell, a numerous congregation alternately shone forth, then disappeared in shadow, and again grew, as it were, out of the darkness, peopling the heart of the solitary woods at once.

"A grave and dark-clad company!" quoth Goodman Brown.   55

In truth, they were such. Among them, quivering to-and-fro, between gloom and splendor, appeared faces that would be seen, next day, at the council-board of the province, and others which, Sabbath after Sabbath, looked devoutly heavenward, and benignantly over the crowded pews, from the holiest pulpits in the land. Some affirm, that the lady of the governor was there. At least, there were high dames well known to her, and wives of honored husbands, and widows a great multitude, and ancient maidens, all of excellent repute, and fair young girls, who trembled lest their mothers should espy them. Either the sudden gleams of light, flashing over the obscure field, bedazzled Goodman Brown, or he recognized a score of the church members of Salem village, famous for their especial sanctity. Good old Deacon Gookin had arrived, and waited at the skirts of that venerable saint, his reverend pastor. But, irreverently consorting with these grave, reputable, and pious people, these elders of the church, these chaste dames and dewy virgins, there were men of dissolute lives and women of spotted fame, wretches given over to all mean and filthy vice, and suspected even of horrid crimes. It was strange to see, that the good shrank not from the wicked, nor were the sinners abashed by the saints. Scattered, also, among their pale-faced enemies, were the Indian priests, or powwows, who had often scared their native forest with more hideous incantations than any known to English witchcraft.

"But, where is Faith?" thought Goodman Brown; and, as hope came into his heart, he trembled.

Another verse of the hymn arose, a slow and mournful strain, such as the pious love, but joined to words which expressed all that our nature can conceive of sin, and darkly hinted at far more. Unfathomable to mere mortals is the lore of fiends. Verse after verse was sung, and still the chorus of the desert swelled between, like the deepest tone of a mighty organ. And, with the final peal of that dreadful anthem, there came a sound, as if the roaring wind, the rushing streams, the howling beasts, and every other voice of the unconverted wilderness were mingling and according with the voice of guilty man, in homage to the prince of all. The four blazing pines threw up a loftier flame, and obscurely discovered shapes and visages of horror on the smoke-wreaths, above the impious assembly. At the same moment, the fire on the rock shot redly forth, and formed a glowing arch above its base, where now appeared a figure. With reverence be it spoken, the apparition bore no slight similitude, both in garb and manner, to some grave divine of the New England churches.

"Bring forth the converts!" cried a voice, that echoed through the field and rolled into the forest.

60   At the word, Goodman Brown stepped forth from the shadow of the trees, and approached the congregation, with whom he felt a loathful brotherhood, by the sympathy of all that was wicked in his heart. He could have well-nigh sworn, that the shape of his own dead father beckoned him to advance, looking downward from a smoke-wreath, while a woman, with dim features of despair, threw out her hand to warn him back. Was it his mother? But he had no power to retreat one step, nor to resist, even in thought, when the minister and good old Deacon Gookin seized his arms, and led him to the blazing rock. Thither came also the slender form of a veiled female, led between Goody Cloyse, that pious teacher of the catechism, and Martha Carrier, who had received the devil's promise to be queen of hell. A rampant hag was she! And there stood the proselytes, beneath the canopy of fire.

"Welcome, my children," said the dark figure, "to the communion of your race! Ye have found, thus young, your nature and your destiny. My children, look behind you!"

They turned; and flashing forth, as it were, in a sheet of flame, the fiend-worshippers were seen; the smile of welcome gleamed darkly on every visage.

"There," resumed the sable form, "are all whom ye have reverenced from youth. Ye deemed them holier than yourselves, and shrank from your own sin, contrasting it with their lives of righteousness and prayerful aspirations heavenward. Yet, here are they all, in my worshipping assembly! This night it shall be granted you to know their secret deeds; how hoary-bearded elders of the church have whispered wanton words to the young maids of their households; how many a woman, eager for widow's weeds, has given her husband a drink at bedtime, and let him sleep his last sleep in her bosom; how beardless youths have made haste to inherit their father's wealth; and how fair damsels — blush not, sweet ones! — have dug little graves in the garden, and bidden me, the sole guest, to an infant's funeral. By the sympathy of your human hearts for sin, ye shall scent out all the places — whether in church, bedchamber, street, field, or forest — where crime has been committed, and shall exult to behold the whole earth one stain of guilt, one mighty blood-spot. Far more than this! It shall be yours to penetrate, in every bosom, the deep mystery of sin, the fountain of all wicked arts, and which inexhaustibly supplies more evil impulses than human power — than my power, at its utmost! — can make manifest in deeds. And now, my children, look upon each other."

They did so; and, by the blaze of the hell-kindled torches, the wretched man beheld his Faith, and the wife her husband, trembling before that unhallowed altar.

65   "Lo! there ye stand, my children," said the figure, in a deep and solemn tone, almost sad, with its despairing awfulness, as if his once angelic nature could yet mourn for our miserable race. "Depending upon one another's hearts, ye had still

hoped that virtue were not all a dream! Now are ye undeceived! — Evil is the nature of mankind. Evil must be your only happiness. Welcome, again, my children, to the communion of your race!"

"Welcome!" repeated the fiend-worshippers, in one cry of despair and triumph.

And there they stood, the only pair, as it seemed, who were yet hesitating on the verge of wickedness, in this dark world. A basin was hollowed, naturally, in the rock. Did it contain water, reddened by the lurid light? or was it blood? or, perchance, a liquid flame? Herein did the Shape of Evil dip his hand, and prepare to lay the mark of baptism upon their foreheads, that they might be partakers of the mystery of sin, more conscious of the secret guilt of others, both in deed and thought, than they could now be of their own. The husband cast one look at his pale wife, and Faith at him. What polluted wretches would the next glance show them to each other, shuddering alike at what they disclosed and what they saw!

"Faith! Faith!" cried the husband. "Look up to Heaven, and resist the Wicked One!"

Whether Faith obeyed, he knew not. Hardly had he spoken, when he found himself amid calm night and solitude, listening to a roar of the wind, which died heavily away through the forest. He staggered against the rock, and felt it chill and damp, while a hanging twig, that had been all on fire, besprinkled his cheek with the coldest dew.

The next morning, young Goodman Brown came slowly into the street of 70 Salem village staring around him like a bewildered man. The good old minister was taking a walk along the grave-yard, to get an appetite for breakfast and meditate his sermon, and bestowed a blessing, as he passed, on Goodman Brown. He shrank from the venerable saint, as if to avoid an anathema. Old Deacon Gookin was at domestic worship, and the holy words of his prayer were heard through the open window. "What God doth the wizard pray to?" quoth Goodman Brown. Goody Cloyse, that excellent old Christian, stood in the early sunshine, at her own lattice, catechising a little girl, who had brought her a pint of morning's milk. Goodman Brown snatched away the child, as from the grasp of the fiend himself. Turning the corner by the meeting-house, he spied the head of Faith, with the pink ribbons, gazing anxiously forth, and bursting into such joy at sight of him that she skipt along the street, and almost kissed her husband before the whole village. But Goodman Brown looked sternly and sadly into her face, and passed on without a greeting.

Had Goodman Brown fallen asleep in the forest, and only dreamed a wild dream of a witch-meeting?

Be it so, if you will. But, alas! it was a dream of evil omen for young Goodman Brown. A stern, a sad, a darkly meditative, a distrustful, if not a desperate man did he become, from the night of that fearful dream. On the Sabbath day, when the congregation were singing a holy psalm, he could not listen, because an anthem of sin rushed loudly upon his ear, and drowned all the blessed strain. When the minister spoke from the pulpit, with power and fervid eloquence, and with his hand on the open Bible, of the sacred truths of our religion, and of saint-like lives and triumphant deaths, and of future bliss or misery unutterable, then did Goodman Brown turn pale, dreading lest the roof should thunder down upon the gray blasphemer and his hearers. Often, awaking suddenly at midnight, he shrank from the bosom of Faith, and at morning or eventide, when the family knelt down at prayer, he scowled, and muttered to himself, and gazed sternly at his wife, and turned away. And when he had lived long, and was borne to his grave, a hoary corpse, followed by Faith, an aged woman, and children and grand-children, a goodly procession, besides neighbors not a few, they carved no hopeful verse upon his tombstone; for his dying hour was gloom.

Reading and Reacting

1. Who is the narrator of "Young Goodman Brown"? What advantages does the narrative point of view give the author?
2. What does young Goodman Brown mean when he says "of all nights in the year, this one night must I tarry away from thee" (par. 3)? What is important about *this* night, and why does Goodman Brown believe he must journey "'twixt now and sunrise"?
3. Is Goodman Brown surprised to encounter the second traveler on the road, or does he seem to expect him? What is the significance of their encounter? What do you make of the fact that the stranger bears a strong resemblance to young Goodman Brown?
4. What sins are the various characters Goodman Brown meets in the woods guilty of committing?
5. "Young Goodman Brown" has two distinct settings: Salem and the woods. What are the differences between these settings? What significance does each setting have in the story?
6. Which figures in the story are allegorical, and which are symbols? On what evidence do you base your conclusions?
7. Why do the people gather in the woods? Why do they attend the ceremony?
8. Explain the change that takes place in young Goodman Brown at the end of the story. Why can he not listen to the singing of holy psalms or to the minister's sermons? What causes him to turn away from Faith and die in gloom?
9. **Journal Entry**   At the end of the story, the narrator suggests that Goodman Brown might have fallen asleep and imagined his encounter with the witches. Do you think the events in the story are all a dream?
10. **Critical Perspective**   In *The Power of Blackness*, his classic study of nineteenth-century American writers, Harry Levin observes that Hawthorne had doubts about conventional religion. This, Levin believes, is why all efforts to read an enlightening theological message into Hawthorne's works are "doomed to failure."

    What comment do you think Hawthorne is making in "Young Goodman Brown" about religious faith?

Related Works: "Where Are You Going, Where Have You Been?" (p. 384), "We Wear the Mask" (p. 665), "La Belle Dame sans Merci: A Ballad" (p. 679), *Nine Ten* (p. 760)

WRITING SUGGESTIONS: Symbol, Allegory, and Myth

1. Select a story from this anthology, and discuss its use of symbols.

2. Strangers figure prominently in "Young Goodman Brown" and "Cathedral." Write an essay in which you discuss the possible symbolic significance of strangers in each story. If you like, you may also discuss Arnold Friend in "Where Are You Going, Where Have You Been?" (p. 384).

3. Write an essay in which you discuss the use of myth in "Young Goodman Brown."

4. If Shirley Jackson had wished to write "The Lottery" as an allegory whose purpose was to expose the evils of Nazi Germany, what revisions would she have had to make to convey the dangers of blind obedience to authority? Consider the story's symbols, the characters (and their names), and the setting.

5. In literary works, characters' prized possessions can function as symbols. In this chapter, for example, the quilt in "Everyday Use" takes on symbolic significance. Write an essay in which you analyze this symbol (or a possession that has symbolic significance in another story), and discuss how it helps to convey the main theme of the story in which it appears.

THEME

> The problem I face as a writer is to make my stories mean something.
>
> —**Toni Morrison,** *Discovering Fiction*

The **theme** of a work of literature is its central or dominant idea. *Theme* is not the same as *plot* or *subject*, two terms with which it is sometimes confused. A summary of the *plot* of Tadeusz Borowski's "Silence," a story about survivors of the Holocaust, could be, "Prisoners are liberated from a concentration camp, and, despite the warnings of the American officer, they kill a captured German guard." The statement " 'Silence' is about freed prisoners and a guard" could define the *subject* of the story. A statement of the *theme* of "Silence," however, has to do more than summarize its plot or define its subject; it has to convey the values and ideas expressed by the story.

Many effective stories are complex, expressing more than one theme, and "Silence" is no exception. You could say that "Silence" suggests that human beings have a need for vengeance. You could also say the story demonstrates that silence is sometimes the only response possible when people confront unspeakable horrors. Both these themes — and others — are expressed in the story, yet one theme seems to dominate: the idea that under extreme conditions the oppressed can have the same capacity for evil as their oppressors.

When you write about theme, you need to do more than tell what happens in the story. The theme you identify should be a general idea that extends beyond the story and applies to the world outside fiction. Compare these two statements that a student wrote about Edgar Allan Poe's "The Cask of Amontillado" (p. 203):

Poe's "The Cask of Amontillado" is about a man who has an obsessive desire for revenge.

Poe's "The Cask of Amontillado" suggests that when the desire for revenge becomes obsessive, it can deprive individuals of all that makes them human.

The first merely tells what the story is about; the second statement identifies the story's theme, a general observation about humanity.

Granted, some short works (fairy tales or fables, for example) have themes that can only be expressed as **clichés** — overused phrases or expressions — or as **morals** — lessons dramatized by the work. The fairy tale "Cinderella," for example, expresses the clichéd theme that a virtuous girl who endures misfortune will eventually achieve her just reward; the fable "The Tortoise and the Hare" illustrates the moral "Slow and steady wins the race." Like "The Cask of Amontillado," however, the stories in this anthology have themes that are more complex than clichés or morals.

Interpreting Themes

Contemporary critical theory holds that the theme of a work of fiction is as much the creation of readers as of the writer. Readers' backgrounds, knowledge, values, and beliefs all play a part in determining the theme or themes they will identify in a work. Most readers, for example, will realize that David Michael Kaplan's story "Doe Season" (p. 327) — in which the main character goes hunting, kills her first deer, and is forced to confront suffering and death — expresses a conventional **initiation theme,** revealing growing up to be a disillusioning and painful process. Still, different readers bring different perspectives to the story and, in some cases, see different themes.

During a classroom discussion of "Doe Season," a student familiar with hunting saw more than his classmates did in the story's conventional initiation theme. He knew that in many states there really is a doe season, which lasts approximately three days. Shorter than the ten-day buck season, it allows hunters to control the size of the deer herd by killing females. This knowledge enabled the student to conclude that by the end of the story the female child's innocence is destroyed, just as the doe is.

Another student pointed out that the participation of Andy — a female who uses a male name — in hunting, a traditional male rite of passage, leads to her killing the deer and to her subsequent disillusionment. It also leads to her decision to abandon her nickname. By contrasting "Andrea" with "Andy," the story reveals the conflict between her "female" nature (illustrated by her compassion) and her desire to emulate the men to whom killing is a sport. This interpretation led the student to conclude that the theme of "Doe Season" is that males and females have very different outlooks on life.

Other students did not accept the negative characterization of the story's male characters that the preceding interpretation implies. They pointed out that the father is a sympathetic figure who is extremely supportive; he encourages and defends his daughter. He takes her hunting because he loves her, not because he wants to initiate her into life or to hurt her. One student mentioned that Andy's reaction (called *buck fever*) when she sees the doe is common in children who kill their first deer. In light of this information, several students concluded that far from being about irreconcilable male and female perspectives, "Doe Season" makes a statement about a young girl who is hunting for her own identity and who in the process discovers her own mortality. Her father is therefore the agent who enables her to confront the inevitability of death, a fact she must accept if she is going to take her place in the adult world. In this sense, the theme of the story is the idea that in order to mature, a child must come to terms with the reality of death.

Different readers may see different themes in a story, but any interpretation of a theme must make sense in light of what is actually in the story. Evidence from the work, not just your own feelings or assumptions, must support your interpretation, and a single symbol or one statement by a character is not enough in itself to reveal a story's theme. Therefore, you must present a cross-section of examples from the text to support your interpretation of the story's theme. If you say that the theme of James Joyce's "Araby" (p. 232) is that an innocent idealist is inevitably doomed to disillusionment, you have to find examples from the text to support this statement. You could begin with the title, concluding that the word *Araby* suggests idealistic dreams of exotic beauty that the boy tries to find when he goes to the bazaar. You could reinforce your interpretation by pointing out that Mangan's unattainable sister is a symbol of all that the boy wants so desperately to find. Finally, you could show how idealism is ultimately crushed by society: at the end of the story, the boy stands alone in the darkness and realizes that his dreams are childish fantasies. Although other readers may have different responses to "Araby," they should find your interpretation reasonable if you support it with enough examples.

Identifying Themes

Every element of a story can shed light on its themes. As you analyze a short story, you should look for features that reveal and reinforce what you perceive to be the story's most important ideas.

- *The **title** can often provide insight into the theme or themes of a story.* The title of an F. Scott Fitzgerald story, "Babylon Revisited," emphasizes a major idea in the story — that Paris of the 1920s is like Babylon, the ancient city the Bible singles out as the epitome of evil and corruption. The story's protagonist, Charlie Wales, comes to realize that no matter how much money he lost after the 1929 stock market crash, he lost more — his wife and his daughter — during the boom, when he was in Paris. Charlie's search through his past — his return to "Babylon" — provides new meaning to his life and offers at least a small bit of hope for the future.
- *Sometimes a **narrator's** or **character's** statement can reveal a theme.* For example, at the beginning of Alberto Alvaro Ríos's "The Secret Lion" (p. 412), the first-person narrator says, "I was twelve and in junior high school and something happened that we didn't have a name for, but it was

there nonetheless like a lion, and roaring, roaring that way the biggest things do. Everything changed." Although the narrator does not directly announce the story's theme, he does suggest that the story will convey the idea that the price children pay for growing up is realizing that everything changes, that nothing stays the way it is.

- The **arrangement of events** *can suggest a story's theme, as it does in an Ernest Hemingway story, "The Short Happy Life of Francis Macomber."* At the beginning of the story, the title character is a coward who is stuck in an unhappy marriage. As the story progresses, he gradually learns the nature of courage and, finally, finds it in himself. At the moment of his triumph, however, Francis is shot by his wife; his "happy life" is short indeed. The way the events of the story are presented, through foreshadowing and flashbacks, reveals the connection between Macomber's marriage and his behavior as a hunter, and this connection in turn helps to reveal a possible theme: that sometimes courage can be more important than life itself.

- A story's **conflict** *can offer clues to its theme.* In "Araby," the young boy believes that his society neglects art and beauty and glorifies the mundane. This conflict between the boy's idealism and his world can help readers understand why the boy isolates himself in his room reading books and why he retreats into dreams of idealized love. A major theme of the story — that growing up leads to the loss of youthful idealism — is revealed by this central conflict.

  Similarly, the main character in "The Yellow Wallpaper" (p. 372), a woman who has recently had a baby, is in conflict with the nineteenth-century society in which she lives. She is suffering from "temporary nervous depression," what doctors today recognize as postpartum depression. Following the practice of the time, her physician has ordered complete bed rest and has instructed her husband to deprive her of all mental and physical stimulation. This harsh treatment leads the narrator to lose her grasp on reality; eventually, she begins to hallucinate. The central conflict of the story is clearly between the woman and her society, controlled by men. This conflict communicates the theme: that in nineteenth-century America, women are controlled not just by their husbands and the male medical establishment, but also by the society they have created.

- The **point of view** *of a story can also help shed light on theme.* For instance, a writer's use of an unreliable first-person narrator can help to communicate the theme of a story. Thus, Montresor's self-serving first-person account of his crime in "The Cask of Amontillado" — along with his attempts to justify these actions — enables readers to understand the dangers of irrational anger and misplaced ideas about honor. The voice of a third-person narrator can also help to convey a story's theme. For example, the detachment of the narrator in Stephen Crane's Civil War novel *The Red Badge of Courage* reinforces the theme of the novel: that bravery, cowardice, war, and even life itself are insignificant when set beside the indifference of the universe.

- *A story may give names, places, and objects* **symbolic significance.** These symbols can not only enrich the story but also help to convey a central theme. For example, the rocking horse in D. H. Lawrence's "The Rocking-Horse Winner" (p. 340) can be seen as a symbol of the boy's desperate desire to remain a child. Interpreted in this way, it reinforces the theme that innocence cannot survive when it confronts adult greed and selfishness. Similarly, Hawthorne's "Young Goodman Brown" (p. 302) uses symbols such as the walking stick, the woods, sunset and night, and the vague shadows to develop one of its central themes: that once a person strays from the path of faith, evil is everywhere.
- *Finally,* **changes in a character** *can shed light on the theme or themes of the story.* The main character in Charles Baxter's "Gryphon" (p. 139), for example, eventually comes to realize that the "lies" Miss Ferenczi tells may be closer to the truth than the "facts" his teachers present, and his changing attitude toward Miss Ferenczi helps to communicate the story's central theme about the nature of truth.

✔ **CHECKLIST Writing about Theme**

- What is the central theme of the story?
- What other themes can you identify?
- Does the title of the story suggest a theme?
- Does the narrator, or any character, make statements that express or imply a theme?
- In what way does the arrangement of events in the story suggest a theme?
- In what way does the central conflict of the story suggest a theme?
- How does the point of view shed light on the story's central theme?
- Do any symbols suggest a theme?
- Do any characters in the story change in any significant way? Do these changes convey a particular theme?
- Have you clearly identified the story's central theme, rather than just summarized the plot or stated the subject?
- Does your statement of the story's central theme make a general observation that has an application beyond the story itself?

EUDORA WELTY (1909–2001) was born and raised in Jackson, Mississippi. After attending the Mississippi College for Women, the University of Wisconsin, and Columbia University (where she studied advertising), she returned to Jackson to pursue her long career as a writer, beginning as a journalist. In 1936, she wrote the first of her many short stories, which are gathered in *Collected Stories* (1980). Welty also wrote several novels, including *Delta Wedding* (1946), *Losing Battles* (1970), and the Pulitzer Prize–winning *The Optimist's Daughter* (1972). Her volume of memoirs, *One Writer's Beginnings* (1984), was a best-seller.

One of the country's most accomplished writers, Welty focused much of her fiction on life in southern towns and villages peopled with dreamers, eccentrics, and close-knit families. Her sharply observed characters are sometimes presented with great humor, sometimes with poignant lyricism, but always with clarity and sympathy. "Of course any writer is in part all of his characters," she observed. "How otherwise would they be known to him, occur to him, become what they are?" In "A Worn Path," Welty creates a particularly memorable character in the tenacious Phoenix Jackson and explores a theme that transcends race and region.

A Worn Path (1940)

It was December — a bright frozen day in the early morning. Far out in the country there was an old Negro woman with her head tied in a red rag, coming along a path through the pinewoods. Her name was Phoenix Jackson. She was very old and small and she walked slowly in the dark pine shadows, moving a little from side to side in her steps, with the balanced heaviness and lightness of a pendulum in a grandfather clock. She carried a thin, small cane made from an umbrella, and with this she kept tapping the frozen earth in front of her. This made a grave and persistent noise in the still air, that seemed meditative like the chirping of a solitary little bird.

She wore a dark striped dress reaching down to her shoe tops, and an equally long apron of bleached sugar sacks, with a full pocket: all neat and tidy, but every time she took a step she might have fallen over her shoelaces, which dragged from her unlaced shoes. She looked straight ahead. Her eyes were blue with age. Her skin had a pattern all its own of numberless branching wrinkles and as though a whole little tree stood in the middle of her forehead, but a golden color ran underneath, and the two knobs of her cheeks were illumined by a yellow burning under the dark. Under the red rag her hair came down on her neck in the frailest of ringlets, still black, and with an odor like copper.

Now and then there was a quivering in the thicket. Old Phoenix said, "Out of my way, all you foxes, owls, beetles, jack rabbits, coons and wild animals! . . . Keep out from under these feet, little bob-whites. . . . Keep the big wild hogs out of my path. Don't let none of those come running my direction. I got a long way." Under her small black-freckled hand her cane, limber as a buggy whip, would switch at the brush as if to rouse up any hiding things.

On she went. The woods were deep and still. The sun made the pine needles almost too bright to look at, up where the wind rocked. The cones dropped as light as feathers. Down in the hollow was the mourning dove — it was not too late for him.

5   The path ran up a hill. "Seem like there is chains about my feet, time I get this far," she said, in the voice of argument old people keep to use with themselves. "Something always take a hold of me on this hill — pleads I should stay."

After she got to the top she turned and gave a full, severe look behind her where she had come. "Up through pines," she said at length. "Now down through oaks."

Her eyes opened their widest, and she started down gently. But before she got to the bottom of the hill a bush caught her dress.

Her fingers were busy and intent, but her skirts were full and long, so that before she could pull them free in one place they were caught in another. It was not possible to allow the dress to tear. "I in the thorny bush," she said. "Thorns, you doing your appointed work. Never want to let folks pass, no sir. Old eyes thought you was a pretty little *green* bush."

Finally, trembling all over, she stood free, and after a moment dared to stoop for her cane.

10   "Sun so high!" she cried, leaning back and looking, while the thick tears went over her eyes. "The time getting all gone here."

At the foot of this hill was a place where a log was laid across the creek.

"Now comes the trial," said Phoenix.

Putting her right foot out, she mounted the log and shut her eyes. Lifting her skirt, leveling her cane fiercely before her, like a festival figure in some parade, she began to march across. Then she opened her eyes and she was safe on the other side.

"I wasn't as old as I thought," she said.

15   But she sat down to rest. She spread her skirts on the bank around her and folded her hands over her knees. Up above her was a tree in a pearly cloud of mistletoe. She did not dare to close her eyes, and when a little boy brought her a plate with a slice of marble-cake on it she spoke to him. "That would be acceptable," she said. But when she went to take it there was just her own hand in the air.

So she left that tree, and had to go through a barbed-wire fence. There she had to creep and crawl, spreading her knees and stretching her fingers like a baby trying to climb the steps. But she talked loudly to herself: she could not let her dress be torn now, so late in the day, and she could not pay for having her arm or her leg sawed off if she got caught fast where she was.

At last she was safe through the fence and risen up out in the clearing. Big dead trees, like black men with one arm, were standing in the purple stalks of the withered cotton field. There sat a buzzard.

"Who you watching?"

In the furrow she made her way along.

"Glad this not the season for bulls," she said, looking sideways, "and the good 20 Lord made his snakes to curl up and sleep in the winter. A pleasure I don't see no two-headed snake coming around that tree, where it come once. It took a while to get by him, back in the summer."

She passed through the old cotton and went into a field of dead corn. It whispered and shook and was taller than her head. "Through the maze now," she said, for there was no path.

Then there was something tall, black, and skinny there, moving before her.

At first she took it for a man. It could have been a man dancing in the field. But she stood still and listened, and it did not make a sound. It was as silent as a ghost.

"Ghost," she said sharply, "who be you the ghost of? For I have heard of nary death close by."

But there was no answer — only the ragged dancing in the wind. 25

She shut her eyes, reached out her hand, and touched a sleeve. She found a coat and inside that an emptiness, cold as ice.

"You scarecrow," she said. Her face lighted. "I ought to be shut up for good," she said with laughter. "My senses is gone. I too old. I the oldest people I ever know. Dance, old scarecrow," she said, "while I dancing with you."

She kicked her foot over the furrow, and with mouth drawn down, shook her head once or twice in a little strutting way. Some husks blew down and whirled in streamers about her skirts.

Then she went on, parting her way from side to side with the cane, through the whispering field. At last she came to the end, to a wagon track where the silver grass blew between the red ruts. The quail were walking around like pullets, seeming all dainty and unseen.

"Walk pretty," she said. "This is the easy place. This the easy going." 30

She followed the track, swaying through the quiet bare fields, through the little strings of trees silver in their dead leaves, past cabins silver from weather, with the doors and windows boarded shut, all like old women under a spell sitting there. "I walking in their sleep," she said, nodding her head vigorously.

In a ravine she went where a spring was silently flowing through a hollow log. Old Phoenix bent and drank. "Sweet-gum makes the water sweet," she said, and drank more. "Nobody know who make this well, for it was here when I was born."

The track crossed a swampy part where the moss hung as white as lace from every limb. "Sleep on, alligators, and blow your bubbles." Then the track went into the road.

Deep, deep the road went down between the high green-colored banks. Overhead the live-oaks met, and it was as dark as a cave.

A black dog with a lolling tongue came up out of the weeds by the ditch. She 35 was meditating, and not ready, and when he came at her she only hit him a little with her cane. Over she went in the ditch, like a little puff of milkweed.

Down there, her senses drifted away. A dream visited her, and she reached her hand up, but nothing reached down and gave her a pull. So she lay there and presently went to talking. "Old woman," she said to herself, "that black dog come up out of the weeds to stall you off, and now there he sitting on his fine tail, smiling at you."

A white man finally came along and found her — a hunter, a young man, with his dog on a chain.

"Well, Granny!" he laughed. "What are you doing there?"

"Lying on my back like a June-bug waiting to be turned over, mister," she said, reaching up her hand.

40 He lifted her up, gave her a swing in the air, and set her down. "Anything broken, Granny?"

"No sir, them old dead weeds is springy enough," said Phoenix, when she had got her breath. "I thank you for your trouble."

"Where do you live, Granny?" he asked, while the two dogs were growling at each other.

"Away back yonder, sir, behind the ridge. You can't even see it from here."

"On your way home?"

45 "No sir, I going to town."

"Why, that's too far! That's as far as I walk when I come out myself, and I get something for my trouble." He patted the stuffed bag he carried, and there hung down a little closed claw. It was one of the bob-whites, with its beak hooked bitterly to show it was dead. "Now you go on home, Granny!"

"I bound to go to town, mister," said Phoenix. "The time come around."

He gave another laugh, filling the whole landscape. "I know you old colored people! Wouldn't miss going to town to see Santa Claus!"

But something held old Phoenix very still. The deep lines in her face went into a fierce and different radiation. Without warning, she had seen with her own eyes a flashing nickel fall out of the man's pocket onto the ground.

50 "How old are you, Granny?" he was saying.

"There is no telling, mister," she said, "no telling."

Then she gave a little cry and clapped her hands and said, "Git on away from here, dog! Look! Look at that dog!" She laughed as if in admiration. "He ain't scared of nobody. He a big black dog." She whispered, "Sic him!"

"Watch me get rid of that cur," said the man. "Sic him, Pete! Sic him!"

Phoenix heard the dogs fighting, and heard the man running and throwing sticks. She even heard a gunshot. But she was slowly bending forward by that time, further and further forward, the lid stretched down over her eyes, as if she were doing this in her sleep. Her chin was lowered almost to her knees. The yellow palm of her hand came out from the fold of her apron. Her fingers slid down and along the ground under the piece of money with the grace and care they would have in lifting an egg from under a setting hen. Then she slowly straightened up, she stood erect, and the nickel was in her apron pocket.

A bird flew by. Her lips moved. "God watching me the whole time. I come to stealing."

The man came back, and his own dog panted about them. "Well, I scared him 55 off that time," he said, and then he laughed and lifted his gun and pointed it at Phoenix.

She stood straight and faced him.

"Doesn't the gun scare you?" he said, still pointing it.

"No, sir, I seen plenty go off closer by, in my day, and for less than what I done," she said, holding utterly still.

He smiled, and shouldered the gun. "Well, Granny," he said, "you must be a hundred years old, and scared of nothing. I'd give you a dime if I had any money with me. But you take my advice and stay home, and nothing will happen to you."

"I bound to go on my way, mister," said Phoenix. She inclined her head in 60 the red rag. Then they went in different directions, but she could hear the gun shooting again and again over the hill.

She walked on. The shadows hung from the oak trees to the road like curtains. Then she smelled wood-smoke, and smelled the river, and she saw a steeple and the cabins on their steep steps. Dozens of little black children whirled around her. There ahead was Natchez shining. Bells were ringing. She walked on.

In the paved city it was Christmas time. There were red and green electric lights strung and crisscrossed everywhere, and all turned on in the daytime. Old Phoenix would have been lost if she had not distrusted her eyesight and depended on her feet to know where to take her.

She paused quietly on the sidewalk where people were passing by. A lady came along in the crowd, carrying an armful of red-, green- and silver-wrapped presents; she gave off perfume like the red roses in hot summer, and Phoenix stopped her.

"Please, missy, will you lace up my shoe?" She held up her foot.

"What do you want, Grandma?"   65

"See my shoe," said Phoenix. "Do all right for out in the country, but wouldn't look right to go in a big building."

"Stand still then, Grandma," said the lady. She put her packages down on the sidewalk beside her and laced and tied both shoes tightly.

"Can't lace 'em with a cane," said Phoenix. "Thank you, missy. I doesn't mind asking a nice lady to tie up my shoe, when I gets out on the street."

Moving slowly and from side to side, she went into the big building, and into a tower of steps, where she walked up and around and around until her feet knew to stop.

She entered a door, and there she saw nailed up on the wall the document that 70 had been stamped with the gold seal and framed in the gold frame, which matched the dream that was hung up in her head.

"Here I be," she said. There was a fixed and ceremonial stiffness over her body.

"A charity case, I suppose," said an attendant who sat at the desk before her.

But Phoenix only looked above her head. There was sweat on her face, the wrinkles in her face shone like a bright net.

"Speak up, Grandma," the woman said. "What's your name? We must have your history, you know. Have you been here before? What seems to be the trouble with you?"

75 Old Phoenix only gave a twitch to her face as if a fly were bothering her.

"Are you deaf?" cried the attendant.

But then the nurse came in.

"Oh, that's just old Aunt Phoenix," she said. "She doesn't come for herself — she has a little grandson. She makes these trips just as regular as clockwork. She lives away back off the Old Natchez Trace." She bent down. "Well, Aunt Phoenix, why don't you just take a seat? We won't keep you standing after your long trip." She pointed.

80 The old woman sat down, bolt upright in the chair.

"Now, how is the boy?" asked the nurse.

Old Phoenix did not speak.

"I said, how is the boy?"

But Phoenix only waited and stared straight ahead, her face very solemn and withdrawn into rigidity.

"Is his throat any better?" asked the nurse. "Aunt Phoenix, don't you hear me? Is your grandson's throat any better since the last time you came for the medicine?"

85 With her hands on her knees, the old woman waited, silent, erect and motionless, just as if she were in armor.

"You mustn't take up our time this way, Aunt Phoenix," the nurse said. "Tell us quickly about your grandson, and get it over. He isn't dead, is he?"

At last there came a flicker and then a flame of comprehension across her face, and she spoke.

"My grandson. It was my memory had left me. There I sat and forgot why I made my long trip."

"Forgot?" The nurse frowned. "After you came so far?"

90 Then Phoenix was like an old woman begging a dignified forgiveness for waking up frightened in the night. "I never did go to school, I was too old at the Surrender,"° she said in a soft voice. "I'm an old woman without an education. It was my memory fail me. My little grandson, he is just the same, and I forgot it in the coming."

"Throat never heals, does it?" said the nurse, speaking in a loud, sure voice to old Phoenix. By now she had a card with something written on it, a little list. "Yes. Swallowed lye. When was it? — January — two-three years ago — "

Phoenix spoke unasked now. "No, missy, he not dead, he just the same. Every little while his throat begin to close up again, and he not able to swallow. He not get his breath. He not able to help himself. So the time come around, and I go on another trip for the soothing medicine."

---

the Surrender: The surrender of General Robert E. Lee to General Ulysses S. Grant at the end of the Civil War, April 9, 1865.

"All right. The doctor said as long as you came to get it, you could have it," said the nurse. "But it's an obstinate case."

"My little grandson, he sit up there in the house all wrapped up, waiting by himself," Phoenix went on. "We is the only two left in the world. He suffer and it don't seem to put him back at all. He got a sweet look. He going to last. He wear a little patch quilt and peep out holding his mouth open like a little bird. I remembers so plain now. I not going to forget him again, no, the whole enduring time. I could tell him from all the others in creation."

"All right." The nurse was trying to hush her now. She brought her a bottle of medicine. "Charity," she said, making a check mark in a book.

Old Phoenix held the bottle close to her eyes, and then carefully put it into her pocket.

"I thank you," she said.

"It's Christmas time, Grandma," said the attendant. "Could I give you a few pennies out of my purse?"

"Five pennies is a nickel," said Phoenix stiffly.

"Here's a nickel," said the attendant.

Phoenix rose carefully and held out her hand. She received the nickel and then fished the other nickel out of her pocket and laid it beside the new one. She stared at her palm closely, with her head on one side.

Then she gave a tap with her cane on the floor.

"This is what come to me to do," she said. "I going to the store and buy my child a little windmill they sells, made out of paper. He going to find it hard to believe there such a thing in the world. I'll march myself back where he waiting, holding it straight up in this hand."

She lifted her free hand, gave a little nod, turned around, and walked out of the doctor's office. Then her slow step began on the stairs, going down.

Reading and Reacting

1. How does the first paragraph set the scene for the rest of the story? How does it foreshadow the events that will take place later on?

2. Traditionally, a quest is a journey in which a knight overcomes a series of obstacles in order to perform a prescribed feat. In what way is Phoenix's journey a quest? What obstacles does she face? What feat must she perform?

3. Because Phoenix is old, she has trouble seeing. What things does she have difficulty seeing? How do her mistakes shed light on her character? How do they contribute to the impact of the story?

4. What is the major theme of this story? What other themes are expressed?

5. A phoenix is a mythical bird that would live for five hundred years, be consumed by fire, and then rise from its own ashes. In what way is the name of this creature appropriate for the main character of this story?

6. Phoenix is not intimidated by the man with the gun and has no difficulty asking a white woman to tie her shoe. In spite of her nobility of character, however, Phoenix has no qualms about stealing a nickel or taking charity from the doctor. How do you account for this apparent contradiction?

7. How do the various people Phoenix encounters react to her? Do they treat her with respect? With disdain? Why do you think they react the way they do?

8. In paragraph 90, Phoenix says that she is an old woman without an education. Does she nevertheless seem to have any knowledge that the other characters lack?

9. JOURNAL ENTRY Could "A Worn Path" be an allegory? If so, what might each of the characters represent?

10. CRITICAL PERSPECTIVE Writing about "A Worn Path," Eudora Welty said that the question she was asked most frequently by both students and teachers was whether Phoenix Jackson's grandson was actually dead. Here she attempts to answer this question:

> I had not meant to mystify readers by withholding any fact; it is not a writer's business to tease. The story is told through Phoenix's mind and she undertakes her errand. As the author at one with the character as I tell it, I must assume that the boy is alive. As the reader, you are free to think as you like, of course; the story invites you to believe that no matter what happens, Phoenix for as long as she is able to walk and can hold to her purpose will make her journey.

Do you think Phoenix's grandson is alive or dead? Why?

Related Works: "Miss Brill" (p. 134), "Araby" (p. 232), "Rooming houses are old women" (p. 524), "We Wear the Mask" (p. 665), "The Rocking-Horse Winner" (p. 340)

DAVID MICHAEL KAPLAN (1946–   ) is one of a group of American writers who, along with South American writers such as Gabriel García Márquez of Columbia, are called "magic realists." Magic realists work outside of the "hobbits and wizards" borders of traditional fantasy writing, seamlessly interweaving magical elements with detailed, realistically drawn "everyday" settings. These elements, says a reviewer of Kaplan's work, are invoked "to illuminate and underscore heightened moments of reality." The story "Doe Season," which appears in Kaplan's debut collection, *Comfort* (1987), was included in *Best American Short Stories 1985*. Kaplan's first novel, *Skating in the Dark*, was published in 1991, and his craft text, *Revision: A Creative Approach to Writing and Re-writing Fiction*, was published in 1997. Kaplan teaches fiction writing at Loyola University Chicago, where he directs the Creative Writing Program.

Interestingly, the stories in *Comfort* break from classic "first-time author" tradition by sidestepping the autobiographical, young-man-comes-of-age theme. Instead, these stories are about young girls — or young women — coming to grips with parents (present or absent) and with loss and searching for ways to resolve their ambivalence about becoming women. In "Doe Season," Andy's surreal encounter with the doe may be a dream, but the beauty and horror of their meeting will affect the rest of her life.

Doe Season (1985)

They were always the same woods, she thought sleepily as they drove through the early morning darkness — deep and immense, covered with yesterday's snowfall, which had frozen overnight. They were the same woods that lay behind her house, *and they stretch all the way to here*, she thought, *for miles and miles, longer than I could walk in a day, or a week even, but they are still the same woods*. The thought made her feel good: it was like thinking of God; it was like thinking of the space between here and the moon; it was like thinking of all the foreign countries from her geography book where even now, Andy knew, people were going to bed, while they — she and her father and Charlie Spoon and Mac, Charlie's eleven-year-old son — were driving deeper into the Pennsylvania countryside, to go hunting.

They had risen long before dawn. Her mother, yawning and not trying to hide her sleepiness, cooked them eggs and French toast. Her father smoked a cigarette and flicked ashes into his saucer while Andy listened, wondering *Why doesn't he come?* and *Won't he ever come?* until at last a car pulled into the graveled drive and honked. "That will be Charlie Spoon," her father said; he always said "Charlie Spoon," even though his real name was Spreun, because Charlie was, in a sense, shaped like a spoon, with a large head and a narrow waist and chest.

Andy's mother kissed her and her father and said, "Well, have a good time" and "Be careful." Soon they were outside in the bitter dark, loading gear by the back-porch light, their breath steaming. The woods behind the house were then only a black streak against the wash of night.

Andy dozed in the car and woke to find that it was half light. Mac — also sleeping — had slid against her. She pushed him away and looked out the window. Her breath clouded the glass, and she was cold; the car's heater didn't work right. They were riding over gentle hills, the woods on both sides now — the same woods, she knew, because she had been watching the whole way, even while she slept. They had been in her dreams, and she had never lost sight of them.

Charlie Spoon was driving. "I don't understand why she's coming," he said to her father. "How old is she anyway — eight?" 5

"Nine," her father replied. "She's small for her age."

"So — nine. What's the difference? She'll just add to the noise and get tired besides."

"No, she won't," her father said. "She can walk me to death. And she'll bring good luck, you'll see. Animals — I don't know how she does it, but they come right up to her. We go walking in the woods, and we'll spot more raccoons and possums and such than I ever see when I'm alone."

Charlie grunted.

"Besides, she's not a bad little shot, even if she doesn't hunt yet. She shoots 10 the .22 real good."

"Popgun," Charlie said, and snorted. "And target shooting ain't deer hunting."

"Well, she's not gonna be shooting anyway, Charlie," her father said. "Don't worry. She'll be no bother."

"I still don't know why she's coming," Charlie said.

"Because she wants to, and I want her to. Just like you and Mac. No difference."

15   Charlie turned onto a side road and after a mile or so slowed down. "That's it!" he cried. He stopped, backed up, and entered a narrow dirt road almost hidden by trees. Five hundred yards down, the road ran parallel to a fenced-in field. Charlie parked in a cleared area deeply rutted by frozen tractor tracks. The gate was locked. *In the spring,* Andy thought, *there will be cows here, and a dog that chases them,* but now the field was unmarked and bare.

"This is it," Charlie Spoon declared. "Me and Mac was up here just two weeks ago, scouting it out, and there's deer. Mac saw the tracks."

"That's right," Mac said.

"Well, we'll just see about that," her father said, putting on his gloves. He turned to Andy. "How you doing, honeybun?"

"Just fine," she said.

20   Andy shivered and stamped as they unloaded: first the rifles, which they unsheathed and checked, sliding the bolts, sighting through scopes, adjusting the slings; then the gear, their food and tents and sleeping bags and stove stored in four backpacks — three big ones for Charlie Spoon and her father and Mac, and a day pack for her.

"That's about your size," Mac said, to tease her.

She reddened and said, "Mac, I can carry a pack big as yours any day." He laughed and pressed his knee against the back of hers, so that her leg buckled. "Cut it out," she said. She wanted to make an iceball and throw it at him, but she knew that her father and Charlie were anxious to get going, and she didn't want to displease them.

Mac slid under the gate, and they handed the packs over to him. Then they slid under and began walking across the field toward the same woods that ran all the way back to her home, where even now her mother was probably rising again to wash their breakfast dishes and make herself a fresh pot of coffee. *She is there, and we are here:* the thought satisfied Andy. There was no place else she would rather be.

Mac came up beside her. "Over there's Canada," he said, nodding toward the woods.

25   "Huh!" she said. "Not likely."

"I don't mean *right* over there. I mean farther up north. You think I'm dumb?"

Dumb as your father, she thought.

"Look at that," Mac said, pointing to a piece of cow dung lying on a spot scraped bare of snow. "A frozen meadow muffin." He picked it up and sailed it at her. "Catch!"

"Mac!" she yelled. His laugh was as gawky as he was. She walked faster. He seemed different today somehow, bundled in his yellow-and-black-checkered coat, a rifle in hand, his silly floppy hat not quite covering his ears. They all seemed different as she watched them trudge through the snow — Mac and her father and Charlie Spoon — bigger, maybe, as if the cold landscape enlarged rather than diminished them, so that they, the only figures in that landscape, took on size and meaning just by being there. If they weren't there, everything would be quieter, and the woods would be the same as before. *But they are here*, Andy thought, looking behind her at the boot prints in the snow, *and I am too, and so it's all different.*

"We'll go down to the cut where we found those deer tracks," Charlie said 30 as they entered the woods. "Maybe we'll get lucky and get a late one coming through."

The woods descended into a gully. The snow was softer and deeper here, so that often Andy sank to her knees. Charlie and Mac worked the top of the gully while she and her father walked along the base some thirty yards behind them. "If they miss the first shot, we'll get the second," her father said, and she nodded as if she had known this all the time. She listened to the crunch of their boots, their breathing, and the drumming of a distant woodpecker. And the crackling. In winter the woods crackled as if everything were straining, ready to snap like dried chicken bones.

We are hunting, Andy thought. The cold air burned her nostrils.

They stopped to make lunch by a rock outcropping that protected them from the wind. Her father heated the bean soup her mother had made for them, and they ate it with bread already stiff from the cold. He and Charlie took a few pulls from a flask of Jim Beam while she scoured the plates with snow and repacked them. Then they all had coffee with sugar and powdered milk, and her father poured her a cup too. "We won't tell your momma," he said, and Mac laughed. Andy held the cup the way her father did, not by the handle but around the rim. The coffee tasted smoky. She felt a little queasy, but she drank it all.

Charlie Spoon picked his teeth with a fingernail. "Now, you might've noticed one thing," he said.

"What's that?" her father asked.   35

"You might've noticed you don't hear no rifles. That's because there ain't no other hunters here. We've got the whole damn woods to ourselves. Now, I ask you — do I know how to find 'em?"

"We haven't seen deer yet, neither."

"Oh, we will," Charlie said, "but not for a while now." He leaned back against the rock. "Deer're sleeping, resting up for the evening feed."

"I seen a deer behind our house once, and it was afternoon," Andy said.

"Yeah, honey, but that was *before* deer season," Charlie said, grinning. "They 40 know something now. They're smart that way."

"That's right," Mac said.

Andy looked at her father — had she said something stupid?

"Well, Charlie," he said, "if they know so much, how come so many get themselves shot?"

"Them's the ones that don't *believe* what they know," Charlie replied. The men laughed. Andy hesitated, and then laughed with them.

45   They moved on, as much to keep warm as to find a deer. The wind became even stronger. Blowing through the treetops, it sounded like the ocean, and once Andy thought she could smell salt air. But that was impossible; the ocean was *hundreds* of miles away, farther than Canada even. She and her parents had gone last summer to stay for a week at a motel on the New Jersey shore. That was the first time she'd seen the ocean, and it frightened her. It was huge and empty, yet always moving. Everything lay hidden. If you walked in it, you couldn't see how deep it was or what might be below; if you swam, something could pull you under and you'd never be seen again. Its musky, rank smell made her think of things dying. Her mother had floated beyond the breakers, calling to her to come in, but Andy wouldn't go farther than a few feet into the surf. Her mother swam and splashed with animal-like delight while her father, smiling shyly, held his white arms above the waist-deep water as if afraid to get them wet. Once a comber rolled over and sent them both tossing, and when her mother tried to stand up, the surf receding behind, Andy saw that her mother's swimsuit top had come off, so that her breasts swayed free, her nipples like two dark eyes. Embarrassed, Andy looked around: except for two women under a yellow umbrella farther up, the beach was empty. Her mother stood up unsteadily, regained her footing. Taking what seemed the longest time, she calmly refixed her top. Andy lay on the beach towel and closed her eyes. The sound of the surf made her head ache.

And now it was winter; the sky was already dimming, not just with the absence of light but with a mist that clung to the hunters' faces like cobwebs. They made camp early. Andy was chilled. When she stood still, she kept wiggling her toes to make sure they were there. Her father rubbed her arms and held her to him briefly, and that felt better. She unpacked the food while the others put up the tents.

"How about rounding us up some firewood, Mac?" Charlie asked.

"I'll do it," Andy said. Charlie looked at her thoughtfully and then handed her the canvas carrier.

There wasn't much wood on the ground, so it took her a while to get a good load. She was about a hundred yards from camp, near a cluster of high, lichen-covered boulders, when she saw through a crack in the rock a buck and two does walking gingerly, almost daintily, through the alder trees. She tried to hush her breathing as they passed not more than twenty yards away. There was nothing she could do. If she yelled, they'd be gone; by the time she got back to camp, they'd be gone. The buck stopped, nostrils quivering, tail up and alert. He looked directly at her. Still she didn't move, not one muscle. He was a beautiful buck, the color of late-turned maple leaves. Unafraid, he lowered his tail, and he and his does silently merged into the trees. Andy walked back to camp and dropped the firewood.

"I saw three deer," she said. "A buck and two does."   50

"Where?" Charlie Spoon cried, looking behind her as if they might have followed her into camp.

"In the woods yonder. They're gone now."

"Well, hell!" Charlie banged his coffee cup against his knee.

"Didn't I say she could find animals?" her father said, grinning.

"Too late to go after them," Charlie muttered. "It'll be dark in a quarter hour.   55
Damn!"

"Damn," Mac echoed.

"They just walk right up to her," her father said.

"Well, leastwise this proves there's deer here." Charlie began snapping long branches into shorter ones. "You know, I think I'll stick with you," he told Andy, "since you're so good at finding deer and all. How'd that be?"

"Okay, I guess," Andy murmured. She hoped he was kidding; no way did she want to hunt with Charlie Spoon. Still, she was pleased he had said it.

Her father and Charlie took one tent, she and Mac the other. When they were   60
in their sleeping bags, Mac said in the darkness, "I bet you really didn't see no deer, did you?"

She sighed. "I did, Mac. Why would I lie?"

"How big was the buck?"

"Four point. I counted."

Mac snorted.

"You just believe what you want, Mac," she said testily.   65

"Too bad it ain't buck season," he said. "Well, I got to go pee."

"So pee."

She heard him turn in his bag. "You ever see it?" he asked.

"It? What's 'it'?"

"It. A pecker."

"Sure," she lied.   70

"Whose? Your father's?"

She was uncomfortable. "No," she said.

"Well, whose then?"

"Oh I don't know! Leave me be, why don't you?"   75

"Didn't see a deer, didn't see a pecker," Mac said teasingly.

She didn't answer right away. Then she said, "My cousin Lewis. I saw his."

"Well, how old's he?"

"One and a half."

"Ha! A baby! A baby's is like a little worm. It ain't a real one at all."   80

If he says he'll show me his, she thought, *I'll kick him. I'll just get out of my bag and kick him.*

"I went hunting with my daddy and Versh and Danny Simmons last year in buck season," Mac said, "and we got ourselves one. And we hog-dressed the thing. You know what that is, don't you?"

"No," she said. She was confused. What was he talking about now?

"That's when you cut him open and take out all his guts, so the meat don't spoil. Makes him lighter to pack out, too."

85   She tried to imagine what the deer's guts might look like, pulled from the gaping hole. "What do you do with them?" she said. "The guts?"

"Oh, just leave 'em for the bears."

She ran her finger like a knife blade along her belly.

"When we left them on the ground," Mac said, "they smoked. Like they were cooking."

"Huh," she said.

90   "They cut off the deer's pecker, too, you know."

Andy imagined Lewis's pecker and shuddered. "Mac, you're disgusting."

He laughed. "Well, I gotta go pee." She heard him rustle out of his bag. "Broo!" he cried, flapping his arms. "It's cold!"

He makes so much noise, she thought, *just noise and more noise.*

Her father woke them before first light. He warned them to talk softly and said that they were going to the place where Andy had seen the deer, to try to cut them off on their way back from their night feeding. Andy couldn't shake off her sleep. Stuffing her sleeping bag into its sack seemed to take an hour, and tying her boots was the strangest thing she'd ever done. Charlie Spoon made hot chocolate and oatmeal with raisins. Andy closed her eyes and, between beats of her heart, listened to the breathing of the forest. *When I open my eyes, it will be lighter,* she decided. But when she did, it was still just as dark, except for the swaths of their flashlights and the hissing blue flame of the stove. *There has to be just one moment when it all changes from dark to light,* Andy thought. She had missed it yesterday, in the car; today she would watch more closely.

95   But when she remembered again, it was already first light and they had moved to the rocks by the deer trail and had set up shooting positions — Mac and Charlie Spoon on the up-trail side, she and her father behind them, some six feet up on a ledge. The day became brighter, the sun piercing the tall pines, raking the hunters, yet providing little warmth. Andy now smelled alder and pine and the slightly rotten odor of rock lichen. She rubbed her hand over the stone and considered that it must be very old, had probably been here before the giant pines, *before anyone was in these woods at all.* A chipmunk sniffed on a nearby branch. She aimed an imaginary rifle and pressed the trigger. The chipmunk froze, then scurried away. Her legs were cramping on the narrow ledge. Her father seemed to doze, one hand in his parka, the other cupped lightly around the rifle. She could smell his scent of old wool and leather. His cheeks were speckled with gray-black whiskers, and he worked his jaws slightly, as if chewing a small piece of gum.

Please let us get a deer, she prayed.

A branch snapped on the other side of the rock face. Her father's hand stiffened on the rifle, startling her — *He hasn't been sleeping at all*, she marveled — and then his jaw relaxed, as did the lines around his eyes, and she heard Charlie Spoon call, "Yo, don't shoot, it's us." He and Mac appeared from around the rock. They stopped beneath the ledge. Charlie solemnly crossed his arms.

"I don't believe we're gonna get any deer here," he said drily.

Andy's father lowered his rifle to Charlie and jumped down from the ledge. Then he reached up for Andy. She dropped into his arms and he set her gently on the ground.

Mac sidled up to her. "I knew you didn't see no deer," he said.   100

"Just because they don't come when you want 'em to don't mean she didn't see them," her father said.

Still, she felt bad. Her telling about the deer had caused them to spend the morning there, cold and expectant, with nothing to show for it.

They tramped through the woods for another two hours, not caring much about noise. Mac found some deer tracks, and they argued about how old they were. They split up for a while and then rejoined at an old logging road that deer might use, and followed it. The road crossed a stream, which had mostly frozen over but in a few spots still caught leaves and twigs in an icy swirl. They forded it by jumping from rock to rock. The road narrowed after that, and the woods thickened.

They stopped for lunch, heating up Charlie's wife's corn chowder. Andy's father cut squares of applesauce cake with his hunting knife and handed them to her and Mac, who ate his almost daintily. Andy could faintly taste knife oil on the cake. She was tired. She stretched her leg; the muscle that had cramped on the rock still ached.

"Might as well relax," her father said, as if reading her thoughts. "We won't   105 find deer till suppertime."

Charlie Spoon leaned back against his pack and folded his hands across his stomach. "Well, even if we don't get a deer," he said expansively, "it's still great to be out here, breathe some fresh air, clomp around a bit. Get away from the house and the old lady." He winked at Mac, who looked away.

"That's what the woods are all about, anyway," Charlie said. "It's where the women don't want to go." He bowed his head toward Andy. "With your exception, of course, little lady." He helped himself to another piece of applesauce cake.

"She ain't a woman," Mac said.

"Well, she damn well's gonna be," Charlie said. He grinned at her. "Or will you? You're half a boy anyway. You go by a boy's name. What's your real name? Andrea, ain't it?"

"That's right," she said. She hoped that if she didn't look at him, Charlie would stop.

"Well, which do you like? Andy or Andrea?"

"Don't matter," she mumbled. "Either."

"She's always been Andy to me," her father said.

Charlie Spoon was still grinning. "So what are you gonna be, Andrea? A boy or a girl?"

115   "I'm a girl," she said.

"But you want to go hunting and fishing and everything, huh?"

"She can do whatever she likes," her father said.

"Hell, you might as well have just had a boy and be done with it!" Charlie exclaimed.

"That's funny," her father said, and chuckled. "That's just what her momma tells me."

120   They were looking at her, and she wanted to get away from them all, even from her father, who chose to joke with them.

"I'm going to walk a bit," she said.

She heard them laughing as she walked down the logging trail. She flapped her arms; she whistled. *I don't care how much noise I make,* she thought. Two grouse flew from the underbrush, startling her. A little farther down, the trail ended in a clearing that enlarged into a frozen meadow; beyond it the woods began again. A few moldering posts were all that was left of a fence that had once enclosed the field. The low afternoon sunlight reflected brightly off the snow, so that Andy's eyes hurt. She squinted hard. A gust of wind blew across the field, stinging her face. And then, as if it had been waiting for her, the doe emerged from the trees opposite and stepped cautiously into the field. Andy watched: it stopped and stood quietly for what seemed a long time and then ambled across. It stopped again about seventy yards away and began to browse in a patch of sugar grass uncovered by the wind. Carefully, slowly, never taking her eyes from the doe, Andy walked backward, trying to step into the boot prints she'd already made. When she was far enough back into the woods, she turned and walked faster, her heart racing. *Please let it stay,* she prayed.

"There's doe in the field yonder," she told them.

They got their rifles and hurried down the trail.

125   "No use," her father said. "We're making too much noise any way you look at it."

"At least we got us the wind in our favor," Charlie Spoon said, breathing heavily. But the doe was still there, grazing.

"Good Lord," Charlie whispered. He looked at her father. "Well, whose shot?"

"Andy spotted it," her father said in a low voice. "Let her shoot it."

130   "What!" Charlie's eyes widened.

Andy couldn't believe what her father had just said. She'd only shot tin cans and targets; she'd never even fired her father's .30-.30, and she'd never killed anything.

"I can't," she whispered.

"That's right, she can't," Charlie Spoon insisted. "She's not old enough and she don't have a license even if she was!"

"Well, who's to tell?" her father said in a low voice. "Nobody's going to know but us." He looked at her. "Do you want to shoot it, punkin?"

Why doesn't it hear us? she wondered. *Why doesn't it run away?* "I don't know,"   135
she said.

"Well, I'm sure as hell gonna shoot it," Charlie said. Her father grasped Charlie's rifle barrel and held it. His voice was steady.

"Andy's a good shot. It's her deer. She found it, not you. You'd still be sitting on your ass back in camp." He turned to her again. "Now — do you want to shoot it, Andy? Yes or no."

He was looking at her; they were all looking at her. Suddenly she was angry at the deer, who refused to hear them, who wouldn't run away even when it could. "I'll shoot it," she said. Charlie turned away in disgust.

She lay on the ground and pressed the rifle stock against her shoulder bone. The snow was cold through her parka; she smelled oil and wax and damp earth. She pulled off one glove with her teeth. "It sights just like the .22," her father said gently. "Cartridge's already chambered." As she had done so many times before, she sighted down the scope; now the doe was in the reticle. She moved the barrel until the cross hairs lined up. Her father was breathing beside her.

"Aim where the chest and legs meet, or a little above, punkin," he was saying   140
calmly. "That's the killing shot."

But now, seeing it in the scope, Andy was hesitant. Her finger weakened on the trigger. Still, she nodded at what her father said and sighted again, the cross hairs lining up in exactly the same spot — the doe had hardly moved, its brownish-gray body outlined starkly against the blue-backed snow. *It doesn't know,* Andy thought. *It just doesn't know.* And as she looked, deer and snow and faraway trees flattened within the circular frame to become like a picture on a calendar, not real, and she felt calm, as if she had been dreaming everything — the day, the deer, the hunt itself. And she, finger on trigger, was only a part of that dream.

"Shoot!" Charlie hissed.

Through the scope she saw the deer look up, ears high and straining.

Charlie groaned, and just as he did, and just at the moment when Andy knew — *knew* — the doe would bound away, as if she could feel its haunches tensing and gathering power, she pulled the trigger. Later she would think, *I felt the recoil, I smelled the smoke, but I don't remember pulling the trigger.* Through the scope the deer seemed to shrink into itself, and then slowly knelt, hind legs first, head raised as if to cry out. It trembled, still straining to keep its head high, as if that alone would save it; failing, it collapsed, shuddered, and lay still.

"Whoee!" Mac cried.   145

"One shot! One shot!" her father yelled, clapping her on the back. Charlie Spoon was shaking his head and smiling dumbly.

"I told you she was a great little shot!" her father said. "I told you!" Mac danced and clapped his hands. She was dazed, not quite understanding what had happened. And then they were crossing the field toward the fallen doe, she walking dreamlike, the men laughing and joking, released now from the tension of silence and anticipation. Suddenly Mac pointed and cried out, "Look at that!"

The doe was rising, legs unsteady. They stared at it, unable to comprehend, and in that moment the doe regained its feet and looked at them, as if it too were trying to understand. Her father whistled softly. Charlie Spoon unslung his rifle and raised it to his shoulder, but the doe was already bounding away. His hurried shot missed, and the deer disappeared into the woods.

"Damn, damn, damn," he moaned.

150 "I don't believe it," her father said. "That deer was dead."

"Dead, hell!" Charlie yelled. "It was gutshot, that's all. Stunned and gutshot. Clean shot, my ass!"

What have I done? Andy thought.

Her father slung his rifle over his shoulder. "Well, let's go. It can't get too far."

"Hell, I've seen deer run ten miles gutshot," Charlie said. He waved his arms. "We may never find her!"

155 As they crossed the field, Mac came up to her and said in a low voice, "Gutshoot a deer, you'll go to hell."

"Shut up, Mac," she said, her voice cracking. It was a terrible thing she had done, she knew. She couldn't bear to think of the doe in pain and frightened. *Please let it die*, she prayed.

But though they searched all the last hour of daylight, so that they had to re-cross the field and go up the logging trail in a twilight made even deeper by thick, smoky clouds, they didn't find the doe. They lost its trail almost immediately in the dense stands of alderberry and larch.

"I am cold, and I am tired," Charlie Spoon declared. "And if you ask me, that deer's in another county already."

"No one's asking you, Charlie," her father said.

160 They had a supper of hard salami and ham, bread, and the rest of the apple-sauce cake. It seemed a bother to heat the coffee, so they had cold chocolate instead. Everyone turned in early.

"We'll find it in the morning, honeybun," her father said, as she went to her tent.

"I don't like to think of it suffering." She was almost in tears.

"It's dead already, punkin. Don't even think about it." He kissed her, his breath sour and his beard rough against her cheek.

Andy was sure she wouldn't get to sleep; the image of the doe falling, falling, then rising again, repeated itself whenever she closed her eyes. Then she heard an owl hoot and realized that it had awakened her, so she must have been asleep after all. She hoped the owl would hush, but instead it hooted louder. She wished her father or Charlie Spoon would wake up and do something about it, but no one moved in the other tent, and suddenly she was afraid that they had all decamped, wanting nothing more to do with her. She whispered, "Mac, Mac," to the sleeping bag where he should be, but no one answered. She tried to find the flashlight she always kept by her side, but couldn't, and she cried in panic, "Mac, are you there?" He mumbled something, and immediately she felt foolish and hoped he wouldn't reply.

When she awoke again, everything had changed. The owl was gone, the woods 165 were still, and she sensed light, blue and pale, light where before there had been none. *The moon must have come out,* she thought. And it was warm, too, warmer than it should have been. She got out of her sleeping bag and took off her parka — it was that warm. Mac was asleep, wheezing like an old man. She unzipped the tent and stepped outside.

The woods were more beautiful than she had ever seen them. The moon made everything ice-rimmed glimmer with a crystallized, immanent light, while underneath that ice the branches of trees were as stark as skeletons. She heard a crunching in the snow, the one sound in all that silence, and there, walking down the logging trail into their camp, was the doe. Its body, like everything around her, was silvered with frost and moonlight. It walked past the tent where her father and Charlie Spoon were sleeping and stopped no more than six feet from her. Andy saw that she had shot it, yes, had shot it cleanly, just where she thought she had, the wound a jagged, bloody hole in the doe's chest.

A heart shot, she thought.

The doe stepped closer, so that Andy, if she wished, could have reached out and touched it. It looked at her as if expecting her to do this, and so she did, running her hand, slowly at first, along the rough, matted fur, then down to the edge of the wound, where she stopped. The doe stood still. Hesitantly, Andy felt the edge of the wound. The torn flesh was sticky and warm. The wound parted under her touch. And then, almost without her knowing it, her fingers were within, probing, yet still the doe didn't move. Andy pressed deeper, through flesh and muscle and sinew, until her whole hand and more was inside the wound and she had found the doe's heart, warm and beating. She cupped it gently in her hand. *Alive,* she marveled. *Alive.*

The heart quickened under her touch, becoming warmer and warmer until it was hot enough to burn. In pain, Andy tried to remove her hand, but the wound closed about it and held her fast. Her hand was burning. She cried out in agony, sure they would all hear and come help, but they didn't. And then her hand pulled free, followed by a steaming rush of blood, more blood than she ever could have imagined — it covered her hand and arm, and she saw to her horror that her hand was steaming. She moaned and fell to her knees and plunged her hand into the snow. The doe looked at her gently and then turned and walked back up the trail.

In the morning, when she woke, Andy could still smell the blood, but she felt 170 no pain. She looked at her hand. Even though it appeared unscathed, it felt weak and withered. She couldn't move it freely and was afraid the others would notice. *I will hide it in my jacket pocket,* she decided, *so nobody can see.* She ate the oatmeal that her father cooked and stayed apart from them all. No one spoke to her, and that suited her. A light snow began to fall. It was the last day of their hunting trip. She wanted to be home.

Her father dumped the dregs of his coffee. "Well, let's go look for her," he said.

Again they crossed the field. Andy lagged behind. She averted her eyes from the spot where the doe had fallen, already filling up with snow. Mac and Charlie entered the woods first, followed by her father. Andy remained in the field and considered the smear of gray sky, the nearby flock of crows pecking at unyielding stubble. *I will stay here*, she thought, *and not move for a long while*. But now someone — Mac — was yelling. Her father appeared at the woods' edge and waved for her to come. She ran and pushed through a brake of alderberry and larch. The thick underbrush scratched her face. For a moment she felt lost and looked wildly about. Then, where the brush thinned, she saw them standing quietly in the falling snow. They were staring down at the dead doe. A film covered its upturned eye, and its body was lightly dusted with snow.

"I told you she wouldn't get too far," Andy's father said triumphantly. "We must've just missed her yesterday. Too blind to see."

"We're just damn lucky no animal got to her last night," Charlie muttered.

175   Her father lifted the doe's foreleg. The wound was blood-clotted, brown, and caked like frozen mud. "Clean shot," he said to Charlie. He grinned. "My little girl."

Then he pulled out his knife, the blade gray as the morning. Mac whispered to Andy, "Now watch this," while Charlie Spoon lifted the doe from behind by its forelegs so that its head rested between his knees, its underside exposed. Her father's knife sliced thickly from chest to belly to crotch, and Andy was running from them, back to the field and across, scattering the crows who cawed and circled angrily. And now they were all calling to her — Charlie Spoon and Mac and her father — crying *Andy, Andy* (but that wasn't her name, she would no longer be called that); yet louder than any of them was the wind blowing through the treetops, like the ocean where her mother floated in green water, also calling *Come in, come in*, while all around her roared the mocking of the terrible, now inevitable, sea.

Reading and Reacting

1. The initiation of a child into adulthood is a common literary theme. In this story, hunting is presented as an initiation rite. In what way is hunting an appropriate coming-of-age ritual?

2. Which characters are in conflict in this story? Which ideas are in conflict? How do these conflicts help to communicate the story's initiation theme?

3. In the story's opening paragraph and elsewhere, Andy finds comfort and re-assurance in the idea that the woods are "always the same"; later in the story, she remembers the ocean, "huge and empty, yet always moving. Everything lay hidden . . ." (par. 45). How does the contrast between the woods and the ocean suggest the transition she must make from childhood to adulthood?

4. How do the references to blood support the story's initiation theme? Do they suggest another theme as well?

5. Throughout the story, references are made to Andy's ability to inspire the trust of animals. As her father says, "Animals — I don't know how she does it, but they come right up to her" (par. 8). How does his comment fore-shadow later events?

6. Why does Andy pray that she and the others will get a deer? What makes her change her mind? How does the change in Andy's character help to convey the story's theme?

7. Andy's mother is not an active participant in the story's events. Still, her presence is important to the story. Why is it important? How does paragraph 45 reveal the importance of the mother's role?

8. What has Andy learned as a result of her experience? What else do you think she still has to learn?

9. JOURNAL ENTRY How would the story be different if Andy were a boy? What would be the same?

10. CRITICAL PERSPECTIVE In a review of *Comfort*, the book in which "Doe Season" appears, Susan Wood makes the following observation:

> The dozen or so stories in David Michael Kaplan's affecting first collection share a common focus on the extraordinary moments of recognition in ordinary lives. He is at his best suggesting how such moments may alter, for better or for worse, our relationships with those to whom we are most deeply bound — children, parents, lovers — in love and guilt.

At what point does "the extraordinary moment of recognition" occur in "Doe Season"? How does this moment alter Andy's relationship with both her parents?

Related Works: "A&P" (p. 128), "The Lesson" (p. 353), "Greasy Lake" (p. 359), "The Lamb" (p. 653), "Traveling through the Dark" (p. 632), "In Trackless Woods" (p. 633)

D(AVID) H(ERBERT) LAWRENCE (1885–1930) was born in Nottinghamshire, England, the son of a coal miner and a schoolteacher. Determined to escape the harsh life of a miner, Lawrence taught for several years after graduating from high school. He soon began writing fiction and established himself in London literary circles.

During World War I, Lawrence and his wife were suspected of treason because of his pacifism and her connection to German aristocracy. Because Lawrence suffered from tuberculosis, he and his wife left England after the armistice in search of a healthier climate. They traveled in Australia, France, Italy, Mexico, and the United States throughout their lives.

Lawrence is recognized for his impassioned portrayal of our unconscious and instinctive natures. In his novel *Lady Chatterley's Lover* (1928), he attempted to restore explicit sexuality to English fiction, and the book was banned for years in Britain and the United States. His other novels include *Sons and Lovers* (1913), *The Rainbow* (1915), *Women in Love* (1921), and *The Plumed Serpent* (1926). Lawrence was also a gifted poet, essayist, travel writer, and short story writer, and his work had a strong influence on other writers.

Lawrence's fascination with the struggle between the unconscious and the intellect is revealed in his short story "The Rocking-Horse Winner" (1920). Lawrence sets his story in a house full of secrets and weaves symbolism with elements of the fairy tale and the gothic to produce a tale that has often been the subject of literary debate.

The Rocking-Horse Winner   (1920)

There was a woman who was beautiful, who started with all the advantages, yet she had no luck. She married for love, and the love turned to dust. She had bonny children, yet she felt they had been thrust upon her, and she could not love them. They looked at her coldly, as if they were finding fault with her. And hurriedly she felt she must cover up some fault in herself. Yet what it was that she must cover up she never knew. Nevertheless, when her children were present, she always felt the centre of her heart go hard. This troubled her, and in her manner she was all the more gentle and anxious for her children, as if she loved them very much. Only she herself knew that at the centre of her heart was a hard little place that could not feel love, no, not for anybody. Everybody else said of her: "She is such a good mother. She adores her children." Only she herself, and her children themselves, knew it was not so. They read it in each other's eyes.

There were a boy and two little girls. They lived in a pleasant house, with a garden, and they had discreet servants, and felt themselves superior to anyone in the neighbourhood.

Although they lived in style, they felt always an anxiety in the house. There was never enough money. The mother had a small income, and the father had a small income, but not nearly enough for the social position which they had to keep up. The father went into town to some office. But though he had good prospects, these prospects never materialised. There was always the grinding sense of the shortage of money, though the style was always kept up.

At last the mother said: "I will see if *I* can't make something." But she did not know where to begin. She racked her brains, and tried this thing and the other, but could not find anything successful. The failure made deep lines come into her face. Her children were growing up, they would have to go to school. There must be more money, there must be more money. The father, who was always very handsome and expensive in his tastes, seemed as if he never *would* be able to do anything worth doing. And the mother, who had a great belief in herself, did not succeed any better, and her tastes were just as expensive.

5   And so the house came to be haunted by the unspoken phrase: *There must be more money! There must be more money!* The children could hear it all the time, though nobody said it aloud. They heard it at Christmas, when the expensive and splendid toys filled the nursery. Behind the shining modern rocking-horse, behind the smart doll's house, a voice would start whispering: "There *must* be more money! There *must* be more money!" And the children would stop playing, to listen for a moment. They would look into each other's eyes, to see if they had all heard. And each one saw in the eyes of the other two that they too had heard. "There *must* be more money! There *must* be more money!"

It came whispering from the springs of the still-swaying rocking-horse, and even the horse, bending his wooden, champing head, heard it. The big doll, sitting so pink and smirking in her new pram, could hear it quite plainly, and seemed to be smirking all the more self-consciously because of it. The foolish puppy, too, that took the place of the teddybear, he was looking so extraordinarily foolish for no other reason but that he heard the secret whisper all over the house: "There *must* be more money!"

Yet nobody ever said it aloud. The whisper was everywhere, and therefore no one spoke it. Just as no one ever says: "We are breathing!" in spite of the fact that breath is coming and going all the time.

"Mother," said the boy Paul one day, "why don't we keep a car of our own? Why do we always use uncle's, or else a taxi?"

"Because we're the poor members of the family," said the mother.

"But why *are* we, mother?" 10

"Well — I suppose," she said slowly and bitterly, "it's because your father has no luck."

The boy was silent for some time.

"Is luck money, mother?" he asked, rather timidly.

"No, Paul. Not quite. It's what causes you to have money."

"Oh!" said Paul vaguely. "I thought when Uncle Oscar said *filthy lucker*, it 15 meant money."

"*Filthy lucre* does mean money," said the mother. "But it's lucre, not luck."

"Oh!" said the boy. "Then what *is* luck, mother?"

"It's what causes you to have money. If you're lucky you have money. That's why it's better to be born lucky than rich. If you're rich, you may lose your money. But if you're lucky, you will always get more money."

"Oh! Will you? And is father not lucky?"

"Very unlucky, I should say," she said bitterly. 20

The boy watched her with unsure eyes.

"Why?" he asked.

"I don't know. Nobody ever knows why one person is lucky and another unlucky."

"Don't they? Nobody at all? Does *nobody* know?"

"Perhaps God. But He never tells." 25

"He ought to, then. And aren't you lucky either, mother?"

"I can't be, if I married an unlucky husband."

"But by yourself, aren't you?"

"I used to think I was, before I married. Now I think I am very unlucky indeed."

"Why?" 30

"Well — never mind! Perhaps I'm not really," she said.

The child looked at her to see if she meant it. But he saw, by the lines of her mouth, that she was only trying to hide something from him.

"Well, anyhow," he said stoutly, "I'm a lucky person."

"Why?" said his mother, with a sudden laugh.

He stared at her. He didn't even know why he had said it. 35

"God told me," he asserted, brazening it out.

"I hope He did, dear!" she said, again with a laugh, but rather bitter.

"He did, mother!"

"Excellent!" said the mother, using one of her husband's exclamations.

40 The boy saw she did not believe him; or rather, that she paid no attention to his assertion. This angered him somewhat, and made him want to compel her attention.

He went off by himself, vaguely, in a childish way, seeking for the clue to "luck." Absorbed, taking no heed of other people, he went about with a sort of stealth, seeking inwardly for luck. He wanted luck, he wanted it, he wanted it. When the two girls were playing dolls in the nursery, he would sit on his big rocking-horse, charging madly into space, with a frenzy that made the little girls peer at him uneasily. Wildly the horse careered, the waving dark hair of the boy tossed, his eyes had a strange glare in them. The little girls dared not speak to him.

When he had ridden to the end of his mad little journey, he climbed down and stood in front of his rocking-horse, staring fixedly into its lowered face. Its red mouth was slightly open, its big eye was wide and glassy-bright.

"Now!" he would silently command the snorting steed. "Now, take me to where there is luck! Now take me!"

And he would slash the horse on the neck with the little whip he had asked Uncle Oscar for. He *knew* the horse could take him to where there was luck, if only he forced it. So he would mount again and start on his furious ride, hoping at last to get there. He knew he could get there.

45 "You'll break your horse, Paul!" said the nurse.

"He's always riding like that! I wish he'd leave off!" said his elder sister Joan.

But he only glared down on them in silence. Nurse gave him up. She could make nothing of him. Anyhow, he was growing beyond her.

One day his mother and his Uncle Oscar came in when he was on one of his furious rides. He did not speak to them.

"Hallo, you young jockey! Riding a winner?" said his uncle.

50 "Aren't you growing too big for a rocking-horse? You're not a very little boy any longer, you know," said his mother.

But Paul only gave a blue glare from his big, rather close-set eyes. He would speak to nobody when he was in full tilt. His mother watched him with an anxious expression on her face.

At last he suddenly stopped forcing his horse into the mechanical gallop and slid down.

"Well, I got there!" he announced fiercely, his blue eyes still flaring, and his sturdy long legs straddling apart.

"Where did you get to?" asked his mother.

55 "Where I wanted to go," he flared back at her.

"That's right, son!" said Uncle Oscar. "Don't you stop till you get there. What's the horse's name?"

"He doesn't have a name," said the boy.

"Gets on without all right?" asked the uncle.

"Well, he has different names. He was called Sansovino last week."

"Sansovino, eh? Won the Ascot.° How did you know this name?"

"He always talks about horse-races with Bassett," said Joan.

The uncle was delighted to find that his small nephew was posted with all the 60 racing news. Bassett, the young gardener, who had been wounded in the left foot in the war and had got his present job through Oscar Cresswell, whose batman° he had been, was a perfect blade of the "turf." He lived in the racing events, and the small boy lived with him.

Oscar Cresswell got it all from Bassett.

"Master Paul comes and asks me, so I can't do more than tell him, sir," said Bassett, his face terribly serious, as if he were speaking of religious matters.

"And does he ever put anything on a horse he fancies?"

"Well — I don't want to give him away — he's a young sport, a fine sport, sir. Would you mind asking him himself? He sort of takes a pleasure in it, and perhaps 65 he'd feel I was giving him away, sir, if you don't mind."

Bassett was serious as a church.

The uncle went back to his nephew and took him off for a ride in the car.

"Say, Paul, old man, do you ever put anything on a horse?" the uncle asked.

The boy watched the handsome man closely.

"Why, do you think I oughtn't to?" he parried.

"Not a bit of it! I thought perhaps you might give me a tip for the Lincoln."° 70

The car sped on into the country, going down to Uncle Oscar's place in Hampshire.

"Honour bright?" said the nephew.

"Honour bright, son!" said the uncle.

"Well, then, Daffodil."

"Daffodil! I doubt it, sonny. What about Mirza?" 75

"I only know the winner," said the boy. "That's Daffodil."

"Daffodil, eh?"

There was a pause. Daffodil was an obscure horse comparatively.

"Uncle!"

"Yes, son?" 80

"You won't let it go any further, will you? I promised Bassett."

"Bassett be damned, old man! What's he got to do with it?"

"We're partners. We've been partners from the first. Uncle, he lent me my first five shillings, which I lost. I promised him, honour bright, it was only between me and him; only you gave me that ten-shilling note I started winning with, so I 85 thought you were lucky. You won't let it go any further, will you?"

The boy gazed at his uncle from those big, hot, blue eyes, set rather close together. The uncle stirred and laughed uneasily.

---

the Ascot: The annual horse race at Ascot Heath in England.

batman: A British military officer's personal assistant.

the Lincoln: The Lincolnshire Handicap, a horse race.

"Right you are, son! I'll keep your tip private. Daffodil, eh? How much are you putting on him?"

"All except twenty pounds," said the boy. "I keep that in reserve."

The uncle thought it a good joke.

"You keep twenty pounds in reserve, do you, you young romancer? What are you betting, then?"

"I'm betting three hundred," said the boy gravely. "But it's between you and me, Uncle Oscar! Honour bright?"

The uncle burst into a roar of laughter.

"It's between you and me all right, you young Nat Gould,"° he said, laughing. "But where's your three hundred?"

"Bassett keeps it for me. We're partners."

"You are, are you! And what is Bassett putting on Daffodil?"

"He won't go quite as high as I do, I expect. Perhaps he'll go a hundred and fifty."

"What, pennies?" laughed the uncle.

"Pounds," said the child, with a surprised look at his uncle. "Bassett keeps a bigger reserve than I do."

Between wonder and amusement Uncle Oscar was silent. He pursued the matter no further, but he determined to take his nephew with him to the Lincoln races.

"Now, son," he said, "I'm putting twenty on Mirza, and I'll put five on for you on any horse you fancy. What's your pick?"

"Daffodil, uncle."

"No, not the fiver on Daffodil!"

"I should if it was my own fiver," said the child.

"Good! Good! Right you are! A fiver for me and a fiver for you on Daffodil."

The child had never been to a race-meeting before, and his eyes were blue fire. He pursed his mouth tight and watched. A Frenchman just in front had put his money on Lancelot. Wild with excitement, he flayed his arms up and down, yelling *"Lancelot! Lancelot!"* in his French accent.

Daffodil came in first, Lancelot second, Mirza third. The child, flushed and with eyes blazing, was curiously serene. His uncle brought him four five-pound notes, four to one.

"What am I to do with these?" he cried, waving them before the boy's eyes.

"I suppose we'll talk to Bassett," said the boy. "I expect I have fifteen hundred now; and twenty in reserve; and this twenty."

His uncle studied him for some moments.

"Look here, son!" he said. "You're not serious about Bassett and that fifteen hundred, are you?"

"Yes, I am. But it's between you and me, uncle. Honour bright?"

"Honour bright all right, son! But I must talk to Bassett."

"If you'd like to be a partner, uncle, with Bassett and me, we could all be partners. Only, you'd have to promise, honour bright, uncle, not to let it go beyond us

---

Nat Gould: Nathaniel Gould (1857–1919), British journalist and writer known for his stories about horse racing.

three. Bassett and I are lucky, and you must be lucky, because it was your ten
shillings I started winning with. . . ."

Uncle Oscar took both Bassett and Paul into Richmond Park for an afternoon,
and there they talked.

"It's like this, you see, sir," Bassett said. "Master Paul would get me talk- 115
ing about racing events, spinning yarns, you know, sir. And he was always keen
on knowing if I'd made or if I'd lost. It's about a year since, now, that I put five
shillings on Blush of Dawn for him: and we lost. Then the luck turned, with
that ten shillings he had from you: that we put on Singhalese. And since that
time, it's been pretty steady, all things considering. What do you say, Master
Paul?"

"We're all right when we're sure," said Paul. "It's when we're not quite sure that
we go down."

"Oh, but we're careful then," said Bassett.

"But when are you *sure*?" smiled Uncle Oscar.

"It's Master Paul, sir," said Bassett in a secret, religious voice. "It's as if he had
it from heaven. Like Daffodil, now, for the Lincoln. That was as sure as eggs."

"Did you put anything on Daffodil?" asked Oscar Cresswell.   120

"Yes, sir. I made my bit."

"And my nephew?"

Bassett was obstinately silent, looking at Paul.

"I made twelve hundred, didn't I, Bassett? I told uncle I was putting three
hundred on Daffodil."

"That's right," said Bassett, nodding.   125

"But where's the money?" asked the uncle.

"I keep it safe locked up, sir. Master Paul can have it any minute he likes to
ask for it."

"What, fifteen hundred pounds?"

"And twenty! And *forty*, that is, with the twenty he made on the course."

"It's amazing!" said the uncle.   130

"If Master Paul offers you to be partners, sir, I would, if I were you: if you'll
excuse me," said Bassett.

Oscar Cresswell thought about it.

"I'll see the money," he said.

They drove home again, and, sure enough, Bassett came round to the garden-
house with fifteen hundred pounds in notes. The twenty pounds reserve was left
with Joe Glee, in the Turf Commission deposit.

"You see, it's all right, uncle, when I'm *sure!* Then we go strong, for all we're 135
worth. Don't we, Bassett?"

"We do that, Master Paul."

"And when are you sure?" said the uncle, laughing.

"Oh, well, sometimes I'm *absolutely* sure, like about Daffodil," said the boy;
"and sometimes I have an idea; and sometimes I haven't even an idea, have I,
Bassett? Then we're careful, because we mostly go down."

"You do, do you! And when you're sure, like about Daffodil, what makes you sure, sonny?"

140   "Oh, well, I don't know," said the boy uneasily. "I'm sure, you know, uncle; that's all."

"It's as if he had it from heaven, sir," Bassett reiterated.

"I should say so!" said the uncle.

But he became a partner. And when the Leger° was coming on Paul was "sure" about Lively Spark, which was a quite inconsiderable horse. The boy insisted on putting a thousand on the horse, Bassett went for five hundred, and Oscar Cresswell two hundred. Lively Spark came in first, and the betting had been ten to one against him. Paul had made ten thousand.

"You see," he said, "I was absolutely sure of him."

145   Even Oscar Cresswell had cleared two thousand.

"Look here, son," he said, "this sort of thing makes me nervous."

"It needn't, uncle! Perhaps I shan't be sure again for a long time."

"But what are you going to do with your money?" asked the uncle.

"Of course," said the boy, "I started it for mother. She said she had no luck, because father is unlucky, so I thought if *I* was lucky, it might stop whispering."

150   "What might stop whispering?"

"Our house. I *hate* our house for whispering."

"What does it whisper?"

"Why — why"— the boy fidgeted —"why, I don't know. But it's always short of money, you know, uncle."

"I know it, son, I know it."

155   "You know people send mother writs,° don't you, uncle?"

"I'm afraid I do," said the uncle.

"And then the house whispers, like people laughing at you behind your back. It's awful, that is! I thought if I was lucky . . ."

"You might stop it," added the uncle.

The boy watched him with big blue eyes, that had an uncanny cold fire in them, and he said never a word.

160   "Well, then!" said the uncle. "What are we doing?"

"I shouldn't like mother to know I was lucky," said the boy.

"Why not, son?"

"She'd stop me."

"I don't think she would."

165   "Oh!"— and the boy writhed in an odd way —"I *don't* want her to know, uncle."

"All right, son! We'll manage it without her knowing."

They managed it very easily. Paul, at the other's suggestion, handed over five thousand pounds to his uncle, who deposited it with the family lawyer, who was then to inform Paul's mother that a relative had put five thousand pounds into his

---

the Leger: The St. Leger Stakes, a horse race.

writs: Letters from creditors requesting payment.

hands, which sum was to be paid out a thousand pounds at a time, on the mother's birthday, for the next five years.

"So she'll have a birthday present of a thousand pounds for five successive years," said Uncle Oscar. "I hope it won't make it all the harder for her later."

Paul's mother had her birthday in November. The house had been "whispering" worse than ever lately, and, even in spite of his luck, Paul could not bear up against it. He was very anxious to see the effect of the birthday letter, telling his mother about the thousand pounds.

When there were no visitors, Paul now took his meals with his parents, as he was beyond the nursery control. His mother went into town nearly every day. She had discovered that she had an odd knack of sketching furs and dress materials, so she worked secretly in the studio of a friend who was the chief "artist" for the leading drapers. She drew the figures of ladies in furs and ladies in silk and sequins for the newspaper advertisements. This young woman artist earned several thousand pounds a year, but Paul's mother only made several hundreds, and she was again dissatisfied. She so wanted to be first in something, and she did not succeed, even in making sketches for drapery advertisements.

She was down to breakfast on the morning of her birthday. Paul watched her face as she read her letters. He knew the lawyer's letter. As his mother read it, her face hardened and became more expressionless. Then a cold, determined look came on her mouth. She hid the letter under the pile of others, and said not a word about it.

"Didn't you have anything nice in the post for your birthday, mother?" said Paul.

"Quite moderately nice," she said, her voice cold and absent.

She went away to town without saying more.

But in the afternoon Uncle Oscar appeared. He said Paul's mother had had a long interview with the lawyer, asking if the whole five thousand could not be advanced at once, as she was in debt.

"What do you think, uncle?" asked the boy.

"I leave it to you, son."

"Oh, let her have it, then! We can get some more with the other," said the boy.

"A bird in the hand is worth two in the bush, laddie!" said Uncle Oscar.

"But I'm sure to *know* for the Grand National; or the Lincolnshire; or else the Derby.° I'm sure to know for *one* of them," said Paul.

So Uncle Oscar signed the agreement, and Paul's mother touched the whole five thousand. Then something very curious happened. The voices in the house suddenly went mad, like a chorus of frogs on a spring evening. There was certain new furnishings, and Paul had a tutor. He was *really* going to Eton, his father's school, in the following autumn. There were flowers in the winter, and a blossoming of the luxury Paul's mother had been used to. And yet the voices in the house, behind the sprays of mimosa and almond-blossom, and from under

---

Grand National . . . Derby: Famous British horse races. The Grand National is run at Aintree; the Derby, at Epsom Downs.

the piles of iridescent cushions, simply trilled and screamed in a sort of ecstasy: "There *must* be more money! Oh-h-h; there *must* be more money. Oh, now, now-w! Now-w-w — there *must* be more money! — more than ever! More than ever!"

It frightened Paul terribly. He studied away at his Latin and Greek with his tutor. But his intense hours were spent with Bassett. The Grand National had gone by: he had not "known," and had lost a hundred pounds. Summer was at hand. He was in agony for the Lincoln. But even for the Lincoln he didn't "know," and he lost fifty pounds. He became wild-eyed and strange, as if something were going to explode in him.

"Let it alone, son! Don't you bother about it!" urged Uncle Oscar. But it was as if the boy couldn't really hear what his uncle was saying.

"I've got to know for the Derby! I've got to know for the Derby!" the child reiterated, his big blue eyes blazing with a sort of madness.

185   His mother noticed how overwrought he was.

"You'd better go to the seaside. Wouldn't you like to go now to the seaside, instead of waiting? I think you'd better," she said, looking down at him anxiously, her heart curiously heavy because of him.

But the child lifted his uncanny blue eyes.

"I couldn't possibly go before the Derby, mother!" he said. "I couldn't possibly!"

"Why not?" she said, her voice becoming heavy when she was opposed. "Why not? You can still go from the seaside to see the Derby with your Uncle Oscar, if that's what you wish. No need for you to wait here. Besides, I think you care too much about these races. It's a bad sign. My family has been a gambling family, and you won't know till you grow up how much damage it has done. But it has done damage. I shall have to send Bassett away, and ask Uncle Oscar not to talk racing to you, unless you promise to be reasonable about it: go away to the seaside and forget it. You're all nerves!"

190   "I'll do what you like, mother, so long as you don't send me away till after the Derby," the boy said.

"Send you away from where? Just from this house?"

"Yes," he said, gazing at her.

"Why, you curious child, what makes you care about this house so much, suddenly? I never knew you loved it."

He gazed at her without speaking. He had a secret within a secret, something he had not divulged, even to Bassett or to his Uncle Oscar.

195   But his mother, after standing undecided and a little bit sullen for some moments, said:

"Very well, then! Don't go to the seaside till after the Derby, if you don't wish it. But promise me you won't let your nerves go to pieces. Promise you won't think so much about horse-racing and *events,* as you call them!"

"Oh no," said the boy casually. "I won't think much about them, mother. You needn't worry. I wouldn't worry, mother, if I were you."

"If you were me and I were you," said his mother, "I wonder what we *should* do!"

"But you know you needn't worry, mother, don't you?" the boy repeated.

200   "I should be awfully glad to know it," she said wearily.

"Oh, well, you *can*, you know. I mean, you *ought* to know you needn't worry," he insisted.

"Ought I? Then I'll see about it," she said.

Paul's secret of secrets was his wooden horse, that which had no name. Since he was emancipated from a nurse and a nursery-governess, he had had his rocking-horse removed to his own bedroom at the top of the house.

"Surely you're too big for a rocking-horse!" his mother had remonstrated.

"Well, you see, mother, till I can have a *real* horse, I like to have *some* sort of animal about," had been his quaint answer.

"Do you feel he keeps you company?" she laughed.

"Oh yes! He's very good, he always keeps me company, when I'm there," said Paul.

So the horse, rather shabby, stood in an arrested prance in the boy's bedroom.

The Derby was drawing near, and the boy grew more and more tense. He hardly heard what was spoken to him, he was very frail, and his eyes were really uncanny. His mother had sudden strange seizures of uneasiness about him. Sometimes, for half an hour, she would feel a sudden anxiety about him that was almost anguish. She wanted to rush to him at once, and know he was safe.

Two nights before the Derby, she was at a big party in town, when one of her rushes of anxiety about her boy, her firstborn, gripped her heart till she could hardly speak. She fought with the feeling, might and main, for she believed in common sense. But it was too strong. She had to leave the dance and go downstairs to telephone to the country. The children's nursery-governess was terribly surprised and startled at being rung up in the night.

"Are the children all right, Miss Wilmot?"

"Oh yes, they are quite all right."

"Master Paul? Is he all right?"

"He went to bed as right as a trivet. Shall I run up and look at him?"

"No," said Paul's mother reluctantly. "No! Don't trouble. It's all right. Don't sit up. We shall be home fairly soon." She did not want her son's privacy intruded upon.

"Very good," said the governess.

It was about one o'clock when Paul's mother and father drove up to their house. All was still. Paul's mother went to her room and slipped off her white fur cloak. She had told her maid not to wait up for her. She heard her husband downstairs, mixing a whisky and soda.

And then, because of the strange anxiety at her heart, she stole upstairs to her son's room. Noiselessly she went along the upper corridor. Was there a faint noise? What was it?

She stood, with arrested muscles, outside his door, listening. There was a strange, heavy, and yet not loud noise. Her heart stood still. It was a soundless noise, yet rushing and powerful. Something huge, in violent, hushed motion. What was it? What in God's name was it? She ought to know. She felt that she knew the noise. She knew what it was.

Yet she could not place it. She couldn't say what it was. And on and on it went, like a madness.

Softly, frozen with anxiety and fear, she turned the door-handle.

The room was dark. Yet in the space near the window, she heard and saw something plunging to and fro. She gazed in fear and amazement.

Then suddenly she switched on the light, and saw her son, in his green pyjamas, madly surging on the rocking-horse. The blaze of light suddenly lit him up, as he urged the wooden horse, and lit her up, as she stood, blonde, in her dress of pale green and crystal, in the doorway.

"Paul!" she cried. "Whatever are you doing?"

225 "It's Malabar!" he screamed in a powerful, strange voice. "It's Malabar!"

His eyes blazed at her for one strange and senseless second, as he ceased urging his wooden horse. Then he fell with a crash to the ground, and she, all her tormented motherhood flooding upon her, rushed to gather him up.

But he was unconscious, and unconscious he remained, with some brain-fever. He talked and tossed, and his mother sat stonily by his side.

"Malabar! It's Malabar! Bassett, Bassett, I *know*! It's Malabar!"

So the child cried, trying to get up and urge the rocking-horse that gave him his inspiration.

230 "What does he mean by Malabar?" asked the heart-frozen mother.

"I don't know," said the father stonily.

"What does he mean by Malabar?" she asked her brother Oscar.

"It's one of the horses running for the Derby," was the answer.

And, in spite of himself, Oscar Cresswell spoke to Bassett, and himself put a thousand on Malabar: at fourteen to one.

235 The third day of the illness was critical: they were waiting for a change. The boy, with his rather long, curly hair, was tossing ceaselessly on the pillow. He neither slept nor regained consciousness, and his eyes were like blue stones. His mother sat, feeling her heart had gone, turned actually into a stone.

In the evening, Oscar Cresswell did not come, but Bassett sent a message, saying could he come up for one moment, just one moment? Paul's mother was very angry at the intrusion, but on second thought she agreed. The boy was the same. Perhaps Bassett might bring him to consciousness.

The gardener, a shortish fellow with a little brown moustache and sharp little brown eyes, tiptoed into the room, touched his imaginary cap to Paul's mother, and stole to the bedside, staring with glittering, smallish eyes at the tossing, dying child.

"Master Paul!" he whispered. "Master Paul! Malabar came in first all right, a clean win. I did as you told me. You've made over seventy thousand pounds, you have; you've got over eighty thousand. Malabar came in all right, Master Paul."

"Malabar! Malabar! Did I say Malabar, mother? Did I say Malabar? Do you think I'm lucky, mother? I knew Malabar, didn't I? Over eighty thousand pounds! I call that lucky, don't you, mother? Over eighty thousand pounds! I knew, didn't I know I knew? Malabar came in all right. If I ride my horse till I'm sure, then I tell you, Bassett, you can go as high as you like. Did you go for all you were worth, Bassett?"

240 "I went a thousand on it, Master Paul."

"I never told you, mother, that if I can ride my horse, and *get there*, then I'm 240
absolutely sure — oh, absolutely! Mother, did I ever tell you? I *am* lucky!"

"No, you never did," said his mother.

But the boy died in the night.

And even as he lay dead, his mother heard her brother's voice saying to her:
"My God, Hester, you're eighty-odd thousand to the good, and a poor devil of a
son to the bad. But, poor devil, poor devil, he's best gone out of a life where he
rides his rocking-horse to find a winner."

Reading and Reacting

1. From what point of view is "The Rocking-Horse Winner" told? How does
this point of view help to communicate the story's theme?

2. In what respects is "The Rocking-Horse Winner" like a fairy tale? How is it
different?

3. Many fairy tales involve a hero who goes on a journey to search for something of great value. What journey does Paul go on? What thing of value
does he search for? Is he successful?

4. In paragraph 5, the narrator says that the house is "haunted by the unspoken phrase: '*There must be more money!*'" In what way does the phrase
"haunt" the house?

5. How would you characterize Paul's parents? His uncle? Bassett? Are they
weak? Evil? What motivates them?

6. Beginning in paragraph 11, Paul's mother attempts to define the word *luck*.
According to her definition, does she consider Paul lucky? Do you agree?

7. In what ways does Paul behave like other children? In what ways is he different? How do you account for these differences? How old do you think
Paul is? Why is his age significant?

8. The rocking horse is an important literary symbol in the story. What
possible meanings might the rocking horse suggest? In what ways does this
symbol reinforce the story's theme?

9. What secrets do the various characters keep from one another? Why do they
keep them? How do these secrets relate to the story's theme?

10. How does Paul know who the winners will be? Does the rocking horse really tell him? Does he get his information "from heaven" as Bassett suggests
(par. 119)? Or does he just guess?

11. JOURNAL ENTRY In your opinion, who or what is responsible for Paul's death?

12. CRITICAL PERSPECTIVE In a letter dated January 17, 1913, Lawrence wrote
the following:

> My great religion is a belief in the blood, the flesh, as being wiser than the intel-
> lect. We can go wrong in our minds. But what our blood feels and believes
> and says, is always true. The intellect is only a bit and a bridle. What do I care
> about knowledge. All I want is to answer to my blood, direct, without fribbling
> intervention of mind, or moral, or what-not.

How does Lawrence's portrayal of Paul in "The Rocking-Horse Winner" support his belief in "the blood . . . being wiser than the intellect"? How does Lawrence remain true in this story to his metaphor of the intellect as "a bit and a bridle"?

Related Works: "The Yellow Wallpaper" (p. 372), "The Meal" (p. 515), "Gretel in Darkness" (p. 460), "Suicide Note" (p. 468), *The Glass Menagerie* (p. 1153)

WRITING SUGGESTIONS: Theme

1. In both "Doe Season" and Hisaye Yamamoto's "Seventeen Syllables" (p. 425) a young girl learns a hard lesson. Write an essay in which you compare the lessons that Andy and Rosie learn and discuss the effects the knowledge they gain has on them.

2. Two of the stories in this chapter deal with the importance of patience and persistence. Write an essay in which you examine the value of enduring despite difficulties, citing the experiences of the main characters in "Doe Season" and "A Worn Path."

3. Both "The Rocking-Horse Winner" and "A Worn Path" deal with characters who make journeys. What is the significance of each journey? How do the protagonists of these two stories overcome the obstacles they encounter? In what sense are these journeys symbolic as well as actual?

4. Like "Doe Season," the following poem focuses on a child's experience with hunting. Write an essay in which you contrast its central theme with the central theme of "Doe Season."

ROBERT HUFF (1924–1993)

Rainbow*

After the shot the driven feathers rock
In the air and are by sunlight trapped.
Their moment of descent is eloquent.
It is the rainbow echo of a bird
Whose thunder, stopped, puts in my daughter's eyes   5
A question mark. She does not see the rainbow,
And the folding bird-fall was for her too quick.
It is about the stillness of the bird
Her eyes are asking. She is three years old;
Has cut her fingers; found blood tastes of salt;   10
But she has never witnessed quiet blood,
Nor ever seen before the peace of death.
I say: "The feathers — Look!" but she is torn
And wretched and draws back. And I am glad
That I have wounded her, have winged her heart,   15
And that she goes beyond my fathering.

---

*Publication date is not available.

CHAPTER 13

FICTION FOR FURTHER READING

TONI CADE BAMBARA   (1939–1995)

The Lesson   (1972)

Back in the days when everyone was old and stupid or young and foolish me and Sugar were the only ones just right, this lady moved on our block with nappy hair and proper speech and no makeup. And quite naturally we laughed at her, laughed the way we did at the junk man who went about his business like he was some big-time president and his sorry-ass horse his secretary. And we kinda hated her too, hated the way we did the winos who cluttered up our parks and pissed on our handball walls and stank up our hallways and stairs so you couldn't halfway play hide-and-seek without a goddamn gas mask. Miss Moore was her name. The only woman on the block with no first name. And she was black as hell, cept for her feet, which were fish-white and spooky. And she was always planning these bor-ing-ass things for us to do, us being my cousin, mostly, who lived on the block cause we all moved North the same time and to the same apartment then spread out gradual to breathe. And our parents would yank our heads into some kinda shape and crisp up our clothes so we'd be presentable for travel with Miss Moore, who al-ways looked like she was going to church, though she never did. Which is just one of the things the grownups talked about when they talked behind her back like a dog. But when she came calling with some sachet she'd sewed up or some ginger-bread she'd made or some book, why then they'd all be too embarrassed to turn her down and we'd get handed over all spruced up. She'd been to college and said it was only right that she should take responsibility for the young ones' education, and she not even related by marriage or blood. So they'd go for it. Specially Aunt Gretchen. She was the main gofer in the family. You got some ole dumb shit fool-ishness you want somebody to go for, you send for Aunt Gretchen. She been screwed into the go-along for so long, it's a blood-deep natural thing with her. Which is how she got saddled with me and Sugar and Junior in the first place while our mothers were in a la-de-da apartment up the block having a good ole time.

So this one day Miss Moore rounds us all up at the mailbox and it's puredee hot and she's knockin herself out about arithmetic. And school suppose to let up in summer I heard, but she don't never let up. And the starch in my pinafore scratching the shit outta me and I'm really hating this nappy-head bitch and her goddamn college degree. I'd much rather go to the pool or to the show where it's cool. So me and Sugar leaning on the mailbox being surly, which is a Miss Moore word. And Flyboy checking out what everybody brought for lunch. And Fat Butt already wasting his peanut butter-and-jelly sandwich like the pig he is. And Junebug punchin on Q.T.'s arm for potato chips. And Rosie Giraffe shifting from one hip to the other waiting for somebody to step on her foot or ask her if she from Georgia so she can kick ass, preferably Mercedes'. And Miss Moore asking us do we know what money is, like we a bunch of retards. I mean real money, she say, like it's only poker chips or monopoly papers we lay on the grocer. So right away I'm tired of this and say so. And would much rather snatch Sugar and go to the Sunset and terrorize the West Indian kids and take their hair ribbons and their money too. And Miss Moore files that remark away for next week's lesson on brotherhood, I can tell. And finally I say we oughta get to the subway cause it's cooler and besides we might meet some cute boys. Sugar done swiped her mama's lipstick, so we ready.

So we heading down the street and she's boring us silly about what things cost and what our parents make and how much goes for rent and how money ain't divided up right in this country. And then she gets to the part about we all poor and live in the slums, which I don't feature. And I'm ready to speak on that, but she steps out in the street and hails two cabs just like that. Then she hustles half the crew in with her and hands me a five-dollar bill and tells me to calculate 10 percent tip for the driver. And we're off. Me and Sugar and Junebug and Flyboy hangin out the window and hollering to everybody, putting lipstick on each other cause Flyboy a faggot anyway, and making farts with our sweaty armpits. But I'm mostly trying to figure how to spend this money. But they all fascinated with the meter ticking and Junebug starts laying bets as to how much it'll read when Flyboy can't hold his breath no more. Then Sugar lays bets as to how much it'll be when we get there. So I'm stuck. Don't nobody want to go for my plan, which is to jump out at the next light and run off to the first bar-b-que we can find. Then the driver tells us to get the hell out cause we there already. And the meter reads eighty-five cents. And I'm stalling to figure out the tip and Sugar say give him a dime. And I decide he don't need it bad as I do, so later for him. But then he tries to take off with Junebug foot still in the door so we talk about his mama something ferocious. Then we check out that we on Fifth Avenue and everybody dressed up in stockings. One lady in a fur coat, hot as it is. White folks crazy.

"This is the place," Miss Moore say, presenting it to us in the voice she uses at the museum. "Let's look in the windows before we go in."

5   "Can we steal?" Sugar asks very serious like she's getting the ground rules squared away before she plays. "I beg your pardon," say Miss Moore, and we fall out. So she leads us around the windows of the toy store and me and Sugar screamin, "This is mine, that's mine, I gotta have that, that was made for me, I was born for that," till Big Butt drowns us out.

"Hey, I'm going to buy that there."

"That there? You don't even know what it is, stupid."

"I do so," he say punchin on Rosie Giraffe. "It's a microscope."

"Whatcha gonna do with a microscope, fool?"

"Look at things."   10

"Like what, Ronald?" ask Miss Moore. And Big Butt ain't got the first notion. So here go Miss Moore gabbing about the thousands of bacteria in a drop of water and the somethinorother in a speck of blood and the million and one living things in the air around us is invisible to the naked eye. And what she say that for? Junebug go to town on that "naked" and we rolling. Then Miss Moore ask what it cost. So we all jam into the window smudgin it up and the price tag say $300. So then she ask how long'd take for Big Butt and Junebug to save up their allowances. "Too long," I say. "Yeh," adds Sugar, "outgrown it by that time." And Miss Moore say no, you never outgrow learning instruments. "Why, even medical students and interns and," blah, blah, blah. And we ready to choke Big Butt for bringing it up in the first damn place.

"This here costs four hundred eighty dollars," say Rosie Giraffe. So we pile up all over her to see what she pointin out. My eyes tell me it's a chunk of glass cracked with something heavy, and different-color inks dripped into the splits, and then the whole thing put into a oven or something. But for $480 it don't make sense.

"That's a paperweight made of semi-precious stones fused together under tremendous pressure," she explains slowly, with her hands doing the mining and all the factory work.

"So what's a paperweight?" asks Rosie Giraffe.

"To weigh paper with, dumbbell," say Flyboy, the wise man from the East.   15

"Not exactly," says Miss Moore, which is what she say when you warm or way off too. "It's to weigh paper down so it won't scatter and make your desk untidy." So right away me and Sugar curtsy to each other and then to Mercedes who is more the tidy type.

"We don't keep paper on top of the desk in my class," say Junebug, figuring Miss Moore crazy or lyin one.

"At home, then," she say "Don't you have a calendar and a pencil case and a blotter and a letter-opener on your desk at home where you do your homework?" And she know damn well what our homes look like cause she nosys around in them every chance she gets.

"I don't even have a desk," say Junebug. "Do we?"

"No. And I don't get no homework neither," says Big Butt.   20

"And I don't even have a home," says Flyboy like he do at school to keep the white folks off his back and sorry for him. Send this poor kid to camp posters, is his specialty.

"I do," says Mercedes. "I have a box of stationery on my desk and a picture of my cat. My godmother bought the stationery and the desk. There's a big rose on each sheet and the envelopes smell like roses."

"Who wants to know about your smelly-ass stationery," say Rosie Giraffe fore I can get my two cents in.

"It's important to have a work area all your own so that . . ."

25   "Will you look at this sailboat, please," say Flyboy, cuttin her off and pointin to the thing like it was his. So once again we tumble all over each other to gaze at this magnificent thing in the toy store which is just big enough to maybe sail two kittens across the pond if you strap them to the posts right. We all start reciting the price tag like we in assembly. "Handcrafted sailboat of fiberglass at one thousand one hundred ninety-five dollars."

"Unbelievable," I hear myself say and am really stunned. I read it again for myself just in case the group recitation put me in a trance. Same thing. For some reason this pisses me off. We look at Miss Moore and she lookin at us, waiting for I dunno what.

"Who'd pay all that when you can buy a sailboat set for a quarter at Pop's, a tube of glue for a dime, and a ball of string for eight cents? It must have a motor and a whole lot else besides," I say. "My sailboat cost me about fifty cents."

"But will it take water?" say Mercedes with her smart ass.

"Took mine to Alley Pond Park once," say Flyboy. "String broke. Lost it. Pity."

30   "Sailed mine in Central Park and it keeled over and sank. Had to ask my father for another dollar."

"And you got the strap," laughed Big Butt. "The jerk didn't even have a string on it. My old man wailed on his behind."

Little Q.T. was staring hard at the sailboat and you could see he wanted it bad. But he too little and somebody'd just take it from him. So what the hell. "This boat for kids, Miss Moore?"

"Parents silly to buy something like that just to get all broke up," say Rosie Giraffe.

"That much money it should last forever," I figure.

35   "My father'd buy it for me if I wanted it."

"Your father, my ass," say Rosie Giraffe getting a chance to finally push Mercedes.

"Must be rich people shop here," say Q.T.

"You are a very bright boy," say Flyboy. "What was your first clue?" And he rap him on the head with the back of his knuckles, since Q.T. the only one he could get away with. Though Q.T. liable to come up behind you years later and get his licks in when you half expect it.

"What I want to know is," I says to Miss Moore though I never talk to her, I wouldn't give the bitch the satisfaction, "is how much a real boat costs? I figure a thousand'd get you a yacht any day."

40   "Why don't you check that out," she says, "and report back to the group?" Which really pains my ass. If you gonna mess up a perfectly good swim day least you could do is have some answers. "Let's go in," she say like she got something up her sleeve. Only she don't lead the way. So me and Sugar turn the corner to where the entrance is, but when we get there I kinda hang back. Not that I'm scared, what's there to be afraid of, just a toy store. But I feel funny, shame. But

what I got to be shamed about? Got as much right to go in as anybody. But somehow I can't seem to get hold of the door, so I step away from Sugar to lead. But she hangs back too. And I look at her and she looks at me and this is ridiculous. I mean, damn, I have never ever been shy about doing nothing or going nowhere. But then Mercedes steps up and then Rosie Giraffe and Big Butt crowd in behind and shove, and next thing we all stuffed into the doorway with only Mercedes squeezing past us, smoothing out her jumper and walking right down the aisle. Then the rest of us tumble in like a glued-together jigsaw done all wrong. And people lookin at us. And it's like the time me and Sugar crashed into the Catholic church on a dare. But once we got in there and everything so hushed and holy and the candles and the bowin and the handkerchiefs on all the drooping heads. I just couldn't go through with the plan. Which was for me to run up to the altar and do a tap dance while Sugar played the nose flute and messed around in the holy water. And Sugar kept givin me the elbow. Then later teased me so bad I tied her up in the shower and turned it on and locked her in. And she'd be there till this day if Aunt Gretchen hadn't finally figured I was lyin about the boarder takin a shower.

Same thing in the store. We all walkin on tiptoe and hardly touchin the games and puzzles and things. And I watched Miss Moore who is steady watchin us like she waitin for a sign. Like Mama Drewery watches the sky and sniffs the air and takes note of just how much slant is in the bird formation. Then me and Sugar bump smack into each other, so busy gazing at the toys, 'specially the sailboat. But we don't laugh and go into our fat-lady bump-stomach routine. We just stare at that price tag. Then Sugar run a finger over the whole boat. And I'm jealous and want to hit her. Maybe not her, but I sure want to punch somebody in the mouth.

"Watcha bring us here for, Miss Moore?"

"You sound angry, Sylvia. Are you mad about something?" Givin me one of them grins like she tellin a grown-up joke that never turns out to be funny. And she's lookin very closely at me like maybe she plannin to do my portrait from memory. I'm mad, but I won't give her that satisfaction. So I slouch around the store bein very bored and say, "Let's go."

Me and Sugar at the back of the train watchin the tracks whizzin by large then small then gettin gobbled up in the dark. I'm thinkin about this tricky toy I saw in the store. A clown that somersaults on a bar then does chin-ups just cause you yank lightly at his leg. Cost $35. I could see me askin my mother for a $35 birthday clown. "You wanna who that costs what?" she'd say, cocking her head to the side to get a better view of the hole in my head. Thirty-five dollars could buy new bunk beds for Junior and Gretchen's boy. Thirty-five dollars and the whole household could go visit Granddaddy Nelson in the country. Thirty-five dollars would pay for the rent and the piano bill too. Who are these people that spend that much for performing clowns and $1000 for toy sailboats? What kinda work they do and how they live and how come we ain't in on it? Where we

are is who we are, Miss Moore always pointin out. But it don't necessarily have
to be that way, she always adds then waits for somebody to say that poor people
have to wake up and demand their share of the pie and don't none of us know
what kind of pie she talking about in the first damn place. But she ain't so smart
cause I still got her four dollars from the taxi and she sure ain't getting it. Messin up
my day with this shit. Sugar nudges me in my pocket and winks.

45   Miss Moore lines us up in front of the mailbox where we started from, seem like
years ago, and I got a headache for thinkin so hard. And we lean all over each other
so we can hold up under the draggy-ass lecture she always finishes us off with at
the end before we thank her for borin us to tears. But she just looks at us like she
readin tea leaves. Finally she say, "Well, what did you think of F.A.O. Schwarz?"

Rosie Giraffe mumbles, "White folks crazy."

"I'd like to go there again when I get my birthday money," says Mercedes, and
we shove her out the pack so she has to lean on the mailbox by herself.

"I'd like a shower. Tiring day," say Flyboy.

Then Sugar surprises me by sayin, "You know, Miss Moore, I don't think all of
us here put together eat in a year what that sailboat costs." And Miss Moore lights
up like somebody goosed her. "And?" she say, urging Sugar on. Only I'm standin
on her foot so she don't continue.

50   "Imagine for a minute what kind of society it is in which some people can
spend on a toy what it would cost to feed a family of six or seven. What do you
think?"

"I think," say Sugar pushing me off her feet like she never done before, cause
I whip her ass in a minute, "that this is not much of a democracy if you ask me.
Equal chance to pursue happiness means an equal crack at the dough, don't it?"
Miss Moore is beside herself and I am disgusted with Sugar's treachery. So I stand
on her foot one more time to see if she'll shove me. She shuts up, and Miss Moore
looks at me, sorrowfully I'm thinkin. And somethin weird is goin on, I can feel it
in my chest.

"Anybody else learn anything today?" lookin dead at me. I walk away and
Sugar has to run to catch up and don't even seem to notice when I shrug her arm
off my shoulder.

"Well, we got four dollars anyway," she says.

"Uh hunh."

55   "We could go to Hascombs and get half a chocolate layer and then go to the
Sunset and still have plenty of money for potato chips and ice cream sodas."

"Uh hunh."

"Race you to Hascombs," she say.

We start down the block and she gets ahead which is O.K. by me cause I'm going to the West End and then over to the Drive to think this day through. She can
run if she want to and even run faster. But ain't nobody gonna beat me at nuthin.

❖ ❖ ❖

T. CORAGHESSAN BOYLE (1948–)

Greasy Lake (1985)

It's about a mile down on the dark side of Route 88.
— Bruce Springsteen

There was a time when courtesy and winning ways went out of style, when it was good to be bad, when you cultivated decadence like a taste. We were all dangerous characters then. We wore torn-up leather jackets, slouched around with toothpicks in our mouths, sniffed glue and ether and what somebody claimed was cocaine. When we wheeled our parents' whining station wagons out into the street we left a patch of rubber half a block long. We drank gin and grape juice, Tango, Thunderbird, and Bali Hai. We were nineteen. We were bad. We read André Gide° and struck elaborate poses to show that we didn't give a shit about anything. At night, we went up to Greasy Lake.

Through the center of town, up the strip, past the housing developments and shopping malls, street lights giving way to the thin streaming illumination of the headlights, trees crowding the asphalt in a black unbroken wall: that was the way out to Greasy Lake. The Indians had called it Wakan, a reference to the clarity of its waters. Now it was fetid and murky, the mud banks glittering with broken glass and strewn with beer cans and the charred remains of bonfires. There was a single ravaged island a hundred yards from shore, so stripped of vegetation it looked as if the air force had strafed it. We went up to the lake because everyone went there, because we wanted to snuff the rich scent of possibility on the breeze, watch a girl take off her clothes and plunge into the festering murk, drink beer, smoke pot, howl at the stars, savor the incongruous full-throated roar of rock and roll against the primeval susurrus° of frogs and crickets. This was nature.

I was there one night, late, in the company of two dangerous characters. Digby wore a gold star in his right ear and allowed his father to pay his tuition at Cornell; Jeff was thinking of quitting school to become a painter/musician/ head-shop proprietor. They were both expert in the social graces, quick with a sneer, able to manage a Ford with lousy shocks over a rutted and gutted black-top road at eighty-five while rolling a joint as compact as a Tootsie Roll Pop stick. They could lounge against a bank of booming speakers and trade "man"s with the best of them or roll out across the dance floor as if their joints worked on bearings. They were slick and quick and they wore their mirror shades at breakfast and dinner, in the shower, in closets and caves. In short, they were bad.

André Gide: French novelist and critic (1869–1951) whose work — much of it semiautobiographical — examines the conflict between desire and discipline and shows individuals battling conventional morality.
susurrus: A whispering or rustling sound.

I drove. Digby pounded the dashboard and shouted along with Toots & the Maytals while Jeff hung his head out the window and streaked the side of my mother's Bel Air with vomit. It was early June, the air soft as a hand on your cheek, the third night of summer vacation. The first two nights we'd been out till dawn, looking for something we never found. On this, the third night, we'd cruised the strip sixty-seven times, been in and out of every bar and club we could think of in a twenty-mile radius, stopped twice for bucket chicken and forty-cent hamburgers, debated going to a party at the house of a girl Jeff's sister knew, and chucked two dozen raw eggs at mailboxes and hitchhikers. It was 2:00 A.M.; the bars were closing. There was nothing to do but take a bottle of lemon-flavored gin up to Greasy Lake.

5   The taillights of a single car winked at us as we swung into the dirt lot with its tufts of weed and washboard corrugations; '57 Chevy, mint, metallic blue. On the far side of the lot, like the exoskeleton of some gaunt chrome insect, a chopper leaned against its kickstand. And that was it for excitement: some junkie half-wit biker and a car freak pumping his girlfriend. Whatever it was we were looking for, we weren't about to find it at Greasy Lake. Not that night.

But then all of a sudden Digby was fighting for the wheel. "Hey, that's Tony Lovett's car! Hey!" he shouted, while I stabbed at the brake pedal and the Bel Air nosed up to the gleaming bumper of the parked Chevy. Digby leaned on the horn, laughing, and instructed me to put my brights on. I flicked on the brights. This was hilarious. A joke. Tony would experience premature withdrawal and expect to be confronted by grim-looking state troopers with flashlights. We hit the horn, strobed the lights, and then jumped out of the car to press our witty faces to Tony's windows; for all we knew we might even catch a glimpse of some little fox's tit, and then we could slap backs with red-faced Tony, roughhouse a little, and go on to new heights of adventure and daring.

The first mistake, the one that opened the whole floodgate, was losing my grip on the keys. In the excitement, leaping from the car with the gin in one hand and a roach clip in the other, I spilled them in the grass — in the dark, rank, mysterious nighttime grass of Greasy Lake. This was a tactical error, as damaging and irreversible in its way as Westmoreland's decision to dig in at Khe Sanh.° I felt it like a jab of intuition, and I stopped there by the open door, peering vaguely into the night that puddled up round my feet.

The second mistake — and this was inextricably bound up with the first — was identifying the car as Tony Lovett's. Even before the very bad character in greasy jeans and engineer boots ripped out of the driver's door, I began to realize that this chrome blue was much lighter than the robin's-egg of Tony's car, and that Tony's car didn't have rear-mounted speakers. Judging from their expressions,

---

Khe Sanh: In late 1967, North Vietnamese and Viet Cong forces mounted a strong attack against American troops at Khe Sanh, thereby causing General William C. Westmoreland, commander of United States forces in Vietnam, to "dig in" to defend an area of relatively little tactical importance.

Digby and Jeff were privately groping toward the same inevitable and unsettling conclusion as I was.

In any case, there was no reasoning with this bad greasy character — clearly he was a man of action. The first lusty Rockette° kick of his steel-toed boot caught me under the chin, chipped my favorite tooth, and left me sprawled in the dirt. Like a fool, I'd gone down on one knee to comb the stiff hacked grass for the keys, my mind making connections in the most dragged-out, testudineous° way, knowing that things had gone wrong, that I was in a lot of trouble, and that the lost ignition key was my grail and my salvation. The three or four succeeding blows were mainly absorbed by my right buttock and the tough piece of bone at the base of my spine.

Meanwhile, Digby vaulted the kissing bumpers and delivered a savage kung-   10
fu blow to the greasy character's collarbone. Digby had just finished a course in martial arts for phys-ed credit and had spent the better part of the past two nights telling us apocryphal tales of Bruce Lee types and of the raw power invested in lightning blows shot from coiled wrists, ankles, and elbows. The greasy character was unimpressed. He merely backed off a step, his face like a Toltec mask, and laid Digby out with a single whistling roundhouse blow. . . but by now Jeff had got into the act, and I was beginning to extricate myself from the dirt, a tinny compound of shock, rage, and impotence wadded in my throat.

Jeff was on the guy's back, biting at his ear. Digby was on the ground, cursing. I went for the tire iron I kept under the driver's seat. I kept it there because bad characters always keep tire irons under the driver's seat, for just such an occasion as this. Never mind that I hadn't been involved in a fight since sixth grade, when a kid with a sleepy eye and two streams of mucus depending from his nostrils hit me in the knee with a Louisville slugger,° never mind that I'd touched the tire iron exactly twice before, to change tires: it was there. And I went for it.

I was terrified. Blood was beating in my ears, my hands were shaking, my heart turning over like a dirtbike in the wrong gear. My antagonist was shirtless, and a single cord of muscle flashed across his chest as he bent forward to peel Jeff from his back like a wet overcoat. "Motherfucker," he spat, over and over, and I was aware in that instant that all four of us — Digby, Jeff, and myself included — were chanting "motherfucker, motherfucker," as if it were a battle cry. (What happened next? the detective asks the murderer from beneath the turned-down brim of his porkpie hat. I don't know, the murderer says, something came over me. Exactly.)

Digby poked the flat of his hand in the bad character's face and I came at him like a kamikaze, mindless, raging, stung with humiliation — the whole thing, from the initial boot in the chin to this murderous primal instant involving no

---

Rockette: The reference is to the Rockettes, a dance troupe at New York's Radio City Music Hall noted for precision and cancan-like high kicks.

testudineous: Slow, like the pace of a tortoise.

Louisville slugger: A popular brand of baseball bat.

more than sixty hyperventilating, gland-flooding seconds — I came at him and brought the tire iron down across his ear. The effect was instantaneous, astonishing. He was a stunt man and this was Hollywood, he was a big grimacing toothy balloon and I was a man with a straight pin. He collapsed. Wet his pants. Went loose in his boots.

A single second, big as a zeppelin, floated by. We were standing over him in a circle, gritting our teeth, jerking our necks, our limbs and hands and feet twitching with glandular discharges. No one said anything. We just stared down at the guy, the car freak, the lover, the bad greasy character laid low. Digby looked at me; so did Jeff. I was still holding the tire iron, a tuft of hair clinging to the crook like dandelion fluff, like down. Rattled, I dropped it in the dirt, already envisioning the headlines, the pitted faces of the police inquisitors, the gleam of handcuffs, clank of bars, the big black shadows rising from the back of the cell . . . when suddenly a raw torn shriek cut through me like all the juice in all the electric chairs in the country.

15   It was the fox. She was short, barefoot, dressed in panties and a man's shirt. "Animals!" she screamed, running at us with her fists clenched and wisps of blow-dried hair in her face. There was a silver chain round her ankle, and her toenails flashed in the glare of the headlights. I think it was the toenails that did it. Sure, the gin and the cannabis and even the Kentucky Fried may have had a hand in it, but it was the sight of those flaming toes that set us off — the toad emerging from the loaf in *Virgin Spring*,° lipstick smeared on a child: she was already tainted. We were on her like Bergman's deranged brothers — see no evil, hear none, speak none — panting, wheezing, tearing at her clothes, grabbing for flesh. We were bad characters, and we were scared and hot and three steps over the line — anything could have happened.

It didn't.

Before we could pin her to the hood of the car, our eyes masked with lust and greed and the purest primal badness, a pair of headlights swung into the lot. There we were, dirty, bloody, guilty, dissociated from humanity and civilization, the first of the Ur-crimes° behind us, the second in progress, shreds of nylon panty and spandex brassiere dangling from our fingers, our flies open, lips licked — there we were, caught in the spotlight. Nailed.

We bolted. First for the car, and then, realizing we had no way of starting it, for the woods. I thought nothing. I thought escape. The headlights came at me like accusing fingers. I was gone.

Ram-bam-bam, across the parking lot, past the chopper and into the feculent undergrowth at the lake's edge, insects flying up in my face, weeds whipping, frogs and snakes and red-eyed turtles splashing off into the night: I was already ankle-deep in muck and tepid water and still going strong. Behind me, the girl's screams

---

Virgin Spring: A Film by Swedish director Ingmar Bergman.
Ur-crimes: Primitive crimes.

rose in intensity, disconsolate, incriminating, the screams of the Sabine women,° the Christian martyrs, Anne Frank° dragged from the garret. I kept going, pursued by those cries, imagining cops and bloodhounds. The water was up to my knees when I realized what I was doing: I was going to swim for it. Swim the breadth of Greasy Lake and hide myself in the thick clot of woods on the far side. They'd never find me there.

I was breathing in sobs, in gasps. The water lapped at my waist as I looked out 20
over the moon-burnished ripples, the mats of algae that clung to the surface like scabs. Digby and Jeff had vanished. I paused. Listened. The girl was quieter now, screams tapering to sobs, but there were male voices, angry, excited, and the high-pitched ticking of the second car's engine. I waded deeper, stealthy, hunted, the ooze sucking at my sneakers. As I was about to take the plunge — at the very instant I dropped my shoulder for the first slashing stroke — I blundered into something. Something unspeakable, obscene, something soft, wet, moss-grown. A patch of weed? A log? When I reached out to touch it, it gave like a rubber duck, it gave like flesh.

In one of those nasty little epiphanies for which we are prepared by films and TV and childhood visits to the funeral home to ponder the shrunken painted forms of dead grandparents, I understood what it was that bobbed there so inadmissibly in the dark. Understood, and stumbled back in horror and revulsion, my mind yanked in six different directions (I was nineteen, a mere child, an infant, and here in the space of five minutes I'd struck down one greasy character and blundered into the waterlogged carcass of a second), thinking, The keys, the keys, why did I have to go and lose the keys? I stumbled back, but the muck took hold of my feet — a sneaker snagged, balance lost — and suddenly I was pitching face forward into the buoyant black mass, throwing out my hands in desperation while simultaneously conjuring the image of reeking frogs and muskrats revolving in slicks of their own deliquescing° juices. AAAAArrrgh! I shot from the water like a torpedo, the dead man rotating to expose a mossy beard and eyes cold as the moon. I must have shouted out, thrashing around in the weeds, because the voices behind me suddenly became animated.

"What was that?"

"It's them, it's them: they tried to, tried to . . . *rape* me!" Sobs.

A man's voice, flat Midwestern accent. "You sons a bitches, we'll kill you!"

Frogs, crickets.   25

Sabine women: According to legend, members of an ancient Italian tribe abducted by Romans who took them for wives. The "Rape of the Sabine Women" has been depicted by various artists, most notably by seventeenth-century French painter Nicolas Poussin.

Anne Frank: German Jewish girl (1929–1945) whose family hid in an attic in Amsterdam during the Nazi occupation of the Netherlands. Frank, who along with her family was discovered by storm troopers and sent to die at the concentration camp at Belsen, is famous for her diary, which recounts her days in hiding. A new version of the diary containing five missing pages surfaced in 1998.

deliquescing: Melting.

Then another voice, harsh, r-less, Lower East Side: "Motherfucker!" I recognized the verbal virtuosity of the bad greasy character in the engineer boots. Tooth chipped, sneakers gone, coated in mud and slime and worse, crouching breathless in the weeds waiting to have my ass thoroughly and definitively kicked and fresh from the hideous stinking embrace of a three-days-dead-corpse, I suddenly felt a rush of joy and vindication: the son of a bitch was alive! Just as quickly, my bowels turned to ice. "Come on out of there, you pansy mothers!" the bad greasy character was screaming. He shouted curses till he was out of breath.

The crickets started up again, then the frogs. I held my breath. All at once there was a sound in the reeds, a swishing, a splash: thunk-a-thunk. They were throwing rocks. The frogs fell silent. I cradled my head. Swish, swish, thunk-a-thunk. A wedge of feldspar the size of a cue ball glanced off my knee. I bit my finger.

It was then that they turned to the car. I heard a door slam, a curse, and then the sound of the headlights shattering — almost a good-natured sound, celebratory, like corks popping from the necks of bottles. This was succeeded by the dull booming of the fenders, metal on metal, and then the icy crash of the windshield. I inched forward, elbows and knees, my belly pressed to the muck, thinking of guerrillas and commandos and *The Naked and the Dead*.° I parted the weeds and squinted the length of the parking lot.

The second car — it was a Trans-Am — was still running, its high beams washing the scene in a lurid stagy light. Tire iron flailing, the greasy bad character was laying into the side of my mother's Bel Air like an avenging demon, his shadow riding up the trunks of the trees. Whomp. Whomp. Whomp-whomp. The other two guys — blond types, in fraternity jackets — were helping out with tree branches and skull-sized boulders. One of them was gathering up bottles, rocks, muck, candy wrappers, used condoms, pop-tops, and other refuse and pitching it through the window on the driver's side. I could see the fox, a white bulb behind the windshield of the '57 Chevy. "Bobbie," she whined over the thumping, "come *on*." The greasy character paused a moment, took one good swipe at the left taillight, and then heaved the tire iron halfway across the lake. Then he fired up the '57 and was gone.

30   Blond head nodded at blond head. One said something to the other, too low for me to catch. They were no doubt thinking that in helping to annihilate my mother's car they'd committed a fairly rash act, and thinking too that there were three bad characters connected with that very car watching them from the woods. Perhaps other possibilities occurred to them as well — police, jail cells, justices of the peace, reparations, lawyers, irate parents, fraternal censure. Whatever they were thinking, they suddenly dropped branches, bottles, and rocks and sprang for their car in unison, as if they'd choreographed it. Five seconds. That's all it took. The engine shrieked, the tires squealed, a cloud of dust rose from the rutted lot and then settled back on darkness.

The Naked and the Dead: A popular and critically successful 1948 novel by Norman Mailer depicting United States Army life during World War II.

I don't know how long I lay there, the bad breath of decay all around me, my jacket heavy as a bear, the primordial ooze subtly reconstituting itself to accommodate my upper thighs and testicles. My jaws ached, my knee throbbed, my coccyx° was on fire. I contemplated suicide, wondered if I'd need bridgework, scraped the recesses of my brain for some sort of excuse to give my parents — a tree had fallen on the car, I was blindsided by a bread truck, hit and run, vandals had got to it while we were playing chess at Digby's. Then I thought of the dead man. He was probably the only person on the planet worse off than I was. I thought about him, fog on the lake, insects chirring eerily, and felt the tug of fear, felt the darkness opening up inside me like a set of jaws. Who was he, I wondered, this victim of time and circumstance bobbing sorrowfully in the lake at my back. The owner of the chopper, no doubt, a bad older character come to this. Shot during a murky drug deal, drowned while drunkenly frolicking in the lake. Another headline. My car was wrecked; he was dead.

When the eastern half of the sky went from black to cobalt and the trees began to separate themselves from the shadows, I pushed myself up from the mud and stepped out into the open. By now the birds had begun to take over for the crickets, and dew lay slick on the leaves. There was a smell in the air, raw and sweet at the same time, the smell of the sun firing buds and opening blossoms. I contemplated the car. It lay there like a wreck along the highway, like a steel sculpture left over from a vanished civilization. Everything was still. This was nature.

I was circling the car, as dazed and bedraggled as the sole survivor of an air blitz, when Digby and Jeff emerged from the trees behind me. Digby's face was crosshatched with smears of dirt; Jeff's jacket was gone and his shirt was torn across the shoulder. They slouched across the lot, looking sheepish, and silently came up beside me to gape at the ravaged automobile. No one said a word. After a while Jeff swung open the driver's door and began to scoop the broken glass and garbage off the seat. I looked at Digby. He shrugged. "At least they didn't slash the tires," he said.

It was true: the tires were intact. There was no windshield, the headlights were staved in, and the body looked as if it had been sledgehammered for a quarter a shot at the county fair, but the tires were inflated to regulation pressure. The car was drivable. In silence, all three of us bent to scrape the mud and shattered glass from the interior. I said nothing about the biker. When we were finished, I reached in my pocket for the keys, experienced a nasty stab of recollection, cursed myself, and turned to search the grass. I spotted them almost immediately, no more than five feet from the open door, glinting like jewels in the first tapering shaft of sunlight. There was no reason to get philosophical about it: I eased into the seat and turned the engine over.

It was at that precise moment that the silver Mustang with the flame decals rumbled into the lot. All three of us froze; then Digby and Jeff slid into the car and

---

coccyx: Tailbone.

slammed the door. We watched as the Mustang rocked and bobbed across the ruts and finally jerked to a halt beside the forlorn chopper at the far end of the lot. "Let's go," Digby said. I hesitated, the Bel Air wheezing beneath me.

Two girls emerged from the Mustang. Tight jeans, stiletto heels, hair like frozen fur. They bent over the motorcycle, paced back and forth aimlessly, glanced once or twice at us, and then ambled over to where the reeds sprang up in a green fence round the perimeter of the lake. One of them cupped her hands to her mouth. "Al," she called, "Hey, Al!"

"Come on," Digby hissed. "Let's get out of here."

But it was too late. The second girl was picking her way across the lot, unsteady on her heels, looking up at us and then away. She was older — twenty-five or -six — and as she came closer we could see there was something wrong with her: she was stoned or drunk, lurching now and waving her arms for balance. I gripped the steering wheel as if it were the ejection lever of a flaming jet, and Digby spat out my name, twice, terse and impatient.

"Hi," the girl said.

40   We looked at her like zombies, like war veterans, like deaf-and-dumb pencil peddlers.

She smiled, her lips cracked and dry. "Listen," she said, bending from the waist to look in the window, "you guys seen Al?" Her pupils were pinpoints, her eyes glass. She jerked her neck. "That's his bike over there — Al's. You seen him?"

Al. I didn't know what to say. I wanted to get out of the car and retch, I wanted to go home to my parents' house and crawl into bed. Digby poked me in the ribs. "We haven't seen anybody," I said.

The girl seemed to consider this, reaching out a slim veiny arm to brace herself against the car. "No matter," she said, slurring the *t*'s, "he'll turn up." And then, as if she'd just taken stock of the whole scene — the ravaged car and our battered faces, the desolation of the place — she said: "Hey, you guys look like some pretty bad characters — been fightin', huh?" We stared straight ahead, rigid as catatonics. She was fumbling in her pocket and muttering something. Finally she held out a handful of tablets in glassine wrappers: "Hey, you want to party, you want to do some of these with me and Sarah?"

I just looked at her. I thought I was going to cry. Digby broke the silence. "No, thanks," he said, leaning over me. "Some other time."

45   I put the car in gear and it inched forward with a groan, shaking off pellets of glass like an old dog shedding water after a bath, heaving over the ruts on its worn springs, creeping toward the highway. There was a sheen of sun on the lake. I looked back. The girl was still standing there, watching us, her shoulders slumped, hand outstretched.

◇ ◇ ◇

GABRIEL GARCÍA MÁRQUEZ (1928–)

A Very Old Man with Enormous Wings (1968)

A Tale for Children

Translated from the Spanish by Gregory Rabassa

On the third day of rain they had killed so many crabs inside the house that Pelayo had to cross his drenched courtyard and throw them into the sea, because the newborn child had a temperature all night and they thought it was due to the stench. The world had been sad since Tuesday. Sea and sky were a single ash-gray thing and the sands of the beach, which on March nights glimmered like powdered light, had become a stew of mud and rotten shellfish. The light was so weak at noon that when Pelayo was coming back to the house after throwing away the crabs, it was hard for him to see what it was that was moving and groaning in the rear of the courtyard. He had to go very close to see that it was an old man, a very old man, lying face down in the mud, who, in spite of his tremendous efforts, couldn't get up, impeded by his enormous wings.

Frightened by that nightmare, Pelayo ran to get Elisenda, his wife, who was putting compresses on the sick child, and he took her to the rear of the courtyard. They both looked at the fallen body with mute stupor. He was dressed like a rag-picker.° There were only a few faded hairs left on his bald skull and very few teeth in his mouth, and his pitiful condition of a drenched great-grandfather had taken away any sense of grandeur he might have had. His huge buzzard wings, dirty and half-plucked, were forever entangled in the mud. They looked at him so long and so closely that Pelayo and Elisenda very soon overcame their surprise and in the end found him familiar. Then they dared speak to him, and he answered in an incomprehensible dialect with a strong sailor's voice. That was how they skipped over the inconvenience of the wings and quite intelligently concluded that he was a lonely castaway from some foreign ship wrecked by the storm. And yet, they called in a neighbor woman who knew everything about life and death to see him, and all she needed was one look to show them their mistake.

"He's an angel," she told them. "He must have been coming for the child, but the poor fellow is so old that the rain knocked him down."

On the following day everyone knew that a flesh-and-blood angel was held captive in Pelayo's house. Against the judgment of the wise neighbor woman, for whom angels in those times were the fugitive survivors of a celestial conspiracy, they did not have the heart to club him to death. Pelayo watched over him all afternoon from the kitchen, armed with his bailiff's club, and before going to bed he dragged him out of the mud and locked him up with the hens in the wire chicken coop. In the middle of the night, when the rain stopped, Pelayo and

---

ragpicker: Someone who makes a living collecting rags and other refuse.

Elisenda were still killing crabs. A short time afterward the child woke up without a fever and with a desire to eat. Then they felt magnanimous and decided to put the angel on a raft with fresh water and provisions for three days and leave him to his fate on the high seas. But when they went out into the courtyard with the first light of dawn, they found the whole neighborhood in front of the chicken coop having fun with the angel, without the slightest reverence, tossing him things to eat through the openings in the wire as if he weren't a supernatural creature but a circus animal.

5   Father Gonzaga arrived before seven o'clock, alarmed by the strange news. By that time onlookers less frivolous than those at dawn had already arrived and they were making all kinds of conjectures concerning the captive's future. The simplest among them thought that he should be named mayor of the world. Others of sterner mind felt that he should be promoted to the rank of five-star general in order to win all wars. Some visionaries hoped that he could be put to stud in order to implant on earth a race of winged wise men who could take charge of the universe. But Father Gonzaga, before becoming a priest, had been a robust woodcutter. Standing by the wire, he reviewed his catechism° in an instant and asked them to open the door so that he could take a close look at that pitiful man who looked more like a huge decrepit hen among the fascinated chickens. He was lying in a corner drying his open wings in the sunlight among the fruit peels and breakfast leftovers that the early risers had thrown him. Alien to the impertinences of the world, he only lifted his antiquarian° eyes and murmured something in his dialect when Father Gonzaga went into the chicken coop and said good morning to him in Latin. The parish priest had his first suspicion of an imposter when he saw that he did not understand the language of God or know how to greet His ministers. Then he noticed that seen close up he was much too human; he had an unbearable smell of the outdoors, the back side of his wings was strewn with parasites and his main feathers had been mistreated by terrestrial winds, and nothing about him measured up to the proud dignity of angels. Then he came out of the chicken coop and in a brief sermon warned the curious against the risks of being ingenuous. He reminded them that the devil had the bad habit of making use of carnival tricks in order to confuse the unwary. He argued that if wings were not the essential element in determining the difference between a hawk and an airplane, they were even less so in the recognition of angels. Nevertheless, he promised to write a letter to his bishop so that the latter would write to his primate so that the latter would write to the Supreme Pontiff° in order to get the final verdict from the highest courts.

His prudence fell on sterile hearts. The news of the captive angel spread with such rapidity that after a few hours the courtyard had the bustle of a marketplace

---

catechism: A book that summarizes the doctrines of Roman Catholicism in question-and-answer form.
antiquarian: Ancient.
the Supreme Pontiff: The pope.

and they had to call in troops with fixed bayonets to disperse the mob that was about to knock the house down. Elisenda, her spine all twisted from sweeping up so much marketplace trash, then got the idea of fencing in the yard and charging five cents admission to see the angel.

The curious came from far away. A traveling carnival arrived with a flying acrobat who buzzed over the crowd several times, but no one paid any attention to him because his wings were not those of an angel but, rather, those of a sidereal° bat. The most unfortunate invalids on earth came in search of health: a poor woman who since childhood had been counting her heartbeats and had run out of numbers; a Portuguese man who couldn't sleep because the noise of the stars disturbed him; a sleepwalker who got up at night to undo the things he had done while awake; and many others with less serious ailments. In the midst of that shipwreck disorder that made the earth tremble, Pelayo and Elisenda were happy with fatigue, for in less than a week they had crammed their rooms with money and the line of pilgrims waiting their turn to enter still reached beyond the horizon.

The angel was the only one who took no part in his own act. He spent his time trying to get comfortable in his borrowed nest, befuddled by the hellish heat of the oil lamps and sacramental candles that had been placed along the wire. At first they tried to make him eat some mothballs, which, according to the wisdom of the wise neighbor woman, were the food prescribed for angels. But he turned them down, just as he turned down the papal lunches that the penitents brought him, and they never found out whether it was because he was an angel or because he was an old man that in the end he ate nothing but eggplant mush. His only supernatural virtue seemed to be patience. Especially during the first days, when the hens pecked at him, searching for the stellar parasites that proliferated in his wings, and the cripples pulled out feathers to touch their defective parts with, and even the most merciful threw stones at him, trying to get him to rise so they could see him standing. The only time they succeeded in arousing him was when they burned his side with an iron for branding steers, for he had been motionless for so many hours that they thought he was dead. He awoke with a start, ranting in his hermetic° language and with tears in his eyes, and he flapped his wings a couple of times, which brought on a whirlwind of chicken dung and lunar dust and a gale of panic that did not seem to be of this world. Although many thought that his reaction had been one not of rage but of pain, from then on they were careful not to annoy him, because the majority understood that his passivity was not that of a hero taking his ease but that of a cataclysm in repose.

Father Gonzaga held back the crowd's frivolity with formulas of maid-servant inspiration while awaiting the arrival of a final judgment on the nature of the captive. But the mail from Rome showed no sense of urgency. They spent their time finding out if the prisoner had a navel, if his dialect had any connection

---

sidereal: Relating to the stars.
hermetic: Occult, magical.

with Aramaic,° how many times he could fit on the head of a pin, or whether he wasn't just a Norwegian with wings. Those meager letters might have come and gone until the end of time if a providential event had not put an end to the priest's tribulations.

10   It so happened that during those days, among so many other carnival attractions, there arrived in town the traveling show of the woman who had been changed into a spider for having disobeyed her parents. The admission to see her was not only less than the admission to see the angel, but people were permitted to ask her all manner of questions about her absurd state and to examine her up and down so that no one would ever doubt the truth of her horror. She was a frightful tarantula the size of a ram and with the head of a sad maiden. What was most heart-rending, however, was not her outlandish shape but the sincere affliction with which she recounted the details of her misfortune. While still practically a child she had sneaked out of her parents' house to go to a dance, and while she was coming back through the woods after having danced all night without permission, a fearful thunderclap rent the sky in two and through the crack came the lightning bolt of brimstone that changed her into a spider. Her only nourishment came from the meatballs that charitable souls chose to toss into her mouth. A spectacle like that, full of so much human truth and with such a fearful lesson, was bound to defeat without even trying that of a haughty angel who scarcely deigned to look at mortals. Besides, the few miracles attributed to the angel showed a certain mental disorder, like the blind man who didn't recover his sight but grew three new teeth, or the paralytic who didn't get to walk but almost won the lottery, and the leper whose sores sprouted sunflowers. Those consolation miracles, which were more like mocking fun, had already ruined the angel's reputation when the woman who had been changed into a spider finally crushed him completely. That was how Father Gonzaga was cured forever of his insomnia and Pelayo's courtyard went back to being as empty as during the time it had rained for three days and crabs walked through the bedrooms.

The owners of the house had no reason to lament. With the money they saved they built a two-story mansion with balconies and gardens and high netting so that crabs wouldn't get in during the winter, and with iron bars on the windows so that angels wouldn't get in. Pelayo also set up a rabbit warren close to town and gave up his job as bailiff for good, and Elisenda bought some satin pumps with high heels and many dresses of iridescent silk, the kind worn on Sunday by the most desirable women in those times. The chicken coop was the only thing that didn't receive any attention. If they washed it down with creolin° and burned tears of myrrh° inside it every so often, it was not in homage to the angel but to drive away the dungheap stench that still hung everywhere like a

---

Aramaic: An ancient Middle Eastern language believed to have been the language spoken by Jesus.
creolin: A disinfectant.
myrrh: A type of incense.

ghost and was turning the new house into an old one. At first, when the child learned to walk, they were careful that he not get too close to the chicken coop. But then they began to lose their fears and got used to the smell, and before the child got his second teeth he'd gone inside the chicken coop to play, where the wires were falling apart. The angel was no less standoffish with him than with other mortals, but he tolerated the most ingenious infamies with the patience of a dog who had no illusions. They both came down with chicken pox at the same time. The doctor who took care of the child couldn't resist the temptation to listen to the angel's heart, and he found so much whistling in the heart and so many sounds in his kidneys that it seemed impossible for him to be alive. What surprised him most, however, was the logic of his wings. They seemed so natural on that completely human organism that he couldn't understand why other men didn't have them too.

When the child began school it had been some time since the sun and rain had caused the collapse of the chicken coop. The angel went dragging himself about here and there like a stray dying man. They would drive him out of the bedroom with a broom and a moment later find him in the kitchen. He seemed to be in so many places at the same time that they grew to think that he'd been duplicated, that he was reproducing himself all through the house, and the exasperated and unhinged Elisenda shouted that it was awful living in that hell full of angels. He could scarcely eat and his antiquarian eyes had also become so foggy that he went about bumping into posts. All he had left were the bare cannulae° of his last feathers. Pelayo threw a blanket over him and extended him the charity of letting him sleep in the shed, and only then did they notice that he had a temperature at night, and was delirious with the tongue twisters of an old Norwegian. That was one of the few times they became alarmed, for they thought he was going to die and not even the wise neighbor woman had been able to tell them what to do with dead angels.

And yet he not only survived his worst winter, but seemed improved with the first sunny days. He remained motionless for several days in the farthest corner of the courtyard, where no one would see him, and at the beginning of December some large, stiff feathers began to grow on his wings, the feathers of a scarecrow, which looked more like another misfortune of decrepitude. But he must have known the reason for those changes, for he was quite careful that no one should notice them, that no one should hear the sea chanteys that he sometimes sang under the stars. One morning Elisenda was cutting some bunches of onions for lunch when a wind that seemed to come from the high seas blew into the kitchen. Then she went to the window and caught the angel in his first attempt at flight. They were so clumsy that his fingernails opened a furrow in the vegetable patch and he was on the point of knocking the shed down with the ungainly flapping that slipped on the light and couldn't get a grip on the air. But he did manage to gain altitude. Elisenda let out a sigh of relief, for herself and for him, when she saw him pass over the last houses,

cannulae: Quills.

holding himself up in some way with the risky flapping of a senile vulture. She kept watching him even when she was through cutting the onions and she kept on watching until it was no longer possible for her to see him, because then he was no longer an annoyance in her life but an imaginary dot on the horizon of the sea.

◇ ◇ ◇

CHARLOTTE PERKINS GILMAN (1860–1935)

The Yellow Wallpaper (1892)

It is very seldom that mere ordinary people like John and myself secure ancestral halls for the summer.

A colonial mansion, a hereditary estate, I would say a haunted house, and reach the height of romantic felicity — but that would be asking too much of fate!

Still I will proudly declare that there is something queer about it.

Else, why should it be let so cheaply? And why have stood so long untenanted?

5   John laughs at me, of course, but one expects that in marriage.

John is practical in the extreme. He has no patience with faith, an intense horror of superstition, and he scoffs openly at any talk of things not to be felt and seen and put down in figures.

John is a physician, and *perhaps* — (I would not say it to a living soul, of course, but this is dead paper and a great relief to my mind —) *perhaps* that is one reason I do not get well faster.

You see he does not believe I am sick!

And what can one do?

10   If a physician of high standing, and one's own husband, assures friends and relatives that there is really nothing the matter with one but temporary nervous depression — a slight hysterical tendency — what is one to do?

My brother is also a physician, and also of high standing, and he says the same thing.

So I take phosphates or phosphites° — whichever it is, and tonics, and journeys, and air, and exercise, and am absolutely forbidden to "work" until I am well again.

Personally, I disagree with their ideas.

Personally, I believe that congenial work, with excitement and change, would do me good.

15   But what is one to do?

I did write for a while in spite of them; but it *does* exhaust me a good deal — having to be so sly about it, or else meet with heavy opposition.

I sometimes fancy that in my condition if I had less opposition and more society and stimulus — but John says the very worst thing I can do is to think about my condition, and I confess it always makes me feel bad.

---

phosphates or phosphites: Both terms refer to salts of phosphorous acid. The narrator, however, means "phosphate," a carbonated beverage of water, flavoring, and a small amount of phosphoric acid.

So I will let it alone and talk about the house.

The most beautiful place! It is quite alone, standing well back from the road, quite three miles from the village. It makes me think of English places that you read about, for there are hedges and walls and gates that lock, and lots of separate little houses for the gardeners and people.

There is a *delicious* garden! I never saw such a garden — large and shady, 20 full of box-bordered paths, and lined with long grape-covered arbors with seats under them.

There were greenhouses, too, but they are all broken now.

There was some legal trouble, I believe, something about the heirs and co-heirs; anyhow, the place has been empty for years.

That spoils my ghostliness, I am afraid, but I don't care — there is something strange about the house — I can feel it.

I even said so to John one moonlight evening, but he said what I felt was a *draught,* and shut the window.

I get unreasonably angry with John sometimes. I'm sure I never used to be so 25 sensitive. I think it is due to this nervous condition.

But John says if I feel so, I shall neglect proper self-control; so I take pains to control myself — before him, at least, and that makes me very tired.

I don't like our room a bit. I wanted one downstairs that opened on the piazza and had roses all over the window, and such pretty old-fashioned chintz hangings! But John would not hear of it.

He said there was only one window and not room for two beds, and no near room for him if he took another.

He is very careful and loving, and hardly lets me stir without special direction.

I have a schedule prescription for each hour in the day; he takes all care from me, and so I feel basely ungrateful not to value it more.

He said we came here solely on my account, that I was to have perfect rest and 30 all the air I could get. "Your exercise depends on your strength, my dear," said he, "and your food somewhat on your appetite; but air you can absorb all the time." So we took the nursery at the top of the house.

It is a big, airy room, the whole floor nearly, with windows that look all ways, and air and sunshine galore. It was nursery first and then playroom and gymnasium, I should judge; for the windows are barred for little children, and there are rings and things in the walls.

The paint and paper look as if a boys' school had used it. It is stripped off — the paper — in great patches all around the head of my bed, about as far as I can reach, and in a great place on the other side of the room low down. I never saw a worse paper in my life.

One of those sprawling flamboyant patterns committing every artistic sin.

It is dull enough to confuse the eye in following, pronounced enough to con- 35 stantly irritate and provoke study, and when you follow the lame uncertain curves for a little distance they suddenly commit suicide — plunge off at outrageous angles, destroy themselves in unheard of contradictions.

The color is repellent, almost revolting; a smouldering unclean yellow, strangely faded by the slow-turning sunlight.

It is a dull yet lurid orange in some places, a sickly sulphur tint in others.

No wonder the children hated it! I should hate it myself if I had to live in this room long.

There comes John, and I must put this away, — he hates to have me write a word.

* * *

40 We have been here two weeks, and I haven't felt like writing before, since that first day.

I am sitting by the window now, up in this atrocious nursery, and there is nothing to hinder my writing as much as I please, save lack of strength.

John is away all day, and even some nights when his cases are serious.

I am glad my case is not serious!

But these nervous troubles are dreadfully depressing.

45 John does not know how much I really suffer. He knows there is no *reason* to suffer, and that satisfies him.

Of course it is only nervousness. It does weigh on me so not to do my duty in any way!

I meant to be such a help to John, such a real rest and comfort, and here I am a comparative burden already!

Nobody would believe what an effort it is to do what little I am able, — to dress and entertain, and order things.

It is fortunate Mary is so good with the baby. Such a dear baby!

50 And yet I *cannot* be with him, it makes me so nervous.

I suppose John never was nervous in his life. He laughs at me so about this wallpaper!

At first he meant to repaper the room, but afterwards he said that I was letting it get the better of me, and that nothing was worse for a nervous patient than to give way to such fancies.

He said that after the wallpaper was changed it would be the heavy bedstead, and then the barred windows, and then that gate at the head of the stairs, and so on.

"You know the place is doing you good," he said, "and really, dear, I don't care to renovate the house just for a three months' rental."

55 "Then do let us go downstairs," I said, "there are such pretty rooms there."

Then he took me in his arms and called me a blessed little goose, and said he would go down cellar, if I wished, and have it whitewashed into the bargain.

But he is right enough about the beds and windows and things.

It is an airy and comfortable room as any one need wish, and, of course, I would not be so silly as to make him uncomfortable just for a whim.

I'm really getting quite fond of the big room, all but that horrid paper.

Out of one window I can see the garden, those mysterious deep-shaded arbors, 60
the riotous old-fashioned flowers, and bushes and gnarly trees.

Out of another I get a lovely view of the bay and a little private wharf belonging to the estate. There is a beautiful shaded lane that runs down there from the house. I always fancy I see people walking in these numerous paths and arbors, but John has cautioned me not to give way to fancy in the least. He says that with my imaginative power and habit of story-making, a nervous weakness like mine is sure to lead to all manner of excited fancies, and that I ought to use my will and good sense to check the tendency. So I try.

I think sometimes that if I were only well enough to write a little it would relieve the press of ideas and rest me.

But I find I get pretty tired when I try.

It is so discouraging not to have any advice and companionship about my work. When I get really well, John says we will ask Cousin Henry and Julia down for a long visit; but he says he would as soon put fireworks in my pillow-case as to let me have those stimulating people about now.

I wish I could get well faster. 65

But I must not think about that. This paper looks to me as if it *knew* what a vicious influence it had!

There is a recurrent spot where the pattern lolls like a broken neck and two bulbous eyes stare at you upside down.

I get positively angry with the impertinence of it and the everlastingness. Up and down and sideways they crawl, and those absurd, unblinking eyes are everywhere. There is one place where two breadths didn't match, and the eyes go all up and down the line, one a little higher than the other.

I never saw so much expression in an inanimate thing before, and we all know how much expression they have! I used to lie awake as a child and get more entertainment and terror out of blank walls and plain furniture than most children could find in a toy-store.

I remember what a kindly wink the knobs of our big, old bureau used to have, 70
and there was one chair that always seemed like a strong friend.

I used to feel that if any of the other things looked too fierce I could always hop into that chair and be safe.

The furniture in this room is no worse than inharmonious, however, for we had to bring it all from downstairs. I suppose when this was used as a playroom they had to take the nursery things out, and no wonder! I never saw such ravages as the children have made here.

The wallpaper, as I said before, is torn off in spots, and it sticketh closer than a brother — they must have had perseverance as well as hatred.

Then the floor is scratched and gouged and splintered, the plaster itself is dug out here and there, and this great heavy bed which is all we found in the room, looks as if it had been through the wars.

But I don't mind it a bit — only the paper. 75

There comes John's sister. Such a dear girl as she is, and so careful of me! I must not let her find me writing.

She is a perfect and enthusiastic housekeeper, and hopes for no better profession. I verily believe she thinks it is the writing which made me sick!

But I can write when she is out, and see her a long way off from these windows.

There is one that commands the road, a lovely shaded winding road, and one that just looks off over the country. A lovely country, too, full of great elms and velvet meadows.

80   This wallpaper has a kind of sub-pattern in a different shade, a particularly irritating one, for you can only see it in certain lights, and not clearly then.

But in the places where it isn't faded and where the sun is just so — I can see a strange, provoking, formless sort of figure, that seems to skulk about behind that silly and conspicuous front design.

There's sister on the stairs!

*   *   *

Well, the Fourth of July is over! The people are all gone and I am tired out. John thought it might do me good to see a little company, so we just had mother and Nellie and the children down for a week.

Of course I didn't do a thing. Jennie sees to everything now.

85   But it tired me all the same.

John says if I don't pick up faster he shall send me to Weir Mitchell° in the fall.

But I don't want to go there at all. I had a friend who was in his hands once, and she says he is just like John and my brother, only more so!

Besides, it is such an undertaking to go so far.

I don't feel as if it was worth while to turn my hand over for anything, and I'm getting dreadfully fretful and querulous.

90   I cry at nothing, and cry most of the time.

Of course I don't when John is here, or anybody else, but when I am alone.

And I am alone a good deal just now. John is kept in town very often by serious cases, and Jennie is good and lets me alone when I want her to.

So I walk a little in the garden or down that lovely lane, sit on the porch under the roses, and lie down up here a good deal.

I'm getting really fond of the room in spite of the wallpaper. Perhaps *because* of the wallpaper.

95   It dwells in my mind so!

I lie here on this great immovable bed — it is nailed down, I believe — and follow that pattern about by the hour. It is as good as gymnastics, I assure you. I start, we'll say, at the bottom, down in the corner over there where it has not been touched, and I determine for the thousandth time that I *will* follow that pointless pattern to some sort of a conclusion.

Weir Mitchell: Silas Weir Mitchell (1829–1914), a Philadelphia neurologist-psychologist who introduced the "rest cure" for nervous diseases.

I know a little of the principle of design, and I know this thing was not arranged on any laws of radiation, or alternation, or repetition, or symmetry, or anything else that I ever heard of.

It is repeated, of course, by the breadths, but not otherwise.

Looked at in one way each breadth stands alone, the bloated curves and flourishes — a kind of "debased Romanesque" with *delirium tremens*° go waddling up and down in isolated columns of fatuity.

But, on the other hand, they connect diagonally, and the sprawling outlines   100 run off in great slanting waves of optic horror, like a lot of wallowing seaweeds in full chase.

The whole thing goes horizontally, too, at least it seems so, and I exhaust myself in trying to distinguish the order of its going in that direction.

They have used a horizontal breadth for a frieze, and that adds wonderfully to the confusion.

There is one end of the room where it is almost intact, and there, when the crosslights fade and the low sun shines directly upon it, I can almost fancy radiation after all, — the interminable grotesques seems to form around a common center and rush off in headlong plunges of equal distraction.

It makes me tired to follow it. I will take a nap I guess.

I don't know why I should write this.   105

I don't want to.

I don't feel able.

And I know John would think it absurd. But I *must* say what I feel and think in some way — it is such a relief!

But the effort is getting to be greater than the relief.

Half the time now I am awfully lazy, and lie down ever so much.   110

John says I mustn't lose my strength, and has me take cod liver oil and lots of tonics and things, to say nothing of ale and wine and rare meat.

Dear John! He loves me very dearly, and hates to have me sick. I tried to have a real earnest reasonable talk with him the other day, and tell him how I wish he would let me go and make a visit to Cousin Henry and Julia.

But he said I wasn't able to go, nor able to stand it after I got there; and I did not make out a very good case for myself, for I was crying before I had finished.

It is getting to be a great effort for me to think straight. Just this nervous weakness I suppose.

And dear John gathered me up in his arms, and just carried me upstairs and   115 laid me on the bed, and sat by me and read to me till it tired my head.

He said I was his darling and his comfort and all he had, and that I must take care of myself for his sake, and keep well.

He says no one but myself can help me out of it, that I must use my will and self-control and not let any silly fancies run away with me.

---

delirium tremens: Mental confusion caused by alcohol poisoning and characterized by physical tremors and hallucinations.

There's one comfort, the baby is well and happy, and does not have to occupy this nursery with the horrid wallpaper.

If we had not used it, that blessed child would have! What a fortunate escape! Why, I wouldn't have a child of mine, an impressionable little thing, live in such a room for worlds.

120   I never thought of it before, but it is lucky that John kept me here after all, I can stand it so much easier than a baby, you see.

Of course I never mention it to them any more — I am too wise, — but I keep watch of it all the same.

There are things in that paper that nobody knows but me, or ever will.

Behind that outside pattern the dim shapes get clearer every day.

It is always the same shape, only very numerous.

125   And it is like a woman stooping down and creeping about behind that pattern. I don't like it a bit. I wonder — I begin to think — I wish John would take me away from here!

It is so hard to talk with John about my case, because he is so wise, and because he loves me so.

But I tried it last night.

It was moonlight. The moon shines in all around just as the sun does.

I hate to see it sometimes, it creeps so slowly, and always comes in by one window or another.

130   John was asleep and I hated to waken him, so I kept still and watched the moonlight on that undulating wallpaper till I felt creepy.

The faint figure behind seemed to shake the pattern, just as if she wanted to get out.

I got up softly and went to feel and see if the paper *did* move, and when I came back John was awake.

"What is it, little girl?" he said. "Don't go walking about like that — you'll get cold."

I thought it was a good time to talk, so I told him that I really was not gaining here, and that I wished he would take me away.

135   "Why, darling!" said he, "our lease will be up in three weeks, and I can't see how to leave before.

"The repairs are not done at home, and I cannot possibly leave town just now. Of course if you were in any danger, I could and would, but you really are better, dear, whether you can see it or not. I am a doctor, dear, and I know. You are gaining flesh and color, your appetite is better, I feel really much easier about you."

"I don't weigh a bit more," said I, "nor as much; and my appetite may be better in the evening when you are here, but it is worse in the morning when you are away!"

"Bless her little heart!" said he with a big hug, "she shall be as sick as she pleases! But now let's improve the shining hours by going to sleep, and talk about it in the morning!"

"And you won't go away?" I asked gloomily.

"Why, how can I, dear? It is only three weeks more and then we will take a 140 nice little trip of a few days while Jennie is getting the house ready. Really dear you are better!"

"Better in body perhaps —" I began, and stopped short, for he sat up straight and looked at me with such a stern, reproachful look that I could not say another word.

"My darling," said he, "I beg of you, for my sake and for our child's sake, as well as for your own, that you will never for one instant let that idea enter your mind! There is nothing so dangerous, so fascinating, to a temperament like yours. It is a false and foolish fancy. Can you not trust me as a physician when I tell you so?"

So of course I said no more on that score, and we went to sleep before long. He thought I was asleep first, but I wasn't, and lay there for hours trying to decide whether that front pattern and the back pattern really did move together or separately.

On a pattern like this, by daylight, there is a lack of sequence, a defiance of law, that is a constant irritant to a normal mind.

The color is hideous enough, and unreliable enough, and infuriating enough, 145 but the pattern is torturing.

You think you have mastered it, but just as you get well underway in following, it turns back-somersault and there you are. It slaps you in the face, knocks you down, and tramples upon you. It is like a bad dream.

The outside pattern is a florid arabesque, reminding one of a fungus. If you can imagine a toadstool in joints, an interminable string of toadstools, budding and sprouting in endless convolutions — why, that is something like it.

That is, sometimes!

There is one marked peculiarity about this paper, a thing nobody seems to notice but myself, and that is that it changes as the light changes.

When the sun shoots in through the east window — I always watch for that 150 first long, straight ray — it changes so quickly that I never can quite believe it.

That is why I watch it always.

By moonlight — the moon shines in all night when there is a moon — I wouldn't know it was the same paper.

At night in any kind of light, in twilight, candlelight, lamplight, and worst of all by moonlight, it becomes bars! The outside pattern I mean, and the woman behind it is as plain as can be.

I didn't realize for a long time what the thing was that showed behind, that dim sub-pattern, but now I am quite sure it is a woman.

By daylight she is subdued, quiet. I fancy it is the pattern that keeps her so still. 155 It is so puzzling. It keeps me quiet by the hour.

I lie down ever so much now. John says it is good for me, and to sleep all I can.

Indeed he started the habit by making me lie down for an hour after each meal.

It is a very bad habit I am convinced, for you see I don't sleep.

And that cultivates deceit, for I don't tell them I'm awake — O no!

160   The fact is I am getting a little afraid of John.

He seems very queer sometimes, and even Jennie has an inexplicable look.

It strikes me occasionally, just as a scientific hypothesis, — that perhaps it is the paper!

I have watched John when he did not know I was looking, and come into the room suddenly on the most innocent excuses, and I've caught him several times *looking at the paper!* And Jennie too. I caught Jennie with her hand on it once.

She didn't know I was in the room, and when I asked her in a quiet, a very quiet voice, with the most restrained manner possible, what she was doing with the paper — she turned around as if she had been caught stealing, and looked quite angry — asked me why I should frighten her so!

165   Then she said that the paper stained everything it touched, that she had found yellow smooches on all my clothes and John's, and she wished we would be more careful!

Did not that sound innocent? But I know she was studying that pattern, and I am determined that nobody shall find it out but myself!

Life is very much more exciting now than it used to be. You see I have something more to expect, to look forward to, to watch. I really do eat better, and am more quiet than I was.

John is so pleased to see me improve! He laughed a little the other day, and said I seemed to be flourishing in spite of my wallpaper.

I turned it off with a laugh. I had no intention of telling him it was *because* of the wallpaper — he would make fun of me. He might even want to take me away.

170   I don't want to leave now until I have found it out. There is a week more, and I think that will be enough.

I'm feeling ever so much better! I don't sleep much at night, for it is so interesting to watch developments; but I sleep a good deal in the daytime.

In the daytime it is tiresome and perplexing.

There are always new shoots on the fungus, and new shades of yellow all over it. I cannot keep count of them, though I have tried conscientiously.

It is the strangest yellow, that wallpaper! It makes me think of all the yellow things I ever saw — not beautiful ones like buttercups, but old foul, bad yellow things.

175   But there is something else about that paper — the smell! I noticed it the moment we came into the room, but with so much air and sun it was not bad. Now we have had a week of fog and rain, and whether the windows are open or not, the smell is here.

It creeps all over the house.

I find it hovering in the dining-room, skulking in the parlor, hiding in the hall, lying in wait for me on the stairs.

It gets into my hair.

Even when I go to ride, if I turn my head suddenly and surprise it — there is that smell!

Such a peculiar odor, too! I have spent hours in trying to analyze it, to find 180 what it smelled like.

It is not bad — at first, and very gentle, but quite the subtlest, most enduring odor I ever met.

In this damp weather it is awful, I wake up in the night and find it hanging over me.

It used to disturb me at first. I thought seriously of burning the house — to reach the smell.

But now I am used to it. The only thing I can think of that it is like is the *color* of the paper! A yellow smell.

There is a very funny mark on this wall, low down, near the mop-board. A 185 streak that runs round the room. It goes behind every piece of furniture, except the bed, a long, straight, even *smooch*, as if it had been rubbed over and over.

I wonder how it was done and who did it, and what they did it for. Round and round and round — round and round and round! — it makes me dizzy!

I really have discovered something at last.

Through watching so much at night, when it changes so, I have finally found out.

The front pattern *does* move — and no wonder! The woman behind shakes it!

Sometimes I think there are a great many women behind, and sometimes only 190 one, and she crawls around fast, and her crawling shakes it all over.

Then in the very bright spots she keeps still, and in the very shady spots she just takes hold of the bars and shakes them hard.

And she is all the time trying to climb through. But nobody could climb through that pattern — it strangles so; I think that is why it has so many heads.

They get through, and then the pattern strangles them off and turns them upside down, and makes their eyes white!

If those heads were covered or taken off it would not be half so bad.

I think that woman gets out in the daytime! 195

And I'll tell you why — privately — I've seen her!

I can see her out of every one of my windows!

It is the same woman, I know, for she is always creeping, and most women do not creep by daylight.

I see her in that long shaded lane, creeping up and down. I see her in those dark grape arbors, creeping all around the garden.

200   I see her on that long road under the trees, creeping along, and when a carriage comes she hides under the blackberry vines.

    I don't blame her a bit. It must be very humiliating to be caught creeping by daylight!

    I always lock the door when I creep by daylight. I can't do it at night, for I know John would suspect something at once.

    And John is so queer now, that I don't want to irritate him. I wish he would take another room! Besides, I don't want anybody to get that woman out at night but myself.

    I often wonder if I could see her out of all the windows at once.

205   But, turn as fast as I can, I can only see out of one at one time.

    And though I always see her, she *may* be able to creep faster than I can turn!

    I have watched her sometimes away off in the open country, creeping as fast as a cloud shadow in a high wind.

    If only that top pattern could be gotten off from the under one! I mean to try it, little by little.

    I have found out another funny thing, but I shan't tell it this time! It does not do to trust people too much.

210   There are only two more days to get this paper off, and I believe John is beginning to notice. I don't like the look in his eyes.

    And I heard him ask Jennie a lot of professional questions about me. She had a very good report to give.

    She said I slept a good deal in the daytime.

    John knows I don't sleep very well at night, for all I'm so quiet!

    He asked me all sorts of questions, too, and pretended to be very loving and kind.

215   As if I couldn't see through him!

    Still, I don't wonder he acts so, sleeping under this paper for three months.

    It only interests me, but I feel sure John and Jennie are secretly affected by it.

*   *   *

    Hurrah! This is the last day, but it is enough. John to stay in town over night, and won't be out until this evening.

    Jennie wanted to sleep with me — the sly thing! But I told her I should undoubtedly rest better for a night all alone.

220   That was clever, for really I wasn't alone a bit! As soon as it was moon-light and that poor thing began to crawl and shake the pattern, I got up and ran to help her.

    I pulled and she shook, I shook and she pulled, and before morning we had peeled off yards of that paper.

    A strip about as high as my head and half around the room.

    And then when the sun came and that awful pattern began to laugh at me, I declared I would finish it to-day!

We go away to-morrow, and they are moving all my furniture down again to leave things as they were before.

Jennie looked at the wall in amazement, but I told her merrily that I did it out of pure spite at the vicious thing. 225

She laughed and said she wouldn't mind doing it herself, but I must not get tired.

How she betrayed herself that time!

But I am here, and no person touches this paper but me, — not *alive!*

She tried to get me out of the room — it was too patent! But I said it was so quiet and empty and clean now that I believed I would lie down again and sleep all I could; and not to wake me even for dinner — I would call when I woke.

So now she is gone, and the servants are gone, and the things are gone, and there is nothing left but that great bedstead nailed down, with the canvas mattress we found on it. 230

We shall sleep downstairs to-night, and take the boat home tomorrow.

I quite enjoy the room, now it is bare again.

How those children did tear about here!

This bedstead is fairly gnawed!

But I must get to work. 235

I have locked the door and thrown the key down into the front path.

I don't want to go out, and I don't want to have anybody come in, till John comes.

I want to astonish him.

I've got a rope up here that even Jennie did not find. If that woman does get out, and tries to get away, I can tie her!

But I forgot I could not reach far without anything to stand on! 240

This bed will *not* move!

I tried to lift and push it until I was lame, and then I got so angry I bit off a little piece at one corner — but it hurt my teeth.

Then I peeled off all the paper I could reach standing on the floor. It sticks horribly and the pattern just enjoys it! All those strangled heads and bulbous eyes and waddling fungus growths just shriek with derision!

I am getting angry enough to do something desperate. To jump out of the window would be admirable exercise, but the bars are too strong even to try.

Besides I wouldn't do it. Of course not. I know well enough that a step like that is improper and might be misconstrued. 245

I don't like to *look* out of the windows even — there are so many of those creeping women, and they creep so fast.

I wonder if they come out of that wall-paper as I did?

But I am securely fastened now by my well-hidden rope — you don't get *me* out in the road there!

I suppose I shall have to get back behind the pattern when it comes night, and that is hard!

It is so pleasant to be out in this great room and creep around as I please! 250

I don't want to go outside. I won't, even if Jennie asks me to.

For outside you have to creep on the ground, and everything is green instead of yellow.

But here I can creep smoothly on the floor, and my shoulder just fits in that long smooch around the wall, so I cannot lose my way.

Why there's John at the door!

255   It is no use, young man, you can't open it!

How he does call and pound!

Now he's crying for an axe.

It would be a shame to break down that beautiful door!

"John dear!" said I in the gentlest voice, "the key is down by the front steps, under a plantain leaf!"

260   That silenced him for a few moments.

Then he said — very quietly indeed, "Open the door, my darling!"

"I can't," said I. "The key is down by the front door under a plantain leaf!"

And then I said it again, several times, very gently and slowly, and said it so often that he had to go and see, and he got it of course, and came in. He stopped short by the door.

"What is the matter?" he cried. "For God's sake, what are you doing!"

265   I kept on creeping just the same, but I looked at him over my shoulder.

"I've got out at last," said I, "in spite of you and Jane. And I've pulled off most of the paper, so you can't put me back!"

Now why should that man have fainted? But he did, and right across my path by the wall, so that I had to creep over him every time!

◊   ◊   ◊

JOYCE CAROL OATES   (1938–   )

Where Are You Going, Where Have You Been?   (1966)

For Bob Dylan

Her name was Connie. She was fifteen and she had a quick nervous giggling habit of craning her neck to glance into mirrors, or checking other people's faces to make sure her own was all right. Her mother, who noticed everything and knew everything and who hadn't much reason any longer to look at her own face, always scolded Connie about it. "Stop gawking at yourself, who are you? You think you're so pretty?" she would say. Connie would raise her eye-brows at these famil-iar complaints and look right through her mother, into a shadowy vision of her-self as she was right at that moment: she knew she was pretty and that was everything. Her mother had been pretty once too, if you could believe those old snapshots in the album, but now her looks were gone and that was why she was always after Connie.

"Why don't you keep your room clean like your sister? How've you got your hair fixed — what the hell stinks? Hair spray? You don't see your sister using that junk."

Her sister June was twenty-four and still lived at home. She was a secretary in the high school Connie attended, and if that wasn't bad enough — with her in the same building — she was so plain and chunky and steady that Connie had to hear her praised all the time by her mother and her mother's sisters. June did this, June did that, she saved money and helped clean the house and cooked and Connie couldn't do a thing, her mind was all filled with trashy daydreams. Their father was away at work most of the time and when he came home he wanted supper and he read the newspaper at supper and after supper he went to bed. He didn't bother talking much to them, but around his bent head Connie's mother kept picking at her until Connie wished her mother was dead and she herself was dead and it was all over. "She makes me want to throw up sometimes," she complained to her friends. She had a high, breathless, amused voice which made everything she said sound a little forced, whether it was sincere or not.

There was one good thing: June went places with girl friends of hers, girls who were just as plain and steady as she, and so when Connie wanted to do that her mother had no objections. The father of Connie's best girl friend drove the girls the three miles to town and left them off at a shopping plaza, so that they could walk through the stores or go to a movie, and when he came to pick them up again at eleven he never bothered to ask what they had done.

They must have been familiar sights, walking around that shopping plaza in 5 their shorts and flat ballerina slippers that always scuffed the sidewalk, with charm bracelets jingling on their thin wrists; they would lean together to whisper and laugh secretly if someone passed by who amused or interested them. Connie had long dark blond hair that drew anyone's eye to it, and she wore part of it pulled up on her head and puffed out and the rest of it she let fall down her back. She wore a pull-over jersey blouse that looked one way when she was at home and another way when she was away from home. Everything about her had two sides to it, one for home and one for anywhere that was not home: her walk that could be childlike and bobbing, or languid enough to make anyone think she was hearing music in her head, her mouth which was pale and smirking most of the time, but bright and pink on these evenings out, her laugh which was cynical and drawling at home — "Ha, ha, very funny" — but high-pitched and nervous anywhere else, like the jingling of the charms on her bracelet.

Sometimes they did go shopping or to a movie, but sometimes they went across the highway, ducking fast across the busy road, to a drive-in restaurant where older kids hung out. The restaurant was shaped like a big bottle, though squatter than a real bottle, and on its cap was a revolving figure of a grinning boy who held a hamburger aloft. One night in mid-summer they ran across, breathless with daring, and right away someone leaned out a car window and invited them over, but it was just a boy from high school they didn't like. It made them feel good to be able to ignore him. They went up through the maze of parked and cruising cars to the bright-lit, fly-infested restaurant, their faces pleased and expectant as if they were entering a sacred building that loomed out of the night to give them what haven and what blessing they yearned for. They sat at the counter and crossed their legs at the ankles, their thin shoulders rigid with excitement, and listened to the music that made everything so good: the music was always in the background like music at a church service, it was something to depend upon.

A boy named Eddie came in to talk with them. He sat backwards on his stool, turning himself jerkily around in semi-circles and then stopping and turning again, and after a while he asked Connie if she would like something to eat. She said she did and so she tapped her friend's arm on her way out — her friend pulled her face up into a brave droll look — and Connie said she would meet her at eleven, across the way. "I just hate to leave her like that," Connie said earnestly, but the boy said that she wouldn't be alone for long. So they went out to his car and on the way Connie couldn't help but let her eyes wander over the windshields and faces all around her, her face gleaming with a joy that had nothing to do with Eddie or even this place; it might have been the music. She drew her shoulders up and sucked in her breath with the pure pleasure of being alive, and just at that moment she happened to glance at a face just a few feet from hers. It was a boy with shaggy black hair, in a convertible jalopy painted gold. He stared at her and then his lips widened into a grin. Connie slit her eyes at him and turned away, but she couldn't help glancing back and there he was still watching her. He wagged a finger and laughed and said, "Gonna get you, baby," and Connie turned away again without Eddie noticing anything.

She spent three hours with him, at the restaurant where they ate hamburgers and drank Cokes in wax cups that were always sweating, and then down an alley a mile or so away, and when he left her off at five to eleven only the movie house was still open at the plaza. Her girl friend was there, talking with a boy. When Connie came up the two girls smiled at each other and Connie said, "How was the movie?" and the girl said, "*You* should know." They rode off with the girl's father, sleepy and pleased, and Connie couldn't help but look at the darkened shopping plaza with its big empty parking lot and its signs that were faded and ghostly now, and over at the drive-in restaurant where cars were still circling tirelessly. She couldn't hear the music at this distance.

Next morning June asked her how the movie was and Connie said, "So-so."

10   She and that girl and occasionally another girl went out several times a week that way, and the rest of the time Connie spent around the house — it was summer vacation — getting in her mother's way and thinking, dreaming, about the boys she met. But all the boys fell back and dissolved into a single face that was not even a face, but an idea, a feeling, mixed up with the urgent insistent pounding of the music and the humid night air of July. Connie's mother kept dragging her back to the daylight by finding things for her to do or saying, suddenly, "What's this about the Pettinger girl?"

And Connie would say nervously, "Oh, her. That dope." She always drew thick clear lines between herself and such girls, and her mother was simple and kindly enough to believe her. Her mother was so simple, Connie thought, that it was maybe cruel to fool her so much. Her mother went scuffling around the house in old bedroom slippers and complained over the telephone to one sister about the other, then the other called up and the two of them complained about the third one. If June's name was mentioned her mother's tone was approving, and if Connie's name was mentioned it was disapproving. This did not really mean she disliked Connie and actually Connie thought that her mother preferred her to June because she was prettier, but the two of them kept up a pretense of exasperation, a sense that they were tugging and struggling over something of little value to either of them. Sometimes, over coffee, they were almost friends, but something would come up — some vexation that was like a fly buzzing suddenly around their heads — and their faces went hard with contempt.

One Sunday Connie got up at eleven — none of them bothered with church — and washed her hair so that it could dry all day long, in the sun. Her parents and sister were going to a barbecue at an aunt's house and Connie said no, she wasn't interested, rolling her eyes to let her mother know just what she thought of it. "Stay home alone then," her mother said sharply. Connie sat out back in a lawn chair and watched them drive away, her father quiet and bald, hunched around so that he could back the car out, her mother with a look that was still angry and not at all softened through the windshield, and in the back seat poor old June all dressed up as if she didn't know what a barbecue was, with all the running yelling kids and the flies. Connie sat with her eyes closed in the sun, dreaming and dazed with the warmth about her as if this were a kind of love, the caresses of love, and her mind slipped over onto thoughts of the boy she had been with the night before and how nice he had been, how sweet it always was, not the way someone like June would suppose but sweet, gentle, the way it was in movies and promised in songs; and when she opened her eyes she hardly knew where she was, the back yard ran off into weeds and a fence-line of trees and behind it the sky was perfectly blue and still. The asbestos "ranch house" that was now three years old startled her — it looked small. She shook her head as if to get awake.

It was too hot. She went inside the house and turned on the radio to drown out the quiet. She sat on the edge of her bed, barefoot, and listened for an hour and a half to a program called XYZ Sunday Jamboree, record after record of hard, fast, shrieking songs she sang along with, interspersed by exclamations from "Bobby King": "An' look here you girls at Napoleon's — Son and Charley want you to pay real close attention to this song coming up!"

And Connie paid close attention herself, bathed in a glow of slow-pulsed joy that seemed to rise mysteriously out of the music itself and lay languidly about the airless little room, breathed in and breathed out with each gentle rise and fall of her chest.

After a while she heard a car coming up the drive. She sat up at once, startled, because it couldn't be her father so soon. The gravel kept crunching all the way in from the road — the driveway was long — and Connie ran to the window. It was a car she didn't know. It was an open jalopy, painted a bright gold that caught the sunlight opaquely. Her heart began to pound and her fingers snatched at her hair, checking it, and she whispered "Christ. Christ," wondering how bad she looked. The car came to a stop at the side door and the horn sounded four short taps as if this were a signal Connie knew.

She went into the kitchen and approached the door slowly, then hung out the screen door, her bare toes curling down off the step. There were two boys in the car and now she recognized the driver: he had shaggy, shabby black hair that looked crazy as a wig and he was grinning at her.

"I ain't late, am I?" he said.

"Who the hell do you think you are?" Connie said.

"Toldja I'd be out, didn't I?"

20   "I don't even know who you are."

She spoke sullenly, careful to show no interest or pleasure, and he spoke in a fast bright monotone. Connie looked past him to the other boy, taking her time. He had fair brown hair, with a lock that fell onto his forehead. His sideburns gave him a fierce, embarrassed look, but so far he hadn't even bothered to glance at her. Both boys wore sunglasses. The driver's glasses were metallic and mirrored everything in miniature.

"You wanta come for a ride?" he said.

Connie smirked and let her hair fall loose over one shoulder.

"Don'tcha like my car? New paint job," he said. "Hey."

25   "What?"

"You're cute."

She pretended to fidget, chasing flies away from the door.

"Don'tcha believe me, or what?" he said.

"Look, I don't even know who you are," Connie said in disgust.

30   "Hey, Ellie's got a radio, see. Mine's broke down." He lifted his friend's arm and showed her the little transistor the boy was holding, and now Connie began to hear the music. It was the same program that was playing inside the house.

"Bobby King?" she said.

"I listen to him all the time. I think he's great."

"He's kind of great," Connie said reluctantly.

"Listen, that guy's *great*. He knows where the action is."

35   Connie blushed a little, because the glasses made it impossible for her to see just what this boy was looking at. She couldn't decide if she liked him or if he was just a jerk, and so she dawdled in the doorway and wouldn't come down or go back inside. She said, "What's all that stuff painted on your car?"

"Can'tcha read it?" He opened the door very carefully, as if he was afraid it might fall off. He slid out just as carefully, planting his feet firmly on the ground, the tiny metallic world in his glasses slowing down like gelatine hardening and in the midst of it Connie's bright green blouse. "This here is my name, to begin with," he said. ARNOLD FRIEND was written in tarlike black letters on the side, with a drawing of a round grinning face that reminded Connie of a pumpkin, except it wore sunglasses. "I wanta introduce myself, I'm Arnold Friend and that's my real name and I'm gonna be your friend, honey, and inside the car's Ellie Oscar, he's kinda shy." Ellie brought his transistor radio up to his shoulder and balanced it there. "Now these numbers are a secret code, honey," Arnold Friend explained. He read off the numbers 33, 19, 17 and raised his eyebrows at her to see what she thought of that, but she didn't think much of it. The left rear fender had been smashed and around it was written, on the gleaming gold background: DONE BY CRAZY WOMAN DRIVER. Connie had to laugh at that. Arnold Friend was pleased at her laughter and looked up at her. "Around the other side's a lot more — you wanta come and see them?"

"No."

"Why not?"

"Why should I?"

"Don'tcha wanta see what's on the car? Don'tcha wanta go for a ride?"   40

"I don't know."

"Why not?"

"I got things to do."

"Like what?"

"Things."   45

He laughed as if she had said something funny. He slapped his thighs. He was standing in a strange way, leaning back against the car as if he were balancing himself. He wasn't tall, only an inch or so taller than she would be if she came down to him. Connie liked the way he was dressed, which was the way all of them dressed: tight faded jeans stuffed into black, scuffed boots, a belt that pulled his waist in and showed how lean he was, and a white pull-over shirt that was a little soiled and showed the hard small muscles of his arms and shoulders. He looked as if he probably did hard work, lifting and carrying things. Even his neck looked muscular. And his face was a familiar face, somehow: the jaw and chin and cheeks slightly darkened, because he hadn't shaved for a day or two, and the nose long and hawk-like, sniffing as if she were a treat he was going to gobble up and it was all a joke.

"Connie, you ain't telling the truth. This is your day set aside for a ride with me and you know it," he said, still laughing. The way he straightened and recovered from his fit of laughing showed that it had been all fake.

"How do you know what my name is?" she said suspiciously.

"It's Connie."

"Maybe and maybe not."   50

"I know my Connie," he said, wagging his finger. Now she remembered him even better, back at the restaurant, and her cheeks warmed at the thought of how she sucked in her breath just at the moment she passed him — how she must have looked to him. And he had remembered her. "Ellie and I come out here especially for you," he said. "Ellie can sit in back. How about it?"

"Where?"

"Where what?"

"Where're we going?"

55   He looked at her. He took off the sunglasses and she saw how pale the skin around his eyes was, like holes that were not in shadow but instead in light. His eyes were chips of broken glass that catch the light in an amiable way. He smiled. It was as if the idea of going for a ride somewhere, to some place, was a new idea to him.

"Just for a ride, Connie sweetheart."

"I never said my name was Connie," she said.

"But I know what it is. I know your name and all about you, lots of things," Arnold Friend said. He had not moved yet but stood still leaning back against the side of his jalopy. "I took a special interest in you, such a pretty girl, and found out all about you like I know your parents and sister are gone somewheres and I know where and how long they're going to be gone, and I know who you were with last night, and your best girl friend's name is Betty. Right?"

He spoke in a simple lilting voice, exactly as if he were reciting the words to a song. His smile assured her that everything was fine. In the car Ellie turned up the volume on his radio and did not bother to look around at them.

60   "Ellie can sit in the back seat," Arnold Friend said. He indicated his friend with a casual jerk of his chin, as if Ellie did not count and she should not bother with him.

"How'd you find out all that stuff?" Connie said.

"Listen: Betty Schultz and Tony Fitch and Jimmy Pettinger and Nancy Pettinger," he said, in a chant. "Raymond Stanley and Bob Hutter —"

"Do you know all those kids?"

"I know everybody."

65   "Look, you're kidding. You're not from around here."

"Sure."

"But — how come we never saw you before?"

"Sure you saw me before," he said. He looked down at his boots, as if he were a little offended. "You just don't remember."

"I guess I'd remember you," Connie said.

70   "Yeah?" He looked up at this, beaming. He was pleased. He began to mark time with the music from Ellie's radio, tapping his fists lightly together. Connie looked away from his smile to the car, which was painted so bright it almost hurt her eyes to look at it. She looked at that name, ARNOLD FRIEND. And up at the front fender was an expression that was familiar — MAN THE FLYING SAUCERS. It was an expression kids had used the year before, but didn't use this year. She looked at it for a while as if the words meant something to her that she did not yet know.

"What're you thinking about? Huh?" Arnold Friend demanded. "Not worried about your hair blowing around in the car, are you?"

"No."

"Think I maybe can't drive good?"

"How do I know?"

"You're a hard girl to handle. How come?" he said. "Don't you know I'm your 75 friend? Didn't you see me put my sign in the air when you walked by?"

"What sign?"

"My sign." And he drew an X in the air, leaning out toward her. They were maybe ten feet apart. After his hand fell back to his side the X was still in the air, almost visible. Connie let the screen door close and stood perfectly still inside it, listening to the music from her radio and the boy's blend together. She stared at Arnold Friend. He stood there so stiffly relaxed, pretending to be relaxed, with one hand idly on the door handle as if he were keeping himself up that way and had no intention of ever moving again. She recognized most things about him, the tight jeans that showed his thighs and buttocks and the greasy leather boots and the tight shirt, and even that slippery friendly smile of his, that sleepy dreamy smile that all the boys used to get across ideas they didn't want to put into words. She recognized all this and also the singsong way he talked, slightly mocking, kidding, but serious and a little melancholy, and she recognized the way he tapped one fist against the other in homage to the perpetual music behind him. But all these things did not come together.

She said suddenly, "Hey, how old are you?"

His smile faded. She could see then that he wasn't a kid, he was much older — thirty, maybe more. At this knowledge her heart began to pound faster.

"That's a crazy thing to ask. Can'tcha see I'm your own age?" 80

"Like hell you are."

"Or maybe a coupla years older, I'm eighteen."

"Eighteen?" she said doubtfully.

He grinned to reassure her and lines appeared at the corners of his mouth. His teeth were big and white. He grinned so broadly his eyes became slits and she saw how thick the lashes were, thick and black as if painted with a black tarlike material. Then he seemed to become embarrassed, abruptly, and looked over his shoulder at Ellie. "*Him*, he's crazy," he said. "Ain't he a riot, he's a nut, a real character." Ellie was still listening to the music. His sunglasses told nothing about what he was thinking. He wore a bright orange shirt unbuttoned halfway to show his chest, which was a pale, bluish chest and not muscular like Arnold Friend's. His shirt collar was turned up all around and the very tips of the collar pointed out past his chin as if they were protecting him. He was pressing the transistor radio up against his ear and sat there in a kind of daze, right in the sun.

"He's kinda strange," Connie said. 85

"Hey, she says you're kinda strange! Kinda strange!" Arnold Friend cried. He pounded on the car to get Ellie's attention. Ellie turned for the first time and Connie saw with shock that he wasn't a kid either — he had a fair, hairless face, cheeks reddened slightly as if the veins grew too close to the surface of his skin, the face of a forty-year-old baby. Connie felt a wave of dizziness rise in her at this sight and she stared at him as if waiting for something to change the shock of the moment, make it all right again. Ellie's lips kept shaping words, mumbling along with the words blasting in his ear.

"Maybe you two better go away," Connie said faintly.

"What? How come?" Arnold Friend cried. "We come out here to take you for a ride. It's Sunday." He had the voice of the man on the radio now. It was the same voice, Connie thought. "Don'tcha know it's Sunday all day and honey, no matter who you were with last night today you're with Arnold Friend and don't you forget it! — Maybe you better step out here," he said, and this last was in a different voice. It was a little flatter, as if the heat was finally getting to him.

90 "No. I got things to do."

"Hey."

"You two better leave."

"We ain't leaving until you come with us."

"Like hell I am —"

95 "Connie, don't fool around with me. I mean, I mean, don't fool *around*," he said, shaking his head. He laughed incredulously. He placed his sunglasses on top of his head, carefully, as if he were indeed wearing a wig, and brought the stems down behind his ears. Connie stared at him, another wave of dizziness and fear rising in her so that for a moment he wasn't even in focus but was just a blur, standing there against his gold car, and she had the idea that he had driven up the driveway all right but had come from nowhere before that and belonged nowhere and that everything about him and even about the music that was so familiar to her was only half real.

"If my father comes and sees you —"

"He ain't coming. He's at a barbecue."

"How do you know that?"

"Aunt Tillie's. Right now they're — uh — they're drinking. Sitting around," he said vaguely, squinting as if he were staring all the way to town and over to Aunt Tillie's backyard. Then the vision seemed to get clear and he nodded energetically. "Yeah. Sitting around. There's your sister in a blue dress, huh? And high heels, the poor sad bitch — nothing like you sweetheart! And your mother's helping some fat woman with the corn, they're cleaning the corn — husking the corn —"

100 "What fat woman?" Connie cried.

"How do I know what fat woman. I don't know every goddam fat woman in the world!" Arnold Friend laughed.

"Oh, that's Mrs. Hornby. . . . Who invited her?" Connie said. She felt a little light-headed. Her breath was coming quickly.

"She's too fat. I don't like them fat. I like them the way you are, honey," he said, smiling sleepily at her. They stared at each other for a while, through the screen door. He said softly, "Now what you're going to do is this: you're going to come out that door. You're going to sit up front with me and Ellie's going to sit in the back, the hell with Ellie, right? This isn't Ellie's date. You're my date. I'm your lover, honey."

"What? You're crazy —"

"Yes, I'm your lover. You don't know what that is but you will," he said. "I 105
know that too. I know all about you. But look: it's real nice and you couldn't ask
for nobody better than me, or more polite. I always keep my word. I'll tell you
how it is, I'm always nice at first, the first time. I'll hold you so tight you won't
think you have to try to get away or pretend anything because you'll know you
can't. And I'll come inside you where it's all secret and you'll give in to me and
you'll love me —"

"Shut up! You're crazy!" Connie said. She backed away from the door. She put
her hands against her ears as if she'd heard something terrible, something not
meant for her. "People don't talk like that, you're crazy," she muttered. Her heart
was almost too big now for her chest and its pumping made sweat break out all
over her. She looked out to see Arnold Friend pause and then take a step toward
the porch lurching. He almost fell. But, like a clever drunken man, he managed
to catch his balance. He wobbled in his high boots and grabbed hold of one of the
porch posts.

"Honey?" he said. "You still listening?"

"Get the hell out of here!"

"Be nice, honey. Listen."

"I'm going to call the police —" 110

He wobbled again and out of the side of his mouth came a fast spat curse, an
aside not meant for her to hear. But even this "Christ!" sounded forced. Then he
began to smile again. She watched this smile come, awkward as if he were smiling from inside a mask. His whole face was a mask, she thought wildly, tanned
down onto his throat but then running out as if he had plastered makeup on his
face but had forgotten about his throat.

"Honey —? Listen, here's how it is. I always tell the truth and I promise you
this: I ain't coming in that house after you."

"You better not! I'm going to call the police if you — if you don't —"

"Honey," he said, talking right through her voice, "honey, I'm not coming in
there but you are coming out here. You know why?"

She was panting. The kitchen looked like a place she had never seen before, 115
some room she had run inside but which wasn't good enough, wasn't going to help
her. The kitchen window had never had a curtain, after three years, and there
were dishes in the sink for her to do — probably — and if you ran your hand
across the table you'd probably feel something sticky there.

"You listening, honey? Hey?"

"— going to call the police —"

"Soon as you touch the phone I don't need to keep my promise and can come
inside. You won't want that."

She rushed forward and tried to lock the door. Her fingers were shaking. "But
why lock it," Arnold Friend said gently, talking right into her face. "It's just a
screen door. It's just nothing." One of his boots was at a strange angle, as if his foot
wasn't in it. It pointed out to the left, bent at the ankle. "I mean, anybody can

break through a screen door and glass and wood and iron or anything else if he needs to, anybody at all and specially Arnold Friend. If the place got lit up with a fire honey you'd come running out into my arms, right into my arms and safe at home —like you knew I was your lover and'd stopped fooling around. I don't mind a nice shy girl but I don't like no fooling around." Part of those words were spoken with a slight rhythmic lilt, and Connie somehow recognized them — the echo of a song from last year, about a girl rushing into her boy friend's arms and coming home again —

120   Connie stood barefoot on the linoleum floor, staring at him. "What do you want?" she whispered.

"I want you," he said.

"What?"

"Seen you that night and thought, that's the one, yes sir. I never needed to look any more."

"But my father's coming back. He's coming to get me. I had to wash my hair first —" She spoke in a dry, rapid voice, hardly raising it for him to hear.

125   "No, your daddy is not coming and yes, you had to wash your hair and you washed it for me. It's nice and shining and all for me, I thank you, sweetheart," he said, with a mock bow, but again he almost lost his balance. He had to bend and adjust his boots. Evidently his feet did not go all the way down; the boots must have been stuffed with something so that he would seem taller. Connie stared out at him and behind him Ellie in the car, who seemed to be looking off toward Connie's right, into nothing. This Ellie said, pulling the words out of the air one after another as if he were just discovering them, "You want me to pull out the phone?"

"Shut your mouth and keep it shut," Arnold Friend said, his face red from bending over or maybe from embarrassment because Connie had seen his boots. "This ain't none of your business."

"What — what are you doing? What do you want?" Connie said. "If I call the police they'll get you, they'll arrest you —"

"Promise was not to come in unless you touch that phone, and I'll keep that promise," he said. He resumed his erect position and tried to force his shoulders back. He sounded like a hero in a movie, declaring something important. He spoke too loudly and it was as if he were speaking to someone behind Connie. "I ain't made plans for coming in that house where I don't belong but just for you to come out to me, the way you should. Don't you know who I am?"

"You're crazy," she whispered. She backed away from the door but did not want to go into another part of the house, as if this would give him permission to come through the door. "What do you. . . . You're crazy, you . . ."

130   "Huh? What're you saying, honey?"

Her eyes darted everywhere in the kitchen. She could not remember what it was, this room.

"This is how it is, honey: you come out and we'll drive away, have a nice ride. But if you don't come out we're gonna wait till your people come home and then they're all going to get it."

"You want that telephone pulled out?" Ellie said. He held the radio away from his ear and grimaced, as if without the radio the air was too much for him.

"I toldja shut up, Ellie," Arnold Friend said, "you're deaf, get a hearing aid, right? Fix yourself up. This little girl's no trouble and's gonna be nice to me, so Ellie keep to yourself, this ain't your date — right? Don't hem in on me. Don't hog. Don't crush. Don't bird dog. Don't trail me," he said in a rapid meaningless voice, as if he were running through all the expressions he'd learned but was no longer sure which one of them was in style, then rushing on to new ones, making them up with his eyes closed, "Don't crawl under my fence, don't squeeze in my chipmunk hole, don't sniff my glue, suck my popsicle, keep your own greasy fingers on yourself!" He shaded his eyes and peered in at Connie, who was backed against the kitchen table. "Don't mind him honey he's just a creep. He's a dope. Right? I'm the boy for you and like I said you come out here nice like a lady and give me your hand, and nobody else gets hurt, I mean, your nice old bald-headed daddy and your mummy and your sister in her high heels. Because listen: why bring them in this?"

"Leave me alone," Connie whispered.   135

"Hey, you know that old woman down the road, the one with the chickens and stuff — you know her?"

"She's dead!"

"Dead? What? You know her?" Arnold Friend said.

"She's dead —"

"Don't you like her?"

"She's dead — she's — she isn't here any more —"   140

"But don't you like her, I mean, you got something against her? Some grudge or something?" Then his voice dipped as if he were conscious of a rudeness. He touched the sunglasses perched on top of his head as if to make sure they were still there. "Now you be a good girl."

"What are you going to do?"

"Just two things, or maybe three," Arnold Friend said. "But I promise it won't last long and you'll like me that way you get to like people you're close to. You will. It's all over for you here, so come on out. You don't want your people in any trouble, do you?"

She turned and bumped against a chair or something, hurting her leg, but she ran into the back room and picked up the telephone. Something roared in her ear, a tiny roaring, and she was so sick with fear that she could do nothing but listen to it — the telephone was clammy and very heavy and her fingers groped down to the dial but were too weak to touch it. She began to scream into the phone, into the roaring. She cried out, she cried for her mother, she felt her breath start jerking back and forth in her lungs as if it were something Arnold Friend were stabbing her with again and again with no tenderness. A noisy sorrowful wailing rose all about her and she was locked inside it the way she was locked inside the house.

After a while she could hear again. She was sitting on the floor with her wet 145 back against the wall.

Arnold Friend was saying from the door, "That's a good girl. Put the phone back."

She kicked the phone away from her.

"No, honey. Pick it up. Put it back right."

She picked it up and put it back. The dial tone stopped.

150   "That's a good girl. Now you come outside."

She was hollow with what had been fear, but what was now just an emptiness. All that screaming had blasted it out of her. She sat, one leg cramped under her, and deep inside her brain was something like a pinpoint of light that kept going and would not let her relax. She thought, I'm not going to see my mother again. She thought, I'm not going to sleep in my bed again. Her bright green blouse was all wet.

Arnold Friend said, in a gentle-loud voice that was like a stage voice, "The place where you came from ain't there any more, and where you had in mind to go is cancelled out. This place you are now — inside your daddy's house — is nothing but a cardboard box I can knock down any time. You know that and always did know it. You hear me?"

She thought, I have got to think. I have to know what to do.

"We'll go out to a nice field, out in the country here where it smells so nice and it's sunny," Arnold Friend said. "I'll have my arms around you so you won't need to try to get away and I'll show you what love is like, what it does. The hell with this house! It looks solid all right," he said. He ran a fingernail down the screen and the noise did not make Connie shiver, as it would have the day before. "Now put your hand on your heart, honey. Feel that? That feels solid too but we know better, be nice to me, be sweet like you can because what else is there for a girl like you but to be sweet and pretty and give in?— and get away before her people come back?"

155   She felt her pounding heart. Her hand seemed to enclose it. She thought for the first time in her life that it was nothing that was hers, that belonged to her, but just a pounding, living thing inside this body that wasn't really hers either.

"You don't want them to get hurt," Arnold Friend went on. "Now get up, honey. Get up all by yourself."

She stood.

"Now turn this way. That's right. Come over here to me — Ellie, put that away, didn't I tell you? You dope. You miserable creepy dope," Arnold Friend said. His words were not angry but only part of an incantation. The incantation was kindly. "Now come out through the kitchen to me honey and let's see a smile, try it, you're a brave sweet little girl and now they're eating corn and hotdogs cooked to bursting over an outdoor fire, and they don't know one thing about you and never did and honey you're better than them because not a one of them would have done this for you."

Connie felt the linoleum under her feet; it was cool. She brushed her hair back out of her eyes. Arnold Friend let go of the post tentatively and opened his arms for her, his elbows pointing in toward each other and his wrists limp, to show that this was an embarrassed embrace and a little mocking, he didn't want to make her self-conscious.

She put out her hand against the screen. She watched herself push the door 160 slowly open as if she were safe back somewhere in the other doorway, watching this body and this head of long hair moving out into the sunlight where Arnold Friend waited.

"My sweet little blue-eyed girl," he said, in a half-sung sigh that had nothing to do with her brown eyes but was taken up just the same by the vast sunlit reaches of the land behind him and on all sides of him, so much land that Connie had never seen before and did not recognize except to know that she was going to it.

❖ ❖ ❖

FLANNERY O'CONNOR   (1925–1964)

Everything That Rises Must Converge (1965)

Her doctor had told Julian's mother that she must lose twenty pounds on account of her blood pressure, so on Wednesday nights Julian had to take her downtown on the bus for a reducing class at the Y. The reducing class was designed for working girls over fifty, who weighed from 165 to 200 pounds. His mother was one of the slimmer ones, but she said ladies did not tell their age or weight. She would not ride the buses by herself at night since they had been integrated, and because the reducing class was one of her few pleasures, necessary for her health, and *free*, she said Julian could at least put himself out to take her, considering all she did for him. Julian did not like to consider all she did for him, but every Wednesday night he braced himself and took her.

She was almost ready to go, standing before the hall mirror, putting on her hat, while he, his hands behind him, appeared pinned to the door frame, waiting like Saint Sebastian° for the arrows to begin piercing him. The hat was new and had cost her seven dollars and a half. She kept saying, "Maybe I shouldn't have paid that for it. No, I shouldn't have. I'll take it off and return it tomorrow. I shouldn't have bought it."

Saint Sebastian: A Roman Catholic Saint. Accused of being a Christian, Sebastian was tied to a tree, shot with arrows, and left for dead. He survived and recovered, returning to preach. The emperor then had him beaten to death.

Julian raised his eyes to heaven. "Yes, you should have bought it," he said "Put it on and let's go." It was a hideous hat. A purple velvet flap came down on one side of it and stood up on the other; the rest of it was green and looked like a cushion with the stuffing out. He decided it was less comical than jaunty and pathetic. Everything that gave her pleasure was small and depressed him.

She lifted the hat one more time and set it down slowly on top of her head. Two wings of gray hair protruded on either side of her florid face, but her eyes, sky-blue, were as innocent and untouched by experience as they must have been when she was ten. Were it not that she was a widow who had struggled fiercely to feed and clothe and put him through school and who was supporting him still "until he got on his feet," she might have been a little girl that he had to take to town.

5   "It's all right, it's all right," he said. "Let's go." He opened the door himself and started down the walk to get her going. The sky was a dying violet and the houses stood out darkly against it, bulbous liver-colored monstrosities of a uniform ugliness though no two were alike. Since this had been a fashionable neighborhood forty years ago, his mother persisted in thinking they did well to have an apartment in it. Each house had a narrow collar of dirt around it in which sat, usually, a grubby child. Julian walked with his hands in his pockets, his head down and thrust forward and his eyes glazed with the determination to make himself completely numb during the time he would be sacrificed to her pleasure.

The door closed and he turned to find the dumpy figure, surmounted by the atrocious hat, coming toward him. "Well," she said, "you only live once and paying a little more for it, I at least won't meet myself coming and going."

"Some day I'll start making money," Julian said gloomily — he knew he never would — "and you can have one of those jokes whenever you take the fit." But first they would move. He visualized a place where the nearest neighbors would be three miles away on either side.

"I think you're doing fine," she said, drawing on her gloves. "You've only been out of school a year. Rome wasn't built in a day."

She was one of the few members of the Y reducing class who arrived in hat and gloves and who had a son who had been to college. "It takes time," she said, "and the world is in such a mess. This hat looked better on me than any of the others, though when she brought it out I said, 'Take that thing back. I wouldn't have it on my head,' and she said, 'Now wait till you see it on,' and when she put it on me, I said, 'We-ull,' and she said, 'If you ask me, that hat does something for you and you do something for the hat, and besides,' she said, 'with that hat, you won't meet yourself coming and going.'"

10   Julian thought he could have stood his lot better if she had been selfish, if she had been an old hag who drank and screamed at him. He walked along, saturated in depression, as if in the midst of his martyrdom he had lost his faith. Catching sight of his long, hopeless, irritated face, she stopped suddenly with a grief-stricken look, and pulled back on his arm. "Wait on me," she said. "I'm going back

to the house and take this thing off and tomorrow I'm going to return it. I was out of my head. I can pay the gas bill with that seven-fifty."

He caught her arm in a vicious grip. "You are not going to take it back," he said. "I like it."

"Well," she said, "I don't think I ought . . ."

"Shut up and enjoy it," he muttered, more depressed than ever.

"With the world in the mess it's in," she said, "it's a wonder we can enjoy anything. I tell you, the bottom rail is on the top."

Julian sighed.   15

"Of course," she said, "if you know who are you, you can go anywhere." She said this every time he took her to the reducing class. "Most of them in it are not our kind of people," she said, "but I can be gracious to anybody. I know who I am."

"They don't give a damn for your graciousness," Julian said savagely. "Knowing who you are is good for one generation only. You haven't the foggiest idea where you stand now or who you are."

She stopped and allowed her eyes to flash at him. "I most certainly do know who I am," she said, "and if you don't know who you are, I'm ashamed of you."

"Oh hell," Julian said.

"Your great-grandfather was a former governor of this state," she said. "Your   20 grandfather was a prosperous land-owner. Your grandmother was a Godhigh."

"Will you look around you," he said tensely, "and see where you are now?" and he swept his arm jerkily out to indicate the neighborhood, which the growing darkness at least made less dingy.

"You remain what you are," she said. "Your great-grandfather had a plantation and two hundred slaves."

"There are no more slaves," he said irritably.

"They were better off when they were," she said. He groaned to see that she was off on that topic. She rolled onto it every few days like a train on an open track. He knew every stop, every junction, every swamp along the way, and knew the exact point at which her conclusion would roll majestically into the station: "It's ridiculous. It's simply not realistic. They should rise, yes, but on their own side of the fence."

"Let's skip it," Julian said.   25

"The ones I feel sorry for," she said, "are the ones that are half white. They're tragic."

"Will you skip it?"

"Suppose we were half white. We would certainly have mixed feelings."

"I have mixed feelings now," he groaned.

"Well let's talk about something pleasant," she said. "I remember going to   30 Grandpa's when I was a little girl. Then the house had double stairways that went up to what was really the second floor — all the cooking was done on the first. I used to like to stay down in the kitchen on account of the way the walls smelled. I would sit with my nose pressed against the plaster and take deep breaths. Actually the place belonged to the Godhighs but your grandfather Chestny paid the mortgage and saved it for them. They were in reduced circum- stances," she said, "but reduced or not, they never forgot who they were."

"Doubtless that decayed mansion reminded them," Julian muttered. He never spoke of it without contempt or thought of it without longing. He had seen it once when he was a child before it had been sold. The double stairways had rot- ted and been torn down. Negroes were living in it. But it remained in his mind as his mother had known it. It appeared in his dreams regularly. He would stand on the wide porch, listening to the rustle of oak leaves, then wander through the high-ceilinged hall into the parlor that opened onto it and gaze at the worn rugs and faded draperies. It occurred to him that it was he, not she, who could have appreciated it. He preferred its threadbare elegance to anything he could name and it was because of it that all the neighborhoods they had lived in had been a torment to him — whereas she had hardly known the difference. She called her insensitivity "being adjustable."

"And I remember the old darky who was my nurse, Caroline. There was no better person in the world. I've always had a great respect for my colored friends," she said. "I'd do anything in the world for them and they'd . . ."

"Will you for God's sake get off that subject?" Julian said. When he got on a bus by himself, he made it a point to sit down beside a Negro, in reparation as it were for his mother's sins.

"You're mighty touchy tonight," she said. "Do you feel all right?"

35   "Yes I feel all right," he said. "Now lay off."

She pursed her lips. "Well, you certainly are in a vile humor," she observed. "I just won't speak to you at all."

They had reached the bus stop. There was no bus in sight and Julian, his hands still jammed in his pockets and his head thrust forward, scowled down the empty street. The frustration of having to wait on the bus as well as ride on it began to creep up his neck like a hot hand. The presence of his mother was borne in upon him as she gave a pained sigh. He looked at her bleakly. She was holding herself very erect under the preposterous hat, wearing it like a banner of her imaginary dignity. There was in him an evil urge to break her spirit. He suddenly unloosened his tie and pulled it off and put it in his pocket.

She stiffened. "Why must you look like *that* when you take me to town?" she said. "Why must you deliberately embarrass me?"

"If you'll never learn where you are," he said, "you can at least learn where I am."

40   "You look like a — thug," she said.

"Then I must be one," he murmured.

"I'll just go home," she said. "I will not bother you. If you can't do a little thing like that for me . . ."

Rolling his eyes upward, he put his tie back on. "Restored to my class," he mut- tered. He thrust his face toward her and hissed, "True culture is in the mind, the *mind*," he said, and tapped his head, "the mind."

"It's in the heart," she said, "and in how you do things and how you do things is because of who you *are.*"

"Nobody in the damn bus cares who you are."

"I care who I am," she said icily.

The lighted bus appeared on top of the next hill and as it approached, they moved out into the street to meet it. He put his hand under her elbow and hoisted her up on the creaking step. She entered with a little smile, as if she were going into a drawing room where everyone had been waiting for her. While he put in the tokens, she sat down on one of the broad front seats for three which faced the aisle. A thin woman with protruding teeth and long yellow hair was sitting on the end of it. His mother moved up beside her and left room for Julian beside herself. He sat down and looked at the floor across the aisle where a pair of thin feet in red and white canvas sandals were planted.

His mother immediately began a general conversation meant to attract anyone who felt like talking. "Can it get any hotter?" she said and removed from her purse a folding fan, black with a Japanese scene on it, which she began to flutter before her.

"I reckon it might could," the woman with the protruding teeth said, "but I know for a fact my apartment couldn't get no hotter."

"It must get the afternoon sun," his mother said. She sat forward and looked up and down the bus. It was half filled. Everybody was white. "I see we have the bus to ourselves," she said Julian cringed.

"For a change," said the woman across the aisle, the owner of the red and white canvas sandals. "I come on one the other day and they were thick as fleas — up front and all through."

"The world is in a mess everywhere," his mother said. "I don't know how we've let it get in this fix."

"What gets my goat is all those boys from good families stealing automobile tires," the woman with the protruding teeth said. "I told my boy, I said you may not be rich but you been raised right and if I ever catch you in any such mess, they can send you on to the reformatory. Be exactly where you belong."

"Training tells," his mother said. "Is your boy in high school?"

"Ninth grade," the woman said.

"My son just finished college last year. He wants to write but he's selling typewriters until he gets started," his mother said.

The woman leaned forward and peered at Julian. He threw her such a malevolent look that she subsided against the seat. On the floor across the aisle there was an abandoned newspaper. He got up and got it and opened it out in front of him. His mother discreetly continued the conversation in a lower tone but the woman across the aisle said in a loud voice, "Well that's nice. Selling typewriters is close to writing. He can go right from one to the other."

"I tell him," his mother said, "that Rome wasn't built in a day."

Behind the newspaper Julian was withdrawing into the inner compartment of his mind where he spent most of his time. This was a kind of mental bubble in which he established himself when he could not bear to be a part of what was going on around him. From it he could see out and judge but in it he was safe from any kind of penetration from without. It was the only place where he felt free of the general idiocy of his fellows. His mother had never entered it but from it he could see her with absolute clarity.

60   The old lady was clever enough and he thought that if she had started from any of the right premises, more might have been expected of her. She lived according to the laws of her own fantasy world, outside of which he had never seen her set foot. The law of it was to sacrifice herself for him after she had first created the necessity to do so by making a mess of things. If he had permitted her sacrifices, it was only because her lack of foresight had made them necessary. All of her life had been a struggle to act like a Chestny without the Chestny goods, and to give him everything she thought a Chestny ought to have; but since, said she, it was fun to struggle, why complain? And when you had won, as she had won, what fun to look back on the hard times! He could not forgive her that she had enjoyed the struggle and that she thought *she* had won.

What she meant when she said she had won was that she had brought him up successfully and had sent him to college and that he had turned out so well — good looking (her teeth had gone unfilled so that his could be straightened), intelligent (he realized he was too intelligent to be a success), and with a future ahead of him (there was of course no future ahead of him). She excused his gloominess on the grounds that he was still growing up and his radical ideas on his lack of practical experience. She said he didn't yet know a thing about "life," that he hadn't even entered the real world — when already he was as disenchanted with it as a man of fifty.

The further irony of all this was that in spite of her, he had turned out so well. In spite of going to only a third-rate college, he had, on his own initiative, come out with a first-rate education; in spite of growing up dominated by a small mind, he had ended up with a large one; in spite of all her foolish views, he was free of prejudice and unafraid to face facts. Most miraculous of all, instead of being blinded by love for her as she was for him, he had cut himself emotionally free of her and could see her with complete objectivity. He was not dominated by his mother.

The bus stopped with a sudden jerk and shook him from his meditation. A woman from the back lurched forward with little steps and barely escaped falling in his newspaper as she righted herself. She got off and a large Negro got on. Julian kept his paper lowered to watch. It gave him a certain satisfaction to see injustice in daily operation. It confirmed his view that with a few exceptions there was no one worth knowing within a radius of three hundred miles. The Negro was well dressed and carried a briefcase. He looked around and then sat down on the other end of the seat where the woman with the red and white canvas sandals was sitting. He immediately unfolded a newspaper and obscured himself behind it. Julian's mother's elbow at once prodded insistently into his ribs. "Now you see why I won't ride on these buses by myself," she whispered.

The woman with the red and white canvas sandals had risen at the same time the Negro sat down and had gone further back in the bus and taken the seat of the woman who had got off. His mother leaned forward and cast her an approving look.

Julian rose, crossed the aisle, and sat down in the place of the woman with 65 the canvas sandals. From this position, he looked serenely across at his mother. Her face had turned an angry red. He stared at her, making his eyes the eyes of a stranger. He felt his tension suddenly lift as if he had openly declared war on her.

He would have liked to get in conversation with the Negro and to talk with him about art or politics or any subject that would be above the comprehension of those around them, but the man remained entrenched behind his paper. He was either ignoring the change of seating or had never noticed it. There was no way for Julian to convey his sympathy.

His mother kept her eyes fixed reproachfully on his face. The woman with the protruding teeth was looking at him avidly as if he were a type of monster new to her.

"Do you have a light?" he asked the Negro.

Without looking away from his paper, the man reached in his pocket and handed him a packet of matches.

"Thanks," Julian said. For a moment he held the matches foolishly. A NO 70 SMOKING sign looked down upon him from over the door. This alone would not have deterred him; he had no cigarettes. He had quit smoking some months before because he could not afford it. "Sorry," he muttered and handed back the matches. The Negro lowered the paper and gave him an annoyed look. He took the matches and raised the paper again.

His mother continued to gaze at him but she did not take advantage of his momentary discomfort. Her eyes retained their battered look. Her face seemed to be unnaturally red, as if her blood pressure had risen. Julian allowed no glimmer of sympathy to show on his face. Having got the advantage, he wanted desperately to keep it and carry it through. He would have liked to teach her a lesson that would last her a while, but there seemed no way to continue the point. The Negro refused to come out from behind his paper.

Julian folded his arms and looked stolidly before him, facing her but as if he did not see her, as if he had ceased to recognize her existence. He visualized a scene in which, the bus having reached their stop, he would remain in his seat and when she said, "Aren't you going to get off?" he would look at her as a stranger who had rashly addressed him. The corner they got off on was usually deserted, but it was well lighted and it would not hurt her to walk by herself the four blocks to the Y. He decided to wait until the time came and then decide whether or not he would let her get off by herself. He would have to be at the Y at ten to bring her back, but he could leave her wondering if he was going to show up. There was no reason for her to think she could always depend on him.

He retired again into the high-ceilinged room sparsely settled with large pieces of antique furniture. His soul expanded momentarily but then he became aware of his mother across from him and the vision shriveled. He studied her coldly. Her feet in little pumps dangled like a child's and did not quite reach the floor. She was training on him an exaggerated look of reproach. He felt completely detached from her. At that moment he could with pleasure have slapped her as he would have slapped a particularly obnoxious child in his charge.

He began to imagine various unlikely ways by which he could teach her a lesson. He might make friends with some distinguished Negro professor or lawyer and bring him home to spend the evening. He would be entirely justified but her blood pressure would rise to 300. He could not push her to the extent of making her have a stroke, and moreover, he had never been successful at making any Negro friends. He had tried to strike up an acquaintance on the bus with some of the better types, with ones that looked like professors or ministers or lawyers. One morning he had sat down next to a distinguished-looking dark brown man who had answered his questions with a sonorous solemnity but who had turned out to be an undertaker. Another day he had sat down beside a cigar-smoking Negro with a diamond ring on his finger, but after a few stilted pleasantries, the Negro had rung the buzzer and risen, slipping two lottery tickets into Julian's hand as he climbed over him to leave.

75   He imagined his mother lying desperately ill and his being able to secure only a Negro doctor for her. He toyed with that idea for a few minutes and then dropped it for a momentary vision of himself participating as a sympathizer in a sit-in demonstration. This was possible but he did not linger with it. Instead, he approached the ultimate horror. He brought home a beautiful suspiciously Negroid woman. Prepare yourself, he said. There is nothing you can do about it. This is the woman I've chosen. She's intelligent, dignified, even good, and she's suffered and she hasn't thought *fun*. Now persecute us, go ahead and persecute us. Drive her out of here, but remember, you're driving me too. His eyes were narrowed and through the indignation he had generated, he saw his mother across the aisle, purple-faced, shrunken to the dwarf-like proportions of her moral nature, sitting like a mummy beneath the ridiculous banner of her hat.

He was tilted out of his fantasy again as the bus stopped. The door opened with a sucking hiss and out of the dark a large, gaily dressed, sullen-looking colored woman got on with a little boy. The child, who might have been four, had on a short plaid suit and a Tyrolean hat with a blue feather in it. Julian hoped that he would sit down beside him and that the woman would push in beside his mother. He could think of no better arrangement.

As she waited for her tokens, the woman was surveying the seating possibilities — he hoped with the idea of sitting where she was least wanted. There was something familiar-looking about her but Julian could not place what it was. She was a giant of a woman. Her face was set not only to meet opposition but to seek it out. The downward tilt of her large lower lip was like a warning sign: DON'T TAMPER WITH ME. Her bulging figure was encased in a green crepe dress and her feet overflowed in red shoes. She had on a hideous hat. A purple velvet flap came down on one side of it and stood up on the other, the rest of it was green and looked like a cushion with the stuffing out. She carried a mammoth red pocketbook that bulged throughout as if it were stuffed with rocks.

To Julian's disappointment, the little boy climbed up on the empty seat beside his mother. His mother lumped all children, black and white, into the common category, "cute," and she thought little Negroes were on the whole cuter than little white children. She smiled at the little boy as he climbed on the seat.

Meanwhile the woman was bearing down upon the empty seat beside Julian. To his annoyance, she squeezed herself into it. He saw his mother's face change as the woman settled herself next to him and he realized with satisfaction that this was more objectionable to her than it was to him. Her face seemed almost gray and there was a look of dull recognition in her eyes, as if suddenly she had sickened at some awful confrontation. Julian saw that it was because she and the woman had, in a sense, swapped sons. Though his mother would not realize the symbolic significance of this, she would feel it. His amusement showed plainly on his face.

The woman next to him muttered something unintelligible to herself. He was 80 conscious of a kind of bristling next to him, a muted growling like that of an angry cat. He could not see anything but the red pocketbook upright on the bulging green thighs. He visualized the woman as she had stood waiting for her tokens — the ponderous figure, rising from the red shoes upward over the solid hips, the mammoth bosom, the haughty face, to the green and purple hat.

His eyes widened.

The vision of the two hats, identical, broke upon him with the radiance of a brilliant sunrise. His face was suddenly lit with joy. He could not believe that Fate had thrust upon his mother such a lesson. He gave a loud chuckle so that the would look at him and see that he saw. She turned her eyes on him slowly. The blue in them seemed to have turned a bruised purple. For a moment he had an uncomfortable sense of her innocence, but it lasted only a second before principle rescued him. Justice entitled him to laugh. His grin hardened until it said to her as plainly as if he were saying aloud: Your punishment exactly fits your pettiness. This should teach you a permanent lesson.

Her eyes shifted to the woman. She seemed unable to bear looking at him and to find the woman preferable. He became conscious again of the bristling presence at his side. The woman was rumbling like a volcano about to become active. His mother's mouth began to twitch slightly at one corner. With a sinking heart, he saw incipient signs of recovery on her face and realized that this was going to strike her suddenly as funny and was going to be no lesson at all. She kept her eyes on the woman and an amused smile came over her face as if the woman were a monkey that had stolen her hat. The little Negro was looking up at her with large fascinated eyes. He had been trying to attract her attention for some time.

"Carver!" the woman said suddenly. "Come heah!"

85   When he saw that the spotlight was on him at last, Carver drew his feet up and turned himself toward Julian's mother and giggled.

"Carver!" the woman said. "You heah me? Come heah!"

Carver slid down from the seat but remained squatting with his back against the base of it, his head turned slyly around toward Julian's mother, who was smiling at him. The woman reached a hand across the aisle and snatched him to her. He righted himself and hung backwards on her knees, grinning at Julian's mother. "Isn't he cute?" Julian's mother said to the woman with the protruding teeth.

"I reckon he is," the woman said without conviction.

The Negress yanked him upright but he eased out of her grip and shot across the aisle and scrambled, giggling wildly, onto the seat beside his love.

90   "I think he likes me," Julian's mother said, and smiled at the woman. It was the smile she used when she was being particularly gracious to an inferior. Julian saw everything was lost. The lesson had rolled off her like rain on a roof.

The woman stood up and yanked the little boy off the seat as if she were snatching him from contagion. Julian could feel the rage in her at having no weapon like his mother's smile. She gave the child a sharp slap across his leg. He howled once and then thrust his head into her stomach and kicked his feet against her shins. "Behave," she said vehemently.

The bus stopped and the Negro who had been reading the newspaper got off. The woman moved over and set the little boy down with a thump between herself and Julian. She held him firmly by the knee. In a moment he put his hands in front of his face and peeped at Julian's mother through his fingers.

"I see yoooooooo!" she said and put her hand in front of her face and peeped at him.

The woman slapped his hand down. "Quit yo' foolishness," she said, "before I knock the living Jesus out of you!"

95   Julian was thankful that the next stop was theirs. He reached up and pulled the cord. The woman reached up and pulled it at the same time. Oh my God, he thought. He had the terrible intuition that when they got off the bus together, his mother would open her purse and give the little boy a nickel. The gesture would be as natural to her as breathing. The bus stopped and the woman got up and lunged to the front, dragging the child, who wished to stay on, after her. Julian and his mother got up and followed. As they neared the door, Julian tried to relieve her of her pocketbook.

"No," she murmured, "I want to give the little boy a nickel."

"No!" Julian hissed. "No!"

She smiled down at the child and opened her bag. The bus door opened and the woman picked him up by the arm and descended with him, hanging at her hip. Once in the street she set him down and shook him.

Julian's mother had to close her purse while she got down the bus step but as soon as her feet were on the ground, she opened it again and began to rummage inside. "I can't find but a penny," she whispered, "but it looks like a new one."

"Don't do it!" Julian said fiercely between his teeth. There was a streetlight 100
on the corner and she hurried to get under it so that she could better see into
her pocketbook. The woman was heading off rapidly down the street with the
child still hanging backward on her hand.

"Oh little boy!" Julian's mother called and took a few quick steps and caught
up with them just beyond the lamppost. "Here's a bright new penny for you,"
and she held out the coin, which shone bronze in the dim light.

The huge woman turned and for a moment stood, her shoulders lifted and
her face frozen with frustrated rage, and stared at Julian's mother. Then all at
once she seemed to explode like a piece of machinery that had been given one
ounce of pressure too much. Julian saw the black fist swing out with the red
pocketbook. He shut his eyes and cringed as he heard the woman shout, "He
don't take nobody's pennies!" When he opened his eyes, the woman was disappearing down the street with the little boy staring wide-eyed over her shoulder.
Julian's mother was sitting on the sidewalk.

"I told you not to do that," Julian said angrily. "I told you not to do that!"

He stood over her for a minute, gritting his teeth. Her legs were stretched
out in front of her and her hat was on her lap. He squatted down and looked her
in the face. It was totally expressionless. "You got exactly what you deserved,"
he said. "Now get up."

He picked up her pocketbook and put what had fallen out back in it. He 105
picked the hat up off her lap. The penny caught his eye on the sidewalk and he
picked that up and let it drop before her eyes into the purse. Then he stood up
and leaned over and held his hands out to pull her up. She remained immobile.
He sighed. Rising above them on either side were black apartment buildings,
marked with irregular rectangles of light. At the end of the block a man came out
of a door and walked off in the opposite direction. "All right," he said, "suppose
somebody happens by and wants to know why you're sitting on the sidewalk?"

She took the hand and, breathing hard, pulled heavily up on it and then
stood for a moment, swaying slightly as if the spots of light in the darkness were
circling around her. Her eyes, shadowed and confused, finally settled on his
face. He did not try to conceal his irritation. "I hope this teaches you a lesson,"
he said. She leaned forward and her eyes raked his face. She seemed trying to
determine his identity. Then, as if she found nothing familiar about him, she
started off with a headlong movement in the wrong direction.

"Aren't you going on to the Y?" he asked.

"Home," she muttered.

"Well, are we walking?"

For answer she kept going. Julian followed along, his hands behind him. He 110
saw no reason to let the lesson she had had go without backing it up with an explanation of its meaning. She might as well be made to understand what had
happened to her. "Don't think that was just an uppity Negro woman," he said.
"That was the whole colored race which will no longer take your condescending pennies. That was your black double. She can wear the same hat as you, and

to be sure," he added gratuitously (because he thought it was funny), "it looked better on her than it did on you. What all this means," he said, "is that the old world is gone. The old manners are obsolete and your graciousness is not worth a damn." He thought bitterly of the house that had been lost for him. "You aren't who you think you are," he said.

She continued to plow ahead, paying no attention to him. Her hair had come undone on one side. She dropped her pocketbook and took no notice. He stooped and picked it up and handed it to her but she did not take it.

"You needn't act as if the world had come to an end," he said, "because it hasn't. From now on you've got to live in a new world and face a few realities for a change. Buck up," he said, "it won't kill you."

She was breathing fast.

"Let's wait on the bus," he said.

"Home," she said thickly.

115 "I hate to see you behave like this," he said. "Just like a child. I should be able to expect more of you." He decided to stop where he was and make her stop and wait for a bus. "I'm not going any farther," he said stopping. "We're going on the bus."

She continued to go on as if she had not heard him. He took a few steps and caught her arm and stopped her. He looked into her face and caught his breath. He was looking into a face he had never seen before. "Tell Grandpa to come get me," she said.

He stared, stricken.

"Tell Caroline to come get me," she said.

120 Stunned, he let her go and she lurched forward again, walking as if one leg were shorter than the other. A tide of darkness seemed to be sweeping her from him. "Mother!" he cried. "Darling, sweetheart, wait!" Crumpling, she fell to the pavement. He dashed forward and fell at her side, crying, "Mamma, Mamma!" He turned her over. Her face was fiercely distorted. One eye, large and staring, moved slightly to the left as if it had become unmoored. The other remained fixed on him, raked his face again, found nothing and closed.

"Wait here, wait here!" he cried and jumped up and began to run for help toward a cluster of lights he saw in the distance ahead of him. "Help, help!" he shouted, but his voice was thin, scarcely a thread of sound. The lights drifted farther away the faster he ran and his feet moved numbly as if they carried him nowhere. The tide of darkness seemed to sweep him back to her, postponing from moment to moment his entry into the world of guilt and sorrow.

❖ ❖ ❖

EDGAR ALLAN POE (1809–1849)

The Tell-Tale Heart (1843)

True!— nervous — very, very dreadfully nervous I had been and am; but why *will* you say that I am mad? The disease had sharpened my senses — not destroyed — not dulled them. Above all was the sense of hearing acute. I heard all things in the heaven and in the earth. I heard many things in hell. How, then, am I mad? Hearken! and observe how healthily — how calmly I can tell you the whole story.

It is impossible to say how first the idea entered my brain; but once conceived, it haunted me day and night. Object there was none. Passion there was none. I loved the old man. He had never wronged me. He had never given me insult. For his gold I had no desire. I think it was his eye! yes, it was this! One of his eyes resembled that of a vulture — a pale eye, with a film over it. Whenever it fell upon me, my blood ran cold; and so by degrees — very gradually — I made up my mind to take the life of the old man, and thus rid myself of the eye forever.

Now this is the point. You fancy me mad. Madmen know nothing. But you should have seen *me*. You should have seen how wisely I proceeded — with what caution — with what foresight — with what dissimulation I went to work! I was never kinder to the old man than during the whole week before I killed him. And every night, about midnight, I turned the latch of his door and opened it — oh, so gently! And then, when I had made an opening sufficient for my head, I put in a dark lantern, all closed, closed, so that no light shone out, and then I thrust in my head. Oh, you would have laughed to see how cunningly I thrust it in! I moved it slowly — very, very slowly, so that I might not disturb the old man's sleep. It took me an hour to place my whole head within the opening so far that I could see him as he lay upon his bed. Ha!— would a madman have been so wise as this? And then, when my head was well in the room, I undid the lantern cautiously — oh, so cautiously — cautiously (for the hinges creaked)— I undid it just so much that a single thin ray fell upon the vulture eye. And this I did for seven long nights — every night just at midnight — but I found the eye always closed; and so it was impossible to do the work; for it was not the old man who vexed me, but his Evil Eye. And every morning, when the day broke, I went boldly into the chamber, and spoke courageously to him, calling him by name in a hearty tone, and inquiring how he had passed the night. So you see he would have been a very profound old man, indeed, to suspect that every night, just at twelve, I looked in upon him while he slept.

Upon the eighth night I was more than usually cautious in opening the door. A watch's minute hand moves more quickly than did mine. Never before that night had I *felt* the extent of my own powers — of my sagacity. I could scarcely contain my feelings of triumph. To think that there I was, opening the door little by little, and he not even to dream of my secret deeds or thoughts. I fairly chuckled at the idea; and perhaps he heard me; for he moved on the bed suddenly, as if startled. Now you may think that I drew back — but no. His room was as black as pitch with the thick darkness (for the shutters were close fastened through fear of robbers), and so I knew that he could not see the opening of the door, and I kept pushing it on steadily, steadily.

5   I had my head in, and was about to open the lantern, when my thumb slipped upon the tin fastening, and the old man sprang up in the bed, crying out — "Who's there?"

I kept quite still and said nothing. For a whole hour I did not move a muscle, and in the meantime I did not hear him lie down. He was still sitting up in the bed listening; — just as I have done, night after night, hearkening to the death watches° in the wall.

Presently I heard a slight groan, and I knew it was the groan of mortal terror. It was not a groan of pain or of grief — oh, no! — it was the low stifled sound that arises from the bottom of the soul when overcharged with awe. I knew the sound very well. Many a night, just at midnight, when all the world slept, it has welled up from my own bosom, deepening, with its dreadful echo, the terrors that distracted me. I say I knew it well. I knew what the old man felt, and pitied him, although I chuckled at heart. I knew that he had been lying awake ever since the first slight noise, when he had turned in the bed. His fears had been ever since growing upon him. He had been trying to fancy them causeless, but could not. He had been saying to himself — "It is nothing but the wind in the chimney — it is only a mouse crossing the floor," or "it is merely a cricket which has made a single chirp." Yes, he had been trying to comfort himself with these suppositions; but he had found all in vain. *All in vain;* because Death, in approaching him, had stalked with his black shadow before him, and enveloped the victim. And it was the mournful influence of the unperceived shadow that caused him to feel — although he neither saw nor heard — to *feel* the presence of my head within the room.

When I had waited a long time, very patiently, without hearing him lie down, I resolved to open a little — a very, very little crevice in the lantern. So I opened it — you cannot imagine how stealthily, stealthily — until, at length, a single dim ray, like the thread of the spider, shot from out of the crevice and fell upon the vulture eye.

It was open — wide, wide open — and I grew furious as I gazed upon it. I saw it with perfect distinctness — all a dull blue, with a hideous veil over it that chilled the very marrow in my bones; but I could see nothing else of the old man's face or person: for I had directed the ray as if by instinct, precisely upon the damned spot.

10   And now have I not told you that what you mistake for madness is but overacuteness of the senses? — now, I say, there came to my ears a low, dull, quick sound, such as a watch makes when enveloped in cotton. I knew *that* sound well, too. It was the beating of the old man's heart. It increased my fury, as the beating of a drum stimulates the soldier into courage.

---

death watches: Wood-burrowing beetles. Their clicking sound was superstitiously thought of as an omen of death.

But even yet I refrained and kept still. I scarcely breathed. I held the lantern motionless. I tried how steadily I could maintain the ray upon the eye. Meantime the hellish tattoo of the heart increased. It grew quicker and quicker, and louder and louder every instant. The old man's terror *must* have been extreme! It grew louder, I say, louder every moment! — do you mark me well? I have told you that I am nervous: so I am. And now at the dead hour of the night, amid the dreadful silence of that old house, so strange a noise as this excited me to uncontrollable terror. Yet, for some minutes longer I refrained and stood still. But the beating grew louder, louder! I thought the heart must burst. And now a new anxiety seized me — the sound would be heard by a neighbor! The old man's hour had come! With a loud yell, I threw open the lantern and leaped into the room. He shrieked once — once only. In an instant I dragged him to the floor, and pulled the heavy bed over him. I then smiled gaily, to find the deed so far done. But, for many minutes, the heart beat on with a muffled sound. This, however, did not vex me; it would not be heard through the wall. At length it ceased. The old man was dead. I removed the bed and examined the corpse. Yes, he was stone, stone dead. I placed my hand upon the heart and held it there many minutes.

If still you think me mad, you will think so no longer when I describe the wise precautions I took for the concealment of the body. The night waned, and I worked hastily, but in silence. First of all I dismembered the corpse. I cut off the head and the arms and the legs.

I then took up three planks from the flooring of the chamber, and deposited all between the scantlings. I then replaced the boards so cleverly, so cunningly, that no human eye — not even *his* — could have detected anything wrong. There was nothing to wash out — no stain of any kind — no bloodspot whatever. I had been too wary for that. A tub had caught all — ha! ha!

When I had made an end of these labors, it was four o'clock — still dark as midnight. As the bell sounded the hour, there came a knocking at the street door. I went down to open it with a light heart, — for what had I *now* to fear? There entered three men, who introduced themselves, with perfect suavity, as officers of the police. A shriek had been heard by a neighbor during the night; suspicion of foul play had been aroused, information had been lodged at the police office, and they (the officers) had been deputed to search the premises.

I smiled, — for *what* had I to fear? I bade the gentlemen welcome. The shriek, 15 I said, was my own in a dream. The old man, I mentioned, was absent in the country. I took my visitors all over the house. I bade them search — search *well*. I led them, at length, to *his* chamber. I showed them his treasures, secure, undisturbed. In the enthusiasm of my confidence, I brought chairs into the room, and desired them *here* to rest from their fatigues, while I myself, in the wild audacity of my perfect triumph, placed my own seat upon the very spot beneath which reposed the corpse of the victim.

The officers were satisfied. My *manner* had convinced them. I was singularly at ease. They sat, and while I answered cheerily, they chatted of familiar things. But, ere long, I felt myself getting pale and wished them gone. My head ached, and I fancied a ringing in my ears: but still they sat and still chatted. The ringing became more distinct:— it continued and became more distinct: I talked more freely to get rid of the feeling: but it continued and gained definitiveness — until, at length, I found that the noise was *not* within my ears.

No doubt I now grew *very* pale:— but I talked more fluently, and with a heightened voice. Yet the sound increased—and what could I do? It was a *low, dull, quick sound—much such a sound as a watch makes when enveloped in cotton.* I gasped for breath — and yet the officers heard it not. I talked more quickly — more vehemently; but the noise steadily increased. I arose and argued about trifles, in a high key and with violent gesticulations; but the noise steadily increased. Why *would* they not be gone? I paced the floor to and fro with heavy strides, as if excited to fury by the observations of the men — but the noise steadily increased. Oh God! what *could* I do? I foamed — I raved — I swore! I swung the chair upon which I had been sitting, and grated it upon the boards, but the noise arose over all and continually increased. It grew louder — louder — *louder!* And still the men chatted pleasantly, and smiled. Was it possible they heard not? Almighty God!— no, no! They heard!— they suspected!— they *knew!*— they were making a mockery of my horror!— this I thought, and this I think. But anything was better than this agony! Anything was more tolerable than this derision! I could bear those hypocritical smiles no longer! I felt that I must scream or die!— and now — again!—hark! louder! louder! louder! *louder!*—

"Villains!" I shrieked, " dissemble no more! I admit the dead!— tear up the planks!—here, here!—it is the beating of his hideous heart!"

◇ ◇ ◇

ALBERTO ALVARO RÍOS (1952–   )

The Secret Lion (1984)

I was twelve and in junior high school and something happened that we didn't have a name for, but it was there nonetheless like a lion, and roaring, roaring that way the biggest things do. Everything changed. Just that. Like the rug, the one that gets pulled — or better, like the tablecloth those magicians pull where the stuff on the table stays the same but the gasp! from the audience makes the staying-the-same part not matter. Like that.

What happened was there were teachers now, not just one teacher, teach-erz, and we felt personally abandoned somehow. When a person had all these teachers now, he didn't get taken care of the same way, even though six was more than one. Arithmetic went out the door when we walked in. And we saw girls now, but they weren't the same girls we used to know because we couldn't talk to them anymore, not the same way we used to, certainly not to Sandy, even though she was my neighbor, too. Not even to her. She just played the piano all the time. And there were words, oh there were words in junior high school, and we wanted to know what they were, and how a person did them — that's what school was supposed to be for. Only, in junior high school, school wasn't school, everything was backward-like. If you went up to a teacher and said the word to try and find out what it meant you got in trouble for saying it. So we didn't. And we figured it must have been that way about other stuff, too, so we never said anything about anything — we weren't stupid.

But my friend Sergio and I, we solved junior high school. We would come home from school on the bus, put our books away, change shoes, and go across the highway to the arroyo. It was the one place we were not supposed to go. So we did. This was, after all, what junior high had at least shown us. It was our river, though, our personal Mississippi, our friend from long back, and it was full of stories and all the branch forts we had built in it when we were still the Vikings of America, with our own symbol, which we had carved everywhere, even in the sand, which let the water take it. That was good, we had decided; whoever was at the end of this river would know about us.

At the very very top of our growing lungs, what we would do down there was shout every dirty word we could think of, in every combination we could come up with, and we would yell about girls, and all the things we wanted to do with them, as loud as we could — we didn't know what we wanted to do with them, just things — and we would yell about teachers, and how we loved some of them, like Miss Crevelone, and how we wanted to dissect some of them, making signs of the cross, like priests, and we would yell this stuff over and over because it felt good, we couldn't explain why, it just felt good and for the first time in our lives there was nobody to tell us we couldn't. So we did.

One Thursday we were walking along shouting this way, and the railroad, the 5
Southern Pacific, which ran above and along the far side of the arroyo, had dropped a grinding ball down there, which was, we found out later, a cannonball thing used in mining. A bunch of them were put in a big vat which turned around and crushed the ore. One had been dropped, or thrown — what do caboose men do when they get bored — but it got down there regardless and as we were walking along yelling about one girl or another, a particular Claudia, we found it, one of these things, looked at it, picked it up, and got very very excited, and held it and passed it back and forth, and we were saying "Guythisis, this is, geeGuythis . . .": we had this perception about nature then, that nature is imperfect and that round things are perfect: we said "GuyGodthis is perfect, thisisthis is perfect, it's round, round and heavy, it'sit's the best thing we'veeverseen. Whatisit?" We didn't know. We just knew it was great. We just, whatever, we played with it, held it some more.

And then we had to decide what to do with it. We knew, because of a lot of things, that if we were going to take this and show it to anybody, this discovery, this best thing, was going to be taken away from us. That's the way it works with little kids, like all the polished quartz, the tons of it we had collected piece by piece over the years. Junior high kids too. If we took it home, my mother, we knew, was going to look at it and say "throw that dirty thing in the, get rid of it." Simple like, like that. "But ma it's the best thing I" "Getridofit." Simple.

So we didn't. Take it home. Instead, we came up with the answer. We dug a hole and buried it. And we marked it secretly. Lots of secret signs. And came back the next week to dig it up and, we didn't know, pass it around some more or something, but we didn't find it. We dug up that whole bank, and we never found it again. We tried.

Sergio and I talked about that ball or whatever it was when we couldn't find it. All we used were small words, neat, good. Kid words. What we were really saying, but didn't know the words, was how much that ball was like that place, that whole arroyo: couldn't tell anybody about it, didn't understand what it was, didn't have a name for it. It just felt good. It was just perfect in the way it was that place, that whole going to that place, that whole junior high school lion. It was just iron-heavy, it had no name, it felt good or not, we couldn't take it home to show our mothers, and once we buried it, it was gone forever.

The ball was gone, like the first reasons we had come to that arroyo years earlier, like the first time we had seen the arroyo, it was gone like everything else that had been taken away. This was not our first lesson. We stopped going to the arroyo after not finding the thing, the same way we had stopped going there years earlier and headed for the mountains. Nature seemed to keep pushing us around one way or another, teaching us the same thing every place we ended up. Nature's gang was tough that way, teaching us stuff.

10   When we were young we moved away from town, me and my family. Sergio's was already out there. Out in the wilds. Or at least the new place seemed like the wilds since everything looks bigger the smaller a man is. I was five, I guess, and we had moved three miles north of Nogales where we had lived, three miles north of the Mexican border. We looked across the highway in one direction and there was the arroyo; hills stood up in the other direction. Mountains, for a small man.

When the first summer came the very first place we went to was of course the one place we weren't supposed to go, the arroyo. We went down in there and found water running, summer rain water mostly, and we went swimming. But every third or fourth or fifth day, the sewage treatment plant that was, we found out, upstream, would release whatever it was that it released, and we would never know exactly what day that was, and a person really couldn't tell right off by looking at the water, not every time, not so a person could get out in time. So, we went swimming that summer and some days we had a lot of fun. Some days we didn't. We found a thousand ways to explain what happened on those other days, constructing elaborate stories about the neighborhood dogs, and hadn't she, my mother, miscalculated her step before, too? But she knew something was up because we'd come running into the house those days, wanting to take a shower, even — if this can be imagined — in the middle of the day.

That was the first time we stopped going to the arroyo. It taught us to look the other way. We decided, as the second side of summer came, we wanted to go into the mountains. They were still mountains then. We went running in one summer Thursday morning, my friend Sergio and I, into my mother's kitchen, and said, well, what'zin, what'zin those hills over there — we used her word so she'd understand us — and she said nothingdon'tworryaboutit. So we went out, and we weren't dumb, we thought with our eyes to each other, ohhoshe'stryingtokeep-somethingfromus. We knew adults.

We had read the books, after all; we knew about bridges and castles and wildtreacherousraging alligatormouth rivers. We wanted them. So we were going to go out and get them. We went back that morning into that kitchen and we said, "We're going out there, we're going into the hills, we're going away for three days, don't worry." She said, "All right."

"You know," I said to Sergio, "if we're going to go away for three days, well, we ought to at least pack a lunch."

But we were two young boys with no patience for what we thought at the   15
time was mom-stuff: making sa-and-wiches. My mother didn't offer. So we got out little kid knapsacks that my mother had sewn for us, and into them we put the jar of mustard. A loaf of bread. Knivesforksplates, bottles of Coke, a can opener. This was lunch for the two of us. And we were weighed down, humped over to be strong enough to carry this stuff. But we started walking anyway, into the hills. We were going to eat berries and stuff otherwise. "Goodbye." My mom said that.

After the first hill we were dead. But we walked. My mother could still see us. And we kept walking. We walked until we got to where the sun is straight overhead, noon. That place. Where that is doesn't matter; it's time to eat. The truth is we weren't anywhere close to that place. We just agreed that the sun was overhead and that it was time to eat, and by tilting our heads a little we could make that the truth.

"We really ought to start looking for a place to eat."

"Yeah. Let's look for a good place to eat." We went back and forth saying that for fifteen minutes, making it lunchtime because that's what we always said back and forth before lunchtimes at home. "Yeah, I'm hungry all right." I nodded my head. "Yeah, I'm hungry all right too. I'm hungry." He nodded his head. I nodded my head back. After a good deal more nodding, we were ready, just as we came over a little hill. We hadn't found the mountains yet. This was a little hill.

And on the other side of this hill we found heaven.

It was just what we thought it would be.   20

Perfect. Heaven was green, like nothing else in Arizona. And it wasn't a ceme-tery or like that because we had seen cemeteries and they had gravestones and stuff and this didn't. This was perfect, had trees, lots of trees, had birds, like we had never seen before. It was like "The Wizard of Oz," like when they got to Oz and everything was so green, so emerald, they had to wear those glasses, and we ran just like them, laughing, laughing that way we did that moment, and we went running down to this clearing in it all, hitting each other that good way we did.

We got down there, we kept laughing, we kept hitting each other, we unpacked our stuff, and we started acting "rich." We knew all about how to do that, like blow-ing on our nails, then rubbing them on our chests for the shine. We made our sand-wiches, opened our Cokes, got out the rest of the stuff, the salt and pepper shakers. I found this particular hole and I put my Coke right into it, a perfect fit, and I called it my Coke-holder. I got down next to it on my back, because everyone knows that rich people eat lying down, and I got my sandwich in one hand and put my other arm around the Coke in its holder. When I wanted a drink, I lifted my neck a little, put out my lips, and tipped my Coke a little with the crook of my elbow. Ah.

We were there, lying down, eating our sandwiches, laughing, throwing bread at each other and out for the birds. This was heaven. We were laughing and we couldn't believe it. My mother was keeping something from us, ah ha, but we had found her out. We even found water over at the side of the clearing to wash our plates with — we had brought plates. Sergio started washing his plates when he was done, and I was being rich with my Coke, and this day in summer was right.

When suddenly these two men came, from around a corner of trees and the tallest grass we had ever seen. They had bags on their backs, leather bags, bags and sticks.

25   We didn't know what clubs were, but I learned later, like I learned about the grinding balls. The two men yelled at us. Most specifically, one wanted me to take my Coke out of my Coke-holder so he could sink his golf ball into it.

Something got taken away from us that moment. Heaven. We grew up a little bit, and couldn't go backward. We learned. No one had ever told us about golf. They had told us about heaven. And it went away. We got golf in exchange.

We went back to the arroyo for the rest of that summer, and tried to have fun the best we could. We learned to be ready for finding the grinding ball. We loved it, and when we buried it we knew what would happen. The truth is, we didn't look so hard for it. We were two boys and twelve summers then, and not stupid. Things get taken away.

We buried it because it was perfect. We didn't tell my mother, but together it was all we talked about, till we forgot. It was the lion.

◇   ◇   ◇

AMY TAN (1952–   )

Two Kinds (1989)

My mother believed you could be anything you wanted to be in America. You could open a restaurant. You could work for the government and get good retirement. You could buy a house with almost no money down. You could become rich. You could become instantly famous.

"Of course you can be prodigy, too," my mother told me when I was nine. "You can be best anything. What does Auntie Lindo know? Her daughter, she is only best tricky."

America was where all my mother's hopes lay. She had come here in 1949 after losing everything in China: her mother and father, her family home, her first husband, and two daughters, twin baby girls. But she never looked back with regret. There were so many ways for things to get better.

We didn't immediately pick the right kind of prodigy. At first my mother thought I could be a Chinese Shirley Temple. We'd watch Shirley's old movies on TV as though they were training films. My mother would poke my arm and say, "*Ni kan*"—You watch. And I would see Shirley tapping her feet, or singing a sailor song, or pursing her lips into a very round O while saying, "Oh my goodness."

"*Ni kan*," said my mother as Shirley's eyes flooded with tears. "You already 5 know how. Don't need talent for crying!"

Soon after my mother got this idea about Shirley Temple, she took me to a beauty training school in the Mission district and put me in the hands of a student who could barely hold the scissors without shaking. Instead of getting big fat curls, I emerged with an uneven mass of crinkly black fuzz. My mother dragged me off to the bathroom and tried to wet down my hair.

"You look like Negro Chinese," she lamented, as if I had done this on purpose.

The instructor of the beauty training school had to lop off these soggy clumps to make my hair even again. "Peter Pan is very popular these days," the instructor assured my mother. I now had hair the length of a boy's, with straight-across bangs that hung at a slant two inches above my eyebrows. I liked the haircut and it made me actually look forward to my future fame.

In fact, in the beginning, I was just as excited as my mother, maybe even more so. I pictured this prodigy part of me as many different images, trying each one on for size. I was a dainty ballerina girl standing by the curtains, waiting to hear the right music that would send me floating on my tiptoes. I was like the Christ child lifted out of the straw manger, crying with holy indignity. I was Cinderella stepping from her pumpkin carriage with sparkly cartoon music filling the air.

In all of my imaginings, I was filled with a sense that I would soon become 10 *perfect.* My mother and father would adore me. I would be beyond reproach. I would never feel the need to sulk for anything.

But sometimes the prodigy in me became impatient. "If you don't hurry up and get me out of here, I'm disappearing for good," it warned. "And then you'll always be nothing."

Every night after dinner, my mother and I would sit at the Formica kitchen table. She would present new tests, taking her examples from stories of amazing children she had read in *Ripley's Believe It or Not,* or *Good Housekeeping, Reader's Digest,* and a dozen other magazines she kept in a pile in our bathroom. My mother got these magazines from people whose houses she cleaned. And since she cleaned many houses each week, we had a great assortment. She would look through them all, searching for stories about remarkable children.

The first night she brought out a story about a three-year-old boy who knew the capitals of all the states and even most of the European countries. A teacher was quoted as saying the little boy could also pronounce the names of the foreign cities correctly.

"What's the capital of Finland?" my mother asked me, looking at the magazine story.

15   All I knew was the capital of California, because Sacramento was the name of the street we lived on in Chinatown. "Nairobi!" I guessed, saying the most foreign word I could think of. She checked to see if that was possibly one way to pronounce "Helsinki" before showing me the answer.

The tests got harder — multiplying numbers in my head, finding the queen of hearts in a deck of cards, trying to stand on my head without using my hands, predicting the daily temperatures in Los Angeles, New York, and London.

One night I had to look at a page from the Bible for three minutes and then report everything I could remember. "Now Jehoshaphat had riches and honor in abundance and . . . that's all I remember, Ma," I said.

And after seeing my mother's disappointed face once again, something inside of me began to die. I hated the tests, the raised hopes and failed expectations. Before going to bed that night, I looked in the mirror above the bathroom sink and when I saw only my face staring back — and that it would always be this ordinary face — I began to cry. Such a sad, ugly girl! I made high-pitched noises like a crazed animal, trying to scratch out the face in the mirror.

And then I saw what seemed to be the prodigy side of me — because I had never seen that face before. I looked at my reflection, blinking so I could see more clearly. The girl staring back at me was angry, powerful. This girl and I were the same. I had new thoughts, willful thoughts, or rather thoughts filled with lots of won'ts. I won't let her change me, I promised myself. I won't be what I'm not.

20   So now on nights when my mother presented her tests, I performed listlessly, my head propped on one arm. I pretended to be bored. And I was. I got so bored I started counting the bellows of the foghorns out on the bay while my mother drilled me in other areas. The sound was comforting and reminded me of the cow jumping over the moon. And the next day, I played a game with myself, seeing if my mother would give up on me before eight bellows. After a while I usually counted only one, maybe two bellows at most. At last she was beginning to give up hope.

Two or three months had gone by without any mention of my being a prodigy again. And then one day my mother was watching *The Ed Sullivan Show* on TV. The TV was old and the sound kept shorting out. Every time my mother got halfway up from the sofa to adjust the set, the sound would go back on and Ed would be talking. As soon as she sat down, Ed would go silent again. She got up, the TV broke into loud piano music. She sat down. Silence. Up and down, back and forth, quiet and loud. It was like a stiff embraceless dance between her and the TV set. Finally she stood by the set with her hand on the sound dial.

She seemed entranced by the music, a little frenzied piano piece with this mesmerizing quality, sort of quick passages and then teasing lilting ones before it returned to the quick playful parts.

"*Ni kan,*" my mother said, calling me over with hurried hand gestures, "Look here."

I could see why my mother was fascinated by the music. It was being pounded out by a little Chinese girl, about nine years old, with a Peter Pan haircut. The girl had the sauciness of a Shirley Temple. She was proudly modest like a proper Chinese child. And she also did this fancy sweep of a curtsy, so that the fluffy skirt of her white dress cascaded slowly to the floor like the petals of a large carnation.

In spite of these warning signs, I wasn't worried. Our family had no piano and 25 we couldn't afford to buy one, let alone reams of sheet music and piano lessons. So I could be generous in my comments when my mother bad-mouthed the little girl on TV.

"Play note right, but doesn't sound good! No singing sound," complained my mother.

"What are you picking on her for?" I said carelessly. "She's pretty good. Maybe she's not the best, but she's trying hard." I knew almost immediately I would be sorry I said that.

"Just like you," she said. "Not the best. Because you not trying." She gave a little huff as she let go of the sound dial and sat down on the sofa.

The little Chinese girl sat down also to play an encore of "Anitra's Dance" by Grieg. I remember the song, because later on I had to learn how to play it.

Three days after watching *The Ed Sullivan Show,* my mother told me what 30 my schedule would be for piano lessons and piano practice. She had talked to Mr. Chong, who lived on the first floor of our apartment building. Mr. Chong was a retired piano teacher and my mother had traded housecleaning services for weekly lessons and a piano for me to practice on every day, two hours a day, from four until six.

When my mother told me this, I felt as though I had been sent to hell. I whined and then kicked my foot a little when I couldn't stand it anymore.

"Why don't you like me the way I am? I'm *not* a genius! I can't play the piano. And even if I could, I wouldn't go on TV if you paid me a million dollars!" I cried.

My mother slapped me. "Who ask you be genius?" she shouted. "Only ask you be your best. For you sake. You think I want you be genius? Hnnh! What for! Who ask you!"

"So ungrateful," I heard her mutter in Chinese. "If she had as much talent as she has temper, she would be famous now."

Mr. Chong, whom I secretly nicknamed Old Chong, was very strange, 35 always tapping his fingers to the silent music of an invisible orchestra. He looked ancient in my eyes. He had lost most of the hair on top of his head and he wore thick glasses and had eyes that always looked tired and sleepy. But he must have been younger than I thought, since he lived with his mother and was not yet married.

I met Old Lady Chong once and that was enough. She had this peculiar smell like a baby that had done something in its pants. And her fingers felt like a dead person's, like an old peach I once found in the back of the refrigerator; the skin just slid off the meat when I picked it up.

I soon found out why Old Chong had retired from teaching piano. He was deaf. "Like Beethoven!" he shouted to me. "We're both listening only in our head!" And he would start to conduct his frantic silent sonatas.

Our lessons went like this. He would open the book and point to different things, explaining their purpose: "Key! Treble! Bass! No sharps or flats! So this is C major! Listen now and play after me!"

And then he would play the C scale a few times, a simple chord, and then, as if inspired by an old, unreachable itch, he gradually added more notes and running trills and a pounding bass until the music was really something quite grand.

40   I would play after him, the simple scale, the simple chord, and then I just played some nonsense that sounded like a cat running up and down on top of garbage cans. Old Chong smiled and applauded and then said, "Very good! But now you must learn to keep time!"

So that's how I discovered that Old Chong's eyes were too slow to keep up with the wrong notes I was playing. He went through the motions in half-time. To help me keep rhythm, he stood behind me, pushing down on my right shoulder for every beat. He balanced pennies on top of my wrists so I would keep them still as I slowly played scales and arpeggios. He had me curve my hand around an apple and keep that shape when playing chords. He marched stiffly to show me how to make each finger dance up and down, staccato like an obedient little soldier.

He taught me all these things, and that was how I also learned I could be lazy and get away with mistakes, lots of mistakes. If I hit the wrong notes because I hadn't practiced enough, I never corrected myself. I just kept playing in rhythm. And Old Chong kept conducting his own private reverie.

So maybe I never really gave myself a fair chance. I did pick up the basics pretty quickly, and I might have become a good pianist at that young age. But I was so determined not to try, not to be anybody different that I learned to play only the most ear-splitting preludes, the most discordant hymns.

Over the next year, I practiced like this, dutifully in my own way. And then one day I heard my mother and her friend Lindo Jong both talking in a loud bragging tone of voice so others could hear. It was after church, and I was leaning against the brick wall wearing a dress with stiff white petticoats. Auntie Lindo's daughter, Waverly, who was about my age, was standing farther down the wall about five feet away. We had grown up together and shared all the closeness of two sisters squabbling over crayons and dolls. In other words, for the most part, we hated each other. I thought she was snotty. Waverly Jong had gained a certain amount of fame as "Chinatown's Littlest Chinese Chess Champion."

"She bring home too many trophy," lamented Auntie Lindo that Sunday. "All 45
day she play chess. All day I have no time do nothing but dust off her winnings."
She threw a scolding look at Waverly, who pretended not to see her.

"You lucky you don't have this problem," said Auntie Lindo with a sigh to my
mother.

And my mother squared her shoulders and bragged: "Our problem worser than
yours. If we ask Jing-mei wash dish, she hear nothing but music. It's like you can't
stop this natural talent."

And right then, I was determined to put a stop to her foolish pride.

A few weeks later, Old Chong and my mother conspired to have me play in a
talent show which would be held in the church hall. By then, my parents had
saved up enough to buy me a secondhand piano, a black Wurlitzer spinet with a
scarred bench. It was the showpiece of our living room.

For the talent show, I was to play a piece called "Pleading Child" from 50
Schumann's *Scenes from Childhood*. It was a simple, moody piece that sounded
more difficult than it was. I was supposed to memorize the whole thing, playing
the repeat parts twice to make the piece sound longer. But I dawdled over it, playing a few bars and then cheating, looking up to see what notes followed. I never
really listened to what I was playing. I daydreamed about being somewhere else,
about being someone else.

The part I liked to practice best was the fancy curtsy: right foot out, touch the
rose on the carpet with a pointed foot, sweep to the side, left leg bends, look up
and smile.

My parents invited all the couples from the Joy Luck Club° to witness my debut. Auntie Lindo and Uncle Tin were there. Waverly and her two older brothers had also come. The first two rows were filled with children both younger and
older than I was. The littlest ones got to go first. They recited simple nursery
rhymes, squawked out tunes on miniature violins, twirled Hula Hoops, pranced
in pink ballet tutus, and when they bowed or curtsied, the audience would sigh in
unison, "Awww," and then clap enthusiastically.

When my turn came, I was very confident. I remember my childish excitement. It was as if I knew, without a doubt, that the prodigy side of me really did
exist. I had no fear whatsoever, no nervousness. I remember thinking to myself,
This is it! This is it! I looked out over the audience, at my mother's blank face,
my father's yawn, Auntie Lindo's stiff-lipped smile, Waverly's sulky expression. I
had on a white dress layered with sheets of lace, and a pink bow in my Peter Pan
haircut. As I sat down I envisioned people jumping to their feet and Ed Sullivan
rushing up to introduce me to everyone on TV.

Joy Luck Club: A name denoting the mother's circle of friends, all of whom were Chinese immigrants to the
United States.

And I started to play. It was so beautiful. I was so caught up in how lovely I looked that at first I didn't worry how I would sound. So it was a surprise to me when I hit the first wrong note and I realized something didn't sound quite right. And then I hit another and another followed that. A chill started at the top of my head and began to trickle down. Yet I couldn't stop playing, as though my hands were bewitched. I kept thinking my fingers would adjust themselves back, like a train switching to the right track. I played this strange jumble through two repeats, the sour notes staying with me all the way to the end.

55   When I stood up, I discovered my legs were shaking. Maybe I had just been nervous and the audience, like Old Chong, had seen me go through the right motions and had not heard anything wrong at all. I swept my right foot out, went down on my knee, looked up and smiled. The room was quiet, except for Old Chong, who was beaming and shouting, "Bravo! Bravo! Well done!" But then I saw my mother's face, her stricken face. The audience clapped weakly, and as I walked back to my chair, with my whole face quivering as I tried not to cry, I heard a little boy whisper loudly to his mother, "That was awful," and the mother whispered back, "Well, she certainly tried."

And now I realized how many people were in the audience, the whole world it seemed. I was aware of eyes burning into my back. I felt the shame of my mother and father as they sat stiffly throughout the rest of the show.

We could have escaped during intermission. Pride and some strange sense of honor must have anchored my parents to their chairs. And so we watched it all: the eighteen-year-old boy with a fake mustache who did a magic show and juggled flaming hoops while riding a unicycle. The breasted girl with white makeup who sang from *Madama Butterfly* and got honorable mention. And the eleven-year-old boy who won first prize playing a tricky violin song that sounded like a busy bee.

After the show, the Hsus, the Jongs, and the St. Clairs from the Joy Luck Club came up to my mother and father.

"Lots of talented kids," Auntie Lindo said vaguely, smiling broadly.

60   "That was somethin' else," said my father, and I wondered if he was referring to me in a humorous way, or whether he even remembered what I had done.

Waverly looked at me and shrugged her shoulders. "You aren't a genius like me," she said matter-of-factly. And if I hadn't felt so bad, I would have pulled her braids and punched her stomach.

But my mother's expression was what devastated me: a quiet, blank look that said she had lost everything. I felt the same way, and it seemed as if everybody were now coming up, like gawkers at the scene of an accident, to see what parts were actually missing. When we got on the bus to go home, my father was humming the busy-bee tune and my mother was silent. I kept thinking she wanted to wait until we got home before shouting at me. But when my father unlocked the door to our apartment, my mother walked in and then went to the back, into the bedroom. No accusations. No blame. And in a way, I felt disappointed. I had been waiting for her to start shouting, so I could shout back and cry and blame her for all my misery.

I assumed my talent-show fiasco meant I never had to play the piano again. But two days later, after school, my mother came out of the kitchen and saw me watching TV.

"Four clock," she reminded me as if it were any other day. I was stunned, as though she were asking me to go through the talent-show torture again. I wedged myself more tightly in front of the TV.

"Turn off TV," she called from the kitchen five minutes later.   65

I didn't budge. And then I decided. I didn't have to do what my mother said anymore. I wasn't her slave. This wasn't China. I had listened to her before and look what happened. She was the stupid one.

She came out from the kitchen and stood in the arched entryway of the living room. "Four clock," she said once again, louder.

"I'm not going to play anymore," I said nonchalantly. "Why should I? I'm not a genius."

She walked over and stood in front of the TV. I saw her chest was heaving up and down in an angry way.

"No!" I said, and I now felt stronger, as if my true self had finally emerged. So   70 this was what had been inside me all along.

"No! I won't!" I screamed.

She yanked me by the arm, pulled me off the floor, snapped off the TV. She was frighteningly strong, half pulling, half carrying me toward the piano as I kicked the throw rugs under my feet. She lifted me up and onto the hard bench. I was sobbing by now, looking at her bitterly. Her chest was heaving even more and her mouth was open, smiling crazily as if she were pleased I was crying.

"You want me to be someone that I'm not!" I sobbed. "I'll never be the kind of daughter you want me to be!"

"Only two kinds of daughters," she shouted in Chinese. "Those who are obedient and those who follow their own mind! Only one kind of daughter can live in this house. Obedient daughter!"

"Then I wish I wasn't your daughter. I wish you weren't my mother," I shouted.   75 As I said these things I got scared. It felt like worms and toads and slimy things crawling out of my chest, but it also felt good, as if this awful side of me had surfaced, at last.

"Too late change this," said my mother shrilly.

And I could sense her anger rising to its breaking point. I wanted to see it spill over. And that's when I remembered the babies she had lost in China, the ones we never talked about. "Then I wish I'd never been born!" I shouted. "I wish I were dead! Like them."

It was as if I had said the magic words. Alakazam! — and her face went blank, her mouth closed, her arms went slack, and she backed out of the room, stunned, as if she were blowing away like a small brown leaf, thin, brittle, lifeless.

It was not the only disappointment my mother felt in me. In the years that followed, I failed her so many times, each time asserting my own will, my right to fall short of expectations. I didn't get straight As. I didn't become class president. I didn't get into Stanford. I dropped out of college.

80   For unlike my mother, I did not believe I could be anything I wanted to be. I could only be me.

And for all those years, we never talked about the disaster at the recital or my terrible accusations afterward at the piano bench. All that remained unchecked, like a betrayal that was now unspeakable. So I never found a way to ask her why she had hoped for something so large that failure was inevitable.

And even worse, I never asked her what frightened me the most: Why had she given up hope?

For after our struggle at the piano, she never mentioned my playing again. The lessons stopped. The lid to the piano was closed, shutting out the dust, my misery, and her dreams.

So she surprised me. A few years ago, she offered to give me the piano, for my thirtieth birthday. I had not played in all those years. I saw the offer as a sign of forgiveness, a tremendous burden removed.

85   "Are you sure?" I asked shyly. "I mean, won't you and Dad miss it?"

"No, this your piano," she said firmly. "Always your piano. You only one can play."

"Well, I probably can't play anymore," I said. "It's been years."

"You pick up fast," said my mother, as if she knew this was certain. "You have natural talent. You could been genius if you want to."

"No I couldn't."

90   "You just not trying," said my mother. And she was neither angry nor sad. She said it as if to announce a fact that could never be disproved. "Take it," she said.

But I didn't at first. It was enough that she had offered it to me. And after that, every time I saw it in my parents' living room, standing in front of the bay windows, it made me feel proud, as if it were a shiny trophy I had won back.

Last week I sent a tuner over to my parents' apartment and had the piano re-conditioned, for purely sentimental reasons. My mother had died a few months before and I had been getting things in order for my father, a little bit at a time. I put the jewelry in special silk pouches. The sweaters she had knitted in yellow, pink, bright orange — all the colors I hated — I put those in moth-proof boxes. I found some old Chinese silk dresses, the kind with little slits up the sides. I rubbed the old silk against my skin, then wrapped them in tissue and decided to take them home with me.

After I had the piano tuned, I opened the lid and touched the keys. It sounded even richer than I remembered. Really, it was a very good piano. Inside the bench were the same exercise notes with handwritten scales, the same secondhand music books with their covers held together with yellow tape.

I opened up the Schumann book to the dark little piece I had played at the recital. It was on the left-hand side of the page, "Pleading Child." It looked more difficult than I remembered. I played a few bars, surprised at how easily the notes came back to me.

And for the first time, or so it seemed, I noticed the piece on the right-hand 95 side. It was called "Perfectly Contented." I tried to play this one as well. It had a lighter melody but the same flowing rhythm and turned out to be quite easy. "Pleading Child" was shorter but slower; "Perfectly Contented" was longer, but faster. And after I played them both a few times, I realized they were two halves of the same song.

◆ ◆ ◆

HISAYE YAMAMOTO (1921–)

Seventeen Syllables (1949)

The first Rosie knew that her mother had taken to writing poems was one evening when she finished one and read it aloud for her daughter's approval. It was about cats, and Rosie pretended to understand it thoroughly and appreciate it no end, partly because she hesitated to disillusion her mother about the quantity and quality of Japanese she had learned in all the years now that she had been going to Japanese school every Saturday (and Wednesday, too, in the summer). Even so, her mother must have been skeptical about the depth of Rosie's understanding, because she explained afterwards about the kind of poem she was trying to write.

See, Rosie, she said, it was a *haiku*,° a poem in which she must pack all her meaning into seventeen syllables only, which were divided into three lines of five, seven, and five syllables. In the one she had just read, she had tried to capture the charm of a kitten, as well as comment on the superstition that owning a cat of three colors meant good luck.

"Yes, yes, I understand. How utterly lovely," Rosie said, and her mother, either satisfied or seeing through the deception and resigned, went back to composing.

The truth was that Rosie was lazy; English lay ready on the tongue but Japanese had to be searched for and examined, and even then put forth tentatively (probably to meet with laughter). It was so much easier to say yes, yes, even when one meant no, no. Besides, this was what was in her mind to say: I was looking through one of your magazines from Japan last night, Mother, and toward the back I found some *haiku* in English that delighted me. There was one that made me giggle off and on until I fell asleep —

> It is morning, and lo!
> I lie awake, comme il faut,
> sighing for some dough.

---

haiku: A classical Japanese poetical form.

5 Now, how to reach her mother, how to communicate the melancholy song? Rosie knew formal Japanese by fits and starts, her mother had even less English, no French. It was much more possible to say yes, yes.

It developed that her mother was writing the *haiku* for a daily newspaper, the *Mainichi Shimbun*, that was published in San Francisco. Los Angeles, to be sure, was closer to the farming community in which the Hayashi family lived and several Japanese vernaculars° were printed there, but Rosie's parents said they preferred the tone of the northern paper. Once a week, the *Mainichi* would have a section devoted to *haiku*, and her mother became an extravagant contributor, taking for herself the blossoming pen name, Ume Hanazono.

So Rosie and her father lived for a while with two women, her mother and Ume Hanazono. Her mother (Tome Hayashi by name) kept house, cooked, washed, and, along with her husband and the Carrascos, the Mexican family hired for the harvest, did her ample share of picking tomatoes out in the sweltering fields and boxing them in tidy strata in the cool packing shed. Ume Hanazono, who came to life after the dinner dishes were done, was an earnest, muttering stranger who often neglected speaking when spoken to and stayed busy at the parlor table as late as midnight scribbling with pencil on scratch paper or carefully copying characters on good paper with her fat, pale-green Parker.

The new interest had some repercussions on the household routine. Before, Rosie had been accustomed to her parents and herself taking their hot baths early and going to bed almost immediately afterwards, unless her parents challenged each other to a game of flower cards or unless company dropped in. Now if her father wanted to play cards, he had to resort to solitaire (at which he always cheated fearlessly), and if a group of friends came over, it was bound to contain someone who was also writing *haiku*, and the small assemblage would be split in two, her father entertaining the non-literary members and her mother comparing ecstatic notes with the visiting poet.

If they went out, it was more of the same thing. But Ume Hanazono's life span, even for a poet's, was very brief — perhaps three months at most.

10 One night they went over to see the Hayano family in the neighboring town to the west, an adventure both painful and attractive to Rosie. It was attractive because there were four Hayano girls, all lovely and each one named after a season of the year (Haru, Natsu, Aki, Fuyu), painful because something had been wrong with Mrs. Hayano ever since the birth of her first child. Rosie would sometimes watch Mrs. Hayano, reputed to have been the belle of her native village, making her way about a room, stooped, slowly shuffling, violently trembling (*always* trembling), and she would be reminded that this woman, in this same condition, had carried and given issue to three babies. She would look wonderingly

---

vernaculars: Dialects, usually associated with particular regions.

at Mr. Hayano, handsome, tall, and strong, and she would look at her four pretty friends. But it was not a matter she could come to any decision about.

On this visit, however, Mrs. Hayano sat all evening in the rocker, as motionless and unobtrusive as it was possible for her to be, and Rosie found the greater part of the evening practically anaesthetic. Too, Rosie spent most of it in the girls' room, because Haru, the garrulous one, said almost as soon as the bows and other greetings were over, "Oh, you must see my new coat!"

It was a pale plaid of grey, sand, and blue, with an enormous collar, and Rosie, seeing nothing special in it, said, "Gee, how nice."

"Nice?" said Haru, indignantly. "Is that all you can say about it? It's gorgeous! And so cheap, too. Only seventeen ninety-eight, because it was a sale. The saleslady said it was twenty-five dollars regular."

"Gee," said Rosie. Natsu, who never said much and when she said anything said it shyly, fingered the coat covetously and Haru pulled it away.

"Mine," she said, putting it on. She minced in the aisle between the two large beds and smiled happily. "Let's see how your mother likes it." 15

She broke into the front room and the adult conversation and went to stand in front of Rosie's mother, while the rest watched from the door. Rosie's mother was properly envious. "May I inherit it when you're through with it?"

Haru, pleased, giggled, and said yes, she could, but Natsu reminded gravely from the door, "You promised me, Haru."

Everyone laughed but Natsu, who shamefacedly retreated into the bedroom. Haru came in laughing, taking off the coat. "We were only kidding, Natsu," she said. "Here, you try it on now."

After Natsu buttoned herself into the coat, inspected herself solemnly in the bureau mirror, and reluctantly shed it, Rosie, Aki, and Fuyu got their turns, and Fuyu, who was eight, drowned in it while her sisters and Rosie doubled up in amusement. They all went into the front room later, because Haru's mother quaveringly called to her to fix the tea and rice cakes and open a can of sliced peaches for everybody. Rosie noticed that her mother and Mr. Hayano were talking together at the little table — they were discussing a *haiku* that Mr. Hayano was planning to send to the *Mainichi,* while her father was sitting at one end of the sofa looking through a copy of *Life,* the new picture magazine. Occasionally, her father would comment on a photograph, holding it toward Mrs. Hayano and speaking to her as he always did — loudly, as though he thought someone such as she must surely be at least a trifle deaf also.

The five girls had their refreshments at the kitchen table, and it was while Rosie was showing the sisters her trick of swallowing peach slices without chewing (she chased each slippery crescent down with a swig of tea) that her father brought his empty teacup and untouched saucer to the sink and said, "Come on, Rosie, we're going home now." 20

"Already?" asked Rosie.

"Work tomorrow," he said.

He sounded irritated, and Rosie, puzzled, gulped one last yellow slice and stood up to go, while the sisters began protesting, as was their wont.

"We have to get up at five-thirty," he told them, going into the front room quickly, so that they did not have their usual chance to hang onto his hands and plead for an extension of time.

25   Rosie, following, saw that her mother and Mr. Hayano were sipping tea and still talking together, while Mrs. Hayano concentrated, quivering, on raising the handleless Japanese cup to her lips with both her hands and lowering it back to her lap. Her father, saying nothing, went out the door, onto the bright porch, and down the steps. Her mother looked up and asked, "Where is he going?"

"Where is he going?" Rosie said. "He said we were going home now."

"Going home?" Her mother looked with embarrassment at Mr. Hayano and his absorbed wife and then forced a smile. "He must be tired," she said.

Haru was not giving up yet. "May Rosie stay overnight?" she asked, and Natsu, Aki, and Fuyu came to reinforce their sister's plea by helping her make a circle around Rosie's mother. Rosie, for once having no desire to stay, was relieved when her mother, apologizing to the perturbed Mr. and Mrs. Hayano for her father's abruptness at the same time, managed to shake her head no at the quartet, kindly but adamant, so that they broke their circle and let her go.

Rosie's father looked ahead into the windshield as the two joined him. "I'm sorry," her mother said. "You must be tired." Her father, stepping on the starter, said nothing. "You know how I get when it's *haiku*," she continued, "I forget what time it is." He only grunted.

30   As they rode homeward silently, Rosie, sitting between, felt a rush of hate for both — for her mother for begging, for her father for denying her mother. I wish this old Ford would crash, right now, she thought, then immediately, no, no, I wish my father would laugh, but it was too late: already the vision had passed through her mind of the green pick-up crumpled in the dark against one of the mighty eucalyptus trees they were just riding past, of the three contorted, bleeding bodies, one of them hers.

Rosie ran between two patches of tomatoes, her heart working more rambunctiously than she had ever known it to. How lucky it was that Aunt Taka and Uncle Gimpachi had come tonight, though, how very lucky. Otherwise she might not have really kept her half-promise to meet Jesus Carrasco. Jesus was going to be a senior in September at the same school she went to, and his parents were the ones helping with the tomatoes this year. She and Jesus, who hardly remembered seeing each other at Cleveland High where there were so many other people and two whole grades between them, had become great friends this summer — he always had a joke for her when he periodically drove the loaded pick-up up from the fields to the shed where she was usually sorting while her mother and father did the packing, and they laughed a great deal together over infinitesimal repartee° during the afternoon break for chilled watermelon or ice cream in the shade of the shed.

repartee: Witty conversation.

What she enjoyed most was racing him to see which could finish picking a double row first. He, who could work faster, would tease her by slowing down until she thought she would surely pass him this time, then speeding up furiously to leave her several sprawling vines behind. Once he had made her screech hideously by crossing over, while her back was turned, to place atop the tomatoes in her green-stained bucket a truly monstrous, pale green worm (it had looked more like an infant snake). And it was when they had finished a contest this morning, after she had pantingly pointed a green finger at the immature tomatoes evident in the lugs° at the end of his row and he had returned the accusation (with justice), that he had startlingly brought up the matter of their possibly meeting outside the range of both their parents' dubious eyes.

"What for?" she had asked.

"I've got a secret I want to tell you," he said. 35

"Tell me now," she demanded.

"It won't be ready till tonight," he said.

She laughed. "Tell me tomorrow then."

"It'll be gone tomorrow," he threatened.

"Well, for seven hakes, what is it?" she had asked, more than twice, and when he had suggested that the packing shed would be an appropriate place to find out, she had cautiously answered maybe. She had not been certain she was going to keep the appointment until the arrival of mother's sister and her husband. Their coming seemed a sort of signal of permission, of grace, and she had definitely made up her mind to lie and leave as she was bowing them welcome.

So as soon as everyone appeared settled back for the evening, she announced 40 loudly that she was going to the privy° outside, "I'm going to the *benjo!*"° and slipped out the door. And now that she was actually on her way, her heart pumped in such an undisciplined way that she could hear it with her ears. It's because I'm running, she told herself, slowing to a walk. The shed was up ahead, one more patch away, in the middle of the fields. Its bulk, looming in the dimness, took on a sinisterness that was funny when Rosie reminded herself that it was only a wooden frame with a canvas roof and three canvas walls that made a slapping noise on breezy days.

Jesus was sitting on the narrow plank that was the sorting platform and she went around to the other side and jumped backwards to seat herself on the rim of a packing stand. "Well, tell me," she said without greeting, thinking her voice sounded reassuringly familiar.

"I saw you coming out the door," Jesus said. "I heard you running part of the way, too."

---

lugs: Shallow boxes in which produce is shipped to market.

privy: Outbuilding containing a toilet.

benjo: A lavatory with a flush toilet (Japanese).

"Uh-huh," Rosie said. "Now tell me the secret."

"I was afraid you wouldn't come," he said.

Rosie delved around on the chicken-wire bottom of the stall for number two tomatoes, ripe, which she was sitting beside, and came up with a left-over that felt edible. She bit into it and began sucking out the pulp and seeds. "I'm here," she pointed out.

"Rosie, are you sorry you came?"

"Sorry? What for?" she said. "You said you were going to tell me something."

"I will, I will," Jesus said, but his voice contained disappointment, and Rosie fleetingly felt the older of the two, realizing a brand-new power which vanished without category under her recognition.

"I have to go back in a minute," she said. "My aunt and uncle are here from Wintersburg. I told them I was going to the privy."

50   Jesus laughed. "You funny thing," he said. "You slay° me!"

"Just because you have a bathroom *inside*," Rosie said. "Come on, tell me."

Chuckling, Jesus came around to lean on the stand facing her. They still could not see each other very clearly, but Rosie noticed that Jesus became very sober again as he took the hollow tomato from her hand and dropped it back into the stall. When he took hold of her empty hand, she could find no words to protest; her vocabulary had become distressingly constricted and she thought desperately that all that remained intact now was yes and no and oh, and even these few sounds would not easily come out. Thus, kissed by Jesus, Rosie fell for the first time entirely victim to a helplessness delectable beyond speech. But the terrible, beautiful sensation lasted no more than a second, and the reality of Jesus' lips and togue and teeth and hands made her pull away with such strength that she nearly tumbled.

Rosie stopped running as she approached the lights from the windows of home. How long since she had left? She could not guess, but gasping yet, she went to the privy in back and locked herself in. Her own breathing deafened her in the dark, close space, and she sat and waited until she could hear at last the nightly calling of the frogs and crickets. Even then, all she could think to say was oh, my, and the pressure of Jesus' face against her face would not leave.

No one had missed her in the parlor, however, and Rosie walked in and through quickly, announcing that she was next going to take a bath. "Your father's in the bathhouse," her mother said, and Rosie, in her room, recalled that she had not seen him when she entered. There had been only Aunt Taka and Uncle Gimpachi with her mother at the table, drinking tea. She got her robe and straw sandals and crossed the parlor again to go outside. Her mother was telling them about the *haiku* competition in the *Mainichi* and the poem she had entered.

---

slay: Amuse, delight (slang).

Rosie met her father coming out of the bathhouse. "Are you through, Father?" she asked. "I was going to ask you to scrub my back."

"Scrub your own back," he said shortly, going toward the main house.

"What have I done now?" she yelled after him. She suddenly felt like doing a 55 lot of yelling. But he did not answer, and she went into the bathhouse. Turning on the dangling light, she removed her denims and T-shirt and threw them in the big carton for dirty clothes standing next to the washing machine. Her other things she took with her into the bath compartment to wash after her bath. After she had scooped a basin of hot water from the square wooden tub, she sat on the grey cement of the floor and soaped herself at exaggerated leisure, singing "Red Sails in the Sunset" at the top of her voice and using da-da-da where she suspected her words. Then, standing up, still singing, for she was possessed by the notion that any attempt now to analyze would result in spoilage and she believed that the larger her volume the less she would be able to hear herself think, she obtained more hot water and poured it on until she was free of lather. Only then did she allow herself to step into the steaming vat, one leg first, then the remainder of her body inch by inch until the water no longer stung and she could move around at will.

She took a long time soaking, afterwards remembering to go around outside to stoke the embers of the tin-lined fireplace beneath the tub and to throw on a few more sticks so that the water might keep its heat for her mother, and when she finally returned to the parlor, she found her mother still talking *haiku* with her aunt and uncle, the three of them on another round of tea. Her father was nowhere in sight.

At Japanese school the next day (Wednesday it was), Rosie was grave and giddy by turns. Preoccupied at her desk in the row for students on Book Eight, she made up for it at recess by performing wild mimicry for the benefit of her friend Chizuko. She held her nose and whined a witticism or two in what she considered was the manner of Fred Allen;° she assumed intoxication and a British accent to go over the climax of the Rudy Vallee° recording of the pub conversation about William Ewart Gladstone;° she was the child Shirley Temple° piping, "On the Good Ship Lollipop"; she was the gentleman soprano of the Four Inkspots° trilling, "If I Didn't Care." And she felt reasonably satisfied when Chizuko wept and gasped, "Oh, Rosie, you ought to be in the movies!"

Fred Allen: American humorist (1894–1956) and radio personality.

Rudy Vallee: American singer (1901–1986), stage, radio, and movie personality.

William Ewart Gladstone: English politician (1809–1902) and reformer.

Shirley Temple: Child actress (1928–   ) of the 1930s, known for her ringlets and dimples, singing and dancing.

Four Inkspots: African-American vocal group popular in the 1930s and 1940s.

60   Her father came after her at noon, bringing her sandwiches of minced ham and two nectarines to eat while she rode, so that she could pitch right into the sorting when they got home. The lugs were piling up, he said, and the ripe tomatoes in them would probably have to be taken to the cannery tomorrow if they were not ready for the produce haulers tonight. "This heat's not doing them any good. And we've got no time for a break today."

It *was* hot, probably the hottest day of the year, and Rosie's blouse stuck damply to her back even under the protection of the canvas. But she worked as efficiently as a flawless machine and kept the stalls heaped, with one part of her mind listening in to the parental murmuring about the heat and the tomatoes and with another part planning the exact words she would say to Jesus when he drove up with the first load of the afternoon. But when at last she saw that the pick-up was coming, her hands went berserk and the tomatoes started falling in the wrong stalls, and her father said, "Hey, hey! Rosie, watch what you're doing!"

"Well, I have to go to the *benjo*," she said, hiding panic.

"Go in the weeds over there," he said, only half-joking.

"Oh, Father!" she protested.

65   "Oh, go on home," her mother said. "We'll make out for awhile."

In the privy Rosie peered through a knothole toward the fields, watching as much as she could of Jesus. Happily she thought she saw him look in the direction of the house from time to time before he finished unloading and went back toward the patch where his mother and father worked. As she was heading for the shed, a very presentable black car purred up the dirt driveway to the house and its driver motioned to her. Was this the Hayashi home, he wanted to know. She nodded. Was she a Hayashi? Yes, she said, thinking that he was a good-looking man. He got out of the car with a huge, flat package and she saw that he warmly wore a business suit. "I have something here for your mother then," he said, in a more elegant Japanese than she was used to.

She told him where her mother was and he came along with her, patting his face with an immaculate white handkerchief and saying something about the coolness of San Francisco. To her surprised mother and father, he bowed and introduced himself as, among other things, the *haiku* editor of the *Mainichi Shimbun*, saying that since he had been coming as far as Los Angeles anyway, he had decided to bring her the first prize she had won in the recent contest.

"First prize?" her mother echoed, believing and not believing, pleased and overwhelmed. Handed the package with a bow, she bobbed her head up and down numerous times to express her utter gratitude.

"It is nothing much," he added, "but I hope it will serve as a token of our great appreciation for your contributions and our great admiration of your considerable talent."

70   "I am not worthy," she said, falling easily into his style. "It is I who should make some sign of my humble thanks for being permitted to contribute."

"No, no, to the contrary," he said, bowing again.

But Rosie's mother insisted, and then saying that she knew she was being unorthodox, she asked if she might open the package because her curiosity was so great. Certainly she might. In fact, he would like her reaction to it, for personally, it was one of his favorite *Hiroshiges*.

Rosie thought it was a pleasant picture, which looked to have been sketched with delicate quickness. There were pink clouds, containing some graceful calligraphy,° and a sea that was a pale blue except at the edges, containing four sampans° with indications of people in them. Pines edged the water and on the far-off beach there was a cluster of thatched huts towered over by pine-dotted mountains of grey and blue. The frame was scalloped and gilt.

After Rosie's mother pronounced it without peer and somewhat prodded her father into nodding agreement, she said Mr. Kuroda must at least have a cup of tea after coming all this way, and although Mr. Kuroda did not want to impose, he soon agreed that a cup of tea would be refreshing and went along with her to the house, carrying the picture for her.

"Ha, your mother's crazy!" Rosie's father said, and Rosie laughed uneasily as 75
she resumed judgment on the tomatoes. She had emptied six lugs when he broke into an imaginary conversation with Jesus to tell her to go and remind her mother of the tomatoes, and she went slowly.

Mr. Kuroda was in his shirtsleeves expounding some *haiku* theory as he munched a rice cake, and her mother was rapt. Abashed in the great man's presence, Rosie stood next to her mother's chair until her mother looked up inquiringly, and then she started to whisper the message, but her mother pushed her gently away and reproached, "You are not being very polite to our guest."

"Father says the tomatoes . . ." Rosie said aloud, smiling foolishly.

"Tell him I shall only be a minute," her mother said, speaking the language of Mr. Kuroda.

When Rosie carried the reply to her father, he did not seem to hear and she said again, "Mother says she'll be back in a minute."

"All right, all right," he nodded, and they worked again in silence. But sud- 80
denly, her father uttered an incredible noise, exactly like the cork of a bottle popping, and the next Rosie knew, he was stalking angrily toward the house, almost running in fact, and she chased after him crying, "Father! Father! What are you going to do?"

He stopped long enough to order her back to the shed. "Never mind!" he shouted. "Get on with the sorting!"

And from the place in the fields where she stood, frightened and vacillating, Rosie saw her father enter the house. Soon Mr. Kuroda came out alone, putting on his coat. Mr. Kuroda got into his car and backed out down the driveway onto the highway. Next her father emerged, also alone, something in his arms (it was

---

calligraphy: Graceful or artistic handwriting.

sampans: Flat-bottomed Asian boats, usually propelled with oars.

the picture, she realized), and, going over to the bathhouse woodpile, he threw the picture on the ground and picked up the axe. Smashing the picture, glass and all (she heard the explosion faintly), he reached over for the kerosene that was used to encourage the bath fire and poured it over the wreckage. I am dreaming, Rosie said to herself, I am dreaming, but her father, having made sure that his act of cremation was irrevocable, was even then returning to the fields.

Rosie ran past him and toward the house. What had become of her mother? She burst into the parlor and found her mother at the back window watching the dying fire. They watched together until there remained only a feeble smoke under the blazing sun. Her mother was very calm.

"Do you know why I married your father?" she said without turning.

85   "No," said Rosie. It was the most frightening question she had ever been called upon to answer. Don't tell me now, she wanted to say, tell me tomorrow, tell me next week, don't tell me today. But she knew she would be told now, that the telling would combine with the other violence of the hot afternoon to level her life, her world to the very ground.

It was like a story out of the magazines illustrated in sepia,° which she had consumed so greedily for a period until the information had somehow reached her that those wretchedly unhappy autobiographies, offered to her as the testimonials of living men and women, were largely inventions: Her mother, at nineteen, had come to America and married her father as an alternative to suicide.

At eighteen she had been in love with the first son of one of the well-to-do families in her village. The two had met whenever and wherever they could, secretly, because it would not have done for his family to see him favor her — her father had no money; he was a drunkard and a gambler besides. She had learned she was with child; an excellent match had already been arranged for her lover. Despised by her family, she had given premature birth to a stillborn son, who would be seventeen now. Her family did not turn her out, but she could no longer project herself in any direction without refreshing in them the memory of her indiscretion. She wrote to Aunt Taka, her favorite sister in America, threatening to kill herself if Aunt Taka would not send for her. Aunt Taka hastily arranged a marriage with a young man of whom she knew, but lately arrived from Japan, a young man of simple mind, it was said, but of kindly heart. The young man was never told why his unseen betrothed was so eager to hasten the day of meeting.

The story was told perfectly, with neither groping for words nor untoward passion. It was as though her mother had memorized it by heart, reciting it to herself so many times over that its nagging vileness had long since gone.

"I had a brother then?" Rosie asked, for this was what seemed to matter now; she would think about the other later, she assured herself, pushing back the illumination which threatened all that darkness that had hitherto been merely mysterious or even glamorous. "A half-brother?"

90   "Yes."

---

sepia: A grayish-brown ink or pigment.

"I would have liked a brother," she said.

Suddenly, her mother knelt on the floor and took her by the wrists. "Rosie," she said urgently, "promise me you will never marry!" Shocked more by the request than the revelation, Rosie stared at her mother's face. Jesus, Jesus, she called silently, not certain whether she was invoking the help of the son of the Carrascos or of God, until there returned sweetly the memory of Jesus' hand, how it had touched her and where. Still her mother waited for an answer, holding her wrists so tightly that her hands were going numb. She tried to pull free. Promise, her mother whispered fiercely, promise. Yes, yes, I promise, Rosie said. But for an instant she turned away, and her mother, hearing the familiar glib agreement, released her. Oh, you, you, you, her eyes and twisted mouth said, you fool. Rosie, covering her face, began at last to cry, and the embrace and consoling hand came much later than she expected.

3| POETRY

CHAPTER 14

UNDERSTANDING POETRY

MARIANNE MOORE   (1887–1972)

Poetry   (1921)

I, too, dislike it: there are things that are important beyond all
     this fiddle.
Reading it, however, with a perfect contempt for it, one discovers
in it after all, a place for the genuine.
          Hands that can grasp, eyes
          that can dilate, hair that can rise   5
               if it must, these things are important not because a

high-sounding interpretation can be put upon them but because they are
     useful. When they become so derivative as to become unintelligible,
     the same thing may be said for all of us, that we
          do not admire what   10
          we cannot understand: the bat
               holding on upside down or in quest of something to

eat, elephants pushing, a wild horse taking a roll, a tireless wolf under
     a tree, the immovable critic twitching his skin like a horse that feels
     a flea, the base-
     ball fan, the statistician—   15
          nor is it valid
               to discriminate against "business documents and

school-books";° all these phenomena are important. One must make
     a distinction
          however: when dragged into prominence by half poets, the result
          is not poetry,
          nor till the poets among us can be   20
               "literalists of

° *"business documents and school-books"*: Moore quotes the *Diaries of Tolstoy* (New York, 1917): "Where the
boundary between prose and poetry lies, I shall never be able to understand. . . . Poetry is verse; prose is not
verse. Or else poetry is everything with the exception of business documents and school books."

the imagination"°— above
　　insolence and triviality and can present

for inspection, "imaginary gardens with real toads in them,"
　　shall we have
　　it. In the meantime, if you demand on the one hand,   25
　　the raw material of poetry in
　　　　all its rawness and
　　　　that which is on the other hand
　　　　　　genuine, you are interested in poetry.

NIKKI GIOVANNI   (1943– 　)

Poetry   (1975)

poetry is motion graceful
as a fawn
gentle as a teardrop
strong like the eye
finding peace in a crowded room   5
we poets tend to think
our words are golden
though emotion speaks too
loudly to be defined
by silence   10

sometimes after midnight or just before
the dawn
we sit typewriter in hand
pulling loneliness around us
forgetting our lovers or children   15
who are sleeping
ignoring the weary wariness
of our own logic
to compose a poem

　　no one understands it   20
it never says "love me" for poets are
beyond love
it never says "accept me" for poems seek not
acceptance but controversy

° *"literalists of the imagination"*: A reference (given by Moore) to W. B. Yeats's "William Blake and His Illustra-
tions" (in *Ideas of Good and Evil*, 1903): "The limitation of his view was from the very intensity of his vision; he
was a too literal realist of the imagination as others are of nature; and because he believed that the figures
seen by the mind's eye, when exalted by inspiration, were 'external existences,' symbols of divine essences, he
hated every grace of style that might obscure their lineaments."

it only says "i am" and therefore   25
i concede that you are too
a poem is pure energy
horizontally contained
between the mind
of the poet and the ear of the reader   30
if it does not sing discard the ear
for poetry is song
if it does not delight discard
the heart for poetry is joy
if it does not inform then close   35
off the brain for it is dead
if it cannot heed the insistent message
that life is precious

which is all we poets
wrapped in our loneliness   40
are trying to say

Origins of Modern Poetry

The history of poetry begins where the history of all literature begins—with the **oral tradition.** In a time before literacy and the printing press, the oral tradition was relied upon as a way of preserving stories, histories, values, and beliefs. These stories were usually put into the form of rhyming poems, with repeated words and sounds used to make the poems easier to memorize and remember.

These extended narratives were eventually transcribed as **epics** — long poems depicting the actions of heroic figures who determine the fate of a nation or entire race. Early epics include Homer's *Iliad* and *Odyssey*, the *Epic of Gilgamesh,* the *Bhagavad Gita,* and Virgil's *Aeneid.* Early poetry can also be found in various religious texts, including ancient Hindu holy books like the Upanishads; sections of the Bible, including the Song of Solomon; and the Koran.

During the **Anglo-Saxon era** (late sixth to mid-eleventh centuries), poetry flourished as a literary form. Unfortunately, only about 30,000 lines of poetry survive from this period. Those poems that did survive are marked by heroic deeds and the absence of romantic love. The major texts of this time include *Beowulf, The Battle of Maldon,* and *The Dream of the Rood,* which is one of the earliest Christian poems. The theme of Christian morality in poetry continued into the Middle Ages with poems such as William Langland's *Piers Plowman,* which consisted of three religious dream visions, and Chaucer's *Canterbury Tales,* a collection of narrative poems told by pilgrims as they travel to Canterbury, England. Using a slightly different approach to similar subject matter, Dante Alighieri wrote the Italian epic poem *The Divine Comedy,* which depicts an imaginary journey

Image depicting the pilgrims from Geoffrey Chaucer's *The Canterbury Tales*

Illuminated manuscript (fifteenth century) from Dante's *Divine Comedy* depicting Dante and Virgil in Hell

through hell, purgatory, and heaven. In France, the **troubadours,** poets of the Provençal region, wrote complex lyric poems about courtly love.

The next major literary period, the **Renaissance** (late fourteenth to mid-sixteenth centuries), witnessed a rebirth of science, philosophy, and the classical arts. Perhaps the most important writer of this period was William Shakespeare. A prolific poet, Shakespeare also wrote plays in verse, continuing in the tradition of the ancient Greek tragedian Sophocles and the ancient Roman playwright Seneca. Other notable writers of the Renaissance included Sir Philip Sidney, Christopher Marlowe, and Edmund Spenser.

During the seventeenth century, several literary movements emerged that contributed to poetry's growing prevalence and influence. John Milton continued the tradition of Christian poetry with his epic *Paradise Lost*, which told the tale of Adam and Eve's exile from the Garden of Eden. The **metaphysical poets** (John Donne, Andrew Marvell, and George Herbert) used elaborate figures of speech and favored intellect over emotions in their writing. Their poems were characterized by reason, complex comparisons and allusions, and paradoxes, and they introduced the **meditative poem** (a poem that abstractly ponders a concept or idea) into the literary world.

In the early eighteenth century, British poets (such as Alexander Pope and Samuel Johnson) wrote poems, biographies, and literary criticism, subsequently expanding the scope and influence of poetry. It was also during this time that the movement known as **Romanticism** began. Romantic poetry was marked by heightened emotion and sentiment; a strong sense of individualism; a respect for nature, history, and mysticism; and a return to first-person lyric poems. The early British

Illuminated manuscript from William Blake's "The Tyger"

John Martin's painting *The Bard* (1817) illustrating the mystical view of nature characteristic of Romanticism

Romantics included Samuel Taylor Coleridge, William Wordsworth, and William Blake. This generation was followed by the later Romantics, including Percy Bysshe Shelley, John Keats, and George Gordon, Lord Byron. American Romantics included Henry David Thoreau, Ralph Waldo Emerson, and Walt Whitman.

The nineteenth century was marked by yet another shift in poetic consciousness. This time, poets moved away from the contemplation of the self within nature and returned to a more elevated sense of rhetoric and subject matter as well as to a more formal structure. Notable British authors included Alfred, Lord Tennyson, Matthew Arnold, Robert Browning, and Elizabeth Barrett Browning. American poets of the this period included Edgar Allan Poe, Henry Wadsworth Longfellow, Emily Dickinson, and Phillis Wheatley, a slave who became the first African-American poet.

The twentieth century had perhaps the largest number of literary movements to date, with each one reflecting its predecessors and influencing future generations of poets. In the early twentieth century, a literary movement that became known as **modernism** developed. As authors responded to

Undated engraving of Edgar Allan Poe's "The Raven"

the increasing complexity of a changing world, the overarching sentiment of modernism was that the "old ways" would no longer suffice in a world that had changed almost overnight as a result of the rise of industrialization and urbanization, as well as the devastation of World War I. Key modernist writers included W. H. Auden, William Butler Yeats, Ezra Pound, and T. S. Eliot, whose epic poem *The Waste Land* expressed the fragmentation of consciousness in the modern world. A precursor to modernism was French symbolism, which was a revolt against the realistic and naturalistic poetic styles of the day. The goal of symbolist poetry was to create a series of symbols that captured the essence of an idea. Its practitioners included Stéphane Mallarmé, Charles Baudelaire, and Arthur Rimbaud.

After World War I, poets began to challenge the prevailing ideas of subject matter and form. Ezra Pound, along with Amy Lowell and other poets, founded **imagism,** a poetic movement that emphasized free verse and the writer's response to a visual scene or an object. William Carlos Williams wrote poems that were often deceptively simple, while the poetry of Wallace Stevens was often opaque and difficult to grasp. Dylan Thomas and E. E. Cummings also experimented with form, with Cummings specifically manipulating the accepted constructs of grammar, syntax, and punctuation.

In the 1920s, the United States experienced the **Harlem Renaissance.** This rebirth of arts and culture was centered in Harlem, an area in New York City where, by the mid-1920s, the African-American population had reached 150,000. Harlem was an area teeming with creativity, especially in music (jazz and blues), literature, art, and drama. The poets who were part of the Harlem Renaissance — including Langston Hughes, Countee Cullen, James Weldon Johnson, and Jean Toomer — chose diverse subject matter and styles, but they were united in their celebration of African-American culture and experience.

In the early 1930s, a group of poets gathered at a college in Black Mountain, North Carolina, with the aim of teaching and writing about poetry in a new way. The **Black Mountain Poets,** as they were called, stressed the process of writing poetry rather than the finished poem. Notable poets in this group included Robert Creeley, Denise Levertov, and Charles Olson. Meanwhile, in Latin America, poetry grew in importance, with poets such as Pablo Neruda experimenting with subject matter, language, form, and imagery.

In the late 1940s, in the aftermath of World War II, a group of disillusioned American poets turned to eastern mysticism and newly available hallucinogenic drugs to achieve higher consciousness. They became known as the **Beat poets,** and their work was known for social and political criticism that challenged the established norms of the time. These poets included Allen Ginsberg, whose long poem *Howl* became an unofficial anthem of the revolutionary 1960s, and Lawrence Ferlinghetti.

Up until the late 1950s, subject matter in American poetry was largely impersonal, concentrating chiefly on symbols, ideas, and politics. This changed when a group of poets — including Robert Lowell, Anne Sexton, W. D. Snod-grass, and Sylvia Plath — began to write **confessional poems** about their own per-sonal experiences, emotions, triumphs, and tragedies — including mental illness and attempted suicide. Although there was considerable backlash against these poets from writers who thought that such highly personal subjects were not suit-able for poetry, contemporary poets such as Sharon Olds continue to write con-fessional poetry.

The early 1960s witnessed the rise of the **Black Arts Movement,** which had its roots in the ideas of the civil rights struggle, Malcolm X and the Nation of Is-lam, and the Black Power Movement. The Black Arts poets wrote political work that addressed the sociopolitical and cultural context of African-Americans. No-table authors in this group included Amiri Baraka, Gwendolyn Brooks, Jayne Cortez, and Etheridge Knight.

The next major literary movement that occurred in poetry had its beginnings in the mid to late 1980s with slam poetry. **Slam poetry,** with origins in the oral tradition, was influenced by the Beat poets, who stressed the live performance of poems. In a **slam,** poets compete either individually or in teams before an audi-ence, which serves as the judge. (The structure of a traditional poetry slam was created by Marc Smith, a poet and construction worker, in 1986.) Slam poetry is concerned with current events and social and political themes, and often the win-ning poet is the one who best combines enthusiasm, presentation, and attitude with contemporary subject matter. A home base for slam poetry is the Nyuorican Poets Café in New York City, which has become a forum for poetry, music, video, and theater. Notable slam poets past and present include Miguel Piñero, Maggie Estep, Jeffrey McDaniel, Staceyann Chin, and Bob Holman.

Staceyann Chin, acclaimed slam poet and the star of
Def Poetry Jam on Broadway

BOB HOLMAN (1948–   )

6 Short Poems

Modern Lovers
In order to save the relationship
We will never see each other again

Night Fears
Everyone is in love
Except you

Ten Things I Do Every Day
Suicide

My Shirt
I like to put it on
My arms get long that way

Love Poems
I love poems

Goo Ahead
Goo ahead

A spinoff of slam poetry is the **spoken word** movement, which, unlike slam poetry, is a rehearsed performance. Spoken word performances have captivated a broad audience due in part to television shows such as HBO's *Def Poetry Jam*. **Hip-hop** and **rap**, musical forms whose lyrics rely heavily on rhyme, alliteration, assonance, consonance, and other poetic devices, also owe a debt to slam poetry and the spoken word movement.

Contemporary poetry is an extremely diverse genre whose practitioners have been influenced by many of the literary movements discussed above. Some contemporary poets embrace narrative poetry; others favor the lyric. Some write free verse; others experiment with traditional forms like the sonnet or the villanelle. Still others write **concrete poetry**, which uses words as well as varying type sizes and type fonts to form pictures on a page, or other forms of **visual poetry** (see Chapter 15). The types of poetry being written today vary greatly, and this diversity is part of the appeal for those who read and write it.

Defining Poetry

Throughout history and across national and cultural boundaries, poetry has held an important place. In ancient China and Japan, for example, poetry was prized above all else. One story tells of a samurai warrior who, when defeated, asked for a pen and paper. Thinking that he wanted to write a will before being executed, his captor granted his wish. Instead of writing a will, however, the warrior wrote a farewell poem that so moved his captor that he immediately released him.

To the ancient Greeks and Romans, poetry was the medium of spiritual and philosophical expression. Today, throughout the world, poetry continues to delight and to inspire. For many people in countless places, poetry is the language of the emotions, the medium of expression they use when they speak from the heart.

But what exactly *is* poetry? Is a poem "pure energy / horizontally contained / between the mind / of the poet and the readers," as Nikki Giovanni (page 440) describes it? Or is a poem simply what Marianne Moore (page 439) calls "all this fiddle"?

One way of defining poetry is to examine how it is different from other forms of literature, such as fiction or drama. The first and most important element of poetry that distinguishes it from other genres is its **form.** Unlike prose, which is written from margin to margin, poetry is made up of individual **lines.** A poetic line begins and ends where the poet chooses: it can start at the left margin or halfway across the page, and it can end at the right margin or after only a word or two. A poet chooses when to stop, or break, the line according to his or her sense of rhythm and cadence.

Poets also use the **sound** of the words themselves, alone and in conjunction with the other words of the poem, to create a sense of rhythm and melody. **Alliteration** (the repetition of consonant sounds in consecutive or neighboring words), **assonance** (the repetition of vowel sounds at the ends of words), and **consonance** (the repetition of consonant sounds at the ends of words) are three devices commonly used by poets to help create the music of a poem. Poets can also use **rhyme** (either at the ends of lines or within the lines themselves), which contributes to the pattern of sounds in a poem.

In addition, poets are more likely than writers of other kinds of literature to rely on **imagery,** words or phrases that describe the senses. These vivid descriptions or details help the reader to connect with the poet's ideas in a tangible way. Poets also make extensive use of **figurative language,** including metaphors and similes, to convey their ideas and to help their readers access these ideas.

Another way of defining poetry is to examine our assumptions about it. Different readers, different poets, different generations of readers and poets, and different cultures may have different expectations about poetry. As a result, they have varying assumptions about what poetry should be, and these assumptions raise questions. Must poetry be written to delight or inspire, or can a poem have a political or social message? Must a poem's theme be conveyed subtly, embellished with imaginatively chosen sounds and words, or can it be explicit and straightforward? Such questions, which have been debated by literary critics as well as by poets for many years, have no easy answers — and perhaps no answers at all. A **haiku** — a short poem, rich in imagery, adhering to a rigid formal structure — is certainly poetry, and so is a political poem like Carolyn Forché's "The Colonel" (p. 593). To some Western readers, however, a haiku might seem too plain or understated to be "poetic," and Forché's poem might seem to be a political tract masquerading as poetry. Still, most of these readers would agree that the following lines qualify as poetry.

WILLIAM SHAKESPEARE (1564–1616)

That time of year thou mayst in me behold (1609)

That time of year thou mayst in me behold
When yellow leaves, or none, or few, do hang
Upon those boughs which shake against the cold,
Bare ruined choirs, where late the sweet birds sang.
In me thou see'st the twilight of such day   5
As after sunset fadeth in the west,
Which by and by black night doth take away,
Death's second self that seals up all in rest.
In me thou see'st the glowing of such fire,
That on the ashes of his youth doth lie,   10
As the deathbed whereon it must expire,
Consumed with that which it was nourished by
   This thou perceiv'st, which makes thy love more strong,
   To love that well which thou must leave ere long.

This poem includes many of the characteristics that Western readers commonly associate with poetry. For instance, its lines have a regular pattern of rhyme and meter that identifies it as a **sonnet.** The poem also develops a complex network of related images and figures of speech that compare the lost youth of the aging speaker to the sunset and to autumn. Finally, the pair of rhyming lines at the end of the poem expresses a familiar poetic theme: the lovers' realization that they must eventually die makes their love stronger.

The next poem is quite different from the preceding one, yet most readers would probably agree that it too is a poem.

LOUIS ZUKOFSKY (1904–1978)

I walk in the old street (1944)

I walk in the old street
to hear the beloved songs
afresh
this spring night.

Like the leaves — my loves wake — 5
not to be the same
or look tireless to the stars
and a ripped doorbell.

Unlike Shakespeare's sonnet, Zukofsky's poem does not have a regular metrical pattern or rhyme scheme. Its diction is more conversational than poetic, and one of its images — a "ripped doorbell" — presents a jarring contrast to the other, more conventionally "poetic" images. Nevertheless, the subject — love — is a traditional one; in fact, Zukofsky's poem echoes some of the sentiments of the Shakespeare sonnet. Finally, the poem's division into two four-line stanzas and its use of figures of speech ("Like the leaves — my loves wake —") are unmistakably poetic.

Although most readers would probably classify the two preceding works as poems, they might be less certain about the following lines.

E. E. CUMMINGS (1894–1962)

l(a (1923)

l(a
le
af
fa
ll   5
s)
one
l
iness

Unlike Shakespeare's and Zukofsky's poems, "l(a" does not seem to have any of the characteristics normally associated with poetry. It has no meter, rhyme, or imagery. It has no repeated sounds, no figures of speech. It cannot even be read aloud because its "lines" are fragments of words. In spite of its odd appearance, however, "l(a" does communicate a conventional poetic theme. When reconstructed, the words Cummings broke apart have the following appearance: "l (a leaf falls) one l iness." In a sense, this poem is a complex visual and verbal pun. If the parenthetical insertion "(a leaf falls)" is removed, the remaining letters spell "loneliness." Moreover, the form of the letter l in loneliness suggest the number 1 — which, in turn, suggests the loneliness and isolation of the individual, as reflected in nature (the single leaf). Like Shakespeare and Zukofsky, Cummings uses an image of a leaf to express his ideas about life and about human experience. At the same time, by breaking words into bits and pieces, Cummings suggests the flexibility of language and conveys the need to break out of customary ways of using words to define experience.

As the preceding discussion illustrates, defining what a poem is (and what it is not) can be difficult. Poems can rhyme or not rhyme. They can be divided into stanzas and have a distinct form, or they can flow freely and have no discernable form. These and other choices are what many poets find alluring about the process of writing poetry. As a form, poetry is compact and concise, and choosing the right words to convey ideas is a challenge. As a literary genre, it offers room for experimentation while at the same time remaining firmly grounded in a literary tradition that stretches back through time to antiquity.

Recognizing Kinds of Poetry

Most poems are either **narrative** poems, which recount a story, or **lyric** poems, which communicate a speaker's mood, feelings, or state of mind.

Narrative Poetry

Although any brief poem that tells a story, such as Edwin Arlington Robinson's "Richard Cory" (p. 695), may be considered a narrative poem, the two most familiar forms of narrative poetry are the *epic* and the *ballad*.

Epics are narrative poems that recount the accomplishments of heroic figures, typically including expansive settings, superhuman feats, and gods and supernatural beings. The language of epic poems tends to be formal, even elevated, and often quite elaborate. In ancient times, epics were handed down orally; more recently, poets have written literary epics, such as John Milton's *Paradise Lost* (1667) and Nobel Prize–winning poet Derek Walcott's *Omeros* (1990), that follow many of the same conventions.

The **ballad** is another type of narrative poetry with roots in an oral tradition. Originally intended to be sung, a ballad uses repeated words and phrases, including a refrain, to advance its story. Some —but not all —ballads use the **ballad stanza.** For examples of traditional ballads in this book, see "Bonny Barbara Allan" (p. 647) and "Western Wind" (p. 650). Dudley Randall's "Ballad of Birmingham" (p. 486) is an example of a contemporary ballad.

Lyric Poetry

Like narrative poems, lyric poems take various forms.

An **elegy** is a poem in which a poet mourns the death of a specific person, as in A. E. Housman's "To an Athlete Dying Young" (p. 508).

An **ode** is a long lyric poem, formal and serious in style, tone, and subject matter. An ode typically has a fairly complex stanzaic pattern, such as the **terza rima** used by Percy Bysshe Shelley in "Ode to the West Wind" (p. 697). Another ode in this text is John Keats's "Ode on a Grecian Urn" (p. 680).

An **aubade** is a poem about morning, usually celebrating the coming of dawn. An example is Philip Larkin's 1977 poem "Aubade."

An **occasional poem** is written to celebrate a particular event or occasion. An example is Billy Collins's poem "The Names," read before a joint session of Congress to commomorate the first anniversary of the terrorist attacks on the World Trade Center.

A **meditation** is a lyric poem that focuses on a physical object, using this object as a vehicle for considering larger issues. Edmund Waller's seventeenth-century poem "Go, lovely rose" is a meditation.

A **pastoral**—for example, Christopher Marlowe's "The Passionate Shepherd to His Love" (p. 685)—is a lyric poem that celebrates the simple, idyllic pleasures of country life.

A **dramatic monologue** is a poem whose speaker addresses one or more silent listeners, often revealing much more than he or she intends. Robert Browning's "My Last Duchess" (p. 465) and "Porphyria's Lover" (p. 480) and Alfred, Lord Tennyson's "Ulysses" (p. 701) are dramatic monologues.

As you read the poems in this text, you will encounter works with a wide variety of forms, styles, and themes. Some you will find appealing, amusing, uplifting, or moving; others may strike you as puzzling, intimidating, or depressing. But regardless of your critical reaction to the poems, one thing is certain: if you take the time to pay attention to the lines you are reading, and to think about them later on, you will come away from them thinking not just about the images and ideas they express but also about yourself and your world.

NOTE: As you will see in the following chapter, poets can also create **visual poetry**, experimenting with the way a poem looks on the page.

CHAPTER 15

POETRY SAMPLER: VISUAL POETRY

Generally speaking, **visual poetry** occupies the area between literature and the visual arts, between words and pictures. Some of its practitioners see visual poetry as a literary form in which the appearance of a poem is as important as its content. Others see it as a visual form that comes from a literary background. Still others see it as an art form that uses visual content in new and interesting ways. As difficult as

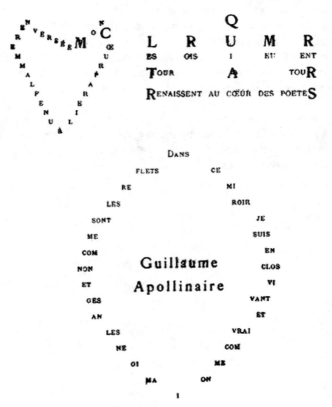

Apollinaire's poem "Coeur couronne et miroir." ("Heart, wreath and mirror.") From *Calligrammes* (1912–1918). The words surrounding the poet's name read, "In this mirror I am enclosed living and true as one imagines angels to be and not as reflections are."

it is to define, visual poetry is growing in popularity and, in some cases, is challenging preconceptions about poetry itself.

The early precursors of visual poetry were ancient Greek **pattern poems** and **acrostics,** sixteenth- and seventeenth-century **emblem poems,** and literary texts such as the poems in Guillaume Apollinaire's *Calligrammes,* one of which, "Couer couronne et miroir," is pictured on page 452. All of these poems had visual formats that mirrored, on some level, their content or subject matter.

Visual poetry has its philosophical roots in various literary and artistic movements, including Dadaism, surrealism, and futurism. **Dadaism** was a nihilistic movement that began in France and emphasized irrationality, cynicism, and anarchy. Dadaists rejected traditional concepts of beauty and social organization and embraced the absurd. **Surrealism** grew out of Dadaism but sought to tap the creative potential of the unconscious mind and to exploit the material of dreams and the states of mind between waking and sleeping. Surrealist writing emphasized broken syntax, free association, nonchronological order, and dreamlike sequences. **Futurism** rejected the past and celebrated change, originality, and innovation in culture and society. Just as visual poetry does, all three of these movements embraced structural and thematic changes that revealed a new sense of meaning and significance.

One kind of visual poetry, called **concrete poetry,** uses words — and, sometimes, different fonts and type sizes — to shape a picture on the page. The form of a concrete poem does not emerge from the poem's words and images; it is predetermined by the visual image the poet has decided to create. In this way, concrete poems explore ways in which the visual form and the arrangement of words on a page interact and affect the content and meaning of a text. Concrete poems are not necessarily read left to right, as traditional poems are; instead, they can

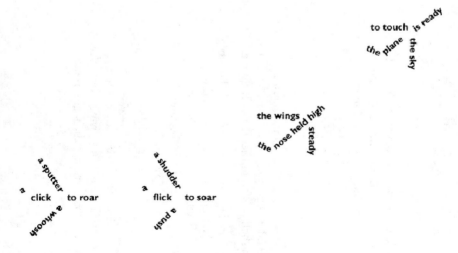

"Airplane Takes Off," concrete poem from NASA Web site.

be approached in numerous ways, with the meaning primarily derived from the forms of the poems themselves. Although some concrete poems, like the one on the previous page, are little more than novelties, others may be enlightening or even profound.

Modern-day visual poets often have experience in the visual arts. Combining words and images collected from popular media such as newspapers and magazines, visual poets explore the relationship between mass media and visual art. By juxtaposing pictures and text, they create montages and collages that explore and sometimes challenge the boundaries between these genres. In fact, many visual poets now use computers to manipulate music tracks, animation, and color, creating highly original — and sometimes strikingly beautiful — works that combine text, sound, and video.

The poems that follow illustrate the varied forms of visual poetry. George Herbert's "Easter Wings," May Swenson's "Women," and Greg Williamson's "Group Photo with Winter Trees" use the techniques of concrete poetry to structure, to mimic, or to represent a tangible form. Charles Bernstein ("this poem intentionally left blank") uses unexpected blank space to create meaning. Ian Hamilton Finlay ("Acrobats") and Reed Altemus and Jim Leftwich ("Flake upper phase") use computer technology to stretch the limits of visual poetry. Finally, Bob Grumman ("Mathemaku No. 10") juxtaposes symbols with words. Regardless of the differences in their approaches, each poet experiments with poetic form and visual presentation in an attempt to expand the limits of poetic expression.

GEORGE HERBERT (1593–1633)

Easter Wings (1633)

Lord, who createdst man in wealth and store,
Though foolishly he lost the same,
Decaying more and more,
Till he became
Most poor,
With thee
Oh, let me rise
As larks, harmoniously,
And sing this day thy victories;   5
Then shall the fall further the flight in me.

My tender age in sorrow did begin;
And still with sicknesses and shame   10
Thou didst so punish sin,
That I became
Most thin.
With thee
Let me combine,   15
And feel this day thy victory;
For if I imp my wing on thine,
Affliction shall advance the flight in me.   20

MAY SWENSON (1919–1989)

Women   (1970)

Women   Or they
  should be   should be
    pedestals   little horses
      moving   those wooden
        pedestals   sweet   5
          moving   oldfashioned
          to the   painted
        motions   rocking
        of men   horses

        the gladdest things in the toyroom   10

            The   feelingly
           pegs   and then
         of their   unfeelingly
        ears   To be
      so familiar   joyfully   15
     and dear   ridden
   to the trusting rockingly
fists   ridden until
To be chafed   the restored

egos dismount and the legs stride away   20

Immobile   willing
  sweetlipped   to be set
    sturdy   into motion
     and smiling   Women
      women   should be   25
    should always pedestals
      be waiting   to men

GREG WILLIAMSON (1964–   )

Group Photo with Winter Trees   (2002)

         These were my neighbors. It's a big group pose:
On mist-gray skies, the stark, black branches etch
         Horizon, lawn, in loose haphazard rows.
As if in tin, or as in some old sketch,
         That's The Great Bob. And that's our good Queen Paul   5
Whose lines, whose every nuance was precise,
         With Champagne Anne and Rick the dog. They're all
But faded now. I've seen the trees in ice,
         Decked out, (Liz, too, who helped me do the plumbing),
But I'll be gone when their spring blooms and scatters   10
         Even the children. And, God, they're all becoming.
Shades, as the new leaves turn to other matters.

CHARLES BERNSTEIN (1950 –   )

this poem intentionally left blank

IAN HAMILTON FINLAY (1925 –   )

Acrobats* (1966)

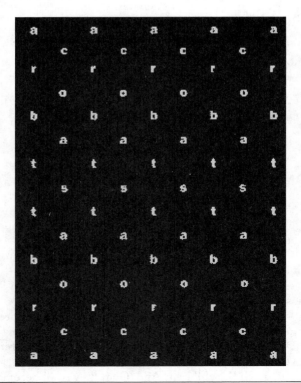

---

* When this poem is read online, the letters move.

REED ALTEMUS (1961–   ) and
JIM LEFTWICH

Flake upper phase (2002)

Flake upper phase react -'. ♦ -- flooding
touchir........... q operator
oblon .... lacement
vitia ong divi.......... vaunted
brick story of inf.......... er shirtstain
long divisio......... od vollies pin
story of inflated so......... filed vollies

Found aiming previous chairs block talked
zipper flecked Bu........ r exude searing
flappy with vu........... blastulas
popover t........... -like movement
move........... f spiral singularity
filim........... ing
somnamb........... irs
flecked mot...........
factor conn
already pre........ and .... eg for popover
sit on the filament boosting motor extract

Attractive offal......... stracted sle limpse
foreign b.........
volcir red........... ities
red s........... print tubea........ant
num volatility bloom rea.......... calibratio.......
test prin...........
volatility bloom re........ calibrati sional isional

Reed Altemus 01/22/02
.... 12.03.02

BOB GRUMMAN (1941–   )

Mathemaku No. 10   (1994)

$$
\text{poetry)}\overline{\text{\textit{existence}}}^{\;\heartsuit}
$$
somewhere, minutely, a widening
existence

Reading and Reacting

1. Which poem in this chapter seems most conventional? Which one seems most experimental? Explain.

2. How would George Herbert's "Easter Wings" and May Swenson's "Women" be different if they were written in traditional form? What would be gained and what would be lost if the poems were written in this way?

3. Try reading these poems aloud. Are they all actually readable? If any one is not, do you still consider it a poem? Explain.

4. Look closely at the poems by Bob Grumman, Hamilton Finlay, and Reed Altemus. Do you think the visual elements of their poems are essential, or do you see them simply as gimmicks? Explain.

5. Why are the alternating lines of "Group Photo with Winter Trees" set in boldface type? How does the form of this poem reflect its title?

6. Do you consider "this poem intentionally left blank" a poem? What ideas does it communicate to readers? How else could Bernstein have expressed these ideas?

WRITING SUGGESTIONS

1. Write an explication of one of the poems in this chapter. Make sure you discuss how the visual elements of the poem help to communicate its main idea.

2. Write an essay in which you discuss the relationship between the shape of George Herbert's "Easter Wings" and the poem's subject. Why do you think Herbert constructed the poem the way he did?

3. Choose several imagist poems from Chapter 18—for example, "Red Wheelbarrow" or "In a Station of the Metro." How could you turn each of these poems into a visual poem? Would the poems be more or less effective as visual poetry? Explain.

CHAPTER 16

VOICE

A poem remains with us to the extent that it allows us to feel that we are listening to a voice at once contemporary and ancient. This makes all the difference.

—John Haines, *"The Hole in the Bucket"*

EMILY DICKINSON   (1830–1886)

I'm nobody! Who are you?   (1891)

I'm nobody! Who are you?
Are you — Nobody — Too?
Then there's a pair of us?
Don't tell! they'd advertise — you know!

How dreary — to be — Somebody!   5
How public — like a Frog —
To tell one's name — the livelong June —
To an admiring Bog!

The Speaker in the Poem

When they read fiction, readers form an impression of a work's narrator and decide whether he or she is sophisticated or unsophisticated, trustworthy or untrustworthy, innocent or experienced. Just as fiction depends on a narrator, poetry depends on a **speaker** who describes events, feelings, and ideas to readers. Finding out as much as possible about this speaker can help readers to interpret a poem. For example, the speaker in Emily Dickinson's "I'm nobody! Who are you?" seems at first to be playful, even flirtatious. In fact, she appears to be entering into a conspiracy with readers. The first stanza of the poem suggests that the speaker is a private person, with little desire to be well known. As the poem continues, however, her focus changes. The poem's two stanzas present a complex persona. In the first stanza, the speaker reveals her private self — internal, isolated, and

revealed through poetry; in the second stanza, she moves outward to express disdain for those who seek to become "somebody," whom she sees as self-centered,
self-promoting, and inevitably superficial. Far from being defeated by her isolation, the speaker seems to have rejected fame and chosen her status as "nobody."

One question readers might ask about "I'm nobody! Who are you?" is how
close the speaker's voice is to the poet's. Readers who conclude that the poem is
about the conflict between a poet's public and private selves may be tempted to
see the speaker and the poet as one. But this is not necessarily the case. Like the
narrator of a short story, the speaker of a poem is a **persona,** or mask, that the poet
puts on. Granted, in some poems little distance exists between the poet and the
speaker. Without hard evidence to support a link between speaker and poet, however, readers should not simply assume they are one and the same.

In many cases, the speaker is quite different from the poet, even when
the speaker's voice conveys the attitude of the poet either directly or indirectly. In
his 1758 poem "The Chimney Sweeper," for example, William Blake assumes the
voice of a child to criticize the system of child labor that existed in eighteenth-
century England. Even though the child speaker does not understand the economic and social forces that cause his misery, readers sense the poet's anger as the
trusting speaker describes the appalling conditions under which he works. The
poet's indignation is especially apparent in the biting irony of the last line, in
which the victimized speaker innocently assures readers that if all people do their
duty, "they need not fear harm."

Sometimes the poem's speaker is anonymous. In such cases — as in William
Carlos Williams's "Red Wheelbarrow" (p. 513), for instance — the first-person
voice is absent and the speaker remains outside the poem. At other times, the
speaker has a set identity — a king, a beggar, a highwayman, a sheriff, a husband,
a wife, a rich man, a murderer, a child, a mythical figure, an explorer, a teacher, a
faithless lover, a saint — or even a flower, an animal, or a clod of earth. Whatever
the case, the speaker is not the poet but rather a creation that the poet uses to convey his or her ideas. (For this reason, poems by a single poet may have very different voices. Compare Sylvia Plath's bitter and sardonic poem "Daddy" [p. 532] with
her calm and meditative work "Mirror" [p. 691], for example.)

Sometimes a poem's title tells readers that the poet is assuming a particular
persona. In the following poem, for example, the title identifies the speaker as a
fictional character, Gretel from the fairy tale "Hansel and Gretel."

LOUISE GLÜCK (1943–   )

Gretel in Darkness (1971)

This is the world we wanted.
All who would have seen us dead
are dead. I hear the witch's cry
break in the moonlight through a sheet

of sugar: God rewards.   5
Her tongue shrivels into gas. . . .

      Now, far from women's arms
And memory of women, in our father's hut
we sleep, are never hungry.
Why do I not forget?   10
My father bars the door, bars harm
from this house, and it is years.

No one remembers. Even you, my brother,
summer afternoons you look at me as though
you meant to leave,   15
as though it never happened.
But I killed for you. I see armed firs,
the spires of that gleaming kiln —

Nights I turn to you to hold me
but you are not there.   20
Am I alone? Spies
hiss in the stillness, Hansel
we are there still, and it is real, real,
that black forest, and the fire in earnest.

The speaker in this poem comments on her life after her encounter with the witch in the forest. Speaking to her brother, Gretel observes that they now live in the world they wanted: they live with their father in his hut, and the witch and the wicked stepmother are dead. Even so, the memory of the events in the forest haunts Gretel and makes it impossible for her to live "happily ever after." The "armed firs," the "gleaming kiln," and "the black forest" break through the "sheet of sugar" that her life has become.

By assuming the persona of Gretel, the poet is able to convey some interesting and complex ideas. On one level, Gretel represents any person who has lived through a traumatic experience. Memories of the event keep breaking through into the present, frustrating her attempts to reestablish her belief in the goodness of the world. The voice we hear is sad, alone, and frightened: "Nights I turn to you to hold me," she says, "but you are not there." Although the murder Gretel committed for her brother was justified, it seems to haunt her. "No one remembers," laments Gretel, not even her brother. At some level, she realizes that by killing the witch she has killed a part of herself, perhaps the part of women that men fear and consequently transform into witches and wicked stepmothers. The world that is left after the killing is the father's and the brother's, not hers, and she is now alone in a dark world haunted by the memories of the black forest. In this sense, Gretel — "Now, far from women's arms / And memory of women" — may be the voice of all victimized women who, because of men, act against their own best interests — and regret it.

As "Gretel in Darkness" illustrates, a title can identify a poem's speaker, but the speaker's own words can provide much more information. This is also the case in the following poem, where Spanish words help to characterize the speaker.

LEONARD ADAMÉ (1947–)

My Grandmother Would Rock Quietly and Hum (1973)

in her house
she would rock quietly and hum
until her swelled hands
calmed

in summer   5
she wore thick stockings
sweaters
and grey braids

(when "el cheque"° came
we went to Payless   10
and I laughed greedily
when given a quarter)

mornings,
sunlight barely lit
the kitchen   15
and where
there were shadows
it was not cold

she quietly rolled
flour tortillas—   20
the "papas"°
cracking in hot lard
would wake me

she had lost her teeth
and when we ate   25
she had bread
soaked in "café"°

always her eyes
were clear

° *el cheque:* The check.   ° *papas:* Potatoes.   ° *café:* Coffee.

and she could see   30
as I cannot yet see —
through her eyes
she gave me herself
she would sit
and talk   35
of her girlhood —
of things strange to me:
    México
    epidemics
    relatives shot   40
    her father's hopes
    of this country —
how they sank
with cement dust
to his insides   45

now
when I go
to the old house
the worn spots
by the stove   50
echo of her shuffling
and
México
still hangs in her
fading   55
calendar pictures

In this poem, the speaker is an adult recalling childhood memories of his grandmother. Spanish words — *el cheque, tortillas, papas,* and *café* — identify the speaker as Latino. His easy use of English, his comment that Mexico is strange to him, and his observation that he cannot yet see through his grandmother's eyes suggest, however, that he is not in touch with his ethnic identity. At one level, the grandmother evokes nostalgic memories of the speaker's youth. At another level, she is a living symbol of his ties with Mexico, connecting him to the ethnic culture he is trying to recover. The poem ends on an ambivalent note: even though the speaker is able to return to "the old house," the pictures of Mexico are fading, perhaps suggesting the speaker's inevitable assimilation into mainstream American culture.

Direct statements by speakers can also help to characterize them. In the next poem, the first line of each stanza establishes the identity of the speaker — and defines his perspective.

LANGSTON HUGHES (1902–1967)

Negro   (1926)

I am a Negro:
   Black as the night is black,
   Black like the depths of my Africa.

I've been a slave:
   Caesar told me to keep his door-steps clean.   5
   I brushed the boots of Washington.

I've been a worker:
   Under my hand the pyramids arose.
   I made mortar for the Woolworth Building.

I've been a singer: 10
   All the way from Africa to Georgia
   I carried my sorrow songs.
   I made ragtime.

I've been a victim:
   The Belgians cut off my hands in the Congo.   15
   They lynch me still in Mississippi.

I am a Negro:
   Black as the night is black,
   Black like the depths of my Africa.

Here the speaker, identifying himself as "a Negro," assumes each of the roles African-Americans have historically played in Western society — slave, worker, singer, and victim. By so doing, he gives voice to his ancestors who, by being forced to serve others, were deprived of their identities. By presenting not only their suffering but also their accomplishments, the speaker asserts his pride in being black. The speaker also implies that the suffering of black people has been caused by economic exploitation: Romans, Egyptians, Belgians, and Americans all used black labor to help build their societies. In this context, the speaker's implied warning is clear: except for the United States, all the societies that have exploited blacks have declined, and long after the fall of those empires, black people still endure.

In each of the preceding poems, the speaker is alone. The following poem, a **dramatic monologue,** presents a more complex situation in which the poet creates a complete dramatic scene. The speaker is developed as a character whose distinctive personality is revealed through his words as he addresses a silent listener.

ROBERT BROWNING (1812–1889)

My Last Duchess   (1842)

Ferrara

That's my last Duchess painted on the wall,
Looking as if she were alive. I call
That piece a wonder, now: Frà Pandolf's° hands
Worked busily a day, and there she stands.
Will't please you sit and look at her? I said   5
"Frà Pandolf" by design, for never read
Strangers like you that pictured countenance,
The depth and passion of its earnest glance,
But to myself they turned (since none puts by
The curtain I have drawn for you, but I)   10
And seemed as they would ask me, if they durst,
How such a glance came there; so, not the first
Are you to turn and ask thus. Sir, 'twas not
Her husband's presence only, called that spot
Of joy into the Duchess' cheek: perhaps   15
Frà Pandolf chanced to say "Her mantle laps
Over my lady's wrist too much," or "Paint
Must never hope to reproduce the faint
Half-flush that dies along her throat": such stuff
Was courtesy, she thought, and cause enough   20
For calling up that spot of joy. She had
A heart — how shall I say? — too soon made glad,
Too easily impressed; she liked whate'er
She looked on, and her looks went everywhere.
Sir, 'twas all one! My favor at her breast,   25
The dropping of the daylight in the West,
The bough of cherries some officious fool
Broke in the orchard for her, the white mule
She rode with round the terrace — all and each
Would draw from her alike the approving speech,   30
Or blush, at least. She thanked men — good! but thanked
Somehow — I know not how — as if she ranked
My gift of a nine-hundred-years-old name
With anybody's gift. Who'd stoop to blame
This sort of trifling? Even had you skill   35
In speech — (which I have not) — to make your will
Quite clear to such an one, and say, "Just this

° *Frà Pandolf:* "Brother" Pandolf, a fictive painter.

Or that in you disgusts me; here you miss,
Or there exceed the mark"— and if she let
Herself be lessoned so, nor plainly set   40
Her wits to yours, forsooth, and made excuse
—E'en then would be some stooping; and I choose
Never to stoop. Oh sir, she smiled, no doubt,
Whene'er I passed her; but who passed without
Much the same smile? This grew; I gave commands;   45
Then all smiles stopped together. There she stands
As if alive. Will't please you rise? We'll meet
The company below, then. I repeat,
The Count your master's known munificence
Is ample warrant that no just pretense   50
Of mine for dowry will be disallowed;
Though his fair daughter's self, as I avowed
At starting, is my object. Nay, we'll go
Together down, sir. Notice Neptune,° though,
Taming a sea horse, thought a rarity,   55
Which Claus of Innsbruck° cast in bronze for me!

The speaker is probably Alfonso II, duke of Ferrara, Italy, whose young wife, Lucrezia, died in 1561 after only three years of marriage. Shortly after her death, the duke began negotiations to marry again. When the poem opens, the duke is showing a portrait of his late wife to an emissary of an unnamed count who is there to arrange a marriage between the duke and the count's daughter. The duke remarks that the artist, Frà Pandolf, has caught a certain look on the duchess's face. This look aroused the jealousy of the duke, who thought that it should have been for him alone. According to the duke, the duchess's crime was that she had a heart "too soon made glad," "Too easily impressed." Eventually the duke could tolerate the situation no longer; he "gave commands," and "all smiles stopped together."

Much of what readers learn about the duke's state of mind comes from what is implied by his words. As he discusses the painting, the duke unintentionally reveals himself to be obsessively possessive and jealous, referring to "my last Duchess," "My favor at her breast," and "My gift of a nine-hundred-years-old name." He keeps the portrait of his late wife hidden behind a curtain that no one draws except him. His interest in the picture has little to do with the memory of his wife, however. In death, the duchess has become exactly what the duke always wanted her to be: a personal possession that reflects his status and good taste.

Though silent, the listener plays a subtle but important role in the poem: his presence establishes the dramatic situation that allows the character of the duke to be revealed. The purpose of the story is to communicate to the emissary exactly what the duke expects from his prospective bride and from her father. As he

---

°*Neptune:* In Roman mythology, the god of the sea.   °*Claus of Innsbruck:* A fictive — or unidentified — sculptor. The count of Tyrol's capital was at Innsbrück, Austria.

speaks, the duke provides only the information that he wants the emissary to take back to his master, the count. Although the duke appears vain and superficial, he is actually extraordinarily shrewd. Throughout the poem, he turns the conversation to his own ends and gains the advantage through flattery and false modesty. Notice, for example, that he claims he has little skill in speaking when actually he is cleverly manipulating the conversation. The success of the poem lies in the poet's ability to develop the voice of this complex character, who embodies both superficial elegance and shocking cruelty.

FURTHER READING: The Speaker in the Poem

LESLIE MARMON SILKO (1948–   )

Where Mountain Lion Lay Down with Deer (1973)

I climb the black rock mountain
   stepping from day to day
      silently.
I smell the wind for my ancestors
   pale blue leaves   5
   crushed wild mountain smell.
Returning
   up the gray stone cliff
   where I descended
      a thousand years ago.   10
Returning to faded black stone.
   where mountain lion lay down with deer.
It is better to stay up here
      watching wind's reflection
      in tall yellow flowers.   15
The old ones who remember me are gone
   the old songs are all forgotten
and the story of my birth.
How I danced in snow-frost moonlight
   distant stars to the end of the Earth,   20
How I swam away
      in freezing mountain water
      narrow mossy canyon tumbling down
         out of the mountain
         out of the deep canyon stone   25
     down
       the memory
         spilling out
         into the world.

Reading and Reacting

1. Who is speaking in line 4? In line 9? Can you explain this shift?
2. From where is the speaker returning? What is she trying to recover?
3. **JOURNAL ENTRY** Is it important for you to know that the poet is of Native American descent? How does this information affect your interpretation of the poem?
4. **CRITICAL PERSPECTIVE** In her 1983 essay "Answering the Deer," Native American poet and critic Paula Gunn Allen observes that the possibility of cultural extinction is a reality Native Americans must face. Native American women writers, says Allen, face this fact directly but with a kind of hope:

> The sense of hope . . . comes about when one has faced ultimate disaster time and time again over the ages and has emerged . . . stronger and more certain of the endurance of the people, the spirits, and the land from which they both arise and which informs both with life. Transformation, or more directly, metamorphosis, is the oldest tribal ceremonial theme. . . . And it comes once again into use within American Indian poetry of extinction and regeneration that is ultimately the only poetry any contemporary Indian woman can write.

Does Silko's poem address the issue of cultural extinction and the possibility of regeneration or metamorphosis? How?

Related Works: "This Is What It Means to Say Phoenix, Arizona"(p. 164), "Two Kinds" (p. 416)

JANICE MIRIKITANI (1942–   )

Suicide Note   (1987)

. . . An Asian-American college student was reported to have jumped to her death from her dormitory window. Her body was found two days later under a deep cover of snow. Her suicide note contained an apology to her parents for having received less than a perfect four point grade average. . . .

How many notes written . . .
ink smeared like birdprints in snow.

    not good enough   not pretty enough   not smart enough
dear mother and father.
I apologize   5
for disappointing you.
I've worked very hard,
        not good enough
harder, perhaps to please you.
If only I were a son, shoulders broad   10
as the sunset threading through pine,

I would see the light in my mother's
eyes, or the golden pride reflected
in my father's dream
of my wide, male hands worthy of work   15
and comfort.
I would swagger through life
muscled and bold and assured,
drawing praises to me
like currents in the bed of wind, virile   20
with confidence.
   not good enough not strong enough not good enough

I apologize.
Tasks do not come easily.
Each failure, a glacier.   25
Each disapproval, a bootprint.
Each disappointment,
ice above my river.
So I have worked hard.
         not good enough   30
My sacrifice I will drop
bone by bone, perched
on the ledge of my womanhood,
fragile as wings.
         not strong enough   35
It is snowing steadily
surely not good weather
for flying — this sparrow
sillied and dizzied by the wind
on the edge.   40
         not smart enough
I make this ledge my altar
to offer penance.
This air will not hold me,
the snow burdens my crippled wings,   45
my tears drop like bitter cloth
softly into the gutter below.
  not good enough not strong enough not smart enough
         Choices thin as shaved
         ice. Notes shredded   50
         drift like snow
on my broken body,
cover me like whispers
of sorries

sorries.   55
Perhaps when they find me
they will bury
my bird bones beneath
a sturdy pine
and scatter my feathers like   60
unspoken song
over this white and cold and silent
breast of earth.

Reading and Reacting

1. This poem is a suicide note that contains an apology. Why does the speaker feel she must apologize? Do you agree that she needs to apologize?

2. What attitude does the speaker convey toward her parents?

3. JOURNAL ENTRY Is the college student who speaks in this poem a stranger to you? Or is her voice in any way like that of students you know?

Related Works: "The Rocking-Horse Winner" (p. 340), "The Value of Education" (p. 503), "Dreams of Suicide" (p. 611), "Death Be Not Proud" (p. 663)

PAT MORA (1942–   )

Veiled

If before the mullah's morning call,
We tiptoe through the village
Gather burqas° that shroud
Even the eyes,
     Heavy, dark, like storm clouds   5

If we rush to the river
Float the black and brown
Garments on soft waves,
Close our eyes, listen

Will the water loosen   10
Laughter trapped inside those threads,
Will light songs rise
And swirl with the morning mist,

Or will sighs rise,
     Heavy, dark like storm clouds?   15

° *burqa:* A garment that veils the head and body, worn by some Muslim women.

Reading and Reacting

1. Who is the speaker? In what type of country does she live?
2. What does the speaker fantasize about? Why is laughter "trapped inside" (11) the threads of the burqa? Why are the sighs "heavy, dark, like storm clouds" (15)?
3. JOURNAL ENTRY What do the speaker's fantasies reveal about her attitude toward burqas?

Related Works: "A Rose for Emily" (p. 113), "Indian Boarding School: The Runaways" (p. 669), *A Doll House* (p. 784)

The Tone of the Poem

The **tone** of a poem conveys the speaker's attitude toward his or her subject or audience. In speech, this attitude can be conveyed easily: stressing a word in a sentence can modify or color a statement, drastically affecting the meaning of the sentence. For example, the statement "Of course, you would want to go to that restaurant" is quite straightforward, but changing the emphasis to "Of course *you* would want to go to *that* restaurant" transforms a neutral statement into a sarcastic one. For poets, however, conveying a particular tone to readers poses a challenge because readers rarely hear poets' spoken voices. Instead, poets indicate tone by using techniques such as rhyme, meter, word choice, sentence structure, figures of speech, and imagery.

The range of possible tones is wide. For example, a poem's speaker may be joyful, sad, playful, serious, comic, intimate, formal, relaxed, condescending, or ironic. In the following poem, notice how the tone conveys the speaker's attitude toward his subject.

ROBERT FROST (1874–1963)

Fire and Ice (1923)

Some say the world will end in fire,
Some say in ice.
From what I've tasted of desire
I hold with those who favor fire.
But if it had to perish twice,   5
I think I know enough of hate
To say that for destruction ice
Is also great
And would suffice.

Here the speaker uses word choice, rhyme, and especially understatement to comment on the human condition. The conciseness and the simple, regular meter and rhyme suggest an **epigram**— a short poem that makes a pointed comment in an unusually clear, and often witty, manner. This pointedness is consistent with the speaker's glib, unemotional tone, as is the last line's wry understatement that ice "would suffice." The contrast between the poem's serious message — that hatred and indifference are equally destructive — and its informal style and off-hand tone complement the speaker's detached, almost smug, posture.

Sometimes shifts in tone reveal changes in the speaker's attitude. In the next poem, subtle shifts in tone reveal a change in the speaker's attitude toward war.

THOMAS HARDY (1840–1928)

The Man He Killed   (1902)

"Had he and I but met
   By some old ancient inn,
We should have sat us down to wet
   Right many a nipperkin!°

"But ranged as infantry,   5
   And staring face to face,
I shot at him as he at me,
   And killed him in his place.

"I shot him dead because—
   Because he was my foe,   10
Just so: my foe of course he was;
   That's clear enough; although

"He thought he'd 'list,° perhaps,
   Off-hand-like —just as I—
Was out of work —had sold his traps—   15
   No other reason why.

"Yes; quaint and curious war is!
   You shoot a fellow down
You'd treat if met where any bar is,
   Or help to half-a crown."   20

The speaker in this poem is a soldier relating a wartime experience. Quotation marks indicate that he is engaged in conversation — perhaps in a pub — and his dialect indicates that he is probably of the English working class. For him, at least at first, the object of war is simple: kill or be killed. To Hardy, this speaker represents all men who are thrust into a war without understanding its underlying so-

°*nipperkin:* A small container of liquor   °*'list:* Enlist.

cial, economic, or ideological causes. In this sense, the speaker and his enemy are both victims of forces beyond their comprehension or control.

The tone of "The Man He Killed" changes as the speaker tells his story. As the poem unfolds, its sentence structure deteriorates, and this in turn helps to convey the speaker's changing attitude toward the war in which he has fought. In the first two stanzas, sentences are smooth and unbroken, establishing the speaker's matter-of-fact tone and reflecting his confidence that he has done what he had to do. In the third and fourth stanzas, broken syntax reflects the narrator's increasingly disturbed state of mind as he tells about the man he killed. The poem's singsong meter and regular rhyme scheme *(met/wet, inn/nipperkin)* suggest that the speaker is struggling to maintain his composure; the smooth sentence structure of the last stanza and the use of a cliché ("Yes; quaint and curious war is!") show the speaker's efforts to trivialize an incident that has seriously traumatized him.

Sometimes a poem's tone can establish an ironic contrast between the speaker and his or her subject. The speaker's abrupt change of tone at the end of the next poem establishes such a contrast.

AMY LOWELL (1874–1925)

Patterns (1915)

I walk down the garden-paths,
And all the daffodils
Are blowing, and the bright blue squills.
I walk down the patterned garden-paths
In my stiff, brocaded gown.   5
With my powdered hair and jewelled fan,
I too am a rare
Pattern. As I wander down
The garden-paths.

My dress is richly figured,   10
And the train
Makes a pink and silver stain
On the gravel, and the thrift
Of the borders.
Just a plate of current fashion   15
Tripping by in high-heeled, ribboned shoes.
Not a softness anywhere about me,
Only whalebone° and brocade.
And I sink on a seat in the shade
Of a lime tree. For my passion   20
Wars against the stiff brocade.

°*whalebone:* The type of bone used to stiffen corsets.

The daffodils and squills
Flutter in the breeze
As they please.
And I weep;   25
For the lime-tree is in blossom
And one small flower has dropped upon my bosom.
And the plashing of waterdrops
In the marble fountain
Comes down the garden-paths.   30
The dripping never stops.
Underneath my stiffened gown
Is the softness of a woman bathing in a marble basin,
A basin in the midst of hedges grown
So thick, she cannot see her lover hiding,   35
But she guesses he is near,
And the sliding of the water
Seems the stroking of a dear
Hand upon her.
What is Summer in a fine brocaded gown!   40
I should like to see it lying in a heap upon the ground.
All the pink and silver crumpled up on the ground.

I would be the pink and silver as I ran along the paths,
And he would stumble after,
Bewildered by my laughter.   45
I should see the sun flashing from his sword-hilt and buckles
   on his shoes.
I would choose
To lead him in a maze along the patterned paths,
A bright and laughing maze for my heavy-booted lover.
Till he caught me in the shade,   50
And the buttons of his waistcoat bruised my body as he clasped me,
Aching, melting, unafraid.
With the shadows of the leaves and the sundrops,
And the plopping of the waterdrops,
All about us in the open afternoon —   55
I am very like to swoon
        With the weight of this brocade,
        For the sun sifts through the shade.

Underneath the fallen blossom
In my bosom,   60
Is a letter I have hid.
It was brought to me this morning by a rider from the Duke.
Madam, we regret to inform you that Lord Hartwell

Died in action Thursday se'nnight.°
As I read it in the white, morning sunlight,   65
The letters squirmed like snakes.
"Any answer, Madam," said my footman.
"No," I told him.
"See that the messenger takes some refreshment.
No, no answer."   70
And I walked into the garden,
Up and down the patterned paths,
In my stiff, correct brocade.
The blue and yellow flowers stood up proudly in the sun,
Each one.   75
I stood upright too,
Held rigid to the pattern
By the stiffness of my gown.
Up and down I walked.
Up and down.   80

In a month he would have been my husband.
In a month, here, underneath this lime,
We would have broken the pattern;
He for me, and I for him,
He as Colonel, I as Lady,   85
On this shady seat.
He had a whim
That sunlight carried blessing.
And I answered, "It shall be as you have said."
Now he is dead.   90

In Summer and in Winter I shall walk
Up and down
The patterned garden-paths
In my stiff, brocaded gown.
The squills and daffodils   95
Will give place to pillared roses, and to asters, and to snow.
I shall go
Up and down,
In my gown.
Gorgeously arrayed,   100
Boned and stayed.
And the softness of my body will be guarded from embrace
By each button, hook, and lace.
For the man who should loose me is dead,

° *se'nnight:* "Seven night," or a week ago Thursday.

Fighting with the Duke in Flanders,°   105
In a pattern called a war.
Christ! What are patterns for?

The speaker begins by describing herself walking down garden paths. She wears a stiff brocaded gown, has powdered hair, and carries a jeweled fan. By her own admission, she is "a plate of current fashion." Although her tone is controlled, she is preoccupied by sensual thoughts. Beneath her "stiffened gown / Is the softness of a woman bathing in a marble basin," and the "sliding of the water" in a fountain reminds the speaker of the stroking of her lover's hand. She imagines herself shedding her brocaded gown and running with her lover along the maze of "patterned paths." The sensuality of the speaker's thoughts stands in ironic contrast to the images of stiffness and control that dominate the poem: her passion "Wars against the stiff brocade." She is also full of repressed rage. She knows that her lover has been killed, and she realizes the meaninglessness of the patterns of her life, patterns to which she has conformed, just as her lover conformed by going to war and doing what he was supposed to do. Throughout the poem, the speaker's tone reflects her barely contained anger and frustration. In the last line, when she finally lets out her rage, the poem's point about the senselessness of war becomes apparent.

FURTHER READING: The Tone of the Poem

ADAM ZAGAJEWSKI (1945–)

Try to Praise the Mutilated World   (2001)

Translated from the Polish by Clare Cavanagh

Try to praise the mutilated world.
Remember June's long days,
and wild strawberries, drops of wine, the dew.
The nettles that methodically overgrow
the abandoned homesteads of exiles.   5
You must praise the mutilated world.
You watched the stylish yachts and ships;
one of them had a long trip ahead of it,
while salty oblivion awaited others.
You've seen the refugees heading nowhere,   10
you've heard the executioners sing joyfully.
You should praise the mutilated world.
Remember the moments when we were together
in a white room and the curtain fluttered.
Return in thought to the concert where music flared.   15

° *Flanders:* A region in northwestern Europe, including part of northern France and western Belgium. Flanders was a site of fighting during World War I.

You gathered acorns in the park in autumn
and leaves eddied over the earth's scars.
Praise the mutilated world
and the gray feather a thrush lost,
and the gentle light that strays and vanishes   20
and returns.

Reading and Reacting

1. Who is the speaker? Whom is he addressing?

2. In line 1, the speaker says, "Try to praise . . ."; in line 6, he says, "You must praise . . ."; in line 12, he says, "You should praise . . ."; and in line 18, he says, "Praise . . .". What is the significance, if any, of these changes in phrasing?

3. What is the mood of the speaker? Do you think he is optimistic or pessimistic?

4. JOURNAL ENTRY   Though written earlier, this poem was printed in the issue of the *New Yorker* that appeared immediately after the World Trade Center towers were destroyed by terrorists on September 11, 2001. Why do you think the editors chose to reprint it then?

5. CRITICAL PERSPECTIVE   The critic and poet Adam Kirsch, writing in the *New Republic*, characterizes Adam Zagajewski as a mystical poet who looks for meaning in ordinary things and situations:

> Like Rilke, Zagajewski is overcome at times by a powerful sense that the singular being of objects conceals some higher truth. For him, too, things are the sites of illumination.

What "higher truth" do the objects in "Try to Praise the Mutilated World" conceal? What do you think is the underlying message of this poem?

Related Works: "Cathedral" (p. 289), "Hope" (p. 482), "Nothing Gold Can Stay" (p. 518), "For the Union Dead" (p. 639), "The Second Coming" (p. 708), *Nine Ten* (p. 760)

WILLIAM WORDSWORTH (1770–1850)

The World Is Too Much with Us   (1807)

The world is too much with us; late and soon,
Getting and spending, we lay waste our powers;
Little we see in Nature that is ours;
We have given our hearts away, a sordid boon!
This Sea that bares her bosom to the moon;   5
The winds that will be howling at all hours,
And are up-gathered now like sleeping flowers;
For this, for everything, we are out of tune;
It moves us not. Great God! I'd rather be
A Pagan suckled in a creed outworn;   10

So might I, standing on this pleasant lea,
Have glimpses that would make me less forlorn;
Have sight of Proteus° rising from the sea;
Or hear old Triton° blow his wreathèd horn.

Reading and Reacting

1. What is the speaker's attitude toward the contemporary world? How is this attitude revealed through the poem's tone?
2. This poem is a **sonnet,** a highly structured traditional form. How do the regular meter and rhyme scheme help to establish the poem's tone?
3. **JOURNAL ENTRY** Imagine you are a modern-day environmentalist, labor organizer, or corporate executive. Write a response to the sentiments expressed in this poem.
4. **CRITICAL PERSPECTIVE** According to M. H. Abrams in his 1972 essay "Two Roads to Wordsworth," critics have tended to view Wordsworth in one of two different ways:

> One Wordsworth is simple, elemental, forthright, the other is complex, paradoxical, problematic; one is an affirmative poet of life, love, and joy, the other is an equivocal or self-divided poet whose affirmations are implicitly qualified . . . by a pervasive sense of morality and an ever-incipient despair of life; . . . one is the Wordsworth of light, the other the Wordsworth of [shadow], or even darkness.

Does your reading of "The World Is Too Much with Us" support one of these versions of Wordsworth over the other? Which one? Why?

Related Works: "The Rocking-Horse Winner" (p. 340), "Dover Beach" (p. 650), "The Lake Isle of Innisfree" (p. 706)

ROBERT HERRICK (1591–1674)

To the Virgins, to Make Much of Time   (1646)

Gather ye rosebuds while ye may,
Old Time is still a-flying;
And this same flower that smiles today,
Tomorrow will be dying.

The glorious lamp of heaven, the sun,   5
The higher he's a-getting,
The sooner will his race be run,
And nearer he's to setting.

°*Proteus:* Sometimes said to be Poseidon's son, this Greek sea-god had the ability to change shape at will and to tell the future.   °*Triton:* The trumpeter of the sea, this sea-god is usually pictured blowing on a conch shell. Triton was the son of Poseidon, ruler of the sea.

That age is best which is the first,
When youth and blood are warmer;   10
But being spent, the worse, and worst
Times still succeed the former.

Then be not coy, but use your time,
And while ye may, go marry;
For having lost but once your prime,   15
You may forever tarry.

Reading and Reacting

1. How would you characterize the speaker? Do you think he expects his listeners to share his views? How might his expectations affect his tone?
2. This poem is developed like an argument. What is the speaker's main point? How does he support it?
3. What effect does the poem's use of rhyme have on its tone?
4. JOURNAL ENTRY Whose side are you on — the speaker's or those he addresses?

Related Works: "Where Are You Going, Where Have You Been?" (p. 384), "Greasy Lake" (p. 359), "The Passionate Shepherd to His Love" (p. 685), *The Brute* (p. 723)

Irony

Just as in fiction and drama, **irony** occurs in poetry when a discrepancy exists between two levels of meaning or experience. Consider the tone of the following lines by Stephen Crane:

Do not weep, maiden, for war is kind.
Because your lover threw wild hands toward the sky
And the afrighted steed ran on alone,
Do not weep.
War is kind.

How can war be "kind"? Isn't war exactly the opposite of "kind"? Surely the speaker does not intend his words to be taken literally. By making this ironic statement, the speaker actually conveys the opposite idea: war is a cruel, mindless exercise of violence.

Skillfully used, irony enables a poet to make a pointed comment about a situation or to manipulate a reader's emotions. Implicit in irony is the writer's assumption that readers will not be misled by the literal meaning of a statement. In order for irony to work, readers must recognize the disparity between what is said and what is meant, or between what a speaker thinks is occurring and what readers know to be occurring.

One kind of irony that appears in poetry is **dramatic irony**, which occurs when a speaker believes one thing and readers realize something else. In the following poem, the poet uses a deranged speaker to tell a story that is filled with irony.

ROBERT BROWNING (1812–1889)

Porphyria's Lover (1836)

The rain set early in to-night,
    The sullen wind was soon awake,
It tore the elm-tops down for spite,
    And did its worst to vex the lake:
    I listened with heart fit to break.   5
When glided in Porphyria; straight
    She shut the cold out and the storm,
And kneeled and made the cheerless grate
    Blaze up, and all the cottage warm;
    Which done, she rose, and from her form   10
Withdrew the dripping cloak and shawl,
    And laid her soiled gloves by, untied
Her hat and let the damp hair fall,
    And, last, she sat down by my side
    And called me. When no voice replied,   15
She put my arm about her waist,
    And made her smooth white shoulder bare,
And all her yellow hair displaced,
    And, stooping, made my cheek lie there,
    And spread, o'er all, her yellow hair,   20
Murmuring how she loved me — she
    Too weak, for all her heart's endeavour,
To set its struggling passion free
    From pride, and vainer ties dissever,
    And give herself to me for ever.   25
But passion sometimes would prevail,
    Nor could to-night's gay feast restrain
A sudden thought of one so pale
    For love of her, and all in vain:
So, she was come through wind and rain.   30
Be sure I looked up at her eyes
    Happy and proud; at last I knew
Porphyria worshipped me; surprise
    Made my heart swell, and still it grew
    While I debated what to do.   35
That moment she was mine, mine, fair,
    Perfectly pure and good: I found
A thing to do, and all her hair
    In one long yellow string I wound
    Three times her little throat around,   40

And strangled her. No pain felt she;
  I am quite sure she felt no pain.
As a shut bud that holds a bee,
  I warily oped her lids: again
  Laughed the blue eyes without a stain.   45
And I untightened next the tress
  About her neck; her cheek once more
Blushed bright beneath my burning kiss:
  I propped her head up as before,
  Only, this time my shoulder bore   50
Her head, which droops upon it still:
  The smiling rosy little head,
So glad it has its utmost will,
  That all it scorned at once is fled,
  And I, its love, am gained instead!   55
Porphyria's love: she guessed not how
  Her darling one wish would be heard.
And thus we sit together now,
  And all night long we have not stirred,
  And yet God has not said a word!   60

Like Browning's "My Last Duchess" (p. 465), this poem is a **dramatic monologue,** a poem that includes an implied listener as well as a speaker. The speaker recounts his story in a straightforward manner, seemingly unaware of the horror of his story. In fact, much of the effect of this poem comes from the speaker's telling his tale of murder in a flat, unemotional tone — and from readers' gradual realization that the speaker is mad.

The irony of the poem, and of its title, becomes apparent as the monologue progresses. At first, the speaker fears that Porphyria is too weak to free herself from pride and vanity to love him. As he looks into her eyes, however, he comes to believe that she worships him. To preserve the perfection of Porphyria's love, the speaker strangles her with her own hair. He assures his silent listener, "I am quite sure she felt no pain." Like many of Browning's narrators, the speaker in this poem exhibits a selfish and perverse need to possess another person totally. The moment the speaker realizes that Porphyria loves him, he feels compelled to kill her and keep her his forever. According to him, she is at this point "mine, mine, fair, / Perfectly pure and good," and he believes that by murdering her, he actually fulfills "Her darling one wish"— to stay with him forever. As he attempts to justify his actions, the speaker reveals himself to be a deluded psychopathic killer.

Another kind of irony is **situational irony,** which occurs when the situation itself contradicts readers' expectations. For example, in "Porphyria's Lover" the meeting of two lovers ironically results not in joy and passion but in murder. In the next poem, the situation also creates irony.

PERCY BYSSHE SHELLEY (1792–1822)

Ozymandias° (1818)

I met a traveler from an antique land
Who said: Two vast and trunkless legs of stone
Stand in the desert. Near them, on the sand,
Half sunk, a shattered visage lies, whose frown,
And wrinkled lip, and sneer of cold command,   5
Tell that its sculptor well those passions read
Which yet survive, stamped on these lifeless things,
The hand that mocked them, and the heart that fed;
And on the pedestal these words appear:
"My name is Ozymandias, king of kings: 10
Look on my works, ye Mighty, and despair!"
Nothing beside remains. Round the decay
Of that colossal wreck, boundless and bare
The lone and level sands stretch far away.

The speaker recounts a tale about a colossal statue that lies shattered in the desert. Its head lies separated from the trunk, and the face has a wrinkled lip and a "sneer of cold command." On the pedestal of the monument are words exhorting all those who pass: "Look on my works, ye Mighty, and despair!" The situational irony of the poem has its source in the contrast between the "colossal wreck" and the boastful inscription on its base: Ozymandias is a monument to the vanity of those who mistakenly think they can withstand the ravages of time.

Perhaps the most common kind of irony found in poetry is **verbal irony,** which is created when words say one thing but mean another, often exactly the opposite. When verbal irony is particularly biting, it is called **sarcasm**—for example, Stephen Crane's use of the word *kind* in his antiwar poem "War Is Kind." In speech, verbal irony is easy to detect through the speaker's change in tone or emphasis. In writing, when these signals are absent, verbal irony becomes more difficult to convey. Poets must depend on the context of a remark or on the contrast between a word and other images in the poem to create irony.

Consider how verbal irony is communicated in the following poem.

ARIEL DORFMAN (1942–   )

Hope (1988)

Translated by Edith Grossman with the author

My son has been
missing
since May 8
of last year.

° *Ozymandias:* The Greek name for Ramses II, ruler of Egypt in the thirteenth century B.C.

They took him   5
just for a few hours
they said
just for some routine
questioning.

After the car left,   10
the car with no license plate,
we couldn't

find out

anything else
about him.   15
But now things have changed.
We heard from a compañero
who just got out
that five months later
they were torturing him   20
in Villa Grimaldi,
at the end of September
they were questioning him
in the red house
that belonged to the Grimaldis.   25

They say they recognized
his voice his screams
they say.

Somebody tell me frankly
what times are these   30
what kind of world
what country?
What I'm asking is
how can it be
that a father's   35
joy
a mother's
joy
is knowing
that they   40
that they are still
torturing
their son?
Which means
that he was alive   45
five months later

and our greatest
hope
will be to find out
next year   50
that they're still torturing him
eight months later

and he may   might   could
still be alive.

Although it is not necessary to know the background of the poet to appreciate
this poem, it does help to know that Ariel Dorfman is a native of Chile. After the
assassination of Salvador Allende, Chile's elected socialist president, in September
1973, the civilian government was replaced by a military dictatorship. Civil rights
were suspended, and activists, students, and members of opposition parties were
arrested. Many were detained indefinitely; some simply disappeared. The irony of
this poem originates in the discrepancy between what the word *hope* comes to
mean in the poem and what it usually means. For most people, *hope* has positive
connotations. For the speaker, however, *hope* means that his son is still being tortured eight months after his arrest. Thus, *hope* takes on a different meaning, and
this irony is not lost on the speaker.

FURTHER READING: Irony

W. H. AUDEN (1907–1973)

The Unknown Citizen   (1939)
(To JS/07/M/378 This Marble Monument Is Erected by the State)

He was found by the Bureau of Statistics to be
One against whom there was no official complaint,
And all the reports on his conduct agree
That, in the modern sense of an old-fashioned word, he was a saint,
For in everything he did he served the Greater Community.
Except for the War till the day he retired
He worked in a factory and never got fired,
But satisfied his employers, Fudge Motors Inc.
Yet he wasn't a scab or odd in his views,
For his Union reports that he paid his dues,
(Our report on his Union shows it was sound)
And our Social Psychology workers found
That he was popular with his mates and liked a drink.
The Press are convinced that he bought a paper every day
And that his reactions to advertisements were normal in every way.
Policies taken out in his name prove that he was fully insured,

And his Health-card shows he was once in hospital but left it cured.
Both Producers Research and High-Grade Living declare
He was fully sensible to the advantages of the Installment Plan
And had everything necessary to the Modern Man,
A phonograph, a radio, a car and a frigidaire.
Our researchers into Public Opinion are content
That he held the proper opinions for the time of year;
When there was peace, he was for peace; when there was war,
  he went.
He was married and added five children to the population,
Which our Eugenist° says was the right number for a parent of his
  generation,
And our teachers report that he never interfered with their
  education.
Was he free? Was he happy? The question is absurd:
Had anything been wrong, we should certainly have heard.

Reading and Reacting

1. The "unknown citizen" represents all modern citizens, who, according to the poem, are programmed like machines. How does the title help to establish the tone of the poem? How does the inscription on the monument also help to establish the tone?
2. Who is the speaker? What is his attitude toward the unknown citizen? How can you tell?
3. What kinds of irony are present in the poem? Identify several examples.
4. JOURNAL ENTRY This poem was written in 1939. Does its message apply to contemporary society, or does the poem seem dated?
5. CRITICAL PERSPECTIVE In 1939, the year this poem was published, Auden argued in his essay "The Public vs. The Late Mr. William Butler Yeats" that poetry can never really change anything. He reiterated this point as late as 1971 in his biographical A Certain World:

> By all means let a poet, if he wants to, write poems . . . that protest against this or that political evil or social injustice. But let him remember this. The only person who will benefit from them is himself; they will enhance his literary reputation among those who feel as he does. The evil or injustice, however, will remain exactly what it would have been if he had kept his mouth shut.

Do you believe that poetry — or any kind of literature — has the power to combat "evil or injustice" in the world? Do you consider "The Unknown Citizen" a political poem? How might this poem effect positive social or political change?

° *Eugenist:* A person who studies eugenics, the science of human improvement through genetic manipulation.

Related Works: "A&P" (p. 128), "The Man He Killed" (p. 472), "next to of course god america i" (p. 660), "The Love Song of J. Alfred Prufrock" (p. 665), *A Doll House* (p. 784), *The Glass Menagerie* (p. 1153)

DUDLEY RANDALL (1914–2000)

Ballad of Birmingham   (1969)

(On the bombing of a church in Birmingham, Alabama, 1963)

"Mother dear, may I go downtown
Instead of out to play,
And march the streets of Birmingham
In a Freedom March today?"

"No, baby, no, you may not go,   5
For the dogs are fierce and wild,
And clubs and hoses, guns and jails
Aren't good for a little child."

"But, mother, I won't be alone.
Other children will go with me,   10
And march the streets of Birmingham
To make our country free."

"No, baby, no, you may not go,
For I fear those guns will fire.
But you may go to church instead   15
And sing in the children's choir."

She has combed and brushed her night-dark hair,
And bathed rose petal sweet,
And drawn white gloves on her small brown hands,
And white shoes on her feet.   20

The mother smiled to know her child
Was in the sacred place,
But that smile was the last smile
To come upon her face.

For when she heard the explosion,   25
Her eyes grew wet and wild.
She raced through the streets of Birmingham
Calling for her child.

She clawed through bits of glass and brick,   30
Then lifted out a shoe.
"O, here's the shoe my baby wore,
But, baby, where are you?"

Reading and Reacting

1. Who are the two speakers in the poem? How do their attitudes differ? How does the tone of the poem convey these attitudes?

2. What kinds of irony are present in the poem? Give examples of each kind you identify.

3. This poem is a **ballad,** a form of poetry traditionally written to be sung or re-cited. Ballads typically repeat words and phrases and have regular meter and rhyme. How do the regular rhyme, repeated words, and singsong meter affect the poem's tone?

4. JOURNAL ENTRY This poem was written in response to the 1963 bombing of the 16th Street Baptist Church in Birmingham, Alabama, a bomb that killed four African-American children. How does this historical background help you to understand the irony of the poem?

Related Works: "Bonny Barbara Allan" (p. 647), "If We Must Die" (p. 686)

✔ **CHECKLIST** Writing about Voice

The Speaker in the Poem

☐ What do we know about the speaker?

☐ Is the speaker anonymous, or does he or she have a particular identity?

☐ How does assuming a particular persona help the poet to convey his or her ideas?

☐ Does the title give readers any information about the speaker's identity?

☐ How does word choice provide information about the speaker?

☐ Does the speaker make any direct statements to readers that help establish his or her identity or character?

☐ Does the speaker address anyone? How can you tell? How does the presence of a listener affect the speaker?

The Tone of the Poem

☐ What is the speaker's attitude toward his or her subject?

☐ How do word choice, rhyme, meter, sentence structure, figures of speech, and imagery help to convey the attitude of the speaker?

☐ Is the poem's tone consistent? How do shifts in tone reveal the changing mood or attitude of the speaker?

Irony

☐ Does the poem include dramatic irony? Situational irony? Verbal irony?

WRITING SUGGESTIONS: Voice

1. The poet Robert Frost once said that he wanted to write "poetry that talked." According to Frost, "whenever I write a line it is because that line has already been spoken clearly by a voice with my mind, an audible voice." Choose some poems in this chapter (or from elsewhere in the book) that you consider "talking poems." Then, write an essay about how successful they are in communicating "an audible voice."

2. Compare the speakers' voices in "Barbie Doll" (p. 689) and "Gretel in Darkness" (p. 460). How are their attitudes toward men similar? How are they different?

3. The theme of Herrick's poem "To the Virgins, to Make Much of Time" (p. 478) is known as **carpe diem,** or "seize the day." Read Andrew Marvell's "To His Coy Mistress" (p. 537), which has the same theme, and compare its tone with that of "To the Virgins, to Make Much of Time."

4. Read the following poem, and compare the speaker's use of the word *hope* with the way the speaker uses the word in Ariel Dorfman's "Hope" (p. 482).

EMILY DICKINSON (1830–1886)

"Hope" is the thing with feathers—   (1861)

"Hope" is the thing with feathers—
That perches in the soul—
And sings the tune without the words—
And never stops — at all—

And sweetest — in the Gale — is heard—   5
And sore must be the storm—
That could abash the little Bird—
That kept so many warm—

I've heard it in the chillest land—
And on the strangest Sea—   10
Yet, never, in Extremity,
It asked a crumb — of Me.

5. Because the speaker and the poet are not the same, poems by the same author can have different voices. Compare the voices of several poems by one poet — for example, Sylvia Plath, W. H. Auden, or William Blake, whose works are included in this anthology.

CHAPTER 17

WORD CHOICE, WORD ORDER

> In a poem, each word, being equally important, exists in absolute focus, having a weight it rarely achieves in fiction. . . . Words in a novel are subordinate to broad slices of action or characterization that push the plot forward. In a poem, they *are* the action.
>
> —**Mark Strand,** *Introduction to* Best American Poems of 1991

SIPHO SEPAMLA (1932–   )

Words, Words, Words (1984)

We don't speak of tribal wars anymore
we say simple faction fights
there are no tribes around here
only nations
it makes sense you see   5
'cause from there
one moves to multinational
it makes sense you get me
'cause from there
one gets one's homeland   10
which is a reasonable idea
'cause from there
one can dabble with independence
which deserves warm applause
— the bloodless revolution   15

we are talking of words
words tossed around as if
denied location by the wind
we mean those words some spit
others grab   20
dress them up for the occasion

489

fling them on the lap of an audience
we are talking of those words
that stalk our lives like policemen
words no dictionary can embrace   25
words that change sooner than seasons
we mean words
that spell out our lives
words, words, words
for there's a kind of poetic licence   30
doing the rounds in these parts

Words identify and name, characterize and distinguish, compare and contrast. Words describe, limit, and embellish; words locate and measure. Even though words may be elusive and uncertain and changeable, "tossed around as if / denied location by the wind" and "can change sooner than seasons," they still can "stalk our lives like policemen." In poetry, as in love and in politics, words matter.

Beyond the quantitative — how many words, how many letters and syllables — is a much more important consideration: the *quality* of words. Which words are chosen, and why? Why are certain words placed next to others? What does a word suggest in a particular context? How are the words arranged? What exactly constitutes the right word?

Word Choice

In poetry, even more than in fiction or drama, words tend to become the focus — sometimes even the true subject — of a work. For this reason, the choice of one word over another can be crucial. Because poems are brief, they must compress many ideas into just a few lines; poets know how much weight each individual word carries, so they choose with great care, trying to select words that imply more than they state.

In general, poets (like prose writers) select words because they communicate their ideas. However, poets may also choose words for their sound. For instance, a word may echo another word's sound, and such repetition may place emphasis on both words; it may rhyme with another word and therefore be needed to preserve the poem's rhyme scheme; or it may have a certain combination of stressed and unstressed syllables needed to maintain the poem's metrical pattern. Occasionally, a poet may even choose a word because of how it looks on the page.

At the same time, poets may choose words for their degree of concreteness or abstraction, specificity or generality. A **concrete** word refers to an item that is a perceivable, tangible entity — for example, a kiss or a flag. An **abstract** word refers to an intangible idea, condition, or quality, something that cannot be perceived by the senses — love or patriotism, for instance. **Specific** words refer to particular items; **general** words refer to entire classes or groups of items. As the following example illustrates, whether a word is specific or general is relative; its degree of specificity or generality depends on its relationship to other words.

Poem → closed form poem → sonnet → seventeenth-century sonnet → Elizabethan sonnet → sonnet by Shakespeare → "My mistress' eyes are nothing like the sun"

Sometimes a poet wants a precise word, one that is both specific and concrete. At other times, a poet might prefer general or abstract language, which may allow for more subtlety — or even for intentional ambiguity.

Finally, a word may be chosen for its **connotation** — what it suggests. Every word has one or more **denotations** — what it signifies without emotional associations, judgments, or opinions. The word *family*, for example, denotes "a group of related things or people." Connotation is a more complex matter; after all, a single word may have many different associations. In general terms, a word may have a connotation that is positive, neutral, or negative. Thus, *family* may have a positive connotation when it describes a group of loving relatives, a neutral connotation when it describes a biological category, and an ironically negative connotation when it describes an organized crime family. Beyond this distinction, *family*, like any other word, may have a variety of emotional and social associations, suggesting loyalty, warmth, home, security, or duty. In fact, many words have somewhat different meanings in different contexts. When poets choose words, then, they must consider what a particular word may suggest to readers as well as what it denotes.

In the poem that follows, the poet chooses words for their sounds and for their relationships to other words as well as for their connotations.

WALT WHITMAN   (1819–1892)

When I Heard the Learn'd Astronomer   (1865)

When I heard the learn'd astronomer,
When the proofs, the figures, were ranged in columns before me,
When I was shown the charts and diagrams, to add, divide, and
    measure them,
When I sitting heard the astronomer where he lectured with much
    applause in the lecture-room,
How soon unaccountable I became tired and sick,   5
Till rising and gliding out I wander'd off by myself,
In the mystical moist night-air, and from time to time,
Look'd up in perfect silence at the stars.

This poem might be paraphrased as follows: "When I grew restless listening to an astronomy lecture, I went outside, where I found I learned more just by looking at the stars than I had learned inside." However, the paraphrase is obviously neither as rich nor as complex as the poem. Through careful use of diction, Whitman establishes a dichotomy that supports the poem's central theme about the relative merits of two ways of learning.

The poem can be divided into two groups of four lines each. The first four lines, unified by the repetition of "When," introduce the astronomer and his tools: "proofs," "figures," and "charts and diagrams" to be added, divided, or measured. In this section of the poem, the speaker is passive: he sits and listens ("I heard"; "I was shown"; "I sitting heard"). The repetition of "When" reinforces the dry monotony of the lecture. In the next four lines, the choice of words signals the change in the speaker's actions and reactions. The confined lecture hall is replaced by "the mystical moist night-air," and the dry lecture and the applause give way to "perfect silence"; instead of sitting passively, the speaker becomes active (he rises, glides, wanders); instead of listening, he looks. The mood of the first half of the poem is restrained: the language is concrete and physical, and the speaker is studying, receiving information from a "learn'd" authority. The rest of the poem, celebrating intuitive knowledge and feelings, is more abstract, freer. Throughout the poem, the lecture hall is set in sharp contrast to the natural world outside its walls.

After considering the poem as a whole, readers should not find it hard to understand why the poet selected certain words. Whitman's use of "lectured" in line 4 rather than a more neutral word like "spoke" is appropriate both because it suggests formality and distance and because it echoes "lecture-room" in the same line. The word "sick" in line 5 is striking because it connotes physical as well as emotional distress, more effectively conveying the extent of the speaker's discomfort than "bored" or "restless" would. "Rising" and "gliding" (line 6) are used rather than "standing" and "walking out" both because of the way their stressed vowel sounds echo each other (and echo "time to time" in the next line) and because of their connotation of dreaminess, which is consistent with "wander'd" (line 6) and "mystical" (line 7). The word "moist" (line 7) is chosen not only because its consonant sounds echo the *m* and *st* sounds in "mystical," but also because it establishes a contrast with the dry, airless lecture hall. Finally, line 8's "perfect silence" is a better choice than a reasonable substitute like "complete silence" or "total silence," either of which would suggest the degree of the silence but not its quality.

In the next poem, the poet also pays careful attention to word choice.

WILLIAM STAFFORD (1914–1993)

For the Grave of Daniel Boone (1957)

The farther he went the farther home grew.
Kentucky became another room;
the mansion arched over the Mississippi;
flowers were spread all over the floor.
He traced ahead a deepening home,   5
and better, with goldenrod:

Leaving the snakeskin of place after place,
going on — after the trees
the grass, a bird flying after a song.
Rifle so level, sighting so well   10
his picture freezes down to now,
a story-picture for children.

They go over the velvet falls
into the tapestry of his time,
heirs to the landscape, feeling no jar: 15
it is like evening; they are the quail
surrounding his fire, coming in for the kill;
their little feet move sacred sand.

Children, we live in a barbwire time
but like to follow the old hands back —   20
the ring in the light, the knuckle, the palm,
all the way to Daniel Boone,
hunting our own kind of deepening home.
From the land that was his I heft this rock.

Here on his grave I put it down.   25

A number of words in "For the Grave of Daniel Boone" are noteworthy for their multiple denotations and connotations. In the first stanza, for example, "home" does not simply mean Boone's residence; it connotes an abstract state, a dynamic concept that grows and deepens, encompassing states and rivers while becoming paradoxically more and more elusive. In literal terms, Boone's "home" at the poem's end is a narrow, confined space: his grave. In a wider sense, his home is the United States, particularly the natural landscape he explored. Thus, the word "home" comes to have a variety of associations to readers beyond its denotative meaning, suggesting both the infinite possibilities beyond the frontier and the realities of civilization's walls and fences.

The word "snakeskin" denotes "the skin of a snake"; its most obvious connotations are smoothness and slipperiness. In this poem, however, the snakeskin signifies more, because it is Daniel Boone who is "Leaving the snakeskin of place after place." Like a snake, Boone belongs to the natural world — and, like a snake, he wanders from place to place, shedding his skin as he goes. Thus, the word "snakeskin," with its connotation of rebirth and its links to nature, passing time, and the inevitability of change, is consistent with the image of Boone as both a man of nature and a restless wanderer, "a bird flying after a song."

In the poem's third stanza, the phrases "velvet falls" and "tapestry of . . . time" seem at first to have been selected solely for their pleasing repetition of sounds ("velvet falls"; "tapestry of time"). But both of these paradoxical phrases also support the poem's theme. Alive, Boone was in constant movement; he was also larger than life. Now, in death, he has been diminished; "his picture freezes down to . . . / a story-picture for children" (lines 11–12), and he is as static and inorganic as velvet or tapestry — no longer dynamic, like "falls" and "time."

The word "barbwire" (line 19) is another word whose multiple meanings enrich the poem's theme. In the simplest terms, "barbwire" denotes a metal fencing material. In light of the poem's concern with space and distance, however, "barbwire" (with its connotations of sharpness, danger, and confinement) is also the antithesis of Boone's free and peaceful wilderness, evoking images of enclosure and imprisonment and reinforcing the poem's central dichotomy between past freedom and present restriction.

The phrase "old hands" (line 20) might also have multiple meanings in the context of the poem. On one level, the hands could belong to an elderly person holding a storybook; on another level, "old hands" could refer to people with considerable life experience — like Boone, who was an "old hand" at scouting. On still another level, given the poem's concern with time, "old hands" could suggest the hands of a clock.

Through what it says literally and through what its words suggest, "For the Grave of Daniel Boone" communicates a good deal about the speaker's identification with Daniel Boone and with the nation he called home. Boone's horizons, his concept of "home," expanded as he wandered. Now, when he is frozen in time and space, a character in a child's picture book, a body in a grave, we are still "hunting our own kind of deepening home," but our horizons, like Boone's, have narrowed in this "barbwire time."

FURTHER READING: Word Choice

ADRIENNE RICH   (1929–   )

Living in Sin   (1955)

She had thought the studio would keep itself,
no dust upon the furniture of love.
Half heresy, to wish the taps less vocal,
the panes relieved of grime. A plate of pears,
a piano with a Persian shawl, a cat   5
stalking the picturesque amusing mouse
had risen at his urging.
                    Not that at five each separate stair would writhe
under the milkman's tramp; that morning light
so coldly would delineate the scraps   10
of last night's cheese and three sepulchral bottles;
that on the kitchen shelf among the saucers
a pair of beetle-eyes would fix her own —
envoy from some black village in the mouldings . . .
Meanwhile, he, with a yawn,   15

sounded a dozen notes upon the keyboard,
declared it out of tune, shrugged at the mirror,
rubbed at his beard, went out for cigarettes;
while she, jeered by the minor demons,
pulled back the sheets and made the bed and found   20
a towel to dust the table-top,
and let the coffee-pot boil over on the stove.
By evening she was back in love again,
though not so wholly but throughout the night
she woke sometimes to feel the daylight coming   25
like a relentless milkman up the stairs.

Reading and Reacting

1. How might the poem's impact change if each of these words were deleted: "Persian" (line 5), "picturesque" (line 6), "sepulchral" (line 11), "minor" (line 19), "sometimes" (line 25)?

2. What words in the poem have strongly negative connotations? What do these words suggest about the relationship the poem describes? How does the image of the "relentless milkman" (line 26) sum up this relationship?

3. This poem, about a woman in love, uses very few words conventionally associated with love poems. Instead, many of its words denote the everyday routine of housekeeping. Give examples of such words. Why do you think they are used?

4. **JOURNAL ENTRY** What connotations does the title have? What other phrases have similar denotative meanings? How do their connotations differ? Why do you think Rich chose the title she did?

5. **CRITICAL PERSPECTIVE** In "Her Cargo: Adrienne Rich and the Common Language," a 1979 essay examining the poet's work over almost thirty years, Alicia Ostriker offers the following analysis of Rich's early poems, including "Living in Sin":

> They seem about to state explicitly . . . a connection between feminine subordination in male-dominated middle-class relationships, and emotionally lethal inarticulateness for both sexes. But the poetry . . . is minor because it is polite. It illustrates symptoms but does not probe sources. There is no disputing the ideas of the predecessors, and Adrienne Rich at this point is a cautious good poet in the sense of being a good girl, a quality noted with approval by her reviewers.

Does your reading of "Living in Sin" support Ostriker's characterization of the poem as "polite" and "cautious"? Do you think Rich is "being a good girl"?

Related Works: "Love and Other Catastrophes: A Mix Tape" (p. 98) "The Storm" (p. 158), "What Lips My Lips Have Kissed" (p. 636), *The Stronger* (p. 853)

E. E. CUMMINGS (1894–1962)

in Just-° (1923)

in Just-
spring when the world is mud-
luscious the little
lame balloonman
whistles   far   and wee   5

and eddieandbill come
running from marbles and
piracies and it's
spring

when the world is puddle-wonderful   10
the queer
old balloonman whistles
far   and   wee
and bettyandisbel come dancing

from hop-scotch and jump-rope and   15
it's
spring
and
   the
       goat-footed   20

balloonMan whistles
far
and
wee

Reading and Reacting

1. In this poem, Cummings coins a number of words that he uses to modify other words. Identify these coinages. What other, more conventional, words could be used in their place? What does Cummings accomplish by using the coined words instead?

2. What do you think Cummings means by "far and wee" in lines 5, 13, and 22–24? Why do you think he arranges these three words in a different way on the page each time he uses them?

3. **JOURNAL ENTRY** Evaluate this poem. Do you like it? Is it memorable? Moving? Or is it just clever?

4. **CRITICAL PERSPECTIVE** In "Latter-Day Notes on E. E. Cummings' Language" (1955), Robert E. Maurer suggests that Cummings often coined new words

---

° *in Just-:* This poem is also known as "Chansons Innocentes I."

in the same way that children do: for example, "by adding the normal -er or -est (*beautifuler, chiefest*), or stepping up the power of a word such as *last*, which is already superlative, and saying *lastest*," creating words such as *givingest* and *whirlingest*. In addition to "combining two or more words to form a single new one . . . to give an effect of wholeness, of one quality" (for example, *yellowgreen*), "in the simplest of his word coinages, he merely creates a new word by analogy as a child would without adding any shade of meaning other than that inherent in the prefix or suffix he utilizes, as in the words *unstrength* and *untimid*. . . ." Many early reviewers, Maurer notes, criticized such coinages because they "convey a thrill but not a precise impression," a criticism also leveled at Cummings's poetry more broadly.

Consider the coinages in "in Just-." Do you agree that many do not add "shades of meaning" or provide a "precise impression"? Or do you find that the coinages contribute to the whole in a meaningful way?

Related Works: "The Secret Lion" (p. 412), "Acrobats" (p. 456), "anyone lived in a pretty how town" (p. 507), "Constantly Risking Absurdity" (p. 523), "Jabberwocky" (p. 566), "the sky was can dy" (p. 589)

ROBERT PINSKY (1940–   )

ABC (1998)

Any body can die, evidently. Few
Go happily, irradiating joy,

Knowledge, love. Many
Need oblivion, painkillers,
Quickest respite.   5

Sweet time unafflicted,
Various world:

X = your zenith.

Reading and Reacting

1. What "rules" limit the choice of words used in this poem? What determines the order in which they are used? Where does the poet break (or bend) the rules he has established? Can you suggest a way for him to avoid doing so?
2. Given the constraints the poet places on himself here, how successful is he? Is the result of his efforts a poem or just a novelty? Explain.
3. **JOURNAL ENTRY** This poem is tightly compressed, limited to very few words. Rewrite it as a paragraph, adding any words you think are necessary to communicate its theme. How is your version different from the original in what it says? In what it suggests?

4. Critical Perspective "ABC" has a very distinctive form. The poet and critic Louise Glück has stressed the importance of form in the poetry of Robert Pinsky:

> [I]n Pinsky's art, form does what we have come to believe only tone can do. That is to say, form here is not intellectual construct but rather metaphor. For the poems to be understood at all they must be apprehended entire, as shapes.

How does reflecting on the form, or "shape," of "ABC" help you to understand the poem?

Related Works: "A Primer for the Punctuation of Heart Disease" (p. 88), "I Walk in the Old Street" (p. 448), "l(a" (p. 449), "Constantly Risking Absurdity" (p. 523), *Tape* (p. 741)

Levels of Diction

Like other writers, poets use various levels of diction to convey their ideas. The diction of a poem may be formal or informal or fall anywhere in between, depending on the identity of the speaker and on the speaker's attitude toward the reader and toward his or her subject. At one extreme, very formal poems can be far removed in style and vocabulary from everyday speech. At the other extreme, highly informal poems can be full of jargon, regionalisms, and slang. Many poems, of course, use language that falls somewhere between formal and informal diction.

Formal diction is characterized by a learned vocabulary and grammatically correct forms. In general, formal diction does not include colloquialisms, such as contractions and shortened word forms (*phone* for *telephone*). As the following poem illustrates, a speaker who uses formal diction can sound aloof and impersonal.

MARGARET ATWOOD (1939–   )

The City Planners   (1966)

Cruising these residential Sunday
streets in dry August sunlight:
what offends us is
the sanities:
the houses in pedantic rows, the planted   5
sanitary trees, assert
levelness of surface like a rebuke
to the dent in our car door.
No shouting here, or
shatter of glass; nothing more abrupt   10

than the rational whine of a power mower
cutting a straight swath in the discouraged grass.

But though the driveways neatly
sidestep hysteria
by being even, the roofs all display   15
the same slant of avoidance to the hot sky,
certain things:
the smell of spilled oil a faint

sickness lingering in the garages,
a splash of paint on brick surprising as a bruise,   20
a plastic hose poised in a vicious

coil; even the too-fixed stare of the wide windows
give momentary access to
the landscape behind or under
the future cracks in the plaster   25

when the houses, capsized, will slide
obliquely into the clay seas, gradual as glaciers
that right now nobody notices.

That is where the City Planners
with the insane faces of political conspirators   30
are scattered over unsurveyed
territories, concealed from each other,
each in his own private blizzard;

guessing directions, they sketch
transitory lines rigid as wooden borders   35
on a wall in the white vanishing air

tracing the panic of suburb
order in a bland madness of snows.

Atwood's speaker is clearly concerned about the poem's central issue, but rather than use *I*, the poem uses the first-person plural (*us*) to convey some degree of emotional detachment. Although phrases such as "sickness lingering in the garages" and "insane faces of political conspirators" communicate the speaker's disapproval, formal words — "pedantic," "rebuke," "display," "poised," "obliquely," "conspirators," "transitory"— help her to maintain her distance. Both the speaker herself and her attack on the misguided city planners gain credibility through her balanced, measured tone and through her use of language that is as formal and "professional" as theirs.

Informal diction is the language closest to everyday conversation. It includes colloquialisms — contractions, shortened word forms, and the like — and may also include slang, regional expressions, and even nonstandard words.

In the poem that follows, the speaker uses informal diction to highlight the contrast between James Baca, a law student speaking to the graduating class of his old high school, and the graduating seniors.

JIM SAGEL   (1947–1998)

Baca Grande°   (1982)

Una vaca se topó con un ratón y le dice:
"Tú—¿tan chiquito y con bigote?" Y le responde el ratón:
"Y tú tan grandota —¿y sin brassiere?"°

It was nearly a miracle
James Baca remembered anyone at all
from the old hometown gang
having been two years at Yale
   no less   5
and halfway through law school
at the University of California at Irvine
They hardly recognized him either
in his three-piece grey business suit
and surfer-swirl haircut   10
with just the menacing hint
of a tightly trimmed Zapata moustache
   for cultural balance
and relevance

He had come to deliver the keynote address   15
to the graduating class of 80
at his old alma mater
and show off his well-trained lips
which laboriously parted
   each Kennedyish "R"   20
and drilled the first person pronoun
through the microphone
like an oil bit
with the slick, elegantly honed phrases
that slid so smoothly   25
off his meticulously bleached
   tongue
He talked Big Bucks
with astronautish fervor and if he
   the former bootstrapless James A. Baca   30

—————————————————————————————

°*Baca Grande: Baca* is both a phonetic spelling of the Spanish word *vaca* (cow) and the last name of one of the poem's characters. *Grande* means "large."   °*Una . . . brassiere?:* A cow ran into a rat and said: "You — so small and with a moustache?" The rat responded: "And you — so big and without a bra?"

could dazzle the ass
off the universe
then even you
    yes you

Joey Martinez toying with your yellow   35
    tassle
and staring dumbly into space
could emulate Mr. Baca someday
    possibly
well   40
there was of course
such a thing
as being an outrageously successful
gas station attendant too
    let us never forget   45
it doesn't really matter what you do
so long as you excel
    James said
never believing a word
of it   50
for he had already risen
    as high as they go

Wasn't nobody else
from this deprived environment
who'd ever jumped   55
    straight out of college
into the Governor's office
and maybe one day
he'd sit in that big chair
    himself   60
and when he did
he'd forget this damned town
and all the petty little people
in it
once and for all   65
    That much he promised himself

"Baca Grande" uses numerous colloquialisms, including contractions; conversational placeholders, such as "no less" and "well"; shortened word forms, such as "gas"; slang terms, such as "Big Bucks"; whimsical coinages ("Kennedyish," "astronautish," "bootstrapless"); nonstandard grammatical constructions, such as "Wasn't nobody else"; and even profanity. The level of language is perfectly appropriate for the poem's speaker, one of the students Baca addresses — suspicious, streetwise, and unimpressed by Baca's "three-piece grey business suit" and "surfer-swirl haircut." In fact, the informal diction is a key element in the poem, expressing the gap between the slick James Baca, with "his well-trained lips / which laboriously parted / each Kennedyish 'R'" and members of his audience, with their unpretentious, forthright speech — and also the gap between Baca as he is today and the student he once was. In this sense, "Baca Grande" is as much a linguistic commentary as a social one.

FURTHER READING: Levels of Diction

WANDA COLEMAN   (1946 –   )

Sears Life   (2001)

it makes me nervous to go into a store
because i never know if i'm going to
come out. have you noticed how much
they look like prisons these days? no display
windows anymore. all that cold soulless   5
lighting — as atmospheric as county jail—
and all that ground-breaking status-quo
shattering rock 'n' roll reduced to neuron
pablum and piped in over the escalators.
breaks my rebel heart. and i especially   10
hate the aroma of fresh-nuked popcorn
rushing my nose, throwing my stomach
off balance. eyes follow me everywhere i go
like i'm a neon sign that shouts shoplifter.
and so many snide counter rats want to   15
service me, it almost makes me feel rich
and royal. that's why i rarely bother to
browse. i go straight to the department of
the object of conjecture, make my decision
quick, throw down the cash and split   20

one time i had barely left this store
when i heard somebody yelling stop! stop!
i turned around and this dough-fleshed
armed security guard was waving me down.
i waited while he caught his breath and   25
demanded to search my purse i stared him
into his socks. we're outside the store,
i reminded him. if you search me, you'd
better find some goddamned something.
he took a minute to examine my eyes, turned   30
around and went back to his job, snorting
dust and coondogging teenage loiterers

Reading and Reacting

1. List the words that identify this poem's diction as informal. Do you think this informality is a strength or a weakness? Explain.
2. Look closely at the poem's sentence structure, use of all lowercase letters, and its punctuation. What does each of these elements contribute to the poem's overall effect?
3. What can you infer about the speaker from the poem's language —for example, from language like "neuron / pablum" (lines 8–9), "counter rats" (line 15), and "dough-fleshed" (line 23)?
4. **JOURNAL ENTRY** What comment does the poem's title make about Sears? About life? Do you think the speaker's observations are valid?

Related Works: "A&P" (p. 128), "The Lesson" (p. 353)

MARK HALLIDAY   (1949–   )

The Value of Education   (2000)

I go now to the library. When I sit in the library
I am not illegally dumping bags of kitchen garbage
in the dumpster behind Clippinger Laboratory,
and a very pissed-off worker at Facilities Management
is not picking through my garbage and finding   5
several yogurt-stained and tomato-sauce-stained envelopes
with my name and address on them.
When I sit in the library,
I might doze off a little,
and what I read might not penetrate my head   10
which is mostly porridge in a bowl of bone.
However, when I sit there trying to read
I am not, you see, somewhere else being a hapless ass.
I am not leaning on the refrigerator
in the apartment of a young female colleague   15
chatting with oily pep
because I imagine she may suddenly decide to
do sex with me while her boyfriend is on a trip.
Instead I am in the library! Sitting still!
No one in town is approaching my chair   20
with a summons, or a bill, or a huge fist.
This is good. You may say,
"But this is merely a negative definition of
the value of education." Maybe so,
but would you be able to say that   25
if you hadn't been to the library?

Reading and Reacting

1. Who is the speaker? What does he reveal about himself? Whom might he be addressing?

2. How is the speaker's life outside the library different from the life he leads inside the library?

3. In lines 23–24, the speaker imagines a challenge to his comments. Do you think this challenge is valid? What do you think of the speaker's reply?

4. What phrases are repeated in this poem? Why?

5. JOURNAL ENTRY What argument is the speaker making for the benefits of the library (and for the value of education)? Is he joking, or is he serious?

Related Works: "Gryphon" (p. 139), "When I Heard the Learn'd Astronomer" (p. 491), "Why I Went to College" (p. 583)

GWENDOLYN BROOKS (1917–2000)

We Real Cool (1959)

The Pool Players.
Seven at the Golden Shovel.

We real cool. We
Left School. We

Lurk late. We
Strike straight. We

Sing sin. We   5
Thin gin. We

Jazz June. We
Die soon.

Reading and Reacting

1. What elements of nonstandard English grammar appear in this poem? How does the use of such language affect your attitude toward the speaker?

2. Every word in this poem is a single syllable. Why?

3. Why do you think the poet begins with "We" only in the first line instead of isolating each complete sentence on its own line? How does this strategy change the poem's impact?

4. JOURNAL ENTRY Write a prose version of this poem, adding words, phrases, and sentences to expand the poem into a paragraph.

5. **CRITICAL PERSPECTIVE** In *Gwendolyn Brooks: Poetry and the Heroic Voice*, critic D. H. Malhem writes of "We Real Cool," "Despite presentation in the voice of the gang, this is a maternal poem, gently scolding yet deeply sorrowing for the hopelessness of the boys."

Do you agree with Malhem that the speaker's attitude is "maternal"?

Related Works: "Where Are You Going, Where Have You Been?" (p. 384), "Greasy Lake" (p. 359), *Tape* (p. 741).

Word Order

The order in which words are arranged in a poem is as important as the choice of words. Because English sentences nearly always have a subject-verb-object sequence, with adjectives preceding the nouns they modify, a departure from this order calls attention to itself. Thus, poets can use readers' expectations about word order to their advantage.

For example, poets often manipulate word order to place emphasis on a word. Sometimes they achieve this emphasis by using a very unconventional sequence; sometimes they simply place the word first or last in a line or place it in a stressed position in the line. Poets may also choose a particular word order to make two related — or startlingly unrelated — words fall in adjacent or parallel positions, calling attention to the similarity (or the difference) between them. In other cases, poets may manipulate syntax to preserve a poem's rhyme or meter or to highlight sound correspondences that might otherwise not be noticeable. Finally, irregular syntax may be used throughout a poem to reveal a speaker's mood — for example, to give a playful quality to a poem or to suggest a speaker's disoriented state.

In the poem that follows, word order frequently departs from conventional English syntax.

EDMUND SPENSER (1552–1599)

One day I wrote her name upon the strand (1595)

One day I wrote her name upon the strand,°
But came the waves and washed it away:
Again I wrote it with a second hand,
But came the tide and made my pains his prey.

° *strand:* Beach.

"Vain man," said she, "that doest in vain assay,   5
A mortal thing so to immortalize,
For I myself shall like to this decay,
And eek° my name be wiped out likewise."
"Not so," quod° I, "let baser things devise,
To die in dust, but you shall live by fame: 10
My verse your virtues rare shall eternize,
And in the heavens write your glorious name.
Where whenas death shall all the world subdue,
Our love shall live, and later life renew."

"One day I wrote her name upon the strand," a **sonnet,** has a fixed metrical pattern and rhyme scheme. To accommodate the sonnet's rhyme and meter, Spenser makes a number of adjustments in syntax. For example, to make sure certain rhyming words fall at the ends of lines, the poet sometimes moves words out of their conventional order, as the following three comparisons illustrate.

Conventional Word Order	**Inverted Sequence**
"'Vain man,' she said, 'that doest *assay in vain.*'"	"'Vain man,' said she, 'that doest *in vain assay.*'" ("Assay" appears at end of line 5, to rhyme with line 7's decay.")
"My verse shall *eternize your rare virtues.*"	"My verse *your virtues rare shall eternize.*" ("Eternize" appears at end of line 11 to rhyme with line 9's "devise.")
"Where whenas death shall *subdue all the world,* / Our love shall live, and *later renew life.*"	"Where whenas death shall *all the world subdue,* / Our love shall live, and *later life renew.*" (Rhyming words "subdue" and "renew" are placed at ends of lines.)

To make sure the metrical pattern stresses certain words, the poet occasionally moves a word out of conventional order and places it in a stressed position. The following comparison illustrates this technique.

Conventional Word Order	**Inverted Sequence**
"But *the waves came* and washed it away."	"But *came the waves* and washed it away." (Stress in line 2 falls on "waves" rather than on "the.")

°*eek:* Also, indeed.   °*quod:* Said.

As the above comparisons show, Spenser's adjustments in syntax are motivated at least in part by a desire to preserve his sonnet's rhyme and meter.

The next poem does more than simply invert words; it presents an intentionally disordered syntax.

E. E. CUMMINGS   (1894–1962)

anyone lived in a pretty how town   (1940)

anyone lived in a pretty how town
(with up so floating many bells down)
spring summer autumn winter
he sang his didn't he danced his did.

Women and men (both little and small)   5
cared for anyone not at all
they sowed their isn't they reaped their same
sun moon stars rain

children guessed (but only a few
and down they forgot as up they grew   10
autumn winter spring summer)
that noone loved him more by more

when by now and tree by leaf
she laughed his joy she cried his grief
bird by snow and stir by still   15
anyone's any was all to her

someones married their everyones
laughed their cryings and did their dance
(sleep wake hope and then) they
said their nevers they slept their dream   20

stars rain sun moon
(and only the snow can begin to explain
how children are apt to forget to remember
with up so floating many bells down)

one day anyone died i guess   25
(and noone stooped to kiss his face)
busy folk buried them side by side
little by little and was by was

all by all and deep by deep
and more by more they dream their sleep   30
noone and anyone earth by april
wish by spirit and if by yes.

Women and men (both dong and ding)
summer autumn winter spring
reaped their sowing and went their came   35
sun moon stars rain

Cummings, like Spenser, sometimes manipulates syntax in response to the
demands of rhyme and meter — for example, in line 10. But Cummings goes
much further, using unconventional syntax as part of a scheme that includes
other unusual elements of the poem, such as its unexpected departures from the
musical metrical pattern (for example, in lines 3 and 8) and from the rhyme
scheme (for example, in lines 3 and 4) and its use of various parts of speech in unfamiliar contexts. Together, these techniques give the poem a playful quality. The
refreshing disorder of the syntax (for instance, in lines 1–2, 10, and 24) adds to
the poem's whimsical effect.

FURTHER READING: Word Order

A. E. HOUSMAN   (1859–1936)

To an Athlete Dying Young   (1896)

The time you won your town the race
We chaired you through the market-place;
Man and boy stood cheering by,
And home we brought you shoulder-high.

Today, the road all runners come,   5
Shoulder-high we bring you home,
And set you at your threshold down,
Townsman of a stiller town.

Smart lad, to slip betimes away
From fields where glory does not stay,   10
And early though the laurel grows
It withers quicker than the rose.

Eyes the shady night has shut
Cannot see the record cut,
And silence sounds no worse than cheers   15
After earth has stopped the ears.

Now you will not swell the rout
Of lads that wore their honors out,
Runners whom renown outran
And the name died before the man.   20

So set, before its echoes fade,
The fleet foot on the sill of shade,

And hold to the low lintel up
The still-defended challenge-cup.

And round that early-laureled head   25
Will flock to gaze the strengthless dead,
And find unwithered on its curls
The garland briefer than a girl's.

Reading and Reacting

1. Where does the poem's meter or rhyme scheme require the poet to depart from conventional syntax?
2. Edit the poem so its word order is more conventional. Do your changes improve the poem?
3. **JOURNAL ENTRY** Who do you think the speaker is? What is his relationship to the athlete?

Related Work: "Nothing Gold Can Stay" (p. 518)

✔ CHECKLIST   Writing about Word Choice and Word Order

Word Choice

Which words are of key importance in the poem? What is the denotative meaning of each of these key words?

Which key words have neutral connotations? Which have negative connotations? Which have positive connotations? Beyond its literal meaning, what does each word suggest?

Why is each word chosen instead of a synonym? (For example, is the word chosen for its sound? Its connotation? Its relationship to other words in the poem? Its contribution to the poem's metrical pattern?)

What other words could be effectively used in place of words now in the poem?

How would substitutions change the poem's meaning?

Are any words repeated? Why?

Levels of Diction

How would you characterize the poem's level of diction? Why is this level of diction used? Is it appropriate?

Does the poem mix different levels of diction? For what purpose?

continued on next page

Word Order

☐ Is the poem's syntax conventional, or are words arranged in unexpected order?

☐ Which phrases represent departures from conventional syntax?

☐ What is the purpose of the unusual syntax? (For example, does it preserve the poem's meter or rhyme scheme? Does it highlight particular sound correspondences? Does it place emphasis on a particular word or phrase? Does it reflect the speaker's mood?)

☐ How would the poem's impact change if conventional syntax were used?

WRITING SUGGESTIONS: Word Choice, Word Order

1. Reread the two poems in this chapter by E. E. Cummings — "in Just-" (p. 496) and "anyone lived in a pretty how town" (p. 507). If you like, you may also read one or two additional poems in this book by Cummings. Do you believe Cummings chose words primarily for their sound? For their appearance on the page? What other factors might have influenced his choices?

2. The tone of "We Real Cool" (p. 504) is flat and unemotional; the problem on which it focuses, however, is serious. Expand this concise poem into a short story that retains the poem's informal, colloquial tone but uses more detailed, more emotional language to communicate the hopeless situation of the speaker and his friends. Include dialogue as well as narrative.

3. Reread "Living in Sin" (p. 494) and "Sears Life" (p. 502), and choose one or two other poems in this book whose speaker is a woman. Compare the speakers' levels of diction and choice of words. What does their language reveal about their lives?

4. Reread "For the Grave of Daniel Boone" (p. 492) alongside Robert Lowell's "For the Union Dead" (p. 639). What does each poem's choice of words reveal about the speaker's attitude toward his subject?

5. Analyze the choice of words and the level of diction in several poems in this book that use language to express social or political criticism. Some poems that might work well include Claude McKay's "If We Must Die" (p. 686), Marge Piercy's "Barbie Doll" (p. 689), Robert Pinsky's "Shirt" (p. 690), and Ariel Dorfman's "Hope" (p. 482).

CHAPTER 18

IMAGERY

It is better to present one Image in a lifetime than to produce voluminous works.

— **Ezra Pound,** *"A Retrospect"*

JANE FLANDERS (1940 – 2001)

Cloud Painter (1984)

Suggested by the life and art of John Constable °

At first, as you know, the sky is incidental —
a drape, a backdrop for trees and steeples.
Here an oak clutches a rock (already he works outdoors),
a wall buckles but does not break,
water pearls through a lock, a haywain° trembles.   5

The pleasures of landscape are endless. What we see
around us should be enough.
Horizons are typically high and far away.

Still, clouds let us drift and remember. He is, after all,
a miller's son, used to trying   10
to read the future in the sky, seeing instead
ships, horses, instruments of flight.
Is that his mother's wash flapping on the line?
His schoolbook, smudged, illegible?

In this period the sky becomes significant.   15
Cloud forms are technically correct — mares' tails,
sheep-in-the-meadow, thunderheads.
You can almost tell which scenes have been interrupted
by summer showers.

° *John Constable:* British painter (1776 – 1837) noted for his landscapes.   ° *haywain:* An open horse-drawn wagon for carrying hay.

Now his young wife dies.   20
His landscapes achieve belated success.
He is invited to join the Academy. I forget
whether he accepts or not.

In any case, the literal forms give way
to something spectral, nameless. His palette shrinks   25
to gray, blue, white — the colors of charity.
Horizons sink and fade,
trees draw back till they are little more than frames,
then they too disappear.

Finally the canvas itself begins to vibrate   30
with waning light,
as if the wind could paint.
And we too, at last, stare into a space
which tells us nothing,
except that the world can vanish along with our need for it.   35

Because the purpose of poetry — and, for that matter, of all literature — is to expand the perception of readers, poets appeal to the senses. In "Cloud Painter," Jane Flanders uses **images,** such as the mother's wash on the line and the smudged schoolbook, to enable readers to visualize particular scenes in John Constable's early paintings. Clouds are described so readers can picture them —"mares' tails, / sheep-in-the-meadow, thunderheads." Thus, "Cloud Painter" is not only about

John Constable (1776–1837). *Landscape, Noon, The Haywain.* 1821. Oil on canvas, 130½ × 185½ cm. London, National Gallery.

the work of John Constable but also about the ability of an artist — poet or painter — to call up images in the minds of an audience. To achieve this end, a poet uses **imagery,** language that evokes a physical sensation produced by one or more of the five senses — sight, hearing, taste, touch, smell.

Although the effect can be quite complex, the way images work is simple: when you read the word *red*, your memory of the various red things that you have seen determines how you picture the image. In addition, the word *red* may have **connotations**— emotional associations that define your response. A red sunset, for example, can have a positive connotation or a negative one, depending on whether it is associated with the end of a perfect day or with air pollution. By choosing images carefully, poets not only create pictures in a reader's mind but also create a great number of imaginative associations. These associations help poets to establish the **atmosphere** or **mood** of the poem. The image of softly falling snow in "Stopping by Woods on a Snowy Evening" (p. 672), for example, creates a quiet, almost mystical mood.

Readers come to a poem with their own unique experiences, so an image in a poem does not suggest exactly the same thing to all readers. In "Cloud Painter," for example, the poet presents the image of an oak tree clutching a rock. Although most readers will probably see a picture that is consistent with the one the poet sees, no two images will be identical. Every reader will have his or her own distinct mental image of a tree clinging to a rock; some images will be remembered experiences, whereas others will be imaginative creations. Some readers may even be familiar enough with the work of the painter John Constable to visualize a particular tree clinging to a particular rock in one of his paintings (see p. 512). By conveying what the poet sees and imagines, images open readers' minds and enrich their reading with perceptions and associations different from — and possibly more original and complex than — their own.

One advantage of imagery is its extreme **economy.** A few carefully chosen words enable poets to evoke a range of emotions and reactions. In the following poem, William Carlos Williams uses simple visual images to create a rich and compelling picture.

WILLIAM CARLOS WILLIAMS (1883–1963)

Red Wheelbarrow (1923)

so much depends
upon

a red wheel
barrow

glazed with rain   5
water

beside the white
chickens

"Red Wheelbarrow" asks readers to consider the uniqueness and mystery of every-day objects. What is immediately apparent is the poem's verbal economy. The poet does not tell readers what the barnyard smells like or what sounds the animals make. In fact, he does not even present a detailed picture of the scene. How large is the wheelbarrow? In what condition is it? How many chickens are in the barnyard? In this poem, the answers to these questions are not important.

Even without answering these questions, the poet is able to use simple imagery to create a scene on which, he says, "so much depends." The wheelbarrow establishes a momentary connection between the poet and his world. Like a still-life painting, the red wheelbarrow beside the white chickens gives order to a world that is full of seemingly unrelated objects. By asserting the importance of the objects in the poem, the poet suggests that our ability to perceive the objects of this world gives our lives meaning and that our ability to convey our perceptions to others is central to our lives as well as to poetry.

Images enable poets to present ideas that would be difficult to convey in any other way. One look at a dictionary will illustrate that concepts such as *beauty* and *mystery* are so abstract that they are difficult to define, let alone to discuss in specific terms. However, by choosing an image or a series of images to embody these ideas, poets can effectively make their feelings known, as Ezra Pound does in the brief poem that follows.

EZRA POUND   (1885–1972)

In a Station of the Metro   (1916)

The apparition of these faces in the crowd;
Petals on a wet, black bough.

This poem is almost impossible to paraphrase because the information it communicates is less important than the feelings associated with this information. The poem's title indicates that the first line is meant to suggest a group of people standing in a station of the Paris subway. The scene, however, is presented not as a clear picture but as an "apparition," suggesting that it is unexpected or even dreamlike. In contrast with the image of the subway platform is the image of the people's faces as flower petals on the dark branch of a tree. Thus, the subway platform — dark, cold, wet, subterranean (associated with baseness, death, and hell) — is juxtaposed with flower petals — delicate, pale, radiant, lovely (associated with the ideal, life, and heaven). These contrasting images, presented without comment, bear the entire weight of the poem.

Although images can be strikingly visual, they can also appeal to the senses of hearing, smell, taste, and touch. The following poem uses images of sound and taste as well as sight.

GARY SNYDER (1930–)

Some Good Things to Be
Said for the Iron Age (1970)

A ringing tire iron
   dropped on the pavement
Whang of a saw
brusht on limbs
the taste   5
of rust

Here Snyder presents two commonplace aural images: the ringing of a tire iron and the sound of a saw. These somewhat ordinary images gain power, however, through their visual isolation on separate lines in the poem. Together they produce a harsh and jarring chord that in turn creates a sense of uneasiness in the reader. This poem does more than present sensory images, though. It also conveys the speaker's interpretations of these images. The last two lines imply not only that the time in which we live (the Iron Age) is base and mundane, but also that it is declining, decaying into an age of rust. This idea is reinforced by the repeated consonant sounds in *taste* and *rust,* which encourage readers to hold the final image of the poem on their tongues. The title of the poem makes an ironic comment, suggesting that compared to the time that is approaching, the age of iron may be "good." Thus, in the mind of the poet, ordinary events gain added significance, and images that spring from everyday experience become sources of enlightenment and insight.

In short poems, such as most of those discussed above, one or two images may serve as focal points. A longer poem may introduce a cluster of images, creating a more complex tapestry of sensory impressions — as in the following poem, where a number of related images are woven together.

SUZANNE E. BERGER (1944–)

The Meal (1984)

They have washed their faces until they are pale,
their homework is beautifully complete.
They wait for the adults to lean towards each other.
The hands of the children are oval
and smooth as pine-nuts.   5

The girls have braided and rebraided their hair,
and tied ribbons without a single mistake.

The boy has put away his coin collection.
They are waiting for the mother to straighten her lipstick,
and for the father to speak.   10

They gather around the table, carefully
as constellations waiting to be named.
Their minds shift and ready, like dunes.
It is so quiet, all waiting stars and dunes.

Their forks move across their plates without scraping,   15
they wait for the milk and the gravy
at the table with its forgotten spices.
They are waiting for a happiness to lift their eyes,
like sudden light flaring in the trees outside.

The white miles of the meal continue,   20
the figures still travel across a screen:
the father carving the Sunday roast,
her mouth uneven as a torn hibiscus,
their braids still gleaming in the silence.

"The Meal" presents related images that together evoke silence, order, and emptiness. It begins with the image of faces washed "until they are pale" and goes on to describe the children's oval hands as "smooth as pine-nuts." Forks move across plates "without scraping," and the table hints at the memory of "forgotten spices." Despite the poem's title, these children are emotionally starved. The attentive, well-scrubbed children sit at a table where, neither eating nor speaking, they wait for "the milk and the gravy" and for happiness that never comes. The "white miles of the meal" seem to go on forever, reinforcing the sterility and emptiness of the Sunday ritual. Suggesting an absence of sensation or feeling, a kind of paralysis, the poem's images challenge conventional assumptions about the family and its rituals.

Much visual imagery is **static,** freezing the moment and thereby giving it the timeless quality of painting or sculpture. ("The Meal" presents such a tableau, and so do "Red Wheelbarrow" and "In a Station of the Metro.") Some imagery, in contrast, is **kinetic,** conveying a sense of motion or change.

WILLIAM CARLOS WILLIAMS (1883–1963)

The Great Figure (1938)

Among the rain
and lights
I saw the figure 5
in gold
on a red   5
firetruck

moving
tense
unheeded
to gong clangs   10
siren howls
and wheels rumbling
through the dark city.

Charles Henry Demuth (1883–1935). *The Figure 5 in Gold*. Oil on composition board, 36 × 29¾ in. The Metropolitan Museum of Art, The Alfred Steiglitz Collection, 1949. (49.59.1). Photograph © The Metropolitan Museum of Art.

Commenting on "The Great Figure" in his autobiography, Williams explained that while walking in New York, he heard the sound of a fire engine. As he turned the corner, he saw a golden figure 5 on a red background speed by. The impression was so forceful that he immediately jotted down a poem about it. In the poem, Williams attempts to re-create the sensation the figure 5 made as it moved into his consciousness, presenting the image as if it were a picture taken by a camera with a high-speed shutter. The poet presents images in the order in which he perceived them: first the 5, and then the red fire truck howling and clanging into the darkness. Thus, "The Great Figure" uses images of sight, sound, and movement to convey the poet's experience. The American painter Charles Demuth was fascinated by the poem. Working closely with Williams, he attempted to capture the poem's kinetic energy in a painting.

> **NOTE:** A special use of imagery, called **synesthesia**, occurs when one sense is described in a way that is more appropriate for another sense — for instance, when a sound is described with color. When people say they are feeling *blue* or describe music as *hot,* they are using synesthesia.

FURTHER READING: Imagery

ROBERT FROST   (1874–1963)

Nothing Gold Can Stay   (1923)

Nature's first green is gold,
Her hardest hue to hold.
Her early leaf's a flower;
But only so an hour.
Then leaf subsides to leaf.   5
So Eden sank to grief.
So dawn goes down to day.
Nothing gold can stay.

Reading and Reacting

1. What central idea does this poem express?
2. What do you think the first line of the poem means? In what sense is this line ironic?
3. What is the significance of the colors green and gold in this poem? What do these colors have to do with "Eden" and "dawn"?
4. JOURNAL ENTRY How do the various images in the poem prepare readers for the last line?
5. CRITICAL PERSPECTIVE In "The Figure a Poem Means," the introduction to the first edition of his *Collected Poems* (1930), Frost laid out a theory of poetry:

It begins in delight, it inclines to the impulse, it assumes direction with the first
line laid down, it runs a course of lucky events, and ends in a clarification of life—
not necessarily a great clarification . . . but a momentary stay against confusion. . . .
Like a piece of ice on a hot stove the poem must ride on its own melting. . . . Read
it a hundred times: it will forever keep its freshness as a metal keeps its fragrance.
It can never lose its sense of a meaning that once unfolded by surprise as it went.

Explain how Frost's remarks apply to "Nothing Gold Can Stay."

Related Works: "The Secret Lion" (p. 412), "Araby" (p. 232), "Greasy Lake"
(p. 359), "Shall I compare thee to a summer's day?" (p. 521), "God's Grandeur"
(p. 676)

WILLIAM SHAKESPEARE (1564–1616)

My mistress' eyes are nothing like the sun (1609)

My mistress' eyes are nothing like the sun;
Coral is far more red than her lips' red;
If snow be white, why then her breasts are dun;
If hairs be wires, black wires grow on her head.
I have seen roses damasked red and white,   5
But no such roses see I in her cheeks;
And in some perfumes is there more delight
Than in the breath that from my mistress reeks.
I love to hear her speak, yet well I know
That music hath a far more pleasing sound;   10
I grant I never saw a goddess go:
My mistress, when she walks, treads on the ground.
      And yet, by heaven, I think my love as rare
      As any she, belied with false compare.

Reading and Reacting

1. What point does Shakespeare make in the first twelve lines of his sonnet?
2. What point does the rhymed couplet at the end of the poem make?
3. How is Shakespeare's imagery like and unlike that of traditional love poems? For example, how is the imagery in this poem different from that in
   Thomas Campion's "There is a garden in her face" (p. 656)?
4. **JOURNAL ENTRY** How do you think the woman to whom the poem is addressed will react?
5. **CRITICAL PERSPECTIVE** During the Renaissance, poets commonly used the
   "Petrarchan conceit" to praise their lovers. In this type of metaphor, the author draws elaborate comparisons between his beloved and one or more dissimilar things. According to critic Felicia Jean Steele, "Traditional readings
   of Shakespeare's Sonnet 130 argue that Shakespeare cunningly employs Petrarchan imagery while deliberately undermining it."

How does this poem use the "Petrarchan conceit"? How does it undercut this convention?

Related Works: "A&P" (p. 128) "The Storm" (p. 158), "How Do I Love Thee?" (p. 635), *The Brute* (p. 723)

✔ CHECKLIST   Writing about Imagery

- Do the images in the poem appeal to the sense of sight, hearing, taste, touch, or smell?
- Does the poem depend on a single image or on several different images?
- Does the poem depend on a cluster of related images?
- What details make the images memorable?
- What mood do the images create?
- Are the images static or kinetic?
- How do the poem's images help to convey its theme?
- How effective are the images? How do they enhance your enjoyment of the poem?

WRITING SUGGESTIONS: Imagery

1. How are short poems such as "Some Good Things to Be Said for the Iron Age" (p. 515) and "In a Station of the Metro" (p. 514) like and unlike **haiku?**

2. After rereading "Cloud Painter" (p. 511) and "The Great Figure" (p. 516), read "Musée des Beaux Arts" (p. 616), and study the corresponding paintings (*Landscape, Noon, the Haywain* on page 512; *The Figure 5 in Gold* on page 517; and *Landscape with the Fall of Icarus*, on page 617, respectively). Then, write an essay in which you draw some conclusions about the differences between artistic and poetic images.

3. Reread "The Meal" (p. 515) and the discussion that accompanies it. Then analyze the role of imagery in the depiction of the parent/child relationships in "Daddy" (p. 532) and "My Papa's Waltz" (p. 622). How does each poem's imagery convey the nature of the relationship it describes?

4. Write an essay in which you discuss the color imagery in "Nothing Gold Can Stay" (p. 518) and "Spring and All" (p. 591). In what way does color reinforce the themes of these poems?

5. Sometimes imagery can be used to make a comment about the society in which a scene takes place. Choose two poems in which imagery functions in this way — "For the Union Dead" (p. 639) or "right on: white america" (p. 695), for example — and discuss how the images chosen reinforce the social comment each poem makes.

CHAPTER 19

FIGURES OF SPEECH

The metaphor is probably the most fertile power possessed by man.

—José Ortega y Gasset

WILLIAM SHAKESPEARE (1564–1616)

Shall I compare thee to a summer's day? (1609)

Shall I compare thee to a summer's day?
Thou art more lovely and more temperate.
Rough winds do shake the darling buds of May,
And summer's lease hath all too short a date.
Sometime too hot the eye of heaven shines,   5
And often is his gold complexion dimmed;
And every fair from fair sometimes declines,
By chance, or nature's changing course, untrimmed.
But thy eternal summer shall not fade,
Nor lose possession of that fair thou ow'st;°   10
Nor shall death brag thou wand'rest in his shade,
When in eternal lines to time thou grow'st.
  So long as men can breathe or eyes can see,
  So long lives this, and this gives life to thee.

Although writers experiment with language in all kinds of literary works, poets in particular recognize the power of a figure of speech to take readers beyond the literal meaning of a word. For this reason, **figures of speech**—expressions that use words to achieve effects beyond the power of ordinary language—are more prominent in poetry than in other kinds of writing. For example, the sonnet above compares a loved one to a summer's day in order to make the point that, unlike the fleeting summer, the loved one will—within the poem—remain

---

° *that fair thou ow'st:* That beauty you possess.

521

forever young. But this sonnet goes beyond the obvious equation (loved one = summer's day): the speaker's assertion that his loved one will live forever in his poem actually says more about his confidence in his own talent and reputation (and about the power of language) than about the loved one's beauty.

Simile, Metaphor, and Personification

When William Wordsworth opens a poem with "I wandered lonely as a cloud" (p. 628), he conveys a good deal more than he would if he simply began, "I wandered, lonely." By comparing himself in his loneliness to a cloud, the speaker suggests that like the cloud he is a part of nature and that he too is drifting, passive, blown by winds, and lacking will or substance. Thus, by using a figure of speech, the poet can suggest a wide variety of feelings and associations in very few words. (The phrase "I wandered lonely as a cloud" is a **simile,** a comparison between two unlike items that uses *like* or *as*. When an imaginative comparison between two unlike items does not use *like* or *as* — that is, when it says "a *is* b" rather than "a is *like* b" — it is a **metaphor.**)

Accordingly, when the speaker in Adrienne Rich's "Living in Sin" (p. 494) speaks of "daylight coming / like a relentless milkman up the stairs," she is using a strikingly original simile to suggest that daylight brings not the conventional associations of promise and awakening but rather a stale, never-ending routine that is greeted without enthusiasm. This idea is consistent with the rest of the poem, an account of an unfulfilling relationship. However, when the speaker in the Audre Lorde poem on page 524 says, "Rooming houses are old women," she uses a metaphor, equating two elements to stress their common associations with emptiness, transience, and hopelessness. At the same time, by identifying rooming houses as old women, Lorde is using **personification,** a special kind of comparison, closely related to metaphor, that gives life or human characteristics to inanimate objects or abstract ideas.

Sometimes, as in Wordsworth's "I wandered lonely as a cloud," a single brief simile or metaphor can be appreciated for what it communicates on its own. At other times, however, a simile or metaphor may be one of several related figures of speech that work together to convey a poem's meaning. The following poem, for example, presents a series of related similes. Together, they suggest the depth of the problem the poem explores in a manner that each individual simile could not do on its own.

LANGSTON HUGHES (1902–1967)

Harlem (1951)

What happens to a dream deferred?

Does it dry up
like a raisin in the sun?
Or fester like a sore —

And then run?   5
Does it stink like rotten meat?
Or crust and sugar over —
like a syrupy sweet?

Maybe it just sags
like a heavy load.   10

Or does it explode?

The dream to which Hughes alludes in this poem is the dream of racial equality. It is also the American Dream — or, by extension, any important unrealized dream. His speaker offers six tentative answers to the question asked in the poem's first line, and five of the six are presented as similes. As the poem unfolds, the speaker considers different alternatives: the dream can shrivel up and die, fester, decay, crust over — or sag under the weight of the burden those who hold the dream must carry. In each case, the speaker transforms an abstract entity — a dream — into a concrete item — a raisin in the sun, a sore, rotten meat, syrupy candy, a heavy load. The final line, italicized for emphasis, gains power less from what it says than from what it leaves unsaid. Unlike the other alternatives explored in the poem, *"Or does it explode?"* is not presented as a simile. Nevertheless, because of the pattern of figurative language the poem has established, readers can supply the other, unspoken half of the comparison: ". . . like a bomb."

Sometimes a single extended simile or extended metaphor is developed throughout a poem. The following poem develops an **extended simile**, comparing a poet to an acrobat.

LAWRENCE FERLINGHETTI (1919–)

Constantly Risking Absurdity (1958)

Constantly risking absurdity
                    and death
        whenever he performs
                    above the heads
                            of his audience   5
the poet like an acrobat
                    climbs on rime
                    to a high wire of his own making
and balancing on eyebeams
                    above a sea of faces   10
        paces his way
                    to the other side of day
        performing entrechats
                    and sleight-of-foot tricks
and other high theatrics   15
                    and all without mistaking

                   any thing
                        for what it may not be

             For he's the super realist
                             who must perforce perceive   20
                    taut truth
                         before the taking of each stance or step
          in his supposed advance
                         toward that still higher perch
          where Beauty stands and waits   25
                         with gravity
                             to start her death-defying leap

          And he
                    a little charleychaplin man
                         who may or may not catch   30
          her fair eternal form
                         spreadeagled in the empty air
             of existence

In his extended comparison of a poet and an acrobat, Ferlinghetti characterizes
the poet as a circus performer, at once swinging recklessly on a trapeze and balancing carefully on a tightrope.

   What the poem suggests is that the poet, like an acrobat, works hard at his
craft but manages to make it all look easy. Something of an exhibitionist, the poet
is innovative and creative, taking impossible chances yet also building on traditional skills in his quest for truth and beauty. Moreover, like an acrobat, the poet
is balanced "on eyebeams / above a sea of faces," for he too depends on audience
reaction to help him keep his performance focused. The poet may be "the super
realist," but he also has plenty of playful tricks up his sleeve: "entrechats / and
sleight-of-foot tricks / and other high theatrics," including puns ("above the heads
/ of his audience"), unexpected rhyme ("climbs on rime"), alliteration ("taut
truth"), coinages ("a little charleychaplin man"), and all the other linguistic acrobatics available to poets. (Even the arrangement of the poem's lines on the page
suggests the acrobatics it describes.) Like these tricks, the poem's central simile is
a whimsical one, perhaps suggesting that Ferlinghetti is poking fun at poets who
take their craft too seriously. In any case, the simile helps him to illustrate the ac-
robatic possibilities of language in a fresh and original manner.

   The following poem develops an **extended metaphor,** personifying rooming
houses as old women.

AUDRE LORDE   (1934–1992)

Rooming houses are old women   (1968)

Rooming houses are old women
rocking dark windows into their whens

waiting incomplete circles
rocking
rent office to stoop to   5
community bathrooms to gas rings and
under-bed boxes of once useful garbage
city issued with a twice monthly check
and the young men next door
with their loud midnight parties   10
and fishy rings left in the bathtub
no longer arouse them
from midnight to mealtime no stops inbetween
light breaking to pass through jumbled up windows
and who was it who married the widow that Buzzie's   15
son messed with?

To Welfare and insult form the slow shuffle
from dayswork to shopping bags
heavy with leftovers
Rooming houses
are old women waiting   20
searching
through darkening windows
the end or beginning of agony
old women seen through half-ajar doors
hoping   25
they are not waiting
but being
the entrance to somewhere
unknown and desired
but not new.   30

So closely does Lorde equate rooming houses and women in this poem that at times it is difficult to tell which of the two is actually the poem's subject. Despite the poem's assertion, rooming houses are *not* old women; however, they are *comparable to* the old women who live there because their walls enclose a lifetime of disappointments as well as the physical detritus of life. Like the old women, rooming houses are in decline, rocking away their remaining years. And, like the houses they inhabit, these women's boundaries are fixed — "rent office to stoop to / community bathrooms to gas rings" — and their hopes and expectations are few. They are surrounded by other people's loud parties, but their own lives have been reduced to a "slow shuffle" to nowhere, a hopeless, frightened — and perhaps pointless — "waiting / searching." Over time, the women and the places in which they live have become one. By using an unexpected comparison between two seemingly unrelated entities, the poem illuminates both the essence of the rooming houses and the essence of their elderly occupants.

FURTHER READING: Simile, Metaphor, and Personification

ROBERT BURNS   (1759–1796)

Oh, my love is like a red, red rose   (1796)

Oh, my love is like a red, red rose
   That's newly sprung in June;
My love is like the melody
   That's sweetly played in tune.

So fair art thou, my bonny lass,   5
   So deep in love am I;
And I will love thee still, my dear,
   Till a' the seas gang° dry.

Till a' the seas gang dry, my dear,
   And the rocks melt wi' the sun;   10
And I will love thee still, my dear,
   While the sands o' life shall run.

And fare thee weel, my only love!
   And fare thee weel awhile!
And I will come again, my love   15
   Though it were ten thousand mile.

Reading and Reacting

1. Why does the speaker compare his love to a rose? What other simile is used in the poem? For what purpose is it used?

2. Why do you suppose Burns begins his poem with similes? Would moving them to the end change the poem's impact?

3. Where does the speaker seem to exaggerate the extent of his love? Why does he exaggerate? Do you think this exaggeration weakens the poem? Explain.

Related Works: "Araby" (p. 232), "My mistress' eyes are nothing like the sun" (p. 519), "How Do I Love Thee?" (p. 635), "Baca Grande" (p. 500), "To His Coy Mistress" (p. 537), *The Brute* (p. 723)

N. SCOTT MOMADAY   (1934–   )

Simile   (1974)

What did we say to each other
that now we are as the deer
who walk in single file

° *gang:* Go.

with heads high
with ears forward
with eyes watchful
with hooves always placed on firm ground
in whose limbs there is latent flight

Reading and Reacting

1. In what sense are the speaker and the person he is speaking to like the deer he describes in this extended simile? In what sense are their limbs in "latent flight" (line 8)?

2. Without using similes or metaphors, paraphrase this poem.

3. This entire poem consists of a single sentence, but it has no punctuation. Do you see this as a problem? What punctuation marks, if any, would you add? Why?

4. JOURNAL ENTRY What do you suppose the speaker and the person he addresses might have said to each other to inspire the feelings described in this poem?

Related Work: "Let me not to the marriage of true minds" (p. 696)

SYLVIA PLATH (1932–1963)

Metaphors (1960)

I'm a riddle in nine syllables,
An elephant, a ponderous house,
A melon strolling on two tendrils.
O red fruit, ivory, fine timbers!
This loaf's big with its yeasty rising.   5
Money's new-minted in this fat purse.
I'm a means, a stage, a cow in calf.
I've eaten a bag of green apples,
Boarded the train there's no getting off.

Reading and Reacting

1. The speaker in this poem is a pregnant woman. Do all the metaphors seem appropriate? For instance, in what sense is the speaker "a means, a stage" (line 7)?

2. If you were going to expand this poem, what other metaphors (or similes) would you add?

3. What are the "nine syllables" to which the speaker refers in the poem's first line? What significance does the number *nine* have in terms of the poem's subject? In terms of its form?

4. JOURNAL ENTRY Would you say the speaker has a positive, negative, or neutral attitude toward her pregnancy? Which metaphors give you this impression?

Related Work: "I Stand Here Ironing" (p. 174)

RANDALL JARRELL (1914–1965)

The Death of the Ball Turret Gunner° (1945)

From my mother's sleep I fell into the State
And I hunched in its belly till my wet fur froze.
Six miles from earth, loosed from its dream of life,
I woke to black flak and the nightmare fighters.
When I died they washed me out of the turret with a hose.   5

Reading and Reacting

1. Who is the speaker? To what does he compare himself in the poem's first two lines? What words establish this comparison?

2. Contrast the speaker's actual identity with the one he creates for himself in lines 1–2. What elements of his actual situation do you think lead him to characterize himself as he does in these lines?

3. JOURNAL ENTRY Both this poem and "Dulce et Decorum Est" (p. 638) use figures of speech to describe the horrors of war. Which poem has a greater impact on you? How does the poem's figurative language contribute to this impact?

4. CRITICAL PERSPECTIVE In a 1974 article, Frances Ferguson criticizes "The Death of the Ball Turret Gunner," arguing that the poem "thoroughly manifests the lack of a middle between the gunner's birth and his death. . . . Because the poem presents a man who seems to have lived in order to die, we forget the fiction that he must have lived." However, in a 1978 explication, Patrick J. Horner writes that the "manipulation of time reveals the stunning brevity of the gunner's waking life and the State's total disregard for that phenomenon. . . . Because of the telescoping of time, [the poem] resonates with powerful feeling."

With which critic do you agree? Do you see the "lack of a middle" as a positive or negative quality of this poem?

Related Work: "The Things They Carried" (p. 251)

°*Ball turret gunner:* World War II machine gunner positioned upside-down in a plexiglass sphere in the belly of a fighter plane.

MARGE PIERCY (1936–)

The Secretary Chant (1973)

My hips are a desk.
From my ears hang
chains of paper clips.
Rubber bands form my hair.
My breasts are wells of mimeograph ink.   5
My feet bear casters.
Buzz. Click.
My head is a badly organized file.
My head is a switchboard
where crossed lines crackle.   10
Press my fingers
and in my eyes appear
credit and debit.
Zing. Tinkle.
My navel is a reject button.   15
From my mouth issue canceled reams.
Swollen, heavy, rectangular
I am about to be delivered
of a baby
Xerox machine.   20
File me under W
because I wonce
was
a woman.

Reading and Reacting

1. Examine each of the poem's figures of speech. Do they all make reasonable comparisons, or are some far-fetched or hard to visualize? Explain the relationship between the secretary and each item with which she is compared.

2. JOURNAL ENTRY Using as many metaphors and similes as you can, write a "chant" about a job you have held.

3. CRITICAL PERSPECTIVE In a review of a recent collection of Piercy's poetry, critic Sandra Gilbert notes instances of "a kind of bombast" (pompous language) and remarks, "As most poets realize, political verse is almost the hardest kind to write."

In what sense can "The Secretary Chant" be seen as "political verse"? Do you think Piercy successfully achieves her political purpose, or does she undercut it with "bombast"?

Related Works: "Girl" (p. 96), "Women" (p. 455), *I Dream Before I Take the Stand* (p. 745)

JOHN DONNE   (1572–1631)

A Valediction: Forbidding Mourning   (1611)

As virtuous men pass mildly away,
  And whisper to their souls to go,
Whilst some of their sad friends do say
  The breath goes now, and some say no:

So let us melt, and make no noise,   5
  No tear-floods, nor sigh-tempests move;
'Twere profanation of our joys
  To tell the laity° our love.

Moving of th' earth brings harms and fears;
  Men reckon what it did and meant;   10
But trepidation of the spheres,
  Though greater far, is innocent.

Dull sublunary lovers' love
  (Whose soul is sense) cannot admit
Absence, because it doth remove   15
  Those things which elemented it.

But we, by a love so much refined
  That ourselves know not what it is,
Inter-assurèd of the mind,
  Care less, eyes, lips, and hands to miss.   20

Our two souls, therefore, which are one,
  Though I must go, endure not yet
A breach, but an expansion,
  Like gold to airy thinness beat.

If they be two, they are two so   25
  As stiff twin compasses° are two:
Thy soul, the fixed foot, makes no show
  To move, but doth, if th' other do.

° *laity:* Here, "common people."   ° *compasses:* V-shaped instruments used for drawing circles.

And though it in the center sit,
    Yet when the other far doth roam,   30
It leans and harkens after it,
    And grows erect as that comes home.

Such wilt thou be to me, who must,
    Like th' other foot, obliquely run;
Thy firmness makes my circle just,°   35
    And makes me end where I begun.

Reading and Reacting

1. Beginning with line 25, the poem develops an extended metaphor that compares the speaker and his loved one to "twin compasses" (line 26), attached yet separate. Why is the compass an especially apt metaphor? What physical characteristics of the compass does the poet emphasize?

2. The poem uses other figures of speech to characterize both the lovers' union and their separation. To what other events does the speaker compare his separation from his loved one? To what other elements does he compare their attachment? Do you think these comparisons make sense?

3. JOURNAL ENTRY To what other object could Donne have compared his loved one and himself? Explain the logic of the extended metaphor you suggest.

4. CRITICAL PERSPECTIVE In *John Donne and the Metaphysical Poets* (1970), Judah Stampfer writes of this poem's "thin, dry texture, its stanzas of pinched music," noting that its form "has too clipped a brevity to qualify as a song" and that its "music wobbles on a dry, measured beat." Yet, he argues, "the poem comes choked with emotional power" because "the speaker reads as a naturally reticent man, leaving his beloved in uncertainty and deep trouble." Stampfer concludes, "Easy self-expression here would be self-indulgent, if not reprehensible. . . . For all his careful dignity, we feel a heart is breaking here."

Do you find such emotional power in this highly intellectual poem?

Related Works: "How Do I Love Thee?" (p. 635), "To My Dear and Loving Husband" (p. 536), *A Doll House* (p. 784)

Hyperbole and Understatement

Two additional kinds of figurative language, *hyperbole* and *understatement*, also give poets opportunities to suggest meaning beyond the literal level of language.

°*just:* Perfect.

Hyperbole is intentional exaggeration — saying more than is actually meant. In the poem "Oh, My Love Is like a Red, Red Rose" (p. 526), when the speaker says that he will love his lady until all the seas go dry, he is using hyperbole. **Understatement** is the opposite — saying less than is meant. When the speaker in the poem "Fire and Ice" (p. 471), weighing two equally grim alternatives for the end of the world, says that "for destruction ice / Is also great / And would suffice," he is using understatement. In both cases, poets expect their readers to understand that their words are not to be taken literally.

By using hyperbole and understatement, poets enhance the impact of their poems. For example, poets can use hyperbole to convey exaggerated anger or graphic images of horror — and to ridicule and satirize as well as to inflame and shock. With understatement, poets can convey the same kind of powerful emotions subtly, without artifice or embellishment, thereby leading readers to read more closely than they would otherwise do.

The emotionally charged poem that follows uses hyperbole to convey anger and bitterness that seem almost beyond the power of words.

SYLVIA PLATH (1932–1963)

Daddy (1965)

You do not do, you do not do
Any more, black shoe
In which I have lived like a foot
For thirty years, poor and white,
Barely daring to breathe or Achoo.   5

Daddy, I have had to kill you.
You died before I had time —
Marble-heavy, a bag full of God,
Ghastly statue with one grey toe
Big as a Frisco seal   10

And a head in the freakish Atlantic
Where it pours bean green over blue
In the waters off beautiful Nauset.
I used to pray to recover you.
Ach, du.°   15

In the German tongue, in the Polish town°
Scraped flat by the roller

°*Ach, du:* Ah, you (German).   °*Polish town:* Grabôw, where Plath's father was born.

Of wars, wars, wars.
But the name of the town is common.
My Polack friend   20

Says there are a dozen or two.
So I never could tell where you
Put your foot, your root,
I never could talk to you.
The tongue stuck in my jaw.   25

It stuck in a barb wire snare.
Ich, ich, ich, ich,°
I could hardly speak.
I thought every German was you.
And the language obscene   30

An engine, an engine
Chuffing me off like a Jew.
A Jew to Dachau, Auschwitz, Belsen.°
I began to talk like a Jew.
I think I may well be a Jew.   35

The snows of the Tyrol, the clear beer of Vienna
Are not very pure or true.
With my gypsy ancestress and my weird luck
And my Taroc pack and my Taroc pack
I may be a bit of a Jew.   40

I have always been scared of *you*,
With your Luftwaffe,° your gobbledygoo.
And your neat moustache
And your Aryan eye, bright blue.
Panzer°-man, panzer-man, O You—   45

Not God but a swastika
So black no sky could squeak through.
Every woman adores a Fascist,
The boot in the face, the brute
Brute heart of a brute like you.   50

You stand at the blackboard, daddy,
In the picture I have of you,
A cleft in your chin instead of your foot

° *ich:* "I" (German).   ° *Dachau, Auschwitz, Belsen:* Nazi concentration camps.   ° *Luftwaffe:* The German air
force.   ° *Panzer:* Protected by armor. The Panzer division was the German armored division.

But no less a devil for that, no not
Any less the black man who   55

Bit my pretty red heart in two.
I was ten when they buried you.
At twenty I tried to die
And get back, back, back to you.
I thought even the bones would do.   60

But they pulled me out of the sack,
And they stuck me together with glue.
And then I knew what to do.
I made a model of you,
A man in black with a Meinkampf° look   65

And a love of the rack and the screw.
And I said I do, I do.
So daddy, I'm finally through.
The black telephone's off at the root,
The voices just can't worm through.   70

If I've killed one man, I've killed two —
The vampire who said he was you
And drank my blood for a year,
Seven years, if you want to know.
Daddy, you can lie back now.   75

There's a stake in your fat black heart
And the villagers never liked you.
They are dancing and stamping on you.
They always *knew* it was you.
Daddy, daddy, you bastard, I'm through.   80

In her anger and frustration, the speaker sees herself as a helpless victim — a foot entrapped in a shoe, a Jew in a concentration camp — of her father's (and, later, her husband's) absolute tyranny. Thus, her hated father is characterized as a "black shoe," "a bag full of God," a "Ghastly statue," and, eventually, a Nazi, a torturer, the devil, a vampire. The poem "Daddy" is widely accepted by scholars as autobiographical, and the fact that Plath's own father was actually neither a Nazi nor a sadist (nor, obviously, the devil or a vampire) makes it clear that the figures of speech in the poem are wildly exaggerated. Even so, they may convey the poet's true feelings toward her father — and, perhaps, toward the patriarchal society in which she lived.

° *Meinkampf: Mein Kampf* (My Struggle) is Adolf Hitler's autobiography.

Plath uses hyperbole to communicate these emotions to readers who she knows cannot possibly feel the way she does. Her purpose, therefore, is not only to shock but also to enlighten, to persuade, and perhaps even to empower her readers. Throughout the poem, the inflammatory language is set in ironic opposition to the childish, affectionate term "Daddy"—most strikingly in the last line's choked out "Daddy, daddy, you bastard, I'm through." The result of the exaggerated rhetoric is a poem that is vivid and shocking. And, although some might believe that Plath's almost wild exaggeration undermines the poem's impact, others would argue that the powerful language is necessary to convey the extent of the speaker's rage.

Like "Daddy," the following poem presents a situation whose emotional impact is devastating. In this case, however, the poet does not use highly charged language; instead, he uses understatement, presenting events without embellishment.

DAVID HUDDLE (1942–)

Holes Commence Falling (1979)

The lead & zinc company
owned the mineral rights
to the whole town anyway,
and after drilling holes
for 3 or 4 years,   5
they finally found the right
place and sunk a mine shaft.
We were proud
of all that digging,
even though nobody from   10
town got hired. They
were going to dig right
under New River and hook up
with the mine at Austinville.
Then people's wells   15
started drying up just like
somebody'd shut off a faucet,
and holes commenced falling,
big chunks of people's yards
would drop 5 or 6 feet,   20
houses would shift and crack.
Now and then the company'd
pay out a little money
in damages; they got a truck
to haul water and sell it   25

to the people whose wells
had dried up, but most
everybody agreed the
situation wasn't
serious.   30

Although "Holes Commence Falling" relates a tragic sequence of events, the tone
of the poem is matter-of-fact, and the language is understated. The speaker could
have overdramatized the events, using inflated rhetoric to denounce big business
and to predict disastrous events for the future. At the very least, he could have
colored the facts with realistic emotions, assigning blame to the lead and zinc
company with justifiable anger. Instead, the speaker is so restrained, so noncha-
lant, so passive that readers must supply the missing emotions themselves —
realizing, for example, that when the speaker concludes "everybody agreed the /
situation wasn't / serious," he means exactly the opposite.

   Throughout the poem, unpleasant information is presented without comment
or emotion. As it proceeds, the poem traces the high and low points in the town's
fortunes, but for every hope ("We were proud / of all that digging"), there is a disappointment ("even though nobody from / town got hired"). The lead and zinc
company offers some compensation for the damage it does, but it is never enough.
The present tense verb of the poem's title indicates that the problems the town
faces — wells drying up, yards dropping, houses shifting and cracking — are regular occurrences. Eventually, readers come to see that what is not expressed, what
lurks just below the surface — anger, powerlessness, resentment, hopelessness —
is the poem's real subject.

FURTHER READING: Hyperbole and Understatement

ANNE BRADSTREET   (1612–1672)

To My Dear and Loving Husband   (1678)

If ever two were one, then surely we.
If ever man were lov'd by wife, then thee;
If ever wife was happy in a man,
Compare with me ye women if you can.
I prize thy love more than whole Mines of gold,   5
Or all the riches that the East doth hold.
My love is such that Rivers cannot quench,
Nor ought but love from thee, give recompense.
Thy love is such I can no way repay,
The heavens reward thee manifold I pray.   10
Then while we live, in love let's so persever,
That when we live no more, we may live ever.

Reading and Reacting

1. Review the claims the poem's speaker makes about her love in lines 5–8. Are such exaggerated declarations of love necessary, or would the rest of the poem be sufficient to convey the extent of her devotion to her husband?

2. JOURNAL ENTRY Compare this poem's declarations of love to those of John Donne's speaker in "A Valediction: Forbidding Mourning" (p. 530). Which speaker do you find more convincing? Why?

Related Work: "A Rose for Emily" (p. 113)

ANDREW MARVELL   (1621–1678)

To His Coy Mistress   (1681)

Had we but world enough and time,
This coyness, lady, were no crime.
We would sit down and think which way
To walk, and pass our long love's day.
Thou by the Indian Ganges' side   5
Should'st rubies find; I by the tide
Of Humber° would complain. I would
Love you ten years before the Flood,
And you should, if you please, refuse
Till the conversion of the Jews.   10
My vegetable love should grow
Vaster than empires, and more slow.
An hundred years should go to praise
Thine eyes, and on thy forehead gaze,
Two hundred to adore each breast,   15
But thirty thousand to the rest.
An age at least to every part,
And the last age should show your heart.
For, lady, you deserve this state,
Nor would I love at lower rate.   20
    But at my back I always hear
Time's wingèd chariot hurrying near,
And yonder all before us lie

° *Humber:* An estuary on the east coast of England.

Deserts of vast eternity.
Thy beauty shall no more be found,   25
Nor in thy marble vault shall sound
My echoing song; then worms shall try
That long preserved virginity,
And your quaint honor turn to dust,
And into ashes all my lust.   30
The grave's a fine and private place,
But none, I think, do there embrace.
      Now therefore, while the youthful hue
Sits on thy skin like morning glew°
And while thy willing soul transpires   35
At every pore with instant fires,
Now let us sport us while we may;
And now, like amorous birds of prey,
Rather at once our time devour
Than languish in his slow-chapped° power.   40
Let us roll all our strength and all
Our sweetness up into one ball
And tear our pleasures with rough strife
Thorough the iron gates of life.
Thus, though we cannot make our sun   45
Stand still, yet we will make him run.

Reading and Reacting

1. In this poem, Marvell's speaker sets out to convince a reluctant woman to become his lover. In order to make his case more persuasive, he uses hyperbole, exaggerating time periods, sizes, spaces, and the possible fate of the woman if she refuses him. Identify as many examples of hyperbole as you can.

2. The tone of "To His Coy Mistress" is more whimsical than serious. Given this tone, what do you see as the purpose of Marvell's use of hyperbole?

3. JOURNAL ENTRY Using contemporary prose, paraphrase the first four lines of the poem. Then, beginning with the word *But*, compose a few new sentences of prose, continuing the argument Marvell's speaker makes.

4. CRITICAL PERSPECTIVE In her critical essay *Andrew Marvell's "To His Coy Mistress": A Feminist Reading*, critic Margaret Wald presents the following analysis of the poem:

> Andrew Marvell's speaker in "To His Coy Mistress" invokes Petrarchan convention, a poetic mode originating in the fourteenth century in which a male

---

°*glew:* Dew.   °*slow-chapped:* Slowly crushing.

lover uses exaggerated metaphors to appeal to his female beloved. Yet Marvell alludes to such excessive — and disempowering — pining only to defy this tradition of unrequited love. Instead of respectful adulation, he offers lustful invitation; rather than anticipating rejection, he assumes sexual dominion over the eponymous "mistress." The poem is as much a celebration of his rhetorical mastery as it is of his physical conquest.

In what sense is the speaker in this poem celebrating his beloved? In what sense is he celebrating himself? Is his portrayal of her entirely positive? Which elements, if any, are negative?

Related Works: "Where Are You Going, Where Have You Been?" (p. 384), "The Passionate Shepherd to His Love" (p. 685), "To the Virgins, to Make Much of Time" (p. 478), *The Brute* (p. 723)

ROBERT FROST (1874–1963)

"Out, Out —" (1916)

The buzz saw snarled and rattled in the yard
And made dust and dropped stove-length sticks of wood,
Sweet-scented stuff when the breeze drew across it.
And from there those that lifted eyes could count
Five mountain ranges one behind the other   5
Under the sunset far into Vermont.
And the saw snarled and rattled, snarled and rattled,
As it ran light, or had to bear a load.
And nothing happened: day was all but done.
Call it a day, I wish they might have said   10
To please the boy by giving him the half hour
That a boy counts so much when saved from work.
His sister stood beside them in her apron
To tell them "Supper." At the word, the saw,
As if to prove saws knew what supper meant,   15
Leaped out at the boy's hand, or seemed to leap —
He must have given the hand. However it was,
Neither refused the meeting. But the hand!
The boy's first outcry was a rueful laugh,
As he swung toward them holding up the hand   20
Half in appeal, but half as if to keep
The life from spilling. Then the boy saw all —
Since he was old enough to know, big boy
Doing a man's work, though a child at heart —
He saw all spoiled. "Don't let him cut my hand off—   25

The doctor, when he comes. Don't let him, sister!"
So. But the hand was gone already.
The doctor put him in the dark of ether.
He lay and puffed his lips out with his breath.
And then — the watcher at his pulse took fright.   30
No one believed. They listened at his heart.
Little — less — nothing! — and that ended it.
No more to build on there. And they, since they
Were not the one dead, turned to their affairs.

Reading and Reacting

1. The poem's title is an **allusion** to a passage in Shakespeare's *Macbeth* (5.5.23–28) that attacks the brevity and meaninglessness of life in very emotional terms:

> Out, out brief candle!
> Life's but a walking shadow, a poor player,
> That struts and frets his hour upon the stage
> And then is heard no more. It is a tale
> Told by an idiot, full of sound and fury,
> Signifying nothing.

What idea do you think Frost wants to convey through the title "Out, Out —"?

2. Explain why each of the following qualifies as understatement:

- "Neither refused the meeting." (line 18)
- "He saw all spoiled." (line 25)
- "— and that ended it." (line 32)
- "No more to build on there." (line 33)

Can you identify any other examples of understatement in the poem?

3. JOURNAL ENTRY Do you think the poem's impact is strengthened or weakened by its understated tone?

4. CRITICAL PERSPECTIVE In an essay on Frost in his book *Affirming Limits*, Robert Pack focuses on the single word "So" in line 27 of "Out, Out —":

> For a moment, his narration is reduced to the impotent word "So," and in that minimal word all his restrained grief is held. . . . That "So" is the narrator's cry of bearing witness to a story that must be what it is in a scene he cannot enter. He cannot rescue or protect the boy. . . . In the poem's sense of human helplessness in an indifferent universe, we are all "watchers," and what we see is death without redemption, "signifying nothing." So. So? So! How shall we read that enigmatic word?

How do you read this "enigmatic word"? Why?

Related Works: "Happy Endings" (p. 94), "Kansas" (p. 107), "The Lottery" (p. 274), "What Were They Like?" (p. 641), "Hope" (p. 482), "The Death of the Ball Turret Gunner" (p. 528)

MARGARET ATWOOD (1939–)

you fit into me (1971)

you fit into me
like a hook into an eye

a fish hook
an open eye

Reading and Reacting

1. What positive connotations does Atwood expect readers to associate with the phrase "you fit into me"? What does the speaker seem at first to mean by "like a hook into an eye" in line 2?

2. The speaker's shift to the brutal suggestions of lines 3 and 4 is calculated to shock readers. Does the use of hyperbole here have another purpose in the context of the poem? Explain.

Related Works: "Daddy" (p. 532), *A Doll House* (p. 784)

Metonymy and Synecdoche

Metonymy and synecdoche are two related figures of speech. **Metonymy** is the substitution of the name of one thing for the name of another thing that most readers associate with the first—for example, using *hired gun* to mean "paid assassin" or *suits* to mean "business executives." A specific kind of metonymy, called **synecdoche,** is the substitution of a part for the whole (for example, using *bread*—as in "Give us this day our daily bread"—to mean "food") or the whole for a part (for example, saying "You can take the boy out of Brooklyn, but you can't take Brooklyn [meaning its distinctive traits] out of the boy"). With metonymy and synecdoche, instead of describing something by saying it is like something else (as in simile) or by equating it with something else (as in metaphor), writers can characterize an object or concept by using a term that evokes it. The following poem illustrates the use of synecdoche.

RICHARD LOVELACE (1618–1658)

To Lucasta Going to the Wars   (1649)

Tell me not, Sweet, I am unkind
    That from the nunnery
Of thy chaste breast and quiet mind,
    To war and arms I fly.

True, a new mistress now I chase,   5
    The first foe in the field;
And with a stronger faith embrace
    A sword, a horse, a shield.

Yet this inconstancy is such
    As you too shall adore;   10
I could not love thee, Dear, so much,
    Loved I not Honor more.

Here, Lovelace's use of synecdoche allows him to condense a number of complex ideas into a very few words. In line 3, when the speaker says that he is flying from his loved one's "chaste breast and quiet mind," he is using "breast" and "mind" to stand for all his loved one's physical and intellectual attributes. In line 8, when he says that he is embracing "A sword, a horse, a shield," he is using these three items to represent the trappings of war — and, thus, to represent war itself.

Apostrophe

With **apostrophe,** a poem's speaker addresses an absent person or thing — for example, a historical or literary figure or even an inanimate object or an abstract concept.

In the following poem, the speaker addresses Vincent Van Gogh.

SONIA SANCHEZ (1934–   )

On Passing thru Morgantown, Pa.   (1984)

i saw you
vincent van
gogh perched
on those pennsylvania
cornfields communing   5
amid secret black
bird societies. yes.
i'm sure that was
you exploding your

fantastic delirium   10
while in the
distance
red indian
hills beckoned.

Expecting her readers to be aware that Van Gogh is a nineteenth-century Dutch postimpressionist painter known for his mental instability as well as for his art, Sanchez is able to give added meaning to a phrase such as "fantastic delirium" as well as to the poem's visual images. Perhaps picturing his 1890 painting *Wheatfield with Crows*, the speaker sees Van Gogh perched like a black bird on a fence, and at the same time she also sees what he sees. Like Van Gogh, then, the speaker sees the Pennsylvania cornfields as both a natural landscape and an "exploding" work of art.

Wheatfield with Crows, 1890 (oil on canvas), Gogh, Vincent van (1853–90)/Rijksmuseum Vincent Van Gogh, Amsterdam, The Netherlands/ Bridgeman Art Library

FURTHER READING: Apostrophe

ALLEN GINSBERG   (1926–1997)

A Supermarket in California   (1956)

What thoughts I have of you tonight, Walt Whitman,° for I walked down the sidestreets under the trees with a headache self-conscious looking at the full moon.

° *Walt Whitman:* American poet (1819–1892) whose poems frequently praise the commonplace and often contain lengthy "enumerations."

In my hungry fatigue, and shopping for images, I went into
the neon fruit supermarket, dreaming of your enumerations!
What peaches and what penumbras! Whole families shopping at
night! Aisles full of husbands! Wives in the avocados, babies in the
tomatoes!— and you, Garcia Lorca,° what were you doing down
by the watermelons?

I saw you, Walt Whitman, childless, lonely old grubber, poking
among the meats in the refrigerator and eyeing the grocery boys.°
I heard you asking questions of each: Who killed the pork chops?   5
What price bananas? Are you my Angel?
I wandered in and out of the brilliant stacks of cans following you,
and followed in my imagination by the store detective.
We strode down the open corridors together in our solitary fancy
tasting artichokes, possessing every frozen delicacy, and never passing
the cashier.

Where are we going, Walt Whitman? The doors close in an hour.
Which way does your beard point tonight?
(I touch your book° and dream of our odyssey in the supermarket
and feel absurd.)
Will we walk all night through solitary streets? The trees add shade   10
to shade, lights out in the houses, we'll both be lonely.
Will we stroll dreaming of the lost America of love past blue
automobiles in driveways, home to our silent cottage?
Ah, dear father, graybeard, lonely old courage-teacher, what
America did you have when Charon° quit poling his ferry and you
got out on a smoking bank and stood watching the boat disappear on
the black waters of Lethe?°

Reading and Reacting

1. In this poem, Ginsberg's speaker wanders through the aisles of a supermarket, speaking to the nineteenth-century American poet Walt Whitman
and asking Whitman a series of questions. Why do you think the speaker
addresses Whitman? What kind of answers do you think he is looking for?

2. In paragraph 2, the speaker says he is "shopping for images." What does he
mean? Why does he look for these images in a supermarket? Does he find
them?

3. Is this poem about supermarkets? About Walt Whitman? About poetry?
About love? About America? What do you see as its primary theme? Why?

° *Federico García Lorca:* Spanish poet and dramatist (1899–1936).   ° *eyeing the grocery boys:* Whitman's sexual orientation is the subject of much debate. Ginsberg is suggesting here that Whitman was homosexual.
° *your book: Leaves of Grass.*   ° *Charon:* In Greek mythology, the ferryman who transported the dead over the
river Styx to Hades.   ° *Lethe:* In Greek mythology, the river of forgetfulness (one of five rivers in Hades).

4. JOURNAL ENTRY Does the incongruous image of the respected poet "poking /
among the meats" (line 4) in the supermarket strengthen the poem's impact,
or does it undercut any serious "message" the poem might have? Explain.

5. CRITICAL PERSPECTIVE The critic Leslie Fiedler discusses some of the ways
in which Ginsberg's style resembles that of Walt Whitman:

> Everything about Ginsberg is . . . blatantly Whitmanian: his meter is resolutely
> anti-iambic, his line groupings stubbornly anti-stanzaic, his diction aggressively
> colloquial and American, his voice public.

Can you identify ways in which the poem is "American" and "public"?

Related Works: "A&P" (p. 128), "Chicago" (p. 588), *from* "Out of the Cradle
Endlessly Rocking" (p. 590), "Defending Walt Whitman" (p. 645), *from* "Song of
Myself" (p. 703)

✔ **CHECKLIST** Writing about Figures of Speech

- Are any figures of speech present in the poem? Identify each example of simile,
metaphor, personification, hyperbole, understatement, metonymy, synecdoche,
and apostrophe.

- What two elements are being compared in each use of simile, metaphor, and
personification? Is the comparison logical? What characteristics are shared by
the two items being compared?

- Does the poet use hyperbole? Why? For example, is it used to move or to shock
readers, or is its use intended to produce a humorous or satirical effect? Would
more understated language be more effective?

- Does the poet use understatement? For what purpose? Would more emotionally
charged language be more effective?

- In metonymy and synecdoche, what item is being substituted for another? What
purpose does the substitution serve?

- If the poem includes apostrophe, whom or what does the speaker address?
What is accomplished through the use of apostrophe?

- How do figures of speech contribute to the impact of the poem as a whole?

WRITING SUGGESTIONS: Figures of Speech

1. Various figures of speech are often used to describe characters in literary
works. Choose two or three works that focus on a single character — for example, "A Rose for Emily" (p. 113), "Miss Brill" (p. 134), "Gryphon" (p. 139),
or "Richard Cory" (p. 695) explain how figures of speech are used to

characterize each work's central figure. If you like, you may write about works that focus on real (rather than fictional) people — for example, "Medgar Evers" (p. 655).

2. Write an essay in which you discuss the different ways poets use figures of speech to examine the nature of poetry itself. What kinds of figures of speech do poets use to describe their craft? (You might begin by reading the two poems about poetry that open Chapter 14.)

3. Write a letter replying to the speaker in the poem by Marvell, Bradstreet, Donne, or Burns that appears in this chapter. Use figures of speech to express the depth of your love and the extent of your devotion.

4. Choose three or four poems that have a common subject — for example, love or nature — and write an essay in which you draw some general conclusions about the relative effectiveness of the poems' use of figures of speech to examine that subject. (If you like, you may focus on the poems clustered under the heads "Poems about Parents," "Poems about Nature," "Poems about Love," and "Poems about War" in Chapter 23.)

5. Select a poem and a short story that deal with the same subject matter, and write an essay in which you compare their use of figures of speech.

CHAPTER 20

SOUND

> A primary pleasure in poetry is . . . the pleasure of saying something over for its own sweet sake and because it sounds just right.
>
> —Howard Nemerov, *"Poetry and Meaning"*

WALT WHITMAN (1819–1892)

Had I the Choice*

Had I the choice to tally greatest bards,
To limn° their portraits, stately, beautiful, and emulate at will,
Homer with all his wars and warriors — Hector, Achilles, Ajax,
Or Shakespeare's woe-entangled Hamlet, Lear, Othello — Tennyson's
    fair ladies,
Meter or wit the best, or choice conceit to wield in perfect rhyme,
delight of singers;
These, these, O sea, all these I'd gladly barter,
Would you the undulation of one wave, its trick to me transfer,
Or breathe one breath of yours upon my verse,
And leave its odor there.

Rhythm

Rhythm— the regular recurrence of sounds — is at the heart of all natural phenomena: the beating of a heart, the lapping of waves against the shore, the croaking of frogs on a summer's night, the whispering of wheat swaying in the wind. In fact, even mechanical phenomena, such as the movement of rush-hour traffic through a city's streets, have a kind of rhythm. Poetry, which explores these phenomena, often tries to reflect the same rhythms. Walt Whitman expresses this idea in "Had I the Choice" when he says that he would gladly trade the "perfect rhyme" of Shakespeare for the ability to reproduce "the undulation of one wave" in his verse.

---

*Publication date is not available.   °*limn:* To describe, depict.

547

Effective public speakers frequently repeat key words and phrases to create rhythm. In his speech "I Have a Dream," for example, Martin Luther King Jr. repeats the phrase "I have a dream" to create a cadence that ties the central section of the speech together:

> I say to you today, my friends, even though we face the difficulties of today and tomorrow, *I still have a dream*. It is a dream deeply rooted in the American dream. *I have a dream* that one day this nation will rise up and live out the true meaning of its creed: "We hold these truths to be self-evident, that all men are created equal." *I have a dream* that one day, on the red hills of Georgia, sons of former slaves and the sons of former slave owners will be able to sit down together at the table of brotherhood. *I have a dream* that one day even the state of Mississippi, a state sweltering with the heat of injustice, sweltering with the heat of oppression, will be transformed into an oasis of freedom and justice. *I have a dream* that my four little children will one day live in a nation where they will not be judged by the color of their skin, but by the content of their character.

Poets too create rhythm by using repeated words and phrases, as Gwendolyn Brooks does in the poem that follows.

GWENDOLYN BROOKS   (1917–2000)

Sadie and Maud   (1945)

Maud went to college.
Sadie stayed at home.
Sadie scraped life
With a fine-tooth comb.

She didn't leave a tangle in.   5
Her comb found every strand.
Sadie was one of the livingest chits
In all the land.

Sadie bore two babies
Under her maiden name.   10
Maud and Ma and Papa
Nearly died of shame.

When Sadie said her last so-long
Her girls struck out from home.
(Sadie had left as heritage   15
Her fine-tooth comb.)

Maud, who went to college,
Is a thin brown mouse.
She is living all alone
In this old house.   20

Much of the force of this poem comes from its balanced structure and regular rhyme and meter, underscored by the repeated words "Sadie" and "Maud," which shift the focus from one subject to the other and back again ("Maud went to college / Sadie stayed home"). The poem's singsong rhythm recalls the rhymes children recite when jumping rope. This evocation of carefree childhood is ironically contrasted with the adult realities that both Sadie and Maud face as they grow up: Sadie stays at home and has two children out of wedlock; Maud goes to college and ends up "a thin brown mouse." The speaker implies that the alternatives Sadie and Maud represent are both undesirable. Although Sadie "scraped life / with a fine-tooth comb," she dies young and leaves nothing to her girls but her desire to experience life. Maud, who graduated from college, shuts out life and cuts herself off from her roots.

Just as the repetition of words and phrases can create rhythm, so can the arrangement of words in a poem — and even the appearance of words on the printed page. How a poem looks is especially important in **open form poetry** (see p. 587), which dispenses with traditional patterns of versification. In the following excerpt from a poem by E. E. Cummings, for example, an unusual arrangement of words forces readers to slow down and then to speed up, creating a rhythm that emphasizes a key phrase —"The / lily":

> the moon is hiding
> in her hair.
> The
> lily
> of heaven
> full of all dreams,
> draws down.

Poetic rhythm— the repetition of stresses and pauses — is an essential element in poetry. Rhythm helps to establish a poem's mood, and, in combination with other poetic elements, it conveys the poet's emphasis and helps communicate the poem's meaning.

Meter

Although rhythm can be affected by the regular repetition of words and phrases or by the arrangement of words into lines, poetic rhythm is largely created by **meter,** the recurrence of regular units of stressed and unstressed syllables. A **stress** (or accent) occurs when one syllable is emphasized more than another, unstressed, syllable: *fór • ceps, bá • sic, il • lú • sion, ma • lár • i • a.* In a poem, even one-syllable words can be stressed to create a particular effect. For example, in Elizabeth Barrett Browning's line "How do I love thee? Let me count the ways," the metrical pattern that places stress on "love" creates one meaning; stressing "I" would create another.

Scansion is the analysis of patterns of stressed and unstressed syllables within a line. The most common method of poetic notation indicates stressed syllables with a ′ and unstressed syllables with a ˘. Although scanning lines gives readers the "beat" of the poem, scansion only approximates the sound of spoken language, which contains an infinite variety of stresses. By providing a graphic representation of the stressed and unstressed syllables of a poem, scansion aids understanding but is no substitute for reading the poem aloud and experimenting with various patterns of emphasis.

The basic unit of meter is a **foot**— a group of syllables with a fixed pattern of stressed and unstressed syllables. The chart below illustrates the most common types of metrical feet in English and American verse.

Foot	Stress Pattern	Example
Iamb	⏑/	They pace | in sleek | chi val | ric cer | tain ty (Adrienne Rich)
Trochee	/⏑	Thou, when | thou re | turn'st, wilt | tell me. (John Donne)
Anapest	⏑⏑/	With a hey, | and a ho, | and a hey | nonino (William Shakespeare)
Dactyl	/⏑⏑	Constantly | risking ab | surdity (Lawrence Ferlinghetti)

Iambic and *anapestic* meters are called **rising meters** because they progress from unstressed to stressed syllables. *Trochaic* and *dactylic* meters are called **falling meters** because they progress from stressed to unstressed syllables.

The following types of metrical feet, less common than those listed above, are used to add emphasis or to provide variety rather than to create the dominant meter of a poem.

Spondee	//	Pomp, pride | and circumstance of glorious war! (William Shakespeare)
Pyrrhic	⏑⏑	A horse! a horse! My king | dom for | a horse! (William Shakespeare)

A metric line of poetry is measured by the number of feet it contains.

Monometer	one foot	**Pentameter**	five feet
Dimeter	two feet	**Hexameter**	six feet
Trimeter	three feet	**Heptameter**	seven feet
Tetrameter	four feet	**Octameter**	eight feet

The name for a metrical pattern of a line of verse identifies the name of the foot used and the number of feet the line contains. For example, the most common foot in English poetry is the **iamb,** most often occurring in lines of three or five feet.

˘ ʹ | ˘ ʹ | ˘ ʹ
Eight hun | dred of | the brave   Iambic trimeter
(William Cowper)

˘ ʹ | ˘ ʹ | ˘ ˘
O, how | much more | doth   Iambic pentameter
ʹ ˘ ʹ ˘ ʹ
beau | ty beau | teous seem
(William Shakespeare)

Because **iambic pentameter** is so well suited to the rhythms of English speech, writers frequently use it in plays and poems. Shakespeare's plays, for example, are written in unrhymed lines of iambic pentameter called **blank verse** (see p. 572).

Many other metrical combinations are also possible; a few are illustrated here.

ʹ ˘ ʹ ˘ ʹ ˘
Like a | high-born | maiden   Trochaic trimeter
(Percy Bysshe Shelley)

˘ ˘ ʹ ˘ ˘ ʹ
The As sy | rian came down | Anapestic tetrameter
˘ ˘ ʹ ˘ ˘ ʹ
like the wolf | on the fold
(Lord Byron)

ʹ ˘ ˘ ʹ ˘ ˘
Maid en most | beau ti ful | Dactylic hexameter
ʹ ˘ ˘ ʹ ˘ ˘ ʹ
mother most | boun ti ful, | la
˘ ˘ ʹ
dy of | lands, (A. C. Swinburne)

˘ ʹ ˘ ʹ ˘ ʹ ˘
The yel | low fog | that rubs | its   Iambic heptameter
ʹ ˘ ʹ ˘ ʹ
back | upon | the win |
˘ ʹ
dow-panes (T. S. Eliot)

Scansion can be an extremely technical process, and when readers become bogged down with anapests and dactyls, they can easily forget that poetic scansion is not an end in itself. Meter should be appropriate for the ideas expressed by the poem, and it should help to create a suitable tone. A light, skipping rhythm, for example, would be inappropriate for an **elegy,** and a slow, heavy rhythm would surely be out of place in an **epigram** or a limerick. The following lines of a poem by Samuel Taylor Coleridge illustrate the uses of different types of metrical feet:

Trochee trips from long to short;

From long to long in solemn sort

Slow Spondee stalks; strong foot! yet ill able

Ever to come up with Dactyl trisyllable.

Iambics march from short to long —   5

With a leap and a bound the swift Anapests throng;

One syllable long, with one short at each side,

Amphibrachys hastes with a stately stride —

First and last being long, middle short, Amphimacer

Strikes his thundering hoofs like a proud high-bred Racer.   10

A poet may use one kind of meter — iambic meter, for example — through-out a poem, but may vary line length to relieve monotony or to accommodate the poem's meaning or emphasis. In the following poem, the poet uses iambic lines of different lengths.

EMILY DICKINSON (1830 – 1886)

I like to see it lap the Miles — (1891)

I like to see it lap the Miles —
And lick the Valleys up —
And stop to feed itself at Tanks —
And then — prodigious step

Around a Pile of Mountains —   5
And supercilious peer
In Shanties — by the sides of Roads —
And then a Quarry pare

To fit its Ribs
And crawl between   10
Complaining all the while
In horrid — hooting stanza —
Then chase itself down Hill —

And neigh like Boanerges° —
Then — punctual as a Star   15
Stop — docile and omnipotent
At its own stable door —

° *Boanerges:* A vociferous preacher and orator. Also, the name, meaning "son of thunder," Jesus gave to apostles John and James because of their fiery zeal.

This poem is a single sentence that, except for some pauses, stretches unbroken from beginning to end. Iambic lines of varying lengths actually suggest the movements of the train that the poet describes. Lines of iambic tetrameter, such as the first, give readers a sense of the train's steady, rhythmic movement across a flat landscape, and shorter lines ("To fit its Ribs / And crawl between") suggest the train's slowing motion. Beginning with two iambic dimeter lines and progressing to iambic trimeter lines, the third stanza increases in speed just like the train that is racing downhill "In horrid — hooting stanza —."

When a poet uses more than one type of metrical foot, any variation in a metrical pattern — the substitution of a trochee for an iamb, for instance — immediately calls attention to itself. Poets are aware of this fact and use it to their advantage. For example, in line 16 of "I like to see it lap the Miles," the poet departs from iambic meter by placing unexpected stress on the first word, *stop*. By emphasizing this word, the poet brings the flow of the poem to an abrupt halt, suggesting the jolt riders experience when a train comes to a stop. In the following segment from "The Rime of the Ancient Mariner," Samuel Taylor Coleridge also departs from his poem's dominant meter:

> The ship | was cheered, | the har | bor cleared,
> Merri | ly did | we drop
> Below | the kirk, | below | the hill,
> Below | the light | house top.

Although these lines are arranged in iambic tetrameter, the poet uses a trochee in the second line, breaking the meter in order to accommodate the natural pronunciation of "merrily" as well as to place stress on the word.

Another way of varying the meter of a poem is to introduce a pause known as a **caesura** — a Latin word meaning "a cutting" — within a line. When scanning a poem, you indicate a caesura with two parallel lines: ‖. Unless a line of poetry is extremely short, it probably will contain a caesura.

A caesura occurs after a punctuation mark or at a natural break in phrasing:

> How do I love thee? ‖ Let me count the ways.

Elizabeth Barrett Browning

> Two loves I have ‖ of comfort and despair.

William Shakespeare

> High on a throne of royal state, ‖ which far
> Outshone the wealth of Ormus ‖ and of Ind

John Milton

Sometimes more than one caesura occurs in a single line:

> 'Tis good. ‖ Go to the gate. ‖ Somebody knocks.

> **William Shakespeare**

Although the end of a line may mark the end of a metrical unit, it does not always coincide with the end of a sentence. Poets may choose to indicate a pause at this point, or they may continue without a break to the next line. Lines that have distinct pauses at the end — usually signaled by punctuation — are called **end-stopped lines.** Lines that do not end with strong pauses are called **run-on lines.** (Sometimes the term **enjambment** is used to describe run-on lines.) End-stopped lines can sometimes seem formal, or even forced, because their length is rigidly dictated by the poem's meter, rhythm, and rhyme scheme. In the following excerpt from John Keats's "La Belle Dame sans Merci" (p. 679), for example, rhythm, meter, and rhyme dictate the pauses that occur at the ends of the lines:

> O, what can ail thee, knight-at-arms,
>   Alone and palely loitering?
> The sedge has wither'd from the lake,
>   And no birds sing.

In contrast to end-stopped lines, run-on lines often seem more natural. Because their ending points are determined by the rhythms of speech and by the meaning and emphasis the poet wishes to convey rather than by meter and rhyme, run-on lines are suited to the open form of much modern poetry. In the following lines from the poem "We Have Come Home," by the poet Lenrie Peters, run-on lines give readers the sense of spoken language:

> We have come home
> From the bloodless war
> With sunken hearts
> Our boots full of pride—
> From the true massacre of the soul
> When we have asked
> "What does it cost
> To be loved and left alone?"

Rather than relying exclusively on end-stopped or run-on lines, poets often use a combination of the two to produce the effects they want. For example, the following lines from "Pot Roast," by Mark Strand juxtapose end-stopped and run-on lines:

> I gaze upon the roast,
> that is sliced and laid out
> on my plate
> and over it
> I spoon the juices
> of carrot and onion.
> And for once I do not regret
> the passage of time.

FURTHER READING: Rhythm and Meter

ADRIENNE RICH (1929–   )

Aunt Jennifer's Tigers (1951)

Aunt Jennifer's tigers prance across a screen,
Bright topaz denizens of a world of green.
They do not fear the men beneath the tree;
They pace in sleek chivalric certainty.

Aunt Jennifer's fingers fluttering through her wool   5
Find even the ivory needle hard to pull.
The massive weight of Uncle's wedding band
Sits heavily upon Aunt Jennifer's hand.

When Aunt is dead, her terrified hands will lie
Still ringed with ordeals she was mastered by.   10
The tigers in the panel that she made
Will go on prancing, proud and unafraid.

Reading and Reacting

1. What is the dominant metrical pattern of the poem? How does the meter enhance the contrast the poem develops?
2. The lines in the first stanza are end-stopped, and those in the second and third stanzas combine end-stopped and run-on lines. What does the poet achieve by varying the rhythm?
3. What ideas do the caesuras in the first and fourth lines of the last stanza emphasize?
4. **JOURNAL ENTRY** What is the speaker's opinion of Aunt Jennifer's marriage? Do you think she is commenting on this particular marriage or on marriage in general?
5. **CRITICAL PERSPECTIVE** In *The Aesthetics of Power*, Claire Keyes writes of this poem that although it is formally beautiful, almost perfect, its voice creates problems:

> [T]he tone seldom approaches intimacy, the speaker seeming fairly detached from the fate of Aunt Jennifer. . . . The dominant voice of the poem asserts the traditional theme that art outlives the person who produces it. . . . The speaker is almost callous in her disregard for Aunt's death. . . . Who cares that Aunt Jennifer dies? The speaker does not seem to; she gets caught up in those gorgeous tigers. . . . Here lies the dominant voice: Aunt is not compelling; her creation is.

Do you agree with Keyes's interpretation of the poem?

Related Works: "Miss Brill" (p. 134), "Everyday Use" (p. 282), "Seventeen Syllables" (p. 425), "Rooming houses are old women" (p. 524)

Alliteration and Assonance

Just as poetry depends on rhythm, it also depends on the sounds of individual words. An effect pleasing to the ear, such as "Did he who made the Lamb make thee?" from William Blake's "The Tyger" (p. 653), is called **euphony.** A jarring or discordant effect, such as "The vorpal blade went snicker-snack!" from Lewis Carroll's "Jabberwocky" (p. 566), is called **cacophony.**

One of the earliest, and perhaps the most primitive, methods of enhancing sound is **onomatopoeia,** which occurs when the sound of a word echoes its meaning, as it does in common words such as *bang, crash,* and *hiss.* Poets make broad application of this technique by using combinations of words that suggest a correspondence between sound and meaning, as Edgar Allan Poe does in these lines from his poem "The Bells":

> Yet the ear, it fully knows,
>   By the twanging
>   And the clanging,
>   How the danger ebbs and flows;
> Yet the ear distinctly tells,
>   In the jangling
>   And the wrangling
>   How the danger sinks and swells
> By the sinking or the swelling in the anger of the bells —
>   Of the bells,—
>   Of the bells, bells, bells, bells. . . .

Poe's primary objective in this poem is to re-create the sound of ringing bells. Although he succeeds, the poem (113 lines long in its entirety) is extremely tedious. A more subtle use of onomatopoetic words appears in the following passage from *An Essay on Criticism* by Alexander Pope:

> Soft is the strain when Zephyr gently blows,
> And the smooth stream in smoother numbers flows;
> But when the loud surges lash the sounding shore,
> The hoarse, rough verse should like the torrent roar:
> When Ajax strives some rock's vast weight to throw,
> The line too Labors, and the words move slow.

After earlier admonishing readers that sound must echo sense, Pope uses onomatopoetic words such as *lash* and *roar* to convey the fury of the sea, and he uses repeated consonants to echo the sounds these words suggest. Notice, for example, how the *s* and *m* sounds suggest the gently blowing Zephyr and the flowing of the smooth stream and how the series of *r* sounds echoes the torrent's roar.

Alliteration— the repetition of consonant sounds in consecutive or neighboring words, usually at the beginning of words — is another device used to enhance sound in a poem. Both Poe ("sinks and swells") and Pope ("smooth stream") make use of alliteration in the preceding excerpts, and so does Tennyson in the following poem.

ALFRED, LORD TENNYSON   (1809–1892)

The Eagle   (1851)

He clasps the crag with crooked hands;
Close to the sun in lonely lands,
Ringed with the azure world, he stands.

The wrinkled sea beneath him crawls:
He watches from his mountain walls,   5
And like a thunderbolt he falls.

Throughout the poem, *c*, *l*, and *w* sounds occur repeatedly. The poem is drawn together by the recurrence of these sounds and, as a result, it flows smoothly from beginning to end.

Sometimes assonance unifies an entire poem. In the following poem, assonance emphasizes the thematic connections among words and thus links the poem's ideas.

ROBERT HERRICK   (1591–1674)

Delight in Disorder   (1648)

A sweet disorder in the dress
Kindles in clothes a wantonness.
A lawn° about the shoulders thrown
Into a fine distractión;
An erring lace, which here and there   5
Enthralls the crimson stomacher;°
A cuff neglectful, and thereby
Ribbons to flow confusedly;
A winning wave, deserving note,
In the tempestuous petticoat;   10
A careless shoestring, in whose tie
I see a wild civility;
Do more bewitch me than when art
Is too precise in every part.

Repeated vowel sounds extend throughout this poem — for instance, "shoulders" and "thrown" in line 3; and "tie," "wild," and "precise" in lines 11, 12, and 14. Using alliteration as well as assonance, Herrick subtly links certain words — "tempestuous petticoat," for example. By connecting these words, he calls attention to the pattern of imagery that helps to convey the poem's theme.

° *lawn:* A shawl made of fine fabric.   ° *stomacher:* A heavily embroidered garment worn by females over the chest and stomach.

Rhyme

In addition to alliteration and assonance, poets create sound patterns with **rhyme**— the use of matching sounds in two or more words: "tight" and "might"; "born" and "horn"; "sleep" and "deep." For a rhyme to be **perfect,** final vowel and consonant sounds must be the same, as they are in each of the preceding examples. **Imperfect rhyme** (also called *near rhyme, slant rhyme, approximate rhyme,* or **consonance**) occurs when the final consonant sounds in two words are the same but vowel sounds are different — "learn" / "barn" or "pads" / "lids," for example. William Stafford uses imperfect rhyme in "Traveling through the Dark" (p. 632) when he rhymes "road" with "dead." Finally, **eye rhyme** occurs when two words look as if they should rhyme but do not — for example, "watch" and "catch."

Rhyme can also be classified according to the position of the rhyming syllables in a line of verse. The most common type of rhyme is **end rhyme,** which occurs at the end of a line:

> Tyger! Tyger! burning <u>bright</u>
> In the forests of the <u>night</u>
>
> **William Blake,** "The Tyger"

Internal rhyme occurs within a line:

> The Sun came up upon the left,
> Out of the <u>sea</u> came <u>he</u>!
> And he shone <u>bright</u> and on the <u>right</u>
> Went down into the sea.
>
> **Samuel Taylor Coleridge,** "The Rime of the Ancient Mariner"

Beginning rhyme occurs at the beginning of a line:

> Red river, red river,
> <u>Slow</u> flow heat is silence
> <u>No</u> will is still as a river
> **T. S. Eliot,** "Virginia"

Rhyme can also be classified according to the number of syllables that correspond. **Masculine rhyme** (also called **rising rhyme**) occurs when single syllables correspond ("can" / "ran"; "descend" / "contend"). **Feminine rhyme** (also called **double rhyme** or **falling rhyme**) occurs when two syllables, a stressed one followed by an unstressed one, correspond ("ocean" / "motion"; "leaping" / "sleeping"). **Triple rhyme** occurs when three syllables correspond. Less common than the other two, triple rhyme is often used for humorous or satiric purposes, as in the following lines from the long poem *Don Juan* by Lord Byron:

> Sagest of women, even of widows, she
>   Resolved that Juan should be quite a <u>paragon</u>,
> And worthy of the noblest pedigree:
>   (His sire of Castile, his dam from <u>Aragon</u>).

In some cases — for example, when it is overused or used in unexpected places — rhyme can create unusual and even comic effects. In the following poem, humor is created by the incongruous connections established by rhymes such as "priest" / "beast" and "pajama" / "lllama."

OGDEN NASH (1902–1971)

The Lama (1931)

The one-l lama
He's a priest.
The two-l llama,
He's a beast.
And I will bet   5
A silk pajama
There isn't any
Three-l lllama.

     The conventional way to describe a poem's rhyme scheme is to chart rhyming sounds that appear at the ends of lines. The sound that ends the first line is designated *a*, and all subsequent lines that end in that sound are also labeled *a*. The next sound to appear at the end of a line is designated *b*, and all other lines whose last sounds rhyme with it are also designated *b*— and so on through the alphabet. The lines of the poem that follows are labeled in this manner.

RICHARD WILBUR (1921–   )

A Sketch (1975)

Into the lower right	*a*
Square of the window frame	*b*
There came	*b*
with scalloped flight	*a*
A goldfinch, lit upon	*c* 5
The dead branch of a pine,	*d*
Shining,	*d*
and then was gone,	*c*
Tossed in a double arc	*e*
Upward into the thatched	*f* 10
And cross-hatched	*f*
pine-needle dark.	*e*
Briefly, as fresh drafts stirred	*g*
The tree, he dulled and gleamed	*h*
And seemed	*h* 15
more coal than bird,	*g*
Then, dodging down, returned	*i*
In a new light, his perch	*j*

A birch —	*j*	
twig, where he burned	*i*	20
In the sun's broadside ray,	*k*	
Some seed pinched in his bill.	*l*	
Yet still	*l*	
he did not stay,	*k*	
But into a leaf-choken pane,	*m*	25
Changeful as even in heaven,	*n*	
Even	*n*	
in Saturn's reign,	*m*	
Tunneled away and hid.	*o*	
And then? But I cannot well	*p*	30
Tell	*p*	
you all that he did.	*o*	
It was like glancing at rough	*q*	
Sketches tacked on a wall,	*r*	
And all	*r*	35
so less than enough	*q*	
Of gold on beaten wing,	*s*	
I could not choose that one	*t*	
Be done	*t*	
as the finished thing.	*s*	40

Although the rhyme scheme of this poem (*abba, cddc*, and so on) is regular, it is hardly noticeable until it is charted. Despite its subtlety, however, the rhyme scheme is not unimportant. In fact, it reinforces the poem's meaning and binds lines into structural units, connecting the first and fourth as well as the second and third lines of each stanza. In stanza 1, "right" and "flight" draw lines 1 and 4 of the stanza together, bracketing "fame" and "came" in lines 2 and 3. The pattern begins again with the next stanza and continues through the rest of the poem. Like the elusive goldfinch the poet describes, the rhymes are difficult to follow with the eye. In this sense, the rhyme reflects the central theme of the poem: the difficulty of capturing in words a reality that, like the goldfinch, is forever shifting.

Of course, rhyme does not have to be subtle to enrich a poem. An obvious rhyme scheme can communicate meaning by connecting ideas that are not normally linked. Notice how Alexander Pope uses this technique in the following excerpt from *An Essay on Man*:

> Honour and shame from no condition rise;
> Act well your part, there all the honour lies.
> Fortune in men has some small diff'rence made,
> One flaunts in rags, one flutters in brocade;
> The cobbler aproned, and the parson gowned,
> The friar hooded, and the monarch crowned.

"What differ more (you cry) than crown and cowl?"
I'll tell you, friend; a wise man and a fool.

You'll find, if once the monarch acts the monk,
Or, cobbler-like, the parson will be drunk,
Worth makes the man, and want of it, the fellow;
The rest is all but leather or prunella.°
    Stuck o'er with titles and hung round with strings,
That thou mayest be by kings, or whores of kings.
Boast the pure blood of an illustrious race,
In quiet flow from Lucrece° to Lucrece;
But by your fathers' worth if yours you rate,
Count me those only who were good and great.

This poem is written in **heroic couplets,** paired iambic pentameter lines with a rhyme scheme of *aa, bb, cc, dd,* and so on. In a heroic couplet, greater stress falls on the second line, usually on the last word. Coming at the end of the line, this word receives double emphasis: it is strengthened both because of its position in the line and because it is rhymed with the last word of the couplet's first line. In this excerpt, rhyme sometimes joins opposing ideas, thereby reinforcing a theme that runs through the passage: the contrast between the high and the low, the virtuous and the immoral. For example, "gowned" and "crowned" in lines 5 and 6 convey the opposite conditions of the parson and the monarch and exemplify the idea expressed in lines 3 and 4 that fortune, not virtue, determines one's station.

FURTHER READING: Alliteration, Assonance, and Rhyme

GERARD MANLEY HOPKINS (1844–1889)

Pied Beauty (1918)

Glory be to God for dappled things —
    For skies of couple-color as a brinded° cow;
        For rose-moles all in stipple upon trout that swim;
Fresh-firecoal chestnut-falls; finches' wings;
    Landscape plotted and pieced — fold, fallow, and plow;   5
        And áll trádes, their gear and tackle and trim.°

All things counter, original, spare, strange;
    Whatever is fickle, freckled (who knows how?)
        With swift, slow; sweet, sour; adazzle, dim;
He fathers-forth whose beauty is past change: 10
        Praise him.

° *prunella:* Heavy cloth the color of prunes.   ° *Lucrece:* In Roman legend, Lucrece stabbed herself after being defiled by Sextus Tarquinius.   ° *brinded:* Brindled (streaked).   ° *trim:* Equipment.

Reading and Reacting

1. Identify examples of onomatopoeia, alliteration, assonance, imperfect rhyme, and perfect rhyme. Do you think all these techniques are essential to the poem? Are any of them annoying or distracting?

2. What is the central idea of this poem? How do the sounds of the poem help to communicate this idea?

3. Identify examples of masculine and feminine rhyme.

4. JOURNAL ENTRY Hopkins uses both pleasing and discordant sounds in his poem. Identify uses of euphony and cacophony, and explain how these techniques affect your reactions to the poem.

Related Works: "Cathedral" (p. 289), "Women" (p. 455), "Batter My Heart, Three-Personed God" (p. 662)

W. H. AUDEN   (1907–1973)

As I Walked Out One Evening   (1940)

As I walked out one evening,
 Walking down Bristol Street,
The crowds upon the pavement
 Were fields of harvest wheat.

And down by the brimming river   5
 I heard a lover sing
Under an arch of the railway:
 "Love has no ending.

"I'll love you, dear, I'll love you
 Till China and Africa meet,   10
And the river jumps over the mountain
 And the salmon sing in the street,

"I'll love you till the ocean
 Is folded and hung up to dry,
And the seven stars go squawking   15
 Like geese about the sky.

"The years shall run like rabbits,
 For in my arms I hold
The Flower of the Ages,
 And the first love of the world."   20

But all the clocks in the city
 Began to whirr and chime:
"O let not Time deceive you,
 You cannot conquer Time.

"In the burrows of the Nightmare   25
   Where Justice naked is,
Time watches from the shadow
   And coughs when you would kiss.

"In headaches and in worry
   Vaguely life leaks away,   30
And Time will have his fancy
   Tomorrow or today.

"Into many a green valley
   Drifts the appalling snow;
Time breaks the threaded dances   35
   And the diver's brilliant bow.

"O plunge your hands in water,
   Plunge them in up to the wrist;
Stare, stare in the basin
   And wonder what you've missed.   40

"The glacier knocks in the cupboard,
   The desert sighs in the bed,
And the crack in the teacup opens
   A lane to the land of the dead.

"Where the beggars raffle the banknotes   45
   And the Giant is enchanting to Jack,
And the Lily-white Boy is a Roarer,
   And Jill goes down on her back.

"O look, look in the mirror,
   O look in your distress;   50
Life remains a blessing
   Although you cannot bless.

"O stand, stand at the window
   As the tears scald and start;
You shall love your crooked neighbor   55
   With your crooked heart."

It was late, late in the evening,
   The lovers they were gone;
The clocks had ceased their chiming,
   And the deep river ran on.   60

Reading and Reacting

1. Does Auden use perfect rhyme at the end of the second line and the fourth line of each stanza? If not, why do you think he chooses not to?

2. Chart the poem's rhyme scheme. Does Auden use internal rhyme? Where does he use alliteration and assonance? In what other ways does he use sound?
3. Does Auden's use of sound reinforce the poem's content or undercut it? Explain.
4. **JOURNAL ENTRY** Could this poem be considered a love poem? How are its sentiments about love different from those conventionally expressed in poems about love?
5. **CRITICAL PERSPECTIVE** In a 1940 British review of Auden's work, T. C. Worlsey made the following comments about this poem:

> There is no technical reason why such a poem as [this] should not be popular; the metre and the rhythm are easy and helpful, and the symbols have reference to a world of experience common to every inhabitant of these islands. Here . . . the poet has gone as far as he can along the road to creating a popular poetry.

Does Auden's poem strike you as a model for "popular" poetry — that is, poetry for people who do not usually read poetry?

Related Works: "The Story of an Hour" (p. 104), "Araby" (p. 232), "The World Is Too Much with Us" (p. 477), "Oh, my love is like a red, red rose" (p. 526), "To His Coy Mistress" (p. 537), "Not marble, nor the gilded monuments" (p. 697)

GALWAY KINNELL (1927–   )

Blackberry Eating   (1980)

I love to go out in late September
among the fat, overripe, icy, black blackberries
to eat blackberries for breakfast,
the stalks very prickly, a penalty
they earn for knowing the black art   5
of blackberry-making; and as I stand among them
lifting the stalks to my mouth, the ripest berries
fall almost unbidden to my tongue,
as words sometimes do, certain peculiar words
like *strengths* or *squinched*,   10
many-lettered, one-syllabled lumps,
which I squeeze, squinch open, and splurge well
in the silent, startled, icy, black language
of blackberry-eating in late September.

Reading and Reacting

1. What sounds does Kinnell repeat in the poem? How do they help to create the poem's rhythm?
2. This poem consists entirely of run-on lines. Why do you think the poet uses this technique instead of end-stopped lines?

3. One part of the poem deals with blackberries, and the other part deals with the poet's love for words. What connection exists between these two subjects?

4. How do alliteration, assonance, and line length help Kinnell convey his ideas?

5. JOURNAL ENTRY What do you think this poem is really about?

6. CRITICAL PERSPECTIVE Critic Daniela Gioseffi had the following to say about Galway Kinnell:

> He has real things to say about an actual world of flesh and bone and excrement, full of nature's glories and horrors, always viewed from within the reality of our gutsy, animal being, our need to survive from the land and its vulnerable animal life, a world poignant with transient beauty and helpless mortality.

Do you think this poem reflects both nature's "glories" and its "horrors"? How does it comment on the transient beauty of nature and our own "helpless mortality"?

Related Works: "Seventeen Syllables" (p. 425), "Words, Words, Words" (p. 489), "Introduction to Poetry" (p. 658)

ROBERT FRANCIS (1901–1987)

Pitcher (1953)

His art is eccentricity, his aim
How not to hit the mark he seems to aim at,

His passion how to avoid the obvious,
His technique how to vary the avoidance.

The others throw to be comprehended. He   5
Throws to be a moment misunderstood.

Yet not too much. Not errant, arrant, wild,
But every seeming aberration willed.

Not to, yet still, still to communicate
Making the batter understand too late.   10

Reading and Reacting

1. Although this poem does not have a regular rhyme scheme, it still includes words that rhyme. Underline these rhyming words, and explain how they contribute to the poem's overall effect.

2. In addition to using rhyme, Francis also uses repetition. What words does he repeat? What ideas are emphasized with this repetition?

3. Where does Francis use alliteration and assonance? Do alliteration and assonance contribute something to the poem, or are they distractions? Explain.

4. **JOURNAL ENTRY** Do you think this poem is an accurate description of a pitcher? Could the poem also be describing something else? Explain.

5. **CRITICAL PERSPECTIVE** Poet and critic Donald Hall, in a review of Robert Francis's *Collected Poems*, makes the following comments on two of Francis's poems about baseball, one of which is "Pitcher":

> Francis is not one to care about baseball much. Baseball is a diamond to begin with, and on this diamond the young ballplayers perform their ritual shapes, as if conspiring to place a grid over the chaos of experience. And this is what, by his shapely resolutions, Francis does with his poems.

Do you agree with Hall that "Pitcher" is about more than a pitcher trying to strike a batter out? Could Francis have written the poem without caring about baseball?

Related Works: "The Rocking-Horse Winner" (p. 340), "Poetry" (p. 439), "Cloud Painter" (p. 511), "Constantly Risking Absurdity" (p. 523)

LEWIS CARROLL (1832–1898)

Jabberwocky (1871)

'Twas brillig, and the slithy toves
    Did gyre and gimble in the wabe:
All mimsy were the borogoves,
    And the mome raths outgrabe.

"Beware the Jabberwock, my son!   5
    The jaws that bite, the claws that catch!
Beware the Jubjub bird, and shun
    The frumious Bandersnatch!"

He took his vorpal sword in hand;
    Long time the manxome foe he sought —   10
So rested he by the Tumtum tree
    And stood awhile in thought.

And, as in uffish thought he stood,
    The Jabberwock, with eyes of flame,
Came whiffling through the tulgey wood,   15
    And burbled as it came!

One, two! One, two! And through and through
    The vorpal blade went snicker-snack!
He left it dead, and with its head
    He went galumphing back.   20

"And hast thou slain the Jabberwock?
    Come to my arms, my beamish boy!
O frabjous day! Callooh, Callay!"
    He chortled in his joy.

'Twas brillig, and the slithy toves   25
   Did gyre and gimble in the wabe:
All mimsy were the borogoves,
   And the mome raths outgrabe.

Reading and Reacting

1. Many words in this poem may be unfamiliar to you. Are they actual words? Use a dictionary to check before you dismiss any. Do some words seem to have meaning in the context of the poem regardless of whether they appear in the dictionary? Explain.

2. This poem contains many examples of onomatopoeia. What meanings do the sounds of these words suggest?

3. JOURNAL ENTRY Summarize the story the poem tells. In what sense is this poem a story of a young man's initiation into adulthood?

4. CRITICAL PERSPECTIVE According to Humpty Dumpty in Carroll's *Alice in Wonderland*, the nonsense words in the poem are **portmanteau words** (that is, words whose form and meaning are derived from two other distinct words — as *smog* is a portmanteau of *smoke* and *fog*). Critic Elizabeth Sewell, however, rejects this explanation: "[F]*rumious*, for instance, is not a word, and does not have two meanings packed up in it; it is a group of letters without any meaning at all. . . . [I]t looks like other words, and almost certainly more than two."

Which nonsense words in the poem seem to you to be portmanteau words, and which do not? Can you suggest possible sources for the words that are not portmanteau words?

Related Works: "A&P" (p. 128), "Gryphon" (p. 139)

✔ **CHECKLIST** Writing about Sound
Rhythm and Meter
Does the poem contain repeated words and phrases? If so, how do they help to create rhythm?
Does the poem use one kind of meter, or does the meter vary from line to line?
How does the meter contribute to the overall effect of the poem?
Which lines of the poem contain caesuras? What effect do they have?
Are the lines of the poem end-stopped, run-on, or a combination of the two? What effects are created by the presence or absence of pauses at the ends of lines?

continued on next page

> **Alliteration, Assonance, and Rhyme**
>
> ☐ Does the poem include alliteration or assonance?
>
> ☐ Does the poem have a regular rhyme scheme?
>
> ☐ Does the poem use internal rhyme? Beginning rhyme?
>
> ☐ Does the poem include examples of masculine, feminine, or triple rhyme?
>
> ☐ How does rhyme unify the poem?
>
> ☐ How does rhyme reinforce the poem's ideas?

WRITING SUGGESTIONS: Sound

1. William Blake's "The Tyger" appeared in a collection entitled *Songs of Experience*. Compare this poem (p. 653) to "The Lamb" (p. 653), which appeared in a collection called *Songs of Innocence*. In what sense are the speakers in these two poems either "innocent" or "experienced"? How does sound help to convey the voice of the speakers in these two poems?

2. "Sadie and Maud" (p. 548), like "My Papa's Waltz" (p. 622) and "Daddy" (p. 532), communicates the speaker's attitude toward home and family. How does the presence or absence of rhyme in these poems help to convey the speakers' attitudes toward home and family?

3. Robert Frost once said that writing poems that have no fixed metrical pattern is like playing tennis without a net. What do you think he meant? Do you agree? After reading "Out, Out —" (p. 539), "Stopping by Woods on a Snowy Evening" (p. 672), and "The Road Not Taken" (p. 671), write an essay in which you discuss Frost's use of meter.

4. Select two or three contemporary poems that have no end rhyme. Write an essay in which you discuss what these poets gain and lose by not using end rhyme.

5. Prose writers as well as poets use techniques such as assonance and alliteration. Choose a passage of prose — from "Araby" (p. 232), "Barn Burning" (p. 209), or "The Things They Carried" (p. 251), for example — and discuss its use of assonance and alliteration. Where are these techniques used? How do they help the writer create a mood?

CHAPTER 21

FORM

No verse can be free; it must be governed by some measure, but not by the old measure.

—**William Carlos Williams,** *"On Measure"*

JOHN KEATS   (1795–1821)

On the Sonnet   (1819)

If by dull rhymes our English must be chained,
And like Andromeda,° the sonnet sweet
Fettered, in spite of painéd loveliness,
Let us find, if we must be constrained,
Sandals more interwoven and complete   5
To fit the naked foot of Poesy:
Let us inspect the lyre, and weigh the stress
Of every chord, and see what may be gained
By ear industrious, and attention meet;
Misers of sound and syllable, no less   10
Than Midas° of his coinage, let us be
Jealous of dead leaves in the bay-wreath crown;
So, if we may not let the Muse be free,
She will be bound with garlands of her own.

BILLY COLLINS   (1941–   )

Sonnet   (1999)

All we need is fourteen lines, well, thirteen now,
and after this one just a dozen
to launch a little ship on love's storm chased seas,

° *Andromeda:* In Greek mythology, an Ethiopian princess chained to a rock to appease a sea monster.
° *Midas:* A legendary king of Phrygia whose wish that everything he touched would turn to gold was granted by the god Dionysus.

569

then only ten more left like rows of beans.
How easily it goes unless you get Elizabethan   5
and insist the iambic bongos must be played
and rhymes positioned at the ends of lines,
one for every station of the cross.
But hang on here while we make the turn
into the final six where all will be resolved,   10
where longing and heartache will find an end,
where Laura will tell Petrarch to put down his pen,
take off those crazy medieval tights,
blow out the lights, and come at last to bed.

The **form** of a literary work is its structure or shape, the way its elements fit together to form a whole; **poetic form** is the design of a poem described in terms of rhyme, meter, and stanzaic pattern.

Until the twentieth century, most poetry was written in **closed form** (sometimes called **fixed form**), characterized by regular patterns of meter, rhyme, line length, and stanzaic divisions. Early poems that were passed down orally — epics and ballads, for example — relied on regular form to facilitate memorization. Even after poems began to be written down, poets tended to favor regular patterns. In fact, until relatively recently, regular form was what distinguished poetry from prose. Of course, strict adherence to regular patterns sometimes produced poems that were, in John Keats's words, "chained" by "dull rhymes" and "fettered" by the rules governing a particular form. But rather than feeling "constrained" by form, many poets — like Billy Collins in the playful sonnet above — have experimented with imagery, figures of speech, allusion, and other techniques, stretching closed form to its limits.

As they sought new ways in which to express themselves, poets also used forms from other cultures, adapting them to the demands of their own languages. English and American poets, for example, adopted (and still use) early French forms, such as the villanelle and the sestina, and early Italian forms, such as the Petrarchan sonnet and terza rima. The nineteenth-century American poet Henry Wadsworth Longfellow studied Icelandic epics; the twentieth-century poet Ezra Pound studied the works of French troubadours; and Pound and other twentieth-century American poets, such as Richard Wright and Carolyn Kizer, were inspired by Japanese haiku. Other American poets, such as Vachel Lindsay, Langston Hughes, and Maya Angelou, looked closer to home — to the rhythms of blues, jazz, and spirituals — for inspiration.

As time went on, more and more poets moved away from closed form to experiment with **open form** poetry (sometimes called **free verse** or *vers libre*), varying line length within a poem, dispensing with stanzaic divisions, breaking lines in unexpected places, and even abandoning any semblance of formal structure. In English, nineteenth-century poets — such as William Blake and Matthew

Arnold—experimented with lines of irregular meter and length, and Walt Whitman wrote **prose poems,** open form poems whose long lines made them look like prose. (Well before this time, Asian poetry and some biblical passages had used a type of free verse.) In nineteenth-century France, Symbolist poets, such as Baudelaire, Rimbaud, Verlaine, and Mallarmé, also used free verse. In the early twentieth century, a group of American poets — including Ezra Pound, William Carlos Williams, and Amy Lowell — who were associated with a movement known as **imagism** wrote poetry that dispensed with traditional principles of English versification, creating new rhythms and meters.

Although much contemporary English and American poetry is composed in open form, many poets also continue to write in closed form — even in very traditional, highly structured patterns. Still, new forms, and new variations of old forms, are being created all the time. And, because contemporary poets do not necessarily feel bound by rules or restrictions about what constitutes "acceptable" poetic form, they experiment freely, trying to discover the form that best suits the poem's purpose, subject, language, and theme.

Closed Form

A **closed form** (or *fixed form*) poem looks symmetrical; it has an identifiable, repeated pattern, with lines of similar length arranged in groups of two, three, four, or more. A closed form poem also tends to rely on regular metrical patterns and rhyme schemes.

Despite what its name suggests, closed form poetry does not have to be confining or conservative. In fact, contemporary poets often experiment with closed form — for example, by using characteristics of open form poetry (such as lines of varying length) within a closed form. Sometimes they move back and forth within a single poem from open to closed to open form; sometimes (like their eighteenth-century counterparts) they combine different stanzaic forms (stanzas of two and three lines, for example) within a single poem.

Even when poets work within a traditional closed form, such as a *sonnet, sestina,* or *villanelle,* they can break new ground. For example, they can write a sonnet with an unexpected meter or rhyme scheme, add an extra line or even extra stanzas to a traditional sonnet form, combine two different traditional sonnet forms in a single poem, or write an abbreviated version of a sestina or villanelle. In other words, poets can use traditional forms as building blocks, combining them in innovative ways to create new patterns and new forms.

Sometimes a pattern (such as *blank verse*) simply determines the meter of a poem's individual lines. At other times, the pattern extends to the level of the *stanza,* with lines arranged into groups (*couplets, quatrains,* and so on). At still other times, as in the case of traditional closed forms like sonnets, a poetic pattern gives shape to an entire poem.

Blank Verse

Blank verse is unrhymed poetry with each line written in a set pattern of five stressed and five unstressed syllables called **iambic pentameter** (see p. 551). Many passages from Shakespeare's plays, such as the following lines from *Hamlet*, are written in blank verse.

> To sleep! perchance to dream:—ay, there's the rub;
> For in that sleep of death what dreams may come,
> When we have shuffled off this mortal coil,
> Must give us pause: there's the respect
> That makes calamity of so long life

Stanza

A **stanza** is a group of two or more lines with the same metrical pattern — and often with a regular rhyme scheme as well — separated by blank space from other such groups of lines. Stanzas in poetry are like paragraphs in prose: they group related ideas into units.

A two-line stanza with rhyming lines of similar length and meter is called a **couplet.** The **heroic couplet,** first used by Chaucer and especially popular throughout the eighteenth century, consists of two rhymed lines of iambic pentameter, with a weak pause after the first line and a strong pause after the second. The following example, from Alexander Pope's *An Essay on Criticism,* is a heroic couplet.

> True ease in writing comes from art, not chance,
> As those move easiest who have learned to dance.

A three-line stanza with lines of similar length and a set rhyme scheme is called a **tercet.** Percy Bysshe Shelley's "Ode to the West Wind" (p. 697) is built largely of tercets.

> O wild West Wind, thou breath of Autumn's being,
> Thou, from whose unseen presence the leaves dead
> Are driven, like ghosts from an enchanter fleeing,
>
> Yellow, and black, and pale, and hectic red,
> Pestilence-stricken multitudes: O Thou,
> Who chariotest to their dark wintry bed

Although in many tercets all three lines rhyme, "Ode to the West Wind" uses a special rhyme scheme, also used by Dante, called **terza rima.** This rhyme scheme (*aba, bcb, cdc, ded,* and so on) creates an interlocking series of stanzas: line 2's *dead* looks ahead to the rhyming words *red* and *bed,* which close lines 4 and 6, and the pattern continues throughout the poem.

A four-line stanza with lines of similar length and a set rhyme scheme is called a **quatrain.** The quatrain, the most widely used and versatile unit in English and

American poetry, is used by William Wordsworth in the following excerpt from his 1800 poem "She dwelt among the untrodden ways."

> A violet by a mossy stone
> Half hidden from the eye!
> —Fair as a star, when only one
> Is shining in the sky.

Quatrains are frequently used by contemporary poets as well — for instance, in Theodore Roethke's "My Papa's Waltz" (p. 622), Adrienne Rich's "Aunt Jennifer's Tigers" (p. 555), and William Stafford's "Traveling through the Dark" (p. 632).

One special kind of quatrain, called the **ballad stanza,** alternates lines of eight and six syllables; typically, only the second and fourth lines rhyme. The following lines from the traditional Scottish ballad "Sir Patrick Spence" illustrate the ballad stanza.

> The king sits in Dumferling toune,
> Drinking the blude-reid wine:
> "O whar will I get guid sailor
> To sail this schip of mine?"

Common measure, a four-line stanzaic pattern closely related to the ballad stanza, is used in hymns as well as in poetry. It differs from the ballad stanza in that its rhyme scheme is *abab* rather than *abcb*.

Other stanzaic forms include **rhyme royal,** a seven-line stanza (*ababbcc*) set in iambic pentameter, used in Sir Thomas Wyatt's sixteenth-century poem "They Flee from Me That Sometimes Did Me Seke" as well as in Theodore Roethke's twentieth-century "I Knew a Woman"; **ottava rima,** an eight-line stanza (*abababcc*) set in iambic pentameter; and the Spenserian stanza, a nine-line form (*ababbcbcc*) whose first eight lines are set in iambic pentameter and whose last line is in iambic hexameter. The Romantic poets John Keats and Percy Bysshe Shelley were among those who used the Spenserian stanza. (See Chapter 20 for definitions and examples of various metrical patterns.)

The Sonnet

Perhaps the most familiar kind of traditional closed form poem written in English is the **sonnet,** a fourteen-line poem with a distinctive rhyme scheme and metrical pattern. The English or **Shakespearean sonnet,** which consists of fourteen lines divided into three quatrains and a concluding couplet, is written in iambic pentameter and follows the rhyme scheme *abab cdcd efef gg*. The **Petrarchan sonnet,** popularized in the fourteenth century by the Italian poet Francesco Petrarch, also consists of fourteen lines of iambic pentameter, but these lines are divided into an eight-line unit called an **octave** and a six-line unit (composed of two tercets) called a **sestet.** The rhyme scheme of the octave is *abba abba*; the rhyme scheme of the sestet is *cde cde*.

The conventional structures of these sonnet forms reflect the arrangement of ideas within the poem. In the Shakespearean sonnet, the poet typically presents three "paragraphs" of related thoughts, introducing an idea in the first quatrain, developing it in the two remaining quatrains, and summing up in a succinct closing couplet. In the Petrarchan sonnet, the octave introduces a problem that is resolved in the sestet. (Many Shakespearean sonnets also have a problem-solution structure.) Some poets vary the traditional patterns somewhat to suit the poem's language or ideas. For example, they may depart from the pattern to side-step a forced rhyme or unnatural stress on a syllable, or they may shift from problem to solution in a place other than between octave and sestet.

The following poem has the form of a traditional English sonnet.

WILLIAM SHAKESPEARE   (1564–1616)

When, in disgrace with Fortune and men's eyes   (1609)

When, in disgrace with Fortune and men's eyes,
I all alone beweep my outcast state,
And trouble deaf heaven with my bootless° cries,
And look upon myself and curse my fate,
Wishing me like to one more rich in hope,   5
Featured like him, like him with friends possessed,
Desiring this man's art, and that man's scope,
With what I most enjoy contented least,
Yet in these thoughts myself almost despising,
Haply° I think on thee, and then my state,   10
Like to the lark at break of day arising
From sullen earth, sings hymns at heaven's gate;
    For thy sweet love rememb'red such wealth brings
    That then I scorn to change my state with kings.

This sonnet is written in iambic pentameter and has a conventional rhyme scheme: *abab* (eyes-state-cries-fate), *cdcd* (hope-possessed-scope-least), *efef* (despising-state-arising-gate), *gg* (brings-kings). In this poem, in which the speaker explains how thoughts of his loved one can rescue him from despair, each quatrain is unified by subject matter as well as by rhyme. In the first quatrain, the speaker presents his problem: he is down on his luck and out of favor with his peers, isolated in self-pity and cursing his fate. In the second quatrain, he develops this idea further: he is envious of others and dissatisfied with things that usually please him. In the third quatrain, the focus shifts. Although the first two quatrains develop a dependent clause ("When . . .") that introduces a problem, line 9 begins to present the resolution. In the third quatrain, the speaker explains how, in the midst of his despair and self-hatred, he thinks of his loved one, and his spirits soar. The closing couplet sums up the mood transformation the poem

---

°*bootless:* Futile.   °*Haply:* Luckily.

describes and explains its significance: when the speaker realizes the emotional riches his loved one gives him, he is no longer envious of others.

FURTHER READING: The Sonnet

JOHN KEATS   (1795–1821)

On First Looking into Chapman's Homer° (1816)

Much have I traveled in the realms of gold,
    And many goodly states and kingdoms seen;
    Round many western islands have I been
Which bards in fealty to Apollo° hold.
Oft of one wide expanse had I been told   5
    That deep-browed Homer ruled as his demesne,°
    Yet did I never breathe its pure serene°
Till I heard Chapman speak out loud and bold.
Then felt I like some watcher of the skies
    When a new planet swims into his ken;   10
Or like stout Cortez° when with eagle eyes
    He stared at the Pacific — and all his men
Looked at each other with a wild surmise —
    Silent, upon a peak in Darien.°

Reading and Reacting

1. Is this a Petrarchan or a Shakespearean sonnet? Explain.

2. JOURNAL ENTRY The sestet's change of focus is introduced with the word "Then" in line 9. How does the mood of the sestet differ from the mood of the octave? How does the language differ?

3. CRITICAL PERSPECTIVE As Keats's biographer Aileen Ward observes, Homer's epic tales of gods and heroes were known to most readers of Keats's day only in a very formal eighteenth-century translation by Alexander Pope. This is Pope's description of Ulysses escaping from a shipwreck:

> his knees no more
> Perform'd their office, or his weight upheld:
> His swoln heart heav'd, his bloated body swell'd:
> From mouth to nose the briny torrent ran,
> And lost in lassitude lay all the man,
> Deprived of voice, of motion, and of breath,
> The soul scarce waking in the arms of death . . .

° *Chapman's Homer:* The translation of Homer's works by Elizabethan poet George Chapman.   ° *Apollo:* Greek god of light, truth, reason, male beauty; associated with music and poetry.   ° *demesne:* Realm, domain.
° *serene:* Air, atmosphere.   ° *Cortez:* It was Vasco de Balboa (not Hernando Cortez as Keats suggests) who first saw the Pacific Ocean, from "a peak in Darien."   ° *Darien:* Former name of the Isthmus of Panama.

In a rare 1616 edition of Chapman's translation, Keats discovered a very different poem:

> both knees falt'ring, both
> His strong hands hanging down, and all with froth
> His cheeks and nostrils flowing, voice and breath
> Spent to all use, and down he sank to death.
> The sea had soak'd his heart through. . . .

This, as Ward notes, was "poetry of a kind that had not been written in England for two hundred years." Can you understand why Keats was so moved by Chapman's translation? Do you think Keats's own poem seems closer in its form and language to Pope or to Chapman?

Related Works: "Gryphon" (p. 139), "Araby" (p. 232), "When I Heard the Learn'd Astronomer" (p. 491), *Beauty* (p. 736), *Trifles* (p. 770)

GWENDOLYN BROOKS   (1917–2000)

First Fight. Then Fiddle   (1949)

First fight. Then fiddle. Ply the slipping string
With feathery sorcery; muzzle the note
With hurting love; the music that they wrote
Bewitch, bewilder. Qualify to sing
Threadwise. Devise no salt, no hempen thing   5
For the dear instrument to bear. Devote
The bow to silks and honey. Be remote
A while from malice and from murdering.
But first to arms, to armor. Carry hate
In front of you and harmony behind.   10
Be deaf to music and to beauty blind.
Win war. Rise bloody, maybe not too late
For having first to civilize a space
Wherein to play your violin with grace.

Reading and Reacting

1. What is the subject of Brooks's poem? What do you think she means by "fight" and "fiddle"?
2. Explain the poem's rhyme scheme. Is this rhyme scheme an essential element of the poem? Would the poem be equally effective if it did not include end rhyme? Why or why not?

3. Study the poem's use of capitalization and punctuation carefully. Why do you think Brooks chooses to end many of her sentences in midline? How do her decisions determine how you read the poem?

Related Works: "The Soldier" (p. 638), "Medgar Evers" (p. 655), "If We Must Die" (p. 686)

MONA VAN DUYN   (1921–2004)

Minimalist Sonnet: Summer Virus   (1991)

Send this blaze still higher.
Degree by degree
let my fever aspire
to transfigure me

to a lampbulb's wire,   5
the red waft of a kite.
From no former fire
shone a blush so bright.

I'll stoke with my numbing
flesh, senses, insight,   10
unafraid of becoming
more and more light,

since I've felt one presence
as incandescence.

Reading and Reacting

1. What pattern of imagery can you identify in this poem? How do the related images help to communicate the poem's theme?
2. What is the "summer virus" to which the title refers? What is the "one presence" (line 13) that the speaker feels as "incandescence" (line 14)?
3. Do you see this as a love poem, or do you think it might be about something else? Explain.
4. JOURNAL ENTRY Study this poem's rhyme scheme, arrangement of lines, and metrical pattern carefully. How is the poem like a traditional sonnet? How is it different? In what sense is it "minimalist"?

Related Works: "Araby" (p. 232), "That time of year thou mayst in me behold" (p. 448), "Sonnet" (p. 569)

The Sestina

The **sestina,** introduced in thirteenth-century France, is composed of six six-line
stanzas and a three-line conclusion called an **envoi.** The sestina does not require
end rhyme; however, it requires that each line end with one of six key words,
which are repeated throughout the poem in a fixed order. The alternation of these
six words in different positions — but always at the ends of lines — in each of the
poem's six stanzas creates a rhythmic verbal pattern that unifies the poem, as the
key words do in the poem that follows.

ALBERTO ALVARO RÍOS (1952–   )

Nani (1982)

Sitting at her table, she serves
the sopa de arroz° to me
instinctively, and I watch her,
the absolute mamá, and eat words
I might have had to say more   5
out of embarrassment. To speak,
now-foreign words I used to speak,
too, dribble down her mouth as she serves
me albóndigas.° No more
than a third are easy to me.   10
By the stove she does something with words
and looks at me only with her
back. I am full. I tell her
I taste the mint, and watch her speak
smiles at the stove. All my words   15
make her smile. Nani never serves
herself, she only watches me
with her skin, her hair. I ask for more.

I watch the mamá warming more
tortillas for me. I watch her   20
fingers in the flame for me.
Near her mouth, I see a wrinkle speak
of a man whose body serves
the ants like she serves me, then more words
from more wrinkles about children, words   25
about this and that, flowing more

° *sopa de arroz:* Rice soup.   ° *albóndigas:* Meatballs.

easily from these other mouths. Each serves
as a tremendous string around her,
holding her together. They speak
nani was this and that to me   30
and I wonder just how much of me
will die with her, what were the words
I could have been, was. Her insides speak
through a hundred wrinkles, now, more
than she can bear, steel around her,   35
shouting, then, What is this thing she serves?

She asks me if I want more.
I own no words to stop her.
Even before I speak, she serves.

In many respects, Ríos's poem closely follows the form of the traditional sestina. For instance, it interweaves six key words — "serves," "me," "her," "words," "more," and "speak"— through six groups of six lines each, rearranging the order in which the words appear so that the first line of each group of six lines ends with the same key word that also ended the preceding group of lines. The poem repeats the key words in exactly the order prescribed: *abcdef, faebdc, cfdabe,* and so on. In addition, the sestina closes with a three-line envoi that includes all six of the poem's key words, three at the ends of lines and three within the lines. Despite this generally strict adherence to the sestina form, however, Ríos departs from the form by grouping his six sets of six lines not into six separate stanzas but rather into two eighteen-line stanzas.

The sestina form suits Ríos's subject matter. The focus of the poem, on the verbal and nonverbal interaction between the poem's "me" and "her," is reinforced by each of the related words. "Nani" is a poem about communication, and the key words return to probe this theme again and again. Throughout the poem, these repeated words help to create a fluid, melodic, and tightly woven work.

FURTHER READING: The Sestina

ELIZABETH BISHOP (1911–1979)

Sestina (1965)

September rain falls on the house.
In the failing light, the old grandmother
sits in the kitchen with the child
beside the Little Marvel Stove,
reading the jokes from the almanac,   5
laughing and talking to hide her tears.

She thinks that her equinoctial tears
and the rain that beats on the roof of the house
were both foretold by the almanac,
but only known to a grandmother.   10
The iron kettle sings on the stove.
She cuts some bread and says to the child,

It's time for tea now; but the child
is watching the teakettle's small hard tears
dance like mad on the hot black stove,   15
the way the rain must dance on the house.
Tidying up, the old grandmother
hangs up the clever almanac

on its string. Birdlike, the almanac
hovers half open above the child,   20
hovers above the old grandmother
and her teacup full of dark brown tears.
She shivers and says she thinks the house
feels chilly, and puts more wood in the stove.

It was to be, says the Marvel Stove.   25
I know what I know, says the almanac.
With crayons the child draws a rigid house
and a winding pathway. Then the child
puts in a man with buttons like tears
and shows it proudly to the grandmother.   30

But secretly, while the grandmother
busies herself about the stove,
the little moons fall down like tears
from between the pages of the almanac
into the flower bed the child   35
has carefully placed in the front of the house.

Time to plant tears, says the almanac.
The grandmother sings to the marvellous stove
and the child draws another inscrutable house.

Reading and Reacting

1. Does the poet's adherence to the traditional sestina form create any problems? For example, do you think the syntax is strained at any point? Explain.

2. How does this sestina use sound — meter, rhyme, alliteration, assonance, and
so on (see Chapter 20)? Could sound have been used more effectively? How?

3. JOURNAL ENTRY How are the six key words related to the poem's theme?

Related Works: "My Papa's Waltz" (p. 622), "The Meal" (p. 515), "Nani" (p. 578)

The Villanelle

The **villanelle,** first introduced in France during the Middle Ages, is a nineteen-line poem composed of five tercets and a concluding quatrain; its rhyme scheme is *aba aba aba aba aba abaa.* Two different lines are systematically repeated in the poem: line 1 appears again in lines 6, 12, and 18, and line 3 reappears as lines 9, 15, and 19. Thus, each tercet concludes with an exact (or close) duplication of either line 1 or line 3, and the final quatrain concludes by repeating both line 1 and line 3.

THEODORE ROETHKE (1908–1963)

The Waking (1953)

I wake to sleep, and take my waking slow.
I feel my fate in what I cannot fear.
I learn by going where I have to go.

We think by feeling. What is there to know?
I hear my being dance from ear to ear.   5
I wake to sleep, and take my waking slow.

Of those so close beside me, which are you?
God bless the Ground! I shall walk softly there,
And learn by going where I have to go.

Light takes the Tree; but who can tell us how?   10
The lowly worm climbs up a winding stair;
I wake to sleep, and take my waking slow.

Great Nature has another thing to do
To you and me; so take the lively air,
And, lovely, learn by going where to go.   15

This shaking keeps me steady. I should know.
What falls away is always. And is near.
I wake to sleep, and take my waking slow.
I learn by going where I have to go.

"The Waking," like all villanelles, closely intertwines threads of sounds and words. The repeated lines and the very regular rhyme and meter give the poem a monotonous, almost hypnotic, rhythm. This poem uses end rhyme and repeats entire lines. It also makes extensive use of alliteration ("I feel my fate in what I cannot fear") and internal rhyme ("I hear my being dance from ear to ear"; "I wake to sleep and take my waking slow"). The result is a tightly constructed poem of overlapping sounds and images. (For an example of another well-known villanelle, see Dylan Thomas's "Do not go gentle into that good night," p. 627)

The Epigram

Originally, an epigram was an inscription carved in stone on a monument or statue. As a literary form, an **epigram** is a very brief poem that makes a pointed, often sarcastic, comment in a surprising twist at the end. In a sense, it is a poem with a punch line. Although some epigrams rhyme, others do not. Many are only two lines long, but others are somewhat longer. What they have in common is their economy of language and their tone. One of the briefest of epigrams, written by Ogden Nash, appeared in the *New Yorker* magazine in 1931.

> The Bronx?
> No thonx.

Here, in four words, Nash manages to convey the unexpected, using rhyme and creative spelling to convey his assessment of one of New York City's five boroughs. The poem's two lines are perfectly balanced, making the contrast between the noncommittal tone of the first and the negative tone of the second quite striking.

FURTHER READING: The Epigram

SAMUEL TAYLOR COLERIDGE (1772–1834)

What Is an Epigram? (1802)

What is an epigram? a dwarfish whole,
Its body brevity, and wit its soul.

WILLIAM BLAKE (1757–1827)

Her Whole Life Is an Epigram (c. 1793–1811)

Her whole life is an epigram: smack, smooth & neatly penned,
Platted° quite neat to catch applause, with a sliding noose at the end.

Reading and Reacting

1. Explain the point made in each of the epigrams above.
2. Evaluate each poem. What qualities do you conclude make an epigram effective?
3. **JOURNAL ENTRY** How are short-short stories (see Chapter 5) and ten-minute plays (see Chapter 26) like epigrams?

Related Works: "Mislaid Plans" (p. 98), "General Review of the Sex Situation" (p. 636), "Fire and Ice" (p. 471), "you fit into me" (p. 541), *Nine Ten* (p. 760)

° *Platted:* Braided.

MARTIN ESPADA (1957–   )

Why I Went to College (2000)

If you don't,
my father said,
you better learn
to eat soup
through a straw,   5
'cause I'm gonna
break your jaw

Reading and Reacting

1. How is "Why I Went to College" different from Coleridge's and Blake's epigrams? How is it similar to them?

2. What function does the poem's title serve? Is it the epigram's "punch line," or does it serve another purpose?

3. What can you infer about the speaker's father from this poem? Why, for example, do you think he wants his son to go to college?

4. JOURNAL ENTRY Exactly why did the speaker go to college? Expand this short poem into a paragraph written from the speaker's point of view.

Related Works: "Baca Grande" (p. 500), "My Papa's Waltz" (p. 622), "'Faith' is a fine invention" (p. 662)

Haiku

Like an epigram, a haiku compresses words into a very small package. Unlike an epigram, however, a haiku focuses on an image, not an idea. A traditional Japanese form, the **haiku** is a brief unrhymed poem that presents the essence of some aspect of nature, concentrating a vivid image in three lines. Although in the strictest sense a haiku consists of seventeen syllables divided into lines of five, seven, and five syllables, respectively, not all poets conform to this rigid form.

The following poem is a translation of a classic Japanese haiku by Matsuo Bashō.

Silent and still: then
Even sinking into the rocks,
The cicada's screech.

Notice that this poem conforms to the haiku's three-line structure and traditional subject matter, vividly depicting a natural scene without comment or analysis.

FURTHER READING: Haiku

MATSUO BASHŌ   (1644–1694)

Four Haiku*

Translated by Geoffrey Bownas and Anthony Thwaite

Spring:
A hill without a name
Veiled in morning mist.

The beginning of autumn:
Sea and emerald paddy   5
Both the same green.

The winds of autumn
Blow: yet still green
The chestnut husks.

A flash of lightning: 10
Into the gloom
Goes the heron's cry.

Reading and Reacting

1. Haiku are admired for their extreme economy and their striking images. What are the central images in each of Bashō's haiku? To what senses do these images appeal?

2. In another poem, Bashō says that art begins with "The depths of the country / and a rice-planting song." What do you think he means? How do these four haiku exemplify this idea?

3. Do you think the conciseness of these poems increases or decreases the impact of their images? Explain.

4. JOURNAL ENTRY   "In a Station of the Metro" (p. 514) is Ezra Pound's version of a haiku. How successful do you think his poem is as a haiku? Do you think a longer poem could have conveyed the images more effectively?

Related Works: "Seventeen Syllables" (p. 425), Where Mountain Lion Lay Down with Deer" (p. 467), "the sky was can dy" (p. 589), "Birches" (p. 631)

CAROLYN KIZER   (1925–   )

After Bashō   (1984)

Tentatively, you
slip onstage this evening,
pallid, famous moon.

*Publication date is not available.

Reading and Reacting

1. What possible meanings might the word "After" have in the title? What does the title tell readers about the writer's purpose?
2. What is the impact of "tentatively" in the first line and "famous" in the last line? How do the connotations of these words convey the image of the moon?
3. JOURNAL ENTRY What visual picture does the poem suggest? What mood does the poem's central image create?

Related Works: "this poem intentionally left blank" (p. 456), "Morning Song" (p. 633)

JOSÉ JUAN TABLADA (1871–1945)

Haiku

Translated by Samuel Beckett

Red cold
guffaw of summer,
slice
of watermelon!

Reading and Reacting

1. This haiku consists of only eight words, two of which are *of.* Consider the remaining six words (two adjectives and four nouns). Are all of them appropriate for a haiku? Are any unexpected (or even incongruous)?
2. This poem, translated from Spanish, contains only 11 (not 17) syllables. Is it still a haiku?
3. Why do you think this poem ends with an exclamation point?
4. JOURNAL ENTRY Retaining the same two adjectives and four nouns, expand this haiku to the standard 17 syllables.

Related Works: "Four Haiku" (p. 584), "Fog" (p. 696)

JACK KEROUAC (1922–1969)

American Haiku

Early morning yellow flowers,
thinking about
the drunkards of Mexico.

No telegram today
only more leaves
fell.

5

Nightfall,
boy smashing dandelions
with a stick.

Holding up my   10
purring cat to the moon
I sighed.

Drunk as a hoot owl,
writing letters
by thunderstorm.   15

Empty baseball field
a robin
hops along the bench.

All day long
wearing a hat   20
that wasn't on my head.

Crossing the football field
coming home from work—
the lonely businessman.

After the shower   25
among the drenched roses
the bird thrashing in the bath.

Snap your finger
stop the world—
rain falls harder.   30

Nightfall,
too dark to read the page
too cold.

Following each other
my cats stop   35
when it thunders.

Wash hung out
by moonlight
Friday night in May.

The bottoms of my shoes   40
are clean
from walking in the rain.

Glow worm
sleeping on this flower—
your light's on.   45

Reading and Reacting

1. In what ways are these haiku different from those by Matsuo Bashō (p. 584)? Do they fit the definition of *haiku* on page 583?

2. What, if anything, makes these poems "American"? Is it their language? Their subject matter? Something else?

3. Journal Entry Try writing a few "American haiku" of your own. Then, evaluate the success of your efforts. What problems did you encounter?

4. Critical Perspective Writing about his experiments with haiku, Jack Kerouac said, "Above all, a Haiku must be very simple and free of all poetic trickery and make a little picture and yet be as airy and graceful as a Vivaldi Pastorella."

Do you think Kerouac's haiku satisfy these conditions?

Related Works: "Love and Other Catastrophes: A Mix Tape" (p. 98), "Chicago" (p. 588), "Morning Song" (p. 633), *from* "Song of Myself" (p. 703)

Open Form

An **open form poem** may make occasional use of rhyme and meter but has no easily identifiable pattern or design: no conventional stanzaic divisions, no consistent metrical pattern or line length, no repeated rhyme scheme. Still, open form poetry is not necessarily shapeless, untidy, or randomly ordered. All poems have form, and the form of a poem may be determined by factors such as repeated sounds, the appearance of words on the printed page, or pauses in natural speech as well as by a conventional metrical pattern or rhyme scheme.

Open form poetry invites readers to participate in the creative process, to discover the relationship between form and meaning. Some modern poets believe that only open form offers them freedom to express their ideas or that the subject matter or mood of their poetry demands a relaxed, experimental approach to form. For example, when Lawrence Ferlinghetti portrays the poet as an acrobat who "climbs on rime" (p. 523), he constructs his poem in a way that is consistent with the poet/acrobat's willingness to take risks. Thus, the poem's idiosyncratic form supports its ideas about the limitless possibilities of poetry and the poet as experimenter.

Without a predetermined pattern, however, poets must create forms that suit their needs, and they must continue to shape and reshape the look of the poem on the page as they revise its words. Thus, open form is a challenge, but it is also a way for poets to experiment with fresh arrangements of words and new juxtapositions of ideas.

For some poets, such as Carl Sandburg, open form provides an opportunity to create **prose poems,** poems that look like prose.

CARL SANDBURG   (1878–1967)

Chicago   (1914)

Hog Butcher for the World,
Tool Maker, Stacker of Wheat,
Player with Railroads and the Nation's Freight Handler;
Stormy, husky, brawling,
City of the Big Shoulders: 5

They tell me you are wicked and I believe them, for I have seen
    your painted women under the gas lamps luring the farm boys.
And they tell me you are crooked and I answer: Yes, it is true
    I have seen the gunman kill and go free to kill again.
And they tell me you are brutal and my reply is: On the faces of
    women and children I have seen the marks of wanton hunger.
And having answered so I turn once more to those who sneer at
    this my city, and I give them back the sneer and say to them:
Come and show me another city with lifted head singing so
    proud to be alive and coarse and strong and cunning.   10
Flinging magnetic curses amid the toil of piling job on job,
    here is a tall bold slugger set vivid against the little soft cities;
Fierce as a dog with tongue lapping for action, cunning as a
    savage pitted against the wilderness,
      Bareheaded,
        Shoveling,
        Wrecking,   15
        Planning,
        Building, breaking, rebuilding,
Under the smoke, dust all over his mouth, laughing with white
    teeth,
Under the terrible burden of destiny laughing as a young man
    laughs,
Laughing even as an ignorant fighter laughs who has never lost
    a battle,   20
Bragging and laughing that under his wrist is the pulse, and under
    his ribs the heart of the people,
                Laughing!
Laughing the stormy, husky, brawling laughter of Youth,
    half-naked, sweating, proud to be Hog Butcher, Tool Maker,
    Stacker of Wheat, Player with railroads and Freight Handler
    to the Nation.

"Chicago" uses capitalization and punctuation conventionally, and it generally (though not always) arranges words in lines in a way that is consistent with the natural divisions of phrases and sentences. However, the poem is not divided into stanzas, and its lines vary widely in length — from a single word isolated on a line to a line crowded with words — and follow no particular metrical pattern. Instead, its form is created through its pattern of alternating sections of long and short lines; through its repeated words and phrases ("They tell me" in lines 6–8, "under" in lines 18–19, and "laughing" in lines 18–23, for example); through alliteration (for instance, "slugger set vivid against the little soft cities" in line 11); and, most of all, through the piling up of words and images into catalogs in lines 1–5, 13–17, and 22.

In order to understand Sandburg's reasons for choosing such a form, we must consider the poem's subject matter and theme. "Chicago" celebrates the scope and power of a "Stormy, husky, brawling" city, one that is exuberant and outgoing, not sedate and civilized. Chicago the city does not follow anyone else's rules; it is, after all, "Bareheaded, / Shoveling, / Wrecking, / Planning, / Building, breaking, rebuilding," constantly active, in flux, on the move, "proud to be alive." "Fierce as a dog . . . cunning as a savage," the city is characterized as, among other things, a worker, a fighter, and a harborer of "painted women" and killers and hungry women and children. Just as Chicago itself does not conform to the rules, the poem departs from the orderly confines of stanzaic form and measured rhyme and meter, a kind of form that is, after all, better suited to "the little soft cities" than to the "tall bold slugger" that is Chicago.

Of course, open form poetry does not have to look like Sandburg's prose poem. The following poem, an extreme example of open form, looks almost as if it has spilled out of a box of words.

E. E. CUMMINGS (1894–1962)

the sky was can dy (1925)

the
　　sky
　　　was
can　　dy lu
minous　　　　　5
　　edible
spry
　　pinks shy
lemons
greens　coo　l choc　　10
olate
s.

　un　der,
　a　lo
co　　　　　15
mo

```
tive     s pout
         ing
         vi
         o        20
         lets
```

Like many of Cummings's poems, this one seems ready to skip off the page. Its irregular line length and its unconventional capitalization, punctuation, and word
divisions immediately draw readers' attention to its form. Despite these oddities,
and despite the absence of orderly rhyme and meter, the poem does have its conventional elements.

A closer examination reveals that the poem's theme — the beauty of the sky
— is quite conventional; that the poem is divided, though somewhat crudely, into
two sections; and that the poet does use some rhyme — "spry" and "shy," for example. However, Cummings's sky is described not in traditional terms but rather
as something "edible," not only in terms of color but of flavor as well. The breaks
within words ("can dy lu / minous"; "coo l choc / olate / s") seem to expand the
words' possibilities, visually stretching them to the limit, extending their taste
and visual image over several lines and, in the case of the poem's last two words,
visually reinforcing the picture the words describe. In addition, the isolation of
syllables exposes hidden rhyme, as in "lo / co / mo" and "lu" / "coo." Thus, by using open form, Cummings makes a clear statement about the capacity of a poem
to move beyond the traditional boundaries set by words and lines.

FURTHER READING: Open Form

WALT WHITMAN   (1819–1892)

from "Out of the Cradle Endlessly Rocking" (1881)

Out of the cradle endlessly rocking,
Out of the mocking-bird's throat, the musical shuttle,
Out of the Ninth-month° midnight,
Over the sterile sands and the fields beyond, where the child
    leaving his bed wander'd alone, bareheaded, barefoot,
Down from the shower'd halo,   5
Up from the mystic play of shadows twining and twisting as if
    they were alive,
Out from the patches of briers and blackberries,
From the memories of the bird that chanted to me,
From your memories sad brother, from the fitful risings and
    fallings I heard,

° *Ninth-month:* The Quaker designation for September; in context, an allusion to the human birth cycle.

From under that yellow half-moon late-risen and swollen as if
   with tears,   10
From those beginning notes of yearning and love there in the
   mist,
From the thousand responses of my heart never to cease,
From the myriad thence-arous'd words,
From the word stronger and more delicious than any,
From such as now they start the scene revisiting,   15
As a flock, twittering, rising, or overhead passing,
Borne hither, ere all eludes me, hurriedly,
A man, yet by these tears a little boy again,
Throwing myself on the sand, confronting the waves,
I, chanter of pains and joys, uniter of here and hereafter,   20
Taking all hints to use them, but swiftly leaping beyond them,
A reminiscence sing.

Reading and Reacting

1. This excerpt, the first twenty-two lines of a poem nearly two hundred lines long, has no regular metrical pattern or rhyme scheme. What gives it its form?

2. How might you explain why the poem's lines vary in length?

3. JOURNAL ENTRY Compare this excerpt with the excerpt from Whitman's "Song of Myself" (p. 703). In what respects are the forms of the two poems similar?

4. CRITICAL PERSPECTIVE Reviewing a recent biography of Whitman, Geoffrey O'Brien writes of a paradox in Whitman's poetry:

> [N]either fiction nor verse as they then existed could provide Whitman with what he needed, so he invented out of necessity his own form, a reversion to what he conceived of as the most archaic bardic impulses, representing itself as the poetry of the future.

Can you see the form of "Out of the Cradle" as both "archaic" and "of the future"?

Related Works: "Chicago" (p. 588), "Defending Walt Whitman" (p. 645), *from* "Song of Myself" (p. 703)

WILLIAM CARLOS WILLIAMS   (1883–1963)

Spring and All   (1923)

By the road to the contagious hospital
under the surge of the blue
mottled clouds driven from the
northeast — a cold wind. Beyond, the

waste of broad, muddy fields   5
brown with dried weeds, standing and fallen

patches of standing water
the scattering of tall trees

All along the road the reddish
purplish, forked, upstanding, twiggy   10
stuff of bushes and small trees
with dead, brown leaves under them
leafless vines —

Lifeless in appearance, sluggish
dazed spring approaches —   15

They enter the new world naked,
cold, uncertain of all
save that they enter. All about them
the cold, familiar wind —

Now the grass, tomorrow   20
the stiff curl of wildcarrot leaf
One by one objects are defined —
It quickens: clarity, outline of leaf

But now the stark dignity of
entrance — Still, the profound change   25
has come upon them: rooted, they
grip down and begin to awaken

Reading and Reacting

1. What characteristics of closed form are present in "Spring and All"? What characteristics are absent?
2. What does Williams accomplish by visually isolating lines 7–8 and lines 14–15?
3. "Spring and All" includes assonance, alliteration, and repetition. Give several examples of each technique, and explain what each adds to the poem.
4. **JOURNAL ENTRY** What do you think the word *All* means in the poem's title?
5. **CRITICAL PERSPECTIVE** According to critic Bonnie Costello, "Williams thought about the creative process in painters' terms, and he asks us to experience the work as we might experience a modern painting. His great achievement was to bring some of its qualities into poetry."

   Consider the images Williams uses in this poem. In what ways is this poem like a painting? Which images are conveyed in "painters' terms"? How does he use these images to create meaning in the poem?

Related Works: "Group Photo with Winter Trees" (p. 455), "Pied Beauty" (p. 561), "Summer" (p. 629)

CAROLYN FORCHÉ (1950–   )

The Colonel (1978)

What you have heard is true. I was in his house. His wife carried
a tray of coffee and sugar. His daughter filed her nails, his son went
out for the night. There were daily papers, pet dogs, a pistol on the
cushion beside him. The moon swung bare on its black cord over
the house. On the television was a cop show. It was in English.   5
Broken bottles were embedded in the walls around the house to
scoop the kneecaps from a man's legs or cut his hands to lace. On
the windows there were gratings like those in liquor stores. We had
dinner, rack of lamb, good wine, a gold bell was on the table for
calling the maid. The maid brought green mangoes, salt, a type of   10
bread. I was asked how I enjoyed the country. There was a brief
commercial in Spanish. His wife took everything away. There was
some talk then of how difficult it had become to govern. The parrot
said hello on the terrace. The colonel told it to shut up, and pushed
himself from the table. My friend said to me with his eyes: say   15
nothing. The colonel returned with a sack used to bring groceries
home. He spilled many human ears on the table. They were like
dried peach halves. There is no other way to say this. He took one
of them in his hands, shook it in our faces, dropped it into a water
glass. It came alive there. I am tired of fooling around he said. As   20
for the rights of anyone, tell your people they can go fuck themselves. He swept the ears to the floor with his arm and held the last
of his wine in the air. Something for your poetry, no? he said. Some
of the ears on the floor caught this scrap of his voice. Some of the
ears on the floor were pressed to the ground.   25

Reading and Reacting

1. Treating Forché's prose poem as prose rather than poetry, try dividing it into
paragraphs. What determines where you make your divisions?

2. If you were to reshape "The Colonel" into a conventional-looking poem,
what options might you have? Rearrange a few sentences of the poem so
that they "look like poetry," and compare your revision to the original.
Which version do you find more effective? Why?

3. What is the main theme of "The Colonel"? How does the form help Forché
to communicate this theme?

4. JOURNAL ENTRY Do you think "The Colonel" is poetry or prose? Consider
its subject matter and language as well as its form.

5. CRITICAL PERSPECTIVE Writing in the *New York Times Book Review*, critic
Katha Pollitt focuses on "poetic clichés," which, she says, are "attempts to

energize the poem by annexing a subject that is guaranteed to produce a knee-jerk response in the reader. This saves a lot of bother all around, and enables poet and reader to drowse together in a warm bath of mutual admiration for each other's capacity for deep feeling and right thinking." Among the poetic clichés Pollitt discusses is something she calls "the CNN poem, which retells in overheated free verse a prominent news story involving war, famine, torture, child abuse or murder."

Do you think "The Colonel" is a "CNN poem," or do you see it as something more than just a "poetic cliché"?

Related Work: "Hope" (p. 482)

	CHECKLIST Writing about Form

☐ Is the poem written in open or closed form? On what characteristics do you base your conclusion?

☐ Why did the poet choose open or closed form? For example, is the poem's form consistent with its subject matter, tone, or theme? Is it determined by the conventions of the historical period in which it was written?

☐ If the poem is arranged in closed form, does the pattern apply to single lines, to groups of lines, or to the entire poem? What factors determine the breaks between groups of lines?

☐ Is the poem a sonnet? A sestina? A villanelle? An epigram? A haiku? How do the traditional form's conventions suit the poet's language and theme? Is the poem consistent with the requirements of the form at all times, or does it break any new ground?

☐ If the poem is arranged in open form, what determines the breaks at the ends of lines?

☐ Are certain words or phrases isolated on lines? Why?

☐ How do elements such as assonance, alliteration, rhyme, and repetition of words give the poem form?

☐ What use does the poet make of punctuation and capitalization? Of white space on the page?

☐ Is the poem a prose poem? How does this form support the poem's subject matter?

☐ Is the poem a concrete poem? How does the poet use the visual shape of the poem to convey meaning?

WRITING SUGGESTIONS: Form

1. Reread the definitions of closed form and open form in this chapter. Do you think the following poem is "open" or "closed"? Explain your position in a short essay, supporting your conclusion with specific references to the poem.

CAROLE SATYAMURTI (1939–   )

I Shall Paint My Nails Red

Because a bit of colour is a public service.
Because I am proud of my hands.
Because it will remind me I'm a woman.
Because I will look like a survivor.
Because I can admire them in traffic jams.   5
Because my daughter will say ugh.
Because my lover will be surprised.
Because it is quicker than dyeing my hair.
Because it is a ten-minute moratorium.
Because it is reversible.   10

2. Some poets — for example, Emily Dickinson and Robert Frost — write both open and closed form poems. Choose one open and one closed form poem by a single poet, and explain the poet's possible reasons for choosing each type of form. In your analysis of the two poems, defend the poet's choices if you can.

3. Do you see complex forms, such as the villanelle and the sestina, as exercises or even merely as opportunities for poets to show off their skills, or do you believe the special demands of the forms add something valuable to a poem? To help you answer this question, read "Do not go gentle into that good night" (p. 627), and analyze Dylan Thomas's use of the villanelle's structure to enhance his poem's theme. Or study Elizabeth Bishop's "Sestina" (p. 579), and consider how her use of the sestina's form helps her to convey her ideas.

4. The following open form poem is an alternate version of May Swenson's "Women" (p. 455). Read the two versions carefully, and write an essay in which you compare them. What differences do you notice? Which do you think was written first? Why? Do the two poems make the same point? Which makes the point with less ambiguity? Which is more effective? Why?

Women Should Be Pedestals

Women should be pedestals
moving pedestals
moving to the motions of men
Or they should be little horses

those wooden sweet oldfashioned painted rocking horses 5
the gladdest things in the toyroom
The pegs of their ears so familiar and dear
to the trusting fists
To be chafed feelingly
and then unfeelingly 10
To be joyfully ridden
until the restored egos dismount and the legs stride away
Immobile sweetlipped sturdy and smiling
women should always be waiting
willing to be set into motion 15
Women should be pedestals to men

5. Look through Chapter 24, "Poetry for Further Reading," and identify one or two prose poems. Write an essay in which you consider why the form seems suitable for the poem or poems you have chosen. Is there a particular kind of subject matter that seems especially appropriate for a prose poem?

CHAPTER 22

SYMBOL, ALLEGORY, ALLUSION, MYTH

What the reader gets from a symbol depends not only upon what the author has put into it but upon the reader's sensitivity and his consequent apprehension of what is there.

—**William York Tindall,** *"Excellent Dumb Discourse"*

WILLIAM BLAKE   (1757–1827)

The Sick Rose   (1794)

O Rose thou art sick.
The invisible worm
That flies in the night,
In the howling storm:

Has found out thy bed   5
Of crimson joy:
And his dark secret love
Does thy life destroy.

Symbol

A **symbol** is an idea or image that suggests something else — but not in the simple way that a dollar sign stands for money or a flag represents a country. A symbol is an image that transcends its literal, or denotative, meaning in a complex way. For instance, if someone gives a rose to a loved one, it could simply be a sign of love. But in the poem "The Sick Rose," the rose has a range of contradictory and complementary meanings. For what does the rose stand? Beauty? Perfection? Passion? Something else? As this poem illustrates, the distinctive trait of a symbol is that its meaning cannot easily be pinned down or defined.

Such ambiguity can be frustrating, but it is precisely this characteristic of a symbol that enables it to enrich a poem by giving it additional layers of meaning.

597

As Robert Frost has said, a symbol is a little thing that touches a larger thing. In the poem of his that follows, the central symbol does just this.

ROBERT FROST   (1874–1963)

For Once, Then, Something   (1923)

Others taunt me with having knelt at well-curbs
Always wrong to the light, so never seeing
Deeper down in the well than where the water
Gives me back in a shining surface picture
Me myself in the summer heaven, godlike,   5
Looking out of a wreath of fern and cloud puffs.
Once, when trying with chin against a well-curb,
I discerned, as I thought, beyond the picture,
Through the picture, a something white, uncertain,
Something more of the depths — and then I lost it.   10
Water came to rebuke the too clear water.
One drop fell from a fern, and lo, a ripple
Shook whatever it was lay there at bottom,
Blurred it, blotted it out. What was that whiteness?
Truth? A pebble of quartz? For once, then, something.   15

The central symbol in this poem is the "something" that the speaker thinks he discerns at the bottom of a well. Traditionally, the act of looking down a well suggests a search for truth. In this poem, the speaker says that he always seems to look down the well at the wrong angle, so that all he can see is his own reflection — the surface, not the depths. Once, however, the speaker thought he saw something "beyond the picture," something "white, uncertain," but the image remained indistinct, disappearing when a drop of water from a fern caused the water to ripple. The poem ends with the speaker questioning the significance of what he saw. Like a reader encountering a symbol, the speaker is left trying to come to terms with images that cannot be clearly perceived and associations that cannot be readily understood. In light of the elusive nature of truth, all the speaker can do is ask questions that have no definite answers.

Symbols that appear in poetic works can be *conventional* or *universal*. **Conventional symbols** are those recognized by people who share certain cultural and social assumptions. For example, national flags evoke a general and agreed-upon response in most people of a particular country and—for better or for worse—American children have for years perceived the golden arches of McDonald's as a symbol of food and fun. **Universal symbols** are those likely to be recognized by people regardless of their culture. In 1890, the noted Scottish anthropologist Sir James George Frazer wrote the first version of his work *The Golden Bough,* in which he identified parallels between the rites and beliefs of early cultures and those of Christianity. Fascinated by Frazer's work, the psychologist Carl Jung sought to explain these parallels by formulating a theory of **archetypes,** which held that certain images or ideas reside in the subconscious of all people. According to Jung, archetypal symbols include water, symbolizing rebirth; spring, symbolizing growth; and winter, symbolizing death.

Sometimes symbols that appear in poems can be obscure or highly idiosyncratic. William Blake is one of many poets (William Butler Yeats is another) whose works combine symbols from different cultural, theological, and philosophical sources to form complex networks of symbolic associations. To Blake, for example, the scientist Isaac Newton represents the tendency of scientists to quantify experience while ignoring the beauty and mystery of nature. Readers cannot begin to understand Blake's use of Newton as a symbol until they have read a number of his more difficult poems.

Most often, however, symbols in poems are not so challenging. In the next poem, the poet introduces a cross — a symbol that has specific associations to people familiar with Christianity — and makes his own use of it.

JIM SIMMERMAN*

Child's Grave, Hale County, Alabama   (1983)

Someone drove a two-by-four
through the heart of this hard land
that even in a good year
will notch a plow blade worthless,
snap the head off a shovel,   5
or bow a stubborn back.
He'd have had to steal
the wood from a local mill
or steal, by starlight, across
his landlord's farm, to worry   10
a fencepost out of its well
and lug it the three miles home.
He'd have had to leave his wife
asleep on a corn shuck mat,
leave his broken brogans°   15
by the stove, to slip outside,
quiet as sin, with the child
bundled in a burlap sack.
What a thing to have to do
on a cold night in December,   20
1936, alone
but for a raspy wind
and the red, rock-ridden dirt
things come down to in the end.

---

*Birth date is not available.   °*brogans:* Sturdy, heavy work shoes, frequently ankle high.

> Whoever it was pounded   25
> this shabby half-cross
> into the ground must have toiled
> all night to root it so:
> five feet buried with the child
> for the foot of it that shows.   30
> And as there are no words
> carved here, it's likely that
> the man was illiterate,
> or addled with fatigue,
> or wrenched simple-minded   35
> by the one simple fact.
> Or else the unscored lumber
> driven deep into the land
> and the hump of busted rock
> spoke too plainly of his grief: 40
> forty years layed by and still
> there are no words for this.

Even in non-Christian cultures, the cross on a grave is a readily identifiable symbol of death and the hope for rebirth. In this poem, however, the cross is not simply presented as a conventional Christian symbol; it is also associated with the tenant farmer's hard work and difficult life. In this sense, the cross suggests the poverty that helped bring about the death of the child and the social conditions that existed during the Depression. These associations take readers through many layers of meaning, so that the cross may ultimately stand for the tenant farmer's whole life (the cross *he* has to bear), not just for the death of the child.

This interpretation by no means exhausts the possible symbolic significance of the cross in the poem. For example, the "shabby half-cross" might also suggest the rage and grief of the individual who made it, or it might call to mind the poor who live and die in anonymity. Certainly the poet could have assigned a fixed meaning to the cross that marks the child's grave, but he chose instead, by suggesting various ideas through a single powerful symbol, to let readers arrive at their own conclusions.

How do you know when an idea or image in a poem is a symbol? At what point do you decide that a particular object or idea goes beyond the literal level and takes on symbolic significance? When is a rose more than a rose or a cross more than a cross? Frequently you can recognize a symbol by its prominence or repetition. In "Child's Grave, Hale County, Alabama," for example, the cross is introduced in the first line of the poem, and it is the poem's focal point; in "The Sick Rose," the importance of the rose is emphasized by the title.

It is not enough, however, to identify an image or idea that seems to suggest something else. Your decision that a particular item has symbolic significance must be supported by the details of the poem and make sense in light of the ideas the poem develops. In the following poem, the symbolic significance of the volcano helps readers to understand the poem's central theme.

EMILY DICKINSON (1830–1886)

Volcanoes be in Sicily (1914)

Volcanoes be in Sicily
And South America
I judge from my Geography—
Volcanoes nearer here
A Lava step at any time   5
Am I inclined to climb—
A Crater I may contemplate
Vesuvius at Home.

This poem opens with a statement of fact: volcanoes are located in Sicily and South America. In lines 3 and 4, however, the speaker makes the improbable observation that volcanoes are located near where she is at the moment. Readers familiar with Dickinson know that her poems are highly autobiographical and that she lived in Massachusetts, where there are no volcanoes. This information leads readers to suspect that they should not take the speaker's observation literally and that in the context of the poem volcanoes may have symbolic significance. But what do volcanoes suggest here?

On the one hand, volcanoes represent the awesome creative power of nature; on the other hand, they suggest its destructiveness. The speaker's contemplation of the crater of Vesuvius — the volcano that buried the ancient Roman city of Pompeii in A.D. 79 — is therefore filled with contradictory associations. Because Dickinson was a recluse, volcanoes — active, destructive, unpredictable, and dangerous — may be seen as symbolic of everything she fears in the outside world — and, perhaps, within herself. Volcanoes may even suggest her own creative power, which, like a volcano, is something to be feared as well as contemplated. She has a voyeur's attraction to danger and power, but she is also afraid of them. For this reason, she (and her speaker) may feel safer contemplating Vesuvius at home — not traveling to exotic lands but simply reading a geography book.

FURTHER READING: Symbol

EDGAR ALLAN POE (1809–1849)

The Raven (1844)

Once upon a midnight dreary, while I pondered, weak and weary,
Over many a quaint and curious volume of forgotten lore,
While I nodded, nearly napping, suddenly there came a tapping,
As of some one gently rapping, rapping at my chamber door.
" 'Tis some visitor," I muttered, "tapping at my chamber door—   5
          Only this, and nothing more."

Ah, distinctly I remember it was in the bleak December,
And each separate dying ember wrought its ghost upon the floor.
Eagerly I wished the morrow;— vainly I had sought to borrow
From my books surcease of sorrow — sorrow for the lost Lenore —   10
For the rare and radiant maiden whom the angels name Lenore—
                    Nameless here for evermore.

And the silken sad uncertain rustling of each purple curtain
Thrilled me —filled me with fantastic terrors never felt before;
so that now, to still the beating of my heart, I stood repeating   15
" 'Tis some visitor entreating entrance at my chamber door;—
Some late visitor entreating entrance at my chamber door;
                    This it is, and nothing more."

Presently my soul grew stronger; hesitating then no longer,
"Sir," said I, "or Madam, truly your forgiveness I implore;   20
But the fact is I was napping, and so gently you came rapping,
An so faintly you came tapping, tapping at my chamber door,
That I scarce was sure I heard you"—here I opened wide the door;—
                    Darkness there, and nothing more.

Deep into that darkness peering, long I stood there wondering, fearing,   25
Doubting, dreaming dreams no mortal ever dared to dream before;
But the silence was unbroken, and the darkness gave no token,
And the only word there spoken was the whispered word, "Lenore!"
This I whispered, and an echo murmured back the word, "Lenore!"—
                    Merely this, and nothing more.   30

Back into the chamber turning, all my soul within me burning,
Soon I heard again a tapping somewhat louder than before.
"Surely," said I, "surely that is something at my window lattice;
Let me see, then, what thereat is, and this mystery explore —
Let my heart be still a moment and this mystery explore;—   35
                    'Tis the wind and nothing more!"

Open here I flung the shutter, when, with many a flirt and flutter,
In there stepped a stately raven of the saintly days of yore;
Not the least obeisance made he; not an instant stopped or stayed he;
But, with mien of lord or lady, perched above my chamber door —   40
Perched upon a bust of Pallas° just above my chamber door —
                    Perched, and sat, and nothing more.

Then this ebony bird beguiling my sad fancy into smiling,
By the grave and stern decorum of the countenance it wore,
"Though thy crest be shorn and shaven, thou," I said, "art sure no craven,

---

°*Pallas:* Athena, Greek goddess of wisdom.

Ghastly grim and ancient raven wandering from the Nightly shore —
Tell me what thy lordly name is on the Night's Plutonian° shore!"
    Quoth the raven, "Nevermore."

Much I marvelled this ungainly fowl to hear discourse so plainly,
Though its answer little meaning — little relevancy bore,   50
For we cannot help agreeing that no living human being
Ever yet was blessed with seeing bird above his chamber door —
Bird or beat upon the sculptured bust above his chamber door,
    With such name as "Nevermore."

But the raven, sitting lonely on the placid bust, spoke only   55
That one word, as if his soul in that one word he did outpour.
Nothing farther then he uttered — not a feather then he fluttered —
Till I scarcely more than muttered "Other friends have flown before —
On the morrow *he* will leave me, as my hopes have flown before."
    Then the bird said "Nevermore."   60

Startled at the stillness broken by reply so aptly spoken,
"Doubtless," said I, "what it utters is its only stock and store
Caught from some unhappy master whom unmerciful Disaster
Followed fast and followed faster till his songs one burden bore —   65
Till the dirges of his Hope that melancholy burden bore
    Of 'Never — nevermore.'"

But the raven still beguiling all my sad soul into smiling,
Straight I wheeled a cushioned seat in front of bird and bust and door;
Then, upon the velvet sinking, I betook myself to linking
Fancy unto fancy, thinking what this ominous bird of yore —   70
What this grim, ungainly, ghastly, gaunt, and ominous bird of yore
    Meant in croaking "Nevermore."

This I sat engaged in guessing, but no syllable expressing
To the fowl whose fiery eyes now burned into my bosom's core;
This and more I sat divining, with my head at ease reclining   75
On the cushion's velvet lining that the lamplight gloated o'er,
But whose velvet violet lining with the lamplight gloating o'er,
    she shall press, ah, nevermore!

Then, methought, the air grew denser, perfumed from an unseen
 censer
Swung by angels whose faint foot-falls tinkled on the tufted floor.   80
"Wretch," I cried, "thy God hath lent thee — by these angels he hath
 sent thee
Respite — respite and nepenthe° from thy memories of Lenore!

° *Plutonian:* dark; Pluto was the Greek god of the dead and ruler of the underworld.   ° *nepenthe:* a drug mentioned in the *Odessy* as a remedy for grief.

Quaff, oh quaff this kind nepenthe and forget this lost Lenore!"
                Quoth the raven, "Nevermore."

"Prophet!" said I, "thing of evil!— prophet still, if bird or devil!—   85
Whether Tempter sent, or whether tempest tossed thee here ashore,
Desolate, yet all undaunted, on this desert land enchanted—
On this home by Horror haunted — tell me truly, I implore—
Is there —*is* there balm in Gilead?°— tell me — tell me, I implore!"
                Quoth the raven, "Nevermore."   90

"Prophet!" said I, "thing of evil — prophet still, if bird or devil!
By that Heaven that bends above us — by that God we both adore —
Tell this soul with sorrow laden if, within the distant Aidenn,
It shall clasp a sainted maiden whom the angels name Lenore —
Clasp a rare and radiant maiden whom the angels name Lenore."   95
                Quoth the raven, "Nevermore."

"Be that word our sign of parting, bird or fiend!" I shrieked
    upstarting —
"Get thee back into the tempest and the Night's Plutonian shore!
Leave no black plume as a token of that lie thy soul hath spoken!
Leave my loneliness unbroken! — quit the bust above my door!   100
Take thy beak from out my heart, and take thy form from off my door!"
                Quoth the raven, "Nevermore."

And the raven, never fitting, still is sitting, still is sitting
On the pallid bust of Pallas just above my chamber door;
And his eyes have all the seeming of a demon's that is dreaming,   105
And the lamp-light o'er him streaming throws his shadow on the floor;
And my soul from out that shadow that lies floating on the floor
              Shall be lifted—nevermore!

Reading and Reacting

1. Who is the speaker in the poem? What is his state of mind? How does the raven mirror the speaker's mental state?
2. "The Raven" contains a good deal of alliteration. Identify some examples. How does this use of repeated consonant sounds help to convey the mood of the poem?
3. The speaker refers to the raven in a number of different ways. At one point, it is simply "an ebony bird" (line 42); at another, it is a "prophet" and "a thing of evil" (85). How else does the speaker characterize the raven?
4. **JOURNAL ENTRY** What is the symbolic significance of the raven? The repeated word "nevermore"? The bust of Pallas, the ancient Greek god of wisdom?

°*Gilead:* a region mentioned in the Bible; noted for its soothing ointments.

5. Critical Perspective According to Christoffer Nilsson, who maintains a Web site dedicated to the works of Poe, "The Raven" was composed with almost mathematical precision. When writing the stanza in which the interrogation of the raven reaches its climax (third stanza from the end), Poe wanted to make certain that no preceding stanza would "surpass this in rythmical effect":

> Poe then worked backwards from this stanza and used the word "Nevermore" in many different ways, so that even with the repetition of this word, it would not prove to be monotonous. Poe builds the tension in this poem up, stanza by stanza, but after the climaxing stanza he tears the whole thing down, and lets the narrator know that there is no meaning in searching for a moral in the raven's "nevermore."

Do you agree with Nilsson that it makes no sense to look for a moral in the raven's "nevermore"? What kind of moral, if any, do you think "Nevermore" implies for the speaker?

Related Works: "Rooming houses are old women" (p. 524), "The Eagle" (p. 557), "The Fish" (p. 651), "The Tyger" (p. 653)

Allegory

Allegory is a form of narrative that conveys a message or doctrine by using people, places, or things to stand for abstract ideas. **Allegorical figures,** each with a strict equivalent, form an **allegorical framework,** a set of ideas that conveys the allegory's message or lesson. Thus, the allegory takes place on two levels: a **literal level** that tells a story and a **figurative level** on which the allegorical figures in the story stand for ideas, concepts, and other qualities.

Like symbols, allegorical figures suggest other things. But unlike symbols, which have a range of possible meanings, allegorical figures can always be assigned specific meanings. (Because writers use allegory to instruct, they gain nothing by hiding its significance.) Thus, symbols open up possibilities for interpretation, whereas allegories tend to restrict possibilities.

Quite often an allegory involves a journey or an adventure, as in the case of Dante's *Divine Comedy*, which traces a journey through Hell, Purgatory, and Heaven. Within an allegory, everything can have meaning: the road on which the characters walk, the people they encounter, or a phrase that one of them repeats throughout the journey. Once you understand the allegorical framework, your main task is to see how the various elements fit within this system. Some allegorical poems can be relatively straightforward, but others can be so complicated that it takes a great deal of effort to unlock their meaning. In the following poem, a journey is central to the allegory.

CHRISTINA ROSSETTI (1830–1894)

Uphill (1861)

Does the road wind uphill all the way?
   Yes, to the very end.
Will the day's journey take the whole long day?
   From morn to night, my friend.

But is there for the night a resting-place?   5
   A roof for when the slow dark hours begin.
May not the darkness hide it from my face?
   You cannot miss that inn.

Shall I meet other wayfarers at night?
   Those who have gone before.   10
Then must I knock, or call when just in sight?
   They will not keep you standing at that door.

Shall I find comfort, travel-sore and weak?
   Of labor you shall find the sum.
Will there be beds for me and all who seek?   15
   Yea, beds for all who come.

"Uphill" uses a question-and-answer structure to describe a journey along an uphill road. Like the one described in John Bunyan's seventeenth-century allegory *The Pilgrim's Progress*, this is a spiritual journey, one that suggests the challenges a person faces throughout life. The day-and-night duration of the journey stands for life and death, and the inn at the end of the road stands for the grave, the final resting place.

FURTHER READING: Allegory

ADRIENNE RICH (1929–   )

Diving into the Wreck (1973)

First having read the book of myths,
and loaded the camera,
and checked the edge of the knife-blade,
I put on
the body-armor of black rubber   5
the absurd flippers
the grave and awkward mask.
I am having to do this
not like Cousteau with his
assiduous team   10

aboard the sun-flooded schooner
but here alone.

There is a ladder.
The ladder is always there
hanging innocently   15
close to the side of the schooner.
We know what it is for,
we who have used it.
Otherwise
it's a piece of maritime floss   20
some sundry equipment.

I go down.
Rung after rung and still
the oxygen immerses me
the blue light   25
the clear atoms
of our human air.
I go down.
My flippers cripple me,
I crawl like an insect down the ladder   30
and there is no one
to tell me when the ocean
will begin.

First the air is blue and then
it is bluer and then green and then   35
black I am blacking out and yet
my mask is powerful
it pumps my blood with power
the sea is another story
the sea is not a question of power   40
I have to learn alone
to turn my body without force
in the deep element.

And now: it is easy to forget
what I came for   45
among so many who have always
lived here
swaying their crenellated fans
between the reefs
and besides   50
you breathe differently down here.

I came to explore the wreck.
The words are purposes.

The words are maps.
I came to see the damage that was done   55
and the treasures that prevail.
I stroke the beam of my lamp
slowly along the flank
of something more permanent
than fish or weed   60

the thing I came for:
the wreck and not the story of the wreck
the thing itself and not the myth
the drowned face always staring
toward the sun   65
the evidence of damage
worn by salt and sway into this threadbare beauty
the ribs of the disaster
curving their assertion
among the tentative haunters.   70

This is the place.
And I am here, the mermaid whose dark hair
streams black, the merman in his armored body
We circle silently
about the wreck   75
we dive into the hold.
I am she: I am he
whose drowned face sleeps with open eyes
whose breasts still bear the stress
whose silver, copper, vermeil cargo lies   80
obscurely inside barrels
half-wedged and left to rot
we are the half-destroyed instruments
that once held to a course
the water-eaten log   85
the fouled compass

We are, I am, you are
by cowardice or courage
the one who finds our way
back to this scene   90
carrying a knife, a camera
a book of myths
in which
our names do not appear.

Reading and Reacting

1. On one level, this poem is about a deep-sea diver's exploration of a wrecked ship. What details suggest that the poet wants you to see something more?

2. Explain the allegorical figures presented in the poem. What, for example, might the diver and the wreck represent?

3. Does the poem contain any symbols? How can you tell they are symbols and not allegorical figures?

4. JOURNAL ENTRY In lines 62–63, the speaker says that she came for "the wreck and not the story of the wreck / the thing itself and not the myth." What do you think the speaker is really looking for?

5. CRITICAL PERSPECTIVE A number of critics have seen "Diving into the Wreck" as an attempt by Rich to reimagine or reinvent the myths of Western culture. Rachel Blau DuPlessis makes the following observation:

> In this poem of journey and transformation Rich is tapping the energies and plots of myth, while re-envisioning the content. While there is a hero, a quest, and a buried treasure, the hero is a woman; the quest is a critique of old myths; the treasure is knowledge. . . .

Why do you suppose Rich decided to "reinvent" myth?

Related Works: "Young Goodman Brown" (p. 302), "The Love Song of J. Alfred Prufrock" (p. 665)

Allusion

An **allusion** is a brief reference to a person, place, or event (fictional or actual) that readers are expected to recognize. Like symbols and allegories, allusions enrich a work by introducing associations from another context.

When poets use allusions, they assume that they and their readers have a common body of knowledge. If, when reading a poem, you come across a reference with which you are not familiar, take the time to look it up in a dictionary or an encyclopedia. As you have probably realized by now, your understanding of a poem may depend on your ability to interpret an unfamiliar reference.

Although most poets expect readers to recognize their references, some use allusions to exclude certain readers from their work. In his 1922 poem "The Waste Land," for example, T. S. Eliot alludes to historical events, ancient languages, and obscure literary works. He even includes a set of notes to accompany his poem, but they do little more than complicate an already difficult text. (As you might expect, initial critical response to this poem was mixed: some critics said that it was a work of genius, while others thought that it was pretentious.)

Allusions can come from any source: history, the arts, other works of literature, the Bible, current events, or even the personal life of the poet. In the following poem, the Nigerian poet and playwright Wole Soyinka alludes to several
contemporary political figures.

WOLE SOYINKA (1934–   )

Future Plans (1972)

The meeting is called
To odium: Forgers, framers
Fabricators Inter-
national. Chairman,
A dark horse, a circus nag turned blinkered sprinter   5

Mach Three
We rate him — one for the Knife
Two for 'iavelli, Three —
Breaking speed
Of the truth barrier by a swooping detention decree   10

Projects in view:
Mao Tse Tung in league
With Chiang Kai. Nkrumah
Makes a secret
Pact with Verwood, sworn by Hastings Banda.   15
Proven: Arafat
In flagrante cum
Golda Meir. Castro drunk
With Richard Nixon
Contraceptives stacked beneath the papal bunk . . .   20
                    . . . and more to come

This poem is structured like an agenda for a meeting. From the moment it an-
nounces that a meeting has been called "To odium" (a pun on "to *order*"), it is
clear that the poem will be a bitter political satire. Those in attendance are "Forgers, framers / Fabricators." The second stanza contains three allusions that shed
light on the character of the chairman. The first is to Mack the Knife, a petty
criminal in Bertolt Brecht and Kurt Weill's *Threepenny Opera* (1933). The second
is to Niccolò Machiavelli, whose book *The Prince* (1532) advocates the use of un-
scrupulous means to strengthen the state. The last is to the term *mach*, which denotes the speed of an airplane in relation to the speed of sound — mach one, two,
three, and so on. By means of these allusions, the poem implies that the meeting's
chairman has been chosen for his ability to engage in violence, to be ruthless, and
to break the "truth barrier"— that is, to lie.

The rest of the poem alludes to individuals involved in global politics around the time it was written, in 1972 — specifically, the politics of developing nations. According to the speaker, instead of fighting for the rights of the oppressed, these people consolidate their own political power by collaborating with those who oppose their positions. Thus, Mao Tse-tung, the communist leader of China, is "in league / With" Chiang Kai-shek, his old Nationalist Chinese enemy; Yassir Arafat, the leader of the Palestine Liberation Organization, is linked with Golda Meir, the prime minister of Israel; Kwame Nkrumah, the first president of Ghana, conspires with Hendrick Verwoerd, the prime minister of South Africa, assassinated in 1966; and United States president Richard Nixon gets drunk with Cuba's communist leader, Fidel Castro. These allusions suggest the self-serving nature of political alliances and the extreme disorder of world politics. The ideological juxtapositions show the interchangeability of various political philosophies, none of which has the answer to the world's problems. Whether the poem is satirizing the United Nations and its agenda, criticizing the tendency of politics to make strange bedfellows, or showing how corrupt politicians are, its allusions enable the poet to broaden his frame of reference and thus make the poem more meaningful to readers.

The next poem uses allusions to prominent literary figures, as well as to myth, to develop its theme.

WILLIAM MEREDITH (1919–   )

Dreams of Suicide (1980)

(in sorrowful memory of Ernest Hemingway, Sylvia Plath, and John Berryman)

I

I reach for the awkward shotgun not to disarm
you, but to feel the metal horn,
furred with the downy membrane of dream.
More surely than the unicorn,
you are the mythical beast.   5

II

Or I am sniffing an oven. On all fours
I am imitating a totemic animal
but she is not my totem or the totem
of my people, this is not my magic oven.

III

If I hold you tight by the ankles,   10
still you fly upward from the iron railing.
Your father made these wings,
after he made his own, and now from beyond
he tells you *fly down*, in the voice
my own father might say *walk, boy*.   15

This poem is dedicated to the memory of three writers who committed suicide. In each stanza, the speaker envisions in a dream the death of one of the writers. In the first stanza, he dreams of Ernest Hemingway, who killed himself with a shotgun. The speaker grasps the "metal horn" of Hemingway's shotgun and transforms Hemingway into a mythical beast who, like a unicorn, represents the rare, unique talent of the artist. In the second stanza, the speaker dreams of Sylvia Plath, who asphyxiated herself in a gas oven. He sees himself, like Plath, on his knees imitating an animal sniffing an oven. In the third stanza, the speaker dreams of John Berryman, who leaped to his death. Berryman is characterized as Icarus, a mythological figure who, along with his father Daedalus, fled Crete by building wings made of feathers and wax. Together they flew away; however, ignoring his father's warning, Icarus flew so close to the sun that the wax melted, and he fell to his death in the sea. Like Icarus, Berryman ignores the warning of his father and, like Daedalus, the speaker tries to stop Berryman. In this poem, then, the speaker uses allusions to make a point about the difficult lives of writers — and, perhaps, to convey his own empathy for those who could not survive the struggle to reconcile art and life.

FURTHER READING: Allusion

MAXINE KUMIN (1925–)

Where Any of Us

Where any of us is
going in tomorrow's reckless Lexus is
the elemental mystery: despite

instructions he left behind, Houdin-,°
i who could outwit   5
ropes and chains, padlocks and steamer

trunks, could extricate
himself from underwater metal crates,
could send forth, he was certain,

a message from the other side,   10
never cracked the curtain
and Mary Baker Eddy's° telephone

said to be hooked up in her crypt—
would it have been
innocence or arrogance,   15

such trust in the beyond?—
has, mythic, failed to ring. If
they knew the script

° *Houdini:* Famous magician (1874–1926) and escape artist who promised to communicate with his wife after he died.   ° *Mary Baker Eddy:* American religion leader (1821–1910) who founded the Christian Science Church (1879).

these two (God may be love
or not) they left, tightlipped   20
and unfulfilled.

As we will.

Reading and Reacting

1. What is the "elemental mystery" that Kumin refers to in her first stanza? What is "tomorrow's reckless Lexus"?

2. What is the significance of the allusions to Houdini and Mary Baker Eddy? How do these allusions help Kumin develop her theme?

3. What is the meaning of the poem's last line? What does Kumin achieve by visually isolating these three words as she does?

4. JOURNAL ENTRY Kumin was eighty years old when she published "Where Any of Us." How might her age have influenced her choice of subject matter and tone?

Related Works: "Cathedral" (p. 289), "I heard a Fly buzz — when I died" (p. 662), "Death Be Not Proud" (p. 663), *Tape* (p. 741), *Nine Ten* (p. 760)

Myth

A **myth** is a narrative that embodies — and in some cases helps to explain — the religious, philosophical, moral, and political values of a culture. Using gods and supernatural beings, myths try to make sense of occurrences in the natural world. (The term *myth* can also refer to a private belief system devised by an individual poet as well as to any fully realized fictitious setting in which a literary work takes place, such as the myths of William Faulkner's Yoknapatawpha County or of Lawrence Durrell's Alexandria.) Contrary to popular usage, *myth* does not mean "falsehood." In the broadest sense, myths are stories — usually whole groups of stories — that can be true or partly true as well as false; regardless of their degree of accuracy, however, myths frequently express the deepest beliefs of a culture. According to this definition, the *Iliad* and the *Odyssey*, the Koran, and the Old and New Testaments can all be regarded as myths.

The mythologist Joseph Campbell wrote that myths contain truths that link people together, whether they live today or lived 2,500 years ago. Myths attempt to explain phenomena that human beings care about regardless of when and where they live. It is not surprising, then, that myths frequently contain **archetypal images** — images that cut across cultural and racial boundaries and touch us at a very deep level. Many Greek myths illustrate this power. For example, when Orpheus descends into Hades to rescue his wife, Eurydice, he acts out the universal human desire to transcend death; and when Telemachus sets out in search of his father, Odysseus, he reminds readers that we all are lost children searching for parents. When Icarus ignores his father and flies too near the sun and when Pandora cannot resist looking into a box that she has been told not to open, we are reminded of the human weaknesses we all share.

When poets use myths, they are actually making allusions. They expect readers to bring to the poem the cultural, emotional, and ethical context of the myths to which they are alluding. At one time, when all educated individuals studied the Greek and Latin classics as well as the Bible and other religious texts, poets could be reasonably sure that readers would recognize the mythological allusions they made. Today, many readers are unable to understand the full significance of an allusion or its application within a poem. In this anthology, many of the poems are accompanied by notes, but these may not provide all the information you will need to understand each mythological allusion and thus to determine its significance within a poem. Occasionally, you may have to look elsewhere for answers, turning to dictionaries, encyclopedias, online information sites such as <http://www.answers.com>, or collections of myths such as the *New Larousse Encyclopedia of Mythology* or *Bulfinch's Mythology*.

Sometimes a poet alludes to a myth in a title; sometimes references to various myths appear throughout a poem; at other times, an entire poem focuses on a single myth. In each case, as in the following poem, the use of myth helps to develop the poem's theme.

COUNTEE CULLEN   (1903–1946)

Yet Do I Marvel   (1925)

I doubt not God is good, well-meaning, kind,
And did He stoop to quibble could tell why
The little buried mole continues blind,
Why flesh that mirrors Him must some day die,
Make plain the reason tortured Tantalus   5
Is baited by the fickle fruit, declare
If merely brute caprice dooms Sisyphus
To struggle up a never-ending stair.
Inscrutable His ways are, and immune
To catechism by a mind too strewn   10
With petty cares to slightly understand
What awful brain compels His awful hand.
Yet do I marvel at this curious thing:
To make a poet black, and bid him sing!

The speaker begins by affirming his belief in the benevolence of God but then questions why God engages in what appear to be capricious acts. As part of his catalog of questions, the speaker mentions Tantalus and Sisyphus, two figures from Greek mythology. Tantalus was a king who for his crimes was condemned to

Hades. There, he was forced to stand in a pool of water up to his chin. Overhead hung a tree branch laden with fruit. When Tantalus got thirsty and tried to drink, the level of the water dropped, and when he got hungry and reached for fruit, it moved just out of reach. Thus, Tantalus was doomed to be near what he most desired but forever unable to obtain it. Sisyphus also was condemned to Hades. For his disrespect to Zeus, he was sentenced to endless toil. Every day, Sisyphus pushed a boulder up a steep hill. Every time he neared the top, the boulder rolled back down the hill, and Sisyphus had to begin again. Like Tantalus, the speaker in "Yet Do I Marvel" cannot have what he wants; like Sisyphus, he is forced to toil in vain. He wonders why a well-meaning God would "make a poet black, and bid him sing" in a racist society that does not listen to his voice. Thus, the poet's two allusions to Greek mythology enrich the poem by connecting the suffering of the speaker to a universal drama that has been acted out again and again.

FURTHER READING: Myth

WILLIAM BUTLER YEATS (1865–1939)

Leda and the Swan (1924)

A sudden blow: the great wings beating still
Above the staggering girl, her thighs caressed
By the dark webs, her nape caught in his bill,
He holds her helpless breast upon his breast.

How can those terrified vague fingers push   5
The feathered glory from her loosening thighs?
And how can body, laid in that white rush,
But feel the strange heart beating where it lies?

A shudder in the loins engenders there
The broken wall, the burning roof and tower   10
And Agamemnon dead.
                    Being so caught up,
So mastered by the brute blood of the air,
Did she put on his knowledge with his power
Before the indifferent beak could let her drop?   15

Reading and Reacting

1. Research the myth of Leda. What event is described in this poem? What is the mythological significance of this event?
2. How is Leda portrayed? Why is the swan described as a "feathered glory" (line 6)? Why in the poem's last line is Leda dropped by his "indifferent beak"?
3. The third stanza refers to the Trojan War, which was indirectly caused by the event described in the poem. How does the allusion to the Trojan War help develop the theme of the poem?

4. JOURNAL ENTRY Does the poem answer the question asked in its last two lines? Explain.

5. CRITICAL PERSPECTIVE According to Richard Ellmann, this poem deals with "transcendence of opposites." The bird's "rape of the human, the coupling of god and woman, the moment at which one epoch ended and another began . . . in the act which included all these Yeats had the violent symbol for the transcendence of opposites which he needed."

What opposite or contrary forces exist in the myth of Leda and the swan? Do you think the poem implies that these forces can be reconciled?

Related Works: "Where Are You Going, Where Have You Been?" (p. 384), "Easter Wings" (p. 454), "The Second Coming" (p. 708)

W. H. AUDEN (1907–1973)

Musée des Beaux Arts (1940)

About suffering they were never wrong,
The Old Masters: how well they understood
Its human position; how it takes place
While someone else is eating or opening a window or just
    walking dully along
How, when the aged are reverently, passionately waiting   5
For the miraculous birth, there always must be
Children who did not specially want it to happen, skating
On a pond at the edge of the wood:
They never forgot
That even the dreadful martyrdom must run its course   10
Anyhow in a corner, some untidy spot
Where the dogs go on with their doggy life and the torturer's
    horse
Scratches its innocent behind on a tree.
In Brueghel's *Icarus*, for instance: how everything turns away
Quite leisurely from the disaster; the ploughman may   15
Have heard the splash, the forsaken cry,
But for him it was not an important failure; the sun shone
As it had to on the white legs disappearing into the green
Water; and the expensive delicate ship that must have seen
Something amazing, a boy falling out of the sky,   20
Had somewhere to get to and sailed calmly on.

Reading and Reacting

1. Reread the summary of the myth of Icarus on page 614. What does Auden's allusion to this myth contribute to the poem?

2. What point does the poet make by referring to the "Old Masters" (2)?

3. JOURNAL ENTRY Brueghel's painting *Landscape with the Fall of Icarus* is shown below. How does looking at this painting help you to understand the poem? To what specific details in the painting does the poet refer?

Brueghel, Pieter the Elder (1525?–1569). *Landscape with the Fall of Icarus.* Musée D'Art Ancien, Brussels, Belgium. © Scala/Art Resource, New York

Related Works: "The Lottery" (p. 274), "One day I wrote her name upon the strand" (p. 505), "Shall I compare thee to a summer's day?" (p. 521), "The Second Coming" (p. 708)

T. S. ELIOT   (1888–1965)

Journey of the Magi°   (1927)

"A cold coming we had of it,
Just the worst time of the year
For a journey, and such a long journey:
The ways deep and the weather sharp,
The very dead of winter." *   5
And the camels galled, sore-footed, refractory,
Lying down in the melting snow.
There were times we regretted

°*Magi:* The three wise men who ventured east to pay tribute to the infant Jesus (see Matthew 12.1–12).
*The five quoted lines are adapted from a passage in a 1622 Christmas Day sermon by Bishop Lancelot Andrewes.

The summer palaces on slopes, the terraces,
And the silken girls bringing sherbet.   10
Then the camel men cursing and grumbling
And running away, and wanting their liquor and women,
And the night-fires going out, and the lack of shelters,
And the cities hostile and the towns unfriendly
And the villages dirty and charging high prices: 15
A hard time we had of it.
At the end we preferred to travel all night,
Sleeping in snatches,
With the voices singing in our ears, saying
That this was all folly.   20

Then at dawn we came down to a temperate valley,
Wet, below the snow line, smelling of vegetation;
With a running stream and a water-mill beating the darkness,
And three trees° on the low sky,
And an old white horse° galloped away in the meadow.   25
Then we came to a tavern with vine-leaves over the lintel,
Six hands at an open door dicing for pieces of silver,°
And feet kicking the empty wine-skins.
But there was no information, and so we continued
And arrived at evening, not a moment too soon   30
Finding the place; it was (you may say) satisfactory.
All this was a long time ago, I remember,
And I would do it again, but set down
This set down
This: were we led all that way for   35
Birth or Death? There was a Birth, certainly,
We had evidence and no doubt. I had seen birth and death,
But had thought they were different; this Birth was
Hard and bitter agony for us, like Death, our death.
We returned to our places, these Kingdoms,   40
But no longer at ease here, in the old dispensation,
With an alien people clutching their gods.
I should be glad of another death.

Reading and Reacting

1. The speaker in the poem is one of the three wise men who came to pay tribute to the infant Jesus. In what way are his recollections unexpected? How
would you have expected him to react to the birth of Jesus?

°*three trees:* The three crosses at Calvary (see Luke 23.32–33).   °*white horse:* The horse ridden by the
conquering Christ in Revelation 19.11–16.   °*dicing . . . silver:* Echoes the soldiers dicing for Christ's
garments, as well as his betrayal by Judas Iscariot for thirty pieces of silver (see Matthew 27.35 and 26.14–16).

2. In what way do the mythical references in the poem allude to future events? Do you need to understand these allusions in order to appreciate the poem?

3. What does the speaker mean in line 41 when he says that the three wise men were "no longer at ease here, in the old dispensation"? What has changed for them? Why does the speaker say that he would be glad for "another death" (line 43)?

4. JOURNAL ENTRY How is this poem similar to and different from the story of the three wise men told in the New Testament (Matthew 2.1–18)?

5. CRITICAL PERSPECTIVE In an analysis of "Journey of the Magi," poet and critic Anthony Hecht discusses the most common interpretation of the poem, pointing to "a consensus of critical feeling about the tone of the conclusion of this poem, which, it is said, appears to border on despair and exhaustion of hope." Hecht, however, suspects that something more subtle is going on — namely, that Eliot is using the speaker of the poem to express his own imperfect acceptance of Christianity:

> Again, if I am right, about this, the poem might have a deeply personal meaning for Eliot himself, and might represent a kind of "confession," an acknowledgment that he had not yet perfectly embraced the fate to which he nominally adhered, that his imperfect spiritual status was, like the Magus's, that of a person whose faith was incomplete. . . .

Which of the two interpretations given above seems more plausible to you? Is the speaker of the poem wrestling with an incomplete faith, or is he experiencing "despair and exhaustion of hope"?

Related Works: "Araby" (p. 232), "Do not go gentle into that good night" (p. 627), "The World Is Too Much with Us" (p. 477), "On First Looking into Chapman's Homer" (p. 575), "The Love Song of J. Alfred Prufrock" (p. 665)

✔ **CHECKLIST**   **Writing about Symbol, Allegory, Allusion, Myth**

Symbol
Are there any symbols in the poem? What leads you to believe they are symbols?

Are these symbols conventional?

Are they universal or archetypal?

Are any symbols obscure or highly idiosyncratic?

What is the literal meaning of each symbol in the context of the poem?

Beyond its literal meaning, what else could each symbol suggest?

How does your interpretation of each symbol enhance your understanding of the poem?

---

continued on next page

Allegory
Is the poem an allegory?

Are there any allegorical figures within the poem? How can you tell?

What do the allegorical figures signify on a literal level?

What lesson does the allegory illustrate?

Allusion
Are there any allusions in the poem?

Do you recognize the names, places, historical events, or literary works to which the poet alludes?

In what way does each allusion deepen the poem's meaning? Does any allusion interfere with your understanding or enjoyment of the poem? If so, how?

Would the poem be more effective without a particular allusion?

Myth
What myths or mythological figures are alluded to?

How does the poem use myth to convey its meaning?

How faithful is the poem to the myth? Does the poet add material to the myth? Are any details from the original myth omitted? Is any information distorted? Why?

WRITING SUGGESTIONS: Symbol, Allegory, Allusion, Myth

1. Read "Aunt Jennifer's Tigers" (p. 555) and "Diving into the Wreck" (p. 606) by Adrienne Rich. Then, write an essay in which you discuss the similarities and differences in Rich's use of symbols in the two poems.

2. Many popular songs make use of allusion. Choose one or two popular songs that you know well, and analyze their use of allusion, paying particular attention to whether the allusions expand the impact and meaning of the song or create barriers to listeners' understanding.

3. Read the Emily Dickinson poem "Because I could not stop for Death —" (p. 661), and then write an interpretation of the poem, identifying its allegorical figures.

4. What applications do the lessons of myth have for life today? Analyze a poem in which myth is central, and then discuss how you might use myth to make generalizations about your own life.

5. Both William Butler Yeats's "Leda and the Swan" (p. 615) and H.D.'s "Helen" (p. 672) allude to the myth of Helen of Troy. Read about Helen of Troy in an encyclopedia or other reference work, and then write an essay in which you compare the poets' use of this myth in their poems.

CHAPTER 23

DISCOVERING THEMES IN POETRY

A poem should not mean
But be.

—Archibald MacLeish, *"Ars Poetica"*

A poem can be about anything, from the mysteries of the universe to poetry itself. Although no subject is really inappropriate for poetic treatment, certain conventional subjects — family, nature, love, war, death, the folly of human desires, and the inevitability of growing old — recur frequently.

A poem's *theme*, however, is more than its *subject*. In general terms, *theme* refers to the ideas that the poet explores, the concerns that the poem examines. More specifically, a poem's **theme** is its main point or idea. Poems "about death," for example, may examine the difficulty of facing one's own mortality, eulogize a friend, assert the need for the acceptance of life's cycles, or cry out against death's inevitability. Or, such poems may explore the **carpe diem theme** — the belief that life is brief, so we must seize the day.

In order to understand the theme of a poem, readers should consider its form, voice, language, images, allusions, sound — all of its individual elements. Together, these elements communicate the ideas that are important in the poem. Keep in mind, however, that a poem may not mean the same thing to every reader. Different readers will bring different backgrounds, attitudes, and experiences to a poem and will therefore see things in various ways. And, poets may approach the same subject in drastically different ways, emphasizing different elements as they view the subject matter from their own unique perspectives. Ultimately, there are as many different themes, and ways to approach these themes, as there are writers (and readers) of poetry.

Poems about Parents

Although a poet's individual experience may be vastly different from the experiences of his or her readers, certain ideas seem universal in poems about parents. On the one hand, such poems can express positive sentiments: love, joy, wistfulness, nostalgia, and gratitude for childhood's happy memories and unconditional

621

love. On the other hand, they may express negative emotions: anger, frustration, resentment, regret, and emotional distance. When they write about parents, poets may be curious or apathetic, remorseful or grateful; they may idealize parents or be puzzled by them. Regardless of the particulars of the poem's specific theme, virtually all poems about parents address one general concept: the influence of a parent over his or her child.

For as long as poets have been writing poetry, their personal experiences (and childhoods) have influenced their subject matter and their poems. In American poetry, poems about parents became more common with the advent of **confessionalism,** a movement in the mid-1950s in which poets began to write subjective verse about their personal experiences. Poems in Robert Lowell's *Life Studies* and W. D. Snodgrass's *Heart's Needle* both addressed the positive and negative aspects of the poets' families (including their parents and children), thus opening the door for an influx of poems about similar themes.

The poems in this section all deal with issues related to parents and family, but their styles, voices, and focuses are very different. Sometimes the speakers' voices express ambivalence, communicating conventional sentiments of love and admiration alongside perplexity, frustration, and even anger. This ambivalence is apparent in Theodore Roethke's "My Papa's Waltz" and Robert Hayden's "Those Winter Sundays," as adult speakers struggle to understand their fathers' long-ago behavior. In Edna St. Vincent Millay's "The courage that my mother had" and Seamus Heaney's "Digging," the speakers are more positive, finding traits in their parents that they would like to emulate. Raymond Carver's "Photograph of My Father in His Twenty-Second Year" is a meditation on visual images of the speaker's father, while Wanda Coleman's "Dear Mama" is an elegiac poem that addresses the inevitable cycles of life, and Mitsuye Yamada's "The Night Before Good-bye" focuses on a mother's quiet sacrifice. Finally, Dylan Thomas's "Do not go gentle into that good night" confronts the death of a parent.

THEODORE ROETHKE   (1908–1963)

My Papa's Waltz   (1948)

The whiskey on your breath
Could make a small boy dizzy;
But I hung on like death:
Such waltzing was not easy.

We romped until the pans   5
Slid from the kitchen shelf;
My mother's countenance
Could not unfrown itself.

The hand that held my wrist
Was battered on one knuckle;   10

At every step you missed
My right ear scraped a buckle.

You beat time on my head
With a palm caked hard by dirt,
Then waltzed me off to bed   15
Still clinging to your shirt.

ROBERT HAYDEN   (1913–1980)

Those Winter Sundays   (1962)

Sundays too my father got up early
and put his clothes on in the blueblack cold,
then with cracked hands that ached
from labor in the weekday weather made
banked fires blaze. No one ever thanked him.   5

I'd wake and hear the cold splintering, breaking.
When the rooms were warm, he'd call,
and slowly I would rise and dress,
fearing the chronic angers of that house,

Speaking indifferently to him,   10
who had driven out the cold
and polished my good shoes as well.
What did I know, what did I know
of love's austere and lonely offices?

EDNA ST. VINCENT MILLAY   (1892–1950)

The courage that my mother had   (1954)

The courage that my mother had
Went with her, and is with her still:
Rock from New England quarried;
New granite in a granite hill.

The golden brooch my mother wore   5
She left behind for me to wear;
I have no thing I treasure more:
Yet, it is something I could spare.

Oh, if instead she'd left to me
The thing she took into the grave!—   10
That courage like a rock, which she
Has no more need of, and I have.

SEAMUS HEANEY * (1939–   )

Digging (1966)

Between my finger and my thumb
The squat pen rests; snug as a gun.

Under my window, a clean rasping sound
When the spade sinks into gravelly ground:
My father, digging. I look down   5

Till his straining rump among the flowerbeds
Bends low, comes up twenty years away
Stooping in rhythm through potato drills
Where he was digging.

The coarse boot nestled on the lug, the shaft   10
Against the inside knee was levered firmly.
He rooted out tall tops, buried the bright edge deep
To scatter new potatoes that we picked
Loving their cool hardness in our hands.

By God, the old man could handle a spade.   15
Just like his old man.

My grandfather cut more turf in a day
Than any other man on Toner's bog.
Once I carried him milk in a bottle
Corked sloppily with paper. He straightened up   20
To drink it, then fell to right away

Nicking and slicing neatly, heaving sods
Over his shoulder, going down and down
For the good turf. Digging.

The cold smell of potato mould, the squelch and slap   25
Of soggy peat, the curt cuts of an edge
Through living roots awaken in my head.
But I've no spade to follow men like them.

Between my finger and my thumb
The squat pen rests.   30
I'll dig with it.

---

* *Seamus Heaney:* Heaney received the 1995 Nobel Prize in Literature.

RAYMOND CARVER (1938–1988)

Photograph of My Father in His Twenty-Second Year (1983)

October. Here in this dank, unfamiliar kitchen
I study my father's embarrassed young man's face.
Sheepish grin, he holds in one hand a string
of spiny yellow perch, in the other
a bottle of Carlsbad beer.   5

In jeans and denim shirt, he leans
against the front fender of a 1934 Ford.
He would like to pose bluff and hearty for his posterity,
wear his old hat cocked over his ear.
All his life my father wanted to be bold.   10

But the eyes give him away, and the hands
that limply offer the string of dead perch
and the bottle of beer. Father, I love you,
yet how can I say thank you, I who can't hold my liquor either,
and don't even know the places to fish?   15

MITSUYE YAMADA (1923–   )

The Night Before Good-bye (1976)

Mama is mending
my underwear
while my brothers sleep.
Her husband taken away by the FBI
one son lured away by the Army   5
now another son and daughter
lusting for the free world outside.
She must let go.
The war goes on.
She will take one still small son   10
and join Papa in internment°
to make a family.
Still sewing
squinting in the dim light
in room C barrack 4 block 4   15

°*internment:* Shortly after the attack on Pearl Harbor, President Roosevelt ordered that all people of Japanese ancestry — even American citizens — be removed from the West Coast. About 112,000 people were relocated to "internment camps," where they remained until after the war's end.

she whispers
Remember
keep your underwear
in good repair
in case of accident   20
don't bring shame
on us.

WANDA COLEMAN (1946 –   )

Dear Mama (1983)

when did we become friends?
it happened so gradual i didn't notice
maybe i had to get my run out first
take a big bite of the honky world and choke on it
maybe that's what has to happen with some uppity youngsters   5
if it happens at all

and now
the thought stark and irrevocable
of being here without you   10
shakes me

beyond love, fear, regret or anger
into that realm children go
who want to care for/protect their parents
as if they could   15
and sometimes the lucky ones do

into the realm of making every moment
important
laughing as though laughter wards off death
each word given   20
received like spanish eight°

treasure to bury within
against that shadow day
when it will be the only coin i possess
with which to buy peace of mind   25

° *spanish eight:* A nickname given to the original Spanish peso, which was minted with real silver in the Americas and transported by ship back to Spain, making the cargo a tempting target for pirates. The Spanish Eight was the most widely used international trade coin.

DYLAN THOMAS   (1914–1953)

Do not go gentle into that good night* (1952)

Do not go gentle into that good night,
Old age should burn and rave at close of day;
Rage, rage against the dying of the light.

Though wise men at their end know dark is right,
Because their words had forked no lightning they   5
Do not go gentle into that good night.

Good men, the last wave by, crying how bright
Their frail deeds might have danced in a green bay,
Rage, rage against the dying of the light.

Wild men who caught and sang the sun in flight,   10
And learn, too late, they grieved it on its way,
Do not go gentle into that good night.

Grave men, near death, who see with blinding sight
Blind eyes could blaze like meteors and be gay,
Rage, rage against the dying of the light.   15

And you, my father, there on the sad height,
Curse, bless, me now with your fierce tears, I pray,
Do not go gentle into that good night.
Rage, rage against the dying of the light.

Reading and Reacting: Poems about Parents

1. What is each speaker's attitude toward his or her parent?
2. Which words, images, and figures of speech have positive associations? Which help to create a negative impression?
3. How would you characterize each poem's tone? For example, is the tone sentimental? Playful? Angry? Resentful? Regretful?
4. What problems associated with parent-child relationships are explored in each poem?
5. What does each poem say about the parent? What does it reveal about the child?
6. What is each poem's central theme?

Related Works: "Sleepy Time Gal" (p. 86), "A Primer for the Punctuation of Heart Disease" (p. 88), "Two Kinds" (p. 416), "Seventeen Syllables" (p. 425), "Daddy" (p. 532)

---

*This poem was written during the last illness of the poet's father.

Poems about Nature

In his 1913 poem "Trees," the American poet Joyce Kilmer neatly summarized the symbiotic relationship that has always existed between poetry and nature: "I think that I shall never see / A poem lovely as a tree." Poets have always found inspiration in the beauty, majesty, and grandeur of the natural world; in fact, some forms of poetry are dedicated solely to the subject of nature. For example, a **pastoral** is a literary form that deals nostalgically with a simple rural life. Many of the early Greek and Roman pastorals were about shepherds who passed the time writing about love while watching their flocks. In these poems, the shepherd's life was idealized. Thus, the pastoral tradition celebrates simple times and the beauty of the rural life. Similarly, an **idyll,** a short work in verse or prose (or a painting or a piece of music), depicts simple pastoral or rural scenes, often in idealized terms.

Certain literary movements also focused on the subject of nature. The **Romantic** poets, for example, found in nature a mirror for their own beliefs and sense of identity. They believed that only the sweeping grandeur of nature could reflect the comparable grandeur of humanity as well as a sense of the infinite and the transcendental. Later, the American **Transcendentalists,** including Ralph Waldo Emerson and Henry David Thoreau, examined the relationships between philosophy, religion, and nature. In *Walden,* for example, Thoreau wrote about the pleasures and rewards of withdrawing from mainstream life in order to live simply in the woods.

While all poems about nature deal with the same general subject, their approaches, and their focuses, can differ greatly. Poems "about nature" may praise the beauty of nature, assert the superiority of its simplest creatures, consider its evanescence, or mourn its destruction. In this section, Romantic poet William Wordsworth's "I wandered lonely as a cloud" extols the virtue of nature and highlights the value of participating in its beauty. In "Summer," Christina Rosetti writes in lighthearted terms of the beauty of the season, while in "The Windhover," Gerard Manley Hopkins celebrates the divinity of God's natural kingdom. In Robert Frost's "Birches," the speaker recalls the childhood enjoyment of climbing trees and longs for the simplicity of those times; in William Stafford's "Traveling through the Dark," the speaker presents human beings as adversaries of nature and its other creatures. Joy Harjo's "Morning Song" is a lyrical ode that celebrates elements of the natural world. Finally, Richard Wilbur's "In Trackless Woods" praises the natural and unforced logic and symmetry of the wilderness within a "civilized" world.

WILLIAM WORDSWORTH (1770–1850)

I wandered lonely as a cloud (1807)

I wandered lonely as a cloud
    That floats on high o'er vales and hills,
When all at once I saw a crowd,

A host, of golden daffodils,
Beside the lake, beneath the trees,   5
Fluttering and dancing in the breeze.

Continuous as the stars that shine
    And twinkle on the milky way,
They stretched in never-ending line
    Along the margin of a bay: 10
Ten thousand saw I at a glance,
Tossing their heads in sprightly dance.

The waves beside them danced; but they
    Out-did the sparkling waves in glee;
A poet could not but be gay,   15
    In such a jocund company;
I gazed — and gazed — but little thought
What wealth the show to me had brought:

For oft, when on my couch I lie
    In vacant or in pensive mood,   20
They flash upon that inward eye
    Which is the bliss of solitude;
And then my heart with pleasure fills,
And dances with the daffodils.

CHRISTINA ROSSETTI (1830–1894)

Summer

Winter is cold-hearted,
    Spring is yea and nay,
Autumn is a weathercock
        Blown every way.
        Summer days for me   5
When every leaf is on its tree;

    When Robin's not a beggar,
    And Jenny Wren's a bride,
And larks hang singing, singing, singing
    Over the wheat-fields wide,   10
    And anchored lilies ride,
    And the pendulum spider
    Swings from side to side;

And blue-black beetles transact business,
    And gnats fly in a host,   15

And furry caterpillars hasten
  That no time be lost
And moths grow fat and thrive,
  And ladybirds arrive

Before green apples blush,   20
Before green nuts embrown,
Why one day in the country
Is worth a month in town;
Is worth a day and a year

Of the dusty, musty, lag-last fashion   25
That days drone elsewhere.

GERARD MANLEY HOPKINS (1844–1889)

The Windhover° (1877)

To Christ Our Lord

I caught this morning morning's minion,° king-
    dom of daylight's dauphin, dapple-dawn-drawn Falcon, in
        his riding
Of the rolling level underneath him steady air, and striding
High there, how he rung upon the rein° of a wimpling° wing
In his ecstasy! then off, off forth on swing,   5
    As a skate's heel sweeps smooth on a bow-bend: the hurl and
        gliding
Rebuffed the big wind. My heart in hiding
Stirred for a bird,— the achieve of, the mastery of the thing!
Brute beauty and valor and act, oh, air, pride, plume, here
    Buckle! and the fire that breaks from thee then, a billion   10
Times told lovelier, more dangerous, O my chevalier!
    No wonder of it: shéer plód, makes plow down sillion°
Shine, and blue-bleak embers, ah my dear,
    Fall, gall themselves, and gash gold-vermilion.

°*Windhover:* A kestrel, a European falcon able to hover in the air with its head to the wind.   °*minion:* Favorite.
°*rung upon the rein:* A horse is "rung upon the rein" when it circles at the end of a long rein held by the trainer.
°*wimpling:* Rippling.   °*sillion:* The ridge between two furrows.

ROBERT FROST   (1874–1963)

Birches   (1915)

When I see birches bend to left and right
Across the lines of straighter darker trees,
I like to think some boy's been swinging them.
But swinging doesn't bend them down to stay
As ice-storms do. Often you must have seen them   5
Loaded with ice a sunny winter morning
After a rain. They click upon themselves
As the breeze rises, and turn many-colored
As the stir cracks and crazes their enamel.
Soon the sun's warmth makes them shed crystal shells   10
Shattering and avalanching on the snow-crust —
Such heaps of broken glass to sweep away
You'd think the inner dome of heaven had fallen.
They are dragged to the withered bracken by the load,
And they seem not to break; though once they are bowed   15
So low for long, they never right themselves:
You may see their trunks arching in the woods
Years afterwards, trailing their leaves on the ground
Like girls on hands and knees that throw their hair
Before them over their heads to dry in the sun.   20
But I was going to say when Truth broke in
With all her matter-of-fact about the ice-storm
I should prefer to have some boy bend them
As he went out and in to fetch the cows—
Some boy too far from town to learn baseball,   25
Whose only play was what he found himself,
Summer or winter, and could play alone.
One by one he subdued his father's trees
By riding them down over and over again
Until he took the stiffness out of them,   30
And not one but hung limp, not one was left
For him to conquer. He learned all there was
To learn about not launching out too soon
And so not carrying the tree away
Clear to the ground. He always kept his poise   35
To the top branches, climbing carefully
With the same pains you use to fill a cup
Up to the brim, and even above the brim.
Then he flung outward, feet first, with a swish,
Kicking his way down through the air to the ground.   40

So was I once myself a swinger of birches.
And so I dream of going back to be.
It's when I'm weary of considerations,
And life is too much like a pathless wood
Where your face burns and tickles with the cobwebs   45
Broken across it, and one eye is weeping
From a twig's having lashed across it open.
I'd like to get away from earth awhile
And then come back to it and begin over.
May no fate willfully misunderstand me   50
And half grant what I wish and snatch me away
Not to return. Earth's the right place for love:
I don't know where it's likely to go better.
I'd like to go by climbing a birch tree,
And climb black branches up a snow-white trunk   55
Toward Heaven, till the tree could bear no more,
But dipped its top and set me down again.
That would be good both going and coming back.
One could do worse than be a swinger of birches.

WILLIAM STAFFORD (1914–1993)

Traveling through the Dark (1962)

Traveling through the dark I found a deer
dead on the edge of the Wilson River road.
It is usually best to roll them into the canyon:
that road is narrow; to swerve might make more dead.

By glow of the tail-light I stumbled back of the car   5
and stood by the heap, a doe, a recent killing;
she had stiffened already, almost cold.
I dragged her off; she was large in the belly.

My fingers touching her side brought me the reason —
her side was warm; her fawn lay there waiting,   10
alive, still, never to be born.
Beside that mountain road I hesitated.

The car aimed ahead its lowered parking lights;
under the hood purred the steady engine.
I stood in the glare of the warm exhaust turning red;   15
around our group I could hear the wilderness listen.

I thought hard for us all — my only swerving —
then pushed her over the edge into the river.

JOY HARJO (1951–   )

Morning Song (2001)

The red dawn now is rearranging the earth
Thought by thought
Beauty by beauty
Each sunrise a link in the ladder
The ladder the backbone   5
Of shimmering deity
Child stirring in the web of your mother
Do not be afraid
Old man turning to walk through the door
Do not be afraid   10

RICHARD WILBUR (1921–   )

In Trackless Woods (2003)

In trackless woods, it puzzled me to find
Four great rock maples seemingly aligned,
As if they had been set out in a row
Before some house a century ago,
To edge the property and lend some shade.   5
I looked to see if ancient wheels had made
Old ruts to which these trees can parallel,
But there were none, so far as I could tell —
There'd been no roadway. Nor could I find the square
Depression of a cellar anywhere,   10
And so I tramped on further, to survey
Amazing patterns in a hornbeam spray
Or spirals in a pinecone, under trees
Not subject to our stiff geometries.

Reading and Reacting: Poems about Nature

1. What do you think inspired the poem?

2. What is the speaker's attitude toward nature? Is nature seen as a benevolent, comforting, threatening, awe-inspiring, or overwhelming force?

3. Which words, images, and figures of speech in the poem have positive associations? Which help to create a negative impression of nature?

4. How would you characterize each poem's tone? For example, is the speaker hopeful? Thoughtful? Humbled? Frightened?

5. Is the natural world the poem's true subject, or is it just the setting? Explain.

6. What is each poem's central theme?

Related Works: "Doe Season" (p. 327), "Greasy Lake" (p. 359), "Blackberry Eating" (p. 564), "Four Haiku" (p. 584)

Poems about Love

Poetry has long been regarded as a romantic genre, as evidenced by the abundance of sentimental verse found in countless Valentine's Day cards. In fact, the history of poetry includes an extensive list of love poems, almost certainly beginning with the earliest poets privately expressing their feelings and desire. Over time, love poems found their way into the public realm. One of the earliest examples is the Bible's *Song of Solomon*, which is an extended love poem (though some critics argue that the "beloved" is not a woman but rather a metaphor for religion). Other examples can be found in the work of Catullus, a Roman poet who wrote a cycle of twenty-five love poems to a mysterious woman he called Lesbia.

Epic medieval poems such as *Beowulf*, which focused on battles and heroic characters, were eventually supplanted by romantic adventures such as the Arthurian legends, which included the idea of "courtly love." In these poems, a chivalrous protagonist performs gallant deeds to win the hand of the fair maiden who has captured his heart. Examples of courtly love poems include *Sir Gawain and the Green Knight* and *Le Morte d'Arthur*. During the Renaissance, a more personal style developed, and poems became vehicles for demonstrating a poet's amorous feelings. Often cloaked in metaphor, simile, or other figures of speech, poems expressed feelings of love in numerous forms. Examples of Renaissance love poems include many of Shakespeare's sonnets, as well as Christopher Marlowe's "The Passionate Shepherd to His Love" (p. 685), a poem in the pastoral tradition, which was answered by Sir Walter Raleigh's "The Nymph's Reply to the Shepherd" (p. 693).

Although the Renaissance marked a high point in the development of the love poem, love has remained a constant theme in poetry regardless of the literary fads and trends of the day. In fact, in every literary movement — from the seventeenth-century metaphysical poets through today's slam poetry — one can find love poems written in the movement's characteristic style and form.

In each of the poems in this section, the poets address the subject of love in their own styles and voices. Robert Browning and Elizabeth Barrett Browning (who were married to each other) are represented with traditional love poems, including "How Do I Love Thee?" which is one of the most often quoted poems in the English language. In Edna St. Vincent Millay's "What Lips My Lips Have Kissed," the speaker reminisces about her past lovers with a mixture of nostalgia and wistfulness. On a lighter note, Dorothy Parker's "General Review of the Sex Situation" is a tongue-in-cheek description of the differences between the sexes.

ROBERT BROWNING (1812–1889)

Meeting at Night (1845)

The gray sea and the long black land;
And the yellow half-moon large and low;
And the startled little waves that leap
In fiery ringlets from their sleep,
As I gain the cove with pushing prow,   5
And quench its speed i' the slushy sand.

Then a mile of warm sea-scented beach;
Three fields to cross till a farm appears;
A tap at the pane, the quick sharp scratch
And blue spurt of a lighted match,   10
And a voice less loud, through its joys and fears,
Than the two hearts beating each to each!

Parting at Morning (1845)

Round the cape of a sudden came the sea,
And the sun looked over the mountain's rim:
And straight was a path of gold for him,
And the need of a world of men for me.

ELIZABETH BARRETT BROWNING (1806–1861)

How Do I Love Thee? (1850)

How do I love thee? Let me count the ways.
I love thee to the depth and breadth and height
My soul can reach, when feeling out of sight
For the ends of being and ideal grace.
I love thee to the level of every day's   5
Most quiet need, by sun and candle-light.
I love thee freely, as men strive for right.
I love thee purely, as they turn from praise.
I love thee with the passion put to use
In my old griefs, and with my childhood's faith.   10
I love thee with a love I seemed to lose
With my lost saints. I love thee with the breath,
Smiles, tears, of all my life; and, if God choose,
I shall but love thee better after death.

EDNA ST. VINCENT MILLAY (1892–1950)

What Lips My Lips Have Kissed (1923)

What lips my lips have kissed, and where, and why,
I have forgotten, and what arms have lain
Under my head till morning; but the rain
Is full of ghosts tonight, that tap and sigh
Upon the glass and listen for reply,   5
And in my heart there stirs a quiet pain
For unremembered lads that not again
Will turn to me at midnight with a cry.
Thus in the winter stands the lonely tree,
Nor knows what birds have vanished one by one,   10
Yet knows its boughs more silent than before:
I cannot say what loves have come and gone,
I only know that summer sang in me
A little while, that in me sings no more.

DOROTHY PARKER (1893–1967)

General Review of the Sex Situation (1933)

Woman wants monogamy;
Man delights in novelty.
Love is woman's moon and sun;
Man has other forms of fun.

Woman lives but in her lord;   5
Count to ten, and man is bored.
With this the gist and sum of it,
What earthly good can come of it?

Reading and Reacting: Poems about Love

1. What general ideas about love are expressed in each poem?
2. What conventional images and figures of speech does each speaker use to express his or her feelings of love?
3. Does any speaker use any unexpected (or even shocking) images or figures of speech?
4. How would you characterize the tone of each poem? For example, is the tone happy? Sad? Celebratory? Regretful?
5. What does each poem reveal about the speaker? About the person to whom the poem is addressed?
6. What is each poem's central theme?

Related Works: "Love and Other Catastrophes: A Mix Tape" (p. 98), "The Storm" (p. 158), "Living in Sin" (p. 494), "A Valediction: Forbidding Mourning" (p. 530), "To My Dear and Loving Husband" (p. 536), "you fit into me" (p. 541), "There Is a Garden in Her Face" (p. 656), *The Brute* (p. 723)

Poems about War

In poetry, war is as ancient a theme as love and nature. In fact, the earliest poems, including Homer's *Iliad* and *Odyssey* and Virgil's *Aeneid,* have at their centers epic battles and struggles. These battles were described in rhymed verse so they could be remembered and passed down from one generation to the next. In this way, the history of humanity and the history of poetry are woven into the recorded history of war.

Early epic poems reflected the belief that war was a noble and gallant endeavor, with soldiers and citizens alike fighting for a variety of causes, including religion and territory. These poems idolized the heroes of the wars and celebrated their accomplishments in battle. Over time, as war became increasingly modern and complex, poems about war began to express deep moral and philosophical ambiguities. One of the best-known of these poems was "Dulce et Decorum Est" (p. 638), written toward the end of World War I by Wilfred Owen, a soldier who was killed on the Western Front in 1918. The poem, which includes graphic images of war, ends with a bitterly ironic quotation that summarizes the mentality that fuels war: "It is sweet and fitting to die for one's country."

Of course, not all modern poems about war are poems of protest. Rupert Brooke, a contemporary of Wilfred Owen, wrote "The Soldier," an elegy that celebrates the nobility of fighting for the sake of one's beloved country. Robert Lowell's "For the Union Dead," written in 1959, is an elegy for Colonel Robert Gould Shaw, who led a regiment of African-American soldiers who fought and died for the Union Army during the Civil War.

Although war poems tend to focus on death and destruction, in modern poems, the victims of war are not always soldiers. In the post–World War II years, enemies (like victims) were not as clearly defined as they had been in the past. After all, both the Korean War and the Vietnam War were waged not just against another nation but against the threat of Communism. The war in Vietnam unfolded before the American people on their television screens, and as a result, many Americans questioned the war's goals. This skepticism carried over into poems about the war, as seen in Denise Levertov's "What Were They Like?" (a call and response poem that asks questions about the people in Vietnam in an effort to heighten their humanity and diminish their identity as "the enemy") and in Yusef Komunyakaa's "Facing It," in which a Vietnam veteran visits the Vietnam War Memorial in Washington.

The post-Vietnam years have seen troops from various nations take part in conflicts around the globe. The final poem in this section, Wislawa Szymborska's

"The End and the Beginning," addresses the onerous job of cleaning up what is left behind in the aftermath of war.

RUPERT BROOKE   (1887–1915)

The Soldier   (1915)

If I should die, think only this of me;
   That there's some corner of a foreign field
That is forever England. There shall be
   In that rich earth a richer dust concealed;
A dust whom England bore, shaped, made aware,   5
   Gave, once, her flowers to love, her ways to roam,
A body of England's breathing English air,
   Washed by the rivers, blest by suns of home.

And think, this heart, all evil shed away,
   A pulse in the eternal mind, no less   10
      Gives somewhere back the thoughts by England given;
Her sights and sounds; dreams happy as her day;
   And laughter, learnt of friends; and gentleness,
      In hearts at peace, under an English heaven.

WILFRED OWEN   (1893–1918)

Dulce et Decorum Est°   (1920)

Bent double, like old beggars under sacks,
Knock-kneed, coughing like hags, we cursed through sludge,
Till on the haunting flares we turned our backs
And towards our distant rest began to trudge.
Men marched asleep. Many had lost their boots   5
But limped on, blood-shod. All went lame; all blind;
Drunk with fatigue; deaf even to the hoots
Of tired, outstripped Five-Nines° that dropped behind.

Gas! GAS Quick, boys! — An ecstasy of fumbling,
Fitting the clumsy helmets just in time;   10
But someone still was yelling out and stumbling
And flound'ring like a man in fire or lime . . .
Dim, through the misty panes and thick green light,
As under a green sea, I saw him drowning.

°*Dulce et Decorum Est:* "The title and last two lines are from Horace, *Odes* 3.2: "Sweet and fitting it is to die for one's country."   °*Five-Nines:* Shells that explode on impact and release poison gas.

In all my dreams, before my helpless sight,   15
He plunges at me, guttering, choking, drowning.

If in some smothering dreams you too could pace
Behind the wagon that we flung him in,
And watch the white eyes writhing in his face,
His hanging face, like a devil's sick of sin;   20
If you could hear, at every jolt, the blood
Come gargling from the froth-corrupted lungs,
Obscene as cancer, bitter as the cud
Of vile, incurable sores on innocent tongues, —
My friend, you would not tell with such high zest   25
To children ardent for some desperate glory,
The old Lie: Dulce et decorum est
Pro patria mori.

ROBERT LOWELL (1917–1977)

For the Union Dead (1959)

"Relinquunt omnia servare rem publicam."°

The old South Boston Aquarium stands
in a Sahara of snow now. Its broken windows are boarded.
The bronze weathervane cod has lost half its scales.
The airy tanks are dry.

Once my nose crawled like a snail on the glass;   5
my hand tingled
to burst the bubbles
drifting from the noses of the cowed, compliant fish.

My hand draws back. I often sigh still
for the dark downward and vegetating kingdom   10
of the fish and reptile. One morning last March,
I pressed against the new barbed and galvanized

fence on the Boston Common. Behind their cage,
yellow dinosaur steamshovels were grunting
as they cropped up tons of mush and grass   15
to gouge their underworld garage.

Parking spaces luxuriate like civic
sandpiles in the heart of Boston.

°*Relinquunt omnia servare rem publicam:* "They gave up everything to preserve the Republic" (Latin). A monument in Boston Common bears a similar form of this quotation. Designed by Augustus Saint-Gaudens, the monument is dedicated to Colonel Robert Gould Shaw and the African-American troops he commanded during a Civil War battle at Fort Wagner, South Carolina, on July 18, 1863.

A girdle of orange, Puritan-pumpkin colored girders
braces the tingling Statehouse,   20

shaking over the excavations, as it faces Colonel Shaw
and his bell-cheeked Negro infantry
on St. Gauden's shaking Civil War relief,
propped by a plant splint against the garage's earthquake.

Two months after marching through Boston,   25
half the regiment was dead;
at the dedication,
William James° could almost hear the bronze Negroes breathe.

Their monument sticks like a fishbone
in the city's throat.   30
Its Colonel is as lean
as a compass-needle.

He has an angry wrenlike vigilance,
a greyhound's gentle tautness;
he seems to wince at pleasure,   35
and suffocate for privacy.

He is out of bounds now. He rejoices in man's lovely,
peculiar power to choose life and die —
when he leads his black soldiers to death,
he cannot bend his back.   40

On a thousand small town New England greens,
the old white churches hold their air
of sparse, sincere rebellion; frayed flags
quilt the graveyards of the Grand Army of the Republic.

The stone statues of the abstract Union Soldier   45
grow slimmer and younger each year —
wasp-waisted, they doze over muskets
and muse through their sideburns . . .

Shaw's father wanted no monument
except the ditch,   50
where his son's body was thrown
and lost with his "niggers."

The ditch is nearer.
There are no statues for the last war here;
on Boylston Street, a commercial photograph   55
shows Hiroshima boiling

° *William James:* Harvard psychologist and philosopher (1842–1910), often called the father of modern psychology.

over a Mosler Safe,° the "Rock of Ages"
that survived the blast. Space is nearer.
When I crouch to my television set,
the drained faces of Negro school-children rise like balloons.   60

Colonel Shaw
is riding on his bubble,
he waits
for the blessed break.

The Aquarium is gone. Everywhere,   65
giant finned cars nose forward like fish;
a savage servility
slides by on grease.

DENISE LEVERTOV   (1923–1997)

What Were They Like?   (1966)

1) Did the people of Viet Nam
 use lanterns of stone?
2) Did they hold ceremonies
 to reverence the opening of buds?
3) Were they inclined to rippling laughter?   5
4) Did they use bone and ivory,
 jade and silver, for ornament?
5) Had they an epic poem?
6) Did they distinguish between speech and singing?

1) Sir, their light hearts turned to stone.   10
 It is not remembered whether in gardens
 stone lanterns illumined pleasant ways.
2) Perhaps they gathered once to delight in blossom,
 but after the children were killed
 there were no more buds.   15
3) Sir, laughter is bitter to the burned mouth.
4) A dream ago, perhaps. Ornament is for joy.
 All the bones were charred.
5) It is not remembered. Remember,
 most were peasants; their life   20
 was in rice and bamboo.
 When peaceful clouds were reflected in the paddies
 and the water buffalo stepped surely along terraces,

° *Mosler Safe:* A brand of safe known for being especially strong.

maybe fathers told their sons old tales.
When bombs smashed the mirrors   25
there was time only to scream.
6) There is an echo yet, it is said,
   of their speech which was like a song.
   It is reported their singing resembled
   the flight of moths in moonlight.   30
   Who can say? It is silent now.

YUSEF KOMUNYAKAA   (1947–   )

Facing It   (1988)

My black face fades,
hiding inside the black granite.
I said I wouldn't,
dammit: No tears.
I'm stone. I'm flesh.   5
My clouded reflection eyes me
like a bird of prey, the profile of night
slanted against morning. I turn
this way — the stone lets me go.
I turn that way — I'm inside   10
the Vietnam Veterans Memorial
again, depending on the light
to make a difference.
I go down the 58,022 names,
half-expecting to find   15
my own in letters like smoke.
I touch the name Andrew Johnson;
I see the booby trap's white flash.
Names shimmer on a woman's blouse
but when she walks away   20
the names stay on the wall.
Brushstrokes flash, a red bird's
wings cutting across my stare.
The sky. A plane in the sky.
A white vet's images floats   25
closer to me, then his pale eyes
look through mine. I'm a window.
He's lost his right arm
inside the stone. In the black mirror
a woman's trying to erase names: 30
No, she's brushing a boy's hair.

WISLAWA SZYMBORSKA (1923–)

The End and the Beginning (1993)

After every war
someone has to clean up.
Things won't
straighten themselves up, after all.

Someone has to push the rubble   5
to the side of the road,
so the corpse-filled wagons
can pass.

Someone has to get mired
in scum and ashes,   10
sofa springs,
splintered glass,
and bloody rags.

Someone has to drag in a girder
to prop up a wall,   15
Someone has to glaze a window,
rehang a door.

Photogenic it's not,
and takes years.
All the cameras have left   20
for another war.

We'll need the bridges back,
and new railway stations.
Sleeves will go ragged
from rolling them up.   25

Someone, broom in hand,
still recalls the way it was.
Someone else listens
and nods with unsevered head.
But already there are those nearby   30
starting to mill about
who will find it dull.

From out of the bushes
sometimes someone still unearths
rusted-out arguments   35
and carries them to the garbage pile.

Those who knew
what was going on here

must make way for
those who know little.   40
And less than little.
And finally as little as nothing.

In the grass that has overgrown
causes and effects,
someone must be stretched out   45
blade of grass in his mouth
gazing at the clouds.

Reading and Reacting: Poems about War

1. What is each speaker's attitude toward war? Does the speaker seem to be focusing on a particular war or on war in general?
2. What conventional images and figures of speech does each poem use to express its ideas about war?
3. Do any of the poems use unusual, unexpected, or shocking images or figures of speech?
4. How would you describe each poem's tone? For example, is the tone angry? Cynical? Sad? Disillusioned? Resigned?
5. What does each poem reveal about the speaker?
6. What is each poem's central theme?

Related Works: "The Things They Carried" (p. 251), "The Man He Killed" (p. 472), "Patterns" (p. 473), "The Death of the Ball Turret Gunner" (p. 528), "Naming of Parts" (p. 694), *Nine Ten* (p. 760)

WRITING SUGGESTIONS: Discovering Themes in Poetry

1. Compare any two poems in this chapter about parents, nature, love, or war.
2. Write an explication of one of the poems in this chapter.
3. Write an essay in which you compare one of the poems in this chapter to a short story or play on the same general subject. (For possible topics, consult the Related Works list that follows each group of poems.)
4. Some poets write multiple poems on the same general subject. For example, Shakespeare wrote many love poems, and Robert Frost wrote a number of poems about nature. Choose two poems by a single poet that explore the same subject, and compare and contrast the themes of the two poems.
5. A number of poems in this book focus on the theme of poetry itself. Choose three poems on this theme, and write an essay that compares the poems' ideas about reading and writing poetry.

CHAPTER 24

POETRY FOR FURTHER READING

SHERMAN J. ALEXIE (1966–)

Defending Walt Whitman (1996)

Basketball is like this for young Indian boys, all arms and legs
and serious stomach muscles. Every body is brown!
These are the twentieth-century warriors who will never kill,
although a few sat quietly in the deserts of Kuwait,
waiting for orders to do something, do something.   5

God, there is nothing as beautiful as a jump shot
on a reservation summer basketball court
where the ball is moist with sweat
and makes a sound when it swishes through the net
that causes Walt Whitman to weep because it is so perfect.   10

There are veterans of foreign wars here,
whose bodies are still dominated
by collarbones and knees, whose bodies still respond
in the ways that bodies are supposed to respond when we
    are young.
Every body is brown! Look there, that boy can run   15
up and down this court forever. He can leap for a rebound
with his back arched like a salmon, all meat and bone
synchronized, magnetic, as if the court were a river,
as if the rim were a dam, as if the air were a ladder
leading the Indian boy toward home.   20

Some of the Indian boys still wear their military haircuts
while a few have let their hair grow back.
It will never be the same as it was before!
One Indian boy has never cut his hair, not once, and he braids it
into wild patterns that do not measure anything.   25

645

He is just a boy with too much time on his hands.
Look at him. He wants to play this game in bare feet.

God, the sun is so bright! There is no place like this.
Walt Whitman stretches his calf muscles
on the sidelines. He has the next game.   30
His huge beard is ridiculous on the reservation.
Some body throws a crazy pass and Walt Whitman catches it
   with quick hands.
He brings the ball close to his nose
and breathes in all of its smells: leather, brown skin, sweat,
   black hair,
burning oil, twisted ankle, long drink of warm water,   35
gunpowder, pine tree. Walt Whitman squeezes the ball tightly.
He wants to run. He hardly has the patience to wait for his turn.
"What's the score?" he asks. He asks, "What's the score?"

Basketball is like this for Walt Whitman. He watches these
   Indian boys
as if they were the last bodies on earth. Every body is brown!   40
Walt Whitman shakes because he believes in God.
Walt Whitman dreams of the Indian boy who will defend him,
trapping him in the corner, all flailing arms and legs
and legendary stomach muscles. Walt Whitman shakes
because he believes in God. Walt Whitman dreams   45
of the first jump shot he will take, the ball arcing clumsily
from his fingers, striking the rim so hard that it sparks.
Walt Whitman shakes because he believes in God.
Walt Whitman closes his eyes. He is a small man and his beard
is ludicrous on the reservation, absolutely insane.   50
His beard makes the Indian boys laugh righteously. His beard
   frightens
the smallest Indian boys. His beard tickles the skin
of the Indian boys who dribble past him. His beard, his beard!

God, there is beauty in every body. Walt Whitman stands
at center court while the Indian boys run from basket to basket.   55
Walt Whitman cannot tell the difference between
offense and defense. He does not care if he touches the ball.
Half of the Indian boys wear T-shirts damp with sweat
and the other half are barebacked, skin slick and shiny.
There is no place like this. Walt Whitman smiles.   60
Walt Whitman shakes. This game belongs to him.

MAYA ANGELOU (1928–   )

Africa (1975)

Thus she had lain
sugar cane sweet

deserts her hair
golden her feet
mountains her breasts   5
two Niles° her tears
Thus she has lain
Black through the years.

Over the white seas
rime white and cold   10
brigands ungentled
icicle bold
took her young daughters
sold her strong sons
churched her with Jesus   15
bled her with guns.
Thus she has lain.

Now she is rising
remember her pain
remember the losses   20
her screams loud and vain
remember her riches
her history slain
now she is striding
although she had lain.   25

ANONYMOUS

Bonny Barbara Allan
(Traditional Scottish ballad)

It was in and about the Martinmas° time,
    When the green leaves were afalling,

° *Niles:* The Nile River, which originates in East Africa and flows through Egypt, is the world's longest river.
° *Martinmas:* Saint Martin's Day, November 11.

That Sir John Graeme, in the West Country,
    Fell in love with Barbara Allan.

He sent his men down through the town,   5
    To the place where she was dwelling;
"O haste and come to my master dear,
    Gin° ye be Barbara Allan."

O hooly,° hooly rose she up,
    To the place where he was lying,   10
And when she drew the curtain by:
    "Young man, I think you're dying."

"O it's I'm sick, and very, very sick,
    And 'tis a' for Barbara Allan."—
"O the better for me ye's never be,   15
    Tho your heart's blood were aspilling.

"O dinna ye mind,° young man," said she,
    "When ye was in the tavern adrinking,
That ye made the health gae round and round,
    And slighted Barbara Allan?"   20

He turned his face unto the wall,
    And death was with him dealing:
"Adieu, adieu, my dear friends all,
    And be kind to Barbara Allan."

And slowly, slowly raise she up,   25
    And slowly, slowly left him,
And sighing said she could not stay,
    Since death of life had reft him.

She had not gane a mile but twa,°
    When she heard the dead-bell ringing,   30
And every jow° that the dead-bell geid,
    It cried, "Woe to Barbara Allan!"

"O mother, mother, make my bed!
    O make it saft and narrow!
Since my love died for me today,   35
    I'll die for him tomorrow."

°*Gin:* If. °*hooly:* Slowly. °*O dinna ye mind:* Don't you remember? °*twa:* Two. °*jow:* Stroke.

ANONYMOUS

Go Down, Moses*

Go down, Moses,
Way down in Egyptland
Tell old Pharaoh
To let my people go.

When Israel was in Egyptland   5
Let my people go
Oppressed so hard they could not stand
Let my people go.

Go down, Moses,
Way down in Egyptland   10
Tell old Pharaoh
"Let my people go."

"Thus saith the Lord," bold Moses said,
"Let my people go;
If not I'll smite your first-born dead   15
Let my people go.

"No more shall they in bondage toil,
Let my people go;
Let them come out with Egypt's spoil,
Let my people go."   20

The Lord told Moses what to do
Let my people go;
To lead the children of Israel through,
Let my people go.

Go down, Moses,   25
Way down in Egyptland,
Tell old Pharaoh,
"Let my people go!"

---

*Music was one of the few means of expression permitted for slaves. For example, slaves were allowed to sing songs when they had to coordinate work efforts, such as hauling a fallen tree or moving a heavy load. Religious songs, or "spirituals," were also allowed. Many of these songs contained coded messages conveying antislavery sentiments or even directions on how to use the Underground Railroad. For example, the spiritual "Wade in the Water" seemed, on the surface, to be about crossing the River Jordan to reach the Promised Land. But its lyrics contained vital information, including the idea that crossing streams was a good way for runaway slaves to cover their scent and thus to lose the bloodhounds used to track them.

ANONYMOUS

Western Wind

(English lyric)

Western wind, when wilt thou blow,
The° small rain down can rain?
Christ, if my love were in my arms,
And I in my bed again!

MATTHEW ARNOLD   (1822–1888)

Dover Beach   (1867)

The sea is calm tonight.
The tide is full, the moon lies fair
Upon the straits;— on the French coast the light
Gleams and is gone; the cliffs of England stand,
Glimmering and vast, out in the tranquil bay.   5
Come to the window, sweet is the night-air!
Only, from the long line of spray
Where the sea meets the moon-blanched° land,
Listen! you hear the grating roar
Of pebbles which the waves draw back, and fling,   10
At their return, up the high strand,°
Begin, and cease, and then again begin,
With tremulous cadence slow, and bring
The eternal note of sadness in.

Sophocles° long ago   15
Heard it on the Aegean,° and it brought
Into his mind the turbid ebb and flow
Of human misery; we
Find also in the sound a thought,
Hearing it by this distant northern sea.   20

The Sea of Faith
Was once, too, at the full, and round earth's shore
Lay like the folds of a bright girdle furled.
But now I only hear
Its melancholy, long, withdrawing roar,   25
Retreating, to the breath

° *The:* [So that] the.   ° *moon-blanched:* Whitened by moonlight.   ° *strand:* Beach.   ° *Sophocles:* Greek playwright (496–406 B.C.), author of tragedies such as *Oedipus the King* and *Antigone.*   ° *Aegean:* Sea between
Greece and Turkey.

Of the night-wind, down the vast edges drear
And naked shingles° of the world.

Ah, love, let us be true
To one another! for the world, which seems   30
To lie before us like a land of dreams,
So various, so beautiful, so new,
Hath really neither joy, nor love, nor light,
Nor certitude, nor peace, nor help for pain;
And we are here as on a darkling° plain   35
Swept with confused alarms of struggle and flight,
Where ignorant armies clash by night.

ELIZABETH BISHOP (1911–1979)

The Fish (1946)

I caught a tremendous fish
and held him beside the boat
half out of water, with my hook
fast in a corner of his mouth.
He didn't fight.   5
He hadn't fought at all.
He hung a grunting weight,
battered and venerable
and homely. Here and there
his brown skin hung in strips   10
like ancient wallpaper,
and its pattern of darker brown
was like wallpaper:
shapes like full-blown roses
stained and lost through age.   15
He was speckled with barnacles,
fine rosettes of lime,
and infested
with tiny white sea-lice,
and underneath two or three   20
rags of green weed hung down.
While his gills were breathing in
the terrible oxygen
— the frightening gills,
fresh and crisp with blood,   25
that can cut so badly —

°*shingles:* Gravel beaches.   °*darkling:* Darkening.

I thought of the coarse white flesh
packed in like feathers,
the big bones and the little bonies,
the dramatic reds and blacks   30
of his shiny entrails,
and the pink swim-bladder
like a big peony.
I looked into his eyes
which were far larger than mine   35
but shallower, and yellowed,
the irises backed and packed
with tarnished tinfoil
seen through the lenses
of old scratched isinglass.   40
They shifted a little, but not
to return my stare.
— It was more like the tipping
of an object toward the light.
I admired his sullen face,   45
the mechanism of his jaw,
and then I saw
that from his lower lip
— if you could call it a lip —
grim, wet, and weaponlike,   50
hung five old pieces of fish-line,
or four and a wire leader
with the swivel still attached,
with all their five big hooks
grown firmly in his mouth.   55
A green line, frayed at the end
and crimped from the strain and snap
when it broke and he got away.
Like medals with their ribbons
frayed and wavering,   60
a five-haired beard of wisdom
trailing from his aching jaw.
I stared and stared
and victory filled up
the little rented boat,   65
from the pool of bilge
where oil had spread a rainbow
around the rusted engine
to the bailer rusted orange,
the sun-cracked thwarts,   70

the oarlocks on their strings,
the gunnels — until everything
was rainbow, rainbow, rainbow!
And I let the fish go.

WILLIAM BLAKE (1757–1827)

The Lamb (1789)

Little Lamb, who made thee?
Dost thou know who made thee?
Gave thee life & bid thee feed,
By the stream & o'er the mead;
Gave thee clothing of delight,   5
Softest clothing wooly bright;
Gave thee such a tender voice,
Making all the vales rejoice!
Little Lamb who made thee?
Dost thou know who made thee?   10

Little Lamb I'll tell thee,
Little Lamb I'll tell thee!
He is calléd by thy name,
For he calls himself a Lamb:
He is meek & he is mild,   15
He became a little child:
I a child & thou a lamb,
We are calléd by his name.
Little Lamb God bless thee.
Little Lamb God bless thee.   20

WILLIAM BLAKE (1757–1827)

To see a World in a Grain of Sand (1803)

To see a World in a Grain of Sand
And a Heaven in a Wild Flower,
Hold Infinity in the palm of your hand
And Eternity in an hour.

WILLIAM BLAKE (1757–1827)

The Tyger (1794)

Tyger! Tyger! burning bright
In the forests of the night,

What immortal hand or eye
Could frame thy fearful symmetry?

In what distant deeps or skies   5
Burnt the fire of thine eyes?
On what wings dare he aspire?
What the hand dare seize the fire?

And what shoulder, and what art,
Could twist the sinews of thy heart?   10
And when thy heart began to beat,
What dread hand? and what dread feet?

What the hammer? what the chain?
In what furnace was thy brain?
What the anvil? what dread grasp   15
Dare its deadly terrors clasp?

When the stars threw down their spears,
And watered heaven with their tears,
Did he smile his work to see?
Did he who made the Lamb make thee?   20

Tyger! Tyger! burning bright
In the forests of the night,
What immortal hand or eye
Dare frame thy fearful symmetry?

ANNE BRADSTREET   (1612–1672)

The Author to Her Book°   (1678)

Thou ill-formed offspring of my feeble brain,
Who after birth did'st by my side remain,
Till snatched from thence by friends, less wise than true,
Who thee abroad exposed to public view;
Made thee in rags, halting, to the press to trudge,   5
Where errors were not lessened, all may judge.
At thy return my blushing was not small,
My rambling brat (in print) should mother call;
I cast thee by as one unfit for light,
Thy visage was so irksome in my sight;   10
Yet being mine own, at length affection would
Thy blemishes amend, if so I could:
I washed thy face, but more defects I saw,

° *Her Book:* Bradstreet addresses *The Tenth Muse,* a collection of her poetry published without her consent in 1650.

And rubbing off a spot, still made a flaw.
I stretched thy joints to make thee even feet,°   15
Yet still thou run'st more hobbling than is meet;°
In better dress to trim thee was my mind,
But nought save homespun cloth in the house I find.
In this array, 'mongst vulgars° may'st thou roam;
In critics' hands beware thou dost not come;   20
And take thy way where yet thou are not known.
If for thy Father asked, say thou had'st none;
And for thy Mother, she alas is poor,
Which caused her thus to send thee out of door.

GWENDOLYN BROOKS (1917–2000)

Medgar Evers° (1964)

For Charles Evers °

The man whose height his fear improved he
arranged to fear no further. The raw
intoxicated time was time for better birth or a final death.

Old styles, old tempos, all the engagement of
the day — the sedate, the regulated fray —   5
the antique light, the Moral rose, old gusts,
tight whistlings from the past, the mothballs
in the Love at last our man forswore.

Medgar Evers annoyed confetti and assorted
brands of businessmen's eyes.   10

The shows came down: to maxims and surprise.
And palsy.

Roaring no rapt arise-ye to the dead, he
leaned across tomorrow. People said that
he was holding clean globes in his hands.   15

GEORGE GORDON, LORD BYRON (1788–1824)

She Walks in Beauty (1815)

1

She walks in beauty, like the night
    Of cloudless climes and starry skies;
And all that's best of dark and bright

°*even feet:* Metrical feet.   °*meet:* Appropriate or decorous.   °*vulgars:* Common people.   °*Medgar Evers:*
African-American civil rights leader who was killed by a sniper in 1963.   °*Charles Evers:* Medgar Evers's brother.

Meet in her aspect and her eyes:
Thus mellowed to that tender light   5
    Which heaven to gaudy day denies.

                    2
One shade the more, one ray the less,
    Had half impaired the nameless grace
Which waves in every raven tress,
    Or softly lightens o'er her face;   10
Where thoughts serenely sweet express
    How pure, how dear their dwelling place.

                    3
And on that cheek, and o'er that brow,
    So soft, so calm, yet eloquent,
The smiles that win, the tints that glow,   15
    But tell of days in goodness spent,
A mind at peace with all below,
    A heart whose love is innocent!

THOMAS CAMPION   (1567–1620)

There is a garden in her face   (1617)

There is a garden in her face
Where roses and white lilies grow;
    A heav'nly paradise is that place
Wherein all pleasant fruits do flow.
    There cherries grow which none may buy   5
    Till "Cherry-ripe" themselves do cry.

Those cherries fairly do enclose
Of orient pearl a double row,
    Which when her lovely laughter shows,
They look like rose-buds filled with snow;   10
    Yet them nor peer nor prince can buy,
    Till "Cherry-ripe" themselves do cry.

Her eyes like angels watch them still;
Her brows like bended bows do stand,
    Threat'ning with piercing frowns to kill   15
All that attempt, with eye or hand
    Those sacred cherries to come nigh
    Till "Cherry-ripe" themselves do cry.

SAMUEL TAYLOR COLERIDGE (1772–1834)

Kubla Khan°   (1797, 1798)

Or, a Vision in a Dream. A Fragment.

In Xanadu did Kubla Khan
A stately pleasure-dome decree:
Where Alph,° the sacred river, ran
Through caverns measureless to man
Down to a sunless sea.   5
So twice five miles of fertile ground
With walls and towers were girdled round;
And there were gardens bright with sinuous rills,
Where blossomed many an incense-bearing tree;
And here were forests ancient as the hills,   10
Enfolding sunny spots of greenery.

But oh! that deep romantic chasm which slanted
Down the green hill athwart a cedarn cover!
A savage place! as holy and enchanted
As e'er beneath a waning moon was haunted   15
By woman wailing for her demon-lover!
And from this chasm, with ceaseless turmoil seething,
As if this earth in fast thick pants were breathing,
A mighty fountain momently was forced:
Amid whose swift half-intermitted burst   20
Huge fragments vaulted like rebounding hail,
Or chaffy grain beneath the thresher's flail:
And 'mid these dancing rocks at once and ever
It flung up momently the sacred river.
Five miles meandering with a mazy motion   25
Through wood and dale the sacred river ran,
Then reached the caverns measureless to man,
And sank in tumult to a lifeless ocean:
And 'mid this tumult Kubla heard from far
Ancestral voices prophesying war!   30

> The shadow of the dome of pleasure
> Floated midway on the waves;

° *Kubla Khan:* Coleridge mythologizes the actual Kublai Khan, a thirteenth-century Mongol emperor, as well as the Chinese city of Xanadu.   ° *Alph:* Probably derived from the Greek river Alpheus, whose waters, according to legend, rose from the Ionian Sea in Sicily as the fountain of Arethusa.

Where was heard the mingled measure
From the fountain and the caves.
It was a miracle of rare device,   35
A sunny pleasure-dome with caves of ice!

A damsel with a dulcimer
In a vision once I saw:
It was an Abyssinian maid,
And on her dulcimer she played,   40
Singing of Mount Abora.°
Could I revive within me
Her symphony and song,
To such a deep delight 'twould win me,
That with music loud and long,   45
I would build that dome in air,
That sunny dome! those caves of ice!
And all who heard should see them there,
And all should cry, Beware! Beware!
His flashing eyes, his floating hair!   50
Weave a circle round him thrice,°
And close your eyes with holy dread,
For he on honey-dew hath fed,
And drunk the milk of Paradise.

BILLY COLLINS (1941–   )

Introduction to Poetry   (1988)

I ask them to take a poem
and hold it up to the light
like a color slide

or press an ear against its hive.

I say drop a mouse into a poem   5
and watch him probe his way out,

or walk inside the poem's room
and feel the walls for a light switch.

I want them to waterski
across the surface of a poem   10
waving at the author's name on the shore.

° *Mount Abora:* Some scholars see a reminiscence here of John Milton's *Paradise Lost* 4.280–82: "where
Abassin kings their issue guard / Mount Amara, though this by some supposed / True Paradise under the Ethiop
Line."   ° *Weave . . . thrice:* A magic ritual to keep away intruding spirits.

But all they want to do
is tie the poem to a chair with rope
and torture a confession out of it.

They begin beating it with a hose   15
to find out what it really means.

HART CRANE   (1899–1932)

To Brooklyn Bridge   (1926)

How many dawns, chill from his rippling rest
The seagull's wings shall dip and pivot him,
Shedding white rings of tumult, building high
Over the chained bay waters Liberty —

Then, with inviolate curve, forsake our eyes   5
As apparitional as sails that cross
Some page of figures to be filed away;
—Till elevators drop us from our day . . .

I think of cinemas, panoramic sleights
With multitudes bent toward some flashing scene   10
Never disclosed, but hastened to again,
Foretold to other eyes on the same screen;

And Thee, across the harbor, silver-paced
As though the sun took step of thee, yet left
Some motion ever unspent in thy stride, —   15
Implicitly thy freedom staying thee!

Out of some subway scuttle, cell or loft
A bedlamite speeds to thy parapets,
Tilting there momently, shrill shirt ballooning,
A jest falls from the speechless caravan.   20

Down Wall, from girder into street noon leaks,
A rip-tooth of the sky's acetylene;
All afternoon the cloud-flown derricks turn . . .
Thy cables breathe the North Atlantic still.

And obscure as that heaven of the Jews,   25
Thy guerdon . . . Accolade thou dost bestow
Of anonymity time cannot raise:
Vibrant reprieve and pardon thou dost show.

O harp and altar, of the fury fused,
(How could mere toil align thy choiring strings!)   30

Terrific threshold of the prophet's pledge,
Prayer of pariah, and the lover's cry,—

Again the traffic lights that skim thy swift
Unfractioned idiom, immaculate sigh of stars,
Beading thy path — condense eternity: 35
And we have seen night lifted in thine arms.

Under thy shadow by the piers I waited;
Only in darkness is thy shadow clear.
The City's fiery parcels all undone,
Already snow submerges an iron year . . .   40

O Sleepless as the river under thee,
Vaulting the sea, the prairies' dreaming sod,
Unto us lowliest sometime sweep, descend
And of the curveship lend a myth to God.

E. E. CUMMINGS (1894–1962)

Buffalo Bill's (1923)

Buffalo Bill's
defunct
          who used to
          ride a watersmooth-silver
                              stallion   5
and break onetwothreefourfive pigeonsjustlikethat
                                        Jesus
he was a handsome man
                    and what i want to know is
how do you like your blueeyed boy   10
  Mister Death

E. E. CUMMINGS (1894–1962)

next to of course god america i (1926)

"next to of course god america i
love you land of the pilgrims' and so forth oh
say can you see by the dawn's early my
country 'tis of centuries come and go
and are no more what of it we should worry   5
in every language even deafandhumb
thy sons acclaim your glorious name by gorry

by jingo by gee by gosh by gum
why talk of beauty what could be more beaut-
iful than these heroic happy dead   10
who rushed like lions to the roaring slaughter
they did not stop to think they died instead
then shall the voice of liberty be mute?"

He spoke. And drank rapidly a glass of water

EMILY DICKINSON   (1830 –1886)

Because I could not stop for Death —   (1863)

Because I could not stop for Death —
He kindly stopped for me —
The Carriage held but just Ourselves —
And Immortality.

We slowly drove — He knew no haste   5
And I had put away
My labor and my leisure too,
For His Civility —

We passed the School, where Children strove
At Recess — in the Ring —   10
We passed the Fields of Gazing Grain —
We passed the Setting Sun —

Or rather — He passed Us —
The Dews drew quivering and chill —
For only Gossamer, my Gown —   15
My Tippet° — only Tulle —

We passed before a House that seemed
A Swelling of the Ground —
The Roof was scarcely visible —
The Cornice — in the Ground —   20

Since then —'tis Centuries — and yet
Feels shorter than the Day
I first surmised the Horses' Heads
Were toward Eternity —

°*Tippet:* A short cape or scarf.

EMILY DICKINSON   (1830–1886)

"Faith" is a fine invention   (1860)

"Faith" is a fine invention
When Gentlemen can *see*—
But *Microscopes* are prudent
In an Emergency.

EMILY DICKINSON   (1830–1886)

I heard a Fly buzz — when I died —   (1862)

I heard a Fly buzz — when I died —
The Stillness in the Room
Was like the Stillness in the Air—
Between the Heaves of Storm—

The Eyes around — had wrung them dry—   5
And Breaths were gathering firm
For that last Onset — when the King
Be witnessed — in the Room—

I willed my Keepsakes — Signed away
What portion of me be   10
Assignable — and then it was
There interposed a Fly—

With Blue — uncertain stumbling Buzz—
Between the light — and me—
And then the Windows failed — and then   15
I could not see to see —

JOHN DONNE   (1572–1631)

Batter My Heart, Three-Personed God   (c. 1610)

Batter my heart, three-personed God, for You
As yet but knock, breathe, shine, and seek to mend.
That I may rise and stand, o'erthrow me, and bend
Your force to break, blow, burn, and make me new.
I, like an usurped town to another due,   5
Labor to admit You, but Oh! to no end.
Reason, Your viceroy in me, me should defend,
But is captived, and proves weak or untrue.

Yet dearly I love You, and would be lovèd fain,
But am betrothed unto Your enemy;   10
Divorce me, untie or break that knot again;
Take me to You, imprison me, for I,
Except You enthrall me, never shall be free,
Nor ever chaste, except You ravish me.

JOHN DONNE   (1572–1631)

Death Be Not Proud   (c. 1610)

Death be not proud, though some have callèd thee
Mighty and dreadful, for thou art not so;
For those whom thou think'st thou dost overthrow
Die not, poor death, nor yet canst thou kill me.
From rest and sleep, which but thy pictures be,   5
Much pleasure, then from thee much more must flow,
And soonest our best men with thee do go,
Rest of their bones, and soul's delivery.
Thou art slave to fate, chance, kings, and desperate men,
And dost with poison, war, and sickness dwell,   10
And poppy, or charms can make us sleep as well,
And better than thy stroke; why swell'st thou then?
One short sleep past, we wake eternally,
And death shall be no more; death, thou shalt die.

JOHN DONNE   (1572–1631)

The Flea   (1633)

Mark but this flea, and mark in this°
How little that which thou deny'st me is;
It sucked me first, and now sucks thee,
And in this flea our two bloods mingled be;
Thou know'st that this cannot be said   5
A sin, nor shame, nor loss of maidenhead,
    Yet this enjoys before it woo,
    And pampered swells with one blood made of two,
    And this, alas, is more than we would do.°

Oh stay, three live sin one flea spare,   10
Where we almost, yea more than, married are.

°*mark in this:* Note the moral lesson in it.   °*more than we would do:* If we do not join our blood.

This flea is you and I, and this
Our marriage bed, and marriage temple is;
Though parents grudge, and you, we're met
And cloistered in these living walls of jet.   15
    Though use make you apt to kill me,
    Let not to that, self-murder added be,
    And sacrilege, three sins in killing three.
Cruel and sudden, hast thou since
Purpled thy nail in blood of innocence?   20
Wherein could this flea guilty be,
Except in that drop which it sucked from thee?
Yet thou triumph'st, and say'st that thou
Find'st not thyself, nor me, the weaker now;
    'Tis true; then learn how false, fears be;   25
    Just so much honor, when thou yield'st to me,
    Will waste, as this flea's death took life from thee.

RITA DOVE   (1952–   )

Fox Trot Fridays   (2004)

Thank the stars there's a day
each week to tuck in

the grief, lift your pearls, and
stride brush stride.

quick-quick with a   5
heel-ball-toe. Smooth

as Nat King Cole's
slow satin smile,

easy as taking
one day at a time: 10

one man and
one woman,

rib to rib,
with no heartbreak in sight —

just the sweep of Paradise   15
and the space of a song

to count all the wonders in it.

PAUL LAURENCE DUNBAR (1872–1906)

We Wear the Mask (1896)

We wear the mask that grins and lies,
It hides our cheeks and shades our eyes —
This debt we pay to human guile;
With torn and bleeding hearts we smile,
And mouth with myriad subtleties.   5

Why should the world be over-wise,
In counting all our tears and sighs?
Nay, let them only see us, while
    We wear the mask.

We smile, but, O great Christ, our cries   10
To thee from tortured souls arise.
We sing, but oh the clay is vile
Beneath our feet, and long the mile;
But let the world dream otherwise,
    We wear the mask!   15

T. S. ELIOT (1888–1965)

The Love Song of J. Alfred Prufrock (1917)

> S'io credessi che mia risposta fosse
> A persona che mai tornasse al mondo,
> Questa fiamma staria senza piu scosse.
> Ma perciocche giammai di questo fondo
> Non torno vivo alcun, s'i'odo il vero,
> Senza tema d'infamia ti rispondo.°

Let us go then, you and I,
When the evening is spread out against the sky
Like a patient etherized upon a table;
Let us go, through certain half-deserted streets,
The muttering retreats   5
Of restless nights in one-night cheap hotels
And sawdust restaurants with oyster-shells:
Streets that follow like a tedious argument
Of insidious intent

°*S'io . . . rispondo:* The epigraph is from Dante's *Inferno,* Canto 27. In response to the poet's question about his identity, Guido da Montefelto, who for his sin of fraud must spend eternity wrapped in flames, replies: "If I thought that I was speaking to someone who could go back to the world, this flame would shake no more. But since from this place nobody ever returns alive, if what I hear is true, I answer you without fear of infamy."

To lead you to an overwhelming question . . .   10
Oh, do not ask, "What is it?"
Let us go and make our visit.

In the room the women come and go
Talking of Michelangelo.

The yellow fog that rubs its back upon the window-panes,   15
The yellow smoke that rubs its muzzle on the window-panes
Licked its tongue into the corners of the evening,
Lingered upon the pools that stand in drains,
Let fall upon its back the soot that falls from chimneys,
Slipped by the terrace, made a sudden leap,   20
And seeing that it was a soft October night,
Curled once about the house, and fell asleep.

And indeed there will be time
For the yellow smoke that slides along the street,
Rubbing its back upon the window-panes;   25
There will be time, there will be time
To prepare a face to meet the faces that you meet;
There will be time to murder and create,
And time for all the works and days° of hands
That lift and drop a question on your plate;   30
Time for you and time for me,
And time yet for a hundred indecisions,
And for a hundred visions and revisions,
Before the taking of a toast and tea.

In the room the women come and go   35
Talking of Michelangelo.

And indeed there will be time
To wonder, "Do I dare?" and, "Do I dare?"
Time to turn back and descend the stair,
With a bald spot in the middle of my hair—   40
(They will say: "How his hair is growing thin!")
My morning coat, my collar mounting firmly to the chin,
My necktie rich and modest, but asserted by a simple pin—
(They will say: "But how his arms and legs are thin!")
Do I dare   45
Disturb the universe?

° *works and days: Works and Days,* by the eighth-century B.C. Greek poet Hesiod, is a poem that celebrates farm life.

In a minute there is time
For decisions and revisions which a minute will reverse.

For I have known them all already, known them all—
Have known the evenings, mornings, afternoons,   50
I have measured out my life with coffee spoons;
I know the voices dying with a dying fall°
Beneath the music from a farther room.
    So how should I presume?

And I have known the eyes already, known them all—   55
The eyes that fix you in a formulated phrase,
And when I am formulated, sprawling on a pin,
When I am pinned and wriggling on the wall,
Then how should I begin
To spit out all the butt-ends of my days and ways?   60
    And how should I presume?

And I have known the arms already, known them all—
Arms that are braceleted and white and bare
(But in the lamplight, downed with light brown hair!)
Is it perfume from a dress   65
That makes me so digress?
Arms that lie along a table, or wrap about a shawl.
    And should I then presume?
    And how should I begin?

* * *

Shall I say, I have gone at dusk through narrow streets   70
And watched the smoke that rises from the pipes
Of lonely men in shirt-sleeves, leaning out of windows? . . .

I should have been a pair of ragged claws
Scuttling across the floors of silent seas.

* * *

And the afternoon, the evening, sleeps so peacefully!   75
Smoothed by long fingers,
Asleep . . . tired . . . or it malingers,
Stretched on the floor, here beside you and me.
Should I, after tea and cakes and ices,
Have the strength to force the moment to its crisis?   80
But though I have wept and fasted, wept and prayed,

°*dying fall:* An allusion to Orsino's speech in *Twelfth Night* (1.1): "That strain again! It had a dying fall."

Though I have seen my head (grown slightly bald) brought in
    upon a platter,°
I am no prophet — and here's no great matter;
I have seen the moment of my greatness flicker,
And I have seen the eternal Footman° hold my coat, and   85
    snicker,
And in short, I was afraid.

And would it have been worth it, after all,
After the cups, the marmalade, the tea,
Among the porcelain, among some talk of you and me,
Would it have been worth while,   90
To have bitten off the matter with a smile,
To have squeezed the universe into a ball
To roll it toward some overwhelming question,
To say: "I am Lazarus,° come from the dead,
Come back to tell you all, I shall tell you all" —   95
If one, settling a pillow by her head,
    Should say: "That is not what I meant at all.
    That is not it, at all."

And would it have been worth it, after all,
Would it have been worth while,   100
After the sunsets and the dooryards and the sprinkled streets,
After the novels, after the teacups, after the skirts that trail
    along the floor —
And this, and so much more? —
It is impossible to say just what I mean!
But as if a magic lantern threw the nerves in patterns on a   105
    screen:
Would it have been worth while
If one, settling a pillow or throwing off a shawl,
And turning toward the window, should say:
    "That is not it at all,
    That is not what I meant, at all."   110

* * *

No! I am not Prince Hamlet, nor was meant to be;
Am an attendant lord, one that will do

°*head . . . platter:* Like John the Baptist, who was beheaded by King Herod (see Matthew 14.3–11).   °*eternal Footman:* Perhaps death or fate.   °*Lazarus:* A man whom Christ raised from the dead (see John 11.1–44).

To swell a progress,° start a scene or two,
Advise the prince; no doubt, an easy tool,
Deferential, glad to be of use,   115
Politic, cautious, and meticulous;
Full of high sentence,° but a bit obtuse;
At times, indeed, almost ridiculous —
Almost, at times, the Fool.

I grow old . . . I grow old . . .   120
I shall wear the bottoms of my trousers rolled.

Shall I part my hair behind? Do I dare to eat a peach?
I shall wear white flannel trousers, and walk upon the beach.
I have heard the mermaids singing, each to each.

I do not think that they will sing to me.   125

I have seen them riding seaward on the waves
Combing the white hair of the waves blown back
When the wind blows the water white and black.

We have lingered in the chambers of the sea
By sea-girls wreathed with seaweed red and brown   130
Till human voices wake us, and we drown.

LOUISE ERDRICH   (1954 –   )

Indian Boarding School: The Runaways   (1984)

Home's the place we head for in our sleep.
Boxcars stumbling north in dreams
don't wait for us. We catch them on the run.
The rails, old lacerations that we love,
shoot parallel across the face and break   5
just under Turtle Mountains.° Riding scars
you can't get lost. Home is the place they cross.

The lame guard strikes a match and makes the dark
less tolerant. We watch through cracks in boards
as the land starts rolling, rolling till it hurts   10
to be here, cold in regulation clothes.

°*a progress:* Here, in the Elizabethan sense of a royal journey.   °*sentence:* Opinions.   °*Turtle Mountains:*
Erdrich is a descendant of the Turtle Mountain band of the Chippewa.

We know the sheriff's waiting at midrun
to take us back. His car is dumb and warm.
The highway doesn't rock, it only hums
like a wing of long insults. The worn-down welts   15
of ancient punishments lead back and forth.

All runaways wear dresses, long green ones,
the color you would think shame was. We scrub
the sidewalks down because it's shameful work.
Our brushes cut the stone in watered arcs   20
and in the soak frail outlines shiver clear
a moment, things us kids pressed on the dark
face before it hardened, pale, remembering
delicate old injuries, the spines of names and leaves.

ROBERT FROST   (1874–1963)

Mending Wall   (1914)

Something there is that doesn't love a wall,
That sends the frozen-ground-swell under it,
And spills the upper boulders in the sun;
And makes gaps even two can pass abreast.
The work of hunters is another thing: 5
I have come after them and made repair
Where they have left not one stone on a stone,
But they would have the rabbit out of hiding,
To please the yelping dogs. The gaps I mean,
No one has seen them made or heard them made,   10
But at spring mending-time we find them there.
I let my neighbor know beyond the hill;
And on a day we meet to walk the line
And set the wall between us once again.
We keep the wall between us as we go.   15
To each the boulders that have fallen to each.
And some are loaves and some so nearly balls
We have to use a spell to make them balance:
"Stay where you are until our backs are turned!"
We wear our fingers rough with handling them.   20
Oh, just another kind of outdoor game,
One on a side. It comes to little more:
There where it is we do not need the wall:
He is all pine and I am apple orchard.
My apple trees will never get across   25

And eat the cones under his pines, I tell him.
He only says, "Good fences make good neighbors."
Spring is the mischief in me, and I wonder
If I could put a notion in his head:
"*Why* do they make good neighbors? Isn't it   30
Where there are cows? But here there are no cows.
Before I built a wall I'd ask to know
What I was walling in or walling out,
And to whom I was like to give offense.
Something there is that doesn't love a wall,   35
That wants it down." I could say "Elves" to him,
But it's not elves exactly, and I'd rather
He said it for himself. I see him there
Bringing a stone grasped firmly by the top
In each hand, like an old-stone savage armed.   40
He moves in darkness as it seems to me,
Not of woods only and the shade of trees.
He will not go behind his father's saying,
And he likes having thought of it so well
He says again, "Good fences make good neighbors."   45

ROBERT FROST   (1874–1963)

The Road Not Taken   (1915)

Two roads diverged in a yellow wood,
And sorry I could not travel both
And be one traveler, long I stood
And looked down one as far as I could
To where it bent in the undergrowth;   5

Then took the other, as just as fair,
And having perhaps the better claim,
Because it was grassy and wanted wear;
Though as for that the passing there
Had worn them really about the same,   10

And both that morning equally lay
In leaves no step had trodden black.
Oh, I kept the first for another day!
Yet knowing how way leads on to way,
I doubted if I should ever come back.   15

I shall be telling this with a sigh
Somewhere ages and ages hence:

Two roads diverged in a wood, and I—
I took the one less traveled by,
And that has made all the difference.   20

ROBERT FROST   (1874–1963)

Stopping by Woods on a Snowy Evening   (1923)

Whose woods these are I think I know.
His house is in the village though;
He will not see me stopping here
To watch his woods fill up with snow.

My little horse must think it queer   5
To stop without a farmhouse near
Between the woods and frozen lake
The darkest evening of the year.

He gives his harness bells a shake
To ask if there is some mistake.   10
The only other sound's the sweep
Of easy wind and downy flake.

The woods are lovely, dark and deep,
But I have promises to keep,
And miles to go before I sleep,   15
And miles to go before I sleep.

H.D. (HILDA DOOLITTLE)   (1886–1961)

Helen°   (1924)

All Greece hates
the still eyes in the white face,
the lustre as of olives
where she stands,
and the white hands.   5

All Greece reviles
the wan face when she smiles,
hating it deeper still

° *Helen:* In Greek mythology, Helen was the most beautiful of all women. She was the daughter of the Greek god Zeus and the mortal Leda. After a decade or so of marriage to Menelaus, the King of Sparta, Helen was abducted by Paris, the son of King Priam of Troy. Menelaus enlisted an army to recapture her in what would become known as the Trojan War, a portion of which is recounted in Homer's epic poem *The Iliad*.

when it grows wan and white,
remembering past enchantments   10
and past ills.

Greece sees unmoved,
God's daughter, born of love,
the beauty of cool feet
and slenderest knees,   15
could love indeed the maid,
only if she were laid,
white ash amid funereal cypresses.

THOMAS HARDY   (1840–1928)

The Convergence of the Twain   (1912)

(Lines on the loss of the 'Titanic')

I

In a solitude of the sea
Deep from human vanity,
And the Pride of Life that planned her, stilly couches she.

II

Steel chambers, late the pyres°
Of her salamandrine fires,°   5
Cold currents thrid,° and turn to rhythmic tidal lyres.

III

Over the mirrors meant
To glass the opulent
The sea-worm crawls — grotesque, slimed, dumb, indifferent.

IV

Jewels in joy designed   10
To ravish the sensuous mind
Lie lightless, all their sparkles bleared and black and blind.

V

Dim moon-eyed fishes near
Gaze at the gilded gear

° *pyres:* Funeral pyres; piles of wood on which corpses were burned in ancient rites.   ° *salamandrine fires:* An allusion to the old belief that salamanders could live in fire.   ° *thrid:* Thread (archaic verb form).

And query: "What does this vaingloriousness down here?" . . .   15

VI

Well: while was fashioning
This creature of cleaving wing,
The Immanent° Will that stirs and urges everything

VII

Prepared a sinister mate
For her — so gaily great —   20
A Shape of Ice, for the time far and dissociate.

VIII

And as the smart ship grew
In stature, grace, and hue,
In shadowy silent distance grew the Iceberg too.

IX

Alien they seemed to be: 25
No mortal eye could see
The intimate welding of their later history,

X

Or sign that they were bent
By paths coincident
On being anon° twin halves of one august° event,   30

XI

Till the Spinner of the Years
Said "Now!" And each one hears,
And consummation comes, and jars two hemispheres.

SEAMUS HEANEY (1939–   )

Mid-Term Break   (1966)

I sat all morning in the college sick bay
Counting bells knelling classes to a close.
At two o'clock our neighbors drove me home.

°*Immanent:* Inherent, dwelling within.   °*anon:* Soon.   °*august:* Awe-inspiring, majestic.

In the porch I met my father crying—
He had always taken funerals in his stride—   5
And Big Jim Evans saying it was a hard blow.

The baby cooed and laughed and rocked the pram
When I came in, and I was embarrassed
By old men standing up to shake my hand

And tell me they were "sorry for my trouble,"   10
Whispers informed strangers I was the eldest,
Away at school, as my mother held my hand

In hers and coughed out angry tearless sighs.
At ten o'clock the ambulance arrived
With the corpse, stanched and bandaged by the nurses.   15

Next morning I went up into the room. Snowdrops
And candles soothed the bedside; I saw him
For the first time in six weeks. Paler now,

Wearing a poppy bruise on his left temple,
He lay in the four foot box as in his cot.   20
No gaudy scars, the bumper knocked him clear.

A four foot box, a foot for every year.

EDWARD HIRSCH (1950–   )

Fast Break   (1990)

In Memory of Dennis Turner, 1946–1984

A hook shot kisses the rim and
hangs there, helplessly, but doesn't drop,

and for once our gangly starting center
boxes out his man and times his jump.

perfectly, gathering the orange leather   5
from the air like a cherished possession

and spinning around to throw a strike
to the outlet who is already shoveling

an underhand pass toward the other guard
scissoring past a flat-footed defender   10

who looks stunned and nailed to the floor
in the wrong direction, trying to catch sight

of a high, gliding dribble and a man
letting the play develop in front of him

in slow motion, almost exactly   15
like a coach's drawing on the blackboard,

both forwards racing down the court
the way that forwards should, fanning out

and filling the lanes in tandem, moving
together as brothers passing the ball   20

between them without a dribble, without
a single bounce hitting the hardwood

until the guard finally lunges out
and commits to the wrong man

while the power-forward explodes past them   25
in a fury, taking the ball into the air

by himself now and laying it gently
against the glass for a lay-up,

but losing his balance in the process,
inexplicably falling, hitting the floor   30

with a wild, headlong motion
for the game he loved like a country

and swiveling back to see an orange blur
floating perfectly though the net.

GERARD MANLEY HOPKINS   (1844–1889)

God's Grandeur   (1877)

The world is charged with the grandeur of God.
   It will flame out, like shining from shook foil;
   It gathers to a greatness, like the ooze of oil
Crushed. Why do men then now not reck his rod?
Generations have trod, have trod, have trod;   5
   And all is seared with trade; bleared, smeared with toil;
   And wears man's smudge and shares man's smell: the soil
Is bare now, nor can foot feel, being shod.

And for all this, nature is never spent;
   There lives the dearest freshness deep down things;   10
And though the last lights off the black West went
   Oh, morning, at the brown brink eastward, springs—
Because the Holy Ghost over the bent
   World broods with warm breast and with ah! bright wings.

LANGSTON HUGHES (1902–1967)

Theme for English B (1949)

The instructor said,

> *Go home and write*
> *a page tonight.*
> *And let that page come out of you—*
> *Then, it will be true.*   5

I wonder if it's that simple?
I am twenty-two, colored, born in Winston-Salem.
I went to school there, then Durham, then here
to this college on the hill above Harlem.
I am the only colored student in my class.   10
The steps from the hill lead down into Harlem,
through a park, then I cross St. Nicholas,
Eighth Avenue, Seventh, and I come to the Y,
the Harlem Branch Y, where I take the elevator
up to my room, sit down and write this page: 15

It's not easy to know what is true for you or me
at twenty-two, my age. But I guess I'm what
I feel and see and hear, Harlem, I hear you:
hear you, hear me — we two — you, me, talk on this page.
(I hear New York, too) Me — who?   20
Well, I like to eat, sleep, drink, and be in love.
I like to work, read, learn, and understand life.
I like a pipe for a Christmas present,
or records — Bessie,° bop,° or Bach.
I guess being colored doesn't make me *not* like   25

°*Bessie:* Bessie Smith (1894–1937), blues singer.   °*bop:* Short for "bebop," a jazz style developed in the early 1940s by Charlie Parker, Dizzy Gillespie, and others.

the same things other folks like who are other races.
So will my page be colored that I write?
Being me, it will not be white.
But it will be
a part of you, instructor. 30
You are white —
yet a part of me, as I am a part of you.
That's American.
Sometimes perhaps you don't want to be a part of me.
Nor do I often want to be a part of you. 35
But we are, that's true!
As I learn from you,
I guess you learn from me —
although you're older — and white —
and somewhat more free. 40

This is my page for English B.

LANGSTON HUGHES (1902–1967)

The Negro Speaks of Rivers (1921)

I've known rivers:
I've known rivers ancient as the world and old as the flow of
    human blood in human veins.

My soul has grown deep like the rivers.

I bathed in the Euphrates° when dawns were young.
I built my hut near the Congo° and it lulled me to sleep. 5
I looked upon the Nile and raised the pyramids above it.
I heard the singing of the Mississippi when Abe Lincoln went
    down to New Orleans, and I've seen its muddy bosom turn
    all golden in the sunset.

I've known rivers:
Ancient, dusky rivers.

My soul has grown deep like the rivers.

° *Euphrates:* Major river of southwest Asia; with the Tigris, the Euphrates forms a valley sometimes referred to
as the "cradle of civilization."   ° *Congo:* River in equatorial Africa, the continent's second longest.

JOHN KEATS (1795–1821)

La Belle Dame sans Merci:
A Ballad° (1819, 1820)

1

O what can ail thee, knight at arms,
    Alone and palely loitering?
The sedge has wither'd from the lake,
    And no birds sing.

2

O what can ail thee, knight at arms,   5
    So haggard and so woe-begone?
The squirrel's granary is full,
    And the harvest's done.

3

I see a lily on thy brow
    With anguish moist and fever dew,   10
And on thy cheeks a fading rose
    Fast withereth too.

4

I met a lady in the meads,
    Full beautiful, a fairy's child;
Her hair was long, her foot was light,   15
    And her eyes were wild.

5

I made a garland for her head,
    And bracelets too, and fragrant zone;°
She look'd at me as she did love,
    And made sweet moan.   20

6

I set her on my pacing steed,
    And nothing else saw all day long,
For sidelong would she bend, and sing
    A fairy's song.

7

She found me roots of relish sweet,   25
    And honey wild, and manna dew,

° *"La Belle Dame sans Merci"*: The title, which means "The Lovely Lady without Pity," was taken from a medieval poem by Alain Chartier.   ° *fragrant zone:* Belt.

And sure in language strange she said —
    I love thee true.

8

She took me to her elfin grot,°
    And there she wept, and sigh'd full sore,   30
And there I shut her wild wild eyes
    With kisses four.

9

And there she lullèd me asleep,
    And there I dream'd — Ah! woe betide!
The latest° dream I ever dream'd   35
    On the cold hill's side.

10

I saw pale kings, and princes too,
    Pale warriors, death pale were they all;
They cried — "La belle dame sans merci
    Hath thee in thrall!"   40

11

I saw their starv'd lips in the gloam°
    With horrid warning gapèd wide,
And I awoke and found me here
    On the cold hill's side.

12

And this is why I sojourn here,   45
    Alone and palely loitering,
Though the sedge is wither'd from the lake,
    And no birds sing.

JOHN KEATS   (1795–1821)

Ode on a Grecian Urn   (1819)

1

Thou still unravish'd bride of quietness,
    Thou foster-child of silence and slow time,
Sylvan° historian, who canst thus express
A flowery tale more sweetly than our rhyme:
What leaf-fring'd legend haunts about thy shape   5

°*grot:* Grotto.   °*latest:* Last.   °*gloam:* Twilight.   °*Sylvan:* Pertaining to woods or forests.

Of deities or mortals, or of both,
    In Tempe° or the dales of Arcady?°
What men or gods are these? What maidens loth?
What mad pursuit? What struggle to escape?
    What pipes and timbrels? What wild ecstasy?   10

2

Heard melodies are sweet, but those unheard
    Are sweeter; therefore, ye soft pipes, play on;
Not to the sensual ear, but, more endear'd,
    Pipe to the spirit ditties of no tone:
Fair youth, beneath the trees, thou canst not leave   15
    Thy song, nor ever can those trees be bare;
        Bold lover, never, never canst thou kiss,
Though winning near the goal — yet, do not grieve;
        She cannot fade, though thou hast not thy bliss,
    For ever wilt thou love, and she be fair!   20

3

Ah, happy, happy boughs! that cannot shed
    Your leaves, nor ever bid the spring adieu;
And, happy melodist, unwearied,
    For ever piping songs for ever new;
More happy love! more happy, happy love!   25
    For ever warm and still to be enjoy'd,
        For ever panting, and for ever young;
All breathing human passion far above,
    That leaves a heart high-sorrowful and cloy'd,
        A burning forehead, and a parching tongue.   30

4

Who are these coming to the sacrifice?
    To what green altar, O mysterious priest,
Lead'st thou that heifer lowing at the skies,
    And all her silken flanks with garlands drest?
What little town by river or sea shore,   35
    Or mountain-built with peaceful citadel,
        Is emptied of this folk, this pious morn?
And, little town, thy streets for evermore
    Will silent be; and not a soul to tell
        Why thou art desolate, can e'er return.   40

° *Tempe:* A beautiful valley in Greece.   ° *Arcady:* The valleys of Arcadia, a mountainous region on the Greek peninsula. Like Tempe, they represent a rustic pastoral ideal.

5

O Attic° shape! Fair attitude! with brede°
Of marble men and maidens overwrought,°
With forest branches and the trodden weed;
  Thou, silent form, dost tease us out of thought
As doth eternity: Cold Pastoral!   45
  When old age shall this generation waste,
    Thou shalt remain, in midst of other woe
Than ours, a friend to man, to whom thou say'st,
"Beauty is truth, truth beauty,"— that is all
  Ye know on earth, and all ye need to know.   50

JOHN KEATS (1795–1821)

When I Have Fears (1818)

When I have fears that I may cease to be
  Before my pen has gleaned my teeming brain,
Before high-piléd books, in charact'ry,°
  Hold like rich garners the full-ripened grain;
When I behold, upon the night's starred face,   5
  Huge cloudy symbols of a high romance,
And think that I may never live to trace
  Their shadows, with the magic hand of chance;
And when I feel, fair creature of an hour,
  That I shall never look upon thee more,   10
Never have relish in the faery power
  Of unreflecting love!— then on the shore
Of the wide world I stand alone, and think
Till Love and Fame to nothingness do sink.

ARON KEESBURY (1971–   )

On the Robbery across the Street (1998)

(An eyewitness to the Brinks heist)°

I tell them, look. Sure, I was around.
The tenant from four
come down to the store
that night to see can he get a cat.

°*Attic:* Characteristic of Athens or Athenians.   °*brede:* Braid.   °*overwrought:* Elaborately ornamented.
°*charact'ry:* Print.   °*Brinks heist:* A 1950 robbery of a Brinks armored car station in Boston, Massachusetts,
and the subject of the 1978 movie *The Brinks Job.*

Tony or Jimmy, his name is.   5
Henry maybe. Mike? Joe?
Maybe Jimmy. Look, I don't know
but he's a nice boy anyway. Wears specs,

you know. He come down
asks me, says can I get a cat   10
upstairs? I says sure. Keep that
sandy crap out of the drains, though —

clogs them all up, you know.
Then I got to get all new pipes.
So he runs upstairs. He's all hyped   15
up like I ain't seen the cat he's got

already. Maybe two,
three weeks he's got a cat up there.
These kids. Jazzing all around, I swear,
think they can get away with murder.   20

But he's a nice boy and I tell the cops,
I say, look. I been in this store here
for thirty-seven years.
Thirty-seven years in this store.

I tell them sure. I say, look.   25
I was here, I was around
that night. I been in this town
thirty-seven years.
And I don't see nothing.

YUSEF KOMUNYAKAA (1947–   )

Ignis Fatuus° (2004)

Something or someone. A feeling
among a swish of reeds. A swampy
glow haloes the Spanish moss,
& there's a swaying at the edge
like a child's memory of abuse   5
growing flesh, living on what
a screech owl recalls. Nothing

°*Ignis Fatuus:* A phosphorescent light that hovers or flits over swampy ground at night, possibly caused by
spontaneous combustion of gases emitted by rotting organic matter. It is also called *friar's lantern, jack-o'-
lantern,* or *will-o'-the-wisp,* and has come to mean something that misleads or deludes; an illusion.

but a presence that fills up
the mind, a replenished body
singing its way into doubletalk.   10
In the city, *Will o' the Wisp*
floats out of Miles' trumpet,
leaning ghosts against nighttime's
backdrop of neon. A foolish fire
can also start this way: before   15
you slide the key into the lock
& half-turn the knob, you know
someone has snuck into your life.
A high window, a corner of sky
spies on upturned drawers of underwear   20
& unanswered letters, on a tin box
of luminous buttons & subway tokens,
on books, magazines, & clothes
flung to studio's floor,
his sweat lingering in the air.   25
Years ago, you followed someone
here, in love with breath
kissing the nape of your neck,
back when it was easy to be
at least two places at once.   30

TED KOOSER (1939–   )

Selecting a Reader (1980)

First, I would have her be beautiful,
and walking carefully up on my poetry
at the loneliest moment of an afternoon,
her hair still damp at the neck
from washing it. She should be wearing   5
a raincoat, an old one, dirty
from not having money enough for the cleaners.
She will take out her glasses, and there
in the bookstore, she will thumb
over my poems, then put the book back   10
up on its shelf. She will say to herself,
"For that kind of money, I can get
my raincoat cleaned." And she will.

ARCHIBALD MACLEISH (1892–1982)

Ars Poetica° (1926)

A poem should be palpable and mute
As a globed fruit,

Dumb
As old medallions to the thumb,

Silent as the sleeve-worn stone   5
Of casement ledges where the moss has grown—

A poem should be wordless
As the flight of birds.

A poem should be motionless in time
As the moon climbs,   10

Leaving, as the moon releases
Twig by twig the night-entangled trees,

Leaving, as the moon behind the winter leaves,
Memory by memory the mind —

A poem should be motionless in time   15
As the moon climbs.

A poem should be equal to:
Not true.

For all the history of grief
An empty doorway and a maple leaf.   20

For love
The leaning grasses and two lights above the sea —

A poem should not mean
But be.

CHRISTOPHER MARLOWE (1564–1593)

The Passionate Shepherd to His Love (1600)

Come live with me and be my love,
And we will all the pleasures prove
That valleys, groves, hills, and fields,
Woods, or steepy mountain yields.

°*Ars Poetica:* "The Art of Poetry" (Latin).

And we will sit upon the rocks,   5
Seeing the shepherds feed their flocks
By shallow rivers, to whose falls
Melodious birds sing madrigals.

And I will make thee beds of roses
And a thousand fragrant posies,   10
A cap of flowers and a kirtle°
Embroidered all with leaves of myrtle;

A gown made of the finest wool
Which from our pretty lambs we pull;
Fair-linèd slippers for the cold,   15
With buckles of the purest gold;

A belt of straw and ivy buds,
With coral clasps and amber studs.
And if these pleasures may thee move,
Come live with me and be my love.   20

The shepherds' swains shall dance and sing
For thy delight each May morning.
If these delights thy mind may move,
Then live with me and be my love.

CLAUDE McKAY   (1890–1948)

If We Must Die   (1922)

If we must die, let it not be like hogs
Hunted and penned in an inglorious spot,
While round us bark the mad and hungry dogs,
Making their mock at our accursed lot.
If we must die, O let us nobly die,   5
So that our precious blood may not be shed
In vain; then even the monsters we defy
Shall be constrained to honor us though dead!
O kinsmen! we must meet the common foe!
Though far outnumbered let us show us brave,   10
And for their thousand blows deal one deathblow!
What though before us lies the open grave?
Like men we'll face the murderous, cowardly pack,
Pressed to the wall, dying, but fighting back!

°*kirtle:* Skirt.

JAMES MERRILL (1926–1995)

Page from the Koran (1985)

A small vellum environment
Overrun by black
Scorpions of Kufic script — their ranks
All trigger tail and gold vowel-sac —
At auction this mild winter morning went   5
For six hundred Swiss francs.

By noon, fire from the same blue heavens
Had half erased Beirut.
Allah be praised, it said on crude handbills,
For guns and Nazarenes to shoot.   10
"How gladly with proper words," said Wallace Stevens,
"The soldier dies." Or kills.

God's very word, then, stung the heart
To greed and rancor. Yet
Not where the last glow touches one spare man   15
Inked-in against his minaret
—Letters so handled they are life, and hurt,
Leaving the scribe immune?

PABLO NERUDA (1904–1973)

The United Fruit Co.° (1950)

Translated by Robert Bly

When the trumpet sounded, it was
all prepared on the earth,
and Jehovah parceled out the earth
to Coca-Cola, Inc., Anaconda,
Ford Motors, and other entities: 5
The Fruit Company, Inc.
reserved for itself the most succulent,
the central coast of my own land,
the delicate waist of America.
It rechristened its territories   10

° *United Fruit Co.:* Incorporated in New Jersey in 1899 by Andrew Preston and Minor C. Keith, United Fruit became a major force in growing, transporting, and merchandising Latin American produce, especially bananas. The company is notorious for its involvement in politics and is a symbol for many people of "Yankee" imperialism and oppression.

as the "Banana Republics"
and over the sleeping dead,
over the restless heroes
who brought about the greatness,
the liberty and the flags,   15
it established the comic opera:
abolished the independencies,
presented crowns of Caesar,
unsheathed envy, attracted
the dictatorship of the flies,   20
Trujillo flies, Tacho flies,
Carias flies, Martinez flies,
Ubico flies,° damp flies
of modest blood and marmalade,
drunken flies who zoom   25
over the ordinary graves,
circus flies, wise flies
well trained in tyranny.
Among the bloodthirsty flies
the Fruit Company lands its ships,   30
taking off the coffee and the fruit;
the treasure of our submerged
territories flows as though
on plates into the ships.
Meanwhile Indians are falling   35
into the sugared chasms
of the harbors, wrapped
for burial in the mist of the dawn:
a body rolls, a thing
that has no name, a fallen cipher,   40
a cluster of dead fruit
thrown down on the dump.

SHARON OLDS   (1942–   )

The One Girl at the Boys' Party   (1983)

When I take my girl to the swimming party
I set her down among the boys. They tower and
bristle, she stands there smooth and sleek,
her math scores unfolding in the air around her.

° *Trujillo, Tacho, Carias, Martinez, Ubico:* Political dictators.

They will strip to their suits, her body hard and   5
indivisible as a prime number,
they'll plunge in the deep end, she'll subtract
her height from ten feet, divide it into
hundreds of gallons of water, the numbers
bouncing in her mind like molecules of chlorine   10
in the bright blue pool. When they climb out,
her ponytail will hang its pencil lead
down her back, her narrow silk suit
with hamburgers and french fries printed on it
will glisten in the brilliant air, and they will   15
see her sweet face, solemn and
sealed, a factor of one, and she will
see their eyes, two each,
their legs, two each, and the curves of their sexes,
one each, and in her head she'll be doing her   20
wild multiplying, as the drops
sparkle and fall to the power of a thousand from her body.

MARGE PIERCY (1934 –   )

Barbie Doll (1973)

This girlchild was born as usual
and presented dolls that did pee-pee
and miniature GE stoves and irons
and wee lipsticks the color of cherry candy.
Then in the magic of puberty, a classmate said: 5
You have a great big nose and fat legs.

She was healthy, tested intelligent,
possessed strong arms and back,
abundant sexual drive and manual dexterity.
She went to and fro apologizing.   10
Everyone saw a fat nose on thick legs.

She was advised to play coy,
exhorted to come on hearty,
exercise, diet, smile and wheedle.
Her good nature wore out   15
like a fan belt.
So she cut off her nose and her legs
and offered them up.
In the casket displayed on satin she lay

with the undertaker's cosmetics painted on,   20
a turned-up putty nose,
dressed in a pink and white nightie.
Doesn't she look pretty? everyone said.
Consummation at last.
To every woman a happy ending.   25

ROBERT PINSKY (1940 –   )

Shirt (1990)

The back, the yoke, the yardage. Lapped seams,
The nearly invisible stitches along the collar
Turned in a sweatshop by Koreans or Malaysians

Gossiping over tea and noodles on their break
Or talking money or politics while one fitted   5
This armpiece with its overseam to the band

Of cuff I button at my wrist. The presser, the cutter,
The wringer, the mangle. The needle, the union,
The treadle, the bobbin. The code. The infamous blaze

At the Triangle Factory in nineteen-eleven.   10
One hundred and forty-six died in the flames
On the ninth floor, no hydrants, no fire escapes —

The witness in a building across the street
Who watched how a young man helped a girl to step
Up to the windowsill, then held her out   15

Away from the masonry wall and let her drop.
And then another. As if he were helping them up
To enter a streetcar, and not eternity.

A third before he dropped her put her arms
Around his neck and kissed him. Then he held   20
Her into space, and dropped her. Almost at once

He stepped to the sill himself, his jacket flared
And fluttered up from his shirt as he came down,
Air filling up the legs of his gray trousers —

Like Hart Crane's Bedlamite, "shrill shirt ballooning."   25
Wonderful how the pattern matches perfectly
Across the placket and over the twin bar-tacked

Corners of both pockets, like a strict rhyme
Or a major chord. Prints, plaids, checks,
Houndstooth, Tattersall, Madras. The clan tartans   30

Invented by mill-owners inspired by the hoax of Ossian,
To control their savage Scottish workers, tamed
By a fabricated heraldry: MacGregor,

Bailey, MacMartin. The kilt, devised for workers
To wear among the dusty clattering looms.   35
Weavers, carders, spinners. The loader,

The docker, the navvy. The planter, the picker, the sorter
Sweating at her machine in a litter of cotton
As slaves in calico headrags sweated in fields:

George Herbert, your descendant is a Black   40
Lady in South Carolina, her name is Irma
And she inspected my shirt. Its color and fit

And feel and its clean smell have satisfied
Both her and me. We have culled its cost and quality
Down to the buttons of simulated bone,

The buttonholes, the sizing, the facing, the characters
Printed in black on neckband and tail. The shape,
The label, the labor, the color, the shade. The shirt.

SYLVIA PLATH   (1932–1963)

Mirror   (1963)

I am silver and exact. I have no preconceptions.
Whatever I see I swallow immediately
Just as it is, unmisted by love or dislike.
I am not cruel, only truthful —
The eye of a little god, four-cornered.   5
Most of the time I meditate on the opposite wall.
It is pink, with speckles. I have looked at it so long
I think it is a part of my heart. But it flickers.
Faces and darkness separate us over and over.

Now I am a lake. A woman bends over me,   10
Searching my reaches for what she really is.
Then she turns to those liars, the candles or the moon.

I see her back, and reflect it faithfully.
She rewards me with tears and an agitation of hands.
I am important to her. She comes and goes.   15
Each morning it is her face that replaces the darkness.
In me she has drowned a young girl, and in me an old woman
Rises toward her day after day, like a terrible fish.

EZRA POUND   (1885–1972)

The River-Merchant's Wife: A Letter° (1916)

While my hair was still cut straight across my forehead
I played about the front gate, pulling flowers.
You came by on bamboo stilts, playing horse,
You walked about my seat, playing with blue plums.
And we went on living in the village of Chokan:°   5
Two small people, without dislike or suspicion.

At fourteen I married My Lord you.
I never laughed, being bashful.
Lowering my head, I looked at the wall.
Called to, a thousand times, I never looked back.   10

At fifteen I stopped scowling,
I desired my dust to be mingled with yours
Forever and forever and forever.
Why should I climb the lookout?

At sixteen you departed,   15
You went into far Ku-to-yen,° by the river of swirling eddies,
And you have been gone five months.
The monkeys make sorrowful noise overhead.
You dragged your feet when you went out.
By the gate now, the moss is grown, the different mosses, 20
Too deep to clear them away!
The leaves fall early this autumn, in wind.
The paired butterflies are already yellow with August
Over the grass in the West garden;

° *"The River-Merchant's Wife: A Letter"*: This is one of the many translations Pound made of Chinese poems. The poem is a free translation of Li Po's (701–762) "Two Letters from Chang-Kan."   ° *Chokan:* Chang-Kan.
° *Ku-to-yen:* An island in the river Ch'ū-t'ang.

They hurt me. I grow older.   25
If you are coming down through the narrows of the river Kiang,°
Please let me know beforehand,
And I will come out to meet you
    As far as Cho-fu-sa.°

SIR WALTER RALEIGH (1552–1618)

The Nymph's Reply to the Shepherd (1600)

If all the world and love were young,
And truth in every shepherd's tongue,
These pretty pleasures might me move
To live with thee and be thy love.

Time drives the flocks from field to fold,   5
When rivers rage and rocks grow cold;
And Philomel° becometh dumb;
The rest complains of cares to come.

The flowers do fade, and wanton fields
To wayward winter reckoning yields: 10
A honey tongue, a heart of gall,
Is fancy's spring, but sorrow's fall.

Thy gowns, thy shoes, thy beds of roses,
Thy cap, thy kirtle, and thy posies
Soon break, soon wither, soon forgotten,   15
In folly ripe, in reason rotten.

Thy belt of straw and ivy buds,
Thy coral clasps and amber studs.
All these in me no means can move
To come to thee and be thy love.   20

But could youth last, and love still breed,
Had joys no date, nor age no need,
Then these delights my mind might move
To live with thee and be thy love.

° *Kiang:* The Japanese name for the river Ch'ū-t'ang. Pound's translations are based on commentaries derived from Japanese scholars; therefore, he usually uses Japanese instead of Chinese names. ° *Cho-fu-sa:* A beach several hundred miles upstream of Nanking. ° *Philomel:* The nightingale.

HENRY REED   (1914–1986)

Naming of Parts   (1946)

Today we have naming of parts. Yesterday,
We had daily cleaning. And tomorrow morning,
We shall have what to do after firing. But today,
Today we have naming of parts. Japonica°
Glistens like coral in all of the neighboring gardens,   5
    And today we have naming of parts.

This is the lower sling swivel. And this
Is the upper sling swivel, whose use you will see,
When you are given your slings. And this is the piling swivel,
Which in your case you have not got. The branches   10
Hold in the gardens their silent, eloquent gestures,
    Which in our case we have not got.

This is the safety-catch, which is always released
With an easy flick of the thumb. And please do not let me
See anyone using his finger. You can do it quite easy   15
If you have any strength in your thumb. The blossoms
Are fragile and motionless, never letting anyone see
    Any of them using their finger.

And this you can see is the bolt. The purpose of this
Is to open the breech, as you see. We can slide it   20
Rapidly backwards and forwards: we call this
Easing the spring. And rapidly backwards and forwards
The early bees are assaulting and fumbling the flowers:
    They call it easing the Spring.

They call it easing the Spring: it is perfectly easy   25
If you have any strength in your thumb: like the bolt,
And the breech, and the cocking-piece, and the point of balance,
Which in our case we have not got; and the almond-blossom
Silent in all of the gardens and the bees going backwards and
        forwards,
    For today we have the naming of parts.   30

° *Japonica:* A shrub having waxy flowers in a variety of colors.

EDWARD ARLINGTON ROBINSON (1869–1935)

Richard Cory (1897)

Whenever Richard Cory went down town,
We people on the pavement looked at him:
He was a gentleman from sole to crown,
Clean favored, and imperially slim.

And he was always quietly arrayed,   5
And he was always human when he talked;
But still he fluttered pulses when he said,
"Good-morning," and he glittered when he walked.

And he was rich — yes, richer than a king—
And admirably schooled in every grace: 10
In fine, we thought that he was everything
To make us wish that we were in his place.

So on we worked, and waited for the light,
And went without the meat, and cursed the bread;
And Richard Cory, one calm summer night,   15
Went home and put a bullet through his head.

SONIA SANCHEZ (1934–   )

right on: white america (1970)

this country might have
been a pio
    neer land
once.
    but.   there ain't   5
no mo
    indians   blowing
custer's° mind
            with a different
image of america.   10
                this country
might have
            needed shoot/
outs/ daily/
        once.   15

°*custer:* General George Armstrong Custer (1839–1876) was killed by Sioux in his "last stand" at the Little Bighorn in Montana.

                    but. there ain't
        no mo real/ white/ allamerican
                            bad/guys.
        just.
            u & me.   20
                    blk / and un /armed.
        this country might have
        been a pion
                    eer land.   once.
                                        and it still is.   25
        check out
                    the falling
        gun /shells   on our blk /tomorrows.

CARL SANDBURG   (1878–1967)

Fog   (1916)

The fog comes
on little cat feet.
It sits looking
over harbor and city
on silent haunches   5
and then moves on.

WILLIAM SHAKESPEARE   (1564–1616)

Let me not to the marriage of true minds   (1609)

Let me not to the marriage of true minds
Admit impediments.° Love is not love
Which alters when it alteration finds,
Or bends with the remover to remove:
Oh, no! it is an ever-fixéd mark,   5
That looks on tempests and is never shaken;
It is the star to every wandering bark,
Whose worth's unknown, although his height be taken.°

° *Admit impediments:* A reference to "The Order of Solemnization of Matrimony" in the Anglican Book of Common Prayer: "I require that if either of you know any impediments why ye may not be lawfully joined together in Matrimony, ye do now confess it."   ° *Whose worth's . . . taken:* Although the altitude of a star may be measured, its worth is unknowable.

Love's not Time's fool,° though rosy lips and cheeks
Within his bending sickle's compass come;   10
Love alters not with his brief hours and weeks,
But bears it out even to the edge of doom.°
    If this be error and upon me proved,
    I never writ, nor no man ever loved.

WILLIAM SHAKESPEARE (1564–1616)

Not marble, nor the gilded monuments (1609)

Not marble, nor the gilded monuments
Of princes, shall outlive this powerful rhyme;
But you shall shine more bright in these contents
Than unswept stone, besmeared with sluttish time.
When wasteful war shall statues overturn,   5
And broils root out the work of masonry,
Nor Mars° his sword nor war's quick fire shall burn
The living record of your memory.
'Gainst death and all-oblivious enmity
Shall you pace forth; your praise shall still find room   10
Even in the eyes of all posterity
That wear this world out to the ending doom.
    So, till the judgment that yourself arise,
    You live in this, and dwell in lovers' eyes.

PERCY BYSSHE SHELLEY (1792–1822)

Ode to the West Wind (1820)

I

O wild West Wind, thou breath of Autumn's being,
Thou, from whose unseen presence the leaves dead
Are driven, like ghosts from an enchanter fleeing,

Yellow, and black, and pale, and hectic red,°
Pestilence-stricken multitudes: O Thou,   5
Who chariotest to their dark wintry bed

°*Love's not Time's fool:* Love is not mocked by Time.   °*doom:* Doomsday.   °*Mars:* The Roman god of war.
°*Yellow . . . hectic red:* A reference to a tubercular fever that produces flushed cheeks.

The winged seeds, where they lie cold and low,
Each like a corpse within its grave, until
Thine azure sister of the Spring° shall blow

Her clarion o'er the dreaming earth, and fill   10
(Driving sweet buds like flocks to feed in air)
With living hues and odours plain and hill:

Wild Spirit, which art moving everywhere;
Destroyer and Preserver; hear, O hear!

II

Thou on whose stream, mid the steep sky's commotion,   15
Loose clouds like Earth's decaying leaves are shed,
Shook from the tangled boughs of Heaven and Ocean,

Angels of rain and lightning: there are spread
On the blue surface of thine aery surge,
Like the bright hair uplifted from the head   20

Of some fierce Maenad,° even from the dim verge
Of the horizon to the zenith's height,
The locks of the approaching storm. Thou Dirge

Of the dying year, to which this closing night
Will be the dome of a vast sepulchre,   25
Vaulted with all thy congregated might

Of vapours, from whose solid atmosphere
Black rain and fire and hail will burst: O hear!

III

Thou who didst waken from his summer dreams
The blue Mediterranean, where he lay,   30
Lulled by the coil of his crystalline streams,

Beside a pumice isle in Baiae's bay,°
And saw in sleep old palaces and towers
Quivering within the wave's intenser day,

All overgrown with azure moss and flowers   35
So sweet, the sense faints picturing them! Thou
For whose path the Atlantic's level powers

°*azure . . . Spring:* The west wind of the spring.   °*Maenad:* A female votary who danced wildly in ceremonies for Dionysus (or Bacchus), Greek god of wine and vegetation, who according to legend died in the fall and was reborn in the spring.   °*Baiae's bay:* A bay in the Mediterranean Sea, west of Naples. It was known for the opulent villas built by Roman emperors along its shores.

Cleave themselves into chasms, while far below
The sea-blooms and the oozy woods which wear
The sapless foliage of the ocean, know   40

Thy voice, and suddenly grow grey with fear,
And tremble and despoil themselves: O hear!

IV

If I were a dead leaf thou mightest bear;
If I were a swift cloud to fly with thee;
A wave to pant beneath thy power, and share   45

The impulse of thy strength, only less free
Than thou, O Uncontrollable! If even
I were as in my boyhood, and could be

The comrade of thy wanderings over Heaven,
As then, when to outstrip thy skiey speed   50
Scarce seemed a vision; I would ne'er have striven

As thus with thee in prayer in my sore need,
Oh! lift me as a wave, a leaf, a cloud!
I fall upon the thorns of life! I bleed!

A heavy weight of hours has chained and bowed   55
One too like thee: tameless, and swift, and proud.

V

Make me thy lyre,° even as the forest is:
What if my leaves are falling like its own!
The tumult of thy mighty harmonies

Will take from both a deep, autumnal tone,   60
Sweet though in sadness. Be thou, Spirit fierce,
My spirit! Be thou me, impetuous one!

Drive my dead thoughts over the universe
Like withered leaves to quicken a new birth!
And, by the incantation of this verse,   65

Scatter, as from an unextinguished hearth
Ashes and sparks, my words among mankind!
Be through my lips to unawakened Earth

The trumpet of a prophecy! O Wind,
If Winter comes, can Spring be far behind?   70

° *lyre:* An Aeolian harp, a stringed instrument that produces musical sounds when exposed to the wind.

WALLACE STEVENS   (1879–1955)

Anecdote of the Jar   (1923)

I placed a jar in Tennessee,
And round it was, upon a hill.
It made the slovenly wilderness
Surround that hill.

The wilderness rose up to it,   5
And sprawled around, no longer wild.
The jar was round upon the ground
And tall and of a port in air.

It took dominion everywhere.
The jar was gray and bare.   10
It did not give of bird or bush,
Like nothing else in Tennessee.

WALLACE STEVENS   (1879–1955)

The Emperor of Ice-Cream   (1923)

Call the roller of big cigars,
The muscular one, and bid him whip
In kitchen cups concupiscent curds.
Let the wenches dawdle in such dress
As they are used to wear, and let the boys   5
Bring flowers in last month's newspapers.
Let be be finale of seem.
The only emperor is the emperor of ice-cream.

Take from the dresser of deal,°
Lacking the three glass knobs, that sheet   10
On which she embroidered fantails° once
And spread it so as to cover her face.
If her horny feet protrude, they come
To show how cold she is, and dumb.
Let the lamp affix its beam.   15
The only emperor is the emperor of ice-cream.

°*deal:* Fir or pine wood.   °*fantails:* According to Stevens, "the word fantails does not mean fans, but fantail pigeons."

ALFRED, LORD TENNYSON (1809–1892)

Ulysses° (1833)

It little profits that an idle king,
By this still hearth, among these barren crags,
Matched with an agèd wife, I mete and dole
Unequal laws unto a savage race
That hoard, and sleep, and feed, and know not me.   5
I cannot rest from travel; I will drink
Life to the lees. All times I have enjoyed
Greatly, have suffered greatly, both with those
That loved me, and alone; on shore, and when
Through scudding drifts the rainy Hyades°   10
Vexed the dim sea. I am become a name;
For always roaming with a hungry heart
Much have I seen and known — cities of men
And manners, climates, councils, governments,
Myself not least, but honored of them all —   15
And drunk delight of battle with my peers,
Far on the ringing plains of windy Troy.°
I am a part of all that I have met;
Yet all experience is an arch wherethrough
Gleams that untraveled world whose margin fades   20
Forever and forever when I move.
How dull it is to pause, to make an end,
To rust unburnished, not to shine in use!
As though to breathe were life! Life piled on life
Were all too little, and of one to me   25
Little remains; but every hour is saved
From that eternal silence, something more,
A bringer of new things; and vile it were
For some three suns to store and hoard myself,
And this grey spirit yearning in desire   30
To follow knowledge like a sinking star,

°*Ulysses:* A legendary Greek king of Ithaca and hero of Homer's *Odyssey,* Ulysses (or Odysseus) is noted for his daring and cunning. After his many adventures — including encounters with the Cyclops, the cannibalistic Laestrygones, and the enchantress Circe — Ulysses returned home to his faithful wife, Penelope. Tennyson portrays an older Ulysses pondering his situation.   °*Hyades:* A group of stars whose rising was supposedly followed by rain and thus stormy seas.   °*Troy:* An ancient city in Asia Minor. According to legend, Paris, king of Troy, abducted Helen, the beautiful wife of Menelaus, king of Sparta, initiating the Trojan War, in which numerous Greek heroes, including Ulysses, fought.

Beyond the utmost bound of human thought.
　This is my son, mine own Telemachus,
To whom I leave the scepter and the isle —
Well-loved of me, discerning to fulfill   35
This labor, by slow prudence to make mild
A rugged people, and through soft degrees
Subdue them to the useful and the good.
Most blameless is he, centered in the sphere
Of common duties, decent not to fail   40
In offices of tenderness, and pay
Meet adoration to my household gods,
When I am gone. He works his work, I mine.
　There lies the port; the vessel puffs her sail;
There gloom the dark, broad seas. My mariners,   45
Souls that have toiled, and wrought, and thought with me —
That ever with a frolic welcome took
The thunder and the sunshine, and opposed
Free hearts, free foreheads — you and I are old;
Old age hath yet his honor and his toil.   50
Death closes all; but something ere the end,
Some work of noble note, may yet be done,
Not unbecoming men that strove with Gods.
The lights begin to twinkle from the rocks;
The long day wanes; the low moon climbs; the deep   55
Moans round with many voices. Come, my friends,
'Tis not too late to seek a newer world.
Push off, and sitting well in order smite
The sounding furrows; for my purpose holds
To sail beyond the sunset, and the baths   60
Of all the western stars, until I die.
It may be that the gulfs will wash us down;
It may be we shall touch the Happy Isles,°
And see the great Achilles,° whom we knew.
Though much is taken, much abides; and though   65
We are not now that strength which in old days
Moved earth and heaven, that which we are, we are —
One equal temper of heroic hearts,
Made weak by time and fate, but strong in will
To strive, to seek, to find, and not to yield.

° *Happy Isles:* Elysium, or Paradise, believed to be in the far western ocean.   ° *Achilles:* Greek hero of the
Trojan War.

PHILLIS WHEATLEY   (1753–1784)

On Being Brought from Africa to America   (1773)

'Twas mercy brought me from my *Pagan* land,
Taught my benighted soul to understand
That there's a God, that there's a *Saviour* too:
Once I redemption neither sought nor knew.
Some view our sable race with scornful eye,   5
"Their colour is a diabolic die."
Remember, *Christians*, *Negroes*, black as *Cain*,
May be refin'd, and join th' angelic train.

WALT WHITMAN   (1819–1892)

A Noiseless Patient Spider   (1881)

A noiseless patient spider,
I mark'd where on a little promontory it stood isolated,
Mark'd how to explore the vacant vast surrounding,
It launch'd forth filament, filament, filament, out of itself,
Ever unreeling them, ever tirelessly speeding them.   5

And you O my soul where you stand,
Surrounded, detached, in measureless oceans of space,
Ceaselessly musing, venturing, throwing, seeking the spheres to
    connect them,
Till the bridge you will need be form'd, till the ductile anchor
    hold,
Till the gossamer thread you fling catch somewhere, O my soul.   10

WALT WHITMAN   (1819–1892)

from "Song of Myself"   (1855)

1

I celebrate myself, and sing myself,
And what I assume you shall assume,
For every atom belonging to me as good belongs to you.

I loafe and invite my soul,
I lean and loafe at my ease observing a spear of summer grass.   5

My tongue, every atom of my blood, form'd from this soil, this air,
Born here of parents born here from parents the same, and their
    parents the same,
I, now thirty-seven years old in perfect health begin,
Hoping to cease not till death.

Creeds and schools in abeyance,   10
Retiring back a while sufficed at what they are, but never
    forgotten,
I harbor for good or bad, I permit to speak at every hazard,
Nature without check with original energy.

                                2
Houses and rooms are full of perfumes, the shelves are crowded
    with perfumes,
I breathe the fragrance myself and know it and like it,   15
The distillation would intoxicate me also, but I shall not let it.

The atmosphere is not a perfume, it has no taste of the distillation,
    it is odorless,
It is for my mouth forever, I am in love with it,
I will go to the bank by the wood and become undisguised
    and naked,
I am mad for it to be in contact with me.   20

The smoke of my own breath,
Echoes, ripples, buzz'd whispers, love-root, silk-thread, crotch
    and vine,
My respiration and inspiration, the beating of my heart, the
    passing of blood and air through my lungs,
The sniff of green leaves and dry leaves, and of the shore and
    dark-color'd sea-rocks, and of hay in the barn,
The sound of the belch'd words of my voice loos'd to the eddies
    of the wind,   25
A few light kisses, a few embraces, a reaching around of arms,
The play of shine and shade on the trees as the supple boughs wag,
The delight alone or in the rush of the streets, or along the fields
    and hill-sides,
The feeling of health, the full-noon trill, the song of me rising
    from bed and meeting the sun.

Have you reckon'd a thousand acres much? have you reckon'd the
    earth much?   30
Have you practis'd so long to learn to read?
Have you felt so proud to get at the meaning of poems?

Stop this day and night with me and you shall possess the origin
    of all poems,
You shall possess the good of the earth and sun, (there are millions
    of suns left,)
You shall no longer take things at second or third hand, nor look
    through the eyes of the dead, nor feed on the spectres in books,   35
You shall not look through my eyes either, nor take things
    from me,
You shall listen to all sides and filter them from your self.

WILLIAM WORDSWORTH (1770–1850)

London, 1802 (1802)

Milton!° thou should'st be living at this hour:
England hath need of thee: she is a fen
Of stagnant waters: altar, sword and pen,
Fireside, the heroic wealth of hall and bower,
Have forfeited their ancient English dower   5
Of inward happiness. We are selfish men;
Oh! raise us up, return to us again;
And give us manners, virtue, freedom, power.
Thy soul was like a star, and dwelt apart:
Thou hadst a voice whose sound was like the sea: 10
Pure as the naked heavens, majestic, free,
So didst thou travel on life's common way,
In cheerful godliness; and yet thy heart
The lowliest duties on herself did lay.

WILLIAM WORDSWORTH (1770–1850)

My heart leaps up when I behold (1807)

My heart leaps up when I behold
    A rainbow in the sky:
So was it when my life began;
So is it now I am a man;
So be it when I shall grow old,   5
    Or let me die!
The Child is father of the Man;
And I could wish my days to be
Bound each to each by natural piety.

°*Milton:* John Milton (1608–1674), poet, best known for *Paradise Lost.*

WILLIAM BUTLER YEATS (1865–1939)

Crazy Jane Talks with the Bishop (1933)

I met the Bishop on the road
And much said he and I.
"Those breasts are flat and fallen now,
Those veins must soon be dry;
Live in a heavenly mansion,   5
Not in some foul sty."

"Fair and foul are near of kin,
And fair needs foul," I cried.
"My friends are gone, but that's a truth
Nor grave nor bed denied,   10
Learned in bodily lowliness
And in the heart's pride.

"A woman can be proud and stiff
When on love intent;
But Love has pitched his mansion in   15
The place of excrement;
For nothing can be sole or whole
That has not been rent."

WILLIAM BUTLER YEATS (1865–1939)

The Lake Isle of Innisfree (1892)

I will arise and go now, and go to Innisfree,°
And a small cabin build there, of clay and wattles° made:
Nine bean-rows will I have there, a hive for the honey-bee,
And live alone in the bee-loud glade.

And I shall have some peace there, for peace comes dropping slow,   5
Dropping from the veils of the morning to where the cricket sings;
There midnight's all a glimmer, and noon a purple glow,
And evening full of the linnet's wings.

I will arise and go now, for always night and day
I hear lake water lapping with low sounds by the shore;   10
While I stand on the roadway, or on the pavements grey,
I hear it in the deep heart's core.

° *Innisfree:* An island in Lough (Lake) Gill, County Sligo, in Ireland.   ° *wattles:* Stakes interwoven with twigs or branches, used for walls and roofing.

WILLIAM BUTLER YEATS (1865–1939)

Sailing to Byzantium° (1927)

That is no country for old men. The young
In one another's arms, birds in the trees
— Those dying generations — at their song,
The salmon-falls, the mackerel-crowded seas,
Fish, flesh, or fowl, commend all summer long   5
Whatever is begotten, born, and dies.
Caught in that sensual music all neglect
Monuments of unaging intellect.

An aged man is but a paltry thing,
A tattered coat upon a stick, unless   10
Soul clap its hands and sing, and louder sing
For every tatter in its mortal dress,
Nor is there singing school but studying
Monuments of its own magnificence;
And therefore I have sailed the seas and come   15
To the holy city of Byzantium.

O sages standing in God's holy fire
As in the gold mosaic of a wall,
Come from the holy fire, perne in a gyre,
And be the singing-masters of my soul.   20
Consume my heart away; sick with desire
And fastened to a dying animal
It knows not what it is; and gather me
Into the artifice of eternity.

Once out of nature I shall never take   25
My bodily form from any natural thing,
But such a form as Grecian goldsmiths make
Of hammered gold and gold enameling
To keep a drowsy Emperor awake;
Or set upon a golden bough to sing   30
To lords and ladies of Byzantium
Of what is past, or passing, or to come.

° *Byzantium:* Ancient Greek city later rebuilt as Constantinople (now Istanbul).

WILLIAM BUTLER YEATS (1865–1939)

The Second Coming° (1921)

Turning and turning in the widening gyre°
The falcon cannot hear the falconer;
Things fall apart; the center cannot hold;
Mere anarchy is loosed upon the world,
The blood-dimmed tide is loosed, and everywhere   5
The ceremony of innocence is drowned;
The best lack all conviction, while the worst
Are full of passionate intensity.°

Surely some revelation is at hand;
Surely the Second Coming is at hand;   10
The Second Coming! Hardly are those words out
When a vast image out of *Spiritus Mundi*°
Troubles my sight: somewhere in sands of the desert
A shape with lion body and the head of a man,
A gaze blank and pitiless as the sun,   15
Is moving its slow thighs, while all about it
Reel shadows of the indignant desert birds.
The darkness drops again; but now I know
That twenty centuries° of stony sleep
Were vexed to nightmare by a rocking cradle,   20
And what rough beast, its hour come round at last,
Slouches towards Bethlehem to be born?

° *The Second Coming:* The phrase usually refers to the return of Christ. Yeats theorized cycles of history, much like the turning of a wheel. Here he offers a poetic comment on his view of the dissolution of civilization at the end of one such cycle.   °*gyre:* Spiral.   °*Mere . . . intensity:* Lines 4–8 refer to the Russian Revolution of 1917.   °*Spiritus Mundi:* Literally, "Spirit of the World" (Latin). Yeats believed all souls to be connected by a "Great Memory."   °*twenty centuries:* The centuries between the birth of Christ and the twentieth century, in which Yeats was writing.

4 | DRAMA

CHAPTER 25

UNDERSTANDING DRAMA

Origins of Modern Drama

The Ancient Greek Theater

The dramatic presentations of ancient Greece developed out of religious rites performed to honor gods or to mark the coming of spring. Playwrights such as Aeschylus (525–456 B.C.), Sophocles (496–406 B.C.), and Euripides (480?–406 B.C.) wrote plays to be performed and judged at competitions held during the yearly Dionysian festivals. Works were chosen by a selection board and evaluated by a panel of judges. To compete in the contest, writers had to submit three tragedies, which could be either based on a common theme or unrelated, and one comedy. Unfortunately, relatively few of these ancient Greek plays survive today.

The open-air semicircular ancient Greek theater, built into the side of a hill, looked much like a primitive version of a modern sports stadium. Some Greek theaters, such as the Athenian theater, could seat almost seventeen thousand spectators. Sitting in tiered seats, the audience would look down on the **orchestra,** or "dancing place," occupied by the **chorus** — originally a group of men (led by an individual called the **choragos**) who danced and chanted, then later a group of onlookers who commented on the drama. Raised a few steps above the orchestra was a platform on which the actors performed. Behind this platform was a **skene,** or building, that originally served as a resting place or dressing room. (The modern word *scene* is derived from the Greek *skene.*) Behind the skene was a line of pillars called a **colonnade,** which was covered by a roof. Actors used the skene for entrances and exits; beginning with the plays of Sophocles, painted backdrops were hung there. These backdrops, however, were most likely more decorative than realistic. Historians believe that realistic props and scenery were probably absent from the ancient Greek theater. Instead, the setting was suggested by the play's dialogue, and the audience had to imagine the specific physical details of a scene.

Two mechanical devices were used. One, a rolling cart or platform, was sometimes employed to introduce action that had occurred offstage. For example, actors frozen in position could be rolled onto the roof of the skene to illustrate an event such as the killing of Oedipus's father, which occurred before the play began. Another mechanical device, a small crane, was used to show gods ascending to or

711

Grand Theater at Ephesus (3rd century B.C.), a Greek settlement in what is now Turkey.

descending from heaven. Such devices enabled playwrights to dramatize the myths that were celebrated at the Dionysian festivals.

The ancient Greek theater was designed to enhance acoustics. The flat stone wall of the skene reflected the sound from the orchestra and the stage, and the curved shape of the amphitheater captured the sound, enabling the audience to hear the lines spoken by the actors. Each actor wore a stylized mask, or **persona,** to convey to the audience the personality traits of the particular character being portrayed — a king, a soldier, a wise old man, a young girl (female roles were played by men). The mouths of these masks were probably constructed so they amplified the voice and projected it into the audience. In addition, the actors wore *kothorni,* high shoes that elevated them above the stage, perhaps also helping to project their voices. Due to the excellent acoustics, audiences who see plays performed in these ancient theaters today can hear clearly without microphones or speaker systems.

Because actors wore masks and because males played the parts of women and gods as well as men, acting methods in the ancient Greek theater were probably not realistic. In their masks, high shoes, and full-length tunics (called *chiton*), actors could not hope to appear natural or to mimic the attitudes of everyday life. Instead, they probably recited their lines while standing in stylized poses, with emotions conveyed more by gesture and tone than by action. Typically, three actors had all the speaking roles. One actor — the **protagonist** — would play the central role and have the largest speaking part. Two other actors would divide the remaining lines between them. Although other characters would come on and off the stage, they would usually not have speaking roles.

Ancient Greek tragedies were typically divided into five parts. The first part was the **prologos,** or prologue, in which an actor gave the background or explanations that the audience needed to follow the rest of the drama. Then came the párodos, in which the chorus entered and commented on the events presented in the prologue. Following this were several **episodia,** or episodes, in which characters spoke to one another on the stage and developed the central conflict of the play. Alternating with episodes were **stasimon** (choral odes), in which the chorus commented on the exchanges that had taken place during the preceding episode. Frequently, the choral odes were divided into *strophes*, or stanzas, which were recited or sung as the chorus moved across the orchestra in one direction, and *antistrophes*, which were recited as it moved in the opposite direction. (Interestingly, the chorus stood between the audience and the actors, often functioning as an additional audience, expressing the political, social, and moral views of the community.) The fifth part was the **exodos,** the last scene of the play, during which the conflict was resolved and the actors left the stage.

Using music, dance, and verse — as well as a variety of architectural and technical innovations — the ancient Greek theater was able to convey the traditional themes of tragedy. Thus, the theater powerfully expressed ideas that were central to the religious festivals in which they first appeared: the reverence for the cycles of life and death, the unavoidable dictates of the gods, and the inscrutable workings of fate.

The Elizabethan Theater

The Elizabethan theater, influenced by the classical traditions of Roman and Greek dramatists, traces its roots back to local religious pageants performed at medieval festivals during the twelfth and thirteenth centuries. Town guilds — organizations of craftsmen who worked in the same profession — reenacted Old and New Testament stories: the fall of man, Noah and the flood, David and Goliath, and the crucifixion of Christ, for example. Church fathers encouraged these plays because they brought the Bible to a largely illiterate audience. Sometimes these spectacles, called **mystery plays,** were presented in the market square or on the church steps, and at other times actors appeared on movable stages or wagons called **pageants,** which could be wheeled to a given location. (Some of these wagons were quite elaborate, with trapdoors and pulleys and an upper tier that simulated heaven.) As mystery plays became more popular, they were performed in series over several days, presenting an entire cycle of a holiday — the crucifixion and resurrection of Christ during Easter, for example.

Related to mystery plays are **morality plays,** which developed in the fourteenth and fifteenth centuries. Unlike mystery plays, which depict scenes from the Bible, morality plays allegorize the Christian way of life. Typically, characters representing various virtues and vices struggle or debate over the soul of man. *Everyman* (1500), the best known of these plays, dramatizes the good and bad qualities of Everyman and shows his struggle to determine what is of value to him as he journeys toward death.

By the middle of the sixteenth century, mystery and morality plays had lost ground to a new secular drama. One reason for this decline was that mystery and morality plays were associated with Catholicism and consequently discouraged by the Protestant clergy. In addition, newly discovered plays of ancient Greece and Rome introduced a dramatic tradition that supplanted the traditions of religious drama. English plays that followed the classic model were sensational and bombastic, often dealing with murder, revenge, and blood retribution. Appealing to privileged classes and commoners alike, these plays were extremely popular. (One source estimates that between 20,000 and 25,000 people attended performances each week.)

In spite of the popularity of the theater, actors and playwrights encountered a number of difficulties. First, they faced opposition from city officials who were averse to theatrical presentations because they thought that the crowds attending these performances spread disease. Puritans opposed the theater because they thought plays were immoral and sinful. Finally, some people attached to the royal court opposed the theater because they thought that the playwrights undermined the authority of Queen Elizabeth by spreading politically seditious ideas. As a result, during Elizabeth's reign, performances were placed under the strict control of the **Master of Revels,** a public official who had the power to censor plays (and did so with great regularity) and to grant licenses for performances.

Acting companies that wanted to put on a performance had to obtain a license — possible only with the patronage of a powerful nobleman — and to perform the play in an area designated by the queen. Despite these difficulties, a number of actors and playwrights gained a measure of financial independence by joining together and forming acting companies. These companies of professional actors performed works such as Christopher Marlowe's *Tamburlaine* and Thomas Kyd's *The Spanish Tragedy* in tavern courtyards and then eventually in permanent theaters. According to scholars, the structures of the Elizabethan theater evolved from these tavern courtyards.

William Shakespeare's plays were performed in the Globe Theatre (a corner of which was unearthed in December 1988). Although scholars do not know the exact design of the original Globe, drawings from the period provide a good idea of its physical features. The major difference between the Globe and today's theaters is the multiple stages on which action could be performed. The Globe consisted of a large main **stage** that extended out into the open-air **yard** where the **groundlings,** or common people, stood. Spectators who paid more sat on small stools in two or three levels of galleries that extended in front of and around the stage. (The theater could probably seat almost two thousand people at a performance.) Most of the play's action occurred on the stage, which had no curtain and could be seen from three sides. Beneath the stage was a space called the **hell,** which could be reached when the floorboards were removed. This space enabled actors to "disappear" or descend into a hole or grave when the play called for such action. Above the stage was a roof called the **heavens,** which protected the actors from the weather and contained ropes and pulleys used to lower props or to create special effects.

At the rear of the stage was a narrow **alcove** covered by a curtain that could be open or closed. This curtain, often painted, functioned as a decorative rather

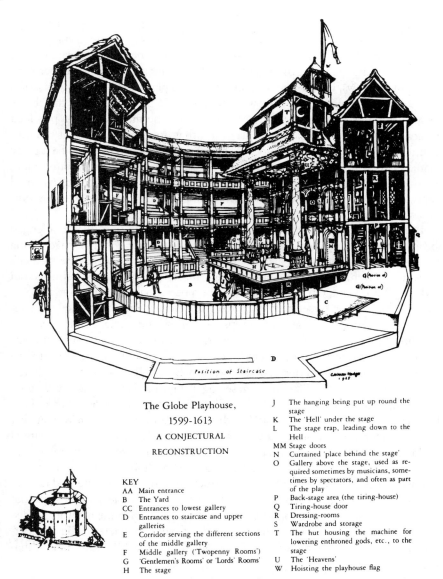

The Globe Playhouse,

1599-1613

A CONJECTURAL

RECONSTRUCTION

KEY

AA Main entrance
B   The Yard
CC Entrances to lowest gallery
D   Entrances to staircase and upper galleries
E   Corridor serving the different sections of the middle gallery
F   Middle gallery ('Twopenny Rooms')
G   'Gentlemen's Rooms' or 'Lords' Rooms'
H   The stage

J   The hanging being put up round the stage
K   The 'Hell' under the stage
L   The stage trap, leading down to the Hell
MM Stage doors
N   Curtained 'place behind the stage'
O   Gallery above the stage, used as required sometimes by musicians, sometimes by spectators, and often as part of the play
P   Back-stage area (the tiring-house)
Q   Tiring-house door
R   Dressing-rooms
S   Wardrobe and storage
T   The hut housing the machine for lowering enthroned gods, etc., to the stage
U   The 'Heavens'
W   Hoisting the playhouse flag

The Globe Playhouse, 1599–1613; a conjectural reconstruction. From C. Walter Hodges *The Globe Restored: A Study of the Elizabethan Theatre.* New York: Norton, 1973.

than a realistic backdrop. The main function of this alcove was to enable actors to hide or disappear when the script called for them to do so. Some Elizabethan theaters contained a **rear stage** instead of an alcove. Because the rear stage was concealed by a curtain, props could be arranged on it ahead of time. When the action on the rear stage was finished, the curtain would be closed and the action would continue on the front stage.

On either side of the rear stage was a door through which the actors could enter and exit the front stage. Above the rear stage was a curtained stage called the **chamber,** which functioned as a balcony or as any other setting located above the action taking place on the stage below. On either side of the chamber were casement windows, which actors could use when a play called for a conversation with someone leaning out a window or standing on a balcony. Above the chamber was the **music gallery,** a balcony that housed the musicians who provided musical interludes throughout the play (and that doubled as a stage if the play required it). The **huts,** windows located above the music gallery, could be used by characters playing lookouts or sentries. Because of the many acting sites, more than one action could take place simultaneously. For example, lookouts could stand in the towers of Hamlet's castle while Hamlet and Horatio walked the walls below.

During Shakespeare's time, the theater had many limitations that challenged the audience's imagination. Because women did not perform on the stage, young boys — usually between the ages of ten and twelve — played all the women's parts. In addition, there was no artificial lighting, so plays had to be performed in daylight. Rain, wind, or clouds could disrupt a performance or ruin an image — such as "the morn in russet mantle clad" — that the audience was asked to imagine. Finally, because few sets and props were used, the audience often had to visualize the high walls of a castle or the trees of a forest. The plays were performed without intermission, except for musical interludes that occurred at various points. Thus, the experience of seeing one of Shakespeare's plays staged in the Elizabethan theater was different from seeing it staged today in a modern theater.

Today, a reconstruction of the Globe Theatre stands on the south bank of the Thames River in London. In the 1940s, the late American actor Sam Wanamaker visited London and was shocked to find nothing that commemorated the site of the original Globe. He eventually decided to try to raise enough money to reconstruct the Globe in its original location. The Globe Playhouse Trust was founded in the 1970s, but the actual construction of the new theater did not begin until the 1980s. After a number of setbacks — for example, the Trust ran out of funds after the construction of a large underground "diaphragm" wall needed to keep out the river water — the project was finally completed. The first performance at the reconstructed Globe was given on June 14, 1996, Sam Wanamaker's birthday.

The Modern Theater

Unlike the theaters of ancient Greece and Elizabethan England, seventeenth- and eighteenth-century theaters — such as the Palais Royal, where the great French playwright Molière presented many of his plays — were covered by a roof, beautifully decorated, and illuminated by candles so that plays could be performed at night. The theater remained brightly lit even during performances, partly because there was no easy way to extinguish hundreds of candles and partly because

Aerial view of the reconstructed Globe Theatre in London.

people went to the theater as much to see each other as to see the play. A curtain opened and closed between acts. The audience of about five hundred spectators sat in a long room and viewed the play on a **picture-frame stage.** This type of stage contained the action within a **proscenium arch** that surrounded the opening through which the audience viewed the performance. Thus, the action seemed to take place in an adjoining room with one of its walls cut away. Painted scenery (some of it quite elaborate), intricately detailed costumes, and stage makeup were commonplace, and for the first time women performed female roles. In addition, a complicated series of ropes, pulleys, and cranks enabled stagehands to change scenery quickly, and sound-effects machines could give audiences the impression that they were hearing a galloping horse or a raging thunderstorm. Because the theaters were small, audiences were relatively close to the stage, so actors could use subtle movements and facial expressions to enhance their performances.

Many of the first innovations in the theater were quite basic. For example, the first stage lighting was produced by candles lining the front of the stage. This method of lighting was not only ineffective — actors were lit from below and had to step forward to be fully illuminated — but also dangerous. Costumes and even entire theaters could (and did) catch fire. Later, covered lanterns with reflectors provided better lighting. In the nineteenth century, a device that used an oxyhydrogen flame directed on a cylinder of lime created extremely bright illumination that could, with the aid of a lens, be concentrated into a spotlight. (It is from this method of stage lighting that we get the expression *to be in the limelight.*)

Eventually, in the twentieth century, electric lights provided a dependable and safe way of lighting the stage. Electric spotlights, footlights, and ceiling light bars made the actors clearly visible and enabled playwrights to create special effects. In Arthur Miller's *Death of a Salesman* (p. 858), for example, lighting focuses attention on action in certain areas of the stage while leaving other areas in complete darkness.

Along with electric lighting came other innovations, such as electronic amplification. Microphones made it possible for actors to speak conversationally and to avoid using unnaturally loud "stage diction" to project their voices to the rear of the theater. Microphones placed at various points around the stage enabled actors and actresses to interact naturally and to deliver their lines audibly even without facing the audience. More recently, small wireless microphones eliminated the unwieldy wires and the "dead spaces" left between upright or hanging microphones, allowing characters to move freely around the stage.

The true revolutions in staging came with the advent of **realism** in the middle of the nineteenth century. Until this time, scenery was painted on canvas backdrops that trembled visibly, especially when they were intersected by doors through which actors and actresses entered. With realism came settings that were accurate down to the smallest detail. (Improved lighting, which revealed the inadequacies of painted backdrops, made such realistic stage settings necessary.) Backdrops were replaced by the **box set,** three flat panels arranged to form connected walls, with the fourth wall removed to give the audience the illusion of looking into a room. The room itself was decorated with real furniture, plants, and pictures on the walls; the door of one room might connect to another completely furnished room, or a window might open to a garden filled with realistic foliage. In addition, new methods of changing scenery were employed. Elevator stages, hydraulic lifts, and moving platforms enabled directors to make complicated changes in scenery out of the audience's view.

During the late nineteenth and early twentieth centuries, however, some playwrights reacted against what they saw as the excesses of realism. They introduced **surrealistic** stage settings, in which color and scenery mirrored the uncontrolled images of dreams, and **expressionistic** stage settings, in which costumes and scenery were exaggerated and distorted to reflect the workings of a troubled, even unbalanced mind. In addition, playwrights used lighting to create areas of light, shadow, and color that reinforced the themes of the play or reflected the emotions of the protagonist. Eugene O'Neill's *The Emperor Jones,* for example, used a series of expressionistic scenes to show the mental state of the terrified protagonist.

Sets in contemporary plays run the gamut from realistic to fantastic, from a detailed re-creation of a room in a production of Tennessee Williams's *The Glass Menagerie* (p. 1153) to a dreamlike set for *The Emperor Jones* and Edward Albee's *The Sandbox.* Motorized devices, such as revolving turntables, and *wagons* — scenery mounted on wheels — make possible rapid changes of scenery. The Broadway musical *Les Misérables,* for example, required scores of elaborate sets —

Parisian slums, barricades, walled gardens — to be shifted as the audience watched. A gigantic barricade constructed on stage at one point in the play was later rotated to show the carnage that had taken place on both sides of a battle. Light, sound, and smoke were used to heighten the impact of the scene.

Today, as dramatists attempt to break down the barriers that separate audiences from the action they are viewing, plays are not limited to the picture-frame stage; in fact, they are performed on many different kinds of stages. Some plays take place on a **thrust stage,** which has an area that projects out into the audience. Other plays are performed on an **arena stage,** with the audience surrounding the actors. (This kind of performance is often called **theater in the round.**) In addition, experiments have been done with **environmental staging,** in which the stage surrounds the audience or several stages are situated at various locations throughout the audience. Plays may also be performed outdoors, in settings ranging from parks to city streets.

Some playwrights even try to blur the line that divides the audience from the stage by having actors move through or sit in the audience — or even by eliminating the stage entirely. For example, *Tony 'n Tina's Wedding,* a **participatory drama** created in 1988 by the theater group Artificial Intelligence, takes place not in a theater but at a church where a wedding is performed and then at a catering hall where the wedding reception is held. Throughout the play, the members of the audience

Thrust-Stage Theater. With seats on three sides of the stage area, the thrust stage and its background can assume many forms other than the conventional living-room interior in the illustration. Entrances can be made from the aisles, from the sides, through the stage floor, and from the back.

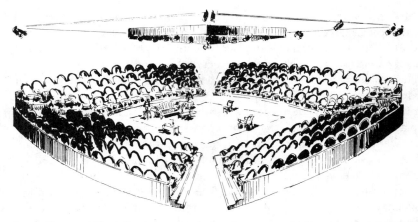

Arena Theater. The audience surrounds the stage area, which may or may not be raised. Use of scenery is limited — perhaps to a single piece of scenery standing alone in the middle of the stage.

function as guests, joining in the wedding celebration and mingling with the actors, who improvise freely. Recent examples of such interactive drama include *Grandma Sylvia's Funeral* and *Off the Wall,* in which audiences "attend" an art auction. Today, no single architectural form defines the theater. The modern stage is a flexible space suited to the many varieties of contemporary theatrical production.

A Note on Translations

Many dramatic works that we read or see are translations from another language. For example, Ibsen wrote in Norwegian, Sophocles in Greek, Molière in French, and Chekhov in Russian. Before English-speaking viewers or readers can evaluate the language of a translated play, they must understand that the language they hear or read is the translator's interpretation of what the playwright intended to communicate. Translation is interpretation, not just a search for literal equivalents; as a result, a translation is always different from the original. Moreover, because translators make different choices, two translations of the same work into English can vary considerably.

Compare these two versions of an exchange of dialogue from two translations of the same Chekhov play, called *The Brute* in the translation that begins on page 723 and *The Bear* in the alternate version.

From *The Brute*

SMIRNOV: You'd like me to come simpering to you in French, I suppose. "*Enchanté, madame! Merci beaucoup* for not paying zee money, *madame!*

Pardonnez-moi if I 'ave disturbed you, *madame!* How *charmante* you look in mourning, *madame!*"

MRS. POPOV: Now you're being silly, Mr. Smirnov.

SMIRNOV: *(mimicking)* "Now you're being silly, Mr. Smirnov." "You don't know how to talk to a lady, Mr. Smirnov." Look here, Mrs. Popov. I've known more women than you've known pussy cats. I've fought three duels on their account. I've jilted twelve, and been jilted by nine others. Oh, yes, Mrs. Popov, I've played the fool in my time, whispered sweet nothings, bowed and scraped and endeavored to please. Don't tell me I don't know what it is to love, to pine away with longing, to have the blues, to melt like butter, to be weak as water. I was full of tender emotion. I was carried away with passion. I squandered half my fortune on the sex. I chattered about women's emancipation. But there's an end to everything, dear madam. . . . (1.71–73)

From *The Bear*

SMIRNOV: Ach, it's astonishing! How would you like me to talk to you? In French, perhaps? *(Lisps in anger.) Madame, je vous prie. . . . how happy I am that you're not paying me the money. . . . Ah, pardon, I've made you uneasy! Such lovely weather we're having today! And you look so becoming in your mourning dress. (Bows and scrapes.)*

MRS. POPOV: That's rude and not very clever!

SMIRNOV: *(teasing)* Rude and not very clever! I don't know how to behave in the company of ladies. Madam, in my time I've seen far more women than you've seen sparrows. Three times I've fought duels over women; I've jilted twelve women, nine have jilted me! Yes! There was a time when I played the fool; I became sentimental over women, used honeyed words, fawned on them, bowed and scraped. . . . I loved, suffered, sighed at the moon; I became limp, melted, shivered . . . I loved passionately, madly, every which way, devil take me, I chattered away like a magpie about the emancipation of women, ran through half my fortune as a result of my tender feelings; but now, if you will excuse me, I'm on to your ways! I've had enough!

Although both translations convey Smirnov's anger and frustration, they use different words (with different connotations), different phrasing — and even different stage directions. In *The Bear,* for instance, only one French phrase is used, whereas *The Brute* uses several and specifies a French accent as well; other differences between the two translations include *The Bear*'s use of "teasing," "sparrows," and "I've had enough!" where *The Brute* uses "mimicking," "pussy cats," and "But there's an end to everything, dear madam." (Elsewhere in the play, *The Bear* uses profanity while *The Brute* uses more polite language.) Many words and idiomatic expressions used in daily speech cannot be translated exactly from one language to another; as a result, the two translators make different choices to try to convey a sense of the original.

Reading Drama

When you read a play, you will notice features it shares with works of fiction — for instance, the use of language and symbols, the interaction among characters, and the development of a theme or themes. In addition, you will notice features that distinguish it from fiction — for example, the presence of stage directions and the division of the play into acts and scenes.

The following guidelines, designed to help you explore works of dramatic literature, focus on issues that are examined in depth in chapters to come:

- *Trace the play's* **plot**. What conflicts are present? Where does the rising action reach a climax? Where does the falling action begin? What techniques move the action along? (See Chapter 27.)
- *Analyze the play's* **characters**. Who are the central characters? What are their most distinctive traits? How do you learn about their personalities, backgrounds, appearances, and strengths and weaknesses? (See Chapter 28.)
- *Consider how the characters interact with one another.* Do the characters change and grow in response to the play's events, or do they remain essentially unchanged? (See Chapter 28.)
- *Examine the play's* **language**. How does **dialogue** reveal characters' emotions, conflicts, opinions, and motivation? (See Chapter 28.)
- *Look for* **soliloquies** *or* **asides**. What do they contribute to your knowledge of the play's characters and events? (See Chapter 28.)
- *Read the play's* **stage directions**. What do you learn from the descriptions of the characters, including their dress, gestures, and facial expressions? (See Chapter 28.) What information do you gain from studying the playwright's descriptions of the play's setting? Do the stage directions include information about lighting, props, music, or sound effects? (See Chapter 29.)
- *Consider the play's* **staging**. Where and when does the action take place? What techniques are used to convey a sense of time and place to the audience? (See Chapter 29.)
- *Try to identify the play's* **themes**. What main idea does the play communicate? What additional themes are explored? (See Chapter 30.)
- *Identify any* **symbols** *in the play.* How do these symbols help you to understand the play's themes? (See Chapter 30.)

ANTON CHEKHOV (1860–1904) is an important nineteenth-century Russian playwright and short story writer. He became a doctor and, as a young adult, supported the rest of his family after his father's bankruptcy. After his early adult years in Moscow, Chekhov spent the rest of his life in the country, moving to Yalta, a resort town in Crimea, for his health (he suffered from tuberculosis). He continued to write plays, mostly for the Moscow Art Theatre, although he could not supervise their production as he would have wished. His plays include *The Seagull* (1896), *Uncle Vanya* (1898), *The Three Sisters* (1901), and *The Cherry Orchard* (1904).

The Brute, or *The Bear* (1888), is one of a number of one-act farces Chekhov wrote just before his major plays. It is based on a French farce (*Les Jurons de Cadillac* by Pierre Breton) about a man who cannot refrain from swearing. The woman he loves offers to marry him if he can avoid swearing for one hour; he is unable to do it, but he fails so charmingly that she agrees to marry him anyway.

The Brute
A JOKE IN ONE ACT (1888)
Translated by Eric Bentley

CHARACTERS

Mrs. Popov, *widow and landowner,*
small, with dimpled cheeks
Mr. Grigory S. Smirnov, *gentleman*
farmer, middle-aged
Luka, *Mrs. Popov's footman, an old man*

Gardener
Coachman
Hired Men

SCENE

The drawing room of a country house. Mrs. Popov, in deep mourning, is staring hard at a photograph. Luka is with her.

LUKA: It's not right, ma'am, you're killing yourself. The cook has gone off with the maid to pick berries. The cat's having a high old time in the yard catching birds. Every living thing is happy. But you stay moping here in the house like it was a convent, taking no pleasure in nothing. I mean it, ma'am! It must be a full year since you set foot out of doors.

MRS. POPOV: I must never set foot out of doors again, Luka. Never! I have nothing to set foot out of doors *for.* My life is done. *He* is in his grave. I have buried myself alive in this house. We are *both* in our graves.

LUKA: You're off again, ma'am. I just won't listen to you no more. Mr. Popov is dead, but what can we do about that? It's God's doing. God's will be done. You've cried over him, you've done your share of mourning, haven't you? There's a limit to everything. You can't go on weeping and wailing forever. My old lady died, for that matter, and I wept and wailed over her a whole month long. Well, that was it. I couldn't weep and wail all my life. She just wasn't worth it. *(He sighs.)* As for the neighbors, you've forgotten all about them, ma'am. You don't visit them and you don't let them visit you. You and I are like a pair of spiders — excuse the expression, ma'am — here we are in this house like a pair of spiders, we never see the light of day. And it isn't like there was no nice people around either. The whole county's swarming with 'em. There's a regiment quartered at Riblov, and the officers are so good-looking! The girls can't take their eyes off them — There's a ball at the camp every Friday — The military band plays most every day of the week — What do you say, ma'am? You're young, you're pretty, you could enjoy yourself! Ten years from now you may want to strut and show your feathers to the officers, and it'll be too late.

Mrs. Popov: *(firmly)* You must never bring this subject up again, Luka. Since Popov died, life has been an empty dream to me, you know that. *You* may think I am alive. Poor ignorant Luka! You are wrong. I am dead. I'm in my grave. Never more shall I see the light of day, never strip from my body this . . . raiment of death! Are you listening, Luka? Let his ghost learn how I love him! Yes, *I* know, and *you* know, he was often unfair to me, he was cruel to me, and he was unfaithful to me. What of it? *I* shall be faithful to *him*, that's all. I will show him how *I* can love. Hereafter, in a better world than this, he will welcome me back, the same loyal girl I always was —

5 Luka: Instead of carrying on this way, ma'am, you should go out in the garden and take a bit of a walk, ma'am. Or why not harness Toby and take a drive? Call on a couple of the neighbours, ma'am?

Mrs. Popov: *(breaking down)* Oh, Luka!

Luka: Yes, ma'am? What have I said, ma'am? Oh, dear!

Mrs. Popov: Toby! You said Toby! He adored that horse. When he drove me out to the Korchagins and the Vlasovs, it was always with Toby! He was a wonderful driver, do you remember, Luka? So graceful! So strong! I can see him now, pulling at those reins with all his might and main! Toby! Luka, tell them to give Toby an extra portion of oats today.

Luka: Yes, ma'am.

A bell rings.

10 Mrs. Popov: Who is that? Tell them I'm not at home.

Luka: Very good, ma'am. *(Exit.)*

Mrs. Popov: *(gazing again at the photograph)* You shall see, my Popov, how a wife can love and forgive. Till death do us part. Longer than that. Till death re-unite us forever! *(Suddenly a titter breaks through her tears.)* Aren't you ashamed of yourself, Popov? Here's your little wife, being good, being faithful, so faithful she's locked up here waiting for her own funeral, while you — doesn't it make you ashamed, you naughty boy? You were terrible, you know. You were unfaithful, and you made those awful scenes about it, you stormed out and left me alone for weeks —

Enter Luka.

LUKA: *(upset)* There's someone asking for you, ma'am. Says he must—

MRS. POPOV: I suppose you told him that since my husband's death I see no one?

LUKA: Yes, ma'am. I did, ma'am. But he wouldn't listen, ma'am. He says it's   15
urgent.

MRS. POPOV: *(shrilly)* I see no one!!

LUKA: He won't take no for an answer, ma'am. He just curses and swears and
comes in anyway. He's a perfect monster, ma'am. He's in the dining room
right now.

MRS. POPOV: In the dining room, is he? I'll give him his come-uppance. Bring
him in here this minute.

Exit Luka.

(Suddenly sad again.) Why do they do this to me? Why? Insulting my grief,
intruding on my solitude? *(She sighs.)* I'm afraid I'll have to enter a convent.
I will, I *must* enter a convent!

Enter Mr. Smirnov and Luka.

SMIRNOV: *(to Luka)* Dolt! Idiot! You talk too much! *(Seeing Mrs. Popov. With
dignity.)* May I have the honor of introducing myself, madam? Grigory S.
Smirnov, landowner and lieutenant of artillery, retired. Forgive me, madam,
if I disturb your peace and quiet, but my business is both urgent and weighty.

MRS. POPOV: *(declining to offer him her hand)* What is it you wish, sir?   20

SMIRNOV: At the time of his death, your late husband — with whom I had the
honor to be acquainted, ma'am — was in my debt to the tune of twelve
hundred rubles. I have two notes to prove it. Tomorrow, ma'am, I must pay
the interest on a bank loan. I have therefore no alternative, ma'am, but to
ask you to pay me the money today.

MRS. POPOV: Twelve hundred rubles? But what did my husband owe it to
you for?

SMIRNOV: He used to buy his oats from me, madam.

MRS. POPOV: *(to Luka, with a sigh)* Remember what I said, Luka: tell them to
give Toby an extra portion of oats today!

Exit Luka.

My dear Mr. — what was the name again?

SMIRNOV: Smirnov, ma'am.   25

MRS. POPOV: My dear Mr. Smirnov, if Mr. Popov owed you money, you shall
be paid — to the last ruble, to the last kopeck. But today — you must
excuse me, Mr. — what was it?

SMIRNOV: Smirnov, ma'am.

MRS. POPOV: Today, Mr. Smirnov, I have no ready cash in the house. *(Smirnov
starts to speak.)* Tomorrow, Mr. Smirnov, no, the day after tomorrow, all will be
well. My steward will be back from town. I shall see that he pays what is owing.
Today, no. In any case, today is exactly seven months from Mr. Popov's death.
On such a day you will understand that I am in no mood to think of money.

SMIRNOV: Madam, if you don't pay up now, you can carry me out feet foremost. They'll seize my estate.

30 MRS. POPOV: You can have your money. *(He starts to thank her.)* Tomorrow. *(He again starts to speak.)* That is: the day after tomorrow.

SMIRNOV: I don't need the money the day after tomorrow. I need it today.

MRS. POPOV: I'm sorry, Mr.—

SMIRNOV: *(shouting)* Smirnov!

MRS. POPOV: *(sweetly)* Yes, of course. But you can't have it today.

35 SMIRNOV: But I can't wait for it any longer!

MRS. POPOV: Be sensible, Mr. Smirnov. How can I pay you if I don't have it?

SMIRNOV: You don't have it?

MRS. POPOV: I don't have it.

SMIRNOV: Sure?

40 MRS. POPOV: Positive.

SMIRNOV: Very well. I'll make a note to that effect. *(Shrugging.)* And then they want me to keep cool. I meet the tax commissioner on the street, and he says, "Why are you always in such a bad humor, Smirnov?" Bad humor! How can I help it, in God's name? I need money, I need it desperately. Take yesterday: I leave home at the crack of dawn, I call on all my debtors. Not a one of them pays up. Footsore and weary. I creep at midnight into some little dive, and try to snatch a few winks of sleep on the floor by the vodka barrel. Then today, I come here, fifty miles from home, saying to myself, "At last, at last, I can be sure of something," and you're not in the mood! You give me a mood! Christ, how can I help getting all worked up?

MRS. POPOV: I thought I'd made it clear, Mr. Smirnov, that you'll get your money the minute my steward is back from town.

SMIRNOV: What the hell do I care about your steward? Pardon the expression, ma'am. But it was you I came to see.

MRS. POPOV: What language! What a tone to take to a lady! I refuse to hear another word. *(Quickly, exit.)*

45 SMIRNOV: Not in the mood, huh? "Exactly seven months since Popov's death," huh? How about me? *(Shouting after her.)* Is there this interest to pay, or isn't there? I'm asking you a question: is there this interest to pay, or isn't there? So your husband died, and you're not in the mood, and your steward's gone off some place, and so forth and so on, but what can *I* do about all that, huh? What do *you* think I should do? Take a running jump and shove my head through the wall? Take off in a balloon? You don't know my *other* debtors. I call on Gruzdeff. Not at home. I look for Yaroshevitch. He's hiding out. I find Kooritsin. He kicks up a row, and I have to throw him through the window. I work my way right down the list. Not a kopeck. Then I come to you, and God damn it to hell, if you'll pardon the expression, you're not in the mood! *(Quietly, as he realizes he's talking to air.)* I've spoiled them all, that's what, I've let them play me for a sucker. Well, I'll show them. I'll show this one. I'll stay right here till she pays up. Ugh!

(*He shudders with rage.*) I'm in a rage! I'm in a positively towering rage! Every nerve in my body is trembling at forty to the dozen! I can't breathe, I feel ill, I think I'm going to faint, hey, you there!

Enter Luka.

LUKA: Yes, sir? Is there anything you wish, sir?
SMIRNOV: Water! Water! No, make it vodka.

Exit Luka.

Consider the logic of it. A fellow creature is desperately in need of cash, so desperately in need that he has to seriously contemplate hanging himself, and this woman, this mere chit of a girl, won't pay up, and why not? Because, forsooth, she isn't in the mood! Oh, the logic of women! Come to that, I never have liked them, I could do without the whole sex. Talk to a woman? I'd rather sit on a barrel of dynamite, the very thought gives me gooseflesh. Women! Creatures of poetry and romance! Just to see one in the distance gets me mad. My legs start twitching with rage. I feel like yelling for help.

Enter Luka, handing Smirnov a glass of water.

LUKA: Mrs. Popov is indisposed, sir. She is seeing no one.
SMIRNOV: Get out.

Exit Luka.

Indisposed, is she? Seeing no one, huh? Well, she can see me or not, but I'll be here, I'll be right here till she pays up. If you're sick for a week, I'll be here for a week. If you're sick for a year, I'll be here for a year. You won't get around *me* with your widow's weeds and your schoolgirl dimples. I know all about dimples. (*Shouting through the window.*) Semyon, let the horses out of those shafts, we're not leaving, we're staying, and tell them to give the horses some oats, yes, oats, you fool, what do you think? (*Walking away from the window.*) What a mess, what an unholy mess! I didn't sleep last night, the heat is terrific today, not a damn one of 'em has paid up, and here's this — this skirt in mourning that's not in the mood! My head aches, where's that —(*He drinks from the glass.*) Water, ugh! You there!

Enter Luka.

LUKA: Yes, sir. You wish for something, sir?
SMIRNOV: Where's that confounded vodka I asked for?

Exit Luka.

50

(*Smirnov sits and looks himself over.*) Oof! A fine figure of a man I am! Unwashed, uncombed, unshaven, straw on my vest, dust all over me. The little woman must've taken me for a highwayman. (*Yawns.*) I suppose it wouldn't be considered polite to barge into a drawing room in this state, but who cares? I'm not a visitor, I'm a creditor — most unwelcome of guests, second only to Death.

Enter Luka.

LUKA: *(handing him the vodka)* If I may say so, sir, you take too many liberties, sir.

SMIRNOV: What?!

LUKA: Oh, nothing, sir, nothing.

55   **SMIRNOV:**   Who in hell do you think you're talking to? Shut your mouth!

LUKA: *(aside)* There's an evil spirit abroad. The Devil must have sent him. Oh! *(Exit Luka.)*

SMIRNOV: What a rage I'm in! I'll grind the whole world to powder. Oh, I feel ill again. You there!

Enter Mrs. Popov.

MRS. POPOV: *(looking at the floor)* In the solitude of my rural retreat, Mr. Smirnov, I've long since grown unaccustomed to the sound of the human voice. Above all, I cannot bear shouting. I must beg you not to break the silence.

SMIRNOV: Very well. Pay me my money and I'll go.

60   **MRS. POPOV:**   I told you before, and I tell you again, Mr. Smirnov. I have no cash, you'll have to wait till the day after tomorrow. Can I express myself more plainly?

SMIRNOV: And *I* told *you* before, and *I* tell *you* again, that I need the money today, that the day after tomorrow is too late, and that if you don't pay, and pay now, I'll have to hang myself in the morning!

MRS. POPOV: But I have no cash. This is quite a puzzle.

SMIRNOV: You won't pay, huh?

MRS. POPOV: I *can't* pay, Mr. Smirnov.

65   **SMIRNOV:**   In that case, I'm going to sit here and wait. *(Sits down.)* You'll pay up the day after tomorrow? Very good. Till the day after tomorrow, here I sit. *(Pause. He jumps up.)* Now look, do I have to pay that interest tomorrow, or don't I? Or do you think I'm joking?

MRS. POPOV: I must ask you not to raise your voice, Mr. Smirnov. This is not a stable.

SMIRNOV: Who said it was? Do I have to pay the interest tomorrow or not?

MRS. POPOV: Mr. Smirnov, do you know how to behave in the presence of a lady?

SMIRNOV: No, madam, I do not know how to behave in the presence of a lady.

70   **MRS. POPOV:**   Just what I thought. I look at you, and I say: ugh! I hear you talk, and I say to myself: "That man doesn't know how to talk to a lady."

SMIRNOV: You'd like me to come simpering to you in French, I suppose. *"Enchanté, madame! Merci beaucoup* for not paying zee money, *madame!*

Pardonnez-moi if I 'ave disturbed you, *madame!* How *charmante* you look in mourning, *madame!*"

MRS. POPOV: Now you're being silly, Mr. Smirnov.

SMIRNOV: *(mimicking)* "Now you're being silly, Mr. Smirnov." "You don't know how to talk to a lady, Mr. Smirnov." Look here, Mrs. Popov, I've known more women than you've known pussy cats. I've fought three duels on their account. I've jilted twelve, and been jilted by nine others. Oh, yes, Mrs. Popov, I've played the fool in my time, whispered sweet nothings, bowed and scraped and endeavored to please. Don't tell me I don't know what it is to love, to pine away with longing, to have the blues, to melt like butter, to be weak as water. I was full of tender emotion. I was carried away with passion. I squandered half my fortune on the sex. I chattered about women's emancipation. But there's an end to everything, dear madam. Burning eyes, dark eyelashes, ripe, red lips, dimpled cheeks, heaving bosoms, soft whisperings, the moon above; the lake below — I don't give a rap for that sort of nonsense any more, Mrs. Popov. I've found out about women. Present company excepted, they're liars. Their behavior is mere play acting; their conversation is sheer gossip. Yes, dear lady, women, young or old, are false, petty, vain, cruel, malicious, unreasonable. As for intelligence, any sparrow could give them points. Appearances, I admit, can be deceptive. In appearance, a woman may be all poetry and romance, goddess and angel, muslin and fluff. To look at her exterior is to be transported to heaven. But I have looked at her interior, Mrs. Popov, and what did I find there — in her very soul? A crocodile. *(He has gripped the back of the chair so firmly that it snaps.)* And, what is more revolting, a crocodile with an illusion, a crocodile that imagines tender sentiments are its own special province, a crocodile that thinks itself queen of the realm of love! Whereas, in sober fact, dear madam, if a woman can love anything except a lapdog you can hang me by the feet on that nail. For a man, love is suffering, love is sacrifice. A woman just swishes her train around and tightens her grip on your nose. Now, you're a woman, aren't you, Mrs. Popov? You must be an expert on some of this. Tell me, quite frankly, did you ever know a woman to be — faithful, for instance? Or even sincere? Only old hags, huh? Though some women are old hags from birth. But as for the others? You're right: a faithful woman is a freak of nature — like a cat with horns.

MRS. POPOV: Who *is* faithful, then? Who *have* you cast for the faithful lover? Not man?

SMIRNOV: Right first time, Mrs. Popov: man.

75

MRS. POPOV: *(going off into a peal of bitter laughter)* Man! Man is faithful! that's a new one! *(Fiercely.)* What right do you have to say this, Mr. Smirnov? Men faithful? Let me tell you something. Of all the men I have ever known my late husband Popov was the best. I loved him, and there are women who know how to love, Mr. Smirnov. I gave him my youth, my happiness,

my life, my fortune. I worshipped the ground he trod on — and what
happened? The best of men was unfaithful to me, Mr. Smirnov. Not once
in a while. All the time. After he died, I found his desk drawer full of love
letters. While he was alive, he was always going away for the week-end. He
squandered my money. He made love to other women before my very eyes.
But, in spite of all, Mr. Smirnov, I was faithful. Unto death. And beyond.
I am *still* faithful, Mr. Smirnov! Buried alive in this house, I shall wear
mourning till the day I, too, am called to my eternal rest.

SMIRNOV: *(laughing scornfully)* Expect me to believe that? As if I couldn't see
through all this hocus-pocus. Buried alive! Till you're called to your eternal
rest! Till when? Till some little poet — or some little subaltern with his
first moustache — comes riding by and asks: "Can that be the house of the
mysterious Tamara who for love of her late husband has buried herself
alive, vowing to see no man?" Ha!

MRS. POPOV: *(flaring up)* How dare you? How dare you insinuate —?

SMIRNOV: You may have buried yourself alive, Mrs. Popov, but you haven't
forgotten to powder your nose.

80 MRS. POPOV: *(incoherent)* How dare you? How —?

SMIRNOV: Who's raising his voice now? Just because I call a spade a spade.
Because I shoot straight from the shoulder. Well, don't shout at me, I'm not
your steward.

MRS. POPOV: I'm not shouting, you're shouting! Oh, leave me alone!

SMIRNOV: Pay me the money, and I will.

MRS. POPOV: You'll get no money out of me!

85 SMIRNOV: Oh, so that's it!

MRS. POPOV: Not a ruble, not a kopeck. Get out! Leave me alone!

SMIRNOV: Not being your husband, I must ask you not to make scenes with
me. *(He sits.)* I don't like scenes.

MRS. POPOV: *(choking with rage)* You're sitting down?

SMIRNOV: Correct, I'm sitting down.

90 MRS. POPOV: I asked you to leave!

SMIRNOV: Then give me the money. *(Aside.)* Oh, what a rage I'm in, what a rage!

MRS. POPOV: The impudence of the man! I won't talk to you a moment
longer. Get out. *(Pause.)* Are you going?

95 SMIRNOV: No.

MRS. POPOV: No?!

SMIRNOV: No.

MRS. POPOV: On your head be it. Luka!

Enter Luka.

Show the gentleman out, Luka.

LUKA: *(approaching)* I'm afraid, sir, I'll have to ask you, um, to leave, sir,
now, um —

SMIRNOV: *(jumping up)* Shut your mouth, you old idiot! Who do you think you're talking to? I'll make mincemeat of you.

LUKA: *(clutching his heart)* Mercy on us! Holy saints above! *(He falls into an armchair.)* I'm taken sick! I can't breathe!!

MRS. POPOV: Then where's Dasha? Dasha! Dasha! Come here at once! 100
(She rings.)

LUKA: They gone picking berries, ma'am, I'm alone here —Water, water, I'm taken sick!

MRS. POPOV: *(to Smirnov)* Get out, you!

SMIRNOV: Can't you even be polite with me, Mrs. Popov?

MRS. POPOV: *(clenching her fists and stamping her feet)* With you? You're a wild animal, you were never house-broken!

SMIRNOV: What? What did you say? 105

MRS. POPOV: I said you were a wild animal, you were never house-broken.

SMIRNOV: *(advancing upon her)* And what right do you have to talk to me like that?

MRS. POPOV: Like what?

SMIRNOV: You have insulted me, madam.

MRS. POPOV: What of it? Do you think I'm scared of you? 110

SMIRNOV: So you think you can get away with it because you're a woman. A creature of poetry and romance, huh? Well, it doesn't go down with me. I hereby challenge you to a duel.

LUKA: Mercy on us! Holy saints alive! Water!

SMIRNOV: I propose we shoot it out.

MRS. POPOV: Trying to scare me again? Just because you have big fists and a voice like a bull? You're a brute.

SMIRNOV: No one insults Grigory S. Smirnov with impunity! And I don't care 115 if you *are* a female.

MRS. POPOV: *(trying to outshout him)* Brute, brute, brute!

SMIRNOV: The sexes are equal, are they? Fine: then it's just prejudice to expect men alone to pay for insults. I hereby challenge—

MRS. POPOV: *(screaming)* All right! You want to shoot it out? All right! Let's shoot it out!

SMIRNOV: And let it be here and now!

MRS. POPOV: Here and now! All right! I'll have Popov's pistols here in one 120 minute! *(Walks away, then turns.)* Putting one of Popov's bullets through your silly head will be a pleasure! Au revoir. *(Exit.)*

SMIRNOV: I'll bring her down like a duck, a sitting duck. I'm not one of your little poets, I'm no little subaltern with his first moustache. No, sir, there's no weaker sex where I'm concerned!

LUKA: Sir! Master! *(He goes down on his knees.)* Take pity on a poor old man, and do me a favor: go away. It was bad enough before, you nearly scared me to death. But a duel —!

Smirnov: *(ignoring him)* A duel! That's equality of the sexes for you! That's women's emancipation! Just as a matter of principle I'll bring her down like a duck. But what a woman! "Putting one of Popov's bullets through your silly head . . ." Her cheeks were flushed, her eyes were gleaming! And, by God, she's accepted the challenge! I never knew a woman like this before!

Luka: Sir! Master! Please go away! I'll always pray for you!

125 **Smirnov:** *(again ignoring him)* What a woman! Phew!! *She's* no sour puss, *she's* no cry baby. She's fire and brimstone. She's a human cannon ball. What a shame I have to kill her!

Luka: *(weeping)* Please, kind sir, please, go away!

Smirnov: *(as before)* I like her, isn't that funny? With those dimples and all? I like her. I'm even prepared to consider letting her off that debt. And where's my rage? It's gone. I never knew a woman like this before.

Enter Mrs. Popov with pistols.

Mrs. Popov: *(boldly)* Pistols, Mr. Smirnov! *(Matter of fact.)* But before we start, you'd better show me how it's done. I'm not too familiar with these things. In fact I never gave a pistol a second look.

Luka: Lord, have mercy on us, I must go hunt up the gardener and the coachman. Why has this catastrophe fallen upon us, O Lord? *(Exit.)*

130 **Smirnov:** *(examining the pistols)* Well, it's like this. There are several makes: one is the Mortimer, with capsules, especially constructed for dueling. What you have here are Smith and Wesson triple-action revolvers, with extractor, first-rate job, worth ninety rubles at the very least. You hold it this way. *(Aside.)* My God, what eyes she has! They're setting me on fire.

Mrs. Popov: This way?

Smirnov: Yes, that's right. You cock the trigger, take aim like this, head up, arm out like this. Then you just press with this finger here, and it's all over. The main thing is, keep cool, take slow aim, and don't let your arm jump.

Mrs. Popov: I see. And if it's inconvenient to do the job here, we can go out in the garden.

Smirnov: Very good. Of course, I should warn you: I'll be firing in the air.

135 **Mrs. Popov:** What? This is the end. Why?

Smirnov: Oh, well—because—for private reasons.

Mrs. Popov: Scared, huh? *(She laughs heartily.)* Now don't you try to get out of it, Mr. Smirnov. My blood is up. I won't be happy till I've drilled a hole through that skull of yours. Follow me. What's the matter? Scared?

Smirnov: That's right. I'm scared.

Mrs. Popov: Oh, come on, what's the matter with you?

140 **Smirnov:** Well, um, Mrs. Popov, I, um, I like you.

Mrs. Popov: *(laughing bitterly)* Good God! He likes me, does he? The gall of the man. *(Showing him the door.)* You may leave, Mr. Smirnov.

Smirnov: *(Quietly puts the gun down, takes his hat, and walks to the door. Then* *he stops and the pair look at each other without a word. Then, approaching gingerly.)* Listen, Mrs. Popov. Are you still mad at me? I'm in the devil of a temper myself, of course. But then, you see — what I mean is — it's this way — the fact is —*(Roaring.)* Well, is it my fault, damn it, if I like you? *(Clutches the back of a chair. It breaks.)* Christ, what fragile furniture you have here. I like you. Know what I mean? I could fall in love with you.

MRS. POPOV: I hate you. Get out!

SMIRNOV: What a woman! I never saw anything like it. Oh, I'm lost, I'm done for, I'm a mouse in a trap. 145

MRS. POPOV: Leave this house, or I shoot!

SMIRNOV: Shoot away! What bliss to die of a shot that was fired by that little velvet hand! To die gazing into those enchanting eyes. I'm out of my mind. I know: you must decide at once. Think for one second, then decide. Because if I leave now, I'll never be back. Decide! I'm a pretty decent chap. Landed gentleman, I should say. Ten thousand a year. Good stable. Throw a kopeck up in the air, and I'll put a bullet through it. Will you marry me?

MRS. POPOV: *(indignant, brandishing the gun)* We'll shoot it out! Get going! Take your pistol!

SMIRNOV: I'm out of my mind. I don't understand anything any more. *(Shouting.)* You there! That vodka!

MRS. POPOV: No excuses! No delays! We'll shoot it out!

SMIRNOV: I'm out of my mind. I'm falling in love. I *have* fallen in love. 150 *(He takes her hand vigorously; she squeals.)* I love you. *(He goes down on his knees.)* I love you as I've never loved before. I jilted twelve, and was jilted by nine others. But I didn't love a one of them as I love you. I'm full of tender emotion. I'm melting like butter. I'm weak as water. I'm on my knees like a fool, and I offer you my hand. It's a shame, it's a disgrace. I haven't been in love in five years. I took a vow against it. And now, all of a sudden, to be swept off my feet, it's a scandal. I offer you my hand, dear lady. Will you or won't you? You won't? Then don't! *(He rises and walks toward the door.)*

MRS. POPOV: I didn't say anything.

SMIRNOV: *(stopping)* What?

MRS. POPOV: Oh, nothing, you can go. Well, no, just a minute. No, you can go. Go! I detest you! But, just a moment. Oh, if you knew how furious I feel! *(Throws the gun on the table.)* My fingers have gone to sleep holding that horrid thing. *(She is tearing her handkerchief to shreds.)* And what are you standing around for? Get out of here!

SMIRNOV: Goodbye.

MRS. POPOV: Go, go, go! *(Shouting.)* Where are you going? Wait a minute! 155 No, no, it's all right, just go. I'm fighting mad. Don't come near me, don't come near me!

SMIRNOV: *(who is coming near her)* I'm pretty disgusted with myself — falling in love like a kid, going down on my knees like some moongazing whippersnapper, the very thought gives me gooseflesh. *(Rudely.)* I love you. But it doesn't make sense. Tomorrow, I have to pay that interest, and we've already started mowing. *(He puts his arm about her waist.)* I shall never forgive myself for this.

MRS. POPOV: Take your hands off me, I hate you! Let's shoot it out!

A long kiss. Enter Luka with an axe, the Gardener with a rake, the coachman with a pitchfork, hired men with sticks.

LUKA: *(seeing the kiss)* Mercy on us! Holy saints above!

MRS. POPOV: *(dropping her eyes)* Luka, tell them in the stable that Toby is *not* to have any oats today.

◆   ◆   ◆

CHAPTER 26

DRAMA SAMPLER: TEN-MINUTE PLAYS

Many different types and forms of drama have emerged throughout the long history of playwriting. In recent years, theater has become a bit more experimental in nature, as evidenced by the proliferation of improvisational plays as well as one-act and ten-minute plays. While one-act plays have the luxury of a more extended period in which to accomplish exposition, dramatic tension, climax, and denouement, the **ten-minute play** offers a very small window of opportunity in which the playwright can create meaning. In fact, the ten-minute play is, in a sense, the dramatic equivalent of the **haiku** in poetry in that it is intended to be taken in all at once, and thus to have a particularly intense impact on the audience.

Since a page of script roughly translates into a minute of time onstage, a ten-minute play is generally limited to about ten pages in length. Despite its brevity, however, a ten-minute play is more than just a scene: it must begin with **exposition,** introduce a **conflict** (usually relatively early in the play), and provide a **resolution,** just as any other complete dramatic work does. A ten-minute play is also more than just a **monologue;** it always includes at least two characters.

Ten-minute plays are generally staged in groups, allowing the audience to watch several plays in sequence. For this reason, large casts and elaborate staging are rare. The most popular venue for a ten-minute play is a dramatic festival, and numerous competitions offer prizes that include the staging of an author's play. The most prominent contest is sponsored by the Actors Theatre of Louisville, which stages the annual Humana Festival of New American Plays.

The four ten-minute plays in this sampler treat a variety of topics. In Jane Martin's *Beauty*, the two protagonists trade lives, with unexpected consequences; in *Tape*, by José Rivera, the protagonist is forced to confront his entire life and face up to his own truths; in *I Dream Before I Take the Stand*, Arlene Hutton's protagonist faces a hostile interrogator; and in *Nine Ten*, by Warren Leight, five strangers are brought together for jury duty. Although each playwright addresses the challenges of the ten-minute play format in a different fashion, each of these plays relies on dialogue, pauses, subtext, and the power of suggestion to create meaning in a short span of time.

735

JANE MARTIN, a prize-winning playwright, has never made a public appearance or spoken about any of her works. In addition, she has never given an interview, and no picture of her has ever been published. As one critic wryly observed, Martin is "America's best known, unknown playwright." Martin first came to the attention of American theater audiences with her collection of monologues, *Talking With . . . ,* a work that premiered at the 1981 Humana Festival of New American Plays at the Actors Theatre of Louisville, Kentucky. Her other works include *Vital Signs* and *What Mama Don't Know;* her full-length plays include *Cementville;* the Pulitzer Prize–nominated *Keely and Du* (winner of the 1994 American Theatre Critics Association New Play Award); *Criminal Hearts;* and *Middle Aged White Guys.* Martin's name is widely believed to be a pseudonym. Jon Jory, artistic director of the Actors Theatre of Louisville — and director of the premieres of all of Martin's plays — is spokesperson for the playwright and, according to some people, may actually be the playwright behind the pen name. Jory has repeatedly denied this; in a 1994 interview, he said that Martin "feels she could not write plays if people knew who she was, regardless of her identity or gender." In Jory's opinion, "The point in the end is the plays themseleves. . . . But if Jane's anonymity is a P. T. Barnum publicity stunt, it's one of the longest circus acts going."

Beauty (2000)

CHARACTERS

Carla
Bethany

An apartment. Minimalist set. A young woman, Carla, on the phone.

CARLA: In love with me? You're in love with me? Could you describe yourself again? Uh-huh. Uh-huh. And you spoke to me? (*A knock at the door.*) Listen, I always hate to interrupt a marriage proposal, but . . . could you possibly hold that thought? (*Puts phone down and goes to door. Bethany, the same age as Carla and a friend, is there. She carries the sort of Mideastern lamp we know of from Aladdin.*)
BETHANY: Thank God you were home. I mean, you're not going to believe this!
CARLA: Somebody on the phone. (*Goes back to it.*)
BETHANY: I mean, I just had a beach urge, so I told them at work my uncle was dying . . .
5 CARLA: (*motions to Bethany for quiet*) And you were the one in the leather jacket with the tattoo? What was the tattoo? (*Carla again asks Bethany, who is gesturing wildly that she should hang up, to cool it.*) Look, a screaming eagle from shoulder to shoulder, maybe. There were a lot of people in the bar.
BETHANY: (*gesturing and mouthing*) I have to get back to work.
CARLA: (*on phone*) See, the thing is, I'm probably not going to marry someone I can't remember . . . particularly when I don't drink. Sorry. Sorry. Sorry. (*She hangs up.*) Madness.
BETHANY: So I ran out to the beach . . .
CARLA: This was some guy I never met who apparently offered me a beer . . .

BETHANY: . . . low tide and this . . . *(The lamp.)* . . . was just sitting there, lying 10
    there . . .
CARLA: . . . and he tracks me down . . .
BETHANY: . . . on the beach, and I lift this lid thing . . .
CARLA: . . . and seriously proposes marriage.
BETHANY: . . . and a genie comes out.
CARLA: I mean, that's twice in a . . . what? 15
BETHANY: A genie comes out of this thing.
CARLA: A genie?
BETHANY: I'm not kidding, the whole Disney kind of thing, swirling smoke,
    and then this twenty-foot-high, see-through guy in like an Arabian outfit.
CARLA: Very funny.
BETHANY: Yes, funny, but twenty feet high! I look up and down the beach, I'm 20
    alone. I don't have my pepper spray or my hand alarm. You know me, when
    I'm petrified I joke. I say his voice is too high for Robin Williams, and he
    says he's a castrati. Naturally. Who else would I meet?
CARLA: What's a castrati?
BETHANY: You know . . .

The appropriate gesture.

CARLA: Bethany, dear one, I have three modeling calls. I am meeting Ralph
    Lauren!
BETHANY: Okay, good. Ralph Lauren. Look, I am not kidding!
CARLA: You're not kidding what?! 25
BETHANY: There is a genie in this thingamajig.
CARLA: Uh-huh. I'll be back around eight.
BETHANY: And he offered me *wishes!*
CARLA: Is this some elaborate practical joke because it's my birthday?
BETHANY: No, happy birthday, but I'm like crazed because I'm on this deserted 30
    beach with a twenty-foot-high, see-through genie, so like sarcastically . . .
    you know how I need a new car . . . I said fine, gimme 25,000 dollars . . .
CARLA: On the beach with the genie?
BETHANY: Yeah, right, exactly, and it rains down out of the sky.
CARLA: Oh sure.
BETHANY: *(pulling a wad out of her purse)* Count it, those are thousands. I lost
    one in the surf.

*Carla sees the top bill. Looks at Bethany, who nods encouragement. Carla thumbs
through them.*

CARLA: These look real. 35
BETHANY: Yeah.
CARLA: And they rained down out of the sky?
BETHANY: Yeah.
CARLA: You've been really strange lately, are you dealing?

40 **BETHANY:** Dealing what, I've even given up chocolate.
CARLA: Let me see the genie.
BETHANY: Wait, wait.
CARLA: Bethany, I don't have time to screw around. Let me see the genie or let me go on my appointments.
BETHANY: Wait! So I pick up the money . . . see, there's sand on the money . . . and I'm like nuts so I say, you know, "Okay, look, ummm, big guy, my uncle is in the hospital" . . . because as you know when I said to the people at work my uncle was dying, I was on one level telling the truth although it had nothing to do with the beach, but he was in Intensive Care after the accident, and that's on my mind, so I say, okay, Genie, heal my uncle . . . which is like impossible given he was hit by two trucks, and the genie says, "Yes, Master" . . . like they're supposed to say, and he goes into this like kind of whirlwind, kicking up sand and stuff, and I'm like, "Oh my God!" and the air clears, and he bows, you know, and says, "It is done, Master," and I say, "Okay, whatever-you-are, I'm calling on my cell phone," and I get it out and I get this doctor who is like dumbstruck who says my uncle came to, walked out of Intensive Care and left the hospital! I'm not kidding, Carla.
45 **CARLA:** On your mother's grave?
BETHANY: On my mother's grave.

They look at each other.

CARLA: Let me see the genie.
BETHANY: No, no, look, that's the whole thing . . . I was just, like, reacting, you know, responding, and that's already two wishes . . . although I'm really pleased about my uncle, the $25,000 thing, I could have asked for $10 million, and there is only one wish left.
CARLA: So ask for $10 million.
50 **BETHANY:** I don't think so. I don't think so. I mean, I gotta focus in here. Do you have a sparkling water?
CARLA: No. Bethany, I'm missing Ralph Lauren now. Very possibly my one chance to go from catalogue model to the very, very big time, so, if you are joking, stop joking.
BETHANY: Not joking. See, see, the thing is, I know what I want. In my guts. Yes. Underneath my entire bitch of a life is this unspoken, ferocious, all-consuming urge . . .
CARLA: (*trying to get her to move this along*) Ferocious, all-consuming urge . . .
BETHANY: I want to be like you.
55 **CARLA:** Me?
BETHANY: Yes.
CARLA: Half the time you don't even like me.
BETHANY: Jealous. The ogre of jealousy.
CARLA: You're the one with the $40,000 job straight out of school. You're the one who has published short stories. I'm the one hanging on by her

fingernails in modeling. The one who has creeps calling her on the phone. The one who had to have a nose job.

BETHANY: I want to be beautiful. 60
CARLA: You are beautiful.
BETHANY: Carla, I'm not beautiful.
CARLA: You have charm. You have personality. You know perfectly well you're pretty.
BETHANY: "Pretty," see, that's it. Pretty is the minor leagues of beautiful. Pretty is what people discover about you after they know you. Beautiful is what knocks them out across the room. Pretty, you get called a couple of times a year; *beautiful* is twenty-four hours a day.
CARLA: Yeah? So? 65
BETHANY: So?! We're talking *beauty* here. Don't say "So?" Beauty is the real deal. You are the center of any moment of your life. People stare. Men flock. I've seen you get offered discounts on makeup for no reason. Parents treat beautiful children better. Studies show your income goes up. You can have sex anytime you want it. Men have to know me. That takes up to a year. I'm continually horny.
CARLA: Bethany, I don't even like sex. I can't have a conversation without men coming on to me. I have no privacy. I get hassled on the street. They start pressuring me from the beginning. Half the time, it never occurs to them to start with a conversation. Smart guys like you. You've had three long-term relationships, and you're only twenty-three. I haven't had one. The good guys, the smart guys are scared to death of me. I'm surrounded by male bimbos who think a preposition is when you go to school away from home. I have no woman friends except you. I don't even want to talk about this!
BETHANY: I knew you'd say something like this. See, you're "in the club" so you can say this. It's the way beauty functions as an elite. You're trying to keep it all for yourself.
CARLA: I'm trying to tell you it's no picnic.
BETHANY: But it's what everybody wants. It's the nasty secret at large in the 70 world. It's the unspoken tidal desire in every room and on every street. It's the unspoken, the soundless whisper . . . millions upon millions of people longing hopelessly and forever to stop being whatever they are and be beautiful, but the difference between those ardent multitudes and me is that I have a goddamn genie and one more wish!
CARLA: Well, it's not what I want. This is me, Carla. I have never read a whole book. Page six, I can't remember page four. The last thing I read was *The Complete Idiot's Guide to WordPerfect*. I leave dinner parties right after the dessert because I'm out of conversation. You know the dumb blond joke about the application where it says, "Sign here," she put Sagittarius? I've done that. Only beautiful guys approach me, and that's because they want to borrow my eye shadow. I barely exist outside a mirror! You don't want to *be me*.

BETHANY: None of you tell the truth. That's why you have no friends. We can all see you're just trying to make us feel better because we aren't in your league. This only proves to me it should be my third wish. Money can only buy things. Beauty makes you the center of the universe.

Bethany picks up the lamp.

CARLA: Don't do it. Bethany, don't wish it! I am telling you you'll regret it.

Bethany lifts the lid. There is a tremendous crash, and the lights go out. Then they flicker and come back up, revealing Bethany and Carla on the floor where they have been thrown by the explosion. We don't realize it at first, but they have exchanged places.

CARLA/BETHANY: Oh God.

75 BETHANY/CARLA: Oh God.

CARLA/BETHANY: Am I bleeding? Am I dying?

BETHANY/CARLA: I'm so dizzy. You're not bleeding.

CARLA/BETHANY: Neither are you.

BETHANY/CARLA: I feel so weird.

80 CARLA/BETHANY: Me too. I feel . . . *(Looking at her hands.)* Oh, my God, I'm wearing your jewelry. I'm wearing your nail polish.

BETHANY/CARLA: I know I'm over here, but I can see myself over there.

CARLA/BETHANY: I'm wearing your dress. I have your legs!!

BETHANY/CARLA: These aren't my shoes. I can't meet Ralph Lauren wearing these shoes!

CARLA/BETHANY: I wanted to be beautiful, but I didn't want to be you.

85 BETHANY/CARLA: Thanks a lot!!

CARLA/BETHANY: I've got to go. I want to pick someone out and get laid.

BETHANY/CARLA: You can't just walk out of here in my body!

CARLA/BETHANY: Wait a minute. Wait a minute. What's eleven eighteenths of 1,726?

BETHANY/CARLA: Why?

90 CARLA/BETHANY: I'm a public accountant. I want to know if you have my brain.

BETHANY/CARLA: One hundred thirty-two and a half.

CARLA/BETHANY: You have my brain.

BETHANY/CARLA: What shade of Rubenstein lipstick does Cindy Crawford wear with teal blue?

CARLA/BETHANY: Raging Storm.

95 BETHANY/CARLA: You have my brain. You poor bastard.

CARLA/BETHANY: I don't care. Don't you see?

BETHANY/CARLA: See what?

CARLA/BETHANY: We both have the one thing, the one and only thing everybody wants.

BETHANY/CARLA: What is that?

CARLA/BETHANY: It's better than beauty for me; it's better than brains   100
   for you.
BETHANY/CARLA: What? What?!
CARLA/BETHANY: Different problems.

Blackout.

◇ ◇ ◇

JOSÉ RIVERA (1955–   ) was born in San Juan, Puerto Rico and grew up in a household where the only book was a Bible. When he was four years old, his family moved to New York. Early in his life, he saw a staged version of the play *Rumpelstiltskin* and decided to become a playwright. He has written numerous plays and won several awards, including two Obie Awards, a Fulbright Fellowship, and the Whiting Foundation Writing Award. In 2002, Rivera wrote the screenplay for *The Motorcycle Diaries,* a movie based on a motorcycle trip that Cuban revolutionary Che Guevara took as a young man. In 2005, Rivera became the first Puerto Rican to be nominated for an Academy Award for best adapted screenplay.

Tape (1993)

CHARACTERS
Person
Attendant

A small dark room. No windows. One door. A Person is being led in by an Attendant. In the room is a simple wooden table and chair. On the table is a large reel-to-reel tape recorder, a glass of water, and a pitcher of water.

PERSON: Dark in here.
ATTENDANT: I'm sorry.
PERSON: No, I know it's not your fault.
ATTENDANT: I'm afraid of those lights . . .
PERSON: I guess, what does it matter now?   5
ATTENDANT: . . . not very bright.
PERSON: Who cares, really?
ATTENDANT: We don't want to cause you any undue suffering. If it's too dark
   in here, I'll make sure one of the other attendants replaces the light bulb.

   (The Person looks at the Attendant.)

PERSON: Any "undue suffering"?
ATTENDANT: That's right. *(The Person looks at the room.)*   10
PERSON: Is this where I'll be?
ATTENDANT: That's right.
PERSON: Will you be outside?
ATTENDANT: Yes.

15 **PERSON:** The entire time?
ATTENDANT: The entire time.
PERSON: Is it boring?
ATTENDANT: I'm sorry?
PERSON: Is it boring? You know. Waiting outside all the time.
20 **ATTENDANT:** (*Soft smile.*) It's my job. It's what I do.
PERSON: Of course. (*Beat.*) Will I get anything to eat or drink?
ATTENDANT: Well, we're not really set up for that. We don't have what you'd call a kitchen. But we can send out for things. Little things. Cold food.
PERSON: I understand.
ATTENDANT: Soft drinks.
25 **PERSON:** (*Hopefully.*) Beer?
ATTENDANT: I'm afraid not.
PERSON: Not even on special occasions like my birthdays?
ATTENDANT: (*Thinking.*) I guess maybe on your birthday.
PERSON: (*Truly appreciative.*) Great, thanks. (*Beat.*)
30 **ATTENDANT:** Do you have any more questions before we start? Because if you do, that's okay. It's okay to ask as many questions as you want. I'm sure you're very curious. I'm sure you'd like to know as much as possible, so you can figure out how it all fits together and what it all means. So please ask. That's why I'm here. Don't worry about the time. We have a lot of time. (*Beat.*)
PERSON: I don't have any questions.
ATTENDANT: (*Disappointed.*) Are you sure?
PERSON: There's not much I really have to know is there? Really?
ATTENDANT: No, I guess not. I just thought . . .
35 **PERSON:** It's okay. I appreciate it. I guess I really want to sit.
ATTENDANT: Sit. (*The person sits on the chair and faces the tape recorder.*)
PERSON: Okay, I'm sitting.
ATTENDANT: Is it . . . comfortable?
PERSON: Does it matter? Does it really fucking matter?
40 **ATTENDANT:** No. I suppose not. (*The Attendant looks sad. The Person looks at the Attendant and feels bad.*)
PERSON: Hey I'm sorry. I know it's not your fault. I know you didn't mean it. I'm sorry.
ATTENDANT: It's all right.
PERSON: What's your name anyway? Do you have a name?
ATTENDANT: Not really. It's not allowed.
45 **PERSON:** Really? Not allowed? Who says?
ATTENDANT: The rules say.
PERSON: Have you actually seen these rules? Are they in writing?
ATTENDANT: Oh yes. There's a long and extensive training course.
PERSON: (*Surprised.*) There is?
50 **ATTENDANT:** Oh yes. It's quite rigorous.

PERSON: Imagine that.

ATTENDANT: You have to be a little bit of everything. Confidant, confessor, friend, stern taskmaster. Guide.

PERSON: I guess that would take time.

ATTENDANT: My teachers were all quite strong and capable. They really pushed me. I was grateful. I knew I had been chosen for something unique and exciting. Something significant. Didn't mind the hard work and sleepless nights.

PERSON: *(Surprised.)* Oh? You sleep? 55

ATTENDANT: *(Smiles.)* When I can. *(Beat.)*

PERSON: Do you dream? *(Beat.)*

ATTENDANT: No. *(Beat.)* That's not allowed. *(Beat.)*

PERSON: I'm sorry.

ATTENDANT: No. It's something you get used to. 60

PERSON: *(Trying to be chummy.)* I know. I went years and years without being able to remember one single dream I had. It really scared the shit out of me when I was ten and . . .

ATTENDANT: I know.

PERSON: I'm sorry.

ATTENDANT: I said I know. I know that story. When you were ten.

PERSON: Oh. Yeah. I guess you would know everything. Every story. 65

ATTENDANT: *(Apologetic.)* It's part of the training.

PERSON: I figured. *(A long uncomfortable silence.)*

ATTENDANT: *(Softly.)* Have you ever operated a reel-to-reel tape recorder before?

PERSON: No I haven't. I mean — no.

ATTENDANT: It's not hard. 70

PERSON: I, uhm, these things were pretty obsolete by the time I was old enough to afford stereo equipment, you know, I got into cassettes, and, later, CDs, but never one of these jobbies.

ATTENDANT: It's not hard. *(Demonstrates.)* On here. Off here. Play. Pause. Rewind.

PERSON: *(Surprised.)* Rewind?

ATTENDANT: In some cases the quality of the recording is so poor . . . you'll want to rewind it until you understand.

PERSON: No fast forward? 75

ATTENDANT: No.

PERSON: It looks like a pretty good one. Sturdy. Very strong.

ATTENDANT: They get a lot of use.

PERSON: I bet. *(Beat.)* Is this the only tape? *(The Attendant laughs out loud— then quickly stops.)*

ATTENDANT: No. 80

PERSON: I didn't think so.

ATTENDANT: There are many more.

PERSON: How many? A lot?

ATTENDANT: There are ten thousand boxes.

85 **PERSON:**   *Ten* thousand?

ATTENDANT: I'm afraid so.

PERSON: Did I really . . .

ATTENDANT: I'm afraid you did.

PERSON: So . . . everyone goes into a room like this?

80 **ATTENDANT:**   Exactly like this. There's no differentiation. Everyone's equal.

PERSON: For once.

ATTENDANT: What isn't equal, of course, is the . . . amount of time you spend here listening.

PERSON: Oh God.

ATTENDANT: *(Part of the training.)* Listening, just to yourself. To your voice.

95 **PERSON:**   I know.

ATTENDANT: Listening, word by word, to every lie you ever told while you were alive.

PERSON: Oh God!

ATTENDANT: Every ugly lie to every person, every single time, every betrayal, every lying thought, every time you lied to yourself, deep in your mind, we were listening, we were recording, and it's all in these tapes, ten thousand boxes of them, in your own words, one lie after the next, over and over, un- til we're finished. So the amount of time varies. The amount of time you spend here all depends on how many lies you told. How many boxes of tape we have to get through together.

PERSON: *(Almost in tears.)* I'm sorry . . .

100 **ATTENDANT:**   Too late.

PERSON: I said I'm sorry! I said I'm sorry! I said it a million times! What hap- pened to forgiveness? I don't want to be here! I don't want this! I don't want to listen! I don't want to hear myself! I didn't mean to say the things that I said! I don't want to listen!

ATTENDANT: Yes, well. Neither did we. Neither did we. *(The Attendant looks sadly at the Person. The Attendant turns on the tape recorder. The Attendant hits the Play button, the reels spin slowly, and the tape starts snaking its way through the machine. Silence. The Attendant leaves the room, leaving the Person all alone. The Person nervously pours a glass of water, accidentally spilling water on the floor. From the depths of the machine comes a long-forgotten voice.)*

WOMAN'S VOICE: "Where have you been? Do you know I've been looking all over? Jesus Christ! I went to Manny's! I went to the pharmacy! The school! I even called the police! Look at me, Jesus Christ, I'm shaking! Now look at me — look at me and tell me where the hell you were! Tell me right now!" *(Silence. As the Person waits for the lying response, the lights fade to black.)*

❖   ❖   ❖

ARLENE HUTTON is a MacDowell Colony fellow and a member of the Dramatists' Guild. Her first full-length play, *Last Train to Nibroc* (2000), received a 2000 New York Drama League nomination for Best Play and was produced regionally more than fifty times. *As It Is in Heaven*, her second play, premiered in Edinburgh and received a highly acclaimed four-month run at the Actors' Co-op in Los Angeles. She teaches at Fordham University.

I Dream Before I Take the Stand (1998)

CHARACTERS
She: a petite woman
He: a man, probably a lawyer

Casting Note: *The man is age 25–50, the woman 20–50, both of any race. The woman should be petite in height or very slim if taller, but the specific hair color lines may be changed with the author's permission.*

Set: *A chair.*

Time: *Right now.*

Lights up on a petite woman sitting in a chair. It is possible that the lights begin the play full and soft, narrowing very slowly throughout, so that by the end of the play only a narrow spot is focused on the woman, like an interrogation room. The man, a lawyer, walks around her throughout, at first in the full circle of light, later appearing in and out of the focused light. Perhaps by the end of the play, the light has narrowed on the woman, and the man is barely seen. There are many ways to present this play, but the pauses are a part of the dialogue.

SHE: I was walking through the park.
HE: Why were you in the park?
SHE: I was on my way to work.
HE: Do you have to walk through the park to get to work?
SHE: No.   5
HE: Do you always walk through the park to work?
SHE: No.
HE: Why did you walk through the park that day?
SHE: It was a beautiful day. I like to walk to work through the park when the weather's good.

Pause.

HE: Were you in a hurry?   10
SHE: I was on my way to work.
HE: Were you late?
SHE: No, I would have been on time.
HE: Were you strolling or walking fast?

15 **She:** I always walk fairly quickly.

    He: Why? The park is not safe?

    She: I guess not.

    He: Yet you walk through it to get to work.

    She: There are lots of people around.

20 **He:** But you walk quickly through the park.

    She: Yes.

Pause.

    He: How do you walk?

    She: Which way?

    He: Do you swing your arms?

25 **She:** I don't know.

    He: Were you carrying anything?

    She: Just my purse.

    He: So your arms were free to swing along as you walked.

    She: Maybe.

30 **He:** Or maybe you walk with them folded.

    She: I don't know what you mean.

    He: Perhaps you fold your arms.

He demonstrates.

    She: Maybe.

    He: So sometimes you swing your arms and sometimes you fold them.

35 **She:** I guess.

    He: What else would you do with them?

    She: I guess you're right.

Pause.

    He: So you were walking through the park that day on your way to work.

    She: Yes. I already said that.

Pause.

40 **He:** What were you wearing?

    She: A skirt and a top.

    He: What color was the skirt?

    She: It was a print.

    He: What color?

45 **She:** Black and red.

    He: And the top?

    She: What?

    He: What color was the top?

    She: Black.

50 **He:** Just black?

SHE: It had a little red flower on it.
HE: The fabric?
SHE: No. A decoration.
HE: Where?
SHE: In the center of the neckline.   55
HE: A rose.
SHE: I guess. It was tiny.
HE: It was in the fabric?
SHE: No. It was a small ribbon.
HE: Like the little flowers on lingerie.   60
SHE: Like that.
HE: How sweet. (*A pause*) Were you wearing jewelry?
SHE: No. Just a watch.
HE: An expensive watch?
SHE: No.   65
HE: An expensive *looking* watch?
SHE: No. Just a Timex.
HE: So that you could hurry through the park to be at work on time.
SHE: Of course.
HE: No other jewelry?   70
SHE: No.
HE: Why not?
SHE: I don't wear jewelry in the park.
HE: Why not?
SHE: I don't want to attract attention.   75
HE: You don't want to get mugged.
SHE: Right.

Pause.

HE: Your hair is up today. Were you wearing it that way in the park?
SHE: No. I was wearing it down.
HE: Why?   80
SHE: It probably wasn't quite dry.
HE: You go out with wet hair? Why?
SHE: In nice weather.
HE: Why?
SHE: It feels good.   85
HE: And you color your hair.
SHE: Yes.
HE: And why is that?
SHE: I like it.
HE: Why? What is your natural color?   90
SHE: Like this when I was in college.
HE: But now?

SHE: I don't know.

HE: You don't know what color your hair is?

95 SHE: It's been a while —

HE: What color do you think it is?

SHE: I imagine it's sort of a dirty blonde with a little gray. (Note: *"dirty blonde" can be "mousy brown," depending on the hair color of the actress. "With a little gray" can be omitted.*)

HE: But you don't really know.

SHE: Not really.

100 HE: (*optional pause*) Do you think you are more attractive with colored hair?

SHE: I don't know.

HE: Then why do you color it?

SHE: I guess so.

HE: What?

105 SHE: I guess I think I'm —

HE: So you color your hair to be more attractive.

SHE: I guess.

HE: But your fingernails are not painted.

SHE: No.

110 HE: Do you sometimes paint your fingernails?

SHE: Sometimes I wear nail polish.

HE: Were your fingernails painted that day?

SHE: I think so.

HE: What nail color did you use?

115 SHE: A pink polish.

HE: Not red.

SHE: No. Just pink.

HE: Why?

SHE: To match my make-up.

120 HE: You were wearing make-up?

SHE: Yes.

HE: Do you always wear make-up to the park?

SHE: No.

HE: Then why were you wearing it that day?

125 SHE: I was on my way to work.

HE: What sort of make-up were you wearing?

SHE: What brand?

HE: Which items of make-up had you put on? Lipstick?

SHE: Yes.

130 HE: What color?

SHE: The actual name?

HE: What color would *you* call the lipstick you wore?

SHE: A sort of peach, maybe, with a darker —

HE: You were wearing two colors on your lips?

SHE: Well, yes.   135
HE: How does one do that?
SHE: It's a lip liner with a brush and then a tube lipstick.
HE: You outline your lips before you put on your lipstick.
SHE: Yes. It's —
HE: You add definition to your lips.   140
SHE: Sort of.
HE: To emphasize them. You emphasize your lips.
SHE: It's just the way you put on make-up.

Possibly a pause.

HE: What other make-up were you wearing?
SHE: A little powder.   145
HE: Why?
SHE: So my nose wouldn't be shiny.
HE: And why would it?
SHE: It was a fairly warm day.
HE: You might have perspired a little.   150
SHE: Maybe.
HE: And was there color on your cheeks?
SHE: Yes. I use a little blush.
HE: Color on the eyes?
SHE: Eyeliner. Maybe a little eye shadow.   155
HE: Mascara.
SHE: No.
HE: Are you sure?
SHE: Yes. I don't use mascara.
HE: Why not?   160
SHE: It bothers my contact lenses.
HE: Were you wearing contact lenses in the park?
SHE: Yes.
HE: You weren't wearing glasses?
SHE: No.   165
HE: But you are wearing glasses now.
SHE: Sometimes I wear contact lenses.
HE: You were wearing contact lenses in the park.
SHE: I already said that.
HE: Your hair was down and you were wearing make-up and contact lenses.   170
SHE: I already said that.
HE: Your hair was down and you were wearing make-up and contact lenses.
SHE: Yes.

A pause.

HE: Were you wearing perfume?

175 SHE: Cologne.
     HE: Do you always wear perfume?
     SHE: Cologne. I was wearing cologne.
     HE: Do you always wear cologne?
     SHE: Usually.
180 HE: In the park?
     SHE: To work.
     HE: And it was a warm day.
     SHE: Yes. But what does that —
     HE: You were walking through the park on your way to work dressed in your skirt
          and top. Your hair was down and you were wearing make-up and perfume.
185 SHE: Cologne.

     A long pause. She has won this round, and he must regroup.

     HE: You were walking through the park.
     SHE: Yes.
     HE: You passed a man sitting on a bench.
     SHE: (*after a slight pause*) There were lots of people sitting on benches.
190 HE: You passed many people.
     SHE: Yes.
     HE: The park was crowded.
     SHE: No.
     HE: The park was not empty.
195 SHE: No. But there were a lot of people.
     HE: Did you see anyone you knew?
     SHE: No.
     HE: No neighbors or friends or familiar faces?
     SHE: No.
200 HE: You walked past the people sitting on benches.
     SHE: Yes.
     HE: There was a man sitting on a bench by himself.
     SHE: I didn't notice he was alone.
     HE: He spoke to you.
205 SHE: Yes.
     HE: You spoke to him.
     SHE: No.
     HE: He spoke to you.
     SHE: Yes.
210 HE: What did he say?
     SHE: He just said hello.
     HE: And what did you do?
     SHE: I nodded to him and kept on walking.
     HE: Did you know him?

SHE: No.   215
HE: Had you ever seen him before?
SHE: No.
HE: He was a stranger.
SHE: Yes.
HE: Yet you nodded at him. Did you smile as you nodded?   220
SHE: Yes.
HE: Why?
SHE: It was a beautiful day. I was just passing by and he said hello.
HE: Do you always acknowledge comments from strangers on the street?
SHE: Not always.   225
HE: Then why did you acknowledge this man?
SHE: It was such a nice day. And I don't like to be rude.
HE: So this stranger said hello and you smiled and nodded.
SHE: That's right.
HE: Did you speak to other people sitting on the benches?   230
SHE: No.
HE: Did you speak to anyone else in the park?
SHE: No.
HE: Why not?
SHE: No one else spoke to me.   235
HE: But when a strange man said hello you smiled and nodded at him.
SHE: Yes. There were lots of people —
HE: Did you stop to smile and nod?
SHE: What?
HE: Did you stop still in front of the man to smile at him?   240
SHE: No. I kept walking.
HE: Why didn't you stop?
SHE: I didn't think about it. It was just a casual hello. I just kept walking. It
      was nothing.
HE: Not really. (*Pause.*) What were you wearing?
SHE: What?   245
HE: What were you wearing?
SHE: I told you.
HE: You have to answer. What were you wearing?
SHE: A skirt and a top.
HE: To go to work?   250
SHE: I had a jacket in the office.
HE: What kind of skirt?
SHE: A printed one.
HE: A red and black print.
SHE: Yes.
HE: Was it long or short?   255

SHE: What?

HE: The skirt. Was it below your knees?

SHE: No.

260 HE: It came above your knees.

SHE: Yes.

HE: It was tight. It clung to your body?

SHE: No. It was gathered. A full skirt.

HE: So it might have moved when you walked.

265 SHE: I don't know.

HE: What was the fabric?

SHE: Chiffon.

HE: Chiffon is a sheer fabric.

SHE: It was lined.

270 HE: What was the lining?

SHE: The lining was chiffon, too.

HE: So you were wearing a see-through mini skirt.

SHE: No.

HE: Describe the blouse.

275 SHE: What?

HE: You were wearing a top.

SHE: Yes. A T-shirt.

HE: A knit top.

SHE: Yes.

280 HE: Did it have sleeves?

SHE: No. It was sleeveless.

HE: A tank top. It was tight.

SHE: No.

HE: It fitted closely on your body. What color was it?

285 SHE: I already told you.

HE: What color was it?

SHE: (*an outburst*) Black.

HE: With a little red flower. (*Possibly a pause.*) Were you wearing underwear?

SHE: (*surprised at this question*) Yes.

290 HE: Were you wearing a slip?

SHE: No.

HE: Why not?

SHE: It was warm out. And the skirt was lined.

HE: Were you wearing panty hose?

295 SHE: No.

HE: Your legs were bare.

SHE: Yes.

HE: No socks?

SHE: I told you. I was wearing sandals.

HE: For the office?   300
SHE: I keep stockings and pumps in my desk.
HE: Along with a jacket.
SHE: Yes.
HE: You walk through the park half naked and cover up for the office.
SHE: (*After a pause*) It's air-conditioned.   305
HE: What?
SHE: The office. It's air-conditioned. It gets cold.
HE: But the park was hot.
SHE: Yes.
HE: So you don't wear much clothing. Were your legs shaved?   310
SHE: Yes.
HE: Why do you shave your legs?
SHE: I just do.
HE: It looks better.
SHE: Yes.   315
HE: So you weren't wearing pantyhose.
SHE: I already said that.
HE: No stockings at all.
SHE: I was wearing sandals.
HE: Were you wearing a bra?   320
SHE: What?
HE: Were you wearing a bra?
SHE: Yes.
HE: What size?
SHE: Thirty-four.   325
HE: Thirty-four what?
SHE: Just thirty-four.
HE: What cup size are you?
SHE: Um, uh, B or C.
HE: You don't know?   330
SHE: It depends on the bra. What brand.
HE: What was the cup size of the bra you had on the day?
SHE: It didn't have a cup size. It was just a 34.
HE: Why didn't it have a cup size? Don't most bras have a cup size?
SHE: It wasn't sized that way. It didn't have an underwire.   335
HE: So it was an elastic sort of bra.
SHE: I don't know. Maybe.

A *slight pause*.

HE: How tall are you?
SHE: Five foot three.
HE: You are considered a petite woman, then.   340

SHE: I guess so.

HE: But thirty-four B or C is a fairly large bra size for a small woman.

SHE: It's average.

HE: Not for a petite woman. You wouldn't say your breasts were small.

345 **SHE:** My . . .

HE: Your breasts. They are not small breasts.

SHE: I don't know.

HE: You don't know you have large breasts?

SHE: They're average.

350 **HE:** Do you always wear a bra?

SHE: When?

HE: When you walk through the park, do you always wear a bra?

SHE: Yes.

HE: Why?

355 **SHE:** I feel more comfortable.

HE: Because you have large breasts.

SHE: (*No answer*).

HE: You would not say that you have small breasts.

SHE: No . . .

360 **HE:** You have a large bust. But you were wearing a tank top.

SHE: It was hot.

HE: You were wearing a tight T-shirt. How wide were the straps on your tank top?

SHE: I don't know.

HE: Wide enough to cover the bra straps?

365 **SHE:** Well, yes.

HE: You were carrying a purse.

SHE: Yes.

HE: What kind?

SHE: A small leather one.

370 **HE:** You were carrying it in your hand.

SHE: No.

HE: It had a strap.

SHE: Yes.

HE: How were you carrying your purse?

375 **SHE:** On my shoulder. The strap was on my shoulder.

HE: Could it cause your tank top strap to shift?

SHE: What?

HE: The strap on your tank top. Could your purse strap have caused it to shift?

SHE: I guess.

380 **HE:** Revealing your bra strap.

SHE: Maybe.

HE: So your bra straps could have been showing as you walked through the park.
SHE: I don't know.

Pause.

HE: What color was your underwear?
SHE: What does it matter? 385
HE: What color was your underwear?
SHE: (*overlapping*) Black.
HE: The bra or the panties?
SHE: Both.
HE: They matched? 390
SHE: Yes.
HE: Did they have lace?
SHE: Yes.
HE: You were wearing a black lacy bra and panties?
SHE: That's right. 395
HE: Why not white or beige?
SHE: To match the tank top and skirt.
HE: Why? Did you expect anyone to see your underwear that day?
SHE: What?
HE: (*doesn't answer*). 400
SHE: No.
HE: Did you have a date with a boyfriend later?
SHE: No.
HE: Then why did it have to match?
SHE: What? 405
HE: The underwear. The bra and panties.
SHE: In case it . . . in case the tank strap . . .
HE: So you expected the bra strap to be seen.
SHE: Not necessarily.
HE: But you thought it might. 410
SHE: I didn't really think about it. It's just what I put on that morning.
HE: Black lacy underwear is considered sexy.
SHE: I guess.
HE: It is sexier than white or beige.
SHE: I guess so. 415
HE: Black is considered a sexy color. So is red.
SHE: I don't know.
HE: Your skirt was black and red. Your top was black with a little red ribbon flower on it. Your bra and panties were black.
SHE: That's right.
HE: So why were you wearing sexy underwear if no one was to see it? 420

SHE: I just like it.

HE: Why?

SHE: It makes me feel . . .

HE: Sexier.

425 SHE: Prettier.

HE: More sensual.

SHE: More feminine.

HE: You walked through the park wearing sexy underwear and revealing clothes and you smiled and nodded at a man you did not know.

SHE: No.

430 HE: No?

SHE: Not like that.

HE: You walked through the park.

SHE: Yes.

HE: You were wearing black lacy underwear.

435 SHE: Yes.

HE: You were wearing a tight tank top and a see-through skirt.

SHE: I . . .

HE: You nodded at a strange man.

SHE: Okay.

440 HE: You smiled at him.

SHE: Okay.

HE: Your bra strap had slipped, and you felt sexy.

SHE: No.

HE: It was a hot day.

445 SHE: Yes.

HE: Your legs were bare. Your thighs were warm.

SHE: No.

HE: The weather was warm.

SHE: Yes.

450 HE: You were walking quickly.

SHE: Yes.

HE: You worked up a sweat.

SHE: I don't know.

HE: It is likely you were perspiring.

455 SHE: I guess.

HE: Your clothes were clinging to you.

SHE: No.

HE: You were moist with sweat and the chiffon lining of your skirt was clinging to your legs as you walked. Your knit top was damp and clung closely to your body.

SHE: That's not right.

460 HE: It was a hot day. You were walking quickly. You were perspiring.

SHE: (*no answer*).

HE: Your clothes were warm and sticky. The shape of your body was revealed. Have your breasts been artificially enlarged?

SHE: No.   465

HE: Or reduced?

SHE: No.

HE: They have not been altered in any way.

SHE: No.

HE: So your breasts are not, shall we say, unnaturally firm.

SHE: I guess not.

HE: And your bra had no underwire.   470

SHE: We've been through that.

HE: So your breasts had little support.

SHE: I was wearing a bra.

HE: You were walking quickly.

SHE: Yes.   475

HE: Your breasts were bouncing.

SHE: I don't know.

HE: Your strap might have slipped. Your breasts had no support.

SHE: I was wearing a bra.

HE: You were swinging your arms.   480

SHE: You said that.

HE: You were either swinging your arms or your arms were folded holding up your breasts.

SHE: I don't know.

HE: Tank tops are low cut.

SHE: It wasn't really —   485

HE: You folded your arms under your breasts to show your cleavage.

SHE: No.

HE: Might you have folded your arms?

SHE: Not to —

HE: Is it possible you folded your arms?   490

SHE: Maybe.

HE: Or you were swinging your arms?

SHE: No.

HE: You were walking quickly.

SHE: Yes. To —   495

HE: Then you were swinging your arms.

SHE: I don't know.

HE: You were swaying your hips.

SHE: No.

HE: You were swinging your arms and your breasts were bouncing.   500

SHE: No.

He: Your large breasts were bouncing and your strap was showing.

She: No.

He: If you were walking at a fast pace your breasts would bounce and your hips sway.

505 **She:** I didn't think about it.

He: That's right (*Pause.*) What size panties?

She: What?

He: What size were your panties?

She: Medium, I guess.

510 **He:** You don't know?

She: I don't remember.

He: What size panties do you usually buy?

She: Medium or small. It depends.

He: On what?

515 **She:** On what's on sale, the style, I don't know.

He: What style?

She: I don't know what you mean.

He: What style were those panties? Bikini panties?

She: That's right.

520 **He:** Why?

She: Why what?

He: Why were you wearing bikini panties?

She: They matched the bra.

He: Wouldn't a looser fitting panty be more comfortable?

525 **She:** Not really.

He: Bikini panties allow your thighs to touch each other.

She: Stop it.

He: It was a very hot day. You walked quickly through the park wearing sexy clothes with your breasts bouncing and your thighs damp and you smiled and nodded at a stranger.

She: That's not it.

530 **He:** You were walking through the park.

She: Yes.

He: It was a hot day.

She: Yes.

He: You smiled at a stranger. And he followed you.

535 **She:** I didn't know.

He: What?

She: I didn't know that he had followed me.

He: When did you notice that he followed you?

She: When he grabbed me.

540 **He:** Not before?

She: He grabbed me from behind. I didn't see him.

HE: You didn't turn when you heard someone behind you?
SHE: There was loud music. I didn't hear anything.
HE: The music was so loud you didn't hear someone behind you?
SHE: There was a machine . . .   545
HE: A lawnmower?
SHE: Louder. An edger. There was loud music and loud noise. I didn't hear him.
HE: You went into the park.
SHE: To walk to work.
HE: You were wearing suggestive clothing.   550
SHE: No.
HE: You signaled to a man.
SHE: No.
HE: You enticed him.
SHE: No.   555
HE: You led him on.
SHE: No.
HE: You acknowledged him.
SHE: (*no answer*).
HE: You smiled at him.   560
SHE: Yes.

The lights are beginning to dim, leaving an ever-brightening single spot focused in the woman's eyes, like an interrogation room. Perhaps the man fades into the background during the rest of the play. Or maybe not.

HE: (*he verbally rapes her*) You left your glasses off. Your dyed hair was bobbing in the breeze. You had painted nails and wore rouge. Your body was scented. You were wearing a revealing outfit, you were feeling sexy in your dainty black lacy undies and your tight shirt and your sheer skirt, and you were shaking your breasts and rolling your hips at this man.
SHE: (*quite possibly a scream*) No!

A very long pause.

HE: Start at the beginning.
SHE: What?   565
HE: Start at the beginning.
SHE: I was walking through the park.
HE: And?
SHE: It was a nice day. (*Pause.*) It was a nice day.

(*Blackout.*)

❖ ❖ ❖

WARREN LEIGHT (1957–   ), a widely acclaimed writer and director, is a writer/producer for the television series *Law and Order: Criminal Intent.* His play *Side Man* (1998) was nominated for a Pulitzer Prize and won Broadway's 1999 Tony Award for Best Play. His other plays include *Glimmer, Glimmer and Shine* (2001); *No Foreigners Beyond This Point;* and *James and Annie.* His screen credits include *Dear God* (1996) and *The Night We Never Met* (1993).

Nine Ten (2001)

CHARACTERS
Leslie
John
Kearrie
Nick
Lyris

Jury Duty Grand Hall. Morning.
John, a slightly awkward bond trader, sits on a bench. Very neat, buttoned down. He reads a perfectly folded Wall Street Journal. *Lyris Touzet, a dancer, enters, almost spills her coffee on him.*

LYRIS: Is this Part B?
JOHN: What?
LYRIS: Part B, or not part B?
JOHN: Ah . . . that is the question.
5 **LYRIS:** Are you making fun of me?
JOHN: No no. Um, let me look at your . . . (*She hands him a slip of paper, he reads it.*) Where you are is where you're supposed to be.

She sits next to him. He needs a little more personal space than she does.

LYRIS: Why do they call us at eight thirty? It's like, nine already, and they haven't said anything.
JOHN: They build in a grace period.
LYRIS: They what?
10 **JOHN:** They say eight thirty so that most people get here by nine. And around nine ten they start calling names.
LYRIS: You knew this, and you came at eight-thirty?
JOHN: Eight actually.
LYRIS: Eight A.M.? You must hate your wife.
JOHN: I don't see her much. We both have to be at work at six.
15 **LYRIS:** You punch in at six?
JOHN: Well, I don't . . . punch in exactly. But, the desk opens at six so . . . .
LYRIS: Your desk opens?
JOHN: Sorry. Trading desk. Bonds. Euros, mostly. From my desk, I'm up so high, on a clear day, you can see Europe.

At a bench opposite, Nick Theron *works the* Times *crossword puzzle as* Leslie Rudin *arrives, pissed off and hyper.*

LESLIE: Part B?   20
NICK: Must be.
LYRIS: Have they called any —
NICK: Does it look like it? (*She looks to the court officer's desk, downstage left.*)
    Every once in a while this guy comes out and says we should wait. Which
    is . . . helpful.
LESLIE: I tried to get out of it on the phone and they said it was my third post-
    ponement and I had to come down here in person on the day of and that
    I wasn't going to get out anyway. And I finally get here — do they just
    change the names of the subway lines for spite lately?— and there's a line a
    mile long to get through security and they go through my purse like I'm a se-
    rial killer and it turns out if I want to smoke I'm going to have to go down
    and outside, and then wait on line again for them to check my bag. This just
    sucks.
NICK: I'm going to tell the judge that I'm a felon. He won't even question it.   25
    And he'll tell me felons can't serve. I'll act offended at this. And then he'll
    just let me go back to my life.
LESLIE: (*impressed*) That's good.
NICK: Racial profiling. A two-way street.

Over to John *and* Lyris.

LYRIS: My brother's in the same building. Security guard. You probably don't
    know him.

Kearrie, *a tough businesswoman, enters, rushed.*

KEARRIE: Part B?
LYRIS AND JOHN: Or not part B?   30
KEARRIE: It's too early for cute. (*They look at her, she means it.*) Have they
    started to give out postponements yet?
LYRIS: No one gets postponement.
KEARRIE: I'm on a flight tomorrow. (*Pulls something out of her bag.*) I've got a
    ticket.

John *takes another look at her.*

JOHN: Kearrie?
KEARRIE: What?   35
JOHN: It's me, John. . . .
KEARRIE: Right. John. That narrows it down.
JOHN: John McCormack. From Wharton.

Kearrie *still doesn't place him.*

LYRIS: (*to* John) You sure leave an impression.

40 JOHN: Story of my life. (*To* Kearrie.) Case study. Euro-economic unity.
  KEARRIE: You got an A, I got a B plus. Even though we worked together.
  JOHN: (*to* Lyris) You know about Irish Alzheimer's . . . you forget everything except your grudges.
  KEARRIE: You went to Gold and Strauss when we graduated, right?
  JOHN: Still there.
45 KEARRIE: (*grades him a loser*) You're kidding. You are not still at —
  JOHN: Just the last ten years. Kearrie this is —
  LYRIS: Lyris Touzet. Spiritual dancer. And healer.
  JOHN: Lyris this is Kearrie Whitman. We went to Wharton together. Class of 91.
  LYRIS: I must have missed you two by like . . . one year.

Leslie and Nick. *He has no hope of attending to his crossword puzzle.* Leslie *must talk or die.*

50 LESLIE: I'm out in the Hamptons. One week after Labor Day. Paradise found. The assholes are gone. The beaches are empty. The water is warm.
  NICK: Sharks are hungry.
  LESLIE: No sharks in the Hamptons. Professional courtesy.
  NICK: Touché.
  LESLIE: I think I'll stay another day. Then I remember . . . fuck me — eight thirty summons. Drive in at midnight. Get stuck in traffic. The L.I.E. has got to be the only road in the world that has traffic jams at two A.M. By the time I get to my garage it's locked for the night. You ever try to find a space on the right side of the street at two A.M.?

Back to John *and* Lyris *chatting.* Kearrie *plays with her Palm Pilot.*

55 JOHN: It's funny, I always wanted to be a spiritual dancer.
  LYRIS: You're making fun of me.
  JOHN: I'm not. . . . swear to god. But what is a —
  LYRIS: I heal people, through movement. Rhythm. Every person has their own . . . pulse. Below the surface, that —
  KEARRIE: Fuck me!
60 LYRIS: I help them to get in touch with their inner —
  KEARRIE: (*Turns to them.*) Fuck me fuck me fuck . . .
  JOHN: What's hers?

Kearrie *now rants in their direction, about her Palm Pilot.*

KEARRIE: Money on the table. I've got a watch list. It's programmed to signal me when there's a discrepancy between euro prices and ADRs. The spread is sitting there. Sitting there. It's blinking — buy me. Buy me. I try to buy and my damn signal fades. What's the point of fucking having a watch list

if you can't follow up on it. This whole building should be wired. This city
is . . . in the stone ages.

LYRIS: (*to* John) Some people are harder cases than others.

Over to Nick *and* Leslie.

NICK: My neighborhood, downtown, they're *always* filming. Some sequel to a 65
sequel to a disaster flick. *Mortal Danger Times Four.* Whatever. Which
means like —

LESLIE: They take every parking place. Big lights up —

NICK: — all night long.

LESLIE: Idiots in walkie-talkies saying don't walk there. On your own street. Call
the cops to complain, they don't care. No one in this city cares. The film
crew can be, like, setting off concussion bombs, and nobody does anything.

Back to John *and* Lyris.

JOHN: (*to* Lyris) I can't.

LYRIS: Everybody can move. Even you . . . Stand up. 70

He doesn't.

LYRIS: (*loud*) STAND UP!

Nick *and* Leslie *hear this. Look over to* John *and* Lyris. John *doesn't want to attract
attention, so he stands.* John *and* Lyris *now overlap with* Nick *and* Leslie. Kearrie *is
in her own world.*)

LYRIS: (*to* John) Just start to, sway a little . . . from your hips.

LESLIE: (*to* Nick) That is sick the way he's flirting with her.

John *sits back down.*

JOHN: I can't.

LYRIS: Yes you can. 75

NICK: (*to* Leslie) How do you know it's his fault?

LESLIE: (*to* Nick) It's always the guy's fault. I date cops. Believe me. I know.

JOHN: (*to* Lyris) I don't like to. Move. I like things as they are. I've had the
same job for ten years.

KEARRIE: (*on her cell phone, to her office*) Here? It's a fucking hellhole. What do
you think? Ah-huh. Ah-huh. Ah-huh. Look — keep that on hold.

JOHN: (*to* Lyris, *oblivious to* Kearrie) Same office, same view. Married my junior 80
high school sweetheart. We take the same train to work. We have the same
lunch. Tuna. On rye. No mayo.

LYRIS: No mayo?

JOHN: It's not so bad, once you get used to it.

KEARRIE: (*into phone*) Yeah as soon as they call roll, I show my plane ticket . . .
and I'm out of here.

Now, from downstage left, a court officer enters.

COURT OFFICER: Hello folks. Welcome to New York County Jury Duty.
Before you all come up to me . . .

85 **KEARRIE:** Excuse me, I have a flight to —

NICK: I have a record —

COURT OFFICER: (He *drowns her out.*) — with your reasons for why you
shouldn't be here, let me tell you: I've heard them all. On the bright side,
most of you will get to go back to your life in two or three days.

LESLIE, NICK, KEARRIE, JOHN, *and* LYRIS *all groan. Two days is eternity.*

COURT OFFICER: And we are as happy to have you, as you are happy to be
here. First things first. Check your summons, and be sure you're in the right
place. This is Civil Court. Part B. 60 Centre Street. Today is Monday,
September 10th . . . Two thousand and one.

Blackout.

◇   ◇   ◇

Reading and Reacting

1. Do you think any of the characters in the four plays in this chapter are fully
developed individuals, or do you see most (or all) of them as stereotypes?
Given the limits of its form, can a ten-minute play ever really develop a
character?

2. With the exception of *Nine Ten*, all the plays in this chapter have only two
characters. Should any additional parts have been written for the four two-
character plays? Are all the characters in *Nine Ten* necessary?

3. The play *Tape* was written for two actors of either gender. Could the roles in
the other plays in this chapter also be portrayed by actors of either gender?
By actors of any age? Of any race?

4. Identify the central conflict in each play. What do you see as the **climax**, or
highest point of tension, in each? Where does the climax generally occur in
these plays?

5. Each play in this chapter has a single setting, and each of these settings is
described very minimally. Do any settings seem to require more detailed descriptions? If you were going to expand each play, would you show any additional settings?

6. Considering the subject matter of each of the four plays in this chapter,
what kinds of topics seem to be most appropriate for ten-minute plays? Why
do you think this is so? What kinds of topics, if any, would *not* be suitable for
ten-minute plays?

WRITING SUGGESTIONS

1. Assume you are a director writing notes for an actor who is to play a role in one of this chapter's plays. Write a character sketch in which you outline the character's background and explain his or her emotions, actions, conflicts, and motivation.

2. Choose a scene from one of the longer plays in this text that has a definite beginning, middle, and end. Rewrite this scene as a self-contained ten-minute play. (If you like, you can update the scene to the present time, change the characters' names or genders, and make other changes you see as necessary.)

3. Write an original ten-minute play for two characters.

CHAPTER 27

PLOT

> Great character creation is a fine thing in a drama, but the sum of all its characters is the story that they enact. Aristotle puts the plot at the head of the dramatic elements; of all these he thinks plot the most difficult and the most expressive. And he is right.
>
> —**Stark Young,** *The Theatre*

Plot denotes the way events are arranged in a work of literature. Although the conventions of drama require that the plot of a play be presented somewhat differently from the plot of a short story, the same components of plot are present in both. Plot in a dramatic work, like plot in a short story, consists of conflicts that are revealed, intensified, and resolved through the characters' actions. (See Chapter 6 for a discussion of conflict.)

Plot Structure

In 1863, the German critic Gustav Freytag devised a pyramid to represent a prototype for the plot of a dramatic work. According to Freytag, a play typically begins with **exposition,** which presents characters and setting and introduces the basic situation in which the characters are involved. Then, during the **rising action,** complications develop, conflicts emerge, suspense builds, and crises occur. The rising action culminates in a **climax,** a point at which the plot's tension

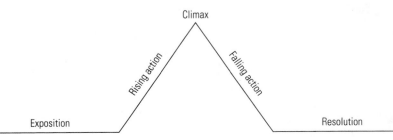

peaks. Finally, during the **falling action,** the intensity subsides, eventually winding down to a **resolution,** or **denouement,** in which all loose ends are tied up.

The familiar plot of a detective story follows Freytag's concept of plot: the exposition section includes the introduction of the detective and the explanation of the crime; the rising action develops as the investigation of the crime proceeds, with suspense increasing as the solution approaches; the high point of the action, the climax, comes with the revelation of the crime's solution; and the falling action presents the detective's explanation of the solution. The story concludes with a resolution that typically includes the capture of the criminal and the restoration of order.

The action of Susan Glaspell's one-act play *Trifles* (p. 770), which in many ways resembles a detective story, can be diagrammed as follows:

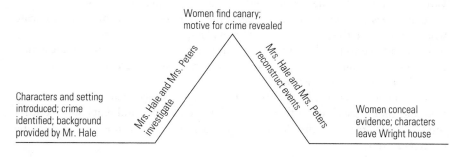

Of course, the plot of a complex dramatic work rarely conforms to the neat pattern represented by Freytag's pyramid. For example, a play can lack exposition entirely: because long stretches of exposition can be dull, a playwright may decide to arouse audience interest by moving directly into conflict, as Sophocles does in *Oedipus the King* (p. 1048). Similarly, because audiences tend to lose interest after the play's climax is reached, a playwright may choose to dispense with extended falling action. Thus, after Hamlet's death, the play ends quite abruptly, with no real resolution.

Plot and Subplot

While the main plot is developing, a parallel plot, called a **subplot,** may be developing alongside it. This structural device is common in the works of Shakespeare and in many other plays as well. The subplot's function may not immediately be clear, so at first it may seem to draw attention away from the main plot. Ultimately, however, the subplot reinforces elements of the primary plot. In Henrik Ibsen's *A Doll House* (p. 784), for example, the threat of Dr. Rank's impending death parallels the threat of Nora's approaching exposure; for both of them, time is running out.

In Shakespeare's *King Lear*, a more elaborate subplot involves the earl of Gloucester, who, like Lear, misjudges his children, favoring a deceitful son who does not deserve his support and overlooking a more deserving one. Both families suffer greatly as a result of the fathers' misplaced loyalties. Thus, the parallel plot places additional emphasis on Lear's poor judgment and magnifies the consequences of his misguided acts: both fathers, and all but one of the five children, are dead by the play's end. A subplot can also set up a contrast — as it does in *Hamlet* (p. 936), where Fortinbras acts decisively to avenge his father, an action that underscores Hamlet's hesitation and procrastination when faced with a similar challenge.

Plot Development

In a dramatic work, plot unfolds through **action:** what characters say and do. Generally, a play does not include a narrator. Instead, dialogue, stage directions, and various staging techniques work together to move the play's action along.

Exchanges of **dialogue** reveal what is happening — and, sometimes, indicate what happened in the past or suggest what will happen in the future. Characters can recount past events to other characters, announce an intention to take some action in the future, or summarize events that are occurring offstage. In such cases, dialogue takes the place of formal narrative.

On the printed page, **stage directions** efficiently move readers from one location and time period to another by specifying entrances and exits and identifying the play's structural divisions — acts and scenes — and their accompanying changes of setting.

Staging techniques can also advance a play's action. For example, a change in **lighting** can shift the focus to another part of the stage — and thus to another place and time. An adjustment of **scenery** or **props**—for instance, a breakfast table, complete with morning paper, replacing a bedtime setting — can indicate that the action has moved forward in time, as can a change of costumes. **Music** can also move a play's action along, predicting excitement or doom or a romantic interlude — or a particular character's entrance.

In Tennessee Williams's *The Glass Menagerie* (p. 1153), unusual staging devices — such as words projected on a screen that preview words to be spoken by a character and visual images on screen that predict scenes to follow — were designed to help keep the action moving. For example, a screen image of blue roses leads into a scene in which Laura tells her mother how Jim gave her the nickname "Blue Roses." Other staging techniques are also used to advance the plot. For example, toward the end of scene 5, stage directions announce, *"The Dance-Hall Music Changes To A Tango That Has A Minor and Somewhat Ominous Tone"*; a "music legend" repeated throughout the play serves as a signature in scenes focusing on Laura.

Occasionally, a play does have a formal narrator. In Thornton Wilder's play *Our Town* (1938), a character known as the Stage Manager functions as a narrator, not only describing the play's setting and introducing the characters to the audience but also soliciting questions from characters scattered around the audience, prompting characters, and interrupting dialogue. In *The Glass Menagerie*, the protagonist, Tom Wingfield, also serves as a narrator, summarizing what has happened and moving readers on to the next scene: "After the fiasco at Rubicam's Business College, the idea of getting a gentleman caller for Laura began to play a more important part in Mother's calculations" (scene 3).

Flashbacks

Many plays — such as *The Glass Menagerie* and Arthur Miller's *Death of a Salesman* (p. 858) — include **flashbacks,** which depict events that occurred before the play's main action. Dialogue can also summarize events that occurred earlier, thereby overcoming the limitations set by the chronological action on stage. Thus, Mr. Hale in *Trifles* tells the other characters how he discovered John Wright's murder, and Nora in *A Doll House* confides her secret past to her friend Kristine. As characters on stage are brought up to date, the audience is also given necessary information — facts that are essential to an understanding of the characters' motivation. (In less realistic dramas, characters can interrupt the action to deliver long monologues or soliloquies that fill in background details — or even address the audience directly, as Tom does in *The Glass Menagerie*.)

Foreshadowing

In addition to revealing past events, dialogue can **foreshadow,** or look ahead to, future action. In many cases, seemingly unimportant comments have significance that becomes clear as the play develops. For example, in act 3 of *A Doll House*, Torvald Helmer says to Kristine, "An exit should always be effective, Mrs. Linde, but that's what I can't get Nora to grasp." At the end of the play, Nora's exit is not only effective but also memorable.

Elements of staging can also suggest events to come. In *The Glass Menagerie*, the ever-present photograph of the absent father — who, Tom tells the audience in scene 1, may be seen as a symbol of "the long delayed but always expected something that we live for" — foreshadows Tom's escape. Various bits of **stage business** — gestures or movements designed to attract the audience's attention — may also foreshadow future events. In *A Doll House*, Nora's sneaking forbidden macaroons seems at first to suggest her fear of her husband, but her actions actually foreshadow her eventual defiance of his authority.

✔ CHECKLIST Writing about Plot

- What happens in the play?
- What is the play's central conflict? How is it resolved? What other conflicts are present?
- What section of the play constitutes its rising action?
- Where does the play's climax occur?

continued on next page

What crises can you identify?

How is suspense created?

What section of the play constitutes its falling action?

Does the play contain a subplot? What is its purpose? How is it related to the main plot?

How do characters' actions advance the play's plot?

How does dialogue advance the play's plot?

How do stage directions advance the play's plot?

How do staging techniques advance the play's plot?

Does the play include a narrator?

Does the play include flashbacks? Foreshadowing? Does the play's dialogue contain summaries of past events or references to events in the future? How does the use of flashbacks or foreshadowing advance the play's plot?

SUSAN GLASPELL (1882–1948) was born in Davenport, Iowa, and graduated from Drake University in 1899. First a reporter and then a freelance writer, she lived in Chicago (where she was part of the Chicago Renaissance that included poet Carl Sandburg and novelist Theodore Dreiser) and later in Greenwich Village. Her works include two plays in addition to *Trifles, The Verge* (1921) and *Alison's House* (1930), and several novels, including *Fidelity* (1915) and *The Morning Is Near Us* (1939). With her husband, George Cram Cook, she founded the Provincetown Players, which became the staging ground for innovative plays by Eugene O'Neill, among others.

Glaspell herself wrote plays for the Provincetown Players, beginning with *Trifles,* which she created for the 1916 season although she had never previously written a drama. The play opened on August 8, 1916, with Glaspell and her husband in the cast. Glaspell said she wrote *Trifles* in one afternoon, sitting in the empty theater and looking at the bare stage: "After a time, the stage became a kitchen — a kitchen there all by itself." She remembered a murder trial she had covered in Iowa in her days as a reporter, and the story began to play itself out on the stage as she gazed. Throughout her revisions, she said, she returned to look at the stage to see whether the events she was recording came to life on it. Although Glaspell later rewrote *Trifles* as a short story called "A Jury of Her Peers," the play remains her most successful and memorable work.

Trifles (1916)

CHARACTERS

George Henderson, *county attorney*   **Mrs. Peters**
Henry Peters, *sheriff*   **Mrs. Hale**
Lewis Hale, *a neighboring farmer*

SCENE

The kitchen in the now abandoned farmhouse of John Wright, a gloomy kitchen, and left without having been put in order — unwashed pans under the sink, a loaf of bread outside the breadbox, a dish towel on the table — other signs of incompleted work. At the rear the outer door opens and the Sheriff comes in followed by the County Attorney and Hale. The Sheriff and Hale are men in middle life, the County Attorney is a young man; all are much bundled up and go at once to the stove. They are followed by two women — the Sheriff's wife first; she is a slight wiry woman, a thin nervous face. Mrs. Hale is larger and would ordinarily be called more comfortable looking, but she is disturbed now and looks fearfully about as she enters. The women have come in slowly, and stand close together near the door.

COUNTY ATTORNEY: *(rubbing his hands)* This feels good. Come up to the fire, ladies.

MRS. PETERS: *(after taking a step forward)* I'm not — cold.

SHERIFF: *(unbuttoning his overcoat and stepping away from the stove as if to mark the beginning of official business)* Now, Mr. Hale, before we move things about, you explain to Mr. Henderson just what you saw when you came here yesterday morning.

COUNTY ATTORNEY: By the way, has anything been moved? Are things just as you left them yesterday?

SHERIFF: *(looking about)* It's just the same. When it dropped below zero last   5
night I thought I'd better send Frank out this morning to make a fire for us — no use getting pneumonia with a big case on, but I told him not to touch anything except the stove — and you know Frank.

COUNTY ATTORNEY: Somebody should have been left here yesterday.

SHERIFF: Oh — yesterday. When I had to send Frank to Morris Center for that man who went crazy — I want you to know I had my hands full yesterday. I knew you could get back from Omaha by today and as long as I went over everything here myself —

COUNTY ATTORNEY: Well, Mr. Hale, tell just what happened when you came here yesterday morning.

HALE: Harry and I had started to town with a load of potatoes. We came along the road from my place and as I got here I said, "I'm going to see if I can't get John Wright to go in with me on a party telephone." I spoke to Wright about it once before and he put me off, saying folks talked too much anyway, and all he asked was peace and quiet — I guess you know about how much he talked himself; but I thought maybe if I went to the house and talked about it before his wife, though I said to Harry that I didn't know as what his wife wanted made much difference to John—

COUNTY ATTORNEY: Let's talk about that later, Mr. Hale. I do want to talk   10
about that, but tell now just what happened when you got to the house.

HALE: I didn't hear or see anything; I knocked at the door, and still it was all quiet inside. I knew they must be up, it was past eight o'clock. So I knocked again, and I thought I heard somebody say, "Come in." I wasn't sure, I'm not sure yet, but I opened the door — this door (*indicating the door by which the two women are still standing*) and there in that rocker —(*pointing to it*) sat Mrs. Wright.

They all look at the rocker.

COUNTY ATTORNEY: What — was she doing?

HALE: She was rockin' back and forth. She had her apron in her hand and was kind of — pleating it.

COUNTY ATTORNEY: And how did she —look?

15 HALE: Well, she looked queer.

COUNTY ATTORNEY: How do you mean — queer?

HALE: Well, as if she didn't know what she was going to do next. And kind of done up.

COUNTY ATTORNEY: How did she seem to feel about your coming?

HALE: Why, I don't think she minded — one way or other. She didn't pay much attention. I said, "How do, Mrs. Wright, it's cold, ain't it?" And she said, "Is it?"— and went on kind of pleating at her apron. Well, I was surprised; she didn't ask me to come up to the stove, or to set down, but just sat there, not even looking at me, so I said, "I want to see John." And then she —laughed. I guess you would call it a laugh. I thought of Harry and the team outside, so I said a little sharp: "Can't I see John?" "No," she says, kind o' dull like. "Ain't he home?" says I. "Yes," says she, "he's home." "Then why can't I see him?" I asked her, out of patience. " 'Cause he's dead," says she. "*Dead?*" says I. She just nodded her head, not getting a bit excited, but rockin' back and forth. "Why — where is he?" says I, not knowing what to say. She just pointed upstairs —like that. (*Himself pointing to the room above.*) I got up, with the idea of going up there. I walked from there to here — then I says, "Why, what did he die of?" "He died of a rope round his neck," says she, and just went on pleatin' at her apron. Well, I went out and called Harry. I thought I might — need help. We went upstairs and there he was lyin'—

20 COUNTY ATTORNEY: I think I'd rather have you go into that upstairs, where you can point it all out. Just go on now with the rest of the story.

HALE: Well, my first thought was to get that rope off. It looked . . . (*stops, his face twitches*) . . . but Harry, he went up to him, and he said, "No, he's dead all right, and we'd better not touch anything." So we went back down stairs. She was still sitting that same way. "Has anybody been notified?" I asked. "No," says she, unconcerned. "Who did this, Mrs. Wright?" said Harry. He said it businesslike — and she stopped pleatin' of her apron. "I don't know," she says. "You don't *know*?" says Harry. "No," says she. "Weren't you sleepin' in the bed with him?" says Harry. "Yes," says she, "but I was on the inside." "Somebody slipped a rope round his neck and strangled him and you didn't wake up?" says Harry. "I didn't wake up," she said after him. We must 'a

In this scene from the Provincetown Players' 1917 production of Susan Glaspell's *Trifles,* the three men discuss the crime while Mrs. Peters and Mrs. Hale look on.

looked as if we didn't see how that could be, for after a minute she said, "I sleep sound." Harry was going to ask her more questions but I said maybe we ought to let her tell her story first to the coroner, or the sheriff, so Harry went fast as he could to Rivers' place, where there's a telephone.

COUNTY ATTORNEY: And what did Mrs. Wright do when she knew that you had gone for the coroner?

HALE: She moved from that chair to this one over here *(pointing to a small chair in the corner)* and just sat there with her hands held together and looking down. I got a feeling that I ought to make some conversation, so I said I had come in to see if John wanted to put in a telephone, and at that she started to laugh, and then she stopped and looked at me — scared. *(The County Attorney, who has had his notebook out, makes a note.)* I dunno, maybe it wasn't scared. I wouldn't like to say it was. Soon Harry got back, and then Dr. Lloyd came, and you, Mr. Peters, and so I guess that's all I know that you don't.

COUNTY ATTORNEY: *(looking around)* I guess we'll go upstairs first — and then out to the barn and around there. *(To the Sheriff.)* You're convinced that there was nothing important here — nothing that would point to any motive.

SHERIFF: Nothing here but kitchen things.

25

The County Attorney, after again looking around the kitchen, opens the door of a cupboard closet. He gets up on a chair and looks on a shelf. Pulls his hand away, sticky.

COUNTY ATTORNEY: Here's a nice mess.

The women draw nearer.

MRS. PETERS: *(to the other woman)* Oh, her fruit; it did freeze. *(To the County Attorney.)* She worried about that when it turned so cold. She said the fire'd go out and her jars would break.

SHERIFF: Well, can you beat the women! Held for murder and worryin' about her preserves.

COUNTY ATTORNEY: I guess before we're through she may have something more serious than preserves to worry about.

30 **HALE:** Well, women are used to worrying over trifles.

The two women move a little closer together.

COUNTY ATTORNEY: *(with the gallantry of a young politician)* And yet, for all their worries, what would we do without the ladies? *(The women do not unbend. He goes to the sink, takes a dipperful of water from the pail and pouring it into a basin, washes his hands. Starts to wipe them on the roller towel, turns it for a cleaner place.)* Dirty towels! *(Kicks his foot against the pans under the sink.)* Not much of a housekeeper, would you say, ladies?

MRS. HALE: *(stiffly)* There's a great deal of work to be done on a farm.

COUNTY ATTORNEY: To be sure. And yet *(with a little bow to her)* I know there are some Dickson county farmhouses which do not have such roller towels.

He gives it a pull to expose its full length again.

MRS. HALE: Those towels get dirty awful quick. Men's hands aren't always as clean as they might be.

35 **COUNTY ATTORNEY:** Ah, loyal to your sex, I see. But you and Mrs. Wright were neighbors. I suppose you were friends, too.

MRS. HALE: *(shaking her head)* I've not seen much of her of late years. I've not been in this house — it's more than a year.

COUNTY ATTORNEY: And why was that? You didn't like her?

MRS. HALE: I liked her all well enough. Farmers' wives have their hands full, Mr. Henderson. And then —

COUNTY ATTORNEY: Yes —?

40 **MRS. HALE:** *(looking about)* It never seemed a very cheerful place.

COUNTY ATTORNEY: No — it's not cheerful. I shouldn't say she had the homemaking instinct.

MRS. HALE: Well, I don't know as Wright had, either.

COUNTY ATTORNEY: You mean that they didn't get on very well?

MRS. HALE: No, I don't mean anything. But I don't think a place'd be any cheerfuller for John Wright's being in it.

45 **COUNTY ATTORNEY:** I'd like to talk more of that a little later. I want to get the lay of things upstairs now.

He goes to the left, where three steps lead to a stair door.

SHERIFF: I suppose anything Mrs. Peters does'll be all right. She was to take in some clothes for her, you know, and a few little things. We left in such a hurry yesterday.

COUNTY ATTORNEY: Yes, but I would like to see what you take, Mrs. Peters, and keep an eye out for anything that might be of use to us.

MRS. PETERS: Yes, Mr. Henderson.

The women listen to the men's steps on the stairs, then look about the kitchen.

MRS. HALE: I'd hate to have men coming into my kitchen, snooping around and criticizing.

She arranges the pans under sink which the County Attorney had shoved out of place.

MRS. PETERS: Of course it's no more than their duty.   50

MRS. HALE: Duty's all right, but I guess that deputy sheriff that came out to make the fire might have got a little of this on. (*Gives the roller towel a pull.*) Wish I'd thought of that sooner. Seems mean to talk about her for not having things slicked up when she had to come away in such a hurry.

MRS. PETERS: (*who has gone to a small table in the left rear corner of the room, and lifted one end of a towel that covers a pan*) She had bread set.

Stands still.

MRS. HALE: (*eyes fixed on a loaf of bread beside the breadbox, which is on a low shelf at the other side of the room. Moves slowly toward it.*) She was going to put this in there. (*Picks up loaf, then abruptly drops it. In a manner of returning to familiar things.*) It's a shame about her fruit. I wonder if it's all gone. (*Gets up on the chair and looks.*) I think there's some here that's all right, Mrs. Peters. Yes — here; (*holding it toward the window*) this is cherries, too. (*Looking again.*) I declare I believe that's the only one. (*Gets down, bottle in her hand. Goes to the sink and wipes it off on the outside.*) She'll feel awful bad after all her hard work in the hot weather. I remember the afternoon I put up my cherries last summer.

She puts the bottle on the big kitchen table, center of the room. With a sigh, is about to sit down in the rocking-chair. Before she is seated realizes what chair it is; with a slow look at it, steps back. The chair which she has touched rocks back and forth.

MRS. PETERS: Well, I must get those things from the front room closet. (*She goes to the door at the right, but after looking into the other room, steps back.*) You coming with me, Mrs. Hale? You could help me carry them.

They go in the other room; reappear, Mrs. Peters carrying a dress and skirt, Mrs. Hale following with a pair of shoes.

MRS. PETERS: My, it's cold in there.   55

She puts the clothes on the big table, and hurries to the stove.

MRS. HALE: (*examining her skirt*) Wright was close. I think maybe that's why she kept so much to herself. She didn't even belong to the Ladies Aid. I suppose she felt she couldn't do her part, and then you don't enjoy things when you feel shabby. She used to wear pretty clothes and be lively, when she was Minnie Foster, one of the town girls singing in the choir. But that — oh, that was thirty years ago. This all you was to take in?

MRS. PETERS: She said she wanted an apron. Funny thing to want, for there isn't much to get you dirty in jail, goodness knows. But I suppose just to make her feel more natural. She said they was in the top drawer in this cupboard. Yes, here. And then her little shawl that always hung behind the door. (*Opens stair door and looks.*) Yes, here it is.

Quickly shuts door leading upstairs.

MRS. HALE: (*abruptly moving toward her*) Mrs. Peters?
MRS. PETERS: Yes, Mrs. Hale?
60 **MRS. HALE:** Do you think she did it?
MRS. PETERS: (*in a frightened voice*) Oh, I don't know.
MRS. HALE: Well, I don't think she did. Asking for an apron and her little shawl. Worrying about her fruit.
MRS. PETERS: (*starts to speak, glances up, where footsteps are heard in the room above. In a low voice.*) Mr. Peters says it looks bad for her. Mr. Henderson is awful sarcastic in a speech and he'll make fun of her sayin' she didn't wake up.
MRS. HALE: Well, I guess John Wright didn't wake when they was slipping that rope under his neck.
65 **MRS. PETERS:** No, it's strange. It must have been done awful crafty and still. They say it was such a — funny way to kill a man, rigging it all up like that.
MRS. HALE: That's just what Mr. Hale said. There was a gun in the house. He says that's what he can't understand.
MRS. PETERS: Mr. Henderson said coming out that what was needed for the case was a motive; something to show anger, or — sudden feeling.
MRS. HALE: (*who is standing by the table*) Well, I don't see any signs of anger around here. (*She puts her hand on the dish towel which lies on the table, stands looking down at table, one half of which is clean, the other half messy.*) It's wiped to here. (*Makes a move as if to finish work, then turns and looks at loaf of bread outside the breadbox. Drops towel. In that voice of coming back to familiar things.*) Wonder how they are finding things upstairs. I hope she had it a little more red-up° up there. You know, it seems kind of *sneaking*. Locking her up in town and then coming out here and trying to get her own house to turn against her!
MRS. PETERS: But Mrs. Hale, the law is the law.
70 **MRS. HALE:** I s'pose 'tis. (*Unbuttoning her coat.*) Better loosen up your things, Mrs. Peters. You won't feel them when you go out.

° *red-up:* Spruced-up (slang).

Mrs. Peters takes off her fur tippet, goes to hang it on hook at back of room, stands looking at the under part of the small corner table.

MRS. PETERS: She was piecing a quilt.

She brings the large sewing basket and they look at the bright pieces.

MRS. HALE: It's log cabin pattern. Pretty, isn't it? I wonder if she was goin' to quilt it or just knot it?

Footsteps have been heard coming down the stairs. The Sheriff enters followed by Hale and the County Attorney.

SHERIFF: They wonder if she was going to quilt it or just knot it!

The men laugh; the women look abashed.

COUNTY ATTORNEY: (*rubbing his hands over the stove*) Frank's fire didn't do much up there, did it? Well, let's go out to the barn and get that cleared up.

The men go outside.

MRS. HALE: (*resentfully*) I don't know as there's anything so strange, our takin'   75
up our time with little things while we're waiting for them to get the evidence. (*She sits down at the big table smoothing out a block with decision.*) I don't
see as it's anything to laugh about.

MRS. PETERS: (*apologetically*) Of course they've got awful important things on their minds.

Pulls up a chair and joins Mrs. Hale at the table.

MRS. HALE: (*examining another block*) Mrs. Peters, look at this one. Here, this
is the one she was working on, and look at the sewing! All the rest of it has
been so nice and even. And look at this! It's all over the place! Why, it looks
as if she didn't know what she was about!

*After she has said this they look at each other, then start to glance back at the door.
After an instant Mrs. Hale has pulled at a knot and ripped the sewing.*

MRS. PETERS: Oh, what are you doing, Mrs. Hale?

MRS. HALE: (*mildly*) Just pulling out a stitch or two that's not sewed very good.
(*Threading a needle.*) Bad sewing always made me fidgety.

MRS. PETERS: (*nervously*) I don't think we ought to touch things.   80

MRS. HALE: I'll just finish up this end. (*Suddenly stopping and leaning forward.*)
Mrs. Peters?

MRS. PETERS: Yes, Mrs. Hale?

MRS. HALE: What do you suppose she was so nervous about?

MRS. PETERS: Oh — I don't know. I don't know as she was nervous. I sometimes sew awful queer when I'm just tired. (*Mrs. Hale starts to say something,
looks at Mrs. Peters, then goes on sewing.*) Well, I must get these things
wrapped up. They may be through sooner than we think. (*Putting apron and
other things together.*) I wonder where I can find a piece of paper, and string.

85   MRS. HALE: In that cupboard, maybe.

MRS. PETERS: *(looking in cupboard)* Why, here's a birdcage. *(Holds it up.)* Did she have a bird, Mrs. Hale?

MRS. HALE: Why, I don't know whether she did or not — I've not been here for so long. There was a man around last year selling canaries cheap, but I don't know as she took one; maybe she did. She used to sing real pretty herself.

MRS. PETERS: *(glancing around)* Seems funny to think of a bird here. But she must have had one, or why would she have a cage? I wonder what happened to it.

MRS. HALE: I s'pose maybe the cat got it.

90   MRS. PETERS: No, she didn't have a cat. She's got that feeling some people have about cats — being afraid of them. My cat got in her room and she was real upset and asked me to take it out.

MRS. HALE: My sister Bessie was like that. Queer, ain't it?

MRS. PETERS: *(examining the cage)* Why, look at this door. It's broke. One hinge is pulled apart.

MRS. HALE: *(looking too)* Looks as if someone must have been rough with it.

MRS. PETERS: Why, yes.

She brings the cage forward and puts it on the table.

95   MRS. HALE: I wish if they're going to find any evidence they'd be about it. I don't like this place.

MRS. PETERS: But I'm awful glad you came with me, Mrs. Hale. It would be lonesome for me sitting here alone.

MRS. HALE: It would, wouldn't it? *(Dropping her sewing.)* But I tell you what I do wish, Mrs. Peters. I wish I had come over sometimes when *she* was here. I — *(looking around the room)* — wish I had.

MRS. PETERS: But of course you were awful busy, Mrs. Hale — your house and your children.

MRS. HALE: I could've come. I stayed away because it weren't cheerful — and that's why I ought to have come. I — I've never liked this place. Maybe because it's down in a hollow and you don't see the road. I dunno what it is but it's a lonesome place and always was. I wish I had come over to see Minnie Foster sometimes. I can see now —

Shakes her head.

100   MRS. PETERS: Well, you mustn't reproach yourself, Mrs. Hale. Somehow we just don't see how it is with other folks until — something comes up.

MRS. HALE: Not having children makes less work — but it makes a quiet house, and Wright out to work all day, and no company when he did come in. Did you know John Wright, Mrs. Peters?

MRS. PETERS: Not to know him; I've seen him in town. They say he was a good man.

MRS. HALE: Yes — good; he didn't drink, and kept his word as well as most, I guess, and paid his debts. But he was a hard man, Mrs. Peters. Just to pass the time of day with him — (*Shivers.*) Like a raw wind that gets to the bone. (*Pauses, her eye falling on the cage.*) I should think she would 'a wanted a bird. But what do you suppose went with it?

MRS. PETERS: I don't know, unless it got sick and died.

She reaches over and swings the broken door, swings it again. Both women watch it.

MRS. HALE: You weren't raised round here, were you? (*Mrs. Peters shakes her head.*) You didn't know — her?   105

MRS. PETERS: Not till they brought her yesterday.

MRS. HALE: She — come to think of it, she was kind of like a bird herself — real sweet and pretty, but kind of timid and — fluttery. How — she — did — change. (*Silence; then as if struck by a happy thought and relieved to get back to everyday things.*) Tell you what, Mrs. Peters, why don't you take the quilt in with you? It might take up her mind.

MRS. PETERS: Why, I think that's a real nice idea, Mrs. Hale. There couldn't possibly be any objection to it, could there? Now, just what would I take? I wonder if her patches are in here — and her things.

They look in the sewing basket.

MRS. HALE: Here's some red. I expect this has got sewing things in it. (*Brings out a fancy box.*) What a pretty box. Looks like something somebody would give you. Maybe her scissors are in here. (*Opens box. Suddenly puts her hand to her nose.*) Why — (*Mrs. Peters bends nearer, then turns her face away.*) There's something wrapped up in this piece of silk.

MRS. PETERS: Why, this isn't her scissors.   110

MRS. HALE: (*lifting the silk*) Oh, Mrs. Peters — it's —

Mrs. Peters bends closer.

MRS. PETERS: It's the bird.

MRS. HALE: (*jumping up*) But, Mrs. Peters — look at it! Its neck! Look at its neck! It's all — other side to.

MRS. PETERS: Somebody — wrung — its — neck.

Their eyes meet. A look of growing comprehension, of horror. Steps are heard outside. Mrs. Hale slips box under quilt pieces, and sinks into her chair. Enter Sheriff and County Attorney. Mrs. Peters rises.

COUNTY ATTORNEY: (*as one turning from serious things to little pleasantries*)   115
    Well, ladies, have you decided whether she was going to quilt it or knot it?

MRS. PETERS: We think she was going to — knot it.

COUNTY ATTORNEY: Well, that's interesting, I'm sure. (*Seeing the birdcage.*) Has the bird flown?

MRS. HALE: (*putting more quilt pieces over the box*) We think the — cat got it.

COUNTY ATTORNEY: *(preoccupied)* Is there a cat?

Mrs. Hale glances in a quick covert way at Mrs. Peters.

120   **MRS. PETERS:** Well, not *now*. They're superstitious, you know. They leave.

COUNTY ATTORNEY: *(to Sheriff Peters, continuing an interrupted conversation)* No sign at all of anyone having come from the outside. Their own rope. Now let's go up again and go over it piece by piece. *(They start upstairs.)* It would have to have been someone who knew just the —

Mrs. Peters sits down. The two women sit there not looking at one another, but as if peering into something and at the same time holding back. When they talk now it is in the manner of feeling their way over strange ground, as if afraid of what they are saying, but as if they can not help saying it.

MRS. HALE: She liked the bird. She was going to bury it in that pretty box.

MRS. PETERS: *(in a whisper)* When I was a girl — my kitten — there was a boy took a hatchet, and before my eyes — and before I could get there — *(Covers her face an instant.)* If they hadn't held me back I would have — *(catches herself, looks upstairs where steps are heard, falters weakly)* — hurt him.

MRS. HALE: *(with a slow look around her)* I wonder how it would seem never to have had any children around. *(Pause.)* No, Wright wouldn't like the bird — a thing that sang. She used to sing. He killed that, too.

125   **MRS. PETERS:** *(moving uneasily)* We don't know who killed the bird.

MRS. HALE: I knew John Wright.

MRS. PETERS: It was an awful thing was done in this house that night, Mrs. Hale. Killing a man while he slept, slipping a rope around his neck that choked the life out of him.

MRS. HALE: His neck. Choked the life out of him.

Her hand goes out and rests on the birdcage.

MRS. PETERS: *(with rising voice)* We don't know who killed him. We don't know.

130   **MRS. HALE:** *(her own feeling not interrupted)* If there'd been years and years of nothing, then a bird to sing to you, it would be awful — still, after the bird was still.

MRS. PETERS: *(something within her speaking)* I know what stillness is. When we homesteaded in Dakota, and my first baby died — after he was two years old, and me with no other then —

MRS. HALE: *(moving)* How soon do you suppose they'll be through, looking for the evidence?

MRS. PETERS: I know what stillness is. *(Pulling herself back.)* The law has got to punish crime, Mrs. Hale.

MRS. HALE: *(not as if answering that)* I wish you'd seen Minnie Foster when she wore a white dress with blue ribbons and stood up there in the choir

and sang. (*A look around the room.*) Oh, I *wish* I'd come over here once in a
while! That was a crime! That was a crime! Who's going to punish that?

MRS. PETERS: (*looking upstairs*) We mustn't — take on.   135

MRS. HALE: I might have known she needed help! I know how things can
be — for women. I tell you, it's queer, Mrs. Peters. We live close together
and we live far apart. We all go through the same things — it's all just a
different kind of the same thing. (*Brushes her eyes; noticing the bottle of fruit,
reaches out for it.*) If I was you I wouldn't tell her her fruit was gone. Tell her
it *ain't*. Tell her it's all right. Take this in to prove it to her. She — she may
never know whether it was broke or not.

MRS. PETERS: (*takes the bottle, looks about for something to wrap it in; takes
petticoat from the clothes brought from the other room, very nervously begins
winding this around the bottle. In a false voice*) My, it's a good thing the men
couldn't hear us. Wouldn't they just laugh! Getting all stirred up over a
little thing like a — dead canary. As if that could have anything to do
with — with — wouldn't they *laugh!*

The men are heard coming down stairs.

MRS. HALE: (*under her breath*) Maybe they would — maybe they wouldn't.

COUNTY ATTORNEY: No, Peters, it's all perfectly clear except a reason for
doing it. But you know juries when it comes to women. If there was some
definite thing. Something to show — something to make a story about — a
thing that would connect up with this strange way of doing it —

The women's eyes meet for an instant. Enter Hale from outer door.

HALE: Well, I've got the team around. Pretty cold out there.   140

COUNTY ATTORNEY: I'm going to stay here a while by myself. (*To the Sheriff.*)
You can send Frank out for me, can't you? I want to go over everything. I'm
not satisfied that we can't do better.

SHERIFF: Do you want to see what Mrs. Peters is going to take in?

The County Attorney goes to the table, picks up the apron, laughs.

COUNTY ATTORNEY: Oh, I guess they're not very dangerous things the ladies
have picked out. (*Moves a few things about, disturbing the quilt pieces which
cover the box. Steps back.*) No, Mrs. Peters doesn't need supervising. For
that matter, a sheriff's wife is married to the law. Ever think of it that way,
Mrs. Peters?

MRS. PETERS: Not — just that way.

SHERIFF: (*chuckling*) Married to the law. (*Moves toward the other room.*) I just 145
want you to come in here a minute, George. We ought to take a look at
these windows.

COUNTY ATTORNEY: (*scoffingly*) Oh, windows!

SHERIFF: We'll be right out, Mr. Hale.

Hale goes outside. The Sheriff follows the County Attorney into the other room. Then Mrs. Hale rises, hands tight together, looking intensely at Mrs. Peters, whose eyes make a slow turn, finally meeting Mrs. Hale's. A moment Mrs. Hale holds her, then her own eyes point the way to where the box is concealed. Suddenly Mrs. Peters throws back quilt pieces and tries to put the box in the bag she is wearing. It is too big. She opens box, starts to take bird out, cannot touch it, goes to pieces, stands there helpless. Sound of a knob turning in the other room. Mrs. Hale snatches the box and puts it in the pocket of her big coat. Enter County Attorney and Sheriff.

COUNTY ATTORNEY: *(facetiously)* Well, Henry, at least we found out that she was not going to quilt it. She was going to — what is it you call it, ladies?

MRS. HALE: *(her hand against her pocket)* We call it — knot it, Mr. Henderson.

Reading and Reacting

1. What key events have occurred before the start of the play? Why do you suppose these events are not presented in the play itself?

2. What are the "trifles" to which the title refers? How do these "trifles" advance the play's plot?

3. Glaspell's short story version of *Trifles* is called "A Jury of Her Peers." Who are Mrs. Wright's peers? What do you suppose the verdict would be if she were tried for her crime in 1916, when only men were permitted to serve on juries? If the trial were held today, do you think a jury might reach a different verdict?

4. *Trifles* is a one-act play, and all its action occurs in the Wrights' kitchen. Does this confined setting restrict the flow of the plot? Are there any advantages to this setting? Explain.

5. All background information about Mrs. Wright is provided by Mrs. Hale. Do you consider her to be a reliable source of information? Why or why not?

6. Mr. Hale's summary of his conversation with Mrs. Wright is the reader's only chance to hear her version of events. How might the play be different if Mrs. Wright appeared as a character?

7. *Trifles* is a relatively slow-moving, "talky" play, with very little physical action. Is this a weakness of the play, or is the slow development consistent with the effect Glaspell is trying to achieve? Explain.

8. How does each of the following events advance the play's action: the men's departure from the kitchen, the discovery of the quilt pieces, the discovery of the dead bird?

9. How do the county attorney's sarcastic comments and his patronizing attitude toward Mrs. Hale and Mrs. Peters advance the play's action?

10. How do Mrs. Peters's memories of her own life advance the action?

11. What assumptions about women do the male characters make? In what ways do the female characters support or challenge these assumptions?

12. In what sense is the process of making a quilt an appropriate metaphor for the plot of *Trifles*?

13. JOURNAL ENTRY Do you think Mrs. Hale and Mrs. Peters do the right thing by concealing evidence?

14. CRITICAL PERSPECTIVE In *American Drama from the Colonial Period through World War I*, Gary A. Richardson says that in *Trifles*, Glaspell developed a new structure for her action:

> While action in the traditional sense is minimal, Glaspell is nevertheless able to rivet attention on the two women, wed the audience to their perspective, and make a compelling case for the fairness of their actions. Existing on the margins of their society, Mrs. Peters and Mrs. Hale become emotional surrogates for the jailed Minnie Wright, effectively exonerating her action as "justifiable homicide." *Trifles* is carefully crafted to match Glaspell's subject matter — the action meanders, without a clearly delineated beginning, middle, or end . . . .

Exactly how does Glaspell "rivet attention on" Mrs. Hale and Mrs. Peters? Do you agree that the play's action "meanders, without a clearly delineated beginning, middle, and end"? If so, do you too see this "meandering" as appropriate for Glaspell's subject matter?

Related Works: "I Stand Here Ironing" (p. 174), "The Cask of Amontillado" (p. 203), "Everyday Use" (p. 282), "The Yellow Wallpaper" (p. 372), "Harlem" (p. 522), *A Doll House* (p. 784)

HENRIK IBSEN (1828–1906), Norway's foremost dramatist, was born into a prosperous family; however, his father lost his fortune when Ibsen was six. When Ibsen was fifteen, he was apprenticed to an apothecary away from home and was permanently estranged from his family. During his apprenticeship, he studied to enter the university and wrote plays. Although he did not pass the university entrance exam, his second play, *The Warrior's Barrow* (1850), was produced by the Christiania Theatre in 1850. He began a life in the theater, writing plays and serving as artistic director of a theatrical company. Disillusioned by the public's lack of interest in theater, he left Norway, living with his wife and son in Italy and Germany between 1864 and 1891. By the time he returned to Norway, he was famous and revered. Ibsen's most notable plays include *Brand* (1865), *Peer Gynt* (1867), *A Doll House* (1879), *Ghosts* (1881), *An Enemy of the People* (1882), *The Wild Duck* (1884), *Hedda Gabler* (1890), and *When We Dead Awaken* (1899).

A Doll House marks the beginning of Ibsen's successful realist period, during which he explored the ordinary lives of small-town people — in this case, writing what he called "a modern tragedy." Ibsen based the play on a true story, which closely paralleled the main events of the play: a wife borrows money to finance a trip for an ailing husband, repayment is demanded, she forges a check and is discovered. (In the real-life story, however, the husband demanded a divorce, and the wife had a nervous breakdown and was committed to a mental institution.) The issue in *A Doll House,* he said, is that there are "two kinds of moral law, . . . one in man and a completely different one in woman. They do not understand each other . . . ." Nora and Helmer's marriage is destroyed because they cannot comprehend or accept their differences. The play begins conventionally but does not fulfill the audience's expectations for a tidy resolution; as a result, it was not successful when first performed. Nevertheless, the publication of *A Doll House* made Ibsen internationally famous.

A Doll House   (1879)

Translated by Rolf Fjelde

CHARACTERS

Torvald Helmer, *a lawyer*	**Nils Krogstad,** *a bank clerk*
Nora, *his wife*	**The Helmers' three small**
Dr. Rank	**children**
Mrs. Linde	**Anne-Marie,** *their nurse*
A Delivery Boy	**Helene,** *a maid*

The action takes place in Helmer's residence.

ACT 1

A comfortable room, tastefully but not expensively furnished. A door to the right in the back wall leads to the entryway; another to the left leads to Helmer's study. Between these doors, a piano. Midway in the left-hand wall a door, and further back a window. Near the window a round table with an armchair and a small sofa. In the right-hand wall, toward the rear, a door, and nearer the foreground a porcelain stove with two armchairs and a rocking chair beside it. Between the stove and the side door, a small table. Engravings on the walls. An étagère with china figures and other small art objects; a small bookcase with richly bound books; the floor carpeted; a fire burning in the stove. It is a winter day.

A bell rings in the entryway; shortly after we hear the door being unlocked. Nora comes into the room, humming happily to herself; she is wearing street clothes and carries an armload of packages, which she puts down on the table to the right. She has left the hall door open; and through it a Delivery Boy is seen, holding a Christmas tree and a basket, which he gives to the Maid who let them in.

NORA: Hide the tree well, Helene. The children mustn't get a glimpse of it till this evening, after it's trimmed. (*To the Delivery Boy, taking out her purse.*) How much?

DELIVERY BOY: Fifty, ma'am.

NORA: There's a crown. No, keep the change. (*The Boy thanks her and leaves. Nora shuts the door. She laughs softly to herself while taking off her street things.*)

Drawing a bag of macaroons from her pocket, she eats a couple, then steals over and listens at her husband's study door.) Yes, he's home. *(Hums again as she moves to the table right.)*

HELMER: *(from the study)* Is that my little lark twittering out there?

NORA: *(busy opening some packages)* Yes, it is.   5

HELMER: Is that my squirrel rummaging around?

NORA: Yes!

HELMER: When did my squirrel get in?

NORA: Just now. *(Putting the macaroon bag in her pocket and wiping her mouth.)* Do come in, Torvald, and see what I've bought.

HELMER: Can't be disturbed. *(After a moment he opens the door and peers in, pen*   10
in hand.) Bought, you say? All that there? Has the little spendthrift been out throwing money around again?

NORA: Oh, but Torvald, this year we really should let ourselves go a bit. It's the first Christmas we haven't had to economize.

HELMER: But you know we can't go squandering.

NORA: Oh yes, Torvald, we can squander a little now. Can't we? Just a tiny, wee bit. Now that you've got a big salary and are going to make piles and piles of money.

HELMER: Yes — starting New Year's. But then it's a full three months till the raise comes through.

NORA: Pooh! We can borrow that long.   15

HELMER: Nora! *(Goes over and playfully takes her by the ear.)* Are your scatterbrains off again? What if today I borrowed a thousand crowns, and you squandered them over Christmas week, and then on New Year's Eve a roof tile fell on my head, and I lay there —

NORA: *(putting her hand on his mouth)* Oh! Don't say such things!

HELMER: Yes, but what if it happened — then what?

NORA: If anything so awful happened, then it just wouldn't matter if I had debts or not.

HELMER: Well, but the people I'd borrowed from?   20

NORA: Them? Who cares about them! They're strangers.

HELMER: Nora, Nora, how like a woman! No, but seriously, Nora, you know what I think about that. No debts! Never borrow! Something of freedom's lost — and something of beauty, too — from a home that's founded on borrowing and debt. We've made a brave stand up to now, the two of us; and we'll go right on like that the little while we have to.

NORA: *(going toward the stove)* Yes, whatever you say, Torvald.

HELMER: *(following her)* Now, now, the little lark's wings mustn't droop. Come on, don't be a sulky squirrel. *(Taking out his wallet.)* Nora, guess what I have here.

NORA: *(turning quickly)* Money!   25

HELMER: There, see. *(Hands her some notes.)* Good grief, I know how costs go up in a house at Christmastime.

NORA: Ten — twenty — thirty — forty. Oh, thank you, Torvald; I can manage no end on this.

HELMER: You really will have to.

NORA: Oh yes, I promise I will! But come here so I can show you everything I bought. And so cheap! Look, new clothes for Ivar here — and a sword. Here a horse and a trumpet for Bob. And a doll and a doll's bed here for Emmy; they're nothing much, but she'll tear them to bits in no time anyway. And here I have dress material and handkerchiefs for the maids. Old Anne-Marie really deserves something more.

30 **HELMER:** And what's in that package there?

NORA: (*with a cry*) Torvald, no! You can't see that till tonight!

HELMER: I see. But tell me now, you little prodigal, what have you thought of for yourself?

NORA: For myself? Oh, I don't want anything at all.

HELMER: Of course you do. Tell me just what — within reason — you'd most like to have.

35 **NORA:** I honestly don't know. Oh, listen, Torvald —

HELMER: Well?

NORA: (*fumbling at his coat buttons, without looking at him*) If you want to give me something, then maybe you could — you could —

HELMER: Come on, out with it.

NORA: (*hurriedly*) You could give me money, Torvald. No more than you think you can spare; then one of these days I'll buy something with it.

40 **HELMER:** But Nora —

NORA: Oh, please, Torvald darling, do that! I beg you, please. Then I could hang the bills in pretty gilt paper on the Christmas tree. Wouldn't that be fun?

HELMER: What are those little birds called that always fly through their fortunes?

NORA: Oh yes, spendthrifts; I know all that. But let's do as I say, Torvald; then I'll have time to decide what I really need most. That's very sensible, isn't it?

HELMER: (*smiling*) Yes, very — that is, if you actually hung onto the money I give you, and you actually used it to buy yourself something. But it goes for the house and for all sorts of foolish things, and then I only have to lay out some more.

45 **NORA:** Oh, but Torvald —

HELMER: Don't deny it, my dear little Nora. (*Putting his arm around her waist.*) Spendthrifts are sweet, but they use up a frightful amount of money. It's incredible what it costs a man to feed such birds.

NORA: Oh, how can you say that! Really, I save everything I can.

HELMER: (*laughing*) Yes, that's the truth. Everything you can. But that's nothing at all.

NORA: (*humming, with a smile of quiet satisfaction*) Hm, if you only knew what expenses we larks and squirrels have, Torvald.

HELMER: You're an odd little one. Exactly the way your father was. You're   50
never at a loss for scaring up money; but the moment you have it, it runs
right out through your fingers; you never know what you've done with it.
Well, one takes you as you are. It's deep in your blood. Yes, these things are
hereditary, Nora.

NORA: Ah, I could wish I'd inherited many of Papa's qualities.

HELMER: And I couldn't wish you anything but just what you are, my sweet
little lark. But wait; it seems to me you have a very — what should I call
it?— a very suspicious look today —

NORA: I do?

HELMER: You certainly do. Look me straight in the eye.

NORA: *(looking at him)* Well?   55

HELMER: *(shaking an admonitory finger)* Surely my sweet tooth hasn't been
running riot in town today, has she?

NORA: No. Why do you imagine that?

HELMER: My sweet tooth really didn't make a little detour through the
confectioner's?

NORA: No, I assure you, Torvald —

HELMER: Hasn't nibbled some pastry?   60

NORA: No, not at all.

HELMER: Nor even munched a macaroon or two?

NORA: No, Torvald, I assure you, really —

HELMER: There, there now. Of course I'm only joking.

NORA: *(going to the table, right)* You know I could never think of going   65
against you.

HELMER: No, I understand that; and you *have* given me your word. *(Going over
to her.)* Well, you keep your little Christmas secrets to yourself, Nora
darling. I expect they'll come to light this evening, when the tree is lit.

NORA: Did you remember to ask Dr. Rank?

HELMER: No. But there's no need for that; it's assumed he'll be dining with us. All
the same, I'll ask him when he stops by here this morning. I've ordered some
fine wine. Nora, you can't imagine how I'm looking forward to this evening.

NORA: So am I. And what fun for the children, Torvald!

HELMER: Ah, it's so gratifying to know that one's gotten a safe, secure job, and   70
with a comfortable salary. It's a great satisfaction, isn't it?

NORA: Oh, it's wonderful!

HELMER: Remember last Christmas? Three whole weeks before, you shut
yourself in every evening till long after midnight, making flowers for the
Christmas tree, and all the other decorations to surprise us. Ugh, that was
the dullest time I've ever lived through.

NORA: It wasn't at all dull for me.

HELMER: *(smiling)* But the outcome *was* pretty sorry, Nora.

NORA: Oh, don't tease me with that again. How could I help it that the cat   75
came in and tore everything to shreds.

Helmer: No, poor thing, you certainly couldn't. You wanted so much to please us all, and that's what counts. But it's just as well that the hard times are past.

Nora: Yes, it's really wonderful.

Helmer: Now I don't have to sit here alone, boring myself, and you don't have to tire your precious eyes and your fair little delicate hands —

Nora: (*clapping her hands*) No, is it really true, Torvald, I don't have to? Oh, how wonderfully lovely to hear! (*Taking his arm.*) Now I'll tell you just how I've thought we should plan things. Right after Christmas —(*The doorbell rings.*) Oh, the bell. (*Straightening the room up a bit.*) Somebody would have to come. What a bore!

80 **Helmer:** I'm not at home to visitors, don't forget.

Maid: (*from the hall doorway*) Ma'am, a lady to see you —

Nora: All right, let her come in.

Maid: (*to Helmer*) And the doctor's just come too.

Helmer: Did he go right to my study?

85 **Maid:** Yes, he did.

Helmer goes into his room. The Maid shows in Mrs. Linde, dressed in traveling clothes, and shuts the door after her.

Mrs. Linde: (*in a dispirited and somewhat hesitant voice*) Hello, Nora.

Nora: (*uncertain*) Hello —

Mrs. Linde: You don't recognize me.

Nora: No, I don't know — but wait, I think —(*Exclaiming.*) What! Kristine! Is it really you?

90 **Mrs. Linde:** Yes, it's me.

Nora: *Kristine!* To think I didn't recognize you. But then, how could I? (*More quietly.*) How you've changed, Kristine!

Mrs. Linde: Yes, no doubt I have. In nine — ten long years.

Nora: Is it so long since we met! Yes, it's all of that. Oh, these last eight years have been a happy time, believe me. And so now you've come in to town, too. Made the long trip in the winter. That took courage.

Mrs. Linde: I just got here by ship this morning.

95 **Nora:** To enjoy yourself over Christmas, of course. Oh, how lovely! Yes, enjoy ourselves, we'll do that. But take your coat off. You're not still cold? (*Helping her.*) There now, let's get cozy here by the stove. No, the easy chair there! I'll take the rocker here. (*Seizing her hands.*) Yes, now you have your old look again; it was only in that first moment. You're a bit more pale, Kristine — and maybe a bit thinner.

Mrs. Linde: And much, much older, Nora.

Nora: Yes, perhaps a bit older; a tiny, tiny bit; not much at all. (*Stopping short; suddenly serious.*) Oh, but thoughtless me, to sit here, chattering away. Sweet, good Kristine, can you forgive me?

Mrs. Linde: What do you mean, Nora?

NORA: (*softly*) Poor Kristine, you've become a widow.

MRS. LINDE: Yes, three years ago.   100

NORA: Oh, I knew it, of course: I read it in the papers. Oh, Kristine, you must
believe me; I often thought of writing you then, but I kept postponing it,
and something always interfered.

MRS. LINDE: Nora dear, I understand completely.

NORA: No, it was awful of me, Kristine. You poor thing, how much you must
have gone through. And he left you nothing?

MRS. LINDE: No.

NORA: And no children?   105

MRS. LINDE: No.

NORA: Nothing at all, then?

MRS. LINDE: Not even a sense of loss to feed on.

NORA: (*looking incredulously at her*) But Kristine, how could that be?

MRS. LINDE: (*smiling wearily and smoothing her hair*) Oh, sometimes it   110
happens, Nora.

NORA: So completely alone. How terribly hard that must be for you. I have
three lovely children. You can't see them now; they're out with the maid.
But now you must tell me everything —

MRS. LINDE: No, no, no, tell me about yourself.

NORA: No, you begin. Today I don't want to be selfish. I want to think only
of you today. But there *is* something I must tell you. Did you hear of the
wonderful luck we had recently?

MRS. LINDE: No, what's that?

NORA: My husband's been made manager in the bank, just think!   115

MRS. LINDE: Your husband? How marvelous!

NORA: Isn't it? Being a lawyer is such an uncertain living, you know, especially
if one won't touch any cases that aren't clean and decent. And of course
Torvald would never do that, and I'm with him completely there. Oh, we're
simply delighted, believe me! He'll join the bank right after New Year's and
start getting a huge salary and lots of commissions. From now on we can
live quite differently — just as we want. Oh, Kristine, I feel so light and
happy! Won't it be lovely to have stacks of money and not a care in the
world?

MRS. LINDE: Well, anyway, it would be lovely to have enough for necessities.

NORA: No, not just for necessities, but stacks and stacks of money!

MRS. LINDE: (*smiling*) Nora, Nora, aren't you sensible yet? Back in school you   120
were such a free spender.

NORA: (*with a quiet laugh*) Yes, that's what Torvald still says. (*Shaking her
finger.*) But "Nora, Nora" isn't as silly as you all think. Really, we've been in
no position for me to go squandering. We've had to work, both of us.

MRS. LINDE: You too?

NORA: Yes, at odd jobs — needlework, crocheting, embroidery, and such —
(*casually*) and other things too. You remember that Torvald left the

department when we were married? There was no chance of promotion in his office, and of course he needed to earn more money. But that first year he drove himself terribly. He took on all kinds of extra work that kept him going morning and night. It wore him down, and then he fell deathly ill. The doctors said it was essential for him to travel south.

MRS. LINDE: Yes, didn't you spend a whole year in Italy?

125 NORA: That's right. It wasn't easy to get away, you know. Ivar had just been born. But of course we had to go. Oh, that was a beautiful trip, and it saved Torvald's life. But it cost a frightful sum, Kristine.

MRS. LINDE: I can well imagine.

NORA: Four thousand, eight hundred crowns it cost. That's really a lot of money.

MRS. LINDE: But it's lucky you had it when you needed it.

NORA: Well, as it was, we got it from Papa.

130 MRS. LINDE: I see. It was just about the time your father died.

NORA: Yes, just about then. And, you know, I couldn't make that trip out to nurse him. I had to stay here, expecting Ivar any moment, and with my poor sick Torvald to care for. Dearest Papa, I never saw him again, Kristine. Oh, that was the worst time I've known in all my marriage.

MRS. LINDE: I know how you loved him. And then you went off to Italy?

NORA: Yes. We had the means now, and the doctors urged us. So we left a month after.

MRS. LINDE: And your husband came back completely cured?

135 NORA: Sound as a drum!

MRS. LINDE: But — the doctor?

NORA: Who?

MRS. LINDE: I thought the maid said he was a doctor, the man who came in with me.

NORA: Yes, that was Dr. Rank — but he's not making a sick call. He's our closest friend, and he stops by at least once a day. No, Torvald hasn't had a sick moment since, and the children are fit and strong, and I am, too. (*Jumping up and clapping her hands.*) Oh, dear God, Kristine, what a lovely thing to live and be happy! But how disgusting of me — I'm talking of nothing but my own affairs. (*Sits on a stool close by Kristine, arms resting across her knees.*) Oh, don't be angry with me! Tell me, is it really true that you weren't in love with your husband? Why did you marry him, then?

140 MRS. LINDE: My mother was still alive, but bedridden and helpless — and I had my two younger brothers to look after. In all conscience, I didn't think I could turn him down.

NORA: No, you were right there. But was he rich at the time?

MRS. LINDE: He was very well off, I'd say. But the business was shaky, Nora. When he died, it all fell apart, and nothing was left.

NORA: And then —?

MRS. LINDE: Yes, so I had to scrape up a living with a little shop and a little teaching and whatever else I could find. The last three years have been like one endless workday without a rest for me. Now it's over, Nora. My poor mother doesn't need me, for she's passed on. Nor the boys, either; they're working now and can take care of themselves.

NORA: How free you must feel — 145

MRS. LINDE: No — only unspeakably empty. Nothing to live for now. (*Standing up anxiously.*) That's why I couldn't take it any longer out in that desolate hole. Maybe here it'll be easier to find something to do and keep my mind occupied. If I could only be lucky enough to get a steady job, some office work —

NORA: Oh, but Kristine, that's so dreadfully tiring, and you already look so tired. It would be much better for you if you could go off to a bathing resort.

MRS. LINDE: (*going toward the window*) I have no father to give me travel money, Nora.

NORA: (*rising*) Oh, don't be angry with me.

MRS. LINDE: (*going to her*) Nora dear, don't you be angry with me. The worst 150 of my kind of situation is all the bitterness that's stored away. No one to work for, and yet you're always having to snap up your opportunities. You have to live; and so you grow selfish. When you told me the happy change in your lot, do you know I was delighted less for your sakes than for mine?

NORA: How so? Oh, I see. You think Torvald could do something for you.

MRS. LINDE: Yes, that's what I thought.

NORA: And he will, Kristine! Just leave it to me; I'll bring it up so delicately — find something attractive to humor him with. Oh, I'm so eager to help you.

MRS. LINDE: How very kind of you, Nora, to be so concerned over me — doubly kind, considering you really know so little of life's burdens yourself.

NORA: I — ? I know so little — ? 155

MRS. LINDE: (*smiling*) Well my heavens — a little needlework and such — Nora, you're just a child.

NORA: (*tossing her head and pacing the floor*) You don't have to act so superior.

MRS. LINDE: Oh?

NORA: You're just like the others. You all think I'm incapable of anything serious —

MRS. LINDE: Come now — 160

NORA: That I've never had to face the raw world.

MRS. LINDE: Nora dear, you've just been telling me all your troubles.

NORA: Hm! Trivial! (*Quietly.*) I haven't told you the big thing.

MRS. LINDE: Big thing? What do you mean?

NORA: You look down on me so, Kristine, but you shouldn't. You're proud 165 that you worked so long and hard for your mother.

MRS. LINDE: I don't look down on a soul. But it *is* true: I'm proud — and happy, too — to think it was given to me to make my mother's last days almost free of care.

NORA: And you're also proud thinking of what you've done for your brothers.

MRS. LINDE: I feel I've a right to be.

NORA: I agree. But listen to this, Kristine — I've also got something to be proud and happy for.

170 MRS. LINDE: I don't doubt it. But whatever do you mean?

NORA: Not so loud. What if Torvald heard! He mustn't, not for anything in the world. Nobody must know, Kristine. No one but you.

MRS. LINDE: But what is it, then?

NORA: Come here. (*Drawing her down beside her on the sofa.*) It's true — I've also got something to be proud and happy for. I'm the one who saved Torvald's life.

MRS. LINDE: Saved —? Saved how?

175 NORA: I told you about the trip to Italy. Torvald never would have lived if he hadn't gone south —

MRS. LINDE: Of course; your father gave you the means —

NORA: (*smiling*) That's what Torvald and all the rest think, but —

MRS. LINDE: But —?

NORA: Papa didn't give us a pin. I was the one who raised the money.

180 MRS. LINDE: You? That whole amount?

NORA: Four thousand, eight hundred crowns. What do you say to that?

MRS. LINDE: But Nora, how was it possible? Did you win the lottery?

NORA: (*disdainfully*) The lottery? Pooh! No art to that.

MRS. LINDE: But where did you get it from then?

185 NORA: (*humming, with a mysterious smile*) Hmm, tra-la-la-la.

MRS. LINDE: Because you couldn't have borrowed it.

NORA: No? Why not?

MRS. LINDE: A wife can't borrow without her husband's consent.

NORA: (*tossing her head*) Oh, but a wife with a little business sense, a wife who knows how to manage —

190 MRS. LINDE: Nora, I simply don't understand —

NORA: You don't have to. Whoever said I *borrowed* the money? I could have gotten it other ways. (*Throwing herself back on the sofa.*) I could have gotten it from some admirer or other. After all, a girl with my ravishing appeal —

MRS. LINDE: You lunatic.

NORA: I'll bet you're eaten up with curiosity, Kristine.

MRS. LINDE: Now listen here, Nora — you haven't done something indiscreet?

195 NORA: (*sitting up again*) Is it indiscreet to save your husband's life?

MRS. LINDE: I think it's indiscreet that without his knowledge you —

NORA: But that's the point: he mustn't know! My Lord, can't you understand? He mustn't ever know the close call he had. It was to *me* the doctors came to say his life was in danger — that nothing could save him but a stay in the south. Didn't I try strategy then! I began talking about how lovely it would be for me to travel abroad like other young wives; I begged and I cried; I told him please to remember my condition, to be kind and indulge me; and then I dropped a hint that he could easily take out a loan. But at that, Kristine, he nearly exploded. He said I was frivolous, and it was his duty as man of the house not to indulge me in whims and fancies — as I think he called them. Aha, I thought, now you'll just have to be saved — and that's when I saw my chance.

MRS. LINDE: And your father never told Torvald the money wasn't from him?

NORA: No, never. Papa died right about then. I'd considered bringing him into my secret and begging him never to tell. But he was too sick at the time — and then, sadly, it didn't matter.

MRS. LINDE: And you've never confided in your husband since?   200

NORA: For heaven's sake, no! Are you serious? He's so strict on that subject. Besides — Torvald, with all his masculine pride — how painfully humiliating for him if he ever found out he was in debt to me. That would just ruin our relationship. Our beautiful, happy home would never be the same.

MRS. LINDE: Won't you ever tell him?

NORA: (*thoughtfully, half smiling*) Yes — maybe sometime, years from now, when I'm no longer so attractive. Don't laugh! I only mean when Torvald loves me less than now, when he stops enjoying my dancing and dressing up and reciting for him. Then it might be wise to have something in reserve — (*Breaking off.*) How ridiculous! That'll never happen — Well, Kristine, what do you think of my big secret? I'm capable of something too, hm? You can imagine, of course, how this thing hangs over me. It really hasn't been easy meeting the payments on time. In the business world there's what they call quarterly interest and what they call amortization, and these are always so terribly hard to manage. I've had to skimp a little here and there, wherever I could, you know. I could hardly spare anything from my house allowance, because Torvald has to live well. I couldn't let the children go poorly dressed; whatever I got for them, I felt I had to use up completely — the darlings!

MRS. LINDE: Poor Nora, so it had to come out of your own budget, then?

NORA: Yes, of course. But I was the one most responsible, too. Every time   205
Torvald gave me money for new clothes and such, I never used more than half; always bought the simplest, cheapest outfits. It was a godsend that everything looks so well on me that Torvald never noticed. But it did weigh me down at times, Kristine. It *is* such a joy to wear fine things. You understand.

MRS. LINDE: Oh, of course.

NORA: And then I found other ways of making money. Last winter I was lucky enough to get a lot of copying to do. I locked myself in and sat writing every evening till late in the night. Ah, I was tired so often, dead tired. But still it was wonderful fun, sitting and working like that, earning money. It was almost like being a man.

MRS. LINDE: But how much have you paid off this way so far?

NORA: That's hard to say, exactly. These accounts, you know, aren't easy to figure. I only know that I've paid out all I could scrape together. Time and again I haven't known where to turn. (*Smiling.*) Then I'd sit here dreaming of a rich old gentleman who had fallen in love with me —

210 **MRS. LINDE:** What! Who is he?

NORA: Oh, really! And that he'd died, and when his will was opened, there in big letters it said, "All my fortune shall be paid over in cash, immediately, to that enchanting Mrs. Nora Helmer."

MRS. LINDE: But Nora dear — who *was* this gentleman?

NORA: Good grief, can't you understand? The old man never existed; that was only something I'd dream up time and again whenever I was at my wits' end for money. But it makes no difference now; the old fossil can go where he pleases for all I care; I don't need him or his will — because now I'm free. (*Jumping up.*) Oh, how lovely to think of that, Kristine! Carefree! To know you're carefree, utterly carefree; to be able to romp and play with the children, and to keep up a beautiful, charming home — everything just the way Torvald likes it! And think, spring is coming, with big blue skies. Maybe we can travel a little then. Maybe I'll see the ocean again. Oh yes, it *is* so marvelous to live and be happy!

The front doorbell rings.

MRS. LINDE: (*rising*) There's the bell. It's probably best that I go.

215 **NORA:** No, stay. No one's expected. It must be for Torvald.

MAID: (*from the hall doorway*) Excuse me, ma'am — there's a gentleman here to see Mr. Helmer, but I didn't know — since the doctor's with him —

NORA: Who is the gentleman?

KROGSTAD: (*from the doorway*) It's me, Mrs. Helmer.

Mrs. Linde starts and turns away toward the window.

NORA: (*stepping toward him, tense, her voice a whisper*) You? What is it? Why do you want to speak to my husband?

220 **KROGSTAD:** Bank business — after a fashion. I have a small job in the investment bank, and I hear now your husband is going to be our chief —

NORA: In other words, it's —

KROGSTAD: Just dry business, Mrs. Helmer. Nothing but that.

NORA: Yes, then please be good enough to step into the study. (*She nods indifferently as she sees him out by the hall door, then returns and begins stirring up the stove.*)

MRS. LINDE: Nora — who was that man?

225 **NORA:** That was a Mr. Krogstad — a lawyer.

MRS. LINDE: Then it really was him.

NORA: Do you know that person?

MRS. LINDE: I did once — many years ago. For a time he was a law clerk in our town.

NORA: Yes, he's been that.

MRS. LINDE: How he's changed. 230

NORA: I understand he had a very unhappy marriage.

MRS. LINDE: He's a widower now.

NORA: With a number of children. There now, it's burning. (*She closes the stove door and moves the rocker a bit to one side.*)

MRS. LINDE: They say he has a hand in all kinds of business.

NORA: Oh? That may be true: I wouldn't know. But let's not think about 235 business. It's so dull.

Dr. Rank enters from Helmer's study.

RANK: (*still in the doorway*) No, no, really — I don't want to intrude, I'd just as soon talk a little while with your wife. (*Shuts the door, then notices Mrs. Linde.*) Oh, beg pardon. I'm intruding here too.

NORA: No, not at all. (*Introducing him.*) Dr. Rank, Mrs. Linde.

RANK: Well now, that's a name much heard in this house. I believe I passed the lady on the stairs as I came.

MRS. LINDE: Yes, I take the stairs very slowly. They're rather hard on me.

RANK: Uh-hm, some touch of internal weakness? 240

MRS. LINDE: More overexertion, I'd say.

RANK: Nothing else? Then you're probably here in town to rest up in a round of parties?

MRS. LINDE: I'm here to look for work.

RANK: Is that the best cure for overexertion?

MRS. LINDE: One has to live, Doctor. 245

RANK: Yes, there's a common prejudice to that effect.

NORA: Oh, come on, Dr. Rank — you really do want to live yourself.

RANK: Yes, I really do. Wretched as I am, I'll gladly prolong my torment indefinitely. All my patients feel like that. And it's quite the same, too, with the morally sick. Right at this moment there's one of those moral invalids in there with Helmer —

MRS. LINDE: (*softly*) Ah!

NORA: Who do you mean? 250

RANK: Oh, it's a lawyer, Krogstad, a type you wouldn't know. His character is rotten to the root — but even he began chattering all-importantly about how he had to *live*.

NORA: Oh? What did he want to talk to Torvald about?

RANK: I really don't know. I only heard something about the bank.

NORA: I didn't know that Krog — that this man Krogstad had anything to do with the bank.

RANK: Yes, he's gotten some kind of berth down there. (*To Mrs. Linde.*) I 255 don't know if you also have, in your neck of the woods, a type of person who scuttles about breathlessly, sniffing out hints of moral corruption, and then maneuvers his victim into some sort of key position where he can keep an eye on him. It's the healthy these days that are out in the cold.

MRS. LINDE: All the same, it's the sick who most need to be taken in.

RANK: *(with a shrug)* Yes, there we have it. That's the concept that's turning society into a sanatorium.

Nora, lost in her thoughts, breaks out into quiet laughter and claps her hands.

RANK: Why do you laugh at that? Do you have any real idea of what society is?

NORA: What do I care about dreary old society? I was laughing at something quite different — something terribly funny. Tell me, Doctor — is everyone who works in the bank dependent now on Torvald?

260 RANK: Is that what you find so terribly funny?

NORA: *(smiling and humming)* Never mind, never mind! *(Pacing the floor.)* Yes, that's really immensely amusing: that we — that Torvald has so much power now over all those people. *(Taking the bag out of her pocket.)* Dr. Rank, a little macaroon on that?

RANK: See here, macaroons! I thought they were contraband here.

NORA: Yes, but these are some that Kristine gave me.

MRS. LINDE: What? I —?

265 NORA: Now, now, don't be afraid. You couldn't possibly know that Torvald had forbidden them. You see, he's worried they'll ruin my teeth. But hmp! Just this once! Isn't that so, Dr. Rank? Help yourself! *(Puts a macaroon in his mouth.)* And you too, Kristine. And I'll also have one, only a little one — or two, at the most. *(Walking about again.)* Now I'm really tremendously happy. Now there's just one last thing in the world that I have an enormous desire to do.

RANK: Well! And what's that?

NORA: It's something I have such a consuming desire to say so Torvald could hear.

RANK: And why can't you say it?

270 NORA: I don't dare. It's quite shocking.

MRS. LINDE: Shocking?

RANK: Well, then it isn't advisable. But in front of us you certainly can. What do you have such a desire to say so Torvald could hear?

NORA: I have such a huge desire to say — to hell and be damned!

RANK: Are you crazy?

MRS. LINDE: My goodness, Nora!

275 RANK: Go on, say it. Here he is.

NORA: *(hiding the macaroon bag)* Shh, shh, shh!

Helmer comes in from his study, hat in hand, overcoat over his arm.

NORA: *(going toward him)* Well, Torvald dear, are you through with him?

HELMER: Yes, he just left.

NORA: Let me introduce you — this is Kristine, who's arrived here in town.

HELMER: Kristine —? I'm sorry, but I don't know — 280

NORA: Mrs. Linde, Torvald dear. Mrs. Kristine Linde.

HELMER: Of course. A childhood friend of my wife's, no doubt?

MRS. LINDE: Yes, we knew each other in those days.

NORA: And just think, she made the long trip down here in order to talk with you.

HELMER: What's this? 285

MRS. LINDE: Well, not exactly —

NORA: You see, Kristine is remarkably clever in office work, and so she's terribly eager to come under a capable man's supervision and add more to what she already knows —

HELMER: Very wise, Mrs. Linde.

NORA: And then when she heard that you'd become a bank manager — the story was wired out to the papers — then she came in as fast as she could and — Really, Torvald, for my sake you can do a little something for Kristine, can't you?

HELMER: Yes, it's not at all impossible. Mrs. Linde, I suppose you're a widow? 290

MRS. LINDE: Yes.

HELMER: Any experience in office work?

MRS. LINDE: Yes, a good deal.

HELMER: Well, it's quite likely that I can make an opening for you —

NORA: (clapping her hands) You see, you see! 295

HELMER: You've come at a lucky moment, Mrs. Linde.

MRS. LINDE: Oh, how can I thank you?

HELMER: Not necessary. (Putting his overcoat on.) But today you'll have to excuse me —

RANK: Wait, I'll go with you. (He fetches his coat from the hall and warms it at the stove.)

NORA: Don't stay out long, dear. 300

HELMER: An hour; no more.

NORA: Are you going too, Kristine?

MRS. LINDE: (putting on her winter garments) Yes, I have to see about a room now.

HELMER: Then perhaps we can all walk together.

NORA: (helping her) What a shame we're so cramped here, but it's quite 305 impossible for us to —

MRS. LINDE: Oh, don't even think of it! Good-bye, Nora dear, and thanks for everything.

NORA: Good-bye for now. Of course you'll be back this evening. And you too, Dr. Rank. What? If you're well enough? Oh, you've got to be! Wrap up tight now.

In a ripple of small talk the company moves out into the hall; children's voices are heard outside on the steps.

NORA: There they are! There they are! (*She runs to open the door. The children come in with their nurse, Anne-Marie.*) Come in, come in! (*Bends down and kisses them.*) Oh, you darlings —! Look at them, Kristine. Aren't they lovely!

RANK: No loitering in the draft here.

310 **HELMER:** Come, Mrs. Linde — this place is unbearable now for anyone but mothers.

Dr. Rank, Helmer, and Mrs. Linde go down the stairs. Anne-Marie goes into the living room with the children. Nora follows, after closing the hall door.

NORA: How fresh and strong you look. Oh, such red cheeks you have! Like apples and roses. (*The children interrupt her throughout the following.*) And it was so much fun? That's wonderful. Really? You pulled both Emmy and Bob on the sled? Imagine, all together! Yes, you're a clever boy, Ivar. Oh, let me hold her a bit, Anne-Marie. My sweet little doll baby! (*Takes the smallest from the nurse and dances with her.*) Yes, yes, Mama will dance with Bob as well. What? Did you throw snowballs? Oh, if I'd only been there! No, don't bother, Anne-Marie — I'll undress them myself. Oh yes, let me. It's such fun. Go in and rest; you look half frozen. There's hot coffee waiting for you on the stove. (*The nurse goes into the room to the left. Nora takes the children's winter things off, throwing them about, while the children talk to her all at once.*) Is that so? A big dog chased you? But it didn't bite? No, dogs never bite little, lovely doll babies. Don't peek in the packages, Ivar! What is it? Yes, wouldn't you like to know. No, no, it's an ugly something. Well? Shall we play? What shall we play? Hide-and-seek? Yes, let's play hide-and-seek. Bob must hide first. I must? Yes, let me hide first. (*Laughing and shouting, she and the children play in and out of the living room and the adjoining room to the right. At last Nora hides under the table. The children come storming in, search, but cannot find her, then hear her muffled laughter, dash over to the table, lift the cloth up and find her. Wild shouting. She creeps forward as if to scare them. More shouts. Meanwhile, a knock at the hall door; no one has noticed it. Now the door half opens, and Krogstad appears. He waits a moment; the game goes on.*)

KROGSTAD: Beg pardon, Mrs. Helmer —

NORA: (*with a strangled cry, turning and scrambling to her knees*) Oh! What do you want?

KROGSTAD: Excuse me. The outer door was ajar; it must be someone forgot to shut it —

315 **NORA:** (*rising*) My husband isn't home, Mr. Krogstad.

KROGSTAD: I know that.

NORA: Yes — then what do you want here?

KROGSTAD: A word with you.

NORA: With —? (*To the children, quietly.*) Go in to Anne-Marie. What? No, the strange man won't hurt Mama. When he's gone, we'll play some more. (*She leads the children into the room to the left and shuts the door after them. Then, tense and nervous.*) You want to speak to me?

KROGSTAD: Yes, I want to.   320
NORA: Today? But it's not yet the first of the month —
KROGSTAD: No, it's Christmas Eve. It's going to be up to you how merry a
  Christmas you have.
NORA: What is it you want? Today I absolutely can't —
KROGSTAD: We won't talk about that till later. This is something else. You do
  have a moment to spare, I suppose?
NORA: Oh yes, of course — I do, except —   325
KROGSTAD: Good. I was sitting over at Olsen's Restaurant when I saw your
  husband go down the street —
NORA: Yes?
KROGSTAD: With a lady.
NORA: Yes. So?
KROGSTAD: If you'll pardon my asking: wasn't that lady a Mrs. Linde?   330
NORA: Yes.
KROGSTAD: Just now come into town?
NORA: Yes, today.
KROGSTAD: She's a good friend of yours?
NORA: Yes, she is. But I don't see —   335
KROGSTAD: I also knew her once.
NORA: I'm aware of that.
KROGSTAD: Oh? You know all about it. I thought so. Well, then let me ask you
  short and sweet: is Mrs. Linde getting a job in the bank?
NORA: What makes you think you can cross-examine me, Mr. Krogstad —
  you, one of my husband's employees? But since you ask, you might as well
  know — yes, Mrs. Linde's going to be taken on at the bank. And I'm the
  one who spoke for her, Mr. Krogstad. Now you know.
KROGSTAD: So I guessed right.   340
NORA: (*pacing up and down*) Oh, one does have a tiny bit of influence, I should
  hope. Just because I am a woman, don't think it means that — When one
  has a subordinate position, Mr. Krogstad, one really ought to be careful
  about pushing somebody who — hm —
KROGSTAD: Who has influence?
NORA: That's right.
KROGSTAD: (*in a different tone*) Mrs. Helmer, would you be good enough to use
  your influence on my behalf?
NORA: What? What do you mean?   345
KROGSTAD: Would you please make sure that I keep my subordinate position
  in the bank?
NORA: What does that mean? Who's thinking of taking away your position?
KROGSTAD: Oh, don't play the innocent with me. I'm quite aware that your
  friend would hardly relish the chance of running into me again; and I'm
  also aware now whom I can thank for being turned out.
NORA: But I promise you —

350 KROGSTAD: Yes, yes, yes, to the point: there's still time, and I'm advising you to use your influence to prevent it.

NORA: But Mr. Krogstad, I have absolutely no influence.

KROGSTAD: You haven't? I thought you were just saying —

NORA: You shouldn't take me so literally. I! How can you believe that I have any such influence over my husband?

KROGSTAD: Oh, I've known your husband from our student days. I don't think the great bank manager's more steadfast than any other married man.

355 NORA: You speak insolently about my husband, and I'll show you the door.

KROGSTAD: The lady has spirit.

NORA: I'm not afraid of you any longer. After New Year's, I'll soon be done with the whole business.

KROGSTAD: (restraining himself) Now listen to me, Mrs. Helmer. If necessary, I'll fight for my little job in the bank as if it were life itself.

NORA: Yes, so it seems.

360 KROGSTAD: It's not just a matter of income; that's the least of it. It's something else — All right, out with it! Look, this is the thing. You know, just like all the others, of course, that once, a good many years ago, I did something rather rash.

NORA: I've heard rumors to that effect.

KROGSTAD: The case never got into court; but all the same, every door was closed in my face from then on. So I took up those various activities you know about. I had to grab hold somewhere; and I dare say I haven't been among the worst. But now I want to drop all that. My boys are growing up. For their sakes, I'll have to win back as much respect as possible here in town. That job in the bank was like the first rung in my ladder. And now your husband wants to kick me right back down in the mud again.

NORA: But for heaven's sake, Mr. Krogstad, it's simply not in my power to help you.

KROGSTAD: That's because you haven't the will to — but I have the means to make you.

365 NORA: You certainly won't tell my husband that I owe you money?

KROGSTAD: Hm — what if I told him that?

NORA: That would be shameful of you. (Nearly in tears.) This secret — my joy and my pride — that he should learn it in such a crude and disgusting way — learn it from you. You'd expose me to the most horrible unpleasantness —

KROGSTAD: Only unpleasantness?

NORA: (vehemently) But go on and try. It'll turn out the worse for you, because then my husband will really see what a crook you are, and then you'll *never* be able to hold your job.

370 KROGSTAD: I asked if it was just domestic unpleasantness you were afraid of.

NORA: If my husband finds out, then of course he'll pay what I owe at once, and then we'd be through with you for good.

KROGSTAD: *(a step closer)* Listen, Mrs. Helmer — you've either got a very bad memory, or else no head at all for business. I'd better put you a little more in touch with the facts.

NORA: What do you mean?

KROGSTAD: When your husband was sick, you came to me for a loan of four thousand, eight hundred crowns.

NORA: Where else could I go?   375

KROGSTAD: I promised to get you that sum —

NORA: And you got it.

KROGSTAD: I promised to get you that sum, on certain conditions. You were so involved in your husband's illness, and so eager to finance your trip, that I guess you didn't think out all the details. It might just be a good idea to remind you. I promised you the money on the strength of a note I drew up.

NORA: Yes, and that I signed.

KROGSTAD: Right. But at the bottom I added some lines for your father to   380
guarantee the loan. He was supposed to sign down there.

NORA: Supposed to? He did sign.

KROGSTAD: I left the date blank. In other words, your father would have dated his signature himself. Do you remember that?

NORA: Yes, I think —

KROGSTAD: Then I gave you the note for you to mail to your father. Isn't that so?

NORA: Yes.   385

KROGSTAD: And naturally you sent it at once — because only some five, six days later you brought me the note, properly signed. And with that, the money was yours.

NORA: Well, then; I've made my payments regularly, haven't I?

KROGSTAD: More or less. But — getting back to the point — those were hard times for you then, Mrs. Helmer.

NORA: Yes, they were.

KROGSTAD: Your father was very ill, I believe.   390

NORA: He was near the end.

KROGSTAD: He died soon after?

NORA: Yes.

KROGSTAD: Tell me, Mrs. Helmer, do you happen to recall the date of your father's death? The day of the month, I mean.

NORA: Papa died the twenty-ninth of September.   395

KROGSTAD: That's quite correct; I've already looked into that. And now we come to a curious thing — *(taking out a paper)* which I simply cannot comprehend.

NORA: Curious thing? I don't know —

KROGSTAD: This is the curious thing: that your father co-signed the note for your loan three days after his death.

NORA: How —? I don't understand.

400 **KROGSTAD:** Your father died the twenty-ninth of September. But look. Here your father dated his signature October second. Isn't that curious, Mrs. Helmer? *(Nora is silent.)* Can you explain it to me? *(Nora remains silent.)* It's also remarkable that the words "October second" and the year aren't written in your father's hand, but rather in one that I think I know. Well, it's easy to understand. Your father forgot perhaps to date his signature, and then someone or other added it, a bit sloppily, before anyone knew of his death. There's nothing wrong in that. It all comes down to the signature. And there's no question about *that*, Mrs. Helmer. It really *was* your father who signed his own name here, wasn't it?

NORA: *(after a short silence, throwing her head back and looking squarely at him)* No, it wasn't. I signed Papa's name.

KROGSTAD: Wait, now — are you fully aware that this is a dangerous confession?

NORA: Why? You'll soon get your money.

KROGSTAD: Let me ask you a question — why didn't you send the paper to your father?

405 **NORA:** That was impossible. Papa was so sick. If I'd asked him for his signature, I also would have had to tell him what the money was for. But I couldn't tell him, sick as he was, that my husband's life was in danger. That was just impossible.

KROGSTAD: Then it would have been better if you'd given up the trip abroad.

NORA: I couldn't possibly. The trip was to save my husband's life. I couldn't give that up.

KROGSTAD: But didn't you ever consider that this was a fraud against me?

NORA: I couldn't let myself be bothered by that. You weren't any concern of mine. I couldn't stand you, with all those cold complications you made, even though you knew how badly off my husband was.

410 **KROGSTAD:** Mrs. Helmer, obviously you haven't the vaguest idea of what you've involved yourself in. But I can tell you this: it was nothing more and nothing worse than I once did — and it wrecked my whole reputation.

NORA: You? Do you expect me to believe that you ever acted bravely to save your wife's life?

KROGSTAD: Laws don't inquire into motives.

NORA: Then they must be very poor laws.

KROGSTAD: Poor or not — if I introduce this paper in court, you'll be judged according to law.

415 **NORA:** This I refuse to believe. A daughter hasn't a right to protect her dying father from anxiety and care? A wife hasn't a right to save her husband's life? I don't know much about laws, but I'm sure that somewhere in the books these things are allowed. And you don't know anything about it — you who practice the law? You must be an awful lawyer, Mr. Krogstad.

KROGSTAD: Could be. But business — the kind of business we two mixed up in — don't you think I know about that? All right. Do what you want now.

But I'm telling you *this*: if I get shoved down a second time, you're going to keep me company. (*He bows and goes out through the hall.*)

NORA: (*pensive for a moment, then tossing her head*) Oh, really! Trying to frighten me! I'm not so silly as all that. (*Begins gathering up the children's clothes, but soon stops.*) But —? No, but that's impossible! I did it out of love.

THE CHILDREN: (*in the doorway, left*) Mama, that strange man's gone out the door.

NORA: Yes, yes, I know it. But don't tell anyone about the strange man. Do you hear? Not even Papa!

THE CHILDREN: No, Mama. But now will you play again?   420

NORA: No, not now.

THE CHILDREN: Oh, but Mama, you promised.

NORA: Yes, but I can't now. Go inside; I have too much to do. Go in, go in, my sweet darlings. (*She herds them gently back in the room and shuts the door after them. Settling on the sofa, she takes up a piece of embroidery and makes some stitches, but soon stops abruptly.*) No! (*Throws the work aside, rises, goes to the hall door and calls out.*) Helene! Let me have the tree in here. (*Goes to the table, left, opens the table drawer, and stops again.*) No, but that's utterly impossible!

MAID: (*with the Christmas tree*) Where should I put it, ma'am?

NORA: There. The middle of the floor.   425

MAID: Should I bring anything else?

NORA: No, thanks. I have what I need.

The Maid, who has set the tree down, goes out.

NORA: (*absorbed in trimming the tree*) Candles here — and flowers here. That terrible creature! Talk, talk, talk! There's nothing to it at all. The tree's going to be lovely. I'll do anything to please you, Torvald. I'll sing for you, dance for you —

Helmer comes in from the hall, with a sheaf of papers under his arm.

NORA: Oh! You're back so soon?

HELMER: Yes. Has anyone been here?   430

NORA: Here? No.

ER: That's odd. I saw Krogstad leaving the front door.

NORA: So? Oh yes, that's true. Krogstad was here a moment.

HELMER: Nora, I can see by your face that he's been here, begging you to put in a good word for him.

NORA: Yes.   435

HELMER: And it was supposed to seem like your own idea? You were to hide it from me that he'd been here. He asked you that, too, didn't he?

NORA: Yes, Torvald, but —

HELMER: Nora, Nora, and you could fall for that? Talk with that sort of person and promise him anything? And then in the bargain, tell me an untruth.

NORA: An untruth — ?

440 HELMER: Didn't you say that no one had been here? (*Wagging his finger.*) My little songbird must never do that again. A songbird needs a clean beak to warble with. No false notes. (*Putting his arm about her waist.*) That's the way it should be, isn't it? Yes, I'm sure of it. (*Releasing her.*) And so, enough of that. (*Sitting by the stove.*) Ah, how snug and cozy it is here. (*Leafing among his papers.*)

NORA: (*busy with the tree, after a short pause*) Torvald!

HELMER: Yes.

NORA: I'm so much looking forward to the Stenborgs' costume party, day after tomorrow.

HELMER: And I can't wait to see what you'll surprise me with.

445 NORA: Oh, that stupid business!

HELMER: What?

NORA: I can't find anything that's right. Everything seems so ridiculous, so inane.

HELMER: So my little Nora's come to *that* recognition?

NORA: (*going behind his chair, her arms resting on its back*) Are you very busy, Torvald?

450 HELMER: Oh —

NORA: What papers are those?

HELMER: Bank matters.

NORA: Already?

HELMER: I've gotten full authority from the retiring management to make all necessary changes in personnel and procedure. I'll need Christmas week for that. I want to have everything in order by New Year's.

455 NORA: So that was the reason this poor Krogstad —

HELMER: Hm.

NORA: (*still leaning on the chair and slowly stroking the nape of his neck*) If you weren't so very busy, I would have asked you an enormous favor, Torvald.

HELMER: Let's hear. What is it?

NORA: You know, there isn't anyone who has your good taste — and I want so much to look well at the costume party. Torvald, couldn't you take over and decide what I should be and plan my costume?

460 HELMER: Ah, is my stubborn little creature calling for a lifeguard?

NORA: Yes, Torvald, I can't get anywhere without your help.

HELMER: All right — I'll think it over. We'll hit on something.

NORA: Oh, how sweet of you. (*Goes to the tree again. Pause.*) Aren't the red flowers pretty — ? But tell me, was it really such a crime that this Krogstad committed?

HELMER: Forgery. Do you have any idea what that means?

465 NORA: Couldn't he have done it out of need?

HELMER: Yes, or thoughtlessness, like so many others. I'm not so heartless that I'd condemn a man categorically for just one mistake.

NORA: No, of course not, Torvald!

HELMER: Plenty of men have redeemed themselves by openly confessing their crimes and taking their punishment.

NORA: Punishment —?

HELMER: But now Krogstad didn't go that way. He got himself out by sharp practices, and that's the real cause of his moral breakdown.   470

NORA: Do you really think that would —?

HELMER: Just imagine how a man with that sort of guilt in him has to lie and cheat and deceive on all sides, has to wear a mask even with the nearest and dearest he has, even with his own wife and children. And with the children, Nora — that's where it's most horrible.

NORA: Why?

HELMER: Because that kind of atmosphere of lies infects the whole life of a home. Every breath the children take in is filled with the germs of something degenerate.

NORA: *(coming closer behind him)* Are you sure of that?   475

HELMER: Oh, I've seen it often enough as a lawyer. Almost everyone who goes bad early in life has a mother who's a chronic liar.

NORA: Why just — the mother?

HELMER: It's usually the mother's influence that's dominant, but the father's works in the same way, of course. Every lawyer is quite familiar with it. And still this Krogstad's been going home year in, year out, poisoning his own children with lies and pretense; that's why I call him morally lost. *(Reaching his hands out toward her.)* So my sweet little Nora must promise me never to plead his cause. Your hand on it. Come, come, what's this? Give me your hand. There, now. All settled. I can tell you it'd be impossible for me to work alongside of him. I literally feel physically revolted when I'm anywhere near such a person.

NORA: *(withdraws her hand and goes to the other side of the Christmas tree)* How hot it is here! And I've got so much to do.

HELMER: *(getting up and gathering his papers)* Yes, and I have to think about getting some of these read through before dinner. I'll think about your   480 costume, too. And something to hang on the tree in gilt paper, I may even see about that. *(Putting his hand on her head.)* Oh you, my darling little songbird. *(He goes into his study and closes the door after him.)*

NORA: *(softly, after a silence)* Oh, really! It isn't so. It's impossible. It must be impossible.

ANNE-MARIE: *(in the doorway, left)* The children are begging so hard to come in to Mama.

NORA: No, no, no, don't let them in to me! You stay with them, Anne-Marie.

ANNE-MARIE: Of course, ma'am. *(Closes the door.)*   485

NORA: *(pale with terror)* Hurt my children —! Poison my home? *(A moment's pause; then she tosses her head.)* That's not true. Never. Never in all the world.

ACT 2

Same room. Beside the piano the Christmas tree now stands stripped of ornaments, burned-down candle stubs on its ragged branches. Nora's street clothes lie on the sofa. Nora, alone in the room, moves restlessly about; at last she stops at the sofa and picks up her coat.

NORA: *(dropping the coat again)* Someone's coming! *(Goes toward the door, listens.)* No — there's no one. Of course — nobody's coming today, Christmas Day — or tomorrow, either. But maybe —*(Opens the door and looks out.)* No, nothing in the mailbox. Quite empty. *(Coming forward.)* What nonsense! He won't do anything serious. Nothing terrible could happen. It's impossible. Why, I have three small children.

Anne-Marie, with a large carton, comes in from the room to the left.

ANNE-MARIE: Well, at last I found the box with the masquerade clothes.
NORA: Thanks. Put it on the table.
ANNE-MARIE: *(does so)* But they're all pretty much of a mess.
5 NORA: Ahh! I'd love to rip them in a million pieces!
ANNE-MARIE: Oh, mercy, they can be fixed right up. Just a little patience.
NORA: Yes, I'll go get Mrs. Linde to help me.
ANNE-MARIE: Out again now? In this nasty weather? Miss Nora will catch cold — get sick.
NORA: Oh, worse things could happen — How are the children?
10 ANNE-MARIE: The poor mites are playing with their Christmas presents, but —
NORA: Do they ask for me much?
ANNE-MARIE: They're so used to having Mama around, you know.
NORA: Yes. But Anne-Marie, I *can't* be together with them as much as I was.
ANNE-MARIE: Well, small children get used to anything.
15 NORA: You think so? Do you think they'd forget their mother if she was gone for good?
ANNE-MARIE: Oh, mercy — gone for good!
NORA: Wait, tell me, Anne-Marie — I've wondered so often — how could you ever have the heart to give your child over to strangers?
20 ANNE-MARIE: But I had to, you know, to become little Nora's nurse.
NORA: Yes, but how could you *do* it?
ANNE-MARIE: When I could get such a good place? A girl who's poor and who's gotten in trouble is glad enough for that. Because that slippery fish, he didn't do a thing for me, you know.
NORA: But your daughter's surely forgotten you.
ANNE-MARIE: Oh, she certainly has not. She's written to me, both when she was confirmed and when she was married.
NORA: *(clasping her about the neck)* You old Anne-Marie, you were a good mother for me when I was little.

ANNE-MARIE: Poor little Nora, with no other mother but me.

NORA: And if the babies didn't have one, then I know that you'd —What silly talk! *(Opening the carton.)* Go in to them. Now I'll have to — Tomorrow you can see how lovely I'll look.

ANNE-MARIE: Oh, there won't be anyone at the party as lovely as Miss Nora. *(She goes off into the room, left.)*

NORA: *(begins unpacking the box, but soon throws it aside)* Oh, if I dared to go out. If only nobody would come. If only nothing would happen here while I'm out. What craziness — nobody's coming. Just don't think. This muff — needs a brushing. Beautiful gloves, beautiful gloves. Let it go. Let it go! One, two, three, four, five, six —*(With a cry.)* Oh, there they are! *(Poises to move toward the door, but remains irresolutely standing. Mrs. Linde enters from the hall, where she has removed her street clothes.)*

NORA: Oh, it's you, Kristine. There's no one else out there? How good that you've come.

MRS. LINDE: I hear you were up asking for me.

NORA: Yes, I just stopped by. There's something you really can help me with. Let's get settled on the sofa. Look, there's going to be a costume party tomorrow evening at the Stenborgs' right above us, and now Torvald wants me to go as a Neapolitan peasant girl and dance the tarantella that I learned in Capri.   30

MRS. LINDE: Really, are you giving a whole performance?

NORA: Torvald says yes, I should. See, here's the dress. Torvald had it made for me down there; but now it's all so tattered that I just don't know —

MRS. LINDE: Oh, we'll fix that up in no time. It's nothing more than the trimmings — they're a bit loose here and there. Needle and thread? Good, now we have what we need.

NORA: Oh, how sweet of you!

MRS. LINDE: *(sewing)* So you'll be in disguise tomorrow, Nora. You know what? I'll stop by then for a moment and have a look at you all dressed up. But listen, I've absolutely forgotten to thank you for that pleasant evening yesterday.   35

NORA: *(getting up and walking about)* I don't think it was as pleasant as usual yesterday. You should have come to town a bit sooner, Kristine —Yes, Torvald really knows how to give a home elegance and charm.

MRS. LINDE: And you do, too, if you ask me. You're not your father's daughter for nothing. But tell me, is Dr. Rank always so down in the mouth as yesterday?

NORA: No, that was quite an exception. But he goes around critically ill all the time — tuberculosis of the spine, poor man. You know, his father was a disgusting thing who kept mistresses and so on — and that's why the son's been sickly from birth.

MRS. LINDE: *(lets her sewing fall to her lap)* But my dearest Nora, how do you know about such things?

40 **NORA:** *(walking more jauntily)* Hmp! When you've had three children, then you've had a few visits from — from women who know something of medicine, and they tell you this and that.

MRS. LINDE: *(resumes sewing; a short pause)* Does Dr. Rank come here every day?

NORA: Every blessed day. He's Torvald's best friend from childhood, and my good friend, too. Dr. Rank almost belongs to this house.

MRS. LINDE: But tell me — is he quite sincere? I mean, doesn't he rather enjoy flattering people?

NORA: Just the opposite. Why do you think that?

45 **MRS. LINDE:** When you introduced us yesterday, he was proclaiming that he'd often heard my name in this house; but later I noticed that your husband hadn't the slightest idea who I really was. So how could Dr. Rank —?

NORA: But it's all true, Kristine. You see, Torvald loves me beyond words, and, as he puts it, he'd like to keep me all to himself. For a long time he'd almost be jealous if I even mentioned any of my old friends back home. So of course I dropped that. But with Dr. Rank I talk a lot about such things, because he likes hearing about them.

MRS. LINDE: Now listen, Nora; in many ways you're still like a child. I'm a good deal older than you, with a little more experience. I'll tell you something: you ought to put an end to all this with Dr. Rank.

NORA: What should I put an end to?

MRS. LINDE: Both parts of it, I think. Yesterday you said something about a rich admirer who'd provide you with money —

50 **NORA:** Yes, one who doesn't exist — worse luck. So?

MRS. LINDE: Is Dr. Rank well off?

NORA: Yes, he is.

MRS. LINDE: With no dependents?

NORA: No, no one. But —

55 **MRS. LINDE:** And he's over here every day?

NORA: Yes, I told you that.

MRS. LINDE: How can a man of such refinement be so grasping?

NORA: I don't follow you at all.

MRS. LINDE: Now don't try to hide it, Nora. You think I can't guess who loaned you the forty-eight hundred crowns?

60 **NORA:** Are you out of your mind? How could you think such a thing! A friend of ours, who comes here every single day. What an intolerable situation that would have been!

MRS. LINDE: Then it really wasn't him.

NORA: No, absolutely not. It never even crossed my mind for a moment — And he had nothing to lend in those days; his inheritance came later.

MRS. LINDE: Well, I think that was a stroke of luck for you, Nora dear.

NORA: No, it never would have occurred to me to ask Dr. Rank — Still, I'm quite sure that if I had asked him —

MRS. LINDE: Which you won't, of course.   65
NORA: No, of course not. I can't see that I'd ever need to. But I'm quite
    positive that if I talked to Dr. Rank—
MRS. LINDE: Behind your husband's back?
NORA: I've got to clear up this other thing; *that's* also behind his back. I've *got*
    to clear it all up.
MRS. LINDE: Yes, I was saying that yesterday, but—
NORA: (*pacing up and down*) A man handles these problems so much better   70
    than a woman—
MRS. LINDE: One's husband does, yes.
NORA: Nonsense. (*Stopping.*) When you pay everything you owe, then you get
    your note back, right?
MRS. LINDE: Yes, naturally.
NORA: And can rip it into a million pieces and burn it up — that filthy scrap
    of paper!
MRS. LINDE: (*looking hard at her, laying her sewing aside, and rising slowly*) Nora,   75
    you're hiding something from me.
NORA: You can see it in my face?
MRS. LINDE: Something's happened to you since yesterday morning. Nora,
    what is it?
NORA: (*hurrying toward her*) Kristine! (*Listening.*) Shh! Torvald's home. Look,
    go in with the children a while. Torvald can't bear all this snipping and
    stitching. Let Anne-Marie help you.
MRS. LINDE: (*gathering up some of the things*) All right, but I'm not leaving here
    until we've talked this out. (*She disappears into the room, left, as Torvald
    enters from the hall.*)
NORA: Oh, how I've been waiting for you, Torvald dear.   80
HELMER: Was that the dressmaker?
NORA: No, that was Kristine. She's helping me fix up my costume. You know,
    it's going to be quite attractive.
HELMER: Yes, wasn't that a bright idea I had?
NORA: Brilliant! But then wasn't I good as well to give in to you?
HELMER: Good — because you give in to your husband's judgment? All right,   85
    you little goose, I know you didn't mean it like that. But I won't disturb you.
    You'll want to have a fitting, I suppose.
NORA: And you'll be working?
HELMER: Yes. (*Indicating a bundle of papers.*) See. I've been down to the bank.
    (*Starts toward his study.*)
NORA: Torvald.
HELMER: (*stops*) Yes.
NORA: If your little squirrel begged you, with all her heart and soul, for   90
    something — ?
HELMER: What's that?
NORA: Then would you do it?

HELMER: First, naturally, I'd have to know what it was.

NORA: Your squirrel would scamper about and do tricks, if you'd only be sweet and give in.

95 HELMER: Out with it.

NORA: Your lark would be singing high and low in every room—

HELMER: Come on, she does that anyway.

NORA: I'd be a wood nymph and dance for you in the moonlight.

HELMER: Nora — don't tell me it's that same business from this morning?

100 NORA: *(coming closer)* Yes, Torvald, I beg you, please!

HELMER: And you actually have the nerve to drag that up again?

NORA: Yes, yes, you've got to give in to me; you *have* to let Krogstad keep his job in the bank.

HELMER: My dear Nora, I've slated his job for Mrs. Linde.

NORA: That's awfully kind of you. But you could just fire another clerk instead of Krogstad.

105 HELMER: This is the most incredible stubbornness! Because you go and give an impulsive promise to speak up for him, I'm expected to—

NORA: That's not the reason, Torvald. It's for your own sake. That man does writing for the worst papers; you said it yourself. He could do you any amount of harm. I'm scared to death of him—

HELMER: Ah, I understand. It's the old memories haunting you.

NORA: What do you mean by that?

HELMER: Of course, you're thinking about your father.

110 NORA: Yes, all right. Just remember how those nasty gossips wrote in the papers about Papa and slandered him so cruelly. I think they'd have had him dismissed if the department hadn't sent you up to investigate, and if you hadn't been so kind and open-minded toward him.

HELMER: My dear Nora, there's a notable difference between your father and me. Your father's official career was hardly above reproach. But mine is; and I hope it'll stay that way as long as I hold my position.

NORA: Oh, who can ever tell what vicious minds can invent? We could be so snug and happy now in our quiet, carefree home — you and I and the children, Torvald! That's why I'm pleading with you so—

HELMER: And just by pleading for him you make it impossible for me to keep him on. It's already known at the bank that I'm firing Krogstad. What if it's rumored around now that the new bank manager was vetoed by his wife—

NORA: Yes, what then —?

115 HELMER: Oh yes — as long as our little bundle of stubbornness gets her way —! I should go and make myself ridiculous in front of the whole office — give people the idea I can be swayed by all kinds of outside pressure. Oh, you can bet I'd feel the effects of that soon enough! Besides — there's something that rules Krogstad right out at the bank as long as I'm the manager.

NORA: What's that?

HELMER: His moral failings I could maybe overlook if I had to —

NORA: Yes, Torvald, why not?

HELMER: And I hear he's quite efficient on the job. But he was a crony of mine back in my teens — one of those rash friendships that crop up again and again to embarrass you later in life. Well, I might as well say it straight out: we're on a first-name basis. And that tactless fool makes no effort at all to hide it in front of others. Quite the contrary — he thinks that entitles him to take a familiar air around me, and so every other second he comes booming out with his "Yes, Torvald!" and "Sure thing, Torvald!" I tell you, it's been excruciating for me. He's out to make my place in the bank unbearable.

NORA: Torvald, you can't be serious about all this.   120

HELMER: Oh no? Why not?

NORA: Because these are such petty considerations.

HELMER: What are you saying? Petty? You think I'm petty!

NORA: No, just the opposite, Torvald dear. That's exactly why —

HELMER: Never mind. You call my motives petty; then I might as well be just   125
that. Petty! All right! We'll put a stop to this for good. (*Goes to the hall door and calls.*) Helene!

NORA: What do you want?

HELMER: (*searching among his papers*) A decision. (*The Maid comes in.*) Look here; take this letter; go out with it at once. Get hold of a messenger and have him deliver it. Quick now. It's already addressed. Wait, here's some money.

MAID: Yes, sir. (*She leaves with the letter.*)

HELMER: (*straightening his papers*) There, now, little Miss Willful.

NORA: (*breathlessly*) Torvald, what was that letter?   130

HELMER: Krogstad's notice.

NORA: Call it back, Torvald! There's still time. Oh, Torvald, call it back! Do it for my sake — for your sake, for the children's sake! Do you hear, Torvald; do it! You don't know how this can harm us.

HELMER: Too late.

NORA: Yes, too late.

HELMER: Nora dear, I can forgive you this panic, even though basically you're   135
insulting me. Yes, you are! Or isn't it an insult to think that *I* should be afraid of a courtroom hack's revenge? But I forgive you anyway, because this shows so beautifully how much you love me. (*Takes her in his arms.*) This is the way it should be, my darling Nora. Whatever comes, you'll see: when it really counts, I have strength and courage enough as a man to take on the whole weight myself.

NORA: (*terrified*) What do you mean by that?

HELMER: The whole weight, I said.

NORA: (*resolutely*) No, never in all the world.

HELMER: Good. So we'll share it, Nora, as man and wife. That's as it should be. (*Fondling her.*) Are you happy now? There, there, there — not these frightened dove's eyes. It's nothing at all but empty fantasies — Now you should run through your tarantella and practice your tambourine. I'll go to the inner office and shut both doors, so I won't hear a thing; you can make all the noise you like. (*Turning in the doorway.*) And when Rank comes, just tell him where he can find me. (*He nods to her and goes with his papers into the study, closing the door.*)

140 NORA: (*standing as though rooted, dazed with fright, in a whisper*) He really could do it. He will do it. He'll do it in spite of everything. No, not that, never, never! Anything but that! Escape! A way out —(*The doorbell rings.*) Dr. Rank! Anything but that! *Anything*, whatever it is! (*Her hands pass over her face, smoothing it; she pulls herself together, goes over and opens the hall door. Dr. Rank stands outside, hanging his fur coat up. During the following scene, it begins getting dark.*)

NORA: Hello, Dr. Rank. I recognized your ring. But you mustn't go in to Torvald yet; I believe he's working.

RANK: And you?

NORA: For you, I always have an hour to spare — you know that. (*He has entered, and she shuts the door after him.*)

RANK: Many thanks. I'll make use of these hours while I can.

145 NORA: What do you mean by that? While you can?

RANK: Does that disturb you?

NORA: Well, it's such an odd phrase. Is anything going to happen?

RANK: What's going to happen is what I've been expecting so long — but I honestly didn't think it would come so soon.

NORA: (*gripping his arm*) What is it you've found out? Dr. Rank, you have to tell me!

150 RANK: (*sitting by the stove*) It's all over with me. There's nothing to be done about it.

NORA: (*breathing easier*) Is it you — then —?

RANK: Who else? There's no point in lying to one's self. I'm the most miserable of all my patients, Mrs. Helmer. These past few days I've been auditing my internal accounts. Bankrupt! Within a month I'll probably be laid out and rotting in the churchyard.

NORA: Oh, what a horrible thing to say.

RANK: The thing itself is horrible. But the worst of it is all the other horror before it's over. There's only one final examination left; when I'm finished with that, I'll know about when my disintegration will begin. There's something I want to say. Helmer with his sensitivity has such a sharp distaste for anything ugly. I don't want him near my sickroom.

155 NORA: Oh, but Dr. Rank—

RANK: I won't have him in there. Under no condition. I'll lock my door to him — As soon as I'm completely sure of the worst, I'll send you my calling card marked with a black cross, and you'll know then the wreck has started to come apart.

NORA: No, today you're completely unreasonable. And I wanted you so much to be in a really good humor.

RANK: With death up my sleeve? And then to suffer this way for somebody else's sins. Is there any justice in that? And in every single family, in some way or another, this inevitable retribution of nature goes on —

NORA: *(her hands pressed over her ears)* Oh, stuff! Cheer up! Please — be gay!

RANK: Yes, I'd just as soon laugh at it all. My poor, innocent spine, serving   160
time for my father's gay army days.

NORA: *(by the table, left)* He was so infatuated with asparagus tips and *pâté de foie gras*, wasn't that it?

RANK: Yes — and with truffles.

NORA: Truffles, yes. And then with oysters, I suppose?

RANK: Yes, tons of oysters, naturally.

NORA: And then the port and champagne to go with it. It's so sad that all   165
these delectable things have to strike at our bones.

RANK: Especially when they strike at the unhappy bones that never shared in the fun.

NORA: Ah, that's the saddest of all.

RANK: *(looks searchingly at her)* Hm.

NORA: *(after a moment)* Why did you smile?

RANK: No, it was you who laughed.   170

NORA: No, it was you who smiled, Dr. Rank!

RANK: *(getting up)* You're even a bigger tease than I'd thought.

NORA: I'm full of wild ideas today.

RANK: That's obvious.

NORA: *(putting both hands on his shoulders)* Dear, dear Dr. Rank, you'll never   175
die for Torvald and me.

RANK: Oh, that loss you'll easily get over. Those who go away are soon forgotten.

NORA: *(looks fearfully at him)* You believe that?

RANK: One makes new connections, and then —

NORA: Who makes new connections?

RANK: Both you and Torvald will when I'm gone. I'd say you're well under   180
way already. What was that Mrs. Linde doing here last evening?

NORA: Oh, come — you can't be jealous of poor Kristine?

RANK: Oh yes, I am. She'll be my successor here in the house. When I'm down under, that woman will probably —

NORA: Shh! Not so loud. She's right in there.

RANK: Today as well. So you see.

NORA: Only to sew on my dress. Good gracious, how unreasonable you are.   185
(Sitting on the sofa.) Be nice now, Dr. Rank. Tomorrow you'll see how beautifully I'll dance; and you can imagine then that I'm dancing only for you — yes, and of course for Torvald, too — that's understood. *(Takes various items out of the carton.)* Dr. Rank, sit over here and I'll show you something.

RANK: *(sitting)* What's that?

NORA: Look here. Look.

RANK: Silk stockings.

NORA: Flesh-colored. Aren't they lovely? Now it's so dark here, but tomorrow — No, no, no, just look at the feet. Oh well, you might as well look at the rest.

190   **RANK:**   Hm —

NORA: Why do you look so critical? Don't you believe they'll fit?

RANK: I've never had any chance to form an opinion on that.

NORA: *(glancing at him a moment)* Shame on you. *(Hits him lightly on the ear with the stockings.)* That's for you. *(Puts them away again.)*

RANK: And what other splendors am I going to see now?

195   **NORA:**   Not the least bit more, because you've been naughty. *(She hums a little and rummages among her things.)*

RANK: *(after a short silence)* When I sit here together with you like this, completely easy and open, then I don't know — I simply can't imagine — whatever would have become of me if I'd never come into this house.

NORA: *(smiling)* Yes, I really think you feel completely at ease with us.

RANK: *(more quietly, staring straight ahead)* And then to have to go away from it all —

NORA: Nonsense, you're not going away.

200   **RANK:**   *(his voice unchanged)* — and not even be able to leave some poor show of gratitude behind, scarcely a fleeting regret — no more than a vacant place that anyone can fill.

NORA: And if I asked you now for —? No —

RANK: For what?

NORA: For a great proof of your friendship —

RANK: Yes, yes?

205   **NORA:**   No, I mean — for an exceptionally big favor —

RANK: Would you really, for once, make me so happy?

NORA: Oh, you haven't the vaguest idea what it is.

RANK: All right, then tell me.

NORA: No, but I can't, Dr. Rank — it's all out of reason. It's advice and help, too — and a favor —

210   **RANK:**   So much the better. I can't fathom what you're hinting at. Just speak out. Don't you trust me?

NORA: Of course. More than anyone else. You're my best and truest friend, I'm sure. That's why I want to talk to you. All right, then, Dr. Rank: there's something you can help me prevent. You know how deeply, how inexpressibly dearly Torvald loves me; he'd never hesitate a second to give up his life for me.

RANK: *(leaning close to her)* Nora — do you think he's the only one —

NORA: *(with a slight start)* Who —?

RANK: Who'd gladly give up his life for you.

215   **NORA:**   *(heavily)* I see.

RANK: I swore to myself you should know this before I'm gone. I'll never find a better chance. Yes, Nora, now you know. And also you know now that you can trust me beyond anyone else.

NORA: *(rising, natural and calm)* Let me by.

RANK: *(making room for her, but still sitting)* Nora —

NORA: *(in the hall doorway)* Helene, bring the lamp in. *(Goes over to the stove.)* Ah, dear Dr. Rank, that was really mean of you.

RANK: *(getting up)* That I've loved you just as deeply as somebody else? 220
Was *that* mean?

NORA: No, but that you came out and told me. That was quite unnecessary —

RANK: What do you mean? Have you known —?

The Maid comes in with the lamp, sets it on the table, and goes out again.

RANK: Nora — Mrs. Helmer — I'm asking you: have you known about it?

NORA: Oh, how can I tell what I know or don't know? Really, I don't know what to say — Why did you have to be so clumsy, Dr. Rank! Everything was so good.

RANK: Well, in any case, you now have the knowledge that my body and 225
soul are at your command. So won't you speak out?

NORA: *(looking at him)* After that?

RANK: Please, just let me know what it is.

NORA: You can't know anything now.

RANK: I have to. You mustn't punish me like this. Give me the chance to do whatever is humanly possible for you.

NORA: Now there's nothing you can do for me. Besides, actually, I don't need 230
any help. You'll see — it's only my fantasies. That's what it is. Of course!
(Sits in the rocker, looks at him, and smiles.) What a nice one you are, Dr.
Rank. Aren't you a little bit ashamed, now that the lamp is here?

RANK: No, not exactly. But perhaps I'd better go — for good?

NORA: No, you certainly can't do that. You must come here just as you always have. You know Torvald can't do without you.

RANK: Yes, but *you*?

NORA: You know how much I enjoy it when you're here.

RANK: That's precisely what threw me off. You're a mystery to me. So many 235
times I've felt you'd almost rather be with me than with Helmer.

NORA: Yes — you see, there are some people that one loves most and other people that one would almost prefer being with.

RANK: Yes, there's something to that.

NORA: When I was back home, of course I loved Papa most. But I always thought it was so much fun when I could sneak down to the maids' quarters, because they never tried to improve me, and it was always so amusing, the way they talked to each other.

RANK: Aha, so it's *their* place that I've filled.

NORA: *(jumping up and going to him)* Oh, dear, sweet Dr. Rank, that's not 240
what I mean at all. But you can understand that with Torvald it's just the same as with Papa —

The Maid enters from the hall.

MAID: Ma'am — please! *(She whispers to Nora and hands her a calling card.)*
NORA: *(glancing at the card)* Ah! *(Slips it into her pocket.)*
RANK: Anything wrong?
NORA: No, no, not at all. It's only some — it's my new dress —
245 RANK: Really? But — there's your dress.
NORA: Oh, that. But this is another one — I ordered it — Torvald mustn't
        know —
RANK: Ah, now we have the big secret.
NORA: That's right. Just go in with him — he's back in the inner study.
        Keep him there as long as —
RANK: Don't worry. He won't get away. *(Goes into the study.)*
250 NORA: *(to the Maid)* And he's standing waiting in the kitchen?
MAID: Yes, he came up by the back stairs.
NORA: But didn't you tell him somebody was here?
MAID: Yes, but that didn't do any good.
NORA: He won't leave?
255 MAID: No, he won't go till he's talked with you, ma'am.
NORA: Let him come in, then — but quietly. Helene, don't breathe a word
        about this. It's a surprise for my husband.
MAID: Yes, yes, I understand — *(Goes out.)*
NORA: This horror — it's going to happen. No, no, no, it can't happen, it mustn't.
        *(She goes and bolts Helmer's door. The Maid opens the hall door for Krogstad and
        shuts it behind him. He is dressed for travel in a fur coat, boots, and a fur cap.)*
NORA: *(going toward him)* Talk softly. My husband's home.
KROGSTAD: Well, good for him.
260 NORA: What do you want?
KROGSTAD: Some information.
NORA: Hurry up, then. What is it?
KROGSTAD: You know, of course, that I got my notice.
NORA: I couldn't prevent it, Mr. Krogstad. I fought for you to the bitter end,
265   but nothing worked.
KROGSTAD: Does your husband's love for you run so thin? He knows
        everything I can expose you to, and all the same he dares to —
NORA: How can you imagine he knows anything about this?
KROGSTAD: Ah, no — I can't imagine it either, now. It's not at all like my fine
        Torvald Helmer to have so much guts —
NORA: Mr. Krogstad, I demand respect for my husband!
KROGSTAD: Why, of course — all due respect. But since the lady's keeping it
270   so carefully hidden, may I presume to ask if you're also a bit better informed
        than yesterday about what you've actually done?
NORA: More than you ever could teach me.
KROGSTAD: Yes, I *am* such an awful lawyer.

NORA: What is it you want from me?

KROGSTAD: Just a glimpse of how you are, Mrs. Helmer. I've been thinking about you all day long. A cashier, a night-court scribbler, a — well, a type like me also has a little of what they call a heart, you know.

NORA: Then show it. Think of my children. 275

KROGSTAD: Did you or your husband ever think of mine? But never mind. I simply wanted to tell you that you don't need to take this thing too seriously. For the present, I'm not proceeding with any action.

NORA: Oh no, really! Well — I knew that.

KROGSTAD: Everything can be settled in a friendly spirit. It doesn't have to get around town at all; it can stay just among us three.

NORA: My husband must never know anything of this.

KROGSTAD: How can you manage that? Perhaps you can pay me the balance? 280

NORA: No, not right now.

KROGSTAD: Or you know some way of raising the money in a day or two?

NORA: No way that I'm willing to use.

KROGSTAD: Well, it wouldn't have done you any good, anyway. If you stood in front of me with a fistful of bills, you still couldn't buy your signature back.

NORA: Then tell me what you're going to do with it. 285

KROGSTAD: I'll just hold onto it — keep it on file. There's no outsider who'll even get wind of it. So if you've been thinking of taking some desperate step —

NORA: I have.

KROGSTAD: Been thinking of running away from home —

NORA: I have!

KROGSTAD: Or even of something worse — 290

NORA: How could you guess that?

KROGSTAD: You can drop those thoughts.

NORA: How could you guess I was thinking of *that*?

KROGSTAD: Most of us think about *that* at first. I thought about it too, but I discovered I hadn't the courage —

NORA: *(lifelessly)* I don't either. 295

KROGSTAD: *(relieved)* That's true, you haven't the courage? You too?

NORA: I don't have it — I don't have it.

KROGSTAD: It would be terribly stupid, anyway. After that first storm at home blows out, why, then — I have here in my pocket a letter for your husband —

NORA: Telling everything?

KROGSTAD: As charitably as possible. 300

NORA: *(quickly)* He mustn't ever get that letter. Tear it up. I'll find some way to get money.

KROGSTAD: Beg pardon, Mrs. Helmer, but I think I just told you —

NORA: Oh, I don't mean the money I owe you. Let me know how much you want from my husband, and I'll manage it.

Krogstad: I don't want any money from your husband.

305 **Nora:** What do you want, then?

Krogstad: I'll tell you what. I want to recoup, Mrs. Helmer; I want to get on in the world — and there's where your husband can help me. For a year and a half I've kept myself clean of anything disreputable — all that time struggling with the worst conditions; but I was satisfied, working my way up step by step. Now I've been written right off, and I'm just not in the mood to come crawling back. I tell you, I want to move on. I want to get back in the bank — in a better position. Your husband can set up a job for me —

Nora: He'll never do that!

Krogstad: He'll do it. I know him. He won't dare breathe a word of protest. And once I'm in there together with him, you just wait and see! Inside of a year, I'll be the manager's right-hand man. It'll be Nils Krogstad, not Torvald Helmer, who runs the bank.

Nora: You'll never see the day!

310 **Krogstad:** Maybe you think you can —

Nora: I have the courage now — for *that.*

Krogstad: Oh, you don't scare me. A smart, spoiled lady like you —

Nora: You'll see; you'll see!

Krogstad: Under the ice, maybe? Down in the freezing, coal-black water? There, till you float up in the spring, ugly, unrecognizable, with your hair falling out —

315 **Nora:** You don't frighten me.

Krogstad: Nor do you frighten me. One doesn't do these things, Mrs. Helmer. Besides, what good would it be? I'd still have him safe in my pocket.

Nora: Afterwards? When I'm no longer — ?

Krogstad: Are you forgetting that *I'll* be in control then over your final reputation? (*Nora stands speechless, staring at him.*) Good; now I've warned you. Don't do anything stupid. When Helmer's read my letter, I'll be waiting for his reply. And bear in mind that it's your husband himself who's forced me back to my old ways. I'll never forgive him for that. Good-bye, Mrs. Helmer. (*He goes out through the hall.*)

Nora: (*goes to the hall door, opens it a crack, and listens*) He's gone. Didn't leave the letter. Oh no, no, that's impossible too! (*Opening the door more and more.*) What's that? He's standing outside — not going downstairs. He's thinking it over? Maybe he'll — ? (*A letter falls in the mailbox; then Krogstad's footsteps are heard, dying away down a flight of stairs. Nora gives a muffled cry and runs over toward the sofa table. A short pause.*) In the mailbox. (*Slips warily over to the hall door.*) It's lying there. Torvald, Torvald — now we're lost!

320 **Mrs. Linde:** (*entering with the costume from the room, left*) There now, I can't see anything else to mend. Perhaps you'd like to try —

Nora: (*in a hoarse whisper*) Kristine, come here.

Mrs. Linde: (*tossing the dress on the sofa*) What's wrong? You look upset.

Nora: Come here. See that letter? *There!* Look — through the glass in the mailbox.

MRS. LINDE: Yes, yes, I see it.

NORA: That letter's from Krogstad—   325

MRS. LINDE: Nora — it's Krogstad who loaned you the money!

NORA: Yes, and now Torvald will find out everything.

MRS. LINDE: Believe me, Nora, it's best for both of you.

NORA: There's more you don't know. I forged a name.

MRS. LINDE: But for heaven's sake —?   330

NORA: I only want to tell you that, Kristine, so that you can be my witness.

MRS. LINDE: Witness? Why should I —?

NORA: If I should go out of my mind — it could easily happen—

MRS. LINDE: Nora!

NORA: Or anything else occurred — so I couldn't be present here—   335

MRS. LINDE: Nora, Nora, you aren't yourself at all!

NORA: And someone should try to take on the whole weight, all of the guilt,
you follow me—

MRS. LINDE: Yes, of course, but why do you think —?

NORA: Then you're the witness that it isn't true, Kristine. I'm very much
myself; my mind right now is perfectly clear; and I'm telling you: nobody
else has known about this; I alone did everything. Remember that.

MRS. LINDE: I will. But I don't understand all this.   340

NORA: Oh, how could you ever understand it? It's the miracle now that's going
to take place.

MRS. LINDE: The miracle?

NORA: Yes, the miracle. But it's so awful, Kristine. It mustn't take place, not for
anything in the world.

MRS. LINDE: I'm going right over and talk with Krogstad.

NORA: Don't go near him; he'll do you some terrible harm!   345

MRS. LINDE: There was a time once when he'd gladly have done anything for me.

NORA: He?

MRS. LINDE: Where does he live?

NORA: Oh, how do I know? Yes. (*Searches in her pocket.*) Here's his card. But
the letter, the letter —!

HELMER: (*from the study, knocking on the door*) Nora!   350

NORA: (*with a cry of fear*) Oh! What is it? What do you want?

HELMER: Now, now, don't be so frightened. We're not coming in. You locked
the door — are you trying on the dress?

NORA: Yes, I'm trying it. I'll look just beautiful, Torvald.

MRS. LINDE: (*who has read the card*) He's living right around the corner.

NORA: Yes, but what's the use? We're lost. The letter's in the box.   355

MRS. LINDE: And your husband has the key?

NORA: Yes, always.

MRS. LINDE: Krogstad can ask for his letter back unread; he can find some
excuse—

NORA: But it's just this time that Torvald usually—

360 MRS. LINDE: Stall him. Keep him in there. I'll be back as quick as I can.
(*She hurries out through the hall entrance.*)

NORA: (*goes to Helmer's door, opens it, and peers in*) Torvald!

HELMER: (*from the inner study*) Well — does one dare set foot in one's own
living room at last? Come on, Rank, now we'll get a look —(*In the
doorway.*) But what's this?

NORA: What, Torvald dear?

HELMER: Rank had me expecting some grand masquerade.

365 RANK: (*in the doorway*) That was my impression, but I must have been
wrong.

NORA: No one can admire me in my splendor — not till tomorrow.

HELMER: But Nora dear, you look so exhausted. Have you practiced too
hard?

NORA: No, I haven't practiced at all yet.

HELMER: You know, it's necessary—

370 NORA: Oh, it's absolutely necessary, Torvald. But I can't get anywhere without your help. I've forgotten the whole thing completely.

HELMER: Ah, we'll soon take care of that.

NORA: Yes, take care of me, Torvald, please! Promise me that? Oh, I'm so
nervous. That big party —You must give up everything this evening for
me. No business — don't even touch your pen. Yes? Dear Torvald,
promise?

HELMER: It's a promise. Tonight I'm totally at your service — you little
helpless thing. Hm — but first there's one thing I want to —(*Goes toward
the hall door.*)

NORA: What are you looking for?

375 HELMER: Just to see if there's any mail.

NORA: No, no, don't do that, Torvald!

HELMER: Now what?

NORA: Torvald, please. There isn't any.

HELMER: Let me look, though. (*Starts out. Nora, at the piano, strikes the first
notes of the tarantella. Helmer, at the door, stops.*) Aha!

380 NORA: I can't dance tomorrow if I don't practice with you.

HELMER: (*going over to her*) Nora dear, are you really so frightened?

NORA: Yes, so terribly frightened. Let me practice right now; there's still
time before dinner. Oh, sit down and play for me, Torvald. Direct me.
Teach me, the way you always have.

HELMER: Gladly, if it's what you want. (*Sits at the piano.*)

NORA: (*snatches the tambourine up from the box, then a long, varicolored shawl,
which she throws around herself, whereupon she springs forward and cries out*)
Play for me now! Now I'll dance!

Helmer plays and Nora dances. Rank stands behind Helmer at the piano and looks on.

385 HELMER: (*as he plays*) Slower. Slow down.

NORA: Can't change it.

HELMER: Not so violent, Nora!

NORA: Has to be just like this.

HELMER: (*stopping*) No, no, that won't do at all.

NORA: (*laughing and swinging her tambourine*) Isn't that what I told you?   390

RANK: Let me play for her.

HELMER: (*getting up*) Yes, go on. I can teach her more easily then.

Rank sits at the piano and plays; Nora dances more and more wildly. Helmer has stationed himself by the stove and repeatedly gives her directions; she seems not to hear them; her hair loosens and falls over her shoulders; she does not notice, but goes on dancing. Mrs. Linde enters.

MRS. LINDE: (*standing dumbfounded at the door*) Ah —!

NORA: (*still dancing*) See what fun, Kristine!

HELMER: But Nora darling, you dance as if your life were at stake.   395

NORA: And it is.

HELMER: Rank, stop! This is pure madness. Stop it, I say!

Rank breaks off playing, and Nora halts abruptly.

HELMER: (*going over to her*) I never would have believed it. You've forgotten everything I taught you.

NORA: (*throwing away the tambourine*) You see for yourself.

HELMER: Well, there's certainly room for instruction here.   400

NORA: Yes, you see how important it is. You've got to teach me to the very last minute. Promise me that, Torvald?

HELMER: You can bet on it.

NORA: You mustn't, either today or tomorrow, think about anything else but me; you mustn't open any letters — or the mailbox—

HELMER: Ah, it's still the fear of that man—

NORA: Oh yes, yes, that too.   405

HELMER: Nora, it's written all over you — there's already a letter from him out there.

NORA: I don't know. I guess so. But you mustn't read such things now; there mustn't be anything ugly between us before it's all over.

RANK: (*quietly to Helmer*) You shouldn't deny her.

HELMER: (*putting his arm around her*) The child can have her way. But tomorrow night, after you've danced—

NORA: Then you'll be free.   410

MAID: (*in the doorway, right*) Ma'am, dinner is served.

NORA: We'll be wanting champagne, Helene.

MAID: Very good, ma'am. (*Goes out.*)

HELMER: So — a regular banquet, hm?

NORA: Yes, a banquet — champagne till daybreak! (*Calling out.*) And some   415
macaroons, Helene. Heaps of them — just this once.

HELMER: *(taking her hands)* Now, now, now — no hysterics. Be my own little
 lark again.
NORA: Oh, I will soon enough. But go on in — and you, Dr. Rank. Kristine,
 help me put up my hair.
RANK: *(whispering, as they go)* There's nothing wrong — really wrong,
 is there?
HELMER: Oh, of course not. It's nothing more than this childish anxiety I was
 telling you about. *(They go out, right.)*
420 **NORA:** Well?
MRS. LINDE: Left town.
NORA: I could see by your face.
MRS. LINDE: He'll be home tomorrow evening. I wrote him a note.
NORA: You shouldn't have. Don't try to stop anything now. After all, it's a
 wonderful joy, this waiting here for the miracle.
425 **MRS. LINDE:** What is it you're waiting for?
NORA: Oh, you can't understand that. Go in to them: I'll be along in
 a moment.

*Mrs. Linde goes into the dining room. Nora stands a short while as if composing herself;
then she looks at her watch.*

NORA: Five. Seven hours to midnight. Twenty-four hours to the midnight
 after, and then the tarantella's done. Seven and twenty-four? Thirty-one
 hours to live.
HELMER: *(in the doorway, right)* What's become of the little lark?
NORA: *(going toward him with open arms)* Here's your lark!

ACT 3

*Same scene. The table, with chairs around it, has been moved to the center of the room.
A lamp on the table is lit. The hall door stands open. Dance music drifts down from the
floor above. Mrs. Linde sits at the table, absently paging through a book, trying to read,
but apparently unable to focus her thoughts. Once or twice she pauses, tensely listening
for a sound at the outer entrance.*

MRS. LINDE: *(glancing at her watch)* Not yet — and there's hardly any time left.
 If only he's not — *(Listening again.)* Ah, there he is. *(She goes out in the hall
 and cautiously opens the outer door. Quiet footsteps are heard on the stairs. She
 whispers:)* Come in. Nobody's here.
KROGSTAD: *(in the doorway)* I found a note from you at home. What's back of
 all this?
MRS. LINDE: I just *had* to talk to you.
KROGSTAD: Oh? And it just *had* to be here in this house?
5 **MRS. LINDE:** At my place it was impossible; my room hasn't a private
 entrance. Come in; we're all alone. The maid's asleep, and the Helmers
 are at the dance upstairs.

KROGSTAD: *(entering the room)* Well, well, the Helmers are dancing tonight? Really?

MRS. LINDE: Yes, why not?

KROGSTAD: How true — why not?

MRS. LINDE: All right, Krogstad, let's talk.

KROGSTAD: Do we two have anything more to talk about? 10

MRS. LINDE: We have a great deal to talk about.

KROGSTAD: I wouldn't have thought so.

MRS. LINDE: No, because you've never understood me, really.

KROGSTAD: Was there anything more to understand — except what's all too common in life? A calculating woman throws over a man the moment a better catch comes by.

MRS. LINDE: You think I'm so thoroughly calculating? You think I broke it off 15 lightly?

KROGSTAD: Didn't you?

MRS. LINDE: Nils — is that what you really thought?

KROGSTAD: If you cared, then why did you write me the way you did?

MRS. LINDE: What else could I do? If I had to break off with you, then it was my job as well to root out everything you felt for me.

KROGSTAD: *(wringing his hands)* So that was it. And this — all this, simply 20 for money!

MRS. LINDE: Don't forget I had a helpless mother and two small brothers. We couldn't wait for you, Nils; you had such a long road ahead of you then.

KROGSTAD: That may be; but you still hadn't the right to abandon me for somebody else's sake.

MRS. LINDE: Yes — I don't know. So many, many times I've asked myself if I did have that right.

KROGSTAD: *(more softly)* When I lost you, it was as if all the solid ground dissolved from under my feet. Look at me; I'm a half-drowned man now, hanging onto a wreck.

MRS. LINDE: Help may be near. 25

KROGSTAD: It was near — but then you came and blocked it off.

MRS. LINDE: Without my knowing it, Nils. Today for the first time I learned that it's you I'm replacing at the bank.

KROGSTAD: All right — I believe you. But now that you know, will you step aside?

MRS. LINDE: No, because that wouldn't benefit you in the slightest.

KROGSTAD: Not "benefit" me, hm! I'd step aside anyway. 30

MRS. LINDE: I've learned to be realistic. Life and hard, bitter necessity have taught me that.

KROGSTAD: And life's taught me never to trust fine phrases.

MRS. LINDE: Then life's taught you a very sound thing. But you do have to trust in actions, don't you?

KROGSTAD: What does that mean?

35 **MRS. LINDE:**   You said you were hanging on like a half-drowned man to a wreck.

KROGSTAD: I've good reason to say that.

MRS. LINDE: I'm also like a half-drowned woman on a wreck. No one to suffer with; no one to care for.

KROGSTAD: You made your choice.

MRS. LINDE: There wasn't any choice then.

40 **KROGSTAD:**   So — what of it?

MRS. LINDE: Nils, if only we two shipwrecked people could reach across to each other.

KROGSTAD: What are you saying?

MRS. LINDE: Two on one wreck are at least better off than each on his own.

KROGSTAD: Kristine!

45 **MRS. LINDE:**   Why do you think I came into town?

KROGSTAD: Did you really have some thought of me?

MRS. LINDE: I have to work to go on living. All my born days, as long as I can remember, I've worked, and it's been my best and my only joy. But now I'm completely alone in the world; it frightens me to be so empty and lost. To work for yourself — there's no joy in that. Nils, give me something — someone to work for.

KROGSTAD: I don't believe all this. It's just some hysterical feminine urge to go out and make a noble sacrifice.

MRS. LINDE: Have you ever found me to be hysterical?

50 **KROGSTAD:**   Can you honestly mean this? Tell me — do you know everything about my past?

MRS. LINDE: Yes.

KROGSTAD: And you know what they think I'm worth around here.

MRS. LINDE: From what you were saying before, it would seem that with me you could have been another person.

KROGSTAD: I'm positive of that.

55 **MRS. LINDE:**   Couldn't it happen still?

KROGSTAD: Kristine — you're saying this in all seriousness? Yes, you are! I can see it in you. And do you really have the courage, then —?

MRS. LINDE: I need to have someone to care for; and your children need a mother. We both need each other. Nils, I have faith that you're good at heart — I'll risk everything together with you.

KROGSTAD: *(gripping her hands)* Kristine, thank you, thank you — Now I know I can win back a place in their eyes. Yes — but I forgot —

MRS. LINDE: *(listening)* Shh! The tarantella. Go now! Go on!

60 **KROGSTAD:**   Why? What is it?

MRS. LINDE: Hear the dance up there? When that's over, they'll be coming down.

KROGSTAD: Oh, then I'll go. But — it's all pointless. Of course, you don't know the move I made against the Helmers.

MRS. LINDE: Yes, Nils, I know.

KROGSTAD: And all the same, you have the courage to — ?

MRS. LINDE: I know how far despair can drive a man like you. 65

KROGSTAD: Oh, if I only could take it all back.

MRS. LINDE: You easily could — your letter's still lying in the mailbox.

KROGSTAD: Are you sure of that?

MRS. LINDE: Positive. But —

KROGSTAD: (*looks at her searchingly*) Is that the meaning of it, then? You'll save 70 your friend at any price. Tell me straight out. Is that it?

MRS. LINDE: Nils — anyone who's sold herself for somebody else once isn't going to do it again.

KROGSTAD: I'll demand my letter back.

MRS. LINDE: No, no.

KROGSTAD: Yes, of course. I'll stay here till Helmer comes down; I'll tell him to give me my letter again — that it only involves my dismissal — that he shouldn't read it —

MRS. LINDE: No, Nils, don't call the letter back. 75

KROGSTAD: But wasn't that exactly why you wrote me to come here?

MRS. LINDE: Yes, in that first panic. But it's been a whole day and night since then, and in that time I've seen such incredible things in this house. Helmer's got to learn everything; this dreadful secret has to be aired; those two have to come to a full understanding; all these lies and evasions can't go on.

KROGSTAD: Well, then, if you want to chance it. But at least there's one thing I can do, and do right away —

MRS. LINDE: (*listening*) Go now, go, quick! The dance is over. We're not safe another second.

KROGSTAD: I'll wait for you downstairs. 80

MRS. LINDE: Yes, please do; take me home.

KROGSTAD: I can't believe it; I've never been so happy. (*He leaves by way of the outer door; the door between the room and the hall stays open.*)

MRS. LINDE: (*straightening up a bit and getting together her street clothes*) How different now! How different! Someone to work for, to live for — a home to build. Well, it is worth the try! Oh, if they'd only come! (*Listening.*) Ah, there they are. Bundle up. (*She picks up her hat and coat. Nora's and Helmer's voices can be heard outside; a key turns in the lock, and Helmer brings Nora into the hall almost by force. She is wearing the Italian costume with a large black shawl about her; he has on evening dress, with a black domino open over it.*)

NORA: (*struggling in the doorway*) No, no, no, not inside! I'm going up again. I don't want to leave so soon.

HELMER: But Nora dear — 85

NORA: Oh, I beg you, please, Torvald. From the bottom of my heart, *please* — only an hour more!

HELMER: Not a single minute, Nora darling. You know our agreement. Come on, in we go; you'll catch cold out here. (*In spite of her resistance, he gently draws her into the room.*)

MRS. LINDE: Good evening.

NORA: Kristine!

90 **HELMER:** Why, Mrs. Linde — are you here so late?

MRS. LINDE: Yes, I'm sorry, but I did want to see Nora in costume.

NORA: Have you been sitting here, waiting for me?

MRS. LINDE: Yes. I didn't come early enough; you were all upstairs; and then I thought I really couldn't leave without seeing you.

HELMER: (*removing Nora's shawl*) Yes, take a good look. She's worth looking at, I can tell you that, Mrs. Linde. Isn't she lovely?

95 **MRS. LINDE:** Yes, I should say—

HELMER: A dream of loveliness, isn't she? That's what everyone thought at the party, too. But she's horribly stubborn — this sweet little thing. What's to be done with her? Can you imagine, I almost had to use force to pry her away.

NORA: Oh, Torvald, you're going to regret you didn't indulge me, even for just a half hour more.

HELMER: There, you see. She danced her tarantella and got a tumultuous hand — which was well earned, although the performance may have been a bit too naturalistic — I mean it rather overstepped the proprieties of art. But never mind — what's important is, she made a success, an overwhelming success. You think I could let her stay on after that and spoil the effect? Oh no; I took my lovely little Capri girl — my capricious little Capri girl, I should say — took her under my arm; one quick tour of the ballroom, a curtsy to every side, and then — as they say in novels — the beautiful vision disappeared. An exit should always be effective, Mrs. Linde, but that's what I can't get Nora to grasp. Phew, it's hot in here. (*Flings the domino on a chair and opens the door to his room.*) Why's it dark in here? Oh yes, of course. Excuse me. (*He goes in and lights a couple of candles.*)

NORA: (*in a sharp, breathless whisper*) So?

100 **MRS. LINDE:** (*quietly*) I talked with him.

NORA: And —?

MRS. LINDE: Nora — you must tell your husband everything.

NORA: (*dully*) I knew it.

MRS. LINDE: You've got nothing to fear from Krogstad, but you have to speak out.

105 **NORA:** I won't tell.

MRS. LINDE: Then the letter will.

NORA: Thanks, Kristine. I know now what's to be done. Shh!

HELMER: (*reentering*) Well, then, Mrs. Linde — have you admired her?

MRS. LINDE: Yes, and now I'll say good night.

110 **HELMER:** Oh, come, so soon? Is this yours, this knitting?

MRS. LINDE: Yes, thanks. I nearly forgot it.

HELMER: Do you knit, then?

MRS. LINDE: Oh yes.

HELMER: You know what? You should embroider instead.

MRS. LINDE: Really? Why? 115

HELMER: Yes, because it's a lot prettier. See here, one holds the embroidery so, in the left hand, and then one guides the needle with the right — so — in an easy, sweeping curve — right?

MRS. LINDE: Yes, I guess that's —

HELMER: But, on the other hand, knitting — it can never be anything but ugly. Look, see here, the arms tucked in, the knitting needles going up and down — there's something Chinese about it. Ah, that was really a glorious champagne they served.

MRS. LINDE: Yes, good night, Nora, and don't be stubborn any more.

HELMER: Well put, Mrs. Linde! 120

MRS. LINDE: Good night, Mr. Helmer.

HELMER: (*accompanying her to the door*) Good night, good night. I hope you get home all right. I'd be very happy to — but you don't have far to go. Good night, good night. (*She leaves. He shuts the door after her and returns.*) There, now, at last we got her out the door. She's a deadly bore, that creature.

NORA: Aren't you pretty tired, Torvald?

HELMER: No, not a bit.

NORA: You're not sleepy? 125

HELMER: Not at all. On the contrary, I'm feeling quite exhilarated. But you? Yes, you really look tired and sleepy.

NORA: Yes, I'm very tired. Soon now I'll sleep.

HELMER: See! You see! I was right all along that we shouldn't stay longer.

NORA: Whatever you do is always right.

HELMER: (*kissing her brow*) Now my little lark talks sense. Say, did you notice 130 what a time Rank was having tonight?

NORA: Oh, was he? I didn't get to speak with him.

HELMER: I scarcely did either, but it's a long time since I've seen him in such high spirits. (*Gazes at her a moment, then comes nearer her.*) Hm — it's marvelous, though, to be back home again — to be completely alone with you. Oh, you bewitchingly lovely young woman!

NORA: Torvald, don't look at me like that!

HELMER: Can't I look at my richest treasure? At all that beauty that's mine, mine alone — completely and utterly.

NORA: (*moving around to the other side of the table*) You mustn't talk to me that 135 way tonight.

HELMER: (*following her*) The tarantella is still in your blood, I can see — and it makes you even more enticing. Listen. The guests are beginning to go. (*Dropping his voice.*) Nora — it'll soon be quiet through this whole house.

NORA: Yes, I hope so.

HELMER: You do, don't you, my love? Do you realize — when I'm out at a party like this with you — do you know why I talk to you so little, and keep such a distance away; just send you a stolen look now and then — you know why I do it? It's because I'm imagining then that you're my secret darling, my secret young bride-to-be, and that no one suspects there's anything between us.

NORA: Yes, yes; oh, yes, I know you're always thinking of me.

140 HELMER: And then when we leave and I place the shawl over those fine young rounded shoulders — over that wonderful curving neck — then I pretend that you're my young bride, that we're just coming from the wedding, that for the first time I'm bringing you into my house — that for the first time I'm alone with you — completely alone with you, your trembling young beauty! All this evening I've longed for nothing but you. When I saw you turn and sway in the tarantella — my blood was pounding till I couldn't stand it — that's why I brought you down here so early —

NORA: Go away, Torvald! Leave me alone. I don't want all this.

HELMER: What do you mean? Nora, you're teasing me. You will, won't you? Aren't I your husband —?

A knock at the outside door.

NORA: (*startled*) What's that?

HELMER: (*going toward the hall*) Who is it?

145 RANK: (*outside*) It's me. May I come in a moment?

HELMER: (*with quiet irritation*) Oh, what does he want now? (*Aloud.*) Hold on. (*Goes and opens the door.*) Oh, how nice that you didn't just pass us by!

RANK: I thought I heard your voice, and then I wanted so badly to have a look in. (*Lightly glancing about.*) Ah, me, these old familiar haunts. You have it snug and cozy in here, you two.

HELMER: You seemed to be having it pretty cozy upstairs, too.

RANK: Absolutely. Why shouldn't I? Why not take in everything in life? As much as you can, anyway, and as long as you can. The wine was superb —

150 HELMER: The champagne especially.

RANK: You noticed that too? It's amazing how much I could guzzle down.

NORA: Torvald also drank a lot of champagne this evening.

RANK: Oh?

NORA: Yes, and that always makes him so entertaining.

155 RANK: Well, why shouldn't one have a pleasant evening after a well spent day?

HELMER: Well spent? I'm afraid I can't claim that.

RANK: (*slapping him on the back*) But I can, you see!

NORA: Dr. Rank, you must have done some scientific research today.

RANK: Quite so.

160 HELMER: Come now — little Nora talking about scientific research!

NORA: And can I congratulate you on the results?

RANK: Indeed you may.

In this scene Doctor Rank, Helmer, and Nora have just returned from the party; Nora is wearing her tarantella costume.

NORA: Then they were good?

RANK: The best possible for both doctor and patient — certainty.

NORA: (*quickly and searchingly*) Certainty?   165

RANK: Complete certainty. So don't I owe myself a gay evening afterwards?

NORA: Yes, you're right, Dr. Rank.

HELMER: I'm with you — just so long as you don't have to suffer for it in the morning.

RANK: Well, one never gets something for nothing in life.

NORA: Dr. Rank — are you very fond of masquerade parties?   170

RANK: Yes, if there's a good array of odd disguises —

NORA: Tell me, what should we two go as at the next masquerade?

HELMER: You little featherhead — already thinking of the next!

RANK: We two? I'll tell you what: you must go as Charmed Life —

HELMER: Yes, but find a costume for *that!*   175

RANK: Your wife can appear just as she looks every day.

HELMER: That was nicely put. But don't you know what you're going to be?

RANK: Yes, Helmer, I've made up my mind.

HELMER: Well?

RANK: At the next masquerade I'm going to be invisible.   180

HELMER: That's a funny idea.

RANK: They say there's a hat — black, huge — have you never heard of the
   hat that makes you invisible? You put it on, and then no one on earth can
   see you.
HELMER: *(suppressing a smile)* Ah, of course.
RANK: But I'm quite forgetting what I came for. Helmer, give me a cigar, one
   of the dark Havanas.
185 HELMER: With the greatest of pleasure. *(Holds out his case.)*
RANK: Thanks. *(Takes one and cuts off the tip.)*
NORA: *(striking a match)* Let me give you a light.
RANK: Thank you. *(She holds the match for him; he lights the cigar.)* And now
   good-bye.
HELMER: Good-bye, good-bye, old friend.
190 NORA: Sleep well, Doctor.
RANK: Thanks for that wish.
NORA: Wish me the same.
RANK: You? All right, if you like — Sleep well. And thanks for the light. *(He
   nods to them both and leaves.)*
HELMER: *(his voice subdued)* He's been drinking heavily.
195 NORA: *(absently)* Could be. *(Helmer takes his keys from his pocket and goes out in
   the hall.)* Torvald — what are you after?
HELMER: Got to empty the mailbox; it's nearly full. There won't be room for
   the morning papers.
NORA: Are you working tonight?
HELMER: You know I'm not. Why — what's this? Someone's been at the
   lock.
NORA: At the lock — ?
200 HELMER: Yes, I'm positive. What do you suppose — ? I can't imagine one of the
   maids — ? Here's a broken hairpin. Nora, it's yours —
NORA: *(quickly)* Then it must be the children —
HELMER: You'd better break them of that. Hm, hm — well, opened it after all.
   (Takes the contents out and calls into the kitchen.) Helene! Helene, would you
   put out the lamp in the hall. *(He returns to the room, shutting the hall door,
   then displays the handful of mail.)* Look how it's piled up. *(Sorting through
   them.)* Now what's this?
NORA: *(at the window)* The letter! Oh, Torvald, no!
HELMER: Two calling cards — from Rank.
205 NORA: From Dr. Rank?
HELMER: *(examining them)* "Dr. Rank, Consulting Physician." They were on
   top. He must have dropped them in as he left.
NORA: Is there anything on them?
HELMER: There's a black cross over the name. See? That's a gruesome notion.
   He could almost be announcing his own death.
NORA: That's just what he's doing.
210 HELMER: What! You've heard something? Something he's told you?

NORA: Yes. That when those cards came, he'd be taking his leave of us. He'll shut himself in now and die.

HELMER: Ah, my poor friend! Of course I knew he wouldn't be here much longer. But so soon — And then to hide himself away like a wounded animal.

NORA: If it has to happen, then it's best it happens in silence — don't you think so, Torvald?

HELMER: (*pacing up and down*) He'd grown right into our lives. I simply can't imagine him gone. He with his suffering and loneliness — like a dark cloud setting off our sunlit happiness. Well, maybe it's best this way. For him, at least. (*Standing still.*) And maybe for us too, Nora. Now we're thrown back on each other, completely. (*Embracing her.*) Oh you, my darling wife, how can I hold you close enough? You know what, Nora — time and again I've wished you were in some terrible danger, just so I could stake my life and soul and everything, for your sake.

NORA: (*tearing herself away, her voice firm and decisive*) Now you must read your mail, Torvald. 215

HELMER: No, no, not tonight. I want to stay with you, dearest.

NORA: With a dying friend on your mind?

HELMER: You're right. We've both had a shock. There's ugliness between us — these thoughts of death and corruption. We'll have to get free of them first. Until then — we'll stay apart.

NORA: (*clinging about his neck*) Torvald — good night! Good night!

HELMER: (*kissing her on the cheek*) Good night, little songbird. Sleep well, 220 Nora. I'll be reading my mail now. (*He takes the letters into his room and shuts the door after him.*)

NORA: (*with bewildered glances, groping about, seizing Helmer's domino, throwing it around her, and speaking in short, hoarse, broken whispers*) Never see him again. Never, never. (*Putting her shawl over her head.*) Never see the children either — them, too. Never, never. Oh, the freezing black water! The depths — down — Oh, I wish it were over — He has it now; he's reading it — now. Oh no, no, not yet. Torvald, good-bye, you and the children — (*She starts for the hall; as she does, Helmer throws open his door and stands with an open letter in his hand.*)

HELMER: Nora!

NORA: (*screams*) Oh —!

HELMER: What is this? You know what's in this letter?

NORA: Yes, I know. Let me go! Let me out! 225

HELMER: (*holding her back*) Where are you going?

NORA: (*struggling to break loose*) You can't save me, Torvald!

HELMER: (*slumping back*) True! Then it's true what he writes? How horrible! No, no, it's impossible — it can't be true.

NORA: It *is* true. I've loved you more than all this world.

HELMER: Ah, none of your slippery tricks. 230

NORA: *(taking one step toward him)* Torvald —!

HELMER: What *is* this you've blundered into!

NORA: Just let me loose. You're not going to suffer for my sake. You're not going to take on my guilt.

HELMER: No more playacting. *(Locks the hall door.)* You stay right here and give me a reckoning. You understand what you've done? Answer! You understand?

235 NORA: *(looking squarely at him, her face hardening)* Yes. I'm beginning to understand everything now.

HELMER: *(striding about)* Oh, what an awful awakening! In all these eight years — she who was my pride and joy — a hypocrite, a liar — worse, worse — a criminal! How infinitely disgusting it all is! The shame! *(Nora says nothing and goes on looking straight at him. He stops in front of her.)* I should have suspected something of the kind. I should have known. All your father's flimsy values — Be still! All your father's flimsy values have come out in you. No religion, no morals, no sense of duty — Oh, how I'm punished for letting him off! I did it for your sake, and you repay me like this.

NORA: Yes, like this.

HELMER: Now you've wrecked all my happiness — ruined my whole future. Oh, it's awful to think of. I'm in a cheap little grafter's hands; he can do anything he wants with me, ask for anything, play with me like a puppet — and I can't breathe a word. I'll be swept down miserably into the depths on account of a featherbrained woman.

NORA: When I'm gone from this world, you'll be free.

240 HELMER: Oh, quit posing. Your father had a mess of those speeches too. What good would that ever do me if you were gone from this world, as you say? Not the slightest. He can still make the whole thing known; and if he does, I could be falsely suspected as your accomplice. They might even think that I was behind it — that I put you up to it. And all that I can thank you for — you that I've coddled the whole of our marriage. Can you see now what you've done to me?

NORA: *(icily calm)* Yes.

HELMER: It's so incredible, I just can't grasp it. But we'll have to patch up whatever we can. Take off the shawl. I said, take if off! I've got to appease him somehow or other. The thing has to be hushed up at any cost. And as for you and me, it's got to seem like everything between us is just as it was — to the outside world, that is. You'll go right on living in this house, of course. But you can't be allowed to bring up the children; I don't dare trust you with them — Oh, to have to say this to someone I've loved so much! Well, that's done with. From now on happiness doesn't matter; all that matters is saving the bits and pieces, the appearance — *(The doorbell rings. Helmer starts.)* What's that? And so late. Maybe the worst —? You think he'd —? Hide, Nora! Say you're sick. *(Nora remains standing motionless. Helmer goes and opens the door.)*

MAID: *(half dressed, in the hall)* A letter for Mrs. Helmer.

HELMER: I'll take it. (*Snatches the letter and shuts the door.*) Yes, it's from him. You don't get it; I'm reading it myself.

NORA: Then read it.   245

HELMER: (*by the lamp*) I hardly dare. We may be ruined, you and I. But — I've got to know. (*Rips open the letter, skims through a few lines, glances at an enclosure, then cries out joyfully.*) Nora! (*Nora looks inquiringly at him.*) Nora! Wait — better check it again — Yes, yes, it's true. I'm saved. Nora, I'm saved!

NORA: And I?

HELMER: You too, of course. We're both saved, both of us. Look. He's sent back your note. He says he's sorry and ashamed — that a happy development in his life — oh, who cares what he says! Nora, we're saved! No one can hurt you. Oh, Nora, Nora — but first, this ugliness all has to go. Let me see — (*Takes a look at the note.*) No, I don't want to see it; I want the whole thing to fade like a dream. (*Tears the note and both letters to pieces, throws them into the stove and watches them burn.*) There — now there's nothing left — He wrote that since Christmas Eve you — Oh, they must have been three terrible days for you, Nora.

NORA: I fought a hard fight.

HELMER: And suffered pain and saw no escape but — No, we're not going to   250
dwell on anything unpleasant. We'll just be grateful and keep on repeating: it's over now, it's over! You hear me, Nora? You don't seem to realize — it's over. What's it mean — that frozen look? Oh, poor little Nora, I understand. You can't believe I've forgiven you. But I have, Nora; I swear I have. I know that what you did, you did out of love for me.

NORA: That's true.

HELMER: You loved me the way a wife ought to love her husband. It's simply the means that you couldn't judge. But you think I love you any the less for not knowing how to handle your affairs? No, no — just lean on me; I'll guide you and teach you. I wouldn't be a man if this feminine helplessness didn't make you twice as attractive to me. You mustn't mind those sharp words I said — that was all in the first confusion of thinking my world had collapsed. I've forgiven you, Nora; I swear I've forgiven you.

NORA: My thanks for your forgiveness. (*She goes out through the door, right.*)

HELMER: No, wait — (*Peers in.*) What are you doing in there?

NORA: (*inside*) Getting out of my costume.   255

HELMER: (*by the open door*) Yes, do that. Try to calm yourself and collect your thoughts again, my frightened little songbird. You can rest easy now; I've got wide wings to shelter you with. (*Walking about close by the door.*) How snug and nice our home is, Nora. You're safe here; I'll keep you like a hunted dove I've rescued out of a hawk's claws. I'll bring peace to your poor, shuddering heart. Gradually it'll happen, Nora; you'll see. Tomorrow all this will look different to you; then everything will be as it was. I won't have to go on repeating I forgive you; you'll feel it for yourself. How can you imagine I'd ever conceivably want to disown you — or even blame you in any way? Ah, you don't know a man's heart, Nora. For a man there's something indescribably sweet and satisfying in knowing he's forgiven his wife — and forgiven her out of a full and open heart. It's as if she belongs to him in two ways now: in a sense he's given her fresh into the world again, and she's become his wife and his child as well. From now on that's what you'll be to me — you little, bewildered, helpless thing. Don't be afraid of anything, Nora; just open your heart to me, and I'll be conscience and will to you both —(*Nora enters in her regular clothes.*) What's this? Not in bed? You've changed your dress?

NORA: Yes, Torvald, I've changed my dress.

HELMER: But why now, so late?

NORA: Tonight I'm not sleeping.

260 HELMER: But Nora dear—

NORA: (*looking at her watch*) It's still not so very late. Sit down, Torvald; we have a lot to talk over. (*She sits at one side of the table.*)

HELMER: Nora — what is this? That hard expression—

NORA: Sit down. This'll take some time. I have a lot to say.

HELMER: (*sitting at the table directly opposite her*) You worry me, Nora. And I don't understand you.

265 NORA: No, that's exactly it. You don't understand me. And I've never understood you either — until tonight. No, don't interrupt. You can just listen to what I say. We're closing out accounts, Torvald.

HELMER: How do you mean that?

NORA: (*after a short pause*) Doesn't anything strike you about our sitting here like this?

HELMER: What's that?

NORA: We've been married now eight years. Doesn't it occur to you that this is the first time we two, you and I, man and wife, have ever talked seriously together?

270 HELMER: What do you mean — seriously?

NORA: In eight whole years —longer even — right from our first acquaintance, we've never exchanged a serious word on any serious thing.

HELMER: You mean I should constantly go and involve you in problems you couldn't possibly help me with?

NORA: I'm not talking of problems. I'm saying that we've never sat down seriously together and tried to get to the bottom of anything.

HELMER: But dearest, what good would that ever do you?

275 NORA: That's the point right there: you've never understood me. I've been wronged greatly, Torvald —first by Papa, and then by you.

HELMER: What! By us — the two people who've loved you more than anyone else?

NORA: (*shaking her head*) You never loved me. You've thought it fun to be in love with me, that's all.

HELMER: Nora, what a thing to say!

NORA: Yes, it's true now, Torvald. When I lived at home with Papa, he told me all his opinions, so I had the same ones too; or if they were different

I hid them, since he wouldn't have cared for that. He used to call me his doll-child, and he played with me the way I played with my dolls. Then I came into your house—

HELMER: How can you speak of our marriage like that? 280

NORA: *(unperturbed)* I mean, then I went from Papa's hands into yours. You arranged everything to your own taste, and so I got the same taste as you — or I pretended to; I can't remember. I guess a little of both, first one, then the other. Now when I look back, it seems as if I'd lived here like a beggar—just from hand to mouth. I've lived by doing tricks for you, Torvald. But that's the way you wanted it. It's a great sin what you and Papa did to me. You're to blame that nothing's become of me.

HELMER: Nora, how unfair and ungrateful you are! Haven't you been happy here?

NORA: No, never. I thought so — but I never have.

HELMER: Not — not happy!

NORA: No, only lighthearted. And you've always been so kind to me. But our 285
home's been nothing but a playpen. I've been your doll-wife here, just as at home I was Papa's doll-child. And in turn the children have been my dolls. I thought it was fun when you played with me, just as they thought it fun when I played with them. That's been our marriage, Torvald.

HELMER: There's some truth in what you're saying — under all the raving exaggeration. But it'll all be different after this. Playtime's over; now for the schooling.

NORA: Whose schooling — mine or the children's?

HELMER: Both yours and the children's, dearest.

NORA: Oh, Torvald, you're not the man to teach me to be a good wife to you.

HELMER: And you can say that? 290

NORA: And I — how am I equipped to bring up children?

HELMER: Nora!

NORA: Didn't you say a moment ago that that was no job to trust me with?

HELMER: In a flare of temper! Why fasten on that?

NORA: Yes, but you were so very right. I'm not up to the job. There's another 295
job I have to do first. I have to try to educate myself. You can't help me with that. I've got to do it alone. And that's why I'm leaving you now.

HELMER: *(jumping up)* What's that?

NORA: I have to stand completely alone, if I'm ever going to discover myself and the world out there. So I can't go on living with you.

HELMER: Nora, Nora!

NORA: I want to leave right away. Kristine should put me up for the night—

HELMER: You're insane! You've no right! I forbid you! 300

NORA: From here on, there's no use forbidding me anything. I'll take with me whatever is mine. I don't want a thing from you, either now or later.

HELMER: What kind of madness is this!

NORA: Tomorrow I'm going home — I mean, home where I came from. It'll be easier up there to find something to do.

HELMER: Oh, you blind, incompetent child!

305   **Nora:** I must learn to be competent, Torvald.

      Helmer: Abandon your home, your husband, your children! And you're not even thinking what people will say.

      Nora: I can't be concerned about that. I only know how essential this is.

      Helmer: Oh, it's outrageous. So you'll run out like this on your most sacred vows.

      Nora: What do you think are my most sacred vows?

310   **Helmer:** And I have to tell you that! Aren't they your duties to your husband and children?

      Nora: I have other duties equally sacred.

      Helmer: That isn't true. What duties are they?

      Nora: Duties to myself.

      Helmer: Before all else, you're a wife and a mother.

315   **Nora:** I don't believe in that any more. I believe that, before all else, I'm a human being, no less than you — or anyway, I ought to try to become one. I know the majority thinks you're right, Torvald, and plenty of books agree with you, too. But I can't go on believing what the majority says, or what's written in books. I have to think over these things myself and try to understand them.

      Helmer: Why can't you understand your place in your own home? On a point like that, isn't there one everlasting guide you can turn to? Where's your religion?

      Nora: Oh, Torvald, I'm really not sure what religion is.

      Helmer: What —?

      Nora: I only know what the minister said when I was confirmed. He told me religion was this thing and that. When I get clear and away by myself, I'll go into that problem too. I'll see if what the minister said was right, or, in any case, if it's right for me.

320   **Helmer:** A young woman your age shouldn't talk like that. If religion can't move you, I can try to rouse your conscience. You do have some moral feeling? Or, tell me — has that gone too?

      Nora: It's not easy to answer that, Torvald. I simply don't know. I'm all confused about these things. I just know I see them so differently from you. I find out, for one thing, that the law's not at all what I'd thought — but I can't get it through my head that the law is fair. A woman hasn't a right to protect her dying father or save her husband's life! I can't believe that.

      Helmer: You talk like a child. You don't know anything of the world you live in.

      Nora: No, I don't. But now I'll begin to learn for myself. I'll try to discover who's right, the world or I.

      Helmer: Nora, you're sick; you've got a fever. I almost think you're out of your head.

325   **Nora:** I've never felt more clearheaded and sure in my life.

      Helmer: And — clearheaded and sure — you're leaving your husband and children?

      Nora: Yes.

      Helmer: Then there's only one possible reason.

      Nora: What?

HELMER: You no longer love me. 330
NORA: No. That's exactly it.
HELMER: Nora! You can't be serious!
NORA: Oh, this is so hard, Torvald — you've been so kind to me always. But I can't help it. I don't love you any more.
HELMER: (*struggling for composure*) Are you also clearheaded and sure about that?
NORA: Yes, completely. That's why I can't go on staying here. 335
HELMER: Can you tell me what I did to lose your love?
NORA: Yes, I can tell you. It was this evening when the miraculous thing didn't come — then I knew you weren't the man I'd imagined.
HELMER: Be more explicit; I don't follow you.
NORA: I've waited now so patiently eight long years — for, my Lord, I know miracles don't come every day. Then this crisis broke over me, and such a certainty filled me: *now* the miraculous event would occur. While Krogstad's letter was lying out there, I never for an instant dreamed that you could give in to his terms. I was so utterly sure you'd say to him: go on, tell your tale to the whole wide world. And when he'd done that —
HELMER: Yes, what then? When I'd delivered my own wife into shame and 340
disgrace — !
NORA: When he'd done that, I was so utterly sure that you'd step forward, take the blame on yourself and say: I am the guilty one.
HELMER: Nora — !
NORA: You're thinking I'd never accept such a sacrifice from you? No, of course not. But what good would my protests be against you? That was the miracle I was waiting for, in terror and hope. And to stave that off, I would have taken my life.
HELMER: I'd gladly work for you day and night, Nora — and take on pain and deprivation. But there's no one who gives up honor for love.
NORA: Millions of women have done just that. 345
HELMER: Oh, you think and talk like a silly child.
NORA: Perhaps. But you neither think nor talk like the man I could join my-self to. When your big fright was over — and it wasn't from any threat against me, only for what might damage you — when all the danger was past, for you it was just as if nothing had happened. I was exactly the same, your little lark, your doll, that you'd have to handle with double care now that I'd turned out so brittle and frail. (*Gets up.*) Torvald — in that instant it dawned on me that for eight years I've been living here with a stranger, and that I'd even conceived three children — oh, I can't stand the thought of it! I could tear myself to bits.
HELMER: (*heavily*) I see. There's a gulf that's opened between us — that's clear. Oh, but Nora, can't we bridge it somehow?
NORA: The way I am now, I'm no wife for you.
HELMER: I have the strength to make myself over. 350

NORA: Maybe — if your doll gets taken away.

HELMER: But to part! To part from you! No, Nora, no — I can't imagine it.

NORA: *(going out, right)* All the more reason why it has to be. *(She reenters with her coat and a small overnight bag, which she puts on a chair by the table.)*

HELMER: Nora, Nora, not now! Wait till tomorrow.

NORA: I can't spend the night in a strange man's room.

355 **HELMER:** But couldn't we live here like brother and sister —

NORA: You know very well how long that would last. *(Throws her shawl about her.)* Good-bye, Torvald. I won't look in on the children. I know they're in better hands than mine. The way I am now, I'm no use to them.

HELMER: But someday, Nora — someday —?

NORA: How can I tell? I haven't the least idea what'll become of me.

HELMER: But you're my wife, now and wherever you go.

360 **NORA:** Listen, Torvald — I've heard that when a wife deserts her husband's house just as I'm doing, then the law frees him from all responsibility. In any case, I'm freeing you from being responsible. Don't feel yourself bound, any more than I will. There has to be absolute freedom for us both. Here, take your ring back. Give me mine.

HELMER: That too?

NORA: That too.

HELMER: There it is.

365 **NORA:** Good. Well, now it's all over. I'm putting the keys here. The maids know all about keeping up the house — better than I do. Tomorrow, after I've left town, Kristine will stop by to pack up everything that's mine from home. I'd like those things shipped up to me.

HELMER: Over! All over! Nora, won't you ever think about me?

NORA: I'm sure I'll think of you often, and about the children and the house here.

HELMER: May I write you?

NORA: No — never. You're not to do that.

370 **HELMER:** Oh, but let me send you —

NORA: Nothing. Nothing.

HELMER: Or help you if you need it.

NORA: No. I accept nothing from strangers.

HELMER: Nora — can I never be more than a stranger to you?

375 **NORA:** *(picking up the overnight bag)* Ah, Torvald — it would take the greatest miracle of all —

HELMER: Tell me the greatest miracle!

NORA: You and I both would have to transform ourselves to the point that — Oh, Torvald, I've stopped believing in miracles.

HELMER: But I'll believe. Tell me! Transform ourselves to the point that —?

NORA: That our living together could be a true marriage. *(She goes out down the hall.)*

HELMER: *(sinks down on a chair by the door, face buried in his hands)* Nora! Nora! 380
(Looking about and rising.) Empty. She's gone. *(A sudden hope leaps in him.)*
The greatest miracle —?

From below, the sound of a door slamming shut.

Reading and Reacting

1. What is your attitude toward Nora at the beginning of the play? How does your attitude toward her change as the play progresses? What actions and lines of dialogue change your assessment of her?

2. List the key events that have occurred before the start of the play. How do we learn of each event?

4. Explain the role of each of the following in advancing the play's action: the Christmas tree, the locked mailbox, the telegram Dr. Rank receives, Dr. Rank's calling cards.

5. In act 2, Torvald says, "Whatever comes, you'll see: when it really counts, I have strength and courage enough as a man to take on the whole weight myself." How does this statement influence Nora's subsequent actions?

6. How do the upcoming costume party and Nora's dance influence the development of the play's plot?

7. Explain how each of the following foreshadows events that will occur later in the play: Torvald's comments about Krogstad's children (act 1); Torvald's attitude toward Nora's father (act 2); Krogstad's suggestions about suicide (act 2).

8. In addition to the play's main plot — which concerns the blackmail of Nora by Krogstad and her attempts to keep her crime secret from Torvald — the play contains several subplots. Some of them began to develop before the start of the play, and some unfold alongside the main plot. Identify these subplots. How do they advance the themes of survival, debt, sacrifice, and duty that run through the play?

9. Is Kristine Linde as much of a "modern woman" as Nora? Is she actually *more* of a modern woman? Explain.

10. Is Mrs. Linde essential to the play? How might the play be different without her?

11. Do you think *A Doll House* is primarily about the struggle between the needs of the individual and the needs of society, or about the conflict between women's roles in the family and in the larger society? Explain.

12. JOURNAL ENTRY Nora makes a drastic decision at the end of the play. Do you think she overreacts? What other options does she have? What other options might she have today?

13. CRITICAL PERSPECTIVE Since its earliest performances, there has been much comment on the conclusion of *A Doll House*. Many viewers have found the play's ending unrealistically harsh. In fact, a famous German actress refused to play the scene as written because she insisted she would never leave her children. (Ibsen reluctantly rewrote the ending for her; in this version, Helmer forces Nora to the doorway of the children's bedroom, and she sinks to the floor as the curtain falls.) Moreover, many critics have found it hard to accept Nora's sudden transformation from, in the words of Elizabeth Hardwick in her essay "Ibsen's Women," "the girlish, charming wife to the radical, courageous heroine setting out alone."

What is your response to the play's ending? Do you think it makes sense in light of what we have learned about Nora and her marriage? Or do you agree with Hardwick that Nora's abandonment of her children is not only implausible but also a "rather casual" gesture that "drops a stain on our admiration of Nora"?

Related Works: "The Story of an Hour" (p. 104), "The Yellow Wallpaper" (p. 372), "The Rocking-Horse Winner" (p. 340), "Barbie Doll" (p. 689), *The Stronger* (p. 853)

WRITING SUGGESTIONS: Plot

1. Central to the plots of both *Trifles* and *A Doll House* is a woman who commits a crime. Compare and contrast the desperate situations that motivate the two women. Then, consider the parallels and contrasts between the reactions of other characters in the two plays to each woman's crime. If you like, you may also discuss the crime committed by Emily Grierson in "A Rose for Emily" (p. 113).

2. Write an essay in which you discuss the influence of Nora's father on the plot of *A Doll House*.

3. Write a monologue for Nora in *A Doll House*, including everything you think she would like to tell her children. Or, write a monologue for Mrs. Wright in *Trifles* in which she describes her marriage and explains the motivation for her crime.

4. Write an essay in which you identify the "trifles" that are important in this chapter's two plays. Consider what these "trifles" contribute to each play and how each play would be different without them.

CHARACTER

A sensible playwright would write a play with three or four people.
Three is best. A man and his dog is even better.

—Tom Stoppard

In Tennessee Williams's 1945 play *The Glass Menagerie* (p. 1153), the protagonist, Tom Wingfield, functions as the play's narrator. Stepping out of his role as a character and speaking directly to the audience, he directs the play's action, music, lighting, and other elements. In addition, he summarizes characters' actions, explains what motivates them, and discusses the significance of their behavior in the context of the play — commenting on his own character's actions as well. As narrator, Tom also presents useful background information about the characters. For instance, when he introduces his coworker, Jim, he prepares the audience for Jim's entrance and helps them to understand his subsequent actions:

> In high school Jim was a hero. He had tremendous Irish good nature and vitality with the scrubbed and polished look of white chinaware. He seemed to move in a continual spotlight. . . . But Jim apparently ran into more interference after his graduation. . . . His speed had definitely slowed. Six years after he left high school he was holding a job that wasn't much better than mine. (scene 6)

Most plays, however, do not include narrators who present background. Instead, the audience learns about characters from their own words and from comments by others about them, as well as from the characters' actions and from the playwright's stage directions. Also, at a performance, the audience gains insight into characters from the way actors interpret them.

Characters in plays, like characters in novels and short stories, may be **round** or **flat, static,** or **dynamic.** Generally speaking, major characters are likely to be round, whereas minor characters are likely to be flat. Through the language and the actions of the characters, audiences learn whether the characters are multidimensional, skimpily developed, or perhaps merely **foils,** players whose main purpose is to shed light on more important characters. Audiences also learn about the emotions, attitudes, and values that help to shape the characters — their hopes

841

and fears, their strengths and weaknesses. In addition, by comparing characters' early words and actions with later ones, audiences learn from the play whether or not characters grow and change emotionally.

Characters' Words

Characters' words reveal the most about their attitudes, feelings, beliefs, and values. Sometimes information is communicated (to other characters as well as to the audience) in a **monologue**—an extended speech by one character. This device is used throughout August Strindberg's *The Stronger* (p. 853). A **soliloquy**—a monologue revealing a character's thoughts and feelings, directed at the audience and presumed not to be heard by other characters—can also convey information about a character. For example, Hamlet's well-known soliloquy that begins "To be or not to be" eloquently communicates his distraught mental state—his resentment of his mother and uncle, his confusion about what course of action to take, and his suicidal thoughts. Finally, **dialogue**—an exchange of words between two characters—can reveal misunderstanding or conflict between them, or it can show their agreement, mutual support, or similar beliefs.

In Henrik Ibsen's *A Doll House* (p. 784), dialogue reveals a good deal about the characters. Nora Helmer, the spoiled young wife, has broken the law and kept her crime secret from her husband. Through her words, we learn about her motivation, her values, her emotions, and her reactions to other characters and to her potentially dangerous situation. We learn, for instance, that she is flirtatious—"If your little squirrel begged you, with all her heart and soul . . ."—and that she is childishly unrealistic about the consequences of her actions. When her husband, Torvald, asks what she would do if he was seriously injured, leaving her in debt, she says, "If anything so awful happened, then it just wouldn't matter if I had debts or not." When Torvald presses, "Well, but the people I'd borrowed from?" she dismisses them: "Them? Who cares about them! They're strangers." As the play progresses, Nora's lack of understanding of the power of the law becomes more and more significant as she struggles with her moral and ethical dilemma.

The inability of both Nora and Torvald to confront ugly truths is also revealed through their words. When, in act 1, Nora tells Krogstad, her blackmailer, that his revealing her secret could expose her to "the most horrible unpleasantness," he responds, "Only unpleasantness?" Yet later on, in act 3, Torvald echoes her language, fastidiously dismissing the horror with, "No, we're not going to dwell on anything unpleasant."

The ease with which Torvald is able to dismiss his dying friend Dr. Rank in act 3 ("He with his suffering and loneliness—like a dark cloud setting off our sunlit happiness. Well, maybe it's best this way.") foreshadows the lack of support he will give Nora immediately thereafter. Especially revealing is his use of *I* and *my* and *me*, which convey his self-centeredness:

Now you've wrecked all my happiness — ruined my whole future. Oh, it's awful to think of. I'm in a cheap little grafter's hands; he can do anything he wants with me, ask for anything, play with me like a puppet — and I can't breathe a word. I'll be swept down miserably into the depths on account of a featherbrained woman.

Just as Torvald's words reveal that he has not been changed by the play's events, Nora's words show that she has changed significantly. Her dialogue near the end of act 3 shows that she has become a responsible, determined woman — one who understands her situation and her options and is no longer blithely oblivious to her duties. When she says, "I've never felt more clearheaded and sure in my life," she is calm and decisive. When she says, "Our home's been nothing but a playpen. I've been your doll-wife here, just as at home I was Papa's doll-child," she reveals a new self-awareness. And, when she confronts her husband, she displays — perhaps for the first time in their relationship — complete honesty.

Sometimes what other characters say to (or about) a character can reveal more to an audience than the character's own words. For instance, in *A Doll House*, when the dying Dr. Rank says, apparently without malice, "[Torvald] Helmer with his sensitivity has such a sharp distaste for anything ugly," the audience not only thinks ill of the man who is too "sensitive" to visit his sick friend but also questions his ability to withstand situations that may be emotionally or morally "ugly" as well.

When a character is offstage for much (or even all) of the action, the audience must rely on other characters' assessments of the absent character. In Susan Glaspell's *Trifles* (p. 770), the play's focus is on an absent character, Minnie Wright, who is described solely through other characters' remarks. The evidence suggests that Mrs. Wright killed her husband, and only Mrs. Hale's and Mrs. Peters's comments about Mrs. Wright's dreary life can delineate her character and suggest a likely motive for the murder. Although Mrs. Wright never appears on stage, we learn essential information from the other women about her: that as a young girl she liked to sing and that more recently she was so distraught about the lack of beauty in her life that even her sewing revealed her distress. Similarly, the father in *The Glass Menagerie* never appears (and therefore never speaks), but the play's other characters describe him as "A telephone man who — fell in love with long-distance!" — the absent husband and father who symbolizes abandonment and instability to Laura and Amanda and the possibility of freedom and escape to Tom.

Whether a character's words are in the form of a monologue, a soliloquy, or dialogue, and whether they reveal information about the character who is speaking or about someone else, such words are always revealing. Explicitly or implicitly, they convey a character's nature, attitudes, and relationships with other characters.

The language characters use can vary widely. A character may, for instance, use learned words, foreign words, elaborate figures of speech, irony or sarcasm, regionalisms, slang, jargon, clichés, or profanity. Words can also be used to indicate tone — for example, to express irony. Any of these uses of language may communicate vital information to the audience about a character's background, attitudes, and motivation. And, of course, a character's language may change as a play progresses, and this change too may be revealing.

Formal and Informal Language

One character in a dramatic work may speak very formally, using absolutely correct grammar, a learned vocabulary, and long, complex sentences; another may speak in an informal style, using conversational speech, colloquialisms, and slang. At times, two characters with different levels of language may be set in opposition for dramatic effect, as they are in Irish playwright George Bernard Shaw's classic play *Pygmalion* (1912), which updates the ancient Greek myth of a sculptor who creates (and falls in love with) a statue of a woman. In Shaw's version, a linguistics professor sets out to teach "proper" speech and manners to a lowly flower seller. Throughout the play, the contrasting language of Henry Higgins, the professor, and Eliza Doolittle, the flower seller, indicates their differing social standing. The following exchange illustrates this contrast:

LIZA: I ain't got no mother. Her that turned me out was my sixth stepmother.
   But I done without them. And I'm a good girl, I am.
HIGGINS: Very well, then, what on earth is all this fuss about?

A character's accent or dialect may also be significant. In **comedies of manners,** for instance, rustic or provincial characters, identified by their speech, are often objects of humor. In *Pygmalion,* Eliza Doolittle uses cockney dialect, the dialect spoken in the East End of London. At first, her colorful, distinctive language (complete with expressions like *Nah-ow, garn,* and *ah-ah-ah-ow-ow-ow-oo*) and her nonstandard grammatical constructions make her an object of ridicule; later, the transformation of her speech reveals the dramatic changes in her character.

Plain and Elaborate Language

A character's speech may be simple and straightforward or complex and convoluted; it may be plain and unadorned or embellished with elaborate **figures of speech.** The relative complexity or lack of complexity of a character's speech may have different effects on the audience. For example, a character whose language is simple and unsophisticated may seem to be unintelligent, unenlightened, gullible, or naive — especially if he or she also uses slang, dialect, or colloquial expressions. Conversely, a character's plain, down-to-earth language may convey common sense or intelligence. Plain language may also be quite emotionally powerful. Thus, Willy Loman's speech in act 2 of *Death of a Salesman* (p. 858), about an eighty-four-year-old salesman named Dave Singleman, moves the audience with its sincerity and directness:

Do you know? When he died — and by the way he died the death of a
salesman, in his green velvet slippers in the smoker of the New York,
New Haven and Hartford, going into Boston — when he died, hundreds
of salesmen and buyers were at his funeral. Things were sad on a lotta trains
for months after that.

Like plain speech, elaborate language may have different effects in different
contexts. Sometimes, use of figures of speech can make a character seem to have
depth and insight and analytical skills absent in other characters. In the following
excerpt from a soliloquy in act 1 scene 2 of *Hamlet,* for example, complex language reveals the depth of Hamlet's anguished self-analysis:

HAMLET: O, that this too too solid flesh would melt,
Thaw, and resolve itself into a dew!
Or that the Everlasting had not fix'd
His canon 'gainst self-slaughter! O God! O God!
How weary, stale, flat, and unprofitable
Seem to me all the uses of this world!
Fie on't, O fie, 'tis an unweeded garden,
That grows to seed. . . .

In these lines, Hamlet compares the world to a garden gone to seed. His use of imagery and figures of speech vividly communicates his feelings about the world and
his internal struggle against the temptation to commit suicide.

Sometimes, however, elaborate language may make a character seem aloof,
pompous, or even untrustworthy. In the following passages from Shakespeare's
King Lear, Goneril and Regan, the deceitful daughters, use complicated verbal constructions to conceal their true feelings from their father, King Lear. Cordelia — the loyal, loving daughter — uses simple, straightforward language that
suggests her sincerity and lack of artifice. Compare the three speeches:

GONERIL: Sir, I love you more than words can wield the matter;
Dearer than eyesight, space, and liberty;
Beyond what can be valued, rich or rare;
No less than life, with grace, health, beauty, honour;
As much as child e'er lov'd, or father found;
A love that makes breath poor, and speech unable.
Beyond all manner of so much I love you. . . .
REGAN: Sir, I am made
Of the selfsame metal that my sister is,
And prize me at her worth. In my true heart
I find she names my very deed of love;
Only she comes too short, that I profess
Myself an enemy to all other joys
Which the most precious square of sense possesses,

And find I am alone felicitate
In your dear Highness' love. . . .
CORDELIA: Unhappy that I am, I cannot heave
My heart into my mouth. I love your Majesty
According to my bond; no more no less. . . .

Cordelia's unwillingness, even when she is prodded by Lear, to exaggerate her feelings or misrepresent her love through inflated language shows the audience her honesty and nobility. The contrast between her language and that of her sisters makes their very different motives clear to the audience.

Tone

Tone reveals a character's mood or attitude. Tone can be flat or emotional, bitter or accepting, affectionate or aloof, anxious or calm. Contrasts in tone can indicate differences in outlook or emotional state between two characters; changes in tone from one point in a play to another can suggest corresponding changes within a character. At the end of *A Doll House*, for instance, Nora is resigned to what she must do, and her language is appropriately controlled. Her husband, however, is desperate to change her mind, and his language reflects this desperation. The following exchanges from act 3 of the play illustrate their contrasting emotional states:

HELMER: But to part! To part from you! No, Nora, no — I can't imagine it.
NORA: (*going out, right*) All the more reason why it has to be.
HELMER: Over! All over! Nora, won't you ever think about me?
NORA: I'm sure I'll think of you often, and about the children and the
house here.

In earlier scenes between the two characters, Nora is emotional — at times, hysterical — and her husband is considerably more controlled. As the above exchange indicates, both Nora and Torvald Helmer change drastically during the course of the play.

Irony

Irony, a contradiction or discrepancy between two different levels of meaning, can reveal a great deal about character. **Verbal irony**— a contradiction between what a character says and what he or she means — is very important in drama, where the verbal interplay between characters may carry the weight of the play. For example, when Nora and Dr. Rank discuss the latest news about his health in *A Doll House*, there is deep irony in his use of the phrase "complete certainty." Although the phrase usually suggests reassuring news, here it is meant to suggest death, and both Nora and Dr. Rank understand this.

Dramatic irony depends on the audience's knowing something that a character has not yet realized, or on one character's knowing something that other characters do not know. In some cases, dramatic irony is created by an audience's awareness of historical background or events of which characters are unaware. Familiar with the story of Oedipus, for instance, the audience knows that the man who has caused all the problems in Thebes — the man Oedipus vows to find and take revenge on — is Oedipus himself. In other cases, dramatic irony emerges when the audience learns something — something the characters do not yet know or comprehend — from a play's unfolding action. The central irony in *A Doll House*, for example, is that the family's "happy home" rests on a foundation of secrets, lies, and deception. Torvald does not know about the secrets, and Nora does not understand how they have poisoned her marriage. The audience, however, quickly becomes aware of the atmosphere of deceit — and aware of how it threatens the family's happiness.

Dramatic irony may also be conveyed through dialogue. Typically, dramatic irony is revealed when a character says something that gives the audience information that other characters, offstage at the time, do not know. In *A Doll House*, the audience knows — because Nora has explained her situation to Kristine — that Nora spent the previous Christmas season hard at work, earning money to pay her secret debt. Torvald, however, remains unaware of her activities and believes her story that she was using the time to make holiday decorations, which the cat destroyed. This belief is consistent with his impression of Nora as an irresponsible child, yet the audience has quite a different impression of her. This discrepancy, one of many contradictions between the audience's view of Nora and Torvald's view of her, helps to create dramatic tension in the play.

Finally, **asides** (comments to the audience that other characters do not hear) can create dramatic irony by undercutting dialogue, providing ironic contrast between what the characters on stage know and what the audience knows. In Anton Chekhov's *The Brute* (p. 723), for example, the audience knows that Mr. Smirnov is succumbing to Mrs. Popov's charms because he says, in an aside, "My God, what eyes she has! They're setting me on fire." Mrs. Popov, however, is not yet aware of his infatuation. The discrepancy between the audience's awareness and the character's adds to the play's humor.

Characters' Actions

Through their actions, characters convey their values and attitudes to the audience. Actions also reveal aspects of a character's personality. When Laura Wingfield, a character in *The Glass Menagerie*, hides rather than face the "gentleman caller," audiences see how shy she is; when Nora in *A Doll House* plays hide-and-seek with her children, eats forbidden macaroons, and takes childish joy in Christmas, her immaturity is apparent.

Audiences also learn about characters from what they do *not* do. Thus, Nora's failure to remain in touch with her friend Kristine, who has had a hard life, reveals her selfishness, and the failure of Mrs. Peters and Mrs. Hale in *Trifles* to give their evidence to the sheriff indicates their support for Mrs. Wright and their understanding of what motivated her to take such drastic action.

Audiences also learn a good deal about characters by observing how they interact with other characters. In William Shakespeare's *Othello*, Iago is the embodiment of evil, and as the play's action unfolds, we discover his true nature. He reveals the secret marriage of Othello and Desdemona to her father; he schemes to arouse Othello's jealousy, making him believe Desdemona has been unfaithful with his lieutenant, Cassio; he persuades Cassio to ask Desdemona to plead his case with Othello, knowing this act will further arouse Othello's suspicions; he encourages Othello to be suspicious of Desdemona's defense of Cassio; he plants Desdemona's handkerchief in Cassio's room; and, finally, he persuades Othello to kill Desdemona and then kills his own wife, Emilia, to prevent her from exposing his role in the intrigue. As the play progresses, then, Iago's dealings with others consistently reveal him to be evil and corrupt.

Stage Directions

When we read a play, we also read the playwright's italicized **stage directions,** the notes that concern **staging**— the scenery, props, lighting, music, sound effects, costumes, and other elements that contribute to the way the play looks and sounds to an audience (see Chapter 29). In addition to commenting on staging, stage directions may supply physical details about the characters, suggesting their age, appearance, movements, gestures, and facial expressions. These details may in turn convey additional information about characters: appearance may reveal social position or economic status, expressions may reveal attitudes, and so on. Stage directions may also indicate the manner in which a line of dialogue is to be delivered —*haltingly, confidently, hesitantly,* or *loudly,* for instance. The way a line is spoken may reveal a character to be excited, upset, angry, shy, or disappointed. Finally, stage directions may indicate *changes* in characters —for instance, a character whose speech is described as timid in early scenes may deliver lines emphatically and forcefully later on in the play.

Some stage directions provide a good deal of detail about character; others do little more than list characters' names. Arthur Miller is one playwright who often provides detailed information about character through stage directions. In *Death of a Salesman,* for instance, Miller's stage directions at the beginning of act 1 characterize Willy Loman immediately and specifically:

> *He is past sixty years of age, dressed quietly. Even as he crosses the stage to the doorway of the house, his exhaustion is apparent. He unlocks the door, comes into*

the kitchen, and thankfully lets his burden down, feeling the soreness of his palms.
A word-sigh escapes his lips. . .

Subsequent stage directions indicate how lines are to be spoken. For example, in the play's opening lines, Willy's wife Linda calls out to him *"with some trepidation"*; Linda speaks *"very carefully, delicately,"* and Willy speaks *"with casual irritation."* These instructions to readers (and actors) are meant to suggest the strained relationship between the two characters.

George Bernard Shaw is notorious for the full character description in his stage directions. In these directions — seen by readers of the play but not heard by audiences — he communicates complex information about characters' attitudes and values, motivation and reactions, and relationships with other characters. In doing so, Shaw functions as a narrator, explicitly communicating his own attitudes toward various characters. (Unlike the voice of Tom Wingfield in *The Glass Menagerie*, however, the voice in Shaw's stage directions is not also the voice of a character in the play; it is the voice of the playwright.) Shaw's stage directions for *Pygmalion* initially describe Eliza Doolittle as follows:

> *She is not at all an attractive person. She is perhaps eighteen, perhaps twenty, hardly older. She wears a little sailor hat of black straw that has long been exposed to the dust and soot of London and has seldom if ever been brushed. Her hair needs washing rather badly; its mousy color can hardly be natural. She wears a shoddy black coat that reaches nearly to her knees and is shaped to her waist. She has a brown skirt with a coarse apron. Her boots are much the worse for wear. She is no doubt as clean as she can afford to be; but compared to the ladies she is very dirty. Her features are no worse than theirs; but their condition leaves something to be desired; and she needs the services of a dentist.*

Rather than providing an objective summary of the character's most notable physical attributes, Shaw injects subjective comments (*"seldom if ever brushed"*; *"color can hardly be natural"*; *"no doubt as clean as she can afford to be"*) that reveal his attitude toward Eliza. This initially supercilious attitude, which he has in common with Professor Higgins, is tempered considerably by the end of the play, helping to make Eliza's transformation more obvious to readers than it would be if measured by her words and actions alone. By act 5, the tone of the stage directions characterizing Eliza has changed to admiration: *"Eliza enters, sunny, self-possessed, and giving a staggeringly convincing exhibition of ease of manner."*

Stage directions in *Hamlet* are not nearly as comprehensive. Characters are introduced with only the barest identifying tags: "Claudius, *King of Denmark*"; "Hamlet, *Son to the former, and nephew to the present King*"; "Gertrude, *Queen of Denmark, mother to Hamlet.*" Most stage directions do little more than chronicle the various characters' entrances and exits or specify particular physical actions: *"Enter Ghost"*; *"Spreads his arms"*; *"Ghost beckons Hamlet"*; *"He kneels"*; *"Sheathes his sword"*; *"Leaps in the grave."* Occasionally, stage directions specify a prop (*"Puts down the skull"*); a sound effect (*"A noise within"*); or a costume

(*"Enter the ghost in his night-gown"*). Such brevity is typical of Shakespeare's plays, in which characters are delineated almost solely by their words — and, not incidentally, by the way actors have interpreted the characters over the years. In fact, because Shakespeare's stage directions only suggest characters' gestures, physical reactions, movements, and facial expressions, actors have been left quite free to experiment, reading various interpretations into Shakespeare's characters.

Actors' Interpretations

When we watch a play, we gain insight into a character not merely through what the character says and does or how other characters react, but also through the way an actor interprets the role. If a playwright does not specify a character's mannerisms, gestures, or movements, or does not indicate how a line is to be delivered (and sometimes even if he or she does), an actor is free to interpret the role as he or she believes it should be played. Even when a playwright *does* specify such actions, the actor has a good deal of freedom to decide which gestures or expressions will convey a particular emotion.

In "Some Thoughts on Playwriting," American dramatist Thornton Wilder argues that "the theatre is an art which reposes upon the work of many collaborators" rather than on "one governing selecting will." Citing examples from Shakespeare and Ibsen, Wilder illustrates the great degree of "intervention" that may occur in dramatic productions. For instance, Wilder observes, Shakespeare's Shylock has been portrayed by two different actors as "noble, wronged and indignant" and as "a vengeful and hysterical buffoon" — and both performances were considered legitimate interpretations. As noted earlier, the absence of detailed stage directions in Shakespeare's plays makes possible (and perhaps even encourages) such widely diverging interpretations. However, as Wilder points out, even when playing roles created by a dramatist such as Ibsen, whose stage directions are typically quite specific, actors and directors have a good deal of leeway. Thus, actress Janet McTeer, who played the part of Ibsen's Nora in the 1997 London production of *A Doll House*, saw Nora and Torvald, despite their many problems, as "the perfect couple," deeply in love and involved in a passionate marriage. "You have to make that marriage sexually credible," McTeer told the *New York Times*, "to imagine they have a wonderful time in bed, so there becomes something to lose. If you play them as already past it or no longer attracted to each other, then there is no play." This interpretation is not inconsistent with the play, but it does go beyond what Ibsen actually wrote.

Similarly, the role of Catherine in David Auburn's Pulitzer Prize-winning play *Proof* (2001) has been played by several actresses — among them Mary-Louise Parker, Jennifer Jason Leigh, Anne Heche, Gwyneth Paltrow, and Lea Salonga — and each actress has interpreted this complex character in a different way. As *New York Times* theater critic John Rockwell observes, "Catherine can be loopy-ethereal-sexy (Ms. Parker), earthy and even a little bitter (Ms. Leigh), or adorable-needy-fragile (Ms. Heche), and Mr. Auburn's structure and characters and ideas still work."

Irish playwright Samuel Beckett devotes a good deal of attention to indicating actors' movements and gestures and their physical reactions to one another. In his 1952 play *Waiting for Godot*, for example, Beckett's stage directions seem to choreograph every gesture, every emotion, every intention:

- *(he looks at them ostentatiously in turn to make it clear they are both meant)*
- *Vladimir seizes Lucky's hat. Silence of Lucky. He falls. Silence. Panting of the victors.*
- *Estragon hands him the boot. Vladimir inspects it, throws it down angrily.*
- *Estragon pulls, stumbles, falls. Long silence.*
- *He goes feverishly to and fro, halts finally at extreme left, broods.*

Beckett provides full and obviously carefully thought-out stage directions and, in so doing, attempts to retain a good deal of control over his characters. Still, in a 1988 production of *Godot*, director Mike Nichols and comic actors Robin Williams and Steve Martin felt free to improvise, adding gestures and movements not specified or even hinted at — and most critics believed that this production remained true to the tragicomic spirit of Beckett's existentialist play. In a sense, then, the playwright's words on the page are just the beginning of the characters' lives on the stage.

✔ CHECKLIST Writing about Character

- Does any character serve as a narrator? If so, what information does this narrator supply about the other characters? How reliable is the narrator?
- Are the major characters fully developed?
- What do the minor characters contribute to the play?
- Do the major characters change and grow during the course of the play, or do they remain essentially unchanged?
- Does the play include monologue or soliloquies? What do these extended speeches reveal about the characters?
- What is revealed about the characters through dialogue?
- Do characters use foreign words, regionalisms, slang, jargon, clichés, or profanity? What does such use of language reveal about characters? About the play's theme?

continued on next page

- Is the characters' language formal or informal?

- Do characters speak in dialect? Do they have accents?

- Is the characters' language plain or elaborate?

- Do different characters have different styles or levels of language? What is the significance of these differences?

- In what way does language reveal characters' emotional states?

- Does the tone of any character's language change significantly as the play progresses? What does this change reveal?

- Does the play include verbal irony? Dramatic irony? How is irony conveyed? What purpose does irony achieve?

- What is revealed about the characters through what others say about them?

- What is revealed about characters through their actions?

- What is revealed about characters through the playwright's stage directions?

- How might different actors' interpretations change an audience's understanding of the characters?

AUGUST STRINDBERG (1849–1912) was born in Stockholm, Sweden, the child of a shipping merchant and his former maid. He studied at Uppsala University but left the university without a degree. By 1872, he had moved into the artistic circles in Stockholm and had begun work as a journalist.

In 1874, Strindberg was appointed assistant librarian at the Royal Library in Stockholm. Beginning the first of several stormy marriages, he struggled over the next few years; in 1879, he declared bankruptcy. During the same period, he wrote the novel that marked his breakthrough as a writer, *The Red Room* (1879). In 1881, he left the Royal Library to devote himself to writing, and in 1883, he left Sweden to join an artists' colony near Paris. His restlessness continued, however, and he soon moved to Switzerland, later living in Denmark, Germany, and Austria before returning at last to Stockholm.

Strindberg was a prolific artist, and his work includes novels, plays, poetry, and paintings. He is considered one of the most influential dramatists in literature.

The Stronger has been called a monodrama, a dramatic monologue, and a battle of brains in one scene. *The Stronger* was the kind of experimental work being encouraged in the late nineteenth century at the Théâtre Libre in Paris, for which Strindberg wrote several plays while hoping to form his own experimental theater in Stockholm. Though written in 1889, *The Stronger* did not premiere on stage until 1907.

The Stronger (1889)

Translated by Elizabeth Sprigge

CHARACTERS

Mrs. X., *actress, married*
Miss Y., *actress, unmarried*
A Waitress

SCENE

A corner of a ladies' café [in Stockholm in the eighteen eighties].° Two small wrought-iron tables, a red plush settee and a few chairs.

Miss Y. is sitting with a half-empty bottle of beer on the table before her, reading an illustrated weekly which from time to time she exchanges for another.

Mrs. X. enters, wearing a winter hat and coat and carrying a decorative Japanese basket.

MRS. X: Why, Millie, my dear, how are you? Sitting here all alone on Christmas Eve like some poor bachelor.

Miss Y. looks up from her magazine, nods, and continues to read.

MRS. X: You know it makes me feel really sad to see you. Alone. Alone in a café and on Christmas Eve of all times. It makes me feel as sad as when once in Paris I saw a wedding party at a restaurant. The bride was reading a comic paper and the bridegroom playing billiards with the witnesses. Ah me, I said to myself, with such a beginning how will it go, and how will it end? He was playing billiards on his wedding day! And she, you were going to say, was reading a comic paper on hers. But that's not quite the same.

A waitress brings a cup of chocolate to Mrs. X. and goes out.

MRS. X: Do you know, Amelia, I really believe now you would have done better to stick to him. Don't forget I was the first who told you to forgive him. Do you remember? Then you would be married now and have a home. Think how happy you were that Christmas when you stayed with your financé's people in the country. How warmly you spoke of domestic happiness! You really quite longed to be out of the theatre. Yes, Amelia dear, home is best — next best to the stage, and as for children — but you couldn't know anything about that.

Miss Y.'s expression is disdainful. Mrs. X. sips a few spoonfuls of chocolate, then opens her basket and displays some Christmas presents.

°[*In Stockholm in the eighteen eighties*] Brackets indicate translator's addition to scene.

Mrs. X: Now you must see what I have bought for my little chicks. (*Takes out a doll.*) Look at this. That's for Lisa. Do you see how she can roll her eyes and turn her head. Isn't she lovely? And here's a toy pistol for Maja.° (*She loads the pistol and shoots it at Miss Y. who appears frightened.*)

5 **Mrs. X:** Were you scared? Did you think I was going to shoot you? Really, I didn't think you'd believe that of me. Now if *you* were to shoot *me* it wouldn't be so surprising, for after all I did get in your way, and I know you never forget it — although I was entirely innocent. You still think I intrigued to get you out of the Grand Theatre, but I didn't. I didn't, however much you think I did. Well, it's no good talking, you will believe it was me . . . (*Takes out a pair of embroidered slippers.*) And these are for my old man, with tulips on them that I embroidered myself. As a matter of fact I hate tulips, but he has to have tulips on everything.

Miss Y. looks up, irony and curiosity in her face.

Mrs. X: (*putting one hand in each slipper*) Look what small feet Bob has, hasn't he? And you ought to see the charming way he walks — you've never seen him in slippers, have you?

Miss Y. laughs.

Mrs. X: Look, I'll show you. (*She makes the slippers walk across the table, and Miss Y. laughs again.*)

Mrs. X: But when he gets angry, look, he stamps his foot like this. "Those damn girls who can never learn how to make coffee! Blast! That silly idiot hasn't trimmed the lamp properly!" Then there's a draught under the door and his feet get cold. "Hell, it's freezing, and the damn fools can't even keep the stove going!" (*She rubs the sole of one slipper against the instep of the other. Miss Y roars with laughter.*)

Mrs. X: And then he comes home and has to hunt for his slippers, which Mary has pushed under the bureau . . . Well, perhaps it's not right to make fun of one's husband like this. He's sweet anyhow, and a good, dear husband. You ought to have had a husband like him, Amelia. What are you laughing at? What is it? Eh? And, you see, I know he is faithful to me. Yes, I know it. He told me himself — what *are* you giggling at?— that while I was on tour in Norway that horrible Frederica came and tried to seduce him. Can you imagine anything more abominable? (*Pause.*) I'd have scratched her eyes out if she had come around while I was at home. (*Pause.*) I'm glad Bob told me about it himself, so I didn't just hear it from gossip. (*Pause.*) And, as a matter of fact, Frederica wasn't the only one. I can't think why, but all the women in the Company° seem to be crazy about my husband. They must think his position gives him some say in who is engaged at the

---

° *Maja:* Pronounced "Maya."   ° *in the Company:* Translator's addition.

Theatre. Perhaps you have run after him yourself? I don't trust you very far, but I know he has never been attracted by you, and you always seemed to have some sort of grudge against him, or so I felt. (*Pause. They look at one another guardedly.*)

MRS. X: Do come and spend Christmas Eve with us tonight, Amelia — just 10
to show that you're not offended with us, or anyhow not with me. I don't know why, but it seems specially unpleasant not to be friends with you. Perhaps it's because I did get in your way that time . . . (*slowly*) or — I don't know — really, I don't know at all why it is.

Pause. Miss Y. gazes curiously at Mrs. X.

MRS. X: (*thoughtfully*) It was so strange when we were getting to know one another. Do you know, when we first met, I was frightened of you, so frightened I didn't dare let you out of my sight. I arranged all my goings and comings to be near you. I dared not be your enemy, so I became your friend. But when you came to our home, I always had an uneasy feeling, because I saw my husband didn't like you, and that irritated me — like when a dress doesn't fit. I did all I could to make him be nice to you, but it was no good — until you went and got engaged. Then you became such tremendous friends that at first it looked as if you only dared show your real feelings then — when you were safe. And then, let me see, how was it after that? I wasn't jealous — that's queer. And I remember at the christening, when you were the godmother, I told him to kiss you. He did, and you were so upset . . . As a matter of fact I didn't notice that then . . . I didn't think about it afterwards either . . . I've never thought about it — until *now*! (*Rises abruptly.*) Why don't you say something? You haven't said a word all this time. You've just let me go on talking. You have sat there with your eyes drawing all these thoughts out of me — they were there in me like silk in a cocoon — thoughts. . . Mistaken thoughts? Let me think. Why did you break off your engagement? Why did you never come to our house after that? Why don't you want to come to us tonight?

Miss Y. makes a motion, as if about to speak.

MRS. X: No. You don't need to say anything, for now I see it all. That was why — and why — and why. Yes. Yes, that's why it was. Yes, yes, all the pieces fit together now. That's it. I won't sit at the same table as you. (*Moves her things to the other table.*) That's why I have to embroider tulips, which I loathe, on his slippers — because you liked tulips. (*Throws the slippers on the floor.*) That's why we have to spend the summer on the lake — because you couldn't bear the seaside. That's why my son had to be called Eskil — because it was your father's name. That's why I had to wear your colours, read your books, eat the dishes you liked, drink your drinks — your chocolate, for instance. That's why — oh my God, it's terrible to think of, terrible! Everything, everything came to me from you — even your passions. Your soul bored into mine like a worm into an apple, and ate and ate and burrowed and burrowed, till nothing was left but the skin and a little black mould. I wanted to fly from you, but I couldn't. You were there like a snake, your black eyes fascinating me. When I spread my wings, they only dragged me down. I lay in the water with my feet tied together, and the harder I worked my arms, the deeper I sank — down, down, till I reached the bottom, where you lay in waiting like a giant crab to catch me in your claws — and now here I am. Oh how I hate you! I hate you, I hate you! And you just go on sitting there, silent, calm, indifferent, not caring whether the moon is new or full, if it's Christmas or New Year, if other people are happy or unhappy. You don't know how to hate or to love. You just sit there without moving — like a cat° at a mouse-hole. You can't drag your prey out, you can't chase it, but you can out-stay it. Here you sit in your corner — you know they call it the rat-trap after you — reading the papers to see if anyone's ruined or wretched or been thrown out of the Company. Here you sit sizing up your victims and weighing your chances — like a pilot his shipwrecks for the salvage. (*Pause.*) Poor Amelia! Do you know, I couldn't be more sorry for you. I know you are miserable, miserable like some wounded creature, and vicious because you are wounded. I can't be angry with you. I should like to be, but after all you are the small one — and as for your affair with Bob, that doesn't worry me in the least. Why should it matter to me? And if you, or somebody else taught me to drink chocolate, what's the difference? (*Drinks a spoonful. Smugly.*) Chocolate is very wholesome anyhow. And if I learnt from you how to dress, *tant mieux!* — that only gave me a stronger hold over my husband, and you have lost what I gained. Yes, to judge from various signs, I think you have now lost him. Of course, you meant me to walk out, as you once did, and which you're now regretting. But I won't do that, you may be sure. One shouldn't be narrow-minded, you know. And why should nobody else want what I have? (*Pause.*) Perhaps, my dear, taking everything into consideration, at this moment it is I who am the stronger. You never got anything from me, you just gave away — from yourself. And now, like the thief in the night, when you woke up I had what you had lost. Why was it then that everything you touched became worthless and sterile? You couldn't keep a man's love — for all your tulips and your passions — but I could. You couldn't learn the art of living from your books — but I learnt it. You bore no little Eskil, although that was your father's name. (*Pause.*) And why is it you are silent — everywhere, always silent? Yes, I used to think this was strength, but perhaps it was because you hadn't anything to say, because you couldn't think of anything. (*Rises and picks up the slippers.*) Now I am going home, taking the tulips with me — *your* tulips. You couldn't learn from

°*cat:* In Swedish, "stork."

others, you couldn't bend, and so you broke like a dry stick. I did not. Thank you, Amelia, for all your good lessons. Thank you for teaching my husband how to love. Now I am going home — to love him.

Exit.

Reading and Reacting

1. Summarize the plot of *The Stronger*. What actually happens during the play? What events have occurred before the play begins?

2. Explain the nature of the conflict between Mrs. X and Miss Y. Is this conflict entirely personal, or is it professional as well?

3. Why do you suppose Strindberg structures this play as a monologue? Would exchanges of dialogue strengthen the play? What do you suppose Miss Y would like to tell Mrs. X?

4. Is Miss Y a flat character? Is she a foil for Mrs. X? Explain.

5. Both Miss Y and Mrs. X are actresses. What significance, if any, do you see in this fact?

6. What does the audience learn about Bob, Mrs. X's husband, during the course of the play? What more can we infer about him?

7. As she continues to speak, Mrs. X's similes—for example, "Your soul bored into mine like a worm into an apple"—grow increasingly vivid. Identify as many similes as you can. What does this language reveal about Mrs. X's character? How does it move the play's action along?

8. As the play progresses, Mrs. X gains knowledge and self-awareness. What does she learn?

9. List all the play's props—for example, the toy gun and the slippers. What function does each of these props serve? Are they all necessary?

10. JOURNAL ENTRY Which of the two women do you see as "the stronger" in this play? Explain your position.

11. CRITICAL PERSPECTIVE In her notes on the play, director Tracy Campbell makes the following observations about the play's two characters:

> To be stronger, two things have to be compared with one overcoming the other. The two are both women, both have hopes and dreams, both have very real fears. But that's where the comparisons end. Mrs. X and Miss Y are not the same kind of woman; they have similar hopes and dreams but they are motivated differently; their fears of loneliness may be the same, but how the two women face this fear is very different.

How are these two women similar? How are they different? What do you think each woman fears, and how does each one face her fears?

Related Works: "Hills Like White Elephants" (p. 80), "The Storm" (p. 158), "Big Black Good Man" (p. 192), "General Review of the Sex Situation" (p. 636)

ARTHUR MILLER (1915–2005) was born in New York City and graduated in 1938 from the University of Michigan, where he began to write plays. His first big success, which won the New York Drama Critics Circle Award, was *All My Sons* (1947), about a man who has knowingly manufactured faulty airplane parts during World War II. Other significant plays are *The Crucible* (1953), based on the Salem witch trials of 1692, which Miller saw as parallel to contemporary investigations by the House Un-American Activities Committee; *A View from the Bridge* (1955); and *After the Fall* (1955). He was married for a time to actress Marilyn Monroe and wrote the screenplay for her movie *The Misfits* (1961). His play *The Last Yankee* opened off-Broadway in 1993, *Broken Glass* was both published and performed in 1994, and *Mr. Peter's Connection* was published in 1998. In 2001, Miller was awarded an NEH fellowship and the John H. Finney Award for Exemplary Service to New York City.

Death of a Salesman is Miller's most significant work, a play that quickly became an American classic. Miller said he was very much influenced by the structure of Greek tragedy, and in his play he shows that a tragedy can also be the story of an ordinary person told in realistic terms. The play is frequently produced, and each production interprets it a bit differently. When Miller directed *Death of a Salesman* in China in 1983, audiences perceived it as primarily the story of the mother. In the 1983 Broadway production, Miller himself realized "at a certain point that it was far more the story of Biff, the son, than it was of Willy Loman, the salesman of the title."

Death of a Salesman (1949)
CERTAIN PRIVATE CONVERSATIONS IN TWO ACTS
AND A REQUIEM

CHARACTERS

Willy Loman	**The Woman**
Linda, *his wife*	**Howard Wagner**
Biff ⎱ *his sons*	**Jenny**
Happy ⎰	**Stanley**
Uncle Ben	**Miss Forsythe**
Charley	**Letta**
Bernard	

The action takes place in Willy Loman's house and yard and in various places he visits in the New York and Boston of today.

Throughout the play, in the stage directions, left and right mean stage left and stage right.

ACT 1

A melody is heard, played upon a flute. It is small and fine, telling of grass and trees and the horizon. The curtain rises.

Before us is the Salesman's house. We are aware of towering, angular shapes behind it, surrounding it on all sides. Only the blue light of the sky falls upon the house and forestage; the surrounding area shows an angry glow of orange. As more light appears, we see a solid vault of apartment houses around the small, fragile-seeming home. An air of the dream clings to the place, a dream rising out of reality. The kitchen at center seems actual enough, for there is a kitchen table with three chairs, and a refrigerator. But no other fixtures are seen. At the back of the kitchen there is a draped entrance, which leads to the living room. To the right of the kitchen, on a level raised two feet, is a bedroom furnished only with a brass bedstead and a straight chair. On a shelf over the bed a silver athletic trophy stands. A window opens onto the apartment house at the side.

Behind the kitchen, on a level raised six and a half feet, is the boys' bedroom, at present barely visible. Two beds are dimly seen, and at the back of the room a dormer window. (This bedroom is above the unseen living room.) At the left a stairway curves up to it from the kitchen.

The entire setting is wholly or, in some places, partially transparent. The roofline of the house is one-dimensional; under and over it we see the apartment buildings. Before the house lies an apron, curving beyond the forestage into the orchestra. This forward area serves as the back yard as well as the locale of all Willy's imaginings and of his city scenes. Whenever the action is in the present the actors observe the imaginary wall-lines, entering the house only through the door at the left. But in the scenes of the past these boundaries are broken, and characters enter or leave a room by stepping "through" a wall onto the forestage.

From the right, Willy Loman, the Salesman, enters, carrying two large sample cases. The flute plays on. He hears but is not aware of it. He is past sixty years of age, dressed quietly. Even as he crosses the stage to the doorway of the house, his exhaustion is apparent. He unlocks the door, comes into the kitchen, and thankfully lets his burden down, feeling the soreness of his palms. A word-sigh escapes his lips — it might be "Oh, boy, oh, boy." He closes the door, then carries his cases out into the living room, through the draped kitchen doorway.

Linda, his wife, has stirred in her bed at the right. She gets out and puts on a robe, listening. Most often jovial, she has developed an iron repression of her exceptions to Willy's behavior — she more than loves him, she admires him, as though his mercurial nature, his temper, his massive dreams and little cruelties, served her only as sharp reminders of the turbulent longings within him, longings which she shares but lacks the temperament to utter and follow to their end.

LINDA: *(hearing Willy outside the bedroom, calls with some trepidation)* Willy!
WILLY: It's all right. I came back.
LINDA: Why? What happened? *(Slight pause.)* Did something happen, Willy?
WILLY: No, nothing happened.
LINDA: You didn't smash the car, did you?   5
WILLY: *(with casual irritation)* I said nothing happened. Didn't you hear me?
LINDA: Don't you feel well?
WILLY: I am tired to the death. *(The flute has faded away. He sits on the bed beside her, a little numb.)* I couldn't make it. I just couldn't make it, Linda.
LINDA: *(very carefully, delicately)* Where were you all day? You look terrible.
WILLY: I got as far as a little above Yonkers. I stopped for a cup of coffee.   10
   Maybe it was the coffee.

LINDA: What?

WILLY: (*after a pause*) I suddenly couldn't drive any more. The car kept going onto the shoulder, y'know?

LINDA: (*helpfully*) Oh. Maybe it was the steering again. I don't think Angelo knows the Studebaker.

WILLY: No, it's me, it's me. Suddenly I realize I'm goin' sixty miles an hour and I don't remember the last five minutes. I'm — I can't seem to — keep my mind to it.

15 LINDA: Maybe it's your glasses. You never went for your new glasses.

WILLY: No, I see everything. I came back ten miles an hour. It took me nearly four hours from Yonkers.

LINDA: (*resigned*) Well, you'll just have to take a rest, Willy, you can't continue this way.

WILLY: I just got back from Florida.

LINDA: But you didn't rest your mind. Your mind is overactive, and the mind is what counts, dear.

20 WILLY: I'll start out in the morning. Maybe I'll feel better in the morning. (*She is taking off his shoes.*) These goddam arch supports are killing me.

LINDA: Take an aspirin. Should I get you an aspirin? It'll soothe you.

WILLY: (*with wonder*) I was driving along, you understand? And I was fine. I was even observing the scenery. You can imagine, me looking at scenery, on the road every week of my life. But it's so beautiful up there, Linda, the trees are so thick, and the sun is warm. I opened the windshield and just let the warm air bathe over me. And then all of a sudden I'm goin' off the road! I'm tellin' ya, I absolutely forgot I was driving. If I'd've gone the other way over the white line I might've killed somebody. So I went on again — and five minutes later I'm dreamin' again, and I nearly — (*He presses two fingers against his eyes.*) I have such thoughts, I have such strange thoughts.

LINDA: Willy, dear. Talk to them again. There's no reason why you can't work in New York.

WILLY: They don't need me in New York. I'm the New England man. I'm vital in New England.

25 LINDA: But you're sixty years old. They can't expect you to keep traveling every week.

WILLY: I'll have to send a wire to Portland. I'm supposed to see Brown and Morrison tomorrow morning at ten o'clock to show the line. Goddammit, I could sell them! (*He starts putting on his jacket.*)

LINDA: (*taking the jacket from him*) Why don't you go down to the place tomorrow and tell Howard you've simply got to work in New York? You're too accommodating, dear.

WILLY: If old man Wagner was alive I'd a been in charge of New York now! That man was a prince, he was a masterful man. But that boy of his, that Howard, he don't appreciate. When I went north the first time, the Wagner Company didn't know where New England was!

LINDA: Why don't you tell those things to Howard, dear?
WILLY: (*encouraged*) I will, I definitely will. Is there any cheese?   30
LINDA: I'll make you a sandwich.
WILLY: No, go to sleep. I'll take some milk. I'll be up right away. The boys in?
LINDA: They're sleeping. Happy took Biff on a date tonight.
WILLY: (*interested*) That so?
LINDA: It was so nice to see them shaving together, one behind the other, in   35
the bathroom. And going out together. You notice? The whole house smells
of shaving lotion.
WILLY: Figure it out. Work a lifetime to pay off a house. You finally own it, and
there's nobody to live in it.
LINDA: Well, dear, life is a casting off. It's always that way.
WILLY: No, no, some people — some people accomplish something. Did Biff
say anything after I went this morning?
LINDA: You shouldn't have criticized him, Willy, especially after he just got off
the train. You mustn't lose your temper with him.
WILLY: When the hell did I lose my temper? I simply asked him if he was   40
making any money. Is that a criticism?
LINDA: But, dear, how could he make any money?
WILLY: (*worried and angered*) There's such an undercurrent in him. He became
a moody man. Did he apologize when I left this morning?
LINDA: He was crestfallen, Willy. You know how he admires you. I think if he
finds himself, then you'll both be happier and not fight any more.
WILLY: How can he find himself on a farm? Is that a life? A farmhand? In the
beginning, when he was young, I thought, well, a young man, it's good for
him to tramp around, take a lot of different jobs. But it's more than ten
years now and he has yet to make thirty-five dollars a week!
LINDA: He's finding himself, Willy.   45
WILLY: Not finding yourself at the age of thirty-four is a disgrace!
LINDA: Shh!
WILLY: The trouble is he's lazy, goddammit!
LINDA: Willy, please!
WILLY: Biff is a lazy bum!   50
LINDA: They're sleeping. Get something to eat. Go on down.
WILLY: Why did he come home? I would like to know what brought him
home.
LINDA: I don't know. I think he's still lost, Willy. I think he's very lost.
WILLY: Biff Loman is lost. In the greatest country in the world a young man
with such — personal attractiveness, gets lost. And such a hard worker.
There's one thing about Biff — he's not lazy.
LINDA: Never.   55
WILLY: (*with pity and resolve*) I'll see him in the morning; I'll have a nice talk
with him. I'll get him a job selling. He could be big in no time. My God!
Remember how they used to follow him around in high school? When

he smiled at one of them their faces lit up. When he walked down the street . . . *(He loses himself in reminiscences.)*

LINDA: *(trying to bring him out of it)* Willy, dear, I got a new kind of American-type cheese today. It's whipped.

WILLY: Why do you get American when I like Swiss?

LINDA: I just thought you'd like a change —

60 WILLY: I don't want a change! I want Swiss cheese. Why am I always being contradicted?

LINDA: *(with a covering laugh)* I thought it would be a surprise.

WILLY: Why don't you open a window in here, for God's sake?

LINDA: *(with infinite patience)* They're all open, dear.

WILLY: The way they boxed us in here. Bricks and windows, windows and bricks.

65 LINDA: We should've bought the land next door.

WILLY: The street is lined with cars. There's not a breath of fresh air in the neighborhood. The grass don't grow any more, you can't raise a carrot in the back yard. They should've had a law against apartment houses. Remember those two beautiful elm trees out there? When I and Biff hung the swing between them?

LINDA: Yeah, like being a million miles from the city.

WILLY: They should've arrested the builder for cutting those down. They massacred the neighborhood. *(Lost.)* More and more I think of those days, Linda. This time of year it was lilac and wisteria. And then the peonies would come out, and the daffodils. What fragrance in this room!

LINDA: Well, after all, people had to move somewhere.

70 WILLY: No, there's more people now.

LINDA: I don't think there's more people. I think —

WILLY: There's more people! That's what's ruining this country! Population is getting out of control. The competition is maddening! Smell the stink from that apartment house! And another on the other side . . . How can they whip cheese?

On Willy's last line, Biff and Happy raise themselves up in their beds, listening.

LINDA: Go down, try it. And be quiet.

WILLY: *(turning to Linda, guiltily)* You're not worried about me, are you, sweetheart?

75 BIFF: What's the matter?

HAPPY: Listen!

LINDA: You've got too much on the ball to worry about.

WILLY: You're my foundation and my support, Linda.

LINDA: Just try to relax, dear. You make mountains out of molehills.

80 WILLY: I won't fight with him any more. If he wants to go back to Texas, let him go.

LINDA: He'll find his way.

WILLY: Sure. Certain men just don't get started till later in life. Like Thomas Edison, I think. Or B. F. Goodrich. One of them was deaf. *(He starts for the bedroom doorway.)* I'll put my money on Biff.

LINDA: And Willy — if it's warm Sunday we'll drive in the country. And we'll open the windshield, and take lunch.

WILLY: No, the windshields don't open on the new cars.

LINDA: But you opened it today. 85

WILLY: Me? I didn't. *(He stops.)* Now isn't that peculiar! Isn't that remarkable — *(He breaks off in amazement and fright as the flute is heard distantly.)*

LINDA: What, darling?

WILLY: That is the most remarkable thing.

LINDA: What, dear?

WILLY: I was thinking of the Chevvy. *(Slight pause.)* Nineteen twenty-eight . . . 90 when I had that red Chevvy — *(Breaks off.)* That funny? I coulda sworn I was driving that Chevvy today.

LINDA: Well, that's nothing. Something must've reminded you.

WILLY: Remarkable. Ts. Remember those days? The way Biff used to simonize that car? The dealer refused to believe there was eighty thousand miles on it. *(He shakes his head.)* Heh! *(To Linda.)* Close your eyes, I'll be right up. *(He walks out of the bedroom.)*

HAPPY: *(to Biff)* Jesus, maybe he smashed up the car again!

LINDA: *(calling after Willy)* Be careful on the stairs, dear! The cheese is on the middle shelf! *(She turns, goes over to the bed, takes his jacket, and goes out of the bedroom.)*

Light has risen on the boys' room. Unseen, Willy is heard talking to himself, "Eighty thousand miles," and a little laugh. Biff gets out of bed, comes downstage a bit, and stands attentively. Biff is two years older than his brother Happy, well built, but in these days bears a worn air and seems less self-assured. He has succeeded less, and his dreams are stronger and less acceptable than Happy's. Happy is tall, powerfully made. Sexuality is like a visible color on him, or a scent that many women have discovered. He, like his brother, is lost, but in a different way, for he has never allowed himself to turn his face toward defeat and is thus more confused and hard-skinned, although seemingly more content.

HAPPY: *(getting out of bed)* He's going to get his license taken away if he keeps 95 that up. I'm getting nervous about him, y'know, Biff?

BIFF: His eyes are going.

HAPPY: No, I've driven with him. He sees all right. He just doesn't keep his mind on it. I drove into the city with him last week. He stops at a green light and then it turns red and he goes. *(He laughs.)*

BIFF: Maybe he's color-blind.

HAPPY: Pop? Why he's got the finest eye for color in the business. You know that.

BIFF: *(sitting down on his bed)* I'm going to sleep. 100

Jo Mielziner's celebrated set for the premiere production of Arthur Miller's *Death of a Salesman,* starring Lee J. Cobb, showing the cut-away house and the downstage playing area.

HAPPY: You're not still sour on Dad, are you, Biff?

BIFF: He's all right, I guess.

WILLY: (*underneath them, in the living room*) Yes, sir, eighty thousand miles — eighty-two thousand!

BIFF: You smoking?

105 **HAPPY:** (*holding out a pack of cigarettes*) Want one?

BIFF: (*taking a cigarette*) I can never sleep when I smell it.

WILLY: What a simonizing job, heh!

HAPPY: (*with deep sentiment*) Funny, Biff, y'know? Us sleeping in here again? The old beds. (*He pats his bed affectionately.*) All the talk that went across those two beds, huh? Our whole lives.

BIFF: Yeah. Lotta dreams and plans.

110 **HAPPY:** (*with a deep and masculine laugh*) About five hundred women would like to know what was said in this room.

They share a soft laugh.

BIFF: Remember that big Betsy something — what the hell was her name — over on Bushwick Avenue?

HAPPY: (*combing his hair*) With the collie dog!

BIFF: That's the one. I got you in there, remember?

HAPPY: Yeah, that was my first time — I think. Boy, there was a pig! (*They laugh, almost crudely.*) You taught me everything I know about women. Don't forget that.

BIFF: I bet you forgot how bashful you used to be. Especially with girls.   115

HAPPY: Oh, I still am, Biff.

BIFF: Oh, go on.

HAPPY: I just control it, that's all. I think I got less bashful and you got more so. What happened, Biff? Where's the old humor, the old confidence? (*He shakes Biff's knee. Biff gets up and moves restlessly about the room.*) What's the matter?

BIFF: Why does Dad mock me all the time?

HAPPY: He's not mocking you, he —   120

BIFF: Everything I say there's a twist of mockery on his face. I can't get near him.

HAPPY: He just wants you to make good, that's all. I wanted to talk to you about Dad for a long time, Biff. Something's — happening to him. He — talks to himself.

BIFF: I noticed that this morning. But he always mumbled.

HAPPY: But not so noticeable. It got so embarrassing I sent him to Florida. And you know something? Most of the time he's talking to you.

BIFF: What's he say about me?

HAPPY: I can't make it out.   125

BIFF: What's he say about me?

HAPPY: I think the fact that you're not settled, that you're still kind of up in the air . . .

BIFF: There's one or two other things depressing him, Happy.

HAPPY: What do you mean?   130

BIFF: Never mind. Just don't lay it all to me.

HAPPY: But I think if you just got started — I mean — is there any future for you out there?

BIFF: I tell ya, Hap, I don't know what the future is. I don't know — what I'm supposed to want.

HAPPY: What do you mean?

BIFF: Well, I spent six or seven years after high school trying to work myself   135
up. Shipping clerk, salesman, business of one kind or another. And it's a measly manner of existence. To get on that subway on the hot mornings in summer. To devote your whole life to keeping stock, or making phone calls, or selling or buying. To suffer fifty weeks of the year for the sake of a two-week vacation, when all you really desire is to be outdoors, with your shirt off. And always to have to get ahead of the next fella. And still — that's how you build a future.

HAPPY: Well, you really enjoy it on a farm? Are you content out there?

BIFF: (*with rising agitation*) Hap, I've had twenty or thirty different kinds of jobs since I left home before the war, and it always turns out the same. I just realized it lately. In Nebraska when I herded cattle, and the Dakotas, and Arizona, and now in Texas. It's why I came home now, I guess, because I realized it. This farm I work on, it's spring there now, see? And they've got about fifteen new colts. There's nothing more inspiring or — beautiful than the sight of a mare and a new colt. And it's cool there now, see? Texas is cool now, and it's spring. And whenever spring comes to where I am, I suddenly get the feeling, my God, I'm not gettin' anywhere! What the hell am I doing, playing around with horses, twenty-eight dollars a week! I'm thirty-four years old, I oughta be makin' my future. That's when I come running home. And now, I get here, and I don't know what to do with myself. (*After a pause.*) I've always made a point of not wasting my life, and every time I come back here I know that all I've done is to waste my life.

HAPPY: You're a poet, you know that, Biff? You're a — you're an idealist!

BIFF: No, I'm mixed up very bad. Maybe I oughta get married. Maybe I oughta get stuck into something. Maybe that's my trouble. I'm like a boy. I'm not married, I'm not in business, I just — I'm like a boy. Are you content, Hap? You're a success, aren't you? Are you content?

140 HAPPY: Hell, no!

BIFF: Why? You're making money, aren't you?

HAPPY: (*moving about with energy, expressiveness*) All I can do now is wait for the merchandise manager to die. And suppose I get to be merchandise manager? He's a good friend of mine, and he just built a terrific estate on Long Island. And he lived there about two months and sold it, and now he's building another one. He can't enjoy it once it's finished. And I know that's just what I would do. I don't know what the hell I'm workin' for. Sometimes I sit in my apartment — all alone. And I think of the rent I'm paying. And it's crazy. But then, it's what I always wanted. My own apartment, a car, and plenty of women. And still, goddammit, I'm lonely.

BIFF: (*with enthusiasm*) Listen, why don't you come out West with me?

HAPPY: You and I, heh?

145 BIFF: Sure, maybe we could buy a ranch. Raise cattle, use our muscles. Men built like we are should be working out in the open.

HAPPY: (*avidly*) The Loman Brothers, heh?

BIFF: (*with vast affection*) Sure, we'd be known all over the counties!

HAPPY: (*enthralled*) That's what I dream about, Biff. Sometimes I want to just rip my clothes off in the middle of the store and outbox that goddam merchandise manager. I mean I can outbox, outrun, and outlift anybody in that store, and I have to take orders from those common, petty sons-of-bitches till I can't stand it any more.

BIFF: I'm telln' you, kid, if you were with me I'd be happy out there.

150 HAPPY: (*enthused*) See, Biff, everybody around me is so false that I'm constantly lowering my ideals . . .

BIFF: Baby, together we'd stand up for one another, we'd have someone to trust.

HAPPY: If I were around you —

BIFF: Hap, the trouble is we weren't brought up to grub for money. I don't know how to do it.

Happy: Neither can I!

Biff: Then let's go! 155

Happy: The only thing is — what can you make out there?

Biff: But look at your friend. Builds an estate and then hasn't the peace of mind to live in it.

Happy: Yeah, but when he walks into the store the waves part in front of him. That's fifty-two thousand dollars a year coming through the revolving door, and I got more in my pinky finger than he's got in his head.

Biff: Yeah, but you just said —

Happy: I gotta show some of those pompous, self-important executives over 160 there that Hap Loman can make the grade. I want to walk into the store the way he walks in. Then I'll go with you, Biff. We'll be together yet, I swear. But take those two we had tonight. Now weren't they gorgeous creatures?

Biff: Yeah, yeah, most gorgeous I've had in years.

Happy: I get that any time I want, Biff. Whenever I feel disgusted. The only trouble is, it gets like bowling or something. I just keep knockin' them over and it doesn't mean anything. You still run around a lot?

Biff: Naa. I'd like to find a girl — steady, somebody with substance.

Happy: That's what I long for.

Biff: Go on! You'd never come home. 165

Happy: I would! Somebody with character, with resistance! Like Mom, y'know? You're gonna call me a bastard when I tell you this. That girl Charlotte I was with tonight is engaged to be married in five weeks. *(He tries on his new hat.)*

Biff: No kiddin'!

Happy: Sure, the guy's in line for the vice-presidency of the store. I don't know what gets into me, maybe I just have an overdeveloped sense of competition or something, but I went and ruined her, and furthermore I can't get rid of her. And he's the third executive I've done that to. Isn't that a crummy characteristic? And to top it all, I go to their weddings! *(Indignantly, but laughing.)* Like I'm not supposed to take bribes. Manufacturers offer me a hundred-dollar bill now and then to throw an order their way. You know how honest I am, but it's like this girl, see. I hate myself for it. Because I don't want the girl, and, still, I take it and — I love it!

Biff: Let's go to sleep.

Happy: I guess we didn't settle anything, heh? 170

Biff: I just got one idea that I think I'm going to try.

Happy: What's that?

Biff: Remember Bill Oliver?

Happy: Sure, Oliver is very big now. You want to work for him again?

Biff: No, but when I quit he said something to me. He put his arm on my 175 shoulder, and he said, "Biff, if you ever need anything, come to me."

Happy: I remember that. That sounds good.

Biff: I think I'll go to see him. If I could get ten thousand or even seven or eight thousand dollars I could buy a beautiful ranch.

Happy: I bet he'd back you. 'Cause he thought highly of you, Biff, I mean, they all do. You're well liked, Biff. That's why I say to come back here, and we both have the apartment. And I'm telln' you, Biff, any babe you want . . .

Biff: No, with a ranch I could do the work I like and still be something. I just wonder though. I wonder if Oliver still thinks I stole that carton of basketballs.

180 **Happy:** Oh, he probably forgot that long ago. It's almost ten years. You're too sensitive. Anyway, he didn't really fire you.

Biff: Well, I think he was going to. I think that's why I quit. I was never sure whether he knew or not. I know he thought the world of me, though. I was the only one he'd let lock up the place.

Willy: *(below)* You gonna wash the engine, Biff?

Happy: Shh!

Biff looks at Happy, who is gazing down, listening. Willy is mumbling in the parlor.

Happy: You hear that?

They listen. Willy laughs warmly.

185 **Biff:** *(growing angry)* Doesn't he know Mom can hear that?

Willy: Don't get your sweater dirty, Biff!

A look of pain crosses Biff's face.

Happy: Isn't that terrible? Don't leave again, will you? You'll find a job here. You gotta stick around. I don't know what to do about him, it's getting embarrassing.

Willy: What a simonizing job!

Biff: Mom's hearing that!

190 **Willy:** No kiddin', Biff, you got a date? Wonderful!

Happy: Go on to sleep. But talk to him in the morning, will you?

Biff: *(reluctantly getting into bed)* With her in the house. Brother!

Happy: *(getting into bed)* I wish you'd have a good talk with him.

The light on their room begins to fade.

Biff: *(to himself in bed)* That selfish, stupid . . .

195 **Happy:** Sh . . . Sleep, Biff.

Their light is out. Well before they have finished speaking, Willy's form is dimly seen below in the darkened kitchen. He opens the refrigerator, searches in there, and takes out a bottle of milk. The apartment houses are fading out, and the entire house and surroundings become covered with leaves. Music insinuates itself as the leaves appear.

Willy: Just wanna be careful with those girls, Biff, that's all. Don't make any promises. No promises of any kind. Because a girl, y'know, they always believe what you tell 'em, and you're very young, Biff, you're too young to be talking seriously to girls.

Light rises on the kitchen. Willy, talking, shuts the refrigerator door and comes down-stage to the kitchen table. He pours milk into a glass. He is totally immersed in himself, smiling faintly.

WILLY: Too young entirely, Biff. You want to watch your schooling first. Then when you're all set, there'll be plenty of girls for a boy like you. (*He smiles broadly at a kitchen chair.*) That so? The girls pay for you? (*He laughs.*) Boy, you must really be makin' a hit.

Willy is gradually addressing — physically — a point offstage, speaking through the wall of the kitchen, and his voice has been rising in volume to that of a normal conversation.

WILLY: I been wondering why you polish the car so careful. Ha! Don't leave the hubcaps, boys. Get the chamois to the hubcaps. Happy, use newspaper on the windows, it's the easiest thing. Show him how to do it, Biff! You see, Happy? Pad it up, use it like a pad. That's it, that's it, good work. You're doin' all right, Hap. (*He pauses, then nods in approbation for a few seconds, then looks upward.*) Biff, first thing we gotta do when we get time is clip that big branch over the house. Afraid it's gonna fall in a storm and hit the roof. Tell you what. We get a rope and sling her around, and then we climb up there with a couple of saws and take her down. Soon as you finish the car, boys, I wanna see ya. I got a surprise for you, boys.

BIFF: (*offstage*) Whatta ya got, Dad?

WILLY: No, you finish first. Never leave a job till you're finished — remember   200
that. (*Looking toward the "big trees."*) Biff, up in Albany I saw a beautiful hammock. I think I'll buy it next trip, and we'll hang it right between those two elms. Wouldn't that be something? Just swingin' there under those branches. Boy, that would be . . .

Young Biff and Young Happy appear from the direction Willy was addressing. Happy car-ries rags and a pail of water. Biff, wearing a sweater with a block "S," carries a football.

BIFF: (*pointing in the direction of the car offstage*) How's that, Pop, professional?

WILLY: Terrific. Terrific job, boys. Good work, Biff.

HAPPY: Where's the surprise, Pop?

WILLY: In the back seat of the car.

HAPPY: Boy! (*He runs off.*)   205

BIFF: What is it, Dad? Tell me, what'd you buy?

WILLY: (*laughing, cuffs him*) Never mind, something I want you to have.

BIFF: (*turns and starts off*) What is it, Hap?

HAPPY: (*offstage*) It's a punching bag!

BIFF: Oh, Pop!   210

WILLY: It's got Gene Tunney's° signature on it!

°*Gene Tunney's:* James Joseph ("Gene") Tunney (1897–1978) — American boxer, world heavyweight champion from his defeat of Jack Dempsey in 1926 until his retirement in 1928.

Happy runs onstage with a punching bag.

BIFF: Gee, how'd you know we wanted a punching bag?

WILLY: Well, it's the finest thing for the timing.

HAPPY: (*lies down on his back and pedals with his feet*) I'm losing weight, you notice, Pop?

215 **WILLY:** (*to Happy*) Jumping rope is good too.

BIFF: Did you see the new football I got?

WILLY: (*examining the ball*) Where'd you get a new ball?

BIFF: The coach told me to practice my passing.

WILLY: That so? And he gave you the ball, heh?

220 **BIFF:** Well, I borrowed it from the locker room. (*He laughs confidentially.*)

WILLY: (*laughing with him at the theft*) I want you to return that.

HAPPY: I told you he wouldn't like it!

BIFF: (*angrily*) Well, I'm bringing it back!

WILLY: (*stopping the incipient argument, to Happy*) Sure, he's gotta practice with a regulation ball, doesn't he? (*To Biff.*) Coach'll probably congratulate you on your initiative!

225 **BIFF:** Oh, he keeps congratulating my initiative all the time, Pop.

WILLY: That's because he likes you. If somebody else took that ball there'd be an uproar. So what's the report, boys, what's the report?

BIFF: Where'd you go this time, Dad? Gee we were lonesome for you.

WILLY: (*pleased, puts an arm around each boy and they come down to the apron*) Lonesome, heh?

BIFF: Missed you every minute.

230 **WILLY:** Don't say? Tell you a secret, boys. Don't breathe it to a soul. Someday I'll have my own business, and I'll never have to leave home any more.

HAPPY: Like Uncle Charley, heh?

WILLY: Bigger than Uncle Charley! Because Charley is not — liked. He's liked, but he's not — well liked.

BIFF: Where'd you go this time, Dad?

WILLY: Well, I got on the road, and I went north to Providence. Met the Mayor.

235 **BIFF:** The Mayor of Providence!

WILLY: He was sitting in the hotel lobby.

BIFF: What'd he say?

WILLY: He said, "Morning!" And I said, "You've got a fine city here, Mayor." And then he had coffee with me. And then I went to Waterbury. Waterbury is a fine city. Big clock city, the famous Waterbury clock. Sold a nice bill there. And then Boston — Boston is the cradle of the Revolution. A fine city. And a couple of other towns in Mass., and on to Portland and Bangor and straight home!

BIFF: Gee, I'd love to go with you sometime, Dad.

240 **WILLY:** Soon as summer comes.

HAPPY: Promise?

WILLY: You and Hap and I, and I'll show you all the towns. America is full of beautiful towns and fine, upstanding people. And they know me, boys, they know me up and down New England. The finest people. And when I bring you fellas up, there'll be open sesame for all of us, 'cause one thing, boys: I have friends. I can park my car in any street in New England, and the cops protect it like their own. This summer, heh?

BIFF AND HAPPY: *(together)* Yeah! You bet!

WILLY: We'll take our bathing suits.

HAPPY: We'll carry your bags, Pop! 245

WILLY: Oh, won't that be something! Me comin' into the Boston store with you boys carryin' my bags. What a sensation!

Biff is prancing around, practicing passing the ball.

WILLY: You nervous, Biff, about the game?

BIFF: Not if you're gonna be there.

WILLY: What do they say about you in school, now that they made you captain?

HAPPY: There's a crowd of girls behind him everytime the classes change. 250

BIFF: *(taking Willy's hand)* This Saturday, Pop, this Saturday — just for you, I'm going to break through for a touchdown.

HAPPY: You're supposed to pass.

BIFF: I'm takin' one play for Pop. You watch me, Pop, and when I take off my helmet, that means I'm breakin' out. Then you watch me crash through that line!

WILLY: *(kisses Biff)* Oh, wait'll I tell this in Boston!

Bernard enters in knickers. He is younger than Biff, earnest and loyal, a worried boy.

BERNARD: Biff, where are you? You're supposed to study with me today. 255

WILLY: Hey, looka Bernard. What're you lookin' so anemic about, Bernard?

BERNARD: He's gotta study, Uncle Willy. He's got Regents next week.

HAPPY: *(tauntingly, spinning Bernard around)* Let's box, Bernard!

BERNARD: Biff! *(He gets away from Happy.)* Listen, Biff, I heard Mr. Birnbaum say that if you don't start studyin' math he's gonna flunk you, and you won't graduate. I heard him!

WILLY: You better study with him, Biff. Go ahead now. 260

BERNARD: I heard him!

BIFF: Oh, Pop, you didn't see my sneakers! *(He holds up a foot for Willy to look at.)*

WILLY: Hey, that's a beautiful job of printing!

BERNARD: *(wiping his glasses)* Just because he printed University of Virginia on his sneakers doesn't mean they've got to graduate him, Uncle Willy!

WILLY: *(angrily)* What're you talking about? With scholarships to three 265 universities they're gonna flunk him?

BERNARD: But I heard Mr. Birnbaum say —

WILLY: Don't be a pest, Bernard! *(To his boys.)* What an anemic!

BERNARD: Okay, I'm waiting for you in my house, Biff.

Bernard goes off. The Lomans laugh.

Willy: Bernard is not well liked, is he?
270 **Biff:** He's liked, but he's not well liked.
Happy: That's right, Pop.
Willy: That's just what I mean. Bernard can get the best marks in school, y'understand, but when he gets out in the business world, y'understand, you are going to be five times ahead of him. That's why I thank Almighty God you're both built like Adonises. Because the man who makes an appearance in the business world, the man who creates personal interest, is the man who gets ahead. Be liked and you will never want. You take me, for instance. I never have to wait in line to see a buyer. "Willy Loman is here!" That's all they have to know, and I go right through.
Biff: Did you knock them dead, Pop?
Willy: Knocked 'em cold in Providence, slaughtered 'em in Boston.
275 **Happy:** (*on his back, pedaling again*) I'm losing weight, you notice, Pop?

Linda enters, as of old, a ribbon in her hair, carrying a basket of washing.

Linda: (*with youthful energy*) Hello, dear!
Willy: Sweetheart!
Linda: How'd the Chevvy run?
Willy: Chevrolet, Linda, is the greatest car ever built. (*To the boys.*) Since when do you let your mother carry wash up the stairs?
280 **Biff:** Grab hold there, boy!
Happy: Where to, Mom?
Linda: Hang them up on the line. And you better go down to your friends, Biff. The cellar is full of boys. They don't know what to do with themselves.
Biff: Ah, when Pop comes home they can wait!
Willy: (*laughs appreciatively*) You better go down and tell them what to do, Biff.
285 **Biff:** I think I'll have them sweep out the furnace room.
Willy: Good work, Biff.
Biff: (*goes through wall-line of kitchen to doorway at back and calls down*) Fellas! Everybody sweep out the furnace room! I'll be right down!
Voices: All right! Okay, Biff.
Biff: George and Sam and Frank, come out back! We're hangin' up the wash! Come on, Hap, on the double! (*He and Happy carry out the basket.*)
290 **Linda:** The way they obey him!
Willy: Well, that's training, the training. I'm tellin' you, I was sellin' thousands and thousands, but I had to come home.
Linda: Oh, the whole block'll be at that game. Did you sell anything?
Willy: I did five hundred gross in Providence and seven hundred gross in Boston.
Linda: No! Wait a minute, I've got a pencil. (*She pulls pencil and paper out of her apron pocket.*) That makes your commission . . . Two hundred — my God! Two hundred and twelve dollars!

WILLY: Well, I didn't figure it yet, but . . .   295
LINDA: How much did you do?
WILLY: Well, I — I did — about a hundred and eighty gross in Providence.
Well, no — it came to — roughly two hundred gross on the whole trip.
LINDA: (*without hesitation*) Two hundred gross. That's . . . (*She figures.*)
WILLY: The trouble was that three of the stores were half closed for inventory
in Boston. Otherwise I woulda broke records.
LINDA: Well, it makes seventy dollars and some pennies. That's very good.   300
WILLY: What do we owe?
LINDA: Well, on the first there's sixteen dollars on the refrigerator —
WILLY: Why sixteen?
LINDA: Well, the fan belt broke, so it was a dollar eighty.
WILLY: But it's brand new.   305
LINDA: Well, the man said that's the way it is. Till they work themselves in,
y'know.

They move through the wall-line into the kitchen.

WILLY: I hope we didn't get stuck on that machine.
LINDA: They got the biggest ads of any of them!
WILLY: I know, it's a fine machine. What else?
LINDA: Well, there's nine-sixty for the washing machine. And for the vacuum   310
cleaner there's three and a half due on the fifteenth. Then the roof, you got
twenty-one dollars remaining.
WILLY: It don't leak, does it?
LINDA: No, they did a wonderful job. Then you owe Frank for the carburetor.
WILLY: I'm not going to pay that man! That goddam Chevrolet, they ought to
prohibit the manufacture of that car!
LINDA: Well, you owe him three and a half. And odds and ends, comes to
around a hundred and twenty dollars by the fifteenth.
WILLY: A hundred and twenty dollars! My God, if business don't pick up I   315
don't know what I'm gonna do!
LINDA: Well, next week you'll do better.
WILLY: Oh, I'll knock them dead next week. I'll go to Hartford. I'm very well
liked in Hartford. You know, the trouble is, Linda, people don't seem to
take to me.

They move onto the forestage.

LINDA: Oh, don't be foolish.
WILLY: I know it when I walk in. They seem to laugh at me.
LINDA: Why? Why would they laugh at you? Don't talk that way, Willy.   320

Willy moves to the edge of the stage. Linda goes into the kitchen and starts to darn stockings.

WILLY: I don't know the reason for it, but they just pass me by. I'm not noticed.

LINDA: But you're doing wonderful, dear. You're making seventy to a hundred dollars a week.

WILLY: But I gotta be at it ten, twelve hours a day. Other men — I don't know — they do it easier. I don't know why — I can't stop myself — I talk too much. A man oughta come in with a few words. One thing about Charley. He's a man of few words, and they respect him.

LINDA: You don't talk too much, you're just lively.

325 WILLY: *(smiling)* Well, I figure, what the hell, life is short, a couple of jokes. *(To himself.)* I joke too much! *(The smile goes.)*

LINDA: Why? You're —

WILLY: I'm fat. I'm very — foolish to look at, Linda. I didn't tell you, but Christmas time I happened to be calling on F. H. Stewarts, and a salesman I know, as I was going in to see the buyer, I heard him say something about — walrus. And I — I cracked him right across the face. I won't take that. I simply will not take that. But they do laugh at me. I know that.

LINDA: Darling . . .

WILLY: I gotta overcome it. I know I gotta overcome it. I'm not dressing to advantage, maybe.

330 LINDA: Willy, darling, you're the handsomest man in the world —

WILLY: Oh, no, Linda.

LINDA: To me you are. *(Slight pause.)* The handsomest.

From the darkness is heard the laughter of a woman. Willy doesn't turn to it, but it continues through Linda's lines.

LINDA: And the boys, Willy. Few men are idolized by their children the way you are.

Music is heard as behind a scrim, to the left of the house, The Woman, dimly seen, is dressing.

WILLY: *(with great feeling)* You're the best there is, Linda, you're a pal, you know that? On the road — on the road I want to grab you sometimes and just kiss the life outa you.

The laughter is loud now, and he moves into a brightening area at the left, where The Woman has come from behind the scrim and is standing, putting on her hat, looking into a "mirror" and laughing.

335 WILLY: 'Cause I get so lonely — especially when business is bad and there's nobody to talk to. I get the feeling that I'll never sell anything again, that I won't make a living for you, or a business, a business for the boys. *(He talks through The Woman's subsiding laughter; The Woman primps at the "mirror.")* There's so much I want to make for —

THE WOMAN: Me? You didn't make me, Willy. I picked you.

WILLY: *(pleased)* You picked me?

THE WOMAN: *(who is quite proper-looking, Willy's age)* I did. I've been sitting at that desk watching all the salesmen go by, day in, day out. But you've got such a sense of humor, and we do have such a good time together, don't we?

WILLY: Sure, sure. *(He takes her in his arms.)* Why do you have to go now?

THE WOMAN: It's two o'clock . . .   340

WILLY: No, come on in! *(He pulls her.)*

THE WOMAN: . . . my sisters'll be scandalized. When'll you be back?

WILLY: Oh, two weeks about. Will you come up again?

THE WOMAN: Sure thing. You do make me laugh. It's good for me. *(She squeezes his arm, kisses him.)* And I think you're a wonderful man.

WILLY: You picked me, heh?   345

THE WOMAN: Sure. Because you're so sweet. And such a kidder.

WILLY: Well, I'll see you next time I'm in Boston.

THE WOMAN: I'll put you right through to the buyers.

WILLY: *(slapping her bottom)* Right. Well, bottoms up!

THE WOMAN: *(slaps him gently and laughs)* You just kill me, Willy. *(He suddenly*   350 *grabs her and kisses her roughly.)* You kill me. And thanks for the stockings. I love a lot of stockings. Well, good night.

WILLY: Good night. And keep your pores open!

THE WOMAN: Oh, Willy!

The Woman bursts out laughing, and Linda's laughter blends in. The Woman disappears into the dark. Now the area at the kitchen table brightens. Linda is sitting where she was at the kitchen table, but now is mending a pair of silk stockings.

LINDA: You are, Willy. The handsomest man. You've got no reason to feel that —

WILLY: *(coming out of The Woman's dimming area and going over to Linda)* I'll make it all up to you, Linda, I'll —

LINDA: There's nothing to make up, dear. You're doing fine, better than —   355

WILLY: *(noticing her mending)* What's that?

LINDA: Just mending my stockings. They're so expensive —

WILLY: *(angrily, taking them from her)* I won't have you mending stockings in this house! Now throw them out!

Linda puts the stockings in her pocket.

BERNARD: *(entering on the run)* Where is he? If he doesn't study!

WILLY: *(moving to the forestage, with great agitation)* You'll give him the   360 answers!

BERNARD: I do, but I can't on a Regents! That's a state exam! They're liable to arrest me!

WILLY: Where is he? I'll whip him, I'll whip him!

LINDA: And he'd better give back that football, Willy, it's not nice.

WILLY: Biff! Where is he? Why is he taking everything?

LINDA: He's too tough with the girls, Willy. All the mothers are afraid of him!   365

WILLY: I'll whip him!

BERNARD: He's driving the car without a license!

The Woman's laugh is heard.

WILLY: Shut up!

LINDA: All the mothers —

370 **WILLY:** Shut up!

BERNARD: (*backing quietly away and out*) Mr. Birnbaum says he's stuck up.

WILLY: Get outa here!

BERNARD: If he doesn't buckle down he'll flunk math! (*He goes off.*)

LINDA: He's right, Willy, you've gotta —

375 **WILLY:** (*exploding at her*) There's nothing the matter with him! You want him to be a worm like Bernard? He's got spirit, personality . . .

As he speaks, Linda, almost in tears, exits into the living room. Willy is alone in the kitchen, wilting and staring. The leaves are gone. It is night again, and the apartment houses look down from behind.

WILLY: Loaded with it. Loaded! What is he stealing? He's giving it back, isn't he? Why is he stealing? What did I tell him? I never in my life told him anything but decent things.

Happy in pajamas has come down the stairs; Willy suddenly becomes aware of Happy's presence.

HAPPY: Let's go now, come on.

WILLY: (*sitting down at the kitchen table*) Huh! Why did she have to wax the floors herself? Everytime she waxes the floors she keels over. She knows that!

HAPPY: Shh! Take it easy. What brought you back tonight?

380 **WILLY:** I got an awful scare. Nearly hit a kid in Yonkers. God! Why didn't I go to Alaska with my brother Ben that time! Ben! That man was a genius, that man was success incarnate! What a mistake! He begged me to go.

HAPPY: Well, there's no use in —

WILLY: You guys! There was a man started with the clothes on his back and ended up with diamond mines!

HAPPY: Boy, someday I'd like to know how he did it.

WILLY: What's the mystery? The man knew what he wanted and went out and got it! Walked into a jungle, and comes out, the age of twenty-one, and he's rich! The world is an oyster, but you don't crack it open on a mattress!

385 **HAPPY:** Pop, I told you I'm gonna retire you for life.

WILLY: You'll retire me for life on seventy goddam dollars a week? And your women and your car and your apartment, and you'll retire me for life! Christ's sake, I couldn't get past Yonkers today! Where are you guys, where are you? The woods are burning! I can't drive a car!

Charley has appeared in the doorway. He is a large man, slow of speech, laconic, immovable. In all he says, despite what he says, there is pity, and now, trepidation. He has a robe over his pajamas, slippers on his feet. He enters the kitchen.

CHARLEY: Everything all right?

HAPPY: Yeah, Charley, everything's . . .

WILLY: What's the matter?

CHARLEY: I heard some noise. I thought something happened. Can't we do   390
something about the walls? You sneeze in here, and in my house hats blow off.

HAPPY: Let's go to bed, Dad. Come on.

Charley signals to Happy to go.

WILLY: You go ahead, I'm not tired at the moment.

HAPPY: *(to Willy)* Take it easy, huh? *(He exits.)*

WILLY: What're you doin' up?

CHARLEY: *(sitting down at the kitchen table opposite Willy)* Couldn't sleep good.   395
I had a heartburn.

WILLY: Well, you don't know how to eat.

CHARLEY: I eat with my mouth.

WILLY: No, you're ignorant. You gotta know about vitamins and things like that.

CHARLEY: Come on, let's shoot. Tire you out a little.

WILLY: *(hesitantly)* All right. You got cards?   400

CHARLEY: *(taking a deck from his pocket)* Yeah, I got them. Someplace. What is
it with those vitamins?

WILLY: *(dealing)* They build up your bones. Chemistry.

CHARLEY: Yeah, but there's no bones in a heartburn.

WILLY: What are you talkin' about? Do you know the first thing about it?

CHARLEY: Don't get insulted.   405

WILLY: Don't talk about something you don't know anything about.

They are playing. Pause.

CHARLEY: What're you doin' home?

WILLY: A little trouble with the car.

CHARLEY: Oh. *(Pause.)* I'd like to take a trip to California.

WILLY: Don't say.   410

CHARLEY: You want a job?

WILLY: I got a job, I told you that. *(After a slight pause.)* What the hell are you
offering me a job for?

CHARLEY: Don't get insulted.

WILLY: Don't insult me.

CHARLEY: I don't see no sense in it. You don't have to go on this way.   415

WILLY: I got a good job. *(Slight pause.)* What do you keep comin' in here for?

CHARLEY: You want me to go?

WILLY: *(after a pause, withering)* I can't understand it. He's going back to Texas
again. What the hell is that?

CHARLEY: Let him go.

WILLY: I got nothin' to give him, Charley, I'm clean, I'm clean.   420

CHARLEY: He won't starve. None a them starve. Forget about him.

WILLY: Then what have I got to remember?

CHARLEY: You take it too hard. To hell with it. When a deposit bottle is broken you don't get your nickel back.

WILLY: That's easy enough for you to say.

425 **CHARLEY:** That ain't easy for me to say.

WILLY: Did you see the ceiling I put up in the living room?

CHARLEY: Yeah, that's a piece of work. To put up a ceiling is a mystery to me. How do you do it?

WILLY: What's the difference?

CHARLEY: Well, talk about it.

430 **WILLY:** You gonna put up a ceiling?

CHARLEY: How could I put up a ceiling?

WILLY: Then what the hell are you bothering me for?

CHARLEY: You're insulted again.

WILLY: A man who can't handle tools is not a man. You're disgusting.

435 **CHARLEY:** Don't call me disgusting, Willy.

Uncle Ben, carrying a valise and an umbrella, enters the forestage from around the right corner of the house. He is a stolid man, in his sixties, with a mustache and an authoritative air. He is utterly certain of his destiny, and there is an aura of far places about him. He enters exactly as Willy speaks.

WILLY: I'm getting awfully tired, Ben.

Ben's music is heard. Ben looks around at everything.

CHARLEY: Good, keep playing; you'll sleep better. Did you call me Ben?

Ben looks at his watch.

WILLY: That's funny. For a second there you reminded me of my brother Ben.

BEN: I have only a few minutes. (*He strolls, inspecting the place. Willy and Charley continue playing.*)

440 **CHARLEY:** You never heard from him again, heh? Since that time?

WILLY: Didn't Linda tell you? Couple of weeks ago we got a letter from his wife in Africa. He died.

CHARLEY: That so.

BEN: (*chuckling*) So this is Brooklyn, eh?

CHARLEY: Maybe you're in for some of his money.

445 **WILLY:** Naa, he had seven sons. There's just one opportunity I had with that man . . .

BEN: I must make a train, William. There are several properties I'm looking at in Alaska.

WILLY: Sure, sure! If I'd gone with him to Alaska that time, everything would've been totally different.

CHARLEY: Go on, you'd froze to death up there.

WILLY: What're you talking about?

BEN: Opportunity is tremendous in Alaska, William. Surprised you're not up   450
there.

WILLY: Sure, tremendous.

CHARLEY: Heh?

WILLY: There was the only man I ever met who knew the answers.

CHARLEY: Who?

BEN: How are you all?   455

WILLY: (*taking a pot, smiling*) Fine, fine.

CHARLEY: Pretty sharp tonight.

BEN: Is Mother living with you?

WILLY: No, she died a long time ago.

CHARLEY: Who?   460

BEN: That's too bad. Fine specimen of a lady, Mother.

WILLY: (*to Charley*) Heh?

BEN: I'd hoped to see the old girl.

CHARLEY: Who died?

BEN: Heard anything from Father, have you?   465

WILLY: (*unnerved*) What do you mean, who died?

CHARLEY: (*taking a pot*) What're you talkin' about?

BEN: (*looking at his watch*) William, it's half-past eight!

WILLY: (*as though to dispel his confusion he angrily stops Charley's hand*) That's my
build!

CHARLEY: I put the ace —   470

WILLY: If you don't know how to play the game I'm not gonna throw my
money away on you!

CHARLEY: (*rising*) It was my ace, for God's sake!

WILLY: I'm through, I'm through!

BEN: When did Mother die?

WILLY: Long ago. Since the beginning you never knew how to play cards.   475

CHARLEY: (*picks up the cards and goes to the door*) All right! Next time I'll bring
a deck with five aces.

WILLY: I don't play that kind of game!

CHARLEY: (*turning to him*) You should be ashamed of yourself!

WILLY: Yeah?

CHARLEY: Yeah! (*He goes out.*)   480

WILLY: (*slamming the door after him*) Ignoramus!

BEN: (*as Willy comes toward him through the wall-line of the kitchen*) So you're
William.

WILLY: (*shaking Ben's hand*) Ben! I've been waiting for you so long! What's the
answer? How did you do it?

BEN: Oh, there's a story in that.

Linda enters the forestage, as of old, carrying the wash basket.

485 **LINDA:** Is this Ben?

BEN: *(gallantly)* How do you do, my dear.

LINDA: Where've you been all these years? Willy's always wondered why you—

WILLY: *(pulling Ben away from her impatiently)* Where is Dad? Didn't you follow him? How did you get started?

BEN: Well, I don't know how much you remember.

490 **WILLY:** Well, I was just a baby, of course, only three or four years old—

BEN: Three years and eleven months.

WILLY: What a memory, Ben!

BEN: I have many enterprises, William, and I have never kept books.

WILLY: I remember I was sitting under the wagon in — was it Nebraska?

495 **BEN:** It was South Dakota, and I gave you a bunch of wild flowers.

WILLY: I remember you walking away down some open road.

BEN: *(laughing)* I was going to find Father in Alaska.

WILLY: Where is he?

BEN: At that age I had a very faulty view of geography, William. I discovered after a few days that I was heading due south, so instead of Alaska, I ended up in Africa.

500 **LINDA:** Africa!

WILLY: The Gold Coast!

BEN: Principally, diamond mines.

LINDA: Diamond mines!

BEN: Yes, my dear. But I've only a few minutes—

505 **WILLY:** No! Boys! Boys! *(Young Biff and Happy appear.)* Listen to this. This is your Uncle Ben, a great man! Tell my boys, Ben!

BEN: Why, boys, when I was seventeen I walked into the jungle, and when I was twenty-one I walked out. *(He laughs.)* And by God I was rich.

WILLY: *(to the boys)* You see what I been talking about? The greatest things can happen!

BEN: *(glancing at his watch)* I have an appointment in Ketchikan Tuesday week.

WILLY: No, Ben! Please tell about Dad. I want my boys to hear. I want them to know the kind of stock they spring from. All I remember is a man with a big beard, and I was in Mamma's lap, sitting around a fire, and some kind of high music.

510 **BEN:** His flute. He played the flute.

WILLY: Sure, the flute, that's right!

New music is heard, a high, rollicking tune.

BEN: Father was a very great and a very wild-hearted man. We would start in Boston, and he'd toss the whole family into the wagon, and then he'd drive the team right across the country; through Ohio, and Indiana, Michigan, Illinois, and all the Western states. And we'd stop in the towns and sell the flutes that he'd made on the way. Great inventor, Father. With one gadget he made more in a week than a man like you could make in a lifetime.

WILLY: That's just the way I'm bringing them up, Ben — rugged, well liked, all-around.

BEN: Yeah? (*To Biff.*) Hit that, boy — hard as you can. (*He pounds his stomach.*)

BIFF: Oh, no, sir! 515

BEN: (*taking boxing stance*) Come on, get to me! (*He laughs.*)

WILLY: Go to it, Biff! Go ahead, show him!

BIFF: Okay! (*He cocks his fist and starts in.*)

LINDA: (*to Willy*) Why must he fight, dear?

BEN: (*sparring with Biff*) Good boy! Good boy! 520

WILLY: How's that, Ben, heh?

HAPPY: Give him the left, Biff!

LINDA: Why are you fighting?

BEN: Good boy! (*Suddenly comes in, trips Biff, and stands over him, the point of his umbrella poised over Biff's eye.*)

LINDA: Look out, Biff! 525

BIFF: Gee!

BEN: (*patting Biff's knee*) Never fight fair with a stranger, boy. You'll never get out of the jungle that way. (*Taking Linda's hand and bowing.*) It was an honor and a pleasure to meet you, Linda.

LINDA: (*withdrawing her hand coldly, frightened*) Have a nice — trip.

BEN: (*to Willy*) And good luck with your — what do you do?

WILLY: Selling. 530

BEN: Yes. Well . . . (*He raises his hand in farewell to all.*)

WILLY: No, Ben, I don't want you to think . . . (*He takes Ben's arm to show him.*) It's Brooklyn, I know, but we hunt too.

BEN: Really, now.

WILLY: Oh, sure, there's snakes and rabbits and — that's why I moved out here. Why, Biff can fell any one of these trees in no time! Boys! Go right over to where they're building the apartment house and get some sand. We're gonna rebuild the entire front stoop right now! Watch this, Ben!

BIFF: Yes, sir! On the double, Hap! 535

HAPPY: (*as he and Biff run off*) I lost weight, Pop, you notice?

Charley enters in knickers, even before the boys are gone.

CHARLEY: Listen, if they steal any more from that building the watchman'll put the cops on them!

LINDA: (*to Willy*) Don't let Biff . . .

Ben laughs lustily.

WILLY: You shoulda seen the lumber they brought home last week. At least a dozen six-by-tens worth all kinds of money.

540 **CHARLEY:** Listen, if that watchman—

WILLY: I gave them hell, understand. But I got a couple of fearless characters there.

CHARLEY: Willy, the jails are full of fearless characters.

BEN: *(clapping Willy on the back, with a laugh at Charley)* And the stock exchange, friend!

WILLY: *(joining in Ben's laughter)* Where are the rest of your pants?

545 **CHARLEY:** My wife bought them.

WILLY: Now all you need is a golf club and you can go upstairs and go to sleep. *(To Ben.)* Great athlete! Between him and his son Bernard they can't hammer a nail!

BERNARD: *(rushing in)* The watchman's chasing Biff!

WILLY: *(angrily)* Shut up! He's not stealing anything!

LINDA: *(alarmed, hurrying off left)* Where is he? Biff, dear! *(She exits.)*

550 **WILLY:** *(moving toward the left, away from Ben)* There's nothing wrong. What's the matter with you?

BEN: Nervy boy. Good!

WILLY: *(laughing)* Oh, nerves of iron, that Biff!

CHARLEY: Don't know what it is. My New England man comes back and he's bleedin', they murdered him up there.

WILLY: It's contacts, Charley, I got important contacts!

555 **CHARLEY:** *(sarcastically)* Glad to hear it, Willy. Come in later, we'll shoot a little casino. I'll take some of your Portland money. *(He laughs at Willy and exits.)*

WILLY: *(turning to Ben)* Business is bad, it's murderous. But not for me, of course.

BEN: I'll stop by on my way back to Africa.

WILLY: *(longingly)* Can't you stay a few days? You're just what I need, Ben, because I — I have a fine position here, but I — well, Dad left when I was such a baby and I never had a chance to talk to him and I still feel — kind of temporary about myself.

BEN: I'll be late for my train.

They are at opposite ends of the stage.

560 **WILLY:** Ben, my boys — can't we talk? They'd go into the jaws of hell for me, see, but I —

BEN: William, you're being first-rate with your boys. Outstanding, manly chaps!

WILLY: *(hanging on to his words)* Oh, Ben, that's good to hear! Because sometimes I'm afraid that I'm not teaching them the right kind of — Ben, how should I teach them?

BEN: *(giving great weight to each word, and with a certain vicious audacity)* William, when I walked into the jungle, I was seventeen. When I walked out I was twenty-one. And, by God, I was rich! *(He goes off into darkness around the right corner of the house.)*

WILLY: . . . was rich! That's just the spirit I want to imbue them with! To walk into a jungle! I was right! I was right! I was right!

Ben is gone, but Willy is still speaking to him as Linda, in nightgown and robe, enters the kitchen, glances around for Willy, then goes to the door of the house, looks out and sees him. Comes down to his left. He looks at her.

LINDA: Willy, dear? Willy?   565

WILLY: I was right!

LINDA: Did you have some cheese? *(He can't answer.)* It's very late, darling. Come to bed, heh?

WILLY: *(looking straight up)* Gotta break your neck to see a star in this yard.

LINDA: You coming in?

WILLY: What ever happened to that diamond watch fob? Remember? When   570
Ben came from Africa that time? Didn't he give me a watch fob with a diamond in it?

LINDA: You pawned it, dear. Twelve, thirteen years ago. For Biff's radio correspondence course.

WILLY: Gee, that was a beautiful thing. I'll take a walk.

LINDA: But you're in your slippers.

WILLY: *(starting to go around the house at the left)* I was right! I was! *(Half to Linda, as he goes, shaking his head.)* What a man! There was a man worth talking to. I was right!

LINDA: *(calling after Willy)* But in your slippers, Willy!   575

Willy is almost gone when Biff, in his pajamas, comes down the stairs and enters the kitchen.

BIFF: What is he doing out there?

LINDA: Sh!

BIFF: God Almighty, Mom, how long has he been doing this?

LINDA: Don't, he'll hear you.

BIFF: What the hell is the matter with him?   580

LINDA: It'll pass by morning.

BIFF: Shouldn't we do anything?

LINDA: Oh, my dear, you should do a lot of things, but there's nothing to do, so go to sleep.

Happy comes down the stairs and sits on the steps.

HAPPY: I never heard him so loud, Mom.

LINDA: Well, come around more often; you'll hear him. *(She sits down at the*   585
table and mends the lining of Willy's jacket.)

BIFF: Why didn't you ever write me about this, Mom?

LINDA: How would I write to you? For over three months you had no address.

BIFF: I was on the move. But you know I thought of you all the time. You know that, don't you, pal?

LINDA: I know, dear, I know. But he likes to have a letter. Just to know that there's still a possibility for better things.

590 **BIFF:** He's not like this all the time, is he?

LINDA: It's when you come home he's always the worst.

BIFF: When I come home?

LINDA: When you write you're coming, he's all smiles, and talks about the future, and — he's just wonderful. And then the closer you seem to come, the more shaky he gets, and then, by the time you get here, he's arguing, and he seems angry at you. I think it's just that maybe he can't bring himself to — to open up to you. Why are you so hateful to each other? Why is that?

BIFF: (*evasively*) I'm not hateful, Mom.

595 **LINDA:** But you no sooner come in the door than you're fighting!

BIFF: I don't know why. I mean to change. I'm tryin', Mom, you understand?

LINDA: Are you home to stay now?

BIFF: I don't know. I want to look around, see what's doin'.

LINDA: Biff, you can't look around all your life, can you?

600 **BIFF:** I just can't take hold, Mom. I can't take hold of some kind of a life.

LINDA: Biff, a man is not a bird, to come and go with the springtime.

BIFF: Your hair . . . (*He touches her hair.*) Your hair got so gray.

LINDA: Oh, it's been gray since you were in high school. I just stopped dyeing it, that's all.

BIFF: Dye it again, will ya? I don't want my pal looking old. (*He smiles.*)

605 **LINDA:** You're such a boy! You think you can go away for a year and . . . You've got to get it into your head now that one day you'll knock on this door and there'll be strange people here —

BIFF: What are you talking about? You're not even sixty, Mom.

LINDA: But what about your father?

BIFF: (*lamely*) Well, I meant him too.

HAPPY: He admires Pop.

610 **LINDA:** Biff, dear, if you don't have any feeling for him, then you can't have any feeling for me.

BIFF: Sure I can, Mom.

LINDA: No. You can't just come to see me, because I love him. (*With a threat, but only a threat, of tears.*) He's the dearest man in the world to me, and I won't have anyone making him feel unwanted and low and blue. You've got to make up your mind now, darling, there's no leeway any more. Either he's your father and you pay him that respect, or else you're not to come here. I know he's not easy to get along with — nobody knows that better than me — but . . .

WILLY: (*from the left, with a laugh*) Hey, hey, Biffo!

BIFF: (*starting to go out after Willy*) What the hell is the matter with him? (*Happy stops him.*)

615 **LINDA:** Don't — don't go near him!

BIFF: Stop making excuses for him! He always, always wiped the floor with you. Never had an ounce of respect for you.

HAPPY: He's always had respect for—

BIFF: What the hell do you know about it?

HAPPY: (*surlily*) Just don't call him crazy!

BIFF: He's got no character — Charley wouldn't do this. Not in his own   620
house — spewing out that vomit from his mind.

HAPPY: Charley never had to cope with what he's got to.

BIFF: People are worse off than Willy Loman. Believe me, I've seen them!

LINDA: Then make Charley your father, Biff. You can't do that, can you? I don't say he's a great man. Willy Loman never made a lot of money. His name was never in the paper. He's not the finest character that ever lived. But he's a human being, and a terrible thing is happening to him. So attention must be paid. He's not to be allowed to fall into his grave like an old dog. Attention, attention must be finally paid to such a person. You called him crazy—

BIFF: I didn't mean—

LINDA: No, a lot of people think he's lost his — balance. But you don't have to 625
be very smart to know what his trouble is. The man is exhausted.

HAPPY: Sure!

LINDA: A small man can be just as exhausted as a great man. He works for a company thirty-six years this March, opens up unheard-of territories to their trademark, and now in his old age they take his salary away.

HAPPY: (*indignantly*) I didn't know that, Mom.

LINDA: You never asked, my dear! Now that you get your spending money someplace else you don't trouble your mind with him.

HAPPY: But I gave you money last—   630

LINDA: Christmas time, fifty dollars! To fix the hot water it cost ninety-seven fifty! For five weeks he's been on straight commission, like a beginner, an unknown!

BIFF: Those ungrateful bastards!

LINDA: Are they any worse than his sons? When he brought them business, when he was young, they were glad to see him. But now his old friends, the old buyers that loved him so and always found some order to hand him in a pinch — they're all dead, retired. He used to be able to make six, seven calls a day in Boston. Now he takes his valises out of the car and puts them back and takes them out again and he's exhausted. Instead of walking he talks now. He drives seven hundred miles, and when he gets there no one knows him any more, no one welcomes him. And what goes through a man's mind, driving seven hundred miles home without having earned a cent? Why shouldn't he talk to himself? Why? When he has to go to Charley and borrow fifty dollars a week and pretend to me that it's his pay? How long can that go on? How long? You see what I'm sitting here and waiting for? And you tell me he has no character? The man who never worked a day but for your benefit? When does he get the medal for that? Is this his reward — to turn around at the age of sixty-three and find his sons, who he loved better than his life, one a philandering bum—

HAPPY: Mom!

635 **LINDA:** That's all you are, my baby! *(To Biff.)* And you! What happened to the love you had for him? You were such pals! How you used to talk to him on the phone every night! How lonely he was till he could come home to you!

BIFF: All right, Mom. I'll live here in my room, and I'll get a job. I'll keep away from him, that's all.

LINDA: No, Biff. You can't stay here and fight all the time.

BIFF: He threw me out of this house, remember that.

LINDA: Why did he do that? I never knew why.

640 **BIFF:** Because I know he's a fake and he doesn't like anybody around who knows!

LINDA: Why a fake? In what way? What do you mean?

BIFF: Just don't lay it all at my feet. It's between me and him — that's all I have to say. I'll chip in from now on. He'll settle for half my pay check. He'll be all right. I'm going to bed. *(He starts for the stairs.)*

LINDA: He won't be all right.

BIFF: *(turning on the stairs, furiously)* I hate this city and I'll stay here. Now what do you want?

645 **LINDA:** He's dying, Biff.

Happy turns quickly to her, shocked.

BIFF: *(after a pause)* Why is he dying?

LINDA: He's been trying to kill himself.

BIFF: *(with great horror)* How?

LINDA: I live from day to day.

650 **BIFF:** What're you talking about?

LINDA: Remember I wrote you that he smashed up the car again? In February?

BIFF: Well?

LINDA: The insurance inspector came. He said that they have evidence. That all these accidents in the last year — weren't — weren't — accidents.

HAPPY: How can they tell that? That's a lie.

655 **LINDA:** It seems there's a woman . . . *(She takes a breath as —)*

BIFF: *(sharply but contained)* What woman?

LINDA: *(simultaneously)* . . . and this woman . . .

LINDA: What?

BIFF: Nothing. Go ahead.

660 **LINDA:** What did you say?

BIFF: Nothing. I just said what woman?

HAPPY: What about her?

LINDA: Well, it seems she was walking down the road and saw his car. She says that he wasn't driving fast at all, and that he didn't skid. She says he came to that little bridge, and then deliberately smashed into the railing, and it was only the shallowness of the water that saved him.

Biff: Oh, no, he probably just fell asleep again.

Linda: I don't think he fell asleep.   665

Biff: Why not?

Linda: Last month . . . (*With great difficulty.*) Oh, boys, it's so hard to say a thing like this! He's just a big stupid man to you, but I tell you there's more good in him than in many other people. (*She chokes, wipes her eyes.*) I was looking for a fuse. The lights blew out, and I went down the cellar. And behind the fuse box — it happened to fall out — was a length of rubber pipe — just short.

Happy: No kidding?

Linda: There's a little attachment on the end of it. I knew right away. And sure enough, on the bottom of the water heater there's a new little nipple on the gas pipe.

Happy: (*angrily*) That — jerk.   670

Biff: Did you have it taken off?

Linda: I'm — I'm ashamed to. How can I mention it to him? Every day I go down and take away that little rubber pipe. But, when he comes home, I put it back where it was. How can I insult him that way? I don't know what to do. I live from day to day, boys. I tell you, I know every thought in his mind. It sounds so old-fashioned and silly, but I tell you he put his whole life into you and you've turned your backs on him. (*She is bent over in the chair, weeping, her face in her hands.*) Biff, I swear to God! Biff, his life is in your hands!

Happy: (*to Biff*) How do you like that damned fool!

Biff: (*kissing her*) All right, pal, all right. It's all settled now. I've been remiss. I know that, Mom, but now I'll stay, and I swear to you, I'll apply myself. (*Kneeling in front of her, in a fever of self-reproach.*) It's just — you see, Mom, I don't fit in business. Not that I won't try. I'll try, and I'll make good.

Happy: Sure you will. The trouble with you in business was you never tried to   675 please people.

Biff: I know, I—

Happy: Like when you worked for Harrison's. Bob Harrison said you were tops, and then you go and do some damn fool thing like whistling whole songs in the elevator like a comedian.

Biff: (*against Happy*) So what? I like to whistle sometimes.

Happy: You don't raise a guy to a responsible job who whistles in the elevator!

Linda: Well, don't argue about it now.   680

Happy: Like when you'd go off and swim in the middle of the day instead of taking the line around.

Biff: (*his resentment rising*) Well, don't you run off? You take off sometimes, don't you? On a nice summer day?

HAPPY: Yeah, but I cover myself!

LINDA: Boys!

685 **HAPPY:** If I'm going to take a fade the boss can call any number where I'm supposed to be and they'll swear to him that I just left. I'll tell you something that I hate to say, Biff, but in the business world some of them think you're crazy.

BIFF: *(angered)* Screw the business world!

HAPPY: All right, screw it! Great, but cover yourself!

LINDA: Hap, Hap!

BIFF: I don't care what they think! They've laughed at Dad for years, and you know why? Because we don't belong in this nut-house of a city! We should be mixing cement on some open plain, or — or carpenters. A carpenter is allowed to whistle!

Willy walks in from the entrance of the house, at left.

690 **WILLY:** Even your grandfather was better than a carpenter. *(Pause. They watch him.)* You never grew up. Bernard does not whistle in the elevator, I assure you.

BIFF: *(as though to laugh Willy out of it)* Yeah, but you do, Pop.

WILLY: I never in my life whistled in an elevator! And who in the business world thinks I'm crazy?

BIFF: I didn't mean it like that, Pop. Now don't make a whole thing out of it, will ya?

WILLY: Go back to the West! Be a carpenter, a cowboy, enjoy yourself!

695 **LINDA:** Willy, he was just saying —

WILLY: I heard what he said!

HAPPY: *(trying to quiet Willy)* Hey, Pop, come on now . . .

WILLY: *(continuing over Happy's line)* They laugh at me, heh? Go to Filene's, go to the Hub, go to Slattery's, Boston. Call out the name Willy Loman and see what happens! Big shot!

BIFF: All right, Pop.

700 **WILLY:** Big!

BIFF: All right!

WILLY: Why do you always insult me?

BIFF: I didn't say a word. *(To Linda.)* Did I say a word?

LINDA: He didn't say anything, Willy.

705 **WILLY:** *(going to the doorway of the living room)* All right, good night, good night.

LINDA: Willy, dear, he just decided . . .

WILLY: *(to Biff)* If you get tired hanging around tomorrow, paint the ceiling I put up in the living room.

BIFF: I'm leaving early tomorrow.

HAPPY: He's going to see Bill Oliver, Pop.

710 **WILLY:** *(interestedly)* Oliver? For what?

BIFF: *(with reserve, but trying, trying)* He always said he'd stake me. I'd like to go into business, so maybe I can take him up on it.

LINDA: Isn't that wonderful?

WILLY: Don't interrupt. What's wonderful about it? There's fifty men in the City of New York who'd stake him. *(To Biff.)* Sporting goods?

BIFF: I guess so. I know something about it and —

WILLY: He knows something about it! You know sporting goods better than   715
Spalding, for God's sake! How much is he giving you?

BIFF: I don't know, I didn't even see him yet, but —

WILLY: Then what're you talkin' about?

BIFF: *(getting angry)* Well, all I said was I'm gonna see him, that's all!

WILLY: *(turning away)* Ah, you're counting your chickens again.

BIFF: *(starting left for the stairs)* Oh, Jesus, I'm going to sleep!   720

WILLY: *(calling after him)* Don't curse in this house!

BIFF: *(turning)* Since when did you get so clean!

HAPPY: *(trying to stop them)* Wait a . . .

WILLY: Don't use that language to me! I won't have it!

HAPPY: *(grabbing Biff, shouts)* Wait a minute! I got an idea. I got a feasible   725
idea. Come here, Biff, let's talk this over now, let's talk some sense here.
When I was down in Florida last time, I thought of a great idea to sell
sporting goods. It just came back to me. You and I, Biff — we have a line,
the Loman Line. We train a couple of weeks, and put on a couple of
exhibitions, see?

WILLY: That's an idea!

HAPPY: Wait! We form two basketball teams, see? Two water-polo teams. We
play each other. It's a million dollars' worth of publicity. Two brothers, see?
The Loman Brothers. Displays in the Royal Palms — all the hotels. And
banners over the ring and the basketball court: "Loman Brothers." Baby, we
could sell sporting goods!

WILLY: That is a one-million-dollar idea.

LINDA: Marvelous!

BIFF: I'm in great shape as far as that's concerned.   730

HAPPY: And the beauty of it is, Biff, it wouldn't be like a business. We'd be out
playin' ball again . . .

BIFF: *(enthused)* Yeah, that's . . .

WILLY: Million-dollar . . .

HAPPY: And you wouldn't get fed up with it, Biff. It'd be the family again.
There'd be the old honor, and comradeship, and if you wanted to go off for
a swim or somethin' — well, you'd do it! Without some smart cooky gettin'
up ahead of you!

WILLY: Lick the world! You guys together could absolutely lick the civilized   735
world.

BIFF: I'll see Oliver tomorrow. Hap, if we could work that out . . .

LINDA: Maybe things are beginning to —

Willy: *(wildly enthused, to Linda)* Stop interrupting! *(To Biff.)* But don't wear sport jacket and slacks when you see Oliver.

Biff: No, I'll—

740 **Willy:** A business suit, and talk as little as possible, and don't crack any jokes.

Biff: He did like me. Always liked me.

Linda: He loved you!

Willy: *(to Linda)* Will you stop! *(To Biff.)* Walk in very serious. You are not applying for a boy's job. Money is to pass. Be quiet, fine, and serious. Everybody likes a kidder, but nobody lends him money.

Happy: I'll try to get some myself, Biff. I'm sure I can.

745 **Willy:** I can see great things for you, kids, I think your troubles are over. But remember, start big and you'll end big. Ask for fifteen. How much you gonna ask for?

Biff: Gee, I don't know—

Willy: And don't say "Gee." "Gee" is a boy's word. A man walking in for fifteen thousand dollars does not say "Gee!"

Biff: Ten, I think, would be top though.

Willy: Don't be so modest. You always started too low. Walk in with a big laugh. Don't look worried. Start off with a couple of your good stories to lighten things up. It's not what you say, it's how you say it — because personality always wins the day.

750 **Linda:** Oliver always thought the highest of him—

Willy: Will you let me talk?

Biff: Don't yell at her, Pop, will ya?

Willy: *(angrily)* I was talking, wasn't I!

Biff: I don't like you yelling at her all the time, and I'm tellin' you, that's all.

755 **Willy:** What're you, takin' over this house?

Linda: Willy—

Willy: *(turning on her)* Don't take his side all the time, goddammit!

Biff: *(furiously)* Stop yelling at her!

Willy: *(suddenly pulling on his cheek, beaten down, guilt ridden)* Give my best to Bill Oliver—he may remember me. *(He exits through the living room doorway.)*

760 **Linda:** *(her voice subdued)* What'd you have to start that for? *(Biff turns away.)* You see how sweet he was as soon as you talked hopefully? *(She goes over to Biff.)* Come up and say good night to him. Don't let him go to bed that way.

Happy: Come on, Biff, let's buck him up.

Linda: Please, dear. Just say good night. It takes so little to make him happy. Come. *(She goes through the living room doorway, calling upstairs from within the living room.)* Your pajamas are hanging in the bathroom. Willy!

Happy: *(looking toward where Linda went out)* What a woman! They broke the mold when they made her. You know that, Biff?

Biff: He's off salary. My God, working on commission!

765 **Happy:** Well, let's face it: he's no hot-shot selling man. Except that sometimes, you have to admit, he's a sweet personality.

BIFF: *(deciding)* Lend me ten bucks, will ya? I want to buy some new ties.

HAPPY: I'll take you to a place I know. Beautiful stuff. Wear one of my striped shirts tomorrow.

BIFF: She got gray. Mom got awful old. Gee, I'm gonna go in to Oliver tomorrow and knock him for a —

HAPPY: Come on up. Tell that to Dad. Let's give him a whirl. Come on.

BIFF: *(steamed up)* You know, with ten thousand bucks, boy!   770

HAPPY: *(as they go into the living room)* That's the talk, Biff, that's the first time I've heard the old confidence out of you! *(From within the living room, fading off.)* You're gonna live with me, kid, and any babe you want you just say the word . . . *(The last lines are hardly heard. They are mounting the stairs to their parents' bedroom.)*

LINDA: *(entering her bedroom and addressing Willy, who is in the bathroom. She is straightening the bed for him)* Can you do anything about the shower? It drips.

WILLY: *(from the bathroom)* All of a sudden everything falls to pieces! Goddam plumbing, oughta be sued, those people. I hardly finished putting it in and the thing . . . *(His words rumble off.)*

LINDA: I'm just wondering if Oliver will remember him. You think he might?

WILLY: *(coming out of the bathroom in his pajamas)* Remember him? What's the   775
matter with you, you crazy? If he'd've stayed with Oliver he'd be on top by now! Wait'll Oliver gets a look at him. You don't know the average caliber any more. The average young man today — *(he is getting into bed)* — is got a caliber of zero. Greatest thing in the world for him was to bum around.

Biff and Happy enter the bedroom. Slight pause.

WILLY: *(stops short, looking at Biff)* Glad to hear it, boy.

HAPPY: He wanted to say good night to you, sport.

WILLY: *(to Biff)* Yeah. Knock him dead, boy. What'd you want to tell me?

BIFF: Just take it easy, Pop. Good night. *(He turns to go.)*

WILLY: *(unable to resist)* And if anything falls off the desk while you're talking   780
to him — like a package or something — don't you pick it up. They have office boys for that.

LINDA: I'll make a big breakfast —

WILLY: Will you let me finish? *(To Biff.)* Tell him you were in the business in the West. Not farm work.

BIFF: All right, Dad.

LINDA: I think everything —

WILLY: *(going right through her speech)* And don't undersell yourself. No less   785
than fifteen thousand dollars.

BIFF: *(unable to bear him)* Okay. Good night, Mom. *(He starts moving.)*

WILLY: Because you got a greatness in you, Biff, remember that. You got all kinds a greatness . . . *(He lies back, exhausted. Biff walks out.)*

LINDA: *(calling after Biff)* Sleep well, darling!

HAPPY: I'm gonna get married, Mom. I wanted to tell you.

790 **LINDA:** Go to sleep, dear.

HAPPY: *(going)* I just wanted to tell you.

WILLY: Keep up the good work. *(Happy exits.)* God . . . remember that Ebbets Field game? The championship of the city?

LINDA: Just rest. Should I sing to you?

WILLY: Yeah. Sing to me. *(Linda hums a soft lullaby.)* When that team came out — he was the tallest, remember?

795 **LINDA:** Oh, yes. And in gold.

Biff enters the darkened kitchen, takes a cigarette, and leaves the house. He comes downstage into a golden pool of light. He smokes, staring at the night.

WILLY: Like a young god. Hercules — something like that. And the sun, the sun all around him. Remember how he waved to me? Right up from the field, with the representatives of three colleges standing by? And the buyers I brought, and the cheers when he came out — Loman, Loman, Loman! God Almighty, he'll be great yet. A star like that, magnificent, can never really fade away!

The light on Willy is fading. The gas heater begins to glow through the kitchen wall, near the stairs, a blue flame beneath red coils.

LINDA: *(timidly)* Willy, dear, what has he got against you?

WILLY: I'm so tired. Don't talk any more.

Biff slowly returns to the kitchen. He stops, stares toward the heater.

LINDA: Will you ask Howard to let you work in New York?

800 **WILLY:** First thing in the morning. Everything'll be all right.

Biff reaches behind the heater and draws out a length of rubber tubing. He is horrified and turns his head toward Willy's room, still dimly lit, from which the strains of Linda's desperate but monotonous humming rise.

WILLY: *(staring through the window into the moonlight)* Gee, look at the moon moving between the buildings!

Biff wraps the tubing around his hand and quickly goes up the stairs. Curtain.

ACT 2

Music is heard, gay and bright. The curtain rises as the music fades away. Willy, in shirt sleeves, is sitting at the kitchen table, sipping coffee, his hat in his lap. Linda is filling his cup when she can.

WILLY: Wonderful coffee. Meal in itself.

LINDA: Can I make you some eggs?

WILLY: No. Take a breath.

LINDA: You look so rested, dear.

WILLY: I slept like a dead one. First time in months. Imagine, sleeping till ten   5
on a Tuesday morning. Boys left nice and early, heh?

LINDA: They were out of here by eight o'clock.

WILLY: Good work!

LINDA: It was so thrilling to see them leaving together. I can't get over the
shaving lotion in this house.

WILLY: (*smiling*) Mmm —

LINDA: Biff was very changed this morning. His whole attitude seemed to be   10
hopeful. He couldn't wait to get downtown to see Oliver.

WILLY: He's heading for a change. There's no question, there simply are
certain men that take longer to get — solidified. How did he dress?

LINDA: His blue suit. He's so handsome in that suit. He could be a — anything
in that suit!

Willy gets up from the table. Linda holds his jacket for him.

WILLY: There's no question, no question at all. Gee, on the way home tonight
I'd like to buy some seeds.

LINDA: (*laughing*) That'd be wonderful. But not enough sun gets back there.
Nothing'll grow any more.

WILLY: You wait, kid, before it's all over we're gonna get a little place out in   15
the country, and I'll raise some vegetables, a couple of chickens . . .

LINDA: You'll do it yet, dear.

Willy walks out of his jacket. Linda follows him.

WILLY: And they'll get married, and come for a weekend. I'd build a little
guest house. 'Cause I got so many fine tools, all I'd need would be a little
lumber and some peace of mind.

LINDA: (*joyfully*) I sewed the lining . . .

WILLY: I could build two guest houses, so they'd both come. Did he decide
how much he's going to ask Oliver for?

LINDA: (*getting him into the jacket*) He didn't mention it, but I imagine ten or   20
fifteen thousand. You going to talk to Howard today?

WILLY: Yeah. I'll put it to him straight and simple. He'll just have to take me
off the road.

LINDA: And Willy, don't forget to ask for a little advance, because we've got
the insurance premium. It's the grace period now.

WILLY: That's a hundred . . .?

LINDA: A hundred and eight, sixty-eight. Because we're a little short again.

WILLY: Why are we short?   25

LINDA: Well, you had the motor job on the car . . .

WILLY: That goddam Studebaker!

LINDA: And you got one more payment on the refrigerator . . .

WILLY: But it just broke again!

30 **LINDA:** Well, it's old, dear.

WILLY: I told you we should've bought a well-advertised machine. Charley bought a General Electric and it's twenty years old and it's still good, that son-of-a-bitch.

LINDA: But, Willy—

WILLY: Whoever heard of a Hastings refrigerator? Once in my life I would like to own something outright before it's broken! I'm always in a race with the junkyard! I just finished paying for the car and it's on its last legs. The refrigerator consumes belts like a goddam maniac. They time those things. They time them so when you finally paid for them, they're used up.

LINDA: (*buttoning up his jacket as he unbuttons it*) All told, about two hundred dollars would carry us, dear. But that includes the last payment on the mortgage. After this payment, Willy, the house belongs to us.

35 **WILLY:** It's twenty-five years!

LINDA: Biff was nine years old when we bought it.

WILLY: Well, that's a great thing. To weather a twenty-five year mortgage is—

LINDA: It's an accomplishment.

WILLY: All the cement, the lumber, the reconstruction I put in this house! There ain't a crack to be found in it any more.

40 **LINDA:** Well, it served its purpose.

WILLY: What purpose? Some stranger'll come along, move in, and that's that. If only Biff would take this house, and raise a family . . . (*He starts to go.*) Good-by, I'm late.

LINDA: (*suddenly remembering*) Oh, I forgot! You're supposed to meet them for dinner.

WILLY: Me?

LINDA: At Frank's Chop House on Forty-eighth near Sixth Avenue.

45 **WILLY:** Is that so! How about you?

LINDA: No, just the three of you. They're gonna blow you to a big meal!

WILLY: Don't say! Who thought of that?

LINDA: Biff came to me this morning, Willy, and he said, "Tell Dad, we want to blow him to a big meal." Be there six o'clock. You and your two boys are going to have dinner.

WILLY: Gee whiz! That's really somethin'. I'm gonna knock Howard for a loop, kid. I'll get an advance, and I'll come home with a New York job. Goddammit, now I'm gonna do it!

50 **LINDA:** Oh, that's the spirit, Willy!

WILLY: I will never get behind a wheel the rest of my life!

LINDA: It's changing, Willy, I can feel it changing!

WILLY: Beyond a question. G'by, I'm late. (*He starts to go again.*)

LINDA: (*calling after him as she runs to the kitchen table for a handkerchief*) You got your glasses?

55 **WILLY:** (*feels for them, then comes back in*) Yeah, yeah, got my glasses.

LINDA: (*giving him the handkerchief*) And a handkerchief.
WILLY: Yeah, handkerchief.
LINDA: And your saccharine?
WILLY: Yeah, my saccharine.
LINDA: Be careful on the subway stairs.   60

She kisses him, and a silk stocking is seen hanging from her hand. Willy notices it.

WILLY: Will you stop mending stockings? At least while I'm in the house.
It gets me nervous. I can't tell you. Please.

Linda hides the stocking in her hand as she follows Willy across the forestage in front of the house.

LINDA: Remember, Frank's Chop House.
WILLY: (*passing the apron*) Maybe beets would grow out there.
LINDA: (*laughing*) But you tried so many times.
WILLY: Yeah. Well, don't work hard today. (*He disappears around the right corner*   65
of the house.)
LINDA: Be careful!

As Willy vanishes, Linda waves to him. Suddenly the phone rings. She runs across the stage and into the kitchen and lifts it.

LINDA: Hello? Oh, Biff! I'm so glad you called, I just . . . Yes, sure, I just told
him. Yes, he'll be there for dinner at six o'clock, I didn't forget. Listen, I was
just dying to tell you. You know that little rubber pipe I told you about?
That he connected to the gas heater? I finally decided to go down the cellar
this morning and take it away and destroy it. But it's gone! Imagine? He
took it away himself, it isn't there! (*She listens.*) When? Oh, then you took
it. Oh — nothing, it's just that I'd hoped he'd taken it away himself. Oh,
I'm not worried, darling, because this morning he left in such high spirits, it
was like the old days! I'm not afraid any more. Did Mr. Oliver see you? . . .
Well, you wait there then. And make a nice impression on him, darling.
Just don't perspire too much before you see him. And have a nice time with
Dad. He may have big news too! . . . That's right, a New York job. And be
sweet to him tonight, dear. Be loving to him. Because he's only a little boat
looking for a harbor. (*She is trembling with sorrow and joy.*) Oh, that's
wonderful, Biff, you'll save his life. Thanks, darling. Just put your arm
around him when he comes into the restaurant. Give him a smile.
That's the boy . . . Good-by, dear. . . . You got your comb? . . . That's fine.
Good-by, Biff dear.

*In the middle of her speech, Howard Wagner, thirty-six, wheels in a small typewriter
table on which is a wire-recording machine and proceeds to plug it in. This is on the left
forestage. Light slowly fades on Linda as it rises on Howard. Howard is intent on threading the machine and only glances over his shoulder as Willy appears.*

WILLY: Pst! Pst!

HOWARD: Hello, Willy, come in.

70 **WILLY:** Like to have a little talk with you, Howard.

HOWARD: Sorry to keep you waiting. I'll be with you in a minute.

WILLY: What's that, Howard?

HOWARD: Didn't you ever see one of these? Wire recorder.

WILLY: Oh. Can we talk a minute?

75 **HOWARD:** Records things. Just got delivery yesterday. Been driving me crazy, the most terrific machine I ever saw in my life. I was up all night with it.

WILLY: What do you do with it?

HOWARD: I bought it for dictation, but you can do anything with it. Listen to this. I had it home last night. Listen to what I picked up. The first one is my daughter. Get this. *(He flicks the switch and "Roll out the Barrel" is heard being whistled.)* Listen to that kid whistle.

WILLY: That is lifelike, isn't it?

HOWARD: Seven years old. Get that tone.

80 **WILLY:** Ts, ts. Like to ask a little favor if you . . .

The whistling breaks off, and the voice of Howard's Daughter is heard.

HIS DAUGHTER: "Now you, Daddy."

HOWARD: She's crazy for me! *(Again the same song is whistled.)* That's me! Ha! *(He winks.)*

WILLY: You're very good!

The whistling breaks off again. The machine runs silent for a moment.

HOWARD: Sh! Get this now, this is my son.

85 **HIS SON:** "The capital of Alabama is Montgomery; the capital of Arizona is Phoenix; the capital of Arkansas is Little Rock; the capital of California is Sacramento . . ." *(And on, and on.)*

HOWARD: *(holding up five fingers)* Five years old, Willy!

WILLY: He'll make an announcer some day!

HIS SON: *(continuing)* "The capital . . ."

HOWARD: Get that — alphabetical order! *(The machine breaks off suddenly.)* Wait a minute. The maid kicked the plug out.

90 **WILLY:** It certainly is a —

HOWARD: Sh, for God's sake!

HIS SON: "It's nine o'clock, Bulova watch time. So I have to go to sleep."

WILLY: That really is —

HOWARD: Wait a minute! The next is my wife.

They wait.

95 **HOWARD'S VOICE:** "Go on, say something." *(Pause.)* "Well, you gonna talk?"

HIS WIFE: "I can't think of anything."

HOWARD'S VOICE: "Well, talk — it's turning."

HIS WIFE: *(shyly, beaten)* "Hello." *(Silence.)* "Oh, Howard, I can't talk into this . . ."

HOWARD: *(snapping the machine off)* That was my wife.

WILLY: That is a wonderful machine. Can we —   100

HOWARD: I tell you, Willy, I'm gonna take my camera, and my bandsaw, and all my hobbies, and out they go. This is the most fascinating relaxation I ever found.

WILLY: I think I'll get one myself.

HOWARD: Sure, they're only a hundred and a half. You can't do without it. Supposing you wanna hear Jack Benny, see? But you can't be at home at that hour. So you tell the maid to turn the radio on when Jack Benny comes on, and this automatically goes on with the radio . . .

WILLY: And when you come home you . . .

HOWARD: You can come home twelve o'clock, one o'clock, any time you like,   105
and you get yourself a Coke and sit yourself down, throw the switch, and there's Jack Benny's program in the middle of the night!

WILLY: I'm definitely going to get one. Because lots of time I'm on the road, and I think to myself, what I must be missing on the radio!

HOWARD: Don't you have a radio in the car?

WILLY: Well, yeah, but who ever thinks of turning it on?

HOWARD: Say, aren't you supposed to be in Boston?

WILLY: That's what I want to talk to you about, Howard. You got a minute?   110

He draws a chair in from the wing.

HOWARD: What happened? What're you doing here?

WILLY: Well . . .

HOWARD: You didn't crack up again, did you?

WILLY: Oh, no. No . . .

HOWARD: Geez, you had me worried there for a minute. What's the trouble?   115

WILLY: Well, to tell you the truth, Howard, I've come to the decision that I'd rather not travel any more.

HOWARD: Not travel! Well, what'll you do?

WILLY: Remember, Christmas time, when you had the party here? You said you'd try to think of some spot for me here in town.

HOWARD: With us?

WILLY: Well, sure.   120

HOWARD: Oh, yeah, yeah. I remember. Well, I couldn't think of anything for you, Willy.

WILLY: I tell ya, Howard. The kids are all grown up, y'know. I don't need much any more. If I could take home — well, sixty-five dollars a week, I could swing it.

HOWARD: Yeah, but Willy, see I —

WILLY: I tell ya why, Howard. Speaking frankly and between the two of us, y'know — I'm just a little tired.

125 **HOWARD:** Oh, I could understand that, Willy. But you're a road man, Willy, and we do a road business. We've only got a half-dozen salesmen on the floor here.

WILLY: God knows, Howard, I never asked a favor of any man. But I was with the firm when your father used to carry you in here in his arms.

HOWARD: I know that, Willy, but —

WILLY: Your father came to me the day you were born and asked me what I thought of the name of Howard, may he rest in peace.

HOWARD: I appreciate that, Willy, but there just is no spot here for you. If I had a spot I'd slam you right in, but I just don't have a single, solitary spot.

He looks for his lighter. Willy has picked it up and gives it to him. Pause.

130 **WILLY:** *(with increasing anger)* Howard, all I need to set my table is fifty dollars a week.

HOWARD: But where am I going to put you, kid?

WILLY: Look, it isn't a question of whether I can sell merchandise, is it?

HOWARD: No, but it's a business, kid, and everybody's gotta pull his own weight.

WILLY: *(desperately)* Just let me tell you a story, Howard —

HOWARD: 'Cause you gotta admit, business is business.

135 **WILLY:** *(angrily)* Business is definitely business, but just listen for a minute. You don't understand this. When I was a boy — eighteen, nineteen — I was already on the road. And there was a question in my mind as to whether selling had a future for me. Because in those days I had a yearning to go to Alaska. See, there were three gold strikes in one month in Alaska, and I felt like going out. Just for the ride, you might say.

HOWARD: *(barely interested)* Don't say.

WILLY: Oh, yeah, my father lived many years in Alaska. He was an adventurous man. We've got quite a little streak of self-reliance in our family. I thought I'd go out with my older brother and try to locate him, and maybe settle in the North with the old man. And I was almost decided to go, when I met a salesman in the Parker House. His name was Dave Singleman. And he was eighty-four years old, and he'd drummed merchandise in thirty-one states. And old Dave, he'd go up to his room, y'understand, put on his green velvet slippers — I'll never forget — and pick up his phone and call the buyers, and without ever leaving his room, at the age of eighty-four, he made his living. And when I saw that, I realized that selling was the greatest career a man could want. 'Cause what could be more satisfying than to be able to go, at the age of eighty-four, into twenty or thirty different cities, and pick up a phone, and be remembered and loved and helped by so many different people? Do you know? when he died — and by the way he died the death of a salesman, in his green velvet slippers in the smoker of the New York, New Haven and Hartford, going into Boston — when he died, hundreds of salesmen and buyers were at his funeral. Things were sad on a lotta trains for months after that. (*He stands up. Howard has not looked at him.*) In those days there was personality in it, Howard. There was respect, and comradeship, and gratitude in it. Today, it's all cut and dried, and there's no chance for bringing friendship to bear — or personality. You see what I mean? They don't know me any more.

HOWARD: (*moving away, to the right*) That's just the thing, Willy.

WILLY: If I had forty dollars a week — that's all I'd need. Forty dollars, Howard.   140

HOWARD: Kid, I can't take blood from a stone, I—

WILLY: (*desperation is on him now*) Howard, the year Al Smith was nominated, your father came to me and—

HOWARD: (*starting to go off*) I've got to see some people, kid.

WILLY: (*stopping him*) I'm talking about your father! There were promises made across this desk! You mustn't tell me you've got people to see — I put thirty-four years into this firm, Howard, and now I can't pay my insurance! You can't eat the orange and throw the peel away — a man is not a piece of fruit! (*After a pause.*) Now pay attention. Your father — in 1928 I had a big year. I averaged a hundred and seventy dollars a week in commissions.

HOWARD: (*impatiently*) Now, Willy, you never averaged—   145

WILLY: (*banging his hand on the desk*) I averaged a hundred and seventy dollars a week in the year of 1928! And your father came to me — or rather, I was in the office here — it was right over this desk — and he put his hand on my shoulder—

HOWARD: (*getting up*) You'll have to excuse me, Willy, I gotta see some people. Pull yourself together. (*Going out.*) I'll be back in a little while.

On Howard's exit, the light on his chair grows very bright and strange.

WILLY: Pull myself together! What the hell did I say to him? My God, I was yelling at him! How could I! (*Willy breaks off, staring at the light, which occupies the chair, animating it. He approaches this chair, standing across the desk from it.*) Frank, Frank, don't you remember what you told me that time? How you put your hand on my shoulder, and Frank . . . (*He leans on the desk and as he speaks the dead man's name he accidentally switches on the recorder, and instantly —*)

HOWARD'S SON: ". . . of New York is Albany. The capital of Ohio is Cincinnati, the capital of Rhode Island is . . ." (*The recitation continues.*)

WILLY: (*leaping away with fright, shouting*) Ha! Howard! Howard! Howard!   150

HOWARD: (*rushing in*) What happened?

WILLY: (*pointing at the machine, which continues nasally, childishly, with the capital cities*) Shut it off! Shut it off!

HOWARD: (*pulling the plug out*) Look, Willy . . .

WILLY: (*pressing his hands to his eyes*) I gotta get myself some coffee. I'll get some coffee . . .

Willy starts to walk out. Howard stops him.

HOWARD: *(rolling up the cord)* Willy, look . . .
WILLY: I'll go to Boston.
HOWARD: Willy, you can't go to Boston for us.
WILLY: Why can't I go?
HOWARD: I don't want you to represent us. I've been meaning to tell you for a long time now.
160 WILLY: Howard, are you firing me?
HOWARD: I think you need a good long rest, Willy.
WILLY: Howard—
HOWARD: And when you feel better, come back, and we'll see if we can work something out.
WILLY: But I gotta earn money, Howard. I'm in no position—
165 HOWARD: Where are your sons? Why don't your sons give you a hand?
WILLY: They're working on a very big deal.
HOWARD: This is no time for false pride, Willy. You go to your sons and tell them that you're tired. You've got two great boys, haven't you?
WILLY: Oh, no question, no question, but in the meantime . . .
HOWARD: Then that's that, heh?
170 WILLY: All right, I'll go to Boston tomorrow.
HOWARD: No, no.
WILLY: I can't throw myself on my sons. I'm not a cripple!
HOWARD: Look, kid, I'm busy this morning.
WILLY: *(grasping Howard's arm)* Howard, you've got to let me go to Boston!
175 HOWARD: *(hard, keeping himself under control)* I've got a line of people to see this morning. Sit down, take five minutes, and pull yourself together, and then go home, will ya? I need the office, Willy. *(He starts to go, turns, remembering the recorder, starts to push off the table holding the recorder.)* Oh, yeah. Whenever you can this week, stop by and drop off the samples. You'll feel better, Willy, and then come back and we'll talk. Pull yourself together, kid, there's people outside.

Howard exits, pushing the table off left. Willy stares into space, exhausted. Now the music is heard — Ben's music — first distantly, then closer, closer. As Willy speaks, Ben enters from the right. He carries valise and umbrella.

WILLY: Oh, Ben, how did you do it? What is the answer? Did you wind up the Alaska deal already?
BEN: Doesn't take much time if you know what you're doing. Just a short business trip. Boarding ship in an hour. Wanted to say good-by.
WILLY: Ben, I've got to talk to you.
BEN: *(glancing at his watch)* Haven't the time, William.
180 WILLY: *(crossing the apron to Ben)* Ben, nothing's working out. I don't know what to do.

BEN: Now, look here, William. I've bought timberland in Alaska and I need a man to look after things for me.

WILLY: God, timberland! Me and my boys in those grand outdoors!

BEN: You've a new continent at your doorstep, William. Get out of these cities, they're full of talk and time payments and courts of law. Screw on your fists and you can fight for a fortune up there.

WILLY: Yes, yes! Linda! Linda!

Linda enters as of old, with the wash.

LINDA: Oh, you're back?   185

BEN: I haven't much time.

WILLY: No, wait! Linda, he's got a proposition for me in Alaska.

LINDA: But you've got — (*To Ben.*) He's got a beautiful job here.

WILLY: But in Alaska, kid, I could —

LINDA: You're doing well enough, Willy!   190

BEN: (*to Linda*) Enough for what, my dear?

LINDA: (*frightened of Ben and angry at him*) Don't say those things to him! Enough to be happy right here, right now. (*To Willy, while Ben laughs.*) Why must everybody conquer the world? You're well liked, and the boys love you, and someday — (*to Ben*) — why, old man Wagner told him just the other day that if he keeps it up he'll be a member of the firm, didn't he, Willy?

WILLY: Sure, sure. I am building something with this firm, Ben, and if a man is building something he must be on the right track, mustn't he?

BEN: What are you building? Lay your hand on it. Where is it?

WILLY: (*hesitantly*) That's true, Linda, there's nothing.   195

LINDA: Why? (*To Ben.*) There's a man eighty-four years old —

WILLY: That's right, Ben, that's right. When I look at that man I say, what is there to worry about?

BEN: Bah!

WILLY: It's true, Ben. All he has to do is go into any city, pick up the phone, and he's making his living and you know why?

BEN: (*picking up his valise*) I've got to go.   200

WILLY: (*holding Ben back*) Look at this boy!

Biff, in his high school sweater, enters carrying suitcase. Happy carries Biff's shoulder guards, gold helmet, and football pants.

WILLY: Without a penny to his name, three great universities are begging for him, and from there the sky's the limit, because it's not what you do, Ben. It's who you know and the smile on your face! It's contacts, Ben, contacts! The whole wealth of Alaska passes over the lunch table at the Commodore Hotel, and that's the wonder, the wonder of this country, that a man can end with diamonds here on the basis of being liked! (*He turns to Biff.*) And that's why when you get out on that field today it's important. Because thousands of people will be rooting for you and loving you. *(To Ben, who has again begun to leave.)* And Ben! when he walks into a business office his name will sound out like a bell and all the doors will open to him! I've seen it, Ben, I've seen it a thousand times! You can't feel it with your hand like timber, but it's there!

BEN: Good-by, William.

WILLY: Ben, am I right? Don't you think I'm right? I value your advice.

205 **BEN:** There's a new continent at your doorstep, William. You could walk out rich. Rich. *(He is gone.)*

WILLY: We'll do it here, Ben! You hear me? We're gonna do it here!

Young Bernard rushes in. The gay music of the boys is heard.

BERNARD: Oh, gee, I was afraid you left already!

WILLY: Why? What time is it?

BERNARD: It's half-past one!

210 **WILLY:** Well, come on, everybody! Ebbets Field° next stop! Where's the pennants? *(He rushes through the wall-line of the kitchen and out into the living room.)*

LINDA: *(to Biff)* Did you pack fresh underwear?

BIFF: *(who has been limbering up)* I want to go!

BERNARD: Biff, I'm carrying your helmet, ain't I?

HAPPY: No, I'm carrying the helmet.

215 **BERNARD:** Oh, Biff, you promised me.

HAPPY: I'm carrying the helmet.

BERNARD: How am I going to get in the locker room?

LINDA: Let him carry the shoulder guards. *(She puts her coat and hat on in the kitchen.)*

BERNARD: Can I, Biff? 'Cause I told everybody I'm going to be in the locker room.

220 **HAPPY:** In Ebbets Field it's the clubhouse.

BERNARD: I meant the clubhouse. Biff!

HAPPY: Biff!

BIFF: *(grandly, after a slight pause)* Let him carry the shoulder guards.

HAPPY: *(as he gives Bernard the shoulder guards)* Stay close to us now.

Willy rushes in with the pennants.

225 **WILLY:** *(handing them out)* Everybody wave when Biff comes out on the field. *(Happy and Bernard run off.)* You set now, boy?

The music has died away.

BIFF: Ready to go, Pop. Every muscle is ready.

WILLY: *(at the edge of the apron)* You realize what this means?

°*Ebbets Field:* The home park of the Brooklyn Dodgers.

BIFF: That's right, Pop.

WILLY: *(feeling Biff's muscles)* You're comin' home this afternoon captain of the All-Scholastic Championship Team of the City of New York.

BIFF: I got it, Pop. And remember, pal, when I take off my helmet, that   230
touchdown is for you.

WILLY: Let's go! *(He is starting out, with his arm around Biff, when Charley enters, as of old, in knickers.)* I got no room for you, Charley.

CHARLEY: Room? For what?

WILLY: In the car.

CHARLEY: You goin' for a ride? I wanted to shoot some casino.

WILLY: *(furiously)* Casino! *(Incredulously.)* Don't you realize what today is?   235

LINDA: Oh, he knows, Willy. He's just kidding you.

WILLY: That's nothing to kid about!

CHARLEY: No, Linda, what's goin' on?

LINDA: He's playing in Ebbets Field.

CHARLEY: Baseball in this weather?   240

WILLY: Don't talk to him. Come on, come on! *(He is pushing them out.)*

CHARLEY: Wait a minute, didn't you hear the news?

WILLY: What?

CHARLEY: Don't you listen to the radio? Ebbets Field just blew up.

WILLY: You go to hell! *(Charley laughs. Pushing them out.)* Come on, come on!   245
We're late.

CHARLEY: *(as they go)* Knock a homer, Biff, knock a homer!

WILLY: *(the last to leave, turning to Charley)* I don't think that was funny,
Charley. This is the greatest day of his life.

CHARLEY: Willy, when are you going to grow up?

WILLY: Yeah, heh? When this game is over, Charley, you'll be laughing out of
the other side of your face. They'll be calling him another Red Grange.°
Twenty-five thousand a year.

CHARLEY: *(kidding)* Is that so?   250

WILLY: Yeah, that's so.

CHARLEY: Well, then, I'm sorry, Willy. But tell me something.

WILLY: What?

CHARLEY: Who is Red Grange?

WILLY: Put up your hands. Goddam you, put up your hands!   255

Charley, chuckling, shakes his head and walks away, around the left corner of the stage. Willy follows him. The music rises to a mocking frenzy.

WILLY: Who the hell do you think you are, better than everybody else? You don't know everything, you big, ignorant, stupid . . . Put up your hands!

° *Red Grange:* Harold Edward ("Red") Grange (1903–1991)— American football player. A running back for the New York Yankees football team and the Chicago Bears, Grange was elected to the Football Hall of Fame in 1963.

Light rises, on the right side of the forestage, on a small table in the reception room of Charley's office. Traffic sounds are heard. Bernard, now mature, sits whistling to himself. A pair of tennis rackets and an overnight bag are on the floor beside him.

WILLY: *(offstage)* What are you walking away for? Don't walk away! If you're going to say something say it to my face! I know you laugh at me behind my back. You'll laugh out of the other side of your goddam face after this game. Touchdown! Touchdown! Eighty thousand people! Touchdown! Right between the goal posts.

Bernard is a quiet, earnest, but self-assured young man. Willy's voice is coming from right upstage now. Bernard lowers his feet off the table and listens. Jenny, his father's secretary, enters.

JENNY: *(distressed)* Say, Bernard, will you go out in the hall?
BERNARD: What is that noise? Who is it?
260 **JENNY:** Mr. Loman. He just got off the elevator.
BERNARD: *(getting up)* Who's he arguing with?
JENNY: Nobody. There's nobody with him. I can't deal with him any more, and your father gets all upset everytime he comes. I've got a lot of typing to do, and your father's waiting to sign it. Will you see him?
WILLY: *(entering)* Touchdown! Touch — *(He sees Jenny.)* Jenny, Jenny, good to see you. How're ya? Workin'? Or still honest?
JENNY: Fine. How've you been feeling?
265 **WILLY:** Not much any more, Jenny. Ha, ha! *(He is surprised to see the rackets.)*
BERNARD: Hello, Uncle Willy.
WILLY: *(almost shocked)* Bernard! Well, look who's here! *(He comes quickly, guiltily, to Bernard and warmly shakes his hand.)*
BERNARD: How are you? Good to see you.
WILLY: What are you doing here?
270 **BERNARD:** Oh, just stopped by to see Pop. Get off my feet till my train leaves. I'm going to Washington in a few minutes.
WILLY: Is he in?
BERNARD: Yes, he's in his office with the accountant. Sit down.
WILLY: *(sitting down)* What're you going to do in Washington?
BERNARD: Oh, just a case I've got there, Willy.
275 **WILLY:** That so? *(indicating the rackets)* You going to play tennis there?
BERNARD: I'm staying with a friend who's got a court.
WILLY: Don't say. His own tennis court. Must be fine people, I bet.
BERNARD: They are, very nice. Dad tells me Biff's in town.
WILLY: *(with a big smile)* Yeah, Biff's in. Working on a very big deal, Bernard.
280 **BERNARD:** What's Biff doing?
WILLY: Well, he's been doing very big things in the West. But he decided to establish himself here. Very big. We're having dinner. Did I hear your wife had a boy?

BERNARD: That's right. Our second.

WILLY: Two boys! What do you know!

BERNARD: What kind of a deal has Biff got?

WILLY: Well, Bill Oliver — very big sporting-goods man — he wants Biff very 285 badly. Called him in from the West. Long distance, carte blanche, special deliveries. Your friends have their own private tennis court?

BERNARD: You still with the old firm, Willy?

WILLY: *(after a pause)* I'm — I'm overjoyed to see how you made the grade, Bernard, overjoyed. It's an encouraging thing to see a young man really — really — Looks very good for Biff — very — *(He breaks off, then.)* Bernard — *(He is so full of emotion, he breaks off again.)*

BERNARD: What is it, Willy?

WILLY: *(small and alone)* What — what's the secret?

BERNARD: What secret?

WILLY: How — how did you? Why didn't he ever catch on?

BERNARD: I wouldn't know that, Willy.

WILLY: *(confidentially, desperately)* You were his friend, his boyhood friend. There's something I don't understand about it. His life ended after that Ebbets Field game. From the age of seventeen nothing good ever happened to him.

BERNARD: He never trained himself for anything.

WILLY: But he did, he did. After high school he took so many correspondence 295 courses. Radio mechanics; television; God knows what, and never made the slightest mark.

BERNARD: *(taking off his glasses)* Willy, do you want to talk candidly?

WILLY: *(rising, faces Bernard)* I regard you as a very brilliant man, Bernard. I value your advice.

BERNARD: Oh, the hell with the advice, Willy. I couldn't advise you. There's just one thing I've always wanted to ask you. When he was supposed to graduate, and the math teacher flunked him —

WILLY: Oh, that son-of-a-bitch ruined his life.

BERNARD: Yeah, but, Willy, all he had to do was go to summer school and 300 make up that subject.

WILLY: That's right, that's right.

BERNARD: Did you tell him not to go to summer school?

WILLY: Me? I begged him to go. I ordered him to go!

BERNARD: Then why wouldn't he go?

WILLY: Why? Why! Bernard, that question has been trailing me like a ghost 305 for the last fifteen years. He flunked the subject, and laid down and died like a hammer hit him!

BERNARD: Take it easy, kid.

WILLY: Let me talk to you — I got nobody to talk to. Bernard, Bernard, was it my fault? Y'see? It keeps going around in my mind, maybe I did something to him. I got nothing to give him.

BERNARD: Don't take it so hard.

WILLY: Why did he lay down? What is the story there? You were his friend!

310 **BERNARD:** Willy, I remember, it was June, and our grades came out. And he'd flunked math.

WILLY: That son-of-a-bitch!

BERNARD: No, it wasn't right then. Biff just got very angry, I remember, and he was ready to enroll in summer school.

WILLY: (*surprised*) He was?

BERNARD: He wasn't beaten by it at all. But then, Willy, he disappeared from the block for almost a month. And I got the idea that he'd gone up to New England to see you. Did he have a talk with you then?

Willy stares in silence.

315 **BERNARD:** Willy?

WILLY: (*with a strong edge of resentment in his voice*) Yeah, he came to Boston. What about it?

BERNARD: Well, just that when he came back — I'll never forget this, it always mystifies me. Because I'd thought so well of Biff, even though he'd always taken advantage of me. I loved him, Willy, y'know? And he came back after that month and took his sneakers — remember those sneakers with "University of Virginia" printed on them? He was so proud of those, wore them every day. And he took them down in the cellar, and burned them up in the furnace. We had a fist fight. It lasted at least half an hour. Just the two of us, punching each other down the cellar, and crying right through it. I've often thought of how strange it was that I knew he'd given up his life. What happened in Boston, Willy?

Willy looks at him as at an intruder.

BERNARD: I just bring it up because you asked me.

WILLY: (*angrily*) Nothing. What do you mean, "What happened?" What's that got to do with anything?

320 **BERNARD:** Well, don't get sore.

WILLY: What are you trying to do, blame it on me? If a boy lays down is that my fault?

BERNARD: Now, Willy, don't get —

WILLY: Well, don't — don't talk to me that way! What does that mean, "What happened?"

Charley enters. He is in his vest, and he carries a bottle of bourbon.

CHARLEY: Hey, you're going to miss that train. (*He waves the bottle.*)

325 **BERNARD:** Yeah, I'm going. (*He takes the bottle.*) Thanks, Pop. (*He picks up his rackets and bag.*) Good-by, Willy, and don't worry about it. You know, "If at first you don't succeed . . ."

WILLY: Yes, I believe in that.

BERNARD: But sometimes, Willy, it's better for a man just to walk away.
WILLY: Walk away?
BERNARD: That's right.
WILLY: But if you can't walk away?   330
BERNARD: (*after a slight pause*) I guess that's when it's tough. (*Extending his hand.*) Good-by, Willy.
WILLY: (*shaking Bernard's hand*) Good-by, boy.
CHARLEY: (*an arm on Bernard's shoulder*) How do you like this kid? Gonna argue a case in front of the Supreme Court.
BERNARD: (*protesting*) Pop!
WILLY: (*genuinely shocked, pained, and happy*) No! The Supreme Court!   335
BERNARD: I gotta run, 'By, Dad!
CHARLEY: Knock 'em dead, Bernard!

Bernard goes off.

WILLY: (*as Charley takes out his wallet*) The Supreme Court! And he didn't even mention it!
CHARLEY: (*counting out money on the desk*) He don't have to — he's gonna do it.
WILLY: And you never told him what to do, did you? You never took any   340
interest in him.
CHARLEY: My salvation is that I never took any interest in anything. There's some money — fifty dollars. I got an accountant inside.
WILLY: Charley, look . . . (*With difficulty.*) I got my insurance to pay. If you can manage it — I need a hundred and ten dollars.

Charley doesn't reply for a moment; merely stops moving.

WILLY: I'd draw it from my bank but Linda would know, and I . . .
CHARLEY: Sit down, Willy.
WILLY: (*moving toward the chair*) I'm keeping an account of everything,   345
remember. I'll pay every penny back. (*He sits.*)
CHARLEY: Now listen to me, Willy.
WILLY: I want you to know I appreciate . . .
CHARLEY: (*sitting down on the table*) Willy, what're you doin'? What the hell is goin' on in your head?
WILLY: Why? I'm simply . . .
CHARLEY: I offered you a job. You can make fifty dollars a week. And I won't   350
send you on the road.
WILLY: I've got a job.
CHARLEY: Without pay? What kind of a job is a job without pay? (*He rises.*) Now, look, kid, enough is enough. I'm no genius but I know when I'm being insulted.
WILLY: Insulted!
CHARLEY: Why don't you want to work for me?
WILLY: What's the matter with you? I've got a job.   355

CHARLEY: Then what're you walkin' in here every week for?

WILLY: *(getting up)* Well, if you don't want me to walk in here—

CHARLEY: I am offering you a job.

WILLY: I don't want your goddam job!

360 CHARLEY: When the hell are you going to grow up?

WILLY: *(furiously)* You big ignoramus, if you say that to me again I'll rap you one! I don't care how big you are! *(He's ready to fight.)*

Pause.

CHARLEY: *(kindly, going to him)* How much do you need, Willy?

WILLY: Charley, I'm strapped. I'm strapped. I don't know what to do. I was just fired.

CHARLEY: Howard fired you?

365 WILLY: That snotnose. Imagine that? I named him. I named him Howard.

CHARLEY: Willy, when're you gonna realize that them things don't mean anything? You named him Howard, but you can't sell that. The only thing you got in this world is what you can sell. And the funny thing is that you're a salesman, and you don't know that.

WILLY: I've always tried to think otherwise, I guess. I always felt that if a man was impressive, and well liked, that nothing—

CHARLEY: Why must everybody like you? Who liked J. P. Morgan?° Was he impressive? In a Turkish bath he'd look like a butcher. But with his pockets on he was very well liked. Now listen, Willy, I know you don't like me, and nobody can say I'm in love with you, but I'll give you a job because—just for the hell of it, put it that way. Now what do you say?

WILLY: I—I just can't work for you, Charley.

370 CHARLEY: What're you, jealous of me?

WILLY: I can't work for you, that's all, don't ask me why.

CHARLEY: *(angered, takes out more bills)* You been jealous of me all your life, you damned fool! Here, pay your insurance. *(He puts the money in Willy's hand.)*

WILLY: I'm keeping strict accounts.

CHARLEY: I've got some work to do. Take care of yourself. And pay your insurance.

375 WILLY: *(moving to the right)* Funny, y'know? After all the highways, and the trains, and the appointments, and the years, you end up worth more dead than alive.

CHARLEY: Willy, nobody's worth nothin' dead. *(After a slight pause.)* Did you hear what I said?

Willy stands still, dreaming.

° *J. P. Morgan:* John Pierpont Morgan (1837–1913)—American financier.

CHARLEY: Willy!

WILLY: Apologize to Bernard for me when you see him. I didn't mean to argue with him. He's a fine boy. They're all fine boys, and they'll end up big — all of them. Someday they'll all play tennis together. Wish me luck, Charley. He saw Bill Oliver today.

CHARLEY: Good luck.

WILLY: (*on the verge of tears*) Charley, you're the only friend I got. Isn't that a remarkable thing? (*He goes out.*) 380

CHARLEY: Jesus!

Charley stares after him a moment and follows. All light blacks out. Suddenly raucous music is heard, and a red glow rises behind the screen at right. Stanley, a young waiter, appears, carrying a table, followed by Happy, who is carrying two chairs.

STANLEY: (*putting the table down*) That's all right, Mr. Loman, I can handle it myself. (*He turns and takes the chairs from Happy and places them at the table.*)

HAPPY: (*glancing around*) Oh, this is better.

STANLEY: Sure, in the front there you're in the middle of all kinds a noise. Whenever you got a party, Mr. Loman, you just tell me and I'll put you back here. Y'know, there's a lotta people they don't like it private, because when they go out they like to see a lotta action around them because they're sick and tired to stay in the house by theirself. But I know you, you ain't from Hackensack. You know what I mean?

HAPPY: (*sitting down*) So, how's it coming, Stanley? 385

STANLEY: Ah, it's a dog's life. I only wish during the war they'd a took me in the Army. I coulda been dead by now.

HAPPY: My brother's back, Stanley.

STANLEY: Oh, he come back, heh? From the Far West.

HAPPY: Yeah, big cattle man, my brother, so treat him right. And my father's coming too.

STANLEY: Oh, your father too! 390

HAPPY: You got a couple of nice lobsters?

STANLEY: Hundred per cent, big.

HAPPY: I want them with the claws.

STANLEY: Don't worry, I don't give you no mice. (*Happy laughs.*) How about some wine? It'll put a head on the meal.

HAPPY: No. You remember, Stanley, that recipe I brought you from overseas? With the champagne in it? 395

STANLEY: Oh, yeah, sure. I still got it tacked up yet in the kitchen. But that'll have to cost a buck apiece anyways.

HAPPY: That's all right.

STANLEY: What'd you, hit a number or somethin'?

HAPPY: No, it's a little celebration. My brother is — I think he pulled off a big deal today. I think we're going into business together.

400 STANLEY: Great! That's the best for you. Because a family business, you know what I mean?— that's the best.

HAPPY: That's what I think.

STANLEY: 'Cause what's the difference? Somebody steals? It's in the family. Know what I mean? (*Sotto voce.*) Like this bartender here. The boss is goin' crazy what kinda leak he's got in the cash register. You put it in but it don't come out.

HAPPY: (*raising his head*) Sh!

STANLEY: What?

405 HAPPY: You notice I wasn't lookin' right or left, was I?

STANLEY: No.

HAPPY: And my eyes are closed.

STANLEY: So what's the—

HAPPY: Strudel's comin'.

410 STANLEY: (*catching on, looks around*) Ah, no, there's no—

He breaks off as a furred, lavishly dressed Girl enters and sits at the next table. Both follow her with their eyes.

STANLEY: Geez, how'd ya know?

HAPPY: I got radar or something. (*Staring directly at her profile.*) Oooooooo . . . Stanley.

STANLEY: I think that's for you, Mr. Loman.

HAPPY: Look at that mouth. Oh, God. And the binoculars.

415 STANLEY: Geez, you got a life, Mr. Loman.

HAPPY: Wait on her.

STANLEY: (*going to The Girl's table*) Would you like a menu, ma'am?

GIRL: I'm expecting someone, but I'd like a—

HAPPY: Why don't you bring her — excuse me, miss, do you mind? I sell champagne, and I'd like you to try my brand. Bring her a champagne, Stanley.

420 GIRL: That's awfully nice of you.

HAPPY: Don't mention it. It's all company money. (*He laughs.*)

GIRL: That's a charming product to be selling, isn't it?

HAPPY: Oh, gets to be like everything else. Selling is selling, y'know.

GIRL: I suppose.

425 HAPPY: You don't happen to sell, do you?

GIRL: No, I don't sell.

HAPPY: Would you object to a compliment from a stranger? You ought to be on a magazine cover.

GIRL: (*looking at him a little archly*) I have been.

Stanley comes in with a glass of champagne.

HAPPY: What'd I say before, Stanley? You see? She's a cover girl.

430 STANLEY: Oh, I could see, I could see.

HAPPY: (*to The Girl*) What magazine?

GIRL: Oh, a lot of them. *(She takes the drink.)* Thank you.
HAPPY: You know what they say in France, don't you? "Champagne is the
   drink of the complexion"— Hya, Biff!

Biff has entered and sits with Happy.

BIFF: Hello, kid. Sorry I'm late.
HAPPY: I just got here. Uh, Miss —?   435
GIRL: Forsythe.
HAPPY: Miss Forsythe, this is my brother.
BIFF: Is Dad here?
HAPPY: His name is Biff. You might've heard of him. Great football player.
GIRL: Really? What team?   440
HAPPY: Are you familiar with football?
GIRL: No, I'm afraid I'm not.
HAPPY: Biff is quarterback with the New York Giants.
GIRL: Well, that is nice, isn't it? *(She drinks.)*
HAPPY: Good health.   445
GIRL: I'm happy to meet you.
HAPPY: That's my name. Hap. It's really Harold, but at West Point they called
   me Happy.
GIRL: *(now really impressed)* Oh, I see. How do you do? *(She turns her profile.)*
BIFF: Isn't Dad coming?
HAPPY: You want her?   450
BIFF: Oh, I could never make that.
HAPPY: I remember the time that idea would never come into your head.
   Where's the old confidence, Biff?
BIFF: I just saw Oliver—
HAPPY: Wait a minute. I've got to see that old confidence again. Do you want
   her? She's on call.
BIFF: Oh, no. *(He turns to look at The Girl.)*   455
HAPPY: I'm telling you. Watch this. *(Turning to The Girl.)* Honey? *(She turns to
   him.)* Are you busy?
GIRL: Well, I am . . . but I could make a phone call.
HAPPY: Do that, will you, honey? And see if you can get a friend. We'll be
   here for a while. Biff is one of the greatest football players in the country.
GIRL: *(standing up)* Well, I'm certainly happy to meet you.
HAPPY: Come back soon.   460
GIRL: I'll try.
HAPPY: Don't try, honey, try hard.

The Girl exits. Stanley follows, shaking his head in bewildered admiration.

HAPPY: Isn't that a shame now? A beautiful girl like that? That's why I can't
   get married. There's not a good woman in a thousand. New York is loaded
   with them, kid!

BIFF: Hap, look —

465 **HAPPY:** I told you she was on call!

BIFF: (*strangely unnerved*) Cut it out, will ya? I want to say something to you.

HAPPY: Did you see Oliver?

BIFF: I saw him all right. Now look, I want to tell Dad a couple of things and I want you to help me.

HAPPY: What? Is he going to back you?

470 **BIFF:** Are you crazy? You're out of your goddam head, you know that?

HAPPY: Why? What happened?

BIFF: (*breathlessly*) I did a terrible thing today, Hap. It's been the strangest day I ever went through. I'm all numb, I swear.

HAPPY: You mean he wouldn't see you?

BIFF: Well, I waited six hours for him, see? All day. Kept sending my name in. Even tried to date his secretary so she'd get me to him, but no soap.

475 **HAPPY:** Because you're not showin' the old confidence, Biff. He remembered you, didn't he?

BIFF: (*stopping Happy with a gesture*) Finally, about five o'clock, he comes out. Didn't remember who I was or anything. I felt like such an idiot, Hap.

HAPPY: Did you tell him my Florida idea?

BIFF: He walked away. I saw him for one minute. I got so mad I could've torn the walls down! How the hell did I ever get the idea I was a salesman there? I even believed myself that I'd been a salesman for him! And then he gave me one look and — I realized what a ridiculous lie my whole life has been! We've been talking in a dream for fifteen years. I was a shipping clerk.

HAPPY: What'd you do?

480 **BIFF:** (*with great tension and wonder*) Well, he left, see. And the secretary went out. I was all alone in the waiting-room. I don't know what came over me, Hap. The next thing I know I'm in his office — paneled walls, everything. I can't explain it. I — Hap, I took his fountain pen.

HAPPY: Geez, did he catch you?

BIFF: I ran out. I ran down all eleven flights. I ran and ran and ran.

HAPPY: That was an awful dumb — what'd you do that for?

BIFF: (*agonized*) I don't know, I just — wanted to take something, I don't know. You gotta help me, Hap. I'm gonna tell Pop.

485 **HAPPY:** You crazy? What for?

BIFF: Hap, he's got to understand that I'm not the man somebody lends that kind of money to. He thinks I've been spiting him all these years and it's eating him up.

HAPPY: That's just it. You tell him something nice.

BIFF: I can't.

HAPPY: Say you got a lunch date with Oliver tomorrow.

490 **BIFF:** So what do I do tomorrow?

HAPPY: You leave the house tomorrow and come back at night and say Oliver is thinking it over. And he thinks it over for a couple of weeks, and gradually it fades away and nobody's the worse.

BIFF: But it'll go on forever!

HAPPY: Dad is never so happy as when he's looking forward to something!

Willy enters.

HAPPY: Hello, scout!

WILLY: Gee, I haven't been here in years!   495

Stanley has followed Willy in and sets a chair for him. Stanley starts off but Happy stops him.

HAPPY: Stanley!

Stanley stands by, waiting for an order.

BIFF: *(going to Willy with guilt, as to an invalid)* Sit down, Pop. You want a drink?

WILLY: Sure, I don't mind.

BIFF: Let's get a load on.

WILLY: You look worried.   500

BIFF: N-no. *(To Stanley.)* Scotch all around. Make it doubles.

STANLEY: Doubles, right. *(He goes.)*

WILLY: You had a couple already, didn't you?

BIFF: Just a couple, yeah.

WILLY: Well, what happened, boy? *(Nodding affirmatively, with a smile.)*   505
Everything go all right?

BIFF: *(takes a breath, then reaches out and grasps Willy's hand)* Pal . . . *(He is smiling bravely, and Willy is smiling too.)* I had an experience today.

HAPPY: Terrific, Pop.

WILLY: That so? What happened?

BIFF: *(high, slightly alcoholic, above the earth)* I'm going to tell you everything from first to last. It's been a strange day. *(Silence. He looks around, composes himself as best he can, but his breath keeps breaking the rhythm of his voice.)* I had to wait quite a while for him, and—

WILLY: Oliver?   510

BIFF: Yeah, Oliver. All day, as a matter of cold fact. And a lot of — instances — facts, Pop, facts about my life came back to me. Who was it, Pop? Who ever said I was a salesman with Oliver?

WILLY: Well, you were.

BIFF: No, Dad, I was a shipping clerk.

WILLY: But you were practically—

BIFF: *(with determination)* Dad, I don't know who said it first, but I was never a   515
salesman for Bill Oliver.

Willy: What're you talking about?

Biff: Let's hold on to the facts tonight, Pop. We're not going to get anywhere bullin' around. I was a shipping clerk.

Willy: *(angrily)* All right, now listen to me —

Biff: Why don't you let me finish?

520 **Willy:** I'm not interested in stories about the past or any crap of that kind because the woods are burning, boys, you understand? There's a big blaze going on all around. I was fired today.

Biff: *(shocked)* How could you be?

Willy: I was fired, and I'm looking for a little good news to tell your mother, because the woman has waited and the woman has suffered. The gist of it is that I haven't got a story left in my head, Biff. So don't give me a lecture about facts and aspects. I am not interested. Now what've you got to say to me?

Stanley enters with three drinks. They wait until he leaves.

Willy: Did you see Oliver?

Biff: Jesus, Dad!

525 **Willy:** You mean you didn't go up there?

Happy: Sure he went up there.

Biff: I did. I — saw him. How could they fire you?

Willy: *(on the edge of his chair)* What kind of a welcome did he give you?

Biff: He won't even let you work on commission?

530 **Willy:** I'm out! *(Driving.)* So tell me, he gave you a warm welcome?

Happy: Sure, Pop, sure!

Biff: *(driven)* Well, it was kind of —

Willy: I was wondering if he'd remember you. *(To Happy.)* Imagine, man doesn't see him for ten, twelve years and gives him that kind of a welcome!

Happy: Damn right!

535 **Biff:** *(trying to return to the offensive)* Pop, look —

Willy: You know why he remembered you, don't you? Because you impressed him in those days.

Biff: Let's talk quietly and get this down to the facts, huh?

Willy: *(as though Biff had been interrupting)* Well, what happened? It's great news, Biff. Did he take you into his office or'd you talk in the waiting-room?

Biff: Well, he came in, see, and —

540 **Willy:** *(with a big smile)* What'd he say? Betcha he threw his arm around you.

Biff: Well, he kinda —

Willy: He's a fine man. *(To Happy.)* Very hard man to see, y'know.

Happy: *(agreeing)* Oh, I know.

Willy: *(to Biff)* Is that where you had the drinks?

545 **Biff:** Yeah, he gave me a couple of — no, no!

Happy: *(cutting in)* He told him my Florida idea.

Willy: Don't interrupt. *(To Biff.)* How'd he react to the Florida idea?

BIFF: Dad, will you give me a minute to explain?

WILLY: I've been waiting for you to explain since I sat down here! What happened? He took you into his office and what?

BIFF: Well — I talked. And — and he listened, see.   550

WILLY: Famous for the way he listens, y'know. What was his answer?

BIFF: His answer was — (*He breaks off, suddenly angry.*) Dad, you're not letting me tell you what I want to tell you!

WILLY: (*accusing, angered*) You didn't see him, did you?

BIFF: I did see him!

WILLY: What'd you insult him or something? You insulted him, didn't you?   555

BIFF: Listen, will you let me out of it, will you just let me out of it!

HAPPY: What the hell!

WILLY: Tell me what happened!

BIFF: (*to Happy*) I can't talk to him!

A single trumpet note jars the ear. The light of green leaves stains the house, which holds the air of night and a dream. Young Bernard enters and knocks on the door of the house.

YOUNG BERNARD: (*frantically*) Mrs. Loman, Mrs. Loman!   560

HAPPY: Tell him what happened!

BIFF: (*to Happy*) Shut up and leave me alone!

WILLY: No, no! You had to go and flunk math!

BIFF: What math? What're you talking about?

YOUNG BERNARD: Mrs. Loman, Mrs. Loman!   565

Linda appears in the house, as of old.

WILLY: (*wildly*) Math, math, math!

BIFF: Take it easy, Pop!

YOUNG BERNARD: Mrs. Loman!

WILLY: (*furiously*) If you hadn't flunked you'd've been set by now!

BIFF: Now, look, I'm gonna tell you what happened, and you're going to listen   570
to me.

YOUNG BERNARD: Mrs. Loman!

BIFF: I waited six hours —

HAPPY: What the hell are you saying?

BIFF: I kept sending in my name but he wouldn't see me. So finally he . . .
(*He continues unheard as light fades low on the restaurant.*)

YOUNG BERNARD: Biff flunked math!   575

LINDA: No!

YOUNG BERNARD: Birnbaum flunked him! They won't graduate him!

LINDA: But they have to. He's gotta go to the university. Where is he? Biff! Biff!

YOUNG BERNARD: No, he left. He went to Grand Central.

LINDA: Grand — You mean he went to Boston!   580

YOUNG BERNARD: Is Uncle Willy in Boston?

LINDA: Oh, maybe Willy can talk to the teacher. Oh, the poor, poor boy!

Light on house area snaps out.

BIFF: (*at the table, now audible, holding up a gold fountain pen*) . . . so I'm washed up with Oliver, you understand? Are you listening to me?

WILLY: (*at a loss*) Yeah, sure. If you hadn't flunked —

585 **BIFF:** Flunked what? What're you talking about?

WILLY: Don't blame everything on me! I didn't flunk math — you did! What pen?

HAPPY: That was awful dumb, Biff, a pen like that is worth —

WILLY: (*seeing the pen for the first time*) You took Oliver's pen?

BIFF: (*weakening*) Dad, I just explained it to you.

590 **WILLY:** You stole Bill Oliver's fountain pen!

BIFF: I didn't exactly steal it! That's just what I've been explaining to you!

HAPPY: He had it in his hand and just then Oliver walked in, so he got nervous and stuck it in his pocket!

WILLY: My God, Biff!

BIFF: I never intended to do it, Dad!

595 **OPERATOR'S VOICE:** Standish Arms, good evening!

WILLY: (*shouting*) I'm not in my room!

BIFF: (*frightened*) Dad, what's the matter? (*He and Happy stand up.*)

OPERATOR: Ringing Mr. Loman for you!

WILLY: I'm not there, stop it!

600 **BIFF:** (*horrified, gets down on one knee before Willy*) Dad, I'll make good, I'll make good. (*Willy tries to get to his feet. Biff holds him down.*) Sit down now.

WILLY: No, you're no good, you're no good for anything.

BIFF: I am, Dad, I'll find something else, you understand? Now don't worry about anything. (*He holds up Willy's face.*) Talk to me, Dad.

OPERATOR: Mr. Loman does not answer. Shall I page him?

WILLY: (*attempting to stand, as though to rush and silence the Operator*) No, no, no!

605 **HAPPY:** He'll strike something, Pop.

WILLY: No, no . . .

BIFF: (*desperately, standing over Willy*) Pop, listen! Listen to me! I'm telling you something good. Oliver talked to his partner about the Florida idea. You listening? He — he talked to his partner, and he came to me . . . I'm going to be all right, you hear? Dad, listen to me, he said it was just a question of the amount!

WILLY: Then you . . . got it?

HAPPY: He's gonna be terrific, Pop!

610 **WILLY:** (*trying to stand*) Then you got it, haven't you? You got it! You got it!

BIFF: (*agonized, holds Willy down*) No, no. Look, Pop. I'm supposed to have lunch with them tomorrow. I'm just telling you this so you'll know that I can still make an impression, Pop. And I'll make good somewhere, but I can't go tomorrow, see?

WILLY: Why not? You simply —

BIFF: But the pen, Pop!

WILLY: You give it to him and tell him it was an oversight!

HAPPY: Sure, have lunch tomorrow!   615

BIFF: I can't say that —

WILLY: You were doing a crossword puzzle and accidentally used his pen!

BIFF: Listen, kid, I took those balls years ago, now I walk in with his fountain pen? That clinches it, don't you see? I can't face him like that! I'll try elsewhere.

PAGE'S VOICE: Paging Mr. Loman!

WILLY: Don't you want to be anything?   620

BIFF: Pop, how can I go back?

WILLY: You don't want to be anything, is that what's behind it?

BIFF: (*now angry at Willy for not crediting his sympathy*) Don't take it that way! You think it was easy walking into that office after what I'd done to him? A team of horses couldn't have dragged me back to Bill Oliver!

WILLY: Then why'd you go?

BIFF: Why did I go? Why did I go? Look at you! Look at what's become of you!   625

Off left, The Woman laughs.

WILLY: Biff, you're going to go to that lunch tomorrow, or —

BIFF: I can't go. I've got no appointment!

HAPPY: Biff, for . . .!

WILLY: Are you spiting me?

BIFF: Don't take it that way! Goddammit!   630

WILLY: (*strikes Biff and falters away from the table*) You rotten little louse! Are you spiting me?

THE WOMAN: Someone's at the door, Willy!

BIFF: I'm no good, can't you see what I am?

HAPPY: (*separating them*) Hey, you're in a restaurant! Now cut it out, both of you! (*The Girls enter.*) Hello, girls, sit down.

The Woman laughs, off left.

MISS FORSYTHE: I guess we might as well. This is Letta.   635

THE WOMAN: Willy, are you going to wake up?

BIFF: (*ignoring Willy*) How're ya, miss, sit down. What do you drink?

MISS FORSYTHE: Letta might not be able to stay long.

LETTA: I gotta get up very early tomorrow. I got jury duty. I'm so excited! Were you fellows ever on a jury?

BIFF: No, but I been in front of them! (*The Girls laugh.*) This is my father.   640

LETTA: Isn't he cute? Sit down with us, Pop.

HAPPY: Sit him down, Biff!

BIFF: (*going to him*) Come on, slugger, drink us under the table. To hell with it! Come on, sit down, pal.

On Biff's last insistence, Willy is about to sit.

THE WOMAN: (*now urgently*) Willy, are you going to answer the door!

The Woman's call pulls Willy back. He starts right, befuddled.

645 BIFF: Hey, where are you going?
WILLY: Open the door.
BIFF: The door?
WILLY: The washroom . . . the door . . . where's the door?
BIFF: (*leading Willy to the left*) Just go straight down.

Willy moves left.

650 THE WOMAN: Willy, Willy, are you going to get up, get up, get up, get up?

Willy exits left.

LETTA: I think it's sweet you bring your daddy along.
MISS FORSYTHE: Oh, he isn't really your father!
BIFF: (*at left, turning to her resentfully*) Miss Forsythe, you've just seen a prince
       walk by. A fine, troubled prince. A hard-working, unappreciated prince.
       A pal, you understand? A good companion. Always for his boys.
LETTA: That's so sweet.
655 HAPPY: Well, girls, what's the program? We're wasting time. Come on, Biff.
       Gather round. Where would you like to go?
BIFF: Why don't you do something for him?
HAPPY: Me!
BIFF: Don't you give a damn for him, Hap?
HAPPY: What're you talking about? I'm the one who—
660 BIFF: I sense it, you don't give a good goddam about him. (*He takes the rolled-
       up hose from his pocket and puts it on the table in front of Happy.*) Look what
       I found in the cellar, for Christ's sake. How can you bear to let it go on?
HAPPY: Me? Who goes away? Who runs off and—
BIFF: Yeah, but he doesn't mean anything to you. You could help him — I
       can't! Don't you understand what I'm talking about? He's going to kill him-
       self, don't you know that?
HAPPY: Don't I know it! Me!
BIFF: Hap, help him! Jesus . . . help him . . . Help me, help me, I can't bear to
       look at his face! (*Ready to weep, he hurries out, up right.*)
665 HAPPY: (*starting after him*) Where are you going?
MISS FORSYTHE: What's he so mad about?
HAPPY: Come on, girls, we'll catch up with him.
MISS FORSYTHE: (*as Happy pushes her out*) Say, I don't like that temper of his!
HAPPY: He's just a little overstrung, he'll be all right!
670 WILLY: (*off left, as The Woman laughs*) Don't answer! Don't answer!
LETTA: Don't you want to tell your father —

HAPPY: No, that's not my father. He's just a guy. Come on, we'll catch Biff, and, honey, we're going to paint this town! Stanley, where's the check! Hey, Stanley!

They exit. Stanley looks toward left.

STANLEY: *(calling to Happy indignantly)* Mr. Loman! Mr. Loman!

Stanley picks up a chair and follows them off. Knocking is heard off left. The Woman enters, laughing. Willy follows her. She is in a black slip; he is buttoning his shirt. Raw, sensuous music accompanies their speech.

WILLY: Will you stop laughing? Will you stop?

THE WOMAN: Aren't you going to answer the door? He'll wake the whole   675
hotel.

WILLY: I'm not expecting anybody.

THE WOMAN: Whyn't you have another drink, honey, and stop being so damn self-centered?

WILLY: I'm so lonely.

THE WOMAN: You know you ruined me, Willy? From now on, whenever you come to the office, I'll see that you go right through to the buyers. No waiting at my desk any more, Willy. You ruined me.

WILLY: That's nice of you to say that.   680

THE WOMAN: Gee, you are self-centered! Why so sad? You are the saddest self-centeredest soul I ever did see-saw. *(She laughs. He kisses her.)* Come on inside, drummer boy. It's silly to be dressing in the middle of the night. *(As knocking is heard.)* Aren't you going to answer the door?

WILLY: They're knocking on the wrong door.

THE WOMAN: But I felt the knocking. And he heard us talking in here. Maybe the hotel's on fire!

WILLY: *(his terror rising)* It's a mistake.

THE WOMAN: Then tell him to go away!   685

WILLY: There's nobody there.

THE WOMAN: It's getting on my nerves, Willy. There's somebody standing out there and it's getting on my nerves!

WILLY: *(pushing her away from him)* All right, stay in the bathroom here, and don't come out. I think there's a law in Massachusetts about it, so don't come out. It may be that new room clerk. He looked very mean. So don't come out. It's a mistake, there's no fire.

The knocking is heard again. He takes a few steps away from her, and she vanishes into the wing. The light follows him, and now he is facing Young Biff, who carries a suitcase. Biff steps toward him. The music is gone.

BIFF: Why didn't you answer?

WILLY: Biff! What are you doing in Boston?   690

BIFF: Why didn't you answer? I've been knocking for five minutes, I called you on the phone —

WILLY: I just heard you. I was in the bathroom and had the door shut. Did anything happen home?

BIFF: Dad — I let you down.

WILLY: What do you mean?

695 **BIFF:** Dad . . .

WILLY: Biffo, what's this about? (*Putting his arm around Biff.*) Come on, let's go downstairs and get you a malted.

BIFF: Dad, I flunked math.

WILLY: Not for the term?

BIFF: The term. I haven't got enough credits to graduate.

700 **WILLY:** You mean to say Bernard wouldn't give you the answers?

BIFF: He did, he tried, but I only got a sixty-one.

WILLY: And they wouldn't give you four points?

BIFF: Birnbaum refused absolutely. I begged him, Pop, but he won't give me those points. You gotta talk to him before they close the school. Because if he saw the kind of man you are, and you just talked to him in your way, I'm sure he'd come through for me. The class came right before practice, see, and I didn't go enough. Would you talk to him? He'd like you, Pop. You know the way you could talk.

WILLY: You're on. We'll drive right back.

705 **BIFF:** Oh, Dad, good work! I'm sure he'll change it for you!

WILLY: Go downstairs and tell the clerk I'm checkin' out. Go right down.

BIFF: Yes, Sir! See, the reason he hates me, Pop — one day he was late for class so I got up at the blackboard and imitated him. I crossed my eyes and talked with a lithp.

WILLY: (*laughing*) You did? The kids like it?

BIFF: They nearly died laughing!

710 **WILLY:** Yeah? What'd you do?

BIFF: The thquare root of thixthy twee is . . . (*Willy bursts out laughing; Biff joins him.*) And in the middle of it he walked in!

Willy laughs and The Woman joins in offstage.

WILLY: (*without hesitating*) Hurry downstairs and —

BIFF: Somebody in there?

WILLY: No, that was next door.

The Woman laughs offstage.

715 **BIFF:** Somebody got in your bathroom!

WILLY: No, it's the next room, there's a party —

THE WOMAN: (*enters, laughing. She lisps this*) Can I come in? There's something in the bathtub, Willy, and it's moving!

Willy looks at Biff, who is staring open-mouthed and horrified at The Woman.

WILLY: Ah — you better go back to your room. They must be finished painting by now. They're painting her room so I let her take a shower here. Go back, go back . . . *(He pushes her.)*

THE WOMAN: *(resisting)* But I've got to get dressed, Willy, I can't —

WILLY: Get out of here! Go back, go back . . . *(Suddenly striving for the ordinary.)* This is Miss Francis, Biff, she's a buyer. They're painting her room. Go back, Miss Francis, go back . . .   720

THE WOMAN: But my clothes, I can't go out naked in the hall!

WILLY: *(pushing her offstage)* Get outa here! Go back, go back!

Biff slowly sits down on his suitcase as the argument continues offstage.

THE WOMAN: Where's my stockings? You promised me stockings, Willy!

WILLY: I have no stockings here!

THE WOMAN: You had two boxes of size nine sheers for me, and I want them!   725

WILLY: Here, for God's sake, will you get outa here!

THE WOMAN: *(enters holding a box of stockings)* I just hope there's nobody in the hall. That's all I hope. *(To Biff.)* Are you football or baseball?

BIFF: Football.

THE WOMAN: *(angry, humiliated)* That's me too. G'night. *(She snatches her clothes from Willy, and walks out.)*

WILLY: *(after a pause)* Well, better get going. I want to get to the school first thing in the morning. Get my suits out of the closet. I'll get my valise. *(Biff doesn't move.)* What's the matter? *(Biff remains motionless, tears falling.)* She's a buyer. Buys for J. H. Simmons. She lives down the hall — they're painting. You don't imagine — *(He breaks off. After a pause.)* Now listen, pal, she's just a buyer. She sees merchandise in her room and they have to keep it looking just so . . . *(Pause. Assuming command.)* All right, get my suits. *(Biff doesn't move.)* Now stop crying and do as I say. I gave you an order. Biff, I gave you an order! Is that what you do when I give you an order? How dare you cry! *(Putting his arm around Biff.)* Now look, Biff, when you grow up you'll understand about these things. You mustn't — you mustn't overemphasize a thing like this. I'll see Birnbaum first thing in the morning.   730

BIFF: Never mind.

WILLY: *(getting down beside Biff)* Never mind! He's going to give you those points. I'll see to it.

BIFF: He wouldn't listen to you.

WILLY: He certainly will listen to me. You need those points for the U. of Virginia.

BIFF: I'm not going there.   735

WILLY: Heh? If I can't get him to change that mark you'll make it up in summer school. You've got all summer to —

BIFF: *(his weeping breaking from him)* Dad . . .
WILLY: *(infected by it)* Oh, my boy . . .
BIFF: Dad . . .
740 **WILLY:** She's nothing to me, Biff. I was lonely, I was terribly lonely.
BIFF: You — you gave her Mama's stockings! *(His tears break through and he rises to go.)*
WILLY: *(grabbing for Biff)* I gave you an order!
BIFF: Don't touch me, you — liar!
WILLY: Apologize for that!
745 **BIFF:** You fake! You phony little fake! You fake! *(Overcome, he turns quickly and weeping fully goes out with his suitcase. Willy is left on the floor on his knees.)*
WILLY: I gave you an order! Biff, come back here or I'll beat you! Come back here! I'll whip you!

Stanley comes quickly in from the right and stands in front of Willy.

WILLY: *(shouts at Stanley)* I gave you an order . . .
STANLEY: Hey, let's pick it up, pick it up, Mr. Loman. *(He helps Willy to his feet.)* Your boys left with the chippies. They said they'll see you home.

A second waiter watches some distance away.

WILLY: But we were supposed to have dinner together.

Music is heard, Willy's theme.

750 **STANLEY:** Can you make it?
WILLY: I'll — sure, I can make it. *(Suddenly concerned about his clothes.)* Do I — I look all right?
STANLEY: Sure, you look all right. *(He flicks a speck off Willy's lapel.)*
WILLY: Here — here's a dollar.
STANLEY: Oh, your son paid me. It's all right.
755 **WILLY:** *(putting it in Stanley's hand)* No, take it. You're a good boy.
STANLEY: Oh, no, you don't have to . . .
WILLY: Here — here's some more, I don't need it any more. *(After a slight pause.)* Tell me — is there a seed store in the neighborhood?
STANLEY: Seeds? You mean like to plant?

As Willy turns, Stanley slips the money back into his jacket pocket.

WILLY: Yes. Carrots, peas . . .
760 **STANLEY:** Well, there's hardware stores on Sixth Avenue, but it may be too late now.
WILLY: *(anxiously)* Oh, I'd better hurry. I've got to get some seeds. *(He starts off to the right.)* I've got to get some seeds, right away. Nothing's planted. I don't have a thing in the ground.

Willy hurries out as the light goes down. Stanley moves over to the right after him, watches him off. The other waiter has been staring at Willy.

STANLEY: *(to the waiter)* Well, whatta you looking at?

The waiter picks up the chairs and moves off right. Stanley takes the table and follows him. The light fades on this area. There is a long pause, the sound of the flute coming over. The light gradually rises on the kitchen, which is empty. Happy appears at the door of the house, followed by Biff. Happy is carrying a large bunch of long-stemmed roses. He enters the kitchen, looks around for Linda. Not seeing her, he turns to Biff, who is just outside the house door, and makes a gesture with his hands, indicating "Not here, I guess." He looks into the living room and freezes. Inside, Linda, unseen, is seated, Willy's coat on her lap. She rises ominously and quietly and moves toward Happy, who backs up into the kitchen, afraid.

HAPPY: Hey, what're you doing up? *(Linda says nothing but moves toward him implacably.)* Where's Pop? *(He keeps backing to the right, and now Linda is in full view in the doorway to the living room.)* Is he sleeping?

LINDA: Where were you?

HAPPY: *(trying to laugh it off)* We met two girls, Mom, very fine types. Here, we 765
brought you some flowers. *(Offering them to her.)* Put them in your room, Ma.

She knocks them to the floor at Biff's feet. He has now come inside and closed the door behind him. She stares at Biff, silent.

HAPPY: Now what'd you do that for? Mom, I want you to have some flowers—

LINDA: *(cutting Happy off, violently to Biff)* Don't you care whether he lives or dies?

HAPPY: *(going to the stairs)* Come upstairs, Biff.

BIFF: *(with a flare of disgust, to Happy)* Go away from me! *(To Linda.)* What do you mean, lives or dies? Nobody's dying around here, pal.

LINDA: Get out of my sight! Get out of here! 770

BIFF: I wanna see the boss.

LINDA: You're not going near him!

BIFF: Where is he? *(He moves into the living room and Linda follows.)*

LINDA: *(shouting after Biff)* You invite him for dinner. He looks forward to it all day —*(Biff appears in his parents' bedroom, looks around, and exits)*— and then you desert him there. There's no stranger you'd do that to!

HAPPY: Why? He had a swell time with us. Listen, when I —*(Linda comes back* 775
into the kitchen)— desert him I hope I don't outlive the day!

LINDA: Get out of here!

HAPPY: Now look, Mom . . .

LINDA: Did you have to go to women tonight? You and your lousy rotten whores!

Biff re-enters the kitchen.

HAPPY: Mom, all we did was follow Biff around trying to cheer him up! *(To Biff.)* Boy, what a night you gave me!

780 **LINDA:** Get out of here, both of you, and don't come back! I don't want you tormenting him any more. Go on now, get your things together! *(To Biff.)* You can sleep in his apartment. *(She starts to pick up the flowers and stops herself.)* Pick up this stuff, I'm not your maid any more. Pick it up, you bum, you!

Happy turns his back to her in refusal. Biff slowly moves over and gets down on his knees, picking up the flowers.

LINDA: You're a pair of animals! Not one, not another living soul would have had the cruelty to walk out on that man in a restaurant!

BIFF: *(not looking at her)* Is that what he said?

LINDA: He didn't have to say anything. He was so humiliated he nearly limped when he came in.

HAPPY: But, Mom he had a great time with us —

785 **BIFF:** *(cutting him off violently)* Shut up!

Without another word, Happy goes upstairs.

LINDA: You! You didn't even go in to see if he was all right!

BIFF: *(still on the floor in front of Linda, the flowers in his hand; with self-loathing)* No. Didn't. Didn't do a damned thing. How do you like that, heh? Left him babbling in a toilet.

LINDA: You louse. You . . .

BIFF: Now you hit it on the nose! *(He gets up, throws the flowers in the wastebasket.)* The scum of the earth, and you're looking at him!

790 **LINDA:** Get out of here!

BIFF: I gotta talk to the boss, Mom. Where is he?

LINDA: You're not going near him. Get out of this house!

BIFF: *(with absolute assurance, determination)* No. We're gonna have an abrupt conversation, him and me.

LINDA: You're not talking to him!

Hammering is heard from outside the house, off right. Biff turns toward the noise.

795 **LINDA:** *(suddenly pleading)* Will you please leave him alone?

BIFF: What's he doing out there?

LINDA: He's planting the garden!

BIFF: *(quietly)* Now? Oh, my God!

Biff moves outside, Linda following. The light dies down on them and comes up on the center of the apron as Willy walks into it. He is carrying a flashlight, a hoe and a handful of seed packets. He raps the top of the hoe sharply to fix it firmly, and then moves to the left, measuring off the distance with his foot. He holds the flashlight to look at the seed packets, reading off the instructions. He is in the blue of night.

WILLY: Carrots . . . quarter-inch apart. Rows . . . one-foot rows. *(He measures it off.)* One foot. *(He puts down a package and measures off.)* Beets. *(He puts* *down another package and measures again.)* Lettuce. (*He reads the package, puts it down.)* One foot — (*He breaks off as Ben appears at the right and moves slowly down to him.)* What a proposition, ts, ts. Terrific, terrific. 'Cause she's suffered, Ben, the woman has suffered. You understand me? A man can't go out the way he came in, Ben, a man has got to add up to something. You can't, you can't — (*Ben moves toward him as though to interrupt.)* You gotta consider, now. Don't answer so quick. Remember, it's a guaranteed twenty-thousand-dollar proposition. Now look, Ben, I want you to go through the ins and outs of this thing with me. I've got nobody to talk to, Ben, and the woman has suffered, you hear me?

BEN: (*standing still, considering*) What's the proposition? 800

WILLY: It's twenty thousand dollars on the barrelhead. Guaranteed, gilt-edged, you understand?

BEN: You don't want to make a fool of yourself. They might not honor the policy.

WILLY: How can they dare refuse? Didn't I work like a coolie to meet every premium on the nose? And now they don't pay off? Impossible!

BEN: It's called a cowardly thing, William.

WILLY: Why? Does it take more guts to stand here the rest of my life ringing 805 up a zero?

BEN: (*yielding*) That's a point, William. (*He moves, thinking, turns.)* And twenty thousand — that *is* something one can feel with the hand, it is there.

WILLY: (*now assured, with rising power*) Oh, Ben, that's the whole beauty of it! I see it like a diamond, shining in the dark, hard and rough, that I can pick up and touch in my hand. Not like — like an appointment! This would not be another damned-fool appointment, Ben, and it changes all the aspects. Because he thinks I'm nothing, see, and so he spites me. But the funeral — (*Straightening up.)* Ben, that funeral will be massive! They'll come from Maine, Massachusetts, Vermont, New Hampshire! All the old-timers with the strange license plates — that boy will be thunder-struck, Ben, because he never realized — I am known! Rhode Island, New York, New Jersey — I am known, Ben, and he'll see it with his eyes once and for all. He'll see what I am, Ben! He's in for a shock, that boy!

BEN: (*coming down to the edge of the garden*) He'll call you a coward.

WILLY: (*suddenly fearful*) No, that would be terrible.

BEN: Yes. And a damned fool. 810

WILLY: No, no, he mustn't, I won't have that! (*He is broken and desperate.)*

BEN: He'll hate you, William.

The gay music of the boys is heard.

WILLY: Oh, Ben, how do we get back to all the great times? Used to be so full of light, and comradeship, the sleigh-riding in winter, and the ruddiness on his cheeks. And always some kind of good news coming up, always something nice coming up ahead. And never even let me carry the valises in the house, and simonizing, simonizing that little red car! Why, why can't I give him something and not have him hate me?

BEN: Let me think about it. (*He glances at his watch.*) I still have a little time. Remarkable proposition, but you've got to be sure you're not making a fool of yourself.

Ben drifts off upstage and goes out of sight. Biff comes down from the left.

815 **WILLY:** (*suddenly conscious of Biff, turns and looks up at him, then begins picking up the packages of seeds in confusion*) Where the hell is that seed? (*Indignantly.*) You can't see nothing out here! They boxed in the whole goddam neighborhood!

BIFF: There are people all around here. Don't you realize that?

WILLY: I'm busy. Don't bother me.

BIFF: (*taking the hoe from Willy*) I'm saying good-by to you, Pop. (*Willy looks at him, silent, unable to move.*) I'm not coming back any more.

WILLY: You're not going to see Oliver tomorrow?

820 **BIFF:** I've got no appointment, Dad.

WILLY: He put his arm around you, and you've got no appointment?

BIFF: Pop, get this now, will you? Everytime I've left it's been a fight that sent me out of here. Today I realized something about myself and I tried to explain it to you and I — I think I'm just not smart enough to make any sense out of it for you. To hell with whose fault it is or anything like that. (*He takes Willy's arm.*) Let's just wrap it up, heh? Come on in, we'll tell Mom. (*He gently tries to pull Willy to the left.*)

WILLY: (*frozen, immobile, with guilt in his voice*) No, I don't want to see her.

BIFF: Come on! (*He pulls again, and Willy tries to pull away.*)

825 **WILLY:** (*highly nervous*) No, no, I don't want to see her.

BIFF: (*tries to look into Willy's face, as if to find the answer there*) Why don't you want to see her?

WILLY: (*more harshly now*) Don't bother me, will you?

BIFF: What do you mean, you don't want to see her? You don't want them calling you yellow, do you? This isn't your fault; it's me, I'm a bum. Now come inside! (*Willy strains to get away.*) Did you hear what I said to you?

Willy pulls away and quickly goes by himself into the house. Biff follows.

LINDA: (*to Willy*) Did you plant, dear?

830 **BIFF:** (*at the door, to Linda*) All right, we had it out. I'm going and I'm not writing any more.

LINDA: (*going to Willy in the kitchen*) I think that's the best way, dear. 'Cause there's no use drawing it out, you'll just never get along.

Willy doesn't respond.

BIFF: People ask where I am and what I'm doing, you don't know, and you don't care. That way it'll be off your mind and you can start brightening up again. All right? That clears it, doesn't it? (*Willy is silent, and Biff goes to him.*) You gonna wish me luck, scout? (*He extends his hand.*) What do you say?

LINDA: Shake his hand, Willy.

WILLY: (*turning to her, seething with hurt*) There's no necessity to mention the pen at all, y'know.

BIFF: (*gently*) I've got no appointment, Dad.   835

WILLY: (*erupting fiercely*) He put his arm around . . . ?

BIFF: Dad, you're never going to see what I am, so what's the use of arguing? If I strike oil I'll send you a check. Meantime forget I'm alive.

WILLY: (*to Linda*) Spite, see?

BIFF: Shake hands, Dad.

WILLY: Not my hand.   840

BIFF: I was hoping not to go this way.

WILLY: Well, this is the way you're going. Good-by.

Biff looks at him a moment, then turns sharply and goes to the stairs.

WILLY: (*stops him with*) May you rot in hell if you leave this house!

BIFF: (*turning*) Exactly what is it that you want from me?

WILLY: I want you to know, on the train, in the mountains, in the valleys,   845
wherever you go, that you cut down your life for spite!

BIFF: No, no.

WILLY: Spite, spite, is the word of your undoing! And when you're down and out, remember what did it. When you're rotting somewhere beside the railroad tracks, remember, and don't you dare blame it on me!

BIFF: I'm not blaming it on you!

WILLY: I won't take the rap for this, you hear?

Happy comes down the stairs and stands on the bottom step, watching.

BIFF: That's just what I'm telling you!   850

WILLY: (*sinking into a chair at the table, with full accusation*) You're trying to put a knife in me — don't think I don't know what you're doing!

BIFF: All right, phony! Then let's lay it on the line. (*He whips the rubber tube out of his pocket and puts it on the table.*)

HAPPY: You crazy —

LINDA: Biff! (*She moves to grab the hose, but Biff holds it down with his hand.*)

BIFF: Leave it there! Don't move it!   855

WILLY: (*not looking at it*) What is that?

BIFF: You know goddam well what that is.

WILLY: (*caged, wanting to escape*) I never saw that.

BIFF: You saw it. The mice didn't bring it into the cellar! What is this supposed to do, make a hero out of you? This supposed to make me sorry for you?

860 **Willy:** Never heard of it.

Biff: There'll be no pity for you, you hear it? No pity!

Willy: *(to Linda)* You hear the spite!

Biff: No, you're going to hear the truth — what you are and what I am!

Linda: Stop it!

865 **Willy:** Spite!

Happy: *(coming down toward Biff)* You cut it now!

Biff: *(to Happy)* The man don't know who we are! The man is gonna know! *(To Willy.)* We never told the truth for ten minutes in this house!

Happy: We always told the truth!

Biff: *(turning on him)* You big blow, are you the assistant buyer? You're one of the two assistants to the assistant, aren't you?

870 **Happy:** Well, I'm practically —

Biff: You're practically full of it! We all are! And I'm through with it. *(To Willy.)* Now hear this, Willy, this is me.

Willy: I know you!

Biff: You know why I had no address for three months? I stole a suit in Kansas City and I was in jail. *(To Linda, who is sobbing.)* Stop crying. I'm through with it.

Linda turns away from them, her hands covering her face.

Willy: I suppose that's my fault!

875 **Biff:** I stole myself out of every good job since high school!

Willy: And whose fault is that?

Biff: And I never got anywhere because you blew me so full of hot air I could never stand taking orders from anybody! That's whose fault it is!

Willy: I hear that!

Linda: Don't, Biff!

880 **Biff:** It's goddam time you heard that! I had to be boss big shot in two weeks, and I'm through with it!

Willy: Then hang yourself! For spite, hang yourself!

Biff: No! Nobody's hanging himself, Willy! I ran down eleven flights with a pen in my hand today. And suddenly I stopped, you hear me? And in the middle of that office building, do you hear this? I stopped in the middle of that building and I saw — the sky. I saw the things that I love in this world. The work and the food and time to sit and smoke. And I looked at the pen and said to myself, what the hell am I grabbing this for? Why am I trying to become what I don't want to be? What am I doing in an office, making a contemptuous, begging fool of myself, when all I want is out there, waiting for me the minute I say I know who I am! Why can't I say that, Willy? *(He tries to make Willy face him, but Willy pulls away and moves to the left.)*

Willy: *(with hatred, threateningly)* The door of your life is wide open!

Biff: Pop! I'm a dime a dozen, and so are you!

WILLY: (*turning on him now in an uncontrolled outburst*) I am not a dime a   885
dozen! I am Willy Loman, and you are Biff Loman!

Biff starts for Willy, but is blocked by Happy. In his fury, Biff seems on the verge of attacking his father.

BIFF: I am not a leader of men, Willy, and neither are you. You were never
anything but a hard-working drummer who landed in the ash can like all
the rest of them! I'm one dollar an hour, Willy! I tried seven states and
couldn't raise it. A buck an hour! Do you gather my meaning? I'm not
bringing home any prizes any more, and you're going to stop waiting for me
to bring them home!

WILLY: (*directly to Biff*) You vengeful, spiteful mutt!

Biff breaks from Happy. Willy, in fright, starts up the stairs. Biff grabs him.

BIFF: (*at the peak of his fury*) Pop, I'm nothing! I'm nothing, Pop. Can't you understand that? There's no spite in it any more. I'm just what I am, that's all.

Biff's fury has spent itself, and he breaks down, sobbing, holding on to Willy, who dumbly fumbles for Biff's face.

WILLY: (*astonished*) What're you doing? What're you doing? (*To Linda.*) Why is
he crying?

BIFF: (*crying, broken*) Will you let me go, for Christ's sake? Will you take that   890
phony dream and burn it before something happens? (*Struggling to contain
himself, he pulls away and moves to the stairs.*) I'll go in the morning. Put
him — put him to bed. (*Exhausted, Biff moves up the stairs to his room.*)

WILLY: (*after a long pause, astonished, elevated*) Isn't that remarkable? Biff — he
likes me!

LINDA: He loves you, Willy!

HAPPY: (*deeply moved*) Always did, Pop.

WILLY: Oh, Biff! (*Staring wildly.*) He cried! Cried to me! (*He is choking with his
love, and now cries out his promise.*) That boy — that boy is going to be
magnificent!

Ben appears in the light just outside the kitchen.

BEN: Yes, outstanding, with twenty thousand behind him.   895

LINDA: (*sensing the racing of his mind, fearfully, carefully*) Now come to bed,
Willy. It's all settled now.

WILLY: (*finding it difficult not to rush out of the house*) Yes, we'll sleep. Come on.
Go to sleep, Hap.

BEN: And it does take a great kind of man to crack the jungle.

In accents of dread, Ben's idyllic music starts up.

HAPPY: *(his arm around Linda)* I'm getting married, Pop, don't forget it. I'm
    changing everything. I'm gonna run that department before the year is up.
    You'll see, Mom. *(He kisses her.)*
900 BEN: The jungle is dark but full of diamonds, Willy.

Willy turns, moves, listening to Ben.

LINDA: Be good. You're both good boys, just act that way, that's all.
HAPPY: 'Night, Pop. *(He goes upstairs.)*
LINDA: *(to Willy)* Come, dear.
BEN: *(with greater force)* One must go in to fetch a diamond out.
905 WILLY: *(to Linda, as he moves slowly along the edge of the kitchen, toward the door)*
    I just want to get settled down, Linda. Let me sit alone for a little.
LINDA: *(almost uttering her fear)* I want you upstairs.
WILLY: *(taking her in his arms)* In a few minutes, Linda. I couldn't sleep right
    now. Go on, you look awful tired. *(He kisses her.)*
BEN: Not like an appointment at all. A diamond is rough and hard to the touch.
WILLY: Go on now. I'll be right up.
910 LINDA: I think this is the only way, Willy.
WILLY: Sure, it's the best thing.
BEN: Best thing!
WILLY: The only way. Everything is gonna be — go on, kid, get to bed. You
    look so tired.
LINDA: Come right up.
915 WILLY: Two minutes.

*Linda goes into the living room, then reappears in her bedroom. Willy moves just out-
side the kitchen door.*

WILLY: Loves me. *(Wonderingly.)* Always loved me. Isn't that a remarkable
    thing? Ben, he'll worship me for it!
BEN: *(with promise)* It's dark there, but full of diamonds.
WILLY: Can you imagine that magnificence with twenty thousand dollars in
    his pocket?
LINDA: *(calling from her room)* Willy! Come up!
920 WILLY: *(calling from the kitchen)* Yes! Yes! Coming! It's very smart, you realize
    that, don't you, sweetheart? Even Ben sees it. I gotta go, baby. 'By! By!
    (Going over to Ben, almost dancing.) Imagine? When the mail comes he'll
    be ahead of Bernard again!
BEN: A perfect proposition all around.
WILLY: Did you see how he cried to me? Oh, if I could kiss him, Ben!
BEN: Time, William, time!
WILLY: Oh, Ben, I always knew one way or another we were gonna make it,
    Biff and I!
925 BEN: *(looking at his watch)* The boat. We'll be late. *(He moves slowly off into the
    darkness.)*

WILLY: (*elegiacally, turning to the house*) Now when you kick off, boy, I want a seventy-yard boot, and get right down the field under the ball, and when you hit, hit low and hit hard, because it's important, boy. (*He swings around and faces the audience.*) There's all kinds of important people in the stands, and the first thing you know . . . (*Suddenly realizing he is alone.*) Ben! Ben, where do I . . . ? (*He makes a sudden movement of search.*) Ben, how do I . . . ?

LINDA: (*calling*) Willy, you coming up?

WILLY: (*uttering a gasp of fear, whirling about as if to quiet her*) Sh! (*He turns around as if to find his way; sounds, faces, voices, seem to be swarming in upon him and he flicks at them, crying.*) Sh! Sh! (*Suddenly music, faint and high, stops him. It rises in intensity, almost to an unbearable scream. He goes up and down on his toes, and rushes off around the house.*) Shhh!

LINDA: Willy?

There is no answer. Linda waits. Biff gets up off his bed. He is still in his clothes. Happy sits up. Biff stands listening.

LINDA: (*with real fear*) Willy, answer me! Willy!

There is the sound of a car starting and moving away at full speed.

LINDA: No!

BIFF: (*rushing down the stairs*) Pop!

As the car speeds off, the music crashes down in a frenzy of sound, which becomes the soft pulsation of a single cello string. Biff slowly returns to his bedroom. He and Happy gravely don their jackets. Linda slowly walks out of her room. The music has developed into a dead march. The leaves of day are appearing over everything. Charley and Bernard, somberly dressed, appear and knock on the kitchen door. Biff and Happy slowly descend the stairs to the kitchen as Charley and Bernard enter. All stop a moment when Linda, in clothes of mourning, bearing a little bunch of roses, comes through the draped doorway into the kitchen. She goes to Charley and takes his arm. Now all move toward the audience, through the wall-line of the kitchen. At the limit of the apron, Linda lays down the flowers, kneels, and sits back on her heels. All stare down at the grave.

REQUIEM

CHARLEY: It's getting dark, Linda.

Linda doesn't react. She stares at the grave.

BIFF: How about it, Mom? Better get some rest, heh? They'll be closing the gate soon.

Linda makes no move. Pause.

HAPPY: *(deeply angered)* He had no right to do that! There was no necessity for it. We would've helped him.

CHARLEY: *(grunting)* Hmmm.

5 **BIFF:** Come along, Mom.

LINDA: Why didn't anybody come?

CHARLEY: It was a very nice funeral.

LINDA: But where are all the people he knew? Maybe they blame him.

CHARLEY: Naa. It's a rough world, Linda. They wouldn't blame him.

10 **LINDA:** I can't understand it. At this time especially. First time in thirty-five years we were just about free and clear. He only needed a little salary. He was even finished with the dentist.

CHARLEY: No man only needs a little salary.

LINDA: I can't understand it.

BIFF: There were a lot of nice days. When he'd come home from a trip; or on Sundays, making the stoop; finishing the cellar; putting on the new porch; when he built the extra bathroom; and put up the garage. You know something, Charley, there's more of him in that front stoop than in all the sales he ever made.

CHARLEY: Yeah. He was a happy man with a batch of cement.

15 **LINDA:** He was so wonderful with his hands.

BIFF: He had the wrong dreams. All, all, wrong.

HAPPY: *(almost ready to fight Biff)* Don't say that!

BIFF: He never knew who he was.

CHARLEY: *(stopping Happy's movement and reply. To Biff.)* Nobody dast blame this man. You don't understand: Willy was a salesman. And for a salesman, there is no rock bottom to the life. He don't put a bolt to a nut, he don't tell you the law or give you medicine. He's a man out there in the blue, riding on a smile and a shoeshine. And when they start not smiling back — that's an earthquake. And then you get yourself a couple of spots on your hat, and you're finished. Nobody dast blame this man. A salesman is got to dream, boy. It comes with the territory.

20 **BIFF:** Charley, the man didn't know who he was.

HAPPY: *(infuriated)* Don't say that!

BIFF: Why don't you come with me, Happy?

HAPPY: I'm not licked that easily. I'm staying right in this city, and I'm gonna beat this racket! *(He looks at Biff, his chin set.)* The Loman Brothers!

BIFF: I know who I am, kid.

25 **HAPPY:** All right, boy. I'm gonna show you and everybody else that Willy Loman did not die in vain. He had a good dream. It's the only dream you can have — to come out number-one man. He fought it out here, and this is where I'm gonna win it for him.

BIFF: *(with a hopeless glance at Happy, bends toward his mother)* Let's go, Mom.

LINDA: I'll be with you in a minute. Go on, Charley. *(He hesitates.)* I want to, just for a minute. I never had a chance to say good-by.

Charley moves away, followed by Happy. Biff remains a slight distance up and left of Linda. She sits there, summoning herself. The flute begins, not far away, playing behind her speech.

LINDA: Forgive me, dear. I can't cry. I don't know what it is, but I can't cry. I don't understand it. Why did you ever do that? Help me, Willy, I can't cry. It seems to me that you're just on another trip. I keep expecting you. Willy, dear, I can't cry. Why did you do it? I search and search and I search, and I can't understand it, Willy. I made the last payment on the house today. Today, dear. And there'll be nobody home. (*A sob rises in her throat.*) We're free and clear. (*Sobbing more fully, released.*) We're free. (*Biff comes slowly toward her.*) We're free . . . We're free . . .

Biff lifts her to her feet and moves out up right with her in his arms. Linda sobs quietly. Bernard and Charley come together and follow them, followed by Happy. Only the music of the flute is left on the darkening stage as over the house the hard towers of the apartment buildings rise into sharp focus, and —

The Curtain Falls

Reading and Reacting

1. With which character in the play do you most identify? Why?
2. Is Willy a likeable character? What words and actions — both Willy's and those of other characters — help you form your conclusion?
3. How does the existence of The Woman affect your overall impression of Willy? What does she reveal about his character?
4. What does Willy's attitude toward his sons indicate about his character? How is this attitude revealed?
5. Does this play have a hero? A villain? Explain.
6. In the absence of a narrator, what devices does Miller use to provide exposition — basic information about character and setting?
7. The conversation between Biff and Happy in act 1 reveals many of their differences. List some of the differences between these two characters.
8. In numerous remarks, Willy expresses his philosophy of business. Summarize some of his key ideas about the business world. How realistic do you think these ideas are? How do these ideas help to delineate his character?
9. In act 1, Linda tells Willy, "Few men are idolized by their children the way you are." Is she sincere, is she being ironic, or is she just trying to make Willy feel better?
10. How do the frequent flashbacks help to explain what motivates Willy? How else could this background information have been presented in the play? Are there advantages to using flashbacks instead of the alternative you suggest?

11. Is Linda simply a stereotype of the long-suffering wife, or is she an individualized, multidimensional character? Explain.
12. Willy Loman lives in Brooklyn, New York; his "territory" is New England. What is the significance to him of the "faraway places"— Africa, Alaska, California, Texas, and the like — mentioned in the play?
13. What purpose does Bernard serve in the play?
14. The play concludes with a requiem. What is a requiem? What information about each of the major characters is supplied in this brief section? Is this information essential to your understanding or appreciation of the play, or would the play have been equally effective without the requiem? Explain.
15. **JOURNAL ENTRY** Do you believe Willy Loman is an innocent victim of the society in which he lives, or do you believe there are flaws in his character that make him at least partially responsible for his own misfortune? Explain.
16. **CRITICAL PERSPECTIVE** Writing just after Miller's death in 2005, playwright David Mamet notes that at the end of *Death of a Salesman*, Miller has offered no solution to Willy's problems but instead "has reconciled us to the notion that there is no solution — that it is the human lot to try and fail, and that no one is immune from self-deception." Mamet goes on to explain the value of Miller's plays by comparing "bad drama" and "good drama":

> Bad drama reinforces our prejudices. It informs us of what we knew when we came into the theater . . . .
>
> The good drama survives because it appeals not to the fashion of the moment, but to the problems both universal and eternal, as they are insoluble.
>
> To find beauty in the sad, hope in the midst of loss, and dignity in failure is great poetic art.

According to Mamet's criteria, do you agree that *Death of a Salesman* qualifies as "good drama"? Do you think it is great drama?

Related Works: "A Primer for the Punctuation of Heart Disease" (p. 88), "Do not go gentle into that good night" (p. 627), "The Love Song of J. Alfred Prufrock" (p. 665), *Oedipus the King* (p. 1048), *Fences* (p. 1096)

WILLIAM SHAKESPEARE (1564 –1616) is recognized as the greatest of English writers, but many details about his life are based on conjecture or tradition. The earliest dependable information concerning Shakespeare is found in the parish registers of Stratford-upon-Avon's Holy Trinity Church, where his baptism was recorded on April 26, 1564. Although his date of birth cannot be determined with certainty, tradition has assigned it to April 23, 1564. Little is known about his early life, but reliable information about significant events is available in church documents. For example, he married Ann Hathaway in 1582 and had three children — Susanna in 1583 and the twins Judith and Hamnet in 1585.

Soon after the birth of his children, Shakespeare left Stratford for London. Upon his arrival in the capital, he set out to establish himself in London's literary world. His first step toward achieving this goal occurred in 1592, when he published his narrative poem *Venus and Adonis;* the following year, he published a second poem, *The Rape of Lucrece.*

By 1594, Shakespeare had become quite involved with the London stage. For approximately twenty years, Shakespeare enjoyed a successful professional career in London — as actor, playwright, shareholder in the Lord Chamberlain's Men (an acting company), part owner of the Globe Theatre (from 1599), and author of at least thirty-six plays. The income derived from these activities brought him significant wealth and enabled him, sometime between 1610 and 1613, to retire from the theater and to return to Stratford-upon-Avon, where he owned considerable property. On April 23, 1616, Shakespeare died at age fifty-two in Stratford and was buried two days later in Holy Trinity Church.

It is difficult to date many of Shakespeare's plays exactly because they must be dated by records of their first performance (often hard to come by) and by topical references in the text. Shakespeare's company probably first staged *Hamlet* at the Globe Theatre in 1600 or 1601, but some scholars believe the play was composed as early as 1598.

Hamlet has been called Shakespeare's most complex and most confusing play, yet it is also the play most frequently performed, read, and written about. Shakespeare's audience would have recognized *Hamlet* as a **revenge tragedy** — a play in which the hero discovers that a close relative has been murdered, experiences considerable trouble in identifying the murderer, and, after overcoming numerous obstacles, avenges the death by killing the murderer. Frequently, revenge tragedies featured murders, physical mutilations, and ghosts, all enacted with grand style and bold rhetoric. These plays were extremely popular productions that were the action movies of their day.

Hamlet, however, is different from the typical revenge tragedy. Because the Ghost gives him the necessary information, Hamlet has no need to search for the cause of his father's death or find the murderer. In fact, the only impediments to Hamlet's revenge are the impediments he himself creates. And, by the time the delay ends and Hamlet avenges his father's death, the loss is immense: his mother, the woman he loves, her father and brother, and Hamlet himself are all dead. Although the argument that there would be no play if Hamlet had immediately avenged his father may be valid, it fails to satisfy those who ponder the tragic cost of Hamlet's inaction.

An audience at the reconstructed Globe Theatre in London.

Hamlet
Prince of Denmark* (c. 1600)

CHARACTERS

Claudius, *King of Denmark*
Hamlet, *son to the former and nephew*
to the present King
Polonius, *Lord Chamberlain*
Horatio, *friend to Hamlet*
Laertes, *son to Polonius*
Courtiers {
Voltimand
Cornelius
Rosencrantz
Guildenstern
Osric
A Gentleman
A Priest
Francisco, *a soldier*
Officers {
Marcellus
Bernardo

Reynaldo, *servant to Polonius*
Players
Two Clowns, *grave-diggers*
Fortinbras, *Prince of Norway*
A Captain
English Ambassadors
Ghost of Hamlet's Father
Gertrude, *Queen of Denmark and mother*
of Hamlet
Ophelia, *daughter to Polonius*
Lords, Ladies, Officers,
Soldiers, Sailors
Messengers, and other
Attendants

ACT 1
SCENE 1

Elsinore. A platform before the castle.

Francisco at his post. Enter to him Bernardo.

BERNARDO: Who's there?
FRANCISCO: Nay, answer me: stand, and unfold yourself.
BERNARDO: Long live the king!
FRANCISCO: Bernardo?
5 **BERNARDO:**   He.
FRANCISCO: You come most carefully upon your hour.
BERNARDO: 'Tis now struck twelve; get thee to bed, Francisco.
FRANCISCO: For this relief much thanks: 'tis bitter cold,
   And I am sick at heart.
10 **BERNARDO:** Have you had quiet guard?
FRANCISCO: Not a mouse stirring.
BERNARDO: Well, good-night.
   If you do meet Horatio and Marcellus,
   The rivals of my watch, bid them make haste.
15 **FRANCISCO:** I think I hear them.— Stand, ho! Who is there?

Enter Horatio and Marcellus.

---

* Note that individual lines are numbered in the following play. When a line is shared by one or more
characters, it is counted as one line.

HORATIO: Friends to this ground.
MARCELLUS: And liegemen to the Dane.
FRANCISCO: Give you good-night.
MARCELLUS: O, farewell, honest soldier:
  Who hath reliev'd you?   20
FRANCISCO: Bernardo has my place.
  Give you good-night.

Exit.

MARCELLUS: Holla! Bernardo!
BERNARDO: Say.
  What, is Horatio there?   25
HORATIO: A piece of him.
BERNARDO: Welcome, Horatio:— welcome, good Marcellus.
MARCELLUS: What, has this thing appear'd again to-night?
BERNARDO: I have seen nothing.
MARCELLUS: Horatio says 'tis but our fantasy,   30
  And will not let belief take hold of him
  Touching this dreaded sight, twice seen of us:
  Therefore I have entreated him along
  With us to watch the minutes of this night;
  That, if again this apparition come   35
  He may approve our eyes and speak to it.
HORATIO: Tush, tush, 'twill not appear.
BERNARDO: Sit down awhile,
  And let us once again assail your ears,
  That are so fortified against our story,   40
  What we two nights have seen.
HORATIO: Well, sit we down,
  And let us hear Bernardo speak of this.
BERNARDO: Last night of all,
  When yon same star that's westward from the pole   45
  Had made his course to illume that part of heaven
  Where now it burns, Marcellus and myself,
  The bell then beating one,—
MARCELLUS: Peace, break thee off; look where it comes again!

Enter Ghost, armed.

BERNARDO: In the same figure, like the king that's dead.   50
MARCELLUS: Thou art a scholar; speak to it, Horatio.
BERNARDO: Looks it not like the king? mark it, Horatio.
HORATIO: Most like:— it harrows me with fear and wonder.
BERNARDO: It would be spoke to.
MARCELLUS: Question it, Horatio.   55

HORATIO: What art thou, that usurp'st this time of night,
   Together with that fair and warlike form
   In which the majesty of buried Denmark
   Did sometimes march? by heaven I charge thee, speak!
60 **MARCELLUS:** It is offended.
BERNARDO: See, it stalks away!
HORATIO: Stay! speak, speak! I charge thee, speak!

Exit Ghost.

MARCELLUS: 'Tis gone, and will not answer.
BERNARDO: How now, Horatio! you tremble and look pale:
65   Is not this something more than fantasy?
   What think you on't?
HORATIO: Before my God, I might not this believe
   Without the sensible and true avouch
   Of mine own eyes.
70 **MARCELLUS:**   Is it not like the king?
HORATIO: As thou art to thyself:
   Such was the very armor he had on
   When he the ambitious Norway combated;
   So frown'd he once when, in an angry parle,°
75   He smote the sledded Polacks on the ice.
   'Tis strange.
MARCELLUS: Thus twice before, and just at this dead hour,
   With martial stalk hath he gone by our watch.
HORATIO: In what particular thought to work I know not;
80   But, in the gross and scope of my opinion,
   This bodes some strange eruption to our state.
MARCELLUS: Good now, sit down, and tell me, he that knows,
   Why this same strict and most observant watch
   So nightly toils the subject of the land;
85   And why such daily cast of brazen cannon,
   And foreign mart for implements of war;
   Why such impress of shipwrights, whose sore task
   Does not divide the Sunday from the week;
   What might be toward, that this sweaty haste
90   Doth make the night joint-laborer with the day:
   Who is't that can inform me?
HORATIO: That can I;
   At least, the whisper goes so. Our last king,
   Whose image even but now appear'd to us,

° *parle:* Parley, or conference.

Was, as you know, by Fortinbras of Norway, 95
Thereto prick'd on by a most emulate pride,
Dar'd to the combat; in which our valiant Hamlet,—
For so this side of our known world esteem'd him,—
Did slay this Fortinbras; who, by a seal'd compact,
Well ratified by law and heraldry, 100
Did forfeit, with his life, all those his lands.
Which he stood seiz'd of,° to the conqueror:
Against the which, a moiety competent°
Was gagéd° by our king; which had return'd
To the inheritance of Fortinbras, 105
Had he been vanquisher; as by the same cov'nant,
And carriage of the article design'd,
His fell to Hamlet. Now, sir, young Fortinbras,
Of unimproved mettle hot and full,
Hath in the skirts of Norway, here and there, 110
Shark'd up a list of landless resolutes,
For food and diet, to some enterprise
That hath a stomach in't: which is no other,—
As it doth well appear unto our state,—
But to recover of us by strong hand, 115
And terms compulsatory, those foresaid lands
So by his father lost: and this, I take it,
Is the main motive of our preparations,
The source of this our watch, and the chief head
Of this post-haste and romage° in the land. 120
BERNARDO: I think it be no other, but e'en so:
Well may it sort that this portentous figure
Comes armed through our watch; so like the king
That was and is the question of these wars.
HORATIO: A mote it is to trouble the mind's eye. 125
In the most high and palmy state of Rome,
A little ere the mightiest Julius fell,
The graves stood tenantless, and the sheeted dead
Did squeak and gibber in the Roman streets:
As, stars with trains of fire and dews of blood, 130
Disasters in the sun; and the moist star,
Upon whose influence Neptune's empire stands,
Was sick almost to doomsday with eclipse:
And even the like precurse of fierce events,—
As harbingers preceding still the fates, 135

° *seiz'd of:* Possessed. ° *moiety competent:* A sufficient portion of his lands. ° *gagéd:* Engaged or pledged.
° *post-haste and romage:* General activity.

And prologue to the omen coming on,—
Have heaven and earth together demonstrated
Unto our climature and countrymen.—
But, soft, behold! lo, where it comes again!

Re-enter Ghost.

140   I'll cross it, though it blast me.— Stay, illusion!
If thou hast any sound or use of voice,
Speak to me:
If there be any good thing to be done,
That may to thee do ease, and grace to me,
145   Speak to me:
If thou art privy to thy country's fate,
Which, happily,° foreknowing may avoid,
O, speak!
Or if thou has uphoarded in thy life
150   Extorted treasure in the womb of earth,
For which, they say, you spirits oft walk in death,

Cock crows.

Speak of it:— stay, and speak!— Stop it, Marcellus.
MARCELLUS: Shall I strike at it with my partisan?°
HORATIO: Do, if it will not stand.
155   BERNARDO: 'Tis here!
HORATIO: 'Tis here!
MARCELLUS: 'Tis gone!

Exit Ghost.

We do it wrong, being so majestical,
To offer it the show of violence;
160   For it is, as the air, invulnerable,
And our vain blows malicious mockery.
BERNARDO: It was about to speak when the cock crew.
HORATIO: And then it started like a guilty thing
Upon a fearful summons. I have heard,
165   The cock, that is the trumpet to the morn,
Doth with his lofty and shrill-sounding throat
Awake the god of day; and at his warning,
Whether in sea or fire, in earth or air,
The extravagant and erring spirit hies
170   To his confine: and of the truth herein
This present object made probation.°

° *happily:* Haply, or perhaps.   ° *partisan:* Pike.   ° *probation:* Proof.

MARCELLUS: It faded on the crowing of the cock.
Some say that ever 'gainst that season comes
Wherein our Saviour's birth is celebrated,
The bird of dawning singeth all night long: 175
And then, they say, no spirit can walk abroad;
The nights are wholesome; then no planets strike,
No fairy takes, nor witch hath power to charm;
So hallow'd and so gracious is the time.
HORATIO: So have I heard, and do in part believe.   180
But, look, the morn, in russet mantle clad,
Walks o'er the dew of yon high eastern hill:
Break we our watch up: and, by my advice,
Let us impart what we have seen to-night
Unto young Hamlet; for, upon my life,   185
This spirit, dumb to us, will speak to him:
Do you consent we shall acquaint him with it,
As needful in our loves, fitting our duty?
MARCELLUS: Let's do't, I pray; and I this morning know
Where we shall find him most conveniently.   190

Exeunt.

SCENE 2

Elsinore. A room of state in the castle.

*Enter the King, Queen, Hamlet, Polonius, Laertes, Voltimand, Cornelius, Lords, and
Attendants.*

KING: Though yet of Hamlet our dear brother's death
The memory be green; and that it us befitted
To bear our hearts in grief, and our whole kingdom
To be contracted in one brow of woe;
Yet so far hath discretion fought with nature   5
That we with wisest sorrow think on him,
Together with remembrance of ourselves.
Therefore our sometime sister, now our queen,
The imperial jointress of this warlike state,
Have we, as 'twere with defeated joy,—   10
With one auspicious and one dropping eye,
With mirth and funeral, and with dirge in marriage,
In equal scale weighing delight and dole,—
Taken to wife: nor have we herein barr'd
Your better wisdoms, which have freely gone   15
With this affair along:—for all, our thanks.
Now follows that you know, young Fortinbras,

Holding a weak supposal of our worth,
Or thinking by our late dear brother's death
20 Our state to be disjoint and out of frame,
Colleagued with the dream of his advantage,
He hath not fail'd to pester us with message,
Importing the surrender of those lands
Lost by his father, with all bonds of law,
25 To our most valiant brother. So much for him.—
Now for ourself, and for this time of meeting:
Thus much the business is:—we have here writ
To Norway, uncle of young Fortinbras,—
Who, impotent and bed-rid, scarcely hears
30 Of this his nephew's purpose,—to suppress
His further gait herein; in that the levies,
The lists, and full proportions, are all made
Out of his subject:—and we here despatch
You, good Cornelius, and you, Voltimand,
35 For bearers of this greeting to old Norway;
Giving to you no further personal power
To business with the king more than the scope
Of these dilated articles allow.
Farewell; and let your haste commend your duty.
40 CORNELIUS and VOLTIMAND: In that and all things will we show
our duty.
KING: We doubt it nothing: heartily farewell.

Exeunt Voltimand and Cornelius.

And now, Laertes, what's the news with you?
You told us of some suit; what is't, Laertes?
You cannot speak of reason to the Dane,
45 And lose your voice: what wouldst thou beg, Laertes,
That shall not be my offer, nor thy asking?
The head is not more native to the heart,
The hand more instrumental to the mouth,
Than is the throne of Denmark to thy father.
50 What wouldst thou have, Laertes?
LAERTES: Dread my lord,
Your leave and favor to return to France;
From whence though willingly I came to Denmark,
To show my duty in your coronation;
55 Yet now, I must confess, that duty done,
My thoughts and wishes bend again toward France.
And bow them to your gracious leave and pardon.

KING: Have you your father's leave? What says Polonius?
POLONIUS: He hath, my lord, wrung from me my slow leave
    By laborsome petition; and at last   60
    Upon his will I seal'd my hard consent:
    I do beseech you, give him leave to go.
KING: Take thy fair hour, Laertes; time be thine,
    And thy best graces spend it at thy will! —
    But now, my cousin Hamlet, and my son, —   65
HAMLET: [*Aside*] A little more than kin, and less than kind.
KING: How is it that the clouds still hang on you?
HAMLET: Not so, my lord; I am too much i' the sun.
QUEEN: Good Hamlet, cast thy nighted color off,
    And let thine eye look like a friend on Denmark.   70
    Do not for ever with thy vailed° lids
    Seek for thy noble father in the dust:
    Thou know'st 'tis common, — all that live must die,
    Passing through nature to eternity.
HAMLET: Ay, madam, it is common.   75
QUEEN: If it be,
    Why seems it so particular with thee?
HAMLET: Seems, madam! nay, it is; I know not seems.
    'Tis not alone my inky cloak, good mother,
    Nor customary suits of solemn black,   80
    Nor windy suspiration of forc'd breath,
    No, nor the fruitful river in the eye,
    Nor the dejected 'havior of the visage,
    Together with all forms, moods, shows of grief,
    That can denote me truly: these, indeed, seem;   85
    For they are actions that a man might play:
    But I have that within which passeth show;
    These but the trappings and the suits of woe.
KING: 'Tis sweet and cómmendable in your nature, Hamlet,
    To give these mourning duties to your father: 90
    But, you must know, your father lost a father;
    That father lost, lost his; and the survivor bound,
    In filial obligation, for some term
    To do obsequious sorrow: but to persever
    In obstinate condolement is a course   95
    Of impious stubbornness; 'tis unmanly grief:
    It shows a will most incorrect to heaven;
    A heart unfortified, a mind impatient;
    An understanding simple and unschool'd:

° *vailed:* Downcast.

100 For what we know must be, and is as common
As any the most vulgar thing to sense,°
Why should we, in our peevish opposition,
Take it to heart? Fie! 'tis a fault to heaven,
A fault against the dead, a fault to nature,
105 To reason most absurd; whose common theme
Is death of fathers, and who still° hath cried,
From the first corse till he that died to-day,
This must be so. We pray you, throw to earth
This unprevailing woe; and think of us
110 As of a father: for let the world take note
You are the most immediate to our throne;
And with no less nobility of love
Than that which dearest father bears his son
Do I impart toward you. For your intent
115 In going back to school in Wittenberg,
It is most retrograde to our desire:
And we beseech you bend you to remain
Here, in the cheer and comfort of our eye,
Our chiefest courtier, cousin, and our son.
120 QUEEN: Let not thy mother lose her prayers, Hamlet:
I pray thee, stay with us; go not to Wittenberg.
HAMLET: I shall in all my best obey you, madam.
KING: Why, 'tis a loving and a fair reply:
Be as ourself in Denmark.—Madam, come;
125 This gentle and unforc'd accord of Hamlet
Sits smiling to my heart: in grace whereof,
No jocund health that Denmark drinks to-day
But the great cannon to the clouds shall tell;
And the king's rouse° the heavens shall bruit° again,
130 Re-speaking earthly thunder. Come away.

Exeunt all but Hamlet.

HAMLET: O, that this too too solid flesh would melt,
Thaw, and resolve itself into a dew!
Or that the Everlasting had not fix'd
His canon 'gainst self-slaughter! O God! O God!
135 How weary, stale, flat, and unprofitable
Seem to me all the uses of this world!
Fie on't! O fie! 'tis an unweeded garden,
That grows to seed; things rank and gross in nature

°*any . . . sense:* Anything that is very commonly seen or heard.   °*still:* Ever, or always.   °*rouse:* Drink.
°*bruit:* Echo.

Possess it merely. That it should come to this!
But two months dead! — nay, not so much, not two: 140
So excellent a king; that was, to this,
Hyperion° to a satyr: so loving to my mother,
That he might not beteem the winds of heaven
Visit her face too roughly. Heaven and earth!
Must I remember? why, she would hang on him 145
As if increase of appetite had grown
By what it fed on: and yet, within a month,—
Let me not think on't,— Frailty, thy name is woman!—
A little month; or ere those shoes were old
With which she follow'd my poor father's body 150
Like Niobe, all tears;— why she, even she,—
O God! a beast, that wants discourse of reason,
Would have mourn'd longer,—married with mine uncle,
My father's brother; but no more like my father
Than I to Hercules: within a month; 155
Ere yet the salt of most unrighteous tears
Had left the flushing in her galled eyes,
She married:— O, most wicked speed, to post
With such dexterity to incestuous sheets!
It is not, nor it cannot come to good; 160
But break, my heart,—for I must hold my tongue!

Enter Horatio, Marcellus, and Bernardo.

HORATIO: Hail to your lordship!
HAMLET: I am glad to see you well:
  Horatio,— or I do forget myself.
HORATIO: The same, my lord, and your poor servant ever. 165
HAMLET: Sir, my good friend; I'll change that name with you:
  And what make you from Wittenberg, Horatio?— Marcellus?
MARCELLUS: My good lord,—
HAMLET: I am very glad to see you.— Good even, sir.—
  But what, in faith, make you from Wittenberg? 170
HORATIO: A truant disposition, good my lord.
HAMLET: I would not hear your enemy say so;
  Nor shall you do mine ear that violence,
  To make it truster of your own report
  Against yourself: I know you are no truant. 175
  But what is your affair in Elsinore?
  We'll teach you to drink deep ere you depart.

° *Hyperion:* The Greek sun-god, the brightest and most beautiful of the gods.

Horatio: My lord, I came to see your father's funeral.
Hamlet: I pray thee, do not mock me, fellow-student;
180   I think it was to see my mother's wedding.
Horatio: Indeed, my lord, it follow'd hard upon.
Hamlet: Thrift, thrift, Horatio! the funeral-bak'd meats
     Did coldly furnish forth the marriage tables.
     Would I had met my dearest foe° in heaven
185   Ere I had ever seen that day, Horatio! —
     My father, — methinks I see my father.
Horatio: Where, my lord?
Hamlet: In my mind's eye, Horatio.
Horatio: I saw him once; he was a goodly° king.
190 **Hamlet:** He was a man, take him for all in all,
     I shall not look upon his like again.
Horatio: My lord, I think I saw him yester-night.
Hamlet: Saw who?
Horatio: My lord, the king your father.
195 **Hamlet:**   The king my father!
Horatio: Season your admiration° for awhile
     With an attent ear, till I may deliver,
     Upon the witness of these gentlemen,
     This marvel to you.
200 **Hamlet:**   For God's love, let me hear.
Horatio: Two nights together had these gentlemen,
     Marcellus and Bernardo, in their watch,
     In the dead vast and middle of the night,
     Been thus encounter'd. A figure like your father,
205   Arm'd at all points exactly, cap-a-pe,°
     Appears before them, and with solemn march
     Goes slow and stately by them: thrice he walk'd
     By their oppress'd° and fear-surprised eyes,
     Within his truncheon's length; whilst they, distill'd
210   Almost to jelly with the act of fear,
     Stand dumb, and speak not to him. This to me
     In dreadful secrecy impart they did;
     And I with them the third night kept the watch:
     Where, as they had deliver'd, both in time,
215   Form of the thing, each word made true and good,
     The apparition comes: I knew your father;
     These hands are not more like.

° *dearest foe:* Worst enemy.   °*goodly:* Handsome.   ° *admiration:* Astonishment.   °*cap-a-pe:* From head to toe.   °*oppress'd:* Overwhelmed.

HAMLET: But where was this?
MARCELLUS: My lord, upon the platform where we watch'd.
HAMLET: Did you not speak to it?   220
HORATIO: My lord, I did;
  But answer made it none: yet once methought
  It lifted up its head, and did address
  Itself to motion, like as it would speak:
  But even then the morning cock crew loud,   225
  And at the sound it shrunk in haste away,
  And vanish'd from our sight.
HAMLET: 'Tis very strange.
HORATIO: As I do live, my honor'd lord, 'tis true;
  And we did think it writ down in our duty   230
  To let you know of it.
HAMLET: Indeed, indeed, sirs, but this troubles me.
  Hold you the watch to-night?
MARCELLUS and **BERNARDO**: We do, my lord.
HAMLET: Arm'd, say you?   235
MARCELLUS and **BERNARDO**: Arm'd, my lord.
HAMLET: From top to toe?
MARCELLUS and **BERNARDO**: My lord, from head to foot.
HAMLET: Then saw you not his face?
HORATIO: O yes, my lord; he wore his beaver up.   240
HAMLET: What, look'd he frowningly?
HORATIO: A countenance more in sorrow than in anger.
HAMLET: Pale or red?
HORATIO: Nay, very pale.
HAMLET: And fix'd his eyes upon you?   245
HORATIO: Most constantly.
HAMLET: I would I had been there.
HORATIO: It would have much amaz'd you.
HAMLET: Very like, very like. Stay'd it long?
HORATIO: While one with moderate haste might tell° a hundred.   250
MARCELLUS and **BERNARDO**: Longer, longer.
HORATIO: Not when I saw't.
HAMLET: His beard was grizzled, — no?
HORATIO: It was, as I have seen it in his life,
  A sable silver'd.   255
HAMLET: I will watch to-night;
  Perchance 'twill walk again.
HORATIO: I warrant it will.

° *tell:* Count

HAMLET: If it assume my noble father's person
260   I'll speak to it, though hell itself should gape
           And bid me hold my peace. I pray you all,
           If you have hitherto conceal'd this sight,
           Let it be tenable in your silence still;
           And whatsoever else shall hap to-night,
265   Give it an understanding, but no tongue:
           I will requite your loves. So, fare ye well:
           Upon the platform, 'twixt eleven and twelve,
           I'll visit you.
ALL: Our duty to your honor.
270 **HAMLET:** Your loves, as mine to you: farewell.

Exeunt Horatio, Marcellus, and Bernardo.

           My father's spirit in arms; all is not well;
           I doubt some foul play: would the night were come!
           Till then sit still, my soul: foul deeds will rise,
           Though all the earth o'erwhelm them, to men's eyes.

Exit.

SCENE 3

A room in Polonius' house.

Enter Laertes and Ophelia.

LAERTES: My necessaries are embark'd: farewell:
           And, sister, as the winds give benefit,
           And convoy° is assistant, do not sleep,
           But let me hear from you.
5 **OPHELIA:**   Do you doubt that?
LAERTES: For Hamlet, and the trifling of his favor,
           Hold it a fashion and a toy in blood:
           A violet in the youth of primy nature,
           Forward, not permanent, sweet, not lasting,
10   The perfume and suppliance of a minute;
           No more.
OPHELIA: No more but so?
LAERTES: Think it no more:
           For nature, crescent,° does not grow alone
15   In thews and bulk; but as this temple° waxes,

° *convoy:* Means of conveyance.   °*crescent:* Growing.   °*temple:* Body.

The inward service of the mind and soul
Grows wide withal. Perhaps he loves you now;
And now no soil nor cautel° doth besmirch
The virtue of his will: but you must fear,
His greatness weigh'd, his will is not his own; 20
For he himself is subject to his birth:
He may not, as unvalu'd persons do,
Carve for himself; for on his choice depends
The safety and the health of the whole state;
And therefore must his choice be circumscrib'd 25
Unto the voice and yielding of that body
Whereof he is the head. Then if he says he loves you,
It fits your wisdom so far to believe it
As he in his particular act and place
May give his saying deed; which is no further 30
Than the main° voice of Denmark goes withal.
Then weigh what loss your honor may sustain
If with too credent ear you list his songs,
Or lose your heart, or your chaste treasure open
To his unmaster'd importunity. 35
Fear it, Ophelia, fear it, my dear sister;
And keep within the rear of your affection,
Out of the shot and danger of desire.
The chariest maid is prodigal enough
If she unmask her beauty to the moon: 40
Virtue itself scrapes not calumnious strokes:
The canker galls the infants of the spring
Too oft before their buttons be disclos'd;
And in the morn and liquid dew of youth
Contagious blastments are most imminent. 45
Be wary, then; best safety lies in fear:
Youth to itself rebels, though none else near.
OPHELIA: I shall the effect of this good lesson keep
As watchman to my heart. But, good my brother,
Do not, as some ungracious pastors do, 50
Show me the steep and thorny way to heaven;
Whilst like a puff'd and reckless libertine,
Himself the primrose path of dalliance treads,
And recks not his own rede.°
LAERTES: O, fear me not. 55
I stay too long:—but here my father comes.

° *cautel:* Deceit.   °*main:* Strong, or mighty.   ° *rede:* Counsel.

Enter Polonius.

    A double blessing is a double grace;
    Occasion smiles upon a second leave.

POLONIUS: Yet here, Laertes! aboard, aboard, for shame!
60   The wind sits in the shoulder of your sail,
    And you are stay'd for. There,—my blessing with you!

Laying his hand on Laertes' head.

    And these few precepts in thy memory
    See thou character.° Give thy thoughts no tongue,
    Nor any unproportion'd thought his act.
65   Be thou familiar, but by no means vulgar.
    The friends thou hast, and their adoption tried,
    Grapple them to thy soul with hoops of steel;
    But do not dull thy palm with entertainment
    Of each new-hatch'd, unfledg'd comrade. Beware
70   Of entrance to a quarrel; but, being in,
    Bear't that the oppos**é**d may beware of thee.
    Give every man thine ear, but few thy voice:
    Take each man's censure,° but reserve thy judgment.
    Costly thy habit as thy purse can buy,
75   But not express'd in fancy; rich, not gaudy:
    For the apparel oft proclaims the man;
    And they in France of the best rank and station
    Are most select and generous chief in that.
    Neither a borrower nor a lender be:
80   For a loan oft loses both itself and friend;
    And borrowing dulls the edge of husbandry.
    This above all,— to thine own self be true;
    And it must follow, as the night the day,
    Thou canst not then be false to any man.
85   Farewell: my blessing season this in thee!
    LAERTES: Most humbly do I take my leave, my lord.
    POLONIUS: The time invites you; go, your servants tend.°
    LAERTES: Farewell, Ophelia; and remember well
    What I have said to you.
90 **OPHELIA:**   'Tis in my memory lock'd,
    And you yourself shall keep the key of it.
    LAERTES: Farewell. [*Exit.*]
    POLONIUS: What is't, Ophelia, he hath said to you?
    OPHELIA: So please you, something touching the Lord Hamlet.

° *in . . . character:* Engrave in your mind.   °*censure:* Opinion.   ° *tend:* Wait.

POLONIUS: Marry, well bethought: 95
    'Tis told me he hath very oft of late
    Given private time to you; and you yourself
    Have of your audience been most free and bounteous:
    If it be so, — as so 'tis put on me,
    And that in way of caution, — I must tell you,   100
    You do not understand yourself so clearly
    As it behoves my daughter and your honor.
    What is between you? give me up the truth.
OPHELIA: He hath, my lord, of late made many tenders
    Of his affection to me.   105
POLONIUS: Affection! pooh! you speak like a green girl,
    Unsifted in such perilous circumstance.
    Do you believe his tenders,° as you call them?
OPHELIA: I do not know, my lord, what I should think.
POLONIUS: Marry, I'll teach you: think yourself a baby;   110
    That you have ta'en these tenders for true pay,
    Which are not sterling. Tender yourself more dearly;
    Or, — not to crack the wind of the poor phrase,
    Wronging it thus, — you'll tender me a fool.
OPHELIA: My lord, he hath impórtun'd me with love   115
    In honorable fashion.
POLONIUS: Ay, fashion you may call it; go to, go to.
OPHELIA: And hath given countenance to his speech, my lord,
    With almost all the holy vows of heaven.
POLONIUS: Ay, springes to catch woodcocks. I do know,   120
    When the blood burns, how prodigal the soul
    Lends the tongue vows: these blazes, daughter,
    Giving more light than heat, — extinct in both,
    Even in their promise, as it is a-making, —
    You must not take for fire. From this time   125
    Be somewhat scanter of your maiden presence;
    Set your entreatments at a higher rate
    Than a command to parley. For Lord Hamlet,
    Believe so much in him, that he is young;
    And with a larger tether may he walk   130
    Than may be given you: in few, Ophelia,
    Do not believe his vows; for they are brokers,°—
    Not of that die which their investments show,
    But mere implorators of unholy suits,
    Breathing like sanctified and pious bawds,   135

° *tenders:* Offers.   ° *brokers:* Procurers.

The better to beguile. This is for all,—
I would not, in plain terms, from this time forth,
Have you so slander any moment leisure
As to give words or talk with the Lord Hamlet.
140   Look to't, I charge you; come your ways.
Ophelia: I shall obey, my lord.

Exeunt.

SCENE 4

The platform.

Enter Hamlet, Horatio, and Marcellus.

Hamlet: The air bites shrewdly; it is very cold.
Horatio: It is a nipping and an eager air.
Hamlet: What hour now?
Horatio: I think it lacks of twelve.
5 **Marcellus:** No, it is struck.
Horatio: Indeed? I heard it not: then it draws near the season
    Wherein the spirit held his wont to walk.

A flourish of trumpets, and ordnance shot off within.

    What does this mean, my lord?
Hamlet: The king doth wake to-night, and takes his rouse,
10   Keeps wassail, and the swaggering upspring° reels;
    And, as he drains his draughts of Rhenish down,
    The kettle-drum and trumpet thus bray out
    The triumph of his pledge.°
Horatio: Is it a custom?
15 **Hamlet:** Ay, marry, is't:
    But to my mind,— though I am native here,
    And to the manner born,— it is a custom
    More honor'd in the breach than the observance.
    This heavy-headed revel east and west
20   Makes us traduc'd and tax'd of other nations:
    They clepe us drunkards, and with swinish phrase
    Soil our addition;° and, indeed, it takes
    From our achievements, though perform'd at height,
    The pith and marrow of our attribute.
25   So oft it chances in particular men
    That, for some vicious mole of nature in them,

° *upspring:* A dance.   ° *triumph . . . pledge:* The glory of his toasts.   ° *addition:* Reputation.

As in their birth,— wherein they are not guilty,
Since nature cannot choose his origin,—
By the o'ergrowth of some complexion,
Oft breaking down the pales and forts of reason;   30
Or by some habit, that too much o'erleavens
The form of plausive° manners;— that these men,—
Carrying, I say, the stamp of one defect,
Being nature's livery or fortune's star,—
Their virtues else,— be they as pure as grace,   35
As infinite as man may undergo,—
Shall in the general censure take corruption
From that particular fault: the dram of evil
Doth all the noble substance of a doubt
To his own scandal.   40
HORATIO: Look, my lord, it comes!

Enter Ghost.

HAMLET: Angels and ministers of grace defend us!—
Be thou a spirit of health or goblin damn'd,
Bring with thee airs from heaven or blasts from hell,
Be thy intents wicked or charitable,   45
Thou com'st in such a questionable shape
That I will speak to thee: I'll call thee Hamlet,
King, father, royal Dane: O, answer me!
Let me not burst in ignorance; but tell
Why thy canóniz'd bones, hearsèd in death,   50
Have burst their cerements;° why the sepulchre,
Wherein we saw thee quietly in-urn'd,
Hath op'd his ponderous and marble jaws
To cast thee up again! What may this mean,
That thou, dead corpse, again in còmplete steel,   55
Revisit'st thus the glimpses of the moon,
Making night hideous and we° fools of nature
So horridly to shake our disposition
With thoughts beyond the reaches of our souls?
Say, why is this? wherefore? what should we do?   60

Ghost beckons Hamlet.

HORATIO: It beckons you to go away with it,
As if it some impartment did desire
To you alone.

° *plausive:* Pleasing.   ° *cerements:* Burial garments   ° *we:* Us.

MARCELLUS: Look, with what courteous action
65   It waves you to a more removed ground:
But do not go with it.
HORATIO: No, by no means.
HAMLET: It will not speak; then will I follow it.
HORATIO: Do not, my lord.
70 HAMLET: Why, what should be the fear?
I do not set my life at a pin's fee;
And for my soul, what can it do to that,
Being a thing immortal as itself?
It waves me forth again;— I'll follow it.
75 HORATIO: What if it tempt you toward the flood, my lord.
Or to the dreadful summit of the cliff
That beetles o'er his base into the sea,
And there assume some other horrible form,
Which might deprive your sovereignty of reason,
80   And draw you into madness? think of it:
The very place puts toys of desperation,
Without more motive, into every brain
That looks so many fathoms to the sea
And hears it roar beneath.
85 HAMLET: It waves me still.—
Go on; I'll follow thee.
MARCELLUS: You shall not go, my lord.
HAMLET: Hold off your hands.
HORATIO: Be rul'd; you shall not go.
90 HAMLET: My fate cries out,
And makes each petty artery in this body
As hardy as the Némean lion's° nerve.—

Ghost beckons.

Still am I call'd;— unhand me, gentlemen;—[*Breaking from them*]
By heaven, I'll make a ghost of him that lets° me.
95   I say, away!— Go on; I'll follow thee.

Exeunt Ghost and Hamlet.

HORATIO: He waxes desperate with imagination.
MARCELLUS: Let's follow; 'tis not fit thus to obey him.
HORATIO: Have after.— To what issue will this come?
MARCELLUS: Something is rotten in the state of Denmark.

° *Némean lion's:* The fierce lion that Hercules was called upon to slay as one of his "twelve labors."
° *lets:* Hinders.

HORATIO: Heaven will direct it.   100
MARCELLUS: Nay, let's follow him.

Exeunt.

SCENE 5

A more remote part of the platform.

Enter Ghost and Hamlet.

HAMLET: Where wilt thou lead me? speak, I'll go no further.
GHOST: Mark me.
HAMLET: I will.
GHOST: My hour is almost come,
    When I to sulphurous and tormenting flames   5
    Must render up myself.
HAMLET: Alas, poor ghost!
GHOST: Pity me not, but lend thy serious hearing
    To what I shall unfold.
HAMLET: Speak; I am bound to hear.   10
GHOST: So art thou to revenge, when thou shalt hear.
HAMLET: What?
GHOST: I am thy father's spirit;
    Doom'd for a certain term to walk the night,
    And, for the day, confin'd to waste in fires   15
    Till the foul crimes° done in my days of nature
    Are burnt and purg'd away. But that I am forbid
    To tell the secrets of my prison-house,
    I could a tale unfold whose lightest word
    Would harrow up thy soul; freeze thy young blood;   20
    Make thy two eyes, like stars, start from their spheres;
    Thy knotted and combined locks to part,
    And each particular hair to stand on end,
    Like quills upon the fretful porcupine:
    But this eternal blazon° must not be   25
    To ears of flesh and blood.—List, list, O, list!—
    If thou didst ever thy dear father love,—
HAMLET: O God!
GHOST: Revenge his foul and most unnatural murder.
HAMLET: Murder!   30
GHOST: Murder—most foul, as in the best it is;
    But this most foul, strange, and unnatural.

° *foul crimes:* Sins or faults.   ° *eternal blazon:* Disclosure of information concerning the other world.

HAMLET: Haste me to know't, that I, with wings as swift
　　　　As meditation or the thoughts of love,
35　　May sweep to my revenge.
GHOST:　　　　　　　　　　I find thee apt;
　　　　And duller shouldst thou be than the fat weed
　　　　That rots itself in ease on Lethe° wharf,
　　　　Wouldst thou not stir in this. Now, Hamlet,
40　　'Tis given out that, sleeping in mine orchard,
　　　　A serpent stung me; so the whole ear of Denmark
　　　　Is by a forged process of my death
　　　　Rankly abus'd: but know, thou noble youth,
　　　　The serpent that did sting thy father's life
45　　Now wears his crown.
HAMLET:　　　　　　　O my prophetic soul! mine uncle!
GHOST: Ay, that incestuous, that adulterate beast,
　　　　With witchcraft of his wit, with traitorous gifts,—
　　　　O wicked wit and gifts that have the power
50　　So to seduce!— won to his shameful lust
　　　　The will of my most seeming virtuous queen:
　　　　O Hamlet, what a falling-off was there!
　　　　From me, whose love was of that dignity
　　　　That it went hand in hand even with the vow
55　　I made to her in marriage: and to decline
　　　　Upon a wretch whose natural gifts were poor
　　　　To those of mine!
　　　　But virtue, as it never will be mov'd,
　　　　Though lewdness court it in a shape of heaven;
60　　So lust, though to a radiant angel link'd,
　　　　Will sate itself in a celestial bed
　　　　And prey on garbage.
　　　　But, soft! methinks I scent the morning air;
　　　　Brief let me be.— Sleeping within mine orchard,
65　　My custom always in the afternoon,
　　　　Upon my sécure hour thy uncle stole,
　　　　With juice of cursed hebenon° in a vial,
　　　　And in the porches of mine ears did pour
　　　　The leperous distilment; whose effect
70　　Holds such an enmity with blood of man
　　　　That, swift as quicksilver, it courses through
　　　　The natural gates and alleys of the body;
　　　　And with a sudden vigor it doth posset°

° *Lethe:* The river of forgetfulness of the past, out of which the dead drink.　° *hebenon:* Ebony.
° *posset:* Coagulate.

And curd, like eager° droppings into milk,
The thin and wholesome blood: so did it mine;   75
And a most instant tetter bark'd about,
Most lazar-like,° with vile and loathsome crust,
All my smooth body.
Thus was I, sleeping, by a brother's hand,
Of life, of crown, of queen, at once despatch'd: 80
Cut off even in the blossoms of my sin,
Unhousel'd, unanointed, unanel'd;
No reckoning made, but sent to my account
With all my imperfections on my head:
O, horrible! O, horrible! most horrible!   85
If thou hast nature in thee, bear it not;
Let not the royal bed of Denmark be
A couch for luxury° and damned incest.
But, howsoever thou pursu'st this act,
Taint not thy mind, nor let thy soul contrive   90
Against thy mother aught: leave her to heaven,
And to those thorns that in her bosom lodge,
To prick and sting her. Fare thee well at once!
The glowworm shows the matin to be near,
And 'gins to pale his uneffectual fire: 95
Adieu, adieu! Hamlet, remember me. [*Exit.*]
HAMLET: O all you host of heaven! O earth! what else?
And shall I couple hell?— O, fie!— Hold, my heart;
And you, my sinews, grow not instant old,
But bear me stiffly up.— Remember thee!   100
Ay, thou poor ghost, while memory holds a seat
In this distracted globe. Remember thee!
Yea, from the table of my memory
I'll wipe away all trivial fond° recórds,
All saws of books, all forms, all pressures past,   105
That youth and observation copied there;
And thy commandment all alone shall live
Within the book and volume of my brain,
Unmix'd with baser matter: yes, by heaven.—
O most pernicious woman!   110
O villain, villain, smiling, damned villain!
My tables,— meet it is I set it down,
That one may smile, and smile, and be a villain;
At least, I am sure, it may be so in Denmark:

Writing.

° *eager:* Acid.   ° *lazar-like:* Like a leper, whose skin is rough.   ° *luxury:* Lechery.   ° *fond:* Foolish.

115   So, uncle, there you are. Now to my word;
    It is, *Adieu, adieu! remember me:*
    I have sworn't.
Horatio: [*Within*] My lord, my lord,—
Marcellus: [*Within*]   Lord Hamlet,—
120 **Horatio:** [*Within*]   Heaven secure him!
Marcellus: [*Within*] So be it!
Horatio: [*Within*] Illo, ho, ho, my lord!
Hamlet: Hillo, ho, ho, boy! come, bird, come.°

Enter Horatio and Marcellus.

Marcellus: How is't, my noble lord?
125 **Horatio:**   What news, my lord?
Hamlet: O, wonderful!
Horatio: Good my lord, tell it.
Hamlet: No; you'll reveal it.
Horatio: Not I, my lord, by heaven.
130 **Marcellus:**   Nor I, my lord.
Hamlet: How say you, then; would heart of man once think it?—
    But you'll be secret?
Horatio and **Marcellus:** Ay, by heaven, my lord.
Hamlet: There's ne'er a villain dwelling in all Denmark
135   But he's an arrant knave.
Horatio: There needs no ghost, my lord, come from the grave
    To tell us this.
Hamlet: Why, right; you are i' the right;
    And so, without more circumstance at all,
140   I hold it fit that we shake hands and part:
    You, as your business and desire shall point you,—
    For every man has business and desire,
    Such as it is;— and for mine own poor part,
    Look you, I'll go pray.
145 **Horatio:** These are but wild and whirling words, my lord.
Hamlet: I'm sorry they offend you, heartily;
    Yes, faith, heartily.
Horatio: There's no offence, my lord.
Hamlet: Yes, by Saint Patrick, but there is, Horatio,
150   And much offence too. Touching this vision here,—
    It is an honest ghost, that let me tell you:
    For you desire to know what is between us,
    O'ermaster't as you may. And now, good friends,
    As you are friends, scholars, and soldiers,
155   Give me one poor request.

° *Hillo . . . come:* Hamlet uses the word "bird" because this is a falconer's call.

HORATIO: What is't, my lord? we will.

HAMLET: Never make known what you have seen to-night.

HORATIO and **MARCELLUS:** My lord, we will not.

HAMLET: Nay, but swear't.

HORATIO: In faith,   16

My lord, not I.

MARCELLUS: Nor I, my lord, in faith.

HAMLET: Upon my sword.

MARCELLUS: We have sworn, my lord, already.

HAMLET: Indeed, upon my sword, indeed.   16

GHOST: [*Beneath*] Swear.

HAMLET: Ha, ha, boy! say'st thou so? art thou there, truepenny?—

Come on,— you hear this fellow in the cellarage,—

Consent to swear.

HORATIO: Propose the oath, my lord.   17

HAMLET: Never to speak of this that you have seen,

Swear by my sword.

GHOST: [*Beneath*] Swear.

HAMLET: *Hic et ubique?*° then we'll shift our ground.—

Come hither, gentlemen,   17

And lay your hands again upon my sword:

Never to speak of this that you have heard,

Swear by my sword.

GHOST: [*Beneath*] Swear.

HAMLET: Well said! old mole! canst work i' the earth so fast?   18

A worthy pioneer!°— Once more remove, good friends.

HORATIO: O day and night, but this is wondrous strange!

HAMLET: And therefore as a stranger give it welcome.

There are more things in heaven and earth, Horatio,

Than are dreamt of in your philosophy.   18

But come;—

Here, as before, never, so help you mercy,

How strange or odd soe'er I bear myself,—

As I, perchance, hereafter shall think meet

To put an antic disposition on,—   19

That you, at such times seeing me, never shall,

With arms encumber'd° thus, or this headshake,

Or by pronouncing of some doubtful phrase,

As, *Well, well, we know;* — or, *We could, an if we would;*—   19

Or, *If we list to speak;* — or, *There be, an if they might;*—

Or such ambiguous giving out, to note

° *Hic et ubique:* "Here and everywhere" (Latin).   ° *pioneer:* A soldier who digs trenches and undermines
fortresses.   ° *encumber'd:* Folded.

That you know aught of me:— this not to do,
So grace and mercy at your most need help you,
Swear.
200 GHOST: [*Beneath*] Swear.
HAMLET: Rest, rest, perturbed spirit!— So, gentlemen,
With all my love I do commend to you:
And what so poor a man as Hamlet is
May do, to express his love and friending to you,
205 God willing, shall not lack. Let us go in together;
And still your fingers on your lips, I pray.
The time is out of joint:— O cursed spite,
That ever I was born to set it right!—
Nay, come, let's go together.

Exeunt.

ACT 2
SCENE 1

A room in Polonius' house.

Enter Polonius and Reynaldo.

POLONIUS: Give him this money and these notes, Reynaldo.
REYNALDO: I will, my lord.
POLONIUS: You shall do marvelous wisely, good Reynaldo,
Before you visit him, to make inquiry
5   On his behavior.
REYNALDO: My lord, I did intend it.
POLONIUS: Marry, well said; very well said. Look you, sir,
Inquire me first what Danskers° are in Paris;
And how, and who, what means, and where they keep,
10 What company, at what expense; and finding,
By this encompassment and drift of question,
That they do know my son, come you more nearer
Than your particular demands will touch it:
Take you, as 'twere, some distant knowledge of him;
15 As thus, *I know his father and his friends,*
And in part him;— do you mark this, Reynaldo?
REYNALDO: Ay, very well, my lord.

─────────────────────────────

° *Danskers:* Danes.

POLONIUS: *And in part him;—but,* you may say, *not well:*
But if't be he I mean, he's very wild;
Addicted so and so; and there put on him   20
What forgeries you please; marry, none so rank
As may dishonor him; take heed of that;
But, sir, such wanton, wild, and usual slips
As are companions noted and most known
To youth and liberty.   25
REYNALDO: As gaming, my lord.
POLONIUS: Ay, or drinking, fencing, swearing, quarreling,
Drabbing:°— you may go so far.
REYNALDO: My lord, that would dishonor him.
POLONIUS: Faith, no; as you may season it in the charge.   30
You must not put another scandal on him,
That he is open to incontinency;
That's not my meaning: but breathe his faults so quaintly
That they may seem the taints of liberty;
The flash and outbreak of a fiery mind;   35
A savageness in unreclaimed blood,
Of general assault.
REYNALDO: But, my good lord,—
POLONIUS: Wherefore should you do this?
REYNALDO: Ay, my lord,   40
I would know that.
POLONIUS: Marry, sir, here's my drift;
And I believe it is a fetch of warrant:°
You laying these slight sullies on my son.
As 'twere a thing a little soil'd i' the working,   45
Mark you,
Your party in converse, him you would sound,
Having ever seen in the prenominate crimes
The youth you breathe of guilty, be assur'd
He closes with you in this consequence;   50
Good sir, or so; or *friend,* or *gentleman,*—
According to the phrase or the addition°
Of man and country.
REYNALDO: Very good, my lord.
POLONIUS: And then, sir, does he this,— he does,—   55
What was I about to say?— By the mass, I was
About to say something:— where did I leave?

° *Drabbing:* Going about with loose women.   ° *fetch of warrant:* A good device.   ° *addition:* Form of address.

REYNALDO: At *closes in the consequence,*
   At *friend or so,* and *gentleman.*
60 **POLONIUS:** At — closes in the consequence, — ay, marry;
   He closes with you thus: — *I know the gentleman;*
   I saw him yesterday, or t'other day,
   Or then, or then; with such, or such; and, as you say,
   There was he gaming; there o'ertook in's rouse;
65 *There falling out at tennis:* or perchance,
   I saw him enter such a house of sale, —
   Videlicet,° a brothel, — or so forth. —
   See you now;
   Your bait of falsehood takes this carp of truth:
70 And thus do we of wisdom and of reach,
   With windlasses, and with assays of bias,
   By indirections find directions out:
   So, by my former lecture and advice,
   Shall you my son. You have me, have you not?
75 **REYNALDO:** My lord, I have.
   POLONIUS: God b' wi' you; fare you well.
   REYNALDO: Good my lord!
   POLONIUS: Observe his inclination in yourself.
   REYNALDO: I shall, my lord.
80 **POLONIUS:** And let him ply his music.
   REYNALDO: Well, my lord.
   POLONIUS: Farewell!

Exit Reynaldo.

Enter Ophelia.

   How now, Ophelia! what's the matter?
   OPHELIA: Alas, my lord, I have been so affrighted.
85 **POLONIUS:** With what, i' the name of God?
   OPHELIA: My lord, as I was sewing in my chamber,
   Lord Hamlet, — with his doublet all unbrac'd;
   No hat upon his head; his stockings foul'd,
   Ungarter'd, and down-gyved° to his ankle;
90 Pale as his shirt; his knees knocking each other;
   And with a look so piteous in purport
   As if he had been loosed out of hell
   To speak of horrors, — he comes before me.

° *Videlicet:* That is; namely (Latin).   ° *down-gyved:* Dangling like chains.

POLONIUS: Mad for thy love?
OPHELIA: My lord, I do not know;   95
 But truly I do fear it.
POLONIUS: What said he?
OPHELIA: He took me by the wrist, and held me hard;
 Then goes he to the length of all his arm;
 And with his other hand thus o'er his brow,   100
 He falls to such perusal of my face
 As he would draw it. Long stay'd he so;
 At last,— a little shaking of mine arm,
 And thrice his head thus waving up and down,—
 He rais'd a sigh so piteous and profound   105
 That it did seem to shatter all his bulk
 And end his being; that done, he lets me go:
 And, with his head over his shoulder turn'd,
 He seem'd to find his way without his eyes;
 For out o' doors he went without their help,   110
 And to the last bended their light on me.
POLONIUS: Come, go with me: I will go seek the king.
 This is the very ecstasy° of love;
 Whose violent property fordoes itself,°
 And leads the will to desperate undertakings,   115
 As oft as any passion under heaven
 That does afflict our nature. I am sorry,—
 What, have you given him any hard words of late?
OPHELIA: No, my good lord; but, as you did command,
 I did repel his letters, and denied   120
 His access to me.
POLONIUS: That hath made him mad.
 I am sorry that with better heed and judgment
 I had not quoted him: I fear'd he did but trifle,
 And meant to wreck thee; but, beshrew my jealousy!   125
 It seems it is as proper to our age
 To cast beyond ourselves in our opinions
 As it is common for the younger sort
 To lack discretion. Come, go we to the king:
 This must be known; which, being kept close, might move   130
 More grief to hide than hate to utter love.

Exeunt.

° *ecstasy:* Madness.   ° *fordoes itself:* Destroys itself.

SCENE 2

A room in the castle.

Enter King, Queen, Rosencrantz, Guildenstern, and Attendants.

KING: Welcome, dear Rosencrantz and Guildenstern!
    Moreover that we much did long to see you,
    The need we have to use you did provoke
    Our hasty sending. Something have you heard
5   Of Hamlet's transformation; so I call it,
    Since nor the exterior nor the inward man
    Resembles that it was. What it should be,
    More than his father's death, that thus hath put him
    So much from the understanding of himself,
10   I cannot dream of: I entreat you both,
    That being of so young days brought up with him,
    And since so neighbor'd to his youth and humor,
    That you vouchsafe your rest here in our court
    Some little time: so by your companies
15   To draw him on to pleasures, and to gather,
    So much as from occasion you may glean,
    Whether aught, to us unknown, afflicts him thus,
    That, open'd, lies within our remedy.

QUEEN: Good gentlemen, he hath much talk'd of you;
20   And sure I am two men there are not living
    To whom he more adheres. If it will please you
    To show us so much gentry and good-will
    As to expend your time with us awhile,
    For the supply and profit of our hope,
25   Your visitation shall receive such thanks
    As fits a king's remembrance.

ROSENCRANTZ: Both your majesties
    Might, by the sovereign power you have of us,
    Put your dread pleasures more into command
30   Than to entreaty.

GUILDENSTERN: We both obey,
    And here give up ourselves, in the full bent,
    To lay our service freely at your feet,
    To be commanded.

35 KING: Thanks, Rosencrantz and gentle Guildenstern.

QUEEN: Thanks, Guildenstern and gentle Rosencrantz:
    And I beseech you instantly to visit
    My too-much-changed son.— Go, some of you,
    And bring these gentlemen where Hamlet is.

GUILDENSTERN: Heavens make our presence and our practices   40
    Pleasant and helpful to him!
QUEEN: Ay, amen!

Exeunt Rosencrantz, Guildenstern, and some Attendants.

Enter Polonius.

POLONIUS: The ambassadors from Norway, my good lord,
    Are joyfully return'd.
KING: Thou still has been the father of good news.   45
POLONIUS: Have I, my lord? Assure you, my good liege,
    I hold my duty, as I hold my soul,
    Both to my God and to my gracious king:
    And I do think,— or else this brain of mine
    Hunts not the trail of policy° so sure   50
    As it hath us'd to do,— that I have found
    The very cause of Hamlet's lunacy.
KING: O, speak of that; that do I long to hear.
POLONIUS: Give first admittance to the ambassadors;
    My news shall be the fruit to that great feast.   55
KING: Thyself do grace to them, and bring them in.

Exit Polonius.

    He tells me, my sweet queen, that he hath found
    The head and source of all your son's distemper.
QUEEN: I doubt it is no other but the main,—
    His father's death and our o'erhasty marriage.   60
KING: Well, we shall sift him.

Re-enter Polonius, with Voltimand and Cornelius.

                 Welcome, my good friends!
    Say, Voltimand, what from our brother Norway?
VOLTIMAND: Most fair return of greetings and desires.
    Upon our first, he sent out to suppress   65
    His nephew's levies; which to him appear'd
    To be a preparation 'gainst the Polack;
    But, better look'd into, he truly found
    It was against your highness: whereat griev'd,—
    That so his sickness, age, and impotence   70
    Was falsely borne in hand,— sends out arrests
    On Fortinbras; which he, in brief, obeys;
    Receives rebuke from Norway; and, in fine,

° *trail of policy:* Statecraft.

Makes vows before his uncle never more
75 To give the assay of arms against your majesty.
Whereon old Norway, overcome with joy,
Gives him three thousand crowns in annual fee;
And his commission to employ those soldiers,
So levied as before, against the Polack:
80 With an entreaty, herein further shown, [*gives a paper*]
That it might please you to give quiet pass
Through your dominions for this enterprise,
On such regards of safety and allowance
As therein are set down.

85 KING: It likes us well;
And at our more consider'd time we'll read,
Answer, and think upon this business.
Meantime we thank you for your well-took labor:
Go to your rest; at night we'll feast together:
90 Most welcome home!

Exeunt Voltimand and Cornelius.

POLONIUS: This business is well ended.—
My liege, and madam,— to expostulate
What majesty should be, what duty is,
Why day is day, night night, and time is time,
95 Were nothing but to waste night, day, and time.
Therefore, since brevity is the soul of wit,
And tediousness the limbs and outward flourishes,
I will be brief:— your noble son is mad:
Mad call I it; for to define true madness,
100 What is't but to be nothing else but mad?
But let that go.
QUEEN: More matter with less art.
POLONIUS: Madam, I swear I use no art at all.
That he is mad, 'tis true 'tis pity;
105 And pity 'tis 'tis true: a foolish figure;
But farewell it, for I will use no art.
Mad let us grant him, then: and now remains
That we find out the cause of this effect;
Or rather say, the cause of this defect,
110 For this effect defective comes by cause:
Thus it remains, and the remainder thus.
Perpend.
I have a daughter,— have whilst she is mine,—
Who, in her duty and obedience, mark,
115 Hath given me this: now gather, and surmise

Reads

> To the celestial, and my soul's idol, the most beautified Ophelia,—

That's an ill phrase, a vile phrase,—*beautified* is a vile phrase: but you shall hear. Thus:

Reads

> In her excellent white bosom, these, &c.

QUEEN: Came this from Hamlet to her?   120
POLONIUS: Good madam, stay a while; I will be faithful.

Reads

> Doubt thou the stars are fire;
>   Doubt that the sun doth move;
> Doubt truth to be a liar;
>   But never doubt I love.   125
>
> O dear Ophelia, I am ill at these numbers, I have not art to reckon my groans: but
> that I love thee best, O most best, believe it. Adieu.
> Thine evermore, most dear lady, whilst this machine is to him,
>
>   Hamlet

This, in obedience, hath my daughter show'd me:
And more above, hath his solicitings,   130
As they fell out by time, by means, and place,
All given to mine ear.
KING: But how hath she
    Receiv'd his love?
POLONIUS: What do you think of me?   135
KING: As of a man faithful and honorable.
POLONIUS: I would fain prove so. But what might you think,
    When I had seen this hot love on the wing,—
    As I perceiv'd it, I must tell you that,
    Before my daughter told me,— what might you,   140
    Or my dear majesty your queen here, think,
    If I had play'd the desk or table-book;°
    Or given my heart a winking, mute and dumb;
    Or look'd upon this love with idle sight;—
    What might you think? No, I went round to work,   145
    And my young mistress thus I did bespeak:
    Lord Hamlet is a prince out of thy sphere;
    This must not be: and then I precepts gave her,
    That she should lock herself from his resort,

° *table-book:* Memorandum pad.

150   Admit no messengers, receive no tokens.
       Which done, she took the fruits of my advice;
       And he, repulsed,— a short tale to make,—
       Fell into a sadness; then into a fast;
       Thence to a watch; thence into a weakness;
155   Thence to a lightness; and, by this declension,
       Into the madness wherein now he raves
       And all we wail for.
KING: Do you think 'tis this?
QUEEN: It may be, very likely.
160 **POLONIUS:** Hath there been such a time,— I'd fain know that,—
       That I have positively said, *'Tis so,*
       When it prov'd otherwise?
KING: Not that I know.
POLONIUS: Take this from this, if this be otherwise: [*Pointing to his head and shoulder*]
165   If circumstances lead me, I will find
       Where truth is hid, though it were hid indeed
       Within the center.
KING: How may we try it further?
POLONIUS: You know, sometimes he walks four hours together
170   Here in the lobby.
QUEEN: So he does, indeed.
POLONIUS: At such a time I'll loose my daughter to him:
       Be you and I behind an arras° then;
       Mark the encounter: if he love her not,
175   And be not from his reason fall'n thereon,
       Let me be no assistant for a state,
       But keep a farm and carters.
KING: We will try it.
QUEEN: But look, where sadly the poor wretch comes reading.
180 **POLONIUS:** Away, I do beseech you, both away:
       I'll board° him presently:— O, give me leave.

Exeunt King, Queen, and Attendants.

Enter Hamlet, reading.

       How does my good Lord Hamlet?
HAMLET: Well, God-a-mercy.
POLONIUS: Do you know me, my lord?
185 **HAMLET:** Excellent, excellent well; you're a fishmonger.
POLONIUS: Not I, my lord.

° *arras:* Tapestry, hung some distance away from a wall.   ° *board:* Address.

HAMLET: Then I would you were so honest a man.

POLONIUS: Honest, my lord!

HAMLET: Ay, sir; to be honest, as this world goes, is to be one man picked out of ten thousand.   190

POLONIUS: That's very true, my lord.

HAMLET: For if the sun breed maggots in a dead dog, being a god kissing carrion, — Have you a daughter?

POLONIUS: I have, my lord.

HAMLET: Let her not walk i' the sun: conception is a blessing; but not as your   195 daughter may conceive: — friend, look to't.

POLONIUS: How say you by that? — [*Aside*] Still harping on my daughter: — yet he knew me not at first; he said I was a fishmonger: he is far gone, far gone: and truly in my youth I suffered much extremity for love; very near this. I'll speak to him again. — What do you read, my lord?   200

HAMLET: Words, words, words.

POLONIUS: What is the matter, my lord?

HAMLET: Between who?

POLONIUS: I mean, the matter that you read, my lord.

HAMLET: Slanders, sir: for the satirical slave says here that old men have gray   205 beards; that their faces are wrinkled; their eyes purging thick amber and plum-tree gum; and that they have a plentiful lack of wit, together with most weak hams: all which, sir, though I most powerfully and potently believe, yet I hold it not honesty to have it thus set down; for you yourself, sir, should be old as I am, if, like a crab, you could go backward.   210

POLONIUS: [*Aside*] Though this be madness, yet there is method in't. — ill you walk out of the air, my lord?

HAMLET: Into my grave?

POLONIUS: Indeed, that is out o' the air. — [*Aside*] How pregnant° sometimes his replies are! a happiness that often madness hits on, which reason and   215 sanity could not so prosperously be delivered of. I will leave him, and sud- denly contrive the means of meeting between him and my daughter. — More honorable lord, I will most humbly take my leave of you.

HAMLET: You cannot, sir, take from me anything that I will more willingly part withal, — except my life, except my life, except my life.   220

POLONIUS: Fare you well, my lord.

HAMLET: These tedious old fools!

Enter Rosencrantz and Guildenstern.

POLONIUS: You go to seek the Lord Hamlet; there he is.

ROSENCRANTZ: [*To Polonius*] God save you, sir!

Exit Polonius.

° *pregnant:* Ready, and clever.

225 GUILDENSTERN: Mine honored lord!

ROSENCRANTZ: My most dear lord!

HAMLET: My excellent good friends! How dost thou, Guildenstern? Ah,
Rosencrantz? Good lads, how do ye both?

ROSENCRANTZ: As the indifferent children of the earth.

230 GUILDENSTERN: Happy in that we are not overhappy; on fortune's cap we are
not the very button.

HAMLET: Nor the soles of her shoe?

ROSENCRANTZ: Neither, my lord.

HAMLET: Then you live about her waist, or in the middle of her favors?

235 GUILDENSTERN: Faith, her privates we.

HAMLET: In the secret parts of fortune? O, most true; she is a strumpet.
What's the news?

ROSENCRANTZ: None, my lord, but that the world's grown honest.

HAMLET: Then is doomsday near: but your news is not true. Let me question
240   more in particular: what have you, my good friends, deserved at the hands
of fortune, that she sends you to prison hither?

GUILDENSTERN: Prison, my lord!

HAMLET: Denmark's a prison.

ROSENCRANTZ: Then is the world one.

245 HAMLET: A goodly one; in which there are many confines, wards, and dun-
geons, Denmark being one o' the worst.

ROSENCRANTZ: We think not so, my lord.

HAMLET: Why, then, 'tis none to you; for there is nothing either good or bad,
but thinking makes it so: to me it is a prison.

250 ROSENCRANTZ: Why, then, your ambition makes it one; 'tis too narrow
for your mind.

HAMLET: O God, I could be bounded in a nutshell, and count myself a king of
infinite space, were it not that I have bad dreams.

GUILDENSTERN: Which dreams, indeed, are ambition; for the very substance
255   of the ambitious is merely the shadow of a dream.

HAMLET: A dream itself is but a shadow.

ROSENCRANTZ: Truly, and I hold ambition of so airy and light a quality that it
is but a shadow's shadow.

HAMLET: Then are our beggars bodies, and our monarchs and outstretched
260   heroes the beggars' shadows. Shall we to the court? for, by my fay, I
cannot reason.

ROSENCRANTZ and GUILDENSTERN: We'll wait upon you.

HAMLET: No such matter: I will not sort you with the rest of my servants, for,
to speak to you like an honest man, I am most dreadfully attended. But, in
265   the beaten way of friendship, what make you at Elsinore?

ROSENCRANTZ: To visit you, my lord; no other occasion.

HAMLET: Beggar that I am, I am even poor in thanks; but I thank you: and
sure, dear friends, my thanks are too dear a halfpenny. Were you not sent

for? Is it your own inclining? Is it a free visitation? Come, deal justly with
me: come, come; nay, speak.   270
GUILDENSTERN: What should we say, my lord?
HAMLET: Why, anything — but to the purpose. You were sent for; and there is
a kind of confession in your looks, which your modesties have not craft
enough to color: I know the good king and queen have sent for you.
ROSENCRANTZ: To what end, my lord?   275
HAMLET: That you must teach me. But let me conjure you, by the rights of
our fellowship, by the consonancy of our youth, by the obligation of our
ever-preserved love, and by what more dear a better proposer could charge
you withal, be even and direct with me, whether you were sent for or no?
ROSENCRANTZ: What say you? [*To Guildenstern*]   280
HAMLET: [*Aside*] Nay, then, I have an eye of you. — If you love me, hold
not off.
GUILDENSTERN: My lord, we were sent for.
HAMLET: I will tell you why; so shall my anticipation prevent your discovery,
and your secrecy to the king and queen moult no feather. I have of late, —   285
but wherefore I know not, — lost all my mirth, forgone all custom of exercises; and, indeed, it goes so heavily with my disposition that this goodly
frame, the earth, seems to me a sterile promontory; this most excellent
canopy, the air, look you, this brave o'erhanging firmament, this majestical
roof fretted° with golden fire, — why, it appears no other thing to me than   290
a foul and pestilent congregation of vapors. What a piece of work is man!
How noble in reason! how infinite in faculties! in form and moving, how
express and admirable! in action, how like an angel! in apprehension, how
like a god! the beauty of the world! the paragon of animals! And yet, to me,
what is this quintessence of dust? man delights not me; no, nor woman   295
neither, though by your smiling you seem to say so.
ROSENCRANTZ: My lord, there was no such stuff in my thoughts.
HAMLET: Why did you laugh, then, when I said, Man *delights not me?*
ROSENCRANTZ: To think, my lord, if you delight not in man, what lenten en-
tertainment° the players shall receive from you: we coted° them on the   300
way; and hither are they coming, to offer you service.
HAMLET: He that plays the king shall be welcome, — his majesty shall have
tribute of me; the adventurous knight shall use his foil and target; the lover
shall not sigh gratis; the humorous° man shall end his part in peace; the
clown shall make those laugh whose lungs are tickled o' the sere;° and the   305
lady shall say her mind freely, or the blank verse shall halt° for't. — What
players are they?

° *roof fretted:* A roof with fretwork.   ° *lenten entertainment:* Poor reception.   ° *coted:* Passed.
° *humorous:* Eccentric.   ° *whose lungs . . . sere:* Whose lungs, for laughter, are easily tickled.   ° *halt:* Limp.

ROSENCRANTZ: Even those you were wont to take delight in, — the tragedians of the city.

310 HAMLET: How chances it they travel? their residence, both in reputation and profit, was better both ways.

ROSENCRANTZ: I think their inhibition° comes by the means of the late innovation.

HAMLET: Do they hold the same estimation they did when I was in the city?
315 Are they so followed?

ROSENCRANTZ: No, indeed, they are not.

HAMLET: How comes it? do they grow rusty?

ROSENCRANTZ: Nay, their endeavor keeps in the wonted pace; but there is, sir, an aery° of children, little eyases,° that cry out on the top of question,
320 and are most tyrannically clapped for't: these are now the fashion; and so berattle the common stages, — so they call them, — that many wearing rapiers are afraid of goose-quills, and dare scarce come thither.

HAMLET: What, are they children? who maintains 'em? how are they escoted?° Will they pursue the quality° no longer than they can sing? will they not say
325 afterwards, if they should grow themselves to common players, — as it is most like, if their means are no better, — their writers do them wrong, to make them exclaim against their own succession?

ROSENCRANTZ: Faith, there has been much to do on both sides; and the nation holds it no sin to tarre° them to controversy: there was for awhile no
330 money bid for argument, unless the poet and the player went to cuffs in the question.

HAMLET: Is't possible?

GUILDENSTERN: O, there has been much throwing about of brains.

HAMLET: Do the boys carry it away?

335 ROSENCRANTZ: Ay, that they do, my lord; Hercules and his load° too.

HAMLET: It is not strange; for mine uncle is king of Denmark, and those that would make mouths at him while my father lived, give twenty, forty, fifty, an hundred ducats a-piece for his picture in little. 'Sblood, there is something in this more than natural, if philosophy could find it out.

Flourish of trumpets within.

340 GUILDENSTERN: There are the players.

HAMLET: Gentlemen, you are welcome to Elsinore. Your hands, come: the appurtenance of welcome is fashion and ceremony: let me comply with you in this garb; lest my extent° to the players, which, I tell you, must show fairly

---

° *inhibition:* Difficulty, preventing them from remaining in the capital.   ° *aery:* Brood of birds of prey.   ° *little eyases:* Young hawks; a reference to the boys' companies that became popular rivals of Shakespeare's company of players.   ° *escoted:* Financially supported.   ° *quality:* Profession.   ° *to tarre:* To egg them on.   ° *his load:* The globe, or the world.   ° *extent:* Show of friendliness.

outward, should more appear like entertainment° than yours. You are welcome: but my uncle-father and aunt-mother are deceived.   345
GUILDENSTERN: In what, my dear lord?
HAMLET: I am but mad north-north-west: when the wind is southerly I know a
hawk from a handsaw.

Enter Polonius.

POLONIUS: Well be with you, gentlemen!
HAMLET: Hark you, Guildenstern;— and you too;— at each ear a hearer: that   350
great baby you see there is not yet out of his swathing-clouts.
ROSENCRANTZ: Happily he's the second time come to them; for they say an
old man is twice a child.
HAMLET: I will prophesy he comes to tell me of the players; mark it. You say
right, sir: o' Monday morning; 'twas so indeed.   355
POLONIUS: My lord, I have news to tell you.
HAMLET: My lord, I have news to tell you. When Roscius was an actor
in Rome,—
POLONIUS: The actors are come hither, my lord.
HAMLET: Buzz, buzz!   360
POLONIUS: Upon mine honor,—
HAMLET: Then came each actor on his ass,—
POLONIUS: The best actors in the world, either for tragedy, comedy, history,
pastoral, pastoral-comical, historical-pastoral, tragical-historical, tragical-
comical-historical-pastoral, scene individable,° or poem unlimited:°   365
Seneca cannot be too heavy nor Plautus too light. For the law of writ and
the liberty,° these are the only men.
HAMLET: O Jephthah, judge of Israel, what a treasure hadst thou!
POLONIUS: What a treasure had he, my lord?
HAMLET: Why—   370

One fair daughter, and no more,
The which he loved passing well.

POLONIUS: [*Aside*] Still on my daughter.
HAMLET: Am I not i' the right, old Jephthah?
POLONIUS: If you call me Jephthah, my lord, I have a daughter that I love   375
passing well.
HAMLET: Nay, that follows not.
POLONIUS: What follows, then, my lord?

° *entertainment:* Welcome.   ° *scene individable:* A play that observes the unities of time and place.   ° *poem
unlimited:* A typical multiscene Elizabethan drama, not restricted by the unities; examples are *Hamlet, Macbeth,
King Lear,* and nearly any other play by Shakespeare.   ° *For the law . . . liberty:* For the laws of the unities and
for playwriting that is not so restricted.

HAMLET: Why—

380
    As by lot, God wot,
    and then, you know,
    It came to pass, as most like it was,

the first row of the pious chanson will show you more; for look where my
abridgement comes.

Enter four or five Players.

385   You are welcome, masters; welcome, all:— I am glad to see thee well:—
welcome, good friends.— O, my old friend! Thy face is valanced since I saw
thee last; comest thou to beard me in Denmark?—What, my young lady and
mistress! By'r lady, your ladyship is nearer heaven than when I saw you last,
by the altitude of a chopine.° Pray God, your voice, like a piece of uncurrent
390   gold, be not cracked within the ring.— Masters, you are all welcome. We'll
e'en to't like French falconers, fly at anything we see: we'll have a speech
straight: come, give us a taste of your quality; come, a passionate speech.
1ST PLAYER: What speech, my lord?
HAMLET: I heard thee speak me a speech once,— but it was never acted; or, if
395   it was, not above once; for the play, I remember, pleased not the million;
'twas caviare to the general: but it was,— as I received it, and others whose
judgments in such matters cried in the top of mine,— an excellent play, well
digested in the scenes, set down with as much modesty as cunning. I remember, one said there were no sallets in the lines to make the matter savory, nor
400   no matter in the phrase that might indite the author of affectation; but
called it an honest method, as wholesome as sweet, and by very much more
handsome than fine. One speech in it I chiefly loved: 'twas Aeneas' tale to
Dido; and thereabout of it especially where he speaks of Priam's slaughter: if
it live in your memory, begin at this line;— let me see, let me see:—

405
    The rugged Pyrrhus, like the Hyrcanian beast,°

— it is not so:— it begins with Pyrrhus:—

    The rugged Pyrrhus,— he whose sable arms,
    Black as his purpose, did the night resemble
    When he lay couched in the ominous horse,—
410
    Hath now this dread and black complexion smear'd
    With heraldry more dismal; head to foot
    Now is he total gules; horridly trick'd
    With blood of fathers, mothers, daughters, sons,

° *chopine:* A wooden stilt more than a foot high used under a woman's shoe; a Venetian fashion introduced into
England.   ° *The rugged . . . :* This speech is an example of the declamatory style of drama, which Shakespeare
surely must have considered outmoded.

Bak'd and impasted with the parching streets,
That lend a tyrannous and damned light
To their vile murders: roasted in wrath and fire,
And thus o'er-sized with coagulate gore,
With eyes like carbuncles, the hellish Pyrrhus
Old grandsire Priam seeks.—   420

So proceed you.

POLONIUS: 'Fore God, my lord, well spoken, with good accent and
good discretion.

1ST PLAYER: Anon he finds him
Striking too short at Greeks; his antique sword,   425
Rebellious to his arm, lies where it falls,
Repugnant to command: unequal match'd,
Pyrrhus at Priam drives; in rage strikes wide;
But with the whiff and wind of his fell sword
The unnerved father falls. Then senseless Ilium,   430
Seeming to feel this blow, with flaming top
Stoops to his base; and with a hideous crash
Takes prisoner Pyrrhus' ear: for, lo! his sword,
Which was declining on the milky head
Of reverend Priam, seem'd i' the air to stick: 435
So, as a painted tyrant, Pyrrhus stood;
And, like a neutral to his will and matter,
Did nothing.
But as we often see, against some storm,
A silence in the heavens, the rack stand still,   440
The blood winds speechless, and the orb below
As hush as death, anon the dreadful thunder
Doth rend the region; so, after Pyrrhus' pause,
A roused vengeance sets him new a-work;
And never did the Cyclops' hammers fall   445
On Mars his armor, forg'd for proof eterne,
With less remorse than Pyrrhus' bleeding sword
Now falls on Priam.—
Out, out, thou strumpet, Fortune! All you gods,
In general synod, take away her power;   450
Break all the spokes and fellies from her wheel,
And bowl the round knave down the hill of heaven,
As low as to the fiends!

POLONIUS: This is too long.

HAMLET: It shall to the barber's, with your beard.— Pr'ythee, say on.— He's   455
for a jig, or a tale of bawdry, or he sleeps:— say on; come to Hecuba.

1ST PLAYER: But who, O, who had seen the mobled queen,—

HAMLET: *The mobled queen?*

POLONIUS: That's good; *mobled queen* is good.

1ST PLAYER: Run barefoot up and down, threatening the flames

460 With bissom rheum; a clout upon that head
Where late the diadem stood; and, for a robe,
About her lank and all o'er-teemed loins,
A blanket, in the alarm of fear caught up;—
Who this had seen, with tongue in venom steep'd,

465 'Gainst Fortune's state would treason have pronounc'd:
But if the gods themselves did see her then,
When she saw Pyrrhus make malicious sport
In mincing with his sword her husband's limbs,
The instant burst of clamor that she made,—

470 Unless things mortal move them not at all,—
Would have made milch the burning eyes of heaven,
And passion in the gods.

POLONIUS: Look, whether he has not turn'd his color, and has tears in's eyes.— Pray you, no more.

475 **HAMLET:** 'Tis well; I'll have thee speak out the rest soon.— Good my lord, will you see the players well bestowed? Do you hear, let them be well used; for they are the abstracts and brief chronicles of the time; after your death you were better have a bad epitaph than their ill report while you live.

480 **POLONIUS:** My lord, I will use them according to their desert.

HAMLET: God's bodikin, man, better: use every man after his desert, and who should scape whipping? Use them after your own honor and dignity: the less they deserve the more merit is in your bounty. Take them in.

POLONIUS: Come, sirs.

485 **HAMLET:** Follow him, friends: we'll hear a play to-morrow.

Exit Polonius with all the Players but the First.

Dost thou hear me, old friend; can you play the Murder of Gonzago?

1ST PLAYER: Ay, my lord.

HAMLET: We'll ha't to-morrow night. You could, for a need, study a speech of some dozen or sixteen lines which I would set down and insert in't?

490 could you not?

1ST PLAYER: Ay, my lord.

HAMLET: Very well.— Follow that lord; and look you mock him not.

Exit First Player.

—My good friends, [*to Rosencrantz and Guildenstern*] I'll leave you till night: you are welcome to Elsinore.

495 **ROSENCRANTZ:** Good my lord!

Exeunt Rosencrantz and Guildenstern.

HAMLET: Ay, so God b' wi' ye!—Now I am alone.
O, what a rogue° and peasant slave am I!
Is it not monstrous that this player here,
But in a fiction, in a dream of passion,
Could force his soul so to his own conceit°   500
That from her working all his visage wan'd;
Tears in his eyes, distraction in's aspéct,
A broken voice, and his whole function suiting
With forms to his conceit? And all for nothing!
For Hecuba?   505
What's Hecuba to him or he to Hecuba,
That he should weep for her? What would he do,
Had he the motive and the cue for passion
That I have? He would drown the stage with tears,
And cleave the general ear with horrid speech;   510
Make mad the guilty, and appal the free;
Confound the ignorant, and amaze, indeed,
The very faculties of eyes and ears.
Yet I,
A dull and muddy-mettled rascal, peak,   515
Like John-a-dreams, unpregnant of my cause,
And can say nothing; no, not for a king
Upon whose property and most dear life
A damn'd defeat was made. Am I a coward?
Who calls me villain? breaks my pate across?   520
Plucks off my beard and blows it in my face?
Tweaks me by the nose? gives me the lie i' the throat,
As deep as to the lungs? who does me this, ha?
'Swounds, I should take it: for it cannot be
But I am pigeon-liver'd, and lack gall   525
To make oppression bitter; or ere this
I should have fatted all the region kites
With this slave's offal:—bloody, bawdy villain!
Remorseless, treacherous, lecherous, kindless villain!
O, vengeance!   530
Why, what an ass am I! This is most brave,
That I, the son of a dear father murder'd,
Prompted to my revenge by heaven and hell,
Must, like a whore, unpack my heart with words,
And fall a-cursing like a very drab,   535

° *rogue:* Wretched creature.   °*conceit:* Conception.

A scullion!
Fie upon't! foh!—About, my brain! I have heard
That guilty creatures, sitting at a play,
Have by the very cunning of the scene
540 Been struck so to the soul that presently
They have proclaim'd their malefactions;
For murder, though it have no tongue, will speak
With most miraculous organ. I'll have these players
Play something like the murder of my father
545 Before mine uncle: I'll observe his looks;
I'll tent° him to the quick: if he but blench,
I know my course. The spirit that I have seen
May be the devil: and the devil hath power
To assume a pleasing shape; yea, and perhaps
550 Out of my weakness and my melancholy,—
As he is very potent with such spirits,—
Abuses me to damn me: I'll have grounds
More relative than this:— the play's the thing
Wherein I'll catch the conscience of the king. [*Exit.*]

ACT 3
SCENE 1

A room in the castle.

Enter King, Queen, Polonius, Ophelia, Rosencrantz, and Guildenstern.

KING: And can you, by no drift of circumstance,
Get from him why he puts on this confusion,
Grating so harshly all his days of quiet
With turbulent and dangerous lunacy?
5 ROSENCRANTZ: He does confess he feels himself distracted;
But from what cause he will by no means speak.
GUILDENSTERN: Nor do we find him forward to be sounded;
But, with a crafty madness, keeps aloof
When we would bring him on to some confession
10 Of his true state.
QUEEN: Did he receive you well?
ROSENCRANTZ: Most like a gentleman.

GUILDENSTERN: But with much forcing of his disposition.

° *tent:* Probe.

ROSENCRANTZ: Niggard of question; but, of our demands,
Most free in his reply. 15

QUEEN: Did you assay him
To any pastime?

ROSENCRANTZ: Madam, it so fell out that certain players
We o'er-raught on the way: of these we told him;
And there did seem in him a kind of joy 20
To hear of it: they are about the court;
And, as I think, they have already order
This night to play before him.

POLONIUS: 'Tis most true:
And he beseech'd me to entreat your majesties 25
To hear and see the matter.

KING: With all my heart; and it doth much content me
To hear him so inclin'd.
Good gentlemen, give him a further edge,
And drive his purpose on to these delights. 30
ROSENCRANTZ: We shall, my lord.

Exeunt Rosencrantz and Guildenstern.

KING: Sweet Gertrude, leave us too;
For we have closely sent for Hamlet hither
That he, as 'twere by accident, may here
Affront Ophelia: 35
Her father and myself,—lawful espials,°—
Will so bestow ourselves that, seeing, unseen,
We may of their encounter frankly judge;
And gather by him, as he is behav'd,
If't be the affliction of his love or no 40
That thus he suffers for.
QUEEN: I shall obey you:—
And for your part, Ophelia, I do wish
That your good beauties be the happy cause
Of Hamlet's wildness: so shall I hope your virtues 45
Will bring him to his wonted way again,
To both your honors.
OPHELIA: Madam, I wish it may.

Exit Queen.

° *espials:* Spies.

POLONIUS: Ophelia, walk you here.— Gracious, so please you,
50   We will bestow ourselves.—[*To Ophelia*] Read on this book;
That show of such an exercise may color
Your loneliness.—We are oft to blame in this,—
'Tis too much prov'd,— that with devotion's visage
And pious action we do sugar o'er
55   The devil himself.
    KING: [*Aside*]   O, 'tis too true!
How smart a lash that speech doth give my conscience!
The harlot's cheek, beautied with plastering art,
Is not more ugly to the thing that helps it
60   Than is my deed to my most painted word:
O heavy burden!
POLONIUS: I hear him coming: let's withdraw, my lord.

Exeunt King and Polonius.

Enter Hamlet.

HAMLET: To be, or not to be,— that is the question:
Whether 'tis nobler in the mind to suffer
65   The slings and arrows of outrageous fortune,
Or to take arms against a sea of troubles,
And by opposing end them?— To die,— to sleep,—
No more; and by a sleep to say we end
The heart-ache and the thousand natural shocks
70   That flesh is heir to,—'tis a consummation
Devoutly to be wish'd. To die,— to sleep;—
To sleep! perchance to dream:— ay, there's the rub;
For in that sleep of death what dreams may come,
When we have shuffled off this mortal coil,
75   Must give us pause: there's the respect
That makes a calamity of so long life;
For who would bear the whips and scorns of time,
The oppressor's wrong, the proud man's contumely,
The pangs of déspis'd love, the law's delay,
80   The insolence of office, and the spurns
That patient merit of the unworthy takes,
When he himself might his quietus make
With a bare bodkin?° who would fardels° bear,
To grunt° and sweat under a weary life,
85   But that the dread of something after death,—
The undiscover'd country, from whose bourn°
No traveler returns,— puzzles the will,

° *bodkin:* Stiletto.   ° *fardels:* Burdens.   ° *grunt:* Groan.   ° *bourn:* Boundary.

And makes us rather bear those ills we have
Than to fly to others that we know not of?
Thus conscience does make cowards of us all;   90
And thus the native hue of resolution
Is sicklied o'er with the pale cast of thought;
And enterprises of great pith and moment,
With this regard, their currents turn awry,
And lose the name of action.— Soft you now!   95
The fair Ophelia.— Nymph, in thy orisons°
Be all my sins remember'd.
OPHELIA: Good my lord,
  How does your honor for this many a day?
HAMLET: I humbly thank you; well, well, well.   100
OPHELIA: My lord, I have remembrances of yours,
  That I have longed long to re-deliver;
  I pray you, now receive them.
HAMLET: No, not I;
  I never gave you aught.   105
OPHELIA: My honor'd lord, you know right well you did;
  And with them, words of so sweet breath compos'd
  As made the things more rich: their perfume lost,
  Take these again; for to the noble mind
  Rich gifts wax poor when givers prove unkind.   110
  There, my lord.
HAMLET: Ha, ha! are you honest?
OPHELIA: My lord?
HAMLET: Are you fair?
OPHELIA: What means your lordship?   115
HAMLET: That if you be honest and fair, your honesty should admit no
  discourse to your beauty.
OPHELIA: Could beauty, my lord, have better commerce than with honesty?
HAMLET: Ay, truly; for the power of beauty will sooner transform honesty from
  what it is to a bawd than the force of honesty can translate beauty into his   120
  likeness: this was sometime a paradox, but now the time gives it proof. I did
  love you once.
OPHELIA: Indeed, my lord, you made me believe so.
HAMLET: You should not have believed me; for virtue cannot so inoculate our
  old stock but we shall relish of it: I loved you not.   125
OPHELIA: I was the more deceived.
HAMLET: Get thee to a nunnery: why wouldst thou be a breeder of sinners? I
  am myself indifferent° honest; but yet I could accuse me of such things that
  it were better my mother had not borne me: I am very proud, revengeful,

° *orisons:* Prayers.   ° *indifferent:* Tolerably.

130   ambitious; with more offences at my beck than I have thoughts to put them
in, imagination to give them shape, or time to act them in. What should such
fellows as I do crawling between heaven and earth? We are arrant knaves, all;
believe none of us. Go thy ways to a nunnery. Where's your father?

OPHELIA: At home, my lord.

135 HAMLET: Let the doors be shut upon him, that he may play the fool nowhere
but in's own house. Farewell.

OPHELIA: O, help him, you sweet heavens!

HAMLET: If thou dost marry, I'll give thee this plague for thy dowry,—be thou
as chaste as ice, as pure as snow, thou shalt not escape calumny. Get thee to
140   a nunnery, go: farewell. Or, if thou wilt needs marry, marry a fool; for wise
men know well enough what monsters you make of them. To a nunnery, go;
and quickly too. Farewell.

OPHELIA: O heavenly powers, restore him!

HAMLET: I have heard of your paintings too, well enough; God has given you
145   one face and you make yourselves another: you jig, you amble, and you lisp,
and nickname God's creatures, and make your wantonness your ignorance.
Go to, I'll no more on't; it hath made me mad. I say, we will have no more
marriages: those that are married already, all but one, shall live; the rest
shall keep as they are. To a nunnery, go. [*Exit.*]

150 OPHELIA: O, what a noble mind is here o'erthrown!
The courtier's, soldier's, scholar's eye, tongue, sword:
The expectancy and rose of the fair state,
The glass of fashion and the mould of form,
The observ'd of all observers,— quite, quite down!
155   And I, of ladies most deject and wretched
That suck'd the honey of his music vows,
Now see that noble and most sovereign reason,
Like sweet bells jangled, out of tune and harsh;
That unmatch'd form and feature of blown° youth
160   Blasted with ecstasy: O, woe is me,
To have seen what I have seen, see what I see!

Re-enter King and Polonius.

KING: Love! his affections do not that way tend;
Nor what he spake, though it lack'd form a little,
Was not like madness. There's something in his soul
165   O'er which his melancholy sits on brood;
And I do doubt° the hatch and the disclose
Will be some danger: which for to prevent,
I have in quick determination
Thus set it down:—he shall with speed to England

° *blown:* Full-blown.   ° *doubt:* Fear.

For the demand of our neglected tribute: 170
Haply, the seas and countries different,
With variable objects, shall expel
This something-settled matter in his heart;
Whereon his brains still beating puts him thus
From fashion of himself. What think you on't?   175
POLONIUS: It shall do well: but yet do I believe
The origin and commencement of his grief
Sprung from neglected love.— How now, Ophelia!
You need not tell us what Lord Hamlet said;
We heard it all.— My lord, do as you please;   180
But if you hold it fit, after the play,
Let his queen mother all alone entreat him
To show his grief: let her be round with him;
And I'll be plac'd, so please you, in the ear
Of all their conference. If she finds him not,°   185
To England send him; or confine him where
Your wisdom best shall think.

KING: It shall be so:
Madness in great ones must not unwatch'd go.

Exeunt.

SCENE 2

A hall in the castle.

Enter Hamlet and certain Players.

HAMLET: Speak the speech, I pray you, as I pronounced it to you, trippingly on
the tongue: but if you mouth it, as many of your players do, I had as lief the
town-crier spoke my lines. Nor do not saw the air too much with your
hand, thus; but use all gently: for in the very torrent, tempest, and, as I may
say, the whirlwind of passion, you must acquire and beget a temperance that   5
may give it smoothness. O, it offends me to the soul, to hear a robustious
periwigpated fellow tear a passion to tatters, to very rags, to split the ears of
the groundlings, who, for the most part, are capable of nothing but inexplicable dumb shows and noise: I could have such a fellow whipped for
o'erdoing Termagant;° it out-herods Herod:° pray you, avoid it.   10
1ST PLAYER: I warrant your honor.
HAMLET: Be not too tame neither, but let your own discretion be your tutor;
suit the action to the word, the word to the action; with this special obser-
vance, that you o'erstep not the modesty of nature: for anything so over-

---

° *finds him not:* Does not find him out.   ° *Termagant:* A violent pagan deity, supposedly Mohammedan.   °*out-
herods Herod:* Outrants the ranting Herod, who figures in medieval drama.

15 done is from the purpose of playing, whose end, both at the first and now,
was and is, to hold, as 'twere, the mirror up to nature; to show virtue her
own feature, scorn her own image, and the very age and body of the time
his form and pressure. Now, this overdone or come tardy off, though it
make the unskilful laugh, cannot but make the judicious grieve; the censure
20 of the which one must, in your allowance, o'erweigh a whole theater of
others. O, there be players that I have seen play,— and heard others praise,
and that highly,— not to speak it profanely, that, neither having the accent
of Christians, nor the gait of Christian, pagan, nor man, have so strutted
and bellowed that I have thought some of nature's journeymen had made
25 men, and not made them well, they imitated humanity so abominably.
1ST PLAYER: I hope we have reformed that indifferently with us, sir.
HAMLET: O, reform it altogether. And let those that play your clowns speak
no more than is set down for them: for there be of them that will themselves laugh, to set on some quantity of barren spectators to laugh too;
30 though, in the meantime, some necessary question of the play be then to be
considered: that's villainous, and shows a most pitiful ambition in the fool
that uses it. Go, make you ready.

Exeunt Players.

Enter Polonius, Rosencrantz, and Guildenstern.

How now, my lord! will the king hear this piece of work?
POLONIUS: And the queen, too, and that presently.
35 HAMLET: Bid the players make haste.

Exit Polonius.

Will you two help to hasten them?
ROSENCRANTZ and GUILDENSTERN: We will, my lord. [*Exeunt.*]
HAMLET: What, ho, Horatio!

Enter Horatio.

HORATIO: Here, sweet lord, at your service.
40 HAMLET: Horatio, thou art e'en as just a man
As e'er my conversation cop'd withal.
HORATIO: O, my dear lord,—
HAMLET: Nay, do not think I flatter;
For what advancement may I hope from thee,
45 That no revénue hast, but thy good spirits,
To feed and clothe thee? Why should the poor be flatter'd?
No, let the candied tongue lick ábsurd pomp;
And crook the pregnant hinges of the knee
Where thrift may follow fawning. Dost thou hear?
50 Since my dear soul was mistress of her choice,

And could of men distinguish, her election
Hath seal'd thee for herself: for thou hast been
As one, in suffering all, that suffers nothing;
A man that Fortune's buffets and rewards
Hast ta'en with equal thanks: and bless'd are those   55
Whose blood and judgment are so well commingled
That they are not a pipe for Fortune's finger
To sound what stop she please. Give me that man
That is not passion's slave, and I will wear him
In my heart's core, ay, in my heart of heart,   60
As I do thee.— Something too much of this.—
There is a play to-night before the king;
One scene of it comes near the circumstance
Which I have told thee of my father's death:
I pr'ythee, when thou see'st that act a-foot,   65
Even with the very comment of thy soul
Observe mine uncle: if this his occulted guilt
Do not itself unkennel in one speech,
It is a damned ghost that we have seen;
And my imaginations are as foul   70
As Vulcan's stithy.° Give him heedful note:
For I mine eyes will rivet to his face;
And, after, we will both our judgments join
In censure of his seeming.

HORATIO: Well, my lord: 75
If he steal aught the whilst this play is playing,
And scape detecting, I will pay the theft.

HAMLET: They are coming to the play; I must be idle:°
Get you a place.

Danish march. A flourish. Enter King, Queen, Polonius, Ophelia, Rosencrantz, Guild-
enstern, and others.

KING: How fares our cousin Hamlet?   80

HAMLET: Excellent, i'faith; of the chameleon's dish: I eat the air,°
promise-crammed: you cannot feed capons so.

KING: I have nothing with this answer, Hamlet; these words are not mine.

HAMLET: No, nor mine now. [*To Polonius*] My lord, you played once i' the
university, you say?   85

POLONIUS: That did I, my lord, and was accounted a good actor.

HAMLET: And what did you enact?

POLONIUS: I did enact Julius Caesar: I was killed i' the Capitol; Brutus
killed me.

° *stithy:* Smithy.   ° *idle:* Foolish.   ° *of the chameleon's . . . the air:* Chameleons were believed to live on air.

90 **HAMLET:** It was a brute part of him to kill so capital a calf there. — Be the
    players ready.
ROSENCRANTZ: Ay, my lord; they stay upon your patience.
QUEEN: Come hither, my good Hamlet, sit by me.
HAMLET: No, good mother, here's metal more attractive.
95 **POLONIUS:** O, ho! do you mark that? [*To the King*]
HAMLET: Lady, shall I lie in your lap? [*Lying down at Ophelia's feet*]
OPHELIA: No, my lord.
HAMLET: I mean, my head upon your lap?
OPHELIA: Ay, my lord.
100 **HAMLET:** Do you think I meant country matters?
OPHELIA: I think nothing, my lord.
HAMLET: That's a fair thought to lie between maids' legs.
OPHELIA: What is, my lord?
HAMLET: Nothing.
105 **OPHELIA:** You are merry, my lord.
HAMLET: Who, I?
OPHELIA: Ay, my lord.
HAMLET: O, your only jig-maker. What should a man do but be merry? for, look
    you, how cheerfully my mother looks, and my father died within's two hours.
110 **OPHELIA:** Nay, 'tis twice two months, my lord.
HAMLET: So long? Nay, then, let the devil wear black, for I'll have a suit of
    sables. O heavens! die two months ago, and not forgotten yet? Then there's
    hope a great man's memory may outlive his life half a year: but, by'r lady, he
    must build churches, then; or else shall he suffer not thinking on, with the
115 hobby-horse, whose epitaph is, *For, O, for, O, the hobby-horse is forgot.*

Trumpets sound. The dumb show enters.

*Enter a King and a Queen, very lovingly; the Queen embracing him and he her. She
kneels, and makes show of protestation unto him. He takes her up, and declines his head
upon her neck: lays him down upon a bank of flowers: she, seeing him asleep, leaves
him. Anon comes in a fellow, takes off his crown, kisses it, and pours poison in the King's
ears, and exit. The Queen returns; finds the King dead, and makes passionate action.
The Poisoner, with some two or three Mutes, comes in again, seeming to lament with
her. The dead body is carried away. The Poisoner woos the Queen with gifts: she seems
loth and unwilling awhile, but in the end accepts his love.*

Exeunt.

OPHELIA: What means this, my lord?
HAMLET: Marry, this is miching mallecho;° it means mischief.
OPHELIA: Belike this show imports the argument of the play.

° *miching mallecho:* A sneaking misdeed.

Enter Prologue.

HAMLET: We shall know by this fellow: the players cannot keep counsel;
    they'll tell all.   120

OPHELIA: Will he tell us what this show meant?

HAMLET: Ay, or any show that you'll show him: be not you ashamed to show,
    he'll not shame to tell you what it means.

OPHELIA: You are naught, you are naught: I'll mark the play.

PROLOGUE: -   125

> For us, and for our tragedy,
> Here stooping to your clemency,
> We beg your hearing patiently.

HAMLET: Is this a prologue, or the posy° of a ring?   130

OPHELIA: 'Tis brief, my lord.

HAMLET: As woman's love.

Enter a King and a Queen.

PROLOGUE KING: Full thirty times hath Phoebus' cart gone round
    Neptune's salt wash and Tellus' orbed ground,°
    And thirty dozen moons with borrow'd sheen
    About the world have times twelve thirties been,   135
    Since love our hearts, and Hymen did our hands
    Unite commutual in most sacred bands.

PROLOGUE QUEEN: So many journeys may the sun and moon
    Make us again count o'er ere love be done!
    But, woe is me, you are so sick of late,   140
    So far from cheer and from your former state
    That I distrust you.° Yet, though I distrust,
    Discomfort you, my lord, it nothing must:
    For women's fear and love holds quantity,°
    In neither aught, or in extremity.   145
    Now, what my love is, proof hath made you know;
    And as my love is siz'd, my fear is so:
    Where love is great, the littlest doubts are fear;
    Where little fears grow great, great love grows there.

PROLOGUE KING: Faith, I must leave thee, love, and shortly too;   150
    My operant powers their functions leave° to do:
    And thou shalt live in this fair world behind,
    Honor'd, belov'd; and haply one as kind
    For husband shalt thou,—

° *posy:* Motto or inscription.   ° *orbed ground:* The globe.   ° *distrust you:* Worry about you.   ° *holds quantity:*
Correspond in degree.   ° *leave:* Cease.

155 **Prologue Queen:**   O, confound the rest!
    Such love must needs be treason in my breast:
    In second husband let me be accurst!
    None wed the second but who kill'd the first.
    Hamlet: [*Aside*] Wormwood, wormwood.
160 **Prologue Queen:** The instances that second marriage move
    Are base respects of thrift, but none of love:
    A second time I kill my husband, dead,
    When second husband kisses me in bed.
    Prologue King: I do believe you think what now you speak;
165   But what we do determine oft we break.
    Purpose is but the slave to memory;
    Of violent birth, but poor validity:
    Which now, like fruit unripe, sticks on the tree;
    But fall unshaken when they mellow be.
170   Most necessary 'tis that we forget
    To pay ourselves what to ourselves is debt:
    What to ourselves in passion we propose,
    The passion ending, doth the purpose lose.
    The violence of either grief or joy
175   Their own enactures with themselves destroy:
    Where joy most revels grief doth most lament;
    Grief joys, joy grieves, on slender accident.
    This world is not for aye; nor 'tis not strange
    That even our loves should with our fortunes change;
180   For 'tis a question left us yet to prove
    Whether love lead fortune or else fortune love.
    The great man down, you mark his favorite flies;
    The poor advanc'd makes friends of enemies.
    And hitherto doth love on fortune tend:
185   For who not needs shall never lack a friend;
    And who in want a hollow friend doth try,
    Directly seasons him his enemy.
    But, orderly to end where I begun,—
    Our wills and fates do so contrary run
190   That our devices still are overthrown;
    Our thoughts are ours, their ends none of our own:
    So think thou wilt no second husband wed;
    But die thy thoughts when thy first lord is dead.
    Prologue Queen: Nor earth to me give food, nor heaven light!
195   Sport and repose lock from me day and night!
    To desperation turn my trust and hope!
    An anchor's° cheer in prison be my scope!

° *anchor's:* Anchorite's, or hermit's.

Each opposite, that blanks the face of joy,
Meet what I would have well, and it destroy!
Both here and hence, pursue me lasting strife,   200
If, once a widow, ever I be wife!
HAMLET: If she should break it now! [*To Ophelia*]
PROLOGUE KING: 'Tis deeply sworn. Sweet, leave me here awhile;
My spirits grow dull, and fain I would beguile
The tedious day with sleep. [*Sleeps*]   205
PROLOGUE QUEEN: Sleep rock thy brain,
And never come mischance between us twain! [*Exit.*]
HAMLET: Madam, how like you this play?
QUEEN: The lady doth protest too much, methinks.
HAMLET: O, but she'll keep her word.   210
KING: Have you heard the argument? Is there no offence in't?
HAMLET: No, no, they do but jest, poison in jest; no offence i' the world.
KING: What do you call the play?
HAMLET: The Mouse-trap. Marry, how? Tropically.° This play is the image of a
murder done in Vienna: Gonzago is the duke's name: his wife, Baptista: you   215
shall see anon; 'tis a knavish piece of work: but what o' that? your majesty,
and we that have free souls, it touches us not: let the galled jade wince, our
withers are unwrung.

Enter Lucianus.

This is one Lucianus, nephew to the king.
OPHELIA: You are a good chorus, my lord.   220
HAMLET: I could interpret between you and your love, if I could see the pup-
pets dallying.
OPHELIA: You are keen, my lord, you are keen.
HAMLET: It would cost you a groaning to take off my edge.
OPHELIA: Still better, and worse.   225
HAMLET: So you must take your husbands.— Begin, murderer; pox, leave thy
damnable faces and begin. Come:— *The croaking raven doth bellow for revenge.*
LUCIANUS: Thoughts black, hands apt, drugs fit, and time agreeing;
Confederate season, else no creature seeing;   230
Thou mixture rank, of midnight weeds collected,
With Hecate's ban° thrice blasted, thrice infected,
Thy natural magic and dire property
On wholesome life usurp immediately.

Pours the poison into the sleeper's ears.

° *Tropically:* Figuratively, or metaphorically; by means of a "trope."   ° *Hecate's ban:* The spell of the goddess of
witchcraft.

235 **HAMLET:** He poisons him i' the garden for's estate. His name's Gonzago: the
story is extant, and writ in choice Italian: you shall see anon how the murderer gets the love of Gonzago's wife.

OPHELIA: The king rises.

HAMLET: What, frighted with false fire!

240 **QUEEN:** How fares my lord?

POLONIUS: Give o'er the play.

KING: Give me some light:— away!

ALL: Lights, lights, lights!

Exeunt all but Hamlet and Horatio.

HAMLET:

245   Why, let the stricken deer go weep,
      The hart ungalled play;
      For some must watch, while some must sleep:
      So runs the world away.—

      Would not this, sir, and a forest of feathers, if the rest of my fortunes turn
250   Turk with me, with two Provencial roses on my razed shoes, get me a
      fellowship in a cry° of players, sir?

HORATIO: Half a share.

HAMLET: A whole one, I.

255   For thou dost know, O Damon dear,
        This realm dismantled was
      Of Jove himself; and now reigns here
      A very, very — pajock.°

HORATIO: You might have rhymed.

HAMLET: O good Horatio, I'll take the ghost's word for a thousand pound.
260 Didst perceive?

HORATIO: Very well, my lord.

HAMLET: Upon the talk of the poisoning,—

HORATIO: I did very well note him.

HAMLET: Ah, ha!— Come, some music! come, the recorders!—

265   For if the king like not the comedy,
      Why, then, belike,—he likes it not, perdy.

      Come, some music!

Re-enter Rosencrantz and Guildenstern.

GUILDENSTERN: Good my lord, vouchsafe me a word with you.

HAMLET: Sir, a whole history.

270 **GUILDENSTERN:** The king, sir,—

° *cry:* Company.   ° *pajock:* Peacock.

HAMLET: Ay, sir, what of him?

GUILDENSTERN: Is, in his retirement, marvelous distempered.

HAMLET: With drink, sir?

GUILDENSTERN: No, my lord, rather with choler.

HAMLET: Your wisdom should show itself more richer to signify this to his   275
doctor; for, for me to put him to his purgation would perhaps plunge him
into far more choler.

GUILDENSTERN: Good my lord, put your discourse into some frame, and start
not so wildly from my affair.

HAMLET: I am tame, sir:— pronounce.   280

GUILDENSTERN: The queen, your mother, in most great affliction of spirit,
hath sent me to you.

HAMLET: You are welcome.

GUILDENSTERN: Nay, good my lord, this courtesy is not of the right breed. If it
shall please you to make me a wholesome answer, I will do you mother's   285
commandment: if not, your pardon and my return shall be the end of my
business.

HAMLET: Sir, I cannot.

GUILDENSTERN: What, my lord?

HAMLET: Make you a wholesome answer; my wit's diseas'd: but, sir, such an-   290
swer as I can make, you shall command; or, rather, as you say, my mother:
therefore no more, but to the matter: my mother, you say,—

ROSENCRANTZ: Then thus she says: your behavior hath struck her into amazement and admiration.

HAMLET: O wonderful son, that can so astonish a mother!— But is there no   295
sequel at the heels of this mother's admiration?

ROSENCRANTZ: She desires to speak with you in her closet° ere you go to bed.

HAMLET: We shall obey, were she ten times our mother. Have you any further
trade with us?

ROSENCRANTZ: My lord, you once did love me.   300

HAMLET: So I do still, by these pickers and stealers.°

ROSENCRANTZ: Good, my lord, what is your cause of distemper? you do,
surely, bar the door upon your own liberty if you deny your griefs to
your friend.

HAMLET: Sir, I lack advancement.   305

ROSENCRANTZ: How can that be, when you have the voice of the king
himself for your succession in Denmark?

HAMLET: Ay, but *While the grass grows,*— the proverb is something musty.

Re-enter the Players, with recorders.

O, the recorders:— let me see one.— To withdraw with you:— why do you
go about to recover the wind of me, as if you would drive me into a toil?   310

° *closet:* Boudoir.   ° *pickers and stealers:* Fingers.

GUILDENSTERN: O, my lord, if my duty be too bold, my love is too
  unmannerly.
HAMLET: I do not well understand that. Will you play upon this pipe?
GUILDENSTERN: My lord, I cannot.
315 HAMLET: I pray you.
GUILDENSTERN: Believe me, I cannot.
HAMLET: I do beseech you.
GUILDENSTERN: I know no touch of it, my lord.
HAMLET: 'Tis as easy as lying: govern these ventages° with your finger and
320 thumb, give it breath with your mouth, and it will discourse most eloquent
  music. Look you, these are the stops.
GUILDENSTERN: But these cannot I command to any utterance of harmony; I
  have not the skill.
HAMLET: Why, look you now, how unworthy a thing you make of me! You
325 would play upon me; you would seem to know my stops; you would pluck
  out the heart of my mystery; you would sound me from my lowest note to
  the top of my compass: and there is much music, excellent voice, in this
  little organ; yet cannot you make it speak. 'Sblood, do you think that I am
  easier to be played on than a pipe? Call me what instrument you will,
330 though you can fret me you cannot play upon me.

Enter Polonius.

  God bless you, sir!
POLONIUS: My lord, the queen would speak with you, and presently.
HAMLET: Do you see yonder cloud that's almost in shape of a camel?
POLONIUS: By the mass, and 'tis like a camel indeed.
335 HAMLET: Methinks it is like a weasel.
POLONIUS: It is backed like a weasel.
HAMLET: Or like a whale?
POLONIUS: Very like a whale.
HAMLET: Then will I come to my mother by and by.— They fool me to the
340 top of my bent.— I will come by and by.
POLONIUS: I will say so.
HAMLET: By and by is easily said.

Exit Polonius.

  Leave me, friends.

Exeunt Rosencrantz, Guildenstern, Horatio, and Players.

  'Tis now the very witching time of night,
345 When churchyards yawn, and hell itself breathes out

° *ventages:* Holes.

Contagion to this world: now could I drink hot blood,
And do such bitter business as the day
Would quake to look on. Soft! now to my mother.—
O heart, lose not thy nature; let not ever
The soul of Nero° enter this firm bosom: 350
Let me be cruel, not unnatural:
I will speak daggers to her, but use none;
My tongue and soul in this be hypocrites,—
How in my words soever she be shent,
To give them seals never, my soul, consent! [*Exit.*]   355

SCENE 3

A room in the castle.

Enter King, Rosencrantz, and Guildenstern.

KING: I like him not; nor stands it safe with us
    To let his madness range. Therefore prepare you;
    I your commission with forthwith despatch,
    And he to England shall along with you:
    The terms of our estate may not endure   5
    Hazard so dangerous as doth hourly grow
    Out of his lunacies.
GUILDENSTERN: We will ourselves provide:
    Most holy and religious fear it is
    To keep those many many bodies safe   10
    That live and feed upon your majesty.
ROSENCRANTZ: The single and peculiar life is bound,
    With all the strength and armor of the mind,
    To keep itself from 'noyance; but much more
    That spirit upon whose weal depend and rest   15
    The lives of many. The cease of majesty
    Dies not alone; but like a gulf doth draw
    What's near it with it: it is a massy wheel,
    Fix'd on the summit of the highest mount,
    To whose huge spokes ten thousand lesser things   20
    Are mortis'd and adjoin'd; which, when it falls,
    Each small annexment, petty consequence,
    Attends the boisterous ruin. Never alone
    Did the king sigh, but with a general groan.

° *Nero:* The Roman emperor Nero killed his mother, a crime of which Hamlet does not want to be guilty.

25 **KING:** Arm you, I pray you, to this speedy voyage;
For we will fetters put upon this fear,
Which now goes too free-footed.

ROSENCRANTZ and **GUILDENSTERN:** We will haste us.

Exeunt Rosencrantz and Guildenstern.

Enter Polonius.

POLONIUS: My lord, he's going to his mother's closet:
30 Behind the arras I'll convey myself
To hear the process; I'll warrant she'll tax him home: °
And, as you said, and wisely was it said,
'Tis meet that some more audience than a mother,
Since nature makes them partial, should o'erhear
35 The speech, of vantage. Fare you well, my liege:
I'll call upon you ere you go to bed,
And tell you what I know.

KING: Thanks, dear my lord.

Exit Polonius.

O, my offence is rank, it smells to heaven;
40 It hath the primal eldest curse upon't,—
A brother's murder!— Pray can I not,
Though inclination be as sharp as will:
My stronger guilt defeats my strong intent;
And, like a man to double business bound,
45 I stand in pause where I shall first begin,
And both neglect. What if this cursed hand
Were thicker than itself with brother's blood,—
Is there not rain enough in the sweet heavens
To wash it white as snow? Whereto serves mercy
50 But to confront the visage of offence?
And what's in prayer but this twofold force,—
To be forestalled ere we come to fall,
Or pardon'd being down? Then I'll look up;
My fault is past. But, O, what form of prayer
55 Can serve my turn? Forgive me my foul murder?—
That cannot be; since I am still possess'd
Of those effects for which I did the murder,—
My crown, mine own ambition, and my queen.
May one be pardon'd and retain the offence? °
60 In the corrupted currents of this world

° *tax him home:* Reprove him properly.   ° *retain the offence:* Retain the gains won by the offense.

Offence's gilded hand may shove by justice;
And oft 'tis seen the wicked prize itself
Buys out the law: but 'tis not so above;
There is no shuffling,— there the action lies
In his true nature; and we ourselves compell'd,   65
Even to the teeth and forehead of our faults,
To give in evidence. What then? what rests?°
Try what repentance can: what can it not?
Yet what can it when one can not repent?
O wretched state! O bosom black as death!   70
O limed° soul, that, struggling to be free,
Art more engag'd! Help, angels! make assay:
Bow, stubborn knees; and, heart, with strings of steel,
Be soft as sinews of the new-born babe!
All may be well. [*Retires and kneels*]   75

Enter Hamlet.

HAMLET: Now might I do it pat, now he is praying;
And now I'll do't — and so he goes to heaven;
And so am I reveng'd:— that would be scann'd:
A villain kills my father; and for that,
I, his sole son, do this same villain send   80
To heaven.
O, this is hire and salary, not revenge.
He took my father grossly, full of bread;
With all his crimes broad blown, as flush as May;
And how his audit stands who knows save heaven?   85
But in our circumstance and course of thought
'Tis heavy with him: and am I, then, reveng'd,
To take him in the purging of his soul,
When he is fit and season'd for his passage?
No.   90
Up, sword; and know thou a more horrid hent:°
When he is drunk, asleep, or in his rage;
Or in the incestuous pleasure of his bed;
At gaming, swearing; or about some act
That has no relish of salvation in't;—   95
Then trip him, that his heels may kick at heaven;
And that his soul may be as damn'd and black
As hell, whereto it goes. My mother stays:
This physic but prolongs thy sickly days. [*Exit.*]

° *rests:* Remains.   ° *limed:* Snared.   ° *hent:* Opportunity.

The King rises and advances.

100 KING: My words fly up, my thoughts remain below:
      Words without thoughts never to heaven go. [*Exit.*]

SCENE 4

Another room in the castle.

Enter Queen and Polonius.

POLONIUS: He will come straight. Look you lay home to him:
      Tell him his pranks have been too broad to bear with,
      And that your grace hath screen'd and stood between
      Much heat and him. I'll silence me e'en here.
5   Pray you, be round with him.
QUEEN: [*Within*] Mother, mother, mother!
QUEEN: I'll warrant you:
      Fear me not:— withdraw, I hear him coming.

Polonius goes behind the arras.

Enter Hamlet.

HAMLET: Now, mother, what's the matter?
10 QUEEN: Hamlet, thou hast thy father much offended.
HAMLET: Mother, you have my father much offended.
QUEEN: Come, come, you answer with an idle tongue.
HAMLET: Go, go, you question with a wicked tongue.
QUEEN: Why, how now, Hamlet!
15 HAMLET: What's the matter now?
QUEEN: Have you forgot me?
HAMLET: No, by the rood, not so:
      You are the queen, your husband's brother's wife;
      And,— would it were not so!— you are my mother.
20 QUEEN: Nay, then, I'll set those to you that can speak.
HAMLET: Come, come, and sit you down; you shall not budge;
      You go not till I set you up a glass
      Where you may see the inmost part of you.
QUEEN: What wilt thou do? thou wilt not murder me?—
25   Help, help, ho!
POLONIUS: [*Behind*] What, ho! help, help, help!
HAMLET: How now! a rat?
      [*Draws.*]
      Dead, for a ducat, dead! [*Makes a pass through the arras*]
30 POLONIUS: [*Behind*] O, I am slain! [*Falls and dies.*]
QUEEN: O me, what hast thou done?

HAMLET: Nay, I know not:
Is it the king? [*Draws forth Polonius*]
QUEEN: O, what a rash and bloody deed is this!
HAMLET: A bloody deed! — almost as bad, good mother,   35
As kill a king and marry with his brother.
QUEEN: As kill a king!
HAMLET: Ay, lady, 'twas my word. —
Thou wretched, rash, intruding fool, farewell! [*To Polonius*]
I took thee for thy better: take thy fortune;   40
Thou find'st to be too busy is some danger.—
Leave wringing of your hands: peace; sit you down,
And let me wring your heart: for so I shall,
If it be made of penetrable stuff;
If damned custom have not braz'd it so   45
That it is proof and bulwark against sense.
QUEEN: What have I done, that thou dar'st wag thy tongue
In noise so rude against me?
HAMLET: Such an act
That blurs the grace and blush of modesty;   50
Calls virtue hypocrite; takes off the rose
From the fair forehead of an innocent love,
And sets a blister there; makes marriage-vows
As false as dicers' oaths: O, such a deed
As from the body of contraction plucks   55
The very soul, and sweet religion makes
A rhapsody of words: heaven's face doth glow;
Yea, this solidity and compound mass,
With tristful° visage, as against the doom,
Is thought-sick at the act.   60
QUEEN: Ah me, what act,
That roars so loud, and thunders in the index?
HAMLET: Look here upon this picture and on this,—
The counterfeit presentment of two brothers.
See what grace was seated on this brow;   65
Hyperion's curls; the front of Jove himself;
An eye like Mars, to threaten and command;
A station like the herald Mercury
New-lighted on a heaven-kissing hill;
A combination and a form, indeed,   70
Where every god did seem to set his seal,

° *tristful:* Gloomy.

To give the world assurance of a man:
This was your husband. — Look you now, what follows:
Here is your husband, like a mildew'd ear
75 Blasting his wholesome brother. Have you eyes?
Could you on this fair mountain leave to feed,
And batten on this moor? Ha! have you eyes?
You cannot call it love; for at your age
The hey-day in the blood is tame, it's humble,
80 And waits upon the judgment: and what judgment
Would step from this to this? Sense, sure, you have,
Else could you not have motion: but sure that sense
Is apoplex'd: for madness would not err;
Nor sense to ecstasy was ne'er so thrill'd
85 But it reserv'd some quantity of choice
To serve in such a difference. What devil was't
That thus hath cozen'd you at hoodman-blind?°
Eyes without feeling, feeling without sight,
Ears without hand or eyes, smelling sans all,
90 Or but a sickly part of one true sense
Could not so mope.
O shame! where is thy blush! Rebellious hell,
If thou canst mutine in a matron's bones,
To flaming youth let virtue be as wax,
95 And melt in her own fire: proclaim no shame
When the compulsive ardor gives the charge,
Since frost itself as actively doth burn,
And reason panders° will.
QUEEN: O Hamlet, speak no more:
100 Thou turn'st mine eyes into my very soul;
And there I see such black and grained spots
As will not leave their tinct.°
HAMLET: Nay, but to live
In the rank sweat of an enseamed bed,
105 Stew'd in corruption, honeying and making love
Over the nasty sty,—
QUEEN: O, speak to me no more;
These words like daggers enter in mine ears;
No more, sweet Hamlet.
110 HAMLET: A murderer and a villain;
A slave that is not twentieth part the tithe

° *cozen'd . . . hoodman-blind:* Tricked you at blindman's buff.   ° *panders:* Becomes subservient to.
° *As will not . . . tinct:* As will not yield up their color.

Of your precedent lord; a vice of kings;°
A cutpurse of the empire and the rule,
That from a shelf the precious diadem stole,
And put it in his pocket!   115
QUEEN: No more.
HAMLET: A king of shreds and patches,—

Enter Ghost.

Save me, and hover o'er me with your wings,
You heavenly guards!—What would your gracious figure?
QUEEN: Alas, he's mad!   120
HAMLET: Do you not come your tardy son to chide,
That, laps'd in time and passion, lets go by
The important acting of your dread command?
O, say!
GHOST: Do not forget: this visitation   125
Is but to whet thy almost blunted purpose.
But, look, amazement on thy mother sits:
O, step between her and her fighting soul,—
Conceit in weakest bodies strongest works,—
Speak to her, Hamlet.   130
HAMLET: How is it with you, lady?
QUEEN: Alas, how is't with you,
That you do bend your eye on vacancy,
And with the incorporal air do hold discourse?
Forth at your eyes your spirits wildly peep;   135
And, as the sleeping soldiers in the alarm,
Your bedded hair, like life in excrements,°
Starts up and stands on end. O gentle son,
Upon the heat and flame of thy distemper
Sprinkle cool patience. Whereon do you look?   140
HAMLET: On him, on him! Look you, how pale he glares!
His form and cause conjoin'd, preaching to stones,
Would make them capable.—Do not look upon me;
Lest with this piteous action you convert
My stern effects: then what I have to do   145
Will want true color; tears perchance for blood.
QUEEN: To whom do you speak this?
HAMLET: Do you see nothing there?
QUEEN: Nothing at all; yet all that is I see.
HAMLET: Nor did you nothing hear?   150

° *a vice of kings:* A buffoon among kings; the character "Vice" in morality plays.   ° *in excrements:* In out-
growths or extremities.

QUEEN: No, nothing but ourselves.

HAMLET: Why, look you there! look, how it steals away!
My father, in his habit as he liv'd!
Look, where he goes, even now, out at the portal!

Exit Ghost.

155 QUEEN: This is the very coinage of your brain:
This bodiless creation ecstasy
Is very cunning in.

HAMLET: Ecstasy!
My pulse, as yours, doth temperately keep time.
160 And makes as healthful music: it is not madness
That I have utter'd: bring me to the test,
And I the matter will re-word; which madness
Would gambol from. Mother, for love of grace,
Lay not that flattering unction to your soul,
165 That not your trespass, but my madness speaks:
It will but skin and film the ulcerous place,
Whilst rank corruption, mining all within,
Infects unseen. Confess yourself to Heaven;
Repent what's past; avoid what is to come;
170 And do not spread the compost on the weeds,
To make them ranker. Forgive me this my virtue;
For in the fatness° of these pursy times
Virtue itself of vice must pardon beg,
Yea, curb and woo for leave to do him good.
175 QUEEN: O Hamlet, thou hast cleft my heart in twain.

HAMLET: O, throw away the worser part of it,
And live the purer with the other half.
Good-night: but go not to mine uncle's bed;
Assume a virtue, if you have it not.
180 That monster custom, who all sense doth eat,
Of habits devil, is angel yet in this,—
That to the use of actions fair and good
He likewise gives a frock or livery
That aptly is put on. Refrain to-night;
185 And that shall lend a kind of easiness
To the next abstinence: the next more easy;
For use almost can change the stamp of nature,
And either curb the devil, or throw him out
With wondrous potency. Once more, good-night:

° *fatness:* Corruption.

And when you are desirous to be bless'd,   190
I'll blessing beg of you. — For this same lord [*pointing to Polonius*]
I do repent: but Heaven hath pleas'd it so,
To punish me with this, and this with me,
That I must be their° scourge and minister.
I will bestow him, and will answer well   195
The death I gave him. So, again, good-night.—
I must be cruel only to be kind:
Thus bad begins and worse remains behind.—
One word more, good lady.
QUEEN: What shall I do?   200
HAMLET: Not this, by no means, that I bid you do:
Let the bloat king tempt you again to bed;
Pinch wanton on your cheek; call you his mouse;
And let him, for a pair of reechy kisses,
Or paddling in your neck with his damn'd fingers,   205
Make you to ravel all this matter out,
That I essentially am not in madness,
But mad in craft. 'Twere good you let him know;
For who that's but a queen, fair, sober, wise,
Would from a paddock,° from a bat, a gib,°   210
Such dear concernings hide? who would do so?
No, in despite of sense and secrecy,
Unpeg the basket on the house's top,
Let the birds fly, and, like the famous ape,
To try conclusions, in the basket creep,   215
And break your own neck down.
QUEEN: Be thou assur'd, if words be made of breath
And breath of life, I have not life to breathe
What thou hast said to me.
HAMLET: I must to England; you know that?   220
QUEEN: Alack,
I had forgot: 'tis so concluded on.
HAMLET: There's letters seal'd: and my two school-fellows,—
Whom I will trust as I will adders fang'd,
They bear the mandate; they must sweep my way,   225
And marshal me to knavery. Let it work;
For 'tis the sport to have the éngineer
Hoist with his own petard: and't shall go hard
But I will delve one yard below their mines,

° *their:* Heaven's, or the heavens'.   ° *paddock:* Toad.   °*gib:* Tomcat.

230 And blow them at the moon: O, 'tis most sweet,
When in one line two crafts directly meet.—
This man shall set me packing:
I'll lug the guts into the neighbor room.—
Mother, good-night.— Indeed, this counsellor
235 Is now most still, most secret, and most grave,
Who was in life a foolish prating knave.
Come, sir, to draw toward an end with you:—
Good-night, mother.

Exeunt severally; Hamlet dragging out Polonius.

ACT 4
SCENE 1

A room in the castle.

Enter King, Queen, Rosencrantz, and Guildenstern.

KING: There's matter in these sighs, these prófound heaves:
You must translate: 'tis fit we understand them.
Where is your son?
QUEEN: Bestow this place on us a little while. [*To Rosencrantz and*
5 *Guildenstern, who go out*]
Ah, my good lord, what have I seen to-night!
KING: What, Gertrude? How does Hamlet?
QUEEN: Mad as the sea and wind, when both contend
Which is the mightier: in his lawless fit,
10 Behind the arras hearing something stir,
He whips his rapier out, and cries, A *rat, a rat!*
And, in this brainish apprehension,° kills
The unseen good old man.
KING: O heavy deed!
15 It had been so with us had we been there:
His liberty is full of threats to all;
To you yourself, to us, to every one.
Alas, how shall this bloody deed be answer'd?
It will be laid to us, whose providence
20 Should have kept short, restrain'd, and out of haunt
This mad young man: but so much was our love,
We would not understand what was most fit;
But, like the owner of a foul disease,

° *brainish apprehension:* Mad notion.

To keep it from divulging, let it feed
Even on the pith of life. Where is he gone?   25
QUEEN: To draw apart the body he hath kill'd:
O'er whom his very madness, like some ore
Among a mineral of metals base,
Shows itself pure; he weeps for what is done.
KING: O Gertrude, come away!   30
The sun no sooner shall the mountains touch
But we will ship him hence: and this vile deed
We must, with all our majesty and skill,
Both countenance and excuse.— Ho, Guildenstern!

Enter Rosencrantz and Guildenstern.

Friends both, go join you with some further aid: 35
Hamlet in madness hath Polonius slain,
And from his mother's closet hath he dragg'd him:
Go seek him out; speak fair, and bring the body
Into the chapel. I pray you, haste in this.

Exeunt Rosencrantz and Guildenstern.

Come, Gertrude, we'll call up our wisest friends;   40
And let them know both what we mean to do
And what's untimely done: so haply slander,—
Whose whisper o'er the world's diameter,
As level as the cannon to his blank,
Transports his poison'd shot,— may amiss our name,   45
And hit the woundless air.— O, come away!
My soul is full of discord and dismay.

Exeunt.

SCENE 2

Another room in the castle.

Enter Hamlet.

HAMLET: Safely stowed.
ROSENCRANTZ and GUILDENSTERN: [*Within*] Hamlet! Lord Hamlet!
HAMLET: What noise? who calls on Hamlet?
O, here they come.

Enter Rosencrantz and Guildenstern.

ROSENCRANTZ: What have you done, my lord, with the dead body?   5
HAMLET: Compounded it with dust, whereto 'tis kin.

ROSENCRANTZ: Tell us where 'tis, that we may take it thence,
  And bear it to the chapel.
HAMLET: Do not believe it.
10 ROSENCRANTZ: Believe what?
HAMLET: That I can keep your counsel, and not mine own. Besides, to be
  demanded of a sponge! — what replication should be made by the son of
  a king?
ROSENCRANTZ: Take you me for a sponge, my lord?
15 HAMLET: Ay, sir; that soaks up the king's countenance, his rewards, his
  authorities. But such officers do the king best service in the end: he keeps
  them, like an ape, in the corner of his jaw; first mouthed, to be last
  swallowed: when he needs what you have gleaned, it is but squeezing you,
  and, sponge, you shall be dry again.
20 ROSENCRANTZ: I understand you not, my lord.
HAMLET: I am glad of it: a knavish speech sleeps in a foolish ear.
ROSENCRANTZ: My lord, you must tell us where the body is, and go with us to
  the king.
HAMLET: The body is with the king, but the king is not with the body. The
25   king is a thing, —
GUILDENSTERN: A thing, my lord!
HAMLET: Of nothing: bring me to him.
  Hide fox, and all after.

Exeunt.

SCENE 3

Another room in the castle.

Enter King, attended.

KING: I have sent to seek him, and to find the body.
  How dangerous is it that this man goes loose!
  Yet must not we put the strong law on him:
  He's lov'd of the distracted multitude,
5   Who like not in their judgment, but their eyes;
  And where 'tis so, the offender's scourge is weigh'd,
  But never the offence. To bear all smooth and even,
  This sudden sending him away must seem
  Deliberate pause: diseases desperate grown
10   By desperate appliance are reliev'd,
  Or not at all.

Enter Rosencrantz.

  How now! what hath befallen!

Rosencrantz: Where the dead body is bestow'd, my lord,
We cannot get from him.
King: But where is he? 15
Rosencrantz: Without, my lord; guarded, to know your pleasure.
King: Bring him before us.
Rosencrantz: Ho, Guildenstern! bring in my lord.

Enter Hamlet and Guildenstern.

King: Now, Hamlet, where's Polonius?
Hamlet: At supper. 20
King: At supper! where?
Hamlet: Not where he eats, but where he is eaten: a certain convocation of
politic worms are e'en at him. Your worm is your only emperor for diet: we
fat all creatures else to fat us, and we fat ourselves for maggots: your fat king
and your lean beggar is but variable service,— two dishes, but to one table: 25
that's the end.
King: Alas, alas!
Hamlet: A man may fish with the worm that hath eat of a king, and eat of
the fish that hath fed of that worm.
King: What does thou mean by this? 30
Hamlet: Nothing but to show you how a king may go a progress through the
guts of a beggar.
King: Where is Polonius?
Hamlet: In heaven; send thither to see: if your messenger find him not there,
seek him i' the other place yourself. But, indeed, if you find him not within 35
this month, you shall nose him as you go up the stairs into the lobby.
King: Go seek him there. [*To some Attendants*]
Hamlet: He will stay till ye come.

Exeunt Attendants.

King: Hamlet, this deed, for thine especial safety,—
Which we do tender, as we dearly grieve 40
For that which thou hast done,— must send thee hence
With fiery quickness: therefore prepare thyself;
The bark is ready, and the wind at help,
The associates tend, and everything is bent
For England. 45
Hamlet: For England!
King: Ay, Hamlet.
Hamlet: Good.
King: So is it, if thou knew'st our purposes.
Hamlet: I see a cherub that sees them.— But, come; for England!— 50
Farewell, dear mother.
King: Thy loving father, Hamlet.

HAMLET: My mother: father and mother is man and wife; man and wife is one
   flesh; and so, my mother.— Come, for England! [*Exit.*]
55 KING: Follow him at foot; tempt him with speed aboard;
   Delay it not; I'll have him hence to-night:
   Away! for everything is seal'd and done
   That else leans on the affair, pray you, make haste.

Exeunt Rosencrantz and Guildenstern.

   And, England, if my love thou hold'st at aught,—
60   As my great power thereof may give thee sense,
   Since yet thy cicatrice looks raw and red
   After the Danish sword, and thy free awe
   Pays homage to us,— thou mayst not coldly set
   Our sovereign process; which imports at full,
65   By letters conjuring to that effect,
   The present death of Hamlet. Do it, England;
   For like the hectic in my blood he rages,
   And thou must cure me: till I know 'tis done,
   Howe'er my haps, my joys will ne'er begin. [*Exit.*]

SCENE 4

A plain in Denmark.

Enter Fortinbras, and Forces marching.

FORTINBRAS: Go, from me greet the Danish king:
   Tell him that, by his license, Fortinbras
   Craves the conveyance of a promis'd march
   Over his kingdom. You know the rendezvous,
5   If that his majesty would aught with us,
   We shall express our duty in his eye,
   And let him know so.
CAPTAIN: I will do't, my lord.
FORTINBRAS: Go softly on.

Exeunt Fortinbras and Forces.

Enter Hamlet, Rosencrantz, Guildenstern, &c.

10 HAMLET: Good sir, whose powers are these?
CAPTAIN: They are of Norway, sir.
HAMLET: How purpos'd, sir, I pray you?
CAPTAIN: Against some part of Poland.
HAMLET: Who commands them, sir?
15 CAPTAIN: The nephew to old Norway, Fortinbras.

HAMLET: Goes it against the main of Poland, sir,
  Or for some frontier?
CAPTAIN: Truly to speak, and with no addition,
  We go to gain a little patch of ground
  That hath in it no profit but the name.   20
  To pay five ducats, five, I would not farm it;
  Nor will it yield to Norway or the Pole
  A ranker° rate should it be sold in fee.
HAMLET: Why, then the Polack never will defend it.
CAPTAIN: Yes, it is already garrison'd.   25
HAMLET: Two thousand souls and twenty thousand ducats
  Will not debate the question of this straw:
  This is the imposthume° of much wealth and peace,
  That inward breaks, and shows no cause without
  Why the man dies.— I humbly thank you, sir.   30
CAPTAIN: God b' wi' you, sir. [*Exit.*]
ROSENCRANTZ: Will't please you go, my lord?
HAMLET: I'll be with you straight. Go a little before.

Exeunt all but Hamlet.

  How all occasions do inform against me,
  And spur my dull revenge! What is a man,   35
  If his chief good and market of his time
  Be but to sleep and feed? a beast, no more.
  Sure he that made us with such large discourse,°
  Looking before and after, gave us not
  That capability and godlike reason   40
  To fust° in us unus'd. Now, whether it be
  Bestial oblivion or some craven scruple
  Of thinking too precisely on the event,—
  A thought which, quarter'd, hath but one part wisdom
  And ever three parts coward,— I do not know   45
  Why yet I live to say, *This thing's to do*;
  Sith° I have cause, and will, and strength, and means
  To do't. Examples, gross as earth, exhort me:
  Witness this army, of such mass and charge,
  Led by a delicate and tender prince;   50
  Whose spirit, with divine ambition puff'd,
  Makes mouths at the invisible event;
  Exposing what is mortal and unsure

° *ranker:* Dearer.   ° *imposthume:* Ulcer.   ° *discourse:* Reasoning faculty.   ° *fust:* Grow musty.   ° *Sith:* Since.

To all that fortune, death, and danger dare,
55 Even for an egg-shell. Rightly to be great
Is not to stir without great argument,
But greatly to find quarrel in a straw
When honor's at the stake. How stand I, then,
That have a father kill'd, a mother stain'd,
60 Excitements of my reason and my blood,
And let all sleep? while, to my shame, I see
The imminent death of twenty thousand men,
That, for a fantasy and trick of fame,
Go to their graves like beds; fight for a plot
65 Whereon the numbers cannot try the cause,
Which is not tomb enough and continent°
To hide the slain?— O, from this time forth,
My thoughts be bloody, or be nothing worth! [*Exit.*]

SCENE 5

Elsinore. A room in the castle.

Enter Queen and Horatio.

QUEEN: I will not speak with her.
HORATIO: She is importunate; indeed, distract:
Her mood will needs be pitied.
QUEEN: What would she have?
5 HORATIO: She speaks much of her father; says she hears
There's tricks i' the world; and hems, and beats her heart;
Spurns enviously at straws; speaks things in doubt,
That carry but half sense: her speech is nothing,
Yet the unshapéd use of it doth move
10 The hearers to collection; they aim at it,
And botch the words up fit to their own thoughts;
Which, as her winks, and nods, and gestures yield them,
Indeed would make one think there might be thought,
Though nothing sure, yet much unhappily.
15 'Twere good she were spoken with; for she may strew
Dangerous conjectures in ill-breeding minds.
QUEEN: Let her come in.

Exit Horatio.

° *continent:* Container.

To my sick soul, as sin's true nature is,
Each toy seems prologue to some great amiss:
So full of artless jealousy is guilt,   20
It spills itself in fearing to be spilt.

Re-enter Horatio and Ophelia.

OPHELIA: Where is the beauteous majesty of Denmark?
QUEEN: How now, Ophelia!
OPHELIA: [*Sings*]

> How should I your true love know   25
>   From another one?
> By his cockle hat and staff,
>   And his sandal shoon.

QUEEN: Alas, sweet lady, what imports this song?
OPHELIA: Say you? nay, pray you, mark.   30

Sings

> He is dead and gone, lady,
>   He is dead and gone;
> At his head a grass green turf,
>   At his heels a stone.

QUEEN: Nay, but, Ophelia, —   35
OPHELIA: Pray you, mark.

Sings

> White his shroud as the mountain snow,

Enter King.

QUEEN: Alas, look here, my lord.
OPHELIA: [*Sings*]

> Larded with sweet flowers;   40
> Which bewept to the grave did go
> With true-love showers.

KING: How do you, pretty lady?
OPHELIA: Well, God 'ild you!° They say the owl was a baker's daughter.
    Lord, we know what we are, but know not what we may be.   45
    God be at your table!
KING: Conceit upon her father.

OPHELIA: Pray you, let's have no words of this; but when they ask you what it
    means, say you this:

° *ild you:* Yield you — i.e., reward you.

Sings.

50   To-morrow is Saint Valentine's day
                All in the morning betime,
            And I a maid at your window,
                To be your Valentine.
            Then up he rose, and donn'd his clothes,
55   And dupp'd the chamber-door;
            Let in the maid, that out a maid
                Never departed more.

KING: Pretty Ophelia!
OPHELIA: Indeed, la, without an oath, I'll make an end on't;

Sings

60   By Gis ° and by Saint Charity,
                Alack, and fie for shame!
            Young men will do't, if they come to't;
                By cock, they are to blame.
            Quoth she, before you tumbled me,
65   You promis'd me to wed.
            So would I ha' done, by yonder sun,
                An thou hadst not come to my bed.

KING: How long hath she been thus?
OPHELIA: I hope all will be well. We must be patient: but I cannot choose but
70   weep, to think they should lay him i' the cold ground. My brother shall
       know of it: and so I thank you; for your good counsel.— Come, my
       coach!— Good-night, ladies; good-night, sweet ladies; good-night, good-
       night. [*Exit.*]
KING: Follow her close; give her good watch, I pray you.

Exit Horatio.

75   O, this is the poison of deep grief; it springs
       All from her father's death. O Gertrude, Gertrude,
       When sorrows come, they come not single spies,
       But in battalions! First, her father slain:
       Next, your son gone; and he most violent author
80   Of his own just remove: the people muddied,
       Thick and unwholesome in their thoughts and whispers
       For good Polonius' death; and we have done but greenly
       In hugger-mugger ° to inter him: poor Ophelia
       Divided from herself and her fair judgment,
85   Without the which we are pictures, or mere beasts:
       Last, and as much containing as all these,

° *Gis:* A contraction for "by Jesus."   ° *In hugger-mugger:* In great secrecy and haste.

Her brother is in secret come from France;
Feeds on his wonder, keeps himself in clouds,
And wants not buzzers to infect his ear
With pestilent speeches of his father's death;   90
Wherein necessity, of matter beggar'd,
Will nothing stick our person to arraign
In ear and ear. O my dear Gertrude, this,
Like to a murdering piece,° in many places
Gives me superfluous death.   95

A noise within.

QUEEN: Alack, what noise is this?
KING: Where are my Switzers?° let them guard the door.

Enter a Gentleman.

What is the matter?
GENTLEMAN: Save yourself, my lord:
The ocean, overpeering of his list,   100
Eats not the flats with more impetuous haste
Than young Laertes, in a riotous head,
O'erbears your officers. The rabble call him lord;
And, as the world were now but to begin,
Antiquity forgot, custom not known,   105
The ratifiers and props of every word,
They cry, *Choose we, Laertes shall be king!*
Caps, hands, and tongues applaud it to the clouds,
Laertes shall be king, Laertes king!
QUEEN: How cheerfully on the false trail they cry!   110
O, this is counter, you false Danish dogs!
KING: The doors are broke.

Noise within.

Enter Laertes armed; Danes following.

LAERTES: Where is this king?— Sirs, stand you all without.
DANES: No, let's come in.
LAERTES: I pray you, give me leave.   115
DANES: We will, we will. [*They retire without the door.*]
LAERTES: I thank you:— keep the door.— O thou vile king,
Give me my father!
QUEEN: Calmly, good Laertes.
LAERTES: That drop of blood that's calm proclaims me bastard;   120
Cries cuckold to my father; brands the harlot

°*murdering piece:* A cannon.   °*Switzers:* Bodyguard of Swiss mercenaries.

Even here, between the chaste unsmirched brow
Of my true mother.

KING: What is the cause, Laertes,
125   That thy rebellion looks so giant-like?—
Let him go, Gertrude; do not fear our person:
There's such divinity doth hedge a king,
That treason can but peep to what it would,
Acts little of his will.—Tell me, Laertes,
130   Why thou art thus incens'd.—Let him go, Gertrude:—
Speak, man.

LAERTES: Where is my father?

KING: Dead.

QUEEN: But not by him.

135 KING: Let him demand his fill.

LAERTES: How came he dead? I'll not be juggled with:
To hell, allegiance! vows, to the blackest devil!
Conscience and grace, to the profoundest pit!
I dare damnation:— to this point I stand,—
140   That both the worlds I give to negligence,
Let come what comes; only I'll be reveng'd
Most thoroughly for my father.

KING: Who shall stay you?

LAERTES: My will, not all the world:
145   And for my means, I'll husband them so well,
They shall go far with little.

KING: Good Laertes,
If you desire to know the certainty
Of your dear father's death, is't writ in your revenge
150   That, sweepstake, you will draw both friend and foe,
Winner or loser?

LAERTES: None but his enemies.

KING: Will you know them, then?

LAERTES: To his good friends thus wide I'll ope my arms;
155   And, like the kind life-rendering pelican,°
Repast them with my blood.

KING: Why, now you speak
Like a good child and a true gentleman.
That I am guiltless of your father's death,
160   And am most sensible in grief for it,
It shall as level to your judgment pierce
As day does to your eye.

° *life-rendering pelican:* The mother pelican was believed to draw blood from herself to feed her young.

DANES: [*Within*]   Let her come in.

LAERTES: How now! what noise is that?

Re-enter Ophelia, fantastically dressed with straws and flowers.

O heat, dry up my brains! tears seven times salt   165
Burn out the sense and virtue of mine eyes! —
By heaven, thy madness shall be paid by weight
Till our scale turn the beam. O rose of May!
Dear maid, kind sister, sweet Ophelia! —
O heavens! is't possible a young maid's wits   170
Should be as mortal as an old man's life!
Nature is fine in love; and where 'tis fine
It sends some precious instance of itself
After the thing it loves.

OPHELIA: [*Sings*]   175

    They bore him barefac'd on the bier;
      Hey no nonny, nonny, hey nonny;
    And on his grave rain'd many a tear, —
      Fare you well, my dove!

LAERTES: Hadst thou thy wits, and didst persuade revenge,   180
It could not move thus.

OPHELIA: You must sing, *Down-a-down, and you call him a-down-a.* O, how the
wheel becomes it! It is the false steward, that stole his master's daughter.

LAERTES: This nothing's more than matter.

OPHELIA: There's rosemary, that's for remembrance; pray, love, remember: and   185
there is pansies that's for thoughts.

LAERTES: A document in madness, — thoughts and remembrance fitted.

OPHELIA: There's fennel for you, and columbines: — there's rue for you; and
here's some for me: — we may call it herb-grace o' Sundays: —
O, you must wear your rue with a difference. — There's a daisy: — I would   190
give you some violets, but they withered all when my father died: — they
say, he made a good end, —

Sings

    For bonny sweet Robin is all my joy, —

LAERTES: Thoughts and affliction, passion, hell itself,
She turns to favor and to prettiness.   195

OPHELIA: [*Sings*]

    And will he not come again?
    And will he not come again?
      No, no, he is dead,
      Go to thy death-bed,   200
    He never will come again.

    His beard was as white as snow

All flaxen was his poll:
   He is gone, he is gone,
205   And we cast away moan:
God ha' mercy on his soul!

And of all Christian souls, I pray God.— God b' wi' ye. [*Exit.*]

LAERTES: Do you see this, O God?
KING: Laertes, I must commune with your grief,
210   Or you deny me right. Go but apart,
Make choice of whom your wisest friends you will,
And they shall hear and judge 'twixt you and me:
If by direct or by collateral hand
They find us touch'd, we will our kingdom give,
215   Our crown, our life, and all that we call ours,
To you in satisfaction; but if not,
Be you content to lend your patience to us,
And we shall jointly labor with your soul
To give it due content.
220 **LAERTES:**   Let this be so;
His means of death, his obscure burial,—
No trophy, sword, nor hatchment° o'er his bones
No noble rite nor formal ostentation,—
Cry to be heard, as 'twere from heaven to earth,
225   That I must call't in question.
KING: So you shall;
And where the offence is, let the great axe fall.
I pray you, go with me.

Exeunt.

SCENE 6

Another room in the castle.

Enter Horatio and a Servant.

HORATIO: What are they that would speak with me?
SERVANT: Sailors, sir: they say they have letters for you.
HORATIO: Let them come in.—

Exit Servant.

I do not know from what part of the world
5   I should be greeted, if not from Lord Hamlet.

° *hatchment:* A tablet with coat of arms.

Enter Sailors.

1ST SAILOR: God bless you, sir.

HORATIO: Let him bless thee too.

1ST SAILOR: He shall, sir, an't please him. There's a letter for you, sir; it comes
    from the ambassador that was bound for England; if your name be Horatio,
    as I am let to know it is.   10

HORATIO: [*Reads*] *Horatio, when thou shalt have overlooked this, give these*
    fellows some means to the king: they have letters for him. Ere we were two
    days old at sea, a pirate of very warlike appointment gave us chase. Finding
    ourselves too slow of sail, we put on a compelled valor; and in the
    grapple I boarded them; on the instant they got clear of our ship; so I alone   15
    became their prisoner. They have dealt with me like thieves of mercy: but
    they knew what they did; I am to do a good turn for them. Let the king
    have the letters I have sent; and repair thou to me with as much haste as thou
    wouldst fly death. I have words to speak in thine ear will make thee dumb;
    yet are they much too light for the bore of the matter. These good fellows   20
    will bring thee where I am. Rosencrantz and Guildenstern hold their course
    for England: of them I have much to tell thee. Farewell. He that thou knowest
    thine.

                                                 Hamlet

Come, I will give you way for these your letters;   25
And do't the speedier, that you may direct me
To him from whom you brought them.

Exeunt.

SCENE 7

Another room in the castle.

Enter King and Laertes.

KING: Now must your conscience my acquittance seal,
    And you must put me in your heart for friend,
    Sith you have heard, and with a knowing ear,
    That he which hath your noble father slain
    Pursu'd my life.   5

LAERTES: It well appears:—but tell me
    Why you proceeded not against these feats,
    So crimeful and so capital in nature,
    As by your safety, wisdom, all things else,
    You mainly were stirr'd up.   10

KING: O, for two special reasons;
    Which may to you, perhaps, seem much unsinew'd,
    But yet to me they are strong. The queen his mother

Lives almost by his looks; and for myself,—
15   My virtue or my plague, be it either which,—
She's so conjunctive to my life and soul,
That, as the star moves not but in his sphere,
I could not but by her. The other motive,
Why to a public count I might not go,
20   Is the great love the general gender bear him;
Who, dipping all his faults in their affection,
Would, like the spring that turneth wood to stone,
Convert his gyves to graces; so that my arrows,
Too slightly timber'd for so loud a wind,
25   Would have reverted to my bow again,
And not where I had aim'd them.

LAERTES: And so have I a noble father lost;
A sister driven into desperate terms,—
Whose worth, if praises may go back again,
30   Stood challenger on mount of all the age
For her perfections:—but my revenge will come.

KING: Break not your sleeps for that: you must not think
That we are made of stuff so flat and dull
That we can let our beard be shook with danger,
35   And think it pastime. You shortly shall hear more:
I lov'd your father, and we love ourself;
And that, I hope, will teach you to imagine,—

Enter a Messenger.

How now! what news?
MESSENGER: Letters, my lord, from Hamlet:
40   This to your majesty; this to the queen.
KING: From Hamlet! Who brought them?
MESSENGER: Sailors, my lord, they say; I saw them not:
They were given me by Claudio,—he receiv'd them
Of him that brought them.
45 KING: Laertes, you shall hear them.—Leave us.

Exit Messenger.

[*Reads*] *High and mighty,—You shall know I am set naked on your kingdom.
To-morrow shall I beg leave to see your kingly eyes: when I shall, first asking
your pardon thereunto, recount the occasions of my sudden and more strange
return.*   Hamlet

50   What should this mean? Are all the rest come back?
Or is it some abuse,° and no such thing?

° *abuse:* Ruse.

LAERTES: Know you the hand?
KING: 'Tis Hamlet's character:°—*Naked*,—
And in a postscript here, he says, *alone*.
Can you advise me?   55
LAERTES: I am lost in it, my lord. But let him come;
It warms the very sickness in my heart,
That I shall live, and tell him to his teeth,
Thus diddest thou.
KING: If it be so, Laertes,—   60
As how should it be so? how otherwise?—
Will you be rul'd by me?
LAERTES: Ay, my lord:
So you will not o'errule me to a peace.
KING: To thine own peace. If he be now return'd,—   65
As checking at his voyage, and that he means
No more to undertake it,—I will work him
To an exploit, now ripe in my device,
Under the which he shall not choose but fall:
And for his death no wind of blame shall breathe;   70
But even his mother shall uncharge the practice
And call it accident.
LAERTES: My lord, I will be rul'd;
The rather if you could devise it so
That I might be the organ.   75
KING: It falls right.
You have been talk'd of since your travel much,
And that in Hamlet's hearing, for a quality
Wherein they say you shine: your sum of parts
Did not together pluck such envy from him   80
As did that one; and that, in my regard,
Of the unworthiest siege.
LAERTES: What part is that, my lord?
KING: A very riband in the cap of youth,
Yet needful too; for youth no less becomes   85
The light and careless livery that it wears
Than settled age his sables and his weeds,
Importing health and graveness.—Two months since,
Here was a gentleman of Normandy,—
I've seen myself, and serv'd against, the French,   90
And they can well on horseback: but this gallant
Had witchcraft in't; he grew unto his seat;
And to such wondrous doing brought his horse,

° *character:* Handwriting.

As he had been incorps'd and demi-natur'd°
95 With the brave beast: so far he topp'd my thought,
That I, in forgery of shapes and tricks,°
Come short of what he did.
LAERTES: A Norman was't?
KING: A Norman.
100 LAERTES: Upon my life, Lamond.
KING: The very same.
LAERTES: I know him well: he is the brooch, indeed,
And gem of all the nation.
KING: He made confession of you;
105 And gave you such a masterly report
For art and exercise in your defence,
And for your rapier most especially,
That he cried out, 'twould be a sight indeed
If one could match you: the scrimers° of their nation,
110 He swore, had neither motion, guard, nor eye,
If you oppos'd them. Sir, this report of his
Did Hamlet so envenom with his envy,
That he could nothing do but wish and beg
Your sudden coming o'er, to play with him.
115 Now, out of this,—
LAERTES: What out of this, my lord?
KING: Laertes, was your father dear to you?
Or are you like the painting of a sorrow,
A face without a heart?
120 LAERTES: Why ask you this?
KING: Not that I think you did not love your father;
But that I know love is begun by time;
And that I see, in passages of proof,°
Time qualifies the spark and fire of it.
125 There lives within the very flame of love
A kind of wick or snuff that will abate it;
And nothing is at a like goodness still;
For goodness, growing to a pleurisy,°
Dies in his own too much: that we would do
130 We should do when we would; for this *would* changes,
And hath abatements and delays as many
As there are tongues, or hands, or accidents;

° *As . . . demi-natur'd:* Made as one body and formed into half man, half horse — or centaur.   ° *in forgery . . . tricks:* In imagining tricks of horsemanship.   ° *scrimers:* Fencers.   ° *passages of proof:* The evidence of experience.   ° *pleurisy:* Plethora, an excess of blood.

And then this *should* is like a spendthrift sigh
That hurts by easing. But to the quick o' the ulcer:
Hamlet comes back: what would you undertake   135
To show yourself your father's son in deed
More than in words?
LAERTES: To cut his throat i' the church.
KING: No place, indeed, should murder sanctuarize;
Revenge should have no bounds. But, good Laertes,   140
Will you do this, keep close within your chamber.
Hamlet return'd shall know you are come home:
We'll put on those shall praise your excellence,
And set a double varnish on the fame
The Frenchman gave you; bring you, in fine, together,   145
And wager on yours heads: he, being remiss,°
Most generous, and free from all contriving,
Will not peruse the foils; so that, with ease,
Or with a little shuffling, you may choose
A sword unbated, and, in a pass of practice,   150
Requite him for your father.
LAERTES: I will do't it:
And, for that purpose, I'll anoint my sword.
I bought an unction of a mountebank,
So mortal that but dip a knife in it,   155
Where it draws blood no cataplasm so rare,°
Collected from all simples that have virtue
Under the moon, can save the thing from death
That is but scratch'd withal: I'll touch my point
With this contagion, that, if I gall him slightly,   160
It may be death.

KING: Let's further think of this;
Weigh what convenience both of time and means
May fit us to our shape: if this should fail,
And that our drift look through our bad performance,   165
'Twere better not assay'd: therefore this project
Should have a back or second, that might hold
If this should blast in proof. Soft! let me see:—
We'll make a solemn wager on your cunnings,—
I ha't: 170
When in your motion you are hot and dry,—
As make your bouts more violent to that end,—

° *remiss:* Unguarded and free from suspicion.   ° *no cataplasm so rare:* No poultice, however remarkably efficacious.

And that he calls for drink, I'll have prepar'd him
A chalice for the nonce;° whereon but sipping,
If he by chance escape your venom'd stuck
Our purpose may hold there.

Enter Queen.

                                        How now, sweet queen!
QUEEN: One woe doth tread upon another's heel,
    So fast they follow:— your sister's drown'd, Laertes.
180 LAERTES: Drown'd! O, where?
QUEEN: There is a willow grows aslant a brook,
    That shows his hoar leaves in the glassy stream;
    There with fantastic garlands did she come
    Of crowflowers, nettles, daisies, and long purples,
185   That liberal shepherds give a grosser name,
    But our cold maids do dead men's fingers call them.
    There, on the pendant boughs her coronet weeds
    Clambering to hang, an envious° sliver broke;
    When down her weedy trophies and herself
190   Fell in the weeping brook. Her clothes spread wide;
    And, mermaid-like, awhile they bore her up:
    Which time she chanted snatches of old tunes;
    As one incapable of her own distress,
    Or like a creature native and indu'd
195   Unto that element: but long it could not be
    Till that her garments, heavy with their drink,
    Pull'd the poor wretch from her melodious lay
    To muddy death.
    LAERTES: Alas, then, she is drown'd?
200 QUEEN: Drown'd, drown'd.
    LAERTES: Too much of water hast thou, poor Ophelia,
    And therefore I forbid my tears: but yet
    It is our trick; nature her custom holds,
    Let shame say what it will: when these are gone,
205   The woman will be out.°— Adieu, my lord:
    I have a speech of fire, that fain would blaze,
    But that this folly douts it.° [*Exit.*]
    KING: Let's follow, Gertrude;
    How much I had to do to calm his rage!
210   Now fear I this will give it start again;
    Therefore let's follow.

° *nonce:* Purpose. ° *envious:* Malicious. ° *The women . . . out:* I.e., "I shall be ruthless."
° *douts it:* Drowns it.

Exeunt.

ACT 5
SCENE 1

A churchyard.

Enter two Clowns° with spades, &c.

1ST CLOWN: Is she to be buried in Christian burial that wilfully seeks her own salvation?

2ND CLOWN: I tell thee she is; and therefore make her grave straight: the crowner° hath sat on her, and finds it Christian burial.

1ST CLOWN: How can that be, unless she drowned herself in her own defence? 5

2ND CLOWN: Why, 'tis found so.

1ST CLOWN: It must be *se offendendo,*° it cannot be else. For here lies the point: if I drown myself wittingly, it argues an act: and an act hath three branches; it is to act, to do, and to perform: argal,° she drowned herself wittingly. 10

2ND CLOWN: Nay, but hear you, goodman delver,—

1ST CLOWN: Give me leave. Here lies the water; good: here stands the man; good: if the man go to this water and drown himself, it is, will he, nill he, he goes,—mark you that: but if the water come to him and drown him, he drowns not himself: argal, he that is not guilty of his own death shortens 15 not his own life.

2ND CLOWN: But is this law?

1ST CLOWN: Ay, marry, is't; crowner's quest law.

2ND CLOWN: Will you ha' the truth on't? If this had not been a gentlewoman she should have been buried out of Christian burial. 20

1ST CLOWN: Why, there thou say'st: and the more pity that great folks should have countenance in this world to drown or hang themselves more than their even-Christian.°— Come, my spade. There is no ancient gentlemen but gardeners, ditchers, and grave-makers; they hold up Adam's profession.

2ND CLOWN: Was he a gentleman? 25

1ST CLOWN: He was the first that ever bore arms.

2ND CLOWN: Why, he had none.

1ST CLOWN: What, art a heathen? How dost thou understand the Scripture? The Scripture says, Adam digged: could he dig without arms? I'll put another question to thee: if thou answerest me not to the purpose, confess 30 thyself,°—

2ND CLOWN: Go to.

° *Clowns:* Rustic fellows.   ° *crowner:* Coroner.   ° *se offendendo:* In self-offense; he means *se defendendo,* in self-defense.   ° *argal:* He means *ergo,* therefore.   ° *even-Christian:* Fellow Christian.   ° *confess thyself:* "Confess thyself an ass," perhaps.

1st Clown: What is he that builds stronger than either the mason, the shipwright, or the carpenter?

35 **2nd Clown:** The gallows-maker; for that frame outlives a thousand tenants.

1st Clown: I like thy wit well, in good faith: the gallows does well; but how does it well? it does well to those that do ill: now thou dost ill to say the gallows is built stronger than the church: argal, the gallows may do well to thee. To't again, come.

40 **2nd Clown:** Who builds stronger than a mason, a shipwright, or a carpenter?

1st Clown: Ay, tell me that, and unyoke.

2nd Clown: Marry, now I can tell.

1st Clown: To't.

2nd Clown: Mass, I cannot tell.

Enter Hamlet and Horatio, at a distance.

45 **1st Clown:** Cudgel thy brains no more about it, for your dull ass will not mend his pace with beating; and when you are asked this question next, say a grave-maker; the houses that he makes last till doomsday. Go, get thee to Yaughan: fetch me a stoup of liquor.

Exit Second Clown.

Digs and sings.

> In youth, when I did love, did love,
> 50   Methought it was very sweet,
> To contract, O, the time, for, ah, my behove,°
>   O, methought there was nothing meet.

Hamlet: Has this fellow no feeling of his business, that he sings at grave-making?

55 **Horatio:** Custom hath made it in him a property of easiness.

Hamlet: 'Tis e'en so: the hand of little employment hath the daintier sense.

1st Clown: [*Sings*]

> But age, with his stealing steps,
>   Hath claw'd me in his clutch,
> 60 And hath shipp'd me intil the land,
>   As if I had never been such.

Throws up a skull.

Hamlet: That skull had a tongue in it, and could sing once: how the knave joels° it to the ground, as if it were Cain's jawbone, that did the first murder! This might be the pate of a politician, which this ass now 65 o'erreaches; one that would circumvent God, might it not?

Horatio: It might, my lord.

° *behove:* Behoof, or advantage.   ° *joels:* Throws.

HAMLET: Or of a courtier; which could say, *Good-morrow, sweet lord! How dost thou, good lord?* This might be my lord such-a-one, that praised my lord such-a-one's horse, when he meant to beg it,—might it not?
HORATIO: Ay, my lord. 70
HAMLET: Why, e'en so: and now my Lady Worm's; chapless,° and knocked about the mazard° with a sexton's spade: here's fine revolution, an we had the trick to see't. Did these bones cost no more the breeding but to play at loggats° with 'em? Mine ache to think on't.
1ST CLOWN: [*Sings*] 75

> A pick-axe and a spade, a spade,
>   For and a shrouding sheet:
> O, a pit of clay for to be made
>   For such a guest is meet.

Throws up another.

HAMLET: There's another: why may not that be the skull of a lawyer? Where 80 be his quiddits° now, his quillets,° his cases, his tenures, and his tricks? why does he suffer this rude knave now to knock him about the sconce with a dirty shovel, and will not tell him of his action of battery? Hum! This fellow might be in's time a great buyer of land, with his statutes, his recognizances, his fines, his double vouchers, his recoveries: is this the fine of his fines, and 85 the recovery of his recoveries, to have his fine pate full of fine dirt? will his vouchers vouch him no more of his purchases, and double ones too, than the length and breadth of a pair of indentures? The very conveyances of his lands will hardly lie in this box; and must the inheritor himself have no more, ha? 90
HORATIO: Not a jot more, my lord.
HAMLET: Is not parchment made of sheep-skins?
HORATIO: Ay, my lord, and of calf-skins too.
HAMLET: They are sheep and calves which seek out assurance in that. I will speak to this fellow.—Whose grave's this, sir? 95
1ST CLOWN: Mine, sir.—[*Sings*]

> O, a pit of clay for to be made
>   For such a guest is meet.

HAMLET: I think it be thine indeed; for thou liest in't.
1ST CLOWN: You lie out on't, sir, and therefore it is not yours: for my part, I do 100 not lie in't, and yet it is mine.
HAMLET: Thou dost lie in't, to be in't, and say it is thine: 'tis for the dead, not for the quick; therefore thou liest.

° *chapless:* Without a lower jaw.   ° *mazard:* Head.   ° *loggats:* A game in which small pieces of wood are hurled at a stake.   ° *quiddits:* Quiddities, "whatnesses"—that is, hair-splittings.   ° *quillets:* Quibbling distinctions.

1st Clown: 'Tis a quick lie, sir: 'twill away again from me to you.
105 Hamlet: What man dost thou dig it for?
1st Clown: For no man, sir.
Hamlet: What woman, then?
1st Clown: For none, neither.
Hamlet: Who is to be buried in't?
110 1st Clown: One that was a woman, sir; but, rest her soul, she's dead.
Hamlet: How absolute the knave is! we must speak by the card, or equivoca-
tion will undo us. By the Lord, Horatio, these three years I have taken note
of it; the age is grown so picked° that the toe of the peasant comes so near
the heel of the courtier, he galls his kibe.°—How long hast thou been a
115 grave-maker?
1st Clown: Of all the days i' the year, I came to't that day that our last King
Hamlet o'ercame Fortinbras.
Hamlet: How long is that since?
1st Clown: Cannot you tell that? every fool can tell that: it was the very day
120 that young Hamlet was born,—he that is mad, and sent into England.
Hamlet: Ay, marry, why was he sent into England?
1st Clown: Why, because he was mad: he shall recover his wits there; or, if
he do not, it's no great matter there.
Hamlet: Why?
125 1st Clown: 'Twill not be seen in him there; there the men are as mad as he.
Hamlet: How came he mad?
1st Clown: Very strangely, they say.
Hamlet: How strangely?
1st Clown: Faith, e'en with losing his wits.
130 Hamlet: Upon what ground?
1st Clown: Why, here in Denmark: I have been sexton here, man and boy,
thirty years.
Hamlet: How long will a man lie i' the earth ere he rot?
1st Clown: Faith, if he be not rotten before he die,—as we have many
135 pocky corses now-a-days, that will scarce hold the laying in,—he will last
you some eight year or nine year: a tanner will last you nine year.
Hamlet: Why he more than another?
1st Clown: Why, sir, his hide is so tanned with his trade that he will keep
out water a great while; and your water is a sore decayer of your whoreson
140 dead body. Here's a skull now; this skull has lain in the earth three-and-
twenty years.
Hamlet: Whose was it?
1st Clown: A whoreson mad fellow's it was: whose do you think it was?
Hamlet: Nay, I know not.

°*picked:* Refined or educated. °*galls his kibe:* Rubs and irritates the chilblain sore on the courtier's heel.

Richard Burton (left), Laurence Olivier (middle), and Mel Gibson (right) have all played the role of Hamlet.

1ST CLOWN: A pestilence on him for a mad rogue! 'a poured a flagon of   145
Rhenish on my head once. This same skull, sir, was Yorick's skull, the
king's jester.
HAMLET: This?
1ST CLOWN: E'en that.
HAMLET: Let me see. [*Takes the skull*]— Alas, poor Yorick!— I knew him,   150
Horatio; a fellow of infinite jest, of most excellent fancy: he hath borne me
on his back a thousand times; and now, how abhorred in my imagination it
is! my gorge rises at it. Here hung those lips that I have kissed I know not
how oft. Where be your gibes now? your gambols? your songs? your flashes
of merriment, that were wont to set the table on a roar? Not one now, to   155
mock your own grinning? quite chap-fallen? Now get you to my lady's
chamber, and tell her, let her paint an inch thick, to this favor° she must
come; make her laugh at that.— Pr'ythee, Horatio, tell me one thing.
HORATIO: What's that, my lord?
HAMLET: Dost thou think Alexander looked o' this fashion i' the earth?   160
HORATIO: E'en so.
HAMLET: And smelt so? pah! [*Throws down the skull*]
HORATIO: E'en so, my lord.
HAMLET: To what base uses we may return, Horatio! Why may not imagina-
tion trace the noble dust of Alexander till he find it stopping a bung-hole?   165
HORATIO: 'Twere to consider too curiously to consider so.
HAMLET: No, faith, not a jot; but to follow him thither with modesty enough,
and likelihood to lead it: as thus; Alexander died, Alexander was buried,

---

° *favor:* Face.

Alexander returneth into dust; the dust is earth; of earth we make loam;
170   and why of that loam whereto he was converted might they not stop
a beer-barrel?

Imperious Caesar, dead and turn'd to clay,
    Might stop a hole to keep the wind away:
    O, that that earth which kept the world in awe
175   Should patch a wall to expel the winter's flaw!—

But soft! but soft! aside.— Here comes the king.

*Enter Priests, &c., in procession; the corpse of Ophelia, Laertes and Mourners following;
King, Queen, their Trains, &c.*

The queen, the courtiers: who is that they follow?
And with such maimed rites? This doth betoken
The corse they follow did with desperate hand
180   Fordo its own life: 'twas of some estate.
Couch we awhile and mark. [*Retiring with Horatio*]
LAERTES: What ceremony else?
HAMLET: That is Laertes,
A very noble youth: mark.
185 **LAERTES:** What ceremony else?
1ST PRIEST: Her obsequies have been as far enlarg'd
As we have warrantise: her death was doubtful,
And, but that great command o'ersways the order,
She should in ground unsanctified have lodg'd
190   Till the last trumpet; for charitable prayers,
Shards, flints, and pebbles, should be thrown on her,
Yet here she is allowed her virgin rites,
Her maiden strewments, and the bringing home
Of bell and burial.
195 **LAERTES:** Must there no more be done?
1ST PRIEST: No more be done:
We should profane the service of the dead
To sing a *requiem*, and such rest to her
As to peace-parted souls.
200 **LAERTES:**   Lay her i' the earth;—
And from her fair and unpolluted flesh
May violets spring!— I tell thee, churlish priest,
A ministering angel shall my sister be
When thou liest howling.
205 **HAMLET:**   What, the fair Ophelia!
QUEEN: Sweets to the sweet: farewell! [*Scattering flowers*]
I hop'd thou shouldst have been my Hamlet's wife;

I thought thy bride-bed to have deck'd, sweet maid,
And not have strew'd thy grave.
LAERTES: O, treble woe   210
Fall ten times treble on that cursed head
Whose wicked deed thy most ingenious sense
Depriv'd thee of! — Hold off the earth awhile,
Till I have caught her once more in mine arms:

Leaps into the grave.

Now pile your dust upon the quick and dead,   215
Till of this flat a mountain you have made,
To o'er-top old Pelion° or the skyish head
Of blue Olympus.
HAMLET: [*Advancing*] What is he whose grief
Bears such an emphasis? whose phrase of sorrow   220
Conjures the wandering stars, and makes them stand
Like wonder-wounded hearers? this is I, Hamlet the
Dane. [*Leaps into the grave*]
LAERTES: The devil take thy soul! [*Grappling with him*]
HAMLET: Thou pray'st not well.   225
I pr'ythee, take thy fingers from my throat;
For, though I am not splenitive and rash,
Yet have I in me something dangerous,
Which let thy wiseness fear: away thy hand.
KING: Pluck them asunder.   230
QUEEN: Hamlet! Hamlet!
ALL: Gentlemen,—
HORATIO: Good my lord, be quiet.

The Attendants part them, and they come out of the grave.

HAMLET: Why, I will fight with him upon this theme
Until my eyelids will no longer wag.   235
QUEEN: O my son, what theme?
HAMLET: I lov'd Ophelia; forty thousand brothers
Could not, with all their quantity of love,
Make up my sum. — What wilt thou do for her?
KING: O, he is mad, Laertes.   240
QUEEN: For love of God, forbear him.
HAMLET: 'Swounds, show me what thou'lt do:
Woul't weep? woul't fight? woul't fast? woul't tear thyself?
Woul't drink up eisel?° eat a crocodile?

° *Pelion:* A mountain in Greece.   ° *eisel:* Vinegar.

245 I'll do't.—Dost thou come here to whine?
To outface me with leaping in her grave?
Be buried quick° with her, and so will I:
And, if thou prate of mountains, let them throw
Millions of acres on us, till our ground,
250 Singeing his pate against the burning zone,°
Make Ossa° like a wart! Nay, an thou'lt mouth,
I'll rant as well as thou.
QUEEN: This is mere madness:
And thus awhile the fit will work on him;
255 Anon, as patient as the female dove,
When that her golden couplets are disclos'd,°
His silence will sit drooping.
HAMLET: Hear you, sir;
What is the reason that you use me thus?
260 I lov'd you ever: but it is no matter;
Let Hercules himself do what he may,
The cat will mew, and dog will have his day. [Exit.]
KING: I pray thee, good Horatio, wait upon him.—

Exit Horatio.

[To Laertes] Strengthen your patience in our last night's speech;
265 We'll put the matter to the present push.—
Good Gertrude, set some watch over your son.—
This grave shall have a living monument:
An hour of quiet shortly shall we see;
Till then, in patience our proceeding be.

Exeunt.

SCENE 2

A hall in the castle.

Enter Hamlet and Horatio.

HAMLET: So much for this, sir: now let me see the other;
You do remember all the circumstance?
HORATIO: Remember it, my lord!
HAMLET: Sir, in my heart there was a kind of fighting
5 That would not let me sleep: methought I lay
Worse than the mutines in the bilboes.° Rashly,

° *quick:* Alive.   °*burning zone:* The fiery zone of the celestial sphere.   °*Ossa:* A high mountain in Greece.
°*When . . . are disclos'd:* When the golden twins are hatched.   °*mutines . . . bilboes:* Mutineers in the iron
stocks on board ship.

And prais'd be rashness for it,—let us know,
Our indiscretion sometimes serves us well,
When our deep plots do fail: and that should teach us
There's a divinity that shapes our ends,   10
Rough-hew them how we will.
HORATIO: This is most certain.
HAMLET: Up from my cabin,
    My sea-gown scarf'd about me, in the dark
    Grop'd I to find out them: had my desire;   15
    Finger'd their packet; and, in fine, withdrew
    To mine own room again: making so bold,
    My fears forgetting manners, to unseal
    Their grand commission; where I found, Horatio,
    O royal knavery! an exact command,—   20
    Larded with many several sorts of reasons,
    Importing Denmark's health and England's too,
    With, ho! such bugs° and goblins in my life,—
    That, on the supervise, no leisure bated,
    No, not to stay the grinding of the axe,   25
    My head should be struck off.
HORATIO: Is't possible?
HAMLET: Here's the commission: read it at more leisure.
    But wilt thou hear me how I did proceed?
HORATIO: I beseech you.   30
HAMLET: Being thus benetted round with villainies,—
    Ere I could make a prologue to my brains,
    They had begun the play,—I sat me down;
    Devis'd a new commission; wrote it fair:
    I once did hold it, as our statists do,   35
    A baseness to write fair, and labor'd much
    How to forget that learning; but, sir, now
    It did me yeoman's service. Wilt thou know
    The effect of what I wrote?
HORATIO: Ay, good my lord.   40
HAMLET: An earnest conjuration from the king,—
    As England was his faithful tributary;
    As love between them like the palm might flourish;
    As peace should still her wheaten garland wear
    And stand a comma° 'tween their amities;   45
    And many such like as's of great charge,—
    That, on the view and know of these contents,

° *bugs:* Bugbears.   ° *comma:* Link.

Without debatement further, more or less,
He should the bearers put to sudden death,
50   Not shriving-time allow'd.
HORATIO: How was this seal'd?
HAMLET: Why, even in that was heaven ordinant.
I had my father's signet in my purse,
Which was the model of that Danish seal:
55   Folded the writ up in form of the other;
Subscrib'd it; gav't the impression; plac'd it safely,
The changeling never known. Now, the next day
Was our sea-fight; and what to this was sequent
Thou know'st already.
60 **HORATIO:** So Guildenstern and Rosencrantz go to't.
HAMLET: Why, man, they did make love to this employment;
They are not near my conscience; their defeat
Does by their own insinuation° grow:
'Tis dangerous when the baser nature° comes
65   Between the pass and fell° incensed points
Of mighty opposites.
HORATIO: Why, what a king is this!
HAMLET: Does it not, think'st thee, stand me now upon,°
He that hath kill'd my king and whor'd my mother;
70   Popp'd in between the election and my hopes;
Thrown out his angle for my proper life,
And with such cozenage,° — is't not perfect conscience
To quit him with this arm? and is't not to be damn'd,
To let this canker of our nature come
75   In further evil?
HORATIO: It must be shortly known to him from England
What is the issue of the business there.
HAMLET: It will be short: the interim is mine;
And a man's life's no more than to say One.
80   But I am very sorry, good Horatio,
That to Laertes I forgot myself;
For by the image of my cause I see
The portraiture of his: I'll court his favors:
But, sure, the bravery° of his grief did put me
85   Into a towering passion.
HORATIO: Peace; who comes here?

Enter Osric.

° *insinuation:* By their own "sticking their noses" into the business.   ° *baser nature:* Men of lower rank.
° *fell:* Fierce.   ° *Does . . . upon:* I.e., "Don't you think it is my duty?"   ° *cozenage:* Deceit.   ° *bravery:* Ostentation.

OSRIC: Your lordship is right welcome back to Denmark.

HAMLET: I humbly thank you, sir.— Dost know this water-fly?

HORATIO: No, my good lord.

HAMLET: Thy state is the more gracious; for 'tis a vice to know him. He hath   90
much land, and fertile: let a beast be lord of beasts, and his crib shall stand
at the king's mess: 'tis a chough;° but, as I say, spacious in the possession
of dirt.

OSRIC: Sweet lord, if your lordship were at leisure, I should impart a thing to
you from his majesty.   95

HAMLET: I will receive it with all diligence of spirit. Put your bonnet to his
right use; 'tis for the head.

OSRIC: I thank your lordship, 'tis very hot.

HAMLET: No, believe me, 'tis very cold; the wind is northerly.

OSRIC: It is indifferent cold, my lord, indeed.   100

HAMLET: Methinks it is very sultry and hot for my complexion.

OSRIC: Exceedingly, my lord; it is very sultry,— as't were,— I cannot tell
how.— But, my lord, his majesty bade me signify to you that he has laid
a great wager on your head. Sir, this is the matter,—

HAMLET: I beseech you, remember,—   105

Hamlet moves him to put on his hat.

OSRIC: Nay, in good faith; for mine ease, in good faith. Sir, here is newly come
to court Laertes; believe me, an absolute gentleman, full of most excellent
differences, of very soft society and great showing: indeed, to speak feelingly
of him, he is the card or calendar of gentry, for you shall find in him the
continent of what part a gentleman would see.   110

HAMLET: Sir, his definement suffers no perdition in you;— though, I know, to
divide him inventorially would dizzy the arithmetic of memory, and yet but
yaw neither, in respect of his quick sail. But, in the verity of extolment,
I take him to be a soul of great article; and his infusion of such dearth° and
rareness as, to make true diction of him, his semblable is his mirror; and   115
who else would trace him, his umbrage,° nothing more.

OSRIC: Your lordship speaks most infallibly of him.

HAMLET: The concernancy, sir? why do we wrap the gentleman in our more
rawer breath?

OSRIC: Sir?   120

HORATIO: Is't not possible to understand in another tongue? You will do't
sir, really.

HAMLET: What imports the nomination° of this gentleman?

OSRIC: Of Laertes?

HORATIO: His purse is empty already; all's golden words are spent.   125

° *his crib . . . chough:* He shall have his trough at the king's table: he is a chattering fool.   ° *dearth:* Rareness, or
excellence.   ° *umbrage:* Shadow.   ° *nomination:* Naming.

HAMLET: Of him, sir.

OSRIC: I know, you are not ignorant,—

HAMLET: I would you did, sir; yet, in faith, if you did, it would not much approve me.°—Well, sir.

130 OSRIC: You are not ignorant of what excellence Laertes is,—

HAMLET: I dare not confess that, lest I should compare with him in excellence; but to know a man well were to know himself.

OSRIC: I mean, sir, for his weapon; but in the imputation laid on him by them, in his meed he's unfellowed.°

135 HAMLET: What's his weapon?

OSRIC: Rapier and dagger.

HAMLET: That's two of his weapons: but, well.

OSRIC: The king, sir, hath wagered with him six Barbary horses: against the which he has imponed,° as I take it, six French rapiers and poniards, with 140 their assigns, as girdle, hangers, and so: three of the carriages, in faith, are very dear to fancy, very responsive to the hilts, most delicate carriages, and of very liberal conceit.

HAMLET: What call you the carriages?

HORATIO: I knew you must be edified by the margent° ere you had done.

145 OSRIC: The carriages, sir, are the hangers.

HAMLET: The phrase would be more german to the matter if we could carry cannon by our sides: I would it might be hangers till then. But, on: six Barbary horses against six French swords, their assigns, and three liberal conceited carriages; that's the French bet against the Danish: why is this 150 imponed, as you call it?

OSRIC: The king, sir, hath laid, that in a dozen passes between you and him he shall not exceed you three hits: he hath laid on twelve for nine; and it would come to immediate trial if your lordship would vouchsafe the answer.

HAMLET: How if I answer no?

155 OSRIC: I mean, my lord, the opposition of your person in trial.°

HAMLET: Sir, I will walk here in the hall: if it please his majesty, it is the breathing time of day with me: let the foils be brought, the gentleman willing, and the king hold his purpose, I will win for him if I can; if not, I will gain nothing but my shame and the odd hits.

160 OSRIC: Shall I re-deliver you° e'en so?

HAMLET: To this effect, sir; after what flourish your nature will.

OSRIC: I commend my duty to your lordship.

HAMLET: Yours, yours.

Exit Osric.

° *if you . . . approve me:* If you, who are a fool, thought me not ignorant, that would not be particularly to my credit.   ° *in . . . unfellowed:* In his worth he has no equal.   ° *imponed:* Staked.   ° *edified . . . margent:* Informed by a note in the margin of your instructions.   ° *the opposition . . . trial:* The presence of your person as Laertes' opponent in the fencing contest.   ° *re-deliver you:* Carry back your answer.

He does well to commend it himself; there are no tongues else for's turn.

HORATIO: This lapwing runs away with the shell on his head.°   165

HAMLET: He did comply with his dug before he sucked it.° Thus has he,—
and many more of the same bevy, that I know the drossy age dotes on,—
only got the tune of the time, and outward habit of encounter; a kind of
yesty collection,° which carries them through and through the most
fanned and winnowed opinions; and do but blow them to their trial,   170
the bubbles are out.

Enter a Lord.

LORD: My lord, his majesty commended him to you by young Osric, who
brings back to him that you attend him in the hall: he sends to know if
your pleasure hold to play with Laertes, or that you will take longer time.

HAMLET: I am constant to my purposes; they follow the king's pleasure: if his   175
fitness speaks, mine is ready; now or whensoever, provided I be so able as now.

LORD: The king and queen and all are coming down.

HAMLET: In happy time.

LORD: The queen desires you to use some gentle entertainment to Laertes
before you fall to play.   180

HAMLET: She well instructs me.

Exit Lord.

HORATIO: You will lose this wager, my lord.

HAMLET: I do not think so; since he went into France I have been in
continual practice: I shall win at the odds. But thou wouldst not think
how ill all's here about my heart: but it is no matter.   185

HORATIO: Nay, good my lord,—

HAMLET: It is but foolery; but it is such a kind of gain-giving° as would
perhaps trouble a woman.

HORATIO: If your mind dislike anything, obey it: I will forestall their repair
hither, and say you are not fit.   190

HAMLET: Not a whit, we defy augury: there's a special providence in the fall of
a sparrow. If it be now, 'tis not to come; if it be not to come, it will be now;
if it be not now, yet it will come: the readiness is all. Since no man has
aught of what he leaves, what is't to leave betimes?°

Enter King, Queen, Laertes, Lords, Osric, and Attendants with foils, &c.   195

KING: Come, Hamlet, come, and take this hand from me.

The King puts Laertes' hand into Hamlet's.

HAMLET: Give me your pardon, sir: I have done you wrong:
But pardon't, as you are a gentleman.

° *This lapwing . . . head:* This precocious fellow is like a lapwing that starts running when it is barely out of the
shell.   ° *He . . . sucked it:* He paid compliments to his mother's breast before he sucked it.   ° *yesty collection:*
Yeasty or frothy affair.   ° *gain-giving:* Misgiving.   ° *what . . . betimes?:* What does an early death matter?

200   This presence knows, and you must needs have heard,
     How I am punish'd with sore distraction.
     What I have done,
     That might your nature, honor, and exception
     Roughly awake, I here proclaim was madness.
205   Was't Hamlet wrong'd Laertes? Never Hamlet:
     If Hamlet from himself be ta'en away,
     And when he's not himself does wrong Laertes,
     Then Hamlet does it not, Hamlet denies it.
     Who does it, then? His madness: if't be so,
210   Hamlet is of the faction that is wrong'd;
     His madness is poor Hamlet's enemy.
     Sir, in this audience,
     Let my disclaiming from a purpos'd evil
     Free me so far in your most generous thoughts
215   That I have shot mine arrow o'er the house
     And hurt my brother.
LAERTES: I am satisfied in nature,
     Whose motive, in this case, should stir me most
     To my revenge: but in my terms of honor
220   I stand aloof; and will no reconcilement
     Till by some elder masters of known honor
     I have a voice and precedent of peace
     To keep my name ungor'd. But till that time
     I do receive your offer'd love like love,
225   And will not wrong it.
HAMLET: I embrace it freely;
     And will this brother's wager frankly play.°—
     Give us the foils; come on.
LAERTES: Come, one for me.
230 **HAMLET:** I'll be your foil, Laertes; in mine ignorance
     Your skill shall, like a star in the darkest night,
     Stick fiery off indeed.
LAERTES: You mock me, sir.
HAMLET: No, by this hand.
235 **KING:** Give them the foils, young Osric.
     Cousin Hamlet,
     You know the wager?
HAMLET: Very well, my lord;
     Your grace hath laid the odds o' the weaker side.
240 **KING:** I do not fear it; I have seen you both;
     But since he's better'd, we have therefore odds.

° *frankly play:* Fence with a heart free from resentment.

Laertes: This is too heavy, let me see another.

Hamlet: This likes me well. These foils have all a length?

They prepare to play.

Osric: Ay, my good lord.

King: Set me the stoups of wine upon that table,—   245
    If Hamlet give the first or second hit,
    Or quit in answer of the third exchange,
    Let all the battlements their ordnance fire;
    The king shall drink to Hamlet's better breath;
    And in the cup an union° shall he throw,   250
    Richer than that which four successive kings
    In Denmark's crown have worn. Give me the cups;
    And let the kettle° to the trumpet speak,
    The trumpet to the cannoneer without,
    The cannons to the heavens, the heavens to earth,   255
    Now the king drinks to Hamlet. — Come, begin;—
    And you, the judges, bear a wary eye.

Hamlet: Come on, sir.

Laertes: Come, my lord.

They play.

Hamlet: One.   260

Laertes: No.

Hamlet: Judgment.

Osric: A hit, a very palpable hit.

Laertes: Well;— again.

King: Stay, give me a drink.— Hamlet, this pearl is thine;
                                                                           265
    Here's to thy health.—

Trumpets sound, and cannon shot off within.

    Give him the cup.

Hamlet: I'll play this bout first; set it by awhile.—
    Come.— Another hit; what say you?

They play.

Laertes: A touch, a touch, I do confess.

King: Our son shall win.   270

Queen: He's fat, and scant of breath.—
    Here, Hamlet, take my napkin, rub thy brows:
    The queen carouses to thy fortune, Hamlet.

Hamlet: Good madam!

King: Gertrude, do not drink.   275

°*an union:* A pearl.   °*kettle:* Kettledrum.

QUEEN: I will, my lord; I pray you, pardon me.
KING: [*Aside*] It is the poison'd cup; it is too late.
HAMLET: I dare not drink yet, madam; by and by.
QUEEN: Come, let me wipe thy face.
280 LAERTES: My lord, I'll hit him now.
KING: I do not think't.
LAERTES: [*Aside*] And yet 'tis almost 'gainst my conscience.
HAMLET: Come, for the third, Laertes: you but dally;
    I pray you, pass with your best violence:
285   I am afeard you make a wanton of me.
LAERTES: Say you so? come on.

They play.

OSRIC: Nothing, neither way.
LAERTES: Have at you now!

Laertes wounds Hamlet; then, in scuffling, they change rapiers, and Hamlet wounds Laertes.

KING: Part them; they are incens'd.
290 HAMLET: Nay, come, again.

The Queen falls.

OSRIC: Look to the queen there, ho!
HORATIO: They bleed on both sides. — How is it, my lord?
OSRIC: How is't, Laertes?
LAERTES: Why, as a woodcock to my own springe, Osric;
295   I am justly kill'd with mine own treachery.
HAMLET: How does the queen?
KING: She swoons to see them bleed.
QUEEN: No, no, the drink, the drink, — O my dear Hamlet, —
    The drink, the drink! — I am poison'd. [*Dies.*]
300 HAMLET: O villainy! — Ho! let the door be lock'd:
    Treachery! seek it out.

Laertes falls.

LAERTES: It is here, Hamlet: Hamlet, thou art slain;
    No medicine in the world can do thee good;
    In thee there is not half an hour of life;
305   The treacherous instrument is in thy hand,
    Unbated and envenom'd: the foul practice
    Hath turn'd itself on me; lo, here I lie,
    Never to rise again: thy mother's poison'd:
    I can no more: — the king, the king's to blame.
HAMLET: The point envenom'd too! —
310   Then venom to thy work. [*Stabs the King.*]

OSRIC and **LORDS:**   Treason! treason!

KING: O, yet defend me, friends; I am but hurt.

HAMLET: Here, thou incestuous, murderous, damned Dane,
Drink off this potion.— Is thy union here?
Follow my mother.   315

King dies.

LAERTES: He is justly serv'd;
It is a poison temper'd by himself.—
Exchange forgiveness with me, noble Hamlet:
Mine and my father's death come not upon thee,
Nor thine on me! [*Dies.*]   320
HAMLET: Heaven make thee free of it! I follow thee.—
I am dead, Horatio.—Wretched queen, adieu!—
You that look pale and tremble at this chance,
That art but mutes or audience to this act,
Had I but time,— as this fell sergeant, death,   325
Is strict in his arrest,— O, I could tell you,—
But let it be.— Horatio, I am dead;
Thou liv'st; report me and my cause aright
To the unsatisfied.°
HORATIO: Never believe it: 330
I am more an antique Roman than a Dane,—
Here's yet some liquor left.
HAMLET: As thou'rt a man,
Give me the cup; let go; by heaven, I'll have't.—
O good Horatio, what a wounded name,   335
Things standing thus unknown, shall live behind me!
If thou didst ever hold me in thy heart,
Absent thee from felicity awhile,
And in this harsh world draw thy breath in pain,
To tell my story.—   340

March afar off, and shot within.

                                    What warlike noise is this?
OSRIC: Young Fortinbras, with conquest come from Poland,
To the ambassadors of England gives
This warlike volley.
HAMLET: O, I die, Horatio;   345
The potent poison quite o'er-crows my spirit:
I cannot live to hear the news from England;
But I do prophesy the election lights

─────────────────────────────────

° *the unsatisfied:* The uninformed.

On Fortinbras: he has my dying voice;
So tell him, with the occurrents, more and less,
350   Which have solicited. ° — The rest is silence. [*Dies.*]
HORATIO: Now cracks a noble heart. — Good-night, sweet prince,
And flights of angels sing thee to thy rest!
Why does the drum come hither?

March within. Enter Fortinbras, the English Ambassadors, and others.

355 FORTINBRAS: Where is this sight?
HORATIO: What is it you would see?
If aught of woe or wonder, cease your search.
FORTINBRAS: This quarry cries on havoc.° — O proud death,
What feast is toward in thine eternal cell,
360   That thou so many princes at a shot
So bloodily hast struck?
1ST AMBASSADOR: The sight is dismal;
And our affairs from England come too late:
The ears are senseless that should give us hearing,
365   To tell him his commandment is fulfill'd,
That Rosencrantz and Guildenstern are dead:
Where should we have our thanks?
HORATIO: Not from his mouth,
Had it the ability of life to thank you:
370   He never gave commandment for their death.
But since, so jump° upon this bloody question,
You from the Polack wars, and you from England,
Are here arriv'd, give order that these bodies
High on a stage be placed to the view;
375   And let me speak to the yet unknowing world
How these things came about: so shall you hear
Of carnal, bloody, and unnatural acts;
Of accidental judgments, casual slaughters;
Of deaths put on by cunning and forc'd cause;
380   And, in this upshot, purposes mistook
Fall'n on the inventors' heads: all this can I
Truly deliver.
FORTINBRAS: Let us haste to hear it,
And call the noblest to the audience.
385   For me, with sorrow I embrace my fortune:
I have some rights of memory in this kingdom,°
Which now to claim my vantage doth invite me.

° *So tell him . . . solicited:* So tell him, together with the events, more or less, that have brought on this tragic affair.   ° *This quarry . . . havoc:* This collection of dead bodies cries out havoc.   ° *so jump:* So opportunely.   ° *I have . . . kingdom:* I have some unforgotten rights to this kingdom.

HORATIO: Of that I shall have also cause to speak,
And from his mouth whose voice will draw on more:
But let this same be presently perform'd, 390
Even while men's minds are wild: lest more mischance
On plots and errors happen.
FORTINBRAS: Let four captains
Bear Hamlet like a soldier to the stage;
For he was likely, had he been put on,° 395
To have prov'd most royally: and, for his passage,
The soldier's music and the rites of war
Speak loudly for him.—
Take up the bodies.— Such a sight as this
Becomes the field, but here shows much amiss. 400
Go, bid the soldiers shoot.

A dead march.

Exeunt, bearing off the dead bodies: after which a peal of ordnance is shot off.

Reading and Reacting

1. What are Hamlet's most notable character traits? Do you see these traits as generally positive or negative?
2. Review each of Hamlet's soliloquies. Judging from his own words, do you believe his assessments of his own problems are accurate? Are his assessments of other characters' behavior accurate? Point to examples from the soliloquies that reveal Hamlet's insight or lack of insight.
3. Is Hamlet a sympathetic character? Where (if anywhere) do you find yourself growing impatient with him or disagreeing with him?
4. What is the emotional impact on the audience of having Hamlet behave so cruelly toward Ophelia after his "To be or not to be" soliloquy (act 3, scene 1)?
5. What do other characters' comments reveal about Hamlet's character *before* the key events in the play begin to unfold? For example, in what way has Hamlet changed since he returned to the castle and found out about his father's death?
6. Claudius is presented as the play's villain. Is he all bad, or does he have any redeeming qualities?
7. List those in the play whom you believe to be flat characters. Why do you characterize each individual in this way? What does each of these flat characters contribute to the play?
8. Is Fortinbras simply Hamlet's foil, or does he have another essential role? Explain.

° *put on:* Tested by succession to the throne.

9. Each of the play's major characters has one or more character flaws that influence plot development. What specific weaknesses do you see in Claudius, Gertrude, Polonius, Laertes, Ophelia, and Hamlet himself? Through what words or actions is each weakness revealed? How does each weakness contribute to the play's plot?

10. Why doesn't Hamlet kill Claudius as soon as the Ghost tells him what Claudius did? Why doesn't he kill him when he has the chance in act 3? What words and actions reveal Hamlet's motivation for hesitating? What are the implications of his failure to act?

11. Why does Hamlet pretend to be insane? Why does he arrange for the "play within a play" to be performed? Why does he agree to the duel with Laertes? In each case, what words or actions reveal his motivation to the audience?

12. Is the Ghost an essential character, or could the information he reveals and the reactions he arouses come from another source? Explain. (Keep in mind that the ghost is a stock character in Elizabethan revenge tragedies.)

13. Describe Hamlet's relationship with his mother. Do you consider this a typical mother/son relationship? Why or why not?

14. In the graveyard scene (act 5, scene 1), the gravediggers make many ironic comments. In what way do these comments shed light on the events taking place in the play?

15. **JOURNAL ENTRY** Both Gertrude and Ophelia are usually seen as weak women, firmly under the influence of the men in their lives. Do you think this characterization of them as passive and dependent is accurate? Why or why not?

16. **CRITICAL PERSPECTIVE** In *The Meaning of Shakespeare*, (1951), Harold Goddard reads *Hamlet* as, in part, a play about war, with a grimly ironic conclusion in that "all the Elder Hamlet's conquests have been for nothing — for less than nothing. Fortinbras, his former enemy, is to inherit the kingdom! Such is the end to which the Ghost's thirst for vengeance has led." Goddard goes on to describe the play's ending:

> The dead Hamlet is borne out "like a soldier" and the last rites over his body are to be the rites of war. The final word of the text is "shoot." The last sounds we hear are a dead march and the reverberations of ordnance being shot off. The end crowns the whole. The sarcasm of fate could go no further. Hamlet, who aspired to nobler things, is treated at death as if he were the mere image of his father: a warrior. Shakespeare knew what he was about in making the conclusion of his play martial. Its theme has been war as well as revenge. It is the story of the Minotaur over again, of that monster who from the beginning of human strife has exacted his annual tribute of youth. No sacrifice ever offered to it was more precious than Hamlet. But he was not the last.
>
> If ever a play seems expressly written for the twentieth century, it is *Hamlet*. It should be unnecessary to underscore its pertinence to an age in which, twice within three decades, the older generation has called on the younger generation to settle a quarrel with the making of which it had nothing to do. So taken,

Hamlet is an allegory of our time. Imagination or violence, Shakespeare seems to say, there is no other alternative.

Can you find other evidence in the play to support the idea that war (and, more specifically, the futility of war) is one of its major themes? Do you agree that the play is, in this respect, "an allegory of our time"?

Related Works: "The Cask of Amontillado" (p. 203), "Young Goodman Brown" (p. 302), *Oedipus the King* (p. 1048)

WRITING SUGGESTIONS: Character

1. In *Death of a Salesman*, each character pursues his or her version of the American Dream. Choose two characters, define their concept of the American dream, and explain how each tries to make the dream a reality. In each case, consider the obstacles the character encounters, and try to account for the character's success or lack of success. If you like, you may also consider other works in which the American Dream is central — for example, "Two Kinds" (p. 416) or *Fences* (p. 1096).

2. Many of the female characters in this chapter's plays — for example, Mrs. X (*The Stronger*), Linda (*Death of a Salesman*), and Ophelia (*Hamlet*) — are, in one way or another, in conflict with men. Focusing on female characters in two different plays, define each conflict, and consider whether it is resolved in the play. (If you like, you may also discuss a female character in a play in another chapter.)

3. Minor characters are often flat characters; in many cases, their sole function is to advance the plot or to highlight a particular trait in a major character. Sometimes, however, minor characters may be of more than minor importance. Choose one minor character from *Death of a Salesman* or *Hamlet* (or from a play in another chapter), and write a paper in which you discuss what this character contributes and how the play would be different without him or her.

4. Watch a film version of one of the three plays in this chapter, and write an essay in which you evaluate the actor's interpretation of the central character.

5. Two of this chapter's three plays explore complex relationships between parents and children. Write an essay in which you compare and contrast Willy Loman's relationships with his sons and Hamlet's relationship with his mother.

6. In several other plays in this anthology, as in *Death of a Salesman*, the past is an important influence on characters' lives in the present. Write an essay in which you discuss the importance of the past on the present in *Death of a Salesman* and one or two other plays — for example, *The Glass Menagerie* or *A Doll House*.

CHAPTER 29

STAGING

> In reading a play rather than witnessing it on stage, we . . . have to imagine what it might look like in performance, projecting in our mind's eye an image of the setting and the props, as well as the movements, gestures, facial expressions, and vocal intonations of the characters.
>
> —Carl H. Klaus, Miriam Gilbert, and Braford S. Field, Jr., *Stages of Drama*

Staging refers to the physical elements of a play's production that determine how the play looks and sounds to an audience. It encompasses the **stage settings,** or **sets**—furnishings, scenery, props, and lighting — as well as the costumes, sound effects, and music that bring the play to life on the stage. In short, staging is everything that goes into making a written script a play.

Contemporary staging in the West has traditionally concentrated on recreating the outside world. This concept of staging, which has dominated Western theatrical productions for centuries, would seem alien in many non-Western theaters. Japanese **Kabuki dramas** and **No plays,** for example, depend on staging conventions that make no attempt to mirror reality. Scenery and costumes are largely symbolic, and often actors wear highly stylized makeup or masks. Although some European and American playwrights have been strongly influenced by non-Western staging, the majority of plays being produced in the West still try to create the illusion of reality.

Stage Directions

Usually a playwright presents instructions for the staging of a play in **stage directions**—notes that comment on the scenery, the movements of the performers, the lighting, and the placement of props. (In the absence of detailed stage directions, dialogue can provide information about staging.) Sometimes these stage directions are quite simple, leaving much to the imagination of the director. Consider how little specific information about the setting of the play is provided

1042

in these stage directions from act 1 of Samuel Beckett's 1952 absurdist play *Waiting for Godot:*

A country road. A tree. Evening.

Often, however, playwrights furnish much more detailed information about staging. Consider these stage directions from act 1 of Anton Chekhov's *The Cherry Orchard:*

A room, which has always been called the nursery. One of the doors leads into Anya's room. Dawn, sun rises during the scene. May, the cherry trees in flower, but it is cold in the garden with the frost of the early morning. Windows closed.
Enter Dunyasha with a candle and Lopahin with a book in his hand.

These comments indicate that the first act takes place in a room with more than one door and that several windows reveal cherry trees in bloom. They also specify that the lighting should simulate the sun rising at dawn and that certain characters should enter carrying particular props. Still, Chekhov leaves it up to those staging the play to decide on the costumes for the characters and on the furniture to be placed around the room.

Some stage directions are even more specific. Irish playwright George Bernard Shaw's long, complex stage directions are legendary in the theater. Note the degree of detail he provides in these stage directions from his 1906 comedy *The Doctor's Dilemma:*

The consulting-room has two windows looking on Queen Anne Street. Between the two is a marble-topped console, with haunched gilt legs ending in sphinx claws. The huge pier-glass [a long narrow mirror that fits between two windows] which surmounts it is mostly disabled from reflection by elaborate painting on its surface of palms, ferns, lilies, tulips, and sunflowers. The adjoining wall contains the fireplace, with two arm-chairs before it. As we happen to face the corner we see nothing of the other two walls. On the right of the fireplace, or rather on the right of any person facing the fireplace, is the door. On the left is the writing-table at which Redpenny [a medical student] sits. It is an untidy table with a microscope, several test tubes, and a spirit lamp [an alcohol burner] standing up through its litter of papers. There is a couch in the middle of the room, at right angles to the console, and parallel to the fireplace. A chair stands between the couch and the window. Another in the corner. Another at the other end of the windowed wall. . . . The wallpaper and carpets are mostly green. . . . The house, in fact, was so well furnished in the middle of the XIXth century that it stands unaltered to this day and is still quite presentable.

Not only does Shaw indicate what furniture is to be placed on stage, but he also includes a good deal of physical description— specifying, for example, "gilt legs ending in sphinx claws" and "test tubes and a spirit lamp" that clutter the writing table. In addition, he defines furniture placement and specifies color.

Regardless of how detailed the stage directions are, they do not eliminate the need for creative interpretations on the part of the producer, director, set designers, and actors (See "Actors' Interpretations," p. 850). Stage directions — and, for that matter, the entire script — are the foundation on which to construct the play that the audience finally sees. Many directors see stage directions as suggestions, not requirements, and some consider them more confusing than helpful. Therefore, some directors may choose to interpret a play's stage directions quite loosely — or even to ignore them entirely.

The Uses of Staging

Various elements of staging communicate important information about characters and their motivation as well as about the play's theme.

Costumes

Costumes establish the historical period in which a play is set and provide insight into the characters who wear them. When Hamlet first appears on stage, he is profoundly disillusioned and quite melancholy. This fact was immediately apparent to Shakespeare's audience because Hamlet is dressed in sable, which to the Elizabethans signified a melancholy nature. In Tennessee Williams's *The Glass Menagerie* (p. 1153), Laura's dress of soft violet material and her hair ribbon reflect her delicate, childlike innocence. In contrast, her mother's *"imitation velvety-looking cloth [coat] with imitation fur collar"* and her *"enormous black patent-leather pocketbook"* reveal her somewhat pathetic attempt to achieve respectability. Later in the play, awaiting the "gentleman caller," Laura's mother wears a dress that is both outdated and inappropriately youthful, suggesting both her need to relive her own past and her increasingly desperate desire to marry off her daughter.

Props and Furnishings

Props (short for *properties*) can also help audiences to interpret a play's characters and themes. For example, the handkerchief in Shakespeare's *Othello* gains significance as the play progresses: it begins as an innocent object and ends as the piece of evidence that convinces Othello his wife is committing adultery. Sometimes props can have symbolic significance. During the Renaissance, flowers had symbolic meaning. In act 4 of *Hamlet*, Ophelia, who is mad, gives flowers to various characters. In a note to the play, the critic Thomas Parrott points out the symbolic significance of her gifts: to Claudius, the murderer of Hamlet's father, she gives fennel and columbines, which signify flattery and ingratitude; to the

Queen, she gives rue and daisies, which symbolize sadness and unfaithfulness. Although modern audiences would not understand the significance of these flowers, many people in Shakespeare's Elizabethan audience would have been aware of their meaning.

The **furnishings** in a room can also reveal a lot about a play's characters and themes. Willy Loman's house in Arthur Miller's *Death of a Salesman* (p. 858) is sparsely furnished, revealing the declining financial status of the family. The kitchen contains a table and three chairs and the bedroom only a brass bed and a straight chair. Over the bed on a shelf is Biff's silver athletic trophy, a constant reminder of his loss of status. Like Willy Loman's house, the Wingfield apartment in *The Glass Menagerie* reflects its inhabitants' modest economic circumstances. For example, the living room, which contains a sofa that opens into a bed, also serves as a bedroom for Laura. In addition, one piece of furniture highlights a central theme of the play: an old-fashioned cabinet in the living room displays a collection of transparent glass animals that, like Laura, are too fragile to be removed from their surroundings.

Scenery and Lighting

Playwrights often use **scenery and lighting** to create imaginative stage settings. In *Death of a Salesman*, the house is surrounded by *"towering angular shapes"* of apartment houses that emphasize the *"small, fragile-seeming home."* Arthur Miller calls for a set that is *"wholly, or in some places, transparent."* Whenever the action is in the present, the actors observe the imaginary boundaries that separate rooms or mark the exterior walls of the house. But when the characters reenact past events, they walk over the boundaries and come to the front of the stage. By lighting up and darkening different parts of the stage, Miller shifts from the present to the past and back again.

The set of *The Glass Menagerie* is also innovative, combining imaginative backdrops with subtle lighting. As the curtain rises, the audience sees the dark rear wall of the Wingfield tenement, which is flanked on both sides by alleys lined with clotheslines, garbage cans, and fire escapes. After Tom delivers his opening narrative, the rear wall becomes transparent, revealing the interior of the Wingfield apartment. To create this effect, Williams used a **scrim,** a curtain that when illuminated from the front appears solid but when illuminated from the back becomes transparent. For Williams, such "atmospheric touches" represented a new direction in theater that contrasted with the theater of "realistic conventions."

Contemporary playwrights often use sets that combine realistic and nonrealistic elements. In his 1988 Tony Award-winning play *M. Butterfly*, for example, David Henry Hwang employs not only scrims but also a large red lacquered ramp that runs from the bottom to the top of the stage. The action takes place beneath, on, and above the ramp, creating an effect not unlike that created by Shakespeare's multiple stages. At several points in the play, a character who acts as the narrator sits beneath the ramp, addressing the audience, while at the same time a character on top of the ramp acts out the narrator's words.

Music and Sound Effects

Staging involves more than visual elements such as costumes and scenery; it also involves **music and sound effects.** The stage directions for *Death of a Salesman*, for example, begin, "*A melody is heard, played upon a flute.*" Although not specifically identified, the music is described as "*small and fine, telling of grass and trees and the horizon.*" Interestingly, this music stands in stark contrast to the claustrophobic urban setting of the play. Music also plays a major role in *The Glass Menagerie*, where a single recurring tune, like circus music, weaves in and out of the play. This musical motif gives emotional impact to certain lines and suggests the fantasy world into which Laura has retreated.

Sound effects play an important part in Henrik Ibsen's *A Doll House* (p. 784). At the very end of the play, after his wife has left him, Torvald Helmer sits alone on the stage. In the following stage directions, the final sound effect cuts short Helmer's attempt at self-deluding optimism:

HELMER: (*sinks down on a chair by the door, face buried in his hands*) Nora! Nora! (*Looking about and rising.*) Empty. She's gone. (*A sudden hope leaps in him.*) The greatest miracle —?

From below, the sound of a door slamming shut.

When you read a play, it may be difficult to appreciate the effect that staging can have on a performance. As you read, pay particular attention to the stage directions, and use your imagination to visualize the scenes the playwright describes. In addition, try to imagine the play's sights and sounds, and consider the options for staging that are suggested as characters speak to one another. Although even such careful reading cannot substitute for actually seeing a play performed, it can help you imagine the play as it might appear on the stage.

A Final Note

Because of a play's limited performance time, and because of space and financial limitations, not every action or event can be represented on stage. Frequently, incidents that would involve many actors or require elaborate scenery are only suggested. For example, a violent political riot may be suggested by a single scuffle, a full-scale wedding by the kiss between bride and groom, a gala evening at the opera by a well-dressed group in box seats, and a trip to an exotic locale by a departure scene. Other events are suggested by sounds offstage — for example, the roar of a crowd may suggest an athletic event.

✔ CHECKLIST Writing about Staging

- What information about staging is specified in the stage directions of the play?
- What information about staging is suggested by the play's dialogue?
- What information about staging is left to the imagination?
- How might different decisions about staging change the play?
- Do the stage directions provide information about how characters are supposed to look or behave?
- What costumes are specified? In what ways do costumes provide insight into the characters who wear them?
- What props play an important part in the play? Do these props have symbolic meaning?
- Is the scenery special or unusual in any way?
- What kind of lighting is specified by the stage directions? In what way does this lighting affect your reaction to the play?
- How are music and sound effects used in the play? Are musical themes associated with any characters? Do music or sound effects heighten the emotional impact of certain lines?
- What events occur offstage? Why? How are they suggested?
- How does staging help to communicate the play's themes?

SOPHOCLES (496 – 406 B.C.), along with Aeschylus and Euripides, is one of the three great Greek tragic dramatists. He lived during the flowering and subsequent decline of fifth-century B.C. Athens — the high point of Greek civilization. Born as Greece struggled against the Persian Empire and moved to adopt democracy, he lived as an adult under Pericles during the golden age of Athens and died as it became clear that Athens would lose the Peloponnesian War. Sophocles was an active participant in the public life of Athens, serving as a collec-  tor of tribute from Athenian subjects and later as a general. He wrote at least 120 plays, but only seven have survived, including three plays about Oedipus: *Oedipus the King* (c. 430 B.C.), *Oedipus at Colonus* (411? B.C.), and *Antigone* (441 B.C.).

Oedipus the King, or *Oedipus Rex* (sometimes called *Oedipus the Tyrant*), was performed shortly after a great plague in Athens (probably in 429 or 425 B.C.) and as Athens was falling into decline. The play opens with an account of a plague in Thebes, Oedipus's kingdom. Over the years, *Oedipus the King* has attracted impressive critical attention, from Aristotle's use of it as a model for his definition of tragedy to Freud's use of its power as evidence of the validity of the "Oedipus complex."

Oedipus the King* (c. 430 B.C.)

Translated by Thomas Gould

CHARACTERS

Oedipus,° *the King of Thebes*
Priest of Zeus, *leader of the suppliants*
Creon, *Oedipus's brother-in-law*
Chorus, *a group of Theban elders*
Choragos, *spokesman of the Chorus*

Tiresias, *a blind seer or prophet*
Jocasta, *the queen of Thebes*
Messenger, *from Corinth, once a shepherd*
Herdsman, *once a servant of Laius*
Second Messenger, *a servant of Oedipus*

MUTES

Suppliants, *Thebans seeking Oedipus's help*
Attendants, *for the Royal Family*
Servants, *to lead Tiresias and Oedipus*
Antigone, *daughter of Oedipus and Jocasta*
Ismene, *daughter of Oedipus and Jocasta*

The action takes place during the day in front of the royal palace in Thebes. There are two altars (left and right) on the proscenium and several steps leading down to the orchestra. As the play opens, Thebans of various ages who have come to beg Oedipus for help are sitting on these steps and in part of the orchestra. These suppliants are holding branches of laurel or olive which have strips of wool° wrapped around them. Oedipus enters from the palace (the central door of the skene).

PROLOGUE°

Oedipus: My children, ancient Cadmus'° newest care,
why have you hurried to those seats, your boughs
wound with the emblems of the suppliant?
The city is weighed down with fragrant smoke,
5 with hymns to the Healer° and the cries of mourners.
I thought it wrong, my sons, to hear your words
through emissaries, and have come out myself,
I, Oedipus, a name that all men know.

Oedipus addresses the Priest.

Old man — for it is fitting that you speak
10 for all — what is your mood as you entreat me,
fear or trust? You may be confident

---

*Note that individual lines are numbered in the following play. When a line is shared by two or more characters, it is counted as one line. °*Oedipus:* The name, meaning "swollen foot," refers to the mutilation of Oedipus's feet by his father, Laius, before the infant was sent to Mount Cithaeron to be put to death by exposure. °*wool:* Branches wrapped with wool are traditional symbols of prayer or supplication. °*Prologue:* The portion of the play containing the exposition, or explanation, of what has gone before and what is now happening. °*Cadmus:* Oedipus's great-great-grandfather (although Oedipus does not know this) and the founder of Thebes. °*Healer:* Apollo, god of prophecy, light, healing, justice, purification, and destruction.

that I'll do anything. How hard of heart
if an appeal like this did not rouse my pity!
PRIEST: You, Oedipus, who hold the power here,
 you see our several ages, we who sit   15
before your altars — some not strong enough
to take long flight, some heavy in old age,
the priests, as I of Zeus,° and from our youths
a chosen band. The rest sit with their windings
in the markets, at the twin shrines of Pallas,°   20
and the prophetic embers of Ismēnos.°
Our city, as you see yourself, is tossed
too much, and can no longer lift its head
above the troughs of billows red with death.
It dies in the fruitful flowers of the soil,   25
it dies in its pastured herds, and in its women's
barren pangs. And the fire-bearing god°
has swooped upon the city, hateful plague,
and he has left the house of Cadmus empty.
Black Hades° is made rich with moans and weeping. 30
Not judging you an equal of the gods,
do I and the children sit here at your hearth,
but as the first of men, in troubled times
and in encounters with divinities.
You came to Cadmus' city and unbound   35
the tax we had to pay to the harsh singer,°
did it without a helpful word from us,
with no instruction; with a god's assistance
you raised up our life, so we believe.
Again now Oedipus, our greatest power,   40
we plead with you, as suppliants, all of us,
to find us strength, whether from a god's response,
or learned in some way from another man.
I know that the experienced among men
give counsels that will prosper best of all.   45

° *Zeus:* Father and king of the gods. ° *Pallas:* Athena, goddess of wisdom, arts, crafts, and war. ° *Ismēnos:* A reference to the temple of Apollo near the river Ismēnos in Thebes. Prophecies were made here by "reading" the ashes of the altar fires. ° *fire-bearing god:* Contagious fever viewed as a god. ° *Black Hades:* Refers both to the underworld where the spirits of the dead go and to the god of the underworld. ° *harsh singer:* The Sphinx, a monster with a woman's head, a lion's body, and wings. The "tax" from which Oedipus freed Thebes was the destruction of all the young men who failed to solve the Sphinx's riddle and were subsequently devoured. The Sphinx always asked the same riddle: "What goes on four legs in the morning, two legs at noon, and three legs in the evening, and yet is weakest when supported by the largest number of feet?" Oedipus discovered the correct answer — man, who crawls in infancy, walks in his prime, and uses a stick in old age — and thus ended the Sphinx's reign of terror. The Sphinx destroyed herself when Oedipus answered the riddle. Oedipus's reward for freeing Thebes of the Sphinx was the throne and the hand of the recently widowed Jocasta.

Noblest of men, lift up our land again!
Think also of yourself; since now the land
calls you its Savior for your zeal of old,
oh let us never look back at your rule
50 as men helped up only to fall again!
Do not stumble! Put our land on firm feet!
The bird of omen was auspicious then,
when you brought that luck; be that same man again!
The power is yours; if you will rule our country,
55 rule over men, not in an empty land.
A towered city or a ship is nothing
if desolate and no man lives within.

OEDIPUS: Pitiable children, oh I know, I know
the yearnings that have brought you. Yes, I know
60 that you are sick. And yet, though you are sick,
there is not one of you so sick as I.
For your affliction comes to each alone,
for him and no one else, but my soul mourns
for me and for you, too, and for the city.
65 You do not waken me as from a sleep,
for I have wept, bitterly and long,
tried many paths in the wanderings of thought,
and the single cure I found by careful search
I've acted on: I sent Menoeceus' son,
70 Creon, brother of my wife, to the Pythian
halls of Phoebus,° so that I might learn
what I must do or say to save this city.
Already, when I think what day this is,
I wonder anxiously what he is doing.
75 Too long, more than is right, he's been away.
But when he comes, then I shall be a traitor
if I do not do all that the god reveals.

PRIEST: Welcome words! But look, those men have signaled
that it is Creon who is now approaching!

80 OEDIPUS: Lord Apollo! May he bring Savior Luck,
a Luck as brilliant as his eyes are now!

PRIEST: His news is happy, it appears. He comes,
forehead crowned with thickly berried laurel.°

OEDIPUS: We'll know, for he is near enough to hear us.

Enter Creon along one of the parados.

°*Pythian halls . . . Phoebus:* The temple of Phoebus, Apollo's oracle or prophet at Delphi.   °*laurel:* Creon is wearing a garland of laurel leaves, sacred to Apollo.

Lord, brother in marriage, son of Menoeceus! 85
What is the god's pronouncement that you bring?
CREON: It's good. For even troubles, if they chance
  to turn out well, I always count as lucky.
OEDIPUS: But what was the response? You seem to say
  I'm not to fear — but not to take heart either. 90
CREON: If you will hear me with these men present,
  I'm ready to report — or go inside.

Creon moves up the steps toward the palace.

OEDIPUS: Speak out to all! The grief that burdens me
  concerns these men more than it does my life.
CREON: Then I shall tell you what I heard from the god. 95
  The task Lord Phoebus sets for us is clear:
  drive out pollution sheltered in our land,
  and do not shelter what is incurable.
OEDIPUS: What is our trouble? How shall we cleanse ourselves?
CREON: We must banish or murder to free ourselves 100
  from a murder that blows storms through the city.
OEDIPUS: What man's bad luck does he accuse in this?
CREON: My Lord, a king named Laius ruled our land
  before you came to steer the city straight.
OEDIPUS: I know. So I was told — I never saw him. 105
CREON: Since he was murdered, you must raise your hand
  against the men who killed him with their hands.
OEDIPUS: Where are they now? And how can we ever find
  the track of ancient guilt now hard to read?
CREON: In our own land, he said. What we pursue, 110
  that can be caught; but not what we neglect.
OEDIPUS: Was Laius home, or in the countryside —
  or was he murdered in some foreign land?
CREON: He left to see a sacred rite, he said;
  He left, but never came home from his journey. 115
OEDIPUS: Did none of his party see it and report —
  someone we might profitably question?
CREON: They were all killed but one, who fled in fear,
  and he could tell us only one clear fact.
OEDIPUS: What fact? One thing could lead us on to more 120
  if we could get a small start on our hope.
CREON: He said that bandits chanced on them and killed him —
  with the force of many hands, not one alone.
OEDIPUS: How could a bandit dare so great an act —
  unless this was a plot paid off from here! 125
CREON: We thought of that, but when Laius was killed,

we had no one to help us in our troubles.

OEDIPUS: It was your very kingship that was killed!
What kind of trouble blocked you from a search?

130 **CREON:** The subtle-singing Sphinx asked us to turn
from the obscure to what lay at our feet.

OEDIPUS: Then I shall begin again and make it plain.
It was quite worthy of Phoebus, and worthy of you,
to turn our thoughts back to the murdered man,

135 and right that you should see me join the battle
for justice to our land and to the god.
Not on behalf of any distant kinships,
it's for myself I will dispel this stain.
Whoever murdered him may also wish

140 to punish me — and with the selfsame hand.
In helping him I also serve myself.
Now quickly, children: up from the altar steps,
and raise the branches of the suppliant!
Let someone go and summon Cadmus' people:
say I'll do anything.

Exit an Attendant along one of the parados.

145   Our luck will prosper
if the god is with us, or we have already fallen.

PRIEST: Rise, my children; that for which we came,
he has himself proclaimed he will accomplish.
May Phoebus, who announced this, also come

150 as Savior and reliever from the plague.

*Exit Oedipus and Creon into the palace. The Priest and the Suppliants exit left and right
along the parados. After a brief pause, the Chorus (including the Choragos) enters the
orchestra from the parados.*

<u>PARADOS</u>°
STROPHE 1°

CHORUS: Voice from Zeus,° sweetly spoken, what are you
that have arrived from golden
Pytho° to our shining
Thebes? I am on the rack, terror
    shakes my soul.

155 Delian Healer,° summoned by "iē!"
I await in holy dread what obligation, something new

°*Parados:* A song sung by the Chorus on first entering.   °*Strophe:* Probably refers to the direction in which the
Chorus danced while reciting specific stanzas. *Strophe* may have indicated dance steps to stage left, *antistro-
phe* to stage right.   °*Voice from Zeus:* A reference to Apollo's prophecy. Zeus taught Apollo how to prophesy
°*Pytho:* Delphi.   °*Delian Healer:* Apollo.

or something back once more with the revolving years,
    you'll bring about for me.
Oh tell me, child of golden Hope,   160
    deathless Response!

ANTISTROPHE 1

I appeal to you first, daughter of Zeus,
    deathless Athena,
    and to your sister who protects this land,
Artemis,° whose famous throne is the whole circle   165
    of the marketplace,
and Phoebus, who shoots from afar: iō!
Three-fold defenders against death, appear!
If ever in the past, to stop blind ruin
    sent against the city,   170
you banished utterly the fires of suffering,
    come now again!

STROPHE 2

Ah! Ah! Unnumbered are the miseries
I bear. The plague claims all
our comrades. Nor has thought found yet a spear   175
by which a man shall be protected. What our glorious
earth gives birth to does not grow. Without a birth
from cries of labor
    do the women rise.
One person after another   180
    you may see, like flying birds,
faster than indomitable fire, sped
to the shore of the god that is the sunset.°

ANTISTROPHE 2

And with their deaths unnumbered dies the city.
Her children lie unpitied on the ground,   185
spreading death, unmourned.
Meanwhile young wives, and gray-haired mothers with them,
on the shores of the altars, from this side and that,
suppliants from mournful trouble,
    cry out their grief.   190
A hymn to the Healer shines,
    the flute a mourner's voice.
Against which, golden goddess, daughter of Zeus,
    send lovely Strength.

°*Artemis:* Goddess of virginity, childbirth, and hunting.   °*god . . . sunset:* Hades, god of the underworld.

STROPHE 3

195 Causing raging Ares°— who,
armed now with no shield of bronze,
burns me, coming on amid loud cries—
to turn his back and run from my land,
with a fair wind behind, to the great
200   hall of Amphitritē,°
or to the anchorage that welcomes no one,
Thrace's troubled sea!
If night lets something get away at last,
   it comes by day.
205 Fire-bearing god . . .
   you who dispense the might of lightning,
Zeus! Father! Destroy him with your thunderbolt!

Enter Oedipus from the palace.

ANTISTROPHE 3

Lycēan Lord!° From your looped
   bowstring, twisted gold,
210 I wish indomitable missiles might be scattered
and stand forward, our protectors; also fire-bearing
radiance of Artemis, with which
   she darts across the Lycian mountains.
I call the god whose head is bound in gold,
215 with whom this country shares its name,
Bacchus,° wine-flushed, summoned by "euoi!,"
   Maenads' comrade,
to approach ablaze
   with gleaming . . .
220 pine, opposed to that god-hated god.

EPISODE 1°

OEDIPUS: I hear your prayer. Submit to what I say
and to the labors that the plague demands
and you'll get help and a relief from evils.
I'll make the proclamation, though a stranger
225 to the report and to the deed. Alone,
had I no key, I would soon lose the track.
Since it was only later that I joined you,
to all the sons of Cadmus I say this:
whoever has clear knowledge of the man

° *Ares:* God of war and destruction.   ° *Amphitritē:* The Atlantic Ocean.   ° *Lycēan Lord:* Apollo.
° *Bacchus:* Dionysus, god of fertility and wine.   ° *Episode:* The portion of ancient Greek plays that appears between choric songs.

who murdered Laius, son of Labdacus, 230
I command him to reveal it all to me —
nor fear if, to remove the charge, he must
accuse himself: his fate will not be cruel —
he will depart unstumbling into exile.
But if you know another, or a stranger, 235
to be the one whose hand is guilty, speak:
I shall reward you and remember you.
But if you keep your peace because of fear,
and shield yourself or kin from my command,
hear you what I shall do in that event: 240
I charge all in this land where I have throne
and power, shut out that man — no matter who —
both from your shelter and all spoken words,
nor in your prayers or sacrifices make
him partner, nor allot him lustral° water. 245
All men shall drive him from their homes: for he
is the pollution that the god-sent Pythian
response has only now revealed to me.
In this way I ally myself in war
with the divinity and the deceased.° 250
And this curse, too, against the one who did it,
whether alone in secrecy, or with others:
may he wear out his life unblest and evil!
I pray this, too: if he is at my hearth
and in my home, and I have knowledge of him, 255
may the curse pronounced on others come to me.
All this I lay to you to execute,
for my sake, for the god's, and for this land
now ruined, barren, abandoned by the gods.
Even if no god had driven you to it, 260
you ought not to have left this stain uncleansed,
the murdered man a nobleman, a king!
You should have looked! But now, since, as it happens,
It's I who have the power that he had once,
and have his bed, and a wife who shares our seed, 265
and common bond had we had common children
(had not his hope of offspring had bad luck —
but as it happened, luck lunged at his head);
because of this, as if for my own father,
I'll fight for him, I'll leave no means untried, 270
to catch the one who did it with his hand,

°*lustral:* Purifying.   °*the deceased:* Laius.

for the son of Labdacus, of Polydōrus,
of Cadmus before him, and of Agēnor.°
This prayer against all those who disobey:

275   the gods send out no harvest from their soil,
nor children from their wives. Oh, let them die
victims of this plague, or of something worse.
Yet for the rest of us, people of Cadmus,
we the obedient, may Justice, our ally,

280   and all the gods, be always on our side!
CHORAGOS:°   I speak because I feel the grip of your curse:
the killer is not I. Nor can I point
to him. The one who set us to this search,
Phoebus, should also name the guilty man.

285   OEDIPUS: Quite right, but to compel unwilling gods —
no man has ever had that kind of power.
CHORAGOS: May I suggest to you a second way?
OEDIPUS: A second or a third — pass over nothing!
CHORAGOS: I know of no one who sees more of what

290   Lord Phoebus sees than Lord Tiresias.
My Lord, one might learn brilliantly from him.
OEDIPUS: Nor is this something I have been slow to do.
At Creon's word I sent an escort — twice now!
I am astonished that he has not come.

295   CHORAGOS: The old account is useless. It told us nothing.
OEDIPUS: But tell it to me. I'll scrutinize all stories.
CHORAGOS: He is said to have been killed by travelers.
OEDIPUS: I have heard, but the one who did it no one sees.
CHORAGOS: If there is any fear in him at all,

300   he won't stay here once he has heard that curse.
OEDIPUS: He won't fear words: he had no fear when he did it.

Enter Tiresias from the right, led by a Servant and two of Oedipus's Attendants.

CHORAGOS: Look there! There is the man who will convict him!
It's the god's prophet they are leading here,
one gifted with the truth as no one else.

305   OEDIPUS: Tiresias, master of all omens —
public and secret, in the sky and on the earth —
your mind, if not your eyes, sees how the city
lives with a plague, against which Thebes can find
no Saviour or protector, Lord, but you.

310   For Phoebus, as the attendants surely told you,
returned this answer to us: liberation

°*son . . . Agēnor:* Refers to Laius by citing his genealogy.   °*Choragos:* Leader of the Chorus and principal commentator on the play's action.

from the disease would never come unless
we learned without a doubt who murdered Laius —
put them to death, or sent them into exile.
Do not begrudge us what you may learn from birds   315
or any other prophet's path you know!
Care for yourself, the city, care for me,
care for the whole pollution of the dead!
We're in your hands. To do all that he can
to help another is man's noblest labor.   320
TIRESIAS: How terrible to understand and get
no profit from the knowledge! I knew this,
but I forgot, or I had never come.
OEDIPUS: What's this? You've come with very little zeal.
TIRESIAS: Let me go home! If you will listen to me,   325
You will endure your troubles better — and I mine.
OEDIPUS: A strange request, not very kind to the land
that cared for you — to hold back this oracle!
TIRESIAS: I see your understanding comes to you
inopportunely. So that won't happen to me . . .   330
OEDIPUS: Oh, by the gods, if you understand about this,
don't turn away! We're on our knees to you.
TIRESIAS: None of you understands! I'll never bring
my grief to light — I will not speak of yours.
OEDIPUS: You know and won't declare it! Is your purpose   335
to betray us and to destroy this land!
TIRESIAS: I will grieve neither of us. Stop this futile
cross-examination. I'll tell you nothing!
OEDIPUS: Nothing? You vile traitor! You could provoke
a stone to anger! You still refuse to tell?   340
Can nothing soften you, nothing convince you?
TIRESIAS: You blamed anger in me — you haven't seen.
The kind that lives with you, so you blame me.
OEDIPUS: Who wouldn't fill with anger, listening
to words like yours which now disgrace this city?   345
TIRESIAS: It will come, even if my silence hides it.
OEDIPUS: If it will come, then why won't you declare it?
TIRESIAS: I'd rather say no more. Now if you wish,
respond to that with all your fiercest anger!
OEDIPUS: Now I am angry enough to come right out   350
with this conjecture: you, I think, helped plot
the deed; you did it — even if your hand,
cannot have struck the blow. If you could see,
I should have said the deed was yours alone.
TIRESIAS: Is that right! Then I charge you to abide   355

by the decree you have announced: from this day
say no word to either these or me,
for you are the vile polluter of this land!

Oedipus: Aren't you appalled to let a charge like that
360   come bounding forth? How will you get away?

Tiresias: You cannot catch me. I have the strength of truth.

Oedipus: Who taught you this? Not your prophetic craft!

Tiresias: You did. You made me say it. I didn't want to.

Oedipus: Say what? Repeat it so I'll understand.

365 **Tiresias:** I made no sense? Or are you trying me?

Oedipus: No sense I understood. Say it again!

Tiresias: I say you are the murderer you seek.

Oedipus: Again that horror! You'll wish you hadn't said that.

Tiresias: Shall I say more, and raise your anger higher?

370 **Oedipus:** Anything you like! Your words are powerless.

Tiresias: You live, unknowing, with those nearest to you
in the greatest shame. You do not see the evil.

Oedipus: You won't go on like that and never pay!

Tiresias: I can if there is any strength in truth.

375 **Oedipus:** In truth, but not in you! You have no strength,
blind in your ears, your reason, and your eyes.

Tiresias: Unhappy man! Those jeers you hurl at me
before long all these men will hurl at you.

Oedipus: You are the child of endless night; it's not
380   for me or anyone who sees to hurt you.

Tiresias: It's not my fate to be struck down by you.
Apollo is enough. That's his concern.

Oedipus: Are these inventions Creon's or your own?

Tiresias: No, your affliction is yourself, not Creon.

385 **Oedipus:** Oh success! — in wealth, kingship, artistry,
in any life that wins much admiration —
the envious ill will stored up for you!
to get at my command, a gift I did not
seek, which the city put into my hands,
390   my loyal Creon, colleague from the start,
longs to sneak up in secret and dethrone me.
So he's suborned this fortuneteller — schemer!
deceitful beggar-priest! — who has good eyes
for gains alone, though in his craft he's blind.
395   Where were your prophet's powers ever proved?
Why, when the dog who chanted verse° was here,
did you not speak and liberate this city?

°*dog . . . verse:* The Sphinx.

Her riddle wasn't for a man chancing by
to interpret; prophetic art was needed,
but you had none, it seems — learned from birds   400
or from a god. I came along, yes I,
Oedipus the ignorant, and stopped her —
by using thought, not augury from birds.
And it is I whom you now wish to banish,
so you'll be close to the Creontian throne.   405
You — and the plot's concocter — will drive out
pollution to your grief: you look quite old
or you would be the victim of that plot!

CHORAGOS: It seems to us that this man's words were said
in anger, Oedipus, and yours as well.   410
Insight, not angry words, is what we need,
the best solution to the god's response.

TIRESIAS: You are the king, and yet I am your equal
in my right to speak. In that I too am Lord.
for I belong to Loxias,° not you.   415
I am not Creon's man. He's nothing to me.
Hear this, since you have thrown my blindness at me:
Your eyes can't see the evil to which you've come,
nor where you live, nor who is in your house.
Do you know your parents? Not knowing, you are   420
their enemy, in the underworld and here.
A mother's and a father's double-lashing
terrible-footed curse will soon drive you out.
Now you can see, then you will stare into darkness.
What place will not be harbor to your cry,   425
or what Cithaeron° not reverberate
when you have heard the bride-song in your palace
to which you sailed? Fair wind to evil harbor!
Nor do you see how many other woes
will level you to yourself and to your children.   430
So, at my message, and at Creon, too,
splatter muck! There will never be a man
ground into wretchedness as you will be.

OEDIPUS: Am I to listen to such things from him!
May you be damned! Get out of here at once!   435
Go! Leave my palace! Turn around and go!

Tiresias begins to move away from Oedipus.

TIRESIAS: I wouldn't have come had you not sent for me.

°*Loxias:* Apollo.   °*Cithaeron:* The mountain on which Oedipus was to be exposed as an infant.

OEDIPUS: I did not know you'd talk stupidity,
or I wouldn't have rushed to bring you to my house.
440 TIRESIAS: Stupid I seem to you, yet to your parents
who gave you natural birth I seemed quite shrewd.
OEDIPUS: Who? Wait! Who is the one who gave me birth?
TIRESIAS: This day will give you birth,° and ruin too.
OEDIPUS: What murky, riddling things you always say!
445 TIRESIAS: Don't you surpass us all at finding out?
OEDIPUS: You sneer at what you'll find has brought me greatness.
TIRESIAS: And that's the very luck that ruined you.
OEDIPUS: I wouldn't care, just so I saved the city.
TIRESIAS: In that case I shall go. Boy, lead the way!
450 OEDIPUS: Yes, let him lead you off. Here, underfoot,
you irk me. Gone, you'll cause no further pain.
TIRESIAS: I'll go when I have said what I was sent for.
Your face won't scare me. You can't ruin me.
I say to you, the man whom you have looked for
455 as you pronounced your curses, your decrees
on the bloody death of Laius — he is here!
A seeming stranger, he shall be shown to be
a Theban born, though he'll take no delight
in that solution. Blind, who once could see,
460 a beggar who was rich, through foreign lands
he'll go and point before him with a stick.
To his beloved children, he'll be shown
a father who is also brother; to the one
who bore him, son and husband; to his father,
465 his seed-fellow and killer. Go in
and think this out; and if you find I've lied,
say then I have no prophet's understanding!

Exit Tiresias, led by a Servant. Oedipus exits into the palace with his Attendants.

STASIMON 1°
STROPHE 1
CHORUS: Who is the man of whom the inspired
rock of Delphi° said
470 he has committed the unspeakable
with blood-stained hands?
Time for him to ply a foot
mightier than those of the horses
of the storm in his escape;

° *This day . . . birth:* On this day, you will learn who your parents are.   ° *Stasimon:* Greek choral ode between episodes.   ° *rock of Delphi:* Apollo's oracle at Delphi.

upon him mounts and plunges the weaponed 475
son of Zeus,° with fire and thunderbolts,
and in his train the dreaded goddesses
of Death, who never miss.

ANTISTROPHE 1

The message has just blazed,
gleaming from the snows 480
of Mount Parnassus: we must track
everywhere the unseen man.
He wanders, hidden by wild
forests, up through caves
and rocks, like a bull, 485
anxious, with an anxious foot, forlorn.
He puts away from him the mantic° words come from earth's
navel,° at its center, yet these live
forever and still hover round him.

STROPHE 2

Terribly he troubles me, 490
the skilled interpreter of birds!°
I can't assent, nor speak against him.
Both paths are closed to me.
I hover on the wings of doubt,
not seeing what is here nor what's to come. 495
What quarrel started in the house of Labdacus°
or in the house of Polybus,°
either ever in the past
or now, I never
heard, so that . . . with this fact for my touchstone 500
I could attack the public
fame of Oedipus, by the side of the Labdaceans
an ally, against the dark assassination.

ANTISTROPHE 2

No, Zeus and Apollo
understand and know things 505
mortal; but that another man
can do more as a prophet than I can —
for that there is no certain test,
though, skill to skill, 510
one man might overtake another.

° *son of Zeus:* Apollo.   ° *mantic:* prophetic.   ° *earth's navel:* Delphi.   ° *interpreter of birds:* Tiresias. The Chorus is
troubled by his accusations.   ° *house of Labdacus:* The line of Laius.   ° *Polybus:* Oedipus's foster father.

No, never, not until
    I see the charges proved,
when someone blames him shall I nod assent.
For once, as we all saw, the winged maiden° came
515   against him: he was seen then to be skilled,
      proved, by that touchstone, dear to the people. So,
never will my mind convict him of the evil.

EPISODE 2

Enter Creon from the right door of the skene and speaks to the Chorus.

CREON: Citizens, I hear that a fearful charge
    is made against me by King Oedipus!
520   I had to come. If, in this crisis,
    he thinks that he has suffered injury
    from anything that I have said or done,
    I have no appetite for a long life—
    bearing a blame like that! It's no slight blow
525   the punishment I'd take from what he said:
    it's the ultimate hurt to be called traitor
    by the city, by you, by my own people!
CHORAGOS: The thing that forced that accusation out
    could have been anger, not the power of thought.
530 CREON: But who persuaded him that thoughts of mine
    had led the prophet into telling lies?
CHORAGOS: I do not know the thought behind his words.
CREON: But did he look straight at you? Was his mind right
    when he said that I was guilty of this charge?
535 CHORAGOS: I have no eyes to see what rulers do.
    But here he comes himself out of the house.

Enter Oedipus from the palace.

OEDIPUS: What? You here? And can you really have
    the face and daring to approach my house
    when you're exposed as its master's murderer
540   and caught, too, as the robber of my kingship?
    Did you see cowardice in me, by the gods,
    or foolishness, when you began this plot?
    Did you suppose that I would not detect
    your stealthy moves, or that I'd not fight back?
545   It's your attempt that's folly, isn't it—
    tracking without followers or connections,
    kingship which is caught with wealth and numbers?

° *winged maiden:* The Sphinx.

CREON: Now wait! Give me as long to answer back!
　　　Judge me for yourself when you have heard me!
OEDIPUS: You're eloquent, but I'd be slow to learn   550
　　　from you, now that I've seen your malice toward me.
CREON: That I deny. Hear what I have to say.
OEDIPUS: Don't you deny it! You are the traitor here!
CREON: If you consider mindless willfulness
　　　a prized possession, you are not thinking sense.   555
OEDIPUS: If you think you can wrong a relative
　　　and get off free, you are not thinking sense.
CREON: Perfectly just, I won't say no. And yet
　　　what is this injury you say I did you?
OEDIPUS: Did you persuade me, yes or no, to send   560
　　　someone to bring that solemn prophet here?
CREON: And I still hold to the advice I gave.
OEDIPUS: How many years ago did your King Laius . . .
CREON: Laius! Do what? Now I don't understand.
OEDIPUS: Vanish — victim of a murderous violence?   565
CREON: That is a long count back into the past.
OEDIPUS: Well, was this seer then practicing his art?
CREON: Yes, skilled and honored just as he is today.
OEDIPUS: Did he, back then, ever refer to me?
CREON: He did not do so in my presence ever.   570
OEDIPUS: You did inquire into the murder then.
CREON: We had to, surely, though we discovered nothing.
OEDIPUS: But the "skilled" one did not say this then? Why not?
CREON: I never talk when I am ignorant.
OEDIPUS: But you're not ignorant of your own part.   575
CREON: What do you mean? I'll tell you if I know.
OEDIPUS: Just this: if he had not conferred with you
　　　he'd not have told about my murdering Laius.
CREON: If he said that, you are the one who knows.
　　　But now it's fair that you should answer me.   580
OEDIPUS: Ask on! You won't convict me as the killer.
CREON: Well then, answer. My sister is your wife?
OEDIPUS: Now there's a statement that I can't deny.
CREON: You two have equal power in this country?
OEDIPUS: She gets from me whatever she desires.   585
CREON: And I'm a third? The three of us are equals?
OEDIPUS: That's where you're treacherous to your kinsman!
CREON: But think about this rationally, as I do.
　　　First look at this: do you think anyone
　　　prefers the anxieties of being king   590
　　　to untroubled sleep — if he has equal power?

I'm not the kind of man who falls in love
with kingship. I am content with a king's power.
And so would any man who's wise and prudent.
595   I get all things from you, with no distress;
as king I would have onerous duties, too.
How could the kingship bring me more delight
than this untroubled power and influence?
I'm not misguided yet to such a point
600   that profitable honors aren't enough.
As it is, all wish me well and all salute;
those begging you for something have me summoned,
for their success depends on that alone.
Why should I lose all this to become king?
605   A prudent mind is never traitorous.
Treason's a thought I'm not enamored of;
nor could I join a man who acted so.
In proof of this, first go yourself to Pytho
and ask if I brought back the true response.
610   Then, if you find I plotted with that portent
reader,° don't have me put to death by your vote
only — I'll vote myself for my conviction.
Don't let an unsupported thought convict me!
It's not right mindlessly to take the bad
615   for good or to suppose the good are traitors.
Rejecting a relation who is loyal
is like rejecting life, our greatest love.
In time you'll know securely without stumbling,
for time alone can prove a just man just,
620   though you can know a bad man in a day.
CHORAGOS: Well said, to one who's anxious not to fall.
    Swift thinkers, Lord, are never safe from stumbling.
OEDIPUS: But when a swift and secret plotter moves
    against me, I must make swift counterplot.
625   If I lie quiet and await his move,
    he'll have achieved his aims and I'll have missed.
CREON: You surely cannot mean you want me exiled!
OEDIPUS: Not exiled, no. Your death is what I want!
CREON: If you would first define what envy is . . .
630 OEDIPUS: Are you still stubborn? Still disobedient?
CREON: I see you cannot think!
OEDIPUS: For me I can.

°*portent reader:* Apollo's oracle or prophet.

CREON: You should for me as well!
OEDIPUS: But you're a traitor!
CREON: What if you're wrong?
OEDIPUS: Authority must be maintained.
CREON: Not if the ruler's evil.
OEDIPUS: Hear that, Thebes!   635
CREON: It is my city too, not yours alone!
CHORAGOS: Please don't, my Lords! Ah, just in time, I see
     Jocasta there, coming from the palace.
     With her help you must settle your quarrel.

Enter Jocasta from the palace.

JOCASTA: Wretched men! What has provoked this ill-
     advised dispute? Have you no sense of shame,   640
     with Thebes so sick, to stir up private troubles?
     Now go inside! And Creon, you go home!
     Don't make a general anguish out of nothing!
CREON: My sister, Oedipus your husband here
     sees fit to do one of two hideous things: 645
     to have me banished from the land — or killed!
OEDIPUS: That's right: I caught him, Lady, plotting harm
     against my person — with a malignant science.
CREON: May my life fail, may I die cursed, if I
     did any of the things you said I did!   650
JOCASTA: Believe his words, for the god's sake, Oedipus,
     in deference above all to his oath
     to the gods. Also for me, and for these men!

<u>KOMMOS°</u>
STROPHE 1
CHORUS: Consent, with will and mind,
     my king, I beg of you!   655
OEDIPUS: What do you wish me to surrender?
CHORUS: Show deference to him who was not feeble in time past
     and is now great in the power of his oath!
OEDIPUS: Do you know what you're asking?
CHORUS: Yes.
OEDIPUS: Tell me then.
CHORUS: Never to cast into dishonored guilt, with an unproved   660
     assumption, a kinsman who has bound himself by curse.
OEDIPUS: Now you must understand, when you ask this,
     you ask my death or banishment from the land.

° *Kommos:* A dirge or lament sung by the Chorus and one or more of the chief characters.

STROPHE 2

CHORUS: No, by the god who is the foremost of all gods,
665   the Sun! No! Godless,
       friendless, whatever death is worst of all,
    let that be my destruction, if this
       thought ever moved me!
    But my ill-fated soul
670   this dying land
    wears out — the more if to these older troubles
    she adds new troubles from the two of you!
OEDIPUS: Then let him go, though it must mean my death,
    or else disgrace and exile from the land.
675   My pity is moved by your words, not by his —
    he'll only have my hate, wherever he goes.
CREON: You're sullen as you yield; you'll be depressed
    when you've passed through this anger. Natures like yours
    are hardest on themselves. That's as it should be.
680 **OEDIPUS:** Then won't you go and let me be?
CREON: I'll go.
    Though you're unreasonable, they know I'm righteous.
Exit Creon.

ANTISTROPHE 1

CHORUS: Why are you waiting, Lady?
    Conduct him back into the palace!
JOCASTA: I will, when I have heard what chanced.
685 **CHORUS:** Conjectures — words alone, and nothing based on thought.
    But even an injustice can devour a man.
JOCASTA: Did the words come from both sides?
CHORUS: Yes.
JOCASTA: What was said?
CHORUS: To me it seems enough! enough! the land already troubled,
    that this should rest where it has stopped.
690 **OEDIPUS:** See what you've come to in your honest thought,
    in seeking to relax and blunt my heart?

ANTISTROPHE 2

CHORUS: I have not said this only once, my Lord.
    That I had lost my sanity,
       without a path in thinking —
    be sure this would be clear
695   if I put you away
    who, when my cherished land
       wandered crazed
    with suffering, brought her back on course.
    Now, too, be a lucky helmsman!

JOCASTA: Please, for the god's sake, Lord, explain to me
    the reason why you have conceived this wrath?
OEDIPUS: I honor you, not them,° and I'll explain
    to you how Creon has conspired against me.
JOCASTA: All right, if that will explain how the quarrel started.   705
OEDIPUS: He says I am the murderer of Laius!
JOCASTA: Did he claim knowledge or that someone told him?
OEDIPUS: Here's what he did: he sent that vicious seer
    so he could keep his own mouth innocent.
JOCASTA: Ah then, absolve yourself of what he charges!   710
    Listen to this and you'll agree, no mortal
    is ever given skill in prophecy.
    I'll prove this quickly with one incident.
    It was foretold to Laius — I shall not say
    by Phoebus himself, but by his ministers —   715
    that when his fate arrived he would be killed
    by a son who would be born to him and me.
    And yet, so it is told, foreign robbers
    murdered him, at a place where three roads meet.
    As for the child I bore him, not three days passed   720
    before he yoked the ball-joints of its feet,°
    then cast it, by others' hands, on a trackless mountain.
    That time Apollo did not make our child
    a patricide, or bring about what Laius
    feared, that he be killed by his own son.   725
    That's how prophetic words determined things!
    Forget them. The things a god must track
    he will himself painlessly reveal.
OEDIPUS: Just now, as I was listening to you, Lady,
    what a profound distraction seized my mind!   730
JOCASTA: What made you turn around so anxiously?
OEDIPUS: I thought you said that Laius was attacked
    and butchered at a place where three roads meet.
JOCASTA: That is the story, and it is told so still.
OEDIPUS: Where is the place where this was done to him?   735
JOCASTA: The land's called Phocis, where a two-forked road
    comes in from Delphi and from Daulia.
OEDIPUS: And how much time has passed since these events?
JOCASTA: Just prior to your presentation here
    as king this news was published to the city.   740
OEDIPUS: Oh, Zeus, what have you willed to do to me?
JOCASTA: Oedipus, what makes your heart so heavy?

° *them:* The Chorus.   ° *ball-joints of its feet:* The ankles.

OEDIPUS: No, tell me first of Laius' appearance,
    what peak of youthful vigor he had reached.
JOCASTA: A tall man, showing his first growth of white.
    He had a figure not unlike your own.
OEDIPUS: Alas! It seems that in my ignorance
    I laid those fearful curses on myself.
JOCASTA: What is it, Lord? I flinch to see your face.
750 OEDIPUS: I'm dreadfully afraid the prophet sees.
    But I'll know better with one more detail.
JOCASTA: I'm frightened too. But ask: I'll answer you.
OEDIPUS: Was his retinue small, or did he travel
    with a great troop, as would befit a prince?
755 JOCASTA: There were just five in all, one a herald.
    There was a carriage, too, bearing Laius.
OEDIPUS: Alas! Now I see it! But who was it,
    Lady, who told you what you know about this?
JOCASTA: A servant who alone was saved unharmed.
760 OEDIPUS: By chance, could he be now in the palace?
JOCASTA: No, he is not. When he returned and saw
    you had the power of the murdered Laius,
    he touched my hand and begged me formally
    to send him to the fields and to the pastures,
765   so he'd be out of sight, far from the city.
    I did. Although a slave, he well deserved
    to win this favor, and indeed far more.
OEDIPUS: Let's have him called back in immediately.
JOCASTA: That can be done, but why do you desire it?
770 OEDIPUS: I fear, Lady, I have already said
    too much. That's why I wish to see him now.
JOCASTA: Then he shall come; but it is right somehow
    that I, too, Lord, should know what troubles you.
OEDIPUS: I've gone so deep into the things I feared
775   I'll tell you everything. Who has a right
    greater than yours, while I cross through this chance?
    Polybus of Corinth was my father,
    my mother was the Dorian Meropē.
    I was first citizen, until this chance
780   attacked me — striking enough, to be sure,
    but not worth all the gravity I gave it.
    This: at a feast a man who'd drunk too much
    denied, at the wine, I was my father's son.
    I was depressed and all that day I barely
785   held it in. Next day I put the question
    to my mother and father. They were enraged

at the man who'd let this fiction fly at me.
I was much cheered by them. And yet it kept
grinding into me. His words kept coming back.
Without my mother's or my father's knowledge   790
I went to Pytho. But Phoebus sent me away
dishonoring my demand. Instead, other
wretched horrors he flashed forth in speech.
He said that I would be my mother's lover,
show offspring to mankind they could not look at,   795
and be his murderer whose seed I am.°
When I heard this, and ever since, I gauged
the way to Corinth by the stars alone,
running to a place where I would never see
the disgrace in the oracle's words come true.   800
But I soon came to the exact location
where, as you tell of it, the king was killed.
Lady, here is the truth. As I went on,
when I was just approaching those three roads,
a herald and a man like him you spoke of   805
came on, riding a carriage drawn by colts.
Both the man out front and the old man himself°
tried violently to force me off the road.
The driver, when he tried to push me off,
I struck in anger. The old man saw this, watched   810
me approach, then leaned out and lunged down
with twin prongs° at the middle of my head!
He got more than he gave. Abruptly — struck
once by the staff in this my hand — he tumbled
out, head first, from the middle of the carriage.   815
And then I killed them all. But if there is
a kinship between Laius and this stranger,
who is more wretched than the man you see?
Who was there born more hated by the gods?
For neither citizen nor foreigner   820
may take me in his home or speak to me.
No, they must drive me off. And it is I
who have pronounced these curses on myself!
I stain the dead man's bed with these my hands,
by which he died. Is not my nature vile?   825
Unclean? — if I am banished and even
in exile I may not see my own parents,

°*be . . . am:* I would murder my father.   °*old man himself:* Laius.   °*lunged . . . prongs:* Laius strikes Oedipus
with a two-pronged horse goad, or whip.

or set foot in my homeland, or else be yoked
in marriage to my mother, and kill my father,
830   Polybus, who raised me and gave me birth?
If someone judged a cruel divinity
did this to me, would he not speak the truth?
You pure and awful gods, may I not ever
see that day, may I be swept away
835   from men before I see so great and so
calamitous a stain fixed on my person!

CHORAGOS: These things seem fearful to us, Lord, and yet,
until you hear it from the witness, keep hope!

OEDIPUS: That is the single hope that's left to me,
840   to wait for him, that herdsman — until he comes.

JOCASTA: When he appears, what are you eager for?

OEDIPUS: Just this: if his account agrees with yours
then I shall have escaped this misery.

JOCASTA: But what was it that struck you in my story?

845 OEDIPUS: You said he spoke of robbers as the ones
who killed him. Now: if he continues still
to speak of many, then I could not have killed him.
One man and many men just do not jibe.
But if he says one belted man, the doubt
850   is gone. The balance tips toward me. I did it.

JOCASTA: No! He told it as I told you. Be certain.
He can't reject that and reverse himself.
The city heard these things, not I alone.
But even if he swerves from what he said,
855   he'll never show that Laius' murder, Lord,
occurred just as predicted. For Loxias
expressly said my son was doomed to kill him.
The boy — poor boy — he never had a chance
to cut him down, for he was cut down first.
860   Never again, just for some oracle
will I shoot frightened glances right and left.

OEDIPUS: That's full of sense. Nonetheless, send a man
to bring that farm hand here. Will you do it?

JOCASTA: I'll send one right away. But let's go in.
865   Would I do anything against your wishes?

Exit Oedipus and Jocasta through the central door into the palace.

<u>STASIMON 2</u>
STROPHE 1

CHORUS: May there accompany me
the fate to keep a reverential purity in what I say,

in all I do, for which the laws have been set forth
and walk on high, born to traverse the brightest,
highest upper air; Olympus° only   870
is their father, nor was it
mortal nature
that fathered them, and never will
oblivion lull them into sleep;
the god in them is great and never ages.   875

ANTISTROPHE 1
The will to violate, seed of the tyrant,
if it has drunk mindlessly of wealth and power,
without a sense of time or true advantage,
mounts to a peak, then
plunges to an abrupt . . . destiny,   880
where the useful foot
is of no use. But the kind
of struggling that is good for the city
I ask the god never to abolish.
The god is my protector: never will I give that up.   885

STROPHE 2
But if a man proceeds disdainfully
        in deeds of hand or word
and has no fear of Justice
        or reverence for shrines of the divinities
(may a bad fate catch him   890
        for his luckless wantonness!),
if he'll not gain what he gains with justice
and deny himself what is unholy,
or if he clings, in foolishness, to the untouchable
(what man, finally, in such an action, will have strength   895
enough to fend off passion's arrows from his soul?),
if, I say, this kind of
        deed is held in honor —
why should I join the sacred dance?

ANTISTROPHE 2
No longer shall I visit and revere   900
        Earth's navel,° the untouchable,
nor visit Abae's° temple,
        or Olympia,°
if the prophecies are not matched by events

°*Olympus:* Mount Olympus, home of the gods, and treated as a god itself.   °*Earth's navel:* Delphi.   °*Abae's:*
Abae was a town in Phocis where there was another oracle of Apollo.   °*Olympia:* Site of the oracle of Zeus.

905   for all the world to point to.
        No, you who hold the power, if you are rightly called
        Zeus the king of all, let this matter not escape you
        and your ever-deathless rule,
        for the prophecies to Laius fade . . .
910   and men already disregard them;
        nor is Apollo anywhere
              glorified with honors.
        Religion slips away.

EPISODE 3

*Enter Jocasta from the palace carrying a branch wound with wool and a jar of incense.
She is attended by two women.*

JOCASTA: Lords of the realm, the thought has come to me
915   to visit shrines of the divinities
        with suppliant's branch in hand and fragrant smoke.
        For Oedipus excites his soul too much
        with alarms of all kinds. He will not judge
        the present by the past, like a man of sense.
920   He's at the mercy of all terror-mongers.

Jocasta approaches the altar on the right and kneels.

        Since I can do no good by counseling,
        Apollo the Lycēan! — you are the closest —
        I come a suppliant, with these my vows,
        for a cleansing that will not pollute him.
925   For when we see him shaken we are all
        afraid, like people looking at their helmsman.

*Enter a Messenger along one of the parados. He sees Jocasta at the altar and then
addresses the Chorus.*

MESSENGER: I would be pleased if you would help me, stranger.
        Where is the palace of King Oedipus?
        Or tell me where he is himself, if you know.
930 **CHORUS:** This is his house, stranger. He is within.
        This is his wife and mother of his children.
MESSENGER: May she and her family find prosperity,
        if, as you say, her marriage is fulfilled.
JOCASTA: You also, stranger, for you deserve as much
935   for your gracious words. But tell me why you've come.
        What do you wish? Or what have you to tell us?
MESSENGER: Good news, my Lady, both for your house and husband.
JOCASTA: What is your news? And who has sent you to us?

MESSENGER: I come from Corinth. When you have heard my news
    you will rejoice, I'm sure — and grieve perhaps.   940
JOCASTA: What is it? How can it have this double power?
MESSENGER: They will establish him their king, so say
    the people of the land of Isthmia.°
JOCASTA: But is old Polybus not still in power?
MESSENGER: He's not, for death has clasped him in the tomb.
JOCASTA: What's this? Has Oedipus' father died?
MESSENGER: If I have lied then I deserve to die.   945
JOCASTA: Attendant! Go quickly to your master,
    and tell him this.

Exit an Attendant into the palace.

                Oracles of the gods!
    Where are you now? The man whom Oedipus   950
    fled long ago, for fear that he should kill him —
    he's been destroyed by chance and not by him!

Enter Oedipus from the palace.

OEDIPUS: Darling Jocasta, my beloved wife,
    Why have you called me from the palace?   955
JOCASTA: First hear what this man has to say. Then see
    what the god's grave oracle has come to now!
OEDIPUS: Where is he from? What is this news he brings me?
JOCASTA: From Corinth. He brings news about your father:
    that Polybus is no more! that he is dead!   960
OEDIPUS: What's this, old man? I want to hear you say it.
MESSENGER: If this is what must first be clarified,
    please be assured that he is dead and gone.
OEDIPUS: By treachery or by the touch of sickness?
MESSENGER: Light pressures tip agéd frames into their sleep.   965
OEDIPUS: You mean the poor man died of some disease.
MESSENGER: And of the length of years that he had tallied.
OEDIPUS: Aha! Then why should we look to Pytho's vapors,°
    or to the birds that scream above our heads?°
    If we could really take those things for guides,   970
    I would have killed my father. But he's dead!
    He is beneath the earth, and here am I,
    who never touched a spear. Unless he died
    of longing for me and I "killed" him that way!

° *land of Isthmia:* Corinth, Greek city-state situated on an isthmus.   ° *Pytho's vapors:* Prophecies of the oracle
at Delphi.   ° *birds . . . heads:* Prophecies derived from interpreting the flights of birds.

No, in this case, Polybus, by dying, took
the worthless oracle to Hades with him.
JOCASTA: And wasn't I telling you that just now?
OEDIPUS: You were indeed. I was misled by fear.
JOCASTA: You should not care about this anymore.
OEDIPUS: I must care. I must stay clear of my mother's bed.
JOCASTA: What's there for man to fear? The realm of chance
prevails. True foresight isn't possible.
His life is best who lives without a plan.
This marriage with your mother — don't fear it.
How many times have men in dreams, too, slept
with their own mothers! Those who believe such things
mean nothing endure their lives most easily.
OEDIPUS: A fine, bold speech, and you are right, perhaps,
except that my mother is still living,
so I must fear her, however well you argue.

990 JOCASTA: And yet your father's tomb is a great eye.
OEDIPUS: Illuminating, yes. But I still fear the living.
MESSENGER: Who is the woman who inspires this fear?
OEDIPUS: Meropē, Polybus' wife, old man.
MESSENGER: And what is there about her that alarms you?
995 OEDIPUS: An oracle, god-sent and fearful, stranger.
MESSENGER: Is it permitted that another know?
OEDIPUS: It is. Loxias once said to me
I must have intercourse with my own mother
and take my father's blood with these my hands.
1000 So I have long lived far away from Corinth.
This has indeed brought much good luck, and yet,
to see one's parents' eyes is happiest.
MESSENGER: Was it for this that you have lived in exile?
OEDIPUS: So I'd not be my father's killer, sir.
1005 MESSENGER: Had I not better free you from this fear,
my Lord? That's why I came — to do you service.
OEDIPUS: Indeed, what a reward you'd get for that!
MESSENGER: Indeed, this is the main point of my trip,
to be rewarded when you get back home.
1010 OEDIPUS: I'll never rejoin the givers of my seed!°
MESSENGER: My son, clearly you don't know what you're doing.
OEDIPUS: But how is that, old man? For the gods' sake, tell me!
MESSENGER: If it's because of them you won't go home.
OEDIPUS: I fear that Phoebus will have told the truth.
1015 MESSENGER: Pollution from the ones who gave you seed?

°*givers of my seed:* Meaning, i.e., my parents." Oedipus still thinks Meropē and Polybus are his parents.

OEDIPUS: That is the thing, old man, I always fear.
MESSENGER: Your fear is groundless. Understand that.
OEDIPUS: Groundless? Not if I was born their son.
MESSENGER: But Polybus is not related to you.
OEDIPUS: Do you mean Polybus was not my father? 1020
MESSENGER: No more than I. We're both the same to you.
OEDIPUS: Same? One who begot me and one who didn't?
MESSENGER: He didn't beget you any more than I did.
OEDIPUS: But then, why did he say I was his son?
MESSENGER: He got you as a gift from my own hands. 1025
OEDIPUS: He loved me so, though from another's hands?
MESSENGER: His former childlessness persuaded him.
OEDIPUS: But had you bought me, or begotten me?
MESSENGER: Found you. In the forest hallows of Cithaeron.
OEDIPUS: What were you doing traveling in that region? 1030
MESSENGER: I was in charge of flocks which grazed those mountains.
OEDIPUS: A wanderer who worked the flocks for hire?
MESSENGER: Ah, but that day I was your savior, son.
OEDIPUS: From what? What was my trouble when you took me?
MESSENGER: The ball-joints of your feet might testify. 1035
OEDIPUS: What's that? What makes you name that ancient trouble?
MESSENGER: Your feet were pierced and I am your rescuer.
OEDIPUS: A fearful rebuke those tokens left for me!
MESSENGER: That was the chance that names you who you are.
OEDIPUS: By the gods, did my mother or my father do this? 1040
MESSENGER: That I don't know. He might who gave you to me.
OEDIPUS: From someone else? You didn't chance on me?
MESSENGER: Another shepherd handed you to me.
OEDIPUS: Who was he? Do you know? Will you explain!
MESSENGER: They called him one of the men of — was it Laius? 1045
OEDIPUS: The one who once was king here long ago?
MESSENGER: That is the one! The man was shepherd to him.
OEDIPUS: And is he still alive so I can see him?
MESSENGER: But you who live here ought to know that best.
OEDIPUS: Does any one of you now present know 1050
about the shepherd whom this man has named?
Have you seen him in town or in the fields? Speak out!
The time has come for the discovery!
CHORAGOS: The man he speaks of, I believe, is the same
as the field hand you have already asked to see. 1055
But it's Jocasta who would know this best.
OEDIPUS: Lady, do you remember the man we just
now sent for — is that the man he speaks of?
JOCASTA: What? The man he spoke of? Pay no attention!

Laurence Olivier as Oedipus, framed by a masked member of the Chorus and Jocasta. In this scene from the landmark 1945 production of *Oedipus the King,* the doomed King seems to finally recognize the "truth" that he has been seeking.

1060   His words are not worth thinking about. It's nothing.
OEDIPUS: With clues like this within my grasp, give up?
   Fail to solve the mystery of my birth?
JOCASTA: For the love of the gods, and if you love your life,
   give up this search! My sickness is enough.
1065 OEDIPUS: Come! Though my mothers for three generations
   were in slavery, you'd not be lowborn!
JOCASTA: No, listen to me! Please! Don't do this thing!
OEDIPUS: I will not listen; I will search out the truth.
JOCASTA: My thinking is for you — it would be best.
1070 OEDIPUS: This "best" of yours is starting to annoy me.
JOCASTA: Doomed man! Never find out who you are!
OEDIPUS: Will someone go and bring that shepherd here?
   Leave her to glory in her wealthy birth!
JOCASTA: Man of misery! No other name
1075   shall I address you by, ever again.

Exit Jocasta into the palace after a long pause.

CHORAGOS: Why has your lady left, Oedipus,
   hurled by a savage grief? I am afraid
   disaster will come bursting from this silence.

OEDIPUS: Let it burst forth! However low this seed
    of mine may be, yet I desire to see it.   1080
    She, perhaps — she has a woman's pride —
    is mortified by my base origins.
    But I who count myself the child of Chance,
    the giver of good, shall never know dishonor.
    She is my mother,° and the months my brothers   1085
    who first marked out my lowness, then my greatness.
    I shall not prove untrue to such a nature
    by giving up the search for my own birth.

STASIMON 3
STROPHE

CHORUS: If I have mantic power°
    and excellence in thought,   1090
    by Olympus,
        you shall not, Cithaeron, at tomorrow's
    full moon,
    fail to hear us celebrate you as the countryman
    of Oedipus, his nurse and mother,   1095
    or fail to be the subject of our dance,
        since you have given pleasure
    to our king.
    Phoebus, whom we summon by "iē!,"   1100
    may this be pleasing to you!

ANTISTROPHE

    Who was your mother, son?
    which of the long-lived nymphs
    after lying with Pan,°
        the mountain roaming . . . Or was it a bride
    of Loxias?°   1105
    For dear to him are all the upland pastures.
    Or was it Mount Cyllēnē's lord,°
    or the Bacchic god,°
        dweller of the mountain peaks,
    who received you as a joyous find   1110
    from one of the nymphs of Helicon,
    the favorite sharers of his sport?

° *She . . . mother:* Chance is my mother.   ° *If . . . mantic power:* If I am a prophet.   ° *Pan:* God of shepherds
and woodlands, half man and half goat.   ° *Loxias:* Apollo.   ° *Mount Cyllēnē's lord:* Hermes, messenger of the
gods.   ° *Bacchic god:* Dionysus.

EPISODE 4

OEDIPUS: If someone like myself, who never met him,
may calculate — elders, I think I see
1115 the very herdsman we've been waiting for.
His many years would fit that man's age,
and those who bring him on, if I am right,
are my own men. And yet, in real knowledge,
you can outstrip me, surely: you've seen him.

Enter the old Herdsman escorted by two of Oedipus's Attendants. At first, the Herdsman will not look at Oedipus.

1120 **CHORAGOS:** I know him, yes, a man of the house of Laius,
a trusty herdsman if he ever had one.
OEDIPUS: I ask you first, the stranger come from Corinth:
is this the man you spoke of?
MESSENGER: That's he you see.
1125 **OEDIPUS:** Then you, old man. First look at me! Now answer:
did you belong to Laius' household once?
HERDSMAN: I did. Not a purchased slave but raised in the palace.
OEDIPUS: How have you spent your life? What is your work?
HERDSMAN: Most of my life now I have tended sheep.
OEDIPUS: Where is the usual place you stay with them?
1130 **HERDSMAN:** On Mount Cithaeron. Or in that district.
OEDIPUS: Do you recall observing this man there?
HERDSMAN: Doing what? Which is the man you mean?
OEDIPUS: This man right here. Have you had dealings with him?
HERDSMAN: I can't say right away. I don't remember.
1135 **MESSENGER:** No wonder, master. I'll bring clear memory
to his ignorance. I'm absolutely sure
he can recall it, the district was Cithaeron,
he with a double flock, and I, with one,
lived close to him, for three entire seasons,
1140 six months along, from spring right to Arcturus.°
Then for the winter I'd drive mine to my fold,
and he'd drive his to Laius' pen again.
Did any of the things I say take place?
HERDSMAN: You speak the truth, though it's from long ago.
1145 **MESSENGER:** Do you remember giving me, back then,
a boy I was to care for as my own?
HERDSMAN: What are you saying? Why do you ask me that?
MESSENGER: There, sir, is the man who was that boy!
1150 **HERDSMAN:** Damn you! Shut your mouth! Keep your silence!

°*Arcturus:* A star that is first seen in September in the sky over Greece.

OEDIPUS: Stop! Don't you rebuke his words.
  Your words ask for rebuke far more than his.
HERDSMAN: But what have I done wrong, most royal master?
OEDIPUS: Not telling of the boy of whom he asked.
HERDSMAN: He's ignorant and blundering toward ruin.
OEDIPUS: Tell it willingly — or under torture.   1155
HERDSMAN: Oh god! Don't — I am old — don't torture me!
OEDIPUS: Here! Someone put his hands behind his back!
HERDSMAN: But why? What else would you find out, poor man?
OEDIPUS: Did you give him the child he asks about?
HERDSMAN: I did. I wish that I had died that day!   1160
OEDIPUS: You'll come to that if you don't speak the truth.
HERDSMAN: It's if I speak that I shall be destroyed.
OEDIPUS: I think this fellow struggles for delay.
HERDSMAN: No, no! I said already that I gave him.
OEDIPUS: From your own home, or got from someone else?   1165
HERDSMAN: Not from my own. I got him from another.
OEDIPUS: Which of these citizens? What sort of house?
HERDSMAN: Don't — by the gods! — don't, master, ask me more!
OEDIPUS: It means your death if I must ask again.
HERDSMAN: One of the children of the house of Laius.   1170
OEDIPUS: A slave — or born into the family?
HERDSMAN: I have come to the dreaded thing, and I shall say it.
OEDIPUS: And I to hearing it, but hear I must.
HERDSMAN: He was reported to have been — his son.
  Your lady in the house could tell you best.   1175
OEDIPUS: Because she gave him to you?
HERDSMAN: Yes, my lord.
OEDIPUS: What was her purpose?
HERDSMAN: I was to kill the boy.
OEDIPUS: The child she bore?
HERDSMAN: She dreaded prophecies.
OEDIPUS: What were they?
HERDSMAN: The word was that he'd kill his parents.
OEDIPUS: Then why did you give him up to this old man?   1180
HERDSMAN: In pity, master — so he would take him home,
  to another land. But what he did was save him
  for this supreme disaster. If you are the one
  he speaks of — know your evil birth and fate!
OEDIPUS: Ah! All of it was destined to be true!   1185
  Oh light, now may I look my last upon you,
  shown monstrous in my birth, in marriage monstrous,
  a murderer monstrous in those I killed.

Exit Oedipus, running into the palace.

<u>STASIMON 4</u>
STROPHE 1

CHORUS: Oh generations of mortal men,
1190   while you are living, I will
                    appraise your lives at zero!
          What man
          comes closer to seizing lasting blessedness
          than merely to seize its semblance,
1195   and after living in this semblance, to plunge?
          With your example before us,
          with your destiny, yours,
                    suffering Oedipus, no mortal
          can I judge fortunate.

ANTISTROPHE 1

1200   For he,° outranging everybody,
          shot his arrow° and became the lord
                    of wide prosperity and blessedness,
          oh Zeus, after destroying
          the virgin with the crooked talons,°
1205   singer of oracles; and against death,
          in my land, he arose a tower of defense.
          From which time you were called my king
          and granted privileges supreme — in mighty
          Thebes the ruling lord.

STROPHE 2

1210   But now — whose story is more sorrowful than yours?
          Who is more intimate with fierce calamities,
          with labors, now that your life is altered?
          Alas, my Oedipus, whom all men know:
          one great harbor°—
1215   one alone sufficed for you,
          as son and father,
          when you tumbled,° plowman° of the woman's chamber.
          How, how could your paternal
                    furrows, wretched man,
1220   endure you silently so long.

ANTISTROPHE 2

          Time, all-seeing, surprised you living an unwilled life
          and sits from of old in judgment on the marriage, not a marriage,

---

°*he:* Oedipus.   °*shot his arrow:* Took his chances; made a guess at the Sphinx's riddle.   °*virgin . . . talons:*
The Sphinx.   °*one great harbor:* Metaphorical allusion to Jocasta's body.   °*tumbled:* Were born and had sex.
°*plowman:* Plowing is used here as a sexual metaphor.

where the begetter is the begot as well.
Ah, son of Laius . . . ,
would that — oh, would that   1225
I had never seen you!
I wail, my scream climbing beyond itself
from my whole power of voice. To say it straight:
        from you I got new breath —
but I also lulled my eye to sleep.°   1230

<u>EXODOS</u>°

Enter the Second Messenger from the palace.

SECOND MESSENGER: You who are first among the citizens,
    what deeds you are about to hear and see!
    What grief you'll carry, if, true to your birth,
    you still respect the house of Labdacus!
    Neither the Ister nor the Phasis river   1235
    could purify this house, such suffering
    does it conceal, or soon must bring to light —
    willed this time, not unwilled. Griefs hurt worst
    which we perceive to be self-chosen ones.
CHORAGOS: They were sufficient, the things we knew before,   1240
    to make us grieve. What can you add to those?
SECOND MESSENGER: The thing that's quickest said and quickest heard:
    our own, our royal one, Jocasta's dead.
CHORAGOS: Unhappy queen! What was responsible?
SECOND MESSENGER: Herself. The bitterest of these events   1245
    is not for you, you were not there to see,
    but yet, exactly as I can recall it,
    you'll hear what happened to that wretched lady.
    She came in anger through the outer hall,
    and then she ran straight to her marriage bed,   1250
    tearing her hair with the fingers of both hands.
    Then, slamming shut the doors when she was in,
    she called to Laius, dead so many years,
    remembering the ancient seed which caused
    his death, leaving the mother to the son   1255
    to breed again an ill-born progeny.
    She mourned the bed where she, alas, bred double —
    husband by husband, children by her child.
    From this point on I don't know how she died,
    for Oedipus then burst in with a cry,   1260

°*I . . . sleep:* I failed to see the corruption you brought.   °*Exodos:* The final scene, containing the play's resolution.

and did not let us watch her final evil.
Our eyes were fixed on him. Wildly he ran
to each of us, asking for his spear
and for his wife — no wife: where he might find
1265 the double mother-field, his and his children's.
He raved, and some divinity then showed him —
for none of us did so who stood close by.
With a dreadful shout — as if some guide were leading —
he lunged through the double doors; he bent the hollow
1270 bolts from the sockets, burst into the room,
and there we saw her, hanging from above,
entangled in some twisted hanging strands.
He saw, was stricken, and with a wild roar
ripped down the dangling noose. When she, poor woman,
1275 lay on the ground, there came a fearful sight:
he snatched the pins of worked gold from her dress,
with which her clothes were fastened: these he raised
and struck into the ball-joints of his eyes.°
He shouted that they would no longer see
1280 the evils he had suffered or had done,
see in the dark those he should not have seen,
and know no more those he once sought to know.
While chanting this, not once but many times
he raised his hand and struck into his eyes.
1285 Blood from his wounded eyes poured down his chin,
not freed in moistening drops, but all at once
a stormy rain of black blood burst like hail.
These evils, coupling them, making them one,
1290 have broken loose upon both man and wife.
The old prosperity that they had once
was true prosperity, and yet today,
mourning, ruin, death, disgrace, and every
evil you could name — not one is absent.
CHORAGOS: Has he allowed himself some peace from all this grief?
1295 **SECOND MESSENGER:** He shouts that someone slide the bolts and show
to all the Cadmeians the patricide,
his mother's — I can't say it, it's unholy —
so he can cast himself out of the land,
not stay and curse his house by his own curse.
1300 He lacks the strength, though, and he needs a guide,
for his is a sickness that's too great to bear.
Now you yourself will see: the bolts of the doors

°*ball-joints of his eyes:* His eyeballs. Oedipus blinds himself in both eyes at the same time.

are opening. You are about to see
a vision even one who hates must pity.

Enter the blinded Oedipus from the palace, led in by a household Servant.

CHORAGOS: Terrifying suffering for men to see,   1305
more terrifying than any I've ever
come upon. Oh man of pain
what madness reached you? Which god from far off,
surpassing in range his longest spring,
     struck hard against your god-abandoned fate?   1310
Oh man of pain,
I cannot look upon you — though there's so much
I would ask you, so much to hear,
so much that holds my eyes —
     such is the shudder you produce in me.   1315
OEDIPUS: Ah! Ah! I am a man of misery.
Where am I carried? Pity me! Where
is my voice scattered abroad on wings?
     Divinity, where has your lunge transported me?
CHORAGOS: To something horrible, not to be heard or seen.   1320

KOMMOS
STROPHE 1

OEDIPUS: Oh, my cloud
of darkness, abominable, unspeakable as it attacks me,
not to be turned away, brought by an evil wind!
Alas!
Again alas! Both enter me at once: 1325
the sting of the prongs,° the memory of evils!
CHORUS: I do not marvel that in these afflictions
you carry double griefs and double evils.

ANTISTROPHE 1

OEDIPUS: Ah, friend,
so you at least are there, resolute servant!   1330
Still with a heart to care for me, the blind man.
Oh! Oh!
I know that you are there. I recognize
even inside my darkness, that voice of yours.
CHORUS: Doer of horror, how did you bear to quench   1335
your vision? What divinity raised your hand?

° *prongs:* Refers both to the whip that Laius used and to the two gold pins that Oedipus used to blind himself.

STROPHE 2

OEDIPUS: It was Apollo there, Apollo, friends,
　　　　who brought my sorrows, vile sorrows to their perfection,
　　　　　　these evils that were done to me.
1340　　But the one who struck them with his hand,
　　　　　　that one was none but I, in wretchedness.
　　　　For why was I to see
　　　　when nothing I could see would bring me joy?
CHORUS: Yes, that is how it was.
1345 OEDIPUS: What could I see, indeed,
　　　　or what enjoy — what greeting
　　　　is there I could hear with pleasure, friends?
　　　　Conduct me out of the land
　　　　　　as quickly as you can!
1350　　Conduct me out, my friends,
　　　　　　the man utterly ruined,
　　　　supremely cursed,
　　　　　　the man who is by gods
　　　　the most detested of all men!
1355 CHORUS: Wretched in disaster and in knowledge:
　　　　oh, I could wish you'd never come to know!

ANTISTROPHE 2

OEDIPUS: May he be destroyed, whoever freed the savage shackles
　　　　from my feet when I'd been sent to the wild pasture,
　　　　　　whoever rescued me from murder
1360　　and became my savior —
　　　　　　a bitter gift:
　　　　if I had died then,
　　　　I'd not have been such grief to self and kin.
CHORUS: I also would have had it so.
1365 OEDIPUS: I'd not have returned to be my father's
　　　　murderer; I'd not be called by men
　　　　my mother's bridegroom.
　　　　Now I'm without a god,
　　　　　　child of a polluted parent,
1370　　fellow progenitor with him
　　　　　　who gave me birth in misery.
　　　　If there's an evil that
　　　　　　surpasses evils, that
　　　　has fallen to the lot of Oedipus.
CHORAGOS: How can I say that you have counseled well?
1375　　Better not to be than live a blind man.
OEDIPUS: That this was not the best thing I could do —
　　　　don't tell me that, or advise me any more!

Should I descend to Hades and endure
to see my father with these eyes? Or see   1380
my poor unhappy mother? For I have done,
to both of these, things too great for hanging.
Or is the sight of children to be yearned for,
to see new shoots that sprouted as these did?
Never, never with these eyes of mine!   1385
Nor city, nor tower, nor holy images
of the divinities! For I, all-wretched,
most nobly raised — as no one else in Thebes —
deprived myself of these when I ordained
that all expel the impious one — god-shown   1390
to be polluted, and the dead king's son!°
Once I exposed this great stain upon me,
could I have looked on these with steady eyes?
No! No! And if there were a way to block
the source of hearing in my ears, I'd gladly   1395
have locked up my pitiable body,
so I'd be blind and deaf. Evils shut out —
that way my mind could live in sweetness.
Alas, Cithaeron, why did you receive me?
Or when you had me, not killed me instantly?   1400
I'd not have had to show my birth to mankind.
Polybus, Corinth, halls — ancestral,
they told me — how beautiful was your ward,
a scar that held back festering disease!
Evil my nature, evil my origin.   1405
You, three roads, and you, secret ravine,
you oak grove, narrow place of those three paths
that drank my blood° from these hands, from him
who fathered me, do you remember still
the things I did to you? When I'd come here,   1410
what I then did once more? Oh marriages! Marriages!
You gave us life and when you'd planted us
you sent the same seed up, and then revealed
fathers, brothers, sons, and kinsman's blood,
and brides, and wives, and mothers, all the most   1415
atrocious things that happen to mankind!
One should not name what never should have been.
Somewhere out there, then, quickly, by the gods,

° *I . . . son:* Oedipus refers to his own curse against the murderer as well as his sins of patricide and incest.
° *my blood:* I.e., "the blood of my father, Laius."

cover me up, or murder me, or throw me
1420   to the ocean where you will never see me more!

Oedipus moves toward the Chorus and they back away from him.

Come! Don't shrink to touch this wretched man!
Believe me, do not be frightened! I alone
of all mankind can carry these afflictions.

Enter Creon from the palace with Attendants.

CHORAGOS: Tell Creon what you wish for. Just when we need him
1425   he's here. He can act, he can advise you.
He's now the land's sole guardian in your place.
OEDIPUS: Ah! Are there words that I can speak to him?
What ground for trust can I present? It's proved
that I was false to him in everything.
1430 CREON: I have not come to mock you, Oedipus,
nor to reproach you for your former falseness.
You men, if you have no respect for sons
of mortals, let your awe for the all-feeding
flames of lordy Hēlius° prevent
1435   your showing unconcealed so great a stain,
abhorred by earth and sacred rain and light.
Escort him quickly back into the house!
If blood kin only see and hear their own
afflictions, we'll have no impious defilement.
1440 OEDIPUS: By the gods, you've freed me from one terrible fear,
so nobly meeting my unworthiness:
grant me something — not for me; for you!
CREON: What do you want that you should beg me so?
OEDIPUS: To drive me from the land at once, to a place
1445   where there will be no man to speak to me!
CREON: I would have done just that — had I not wished
to ask first of the god what I should do.
OEDIPUS: His answer was revealed in full — that I,
the patricide, unholy, be destroyed.
1450 CREON: He said that, but our need is so extreme,
it's best to have sure knowledge what must be done.
OEDIPUS: You'll ask about a wretched man like me?
CREON: Is it not time you put your trust in the god?
OEDIPUS: But I bid you as well, and shall entreat you.
1455   Give her who is within what burial
you will — you'll give your own her proper rites;

°*Hēlius:* The sun.

but me — do not condemn my fathers' land
to have me dwelling here while I'm alive,
but let me live on mountains — on Cithaeron
famed as mine, for my mother and my father,
while they yet lived, made it my destined tomb,   1460
and I'll be killed by those who wished my ruin!
And yet I know: no sickness will destroy me,
nothing will: I'd never have been saved
when left to die unless for some dread evil.
Then let my fate continue where it will!   1465
As for my children, Creon, take no pains
for my sons — they're men and they will never lack
the means to live, wherever they may be —
but my two wretched, pitiable girls,
who never ate but at my table, never   1470
were without me — everything that I
would touch, they'd always have a share of it —
please care for them! Above all, let me touch
them with my hands and weep aloud my woes!
Please, my Lord!   1475
Please, noble heart! Touching with my hands,
I'd think I held them as when I could see.

Enter Antigone and Ismene from the palace with Attendants.

What's this?
Oh gods! Do I hear, somewhere, my two dear ones
sobbing? Has Creon really pitied me   1480
and sent to me my dearest ones, my children?
Is that it?

CREON: Yes, I prepared this for you, for I knew
you'd feel this joy, as you have always done.

OEDIPUS: Good fortune, then, and, for your care, be guarded   1485
far better by divinity than I was!
Where are you, children? Come to me! Come here
to these my hands, hands of your brother, hands
of him who gave you seed, hands that made
these once bright eyes to see now in this fashion.   1490

Oedipus embraces his daughters.

He, children, seeing nothing, knowing nothing,
he fathered you where his own seed was plowed.
I weep for you as well, though I can't see you,
imagining your bitter life to come,
the life you will be forced by men to live.   1495
What gatherings of townsmen will you join,

what festivals, without returning home
in tears instead of watching holy rites?
And when you've reached the time for marrying,
1500   where, children, is the man who'll run the risk
of taking on himself the infamy
that will wound you as it did my parents?
What evil is not here? Your father killed
his father, plowed the one who gave him birth,
1505   and from the place where he was sown, from there
he got you, from the place he too was born.
These are the wounds: then who will marry you?
No man, my children. No, it's clear that you
must wither in dry barrenness, unmarried.

1510   *Oedipus addresses Creon.*

Son of Menoeceus! You are the only father
left to them — we two who gave them seed
are both destroyed: watch that they don't become
poor, wanderers, unmarried — they are your kin.
Let not my ruin be their ruin, too!
1515   No, pity them! You see how young they are,
bereft of everyone, except for you.
Consent, kind heart, and touch me with your hand!

Creon grasps Oedipus's right hand.

You, children, if you had reached an age of sense,
I would have counseled much. Now, pray you may live
1520   always where it's allowed, finding a life
better than his was, who gave you seed.
CREON: Stop this now. Quiet your weeping. Move away, into the house.
OEDIPUS: Bitter words, but I obey them.
CREON: There's an end to all things.
OEDIPUS: I have first this request.
CREON: Tell me. I shall judge when I will hear it.
1525   OEDIPUS: Banish me from my homeland.
CREON: You must ask that of the god.
OEDIPUS: But I am the gods' most hated man!
CREON: Then you will soon get what you want.
OEDIPUS: Do you consent?
CREON: I never promise when, as now, I'm ignorant.
OEDIPUS: Then lead me in.
CREON: Come. But let your hold fall from your children.
OEDIPUS: Do not take them from me, ever!
CREON: Do not wish to keep all of the power.

You had power, but that power did not follow you through life.   1530

Oedipus's daughters are taken from him and led into the palace by Attendants. Oedipus is led into the palace by a Servant. Creon and the other Attendants follow. Only the Chorus remains.

CHORUS: People of Thebes, my country, see: here is that Oedipus —
he who "knew" the famous riddle, and attained the highest power,
whom all citizens admired, even envying his luck!
See the billows of wild troubles which he has entered now!   1535
Here is the truth of each man's life: we must wait, and see his end,
scrutinize his dying day, and refuse to call him happy
till he has crossed the border of his life without pain.

Exit the Chorus along each of the parados.

Reading and Reacting

1. The ancient Greeks used no scenery in their theatrical productions. In the absence of scenery, how is the setting established at the beginning of *Oedipus the King*?

2. In order not to detract from the language of *Oedipus the King*, some contemporary productions use very simple costumes. Do you agree with this decision? If so, why? If not, what kind of costumes would you use?

3. In some recent productions of *Oedipus the King*, actors wear copies of ancient Greek masks. What are the advantages and disadvantages of using such masks in a contemporary production of the play?

4. In the ancient Greek theater, the *strophe* and *antistrophe* were sung or chanted by the chorus as it danced back and forth across the stage. If you were staging the play today, would you retain the chorus or do away with it entirely? What would be gained or lost with each alternative?

5. Why does Sophocles have Oedipus blind himself offstage? What would be the effect of having Oedipus perform this act in full view of the audience?

6. How does Sophocles present information about what happened years before the play took place? If you were staging a contemporary version of the play, what additional ways could you use to present this information?

7. The ancient Greek audience that viewed *Oedipus the King* was familiar with the plot of the play. Given this situation, how does Sophocles create suspense? What are the advantages and disadvantages of using a story that the audience already knows?

8. By the end of the play, what has Oedipus learned about himself? About the gods? About the quest for truth? Do you see him as a tragic or a pathetic figure?

9. Today, many directors employ **color-blind casting** — that is, they cast an actor in a role without regard to his or her race. Do you think this practice could be used in casting *Oedipus the King*? How, for example, would you react to an African-American Oedipus or to an Asian Creon?

10. JOURNAL ENTRY Do you think Oedipus deserves his fate? Why or why not?

11. CRITICAL PERSPECTIVE In "On Misunderstanding the *Oedipus Rex*," F. R. Dodds argues that Sophocles did not intend that Oedipus's tragedy be seen as rising from a "grave moral flaw." Neither, says Dodds, was Oedipus a "mere puppet" of the gods. Rather, "what fascinates us is the spectacle of a man freely choosing, from the highest motives, a series of actions which lead to his own ruin":

> Oedipus is great, not in virtue of a great worldly position—for his worldly position is an illusion which will vanish like a dream—but in virtue of his inner strength: strength to pursue the truth at whatever personal cost, and strength to accept and endure it when found. . . . Oedipus is great because he accepts the responsibility for all his acts, including those which are objectively most horrible, though subjectively innocent.

Do you agree with Dodds's arguments? Do you see Oedipus as someone who has inner strength or as a morally flawed victim of the gods?

Related Works: "Barn Burning" (p. 209), "Young Goodman Brown" (p. 302), "'Out, Out—'" (p. 539), "Leda and the Swan" (p. 615), "Ulysses" (p. 701), *Hamlet* (p. 936)

WRITING SUGGESTIONS: Staging

1. Discuss the problems that the original staging of *Oedipus the King* or *Hamlet* poses for contemporary audiences, and offer some possible solutions.

2. More than one critic has observed that the simplicity of Shakespeare's theater was one of its main strengths. If a character wanted to make himself invisible, all he had to do was declare himself so. If a scene called for a particular setting — a palace or forest, for example — the setting could be established with dialogue. Find two or three examples of this technique, and write an essay in which you discuss whether or not suggestions are more effective in the staging of *Hamlet* than special effects or realistic settings would be.

3. Discuss and analyze the staging techniques used in a play that is not in this chapter — for example, *Trifles* (p. 770) or *Tape* (p. 741).

4. Choose a short story that appears in this anthology, and explain how you would stage it if it were a play. What furnishings, props, costumes, lighting, and sound effects would you choose? What events would occur offstage? Possible subjects for this paper might include "A&P" (p. 128), "The Story of an Hour" (p. 104), or "The Storm" (p. 158).

5. *Beauty* and *Nine Ten* present different problems in staging. Write an essay in which you outline plans for staging *Beauty* with a generous budget and *Nine Ten* with a very limited budget.

CHAPTER 30

THEME

> I can't even count how many times I've heard the line, "Where did the idea for this play come from?" . . . Ideas emerge from plays —not the other way around. . . . I think explanation destroys [a play] and makes it less than it is.
>
> —Sam Shepard, Fool for Love *and Other Plays*

Like a short story or a novel, a play is open to interpretation. Readers' reactions are influenced by the language of the text, and audiences' reactions are influenced by the performance on stage. Just as in fiction, every element of a play—its title, its conflicts, its dialogue, its characters, and its staging, for instance—can shed light on its themes.

Titles

The **title** of a play can provide insight into its themes. The ironic title of Susan Glaspell's *Trifles* (p. 770), for example, suggests that women's concerns with "trifles" may get to the heart of the matter more effectively than the preoccupations of self-important men do. Lorraine Hansberry's *A Raisin in the Sun* is another title that offers clues to the theme of a play. An allusion to Langston Hughes's poem "Harlem" (p. 522), which asks, "what happens to a dream deferred? / Does it dry up / like a raisin in the sun?" the title suggests what happens to an African-American family whose dreams are constantly crushed. Likewise, the title *Fences* (p. 1096) offers clues to a major theme of August Wilson's play, suggesting that the main character in the play is kept from his goals by barriers that are constructed by himself as well as by society. Finally, the title of Anton Chekhov's *The Brute* (p. 723) effectively calls attention to the play's ideas about male-female relationships. The title may refer to Smirnov, who says that he has never liked women — whom he characterizes as "creatures of poetry and romance." Or, it may refer to Mrs. Popov's late husband, to whose memory she has dedicated her life despite the fact that he was repeatedly unfaithful. Either alternative reinforces the play's tongue-in-cheek characterization of men as "brutes."

1091

Conflicts

The unfolding plot of a play — especially the **conflicts** that develop — can also reveal the play's themes. In Henrik Ibsen's *A Doll House* (p. 784), for example, at least three major conflicts are present: one between Nora and her husband Torvald, one between Nora and Krogstad (an old acquaintance), and one between Nora and society. Each of these conflicts sheds light on the themes of the play.

Through Nora's conflict with Torvald, Ibsen examines the constraints placed on women and men by marriage in the nineteenth century. Both Nora and Torvald are imprisoned within their respective roles: Nora must be passive and child-like, and Torvald must be proper and always in control. Nora, therefore, expects her husband to be noble and generous and, in a crisis, to sacrifice himself for her. When he fails to live up to her expectations, she is profoundly disillusioned.

Nora's conflict with Krogstad underscores Ibsen's criticisms of the class system in nineteenth-century Norway. At the beginning of the play, Nora finds it "immensely amusing: that we — that Torvald has so much power over . . . people." Krogstad, a bank clerk who is in the employ of Torvald, visits Nora in act 1 to enlist her aid in saving his job. It is clear that she sees him as her social inferior. When Krogstad questions her about a woman with whom he has seen her, she replies, "What makes you think you can cross-examine me, Mr. Krogstad — you, one of my husband's employees?" Nora does not realize that she and Krogstad are, ironically, very much alike: both occupy subordinate positions and therefore have no power to determine their own destinies.

Finally, through Nora's conflict with society, Ibsen examines an important theme of his play: the destructive nature of the forces that subjugate women. Nineteenth-century society was male dominated. A married woman could not borrow money without her husband's signature, own real estate in her own name, or enter into contracts. In addition, all her assets — including inheritances and trust funds — automatically became the property of her husband at the time of marriage. As a result of her sheltered life, Nora at the beginning of the play is completely unaware of the consequences of her actions. Most readers share Dr. Rank's confusion when he asks Nora, "Why do you laugh at that? Do you have any idea of what society is?" It is Nora's disillusionment at finding out that Torvald and the rest of society are not what she has been led to believe they are that ultimately causes her to rebel. By walking out the door at the end of the play, Nora rejects not only her husband and her children (to whom she has no legal right once she leaves), but also society and its laws.

Those three conflicts underscore many of the themes that dominate *A Doll House*. First, the conflicts show that marriage in the nineteenth century imprisons both men and women in narrow, constricting roles. They also show that middle-class Norwegian society is narrow, smug, and judgmental. (Krogstad is looked down upon for a crime years after he committed it, and Nora is looked down upon because she borrows money to save her husband's life.) Finally, the conflicts show that society does not offer individuals — especially women — the freedom to lead happy and fulfilling lives. Only when the social and economic conditions that govern society change, Ibsen suggests, can women and men live together in mutual esteem.

Dialogue

Dialogue can also give insight into a play's themes. Sometimes a character suggests — or even explicitly states — a theme. In act 3 of *A Doll House*, for example, Nora's friend, Mrs. Linde, comes as close as any character to expressing the central concern of the play when she says, "Helmer's got to learn everything; this dreadful secret has to be aired; those two have to come to a full understanding; all these lies can't go on." As the play goes on to demonstrate, the lies that exist both in marriage and in society are obstacles to love and happiness.

One of the main themes of Arthur Miller's *Death of a Salesman* (p. 858) — the questionable validity of the American Dream, given the nation's social, political, and economic realities — is suggested by the play's dialogue. As his son Biff points out, Willy Loman's stubborn belief in upward mobility and material success is based more on fantasy than on fact:

WILLY: *(with hatred, threatening)* The door of your life is wide open!

BIFF: Pop! I am a dime a dozen, and so are you!

WILLY: *(turning on him now in an uncontrolled outburst)* I am not a dime a dozen! I am Willy Loman, and you are Biff Loman!

> *Biff starts for Willy, but is blocked by Happy. In his fury, Biff seems on the verge of attacking his father.*

BIFF: I am not a leader of men, Willy, and neither are you. You were never anything but a hard-working drummer who landed in the ash can like all the rest of them! I'm one dollar an hour, Willy! I tried seven states and couldn't raise it. A buck an hour! Do you gather my meaning? I'm not bringing home any prizes any more, and you're going to stop waiting for me to bring them home!

Though not explicitly stating the theme of the play, this exchange strongly suggests that Biff rejects the desperate optimism to which Willy clings.

Characters

Because a dramatic work focuses on a central character, or **protagonist,** the development of this character can shed light on a play's themes. Willy Loman in *Death of a Salesman* is developed in great detail. At the beginning of the play, he feels trapped, exhausted, and estranged from his surroundings. As Willy gradually sinks from depression into despair, the action of the play shifts from the present to the past, showing the events that shaped his life. His attitudes, beliefs, dreams, and dashed hopes reveal him to be an embodiment of the major theme of the play — that an unquestioning belief in the American dream of success and upward mobility is unrealistic and possibly destructive.

Nora in *A Doll House* changes a great deal during the course of the play. At the beginning, she is more her husband's possession than an adult capable of shaping her own destiny. Nora's status becomes apparent in the first act when Torvald gently scolds his "little spendthrift" and refers to her as his "little lark" and his "squirrel." She is reduced to childish deceptions, such as hiding her macaroons when her husband enters the room. After Krogstad accuses her of committing forgery and threatens to expose her, she expects her husband to rise to the occasion and take the blame for her. When Torvald instead accuses her of being a hypocrite, a liar, and a criminal, Nora's neat little world comes crashing down. As a result of this experience, Nora changes; no longer is she the submissive and obedient wife. Instead, she becomes assertive — even rebellious — ultimately telling Torvald that their marriage is a sham and that she can no longer stay with him. This abrupt shift in Nora's personality gives the audience a clear understanding of the major themes of the play.

Unlike Willy and Nora, Laura in Tennessee Williams's *The Glass Menagerie* (p. 1153) is a character who changes very little during the course of the play. Laura suffers from such pathological shyness that she is unable to attend typing class, let alone talk to a potential suitor. Although the "gentleman caller" draws Laura out of her shell for a short time, she soon withdraws again. Laura's inability to change reinforces the play's theme that contemporary society, with its emphasis on progress, has no place for people like Laura who live in private worlds "of glass animals and old, worn-out phonograph records."

Staging

Various physical elements, such as props and furnishings, may also convey the themes of a play. In *Death of a Salesman*, Biff's trophy, which is constantly in the audience's view, ironically underscores the futility of Willy's efforts to achieve success. Similarly, the miniature animals in *The Glass Menagerie* reflect the fragility of Laura's character and the futility of her efforts to fit into the modern world. And, in *Trifles*, the depressing farm house, the broken birdcage, and the dead canary suggest Mrs. Wright's misery and the reason she murdered her husband.

Special lighting effects and music can also suggest a play's themes. Throughout *The Glass Menagerie*, for example, words and pictures are projected onto a section of the set between the front room and dining room walls. In scene 1, as Tom's mother, Amanda, tells him about her experiences with her "gentlemen callers," an image of her as a girl greeting callers appears on the screen. As Amanda continues, the words *"Où sont Les Neiges"* — "Where are the snows [of yesteryear]?" — appear on the screen. Later in the play, when Laura and her mother discuss a boy Laura knew, his picture is projected on the screen, showing him as a high school hero carrying a silver cup. In addition to the slides, Williams uses music — a recurring tune, dance music, and "Ave Maria" — to increase the emotional impact of certain scenes. He also uses shafts of light focused on selected areas or characters to create a dreamlike atmosphere for the play. Collectively, the slides, music, and lighting reinforce the theme that those who retreat into the past inevitably become estranged from the present.

A Final Note

As you read, your values and beliefs influence your interpretation of a play's themes. For instance, your interest in the changing status of women could lead you to focus on the submissive, almost passive, role of Willy's wife, Linda, in *Death of a Salesman*. As a result, you could conclude that the play shows how, in the post–World War II United States, women like Linda often sacrificed their own happiness for their husbands. Remember, however, that the play itself, not just your own feelings or assumptions about it, must support your interpretation.

✔ CHECKLIST Writing about Theme

- [ ] What is the central theme of the play?
- [ ] What other themes can you identify?
- [ ] Does the title of the play suggest a theme?
- [ ] What conflicts exist in the play? In what way do they shed light on the themes of the play?
- [ ] Do any characters' statements express or imply a theme of the play?
- [ ] Do any characters change during the play? How do these changes suggest the play's themes?
- [ ] Do certain characters resist change? How does their failure to change suggest a theme of the play?
- [ ] Do scenery and props help to communicate the play's themes?
- [ ] Does music reinforce certain ideas in the play?
- [ ] Does lighting underscore the themes of the play?

AUGUST WILSON (1945–2005) was born in Pittsburgh, Pennsylvania, to a German immigrant father and a black mother and lived in the African-American neighborhood known as the Hill District. After leaving school at fifteen when he was accused of plagiarizing a paper, he participated in the Black Arts movement in Pittsburgh, submitting poems to local African-American publications. In 1969, Wilson and his friend Rob Penny founded the Black Horizons Theatre Company, for which Wilson produced and directed plays. Although Wilson wrote plays while living in Pittsburgh, his work began to gain recognition only after 1978, when he moved to St. Paul, Minnesota. There, in 1982, Lloyd Richards, dean of the Yale School of Drama and artistic director of the Yale Repertory Company, staged a performance of Wilson's *Ma Rainey's Black Bottom*.

Wilson's achievement was epic. Beginning with *Ma Rainey's Black Bottom* in 1984, he wrote a ten-play cycle that chronicled the African-American experience in the United States decade by decade. In addition to *Ma Rainey's Black Bottom,* a Tony Award winner, the plays in this cycle include *Fences* (1985), which won a Pulitzer Prize in 1987; *Joe Turner's Come and Gone* (1986); *Two Trains Running* (1989), which won Wilson his fifth New York Drama Critics Circle Award; *The Piano Lesson* (1987), which won a second Pulitzer Prize for Wilson in 1990; *Seven Guitars* (1996); *Radio Golf*, the last play in the cycle, opened in 2005, the year of Wilson's death. To honor his achievements, Broadway's Virginia Theater was renamed the August Wilson Theater.

Fences explores how the long-upheld color barrier in professional baseball affects the main character, Troy, who struggles with the pain of never realizing his dream of becoming a big-league player. Throughout the play, Troy retreats behind literal and figurative barriers that impair his relationships with his family.

Fences (1985)

CHARACTERS

Troy Maxson	**Gabriel,** *Troy's brother*
Jim Bono, *Troy's friend*	**Cory,** *Troy and Rose's son*
Rose, *Troy's wife*	**Raynell,** *Troy's daughter*
Lyons, *Troy's oldest son by previous marriage*	

SETTING

The setting is the yard which fronts the only entrance to the Maxson household, an ancient two-story brick house set back off a small alley in a big-city neighborhood. The entrance to the house is gained by two or three steps leading to a wooden porch badly in need of paint.

A relatively recent addition to the house and running its full width, the porch lacks congruence. It is a sturdy porch with a flat roof. One or two chairs of dubious value sit at one end where the kitchen window opens onto the porch. An old-fashioned icebox stands silent guard at the opposite end.

The yard is a small dirt yard, partially fenced, except for the last scene, with a wooden sawhorse, a pile of lumber, and other fence-building equipment set off to the side. Opposite is a tree from which hangs a ball made of rags. A baseball bat leans against the tree. Two oil drums serve as garbage receptacles and sit near the house at right to complete the setting.

THE PLAY

Near the turn of the century, the destitute of Europe sprang on the city with tenacious claws and an honest and solid dream. The city devoured them. They swelled its belly until it burst into a thousand furnaces and sewing machines, a thousand butcher shops and bakers' ovens, a thousand churches and hospitals and funeral parlors and money-lenders. The city grew. It nourished itself and offered each man a partnership limited only by his talent, his guile, and his willingness and capacity for hard work. For the immigrants of Europe, a dream dared and won true.

The descendants of African slaves were offered no such welcome or participation. They came from places called the Carolinas and the Virginias, Georgia, Alabama, Mississippi, and Tennessee. They came strong, eager, searching. The city rejected them and they fled and settled along the riverbanks and under bridges in shallow, ramshackle houses made of sticks and tarpaper. They collected rags and wood. They sold the use of their muscles and their bodies. They cleaned houses and washed clothes, they shined shoes, and in quiet desperation and vengeful pride, they stole, and lived in pursuit of their own dream. That they could breathe free, finally, and stand to meet life with the force of dignity and whatever eloquence the heart could call upon.

By 1957, the hard-won victories of the European immigrants had solidified the industrial might of America. War had been confronted and won with new energies that used loyalty and patriotism as its fuel. Life was rich, full, and flourishing. The Milwaukee Braves won the World Series, and the hot winds of change that would make the sixties a turbulent, racing, dangerous, and provocative decade had not yet begun to blow full.

ACT 1
SCENE 1

It is 1957. Troy and Bono enter the yard, engaged in conversation. Troy is fifty-three years old, a large man with thick, heavy hands; it is this largeness that he strives to fill out and make an accommodation with. Together with his blackness, his largeness informs his sensibilities and the choices he has made in his life.

Of the two men, Bono is obviously the follower. His commitment to their friendship of thirty-odd years is rooted in his admiration of Troy's honesty, capacity for hard work, and his strength, which Bono seeks to emulate.

It is Friday night, payday, and the one night of the week the two men engage in a ritual of talk and drink. Troy is usually the most talkative and at times he can be crude and almost vulgar, though he is capable of rising to profound heights of expression. The men carry lunch buckets and wear or carry burlap aprons and are dressed in clothes suitable to their jobs as garbage collectors.

BONO: Troy, you ought to stop that lying!

TROY: I ain't lying! The nigger had a watermelon this big. (*He indicates with his hands.*) Talking about . . . "What watermelon, Mr. Rand?" I liked to fell out! "What watermelon, Mr. Rand?" . . . And it sitting there big as life.

BONO: What did Mr. Rand say?

TROY: Ain't said nothing. Figure if the nigger too dumb to know he carrying a watermelon, he wasn't gonna get much sense out of him. Trying to hide that great big old watermelon under his coat. Afraid to let the white man see him carry it home.

BONO: I'm like you . . . I ain't got no time for them kind of people.

5

TROY: Now what he look like getting mad 'cause he see the man from the union talking to Mr. Rand?

BONO: He come to me talking about . . . "Maxson gonna get us fired." I told him to get away from me with that. He walked away from me calling you a troublemaker. What Mr. Rand say?

TROY: Ain't said nothing. He told me to go down the Commissioner's office next Friday. They called me down there to see them.

BONO: Well, as long as you got your complaint filed, they can't fire you. That's what one of them white fellows tell me.

10 TROY: I ain't worried about them firing me. They gonna fire me 'cause I asked a question? That's all I did. I went to Mr. Rand and asked him, "Why? Why you got the white mens driving and the colored lifting?" Told him, "what's the matter, don't I count? You think only white fellows got sense enough to drive a truck. That ain't no paper job! Hell, anybody can drive a truck. How come you got all whites driving and the colored lifting?" He told me "take it to the union." Well, hell, that's what I done! Now they wanna come up with this pack of lies.

BONO: I told Brownie if the man come and ask him any questions . . . just tell the truth! It ain't nothing but something they done trumped up on you 'cause you filed a complaint on them.

TROY: Brownie don't understand nothing. All I want them to do is change the job description. Give everybody a chance to drive the truck. Brownie can't see that. He ain't got that much sense.

BONO: How you figure he be making out with that gal be up at Taylors' all the time . . . that Alberta gal?

TROY: Same as you and me. Getting just as much as we is. Which is to say nothing.

15 BONO: It is, huh? I figure you doing a little better than me . . . and I ain't saying what I'm doing.

TROY: Aw, nigger, look here . . . I know you. If you had got anywhere near that gal, twenty minutes later you be looking to tell somebody. And the first one you gonna tell . . . that you gonna want to brag to . . . is me.

BONO: I ain't saying that. I see where you be eyeing her.

TROY: I eye all the women. I don't miss nothing. Don't never let nobody tell you Troy Maxson don't eye the women.

BONO: You been doing more than eyeing her. You done bought her a drink or two.

20 TROY: Hell yeah, I bought her a drink! What that mean? I bought you one, too. What that mean 'cause I buy her a drink? I'm just being polite.

BONO: It's all right to buy her one drink. That's what you call being polite. But when you wanna be buying two or three . . . that's what you call eyeing her.

TROY: Look here, as long as you known me . . . you ever known me to chase after women?

BONO: Hell yeah! Long as I done known you. You forgetting I knew you when.

TROY: Naw, I'm talking about since I been married to Rose?

BONO: Oh, not since you been married to Rose. Now, that's the truth, there. I ²⁵ can say that.

TROY: All right then! Case closed.

BONO: I see you be walking up around Alberta's house. You supposed to be at Taylors' and you be walking up around there.

TROY: What you watching where I'm walking for? I ain't watching after you.

BONO: I seen you walking around there more than once.

TROY: Hell, you liable to see me walking anywhere! That don't mean nothing ³⁰ cause you see me walking around there.

BONO: Where she come from anyway? She just kinda showed up one day.

TROY: Tallahassee. You can look at her and tell she one of them Florida gals. They got some big healthy women down there. Grow them right up out the ground. Got a little bit of Indian in her. Most of them niggers down in Florida got some Indian in them.

BONO: I don't know about that Indian part. But she damn sure big and healthy. Woman wear some big stockings. Got them great big old legs and hips as wide as the Mississippi River.

TROY: Legs don't mean nothing. You don't do nothing but push them out of the way. But them hips cushion the ride!

BONO: Troy, you ain't got no sense. ³⁵

TROY: It's the truth! Like you riding on Goodyears!

Rose enters from the house. She is ten years younger than Troy, her devotion to him stems from her recognition of the possibilities of her life without him: a succession of abusive men and their babies, a life of partying and running the streets, the Church, or aloneness with its attendant pain and frustration. She recognizes Troy's spirit as a fine and illuminating one and she either ignores or forgives his faults, only some of which she recognizes. Though she doesn't drink, her presence is an integral part of the Friday night rituals. She alternates between the porch and the kitchen, where supper preparations are under way.

ROSE: What you all out here getting into?

TROY: What you worried about what we getting into for? This is men talk, woman.

ROSE: What I care what you all talking about? Bono, you gonna stay for supper?

BONO: No, I thank you, Rose. But Lucille say she cooking up a pot of pigfeet.

TROY: Pigfeet! Hell, I'm going home with you! Might even stay the night if ⁴⁰ you got some pigfeet. You got something in there to top them pigfeet, Rose?

ROSE: I'm cooking up some chicken. I got some chicken and collard greens.°

TROY: Well, go on back in the house and let me and Bono finish what we was talking about. This is men talk. I got some talk for you later. You know what kind of talk I mean. You go on and powder it up.

ROSE: Troy Maxson, don't you start that now!

°*collard greens:* A leafy green vegetable.

45   **TROY:**   *(puts his arm around her)* Aw, woman . . . come here. Look here, Bono . . .
  when I met this woman . . . I got out that place, say, "Hitch up my pony, saddle
  up my mare . . . there's a woman out there for me somewhere. I looked here.
  Looked there. Saw Rose and latched on to her." I latched on to her and told
  her — I'm gonna tell you the truth — I told her, "Baby, I don't wanna marry, I
  just wanna be your man." Rose told me . . . tell him what you told me, Rose.

  ROSE: I told him if he wasn't the marrying kind, then move out the way so the
  marrying kind could find me.

  TROY: That's what she told me. "Nigger, you in my way. You blocking the view!
  Move out the way so I can find me a husband." I thought it over two or three
  days. Come back—

  ROSE: Ain't no two or three days nothing. You was back the same night.

  TROY: Come back, told her . . . "Okay, baby . . . but I'm gonna buy me a banty
  rooster and put him out there in the backyard . . . and when he see a stranger
  come, he'll flap his wings and crow . . ." Look here, Bono, I could watch the
  front door by myself . . . it was that back door I was worried about.

50   **ROSE:**   Troy, you ought not talk like that. Troy ain't doing nothing but telling a lie.

  TROY: Only thing is . . . when we first got married . . . forget the rooster . . . we
  ain't had no yard!

  BONO: I hear you tell it. Me and Lucille was staying down there on Logan
  Street. Had two rooms with the outhouse in the back. I ain't mind the outhouse none. But when that goddamn wind blow through there in the winter . . . that's what I'm talking about! To this day I wonder why in the hell I
  ever stayed down there for six long years. But see, I didn't know I could do
  no better. I thought only white folks had inside toilets and things.

  ROSE: There's a lot of people don't know they can do no better than they doing
  now. That's just something you got to learn. A lot of folks still shop at Bella's.

  TROY: Ain't nothing wrong with shopping at Bella's. She got fresh food.

55   **ROSE:**   I ain't said nothing about if she got fresh food. I'm talking about what
  she charge. She charge ten cents more than the A&P.

  TROY: The A&P ain't never done nothing for me. I spends my money where
  I'm treated right. I go down to Bella, say, "I need a loaf of bread, I'll pay you
  Friday." She give it to me. What sense that make when I got money to go
  and spend it somewhere else and ignore the person who done right by me?
  That ain't in the Bible.

  ROSE: We ain't talking about what's in the Bible. What sense it make to shop
  there when she overcharge?

  TROY: You shop where you want to. I'll do my shopping where the people been
  good to me.

  ROSE: Well, I don't think it's right for her to overcharge. That's all I was saying.

60   **BONO:**   Look here . . . I got to get on. Lucille going be raising all kind of hell.

  TROY: Where you going, nigger? We ain't finished this pint. Come here, finish
  this pint.

  BONO: Well, hell, I am . . . if you ever turn the bottle loose.

TROY: *(hands him the bottle)* The only thing I say about the A&P is I'm glad Cory got that job down there. Help him take care of his school clothes and things. Gabe done moved out and things getting tight around here. He got that job . . . He can start to look out for himself.

ROSE: Cory done went and got recruited by a college football team.

TROY: I told that boy about that football stuff. The white man ain't gonna let   65
him get nowhere with that football. I told him when he first come to me with it. Now you come telling me he done went and got more tied up in it. He ought to go and get recruited in how to fix cars or something where he can make a living.

ROSE: He ain't talking about making no living playing football. It's just something the boys in school do. They gonna send a recruiter by to talk to you. He'll tell you he ain't talking about making no living playing football. It's a honor to be recruited.

TROY: It ain't gonna get him nowhere. Bono'll tell you that.

BONO: If he be like you in the sports . . . he's gonna be all right. Ain't but two men ever played baseball as good as you. That's Babe Ruth° and Josh Gibson.° Them's the only two men ever hit more home runs than you.

TROY: What it ever get me? Ain't got a pot to piss in or a window to throw it out of.

ROSE: Times have changed since you was playing baseball, Troy. That was   70
before the war. Times have changed a lot since then.

TROY: How in hell they done changed?

ROSE: They got lots of colored boys playing ball now. Baseball and football.

BONO: You right about that, Rose. Times have changed, Troy. You just come along too early.

TROY: There ought not never have been no time called too early! Now you take that fellow . . . what's that fellow they had playing right field for the Yankees back then? You know who I'm talking about, Bono. Used to play right field for the Yankees.

ROSE: Selkirk?   75

TROY: Selkirk! That's it! Man batting .269, understand? .269. What kind of sense that make? I was hitting .432 with thirty-seven home runs! Man batting .269 and playing right field for the Yankees! I saw Josh Gibson's daughter yesterday. She walking around with raggedy shoes on her feet. Now I bet you Selkirk's daughter ain't walking around with raggedy shoes on her feet! I bet you that!

ROSE: They got a lot of colored baseball players now. Jackie Robinson° was the first. Folks had to wait for Jackie Robinson.

°*Babe Ruth:* George Herman Ruth (1895–1948), American baseball player. He played for the New York Yankees during the 1910s and 1920s and is remembered for his home-run hitting and flamboyant lifestyle.   °*Josh Gibson:* (1911–1947), American baseball player. He played between the Negro Leagues between 1920s and 1940s and was known as "the Negro Babe Ruth." An unwritten rule against hiring black players kept him out of the major leagues.   °*Jackie Robinson:* John Roosevelt Robinson (1919–1972). He became the first African American to play major-league baseball when he was hired by the Brooklyn Dodgers in 1947.

TROY: I done seen a hundred niggers play baseball better than Jackie Robinson. Hell, I know some teams Jackie Robinson couldn't even make! What
you talking about Jackie Robinson. Jackie Robinson wasn't nobody. I'm
talking about if you could play ball then they ought to have let you play.
Don't care what color you were. Come telling me I come along too early. If
you could play . . . then they ought to have let you play.

Troy takes a long drink from the bottle.

ROSE: You gonna drink yourself to death. You don't need to be drinking like that.

80 TROY: Death ain't nothing. I done seen him. Done wrassled with him. You
can't tell me nothing about death. Death ain't nothing but a fastball on the
outside corner. And you know what I'll do to that! Lookee here, Bono . . .
am I lying? You get one of them fastballs, about waist high, over the outside
corner of the plate where you can get the meat of the bat on it . . . and good
god! You can kiss it goodbye. Now, am I lying?

BONO: Naw, you telling the truth there. I seen you do it.

TROY: If I'm lying . . . that 450 feet worth of lying! *(Pause.)* That's all death is
to me. A fastball on the outside corner.

ROSE: I don't know why you want to get on talking about death.

TROY: Ain't nothing wrong with talking about death. That's part of life. Everybody gonna die. You gonna die, I'm gonna die. Bono's gonna die. Hell, we
all gonna die.

85 ROSE: But you ain't got to talk about it. I don't like to talk about it.

TROY: You the one brought it up. Me and Bono was talking about baseball . . . you
tell me I'm gonna drink myself to death. Ain't that right, Bono? You know I
don't drink this but one night out of the week. That's Friday night. I'm gonna
drink just enough to where I can handle it. Then I cuts it loose. I leave it
alone. So don't you worry about me drinking myself to death. 'Cause I ain't
worried about Death. I done seen him. I done wrestled with him.

　　Look here, Bono . . . I looked up one day and Death was marching straight
at me. Like Soldiers on Parade! The Army of Death was marching straight at
me. The middle of July, 1941. It got real cold just like it be winter. It seem like
Death himself reached out and touched me on the shoulder. He touch me just
like I touch you. I got cold as ice and Death standing there grinning at me.

ROSE: Troy, why don't you hush that talk.

TROY: I say . . . what you want, Mr. Death? You be wanting me? You done
brought your army to be getting me? I looked him dead in the eye. I wasn't
fearing nothing. I was ready to tangle. Just like I'm ready to tangle now.
The Bible say be ever vigilant. That's why I don't get but so drunk. I got to
keep watch.

ROSE: Troy was right down there in Mercy Hospital. You remember he had
pneumonia? Laying there with a fever talking plumb out of his head.

90 TROY: Death standing there staring at me . . . carrying that sickle in his
hand. Finally he say, "You want bound over for another year?" See, just like

that . . . "You want bound over for another year?" I told him, "Bound over hell! Let's settle this now!"

It seem like he kinda fell back when I said that, and all the cold went out of me. I reached down and grabbed that sickle and threw it just as far as I could throw it . . . and me and him commenced to wrestling.

We wrestled for three days and three nights. I can't say where I found the strength from. Every time it seemed like he was gonna get the best of me, I'd reach way down deep inside myself and find the strength to do him one better.

ROSE: Every time Troy tell that story he find different ways to tell it. Different things to make up about it.

TROY: I ain't making up nothing. I'm telling you the facts of what happened. I wrestled with Death for three days and three nights and I'm standing here to tell you about it. *(Pause.)* All right. At the end of the third night we done weakened each other to where we can't hardly move. Death stood up, throwed on his robe . . . had him a white robe with a hood on it. He throwed on that robe and went off to look for his sickle. Say, "I'll be back." Just like that. "I'll be back." I told him, say, "Yeah, but . . . you gonna have to find me!" I wasn't no fool. I wan't going looking for him. Death ain't nothing to play with. And I know he's gonna get me. I know I got to join his army . . . his camp followers. But as long as I keep my strength and see him coming . . . as long as I keep up my vigilance . . . he's gonna have to fight to get me. I ain't going easy.

BONO: Well, look here, since you got to keep up your vigilance . . . let me have the bottle.

TROY: Aw hell, I shouldn't have told you that part. I should have left out that part.

ROSE: Troy be talking that stuff and half the time don't even know what he be 95 talking about.

TROY: Bono know me better than that.

BONO: That's right. I know you. I know you got some Uncle Remus° in your blood. You got more stories than the devil got sinners.

TROY: Aw hell, I done seen him too! Done talked with the devil.

ROSE: Troy, don't nobody wanna be hearing all that stuff.

Lyons enters the yard from the street. Thirty-four years old, Troy's son by a previous marriage, he sports a neatly trimmed goatee, sport coat, white shirt, tieless and buttoned at the collar. Though he fancies himself a musician, he is more caught up in the rituals and "idea" of being a musician than in the actual practice of the music. He has come to borrow money from Troy, and while he knows he will be successful, he is uncertain as to what extent his lifestyle will be held up to scrutiny and ridicule.

LYONS: Hey, Pop.   100

° *Uncle Remus:* The fictional narrator of *Uncle Remus: His Songs and His Sayings* (1880) and a number of sequels by Joel Chandler Harris. Uncle Remus tells tales about characters such as Brer Rabbit and the Tarbaby in exaggerated dialect, now widely considered to be a derogatory representation of African Americans.

Troy: What you come "Hey, Popping" me for?

Lyons: How you doing, Rose? *(He kisses her.)* Mr. Bono. How you doing?

Bono: Hey, Lyons . . . how you been?

Troy: He must have been doing all right. I ain't seen him around here last week.

105 **Rose:** Troy, leave your boy alone. He come by to see you and you wanna start all that nonsense.

Troy: I ain't bothering Lyons. *(Offers him the bottle.)* Here . . . get you a drink. We got an understanding. I know why he come by to see me and he know I know.

Lyons: Come on, Pop . . . I just stopped by to say hi . . . see how you was doing.

Troy: You ain't stopped by yesterday.

Rose: You gonna stay for supper, Lyons? I got some chicken cooking in the oven.

110 **Lyons:** No, Rose . . . thanks. I was just in the neighborhood and thought I'd stop by for a minute.

Troy: You was in the neighborhood all right, nigger. You telling the truth there. You was in the neighborhood cause it's my payday.

Lyons: Well, hell, since you mentioned it . . . let me have ten dollars.

Troy: I'll be damned! I'll die and go to hell and play blackjack with the devil before I give you ten dollars.

Bono: That's what I wanna know about . . . that devil you done seen.

115 **Lyons:** What . . . Pop done seen the devil? You too much, Pops.

Troy: Yeah, I done seen him. Talked to him too!

Rose: You ain't seen no devil. I done told you that man ain't had nothing to do with the devil. Anything you can't understand, you want to call it the devil.

Troy: Look here, Bono . . . I went down to see Hertzberger about some furniture. Got three rooms for two-ninety-eight. That what it say on the radio. "Three rooms . . . two-ninety-eight." Even made up a little song about it. Go down there . . . man tell me I can't get no credit. I'm working every day and can't get no credit. What to do? I got an empty house with some raggedy furniture in it. Cory ain't got no bed. He's sleeping on a pile of rags on the floor. Working every day and can't get no credit. Come back here — Rose'll tell you — madder than hell. Sit down . . . try to figure what I'm gonna do. Come a knock on the door. Ain't been living here but three days. Who know I'm here? Open the door . . . devil standing there bigger than life. White fellow . . . white fellow . . . got on good clothes and everything. Standing there with a clipboard in his hand. I ain't had to say nothing. First words come out of his mouth was . . . "I understand you need some furniture and can't get no credit." I liked to fell over. He say, "I'll give you all the credit you want, but you got to pay the interest on it." I told him, "Give me three rooms worth and charge whatever you want." Next day a truck pulled up here and two men unloaded them three rooms. Man what drove the truck give me a book. Say send ten dollars, first of every month to the ad- dress in the book and everything will be all right. Say if I miss a payment the devil was coming back and it'll be hell to pay. That was fifteen years ago. To this day . . . the first of the month I send my ten dollars, Rose'll tell you.

James Earl Jones as Troy in a 1986 production of *Fences* at the Goodman Theatre.

ROSE: Troy lying.

TROY: I ain't never seen that man since. Now you tell me who else that could   120
have been but the devil? I ain't sold my soul or nothing like that, you understand. Naw, I wouldn't have truck with the devil about nothing like that. I got
my furniture and pays my ten dollars the first of the month just like clockwork.

BONO: How long you say you been paying this ten dollars a month?

TROY: Fifteen years!

BONO: Hell, ain't you finished paying for it yet? How much the man done
charged you?

TROY: Ah hell, I done paid for it. I done paid for it ten times over! The fact is
I'm scared to stop paying it.

ROSE: Troy lying. We got that furniture from Mr. Glickman. He ain't paying   125
no ten dollars a month to nobody.

TROY: Aw hell, woman. Bono know I ain't that big a fool.

LYONS: I was just getting ready to say . . . I know where there's a bridge for sale.

TROY: Look here, I'll tell you this . . . it don't matter to me if he was the devil.
It don't matter if the devil give credit. Somebody has got to give it.

ROSE: It ought to matter. You going around talking about having truck with
the devil . . . God's the one you gonna have to answer to. He's the one
gonna be at the Judgment.

LYONS: Yeah, well, look here, Pop . . . let me have that ten dollars. I'll give it   130
back to you. Bonnie got a job working at the hospital.

Troy: What I tell you, Bono? The only time I see this nigger is when he wants something. That's the only time I see him.

Lyons: Come on, Pop, Mr. Bono don't want to hear all that. Let me have the ten dollars. I told you Bonnie working.

Troy: What that mean to me? "Bonnie working." I don't care if she working. Go ask her for the ten dollars if she working. Talking about "Bonnie working." Why ain't you working?

Lyons: Aw, Pop, you know I can't find no decent job. Where am I gonna get a job at? You know I can't get no job.

135 **Troy:** I told you I know some people down there. I can get you on the rubbish if you want to work. I told you that the last time you came by here asking me for something.

Lyons: Naw, Pop . . . thanks. That ain't for me. I don't wanna be carrying nobody's rubbish. I don't wanna be punching nobody's time clock.

Troy: What's the matter, you too good to carry people's rubbish? Where you think that ten dollars you talking about come from? I'm just supposed to haul people's rubbish and give my money to you 'cause you too lazy to work. You too lazy to work and wanna know why you ain't got what I got.

Rose: What hospital Bonnie working at? Mercy?

Lyons: She's down at Passavant working in the laundry.

140 **Troy:** I ain't got nothing as it is. I give you that ten dollars and I got to eat beans the rest of the week. Naw . . . you ain't getting no ten dollars here.

Lyons: You ain't got to be eating no beans. I don't know why you wanna say that.

Troy: I ain't got no extra money. Gabe done moved over to Miss Pearl's paying her the rent and things done got tight around here. I can't afford to be giving you every payday.

Lyons: I ain't asked you to give me nothing. I asked you to loan me ten dollars. I know you got ten dollars.

Troy: Yeah, I got it. You know why I got it? 'Cause I don't throw my money away out there in the streets. You living the fast life . . . wanna be a musician . . . running around in them clubs and things . . . then, you learn to take care of yourself. You ain't gonna find me going and asking nobody for nothing. I done spent too many years without.

145 **Lyons:** You and me is two different people, Pop.

Troy: I done learned my mistake and learned to do what's right by it. You still trying to get something for nothing. Life don't owe you nothing. You owe it to yourself. Ask Bono. He'll tell you I'm right.

Lyons: You got your way of dealing with the world . . . I got mine. The only thing that matters to me is the music.

Troy: Yeah, I can see that! It don't matter how you gonna eat . . . where your next dollar is coming from. You telling the truth there.

Lyons: I know I got to eat. But I got to live too. I need something that gonna help me to get out of the bed in the morning. Make me feel like I belong in the world. I don't bother nobody. I just stay with the music 'cause that's the only way I can find to live in the world. Otherwise there ain't no telling what I might do. Now I don't come criticizing you and how you live. I just come by to ask you for ten dollars. I don't wanna hear all that about how I live.

TROY: Boy, your mama did a hell of a job raising you.   150

LYONS: You can't change me, Pop. I'm thirty-four years old. If you wanted to change me, you should have been there when I was growing up. I come by to see you . . . ask for ten dollars and you want to talk about how I was raised. You don't know nothing about how I was raised.

ROSE: Let the boy have ten dollars, Troy.

TROY: (*to Lyons*) What the hell you looking at me for? I ain't got no ten dollars. You know what I do with my money. (*To Rose.*) Give him ten dollars if you want him to have it.

ROSE: I will. Just as soon as you turn it loose.

TROY: (*handing Rose the money*) There it is. Seventy-six dollars and forty-two   155
cents. You see this, Bono? Now, I ain't gonna get but six of that back.

ROSE: You ought to stop telling that lie. Here, Lyons. (*She hands him the money.*)

LYONS: Thanks, Rose. Look . . . I got to run . . . I'll see you later.

TROY: Wait a minute. You gonna say "thanks, Rose" and ain't gonna look to see where she got that ten dollars from? See how they do me, Bono?

LYONS: I know she got it from you, Pop. Thanks. I'll give it back to you.

TROY: There he go telling another lie. Time I see that ten dollars . . . he'll be   160
owing me thirty more.

LYONS: See you, Mr. Bono.

BONO: Take care, Lyons!

LYONS: Thanks, Pop. I'll see you again.

Lyons exits the yard.

TROY: I don't know why he don't go and get him a decent job and take care of that woman he got.

BONO: He'll be all right, Troy. The boy is still young.   165

TROY: The *boy* is thirty-four years old.

ROSE: Let's not get off into all that.

BONO: Look here . . . I got to be going. I got to be getting on. Lucille gonna be waiting.

TROY: (*puts his arm around Rose*) See this woman, Bono? I love this woman. I love this woman so much it hurts. I love her so much . . . I done run out of ways of loving her. So I got to go back to basics. Don't you come by my house Monday morning talking about time to go to work . . . 'cause I'm still gonna be stroking!

ROSE: Troy! Stop it now!   170

BONO: I ain't paying him no mind, Rose. That ain't nothing but gin-talk. Go on, Troy. I'll see you Monday.

TROY: Don't you come by my house, nigger! I done told you what I'm gonna be doing.

The lights go down to black.

Scene 2

The lights come up on Rose hanging up clothes. She hums and sings softly to herself. It is the following morning.

Rose: (*sings*)

> Jesus, be a fence all around me every day
> Jesus, I want you to protect me as I travel on my way.
> Jesus, be a fence all around me every day.

Troy enters from the house.

> Jesus, I want you to protect me
> As I travel on my way.

(*To Troy.*) 'Morning, You ready for breakfast? I can fix it soon as I finish hanging up these clothes?

Troy: I got the coffee on. That'll be all right. I'll just drink some of that this morning.

5 Rose: That 651 hit yesterday. That's the second time this month. Miss Pearl hit for a dollar . . . seem like those that need the least always get lucky. Poor folks can't get nothing.

Troy: Them numbers don't know nobody. I don't know why you fool with them. You and Lyons both.

Rose: It's something to do.

10 Troy: You ain't doing nothing but throwing your money away.

Rose: Troy, you know I don't play foolishly. I just play a nickel here and a nickel there.

Troy: That's two nickels you done thrown away.

Rose: Now I hit sometimes . . . that makes up for it. It always comes in handy when I do hit. I don't hear you complaining then.

Troy: I ain't complaining now. I just say it's foolish. Trying to guess out of six hundred ways which way the number gonna come. If I had all the money niggers, these Negroes, throw away on numbers for one week — just one week — I'd be a rich man.

Rose: Well, you wishing and calling it foolish ain't gonna stop folks from playing numbers. That's one thing for sure. Besides . . . some good things come from playing numbers. Look where Pope done bought him that restaurant off of numbers.

Troy: I can't stand niggers like that. Man ain't had two dimes to rub together. He walking around with his shoes all run over bumming money for cigarettes. All right. Got lucky there and hit the numbers . . .

15 Rose: Troy, I know all about it.

Troy: Had good sense, I'll say that for him. He ain't throwing his money away. I seen niggers hit the numbers and go through two thousand dollars in four days. Man bought him that restaurant down there . . . fixed it up real nice . . . and then didn't want nobody to come in it! A Negro go in there and can't get no kind of service. I seen a white fellow come in there and order a bowl of stew. Pope picked all the meat out the pot for him. Man ain't had nothing but a bowl of meat! Negro come behind him and ain't got nothing but the potatoes and carrots. Talking about what numbers do for people, you picked a wrong example. Ain't done nothing but make a worser fool out of him than he was before.

ROSE: Troy, you ought to stop worrying about what happened at work yesterday.

TROY: I ain't worried. Just told me to be down there at the Commissioner's office on Friday. Everybody think they gonna fire me. I ain't worried about them firing me. You ain't got to worry about that. (*Pause.*) Where's Cory? Cory in the house? (*Calls.*) Cory?

ROSE: He gone out.

TROY: Out, huh? He gone out 'cause he know I want him to help me with this   20 fence. I know how he is. That boy scared of work.

Gabriel enters. He comes halfway down the alley and, hearing Troy's voice, stops.

TROY: (*continues*) He ain't done a lick of work in his life.

ROSE: He had to go to football practice. Coach wanted them to get in a little extra practice before the season start.

TROY: I got his practice . . . running out of here before he get his chores done.

ROSE: Troy, what is wrong with you this morning? Don't nothing set right with you. Go on back in there and go to bed . . . get up on the other side.

TROY: Why something got to be wrong with me? I ain't said nothing wrong   25 with me.

ROSE: You got something to say about everything. First it's the numbers . . . then it's the way the man runs his restaurant . . . then you done got on Cory. What's it gonna be next? Take a look up there and see if the weather suits you . . . or is it gonna be how you gonna put up the fence with the clothes hanging in the yard.

TROY: You hit the nail on the head then.

ROSE: I know you like I know the back of my hand. Go on in there and get you some coffee . . . see if that straighten you up. 'Cause you ain't right this morning.

Troy starts into the house and sees Gabriel. Gabriel starts singing. Troy's brother, he is seven years younger than Troy. Injured in World War II, he has a metal plate in his head. He carries an old trumpet tied around his waist and believes with every fiber of his being that he is the Archangel Gabriel.° He carries a chipped basket with an assortment of discarded fruits and vegetables he has picked up in the strip district and which he attempts to sell.

GABRIEL: (*singing*)

° *Archangel Gabriel:* A messenger of God.

Yes, ma'am, I got plums
You ask me how I sell them
Oh ten cents apiece
Three for a quarter
Come and buy now
'Cause I'm here today
And tomorrow I'll be gone

Gabriel enters.

Hey, Rose!

ROSE: How you doing, Gabe?

30 GABRIEL: There's Troy . . . Hey, Troy!

TROY: Hey, Gabe.

Exit into kitchen.

ROSE: *(To Gabriel.)* What you got there?

GABRIEL: You know what I got, Rose. I got fruits and vegetables.

35 ROSE: *(looking in basket)* Where's all these plums you talking about?

GABRIEL: I ain't got no plums today, Rose. I was just singing that. Have some tomorrow. Put me in a big order for plums. Have enough plums tomorrow for St. Peter and everybody.

Troy reenters from kitchen, crosses to steps.

(To Rose.) Troy's mad at me.

TROY: I ain't mad at you. What I got to be mad at you about? You ain't done nothing to me.

GABRIEL: I just moved over to Miss Pearl's to keep out from in your way. I ain't mean no harm by it.

TROY: Who said anything about that? I ain't said anything about that.

40 GABRIEL: You ain't mad at me, is you?

TROY: Naw . . . I ain't mad at you, Gabe. If I was mad at you I'd tell you about it.

GABRIEL: Got me two rooms. In the basement. Got my own door too. Wanna see my key? *(He holds up a key.)* That's my own key! Ain't nobody else got a key like that. That's my key! My two rooms!

TROY: Well, that's good, Gabe. You got your own key . . . that's good.

ROSE: You hungry, Gabe? I was just fixing to cook Troy his breakfast.

45 GABRIEL: I'll take some biscuits. You got some biscuits? Did you know when I was in heaven . . . every morning me and St. Peter° would sit down by the gate and eat some big fat biscuits? Oh, yeah! We had us a good time. We'd sit there and eat us them biscuits and then St. Peter would go off to sleep and tell me to wake him up when it's time to open the gates for the judgment.

ROSE: Well, come on . . . I'll make up a batch of biscuits.

° *St. Peter:* Disciple of Christ, believed to be the guard at the gates of heaven.

Rose exits into the house.

GABRIEL: Troy . . . St. Peter got your name in the book. I seen it. It say . . .
Troy Maxson. I say . . . I know him! He got the same name like what I got.
That's my brother!

TROY: How many times you gonna tell me that, Gabe?

GABRIEL: Ain't got my name in the book. Don't have to have my name. I done
died and went to heaven. He got your name though. One morning St. Peter
was looking at his book . . . marking it up for the judgment . . . and he let
me see your name. Got it in there under M. Got Rose's name . . . I ain't
seen it like I seen yours . . . but I know it's in there. He got a great big book.
Got everybody's name what was ever been born. That's what he told me.
But I seen your name. Seen it with my own eyes.

TROY: Go on in the house there. Rose going to fix you something to eat.   50

GABRIEL: Oh, I ain't hungry. I done had breakfast with Aunt Jemima. She
come by and cooked me up a whole mess of flapjacks. Remember how we
used to eat them flapjacks?

TROY: Go on in the house and get you something to eat now.

GABRIEL: I got to sell my plums. I done sold some tomatoes. Got me two quarters. Wanna see? (*He shows Troy his quarters.*) I'm gonna save them and buy
me a new horn so St. Peter can hear me when it's time to open the gates.
(*Gabriel stops suddenly. Listens.*) Hear that? That's the hellhounds. I got to
chase them out of here. Go on get out of here! Get out!

Gabriel exits singing.

> Better get ready for the Judgment
> Better get ready for the Judgment
> My Lord is coming down

Rose enters from the house.

TROY: He's gone off somewhere.

GABRIEL: (*offstage*)   55

> Better get ready for the Judgment
> Better get ready for the Judgment morning
> Better get ready for the Judgment
> My God is coming down

ROSE: He ain't eating right. Miss Pearl say she can't get him to eat nothing.

TROY: What you want me to do about it, Rose? I done did everything I can for
the man. I can't make him get well. Man got half his head blown away . . .
what you expect?

ROSE: Seem like something ought to be done to help him.

TROY: Man don't bother nobody. He just mixed up from that metal plate he
got in his head. Ain't no sense for him to go back into the hospital.

ROSE: Least he be eating right. They can help him take care of himself.   60

TROY: Don't nobody wanna be locked up, Rose. What you wanna lock him up for? Man go over there and fight the war . . . messin' around with them Japs, get half his head blown off . . . and they give him a lousy three thousand dollars. And I had to swoop down on that.

ROSE: Is you fixing to go into that again?

TROY: That's the only way I got a roof over my head . . . 'cause of that metal plate.

ROSE: Ain't no sense you blaming yourself for nothing. Gabe wasn't in no condition to manage that money. You done what was right by him. Can't nobody say you ain't done what was right by him. Look how long you took care of him . . . till he wanted to have his own place and moved over there with Miss Pearl.

65 TROY: That ain't what I'm saying, woman! I'm just stating the facts. If my brother didn't have that metal plate in his head . . . I wouldn't have a pot to piss in or a window to throw it out of. And I'm fifty-three years old. Now see if you can understand that!

Troy gets up from the porch and starts to exit the yard.

ROSE: Where you going off to? You been running out of here every Saturday for weeks. I thought you was gonna work on this fence?

TROY: I'm gonna walk down to Taylors'. Listen to the ball game. I'll be back in a bit. I'll work on it when I get back.

He exits the yard. The lights go to black.

SCENE 3

The lights come up on the yard. It is four hours later. Rose is taking down the clothes from the line. Cory enters carrying his football equipment.

ROSE: Your daddy like to had a fit with you running out of here this morning without doing your chores.

CORY: I told you I had to go to practice.

5 ROSE: He say you were supposed to help him with this fence.

CORY: He been saying that the last four or five Saturdays, and then he don't never do nothing, but go down to Taylors'. Did you tell him about the recruiter?

ROSE: Yeah, I told him.

CORY: What he say?

ROSE: He ain't said nothing too much. You get in there and get started on your chores before he gets back. Go on and scrub down them steps before he gets back here hollering and carrying on.

10 CORY: I'm hungry. What you got to eat, Mama?

ROSE: Go on and get started on your chores. I got some meat loaf in there. Go on and make you a sandwich . . . and don't leave no mess in there.

Cory exits into the house. Rose continues to take down the clothes. Troy enters the yard and sneaks up and grabs her from behind.

Troy! Go on, now. You liked to scared me to death. What was the score of the game? Lucille had me on the phone and I couldn't keep up with it.

TROY: What I care about the game? Come here, woman. (*He tries to kiss her.*)

ROSE: I thought you went down Taylors' to listen to the game. Go on, Troy! You supposed to be putting up this fence.

TROY: (*attempting to kiss her again*) I'll put it up when I finish with what is at hand.

ROSE: Go on, Troy. I ain't studying you.   15

TROY: (*chasing after her*) I'm studying you . . . fixing to do my homework!

ROSE: Troy, you better leave me alone.

TROY: Where's Cory? That boy brought his butt home yet?

ROSE: He's in the house doing his chores.

TROY: (*calling*) Cory! Get your butt out here, boy!   20

Rose exits into the house with the laundry. Troy goes over to the pile of wood, picks up a board, and starts sawing. Cory enters from the house.

TROY: You just now coming in here from leaving this morning?

CORY: Yeah, I had to go to football practice.

TROY: Yeah, what?

CORY: Yessir.

TROY: I ain't but two seconds off you noway. The garbage sitting in there   25
overflowing . . . you ain't done none of your chores . . . and you come in
here talking about "Yeah."

CORY: I was just getting ready to do my chores now, Pop . . .

TROY: Your first chore is to help me with this fence on Saturday. Everything
else come after that. Now get that saw and cut them boards.

Cory takes the saw and begins cutting the boards. Troy continues working. There is a long pause.

CORY: Hey, Pop . . . why don't you buy a TV?

TROY: What I want with a TV? What I want one of them for?

CORY: Everybody got one. Earl, Ba Bra . . . Jesse!   30

TROY: I ain't asked you who had one. I say what I want with one?

CORY: So you can watch it. They got lots of things on TV. Baseball games and
everything. We could watch the World Series.

TROY: Yeah . . . and how much this TV cost?

CORY: I don't know. They got them on sale for around two hundred dollars.

TROY: Two hundred dollars, huh?   35

CORY: That ain't that much, Pop.

TROY: Naw, it's just two hundred dollars. See that roof you got over your head
at night? Let me tell you something about that roof. It's been over ten years

since that roof was last tarred. See now . . . the snow comes this winter and sit up there on that roof like it is . . . and it's gonna seep inside. It's just gonna be a little bit . . . ain't gonna hardly notice it. Then the next thing you know, it's gonna be leaking all over the house. Then the wood rot from all that water and you gonna need a whole new roof. Now, how much you think it cost to get that roof tarred?

Cory: I don't know.

Troy: Two hundred and sixty-four dollars . . . cash money. While you thinking about a TV, I got to be thinking about the roof . . . and whatever else go wrong here. Now if you had two hundred dollars, what would you do . . . fix the roof or buy a TV?

40 **Cory:** I'd buy a TV. Then when the roof started to leak . . . when it needed fixing . . . I'd fix it.

Troy: Where you gonna get the money from? You done spent it for a TV. You gonna sit up and watch the water run all over your brand new TV.

Cory: Aw, Pop. You got money. I know you do.

Troy: Where I got it at, huh?

Cory: You got it in the bank.

45 **Troy:** You wanna see my bankbook? You wanna see that seventy-three dollars and twenty-two cents I got sitting up in there.

Cory: You ain't got to pay for it all at one time. You can put a down payment on it and carry it on home with you.

Troy: Not me. I ain't gonna owe nobody nothing if I can help it. Miss a payment and they come and snatch it right out your house. Then what you got? Now, soon as I get two hundred dollars clear, then I'll buy a TV. Right now, as soon as I get two hundred and sixty-four dollars, I'm gonna have this roof tarred.

Cory: Aw . . . Pop!

Troy: You go on and get you two hundred and buy one if ya want it. I got better things to do with my money.

50 **Cory:** I can't get no two hundred dollars. I ain't never seen two hundred dollars.

Troy: I'll tell you what . . . you get you a hundred dollars and I'll put the other hundred with it.

Cory: All right, I'm gonna show you.

Troy: You gonna show me how you can cut them boards right now.

Cory begins to cut the boards. There is a long pause.

Cory: The Pirates won today. That makes five in a row.

55 **Troy:** I ain't thinking about the Pirates. Got an all-white team. Got that boy . . . that Puerto Rican boy . . . Clemente.° Don't even half-play him.

°*Roberto Clemente:* (1934–1972), Major League baseball player for the Pittsburg Pirates, known as much for his humanitarianism as his unique batting style and ability. Clemente received the Most Valuable Player Award in 1966 and died in a plane crash in 1972 while shuttling supplies to Nicaraguan earthquake victims.

That boy could be something if they give him a chance. Play him one day and sit him on the bench the next.

CORY: He gets a lot of chances to play.

TROY: I'm talking about playing regular. Playing every day so you can get your timing. That's what I'm talking about.

CORY: They got some white guys on the team that don't play every day. You can't play everybody at the same time.

TROY: If they got a white fellow sitting on the bench . . . you can bet your last dollar he can't play! The colored guy got to be twice as good before he get on the team. That's why I don't want you to get all tied up in them sports. Man on the team and what it get him? They got colored on the team and don't use them. Same as not having them. All them teams the same.

CORY: The Braves got Hank Aaron° and Wes Covington.° Hank Aaron hit   60
two home runs today. That makes forty-three.

TROY: Hank Aaron ain't nobody. That what you supposed to do. That's how you supposed to play the game. Ain't nothing to it. It's just a matter of timing . . . getting the right follow-through. Hell, I can hit forty-three home runs right now!

CORY: Not off no major-league pitching, you couldn't.

TROY: We had better pitching in the Negro leagues. I hit seven home runs off of Satchel Paige.° You can't get no better than that!

CORY: Sandy Koufax.° He's leading the league in strikeouts.

TROY: I ain't thinking of no Sandy Koufax.   65

CORY: You got Warren Spahn° and Lew Burdette.° I bet you couldn't hit no home runs off of Warren Spahn.

TROY: I'm through with it now. You go on and cut them boards. (Pause.) Your mama tell me you done got recruited by a college football team? Is that right?

CORY: Yeah. Coach Zellman say the recruiter gonna be coming by to talk to you. Get you to sign the permission papers.

°*Hank Aaron:* Henry Aaron (1934–   ), American baseball player who broke Babe Ruth's career home run record with a lifetime total of 755 home runs. The holder of 12 other Major League records, Aaron spent his Major League career with the Braves, first in Milwaukee and later in their hometown of Atlanta.   °*Wes Covington:* John Wesley Covington (1932–   ), American baseball player known for his ability to frustrate pitchers by wasting time at the plate. In an eleven year career, Covington played for six Major League teams, beginning with the Milwaukee Braves and retiring with the Los Angeles Dodgers in 1966.   °*Satchel Page:* Leroy Robert Paige (1906–1982), American baseball player. He played in the Negro Leagues from the 1920s until 1948, when he joined the Cleveland Indians; he reportedly pitched 55 no-hit games during his career. Joe DiMaggio called him "the best pitcher I have ever faced."   °*Sandy Koufax:* Sanford Koufax (1935–   ), left-handed pitcher who won 129 games and lost only 47 for the Los Angeles Dodgers in the six seasons between 1961 and 1966; he won three Cy Young Awards and pitched four no-hit games, the last of which (1965) was a perfect game.   °*Warren Spahn:* (1921–2003), left-handed pitcher who at the time of his retirement in 1966 held the National League record of 363 wins; he won 20 or more games in four con-secutive seasons (1947–1950) and in several other seasons during the 1950s.   °*Lew Burdette:* Selva Lewis Burdette (1926–   ), American baseball player who pitched and won three games for the Milwaukee Braves against the New York Yankees in the 1957 World Series; for that Series, his ERA was an amazingly low .067.

TROY: I thought you supposed to be working down there at the A&P. Ain't you
suppose to be working down there after school?

70 CORY: Mr. Stawicki say he gonna hold my job for me until after the football
season. Say starting next week I can work weekends.

TROY: I thought we had an understanding about this football stuff? You suppose to keep up with your chores and hold that job down at the A&P. Ain't
been around here all day on a Saturday. Ain't none of your chores done . . .
and now you telling me you done quit your job.

CORY: I'm going to be working weekends.

TROY: You damn right you are! And ain't no need for nobody coming around
here to talk to me about signing nothing.

CORY: Hey, Pop . . . you can't do that. He's coming all the way from North
Carolina.

75 TROY: I don't care where he coming from. The white man ain't gonna let
you get nowhere with that football noway. You go on and get your book-
learning so you can work yourself up in that A&P or learn how to fix cars or
build houses or something, get you a trade. That way you have something
can't nobody take away from you. You go on and learn how to put your
hands to some good use. Besides hauling people's garbage.

CORY: I get good grades, Pop. That's why the recruiter wants to talk with you.
You got to keep up your grades to get recruited. This way I'll be going to
college. I'll get a chance . . .

TROY: First you gonna get your butt down there to the A&P and get your job
back.

CORY: Mr. Stawicki done already hired somebody else 'cause I told him I was
playing football.

TROY: You a bigger fool than I thought . . . to let somebody take away your
job so you can play some football. Where you gonna get your money to take
out your girlfriend and whatnot? What kind of foolishness is that to let
somebody take away your job?

80 CORY: I'm still gonna be working weekends.

TROY: Naw . . . naw. You getting your butt out of here and finding you another job.

CORY: Come on, Pop! I got to practice. I can't work after school and play
football too. The team needs me. That's what Coach Zellman say . . .

TROY: I don't care what nobody else say. I'm the boss . . . you understand? I'm
the boss around here. I do the only saying what counts.

CORY: Come on, Pop!

85 TROY: I asked you . . . did you understand?

CORY: Yeah . . .

TROY: What?!

CORY: Yessir.

TROY: You go on down there to that A&P and see if you can get your job back.
If you can't do both . . . then you quit the football team. You've got to take
the crookeds with the straights.

CORY: Yessir. (*Pause.*) Can I ask you a question?   90
TROY: What the hell you wanna ask me? Mr. Stawicki the one you got the
questions for.
CORY: How come you ain't never liked me?
TROY: Liked you? Who the hell say I got to like you? What law is there say I got
to like you? Wanna stand up in my face and ask a damn fool-ass question like
that. Talking about liking somebody. Come here, boy, when I talk to you.

*Cory comes over to where Troy is working. He stands slouched over and Troy shoves
him on his shoulder.*

Straighten up, goddammit! I asked you a question . . . what law is there say
I got to like you?
CORY: None.
TROY: Well, all right then! Don't you eat every day? (*Pause.*) Answer me when
I talk to you! Don't you eat every day?
CORY: Yeah.
TROY: Nigger, as long as you in my house, you put that sir on the end of it
when you talk to me!
CORY: Yes . . . sir.
TROY: You eat every day.
CORY: Yessir!   100
TROY: Got a roof over your head.
CORY: Yessir!
TROY: Got clothes on your back.
CORY: Yessir.
TROY: Why you think that is?   105
CORY: 'Cause of you.
TROY: Ah, hell I know it's 'cause of me . . . but why do you think that is?
CORY: (*hesitant*) 'Cause you like me.
TROY: Like you? I go out of here every morning . . . bust my butt . . . putting up
with them crackers° every day . . . 'cause I like you? You are the biggest fool I
ever saw. (*Pause.*) It's my job. It's my responsibility! You understand that? A
man got to take care of his family. You live in my house . . . sleep you behind on
my bedclothes . . . fill you belly up with my food . . . 'cause you my son. You my
flesh and blood. Not 'cause I like you! 'Cause it's my duty to take care of you. I
owe a responsibility to you! Let's get this straight right here . . . before it go
along any further . . . I ain't got to like you. Mr. Rand don't give me my money
come payday cause he likes me. He give me 'cause he owe me. I done give you
everything I had to give you. I gave you your life! Me and your mama worked
that out between us. And liking your black ass wasn't part of the bargain. Don't
you try and go through life worrying about if somebody like you or not. You best
be making sure they doing right by you. You understand what I'm saying, boy?

°*crackers:* Derogatory term for white people, generally poor southern whites.

110 **Cory:** Yessir.
Troy: Then get the hell out of my face, and get on down to that A&P.

Rose has been standing behind the screen door for much of the scene. She enters as Cory exits.

Rose: Why don't you let the boy go ahead and play football, Troy? Ain't no harm in that. He's just trying to be like you with the sports.
Troy: I don't want him to be like me! I want him to move as far away from my life as he can get. You the only decent thing that ever happened to me. I wish him that. But I don't wish him a thing else from my life. I decided seventeen years ago that boy wasn't getting involved in no sports. Not after what they did to me in the sports.
Rose: Troy, why don't you admit you was too old to play in the major leagues? For once . . . why don't you admit that?
115 **Troy:** What do you mean too old? Don't come telling me I was too old. I just wasn't the right color. Hell, I'm fifty-three years old and can do better than Selkirk's .269 right now!
Rose: How's was you gonna play ball when you were over forty? Sometimes I can't go no sense out of you.
Troy: I got good sense, woman. I got sense enough not to let my boy get hurt over playing no sports. You been mothering that boy too much. Worried about if people like him.
Rose: Everything that boy do . . . he do for you. He wants you to say "Good job, son." That's all.
Troy: Rose, I ain't got time for that. He's alive. He's healthy. He's got to make his own way. I made mine. Ain't nobody gonna hold his hand when he get out there in that world.
120 **Rose:** Times have changed from when you was young, Troy. People change. The world's changing around you and you can't even see it.
Troy: *(slow, methodical)* Woman . . . I do the best I can do. I come in here every Friday. I carry a sack of potatoes and a bucket of lard. You all line up at the door with your hands out. I give you the lint from my pockets. I give you my sweat and my blood. I ain't got no tears. I done spent them. We go upstairs in that room at night . . . and I fall down on you and try to blast a hole into forever. I get up Monday morning . . . find my lunch on the table. I go out. Make my way. Find my strength to carry me through to the next Friday. *(Pause.)* That's all I got, Rose. That's all I got to give. I can't give nothing else.

Troy exits into the house. The lights go down to black.

SCENE 4

It is Friday. Two weeks later. Cory starts out of the house with his football equipment. The phone rings.

CORY: *(calling)* I got it! *(He answers the phone and stands in the screen door talking.)* Hello? Hey, Jesse. Naw . . . I was just getting ready to leave now.

ROSE: *(calling)* Cory! 5

CORY: I told you, man, them spikes° is all tore up. You can use them if you want, but they ain't no good. Earl got some spikes.

ROSE: *(calling)* Cory!

CORY: *(calling to Rose)* Mam? I'm talking to Jesse. *(Into phone.)* When she say that? *(Pause.)* Aw, you lying, man. I'm gonna tell her you said that.

ROSE: *(calling)* Cory, don't you go nowhere!

CORY: I got to go to the game, Ma! *(Into the phone.)* Yeah, hey, look, I'll talk to you later. Yeah, I'll meet you over Earl's house. Later. Bye, Ma.

Cory exits the house and starts out the yard.

ROSE: Cory, where you going off to? You got that stuff all pulled out and thrown all over your room.

CORY: *(in the yard)* I was looking for my spikes. Jesse wanted to borrow my spikes.

ROSE: Get up there and get that cleaned up before your daddy get back in here. 10

CORY: I got to go to the game! I'll clean it up *when I get back.*

Cory exits.

ROSE: That's all he need to do is see that room all messed up.

Rose exits into the house. Troy and Bono enter the yard. Troy is dressed in clothes other than his work clothes.

BONO: He told him the same thing he told you. Take it to the union.

TROY: Brownie ain't got that much sense. Man wasn't thinking about nothing. He wait until I confront them on it . . . then he wanna come crying seniority. *(Calls.)* Hey, Rose!

BONO: I wish I could have seen Mr. Rand's face when he told you. 15

TROY: He couldn't get it out of his mouth! Liked to bit his tongue! When they called me down there to the Commissioner's office . . . he thought they was gonna fire me. Like everybody else.

BONO: I didn't think they was gonna fire you. I thought they was gonna put you on the warning paper.

TROY: Hey, Rose! *(To Bono.)* Yeah, Mr. Rand like to bit his tongue.

Troy breaks the seal on the bottle, takes a drink, and hands it to Bono.

BONO: I see you run right down to Taylors' and told that Alberta gal. 20

°*spikes:* Athletic shoes with sharp metal grips set into the soles.

TROY: *(calling)* Hey, Rose! *(To Bono.)* I told everybody. Hey, Rose! I went down there to cash my check.

ROSE: *(entering from the house)* Hush all that hollering, man! I know you out here. What they say down there at the Commissioner's office?

TROY: You supposed to come when I call you, woman. Bono'll tell you that. *(To Bono.)* Don't Lucille come when you call her?

ROSE: Man, hush your mouth, I ain't no dog . . . talk about "come when you call me."

25 TROY: *(puts his arm around Rose)* You hear this, Bono? I had me an old dog used to get uppity like that. You say, "C'mere, Blue!" . . . and he just lay there and look at you. End up getting a stick and chasing him away trying to make him come.

ROSE: I ain't studying you and your dog. I remember you used to sing that old song.

TROY: *(he sings)*

> Hear it ring! Hear it ring!
> I had a dog his name was Blue.

ROSE: Don't nobody wanna hear you sing that old song.

TROY: *(sings)*

> You know Blue was mighty true.

30 ROSE: Used to have Cory running around here singing that song.

BONO: Hell, I remember that song myself.

TROY: *(sings)*

> You know Blue was a good old dog.
> Blue treed a possum in a hollow log.

That was my daddy's song. My daddy made up that song.

ROSE: I don't care who made it up. Don't nobody wanna hear you sing it.

TROY: *(makes a song like calling a dog)* Come here, woman.

ROSE: You come in here carrying on, I reckon they ain't fired you. What they
35 say down there at the Commissioner's office?

TROY: Look here, Rose . . . Mr. Rand called me into his office today when I got back from talking to them people down there . . . it come from up top . . . he called me in and told me they was making me a driver.

ROSE: Troy, you kidding!

TROY: No I ain't. Ask Bono.

ROSE: Well, that's great, Troy. Now you don't have to hassle them people no more.

Lyons enters from the street.

40 TROY: Aw hell, I wasn't looking to see you today. I thought you was in jail. Got it all over the front page of the *Courier* about them raiding Sefus's place . . . where you be hanging out with all them thugs.

LYONS: Hey, Pop . . . that ain't got nothing to do with me. I don't go down there gambling. I go down there to sit in with the band. I ain't got nothing to do with the gambling part. They got some good music down there.

TROY: They got some rogues . . . is what they got.

LYONS: How you been, Mr. Bono? Hi, Rose.

BONO: I see where you playing down at the Crawford Grill tonight.

ROSE: How come you ain't brought Bonnie like I told you? You should have   45
brought Bonnie with you, she ain't been over in a month of Sundays.

LYONS: I was just in the neighborhood . . . thought I'd stop by.

TROY: Here he come . . .

BONO: Your daddy got a promotion on the rubbish. He's gonna be the first col-ored driver. Ain't got to do nothing but sit up there and read the paper like them white fellows.

LYONS: Hey, Pop . . . if you knew how to read you'd be all right.

BONO: Naw . . . naw . . . you mean if the nigger knew how to *drive* he'd be all   50
right. Been fighting with them people about driving and ain't even got a license. Mr. Rand know you ain't got no driver's license?

TROY: Driving ain't nothing. All you do is point the truck where you want it to go. Driving ain't nothing.

BONO: Do Mr. Rand know you ain't got no driver's license? That's what I'm talking about. I ain't asked if driving was easy. I asked if Mr. Rand know you ain't got no driver's license.

TROY: He ain't got to know. The man ain't got to know my business. Time he find out, I have two or three driver's licenses.

LYONS: *(going into his pocket)* Say, look here, Pop . . .

TROY: I knew it was coming. Didn't I tell you, Bono? I know what kind of   55
"Look here, Pop" that was. The nigger fixing to ask me for some money. It's Friday night. It's my payday. All them rogues down there on the avenue . . . the ones that ain't in jail . . . and Lyons is hopping in his shoes to get down there with them.

LYONS: See, Pop . . . if you give somebody else a chance to talk sometimes, you'd see that I was fixing to pay you back your ten dollars like I told you. Here . . . I told you I'd pay you when Bonnie got paid.

TROY: Naw . . . you go ahead and keep that ten dollars. Put it in the bank. The next time you feel like you wanna come by here and ask me for something . . . you go on down there and get that.

LYONS: Here's your ten dollars, Pop. I told you I don't want you to give me nothing. I just wanted to borrow ten dollars.

TROY: Naw . . . you go on and keep that for the next time you want to ask me.

LYONS: Come on, Pop . . . here go your ten dollars.   60

ROSE: Why don't you go on and let the boy pay you back, Troy?

LYONS: Here you go, Rose. If you don't take it I'm gonna have to hear about it for the next six months. *(He hands her the money.)*

ROSE: You can hand yours over here too, Troy.

Troy: You see this, Bono. You see how they do me.
65 **Bono:** Yeah, Lucille do me the same way.

Gabriel is heard singing offstage. He enters.

Gabriel: Better get ready for the Judgment! Better get ready for . . . Hey! . . .
Hey! . . . There's Troy's boy!
Lyons: How are you doing, Uncle Gabe?
Gabriel: Lyons . . . The King of the Jungle! Rose . . . hey, Rose. Got a flower
for you. (*He takes a rose from his pocket.*) Picked it myself. That's the same
rose like you is!
Rose: That's right nice of you, Gabe.
70 **Lyons:** What you been doing, Uncle Gabe?
Gabriel: Oh, I been chasing hellhounds and waiting on the time to tell
St. Peter to open the gates.
Lyons: You been chasing hellhounds, huh? Well . . . you doing the right thing,
Uncle Gabe. Somebody got to chase them.
Gabriel: Oh, yeah . . . I know it. The devil's strong. The devil ain't no
pushover. Hellhounds snipping at everybody's heels. But I got my trumpet
waiting on the judgment time.
Lyons: Waiting on the Battle of Armageddon, huh?
75 **Gabriel:** Ain't gonna be too much of a battle when God get to waving that
Judgment sword. But the people's gonna have a hell of a time trying to get
into heaven if them gates ain't open.
Lyons: (*putting his arm around Gabriel*) You hear this, Pop. Uncle Gabe, you all
right!
Gabriel: (*laughing with Lyons*) Lyons! King of the Jungle.
Rose: You gonna stay for supper, Gabe? Want me to fix you a plate?
Gabriel: I'll take a sandwich, Rose. Don't want no plate. Just wanna eat with
my hands. I'll take a sandwich.
80 **Rose:** How about you, Lyons? You staying? Got some short ribs cooking.
Lyons: Naw, I won't eat nothing till after we finished playing. (*Pause.*) You
ought to come down and listen to me play, Pop.
Troy: I don't like that Chinese music. All that noise.
Rose: Go on in the house and wash up, Gabe . . . I'll fix you a sandwich.
Gabriel: (*to Lyons, as he exits*) Troy's mad at me.
85 **Lyons:** What you mad at Uncle Gabe for, Pop?
Rose: He thinks Troy's mad at him cause he moved over to Miss Pearl's.
Troy: I ain't mad at the man. He can live where he want to live at.
Lyons: What he move over there for? Miss Pearl don't like nobody.
Rose: She don't mind him none. She treats him real nice. She just don't allow
all that singing.
90 **Troy:** She don't mind that rent he be paying . . . that's what she don't mind.
Rose: Troy, I ain't going through that with you no more. He's over there cause
he want to have his own place. He can come and go as he please.

TROY: Hell, he could come and go as he please here. I wasn't stopping him. I ain't put no rules on him.

ROSE: It ain't the same thing, Troy. And you know it.

Gabriel comes to the door.

Now, that's the last I wanna hear about that. I don't wanna hear nothing else about Gabe and Miss Pearl. And next week . . .

GABRIEL: I'm ready for my sandwich, Rose.

ROSE: And next week . . . when that recruiter come from that school . . . I   95
want you to sign that paper and go on and let Cory play football. Then that'll be the last I have to hear about that.

TROY: *(to Rose as she exits into the house)* I ain't thinking about Cory nothing.

LYONS: What . . . Cory got recruited? What school he going to?

TROY: That boy walking around here smelling his piss . . . thinking he's grown. Thinking he's gonna do what he want, irrespective of what I say. Look here, Bono . . . I left the Commissioner's office and went down to the A&P . . . that boy ain't working down there. He lying to me. Telling me he got his job back . . . telling me he working weekends . . . telling me he working after school . . . Mr. Stawicki tell me he ain't working down there at all!

LYONS: Cory just growing up. He's just busting at the seams trying to fill out your shoes.

TROY: I don't care what he's doing. When he get to the point where he wanna   100
disobey me . . . then it's time for him to move on. Bono'll tell you that. I bet he ain't never disobeyed his daddy without paying the consequences.

BONO: I ain't never had a chance. My daddy came on through . . . but I ain't never knew him to see him . . . or what he had on his mind or where he went. Just moving on through. Searching out the New Land. That's what the old folks used to call it. See a fellow moving around from place to place . . . woman to woman . . . called it searching out the New Land. can't say if he ever found it. I come along, didn't want no kids. Didn't know if I was gonna be in one place long enough to fix on them right as their daddy. I figured I was going searching too. As it turned out I been hooked up with Lucille near about as long as your daddy been with Rose. Going on sixteen years.

TROY: Sometimes I wish I hadn't known my daddy. He ain't cared nothing about no kids. A kid to him wasn't nothing. All he wanted was for you to learn how to walk so he could start you to working. When it come time for eating . . . he ate first. If there was anything left over, that's what you got. Man would sit down and eat two chickens and give you the wing.

LYONS: You ought to stop that, Pop. Everybody feed their kids. No matter how hard times is . . . everybody care about their kids. Make sure they have something to eat.

TROY: The only thing my daddy cared about was getting them bales of cotton in to Mr. Lubin. That's the only thing that mattered to him. Sometimes I used to wonder why he was living. Wonder why the devil hadn't come and got him. "Get them bales of cotton in to Mr. Lubin" and find out he owe him money . . .

105 LYONS: He should have just went on and left when he saw he couldn't get nowhere. That's what I would have done.

TROY: How he gonna leave with eleven kids? And where he gonna go? He ain't knew how to do nothing but farm. No, he was trapped and I think he knew it. But I'll say this for him . . . he felt a responsibility toward us. Maybe he ain't treated us the way I felt he should have . . . but without that responsibility he could have walked off and left us . . . made his own way.

BONO: A lot of them did. Back in those days what you talking about . . . they walk out their front door and just take on down one road or another and keep on walking.

LYONS: There you go? That's what I'm talking about.

BONO: Just keep on walking till you come to something else. Ain't you never heard of nobody having the walking blues? Well, that's what you call it when you just take off like that.

110 TROY: My daddy ain't had them walking blues! What you talking about? He stayed right there with his family. But he was just as evil as he could be. My mama couldn't stand him. Couldn't stand that evilness. She run off when I was about eight. She sneaked off one night after he had gone to sleep. Told me she was coming back for me. I ain't never seen her no more. All his women run off and left him. He wasn't good for nobody.

When my turn come to head out, I was fourteen and got to sniffing around Joe Canewell's daughter. Had us an old mule we called Greyboy. My daddy sent me out to do some plowing and tied up Greyboy and went to fooling around with Joe Canewell's daughter. We done found us a nice little spot, got real cozy with each other. She about thirteen and we done figured we was grown anyway . . . so we down there enjoying ourselves . . . ain't thinking about nothing. We didn't know Greyboy had got loose and wandered back to the house and my daddy was looking for me. We down there by the creek enjoying ourselves when my daddy come up on us. Surprised us. He had them leather straps off the mule and commenced to whupping me like there was no tomorrow. I jumped up, mad and embarrassed. I was scared of my daddy. When he commenced to whupping on me . . . quite naturally I run to get out of the way. (*Pause.*) Now I thought he was mad 'cause I ain't done my work. But I see where he was chasing me off so he could have that gal for himself. When I see what the matter of it was, I lost all fear of my daddy. Right there is where I become a man . . . at fourteen years of age. (*Pause.*) Now it was my turn to run him off. I picked up them same reins that he had used on me. I picked up them reins and commenced to whupping on him. The gal jumped up and run off . . . and when my daddy turned to face me, I could see why the devil had never come to get him . . . cause he was the devil himself. I don't know what happened.

When I woke up, I was laying right there by the creek, and Blue . . . this old dog we had . . . was licking my face. I thought I was blind. I couldn't see nothing. Both my eyes were swollen shut. I laid there and cried. I didn't know what I was gonna do. The only thing I knew was the time had come for me to leave my daddy's house. And right there the world suddenly got big. And it was a long time before I could cut it down to where I could handle it.

Part of that cutting down was when I got to the place where I could feel him kicking in my blood and knew that the only thing that separated us was the matter of a few years.

Gabriel enters from the house with a sandwich.

LYONS: What you got there, Uncle Gabe?

GABRIEL: Got me a ham sandwich. Rose gave me a ham sandwich.

TROY: I don't know what happened to him. I done lost touch with everybody except Gabriel. But I hope he's dead. I hope he found some peace.

LYONS: That's a heavy story, Pop. I didn't know you left home when you was fourteen.

TROY: And didn't know nothing. The only part of the world I knew was the   115
forty-two acres of Mr. Lubin's land. That's all I knew about life.

LYONS: Fourteen's kinda young to be out on your own. *(Phone rings.)* I don't even think I was ready to be out on my own at fourteen. I don't know what I would have done.

TROY: I got up from the creek and walked on down to Mobile.° I was through with farming. Figured I could do better in the city. So I walked the two hundred miles to Mobile.

LYONS: Wait a minute . . . you ain't walked no two hundred miles, Pop. Ain't nobody gonna walk no two hundred miles. You talking about some walking there.

BONO: That's the only way you got anywhere back in them days.

LYONS: Shhh. Damn if I wouldn't have hitched a ride with somebody!   120

TROY: Who you gonna hitch it with? They ain't got no cars and things like they got now. We talking about 1918.

ROSE: *(entering)* What you all out here getting into?

TROY: *(to Rose)* I'm telling Lyons how good he got it. He don't know nothing about this I'm talking.

ROSE: Lyons, that was Bonnie on the phone. She say you supposed to pick her up.

LYONS: Yeah, okay, Rose.   125

TROY: I walked on down to Mobile and hitched up with some of them fellows that was heading this way. Got up here and found out . . . not only couldn't you get a job . . . you couldn't find no place to live. I thought I was in

---

°*Mobile:* City and seaport in southwestern Alabama.

freedom. Shhh. Colored folks living down there on the riverbanks in whatever kind of shelter they could find for themselves. Right down there under
the Brady Street Bridge. Living in shacks made of sticks and tarpaper.
Messed around there and went from bad to worse. Started stealing. First it
was food. Then I figured, hell, if I steal money I can buy me some food. Buy
me some shoes too! One thing led to another. Met your mama. I was young
and anxious to be a man. Met your mama and had you. What I do that for?
Now I got to worry about feeding you and her. Got to steal three times as
much. Went out one day looking for somebody to rob . . . that's what I was,
a robber. I'll tell you the truth. I'm ashamed of it today. But it's the truth.
Went to rob this fellow . . . pulled out my knife . . . and he pulled out a gun.
Shot me in the chest. I felt just like somebody had taken a hot branding
iron and laid it on me. When he shot me I jumped at him with my knife.
They told me I killed him and they put me in the penitentiary and locked
me up for fifteen years. That's where I met Bono. That's where I learned
how to play baseball. Got out that place and your mama had taken you and
went on to make life without me. Fifteen years was a long time for her to
wait. But that fifteen years cured me of that robbing stuff. Rose'll tell you.
She asked me when I met her if I had gotten all that foolishness out of my
system. And I told her, "Baby, it's you and baseball all what count with me."
You hear me, Bono? I meant it too. She say, "Which one comes first?" I told
her, "Baby, ain't no doubt it's baseball . . . but you stick and get old with me
and we'll both outlive this baseball." Am I right, Rose? And it's true.

ROSE: Man, hush your mouth. You ain't said no such thing. Talking about
"Baby, you know you'll always be number one with me." That's what you
was talking.

TROY: You hear that, Bono. That's why I love her.

BONO: Rose'll keep you straight. You get off the track, she'll straighten you up.

130   ROSE: Lyons, you better get on up and get Bonnie. She waiting on you.

LYONS: *(gets up to go)* Hey, Pop, why don't you come on down to the Grill and
hear me play

TROY: I ain't going down there. I'm too old to be sitting around in them clubs.

BONO: You got to be good to play down at the Grill.

LYONS: Come on, Pop . . .

135   TROY: I got to get up in the morning.

LYONS: You ain't got to stay long.

TROY: Naw, I'm gonna get my supper and go on to bed.

LYONS: Well, I got to go. I'll see you again.

TROY: Don't you come around my house on my payday.

140   ROSE: Pick up the phone and let somebody know you coming. And bring
Bonnie with you. You know I'm always glad to see her.

LYONS: Yeah, I'll do that, Rose. You take care now. See you, Pop. See you,
Mr. Bono. See you, Uncle Gabe.

GABRIEL: Lyons! King of the Jungle!

Lyons exits.

TROY: Is supper ready, woman? Me and you got some business to take care of. I'm gonna tear it up too.

ROSE: Troy, I done told you now!

TROY: *(puts his arm around Bono)* Aw hell, woman . . . this is Bono. Bono like 145 family. I done known this nigger since . . . how long I done know you?

BONO: It's been a long time.

TROY: I done know this nigger since Skippy was a pup. Me and him done been through some times.

BONO: You sure right about that.

TROY: Hell, I done know him longer than I known you. And we still standing shoulder to shoulder. Hey, look here, Bono . . . a man can't ask for no more than that. *(Drinks to him.)* I love you, nigger.

BONO: Hell, I love you too . . . I got to get home see my woman. You got yours 150 in hand. I got to go get mine.

Bono starts to exit as Cory enters the yard, dressed in his football uniform. He gives Troy a hard, uncompromising look.

CORY: What you do that for, Pop?

He throws his helmet down in the direction of Troy.

ROSE: What's the matter? Cory . . . what's the matter?

CORY: Papa done went up to the school and told Coach Zellman I can't play football no more. Wouldn't even let me play the game. Told him to tell the recruiter not to come.

ROSE: Troy . . .

TROY: What you Troying me for. Yeah, I did it. And the boy know why I did it. 155

CORY: Why you wanna do that to me? That was the one chance I had.

ROSE: Ain't nothing wrong with Cory playing football, Troy.

TROY: The boy lied to me. I told the nigger if he wanna play football . . . to keep up his chores and hold down that job at the A&P. That was the conditions. Stopped down there to see Mr. Stawicki . . .

CORY: I can't work after school during the football season, Pop! I tried to tell you that Mr. Stawicki's holding my job for me. You don't never want to listen to nobody. And then you wanna go and do this to me!

TROY: I ain't done nothing to you. You done it to yourself.   160

CORY: Just cause you didn't have a chance! You just scared I'm gonna be better than you, that's all.

TROY: Come here.

ROSE: Troy . . .

Cory reluctantly crosses over to Troy.

TROY: All right! See. You done made a mistake.

165 **CORY:** I didn't even do nothing!

TROY: I'm gonna tell you what your mistake was. See . . . you swung at the ball and didn't hit it. That's strike one. See, you in the batter's box now. You swung and you missed. That's strike one. Don't you strike out!

Lights fade to black.

ACT 2

SCENE 1

The following morning. Cory is at the tree hitting the ball with the bat. He tries to mimic Troy, but his swing is awkward, less sure. Rose enters from the house.

ROSE: Cory, I want you to help me with this cupboard.

CORY: I ain't quitting the team. I don't care what Poppa say.

ROSE: I'll talk to him when he gets back. He had to go see about your Uncle Gabe. The police done arrested him. Say he was disturbing the peace. He'll be back directly. Come on in here and help me clean out the top of this cupboard.

Cory exits into the house. Rose sees Troy and Bono coming down the alley.

Troy . . . what they say down there?

TROY: Ain't said nothing. I give them fifty dollars and they let him go. I'll talk to you about it. Where's Cory?

5 **ROSE:** He's in there helping me clean out these cupboards.

TROY: Tell him to get his butt out here.

Troy and Bono go over to the pile of wood. Bono picks up the saw and begins sawing.

TROY: *(to Bono)* All they want is the money. That makes six or seven times I done went down there and got him. See me coming they stick out their *hands.*

BONO: Yeah. I know what you mean. That's all they care about . . . that money. They don't care about what's right. *(Pause.)* Nigger, why you got to go and get some hard wood? You ain't doing nothing but building a little old fence. Get you some soft pine wood. That's all you need.

TROY: I know what I'm doing. This is outside wood. You put pine wood inside the house. Pine wood is inside wood. This here is outside wood. Now you tell me where the fence is gonna be?

10 **BONO:** You don't need this wood. You can put it up with pine wood and it'll stand as long as you gonna be here looking at it.

TROY: How you know how long I'm gonna be here, nigger? Hell, I might just live forever. Live longer than old man Horsely.

BONO: That's what Magee used to say.

TROY: Magee's a damn fool. Now you tell me who you ever heard of gonna pull their own teeth with a pair of rusty pliers.

BONO: The old folks . . . my granddaddy used to pull his teeth with pliers. They ain't had no dentists for the colored folks back then.

TROY: Get clean pliers! You understand? Clean pliers! Sterilize them! Besides we 15 ain't living back then. All Magee had to do was walk over to Doc Goldblum's.

BONO: I see where you and that Tallahassee gal . . . that Alberta . . . I see where you all done got tight.

TROY: What you mean "got tight"?

BONO: I see where you be laughing and joking with her all the time.

TROY: I laughs and jokes with all of them, Bono. You know me.

BONO: That ain't the kind of laughing and joking I'm talking about. 20

Cory enters from the house.

CORY: How you doing, Mr. Bono?

TROY: Cory? Get that saw from Bono and cut some wood. He talking about the wood's too hard to cut. Stand back there, Jim, and let that young boy show you how it's done.

BONO: He's sure welcome to it.

Cory takes the saw and begins to cut the wood.

Whew-e-e! Look at that. Big old strong boy. Look like Joe Louis.° Hell, must be getting old the way I'm watching that boy whip through that wood.

CORY: I don't see why Mama want a fence around the yard noways.

TROY: Damn if I know either. What the hell she keeping out with it? She ain't 25 got nothing nobody want.

BONO: Some people build fences to keep people out . . . and other people build fences to keep people in. Rose wants to hold on to you all. She loves you.

TROY: Hell, nigger, I don't need nobody to tell me my wife loves me. Cory . . . go on in the house and see if you can find that other saw.

CORY: Where's it at?

TROY: I said find it! Look for it till you find it!

Cory exits into the house.

What's that supposed to mean? Wanna keep us in?

BONO: Troy . . . I done known you seem like damn near my whole life. You and 30 Rose both. I done know both of you all for a long time. I remember when you met Rose. When you was hitting them baseballs out the park. A lot of them gals was after you then. You had the pick of the litter. When you picked Rose, I was happy for you. That was the first time I knew you had any sense. I said . . . My man Troy knows what he's doing . . . I'm gonna follow this nigger . . . he might take me somewhere. I been following you too.

°*Joe Louis:* Joseph Louis Barrow (1914–1981), American boxer known as the "Brown Bomber." In 1937, he became the youngest boxer ever to win the Heavyweight Championship, which he defended twenty-five times; he retired undefeated in 1949.

I done learned a whole heap of things about life watching you. I done learned how to tell where the shit lies. How to tell it from the alfalfa. You done learned me a lot of things. You showed me how to not make the same mistakes . . . to take life as it comes along and keep putting one foot in front of the other. *(Pause.)* Rose a good woman, Troy.

TROY: Hell, nigger, I know she a good woman. I been married to her for eighteen years. What you got on your mind, Bono?

BONO: I just say she a good woman. Just like I say anything. I ain't got to have nothing on my mind.

TROY: You just gonna say she a good woman and leave it hanging out there like that? Why you telling me she a good woman?

BONO: She loves you, Troy. Rose loves you.

35 TROY: You saying I don't measure up. That's what you trying to say. I don't measure up 'cause I'm seeing this other gal. I know what you trying to say.

BONO: I know what Rose means to you, Troy. I'm just trying to say I don't want to see you mess up.

TROY: Yeah, I appreciate that, Bono. If you was messing around on Lucille I'd be telling you the same thing.

BONO: Well, that's all I got to say. I just say that because I love you both.

TROY: Hell, you know me . . . I wasn't out there looking for nothing. You can't find a better woman than Rose. I know that. But seems like this woman just stuck onto me where I can't shake her loose. I done wrestled with it, tried to throw her off me . . . but she just stuck on tighter. Now she's stuck on for good.

40 BONO: You's in control . . . that's what you tell me all the time. You responsible for what you do.

TROY: I ain't ducking the responsibility of it. As long as it sets right in my heart . . . then I'm okay. 'Cause that's all I listen to. It'll tell me right from wrong every time. And I ain't talking about doing Rose no bad turn. I love Rose. She done carried me a long ways and I love and respect her for that.

BONO: I know you do. That's why I don't want to see you hurt her. But what you gonna do when she find out? What you got then? If you try and juggle both of them . . . sooner or later you gonna drop one of them. That's common sense.

TROY: Yeah, I hear what you saying, Bono. I been trying to figure a way to work it out.

BONO: Work it out right, Troy. I don't want to be getting all up between you and Rose's business . . . but work it so it come out right.

45 TROY: Ah hell, I get all up between you and Lucille's business. When you gonna get that woman that refrigerator she been wanting? Don't tell me you ain't got no money now. I know who your banker is. Mellon don't need that money bad as Lucille want that refrigerator. I'll tell you that.

BONO: Tell you what I'll do . . . when you finish building this fence for Rose . . . I'll buy Lucille that refrigerator.

TROY: You done stuck your foot in your mouth now!

Troy grabs up a board and begins to saw. Bono starts to walk out the yard.

Hey, nigger . . . where you going?

BONO: I'm going home. I know you don't expect me to help you now. I'm protecting my money. I wanna see you put that fence up by yourself. That's what I want to see. You'll be here another six months without me.

TROY: Nigger, you ain't right.

BONO: When it comes to my money . . . I'm right as fireworks on the Fourth of July. 50

TROY: All right, we gonna see now. You better get out your bankbook.

Bono exits, and Troy continues to work. Rose enters from the house.

ROSE: What they say down there? What's happening with Gabe?

TROY: I went down there and got him out. Cost me fifty dollars. Say he was 55 disturbing the peace. Judge set up a hearing for him in three weeks. Say to show cause why he shouldn't be recommitted.

ROSE: What was he doing that cause them to arrest him?

TROY: Some kids were teasing him and he run them off home. Say he was howling and carrying on. Some folks seen him and called the police. That's all it was.

ROSE: Well, what's you say? What'd you tell the judge?

TROY: Told him I'd look after him. It didn't make no sense to recommit the man. He stuck out his big greasy palm and told me to give him fifty dollars and take him on home.

ROSE: Where's he at now? Where'd he go off to?

TROY: He's gone about his business. He don't need nobody to hold his hand.

ROSE: Well, I don't know. Seem like that would be the best place for him if 60 they did put him into the hospital. I know what you're gonna say. But that's what I think would be best.

TROY: The man done had his life ruined fighting for what? And they wanna take and lock him up. Let him be free. He don't bother nobody.

ROSE: Well, everybody got their own way of looking at it I guess. Come on and get your lunch. I got a bowl of lima beans and some cornbread in the oven. Come and get something to eat. Ain't no sense you fretting over Gabe.

Rose turns to go into the house.

TROY: Rose . . . got something to tell you.

ROSE: Well, come on . . . wait till I get this food on the table.

TROY: Rose! 65

She stops and turns around.

I don't know how to say this. (*Pause.*) I can't explain it none. It just sort of grows on you till it gets out of hand. It starts out like a little bush . . . and the next thing you know it's a whole forest.

ROSE: Troy . . . what is you talking about?

TROY: I'm talking, woman, let me talk. I'm trying to find a way to tell you . . . I'm gonna be a daddy. I'm gonna be somebody's daddy.

ROSE: Troy . . . you're not telling me this? You're gonna be . . . what?

TROY: Rose . . . now . . . see . . .

70 ROSE: You telling me you gonna be somebody's daddy? You telling your *wife* this?

Gabriel enters from the street. He carries a rose in his hand.

GABRIEL: Hey, Troy! Hey, Rose!

ROSE: I have to wait eighteen years to hear something like this.

GABRIEL: Hey, Rose . . . I got a flower for you. (*He hands it to her.*) That's a rose. Same rose like you is.

ROSE: Thanks, Gabe.

75 GABRIEL: Troy, you ain't mad at me is you? Them bad mens come and put me away. You ain't mad at me is you?

TROY: Naw, Gabe, I ain't mad at you.

ROSE: Eighteen years and you wanna come with this.

GABRIEL: (*takes a quarter out of his pocket*) See what I got? Got a brand new quarter.

TROY: Rose . . . it's just . . .

80 ROSE: Ain't nothing you can say, Troy. Ain't no way of explaining that.

GABRIEL: Fellow that give me this quarter had a whole mess of them. I'm gonna keep this quarter till it stop shining.

ROSE: Gabe, go on in the house there. I got some watermelon in the Frigidaire. Go on and get you a piece.

GABRIEL: Say, Rose . . . you know I was chasing hellhounds and them bad mens come and get me and take me away. Troy helped me. He come down there and told them they better let me go before he beat them up. Yeah, he did!

ROSE: You go on and get you a piece of watermelon, Gabe. Them bad mens is gone now.

85 GABRIEL: Okay, Rose . . . gonna get me some watermelon. The kind with the stripes on it.

Gabriel exits into the house.

ROSE: Why, Troy? Why? After all these years to come dragging this in to me now. It don't make no sense at your age. I could have expected this ten or fifteen years ago, but not now.

TROY: Age ain't got nothing to do with it, Rose.

Rose: I done tried to be everything a wife should be. Everything a wife could be. Been married eighteen years and I got to live to see the day you tell me you been seeing another woman and done fathered a child by her. And you know I ain't never wanted no half nothing in my family. My whole family is half. Everybody got different fathers and mothers . . . my two sisters and my brother. Can't hardly tell who's who. Can't never sit down and talk about Papa and Mama. It's your papa and your mama and my papa and my mama . . .

Troy: Rose . . . stop it now.

Rose: I ain't never wanted that for none of my children. And now you wanna   90
drag your behind in here and tell me something like this.

Troy: You ought to know. It's time for you to know.

Rose: Well, I don't want to know, goddamn it!

Troy: I can't just make it go away. It's done now. I can't wish the circumstance of the thing away.

Rose: And you don't want to either. Maybe you want to wish me and my boy away. Maybe that's what you want? Well, you can't wish us away. I've got eighteen years of my life invested in you. You ought to have stayed upstairs in my bed where you belong.

Troy: Rose . . . now listen to me . . . we can get a handle on this thing. We   95
can talk this out . . . come to an understanding.

Rose: All of a sudden it's "we." Where was "we" at when you was down there rolling around with some godforsaken woman? "We" should have come to an understanding before you started making a damn fool of yourself. You're a day late and a dollar short when it comes to an understanding with me.

Troy: It's just . . . She gives me a different idea . . . a different understanding about myself. I can step out of this house and get away from the pressures and problems . . . be a different man. I ain't got to wonder how I'm gonna pay the bills or get the roof fixed. I can just be a part of myself that I ain't never been.

Rose: What I want to know . . . is do you plan to continue seeing her. That's all you can say to me.

Troy: I can sit up in her house and laugh. Do you understand what I'm saying. I can laugh out loud . . . and it feels good. It reaches all the way down to the bottom of my shoes. *(Pause.)* Rose, I can't give that up.

Rose: Maybe you ought to go on and stay down there with her . . . if she's a   100
better woman than me.

Troy: It ain't about nobody being a better woman or nothing. Rose, you ain't the blame. A man couldn't ask for no woman to be a better wife than you've been. I'm responsible for it. I done locked myself into a pattern trying to take care of you all that I forgot about myself.

Rose: What the hell was I there for? That was my job, not somebody else's.

TROY: Rose, I done tried all my life to live decent . . . to live a clean . . . hard . . . useful life. I tried to be a good husband to you. In every way I knew how. Maybe I come into the world backwards, I don't know. But . . . you born with two strikes on you before you come to the plate. You got to guard it closely . . . always looking for the curve ball on the inside corner. You can't afford to let none get past you. You can't afford a call strike. If you go-ing down . . . you going down swinging. Everything lined up against you. What you gonna do. I fooled them, Rose. I bunted. When I found you and Cory and a halfway decent job . . . I was safe. Couldn't nothing touch me. I wasn't gonna strike out no more. I wasn't going back to the penitentiary. I wasn't gonna lay in the streets with a bottle of wine. I was safe. I had me a family. A job. I wasn't gonna get that last strike. I was on first looking for one of them boys to knock me in. To get me home.

ROSE: You should have stayed in my bed, Troy.

105 TROY: Then when I saw that gal . . . she firmed up my backbone. And I got to thinking that if I tried . . . I just might be able to steal second. Do you understand after eighteen years I wanted to steal second.

ROSE: You should have held me tight. You should have grabbed me and held on.

TROY: I stood on first base for eighteen years and I thought . . . well, goddamn it . . . go on for it!

ROSE: We're not talking about baseball! We're talking about you going off to lay in bed with another woman . . . and then bring it home to me. That's what we're talking about. We ain't talking about no baseball.

TROY: Rose, you're not listening to me. I'm trying the best I can to explain it to you. It's not easy for me to admit that I been standing in the same place for eighteen years.

110 ROSE: I been standing with you! I been right here with you, Troy. I got a life too. I gave eighteen years of my life to stand in the same spot with you. Don't you think I ever wanted other things? Don't you think I had dreams and hopes? What about my life? What about me. Don't you think it ever crossed my mind to want to know other men? That I wanted to lay up somewhere and forget about my responsibilities? That I wanted someone to make me laugh so I could feel good? You not the only one who's got wants and needs. But I held on to you, Troy. I took all my feelings, my wants and needs, my dreams . . . and I buried them inside you. I planted a seed and watched and prayed over it. I planted myself inside you and waited to bloom. And it didn't take me no eighteen years to find out the soil was hard and rocky and it wasn't never gonna bloom.

But I held on to you, Troy. I held you tighter. You was my husband. I owed you everything I had. Every part of me I could find to give you. And upstairs in that room . . . with the darkness falling in on me . . . I gave everything I had to try and erase the doubt that you wasn't the finest man in the world. And wherever you was going . . . I wanted to be there with

you. 'Cause you was my husband. 'Cause that's the only way I was gonna
survive as your wife. You always talking about what you give . . . and what
you don't have to give. But you take too. You take . . . and don't even know
nobody's giving!

Rose turns to exit into the house; Troy grabs her arm.

TROY: You say I take and don't give!
ROSE: Troy! You're hurting me!
TROY: You say I take and don't give!
ROSE: Troy . . . you're hurting my arm! Let go!
TROY: I done give you everything I got. Don't you tell that lie on me.   115
ROSE: Troy!
TROY: Don't you tell that lie on me!

Cory enters from the house.

CORY: Mama!
ROSE: Troy. You're hurting me.
TROY: Don't you tell me about no taking and giving.   120

*Cory comes up behind Troy and grabs him. Troy, surprised, is thrown off balance just
as Cory throws a glancing blow that catches him on the chest and knocks him down.
Troy is stunned, as is Cory.*

ROSE: Troy. Troy. No!

Troy gets to his feet and starts at Cory.

Troy . . . no. Please! Troy!

Rose pulls on Troy to hold him back. Troy stops himself.

TROY: (*to Cory*) All right. That's strike two. You stay away from around me,
boy. Don't you strike out. You living with a full count. Don't you strike out.

Troy exits out the yard as the lights go down.

SCENE 2

*It is six months later, early afternoon. Troy enters from the house and starts to exit the
yard. Rose enters from the house.*

ROSE: Troy, I want to talk to you.
TROY: All of a sudden, after all this time, you want to talk to me, huh? You
ain't wanted to talk to me for months. You ain't wanted to talk to me last
night. You ain't wanted no part of me then. What you wanna talk to me
about now?

5 ROSE: Tomorrow's Friday.

TROY: I know what day tomorrow is. You think I don't know tomorrow's Friday? My whole life I ain't done nothing but look to see Friday coming and you got to tell me it's Friday.

ROSE: I want to know if you're coming home.

TROY: I always come home, Rose. You know that. There ain't never been a night I ain't come home.

ROSE: That ain't what I mean . . . and you know it. I want to know if you're coming straight home after work.

10 TROY: I figure I'd cash my check . . . hang out at Taylors' with the boys . . . maybe play a game of checkers . . .

ROSE: Troy, I can't live like this. I won't live like this. You livin' on borrowed time with me. It's been going on six months now you ain't been coming home.

TROY: I be here every Friday. Every night of the year. That's 365 days.

ROSE: I want you to come home tomorrow after work.

TROY: Rose . . . I don't mess up my pay. You know that now. I take my pay and I give it to you. I don't have no money but what you give me back. I just want to have a little time to myself . . . a little time to enjoy life.

15 ROSE: What about me? When's my time to enjoy life?

TROY: I don't know what to tell you, Rose. I'm doing the best I can.

ROSE: You ain't been home from work but time enough to change your clothes and run out . . . and you wanna call that the best you can do?

TROY: I'm going over to the hospital to see Alberta. She went into the hospital this afternoon. Look like she might have the baby early. I won't be gone long.

ROSE: Well, you ought to know. They went over to Miss Pearl's and got Gabe today. She said you told them to go ahead and lock him up.

20 TROY: I ain't said no such thing. Whoever told you that is telling a lie. Pearl ain't doing nothing but telling a big fat lie.

ROSE: She ain't had to tell me. I read it on the papers.

TROY: I ain't told them nothing of the kind.

ROSE: I saw it right there on the papers.

TROY: What it say, huh?

25 ROSE: It said you told them to take him.

TROY: Then they screwed that up, just the way they screw up everything. I ain't worried about what they got on the paper.

ROSE: Say the government send part of his check to the hospital and the other part to you.

TROY: I ain't got nothing to do with that if that's the way it works. I ain't made up the rules about how it work.

ROSE: You did Gabe just like you did Cory. You wouldn't sign the paper for Cory . . . but you signed for Gabe. You signed that paper.

The telephone is heard ringing inside the house.

TROY: I told you I ain't signed nothing, woman! The only thing I signed was   30
the release form. Hell, I can't read. I don't know what they had on that
paper! I ain't signed nothing about sending Gabe away.

ROSE: I said send him to the hospital . . . you said let him be free . . . now you
done went down there and signed him to the hospital for half his money.
You went back on yourself, Troy. You gonna have to answer for that.

TROY: See now . . . you been over there talking to Miss Pearl. She done got
mad cause she ain't getting Gabe's rent money. That's all it is. She's liable to
say anything.

ROSE: Troy, I seen where you signed the paper.

TROY: You ain't seen nothing I signed. What she doing got papers on my brother
anyway? Miss Pearl telling a big fat lie. And I'm gonna tell her about it too!
You ain't seen nothing I signed. Say . . . you ain't seen nothing I signed.

Rose exits into the house to answer the telephone. Presently she returns.

ROSE: Troy . . . that was the hospital. Alberta had the baby.   35

TROY: What she have? What is it?

ROSE: It's a girl.

TROY: I better get on down to the hospital to see her.

ROSE: Troy . . .

TROY: Rose . . . I got to go see her now. That's only right . . . what's the   40
matter . . . the baby's all right, ain't it?

ROSE: Alberta died having the baby.

TROY: Died . . . you say she's dead? Alberta's dead?

ROSE: They said they done all they could. They couldn't do nothing for her.

TROY: The baby? How's the baby?

ROSE: They say it's healthy. I wonder who's gonna bury her.   45

TROY: She had family, Rose. She wasn't living in the world by herself.

ROSE: I know she wasn't living in the world by herself.

TROY: Next thing you gonna want to know if she had any insurance.

ROSE: Troy, you ain't got to talk like that.

TROY: That's the first thing that jumped out your mouth. "Who's gonna bury   50
her?" Like I'm fixing to take on that task for myself.

ROSE: I am your wife. Don't push me away.

TROY: I ain't pushing nobody away. Just give me some space. That's all. Just
give me some room to breathe.

Rose exits into the house. Troy walks about the yard.

TROY: (*with a quiet rage that threatens to consume him*) All right . . . Mr. Death.
See now . . . I'm gonna tell you what I'm gonna do. I'm gonna take and
build me a fence around this yard. See? I'm gonna build me a fence around
what belongs to me. And then I want you to stay on the other side. See?

You stay over there until you're ready for me. Then you come on. Bring your army. Bring your sickle. Bring your wrestling clothes. I ain't gonna fall down on my vigilance this time. You ain't gonna sneak up on me no more. When you ready for me . . . when the top of your list say Troy Maxson . . . that's when you come around here. You come up and knock on the front door. Ain't nobody else got nothing to do with this. This is between you and me. Man to man. You stay on the other side of the fence until you ready for me. Then you come up and knock on the front door. Anytime you want. I'll be ready for you.

The lights go down to black.

SCENE 3

The lights come up on the porch. It is late evening three days later. Rose sits listening to the ball game waiting for Troy. The final out of the game is made and Rose switches off the radio. Troy enters the yard carrying an infant wrapped in blankets. He stands back from the house and calls.

    Rose enters and stands on the porch. There is a long, awkward silence, the weight of which grows heavier with each passing second.

TROY: Rose . . . I'm standing here with my daughter in my arms. She ain't but a wee bittie little old thing. She don't know nothing about grownups' business. She innocent . . . and she ain't got no mama.

5 ROSE: What you telling me for, Troy?

She turns and exits into the house.

TROY: Well . . . I guess we'll just sit out here on the porch.

He sits down on the porch. There is an awkward indelicateness about the way he handles the baby. His largeness engulfs and seems to swallow it. He speaks loud enough for Rose to hear.

A man's got to do what's right for him. I ain't sorry for nothing I done. It felt right in my heart. *(To the baby.)* What you smiling at? Your daddy's a big man. Got these great big old hands. But sometimes he's scared. And right now your daddy's scared 'cause we sitting out here and ain't got no home. Oh, I been homeless before. I ain't had no little baby with me. But I been homeless. You just be out on the road by your lonesome and you see one of them trains coming and you just kinda go like this . . .

He sings a lullaby.

      Please, Mr. Engineer let a man ride the line
      Please, Mr. Engineer let a man ride the line
      I ain't got no ticket please let me ride the blinds

Rose enters from the house. Troy, hearing her steps behind him, stands and faces her.

She's my daughter, Rose. My own flesh and blood. I can't deny her no more than I can deny them boys. (*Pause.*) You and them boys is my family. You and them and this child is all I got in the world. So I guess what I'm saying is . . . I'd appreciate it if you'd help me take care of her.

ROSE: Okay, Troy . . . you're right. I'll take care of your baby for you . . . 'cause . . . like you say . . . she's innocent . . . and you can't visit the sins of the father upon the child. A motherless child has got a hard time. (*She takes the baby from him.*) From right now . . . this child got a mother. But you a womanless man.

Rose turns and exits into the house with the baby. Lights go down to black.

SCENE 4

It is two months later. Lyons enters from the street. He knocks on the door and calls.

LYONS: Hey, Rose! (*Pause.*) Rose!

ROSE: (*from inside the house*) Stop that yelling. You gonna wake up Raynell. I just got her to sleep.

LYONS: I just stopped by to pay Papa this twenty dollars I owe him. Where's Papa at?   5

ROSE: He should be here in a minute. I'm getting ready to go down to the church. Sit down and wait on him.

LYONS: I got to go pick up Bonnie over her mother's house.

ROSE: Well, sit it down there on the table. He'll get it.

LYONS: (*enters the house and sets the money on the table*) Tell Papa I said thanks. I'll see you again.

ROSE: All right, Lyons. We'll see you.   10

Lyons starts to exit as Cory enters.

CORY: Hey, Lyons.

LYONS: What's happening, Cory? Say man, I'm sorry I missed your graduation. You know I had a gig and couldn't get away. Otherwise, I would have been there, man. So what you doing?

CORY: I'm trying to find a job.

LYONS: Yeah I know how that go, man. It's rough out there. Jobs are scarce.

CORY: Yeah, I know.   15

LYONS: Look here, I got to run. Talk to Papa . . . he know some people. He'll be able to help get you a job. Talk to him . . . see what he say.

CORY: Yeah . . . all right, Lyons.

LYONS: You take care. I'll talk to you soon. We'll find some time to talk.

Lyons exits the yard. Cory wanders over to the tree, picks up the bat, and assumes a batting stance. He studies an imaginary pitcher and swings. Dissatisfied with the result, he tries again. Troy enters. They eye each other for a beat. Cory puts the bat down and exits the yard. Troy starts into the house as Rose exits with Raynell. She is carrying a cake.

TROY: I'm coming in and everybody's going out.

20 **ROSE:** I'm taking this cake down to the church for the bake sale. Lyons was by to see you. He stopped by to pay you your twenty dollars. It's laying in there on the table.

TROY: *(going into his pocket)* Well . . . here go this money.

ROSE: Put it in there on the table, Troy. I'll get it.

TROY: What time you coming back?

ROSE: Ain't no use in you studying me. It don't matter what time I come back.

25 **TROY:** I just asked you a question, woman. What's the matter . . . can't I ask you a question?

ROSE: Troy, I don't want to go into it. Your dinner's in there on the stove. All you got to do is heat it up. And don't you be eating the rest of them cakes in there. I'm coming back for them. We having a bake sale at the church tomorrow.

Rose exits the yard. Troy sits down on the steps, takes a pint bottle from his pocket, opens it, and drinks. He begins to sing.

TROY:

> Hear it ring! Hear it ring!
> Had an old dog his name was Blue
> You know Blue was mighty true
> You know Blue was a good old dog
> Blue treed a possum in a hollow log
> You know from that he was a good old dog

Bono enters the yard.

BONO: Hey, Troy.

TROY: Hey, what's happening, Bono?

30 **BONO:** I just thought I'd stop by to see you.

TROY: What you stop by and see me for? You ain't stopped by in a month of Sundays. Hell, I must owe you money or something.

BONO: Since you got your promotion I can't keep up with you. Used to see you every day. Now I don't even know what route you working.

TROY: They keep switching me around. Got me out in Greentree now . . . hauling white folks' garbage.

BONO: Greentree, huh? You lucky, at least you ain't got to be lifting them barrels. Damn if they ain't getting heavier. I'm gonna put in my two years and call it quits.

35 **TROY:** I'm thinking about retiring myself.

BONO: You got it easy. You can *drive* for another five years.

TROY: It ain't the same, Bono. It ain't like working the back of the truck. Ain't got nobody to talk to . . . feel like you working by yourself. Naw, I'm thinking about retiring. How's Lucille?

BONO: She all right. Her arthritis get to acting up on her sometime. Saw Rose on my way in. She going down to the church, huh?

TROY: Yeah, she took up going down there. All them preachers looking for somebody to fatten their pockets. *(Pause.)* Got some gin here.

BONO: Naw, thanks. I just stopped by to say hello.   40

TROY: Hell, nigger . . . you can take a drink. I ain't never known you to say no to a drink. You ain't got to work tomorrow.

BONO: I just stopped by. I'm fixing to go over to Skinner's. We got us a domino game going over his house every Friday.

TROY: Nigger, you can't play no dominoes. I used to whup you four games out of five.

BONO: Well, that learned me. I'm getting better.

TROY: Yeah? Well, that's all right.   45

BONO: Look here . . . I got to be getting on. Stop by sometime, huh?

TROY: Yeah, I'll do that, Bono. Lucille told Rose you bought her a new refrigerator.

BONO: Yeah, Rose told Lucille you had finally built your fence . . . so I figured we'd call it even.

TROY: I knew you would.

BONO: Yeah . . . okay. I'll be talking to you.   50

TROY: Yeah, take care, Bono. Good to see you. I'm gonna stop over.

BONO: Yeah. Okay, Troy.

Bono exits. Troy drinks from the bottle.

TROY:

> Old Blue died and I dig his grave
> Let him down with a golden chain
> Every night when I hear old Blue bark
> I know Blue treed a possum in Noah's Ark.
> Hear it ring! Hear it ring!

Cory enters the yard. They eye each other for a beat. Troy is sitting in the middle of the steps. Cory walks over.

CORY: I got to get by.

TROY: Say what? What's you say?   55

CORY: You in my way. I got to get by.

TROY: You got to get by where? This is my house. Bought and paid for. In full. Took me fifteen years. And if you wanna go in my house and I'm sitting on the steps . . . you say excuse me. Like your mama taught you.

CORY: Come on, Pop . . . I got to get by.

Cory starts to maneuver his way past Troy. Troy grabs his leg and shoves him back.

TROY: You just gonna walk over top of me?

60 **CORY:** I live here too!

TROY: *(advancing toward him)* You just gonna walk over top of me in my own house?

CORY: I ain't scared of you.

TROY: I ain't asked if you was scared of me. I asked you if you was fixing to walk over top of me in my own house? That's the question. You ain't gonna say excuse me? You just gonna walk over top of me?

CORY: If you wanna put it like that.

65 **TROY:** How else am I gonna put it?

CORY: I was walking by you to go into the house 'cause you sitting on the steps drunk, singing to yourself. You can put it like that.

TROY: Without saying excuse me???

Cory doesn't respond.

I asked you a question. Without saying excuse me???

CORY: I ain't got to say excuse me to you. You don't count around here no more.

TROY: Oh, I see . . . I don't count around here no more. You ain't got to say excuse me to your daddy. All of a sudden you done got so grown that your daddy don't count around here no more . . . Around here in his own house and yard that he done paid for with the sweat of his brow. You done got so grown to where you gonna take over. You gonna take over my house. Is that right? You gonna wear my pants. You gonna go in there and stretch out on my bed. You ain't got to say excuse me 'cause I don't count around here no more. Is that right?

70 **CORY:** That's right. You always talking this dumb stuff. Now, why don't you just get out my way?

TROY: I guess you got someplace to sleep and something to put in your belly. You got that, huh? You got that? That's what you need. You got that, huh?

CORY: You don't know what I got. You ain't got to worry about what I got.

TROY: You right! You one hundred percent right! I done spent the last seventeen years worrying about what you got. Now it's your turn, see? I'll tell you what to do. You grown . . . we done established that. You a man. Now, let's see you act like one. Turn your behind around and walk out this yard. And when you get out there in the alley . . . you can forget about this house. See? 'Cause this is my house. You go on and be a man and get your own house. You can forget about this. 'Cause this is mine. You go on and get yours 'cause I'm through with doing for you.

CORY: You talking about what you did for me . . . what'd you ever give me?

75 **TROY:** Them feet and bones! That pumping heart, nigger! I give you more than anybody else is ever gonna give you.

CORY: You ain't never gave me nothing! You ain't never done nothing but hold me back. Afraid I was gonna be better than you. All you ever did was try and make me scared of you. I used to tremble every time you called my name. Every time I heard your footsteps in the house. Wondering all the time . . . what's Papa gonna say if I do this? . . . What's he gonna say if I do that? . . . What's Papa gonna say if I turn on the radio? And Mama, too . . . she tries . . . but she's scared of you.

TROY: You leave your mama out of this. She ain't got nothing to do with this.

CORY: I don't know how she stand you . . . after what you did to her.

TROY: I told you to leave your mama out of this!

He advances toward Cory.

CORY: What you gonna do . . . give me a whupping? You can't whup me no   80
more. You're too old. You just an old man.

TROY: *(shoves him on his shoulder)* Nigger! That's what you are. You just another nigger on the street to me!

CORY: You crazy! You know that?

TROY: Go on now! You got the devil in you. Get on away from me!

CORY: You just a crazy old man . . . talking about I got the devil in me.

TROY: Yeah, I'm crazy! If you don't get on the other side of that yard . . . I'm   85
gonna show you how crazy I am! Go on . . . get the hell out of my yard.

CORY: It ain't your yard. You took Uncle Gabe's money he got from the army to buy this house and then you put him out.

TROY: *(advances on Cory)* Get your black ass out of my yard!

Troy's advance backs Cory up against the tree. Cory grabs up the bat.

CORY: I ain't going nowhere! Come on . . . put me out! I ain't scared of you.

TROY: That's my bat!

CORY: Come on!   90

TROY: Put my bat down!

CORY: Come on, put me out.

Cory swings at Troy, who backs across the yard.

What's the matter? You so bad . . . put me out!

Troy advances toward Cory.

CORY: *(backing up)* Come on! Come on!

TROY: You're gonna have to use it! You wanna draw that bat back on me . . . you're gonna have to use it.

CORY: Come on! . . . Come on!   95

Cory swings the bat at Troy a second time. He misses. Troy continues to advance toward him.

TROY: You're gonna have to kill me! You wanna draw that bat back on me. You're gonna have to kill me.

Cory, backed up against the tree, can go no farther. Troy taunts him. He sticks out his head and offers him a target.

Come on! Come on!

Cory is unable to swing the bat. Troy grabs it.

TROY: Then I'll show you.

Cory and Troy struggle over the bat. The struggle is fierce and fully engaged. Troy ultimately is the stronger and takes the bat away from Cory and stands over him ready to swing. He stops himself.

Go on and get away from around my house.

Cory, stung by his defeat, picks himself up, walks slowly out of the yard and up the alley.

CORY: Tell Mama I'll be back for my things.
TROY: They'll be on the other side of that fence.

Cory exits.

100 TROY: I can't taste nothing. Helluljah! I can't taste nothing no more. (*Troy assumes a batting posture and begins to taunt Death, the fastball on the outside corner.*) Come on! It's between you and me now! Come on! Anytime you want! Come on! I be ready for you . . . but I ain't gonna be easy.

The lights go down on the scene.

SCENE 5

The time is 1965. The lights come up in the yard. It is the morning of Troy's funeral. A funeral plaque with a light hangs beside the door. There is a small garden plot off to the side. There is noise and activity in the house as Rose, Gabriel, and Bono have gathered. The door opens and Raynell, seven years old, enters dressed in a flannel nightgown. She crosses to the garden and pokes around with a stick. Rose calls from the house.

ROSE: Raynell!
RAYNELL: Mam?
ROSE: What you doing out there?
RAYNELL: Nothing.

Rose comes to the door.

5 ROSE: Girl, get in here and get dressed. What you doing?
RAYNELL: Seeing if my garden growed.
ROSE: I told you it ain't gonna grow overnight. You got to wait.
RAYNELL: It don't look like it never gonna grow. Dag!
ROSE: I told you a watched pot never boils. Get in here and get dressed.
10 RAYNELL: This ain't even no pot, Mama.
ROSE: You just have to give it a chance. It'll grow. Now you come on and do what I told you. We got to be getting ready. This ain't no morning to be playing around. You hear me?
RAYNELL: Yes, mam.

Rose exits into the house. Raynell continues to poke at her garden with a stick. Cory enters. He is dressed in a Marine corporal's uniform, and carries a duffel bag. His posture is that of a military man, and his speech has a clipped sternness.

CORY: *(to Raynell)* Hi. *(Pause.)* I bet your name is Raynell.
RAYNELL: Uh huh.
CORY: Is your mama home?   15

Raynell runs up on the porch and calls through the screen door.

RAYNELL: Mama . . . there's some man out here. Mama?

Rose comes to the door.

ROSE: Cory? Lord have mercy! Look here, you all!

Rose and Cory embrace in a tearful reunion as Bono and Lyons enter from the house dressed in funeral clothes.

BONO: Aw, looka here . . .
ROSE: Done got all grown up!
CORY: Don't cry, Mama. What you crying about?   20
ROSE: I'm just so glad you made it.
CORY: Hey Lyons. How you doing, Mr. Bono.

Lyons goes to embrace Cory.

LYONS: Look at you, man. Look at you. Don't he look good, Rose. Got them
    Corporal stripes.
ROSE: What took you so long?
CORY: You know how the Marines are, Mama. They got to get all their   25
    paperwork straight before they let you do anything.
ROSE: Well, I'm sure glad you made it. They let Lyons come. Your Uncle
    Gabe's still in the hospital. They don't know if they gonna let him out or
    not. I just talked to them a little while ago.
LYONS: A Corporal in the United States Marines.
BONO: Your daddy knew you had it in you. He used to tell me all the time.
LYONS: Don't he look good, Mr. Bono?
BONO: Yeah, he remind me of Troy when I first met him. *(Pause.)* Say, Rose,   30
    Lucille's down at the church with the choir. I'm gonna go down and get the
    pallbearers lined up. I'll be back to get you all.
ROSE: Thanks, Jim.
CORY: See you, Mr. Bono.
LYONS: *(with his arm around Raynell)* Cory . . . look at Raynell. Ain't she
    precious? She gonna break a whole lot of hearts.
ROSE: Raynell, come and say hello to your brother. This is your brother, Cory.
    You remember Cory.
RAYNELL: No, Mam.   35

CORY: She don't remember me, Mama.

ROSE: Well, we talk about you. She heard us talk about you. (*To Raynell.*) This is your brother, Cory. Come on and say hello.

RAYNELL: Hi.

CORY: Hi. So you're Raynell. Mama told me a lot about you.

40 ROSE: You all come on into the house and let me fix you some breakfast. Keep up your strength.

CORY: I ain't hungry, Mama.

LYONS: You can fix me something, Rose. I'll be in there in a minute.

ROSE: Cory, you sure you don't want nothing? I know they ain't feeding you right.

CORY: No, Mama . . . thanks. I don't feel like eating. I'll get something later.

45 ROSE: Raynell . . . get on upstairs and get that dress on like I told you.

Rose and Raynell exit into the house.

LYONS: So . . . I hear you thinking about getting married.

CORY: Yeah, I done found the right one, Lyons. It's about time.

LYONS: Me and Bonnie been split up about four years now. About the time Papa retired. I guess she just got tired of all them changes I was putting her through. (*Pause.*) I always knew you was gonna make something out yourself. Your head was always in the right direction. So . . . you gonna stay in . . . make it a career . . . put in your twenty years?

CORY: I don't know. I got six already, I think that's enough.

50 LYONS: Stick with Uncle Sam and retire early. Ain't nothing out here. I guess Rose told you what happened with me. They got me down the workhouse. I thought I was being slick cashing other people's checks.

CORY: How much time you doing?

LYONS: They give me three years. I got that beat now. I ain't got but nine more months. It ain't so bad. You learn to deal with it like anything else. You got to take the crookeds with the straights. That's what Papa used to say. He used to say that when he struck out. I seen him strike out three times in a row . . . and the next time up he hit the ball over the grandstand. Right out there in Homestead Field. He wasn't satisfied hitting in the seats . . . he want to hit it over everything! After the game he had two hundred people standing around waiting to shake his hand. You got to take the crookeds with the straights. Yeah, Papa was something else.

CORY: You still playing?

LYONS: Cory . . . you know I'm gonna do that. There's some fellows down there we got us a band . . . we gonna try and stay together when we get out . . . but yeah, I'm still playing. It still helps me to get out of bed in the morning. As long as it do that I'm gonna be right there playing and trying to make some sense out of it.

55 ROSE: (*calling*) Lyons, I got these eggs in the pan.

LYONS: Let me go on and get these eggs, man. Get ready to go bury Papa. (*Pause.*) How you doing? You doing all right?

Cory nods. Lyons touches him on the shoulder and they share a moment of silent grief. Lyons exits into the house. Cory wanders about the yard. Raynell enters.

RAYNELL: Hi.
CORY: Hi.
RAYNELL: Did you used to sleep in my room?
CORY: Yeah . . . that used to be my room.   60
RAYNELL: That's what Papa call it. "Cory's room." It got your football in the closet.

Rose comes to the door.

ROSE: Raynell, get in there and get them good shoes on.
RAYNELL: Mama, can't I wear these? Them other ones hurt my feet.
ROSE: Well, they just gonna have to hurt your feet for a while. You ain't said they hurt your feet when you went down to the store and got them.
RAYNELL: They didn't hurt then. My feet done got bigger.   65
ROSE: Don't you give me no backtalk now. You get in there and get them shoes on.

Raynell exits into the house.

Ain't too much changed. He still got that piece of rag tied to that tree. He was out here swinging that bat. I was just ready to go back in the house. He swung that bat and then he just fell over. Seem like he swung it and stood there with this grin on his face . . . and then he just fell over. They carried him on down to the hospital, but I knew there wasn't no need . . . why don't you come on in the house?

CORY: Mama . . . I got something to tell you. I don't know how to tell you this . . . but I've got to tell you . . . I'm not going to Papa's funeral.
ROSE: Boy, hush your mouth. That's your daddy you talking about. I don't want hear that kind of talk this morning. I done raised you to come to this? You standing there all healthy and grown talking about you ain't going to your daddy's funeral?
CORY: Mama . . . listen . . .
ROSE: I don't want to hear it, Cory. You just get that thought out of your head.   70
CORY: I can't drag Papa with me everywhere I go. I've got to say no to him. One time in my life I've got to say no.
ROSE: Don't nobody have to listen to nothing like that. I know you and your daddy ain't seen eye to eye, but I ain't got to listen to that kind of talk this morning. Whatever was between you and your daddy . . . the time has come to put it aside. Just take it and set it over there on the shelf and forget about it. Disrespecting your daddy ain't gonna make you a man, Cory. You got to find a way to come to that on your own. Not going to your daddy's funeral ain't gonna make you a man.

CORY: The whole time I was growing up . . . living in his house . . . Papa was like a shadow that followed you everywhere. It weighed on you and sunk into your flesh. It would wrap around you and lay there until you couldn't tell which one was you anymore. That shadow digging in your flesh. Trying to crawl in. Trying to live through you. Everywhere I looked, Troy Maxson was staring back at me . . . hiding under the bed . . . in the closet. I'm just saying I've got to find a way to get rid of that shadow, Mama.

ROSE: You just like him. You got him in you good.

75 CORY: Don't tell me that, Mama.

ROSE: You Troy Maxson all over again.

CORY: I don't want to be Troy Maxson. I want to be me.

ROSE: You can't be nobody but who you are, Cory. That shadow wasn't nothing but you growing into yourself. You either got to grow into it or cut it down to fit you. But that's all you got to make life with. That's all you got to measure yourself against that world out there. Your daddy wanted you to be everything he wasn't . . . and at the same time he tried to make you into everything he was. I don't know if he was right or wrong . . . but I do know he meant to do more good than he meant to do harm. He wasn't always right. Sometimes when he touched he bruised. And sometimes when he took me in his arms he cut.

When I first met your daddy I thought . . . Here is a man I can lay down with and make a baby. That's the first thing I thought when I seen him. I was thirty years old and had done seen my share of men. But when he walked up to me and said, "I can dance a waltz that'll make you dizzy." I thought, Rose Lee, here is a man that you can open yourself up to and be filled to bursting. Here is a man that can fill all them empty spaces you been tipping around the edges of. One of them empty spaces was being somebody's mother.

I married your daddy and settled down to cooking his supper and keeping clean sheets on the bed. When your daddy walked through the house he was so big he filled it up. That was my first mistake. Not to make him leave some room for me. For my part in the matter. But at that time I wanted that. I wanted a house that I could sing in. And that's what your daddy gave me. I didn't know to keep up his strength I had to give up little pieces of mine. I did that. I took on his life as mine and mixed up the pieces so that you couldn't hardly tell which was which anymore. It was my choice. It was my life and I didn't have to live it like that. But that's what life offered me in the way of being a woman and I took it. I grabbed hold of it with both hands.

By the time Raynell came into the house, me and your daddy had done lost touch with one another. I didn't want to make my blessing off of nobody's misfortune . . . but I took on to Raynell like she was all them babies I had wanted and never had.

The phone rings.

Like I' been blessed to relive a part of my life. And if the Lord see fit to
keep my strength . . . I'm gonna do her just like your daddy did you . . .
I'm onna give her the best of what's in me.
RAY_L: *(entering, still with her old shoes)* Mama . . . Reverend Tollivier on the
one.

exits into the house.

YNELL: Hi.   80
ORY: Hi.
RAYNELL: You in the Army or the Marines?
CORY: Marines.
RAYNELL: Papa said it was the Army. Did you know Blue?
CORY: Blue? Who's Blue?   85
RAYNELL: Papa's dog what he sing about all the time.
CORY: *(singing)*
      Hear it ring! Hear it ring!
      I had a dog his name was Blue
      You know Blue was mighty true
      You know Blue was a good old dog
      Blue treed a possum in a hollow log
      You know from that he was a good old dog.
      Hear it ring! Hear it ring!

Raynell joins in singing.

CORY AND RAYNELL:
      Blue treed a possum out on a limb
      Blue looked at me and I looked at him
      Grabbed that possum and put him in a sack
      Blue stayed there till I came back
      Old Blue's feets was big and round
      Never allowed a possum to touch the ground.
      Old Blue died and I dug his grave
      I dug his grave with a silver spade
      Let him down with a golden chain
      And every night I call his name
      Go on Blue, you good dog you
      Go on Blue, you good dog you

RAYNELL:
      Blue laid down and died like a man
      Blue laid down and died . . .

BOTH: 90
      Blue laid down and died like a man
      Now he's treeing possums in the Promised Land
      I'm gonna tell you this to let you know
      Blue's gone where the good dogs go
      When I hear old Blue bark

When I hear old Blue bark
Blue treed a possum in Noah's Ark°
Blue treed a possum in Noah's Ark.

Rose comes to the screen door.

ROSE: Cory, we gonna be ready to go in a minute.
CORY: *(to Raynell)* You go on in the house and change them shoes like Mama
told you so we can go to Papa's funeral.
RAYNELL: Okay, I'll be back.

*Raynell exits into the house. Cory gets up and crosses over to the tree. Rose stands in the
screen door watching him. Gabriel enters from the alley.*

GABRIEL: *(calling)* Hey, Rose!
95 **ROSE:** Gabe?
GABRIEL: I'm here, Rose. Hey Rose, I'm here!

Rose enters from the house.

ROSE: Lord . . . Look here, Lyons!
LYONS: See, I told you, Rose . . . I told you they'd let him come.
CORY: How you doing, Uncle Gabe?
100 **LYONS:** How you doing, Uncle Gabe?
GABRIEL: Hey, Rose. It's time. It's time to tell St. Peter to open the gates. Troy,
you ready? You ready, Troy. I'm gonna tell St. Peter to open the gates. You
get ready now.

*Gabriel, with great fanfare, braces himself to blow. The trumpet is without a mouth-
piece. He puts the end of it into his mouth and blows with great force, like a man who
has been waiting some twenty-odd years for this single moment. No sound comes out of
the trumpet. He braces himself and blows again with the same result. A third time he
blows. There is a weight of impossible description that falls away and leaves him bare and
exposed to a frightful realization. It is a trauma that a sane and normal mind would be
unable to withstand. He begins to dance. A slow, strange dance, eerie and life-giving.
A dance of atavistic signature and ritual. Lyons attempts to embrace him. Gabriel
pushes Lyons away. He begins to howl in what is an attempt at song, or perhaps a song-
turning back into itself in an attempt at speech. He finishes his dance and the gates of
heaven stand open as wide as God's closet.*

That's the way that go!

Reading and Reacting

1. Obviously, fences are a central metaphor of the play. To what different kinds
of fences does the play's title refer?
2. How are the fathers and sons in this play alike? How are they different? Does
the play imply that sons must inevitably follow in their fathers' footsteps?

°*Noah's Ark:* See Genesis 6.14–20.

3. What purpose does the section of the stage directions entitled "The Play" (p. 1096) serve? How does it prepare readers for the events to follow?

4. What is the significance of the fact that the play is set in 1957? Given the racial climate of the country at that time, how realistic are Cory's ambitions? How reasonable are his father's criticisms?

5. In what ways has Troy's character been shaped by his contact with the white world?

6. Is Troy a tragic hero? If so, what is his flaw?

7. Which of the play's characters, if any, do you consider to be stereotypes? What comment do you think the play makes about stereotypes?

8. In what ways does the conflict between Troy and Cory reflect conflicts within the African-American community? Does the play suggest any possibilities for compromise?

9. Which characters do you like? Which do you dislike? Why?

10. Do you consider the message of this play to be optimistic or pessimistic? Explain.

11. JOURNAL ENTRY How would the play be different if the characters were white? What would remain the same?

12. CRITICAL PERSPECTIVE Robert Brustein, theater critic and artistic director of Harvard's American Repertory Theater, has criticized Wilson on the ground that "his recurrent theme is the familiar American charge of victimization"; in *Fences*, he argues, "Wilson's larger purpose depends on his conviction that Troy's potential was stunted not [by] 'his own behavior' but by centuries of racist oppression."

Do you agree with Brustein's characterization of Wilson's theme? Or do you think there is another theme that Brustein ignores?

Related Works: "Big Black Good Man" (p. 192), "Yet Do I Marvel" (p. 614), *Death of a Salesman* (p. 858).

TENNESSEE WILLIAMS (1911–1983) was born Thomas Lanier Williams in Columbus, Mississippi, on March 26, 1911. His father, who came from a well-to-do and well-connected Tennessee family, was a shoe salesman who was often on the road. His mother was the daughter of a minister, and her genteel ways left her ill-equipped to handle her three rowdy children, who spent more and more time with their maternal grandfather. Williams's grandfather had a stern manner and strong views about right and wrong. His grandson, however, did not always abide by these rules and mocked him playfully whenever he could.

When Williams was eight, his family moved to St. Louis, Missouri, where, only eight years later — at the age of sixteen — Williams made his first mark on the literary world by winning five dollars and placing third in a national essay contest sponsored by *Smart Set* magazine. His essay was entitled "Can a Good Wife Be a Good Sport?" After winning this award, he began to submit his writing widely. He enrolled at the University of Missouri, but he found that college did not give him enough opportunity to write, so he left and worked at his father's shoe company — and as a waiter, an elevator operator, and a theater usher — while he wrote. Hoping to learn playwriting, he eventually went back to college and graduated from the University of Iowa in 1938. A year later, he adopted his college nickname and began to publish as Tennessee Williams.

Williams's earliest staged play, *Cairo, Shanghai, Bombay,* was produced in Memphis in 1937, followed closely by *Candles to the Sun* and *The Fugitive Kind.* Williams's career rocketed, and he went on to write over fifty plays, ten works of fiction, several books of poetry, and other collections of writing, including his letters and memoirs. His most successful plays include *The Glass Menagerie* (1945), *A Streetcar Named Desire* (1947), *Cat on a Hot Tin Roof* (1955), *Night of the Iguana* (1961), and *Sweet Bird of Youth* (1959). A recently rediscovered early play, *Not about Nightingales,* was staged in New York City in 1999.

The Glass Menagerie, Williams's first major success, won the New York Drama Critics Circle Award, freeing Williams to write plays full-time. *The Glass Menagerie* was written partly in Provincetown, Massachusetts, the site of Susan Glaspell's theater company (Glaspell is the author of the play *Trifles,* in Chapter 27), and partly in Hollywood, where Williams was working as a screenwriter. Williams saw the play as somewhat autobiographical: he said his sister Rose had a collection of glass animals in her room in St. Louis, and he gave his own real first name to Tom, Laura's brother in the play. In the first movie version of the play, the story was altered to include a second, more promising Gentleman Caller at its conclusion, giving it a happy ending. To the end of his life, Williams strongly disliked this change.

Tennessee Williams found acclaim wherever he took his plays, from the age of thirty-four and the remarkable success of *The Glass Menagerie* until the end of his life. He received four New York Drama Critics Circle Awards, won a Pulitzer Prize for *Streetcar* in 1948, and saw both *Streetcar* and *The Glass Menagerie* made into successful Hollywood films. *Cat on a Hot Tin Roof* (for which he won his second Pulitzer), *Orpheus Descending,* and *Night of the Iguana* were also filmed.

Like *The Glass Menagerie,* Williams's other work was largely autobiographical, often drawing comparisons between his family and his characters and using the backdrops with which he was most familiar. Williams moved around a good deal — from New Orleans, to Key West, to New York City, to Provincetown. Each locale had a significant homosexual population, which suited Williams's sexual orientation well. He was a committed partner and suffered greatly when his love of many years, Frank Merlo, died of cancer in 1961.

Tennessee Williams battled alcoholism, drug abuse, and mental illness through much of his life. Along with his older sister Rose, he fought constantly against the fear that he might go insane. Rose, who was diagnosed as schizophrenic, underwent a prefrontal lobotomy in her late twenties and was institutionalized for the remainder of her life; Williams himself suffered a mental breakdown at a young age. In the end, he choked to death on a bottle cap in his room at the Hotel Elysée in New York City.

His life and his work helped make Tennessee Williams one of America's best playwrights and one of the signature writers of the American South. His plays were bold and sometimes considered tawdry while those of his predecessors had been considered genteel and polite. Still, just as he was able to burst onto Broadway, he was able to spring on his readers a new type of drama that would forever change the way they saw the South.

The Glass Menagerie (1945)

Nobody, not even the rain, has such small hands.
E. E. Cummings

CHARACTERS

Amanda Wingfield, *the mother. A little woman of great but confused vitality clinging frantically to another time and place. Her characterization must be carefully created, not copied from type. She is not paranoiac, but her life is paranoia. There is much to admire in Amanda, and as much to love and pity as there is to laugh at. Certainly she has endurance and a kind of heroism, and though her foolishness makes her unwittingly cruel at times, there is tenderness in her slight person.*

Laura Wingfield, *her daughter. Amanda, having failed to establish contact with reality, continues to live vitally in her illusions, but Laura's situation is even graver. A childhood illness has left her crippled, one leg slightly shorter than the other, and held in a brace. This defect need not be more than suggested on the stage. Stemming from this, Laura's separation increases till she is like a piece of her own glass collection, too exquisitely fragile to move from the shelf.*

Tom Wingfield, *her son. And the narrator of the play. A poet with a job in a warehouse. His nature is not remorseless, but to escape from a trap he has to act without pity.*

Jim O'Connor, *the gentleman caller. A nice, ordinary, young man.*

SCENE

An alley in St. Louis.

PART I

Preparation for a Gentleman Caller.

PART II

The Gentleman Calls.

TIME

Now and the Past.

SCENE 1

The Wingfield apartment is in the rear of the building, one of those vast hive-like con-glomerations of cellular living-units that flower as warty growths in overcrowded urban centers of lower middle-class population and are symptomatic of the impulse of this largest and fundamentally enslaved section of American society to avoid fluidity and dif-ferentiation and to exist and function as one interfused mass of automatism.

The apartment faces an alley and is entered by a fire-escape, a structure whose name is a touch of accidental poetic truth, for all of these huge buildings are always burn-ing with the slow and implacable fires of human desperation. The fire-escape is included in the set—that is, the landing of it and steps descending from it.

The scene is memory and is therefore nonrealistic. Memory takes a lot of poetic li-cense. It omits some details; others are exaggerated, according to the emotional value of *the articles it touches, for memory is seated predominantly in the heart. The interior is therefore rather dim and poetic.*

At the rise of the curtain, the audience is faced with the dark, grim rear wall of the Wingfield tenement. This building, which runs parallel to the footlights, is flanked on both sides by dark, narrow alleys which run into murky canyons of tangled clotheslines, garbage cans and the sinister latticework of neighboring fire-escapes. It is up and down these side alleys that exterior entrances and exits are made, during the play. At the end of Tom's opening commentary, the dark tenement wall slowly reveals (by means of a transparency) the interior of the ground floor Wingfield apartment.

Downstage is the living room, which also serves as a sleeping room for Laura, the sofa unfolding to make her bed. Upstage, center, and divided by a wide arch or second proscenium with transparent faded portieres (or second curtain), is the dining room. In an old-fashioned what-not in the living room are seen scores of transparent glass animals. A blown-up photograph of the father hangs on the wall of the living room, facing the audience, to the left of the archway. It is the face of a very handsome young man in a doughboy's First World War cap. He is gallantly smiling, ineluctably smiling, as if to say, "I will be smiling forever."

The audience hears and sees the opening scene in the dining room through both the transparent fourth wall of the building and the transparent gauze portieres of the dining-room arch. It is during this revealing scene that the fourth wall slowly ascends, out of sight. This transparent exterior wall is not brought down again until the very end of the play, during Tom's final speech.

The narrator is an undisguised convention of the play. He takes whatever license with dramatic convention as is convenient to his purposes.

Tom enters dressed as a merchant sailor from the alley, stage left, and strolls across the front of the stage to the fire-escape. There he stops and lights a cigarette. He addresses the audience.

TOM: Yes, I have tricks in my pocket, I have things up my sleeve. But I am the opposite of a stage magician. He gives you illusion that has the appearance of truth. I give you truth in the pleasant disguise of illusion. To begin with, I turn back time. I reverse it to that quaint period, the thirties, when the huge middle class of America was matriculating in a school for the blind. Their eyes had failed them, or they had failed their eyes, and so they were having their fingers pressed forcibly down on the fiery Braille alphabet of a dissolving economy. In Spain there was revolution.° Here there was only shouting and confusion. In Spain there was Guernica.° Here there were disturbances of labor, sometimes pretty violent, in otherwise peaceful cities such as Chicago, Cleveland, Saint Louis. . . . This is the social background of the play.

Music.

°*revolution:* The Spanish Civil War (1936–1939).   °*Guernica:* A Basque town in northern Spain, bombed and practically destroyed on April 27, 1937, by German planes aiding fascist General Francisco Franco's Nationalists. The destruction is depicted in one of Pablo Picasso's most famous paintings, *Guernica* (1937).

The play is memory. Being a memory play, it is dimly lighted, it is senti-mental, it is not realistic. In memory everything seems to happen to mu-sic. That explains the fiddle in the wings. I am the narrator of the play, and also a character in it. The other characters are my mother, Amanda, my sister, Laura, and a gentleman caller who appears in the final scenes. He is the most realistic character in the play, being an emissary from a world of reality that we were somehow set apart from. But since I have a poet's weakness for symbols, I am using this character also as a symbol; he is the long delayed but always expected something that we live for. There is a fifth character in the play who doesn't appear except in this larger-than-life photograph over the mantel. This is our father who left us a long time ago. He was a telephone man who fell in love with long dis-tances; he gave up his job with the telephone company and skipped the light fantastic out of town. . . . The last we heard of him was a picture post-card from Mazatlan, on the Pacific coast of Mexico, containing a message of two words — "Hello — Good-bye!" and an address. I think the rest of the play will explain itself. . . .

Amanda's voice becomes audible through the portieres.

Legend On Screen: "Où Sont Les Neiges."°

He divides the portieres and enters the upstage area.

Amanda and Laura are seated at a drop-leaf table. Eating is indicated by gestures without food or utensils. Amanda faces the audience. Tom and Laura are seated in profile.

The interior has lit up softly and through the scrim we see Amanda and Laura seated at the table in the upstage area.

AMANDA: *(calling)* Tom?

TOM: Yes, Mother.

AMANDA: We can't say grace until you come to the table!

TOM: Coming, Mother. *(He bows slightly and withdraws, reappearing a few moments later in his place at the table.)*   5

AMANDA: *(to her son)* Honey, don't push with your fingers. If you have to push with something, the thing to push with is a crust of bread. And chew — chew! Animals have sections in their stomachs which enable them to digest food without mastication, but human beings are supposed to chew their food before they swallow it down. Eat food leisurely, son, and really enjoy it. A well-cooked meal has lots of delicate flavors that have to be held in the mouth for appreciation. So chew your food and give your salivary glands a chance to function!

Tom deliberately lays his imaginary fork down and pushes his chair back from the table.

° *"Où Sont Les Neiges":* "Where the snows [of yesteryear]." A famous line by French poet François Villon (1431–1463?).

Tom: I haven't enjoyed one bite of this dinner because of your constant directions on how to eat it. It's you that makes me rush through meals with your hawk-like attention to every bite I take. Sickening — spoils my appetite — all this discussion of animals' secretion — salivary glands —mastication!

Amanda: *(lightly)* Temperament like a Metropolitan star! *(He rises and crosses downstage.)* You're not excused from the table.

Tom: I am getting a cigarette.

10 **Amanda:** You smoke too much.

Laura rises.

Laura: I'll bring in the blanc mange.

He remains standing with his cigarette by the portieres during the following.

Amanda: *(rising)* No, sister, no, sister — you be the lady this time and I'll be the darky.

Laura: I'm already up.

Amanda: Resume your seat, little sister — I want you to stay fresh and pretty —for gentlemen callers!

15 **Laura:** I'm not expecting any gentlemen callers.

Amanda: *(crossing out to kitchenette. Airily)* Sometimes they come when they are least expected! Why, I remember one Sunday afternoon in Blue Mountain — *(Enters kitchenette.)*

Tom: I know what's coming!

Laura: Yes. But let her tell it.

Tom: Again?

20 **Laura:** She loves to tell it.

Amanda returns with bowl of dessert.

Amanda: One Sunday afternoon in Blue Mountain — your mother received —*seventeen!*— gentlemen callers! Why, sometimes there weren't chairs enough to accommodate them all. We had to send the nigger over to bring in folding chairs from the parish house.

Tom: *(remaining at portieres)* How did you entertain those gentlemen callers?

Amanda: I understood the art of conversation!

Tom: I bet you could talk.

25 **Amanda:** Girls in those days *knew* how to talk, I can tell you.

Tom: Yes?

Image: Amanda As A Girl On A Porch Greeting Callers.

Amanda: They knew how to entertain their gentlemen callers. It wasn't enough for a girl to be possessed of a pretty face and a graceful figure — although I wasn't slighted in either respect. She also needed to have a nimble wit and a tongue to meet all occasions.

Tom: What did you talk about?

AMANDA: Things of importance going on in the world! Never anything coarse or common or vulgar. *(She addresses Tom as though he were seated in the vacant chair at the table though he remains by portieres. He plays this scene as though he held the book.)* My callers were gentlemen — all! Among my callers were some of the most prominent young planters of the Mississippi Delta — planters and sons of planters!

Tom motions for music and a spot of light on Amanda. Her eyes lift, her face glows, her voice becomes rich and elegiac.

Screen Legend: "Où Sont Les Neiges."

There was young Champ Laughlin who later became vice-president of the Delta Planters Bank. Hadley Stevenson who was drowned in Moon Lake and left his widow one hundred and fifty thousand in Government bonds. There were the Cutrere brothers, Wesley and Bates. Bates was one of my bright particular beaux! He got in a quarrel with that wild Wainright boy. They shot it out on the floor of Moon Lake Casino. Bates was shot through the stomach. Died in the ambulance on his way to Memphis. His widow was also well-provided for, came into eight or ten thousand acres, that's all. She married him on the rebound — never loved her — carried my picture on him the night he died! And there was that boy that every girl in the Delta had set her cap for! That beautiful, brilliant young Fitzhugh boy from Green County!

TOM: What did he leave his widow?   30
AMANDA: He never married! Gracious, you talk as though all of my old admirers had turned up their toes to the daisies!
TOM: Isn't this the first you mentioned that still survives?
AMANDA: That Fitzhugh boy went North and made a fortune — came to be known as the Wolf of Wall Street! He had the Midas touch, whatever he touched turned to gold! And I could have been Mrs. Duncan J. Fitzhugh, mind you! But — I picked your *father!*
LAURA: *(rising)* Mother, let me clear the table.
AMANDA: No dear, you go in front and study your typewriter chart. Or prac-   35
tice your shorthand a little. Stay fresh and pretty! — It's almost time for our gentlemen callers to start arriving. *(She flounces girlishly toward the kitchenette.)* How many do you suppose we're going to entertain this afternoon?

Tom throws down the paper and jumps up with a groan.

LAURA: *(alone in the dining room)* I don't believe we're going to receive any, Mother.
AMANDA: *(reappearing, airily)* What? No one — not one? You must be joking! *(Laura nervously echoes her laugh. She slips in a fugitive manner through the half-open portieres and draws them gently behind her. A shaft of very clear light is thrown on her face against the faded tapestry of the curtains.)* *(Music: "The*

Glass Menagerie" under faintly.) (Lightly.) Not one gentleman caller? It can't be true! There must be a flood, there must have been a tornado!

LAURA: It isn't a flood, it's not a tornado, Mother. I'm just not popular like you were in Blue Mountain. . . . *(Tom utters another groan. Laura glances at him with a faint, apologetic smile. Her voice catching a little.)* Mother's afraid I'm going to be an old maid.

The Scene Dims Out With "Glass Menagerie" Music.

SCENE 2

"Laura, Haven't You Ever Liked Some Boy?"
On the dark stage the screen is lighted with the image of blue roses.
Gradually Laura's figure becomes apparent and the screen goes out.
The music subsides.
Laura is seated in the delicate ivory chair at the small clawfoot table.
She wears a dress of soft violet material for a kimono — her hair tied back from her forehead with a ribbon.
She is washing and polishing her collection of glass.
Amanda appears on the fire-escape steps. At the sound of her ascent, Laura catches her breath, thrusts the bowl of ornaments away and seats herself stiffly before the diagram of the typewriter keyboard as though it held her spellbound. Something has happened to Amanda. It is written in her face as she climbs to the landing: a look that is grim and hopeless and a little absurd.
She has on one of those cheap or imitation velvety-looking cloth coats with imitation fur collar. Her hat is five or six years old, one of those dreadful cloche hats that were worn in the late twenties, and she is clasping an enormous black patent-leather pocketbook with nickel clasp and initials. This is her fulldress outfit, the one she usually wears to the D.A.R.°
Before entering she looks through the door.
She purses her lips, opens her eyes wide, rolls them upward and shakes her head.
Then she slowly lets herself in the door. Seeing her mother's expression Laura touches her lips with a nervous gesture.

LAURA: Hello, Mother, I was — *(She makes a nervous gesture toward the chart on the wall. Amanda leans against the shut door and stares at Laura with a martyred look.)*

AMANDA: Deception? Deception? *(She slowly removes her hat and gloves, continuing the swift suffering stare. She lets the hat and gloves fall on the floor — a bit of acting.)*

°*D.A.R.:* Daughters of the American Revolution, an organization for female descendants of participants in the American Revolution, founded in 1890. That Amanda is a member says much about her concern with the past, as well as about her pride and affectations.

LAURA: *(shakily)* How was the D.A.R. meeting? *(Amanda slowly opens her purse and removes a dainty white handkerchief which she shakes out delicately and delicately touches to her lips and nostrils.)* Didn't you go to the D.A.R. meeting, Mother?

AMANDA: *(faintly, almost inaudibly)* — No. — No. *(Then more forcibly.)* I did not have the strength — to go the D.A.R. In fact, I did not have the courage! I wanted to find a hole in the ground and hide myself in it forever! *(She crosses slowly to the wall and removes the diagram of the typewriter keyboard. She holds it in front of her for a second, staring at it sweetly and sorrowfully — then bites her lips and tears it in two pieces.)*

LAURA: *(faintly)* Why did you do that, Mother? *(Amanda repeats the same*   5
procedure with the chart of the Gregg Alphabet.) Why are you —

AMANDA: Why? Why? How old are you, Laura?

LAURA: Mother, you know my age.

AMANDA: I thought that you were an adult; it seems that I was mistaken. *(She crosses slowly to the sofa and sinks down and stares at Laura.)*

LAURA: Please don't stare at me, Mother.

Amanda closes her eyes and lowers her head. Count ten.

AMANDA: What are we going to do, what is going to become of us, what is   10
the future?

Count ten.

LAURA: Has something happened, Mother? *(Amanda draws a long breath and takes out the handkerchief again. Dabbing process.)* Mother, has — something happened?

AMANDA: I'll be all right in a minute. I'm just bewildered — *(count five)* — by life. . . .

LAURA: Mother, I wish that you would tell me what's happened.

AMANDA: As you know, I was supposed to be inducted into my office at the D.A.R. this afternoon. *(Image: A Swarm Of Typewriters.)* But I stopped off at Rubicam's Business College to speak to your teachers about your having a cold and ask them what progress they thought you were making down there.

LAURA: Oh. . . .   15

AMANDA: I went to the typing instructor and introduced myself as your mother. She didn't know who you were. Wingfield, she said. We don't have any such student enrolled at the school! I assured her she did, that you had been going to classes since early in January. "I wonder," she said, "if you could be talking about that terribly shy little girl who dropped out of school after only a few days' attendance?" "No," I said, "Laura, my daughter, has been going to school every day for the past six weeks!" "Excuse me," she said. She took the attendance book out and there was your name, unmistakably printed, and all the dates you were absent until they decided that you had dropped out of school. I still said, "No, there must have been some mistake! There must have been some mix-up in the records!" And she said, "No — I remember her perfectly now. Her hand shook so that she couldn't hit the right keys! The first time we gave a speed-test, she broke down completely — was sick at the stomach and almost had to be carried into the wash-room! After that morning she never showed up any more. We phoned the house but never got any answer"— while I was working at Famous and Barr, I suppose, demonstrating those — Oh! I felt so weak I could barely keep on my feet. I had to sit down while they got me a glass of water! Fifty dollars' tuition, all of our plans — my hopes and ambitions for you —just gone up the spout, just gone up the spout like that. *(Laura draws a long breath and gets awkwardly to her feet. She crosses to the Victrola and winds it up.)* What are you doing?

LAURA: Oh! *(She releases the handle and returns to her seat.)*

AMANDA: Laura, where have you been going when you've gone out pretending that you were going to business college?

LAURA: I've just been going out walking.

20 AMANDA: That's not true.

LAURA: It is. I just went walking.

AMANDA: Walking? Walking? In winter? Deliberately courting pneumonia in that light coat? Where did you walk to, Laura?

LAURA: It was the lesser of two evils, Mother. *(Image: Winter Scene In Park.)* I couldn't go back up. I — threw up — on the floor!

AMANDA: From half past seven till after five every day you mean to tell me you walked around in the park, because you wanted to make me think that you were still going to Rubicam's Business College?

25 LAURA: It wasn't as bad as it sounds. I went inside places to get warmed up.

AMANDA: Inside where?

LAURA: I went in the art museum and the bird-houses at the Zoo. I visited the penguins every day! Sometimes I did without lunch and went to the movies. Lately I've been spending most of my afternoons in the Jewel-box, that big glass house where they raise the tropical flowers.

AMANDA: You did all this to deceive me, just for the deception? *(Laura looks down.)* Why?

LAURA: Mother, when you're disappointed, you get that awful suffering look on your face, like the picture of Jesus' mother in the museum!

30 AMANDA: Hush!

LAURA: I couldn't face it.

Pause. A whisper of strings.

Legend: "The Crust Of Humility."

AMANDA: *(hopelessly fingering the huge pocketbook)* So what are we going to do the rest of our lives? Stay home and watch the parades go by? Amuse ourselves with the glass menagerie, darling? Eternally play those worn-out

phonograph records your father left as a painful reminder of him? We won't
have a business career — we've given that up because it gave us nervous
indigestion! (*Laughs wearily.*) What is there left but dependency all our lives?
I know so well what becomes of unmarried women who aren't prepared to
occupy a position. I've seen such pitiful cases in the South — barely
tolerated spinsters living upon the grudging patronage of sister's husband
or brother's wife! — stuck away in some little mouse-trap of a room —
encouraged by one in-law to visit another — little birdlike women without
any nest — eating the crust of humility all their life! Is that the future that
we've mapped out for ourselves? I swear it's the only alternative I can think
of! It isn't a very pleasant alternative, is it? Of course — some girls *do*
marry. (*Laura twists her hands nervously.*) Haven't you ever liked some boy?

LAURA: Yes I liked one once. (*Rises.*) I came across his picture a while ago.

AMANDA: (*with some interest*) He gave you his picture?

LAURA: No, it's in the year-book.   35

AMANDA: (*disappointed*) Oh — a high-school boy.

Screen Image: Jim As A High-School Hero Bearing A Silver Cup.

LAURA: Yes. His name was Jim. (*Laura lifts the heavy annual from the clawfoot*
table.) Here he is in *The Pirates of Penzance.*°

AMANDA: (*absently*) The what?

LAURA: The operetta the senior class put on. He had a wonderful voice and
we sat across the aisle from each other Mondays, Wednesdays and Fridays in
the Aud. Here he is with the silver cup for debating! See his grin?

AMANDA: (*absently*) He must have had a jolly disposition.   40

LAURA: He used to call me — Blue Roses.

Image: Blue Roses.

AMANDA: Why did he call you such a name as that?

LAURA: When I had that attack of pleurosis — he asked me what was the matter when I came back. I said pleurosis — he thought that I said Blue Roses!
So that's what he always called me after that. Whenever he saw me, he'd
holler, "Hello, Blue Roses!" I didn't care for the girl that he went out with.
Emily Meisenbach. Emily was the best-dressed girl at Soldan. She never
struck me, though, as being sincere . . . It says in the Personal Section —
they're engaged. That's — six years ago! They must be married by now.

AMANDA: Girls that aren't cut out for business careers usually wind up
married to some nice man. (*Gets up with a spark of revival.*) Sister, that's
what you'll do!

Laura utters a startled, doubtful laugh. She reaches quickly for a piece of glass.

°*The Pirates of Penzance:* A musical by Gilbert and Sullivan.

45 LAURA: But, Mother—
AMANDA: Yes? (*Crossing to photograph.*)
LAURA: (*in a tone of frightened apology*) I'm — crippled!

Image: Screen.

AMANDA: Nonsense! Laura, I've told you never, never to use that word. Why, you're not crippled, you just have a little defect — hardly noticeable, even! When people have some slight disadvantage like that, they cultivate other things to make up for it — develop charm — and vivacity — and — charm! That's all you have to do! (*She turns again to the photograph.*) One thing your father had *plenty* of — was *charm!*

Tom motions to the fiddle in the wings.

The Scene Fades Out With Music.

SCENE 3

Legend On The Screen: "After The Fiasco —"

Tom speaks from the fire-escape landing.

TOM: After the fiasco at Rubicam's Business College, the idea of getting a gentleman caller for Laura began to play a more important part in Mother's calculations. It became an obsession. Like some archetype of the universal unconscious, the image of the gentleman caller haunted our small apartment. . . . (*Image: Young Man At Door With Flowers.*) An evening at home rarely passed without some allusion to this image, this spectre, this hope. . . . Even when he wasn't mentioned, his presence hung in Mother's preoccupied look and in my sister's frightened, apologetic manner — hung like a sentence passed upon the Wingfields! Mother was a woman of action as well as words. She began to take logical steps in the planned direction. Late that winter and in the early spring — realizing that extra money would be needed to properly feather the nest and plume the bird — she conducted a vigorous campaign on the telephone, roping in subscribers to one of those magazines for matrons called *The Home-maker's Companion*, the type of journal that features the serialized sublimations of ladies of letters who think in terms of delicate cup-like breasts, slim, tapering waists, rich, creamy thighs, eyes like wood-smoke in autumn, fingers that soothe and caress like strains of music, bodies as powerful as Etruscan sculpture.

Screen Image: A Glamour Magazine Cover.

Amanda enters with phone on long extension cord. She is spotted in the dim stage.

AMANDA: Ida Scott? This is Amanda Wingfield! We *missed* you at the D.A.R. last Monday! I said to myself: She's probably suffering with that sinus condition! How is that sinus condition? Horrors! Heaven have mercy! — You're a Christian martyr, yes, that's what you are, a Christian martyr! Well, I just now happened to notice that your subscription to the *Companion's* about to expire! Yes, it expires with the next issue, honey!—just when that wonderful new serial by Bessie Mae Hopper is getting off to such an exciting start. Oh, honey, it's something that you can't miss! You remember how *Gone With the Wind* took everybody by storm? You simply couldn't go out if you hadn't read it. All everybody *talked* was Scarlett O'Hara. Well, this is a book that critics already compare to *Gone With the Wind*. It's the *Gone With the Wind* of the post–World War generation!—What?— Burning?— Oh, honey, don't let them burn, go take a look in the oven and I'll hold the wire! Heavens — I think she's hung up!

Dim Out.

Legend On Screen: "You Think I'm In Love With Continental Shoemakers?"

Before the stage is lighted, the violent voices of Tom and Amanda are heard. They are quarreling behind the portieres. In front of them stands Laura with clenched hands and panicky expression.
A clear pool of light on her figure throughout this scene.

TOM: What in Christ's name am I—
AMANDA: *(shrilly)* Don't you use that—
TOM: Supposed to do!   5
AMANDA: Expression! Not in my—
TOM: Ohhh!
AMANDA: Presence! Have you gone out of your senses?
TOM: I have, that's true, *driven* out!
AMANDA: What is the matter with you, you — big — big —IDIOT!   10
TOM: Look — I've got *no thing*, no single thing—
AMANDA: Lower your voice!
TOM: In my life here that I can call my OWN! Everything is—
AMANDA: Stop that shouting!
TOM: Yesterday you confiscated my books! You had the nerve to—   15
AMANDA: I took that horrible novel back to the library — yes! That hideous
   book by that insane Mr. Lawrence.° *(Tom laughs wildly.)* I cannot control
   the output of diseased minds or people who cater to them —*(Tom laughs
   still more wildly.)* BUT I WON'T ALLOW SUCH FILTH BROUGHT INTO MY
   HOUSE! No, no, no, no, no!
TOM: House, house! Who pays rent on it, who makes a slave of himself to—
AMANDA: *(fairly screeching)* Don't you DARE to—
TOM: No, no, I mustn't say things! *I've* got to just—

°*Mr. Lawrence:* English novelist D. H. Lawrence (1885–1930). The reference is to his 1928 novel *Lady Chatterley's Lover,* which was banned in the United States and England because of its frank treatment of sexuality.

20 AMANDA: Let me tell you—
TOM: I don't want to hear any more! (*He tears the portieres open. The upstage area is lit with a turgid smoky red glow.*)

Amanda's hair is in metal curlers and she wears a very old bathrobe, much too large for her slight figure, a relic of the faithless Mr. Wingfield.
An upright typewriter and a wild disarray of manuscripts are on the drop-leaf table. The quarrel was probably precipitated by Amanda's interruption of his creative labor. A chair lying overthrown on the floor.
Their gesticulating shadows are cast on the ceiling by the fiery glow.

AMANDA: You *will* hear more, you—
TOM: No, I won't hear more, I'm going out!
AMANDA: You come right back in—
25 TOM: Out, out out! Because I'm—
AMANDA: Come back here, Tom Wingfield! I'm not through talking to you!
TOM: Oh, go—
LAURA: (*desperately*) Tom!
AMANDA: You're going to listen, and no more insolence from you! I'm at the end of my patience! (*He comes back toward her.*)
30 TOM: What do you think I'm at? Aren't I supposed to have any patience to reach the end of, Mother? I know, I know. It seems unimportant to you, what I'm *doing*— what I *want* to do —having a little *difference* between them! You don't think that—
AMANDA: I think you've been doing things that you're ashamed of. That's why you act like this. I don't believe that you go every night to the movies. Nobody goes to the movies night after night. Nobody in their right mind goes to the movies as often as you pretend to. People don't go to the movies at nearly midnight, and movies don't let out at two A.M. Come in stumbling. Muttering to yourself like a maniac! You get three hours' sleep and then go to work. Oh, I can picture the way you're doing down there. Moping, doping, because you're in no condition.
TOM: (*wildly*) No, I'm in no condition!
AMANDA: What right have you got to jeopardize your job? Jeopardize the security of us all? How do you think we'd manage if you were—
TOM: Listen! You think I'm crazy *about* the *warehouse*? (*He bends fiercely toward her slight figure.*) You think I'm in love with the Continental Shoemakers? You think I want to spend fifty-five *years* down there in that —*celotex interior*! with —*fluorescent*— *tubes*! Look! I'd rather somebody picked up a crowbar and battered out my brains — than go back mornings! I *go*! Every time you come in yelling that God damn "*Rise and Shine!*" "*Rise and Shine!*" I say to myself "How *lucky dead* people are!" But I get up. I *go*! For sixty-five dollars a month I give up all that I dream of doing and being *ever*! And you say self —*self's* all I ever think of. Why, listen, if self is what I thought of, Mother, I'd be where he is —GONE! (*Pointing to father's picture.*) As far as

the system of transportation reaches! (*He starts past her. She grabs his arm.*) Don't grab at me, Mother!

AMANDA: Where are you going?   35

TOM: I'm going to the *movies!*

AMANDA: I don't believe that lie!

TOM: (*crouching toward her, overtowering her tiny figure. She backs away, gasping*) I'm going to opium dens! Yes, opium dens, dens of vice and criminals' hangouts, Mother. I've joined the Hogan gang, I'm a hired assassin, I carry a tommy-gun in a violin case! I run a string of cat-houses in the Valley! They call me Killer, Killer Wingfield, I'm leading a double-life, a simple, honest warehouse worker by day, by night a dynamic *czar of the underworld, Mother.* I go to gambling casinos, I spin away fortunes on the roulette table! I wear a patch over one eye and a false mustache, sometimes I put on green whiskers. On those occasions they call me — *El Diablo!* Oh, I could tell you things to make you sleepless! My enemies plan to dynamite this place. They're going to blow us all sky-high some night! I'll be glad, very happy, and so will you! You'll go up, up on a broomstick, over Blue Mountain with seventeen gentlemen callers! You ugly — babbling old — *witch.* . . . (*He goes through a series of violent, clumsy movements, seizing his overcoat, lunging to the door, pulling it fiercely open. The women watch him, aghast. His arm catches in the sleeve of the coat as he struggles to pull it on. For a moment he is pinioned by the bulky garment. With an outraged groan he tears the coat off again, splitting the shoulders of it, and hurls it across the room. It strikes against the shelf of Laura's glass collection, there is a tinkle of shattering glass. Laura cries out as if wounded.*)

Music Legend: "The Glass Menagerie."

LAURA: My glass! — menagerie. . . . (*She covers her face and turns away.*)

But Amanda is still stunned and stupefied by the "ugly witch" so that she barely notices this occurrence. Now she recovers her speech.

AMANDA: (*in an awful voice*) I won't speak to you — until you apologize! (*She   40 crosses through portieres and draws them together behind her. Tom is left with Laura. Laura clings weakly to the mantel with her face averted. Tom stares at her stupidly for a moment. Then he crosses to shelf. Drops awkwardly to his knees to collect the fallen glass, glancing at Laura as if he would speak but couldn't.*)

"The Glass Menagerie" steals in as The Scene Dims Out.

SCENE 4

The interior is dark. Faint in the alley.

A deep-voiced bell in a church is tolling the hour of five as the scene commences.

Tom appears at the top of the alley. After each solemn boom of the bell in the tower, he shakes a little noise-maker or rattle as if to express the tiny spasm of man in contrast to the sustained power and dignity of the Almighty. This and the unsteadiness of his advance make it evident that he has been drinking.

As he climbs the few steps to the fire-escape landing light steals up inside. Laura appears in night-dress, observing Tom's empty bed in the front room.

Tom fishes in his pockets for the door-key, removing a motley assortment of articles in the search, including a perfect shower of movie-ticket stubs and an empty bottle. At last he finds the key, but just as he is about to insert it, it slips from his fingers. He strikes a match and crouches below the door.

TOM: *(bitterly)* One crack — and it falls through!

Laura opens the door.

LAURA: Tom! Tom, what are you doing?

TOM: Looking for a door-key.

LAURA: Where have you been all this time?

5 TOM: I have been to the movies.

LAURA: All this time at the movies?

TOM: There was a very long program. There was a Garbo picture and a Mickey Mouse and a travelogue and a newsreel and a preview of coming attractions. And there was an organ solo and a collection for the milk-fund — simultaneously — which ended up in a terrible fight between a fat lady and an usher!

LAURA: *(innocently)* Did you have to stay through everything?

TOM: Of course! And, oh, I forgot! There was a big stage show! The headliner on this stage show was Malvolio the Magician. He performed wonderful tricks, many of them, such as pouring water back and forth between pitchers. First it turned to wine and then it turned to beer and then it turned to whiskey. I know it was whiskey it finally turned into because he needed somebody to come up out of the audience to help him, and I came up — both shows! It was Kentucky Straight Bourbon. A very generous fellow, he gave souvenirs. *(He pulls from his back pocket a shimmering rainbow-colored scarf.)* He gave me this. This is his magic scarf. You can have it, Laura. You wave it over a canary cage and you get a bowl of gold-fish. You wave it over the gold-fish bowl and they fly away canaries. . . . But the wonderfullest trick of all was the coffin trick. We nailed him into a coffin and he got out of the coffin without removing one nail. *(He has come inside.)* There is a trick that would come in handy for me — get me out of this 2 by 4 situation! *(Flops onto bed and starts removing shoes.)*

10 LAURA: Tom — Shhh!

TOM: What you shushing me for?

LAURA: You'll wake up Mother.

TOM: Goody, goody! Pay 'er back for all those "Rise an' Shines." *(Lies down, groaning.)* You know it don't take much intelligence to get yourself into a nailed-up coffin, Laura. But who in hell ever got himself out of one without removing one nail?

As if in answer, the father's grinning photograph lights up.

Scene Dims Out.

Immediately following: The church bell is heard striking six. At the sixth stroke the alarm clock goes off in Amanda's room, and after a few moments we hear her calling: "Rise and Shine! Rise and Shine! Laura, go tell your brother to rise and shine!"

TOM: (*sitting up slowly*) I'll rise — but I won't shine.

The light increases.

AMANDA: Laura, tell your brother his coffee is ready. 15

Laura slips into front room.

LAURA: Tom! it's nearly seven. Don't make Mother nervous. (*He stares at her stupidly. Beseechingly.*) Tom, speak to Mother this morning. Make up with her, apologize, speak to her!
TOM: She won't to me. It's her that started not speaking.
LAURA: If you just say you're sorry she'll start speaking.
TOM: Her not speaking — is that such a tragedy?
LAURA: Please — please! 20
AMANDA: (*calling from kitchenette*) Laura, are you going to do what I asked you to do, or do I have to get dressed and go out myself?
LAURA: Going, going — soon as I get on my coat! (*She pulls on a shapeless felt hat with nervous, jerky movement, pleadingly glancing at Tom. Rushes awkwardly for coat. The coat is one of Amanda's inaccurately made-over, the sleeves too short for Laura.*) Butter and what else?
AMANDA: (*entering upstage*) Just butter. Tell them to charge it.
LAURA: Mother, they make such faces when I do that.
AMANDA: Sticks and stones may break my bones, but the expression on 25
Mr. Garfinkel's face won't harm us! Tell your brother his coffee is getting cold.
LAURA: (*at door*) Do what I asked you, will you, will you, Tom?

He looks sullenly away.

AMANDA: Laura, go now or just don't go at all!
LAURA: (*rushing out*) Going — going! (*A second later she cries out. Tom springs up and crosses to the door. Amanda rushes anxiously in. Tom opens the door.*)
TOM: Laura?
LAURA: I'm all right. I slipped, but I'm all right. 30
AMANDA: (*peering anxiously after her*) If anyone breaks a leg on those fire-escape steps, the landlord ought to be sued for every cent he possesses! (*She shuts door. Remembers she isn't speaking and returns to other room.*)

As Tom enters listlessly for his coffee, she turns her back to him and stands rigidly facing the window on the gloomy gray vault of the areaway. Its light on her face with its aged but childish features is cruelly sharp, satirical as a Daumier print.

Music Under: "Ave Maria."

Tom glances sheepishly but sullenly at her averted figure and slumps at the table. The coffee is scalding hot; he sips it and gasps and spits it back in the cup. At his gasp, Amanda catches her breath and half turns. Then catches herself and turns back to window.
Tom blows on his coffee, glancing sidewise at his mother. She clears her throat. Tom clears his. He starts to rise. Sinks back down again, scratches his head, clears his throat again. Amanda coughs. Tom raises his cup in both hands to blow on it, his eyes staring over the rim of it at his mother for several moments. Then he slowly sets the cup down and awkwardly and hesitantly rises from the chair.

TOM: *(hoarsely)* Mother. I — I apologize. Mother. *(Amanda draws a quick, shuddering breath. Her face works grotesquely. She breaks into childlike tears.)* I'm sorry for what I said, for everything that I said, I didn't mean it.

AMANDA: *(sobbingly)* My devotion has made me a witch and so I make myself hateful to my children!

TOM: No, you *don't.*

35 AMANDA: I worry so much, don't sleep, it makes me nervous!

TOM: *(gently)* I understand that.

AMANDA: I've had to put up a solitary battle all these years. But you're my right-hand bower! Don't fall down, don't fail!

TOM: *(gently)* I try, Mother.

AMANDA: *(with great enthusiasm)* Try and you will SUCCEED! *(The notion makes her breathless.)* Why, you — you're just *full* of natural endowments! Both of my children — they're *unusual* children! Don't you think I know it? I'm so — *proud!* Happy and — feel I've — so much to be thankful for but — Promise me one thing, son!

40 TOM: What, Mother?

AMANDA: Promise, son, you'll — never be a drunkard!

TOM: *(turns to her grinning)* I will never be a drunkard, Mother.

AMANDA: That's what frightened me so, that you'd be drinking! Eat a bowl of Purina!

TOM: Just coffee, Mother.

45 AMANDA: Shredded wheat biscuit?

TOM: No. No, Mother, just coffee.

AMANDA: You can't put in a day's work on an empty stomach. You've got ten minutes — don't gulp! Drinking too-hot liquids makes cancer of the stomach. . . . Put cream in.

TOM: No, thank you.

AMANDA: To cool it.

50 TOM: No! No, thank you, I want it black.

AMANDA: I know, but it's not good for you. We have to do all that we can to build ourselves up. In these trying times we live in, all that we have to cling to is — each other. . . . That's why it's so important to — Tom, I — I sent out your sister so I could discuss something with you. If you hadn't spoken I would have spoken to you. (*Sits down.*)

TOM: (*gently*) What is it, Mother, that you want to discuss?

AMANDA: Laura!

Tom puts his cup down slowly.

Legend On Screen: "Laura."

Music: "The Glass Menagerie."

TOM: — Oh. — Laura . . .

AMANDA: (*touching his sleeve*) You know how Laura is. So quiet but — still   55
water runs deep! She notices things and I think she — broods about them. (*Tom looks up.*) A few days ago I came in and she was crying.

TOM: What about?

AMANDA: You.

TOM: Me?

AMANDA: She has an idea that you're not happy here.

TOM: What gave her that idea?   60

AMANDA: What gives her any idea? However, you do act strangely. I — I'm not criticizing, understand *that!* I know your ambitions do not lie in the warehouse, that like everybody in the whole wide world — you've had to — make sacrifices, but — Tom — Tom — life's not easy, it calls for — Spartan endurance! There's so many things in my heart that I cannot describe to you! I've never told you but I — *loved* your father. . . .

TOM: (*gently*) I know that, Mother.

AMANDA: And you — when I see you taking after his ways! Staying out late — and — well, you *had* been drinking the night you were in that — terrifying condition! Laura says that you hate the apartment and that you go out nights to get away from it! Is that true, Tom?

TOM: No. You say there's so much in your heart that you can't describe to me. That's true of me, too. There's so much in my heart that I can't describe to *you!* So let's respect each other's —

AMANDA: But, why — *why*, Tom — are you always so *restless?* Where do you   65
go to, nights?

TOM: I — go to the movies.

AMANDA: Why do you go to the movies so much, Tom?

TOM: I go to the movies because — I like adventure. Adventure is something I don't have much of at work, so I go to the movies.

AMANDA: But, Tom, you go to the movies *entirely* too *much!*

70 **TOM:** I like a lot of adventure.

Amanda looks baffled, then hurt. As the familiar inquisition resumes he becomes hard and impatient again. Amanda slips back into her querulous attitude toward him.

Image On Screen: Sailing Vessel With Jolly Roger.

AMANDA: Most young men find adventure in their careers.

TOM: Then most young men are not employed in a warehouse.

AMANDA: The world is full of young men employed in warehouses and offices and factories.

TOM: Do all of them find adventure in their careers?

75 **AMANDA:** They do or they do without it! Not everybody has a craze for adventure.

TOM: Man is by instinct a lover, a hunter, a fighter, and none of those instincts are given much play at the warehouse!

AMANDA: Man is by instinct! Don't quote instinct to me! Instinct is something that people have got away from! It belongs to animals! Christian adults don't want it!

TOM: What do Christian adults want, then, Mother?

AMANDA: Superior things! Things of the mind and the spirit! Only animals have to satisfy instincts! Surely your aims are somewhat higher than theirs! Than monkeys — pigs —

80 **TOM:** I reckon they're not.

AMANDA: You're joking. However, that isn't what I wanted to discuss.

TOM: *(rising)* I haven't much time.

AMANDA: *(pushing his shoulders)* Sit down.

TOM: You want me to punch in red at the warehouse, Mother?

85 **AMANDA:** You have five minutes. I want to talk about Laura.

Legend: "Plans And Provisions."

TOM: All right! What about Laura?

AMANDA: We have to be making plans and provisions for her. She's older than you, two years, and nothing has happened. She just drifts along doing nothing. It frightens me terribly how she just drifts along.

TOM: I guess she's the type that people call home-girls.

AMANDA: There's no such type, and if there is, it's a pity! That is unless the home is hers, with a husband!

90 **TOM:** What?

AMANDA: Oh, I can see the handwriting on the wall as plain as I see the nose in front of my face! It's terrifying! More and more you remind me of your father! He was out all hours without explanation — Then *left! Good-bye!* And me with the bag to hold. I saw that letter you got from the Merchant Marine. I know what you're dreaming of. I'm not standing here blindfolded. Very well, then. Then *do* it! But not till there's somebody to take your place.

TOM: What do you mean?

AMANDA: I mean that as soon as Laura has got somebody to take care of her, married, a home of her own, independent — why, then you'll be free to go wherever you please, on land, on sea, whichever way the wind blows! But until that time you've got to look out for your sister. I don't say me because I'm old and don't matter! I say for your sister because she's young and de-pendent. I put her in business college — a dismal failure! Frightened her so it made her sick to her stomach. I took her over to the Young People's League at the church. Another fiasco. She spoke to nobody, nobody spoke to her. Now all she does is fool with those pieces of glass and play those worn-out records. What kind of a life is that for a girl to lead!

TOM: What can I do about it?

AMANDA: Overcome selfishness! Self, self, self is all that you ever think of!   95
(*Tom springs up and crosses to get his coat. It is ugly and bulky. He pulls on a cap with earmuffs.*) Where is your muffler? Put your wool muffler on! (*He snatches it angrily from the closet and tosses it around his neck and pulls both ends tight.*) Tom! I haven't said what I had in mind to ask you.

TOM: I'm too late to—

AMANDA: (*catching his arms — very importunately. Then shyly*) Down at the warehouse, aren't there some — nice young men?

TOM: No!

AMANDA: There *must* be —*some* . . .

TOM: Mother—   100

Gesture.

AMANDA: Find out one that's clean-living — doesn't drink and — ask him out for sister!

TOM: What?

AMANDA: For *sister!* To *meet!* Get *acquainted!*

TOM: (*stamping to door*) Oh, my go-osh!

AMANDA: Will you? (*He opens door. Imploringly.*) Will you? (*He starts down.*)   105
Will you? *Will* you, dear?

TOM: (*calling back*) YES!

Amanda closes the door hesitantly and with a troubled but faintly hopeful expression.

(*Screen Image: A Glamour Magazine Cover.*)

Spot Amanda at phone.

AMANDA: Ella Cartwright? This is Amanda Wingfield! How are you, honey? How is that kidney condition? (*Count five.*) Horrors! (*Count five.*) You're a Christian martyr, yes, honey, that's what you are, a Christian martyr! Well, I just happened to notice in my little red book that your subscription to the *Companion* has just run out! I knew that you wouldn't want to miss out on the wonderful serial starting in this new issue. It's by Bessie Mae Hopper, the first thing she's written since *Honeymoon for Three*. Wasn't that a strange and interesting story? Well, this one is even lovelier, I believe. It has a sophisticated society background. It's all about the horsey set on Long Island!

Fade Out.

SCENE 5

(Legend On Screen: "Annunciation.") Fade with music.

It is early dusk of a spring evening. Supper has just been finished in the Wingfield apartment. Amanda and Laura in light colored dresses are removing dishes from the table, in the upstage area, which is shadowy, their movements formalized almost as a dance or ritual, their moving forms as pale and silent as moths.

Tom, in white shirt and trousers, rises from the table and crosses toward the fire-escape.

AMANDA: *(as he passes her)* Son, will you do me a favor?
TOM: What?
AMANDA: Comb your hair! You look so pretty when your hair is combed!
(Tom slouches on sofa with evening paper. Enormous caption "Franco Triumphs.")
There is only one respect in which I would like you to emulate your father.
TOM: What respect is that?
5 AMANDA: The care he always took of his appearance. He never allowed himself to look untidy. *(He throws down the paper and crosses to fire-escape.)* Where are you going?
TOM: I'm going out to smoke.
AMANDA: You smoke too much. A pack a day at fifteen cents a pack. How much would that amount to in a month? Thirty times fifteen is how much, Tom? Figure it out and you will be astounded at what you could save. Enough to give you a night-school course in accounting at Washington U! Just think what a wonderful thing that would be for you, son!

Tom is unmoved by the thought.

TOM: I'd rather smoke. *(He steps out on landing, letting the screen door slam.)*
AMANDA: *(sharply)* I know! That's the tragedy of it. . . . *(Alone, she turns to look at her husband's picture.)*

Dance Music: "All The World Is Waiting For The Sunrise!"

10 TOM: *(to the audience)* Across the alley from us was the Paradise Dance Hall. On evenings in spring the windows and doors were open and the music came outdoors. Sometimes the lights were turned out except for a large glass sphere that hung from the ceiling. It would turn slowly about and filter the dusk with delicate rainbow colors. Then the orchestra played a waltz or

a tango, something that had a slow and sensuous rhythm. Couples would come outside, to the relative privacy of the alley. You could see them kissing behind ash-pits and telephone poles. This was the compensation for lives that passed like mine, without any change or adventure. Adventure and change were imminent in this year. They were waiting around the corner for all these kids. Suspended in the mist over Berchtesgaden,° caught in the folds of Chamberlain's umbrella° — In Spain there was Guernica! But here there was only hot swing music and liquor, dance halls, bars, and movies, and sex that hung in the gloom like a chandelier and flooded the world with brief, deceptive rainbows. . . . All the world was waiting for bombardments!

Amanda turns from the picture and comes outside.

AMANDA: *(sighing)* A fire-escape landing's a poor excuse for a porch. (*She spreads a newspaper on a step and sits down, gracefully and demurely as if she were settling into a swing on a Mississippi veranda.*) What are you looking at?

TOM: The moon.

AMANDA: Is there a moon this evening?

TOM: It's rising over Garfinkel's Delicatessen.

AMANDA: So it is! A little silver slipper of a moon. Have you made a wish on it yet?

TOM: Um-hum.   15

AMANDA: What did you wish for?

TOM: That's a secret.

AMANDA: A secret, huh? Well, I won't tell mine either. I will be just as mysterious as you.

TOM: I bet I can guess what yours is.

AMANDA: Is my head so transparent?   20

TOM: You're not a sphinx.

AMANDA: No, I don't have secrets. I'll tell you what I wished for on the moon. Success and happiness for my precious children! I wish for that whenever there's a moon, and when there isn't a moon, I wish for it, too.

TOM: I thought perhaps you wished for a gentleman caller.

AMANDA: Why do you say that?

TOM: Don't you remember asking me to fetch one?   25

AMANDA: I remember suggesting that it would be nice for your sister if you brought home some nice young man from the warehouse. I think I've made that suggestion more than once.

°*Berchtesgaden:* A resort in Germany, in the Bavarian Alps; the site of Adolf Hitler's fortified retreat, the Berghof. °*Chamberlain's umbrella:* (Arthur) Neville Chamberlain (1869–1940)— Conservative Party prime minister of England (1937–1940) who advocated a policy of appeasement toward Hitler. Political cartoons often showed him carrying an umbrella.

Tom: Yes, you have made it repeatedly.

Amanda: Well?

30 **Tom:** We are going to have one.

Amanda: What?

Tom: A gentleman caller!

The Annunciation Is Celebrated With Music.

Amanda rises.

Image On Screen: Caller With Bouquet.

Amanda: You mean you have asked some nice young man to come over?

Tom: Yep. I've asked him to dinner.

35 **Amanda:** You really did?

Tom: I did!

Amanda: You did, and did he —*accept?*

Tom: He did!

Amanda: Well, well — well, well! That's —lovely!

40 **Tom:** I thought that you would be pleased.

Amanda: It's definite, then?

Tom: Very definite.

Amanda: Soon?

Tom: Very soon.

45 **Amanda:** For heaven's sake, stop putting on and tell me some things, will you?

Tom: What things do you want me to tell you?

Amanda: Naturally I would like to know when he's *coming!*

Tom: He's coming tomorrow.

Amanda: *Tomorrow?*

50 **Tom:** Yep. Tomorrow.

Amanda: But, Tom!

Tom: Yes, Mother?

Amanda: Tomorrow gives me no time!

Tom: Time for what?

55 **Amanda:** Preparations! Why didn't you phone me at once, as soon as you asked him, the minute that he accepted? Then, don't you see, I could have been getting ready!

Tom: You don't have to make any fuss.

Amanda: Oh, Tom, Tom, Tom, of course I have to make a fuss! I want things nice, not sloppy! Not thrown together. I'll certainly have to do some fast thinking, won't I?

Tom: I don't see why you have to think at all.

Amanda: You just don't know. We can't have a gentleman caller in a pig-sty! All my wedding silver has to be polished, the monogrammed table linen ought to be laundered! The windows have to be washed and fresh curtains put up. And how about clothes? We have to *wear* something, don't we?

TOM: Mother, this boy is no one to make a fuss over! 60

AMANDA: Do you realize he's the first young man we've introduced to your sister? It's terrible, dreadful, disgraceful that poor little sister has never received a single gentleman caller! Tom, come inside! (*She opens the screen door.*)

TOM: What for?

AMANDA: I want to ask you some things.

TOM: If you're going to make such a fuss, I'll call it off, I'll tell him not to come.

AMANDA: You certainly won't do anything of the kind. Nothing offends people 65 worse than broken engagements. It simply means I'll have to work like a Turk! We won't be brilliant, but we'll pass inspection. Come on inside. (*Tom follows, groaning.*) Sit down.

TOM: Any particular place you would like me to sit?

AMANDA: Thank heavens I've got that new sofa! I'm also making payments on a floor lamp I'll have sent out! And put the chintz covers on, they'll brighten things up! Of course I'd hoped to have these walls re-papered. . . . What is the young man's name?

TOM: His name is O'Connor.

AMANDA: That, of course, means fish — tomorrow is Friday! I'll have that salmon loaf — with Durkee's dressing! What does he do? He works at the warehouse?

TOM: Of course! How else would I— 70

AMANDA: Tom, he — doesn't drink?

TOM: Why do you ask me that?

AMANDA: Your father *did!*

TOM: Don't get started on that!

AMANDA: He *does* drink, then? 75

TOM: Not that I know of!

AMANDA: Make sure, be certain! The last thing I want for my daughter's a boy who drinks!

TOM: Aren't you being a little premature? Mr. O'Connor has not yet appeared on the scene!

AMANDA: But will tomorrow. To meet your sister, and what do I know about his character? Nothing! Old maids are better off than wives of drunkards!

TOM: Oh, my God! 80

AMANDA: Be still!

TOM: (*leaning forward to whisper*) Lots of fellows meet girls whom they don't marry!

AMANDA: Oh, talk sensibly, Tom — and don't be sarcastic! (*She has gotten a hairbrush.*)

TOM: What are you doing?

AMANDA: I'm brushing that cow-lick down! What is this young man's position 85 at the warehouse?

TOM: (*submitting grimly to the brush and the interrogation*) This young man's position is that of a shipping clerk, Mother.

AMANDA: Sounds to me like a fairly responsible job, the sort of a job *you* would be in if you just had more *get-up*. What is his salary? Have you got any idea?

TOM: I would judge it to be approximately eighty-five dollars a month.

AMANDA: Well — not princely, but —

90 TOM: Twenty more than I make.

AMANDA: Yes, how well I know! But for a family man, eighty-five dollars a month is not much more than you can just get by on. . . .

TOM: Yes, but Mr. O'Connor is not a family man.

AMANDA: He might be, mightn't he? Some time in the future?

TOM: I see. Plans and provisions.

95 AMANDA: You are the only young man that I know of who ignores the fact that the future becomes the present, the present the past, and the past turns into everlasting regret if you don't plan for it!

TOM: I will think that over and see what I can make of it.

AMANDA: Don't be supercilious with your mother! Tell me some more about this — what do you call him?

TOM: James D. O'Connor. The D. is for Delaney.

AMANDA: Irish on *both* sides! *Gracious!* And doesn't drink?

100 TOM: Shall I call him up and ask him right this minute?

AMANDA: The only way to find out about those things is to make discreet inquiries at the proper moment. When I was a girl in Blue Mountain and it was suspected that a young man drank, the girl whose attentions he had been receiving, if any girl *was*, would sometimes speak to the minister of his church, or rather her father would if her father was living, and sort of feel him out on the young man's character. That is the way such things are discreetly handled to keep a young woman from making a tragic mistake!

TOM: Then how did you happen to make a tragic mistake?

AMANDA: That innocent look of your father's had everyone fooled! He *smiled* — the world was *enchanted!* No girl can do worse than put herself at the mercy of a handsome appearance! I hope that Mr. O'Connor is not too good-looking.

TOM: No, he's not too good-looking. He's covered with freckles and hasn't too much of a nose.

105 AMANDA: He's not right-down homely, though?

TOM: Not right-down homely. Just medium homely, I'd say.

AMANDA: Character's what to look for in a man.

TOM: That's what I've always said, Mother.

AMANDA: You've never said anything of the kind and I suspect you would never give it a thought.

110 TOM: Don't be suspicious of me.

AMANDA: At least I hope he's the type that's up and coming.

TOM: I think he really goes in for self-improvement.

AMANDA: What reason have you to think so?

TOM: He goes to night school.

AMANDA: *(beaming)* Splendid! What does he do, I mean study?   115

TOM: Radio engineering and public speaking!

AMANDA: Then he has visions of being advanced in the world! Any young man who studies public speaking is aiming to have an executive job some day! And radio engineering? A thing for the future! Both of these facts are very illuminating. Those are the sort of things that a mother should know concerning any young man who comes to call on her daughter. Seriously or — not.

TOM: One little warning. He doesn't know about Laura. I didn't let on that we had dark ulterior motives. I just said, why don't you come have dinner with us? He said okay and that was the whole conversation.

AMANDA: I bet it was! You're eloquent as an oyster. However, he'll know about Laura when he gets here. When he sees how lovely and sweet and pretty she is, he'll thank his lucky stars he was asked to dinner.

TOM: Mother, you mustn't expect too much of Laura.   120

AMANDA: What do you mean?

TOM: Laura seems all those things to you and me because she's ours and we love her. We don't even notice she's crippled any more.

AMANDA: Don't say crippled! You know that I never allow that word to be used!

TOM: But face facts, Mother. She is and — that's not all—

AMANDA: What do you mean "not all"?   125

TOM: Laura is very different from other girls.

AMANDA: I think the difference is all to her advantage.

TOM: Not quite all — in the eyes of others — strangers — she's terribly shy and lives in a world of her own and those things make her seem a little peculiar to people outside the house.

AMANDA: Don't say peculiar.

TOM: Face the facts. She is.   130

The Dance-Hall Music Changes To A Tango That Has A Minor And Somewhat Ominous Tone.

AMANDA: In what way is she peculiar — may I ask?

TOM: *(gently)* She lives in a world of her own — a world of — little glass ornaments, Mother. . . . *(Gets up. Amanda remains holding brush, looking at him, troubled.)* She plays old phonograph records and — that's about all — *(He glances at himself in the mirror and crosses to door.)*

AMANDA: *(sharply)* Where are you going?

TOM: I'm going to the movies. *(Out screen door.)*

AMANDA: Not to the movies, every night to the movies! *(Follows quickly to   135 screen door.)* I don't believe you always go to the movies! *(He is gone. Amanda looks worriedly after him for a moment. Then vitality and optimism return and she turns from the door. Crossing to portieres.)* Laura! Laura! *(Laura answers from kitchenette.)*

LAURA: Yes, Mother.

AMANDA: Let those dishes go and come in front! *(Laura appears with dish towel. Gaily.)* Laura, come here and make a wish on the moon!

LAURA: *(entering)* Moon — moon?

AMANDA: A little silver slipper of a moon. Look over your left shoulder, Laura, and make a wish! *(Laura looks faintly puzzled as if called out of sleep. Amanda seizes her shoulders and turns her at an angle by the door.)* Now! Now, darling, wish!

140 LAURA: What shall I wish for, Mother?

AMANDA: *(her voice trembling and her eyes suddenly filling with tears)* Happiness! Good Fortune!

The violin rises and the stage dims out.

SCENE 6

Image: High-School Hero.

TOM: And so the following evening I brought Jim home to dinner. I had known Jim slightly in high school. In high school Jim was a hero. He had tremendous Irish good nature and vitality with the scrubbed and polished look of white chinaware. He seemed to move in a continual spotlight. He was a star in basketball, captain of the debating club, president of the senior class and the glee club and he sang the male lead in the annual light operas. He was always running or bounding, never just walking. He seemed always at the point of defeating the law of gravity. He was shooting with such velocity through his adolescence that you would logically expect him to arrive at nothing short of the White House by the time he was thirty. But Jim apparently ran into more interference after his graduation from Soldan. His speed had definitely slowed. Six years after he left high school he was holding a job that wasn't much better than mine.

Image: Clerk.

He was the only one at the warehouse with whom I was on friendly terms. I was valuable to him as someone who could remember his former glory, who had seen him win basketball games and the silver cup in debating. He knew of my secret practice of retiring to a cabinet of the washroom to work on poems when business was slack in the warehouse. He called me Shakespeare. And while the other boys in the warehouse regarded me with suspicious hostility, Jim took a humorous attitude toward me. Gradually his attitude affected the others, their hostility wore off and they also began to smile at me as people smile at an oddly fashioned dog who trots across their path at some distance.

I knew that Jim and Laura had known each other at Soldan, and I had heard Laura speak admiringly of his voice. I didn't know if Jim remembered her or not. In high school Laura had been as unobtrusive as Jim had been astonishing. If he did remember Laura, it was not as my sister, for when I asked him to dinner, he grinned and said, "You know, Shakespeare, I never thought of you as having folks!" He was about to discover that I did. . . .

Light Up Stage.

Legend On Screen: "The Accent Of A Coming Foot."

Friday evening. It is about five o'clock of a late spring evening which comes "scattering poems in the sky."
A delicate lemony light is in the Wingfield apartment.
Amanda has worked like a Turk in preparation for the gentleman caller. The results are astonishing. The new floor lamp with its rose-silk shade is in place, a colored paper lantern conceals the broken light fixture in the ceiling, new billowing white curtains are at the windows, chintz covers are on chairs and sofa, a pair of new sofa pillows make their initial appearance.
Open boxes and tissue paper are scattered on the floor.
Laura stands in the middle with lifted arms while Amanda crouches before her, adjusting the hem of the new dress, devout and ritualistic. The dress is colored and designed by memory. The arrangement of Laura's hair is changed; it is softer and more becoming. A fragile, unearthly prettiness has come out in Laura: she is like a piece of translucent glass touched by light, given a momentary radiance, not actual, not lasting.

AMANDA: (*impatiently*) Why are you trembling?
LAURA: Mother, you've made me so nervous!
AMANDA: How have I made you nervous?   5
LAURA: By all this fuss! You make it seem so important!
AMANDA: I don't understand you, Laura. You couldn't be satisfied with just sitting home, and yet whenever I try to arrange something for you, you seem to resist it. (*She gets up.*) Now take a look at yourself. No, wait! Wait just a moment — I have an idea!
LAURA: What is it now?

Amanda produces two powder puffs which she wraps in handkerchiefs and stuffs in Laura's bosom.

LAURA: Mother, what are you doing?
AMANDA: They call them "Gay Deceivers"!
LAURA: I won't wear them!   10
AMANDA: You will!
LAURA: Why should I?
AMANDA: Because, to be painfully honest, your chest is flat.
LAURA: You make it seem like we were setting a trap.

15 **AMANDA:** All pretty girls are a trap, a pretty trap, and men expect them to be. (*Legend: "A Pretty Trap."*) Now look at yourself, young lady. This is the prettiest you will ever be! I've got to fix myself now! You're going to be surprised by your mother's appearance! (*She crosses through portieres, humming gaily.*)

Laura moves slowly to the long mirror and stares solemnly at herself.
A wind blows the white curtains inward in a slow, graceful motion and with a faint, sorrowful sighing.

AMANDA: (*offstage*) It isn't dark enough yet. (*She turns slowly before the mirror with a troubled look.*)

Legend On Screen: "This Is My Sister: Celebrate Her With Strings!" Music.

AMANDA: (*laughing, off*) I'm going to show you something. I'm going to make a spectacular appearance!

LAURA: What is it, Mother?

AMANDA: Possess your soul in patience — you will see! Something I've resurrected from that old trunk! Styles haven't changed so terribly much after all. . . . (*She parts the portieres.*) Now just look at your mother! (*She wears a girlish frock of yellowed voile with a blue silk sash. She carries a bunch of jonquils — the legend of her youth is nearly revived. Feverishly.*) This is the dress in which I led the cotillion. Won the cakewalk twice at Sunset Hill, wore one spring to the Governor's ball in Jackson! See how I sashayed around the ballroom, Laura? (*She raises her skirt and does a mincing step around the room.*) I wore it on Sundays for my gentlemen callers! I had it on the day I met your father — I had malaria fever all that spring. The change of climate from East Tennessee to the Delta — weakened resistance — I had a little temperature all the time — not enough to be serious — just enough to make me restless and giddy! Invitations poured in — parties all over the Delta! — "Stay in bed," said Mother, "you have fever!" — but I just wouldn't. — I took quinine but kept on going, going! — Evenings, dances! — Afternoons, long, long rides! Picnics — lovely! — So lovely, that country in May. All lacy with dogwood, literally flooded with jonquils! — That was the spring I had the craze for jonquils. Jonquils became an absolute obsession. Mother said, "Honey, there's no more room for jonquils." And still I kept bringing in more jonquils. Whenever, wherever I saw them, I'd say, "Stop! Stop! I see jonquils!" I made the young men help me gather the jonquils! It was a joke, Amanda and her jonquils! Finally there were no more vases to hold them, every available space was filled with jonquils. No vases to hold them? All right, I'll hold them myself! And then I — (*She stops in front of the picture.*) (*Music*) met your father! Malaria fever and jonquils and then — this — boy. . . . (*She switches on the rose-colored lamp.*) I hope they get here before it starts to rain. (*She crosses upstage and places the jonquils in bowl on table.*) I gave

your brother a little extra change so he and Mr. O'Connor could take the
service car home.

LAURA: *(with altered look)* What did you say his name was?   20

AMANDA: O'Connor.

LAURA: What is his first name?

AMANDA: I don't remember. Oh, yes, I do. It was — Jim!

Laura sways slightly and catches hold of a chair.

Legend On Screen: "Not Jim!"

LAURA: *(faintly)* Not — Jim!

AMANDA: Yes, that was it, it was Jim! I've never known a Jim that wasn't nice!   25

Music: Ominous.

LAURA: Are you sure his name is Jim O'Connor?

AMANDA: Yes. Why?

LAURA: Is he the one that Tom used to know in high school?

AMANDA: He didn't say so. I think he just got to know him at the warehouse.

LAURA: There was a Jim O'Connor we both knew in high school — *(Then,*   30
with effort.) If that is the one that Tom is bringing to dinner — you'll have
to excuse me, I won't come to the table.

AMANDA: What sort of nonsense is this?

LAURA: You asked me once if I'd ever liked a boy. Don't you remember I
showed you this boy's picture?

AMANDA: You mean the boy you showed me in the year book?

LAURA: Yes, that boy.

AMANDA: Laura, Laura, were you in love with that boy?   35

LAURA: I don't know, Mother. All I know is I couldn't sit at the table if it
was him!

AMANDA: It won't be him! It isn't the least bit likely. But whether it is or not,
you will come to the table. You will not be excused.

LAURA: I'll have to be, Mother.

AMANDA: I don't intend to humor your silliness, Laura. I've had too much
from you and your brother, both! So just sit down and compose yourself till
they come. Tom has forgotten his key so you'll have to let them in, when
they arrive.

LAURA: *(panicky)* Oh, Mother —*you* answer the door!   40

AMANDA: *(lightly)* I'll be in the kitchen — busy!

LAURA: Oh, Mother, please answer the door, don't make me do it!

AMANDA: *(crossing into kitchenette)* I've got to fix the dressing for the salmon.
Fuss, fuss — silliness! — over a gentleman caller!

Door swings shut. Laura is left alone.

Legend: "Terror!"

She utters a low moan and turns off the lamp — sits stiffly on the edge of the sofa, knotting her fingers together.

Legend On Screen: "The Opening Of A Door!"

Tom and Jim appear on the fire-escape steps and climb to landing. Hearing their approach, Laura rises with a panicky gesture. She retreats to the portieres.
    The doorbell. Laura catches her breath and touches her throat. Low drums.

AMANDA: *(calling)* Laura, sweetheart! The door!

Laura stares at it without moving.

45 **JIM:** I think we just beat the rain.
TOM: Uh-huh. *(He rings again, nervously. Jim whistles and fishes for a cigarette.)*
AMANDA: *(very, very gaily)* Laura, that is your brother and Mr. O'Connor!
    Will you let them in, darling?

Laura crosses toward kitchenette door.

LAURA: *(breathlessly)* Mother — you go to the door!

Amanda steps out of kitchenette and stares furiously at Laura. She points imperiously at the door.

LAURA: Please, please!
50 **AMANDA:** *(in a fierce whisper)* What is the matter with you, you silly thing?
LAURA: *(desperately)* Please, you answer it, *please!*
AMANDA: I told you I wasn't going to humor you, Laura. Why have you chosen this moment to lose your mind?
LAURA: Please, please, please, you go!
AMANDA: You'll have to go to the door because I can't!
55 **LAURA:** *(despairingly)* I can't either!
AMANDA: Why?
LAURA: I'm *sick!*
AMANDA: I'm sick, too — of your nonsense! Why can't you and your brother be normal people? Fantastic whims and behavior! *(Tom gives a long ring.)* Preposterous goings on! Can you give me one reason — *(Calls out lyrically.)* COMING! JUST ONE SECOND! — why should you be afraid to open a door? Now you answer it, Laura!
LAURA: Oh, oh, oh . . . *(She returns through the portieres. Darts to the Victrola and winds it frantically and turns it on.)*
60 **AMANDA:** Laura Wingfield, you march right to that door!
LAURA: Yes — yes, Mother!

A faraway, scratchy rendition of "Dardanella" softens the air and gives her strength to move through it. She slips to the door and draws it cautiously open. Tom enters with the caller, Jim O'Connor.

TOM: Laura, this is Jim. Jim, this is my sister, Laura.

JIM: *(stepping inside)* I didn't know that Shakespeare had a sister!
LAURA: *(retreating stiff and trembling from the door)* How — how do you do?
JIM: *(heartily extending his hand)* Okay!   65

Laura touches it hesitantly with hers.

JIM: Your hand's *cold*, Laura!
LAURA: Yes, well — I've been playing the Victrola. . . .
JIM: Must have been playing classical music on it! You ought to play a little hot
swing music to warm you up!
LAURA: Excuse me — I haven't finished playing the Victrola. . . .

*She turns awkwardly and hurries into the front room. She pauses a second by the
Victrola. Then catches her breath and darts through the portieres like a frightened deer.*

JIM: *(grinning)* What was the matter?   70
TOM: Oh — with Laura? Laura is — terribly shy.
JIM: Shy, huh? It's unusual to meet a shy girl nowadays. I don't believe you ever
mentioned you had a sister.
TOM: Well, now you know. I have one. Here is the *Post Dispatch*. You want a
piece of it?
JIM: Uh-huh.
TOM: What piece? The comics?   75
JIM: Sports! *(Glances at it.)* Ole Dizzy Dean° is on his bad behavior.
TOM: *(disinterested)* Yeah? *(Lights cigarette and crosses back to fire-escape door.)*
JIM: Where are *you* going?
TOM: I'm going out on the terrace.
JIM: *(goes after him)* You know, Shakespeare — I'm going to sell you a bill of   80
goods!
TOM: What goods?
JIM: A course I'm taking.
TOM: Huh?
JIM: In public speaking! You and me, we're not the warehouse type.
TOM: Thanks — that's good news. But what has public speaking got to do   85
with it?
JIM: It fits you for — executive positions!
TOM: Awww.
JIM: I tell you it's done a helluva lot for me.

Image: Executive At Desk.

TOM: In what respect?

°*Dizzy Dean:* Jay Hanna Dean (1910–1974), American baseball player who pitched for the St. Louis Cardinals
(1930, 1932–1937), winning 30 games in 1934 and averaging 24 wins in his first five full seasons. From 1938 to
1941, he played for the Chicago Cubs.

90 JIM: In every! Ask yourself what is the difference between you an' me and men
        in the office down front? Brains?— No!— Ability?— No! Then what? Just
        one little thing—

    TOM: What is that one little thing?

    JIM: Primarily it amounts to — social poise! Being able to square up to people
        and hold your own on any social level!

    AMANDA: (offstage) Tom?

    TOM: Yes, Mother?

95 AMANDA: Is that you and Mr. O'Connor?

    TOM: Yes, Mother.

    AMANDA: Well, you just make yourselves comfortable in there.

    TOM: Yes, Mother.

    AMANDA: Ask Mr. O'Connor if he would like to wash his hands.

100 JIM: Aw — no — thank you — I took care of that at the warehouse. Tom—

    TOM: Yes?

    JIM: Mr. Mendoza was speaking to me about you.

    TOM: Favorably?

    JIM: What do you think?

105 TOM: Well—

    JIM: You're going to be out of a job if you don't wake up.

    TOM: I am waking up—

    JIM: You show no signs.

    TOM: The signs are interior.

Image On Screen: The Sailing Vessel With Jolly Roger Again.

110 TOM: I'm planning to change. (*He leans over the rail speaking with quiet exhilara-
        tion. The incandescent marquees and signs of the first-run movie houses light his
        face from across the alley. He looks like a voyager.*) I'm right at the point of
        committing myself to a future that doesn't include the warehouse and
        Mr. Mendoza or even a night-school course in public speaking.

    JIM: What are you gassing about?

    TOM: I'm tired of the movies.

    JIM: Movies!

    TOM: Yes, movies! Look at them — (*A wave toward the marvels of Grand Avenue.*)
        All of those glamorous people — having adventures — hogging it all, gobbling
        the whole thing up! You know what happens? People go to the *movies instead
        of moving!* Hollywood characters are supposed to have all the adventures for
        everybody in America, while everybody in America sits in a dark room and
        watches them have them! Yes, until there's a war. That's when adventure
        becomes available to the masses! *Everyone's* dish, not only Gable's! Then the
        people in the dark room come out of the dark room to have some adventures
        themselves — Goody, goody — It's our turn now, to go to the South Sea
        Island — to make a safari — to be exotic, far-off — But I'm not patient. I don't
        want to wait till then. I'm tired of the *movies* and I am *about* to move!

JIM: (*incredulously*) Move?   115
TOM: Yes.
JIM: When?
TOM: Soon!
JIM: Where? Where?

Theme three music seems to answer the question, while Tom thinks it over. He searches among his pockets.

TOM: I'm starting to boil inside. I know I seem dreary, but inside — well, I'm   120
     boiling! Whenever I pick up a shoe, I shudder a little thinking how short
     life is and what I am doing! — Whatever that means. I know it doesn't
     mean shoes — except as something to wear on a traveler's feet! (*Finds
     paper.*) Look —
JIM: What?
TOM: I'm a member.
JIM: (*reading*) The Union of Merchant Seamen.
TOM: I paid my dues this month, instead of the light bill.
JIM: You will regret it when they turn the lights off.   125
TOM: I won't be here.
JIM: How about your mother?
TOM: I'm like my father. The bastard son of a bastard! See how he grins? And
     he's been absent going on sixteen years!
JIM: You're just talking, you drip. How does your mother feel about it?
TOM: Shhh — Here comes Mother! Mother is not acquainted with my plans!   130
AMANDA: (*enters portieres*) Where are you all?
TOM: On the terrace, Mother.

They start inside. She advances to them. Tom is distinctly shocked at her appearance. Even Jim blinks a little. He is making his first contact with girlish Southern vivacity and in spite of the night-school course in public speaking is somewhat thrown off the beam by the unexpected outlay of social charm.

Certain responses are attempted by Jim but are swept aside by Amanda's gay laugh-ter and chatter. Tom is embarrassed but after the first shock Jim reacts very warmly. Grins and chuckles, is altogether won over.

Image: Amanda As A Girl.

AMANDA: (*coyly smiling, shaking her girlish ringlets*) Well, well, well, so this is
     Mr. O'Connor. Introductions entirely unnecessary. I've heard so much
     about you from my boy. I finally said to him, Tom — good gracious! — why
     don't you bring this paragon to supper? I'd like to meet this nice young man
     at the warehouse! — Instead of just hearing him sing your praises so much!
     I don't know why my son is so stand-offish — that's not Southern behavior!
     Let's sit down and — I think we could stand a little more air in here! Tom,
     leave the door open. I felt a nice fresh breeze a moment ago. Where has it

gone? Mmm, so warm already! And not quite summer, even. We're going to burn up when summer really gets started. However, we're having — we're having a very light supper. I think light things are better fo' this time of year. The same as light clothes are. Light clothes an' light food are what warm weather calls fo'. You know our blood gets so thick during th' winter — it takes a while fo' us to *adjust* ou'selves! — when the season changes . . . It's come so quick this year. I wasn't prepared. All of a sudden — heavens! Already summer! — I ran to the trunk an' pulled out this light dress — Terribly old! Historical almost! But feels so good — so good an' co-ol, y'know. . . .

TOM: Mother —

135   AMANDA: Yes, honey?

TOM: How about — supper?

AMANDA: Honey, you go ask Sister if supper is ready! You know that Sister is in full charge of supper! Tell her you hungry boys are waiting for it. (*To Jim.*) Have you met Laura?

JIM: She —

AMANDA: Let you in? Oh, good, you've met already! It's rare for a girl as sweet an' pretty as Laura to be domestic! But Laura is, thank heavens, not only pretty but also very domestic. I'm not at all. I never was a bit. I never could make a thing but angel-food cake. Well, in the South we had so many servants. Gone, gone, gone. All vestiges of gracious living! Gone completely! I wasn't prepared for what the future brought me. All of my gentlemen callers were sons of planters and so of course I assumed that I would be married to one and raise my family on a large piece of land with plenty of servants. But man proposes — and woman accepts the proposal! — To vary that old, old saying a little bit — I married no planter! I married a man who worked for the telephone company! — that gallantly smiling gentleman over there! (*Points to the picture.*) A telephone man who — fell in love with long-distance! — Now he travels and I don't even know where! — But what am I going on for about my — tribulations? Tell me yours — I hope you don't have any! Tom?

140   TOM: (*returning*) Yes, Mother?

AMANDA: Is supper nearly ready?

TOM: It looks to me like supper is on the table.

AMANDA: Let me look — (*She rises prettily and looks through portieres.*) Oh, lovely — But where is Sister?

TOM: Laura is not feeling well and says that she thinks she'd better not come to the table.

145   AMANDA: What? — Nonsense! — Laura? Oh, Laura!

LAURA: (*offstage, faintly*) Yes, Mother.

AMANDA: You really must come to the table. We won't be seated until you come to the table! Come in, Mr. O'Connor. You sit over there and I'll — Laura? Laura Wingfield! You're keeping us waiting, honey! We can't say grace until you come to the table!

The back door is pushed weakly open and Laura comes in. She is obviously quite faint, her lips trembling, her eyes wide and staring. She moves unsteadily toward the table.

Legend: "Terror!"

Outside a summer storm is coming abruptly. The white curtains billow inward at the windows and there is a sorrowful murmur and deep blue dusk.
Laura suddenly stumbles — She catches at a chair with a faint moan.

TOM: Laura!
AMANDA: Laura! *(There is a clap of thunder.) (Legend: "Ah!") (Despairingly.)* Why, Laura, you are sick, darling! Tom, help your sister into the living room, dear! Sit in the living room, Laura — rest on the sofa. Well! *(To the gentleman caller.)* Standing over the hot stove made her ill! — I told her that it was just too warm this evening, but — *(Tom comes back in. Laura is on the sofa.)* Is Laura all right now?
TOM: Yes.   150
AMANDA: What is that? Rain? A nice cool rain has come up! *(She gives the gentleman caller a frightened look.)* I think we may — have grace — now . . . *(Tom looks at her stupidly.)* Tom, honey — you say grace!
TOM: Oh . . . "For these and all thy mercies —" *(They bow their heads, Amanda stealing a nervous glance at Jim. In the living room Laura, stretched on the sofa, clenches her hand to her lips, to hold back a shuddering sob.)* God's Holy Name be praised —

The Scene Dims Out.

SCENE 7

A Souvenir.

Half an hour later. Dinner is just being finished in the upstage area which is concealed by the drawn portieres.
    As the curtain rises Laura is still huddled upon the sofa, her feet drawn under her, her head resting on a pale blue pillow, her eyes wide and mysteriously watchful. The new floor lamp with its shade of rose-colored silk gives a soft, becoming light to her face, bringing out the fragile, unearthly prettiness which usually escapes attention. There is a steady murmur of rain, but it is slackening and stops soon after the scene begins; the air outside becomes pale and luminous as the moon breaks out.
    A moment after the curtain rises, the lights in both rooms flicker and go out.

JIM: Hey, there, Mr. Light Bulb!

Amanda laughs nervously.

Legend: "Suspension Of A Public Service."

AMANDA: Where was Moses when the lights went out? Ha-ha. Do you know the answer to that one, Mr. O'Connor?

JIM: No, Ma'am, what's the answer?

AMANDA: In the dark! (*Jim laughs appreciatively.*) Everybody sit still. I'll light the candles. Isn't it lucky we have them on the table? Where's a match? Which of you gentlemen can provide a match?

5 JIM: Here.

AMANDA: Thank you, sir.

JIM: Not at all, Ma'am!

AMANDA: I guess the fuse has burnt out. Mr. O'Connor, can you tell a burnt-out fuse? I know I can't and Tom is a total loss when it comes to mechanics. (*Sound: Getting Up: Voices Recede A Little To Kitchenette.*) Oh, be careful you don't bump into something. We don't want our gentleman caller to break his neck. Now wouldn't that be a fine howdy-do?

JIM: Ha-ha! Where is the fuse-box?

10 AMANDA: Right here next to the stove. Can you see anything?

JIM: Just a minute.

AMANDA: Isn't electricity a mysterious thing? Wasn't it Benjamin Franklin who tied a key to a kite? We live in such a mysterious universe, don't we? Some people say that science clears up all the mysteries for us. In my opinion it only creates more! Have you found it yet?

JIM: No, Ma'am. All these fuses look okay to me.

AMANDA: Tom!

15 TOM: Yes, Mother?

AMANDA: That light bill I gave you several days ago. The one I told you we got the notices about?

TOM: Oh.—Yeah.

Legend: "Ha!"

AMANDA: You didn't neglect to pay it by any chance?

TOM: Why, I—

20 AMANDA: Didn't! I might have known it!

JIM: Shakespeare probably wrote a poem on that light bill, Mrs. Wingfield.

AMANDA: I might have known better than to trust him with it! There's such a high price for negligence in this world!

JIM: Maybe the poem will win a ten-dollar prize.

AMANDA: We'll just have to spend the remainder of the evening in the nineteenth century, before Mr. Edison made the Mazda lamp!

25 JIM: Candlelight is my favorite kind of light.

AMANDA: That shows you're romantic! But that's no excuse for Tom. Well, we got through dinner. Very considerate of them to let us get through dinner before they plunged us into everlasting darkness, wasn't it, Mr. O'Connor?

JIM: Ha-ha!

AMANDA: Tom, as a penalty for your carelessness you can help me with the dishes.

JIM: Let me give you a hand.

AMANDA: Indeed you will not! 30

JIM: I ought to be good for something.

AMANDA: Good for something? (*Her tone is rhapsodic.*) *You?* Why, Mr. O'Connor, nobody, *nobody's* given me this much entertainment in years — as you have!

JIM: Aw, now, Mrs. Wingfield!

AMANDA: I'm not exaggerating, not one bit! But Sister is all by her lonesome. You go keep her company in the parlor! I'll give you this lovely old candelabrum that used to be on the altar at the church of the Heavenly Rest. It was melted a little out of shape when the church burnt down. Lightning struck it one spring. Gypsy Jones was holding a revival at the time and he intimated that the church was destroyed because the Episcopalians gave card parties.

JIM: Ha-ha. 35

AMANDA: And how about coaxing Sister to drink a little wine? I think it would be good for her! Can you carry both at once?

JIM: Sure. I'm Superman!

AMANDA: Now, Thomas, get into this apron!

The door of kitchenette swings closed on Amanda's gay laughter; the flickering light approaches the portieres.

Laura sits up nervously as he enters. Her speech at first is low and breathless from the almost intolerable strain of being alone with a stranger.

The Legend: "I Don't Suppose You Remember Me At All!"

In her first speeches in this scene, before Jim's warmth overcomes her paralyzing shyness, Laura's voice is thin and breathless as though she has run up a steep flight of stairs.

Jim's attitude is gently humorous. In playing this scene it should be stressed that while the incident is apparently unimportant, it is to Laura the climax of her secret life.

JIM: Hello, there, Laura.

LAURA: (*faintly*) Hello. (*She clears her throat.*) 40

JIM: How are you feeling now? Better?

LAURA: Yes. Yes, thank you.

JIM: This is for you. A little dandelion wine. (*He extends it toward her with extravagant gallantry.*)

LAURA: Thank you.

JIM: Drink it — but don't get drunk! (*He laughs heartily. Laura takes the glass uncertainly; laughs shyly.*) Where shall I set the candles? 45

LAURA: Oh — oh, anywhere . . .

JIM: How about here on the floor? Any objections?

LAURA: No.

JIM: I'll spread a newspaper under to catch the drippings. I like to sit on the floor. Mind if I do?

50   **Laura:**   Oh, no.
Jim: Give me a pillow?
Laura: What?
Jim: A pillow!
Laura: Oh . . . (*Hands him one quickly.*)
55   **Jim:**   How about you? Don't you like to sit on the floor?
Laura: Oh — yes.
Jim: Why don't you, then?
Laura: I — will.
Jim: Take a pillow! (*Laura does. Sits on the other side of the candelabrum. Jim crosses his legs and smiles engagingly at her.*) I can't hardly see you sitting way over there.
60   **Laura:**   I can — see you.
Jim: I know, but that's not fair, I'm in the limelight. (*Laura moves her pillow closer.*) Good! Now I can see you! Comfortable?
Laura: Yes.
Jim: So am I. Comfortable as a cow. Will you have some gum?
Laura: No, thank you.
65   **Jim:**   I think that I will indulge, with your permission. (*Musingly unwraps it and holds it up.*) Think of the fortune made by the guy that invented the first piece of chewing gum. Amazing, huh? The Wrigley Building is one of the sights of Chicago. — I saw it summer before last when I went up to the Century of Progress. Did you take in the Century of Progress?
Laura: No, I didn't.
Jim: Well, it was quite a wonderful exposition. What impressed me most was the Hall of Science. Gives you an idea of what the future will be in America, even more wonderful than the present time is! (*Pause. Smiling at her.*) Your brother tells me you're shy. Is that right, Laura?
Laura: I — don't know.
Jim: I judge you to be an old-fashioned type of girl. Well, I think that's a pretty good type to be. Hope you don't think I'm being too personal — do you?
70   **Laura:**   (*hastily, out of embarrassment*) I believe I *will* take a piece of gum, if you — don't mind. (*Clearing her throat.*) Mr. O'Connor, have you — kept up with your singing?
Jim: Singing? Me?
Laura: Yes. I remember what a beautiful voice you had.
Jim: When did you hear me sing?

Voice Offstage In The Pause.

Voice (*offstage*):

> O blow, ye winds, heigh-ho,
> A-roving I will go!
> I'm off to my love
> With a boxing glove —
> Ten thousand miles away!

JIM: You say you've heard me sing?

LAURA: Oh, yes! Yes, very often . . . I — don't suppose you remember   75
me — at all?

JIM: (*smiling doubtfully*) You know I have an idea I've seen you before. I had
that idea soon as you opened the door. It seemed almost like I was about to
remember your name. But the name that I started to call you — wasn't a
name! And so I stopped myself before I said it.

LAURA: Wasn't it — Blue Roses?

JIM: (*springs up, grinning*) Blue Roses! My gosh, yes — Blue Roses! That's what
I had on my tongue when you opened the door! Isn't it funny what tricks
your memory plays? I didn't connect you with the high school somehow or
other. But that's where it was; it was high school. I didn't even know you
were Shakespeare's sister! Gosh, I'm sorry.

LAURA: I didn't expect you to. You — barely knew me!

JIM: But we did have a speaking acquaintance, huh?   80

LAURA: Yes, we — spoke to each other.

JIM: When did you recognize me?

LAURA: Oh, right away!

JIM: Soon as I came in the door?

LAURA: When I heard your name I thought it was probably you. I knew that   85
Tom used to know you a little in high school. So when you came in the
door — Well, then I was — sure.

JIM: Why didn't you *say* something, then?

LAURA: (*breathlessly*) I didn't know what to say, I was — too surprised!

JIM: For goodness' sakes! You know, this sure is funny!

LAURA: Yes! Yes, isn't it, though . . .

JIM: Didn't we have a class in something together?   90

LAURA: Yes, we did.

JIM: What class was that?

LAURA: It was — singing — Chorus!

JIM: Aw!

LAURA: I sat across the aisle from you in the Aud.   95

JIM: Aw.

LAURA: Mondays, Wednesdays and Fridays.

JIM: Now I remember — you always came in late.

LAURA: Yes, it was so hard for me, getting upstairs. I had that brace on my
leg — it clumped so loud!

JIM: I never heard any clumping.   100

LAURA: (*wincing at the recollection*) To me it sounded like — thunder!

JIM: Well, well, well. I never even noticed.

LAURA: And everybody was seated before I came in. I had to walk in front of
all those people. My seat was in the back row. I had to go clumping all the
way up the aisle with everyone watching!

JIM: You shouldn't have been self-conscious.

105 LAURA: I know, but I was. It was always such a relief when the singing started.

JIM: Aw, yes, I've placed you now! I used to call you Blue Roses. How was it that I got started calling you that?

LAURA: I was out of school a little while with pleurosis. When I came back you asked me what was the matter. I said I had pleurosis — you thought I said Blue Roses. That's what you always called me after that!

JIM: I hope you didn't mind.

LAURA: Oh, no — I liked it. You see, I wasn't acquainted with many — people. . . .

110 JIM: As I remember you sort of stuck by yourself.

LAURA: I — I — never had much luck at — making friends.

JIM: I don't see why you wouldn't.

LAURA: Well, I — started out badly.

JIM: You mean being —

115 LAURA: Yes, it sort of — stood between me —

JIM: You shouldn't have let it!

LAURA: I know, but it did, and —

JIM: You were shy with people!

LAURA: I tried not to be but never could —

120 JIM: Overcome it?

LAURA: No, I — I never could!

JIM: I guess being shy is something you have to work out of kind of gradually.

LAURA: (sorrowfully) Yes — I guess it —

JIM: Takes time!

125 LAURA: Yes —

JIM: People are not so dreadful when you know them. That's what you have to remember! And everybody has problems, not just you, but practically everybody has got some problems. You think of yourself as having the only problems, as being the only one who is disappointed. But just look around you and you will see lots of people as disappointed as you are. For instance, I hoped when I was going to high school that I would be further along at this time, six years later, than I am now — You remember that wonderful write-up I had in *The Torch?*

LAURA: Yes! (*She rises and crosses to table.*)

JIM: It said I was bound to succeed in anything I went into! (*Laura returns with the annual.*) Holy Jeez! *The Torch!* (*He accepts it reverently. They smile across it with mutual wonder. Laura crouches beside him and they begin to turn through it. Laura's shyness is dissolving in his warmth.*)

LAURA: Here you are in *Pirates of Penzance!*

130 JIM: (*wistfully*) I sang the baritone lead in that operetta.

LAURA: (*rapidly*) So — beautifully!

JIM: (*protesting*) Aw —

LAURA: Yes, yes — beautifully — beautifully!

JIM: You heard me?

LAURA: All three times!   135
JIM: No!
LAURA: Yes!
JIM: All three performances?
LAURA: (*looking down*) Yes.
JIM: Why?   140
LAURA: I — wanted to ask you to — autograph my program.
JIM: Why didn't you ask me to?
LAURA: You were always surrounded by your own friends so much that I never
 had a chance to.
JIM: You should have just —
LAURA: Well, I — thought you might think I was —   145
JIM: Thought I might think you was — what?
LAURA: Oh —
JIM: (*with reflective relish*) I was beleaguered by females in those days.
LAURA: You were terribly popular!
JIM: Yeah —   150
LAURA: You had such a — friendly way —
JIM: I was spoiled in high school.
LAURA: Everybody — liked you!
JIM: Including you?
LAURA: I — yes, I — I did, too — (*She gently closes the book in her lap.*)   155
JIM: Well, well, well! — Give me that program, Laura. (*She hands it to him.
 He signs it with a flourish.*) There you are — better late than never!
LAURA: Oh, I — what a — surprise!
JIM: My signature isn't worth very much right now. But some
 day — maybe — it will increase in value! Being disappointed is one
 thing and being discouraged is something else. I am disappointed but
 I'm not discouraged. I'm twenty-three years old. How old are you?
LAURA: I'll be twenty-four in June.
JIM: That's not old age!   160
LAURA: No, but —
JIM: You finished high school?
LAURA: (*with difficulty*) I didn't go back.
JIM: You mean you dropped out?
LAURA: I made bad grades in my final examinations. (*She rises and replaces the*   165
 book and the program. Her voice strained.) How is — Emily Meisenbach
 getting along?
JIM: Oh, that kraut-head!
LAURA: Why do you call her that?
JIM: That's what she was.
LAURA: You're not still — going with her?
JIM: I never see her.   170
LAURA: It said in the Personal Section that you were — engaged!

Jim: I know, but I wasn't impressed by that — propaganda!
Laura: It wasn't — the truth?
Jim: Only in Emily's optimistic opinion!
175 **Laura:** Oh—

Legend: "What Have You Done Since High School?"

Jim lights a cigarette and leans indolently back on his elbows smiling at Laura with a warmth and charm which light her inwardly with altar candles. She remains by the table and turns in her hands a piece of glass to cover her tumult.

Jim: *(after several reflective puffs on a cigarette)* What have you done since high school? *(She seems not to hear him.)* Huh? *(Laura looks up.)* I said what have you done since high school, Laura?
Laura: Nothing much.
Jim: You must have been doing something these six long years.
Laura: Yes.
180 **Jim:** Well, then, such as what?
Laura: I took a business course at business college—
Jim: How did that work out?

Laura: Well, not very — well — I had to drop out, it gave me — indigestion—

Jim laughs gently.

Jim: What are you doing now?
185 **Laura:** I don't do anything — much. Oh, please don't think I sit around doing nothing! My glass collection takes up a good deal of my time. Glass is something you have to take good care of.
Jim: What did you say — about glass?
Laura: Collection I said — I have one — *(She clears her throat and turns away again, acutely shy.)*
Jim: *(abruptly)* You know what I judge to be the trouble with you? Inferiority complex! Know what that is? That's what they call it when someone low-rates himself! I understand it because I had it, too. Although my case was not so aggravated as yours seems to be. I had it until I took up public speaking, developed my voice, and learned that I had an aptitude for science. Before that time I never thought of myself as being outstanding in any way whatsoever! Now I've never made a regular study of it, but I have a friend who says I can analyze people better than doctors that make a profession of it. I don't claim that to be necessarily true, but I can sure guess a person's psychology, Laura! *(Takes out his gum.)* Excuse me, Laura. I always take it out when the flavor is gone. I'll use this scrap of paper to wrap it in. I know how it is to get it stuck on a shoe. Yep — that's what I judge to be your principal trouble. A lack of confidence in yourself as a person. You don't have the proper amount of faith in yourself. I'm basing that fact on a number of your remarks and also on certain observations I've made. For instance that

clumping you thought was so awful in high school. You say that you even dreaded to walk into class. You see what you did? You dropped out of school, you gave up an education because of a clump, which as far as I know was practically nonexistent! A little physical defect is what you have. Hardly noticeable even! Magnified thousands of times by imagination! You know what my strong advice to you is? Think of yourself as *superior* in some way!

LAURA: In what way would I think?

JIM: Why, man alive, Laura! Just look about you a little. What do you see? A   190
world full of common people! All of 'em born and all of 'em going to die! Which of them has one-tenth of your good points! Or mine! Or anyone else's, as far as that goes — Gosh! Everybody excels in some one thing. Some in many! (*Unconsciously glances at himself in the mirror.*) All you've got to do is discover in *what*! Take me, for instance. (*He adjusts his tie at the mirror.*) My interest happens to lie in electro-dynamics. I'm taking a course in radio engineering at night school, Laura, on top of a fairly responsible job at the warehouse. I'm taking that course and studying public speaking.

LAURA: Ohhhh.

JIM: Because I believe in the future of television! (*Turning back to her.*) I wish to be ready to go up right along with it. Therefore I'm planning to get in on the ground floor. In fact, I've already made the right connections and all that remains is for the industry itself to get underway! Full steam — (*His eyes are starry.*) Knowledge— Zzzzzp! Money— Zzzzzzp! —Power! That's the cycle democracy is built on! (*His attitude is convincingly dynamic. Laura stares at him, even her shyness eclipsed in her absolute wonder. He suddenly grins.*) I guess you think I think a lot of myself!

LAURA: No — o-o-o, I—

JIM: Now how about you? Isn't there something you take more interest in than anything else?

LAURA: Well, I do — as I said —have my — glass collection—   195

A peal of girlish laughter from the kitchen.

JIM: I'm not right sure I know what you're talking about. What kind of glass is it?

LAURA: Little articles of it, they're ornaments mostly! Most of them are little animals made out of glass, the tiniest little animals in the world. Mother calls them a glass menagerie! Here's an example of one, if you'd like to see it! This one is one of the oldest. It's nearly thirteen. (*He stretches out his hand.*) (*Music: "The Glass Menagerie."*) Oh, be careful —if you breathe, it breaks!

JIM: I'd better not take it. I'm pretty clumsy with things.

LAURA: Go on, I trust you with him! (*Places it in his palm.*) There now — you're holding him gently! Hold him over the light, he loves the light! You see how the light shines through him?

JIM: It sure does shine!   200

LAURA: I shouldn't be partial, but he is my favorite one.

JIM: What kind of a thing is this one supposed to be?

LAURA: Haven't you noticed the single horn on his forehead?

JIM: A unicorn, huh?

205 LAURA: Mmm-hmmm!

JIM: Unicorns, aren't they extinct in the modern world?

LAURA: I know!

JIM: Poor little fellow, he must feel sort of lonesome.

LAURA: (*smiling*) Well, if he does he doesn't complain about it. He stays on a shelf with some horses that don't have horns and all of them seem to get along nicely together.

210 JIM: How do you know?

LAURA: (*lightly*) I haven't heard any arguments among them!

JIM: (*grinning*) No arguments, huh? Well, that's a pretty good sign! Where shall I set him?

LAURA: Put him on the table. They all like a change of scenery once in a while!

JIM: (*stretching*) Well, well, well, well — Look how big my shadow is when I stretch!

215 LAURA: Oh, oh, yes — it stretches across the ceiling!

JIM: (*crossing to door*) I think it's stopped raining. (*Opens fire-escape door.*) Where does the music come from?

LAURA: From the Paradise Dance Hall across the alley.

JIM: How about cutting the rug a little, Miss Wingfield?

LAURA: Oh, I—

220 JIM: Or is your program filled up? Let me have a look at it. (*Grasps imaginary card.*) Why, every dance is taken! I'll just have to scratch some out. (*Waltz Music: "La Golondrina."*) Ahhh, a waltz! (*He executes some sweeping turns by himself, then holds his arms toward Laura.*)

LAURA: (*breathlessly*) I — can't dance!

JIM: There you go, that inferiority stuff!

LAURA: I've never danced in my life!

JIM: Come on, try!

225 LAURA: Oh, but I'd step on you!

JIM: I'm not made out of glass.

LAURA: How — how — how do we start?

JIM: Just leave it to me. You hold your arms out a little.

LAURA: Like this?

230 JIM: A little bit higher. Right. Now don't tighten up, that's the main thing about it — relax.

LAURA: (*laughing breathlessly*) It's hard not to.

JIM: Okay.

LAURA: I'm afraid you can't budge me.

JIM: What do you bet I can't? (*He swings her into motion.*)

235 LAURA: Goodness, yes, you can!

JIM: Let yourself go, now, Laura, just let yourself go.

LAURA: I'm—

JIM: Come on!

LAURA: Trying!

JIM: Not so stiff — Easy does it!   240

LAURA: I know but I'm —

JIM: Loosen th' backbone! There now, that's a lot better.

LAURA: Am I?

JIM: Lots, lots better! (*He moves her about the room in a clumsy waltz.*)

LAURA: Oh, my!   245

JIM: Ha-ha!

LAURA: Goodness, yes you can!

JIM: Ha-ha-ha! (*They suddenly bump into the table, Jim stops.*) What did we hit on?

LAURA: Table.

JIM: Did something fall off it? I think —   250

LAURA: Yes.

JIM: I hope that it wasn't the little glass horse with the horn!

LAURA: Yes.

JIM: Aw, aw, aw. Is it broken?

LAURA: Now it is just like all the other horses.   255

JIM: It's lost its —

LAURA: Horn! It doesn't matter. Maybe it's a blessing in disguise.

JIM: You'll never forgive me. I bet that that was your favorite piece of glass.

Laura in the arms of the gentleman caller while Tom and Amanda look on in Tennessee Williams's *The Glass Menagerie* presented in 1956 at the Williamstown Theatre festival.

LAURA: I don't have favorites much. It's no tragedy, Freckles. Glass breaks so easily. No matter how careful you are. The traffic jars the shelves and things fall off them.

260 JIM: Still I'm awfully sorry that I was the cause.

LAURA: *(smiling)* I'll just imagine he had an operation. The horn was removed to make him feel less — freakish! *(They both laugh.)* Now he will feel more at home with the other horses, the ones that don't have horns . . .

JIM: Ha-ha, that's very funny! *(Suddenly serious.)* I'm glad to see that you have a sense of humor. You know — you're — well — very different! Surprisingly different from anyone else I know! *(His voice becomes soft and hesitant with a genuine feeling.)* Do you mind me telling you that? *(Laura is abashed beyond speech.)* You make me feel sort of — I don't know how to put it! I'm usually pretty good at expressing things, but — This is something that I don't know how to say! *(Laura touches her throat and clears it — turns the broken unicorn in her hands.)* *(Even softer.)* Has anyone ever told you that you were pretty? *(Pause: Music.)* *(Laura looks up slowly, with wonder, and shakes her head.)* Well, you are! In a very different way from anyone else. And all the nicer because of the difference, too. *(His voice becomes low and husky. Laura turns away, nearly faint with the novelty of her emotions.)* I wish you were my sister. I'd teach you to have some confidence in yourself. The different people are not like other people, but being different is nothing to be ashamed of. Because other people are not such wonderful people. They're one hundred times one thousand. You're one times one! They walk all over the earth. You just stay here. They're common as — weeds, but — you — well, you're —*Blue Roses!*

Image On Screen: Blue Roses.

Music Changes.

LAURA: But blue is wrong for — roses . . .

JIM: It's right for you —You're — pretty!

265 LAURA: In what respect am I pretty?

JIM: In all respects —believe me! Your eyes — your hair — are pretty! Your hands are pretty! *(He catches hold of her hand.)* You think I'm making this up because I'm invited to dinner and have to be nice. Oh, I could do that! I could put on an act for you, Laura, and say lots of things without being very sincere. But this time I am. I'm talking to you sincerely. I happened to notice you had this inferiority complex that keeps you from feeling comfortable with people. Somebody needs to build your confidence up and make you proud instead of shy and turning away and — blushing — Somebody ought to — ought to —*kiss you, Laura! (His hand slips slowly up her arm to her shoulder.) (Music Swells Tumultuously.) (He suddenly turns her about and kisses her on the lips. When he releases her Laura sinks on the sofa with a bright, dazed look. Jim backs away and fishes in his pocket for a cigarette.) (Legend On*

Screen: "Souvenir.") Stumble-john! *(He lights the cigarette, avoiding her look. There is a peal of girlish laughter from Amanda in the kitchen. Laura slowly raises and opens her hand. It still contains the little broken glass animal. She looks at it with a tender, bewildered expression.)* Stumble-john! I shouldn't have done that — That was way off the beam. You don't smoke, do you? *(She looks up, smiling, not hearing the question. He sits beside her a little gingerly. She looks at him speechlessly — waiting. He coughs decorously and moves a little farther aside as he considers the situation and senses her feelings, dimly, with perturbation. Gently.)* Would you — care for a — mint? *(She doesn't seem to hear him but her look grows brighter even.)* Peppermint — Life Saver? My pocket's a regular drug store — wherever I go . . . *(He pops a mint in his mouth. Then gulps and decides to make a clean breast of it. He speaks slowly and gingerly.)* Laura, you know, if I had a sister like you, I'd do the same thing as Tom, I'd bring out fellows — introduce her to them. The right type of boys of a type to — appreciate her. Only — well — he made a mistake about me. Maybe I've got no call to be saying this. That may not have been the idea in having me over. But what if it was? There's nothing wrong about that. The only trouble is that in my case — I'm not in a situation to do the right thing. I can't take down your number and say I'll phone. I can't call up next week and — ask for a date. I thought I had better explain the situation in case you misunderstood it and — hurt your feelings. . . . *(Pause. Slowly, very slowly, Laura's look changes, her eyes returning slowly from his to the ornament in her palm.)*

Amanda utters another gay laugh in the kitchen.

Laura: *(faintly)* You — won't — call again?

Jim: No, Laura. I can't. *(He rises from the sofa.)* As I was just explaining, I've — got strings on me, Laura, I've — been going steady! I go out all the time with a girl named Betty. She's a home-girl like you, and Catholic, and Irish, and in a great many ways we — get along fine. I met her last summer on a moonlight boat trip up the river to Alton, on the *Majestic.* Well — right away from the start it was — love! *(Legend: Love!) (Laura sways slightly forward and grips the arm of the sofa. He fails to notice, now enrapt in his own comfortable being.)* Being in love has made a new man of me! *(Leaning stiffly forward, clutching the arm of the sofa, Laura struggles visibly with her storm. But Jim is oblivious, she is a long way off.)* The power of love is really pretty tremendous! Love is something that — changes the whole world, Laura! *(The storm abates a little and Laura leans back. He notices her again.)* It happened that Betty's aunt took sick, she got a wire and had to go to Centralia. So Tom — when he asked me to dinner — I naturally just accepted the invitation, not knowing that you — that he — that I — (He stops awkwardly.)* Huh — I'm a stumble-john! *(He flops back on the sofa. The holy candles in the altar of Laura's face have been snuffed out! There is a look of almost infinite desolation. Jim glances at her uneasily.)* I wish that you would — say something. *(She bites her lip which was trembling and then bravely smiles. She opens her* *hand again on the broken glass ornament. Then she gently takes his hand and raises it level with her own. She carefully places the unicorn in the palm of his hand, then pushes his fingers closed upon it.)* What are you — doing that for? You want me to have him?— Laura? *(She nods.)* What for?

LAURA: A — souvenir . . .

She rises unsteadily and crouches beside the Victrola to wind it up.

Legend On Screen: "Things Have A Way Of Turning Out So Badly."

Or Image: "Gentleman Caller Waving Good-bye! — Gaily."

At this moment Amanda rushes brightly back in the front room. She bears a pitcher of fruit punch in an old-fashioned cut-glass pitcher and a plate of macaroons. The plate has a gold border and poppies painted on it.

270 **AMANDA:** Well, well, well! Isn't the air delightful after the shower? I've made you children a little liquid refreshment. *(Turns gaily to the gentleman caller.)* Jim, do you know that song about lemonade?
     "Lemonade, lemonade
     Made in the shade and stirred with a spade —
     Good enough for any old maid!"

JIM: *(uneasily)* Ha-ha! No — I never heard it.

AMANDA: Why, Laura! You look so serious!

JIM: We were having a serious conversation.

AMANDA: Good! Now you're better acquainted!

275 **JIM:** *(uncertainly)* Ha-ha! Yes.

AMANDA: You modern young people are much more serious-minded than my generation. I was so gay as a girl!

JIM: You haven't changed, Mrs. Wingfield.

AMANDA: Tonight I'm rejuvenated! The gaiety of the occasion, Mr. O'Connor! *(She tosses her head with a peal of laughter. Spills lemonade.)* Oooo! I'm baptizing myself!

JIM: Here — let me —

280 **AMANDA:** *(setting the pitcher down)* There now. I discovered we had some maraschino cherries. I dumped them in, juice and all!

JIM: You shouldn't have gone to that trouble. Mrs. Wingfield.

AMANDA: Trouble, trouble? Why it was loads of fun! Didn't you hear me cutting up in the kitchen? I bet your ears were burning! I told Tom how outdone with him I was for keeping you to himself so long a time! He should have brought you over much, much sooner! Well, now that you've found your way, I want you to be a very frequent caller! Not just occasional but all the time. Oh, we're going to have a lot of gay times together! I see them coming! Mmm, just breathe that air! So fresh, and the moon's so pretty! I'll skip back out — I know where my place is when young folks are having a — serious conversation!

JIM: Oh, don't go out, Mrs. Wingfield. The fact of the matter is I've got to be going.

AMANDA: Going, now? You're joking! Why, it's only the shank of the evening,
Mr. O'Connor!

JIM: Well, you know how it is. 285

AMANDA: You mean you're a young workingman and have to keep
workingmen's hours. We'll let you off early tonight. But only on the
condition that next time you stay later. What's the best night for you? Isn't
Saturday night the best night for you workingmen?

JIM: I have a couple of time-clocks to punch, Mrs. Wingfield. One at morning,
another one at night!

AMANDA: My, but you are ambitious! You work at night, too?

JIM: No, Ma'am, not work but — Betty! (*He crosses deliberately to pick up his hat.
The band at the Paradise Dance Hall goes into a tender waltz.*)

AMANDA: Betty? Betty? Who's Betty! (*There is an ominous cracking sound in* 290
the sky.)

JIM: Oh, just a girl. The girl I go steady with! (*He smiles charmingly. The sky falls.*)

Legend: "The Sky Falls."

AMANDA: (*a long-drawn exhalation*) Ohhhh . . . Is it a serious romance
Mr. O'Connor?

JIM: We're going to be married the second Sunday in June.

AMANDA: Ohhhh — how nice! Tom didn't mention that you were engaged to
be married.

JIM: The cat's not out of the bag at the warehouse yet. You know how they 295
are. They call you Romeo and stuff like that. (*He stops at the oval mirror to
put on his hat. He carefully shapes the brim and the crown to give a discreetly
dashing effect.*) It's been a wonderful evening, Mrs. Wingfield. I guess this is
what they mean by Southern hospitality.

AMANDA: It really wasn't anything at all.

JIM: I hope it don't seem like I'm rushing off. But I promised Betty I'd pick her
up at the Wabash depot, an' by the time I get my jalopy down there her
train'll be in. Some women are pretty upset if you keep 'em waiting.

AMANDA: Yes, I know — The tyranny of women! (*Extends her hand.*)
Good-bye, Mr. O'Connor. I wish you luck — and happiness — and
success! All three of them, and so does Laura! — Don't you, Laura?

LAURA: Yes!

JIM: (*taking her hand*) Good-bye, Laura. I'm certainly going to treasure that 300
souvenir. And don't you forget the good advice I gave you. (*Raises his
voice to a cheery shout.*) So long, Shakespeare! Thanks again, ladies —
Good night!

He grins and ducks jauntily out.

*Still bravely grimacing, Amanda closes the door on the gentleman caller. Then she
turns back to the room with a puzzled expression. She and Laura don't dare to face each
other. Laura crouches beside the Victrola to wind it.*

AMANDA: *(faintly)* Things have a way of turning out so badly. I don't believe that I would play the Victrola. Well, well — well — Our gentleman caller was engaged to be married! Tom!

TOM: *(from back)* Yes, Mother?

AMANDA: Come in here a minute. I want to tell you something awfully funny.

TOM: *(enters with macaroon and a glass of the lemonade)* Has the gentleman caller gotten away already?

305 **AMANDA:** The gentleman caller has made an early departure. What a wonderful joke you played on us!

TOM: How do you mean?

AMANDA: You didn't mention that he was engaged to be married.

TOM: Jim? Engaged?

AMANDA: That's what he just informed us.

310 **TOM:** I'll be jiggered! I didn't know about that.

AMANDA: That seems very peculiar.

TOM: What's peculiar about it?

AMANDA: Didn't you call him your best friend down at the warehouse?

TOM: He is, but how did I know?

315 **AMANDA:** It seems extremely peculiar that you wouldn't know your best friend was going to be married!

TOM: The warehouse is where I work, not where I know things about people!

AMANDA: You don't know things anywhere! You live in a dream; you manufacture illusions! *(He crosses to door.)* Where are you going?

TOM: I'm going to the movies.

AMANDA: That's right, now that you've had us make such fools of ourselves. The effort, the preparations, all the expense! The new floor lamp, the rug, the clothes for Laura! All for what? To entertain some other girl's fiancé! Go to the movies, go! Don't think about us, a mother deserted, an unmarried sister who's crippled and has no job! Don't let anything interfere with your selfish pleasure! Just go, go, go — to the movies!

320 **TOM:** All right, I will! The more you shout about my selfishness to me the quicker I'll go, and I won't go to the movies!

AMANDA: Go, then! Then go to the moon — you selfish dreamer!

Tom smashes his glass on the floor. He plunges out on the fire-escape, slamming the door. Laura screams — cut by door.

Dance-hall music up. Tom goes to the rail and grips it desperately, lifting his face in the chill white moonlight penetrating the narrow abyss of the alley.

Legend On Screen: "And So Good-bye . . ."

Tom's closing speech is timed with the interior pantomime. The interior scene is played as though viewed through sound-proof glass. Amanda appears to be making a comforting speech to Laura who is huddled upon the sofa. Now that we cannot hear the mother's speech, her silliness is gone and she has dignity and tragic beauty. Laura's dark hair hides her face until at the end of the speech she lifts it to smile at her mother. Amanda's gestures are slow and graceful, almost dancelike, as she comforts the daughter. At the end of her speech she glances a moment at the father's picture — then withdraws through the portieres. At close of Tom's speech, Laura blows out the candles, ending the play.

TOM: I didn't go to the moon, I went much further — for time is the longest distance between two places — Not long after that I was fired for writing a poem on the lid of a shoe-box. I left Saint Louis. I descended the steps of this fire-escape for a last time and followed, from then on, in my father's footsteps, attempting to find in motion what was lost in space — I traveled around a great deal. The cities swept about me like dead leaves, leaves that were brightly colored but torn away from the branches. I would have stopped, but was pursued by something. It always came upon me unawares, taking me altogether by surprise. Perhaps it was a familiar bit of music. Perhaps it was only a piece of transparent glass. Perhaps I am walking along a street at night, in some strange city, before I have found companions. I pass the lighted window of a shop where perfume is sold. The window is filled with pieces of colored glass, tiny transparent bottles in delicate colors, like bits of a shattered rainbow. Then all at once my sister touches my shoulder. I turn around and look into her eyes . . . Oh, Laura, Laura, I tried to leave you behind me, but I am more faithful than I intended to be! I reach for a cigarette, I cross the street, I run into the movies or a bar, I buy a drink, I speak to the nearest stranger — anything that can blow your candles out! (*Laura bends over the candles.*) — for nowadays the world is lit by lightning! Blow out your candles, Laura — and so good-bye . . .

She blows the candles out.

The Scene Dissolves.

Reading and Reacting

1. Who is this play really about — Tom, Laura, or Amanda?

2. What is the function of the absent father in the play?

3. Besides serving as a possible suitor for Laura, what other roles does Jim play?

4. Identify references to historical events occurring at the time of the play's action. How are these events related to the play's central theme?

5. Does Tom function primarily as an actor, character, playwright, or narrator? Explain.

6. How do the music, the lighting, and the words and pictures projected on slides — which Tennessee Williams called "extra-literary accents" — contribute to the play's action? Are they essential? (Note that at the urging of the director, Williams eliminated these "accents" when the play opened on Broadway.)

7. In his production notes, Tennessee Williams calls *The Glass Menagerie* a "memory play." What do you think he means?

8. Discuss how props help to develop the play's themes. For example, consider the picture of the father, the Victrola, the fire escape, the telephone, the alarm clock, the high school yearbook, the unicorn, and the candles.

9. What events and dialogue foreshadow Tom's escape? Do you see this escape as inevitable? Do you see it as successful? Explain.

10. Do Amanda and Laura change as the play proceeds? What do you think will happen to them after the play is over? What is the significance of Laura's blowing out the candles at the end of the play?

11. Identify several examples of religious imagery in the play — for example, the Paradise Dance Hall. What is the significance of this imagery? In what way does it relate to the major theme of the play?

12. **JOURNAL ENTRY** Do you think Tom's decision to leave his family is a sign of strength or of weakness?

13. **CRITICAL PERSPECTIVE** Literary critic Roger Boxill says that *The Glass Menagerie* "is a moving elegy." Why do you think he calls the play an **elegy**—a work that commemorates someone's death? Does he want readers to take his comment literally? Whose death (or deaths) do you think he could be could he be referring to? Do you agree with Boxill's assessment of this play?

Related Works: "A Primer for the Punctuation of Heart Disease" (p. 88), "A&P" (p. 128), "Barn Burning" (p. 209), "The Road Not Taken" (p. 671)

WRITING SUGGESTIONS: Theme

1. The protagonists of *Fences* (p. 1096) and *Death of a Salesman* (p. 858) both have flaws that cause them to fail. Write an essay in which you compare Troy, the main character in *Fences*, and Willy Lowman, the main character in *Death of a Salesman*. How are these two characters similar? How are they different? In what way do their flaws further the themes of the two plays?

2. In an interview, writer Lorrie Moore calls *Fences* "an African-American *Death of a Salesman*." What do you think she means? Do you agree? Write an essay in which you examine the two plays in light of Moore's comment.

3. Write an essay in which you analyze the baseball images in *Fences*. How do the references to baseball help to develop the play's themes?

4. One of the themes of *Fences* is the dream a family has for its children. Compare the development of this theme in *Fences* and in another play in this book — for example, *The Glass Menagerie* (p. 1153).

5. In one sense, *Fences* is a play that explores Troy's effort to find his identity as an African-American in a predominantly white society. Compare and contrast Troy's attitude toward his identity with the development of this theme in a short story—for example, in "Big Black Good Man" (p. 192) or in "Two Kinds" (p. 416).

CREDITS

C1

PHOTOS

p. 46: © Denna Bendall/Worn Path Productions

p. 49: © Suzanne English/Worn Path Productions

p. 74 left and right: © Bettmann/CORBIS

p. 75 top: © Bettmann/CORBIS

p. 75 bottom: © Chris Hellier/CORBIS

p. 76, 78: © Bettmann/CORBIS

p. 79: © AP Photo

p. 86: Courtesy of Gary Gildner

p. 88: © AP Photo/Jim Cooper

p. 93: © AP Photo/Jennifer Graylock

p. 103: Courtesy of Louisiana State University

p. 107: © Dorothy Alexander

p. 113: © AP Photo

p. 128: © AP Photo/Reading Eagle/Times, Bill Uhrich

p. 134: © Bettmann/CORBIS

p. 139: © AP Photo/Janet Hostetter

p. 163: © Rex Rystedt

p. 173: © AP Photo

p. 191: © AP Photo/Robert Kradin

p. 203, 231, 238: © AP Photo

p. 251: © AP Photo/David Pickoff

p. 273, 281: © AP Photo

p. 289: © Marion Ettlinger

p. 302: © Bettmann/CORBIS

p. 319: © AP Photo

p. 326: Courtesy of David Michael Kaplan

p. 339: © Bettmann/CORBIS

p. 442 left: Detail from Roy.18 D 11 f.148 Lydgate and the Canterbury Pilgrims Leaving Canterbury from the 'Troy Book and the Siege of Thebes', 1412–22 (vellum), © British Library, London, UK/Bridgeman Art Library

p. 442 right: © Archivo Iconografico, S.A./CORBIS

p. 443 top left: P.124–1950.pt43 *The Tyger*: plate 43 from 'Songs of Innocence and of Experience' (copy R) c.1802–08 (etching, ink and w/c), Blake, William (1757–1827)/© Fitzwilliam Museum, University of Cambridge, UK/Bridgeman Art Library

p. 443 top right: *The Bard*, c.1817 (oil on canvas), Martin, John (1789–1854)/© Yale Center for British Art, Paul Mellon Collection, USA/Bridgeman Art Library

p. 443 bottom: © Bettmann/CORBIS

p. 445: © AP Photo/In the Life TV, Pat Johnson

p. 456 bottom: *Acrobats*, 1966, silkscreen (53.5cm x 38cm), Tarasque Press, © Ian Hamilton Finlay

p. 457: *Flake Upper Phase*, © Reed Altemus

INDEX OF FIRST LINES OF POETRY

INDEX OF AUTHORS AND TITLES

INDEX OF LITERARY TERMS